EUROPEAN IMMIGRATION
and ETHNICITY
in the United States and Canada

Clio Bibliography Series No. 7

Eric H. Boehm, Editor
Gail Schlachter, Executive Editor
Pamela R. Byrne, Associate Editor

Users of the Clio Bibliography Series may refer to current issues of
America: History and Life *and* Historical Abstracts
*for continuous bibliographic coverage of the subject areas
treated by each individual volume in the series.*

EUROPEAN IMMIGRATION and ETHNICITY in the United States and Canada

A Historical Bibliography

David L. Brye

Editor

Santa Barbara, California
Oxford, England

© 1983 by ABC-Clio Information Services, Inc.

ISBN 0-87436-258-X

American Bibliographical Center—Clio Press, Inc.
2040 Alameda Padre Serra
Santa Barbara, California

European Bibliographical Center—Clio Press
Woodside House, Hinksey Hill
Oxford OXI 5BE, England

Printed and bound in the United States of America

Cover design by Lance Klass from an original photograph of East European immigrants landing at Ellis Island, New York.

TABLE OF CONTENTS

United States

Canada

PREFACE

The earliest written materials about immigrants and the immigrant experience in America were probably the first entries in a Virginian's diary and the first letters home from New England Puritans. Large-scale immigration from Europe in the nineteenth and early twentieth centuries brought with it both written attacks on immigrants and defensive writings by members of specific ethnic or religious groups. In the twentieth century, a more dispassionate approach to immigrants came with the work of scholars such as Marcus Lee Hansen, Oscar Handlin, and many others. Due to the increased attention paid to ethnicity under the impact of the new political and social history within the historical profession and the "new ethnicity" outside the profession, recent years have seen an explosion of articles, essays, and monographs either discussing specific groups or using ethnicity as a major variable to explain political and social behavior.

This bibliography, an effort to pull all this material together, grew out of the experiences of the editor in researching the ethnic dimensions of American history in a National Endowment for the Humanities seminar for American historians, held at the University of Michigan in 1975-76. The need for more bibliographic aids in the field of immigrant-ethnic history soon became obvious. Encouragement from Joyce Duncan Falk, then director of the American Bibliographical Center and executive editor of the Clio Bibliography Series, led ultimately to the present work.

As is true of all volumes in the Clio Bibliography Series, this work is derived from the abstracts data base of *America: History and Life* — in this case, abstracts published in volumes 11 through 17, covering 1973 to 1979. A total of 4,066 abstracts of articles in some 585 periodicals were selected for the bibliography. The range of articles goes well beyond the usual historical categories to include writings in political science, sociology, economics, psychology, health sciences, and literature. A complete list of the journals from which articles have been selected appears at the end of this volume.

Essential to any bibliography is an explanation of the criteria for selection and the method of categorization. This bibliography is limited to European immigration to the United States and Canada from the colonial period to the present. Because it would have meant selecting material on almost all of American history, English settlement before 1783 was not included for either the United States or Canada. Early Spanish immigration to the New World was also excluded since it more properly belongs in a projected volume on Hispanic immigration to the United States and Canada.

Once the 4,066 entries were selected (out of a total of 57,748 in ABC-Clio's data base for 1973 to 1979), the more difficult task of categorizing began. The most obvious division was between the United States (entries 1-3,012) and Canada (3,013-4,066). To avoid a third major category, entries dealing with both countries were included under the United States, unless primarily in Canada.

The second major decision was to place all articles on a single ethnic group, regardless of topic, under the nationality category. Thus "Immigrants and Ethnics, By Groups" (Sections III and IX) includes 32 different groups with 1,892 out of 3,012 United States entries and 517 out of 1,054 Canadian entries appearing under this heading. While there are 126 entries under French and Canadians in the United States, 167 under Germans in the United States, and over 100 in the Irish, Italian, Swedish, and Polish ethnic categories, only the 751 under Jewish immigrants in the United States justified further subdividing. The subdivisions under the two main sections, United States and Canada, are the same except for the addition of Canada to the United States section and United States (including Loyalists) to the Canadian section, and the omission of some smaller groups from the Canadian list. The French sub-section for the main section on the United States includes French Canadians. So, too, Scottish and Scotch-Irish are categorized together, Russian Germans are included with Germans, Swedish Finns with Finns, and Ukrainians with Russians. While these combinations may offend ethnic purists, the numbers involved in each case are small enough to be easily sorted out. Biographical articles on individual members of ethnic groups were generally included if the discussion involved the person's ethnicity in a significant way. The remaining entries, including those covering several ethnic groups were assigned according to topics.

Specific criteria on assignment of abstracts to particular sections and sub-sections are as follows: Sections I and VI: Resources and General Studies (U.S.: 170 entries, Canada: 31): This heading for both the United States and Canadian sections includes historiography, primary sources, and settlement patterns. Sections II and VIII: Response to Immigration (U.S.: 95 entries, Canada: 29): This section includes such topics as nativism and legislation restricting immigration. Anti-Semitism, however, is included as a sub-topic under Jewish, and general articles on anti-Catholicism are included under Catholic. Sections IV and X: Immigrants and Ethnics: By Topics (U.S.: 775 entries, Canada: 229): This is the second most important part of the bibliography. The section on religion includes general articles on ethnicity and religion as well as articles on ethnically-oriented churches not tied to a specific ethnic group. (Thus, articles on Norwegian Lutherans are categorized under Norwegian, not under Lutheran.) Articles on Judaism are included under "Immigrant Groups: Jewish" if they have a clear ethnic orientation. Articles on political elites, voting behavior, and social mobility are in categories that would scarcely have appeared in a bibliography on immigration and ethnicity twenty years ago, before the introduction of the new political and social history with their ethnic emphases. Obviously, many of the articles that appear under "Immigrants and Ethnics: By Groups" could also appear in this section of the bibliography. Use of the index will greatly enhance access to the topics in this section. Section V: Contemporary Ethnicity (U.S.: 80 entries) and Section XI: French-English Relations (Canada: 234 entries): These sections have comparable but different foci. For the United States, articles on assimilation, group relations, and the "new ethnicity" form the core of the section; the Canada section concentrates on the conflicts between English-speaking and French-speaking areas of the nation, including the current struggles over Quebec separatism and bilingualism.

Not everyone will agree with this method of categorizing the vast number of articles and essays that have appeared on immigration and ethnicity during these seven years. Users of the bibliography will want to delve deeply into the index for additional articles on the topics included here and on a myriad of others ranging from abolition movements to Zionism. The abstracts are expertly indexed by editor/indexers, using the American Bibliographical Center's Subject Profile Index System (ABC-SPIndex). The subjects of each entry are indexed as a set of terms (an index string) that provides a complete profile of the subject matter of the cited article — in effect giving the user an abstract of the abstract. By spending a few minutes perusing the index profiles, the researcher should be able to reduce considerably the time that must be spent finding relevant articles. See the explanatory note at the beginning of the index for more information about ABC-SPIndex.

Pamela R. Byrne, Associate Editor of the Clio Bibliography Series, directed and participated in every phase of the project, from the initial planning stage through the complex editorial processes of the computer-assisted indexing system and machine-readable data base, to the final design and production of the book. Assistant Editors Suzanne Robitaille Ontiveros, Robert DeV. Brunkow, Paula May Cohen, David J. Valiulis, and Lance Klass provided editorial support at crucial stages of the project. The Data Processing Services Department under the supervision of Kenneth H. Baser, Director, Deborah Looker, Production Supervisor, and Cathy Clements, Applications Programmer, provided the technical expertise required to tap the *America: History and Life* data base and reprocess the material according to editorial specifications. I especially want to acknowledge the contribution of all those individuals in the academic and library communities who prepared the abstracts used in this volume. Their names are listed at the end of the volume.

Luther College   David L. Brye
Decorah, Iowa

UNITED STATES

1. RESOURCES AND GENERAL STUDIES OF IMMIGRATION

Historiography and General Studies

1. Adams, Pauline and Appel, John J. IMMIGRANTS SOUND OFF: THE IMMIGRANT EXPERIENCE ON TAPE. *Immigration Hist. Newsletter 1978 10(1): 8-12.* Cassette tapes available through Pacifica Programs and Sourcetape Programs are intended for classroom instruction relating to ethnic groups in the United States, including Asian Americans, Jews, Hispanics, Mexicans, Irish, Italians, Cubans, Polish, Germans, Greeks, Hungarians, and Scandinavians, and to immigration and immigrants' participation in labor movements.

2. Billington, Ray Allen. FRANKLIN D. SCOTT: TEACHER, SCHOLAR, AND AMBASSADOR OF INTERNATIONAL GOOD WILL. *Swedish Pioneer Hist. Q. 1974 25(3/4): 169-182.* Biography of Franklin D. Scott, historian and scholar. Based on unpublished reminiscences and information from friends of F. D. Scott; photo.
K. J. Puffer

3. Bleda, Sharon Estee. INTERGENERATIONAL DIFFERENCES IN PATTERNS AND BASES OF ETHNIC RESIDENTIAL DISSIMILARITY. *Ethnicity 1978 5(2): 91-107.* Attempts to assess the importance of five variables (education, income, occupation, age structure, and mother tongue) in explaining residential dissimilarity 1) between immigrants and native whites of native parentage, 2) between the latter and children of immigrants or of mixed parentage, and 3) between the first and second generations. The importance of each variable in determining each index of dissimilarity is assessed by means of indirect standardization and stated as a ratio of the dissimilarity resulting with all other variables held constant to the actual dissimilarity. The 15 ratios are determined separately for 11 nationalities and for 15 Standard Metropolitan Statistical Areas. Mother tongue (the first language learned in infancy) is consistently found to be the most important variable, except in the case of English-speaking nationalities. Based on data from the 1970 census, plus secondary sources; 5 tables, 12 ref., 3 notes.
L. W. Van Wyk

4. Chałasiński, Józef. CYWILIZACJA AMERYKAŃSKA I ROLA EMIGRACJI W JEJ ROZWOJU [American civilization and the role of emigration in its development]. *Kultura i Społeczeństwo [Poland] 1974 18(4): 53-70.* Many authors such as Oscar Handlin, Charles and Mary Beard, Max Lerner, Edward Sapir, Franz Boas, and R. H. Gabriel, writing on cultural anthropology, dispute the myth of Anglo-Saxonism in the formation of American civilization. They stress the huge role of European immigration in the development of humanistic studies, mass culture, and mass society in America. By the same token, one no longer speaks of only the assimilation of Poles to American culture, but of their contributions as well.
M. Swiecicka-Ziemianek

5. Christian, Henry A. FROM TWO HOMELANDS TO ONE WORLD: LOUIS ADAMIC'S SEARCH FOR UNITY. *Papers in Slovene Studies 1975 : 133-144.* Louis Adamic (b. 1898 in Blato, Slovenia) was an American writer who realized that to be Americanized was to suffer the loss of valuable traditions, but that to remain totally foreign meant isolation. In an attempt to make America one nation, he began to concentrate on what he called the unity in diversity. His quest for unity in diversity was implicit in *Grandsons* (1935), made up a portion of *My America* (1938), and was the basis of his Nation of Nations series: *From Many Lands* (1940), *Two-Way Passage* (1941), *What's Your Name?* (1942), and *A Nation of Nations* (1945). 20 notes.
T. Hočevar

6. Christian, Henry A. LOUIS ADAMIC AND THE AMERICAN DREAM. *J. of General Educ. 1975 27(2): 113-123.* In 1913 Yugoslavian-born Louis Adamic (1898-1951) immigrated to Washington, D. C., where, as an author, lecturer, and adviser on immigrant problems, he

delved into many aspects of American life. His writings define and explain the immigrant, reflect the identity crisis of minorities, and develop his quest for unity within diversity—still a social concern in our society today. Based on secondary sources; 15 notes.
N. A. Williamson

7. Cross, Robert D. HOW HISTORIANS HAVE LOOKED AT IMMIGRANTS TO THE UNITED STATES. *Int. Migration Rev. 1973 7(1): 4-13.* Examines historians' attitudes toward immigration and assimilation in the United States in the 19th and 20th centuries; includes their attention to specific ethnic groups.

8. Dennis, Lee. DOORWAY TO AMERICA. *Hist. Preservation 1978 30(2): 12-19.* Traces the history of Ellis Island in upper New York City Bay from mid-17th century to the present. Discusses various historic preservation efforts since 1954 when immigration processing ceased, particularly the Restore Ellis Island Committee formed in 1974. 9 photos.
R. M. Frame, III

9. Dunlevy, James A. and Gemery, Henry A. ECONOMIC OPPORTUNITY AND THE RESPONSE OF "OLD" AND "NEW" MIGRANTS TO THE UNITED STATES. *J. of Econ. Hist. 1978 38(4): 901-917.* The hostile and patronizing attitudes of native[-born] Americans toward the increasing number of immigrants from southern and eastern Europe at the turn of the century raise a number of issues that bear on the history of US immigration policy and on other matters. Utilizing Zellner's SUR technique, a model of settlement patterns of ten immigrant nationalities is estimated, and the appropriate F-statistics are generated to test several of these issues: 1) Did "new" immigrants behave as purposefully as contemporaneous "old" migrants from northwestern Europe? 2) Did they react as did the old migrants to a variety of socioeconomic factors? 3) Were the new migrants more dependent on the cultural support of earlier migrated countrymen? The findings indicate diverse, but purposeful, behavior within both the new and the old migrant groups with few systematic differences between them.
J

10. Gallaway, Lowell E.; Vedder, Richard K.; and Shukla, Vishwa. THE DISTRIBUTION OF THE IMMIGRANT POPULATION IN THE UNITED STATES, AN ECONOMIC ANALYSIS. *Explorations in Econ. Hist. 1974 11(3): 213-226.* Immigrant settlement patterns of 1900 show that immigrants entered the country with relatively accurate information about economic conditions in various parts of the United States. As a result they generally settled in urbanized rather than sparsely populated areas. This was consistent with an optimal allocation of labor resources. Based on published statistics and secondary accounts.
P. J. Coleman

11. Galush, William. ESSAYS ON ETHNIC HISTORY. *Mid-America 1978 60(1): 48-52.* Review article prompted by four books on American immigration history of the late 19th century. *The Immigrant Church,* by Jay P. Dolan, analyzes Irish and German impact on the Catholic Church in the United States. *For God and Country,* by Victor Greene, looks into Polish and Lithuanian conflict in Chicago Catholic parishes and how these two groups adjusted to each other and to American Catholic institutions. Edward Kantowisc studies Poles in Chicago in *Polish-American Politics in Chicago.* He concludes that Polish Americans never were effective enough to be politically influential or dominant. *Immigrants and the City,* by Dean R. Esslinger, looks at South Bend, Indiana, as an ethnic melting pot. It is more valuable as urban, rather than immigrant, history.
J. M. Lee

12. Harris, R. Cole. THE HISTORICAL GEOGRAPHY OF NORTH AMERICAN REGIONS. *Am. Behavioral Scientist 1979 22(1): 115-130.* Discusses themes and ideas in the recent historical geographical literature on North America which interprets European settlement on the continent during 17th-19th centuries.

13. Hershberg, Theodore. TOWARD THE HISTORICAL STUDY OF ETHNICITY. *J. of Ethnic Studies 1973 1(1): 1-5.* Notes the growing interest in the study of ethnicity and urges development and expansion of ethnic study programs. The field of ethnic studies is a prime example of the need for greater interdisciplinary research and collaboration. Departmental provincialism and the emphasis on individual rather than group research hinder better scholarship in ethnic studies and other subjects. Illustrates the importance of examining population subgroups by showing that each racial-ethnic group varied in its pattern of employment and ability to acquire real property. Describes the Philadelphia Social History Project, a quantitative study of the social structure and mobility of blacks, Irish, Germans, and "native white Americans" in Philadelphia 1850-80.   T. W. Smith

14. Hvidt, Kristian. EMIGRATION AGENTS: THE DEVELOPMENT OF A BUSINESS AND ITS METHODS. *Scandinavian J. of Hist. [Sweden] 1978 3(2): 179-203.* Analyzes the nature and development of the 19th-century emigration agent system, its links with steamship companies, and the methods of salesmanship. The American Dillingham Commission of 1911 argued that the old migration from northwest Europe was spontaneous as compared to the new Slavic migration which was artificially stimulated by the emigration agents. The sales promotion system was operating in the 1860's at the time of the old migration, but price competition between companies did not have any direct effect on the flow of emigration. However, lower fares and a general rise in wages created new potential emigrants. Based on Danish sources and the Uppsala Project (Sweden); 2 tables, 70 notes.   P. J. Beck

15. Kessler-Harris, Alice and Yans-McLaughlin, Virginia. EUROPEAN IMMIGRANT GROUPS. Sowell, Thomas, ed. *Essays and Data on American Ethnic Groups* (Washington, D.C.: Urban Inst. Pr., 1978): 107-137. Analyzes the differences in social mobility patterns among the Irish, Italians, and Jews. Between 1820 and 1950, 4.5 million Irish, 5 million Italians, and 3 million Russians, mostly Jews, entered the United States. The Irish and Jews viewed their immigration as permanent, whereas the Italians often came to the New World to accumulate money to buy land in the old. Arriving when the United States had a largely agrarian economy, the Irish generally were unskilled laborers. The Italians and Jews, arriving later, moved into more professional occupations. Relative living conditions, community cohesion, politics, intermarriage, family structure, and education are discussed, as is discrimination in housing and employment. Primary and secondary sources; 2 tables, 86 notes.   K. A. Talley

16. Mendel, Roberta. CARL FREDERICK WITTKE: VERSATILE HUMANIST. *Ohio Hist. 1975 84(1&2): 78-91.* Though best known as an immigrant historian and civil libertarian, Carl Frederick Wittke was also a baseball enthusiast and administrator. He insisted upon a "scholar's balance" and excellence. He helped make state and local history respectable, stressed the importance of the foreign language press, and the concept of "cultural blending." Primary and secondary sources; 3 illus., 34 notes, biblio.   S. S. Sprague

17. Morse, Richard M. THE AMERICANIZATION OF LANGUAGES OF THE NEW WORLD. *Cultures [France] 1976 3(3): 28-53.* Discusses linguistic changes in the New World (19th and 20th centuries) following revolutionary breaks with colonial powers, especially the Americanization of English and Spanish; Portuguese is discussed to some extent.

18. Nelson, Murry. ETHNIC STUDIES PROGRAMS: SOME HISTORICAL ANTECEDENTS. *Social Studies 1977 68(3): 104-108.* Interest in ethnic groups and minorities is documented in public school curricula from 1913, journal articles from 1908, and in books from 1940's.

19. Palmer, Howard. MOSAIC VERSUS MELTING POT?: IMMIGRATION AND ETHNICITY IN CANADA AND THE UNITED STATES. *Int. J. [Canada] 1976 31(3): 488-528.* Stresses the similarities rather than the differences in immigration policy and attitudes to immigrants in the two countries. 2 tables, 81 notes.   R. V. Kubicek

20. Parkin, Andrew. ETHNIC POLITICS: A COMPARATIVE STUDY OF TWO IMMIGRANT SOCIETIES, AUSTRALIA AND THE UNITED STATES. *J. of Commonwealth and Comparative Pol.*

[Great Britain] 1977 15(1): 22-38. Traces the patterns of immigration in Australia and the United States since the early 19th century. Outlines the processes of assimilation, the economic repercussions, and the political implications inherent in a multiracial society. Compares historic government and social attitudes toward immigration and immigrants in both countries. Secondary sources; 82 notes.   C. Anstey

21. Pierson, George W. THE SHAPING OF A PEOPLE: THE UNITED STATES OF AMERICA. *Cultures [France] 1976 3(3): 13-27.* Examines the shaping of the American national character during 1776-1976; Thomas Jefferson Wertenberger in *The First Americans* (1929) posits four determinants: inheritance, the melting pot, the environment, and continued European contacts; the author offers four additional factors: migration, choice, accident, and repetition.

22. Poulson, Barry W. and Holyfield, James, Jr. A NOTE ON EUROPEAN MIGRATION TO THE UNITED STATES: A CROSS SPECTRAL ANALYSIS. *Explorations in Econ. Hist. 1974 11(3): 299-310.* Tests the relative importance of the push of European and the pull of American economic conditions in explaining fluctuations in migration rates, particularly for the United Kingdom and generally for the period from 1840 to 1950. Based on published statistics and secondary accounts.   P. J. Coleman

23. Raitz, Karl B. ETHNIC MAPS OF NORTH AMERICA. *Geographical Rev. 1978 68(3): 335-350.* Reviews the methods of mapping American cultural or ethnic groups that indicate major trends in ethnic research. Because ethnicity has a number of forms, the most difficult methodological problems in the United States and Canada are to define ethnicity and to find reliable data sources. The most innovative techniques have been developed by those who make medium and large-scale maps based on several types of information. The most useful maps sometimes require accuracy in a distance as short as a street width, and they involve a considerable amount of fieldwork. Based on maps and on secondary sources; 59 notes.   W. R. Hively

24. Shergold, Peter R. THE WALKER THESIS REVISITED: IMMIGRATION AND WHITE AMERICAN FERTILITY, 1800-60. *Australian Econ. Hist. R. 1974 14(2): 168-189.* Analyzes the thesis presented in the late 19th century by Francis A. Walker, Superintendent of the American Census, that the momentous influx of foreign labor in the United States, 1800-60, caused a reduction in white native fertility, even to the extent that the growth in American population was no greater with immigration than it would have been without it. Based on secondary sources; table, 63 notes.   R. B. Orr

25. Stipanovich, Joseph. IMMIGRATION AND AMERICAN SOCIAL HISTORY. *J. of Urban Hist. 1978 5(1): 133-142.* Review article prompted by Herbert G. Gutman's *Work, Culture, and Society in Industrializing America,* Victor Green's *For God and Country: The Rise of Polish and Lithuanian Ethnic Consciousness in America, 1860-1910,* Edward R. Kantowicz's *Polish-American Politics in Chicago, 1888-1940* and Thomas Kessner's *The Golden Door: Italian and Jewish Immigrant Mobility in New York City, 1880-1915.* Gutman takes the Thompsonian approach to the study of industrialization while Kessner follows in the footsteps of Thernstrom. Green and Kantowicz do case studies of the assimilation of particular ethnic groups. Despite these diverse approaches they all examine the role of ethnicity and industrialization in shaping modern America. 9 notes.   T. W. Smith

26. Strave, Bruce M. A CONVERSATION WITH OSCAR HANDLIN. *J. of Urban Hist. 1977 3(1): 119-130.* Interviews Oscar Handlin, who brought ethnic history and local history to the mainstream of social history. 12 notes, biblio.   T. W. Smith

27. Vecoli, Rudolph J. THE IMMIGRANT EXPERIENCE: NEW PERSPECTIVES AND OLD PREJUDICES. *Rev. in Am. Hist. 1979 7(1): 43-50.* Review article prompted by John W. Briggs's *An Italian Passage: Immigrants to Three American Cities, 1890-1930* (New Haven, Conn.: Yale U. Pr., 1978) and Caroline Golab's *Immigrant Destinations* (Philadelphia: Temple U. Pr., 1977).

28. Vecoli, Rudolph J. THE RESURGENCE OF AMERICAN IMMIGRATION HISTORY. *Am. Studies Int. 1979 17(2): 46-66.* The

current emphasis on ethnicity brought immigration history to the fore. Governmental and private agencies created an infrastructure of facilities and resources—research centers and collections, microform and reprint editions, reference tools, historical societies, and publications. Recent immigration scholarship examines the causes of mass migrations, the experiences of particular groups including some hitherto neglected, and the ethnic diversity of particular states and regions; it employs theories of modernization, cliometrics, and oral history, and emphasizes the persistence of ethnic cultures. It presages a rewriting of US history which will be multiethnic, multiracial, and multilingual. 3 photos, 31 notes.

R. E. Noble

29. Weinberg, Daniel E. VIEWING THE IMMIGRANT EXPERIENCE IN AMERICA THROUGH FICTION AND AUTOBIOGRAPHY—WITH A SELECT BIBLIOGRAPHY. *Hist. Teacher 1976 9(3): 409-432.* Discusses the use of autobiography and fiction in teaching the immigrant experience in America. These sources, used critically, constitute an important teaching aid. Discusses two examples. Based on primary and secondary sources; 8 illus., 25 notes, biblio.

P. W. Kennedy

30. Williamson, Jeffrey G. MIGRATION TO THE NEW WORLD: LONG TERM INFLUENCES AND IMPACT. *Explorations in Econ. Hist. 1974 11(4): 357-389.* Analyzes the conflicting explanations for migration (mainly "push/pull" interpretations) and argues that the soundest explanation lies in the relative rates of industrialization and economic growth in the trans-Atlantic economy. Immigration fostered industrialization in the New World and suppressed real wage improvement, but did not have a very significant effect on aggregate growth as measured by real GNP per capita indices. Based on published data and secondary accounts.

P. J. Coleman

31. Unsigned. FRANKLIN D. SCOTT: A BIBLIOGRAPHY OF HIS WORK (THROUGH MARCH 1974). *Swedish Pioneer Hist. Q. 1974 25(3/4): 271-276.* A chronological listing, by categories, of the publications of Franklin D. Scott (b. 1901). Categories include books and monographs, articles, briefer articles, encyclopedia articles, and editorial work. Gives a list of the periodicals in which Scott's 150 book reviews have appeared.

K. J. Puffer

Primary Sources

32. Juliani, Richard N. THE USE OF ARCHIVES IN THE STUDY OF IMMIGRATION AND ETHNICITY. *Am. Archivist 1976 39(4): 469-477.* Current research trends in the study of ethnic groups have important implications for archival research. Although there is increased emphasis on quantitative techniques, limitations inherent in such studies require the complementary use of archival sources. Oral history interviews, parish records, voluntary association records and business archives are important qualitative sources for documenting the content of ethnic cultures. 22 notes.

J. A. Benson

33. Lehmann, Ingrid. DAS "CENTER FOR IMMIGRATION STUDIES" UND DAS IMMIGRANTENARCHIV AN DER UNIVERSITY OF MINNESOTA [The Center for Immigration Studies and the immigrant archive at the University of Minnesota]. *Internationale wissenschaftliche Korrespondenz zur Geschichte der deutschen Arbeiterbewegung [West Germany] 1974 10(4): 496-497.* Describes the work and holdings of the Immigration History Research Center at the University of Minnesota (St. Paul), which has collected well over 20,000 volumes of ethnic pamphlets, newspapers, and manuscripts of the post-1890 wave of primarily south and east European and Near Eastern immigrants. Especially the Finnish and Italian collections yield much valuable source material for labor history. 3 notes.

D. Prowe

34. Minto, Mary. SAN FRANCISCO FOREIGN AND ETHNIC COLLECTIONS AND LIBRARIES. *California Lib. 1977 38(4): 17-28.* Surveys foreign and ethnic collections in libraries throughout San Francisco, including French, American Indian, Arabic, Australian, British, Chinese, Canadian, Filipino, Jewish, Japanese, Indian, Russian, Polish, Dutch, African, Nigerian, Irish, Western American, world trade, and business libraries.

35. Montalto, Nicholas V. THE CHALLENGE OF PRESERVATION IN A PLURALISTIC SOCIETY. *Am. Archivist 1978 41(4): 399-404.* Two new projects of the Immigration History Research Center of the University of Minnesota have been developed to encourage a national effort for preservation of immigrant resources. The Ethnic Fraternal Project is designed to ensure preservation of the records of fraternal benefit societies which assured financial security for immigrants in time of need and later developed into ethnic cultural organizations. The International Institutes Project is an attempt to locate, survey, and preserve records of agencies originally founded by the YWCA to assist immigrants with social, legal, personal, and educational problems. 9 notes.

G.-A. Patzwald

36. Mulder, William. MORMON SOURCES FOR IMMIGRATION HISTORY. *Immigration Hist. Newsletter 1978 10(2): 1-8.* As an offspring from a basic religious tenet, the library at Brigham Young University (associated with the Mormon Church) contains extensive research and genealogical materials with important source material for immigration studies.

37. O'Toole, James M. CATHOLIC CHURCH RECORDS: A GENEALOGICAL AND HISTORICAL RESOURCE. *New England Hist. and Geneal. Register 1978 132(Oct): 251-263.* In contrast to individual Protestants, Roman Catholics have more frequently relied on the church to keep genealogical records. Describes how church records have been kept at parish and diocesan levels and by interconnecting agencies such as cemeteries, orphanages, schools, welfare agencies, and hospitals. Diaries and papers of priests and bishops often provide additional information on parishioners. Most records which were not lost or destroyed are now preserved in institutional archives. 10 notes. A. E. Huff

38. Warner, Robert M. and Blouin, Francis X., Jr. DOCUMENTING THE GREAT MIGRATIONS AND A CENTURY OF ETHNICITY IN AMERICA. *Am. Archivist 1976 39(3): 319-328.* In building immigration or ethnic collections, archivists should consider the dimensions of the field, the variety of sources available, and the likelihood that immigration sources are available in more general subject collections. The Bentley Library at the University of Michigan has engaged in active overseas collection of immigration and ethnic materials. Difficulties involving expense, languages, and bulk of collections require cooperation in efforts to acquire foreign materials. 22 notes.

J. A. Benson

Settlement

Early Settlement

39. Anderson-Green, Paula Hathaway. THE NEW RIVER FRONTIER SETTLEMENT ON THE VIRGINIA-NORTH CAROLINA BORDER 1760-1820. *Virginia Mag. of Hist. and Biography 1978 86(4): 413-431.* Attempts to describe the nature of emigration to, and economic and social development in this geographically discrete area of western Virginia and North Carolina. Compares findings with some generalizations of regional and national frontier writers. Concludes that the settlers, both native Americans and European immigrants, often consisted of extended families that maintained close ties as they developed largely self-sufficient farms in considerable isolation. Public records and secondary sources; 78 notes.

P. J. Woehrmann

40. Becker, M. J. "SWEDISH" COLONIAL YELLOW BRICKS: NOTES ON THEIR USES AND POSSIBLE ORIGINS IN 17TH CENTURY AMERICA. *Hist. Archaeology 1977 11: 112-118.* Small yellow bricks are often found at early colonial sites along the eastern seaboard. These building elements are usually associated with Swedish and Dutch constructions of the 17th century. Despite their frequent appearance, there has been little research on these bricks. Presents information from excavations on a 1643 house foundation in Governor Pritz State Park (36DE3), Pennsylvania, believed to be the earliest European settlement in Pennsylvania.

J/S

41. Bridenbaugh, Carl. THE OLD AND NEW SOCIETIES OF THE DELAWARE VALLEY IN THE SEVENTEENTH CENTURY.

Pennsylvania Mag. of Hist. and Biog. 1976 100(2): 143-172. From 1600 to 1700, the Delaware Valley "formed a single geographical unit of greater historical importance than the sum of the four political divisions that comprise it taken together—Cecil County in Maryland, the Lower Counties on the Delaware, Pennsylvania, and West New Jersey." Before 1610, the valley was inhabited by the Lenni Lenape or Delawares. By 1638, the Indian society had collapsed under the impact of the Dutch fur trade, disease, and alcohol. The Dutch were joined after 1638 by the Swedes and Finns. Between 1638 and 1673, these Europeans cleared the land, fenced fields, built houses, erected courts of law, and formed towns. After 1675, this European influence was supplanted by the Quakers under Penn. "The Englishing of this rich region was, from the economic and social point of view, as profound an influence in American colonial history as Puritanism." Based on primary and secondary sources; 48 notes.
E. W. Carp

42. Chardon, Roland E. THE CAPE FLORIDA SOCIETY OF 1773. *Tequesta 1975 35: 1-36.* In 1773 the Cape Florida Society was organized in Great Britain in an unsuccessful effort to settle about 20 European families on 6,000 acres of land in southeastern Florida. The society was largely organized by Lord Dartmouth, William Gerard De Brahm, and two Swiss entrepreneurs. The Society, however, was never formally incorporated. Based on primary and secondary sources; 58 notes.
H. S. Marks

43. Din, Gilbert C. SPAIN'S IMMIGRATION POLICY IN LOUISIANA AND THE AMERICAN PENETRATION, 1792-1803. *Southwestern Hist. Q. 1973 76(3): 255-276.* The unreliability of Anglo-American settlers in Spanish Louisiana, who had been encouraged to settle, led to a reversal of Spain's immigration policy in 1792. Hoping to secure a loyal European Catholic population compatible with Spanish monarchical rule, Louisiana sought French émigrés and Irish, Flemish, and German immigrants. Failure to attract large numbers and Anglo-American penetration at will contributed to Spain's accord with the United States in 1795 and retrocession of Louisiana to France in 1801. 59 notes.
D. L. Smith

44. Hale, Richard W., Jr. THE FRENCH SIDE OF THE "LOG CABIN MYTH." *Massachusetts Hist. Soc. Pro. 1957-60 72: 118-125.* Discusses the spread and evolution of the log cabin in America, following a book on the origins of the log cabin entitled *The Log Cabin Myth,* written in 1939 by Harold R. Shurtleff.

45. Wakely, Francis E. MISSION ACTIVITY AMONG THE IROQUOIS, 1642-1719. *Rochester Hist. 1976 38(4): 1-24.* Examines the efforts of French Jesuits to convert Iroquois Indians in the New World (primarily New York) to Catholicism, and the response from Dutch and British colonizers, 1642-1719.

The Movement West and State Studies

46. Cohen, Bronwen J. NATIVISM AND WESTERN MYTH: THE INFLUENCE OF NATIVIST IDEAS ON THE AMERICAN SELF-IMAGE. *J. of Am. Studies [Great Britain] 1974 8(1): 23-39.* Analyzes the "mythology" in which American nativists shrouded the development of the American West. Nativists claimed that the westward movement involved only "old-stock" Americans while immigrants eschewed pioneering to settle in the cities. Many Americans found comforting the "self-image" provided by nativist interpretations. Primary and secondary sources; 56 notes.
H. T. Lovin

47. Demaree, L. Steven. POST-CIVIL WAR IMMIGRATION TO SOUTHWEST MISSOURI, 1865-1873. *Missouri Hist. R. 1975 69(2): 169-190.* During 1865-73 immigrants from Europe and the East were drawn to southwest Missouri by the efforts of individuals and business enterprises. The first regional and county organizations to attract immigrants did not appear before 1878. The immigrants influenced the economic and political development of the region, and they probably influenced social changes, religious configurations, and landowning patterns. Based on primary and secondary material; 2 tables, 67 notes.
W. F. Zornow

48. Doran, Michael F. POPULATION STATISTICS OF NINETEENTH CENTURY INDIAN TERRITORY. *Chronicles of Oklahoma 1975-76 53(4): 492-515.* Presents an approximation of population changes in Indian Territory during the 19th century. Charts the population decline of the Five Civilized Tribes following removal, origins of white immigration into the territory, population shifts within the Indian Nations, and the increasing ratio of alien immigrants compared to Indian residents. Primary and secondary sources; 9 maps, 9 tables, 31 notes.
M. L. Tate

49. Forsythe, James L. ENVIRONMENTAL CONSIDERATIONS IN THE SETTLEMENT OF ELLIS COUNTY, KANSAS. *Agric. Hist. 1977 51(1): 38-50.* Environment played an important role in Ellis County, Kansas, settlement. Early settlers favored lands near transportation, such as creeks and the Kansas Pacific Railroad. Livestock farmers looked for rolling hills, grain farmers for flat, rich soil. Other factors such as the availability of water also influenced settlement. Early arrivals in Ellis County included English and Russian colonists and farmers from Pennsylvania, Ohio, and Illinois. 36 notes.
D. E. Bowers

50. Gerlach, Russell L. POPULATION ORIGINS IN RURAL MISSOURI. *Missouri Hist. Rev. 1976 71(1): 1-21.* Presents a map based on the US census manuscript schedule of population, to describe the broad pattern of settlement of both foreign- and native-born settlers by country and state of origin. Discusses the unique contribution of each group to the character of present-day rural Missouri. Based on primary and secondary sources; illus., map, 57 notes.
W. F. Zornow

51. Hackett, D. L. A. THE SOCIAL STRUCTURE OF JACKSONIAN LOUISIANA. *Louisiana Studies 1973 12(1): 325-353.* Attempts to correct inadequate analysis of the social structure of Louisiana 1830-60 by presenting economic and social changes. Uses tables and graphs to show ethnic changes, relationships of slaves to whites, native-born to foreign-born, comparative numbers of Anglo-Saxon and French parishes, parishes with the highest and lowest percentages of slaves, agricultural crops (sugar cane and cotton), general farming in each parish, and the ratio of slave holders to total number of families. The parishes are ranked according to individual wealth and family income. These and other data are utilized in analyzing Louisiana religion, politics, economics, and education. 18 tables, 36 notes.
G. W. McGinty

52. Hale, Douglas. EUROPEAN IMMIGRANTS IN OKLAHOMA: A SURVEY. *Chronicles of Oklahoma 1975 53(2): 179-203.* Traces the significant immigration patterns of Europeans within Oklahoma by focusing on the major ethnic groups, their origins, and population densities. This preliminary study is confined to immigrants from Germany, Russia, Poland, Austria-Hungary, Italy, Sweden, Ireland, and Britain during 1890-1920. Mentions subgroups such as Jews and Russian Mennonites and makes methodological suggestions for future detailed studies of Oklahoma immigrants. Based on primary and secondary sources; 6 charts, 9 population maps, 56 notes.
M. L. Tate

53. Hudson, John C. MIGRATION TO AN AMERICAN FRONTIER. *Ann. of the Assoc. of Am. Geographers 1976 66(2): 242-265.* Examines 1,000 autobiographies written by North Dakota pioneers during the late 1930's, which reveal cultural and economic patterns of settlement by people of German, German Russian, and Scandinavian descent (1875-1915).

54. Johnson, Dorothy M. THE FOREIGNERS. *Montana 1976 26(3): 62-67.* Recollections of childhood experiences with non-English speaking neighbors in Montana towns in the era before World War I. Human warmth overcame difficulties in communication and differences in lifestyles.
S. R. Davison

55. Lamar, Howard R. PUBLIC VALUES AND PRIVATE DREAMS: SOUTH DAKOTA'S SEARCH FOR IDENTITY, 1850-1900. *South Dakota Hist. 1978 8(2): 117-142.* The history of the last half of the 19th century is first analyzed with regard to the traditional traders, missionaries, and settlers. A Missouri mercantile tradition was established, only to be blunted by the Civil War, decline of steamboat transportation, and the railroad companies' choice of routes south of Dakota. Missionary work in southern Dakota brought not only Protestantism but also other elements of cultural New England. The settlers

who formed much of the territory's heritage were also of New England-Yankee origins. Additionally, the established cultures appeared attractive to European religious groups who sought out Dakota, especially during the last three decades of the 19th century. By the time of statehood, South Dakota's public and private values had also included vigorous but sometimes corrupt politics and a proud rural, agrarian economy. Secondary sources; 7 photos, map, 59 notes.   A. J. Larson

56. Lang, Herbert H. THE NEW MEXICO BUREAU OF IMMIGRATION, 1880-1912. *New Mexico Hist. Rev. 1976 51(3): 193-214.* New Mexico, upon becoming a part of the United States, had large mineral resources, but lacked the men and finances to develop them. In 1880 a Bureau of Immigration was established. Some members of the legislature were hostile to the Bureau. During the Bureau's 32 years several hundred men served as commissioners; many were not native New Mexicans. The man who did most for the bureau was Max Frost. He resorted to advertising to attract settlers to New Mexico.
J. H. Krenkel

57. Levernier, James A. THE CAPTIVITY NARRATIVE AS REGIONAL, MILITARY, AND ETHNIC HISTORY. *Research Studies 1977 45(1): 30-37.* Presents a catalogue of Indian captivities in the 19th century, examining them as representatives of local, regional, military, and ethnic history; 21 notes.

58. Luebke, Frederick C. ETHNIC GROUP SETTLEMENT ON THE GREAT PLAINS. *Western Hist. Q. 1977 8(4): 405-430.* Foreign-born people and their children often constituted the majority of the Great Plains frontier population in the mid-19th century. The greatest number were German; English-speaking people were the second largest group. Most were farmers, who, after working in eastern urban occupations to accumulate enough money to start anew on the western frontier, migrated in family units, with relatives and neighbors coming later. Although typical "old-stock" Americans had little appreciation of the problems faced by the immigrants, most ethnic groups were eagerly welcomed to help populate the Great Plains. 33 notes.   D. L. Smith

59. Maluy, Dale C. BOER COLONIZATION IN THE SOUTHWEST. *New Mexico Hist. Rev. 1977 52(2): 93-110.* As a result of the South African War during 1889-1902, refugees who did not wish to live under British rule fled to New Mexico where they established the village of Chamberino. These farmers, known as Boers, were of Dutch, French Huguenot, and German ancestry. The first Boer officer to arrive in the United States was General William D. Snyman. The English offered 10,000 pounds for his capture. The settlement in New Mexico prospered despite annual flooding by the Rio Grande. The lush farms of the Boers resulted in a good increase in land prices in the Mesilla Valley. 3 illus., map, 66 notes.   J. H. Krenkel

60. McDonald, Forrest. THE ETHNIC FACTOR IN ALABAMA HISTORY: A NEGLECTED DIMENSION. *Alabama Rev. 1978 31(4): 256-265.* Argues that the predominant ethnic influence in Alabama (and possibly the South) is not WASP, but Celtic. Alabama history has been affected by inherent resistance to change, a tendency towards political as opposed to legal action, and a deep-seated antipathy to other ethnic groups, notably Germans. Primary and secondary sources; 5 notes.
J. F. Vivian

61. McWilliams, Carey. AND THE PEOPLE CAME. *Westways 1976 68(7): 38-49.* Discusses immigration to California, including the variety of ethnic groups in the state and the effect these groups have had on California's character, 1850-1976.

62. Miller, Randall M. IMMIGRANTS IN THE OLD SOUTH. *Immigration Hist. Newsletter 1978 10(2): 8-14.* Examines the impact of Northern European ethnic groups and religious sects on the formation of southern culture, 1820's-50's.

63. Nadeau, Josephine E. RIPON: ETHNIC AND GENERAL DEVELOPMENT. *Pacific Historian 1976 20(1): 52-66; 1978 22(2): 160-169.* Part II. Presents the history of Ripon, California, from the end of conflicts with Indians to the 20th century. Pays special attention to the arrival of representatives of various national and ethnic groups (the Americans Jedediah Smith and John C. Frémont, French Canadian trap-

pers, "49er's," Irish, and Welsh). Also notes other important individuals. Primary and secondary sources; 4 illus., 35 notes. Part VI. Enumerates nationalities and occupations of the original residents of Ripon, California. Mentions, among others, those who were to start Franzia Winery, Bella Napoli Winery, and the Canaan Vineyards. 14 notes.
G. L. Olson/R. S. Barnard

64. Notarianni, Philip F. UTAH'S ELLIS ISLAND: THE DIFFICULT "AMERICANIZATION" OF CARBON COUNTY. *Utah Hist. Q. 1979 47(2): 178-193.* Carbon County's ethnic diversity is a result of immigrants brought in to work in the coal industry. Congregation with others of the same nationality for security tended to accentuate cultural differences. Forced Americanization after World War I represented to many a stripping away of cultural differences. Gradual changes occurred as immigrants came into contact with American institutions and ideas, intermarried, unionized, and entered business. Cultural traits were modified in the accommodation process, but cultural maintenance was not lost. 10 illus., 34 notes.   J. L. Hazelton

65. Powell, William E. EUROPEAN SETTLEMENT IN THE CHEROKEE-CRAWFORD COAL FIELD OF SOUTHEASTERN KANSAS. *Kansas Hist. Q. 1975 41(2): 150-165.* Underground coal mining started in southeastern Kansas during the 1870's reached a peak during 1890-1920. Adverse conditions in Europe, coupled with economic opportunity and lax immigration laws, drew large numbers of immigrants from Europe and Canada to Kansas coal fields, where they settled in existing towns or company mining camps. When the mines declined after 1920 many immigrants moved to northern industrial cities. Based on primary and secondary sources; 3 photos, 2 tables, fig., 51 notes.
W. F. Zornow

66. Pozzetta, George E. FOREIGN COLONIES IN SOUTH FLORIDA, 1865-1910. *Tequesta 1974 (34): 45-56.* Immigrant colonies were sought by land promoters in south Florida, for large tracts of land could be sold and prices on remaining tracts would be enhanced. Many of the transactions were clouded because of nefarious activities by promoters, but the Florida East Coast Railway and Henry Flagler were honest in their relations with immigrant colonists. Discusses the Scottish colony at Sarasota, the Danish colony of White City in St. Lucie County, Dania and Hallendale (designed for Swedish immigrants) in Dade County, and a Japanese settlement near Boca Raton in Broward County. Based on primary and secondary sources; 21 notes.   H. S. Marks

67. Pozzetta, George E. FOREIGNERS IN FLORIDA: A STUDY OF IMMIGRATION PROMOTION, 1865-1910. *Florida Hist. Q. 1974 53(2): 164-180.* For many years following the Civil War much attention was given to attracting settlers as a means of building the economy of the state. Convinced that blacks were undependable as a labor force, Florida looked hopefully to immigrants. Various methods were used to attract them, but in the early 20th century, the tide of sentiment changed to opposition largely because of changes produced by southern Europeans in such areas as politics, religion, and culture. 2 photos, 45 notes.   R. V. Ritter

68. Rice, John G. THE EFFECT OF LAND ALIENATION ON SETTLEMENT. *Ann. of the Assoc. of Am. Geographers 1978 68(1): 61-72.* The process of land alienation involves the disposal of the public domain by the federal government and the acquisition of land by settlers. Land alienation policies affected the way in which the land was settled. Homesteads, railroad grants, purchase via scrip, and state grants all played a role in the settlement of Kandiyohi County, central Minnesota, during the latter half of the nineteenth century. Dutch and Swedish settlers took up land in restricted areas of the county because of the pattern of available land resulting from the various policies. Homestead entries contained the largest proportion of original farmsteads in the mid-1880's. These patterns resulting from initial settlement conditions are still observable.   J

69. Shanabruch, Charles. THE LOUISIANA IMMIGRATION MOVEMENT, 1891-1907: AN ANALYSIS OF EFFORTS, ATTITUDES, AND OPPORTUNITIES. *Louisiana Hist. 1977 18(2): 203-226.* Analyzes efforts to stimulate immigration in Louisiana during 1891-1907, and obstacles and opposition to those efforts. Concludes that the efforts were generally unsuccessful because of natural impediments,

the state's rigid rural economy, political tensions, violence, poor education and poor timing. Primary sources; table, 117 notes.

R. L. Woodward, Jr.

70. Sherman, William C. ETHNIC DISTRIBUTION IN WESTERN NORTH DAKOTA. *North Dakota Hist. 1979 46(1): 4-12.* Based on interviews with longtime rural property owners in the 14 county area of western North Dakota, a map was constructed indicating the distribution of ethnic groups as of 1965. Evidence indicated the past settlement in this region of clusters of Anglo-Americans, blacks, Bohemians, and Estonians from the Crimea, Bohemians, Dutch, Finns, French, Germans, Jews, German-Hungarians, Russian-Germans, Indians, Irish, Norwegians, Swedes, Polish, Syrians, Ukrainians and Russians in southwest North Dakota. Over the generations many of these groups have disappeared owing to outward migration. Significant groupings of some ethnic folk remain, especially Russian-Germans, Ukrainians, Bohemians, German-Hungarians. Article accompanied by a map illustrating ethnic population distribution in the southwest section of North Dakota as of 1965.

N. Lederer

71. Sprunk, Larry J. HAROLD G. AUREN—COOPERSTOWN. *North Dakota Hist. 1977 44(4): 80-81.* Interviews retired farmer Harold G. Auren. Many early residents of Griggs County, North Dakota, lived in dugouts and sod houses until lumber could be obtained to build surface, free-standing dwellings. Despite these primitive conditions the settlers, many of them immigrants, enjoyed themselves from time to time by playing cards and drinking whiskey. The winter of 1897 was the worst one in memory.

N. Lederer

72. Sutherland, Daniel E. MICHIGAN EMIGRANT AGENT: EDWARD H. THOMSON. *Michigan Hist. 1975 59(1-2): 3-37.* Edward H. Thomson was appointed Michigan's emigrant agent in 1849 and pioneered the role of that office. He overcame unenthusiastic legislative support, slurs by other agents, lack of funds, and maneuvering by his political enemies, and also raised money, prepared a pamphlet which introduced Michigan to potential immigrants, contacted merchants and European consuls, and received endorsement from New York City officials. Thomson regarded his job as more than a political plum and worked extremely hard. While revolutionary events in Europe actually caused migration, Thomson was effective in attracting many immigrants—chiefly Protestant and often wealthy—to Michigan. Primary and secondary sources; 9 illus., photo, map, 76 notes.

D. W. Johnson

73. Tjarks, Alicia V. COMPARATIVE DEMOGRAPHIC ANALYSIS OF TEXAS, 1777-1793. *Southwestern Hist. Q. 1974 77(3): 291-338.* Using the 12 general and local censuses taken in Spanish Texas in 1777-93 as a resource, discusses the problems of demographic methodology and analysis. Although there was small growth, mission population decreased markedly. New urban centers developed in east Texas because of proximity to Louisiana, not to expand Texas. Internal shifts and migrations had a positive effect on Texas. The absence of pronounced racial and social discrimination made Texas a melting pot of races and cultures. Map, 24 tables, 2 graphs, 54 notes.

D. L. Smith

74. Watkins, Beverly. EFFORTS TO ENCOURAGE IMMIGRATION TO ARKANSAS, 1865-1874. *Arkansas Hist. Q. 1979 38(1): 32-62.* During Reconstruction Arkansans attempted to encourage immigration to their state. Legislation was introduced, immigration societies were formed, grandiose plans were made, and books and pamphlets were published, but little was actually accomplished. The state population grew, but few foreigners were attracted to it. Primary and some secondary sources; 88 notes.

G. R. Schroeder

75. Williams, E. Russ, Jr. LOUISIANA'S PUBLIC AND PRIVATE IMMIGRATION ENDEAVORS: 1866-1893. *Louisiana Hist. 1974 15(2): 153-174.* Examines societies formed in Louisiana following the Civil War in the hopes of attracting immigrants to settle, 1866-93.

76. —. THE EMIGRANT'S PROGRESS. *Am. West 1975 12(3): 32-39.* Nine sketches and several excerpts from pictorial journals and books of the last half of the 19th century portray the difficulties of millions of immigrants, from their embarkation at European ports to their arrival in the American West.

D. L. Smith

Rural

77. Coffey, Brian. NINETEENTH-CENTURY BARNS OF GEAUGA COUNTY, OHIO. *Pioneer Am. 1978 10(2): 53-63.* The 19th-century barns in Geauga County of northeastern Ohio present a partial record of the relationship of barns to ethnicity and agricultural practices in an area that is losing its rural character. Of the four dominant barn types, three types (English, basement, and three-gable) account for more than four-fifths of all barns investigated in a 1975 survey. These types were generally associated with Anglo-Saxon culture. Secondary sources and field work; map, 3 tables, 9 fig., 12 notes.

C. R. Gunter, Jr.

78. Jordan, Terry G. EVOLUTION OF THE AMERICAN WINDMILL: A STUDY IN DIFFUSION AND MODIFICATION. *Pioneer Am. 1973 5(2): 3-12.* Traces the immediate ancestry of the American windmill from a widely distributed area of the Old World to North America. The American windmill, once a highly visible aspect of the cultural landscape of the United States, is now becoming a part of vanishing Americana. Windmill concentrations developed along the eastern seabord of North America, but failed to penetrate extensively the interior of the United States because of lower wind velocities in the heavily-wooded sections. Evidence suggests that the American windmill has evolved from the European tower windmill. Secondary sources; 3 illus., 2 maps, 5 photos, 1 fig., 19 notes.

C. R. Gunter, Jr.

79. Lord, Arthur C. THE PRE-REVOLUTIONARY AGRICULTURE OF LANCASTER COUNTY, PENNSYLVANIA. *J. of the Lancaster County Hist. Soc. 1975 79(1): 23-42.* Describes and gives data concerning Pre-Revolutionary agriculture in Lancaster County, Pennsylvania, noting the geographic and ethnic variables behind a general farming pattern that was to be "transferred to the Mid-West as the feed grain-livestock system of the Corn Belt." 6 tables.

80. McHenry, Stewart G. VERMONT BARNS: A CULTURAL LANDSCAPE ANALYSIS. *Vermont Hist. 1978 46(3): 151-156.* Mapping distinctive features of 4,165 barns in 141 towns reveals subcultural areas: Dutch dimensions in the southwest, covered ramps in areas of Scottish settlement, a few clerestory ventilators from Rhode Island in the Winooski Valley, the attached barn with diamond windows where the builders came from New Hampshire or Massachusetts, and near the Canadian border, signs of the Franco-American preference for color and exterior murals. 6 photos, 4 maps.

T. D. S. Bassett

81. McQuillan, D. Aidan. FARM SIZE AND WORK ETHIC: MEASURING THE SUCCESS OF IMMIGRANT FARMERS ON THE AMERICAN GRASSLANDS, 1875-1925. *J. of Hist. Geography 1978 4(1): 57-76.* In America farm size is often seen as an indicator of farming success. To test this assumption, colonies of French Canadians, Mennonites, and Swedish Americans were studied in Kansas. Although the Swedish farms were largest, they were the least productive, while the Mennonites with the smallest farms were the most productive because they were the most labor-intensive farmers of the three groups. The poor reputation of French Canadian farmers in Canada was not earned in Kansas. Based on Kansas township records and on secondary sources; map, 3 tables, 6 graphs, 32 notes.

F. N. Egerton

82. McQuillan, D. Aidan. THE MOBILITY OF IMMIGRANTS AND AMERICANS: A COMPARISON OF FARMERS ON THE KANSAS FRONTIER. *Agric. Hist. 1979 53(3): 576-596.* Kansas immigrant farmers showed about the same mobility rates between 1875 and 1925 as those born in the United States. Mobility was high both in the pioneer period and later. In general the most persistent farmers were older ones with greater wealth and larger families, though it is difficult to form a model to predict who would stay the longest. Based on census data from six Kansas townships with American, Mennonite, Swedish and French Canadian farmers; map, 4 charts, 2 tables, 24 notes.

D. E. Bowers

83. Noble, Allen G. BARNS AND SQUARE SILOS IN NORTHEAST OHIO. *Pioneer Am. 1974 6(2): 12-21.* Investigates 19th-century barns and silos extant in northeastern Ohio. Several basic barn types occur in the area, including the English-style barn, or three-bay barn.

Other major barn styles observed include the German bank barn, transverse gable barn, and gambrel roof barn. The latter two barn types appeared after 1875 as a result of emphasis upon scientific farming. The construction of silos also appeared at this time and was quickly adopted by local farmers. Early silos were patterned after European models, but many modifications were made during the 19th century. Continued study hopefully will shed light on a portion of the cultural diffusion process in this region. Based on field observation and secondary sources; 3 photos, 2 maps, 6 figs., 16 notes.   C. R. Gunter, Jr.

84.   Paul, Rodman.   IMMIGRANT GROUPS IN WESTERN AGRICULTURE: A COMMENT.   *Agric. Hist. 1975 49(1): 216-219.* Surveys the great diversity of California agriculture, including comments on large scale farming and immigration. Based on secondary sources; 4 notes.
                                                           R. T. Fulton

85.   Salamon, Sonya and O'Reilly, Shirley M.   FAMILY LAND AND DEVELOPMENTAL CYCLES AMONG ILLINOIS FARMERS. *Rural Sociol. 1979 44(3): 525-542.* A 1975-77 study involving an ethnic community of farmers revealed that four types of family land developmental cycles (expander, conservator, pragmatist, and convertor) are related to land transfer and overall farm management.

86.   Saloutos, Theodore.   AN HISTORIOGRAPHICAL ESSAY: IMMIGRANTS IN AGRICULTURE.   *Immigration Hist. Newsletter 1979 11(1): 1-4.* Evaluates 20th-century articles, essays, and books on 19th-20th centuries.

87.   Saloutos, Theodore.   THE IMMIGRANT CONTRIBUTION TO AMERICAN AGRICULTURE.   *Agric. Hist. 1976 50(1): 45-67.* Farmers from many immigrant groups contributed to the United States. As a result, America's agricultural production is high. Based on primary and secondary sources; 2 tables, 91 notes.   R. T. Fulton

88.   Saloutos, Theodore.   THE IMMIGRANT IN PACIFIC COAST AGRICULTURE, 1880-1940.   *Agric. Hist. 1975 49(1): 182-201.* Identifies and quantifies ethnic groups, both foreign born and domestic, practicing agriculture in California from 1880-1940. Covers the Exclusion Act of 1882 and the California Alien Land Laws of 1913. Also deals with the various communal and cooperative enterprises that have existed in California agriculture. Primary and secondary sources; 4 tables, 71 notes.
                                                           R. T. Fulton

89.   Simms, L. Moody, Jr.   RICHARD MALCOLM JOHNSTON ON RURAL LIFE IN MIDDLE GEORGIA.   *Georgia Hist. Q. 1974 58(Supplement): 181-192.* Middle Georgia was composed of Putman county and those surrounding it. It was an area composed of immigrants from western Europe except Britain. The culture of the area was rustic, and the humor unique. Although slavery was practiced, it did not inhibit a positive relationship between slave and master which led to an extension of the regional humor. The rural humor and careless speech patterns of the area erroneously led outsiders to assume that middle Georgians were ignorant, but the misconception was more likely due to a failure to understand the culture of the region. Primary and secondary sources; 5 notes.   M. R. Gillam

90.   Taylor, Paul S.   IMMIGRANT GROUPS IN WESTERN CULTURE.   *Agric. Hist. 1975 49(1): 179-181.* Surveys the entire western agricultural experience, from international immigration to agribusiness in California, as the introduction to a session on immigration in the West.
                                                           R. T. Fulton

91.   Tishler, William H.   THE SITE ARRANGEMENT OF RURAL FARMSTEADS.   *APT Bull. [Canada] 1978 10(1): 63-78.* Describes European influences on the arrangement of farms making up rural farmsteads which exemplify important values and elements of the built environment, 18th-19th centuries.

Urban

92.   Abbott, Carl.   SUBURB AND CITY: CHANGING PATTERNS OF SOCIOECONOMIC STATUS IN METROPOLITAN DENVER SINCE 1940.   *Social Sci. Hist. 1977 2(1): 53-71.* Assesses population redistribution trends among ethnic and socioeconomic groups in Denver, Colorado, 1940-77.

93.   Anderson, Glenn F.   THE SOCIAL EFFECTS OF THE CONSTRUCTION OF THE WACHUSETT RESERVOIR ON BOYLSTON AND WEST BOYLSTON.   *Hist. J. of Western Massachusetts 1974 3(1): 51-58.* Consequences were severe—West Boylston's population was halved during 1895-1908 and Boylston lost 2761 acres of land. Industry was totally destroyed and the inhabitants (70% native Americans and 30% French Canadians) expressed a marked distaste for the Italian and Hungarian workforce. Primary and secondary sources, 2 illus., table, 28 notes.   S. S. Sprague

94.   Bodnar, John.   THE IMMIGRANT AND THE AMERICAN CITY.   *J. of Urban Hist. 1977 3(2): 241-249.* Review article prompted by four recent works in ethnic history: Josef J. Barton, *Peasants and Strangers, Italians, Rumanians, and Slovaks in an American City, 1890-1950,* Leonard Dinnerstein and David M. Reimers, *Ethnic Americans: A History of Immigration and Assimilation,* Dean R. Esslinger, *Immigrants and the City: Ethnicity and Mobility in a Nineteenth Century Midwestern City,* and Kristian Hvidt, *Flight to America: The Social Background of 300,000 Danish Emigrants.* Each work approaches immigrants from a different angle. Hvidt looks at them from the mother country, Barton examines their experience in both the old and the new world, Esslinger picks up the story deep in the heartland of the New World, and Dinnerstein and Reimers overview the entire process. 12 notes.   T. W. Smith

95.   Bolin, Winifred D. Wandersee.   HEATING UP THE MELTING POT: SETTLEMENT WORK AND AMERICANIZATION IN NORTHEAST MINNEAPOLIS.   *Minnesota Hist. 1976 45(2): 58-70.* Since the turn of the century northeast Minneapolis has remained an Eastern European ethnic enclave. Middle-class Progressive reformers were concerned about the slow assimilation of these mainly Roman and Eastern Catholic groups. From a survey of the neighborhood emerged in January 1915 the North East Neighborhood House, headed by Robbins Gilman and his wife, Catheryne Cooke Gilman. The venture offered social, civic, and economic opportunities to adults and children. Initial projects such as job search aid and a day nursery were supplemented during World War I by help for men registering for the draft, Red Cross courses in a variety of subjects, recreation facilities for servicemen, and coordinating the sale of thrift stamps and war bonds to the people of the neighborhood. By 1918, the neighborhood was a scene of ethnic cooperation rather than antagonism. In the 1920's the settlement house became a center of Americanization and moral uplift efforts in the neighborhood.
                                                           N. Lederer

96.   Borodkin, L. I. and Selunskaia, N. B.   METODY IZUCHENIIA SOTSIALNOI ISTORII V AMERIKANSKOI ISTORIOGRAFII [Methods of studying social history in American historiography]. *Istoriia SSSR [USSR] 1978 (2): 217-225.* Analyzes American study of social history with particular reference to the Philadelphia Social History Project, considering the role and significance of social history, the adoption of new historiographical approaches, and the usual method of analysis. Compares the work of American and Soviet historians on similar topics, and considers the work of individual American historians and presentation of official government reports, stressing the differences in factual and analytical approach. Based on American and Soviet secondary works; 17 notes.   L. Smith

97.   Chudacoff, Howard P.   THE NEW IMMIGRATION HISTORY. *Rev. in Am. Hist. 1976 4(1): 99-104.* Review article prompted by Josef J. Barton's *Peasants and Strangers: Italians, Rumanians, and Slovaks in an American City, 1890-1950* (Cambridge, Massachusetts: Harvard U. Pr., 1975) and Edward R. Kantowicz's *Polish-American Politics in Chicago, 1888-1940* (Chicago: U. of Chicago Pr., 1975).

98. Chudacoff, Howard P. A NEW LOOK AT ETHNIC NEIGH-BORHOODS: RESIDENTIAL DISPERSION AND THE CONCEPT OF VISIBILITY IN A MEDIUM-SIZED CITY. *J. of Am. Hist. 1973 60(1): 76-93.* Compares foreign-born and native residential patterns in Omaha 1880-1920. Contrary to popular belief, there was no significant concentration of foreign-born residents in particular districts. Like native Americans, few foreign-born residents remained at the same address for 20 years. The same percentages of foreign-born and native residents tended to emigrate from the city, and those remaining made about the same number of moves. Moreover, the same volatility was found among upper and middle classes as among the poor, and among the "new immigrants" as among the old. Certain areas were still designated as "Bohemiantown" and the "Jewish section," not because of residential concentration but because of the visibility of ethnic churches, businesses, and social institutions. 8 tables, 28 notes. K. B. West

99. Conzen, Kathleen Neils. APPROACHES TO EARLY MIL-WAUKEE COMMUNITY HISTORY. *Milwaukee Hist. 1978 1(1-2): 4-12.* Several approaches to the early history of Milwaukee use earlier means of documenting community history to explore such areas as family structure, social mobility, and prestige.

100. Conzen, Kathleen Neils. IMMIGRANTS, IMMIGRANT NEIGHBORHOODS, AND ETHNIC IDENTITY: HISTORICAL IS-SUES. *J. of Am. Hist. 1979 66(3): 603-615.* Analyzes various interpretations attempting to explain the relationship between ethnic identity, neighborhood residence, and acculturation for immigrants, especially Germans, in eastern and midwestern American cities. Although scholars must abandon old assumptions about straight-line relationships between residence, assimilation, and cultural maintenance, they cannot afford to discount the potential role of the immigrant neighborhood itself in the process of immigrant adaptation. 37 notes. T. P. Linkfield

101. Cybriwsky, Roman A. SOCIAL ASPECTS OF NEIGHBOR-HOOD CHANGE. *Ann. of the Assoc. of Am. Geographers 1978 68(1): 17-33.* During the last decade, Fairmount, a small area in Philadelphia's inner city, has changed from a working-class neighborhood with a strong European-ethnic flavor to a revitalized, "fashionable" area with many young professionals. One step in the transition was the exclusion of blacks from the neighborhood. The influx of newcomers to Fairmount has altered traditional social patterns, and for some residents resulted in a declining quality of neighborhood life. J

102. Driedger, Leo. ETHNIC BOUNDARIES: A COMPARISON OF TWO URBAN NEIGHBORHOODS. *Sociol. and Social Res. 1978 62(2): 193-211.* This study in metropolitan Winnipeg shows that St. Boniface and the North End represent two "natural ethnic areas" with distinct urban boundaries. Territory, institutions, and culture were important boundary maintenance factors. The community of the North End, originally dominated by East European Jews, Ukrainians, and Poles is experiencing the process of invasion and succession as has been demonstrated in many other urban community studies. The Jews have moved to the suburbs taking their culture and institutions with them; the Ukrainians and Poles are also changing and adjusting to newcomers. The East European ethnic boundaries are giving way to a more heterogeneous, multi-ethnic invasion by native Indian and south European newcomers. In contrast, the community of north St. Boniface has remained essentially a French urban neighborhood for 160 years. The urban French community by means of residential segregation, with limited out mobility, has maintained a French culture within a fairly complete ethnic institutional framework. The unique French St. Boniface urban community does not follow the numerous other invasion-succession patterns which have been reported. This paper explores possible reasons for the two differential community change patterns within the same metropolitan area. J

103. Duis, Perry. THE SALOON IN A CHANGING CHICAGO. *Chicago Hist. 1975-76 4(4): 214-224.* Describes the ups and downs of the liquor industry and Chicago saloons until prohibition (1920).

104. Fisher, Robert. COMMUNITY ORGANIZING AND CITI-ZEN PARTICIPATION: THE EFFORTS OF THE PEOPLE'S INSTI-TUTE IN NEW YORK CITY, 1910-1920. *Social Service Rev. 1977 51(3): 474-490.* Analyzes the goals, methods, and organizational structure of the People's Institute of New York City, an urban reform group which sought, 1910-20, to organize working class immigrants on the neighborhood level as part of a larger national organization seeking to employ public schools as community centers.

105. Garonzik, Joseph. THE RACIAL AND ETHNIC MAKE-UP OF BALTIMORE NEIGHBORHOODS, 1850-1870. *Maryland Hist. Mag. 1976 71(3): 392-402.* Analyzes the significant changes in Baltimore's economy and population and the effects on spatial patterns. Along with a great influx of immigrants after 1865, mainly of German stock, Baltimore had more blacks than any northern city, proximity according to ethnicity apparently having little to do with choice of residence. Occupational proximity was more important, and with the increasing differentiation of the city into a central industrial district and areas of specialized production, working class, commercial, and professional people grouped themselves accordingly. Residential analysis shows that by 1870 a householder's residence, occupation, and ethnic origin were more closely related than origin and residence alone. Baltimore remained a patchwork of nationalities with white natives, Germans, Irish, and blacks scattered throughout the "social quilt" in heterogeneous neighborhoods. Not until the "new immigration" arrived did the city lose this integrated character. From the author's 1974 thesis at SUNY, Stony Brook, and secondary works; 2 tables, 20 notes. G. J. Bobango

106. Goetze, Rolf. URBAN NEIGHBORHOODS IN TRANSI-TION. *Social Policy 1979 10(2): 53-57.* Discusses housing demands and availability, and changes in urban neighborhoods since 1890, and their relationship to populations, using this information to predict trends and the role of public policy in city planning.

107. Greeley, Andrew M. AN IRISH-ITALIAN? *Italian Americana 1975 1(2): 239-245.* An Irish American priest who grew up on the West Side of Chicago during the 1920's reminisces about the coming of Italian Americans to his neighborhood, discusses negative ethnic stereotypes, and offers a corrective sociological profile of these immigrants. S

108. Greer, Edward. MONOPOLY AND COMPETITIVE CAPI-TAL IN THE MAKING OF GARY, INDIANA. *Sci. and Soc. 1976-77 40(4): 465-478.* Gary, Indiana, was not a company town in the historically accepted definition of the term. The planners of US Steel Corporation tried to create a community in which labor unrest would be subdued owing to the position of dependency on the corporation by its skilled workers. The corporation preferred control of Gary by respectable middle class elements rather than direct company control. The growth of an urban bourgeois class of many ethnic origins caused the corporation to compromise its position on at least peripheral matters in order to maintain its basic pervasive and immensely influential position in the city. N. Lederer

109. Guest, Avery M. and Weed, James A. ETHNIC RESIDEN-TIAL SEGREGATION: PATTERNS OF CHANGE. *Am. J. of Sociol. 1976 81(5): 1088-1111.* This study traces changes in patterns of ethnic residential segregation for Cleveland from 1930 to 1970 and for Boston and Seattle from 1960 to 1970. For Cleveland the data indicate some clear declines in residential segregation since 1930 for "new" southern and eastern European ethnic groups; "old" groups, however, actually increased in segregation. Between 1960 and 1970, we could find few changes in patterns of ethnic segregation for Boston, Cleveland, and Seattle. On the whole, we found that differences in residential segregation among ethnic groups, both cross-sectionally and over time, were highly related to differences in social status. It is clear, nevertheless, that ethnic segregation would continue to exist even if social status differences among ethnic groups disappeared. J

110. Hawkes, Roland K. SPATIAL PATTERNING OF URBAN POPULATION CHARACTERISTICS. *Am. J. of Sociol. 1973 78(5): 1216-1235.* "This paper develops a mathematical expression of the classic zone and sector phenomena in the distribution of residential neighborhood characteristics in urban areas. Problems of evaluation are discussed, and the use of the model is illustrated with the 1960 census tract statistics for Baltimore, Maryland." J

111. Hershberg, Theodore; Burstein, Alan N.; Ericksen, Eugene P.; Greenberg, Stephanie; and Yancey, William L. A TALE OF THREE

CITIES: BLACKS AND IMMIGRANTS IN PHILADELPHIA: 1850-1880, 1930 AND 1970. *Ann. of the Am. Acad. of Pol. and Social Sci. 1979 441: 55-81.* Determining whether the black experience was unique, or similar to that of earlier white immigrant groups, is central to the debate over whether blacks should be the beneficiaries of special compensatory legislation in the present. To answer this question requires interdisciplinary research that combines a comparative ethnic, an urban, and a historical perspective. Thus we observe the experience of three waves of immigrants to Philadelphia: the Irish and Germans who settled in the "Industrializing City" of the mid-to-late 19th century; the Italians, Poles and Russian Jews who came to the "Industrial City" at the turn of the 20th century; and blacks who arrived in the "Post-Industrial City" in their greatest numbers after World War II. Analysis of the city's changing opportunity structure and ecological form, and the racial discrimination encountered shows the black experience to be unique in kind and degree. Significant changes in the structures that characterized each of the "three cities" call into question our standing notion of the assimilation process.
J

112. Holt, Glen E. ST. LOUIS OBSERVED "FROM TWO DIFFERENT WORLDS": AN EXPLORATION OF THE CITY THROUGH FRENCH AND ENGLISH TRAVELERS' ACCOUNTS, 1874-1889. *Missouri Hist. Soc. Bull. 1973 29(2): 63-87.* Analyzes the impressions of French and English visitors to St. Louis. British and French visitors alike were favorably impressed by the Eads Bridge and other engineering achievements, and by the city's burgeoning commerce and its "many fine residential sections." French and English visitors responded differently to the social and cultural *milieu.* British visitors tended to accept the city "on its own terms," while the French probed more deeply and critically into ethnic, racial, and religious matters. 104 notes.
H. T. Lovin

113. Hunter, Albert. THE URBAN NEIGHBORHOOD: ITS ANALYTICAL AND SOCIAL CONTEXTS. *Urban Affairs Q. 1979 14(3): 267-288.* Each of the articles in this issue of *Urban Affairs Quarterly* devoted to neighborhoods casts them as unique spatial/social links between people and the larger forces of society. Concludes that the importance of each of the neighborhood typologies may be their academic and policy utility. The author's analysis of the stages of neighborhood evolution suggests that they are residues of urban macroforces, but he finds that they still function independently in such areas as political organization, socialization, and sociability. Suspects that future scholarship will focus on neighborhoods as a component in national political federations and as an emotional base in an increasingly narrow unrooted society. Biblio.
L. N. Beecher

114. Janis, Ralph. FLIRTATION AND FLIGHT: ALTERNATIVES TO ETHNIC CONFRONTATION IN WHITE ANGLO-AMERICAN PROTESTANT DETROIT, 1880-1940. *J. of Ethnic Studies 1978 6(2): 1-17.* Examines a large sampling of marriage and baptismal registers, membership rosters, and officer lists of Detroit churches to demonstrate the changing class, cultural, and spatial composition of church-related social organizations over two generations. Solid social interdicts existed against ethnic mixture in 1880. Ethnic uniformity in marriage and membership had declined by 1906, but was resurrected after this by the impact of the auto boom. Ethnocentrism, however, represented a rational 19th-century-rooted search for order by the large majority, who sought viable "acts of adjustment to urban change." Vigilantism, Klanism, and demagoguery were the exception, not the rule, of Detroit Protestants, in their search for "the creative use of social distance, not confrontation," in making the transition to new and modified social boundaries. Primary and secondary research; 2 tables, 26 notes.
G. J. Bobango

115. Jarrett, Walter. [FROM NEW AMSTERDAM TO THE BIG APPLE].
NEW YORK. PART I: WHEN THE BIG APPLE WAS NEW AMSTERDAM. *Mankind 1975 5(3): 10-13, 52-55.*
NEW YORK. PART II: FROM THE REVOLUTION TO FUN CITY. *Mankind 1975 5(4): 10-13, 60-63.*
The political, economic, and social history of New York City in the 17th-20th centuries includes the colonial governments of the Netherlands and Great Britain, the divided loyalties during the American Revolution, the impact of immigration, and the fortunes and innovations of businessmen.

116. Kantrowitz, Nathan. RACIAL AND ETHNIC RESIDENTIAL SEGREGATION: BOSTON, 1830-1970. *Ann. of the Am. Acad. of Pol. and Social Sci. 1979 441: 41-54.* Residential segregation in Boston between European ethnic population has declined little during the 20th century. Racial segregation rose during the 19th and early 20th century, but has remained stable since about 1940, prior to the expansion of the city's Negro population. These conclusions indicate that racial segregation is but an extension of the pattern of ethnic separation, especially since Asian and Latin ethnics show similar patterns in the contemporary city. Moreover, segregation levels are only slightly lower in the 1970 SMSA suburban ring than they are in the central city. We suggest that this demographic record is relevant to issues of Boston's public school desegregation controversy.
J

117. Katz, Harriet. WORKERS' EDUCATION OR EDUCATION FOR THE WORKER? *Social Service Rev. 1978 52(2): 265-274.* Jane Addams's Hull House educational programs for the working class in Chicago stressed humanities, fine arts, and folk handicrafts and reflected her educational philosophy of enrichment of social relations and human existence, 1890's.

118. Kingsdale, Jon M. THE "POOR MAN'S CLUB": SOCIAL FUNCTIONS OF THE URBAN WORKING-CLASS SALOON. *Am. Q. 1973 25(4): 472-489.* Turn-of-the-century saloons provided an all-male neighborhood social and political center for urban industrial and ethnic groups conserving and reinforcing working-class and ethnic values. Saloons retarded assimilation toward the Anglo-Saxon Protestant ideal and were, therefore, more than symbolic enemies to Prohibitionists concerned with conserving traditional American values and family life. Based on secondary sources; 65 notes.
W. D. Piersen

119. Kocolowski, Gary P. STABILIZING MIGRATION TO LOUISVILLE AND CINCINNATI, 1865-1901. *Cincinnati Hist. Soc. Bull. 1979 37(1): 23-47.* Describes efforts to regulate urban migration patterns of immigrants to Louisville and Cincinnati.

120. Kopf, Edward. UNTARNISHING THE DREAM: MOBILITY, OPPORTUNITY, AND ORDER IN MODERN AMERICA. *J. of Social Hist. 1977 11(2): 206-227.* Most quantitative studies of 19th- and 20th-century communities have demonstrated that high levels of personal residential mobility have been common in American life. A study of Chelsea, Massachusetts, focusing on 1915, indicates a high degree of mobility, but much of it within ethnic neighborhoods. There was also substantial external migration, but Chelsea contained a highly stable adult population. This study indicates that more research is needed concerning how geographic mobility affected social integration, not social disintegration. 3 maps, 10 tables, 39 notes.
L. E. Ziewacz

121. Korman, Gerd. HISTORY FOR SOCIAL SCIENCE. *Rev. in Am. Hist. 1978 6(1): 68-71.* Review article prompted by Kathleen Neils Conzen's *Immigrant Milwaukee, 1836-1860: Accommodation and Community in a Frontier City* (Cambridge, Mass.: Harvard U. Pr., 1976).

122. Lawson, Michael L. OMAHA, A CITY OF FERMENT: SUMMER OF 1919. *Nebraska Hist. 1977 58(3): 395-417.* Examines the tensions and frustrations accompanying peacetime adjustment in Omaha. Mentions inflation, the lifting of a wartime strike ban, ethnic and racial tensions, prohibition, woman suffrage, municipal corruption, and returning veterans. This places the September race riot in a meaningful context.
R. Lowitt

123. Leonard, Henry B. THE IMMIGRANTS' PROTECTIVE LEAGUE OF CHICAGO, 1908-1921. *J. of the Illinois State Hist. Soc. 1973 66(3): 271-284.* The unprecedented numbers of immigrants from southern and eastern Europe were called racially inferior by people descended from northwestern Europeans. The Immigrants' Protective League, founded in Chicago in 1908 by Jane Addams and other reformers, helped the new immigrants in urban-industrial American life. The league sought broad government intervention to protect the immigrants in employment, education, and the courts. Despite some failures, the league guided immigrants in an imaginative, enlightened, and humane way that acquainted the public with their problems. Based on the league's annual reports and papers in the manuscript division of the Library of the University of Illinois, Chicago Circle; 2 photos, 34 notes.
A. C. Aimone

124. Leonard, Stephen J. THE IRISH, ENGLISH AND GERMANS IN DENVER, 1860-1890. *Colorado Mag. 1977 54(2): 126-153.* During 1860-90, Irish, English, and German Americans were consistently among Denver's larger nationality groups. The Germans had both community solidarity and skills the other nationalities lacked. Denver was faster than larger American cities in acculturation, possibly because of small numbers of immigrants and their familiarity with English. Toleration persisted through the 1880's. Primary sources; 12 illus., 121 notes.
O. H. Zabel

125. Luckingham, Bradford. IMMIGRANT LIFE IN EMERGENT SAN FRANCISCO. *J. of the West 1973 12(4): 600-617.* San Francisco was unrivalled in its attraction of immigrant groups during the gold rush era. Religious, racial, ethnic, and regional groups tended to settle in clusters in the city. Each group attempted to be self-contained, united, and more or less unfriendly to everyone else. The strength of unity often determined the success or failure of the group. Group policies gradually coalesced under one of the major political parties. The Vigilance Committees were in part politically oriented. The establishment of a city government was inspired by the desire to contain the growing power of immigrant groups. 31 notes.
V. L. Human

126. Luker, Ralph E. RELIGION AND SOCIAL CONTROL IN THE NINETEENTH-CENTURY AMERICAN CITY. *J. of Urban Hist. 1976 2(3): 363-368.* In earlier years, historians assumed that clergymen and religiously aroused laypeople forged and led reform movements because it was their innate nature to do good and help their fellow man. Current literature, such as in Nathan L. Huggins' *Protestants Against Poverty: Boston's War on Poverty, 1870-1900,* David J. Pivar's *Purity Crusade: Sexual Morality and Social Control, 1868-1900,* and Carroll Smith Rosenberg's *Religion and the Rise of the American City: The New York City Mission Movement, 1812-1870,* shows the religious reformers to be conservatives interested primarily in social control and the preservation of established moral and social values. Examines this social control thesis and the scholarly merits of the works reviewed. Concludes that 19th-century religious reform was not aimed simply at social control or social liberation but at striking a new balance between the two. 8 notes.
T. W. Smith

127. Margon, Arthur. INDIANS AND IMMIGRANTS: A COMPARISON OF GROUPS NEW TO THE CITY. *J. of Ethnic Studies 1977 4(4): 17-28.* Questions the widespread view that "Native Americans are beset with special, nearly insurmountable difficulties because of the dissonance between their traditional cultures and the demands and patterns of modern urban living." At issue is how much group experience is the special provenance of the group and how much an aspect of the process of moving to and coping with an alien environment. Federally assisted Indian relocatees make up, at best, only one-third of urban Indians, so research efforts must be redirected. "There is evidence that many Native Americans migrate . . . and adapt quite successfully to urban life." This is because migration is not directly from reservation to city, but involves a set of "intermediate steps" to small town, small city, and large city. A 50% return rate to the reservation is no more extreme than that of many other immigrant groups. The whites' labeling of all Indians as "Indians" regardless of tribal differences is the same process of ignoring intragroup differences that Italians or Jews experienced. Native Americans face a situation no different from that faced before World War II by the still unhomogenized members of European ethnic groups. Secondary sources; 21 notes.
G. J. Bobango

128. Marsh, Margaret Sammartino. SUBURBANIZATION AND THE SEARCH FOR COMMUNITY: RESIDENTIAL DECENTRALIZATION IN PHILADELPHIA, 1880-1900. *Pennsylvania Hist. 1977 44(2): 99-116.* During 1880-1900, peripheral settlements in northwest Philadelphia began to become modern suburban areas. Reformers then considered suburbanization a panacea for many social problems. With the exception of Overbrook Farms, the area saw haphazard residential development. Overbrook Farms was a planned community for lower upper class families. In 1880, the typical resident of northwest Philadelphia was a laborer living near his place of employment. The area had relatively few churches and social institutions. By 1900, population had grown from 14,250 to 43,708, and mostly middle class and working class families had moved into the area. The many churches and social institutions provided cultural separation in a community that generally was not characterized by physical segregation. Primary sources; photo, map, 2 tables, 33 notes.
D. C. Swift

129. McClymer, John F. THE PITTSBURGH SURVEY, 1907-1914: FORGING AN IDEOLOGY IN THE STEEL DISTRICT. *Pennsylvania Hist. 1974 41(2): 169-186.* The *Pittsburgh Survey,* first published in 1909 in three issues of *Charities and the Commons,* was undertaken in 1907 by professors, social workers, charitable societies, and ethnic associations. It reflects the essentially moderate attitudes of a new class of social engineers who thought it possible to accurately measure the social effects of industrialization and to suggest viable remedies. Surveys of other industrial cities were modelled on this effort. Illus., 52 notes.
D. C. Swift

130. McIlwain, Josephine. TWELVE BLOCKS: A STUDY OF ONE SEGMENT OF PITTSBURGH'S SOUTH SIDE, 1880-1915. *Western Pennsylvania Hist. Mag. 1977 60(4): 351-370.* Examines population changes in the Twenty-sixth Ward of Pittsburgh, Pennsylvania, 1880-1915, due to changes in industrial focus from the iron and glass industries (requiring skilled laborers) to the steel industry (requiring unskilled laborers).

131. McTigue, Geraldine. PATTERNS OF RESIDENCE: HOUSING DISTRIBUTION BY COLOR IN TWO LOUISIANA TOWNS, 1860-1880. *Louisiana Studies 1976 15(4): 345-388.* Examines housing patterns in Opelousas, the parish (county) seat, and Washington, the main port, of St. Landry Parish. Each had a population of about 600 persons. No strict dichotomy of integration-segregation existed in either town. Foreign-born Caucasians were much more apt to live in integrated areas than were native-born whites. Both towns were somewhat integrated in 1860; by 1880 all integration had disappeared in Washington and the percentage had declined in Opelousas. Economics was not the determining factor; rather it was the rate at which blacks entered the community. Concludes that integration was possible though status was fixed; with growing numbers and fuller freedom, integration declined. Based on US Census Reports and secondary sources; 24 tables, 32 notes.
J. Buschen

132. Merriam, Paul G. THE "OTHER PORTLAND": A STATISTICAL NOTE ON FOREIGN-BORN, 1860-1910. *Oregon Hist. Q. 1979 80(3): 258-268.* Portland has long been characterized as a transplanted New England commercial city. However, demographic statistics convincingly shatter this myth and demonstrate that Portland was built and populated by numerous ethnic groups. By 1860, one-quarter of the city's population was foreign-born. The percentage rose to 31.1 by 1870. 3 illus., 4 tables, 12 notes.
D. R. McDonald

133. Montgomery, David. THE NEW URBAN HISTORY. *Rev. in Am. Hist. 1974 2(4): 498-504.* Review article prompted by Dennis Clark's *The Irish in Philadelphia: Ten Generations of Urban Experience* (Philadelphia: Temple U. Pr., 1973), Allen F. Davis and Mark H. Haller's *The Peoples of Philadelphia: A History of Ethnic Groups and Lower-Class Life, 1790-1940* (Philadelphia: Temple U. Pr., 1973), and Estelle F. Feinstein's *Stamford in the Gilded Age: The Political Life of a Connecticut Town 1868-1893* (Stamford, Conn.: The Stamford Historical Society, 1973) which outlines the books' contents, discusses the books' relation to the "new urban history," mentions the authors' methodologies, use of data, theoretical assumptions, and historical assumptions, and assesses the books' contributions to understanding the history of "ordinary people" living in American cities.

134. Noel, Thomas J. THE IMMIGRANT SALOON IN DENVER. *Colorado Mag. 1977 54(3): 200-219.* From the Civil War through Prohibition, Denver's immigrant population relied on saloons as haven for old world culture and introduction to the new home. German, Irish, Jewish, Italian, and Slavic immigrants relied on taverns as important community centers to stimulate social, political, and economic activities. Primary and secondary sources; 7 illus., 51 notes.
D. A. Hartford

135. Passi, Michael M. IMMIGRANTS AND THE CITY: PROBLEMS OF INTERPRETATION AND SYNTHESIS IN RECENT WHITE ETHNIC HISTORY. *J. of Ethnic Studies 1976 4(2): 61-72.* A review essay prompted by three ethnic studies: Dean R. Esslinger's *Immigrants and the City: Ethnicity and Mobility in a Nineteenth Century*

Midwestern City; Edward R. Kantowicz' *Polish-American Politics in Chicago, 1880-1940*; and Josef J. Barton's *Peasants and Strangers: Italians, Rumanians, and Slovaks in an American City, 1890-1950*. All are products of the academic trends and ferment in ethnic history since 1960. Esslinger's study is "new urban history" on social mobility in South Bend, Indiana, with "no surprises in its methodology or in its findings," but with "an excessive faith in quantitative methods" and some serious flaws in conceptual design. Kantowicz' book "demonstrates the limits of old-fashioned narrative history in writing about ethnicity," and offers at bottom only the standard chronicle of leaders and elections. Barton's work is the most genuine accomplishment, although an ultimately disappointing book by its leap to the triple-melting pot notion as a conclusion and its sparse attention to second-generation family formation. All of the studies show the need to get beyond the unilinear theories of cultural change and recognize the dialectical relationship between the immigrant and American society.

G. J. Bobango

136. Pessen, Edward. FRUITS OF THE NEW URBAN HISTORY: THE SOCIOLOGY OF SMALL NINETEENTH-CENTURY CITIES. *J. of Urban Hist. 1978 5(1): 93-108*. Review article prompted by Kathleen Conzen's *Immigrant Milwaukee, 1836-1860*; Alan Dawley's *Class and Community: The Industrial Revolution in Lynn*; Michael B. Katz's *The People of Hamilton, Canada West*; Eric H. Monkkonen's *The Dangerous Class: Crime and Poverty in Columbus Ohio 1860-1865*; and Michael P. Weber's *Social Change in an Industrial Town: Patterns of Progress in Warren, Pennsylvania, From Civil War to World War I*. Includes detailed critiques of each work and considers their shared features. All tend to embrace some form of "new urban history" usually either of the Thernstrom or Thompson mold and all tend to neglect or to subordinate politics. Sadly for comparative purposes all use sufficiently different techniques so that their precise findings are not easily comparable. 7 notes.

T. W. Smith

137. Power, Mary G. ETHNIC CONCENTRATION AND SOCIO-ECONOMIC STATUS IN METROPOLITAN AREAS. *Ethnicity 1978 5(3): 266-273*. Examination of data derived from standard metropolitan statistical areas (SMSA) indicates confirmation of R. Breton's findings that the institutional completeness of large ethnic communities attracts and holds those ethnic group members with the lowest education levels and skills. Those SMSA's having the lowest concentration of foreign stock residents are also those in which the latter hold the highest socioeconomic status. On the other hand, in all SMSA's the socioeconomic status of native whites of native parentage and nonwhites was highest in areas having the largest foreign stock concentration. 5 tables.

N. Lederer

138. Prior, Moody E. LOST (AND FOUND) CITIES. *Am. Scholar 1976-77 46(4): 506-513*. Uses Chicago as a model of the American city. Traces architectural and ethnic epochs since its beginning.

F. F. Harling

139. Renshaw, Patrick. THE BLACK GHETTO 1890-1940. *J. of Am. Studies [Great Britain] 1974 8(1): 41-59*. Surveys the "ghetto experience" of Negroes to 1940. When Negroes migrated from the rural South to cities, their experiences differed markedly from the experiences of European immigrants in the same urban centers. By 1940, blacks became "locked in" and were unable to escape urban ills in the ways that other ethnic groups had overcome the shortcomings of the urban situation. Based on secondary sources; 51 notes.

H. T. Lovin

140. Rogers, Theresa F. and Friedman, Nathalie. DECENTRALIZING CITY GOVERNMENT: THE CITIZEN SURVEY AS A GUIDE FOR PLANNING AND IMPLEMENTING INSTITUTIONAL CHANGE. *Administration and Soc. 1978 10(2): 177-202*. Assesses reactions to city government decentralization plans in New York City according to responders' ethnicity, the sociopolitical composition of their neighborhoods, and their appraisal of city services, 1974.

141. Schwartz, Joel. MORRISANIA'S VOLUNTEER FIREMEN, 1848-1874: THE LIMITS OF LOCAL INSTITUTIONS IN A METROPOLITAN AGE. *New York Hist. 1974 55(2): 159-178*. Morrisania, now a neighborhood in the South Bronx, was an independent township until its annexation by New York City in 1874. One of the primary factors in Morrisania's desire for annexation was that its volunteer fire depart-

ment had degenerated into a rowdy and criminal element. Instead of fighting fires, Morrisania's Irish and German fire companies often fought each other in the streets of Morrisania. The appeal of New York City's professional and technologically modern fire department persuaded Morrisania's business community that merger with New York City was in their economic interest. Based on primary and secondary works; 5 illus., 40 notes.

G. Kurland

142. Shapiro, Edward S. ROBERT A. WOODS AND THE SETTLEMENT HOUSE IMPULSE. *Social Service Rev. 1978 52(2): 215-226*. Initially suspected by Catholics as an agency of Protestant proselytization, Boston's South End House, founded by Robert A. Woods, was intended to slow the city's growing religious, ethnic, and social heterogeneity by providing a sense of community; covers 1891-1900's.

143. Starr, Stephen Z. PROSIT!!!!: A NON-COSMIC TOUR OF THE CINCINNATI SALOON. *Cincinnati Hist. Soc. Bull. 1978 36(3): 175-191*. Describes saloons in Cincinnati, Ohio, 1840-1920, and the growth of lager beer breweries.

144. Still, Bayrd. MILWAUKEE REVISITED: A REVIEW ESSAY. *Wisconsin Mag. of Hist. 1977 60(4): 330-333* Review article prompted by *Immigrant Milwaukee, 1836-1860: Accommodation and Community in a Frontier City* (1976) by Kathleen Neils Conzen, *Technology and Reform: Street Railways and the Growth of Milwaukee, 1887-1900* (1974) by Clay McShane, *Milwaukee: A Contemporary Urban Profile* (1971) by Henry J. Schmandt, John C. Goldbach, and Donald Vogel, *Yesterday's Milwaukee* (1976) by Robert W. Wells, and an article, "Housing and Services in an Immigrant Neighborhood: Milwaukee's Ward 14," by Roger D. Simon in the *Journal of Urban History,* 1976. Conzen's book is a study of the Germans, while Simon's article analyzes the Poles. Wells's is a pictorial history.

N. C. Burckel

145. Stolarik, Mark. AN ANALYSIS—ETHNIC NEIGHBORHOODS. *Jednota Annual Furdek 1976 15: 54-58*. Contrasts the WASP concept of social mobility with that of white, ethnic, urban Catholics, suggesting that opposition to integration is not racism but a defense by ethnic Catholics of their way of life, which, unlike the Protestant ethic, gives stability to American society.

146. Sullivan, Margaret Lo Piccolo. ST. LOUIS ETHNIC NEIGHBORHOODS, 1850-1930: AN INTRODUCTION. *Missouri Hist. Soc. Bull. 1977 33(2): 64-76*. Traces the development of ethnic neighborhoods, in St. Louis, Missouri, in which persons of French, German, Irish, and South and East European origins lived. German and Irish immigrants to St. Louis predominated during 1820-60. Substantial migrations of South and East Europeans occurred during 1900-30 and were followed by major Negro migrations after 1930. Formation of Black ghettos was hastened by the passage of a segregation ordinance in 1916. Based on secondary works and government documents; 3 photos, 40 notes.

H. T. Lovin

147. Sutherland, John F. THE ORIGINS OF PHILADELPHIA'S OCTAVIA HILL ASSOCIATION: SOCIAL REFORM IN THE "CONTENTED" CITY. *Pennsylvania Mag. of Hist. and Biog. 1975 99(1): 20-44*. An analysis of the philosophy, works, and influence of the Octavia Hill Association, a private reform group in Philadelphia dedicated to the improvement of the lot of the urban poor. The association purchased and improved homes, introduced strict sanitation measures, and meticulously avoided disrupting established neighborhoods. Its members lived in the affected neighborhoods but were socially not part of them. Their efforts were handicapped by the philosophy of the time but eventually led to governmental reform programs which enjoyed some success. 46 notes.

V. L. Human

148. Thernstrom, Stephan T. THE NEW URBAN HISTORY. Delzell, Charles F., ed. *The Future of History: Essays in the Vanderbilt University Centennial Symposium* (Nashville: Vanderbilt U. Pr., 1977): 43-51. The term "new urban history," first employed in 1969, is misleading because it extends back to the 1930's. Major early contributions in the field included Oscar Handlin's *Boston's Immigrants* (1941) and Frank and Harriet Owsley's *Plain Folk of the Old South* (1949). During the 1950's works of this genre often were overlooked or quickly forgotten. For

the future, the geographical and temporal scopes of urban inquiries should be broadened. The blue collar-white collar delineation of stratification must be made less crude, and less emphasis should be placed on male heads of households. A greater awareness of migration is needed. In addition, the pitfalls of quantification must be avoided; the most thorough mastery of the new methods is not sufficient to make a good historian. 15 notes.   P. L. Solodkin

149. Travis, Anthony R. ESSAYS ON ETHNIC HISTORY. *Mid-America 1978 60(1): 43-48.* Review article prompted by three works on minority and ethnic groups in New York City and Chicago. *The Golden Door,* by Thomas Kessner, compares Italian and Jewish immigrants in New York City and concludes that Jewish immigrants were better skilled to show upward social mobility than were their Italian counterparts. *The Education of an Urban Minority,* by James W. Sanders, investigates public education and its impact on Catholic Church members in Chicago. To most Catholics of the past 150 years, Chicago public schools showed an anti-Catholic and anti-European bias. *Culture and the City,* by Helen Horowitz, analyzes cultural philanthropy in Chicago from 1880 to World War I, and shows the relations of the business and financial elite to culture and philanthropy.
                                                                    J. M. Lee

150. Vinyard, JoEllen McNergney. ON THE FRINGE IN PHILADELPHIA. *J. of Urban Hist. 1975 1(4): 492-498.* Review article prompted by Dennis Clark's *The Irish in Philadelphia: Ten Generations of Urban Experience* (Philadelphia: Temple U. Pr., 1973) and Allen F. Davis and Mark H. Haller's *The Peoples of Philadelphia: History of Ethnic Groups and Lower-Class Life* 1790-1940 (Philadelphia: Temple U. Pr., 1973).

151. Walch, Timothy. CATHOLIC SOCIAL INSTITUTIONS AND URBAN DEVELOPMENTS: THE VIEW FROM NINETEENTH-CENTURY CHICAGO AND MILWAUKEE. *Catholic Hist. Rev. 1978 64(1): 16-32.* The Catholic Church committed itself to the improvement of American life by establishing a variety of urban social institutions, including schools, hospitals, and asylums. The impact of the Church's efforts, however, varied from one city to the next. In Eastern cities, Catholic institutions served immigrants almost exclusively. But the newness of Chicago and Milwaukee and their drastic need for social institutions precipitated a different kind of experience for the Catholic Church in the Midwest. The Church mobilized quickly and offered these cities needed hospitals, asylums and schools. Non-Catholic leaders in Chicago and Milwaukee accepted these institutions with gratitude because they made their cities more attractive and helped to insure future growth. The story of Catholic social institutions in Chicago and Milwaukee highlights the complexity of relations between Catholics and non-Catholics in urban areas and emphasizes the need to look at the Church in a number of regional settings to gain a balanced picture of the American Catholic experience.   A

152. Waltzer, Kenneth. URBAN AMERICA: BOILING POT AND MELTING POT. *Rev. in Am. Hist. 1979 7(2): 241-246.* Review article prompted by Ronald H. Bayor's *Neighbors in Conflict: The Irish, Germans, Jews, and Italians of New York City, 1929-1941* (Baltimore, Md.: The Johns Hopkins U. Pr., 1978).

153. Weiner, Lynn. "OUR SISTER'S KEEPERS": THE MINNEAPOLIS WOMAN'S CHRISTIAN ASSOCIATION AND HOUSING FOR WORKING WOMEN. *Minnesota Hist. 1979 46(5): 189-200.* In the late 19th century, many young women made their way to Minneapolis to find work, coming from rural areas and from Europe. The paucity of inexpensive boardinghouses available to these women and the consequent fear that poverty would drive the women into prostitution and other forms of criminal behavior, generated an effort on the part of middle and upper class Minneapolis women to provide suitable, safe and cheap housing for women. Various buildings were donated to the Women's Christian Association (WCA) for this purpose, and both long-term and temporary housing arrangements were made available. The boardinghouses sponsored by the WCA were run along rather puritanical lines but seemed to fill the needs of generations of female sojourners in the city. The WCA also sponsored Travelers' Aid efforts in which young women arriving via train were met by agents and were given advice and assistance. By the end of World War I large-scale migration into Minneapolis had ended and the efforts of the WCA tapered off but did not die out.   N. Lederer

154. Wilkenfeld, Bruce M. NEW YORK CITY NEIGHBORHOODS, 1730. *New York Hist. 1976 57(2): 165-182.* Analyzes New York City tax lists and other statistical records of 1730 and reveals that the city's population was clustered in socioeconomically, ethnically, and religiously differentiated neighborhoods in the early 18th century. The author suggests that the patterns of residential clustering in American cities, generally believed to be indicative of change in the late 18th and 19th centuries, had begun in the early colonial cities. Map, 3 tables, 27 notes.   R. N. Lokken

155. Woods, Joseph Gerald. ON AMERICAN URBAN HISTORY. *Queen's Q. [Canada] 1976 83(3): 483-487.* A review article prompted by Adrian Cook's *The Arms of the Streets: The New York City Draft Riots of 1863* (Lexington: The U. Pr. of Kentucky, 1975) and Howard M. Gitelman's *The Workingmen of Waltham: Mobility in American Urban Industrial Development 1850-1890* (Baltimore: John Hopkins U. Pr., 1975), which are typical of the tendency to examine relatively small, isolated topics, in view of our inability to define urban history. Both studies make significant contributions, Cook's more traditional, Gitelman's a quantitative analysis of mobility, typifying the differences of subject matter and method which make consensus difficult.
                                                                    R. V. Ritter

156. Zunz, Olivier. DETROIT EN 1880: ESPACE ET SÉGRÉGATION [Detroit in 1880: Spatial clustering and segregation]. *Ann.: Écon., Soc., Civilisations [France] 1977 32(1): 106-136.* This study examines the population of neighborhoods sampled in Detroit in 1880. It determines the different forms of spatial clustering when Detroit was developing into a metropolis. Ethnic and social groups are identified in their physical environments; their characteristics and their distribution in the city are examined. The respective roles of ethnic and social factors as they contributed to the formation of clusters in the urban environment are measured. The data were collected from the first real estate atlas of the city of Detroit in 1885 and the census manuscript of 1880. A chi-squared statistic approach was developed for measuring and testing geographic clustering.   J

157. Zunz, Olivier. THE ORGANIZATION OF THE AMERICAN CITY IN THE LATE NINETEENTH CENTURY: ETHNIC STRUCTURE AND SPATIAL ARRANGEMENT IN DETROIT. *J. of Urban Hist. 1977 3(4): 443-466.* Examines a sample of blocks from the 1880 census of Detroit, Michigan, and analyzes the spatial organization of the city. Finds that there was strong ethnic-racial and occupational clustering. This clustering was weakest both in the center and at the periphery. A factoral analysis of the data revealed five cluster types: central area, residential center, east side, west sides, and peripheral area. 6 maps, 6 tables, 20 notes.   T. W. Smith

158. Zunz, Olivier; Ericson, William A.; and Fox, Daniel J. SAMPLING FOR A STUDY OF THE POPULATION AND LAND USE OF DETROIT IN 1880-1885. *Social Sci. Hist. 1977 1(3): 307-332.* One major problem of historical urban population studies has been that of sampling. To study the relationships of urban populations and space, either investigations of gross patterns of urban land use or intensive studies of neighborhoods or social groups have been undertaken. The goals of this study of Detroit in 1880 and 1885 were to represent the demographic, ethnic, and occupational make-up of Detroit, the geographic clustering in neighborhoods, and the interplay between various populations and land use. Presents a new sampling system they devised to overcome traditional sampling problems, and demonstrates its use in a pilot study. Based on the 1880 manuscript United States Census, an 1885 city atlas, and secondary sources; map, 6 tables, 7 fig., 25 notes.
                                                                    T. L. Savitt

Recent Immigration

159. Abrams, Elliott and Abrams, Franklin S. IMMIGRATION POLICY—WHO GETS IN AND WHY? *Public Interest 1975 (38): 3-29.* Analyzes the effects of the Immigration and Nationality Act, 1965, one of the most liberal immigration policies in the world.   S

160. Bernard, William S.   IMMIGRANTS AND REFUGEES: THEIR SIMILARITIES, DIFFERENCES, AND NEEDS.   *Int. Migration [Netherlands] 1976 14(4): 267-281.* Compares immigrants and refugees to determine their similarities, differences, and needs. Analyzes common factors affecting migrants, including reasons for resettlement, social and demographic characteristics, and problems relating to adjustment in a new environment. Similarities between immigrants and refugees are greater than their differences. Migrants face many problems after their arrival and few nations provide comprehensive programs for their special needs. Biblio.   R. C. Alltmont

161.   Chaney, Elsa M.   THE WORLD ECONOMY AND CONTEMPORARY MIGRATION.   *Int. Migration Rev. 1979 13(2): 204-212.* Surveys the literature on immigration from 1955 to 1976, noting that there is a growing tendency of migration to be considered temporary by the migrators, who now frequently have relatively short, inexpensive journeys between homeland and new residence.

162.   Donnelly, J. B.   THE VISION OF SCHOLARSHIP: JOHNS HOPKINS AFTER THE WAR.   *Maryland Hist. Mag. 1978 73(2): 137-162.* Reminisces on the unique combination of refugee professors and returning veterans at Johns Hopkins University in the postwar 1940's, the latter seen as the "most worldy wise and motivated generation ever to enter college in this country." The stern character of president Isaiah Bowman, from the workhorse branch of the genteel tradition, coincided with the intense traditionalist scholarship of the faculty and the seriousness of the vets to make Hopkins "a school for grinding." Offers vignettes of fabled professors such as the Sanskrit scholar Paul Dumont, Weimar Germany's Arno C. Schirokauer, pianist Artur Schnabel, philologist Leo Spitzer, philosopher Arthur Oncken Lovejoy and his disciple George Boas. The recession of 1949-50 and the outbreak of the Korean War meant an end to this singular era at Hopkins, but the heritage of learning and the example it provided of the "vision of scholarship" continue to influence countless lives. Primary writings, conversations, secondary works; 105 notes.   G. J. Bobango

163.   Iwańska, Alicja.   MODERN EXILES: SPANISH, POLISH, AMERICAN.   *Polish Rev. 1978 23(3): 47-61.* Analyzes within similar frames of reference exiles from Franco's Spain, Polish exiles from Nazi and Soviet occupation, and American exiles, mainly in Canada (Vietnam War draft resisters). Also, there are the political organizational structures taking the form of a "government in exile"; this category is of course less formal with the Americans. 34 notes.   R. V. Ritter

164.   Jackman, Jarrell C.   EXILES IN PARADISE: GERMAN EMIGRES IN SOUTHERN CALIFORNIA, 1933-1950.   *Southern California Q. 1979 61(2): 183-205.* During 1930's-40's hundreds of Jewish and non-Jewish Germans emigrated to southern California. They were mostly intellectuals and artists. Composers and musicians adjusted more easily than authors who faced the language barrier and the loss of their reading audience. Although literary figures such as Thomas Mann, Bertolt Brecht, and Franz Werfel enjoyed continuing career success, most author-exiles found it difficult to adapt to southern California's climate and life-style. They missed the seasonal changes, the pastime of walking, and the intellectual exchanges in coffeehouses. Finding employment was difficult, although the motion picture industry provided jobs for many exiles. Successful exiles in films organized the European Film Fund which aided émigrés in need. The misery of exile was a problem of the mind, for there were few physical discomforts. The main problem was adaptation to a foreign environment. After the war many émigrés left, having found their years in California less a time in paradise than a bearable

existence in a region known for its imperative uniqueness. Primary and secondary sources; 59 notes.   A. Hoffman

165.   Petrie, Graham.   EUROPEANS IN HOLLYWOOD: SUCCESS, FAILURE AND FRUSTRATION.   *Can. Rev. of Am. Studies [Canada] 1978 9(1): 125-128.* Two recent works survey the impact of European cinema artists and directors on American films and film making since 1920. Heavy foreign influxes to Hollywood came during the 1920's, near the end of the 1930's when artists fled from the Nazis, and lastly during the 1960's. The new volumes are: *Passport to Hollywood* (New York: McGraw Hill, 1976) by Don Whittemore and Philip Alan Cecchettini; and *The Hollywood Exiles* (London: Macdonald and Jane's, 1976) by John Baxter. 3 notes.   H. T. Lovin

166.   Tuttle, William M., Jr.   AMERICAN HIGHER EDUCATION AND THE NAZIS: THE CASE OF JAMES B. CONANT AND HARVARD UNIVERSITY'S "DIPLOMATIC RELATIONS" WITH GERMANY.   *Am. Studies (Lawrence, KS) 1979 20(1): 49-70.* Surveys some current efforts by foreign governments to influence American college education, and then traces Nazi efforts to propagandize their sentiments in the 1930's at Harvard University. For Harvard and its president, James B. Conant, this presented a dilemma for those who admired Germany but detested Hitler. The plight of displaced German academics added to this dilemma, for Harvard refused to accept any and this further encouraged the Nazis. By the mid-1930's Conant and Harvard, to quell mounting criticism, finally denounced Nazism. Primary and secondary sources; illus., 78 notes.   J. A. Andrew

167.   Veysey, Laurence.   FROM GERMANY TO AMERICA.   *Hist. of Educ. Q. 1973 13(4): 401-407.* Discusses the interrelationship of German and American intellectual life ca. 1917-60; refers to eight books on the subject.

168.   Wareing, J.   THE CHANGING PATTERN OF IMMIGRATION INTO THE UNITED STATES, 1956-1975.   *Geography [Great Britain] 1978 63(3): 220-224.* The Immigration and Nationality Act (US, 1965) was a turning point in US immigration laws. By 1968, the quota system of allocating visas was abolished, and replaced with a first-come first-served system, with quotas used only on a hemisphere-wide basis. One unexpected result was to increase the number of illegal aliens entering the United States. Immigrants were required to have jobs waiting for them in the United States, and Latin Americans were restricted by the Western Hemisphere quota. Illegal immigration into the United States, particularly from Mexico, has risen sharply since the passage of the 1965 act, and shows no signs of diminishing. In addition, the 1965 act resulted in increased immigration from southern Europe and Asia. Despite some flaws, the main problems with the 1965 act and US immigration policies in general, are caused by illegal aliens—a problem which, by its nature, cannot be directly affected by legislation. Table, 3 fig.

J. W. Leedom

Outmigration

169.   Finifter, Ada W.   AMERICAN EMIGRATION.   *Society 1976 13(5): 30-36.* Discusses political and economic aspects of emigration and expatriation from the United States 1946-70's.

170.   Pemberton, John R.   DIGGING DOWN UNDER.   *Colorado Q. 1976 24(3): 261-273.* The discovery of gold in Australia in the 1850's attracted many Americans, among them merchant George Francis Train.

2. THE RESPONSE TO IMMIGRATION

General

171.   Clark, Malcolm, Jr.   THE BIGOT DISCLOSED: 90 YEARS OF NATIVISM. *Oregon Hist. Q. 1974 75(2): 108-190.* A history of bigotry in the Pacific Northwest, illustrated in the nativism of the period on the religious, social, and political scenes. Extreme religious sectarianism was evident at a very early date, exemplified by strong anti-Catholicism. The treatment of Chinese laborers was equally shameful, and became the subject of inflammatory journalism and oratory. Henry Francis Bowers and his American Protective Association brought bigotry into the political arena, followed in turn by the Guardians of Liberty, and the revived Ku Klux Klan under the leadership of Edward Young Clark. The latter organization had phenomenal growth and influence in the 1920's, with Fred L. Gifford becoming the political boss of Oregon. Despite the Klan's demise, nativism unfortunately is not dead. 17 photos, 179 notes.
R. V. Ritter

172.   Garcia, Sandra A.   INSIDE THE MELTING POT AND PRESSURE COOKER. *J. of Intergroup Relations 1978 6(3): 3-18.* Compares attempts at assimilation of ethnic groups in the United States to that of Oriental (or "Black") Jews in Israel, 1954-77, comparing each country in terms of the nature and degree of racial and ethnic prejudice, the intent and the results of mass immigration, how prejudices are acted out in each country, and the strategies for survival and development of the dominant culture.

173.   Glazer, Nathan.   FEDERALISM AND ETHNICITY: THE EXPERIENCE OF THE UNITED STATES. *Publius 1977 7(4): 71-87.* The United States has met with mixed success in satisfying the interests of the many diverse ethnic groups in the nation. Three phases have occurred chronologically in the relationship between ethnicity and federalism: dominance of white, English-origin pioneers and settlers; numerous and politically active ethnic groups expressing their interests through state power; and federal standards for the protection of minority group and ethnic group rights. Federalism, while successful in preventing action against ethnic groups, has inhibited adoption of policies which would better suit the ethnic mix. 10 notes.
R. S. Barnard

174.   Gollobin, Ira.   THE BILL OF RIGHTS AND THE FOREIGN BORN. *Worldview 1975 18(7-8): 31-35.* Discusses provisions in the Bill of Rights and Constitutional law regarding the residency rights of foreign-born citizens, 1798-1970's, including issues in deportation during the Nixon Administration.

175.   Nord, Douglas C.   THE "PROBLEM" OF IMMIGRATION: THE CONTINUING PRESENCE OF THE STRANGER WITHIN OUR GATES. *Am. Rev. of Can. Studies 1978 8(2): 116-133.* In their studies of American and Canadian attitudes toward immigration, Louis Hartz and John Higham identified a generally-accepted "founding ideology" which provided for both "inclusionist" and "exclusionist" sentiments. This has resulted in shifting immigration policies. Generally, both countries have favored immigration as long as the immigrant groups readily adopted the "founding ideology" and were assimilated. In the 1880's and again in the 1970's, when groups such as Asians and Hispanics have appeared to reject assimilation, opposition to immigration has developed. Secondary sources and newspaper accounts; 43 notes.
G.-A. Patzwald

176.   Perlmutter, Philip.   THE AMERICAN STRUGGLE WITH ETHNIC SUPERIORITY. *J. of Intergroup Relations 1977 6(2): 31-56.* Surveys the American tradition of xenophobia and discrimination against different religions and ethnic groups, from the Mayflower Compact to the 1965 immigration law reform.

177.   Walker, Gerda S.   NATURALIZATION RECORDS IN GENEALOGICAL RESEARCH. *J. of the Am. Hist. Soc. of Germans from Russia 1978 1(2): 20-24.* Describes the history of naturalization laws in the United States, giving 1673 as the date of the first known foreigner to become a naturalized citizen.

The Early Period

178.   Agonito, Joseph.   ECUMENICAL STIRRINGS: CATHOLIC-PROTESTANT RELATIONS DURING THE EPISCOPACY OF JOHN CARROLL. *Church Hist. 1976 45(3): 358-373.* John Carroll became the first Roman Catholic Bishop of Baltimore in 1790. During his episcopacy, Catholic-Protestant relations were better than they had been during the colonial period and less violent than they would be during the mid-19th century nativist period. During Carroll's episcopacy, Protestants tempered their anti-Catholic sentiments and Catholics found that their separated brethren were not so bad. Carroll and other Catholic leaders hoped that this period was a prediction of future Protestant-Catholic relationships. Such hopes were dashed when the anti-Catholic sentiment was stirred up once more as waves of Catholic immigrants poured into this country. 116 notes.
M. D. Dibert

The Nineteenth-Century Response

179.   Baum, Dale.   KNOW-NOTHINGISM AND THE REPUBLICAN MAJORITY IN MASSACHUSETTS: THE POLITICAL REALIGNMENT OF THE 1850'S. *J. of Am. Hist. 1978 64(4): 959-986.* During the 1850's in Massachusetts, nativism and antislavery were distinct as political forces. The success of the Republican Party in Massachusetts after 1855 did not depend significantly upon attracting former Know-Nothing voters. Even though the Native American Party enjoyed a brief and phenomenal success in the state, it still represented only a temporary stop for many voters searching for a true antislavery party. The Know-Nothing Party played a minor role in the transition from a Whig to a Republican Party in Massachusetts politics. Uses ecological regression to trace voters' transitions and alignments during the 1850's. 25 tables, 53 notes.
T. P. Linkfield

180.   Camposeo, James M.   ANTI-CATHOLIC PREJUDICE IN EARLY NEW ENGLAND: THE DALEY-HALLIGAN MURDER TRIAL. *Hist. J. of Western Massachusetts 1978 6(2): 5-17.* In April 1806 Irish Catholic immigrants Dominic Daley and James Halligan were convicted (with virtually no defense and on a 13-year-old's shaky testimony) in Northampton, Massachusetts, of the murder in 1805 of Marcus Lyon. They were executed in June after hearing Mass and receiving extreme unction from Father (later Cardinal) Jean Louis Lefebvre de Cheverus, who in a sermon to some of the 15,000 people gathered for the execution tried to diminish the great deal of anti-Irish and anti-Catholic feeling among the people of Massachusetts. 4 illus., 70 notes.
W. H. Mulligan, Jr./S

181.   Cassell, Frank A.   THE GREAT BALTIMORE RIOT OF 1812. *Maryland Hist. Mag. 1975 70(3): 241-259.* Uncontrolled armed warfare between a Republican mob and a group of Federalist zealots barricaded in a Baltimore house during 26-29 July 1812 "demonstrated profound political and social divisions in Maryland" and showed "flaws in the American . . . character" such as intolerance, "uncompromising ideological confrontation, and . . . acceptance of violence as a substitute for constitutional process." Alexander Contee Hanson, editor of the *Federal Republican*, led in opposing war with Britain, blaming war fever on Irish immigrants and the "European rabble" which made up the Republican ultrapatriots, who destroyed his press late in June. Hanson organized a little band of partisans, including "Light-Horse Harry" Lee and General James Lingan, to secretly reenter the city and defy their opponents. The ensuing armed battles at the Charles Street House and the jail saw several killed and maimed and others ruthlessly beaten and tortured, while the authorities did almost nothing. Sympathy turned "almost overnight" against the Republicans, and Federalists won massive majorities later that year, ending a decade of state control by the Jeffersonians. Primary and secondary sources; 52 notes.
G. J. Bobango

182. Clark, Andrienne G. WHO MURDERED MARCUS LYON? *New-England Galaxy 1977 19(2): 15-21.* In strongly anti-Catholic, anti-Irish, and anti-immigrant Northampton, Massachusetts, Irish immigrants Dominic Daley and James Halligan were convicted with little defense and on doubtful evidence in April 1806, and hanged in June, for the murder of Marcus Lyon in November 1805. Father (later Cardinal) Jean Louis Lefebvre de Cheverus, in an eloquent sermon to Protestants waiting for the hanging, attempted to diminish their prejudice.
D. J. Engler

183. Clark, Dennis. INVENTION AND CONTENTION IN THE QUAKER CITY. *J. of Urban Hist. 1979 5(2): 265-271.* Review article prompted by Richard G. Miller, *Philadelphia—The Federalist City: A Study in Urban Politics, 1789-1801,* Bruce Sinclair, *Philadelphia's Philosopher Mechanics: A History of the Franklin Institute, 1824-1865,* Michael Feldberg, *The Philadelphia Riots of 1844: A Study of Ethnic Conflict,* and Philip S. Benjamin, *The Philadelphia Quakers in the Industrial Age, 1865-1920.* These books examine three great city-shaping forces: politics, religion, and technology. Their limitation is that they describe and explain the particular rather than the overall structure and complexity of the city. 9 notes.
T. W. Smith

184. Di Nunzio, Mario R. and Galkowski, Jan T. POLITICAL LOYALTY IN RHODE ISLAND—A COMPUTER STUDY OF THE 1850'S. *Rhode Island Hist. 1977 36(3): 93-95.* Whig leaders shifted their allegience to nativist and antislavery parties, though most conservatives were unwilling to support radical Republicans in the 1860-61 gubernatorial elections. Democratic leaders remained loyal to their party. Based on published documents. newspapers, and secondary accounts; table, 8 notes.
P. J. Coleman

185. George, Joseph, Jr. THE LINCOLN WRITINGS OF CHARLES P. T. CHINIQUY. *J. of the Illinois State Hist. Soc. 1976 69(1): 17-25.* Examines the claims of the anti-Catholic Charles P. T. Chiniquy (1809-99), a client of Abraham Lincoln in 1856 who later claimed to be a friend of Lincoln and an authority on his religious beliefs, particularly his alleged anti-Catholicism. Chiniquy's claims of a Catholic plot to assassinate Lincoln are false, but several historians have accepted his less sensational but equally unfounded writings about Lincoln's religion. Chiniquy autobiography, Lincoln's *Collected Works,* court records; 2 illus., 45 notes.
J/S

186. Gudelunas, William, Jr. NATIVISM AND THE DEMISE OF SCHUYLKILL COUNTY WHIGGERY: ANTI-SLAVERY OR ANTI-CATHOLICISM. *Pennsylvania Hist. 1978 45(3): 225-236.* The Schuylkill County, Pennsylvania, Whigs disintegrated in 1853-54 because they were not the strong anti-Catholic and prohibitionist force that potential supporters wanted. The Kansas-Nebraska Act was not an important factor in the demise of the party in this farming and mining county. Benjamin Bannan, editor of the *Pottsville Miners' Journal,* played a major role in bringing about a coalition of prohibitionist and anti-Catholic forces. Uses quantitative methods based on newspapers and other primary and secondary sources; photo, 3 tables, 48 notes.
D. C. Swift

187. Hammett, Theodore M. TWO MOBS OF JACKSONIAN BOSTON: IDEOLOGY AND INTEREST. *J. of Am. Hist. 1976 62(4): 845-868.* Using two dissimilar mob actions occurring in Boston, discusses the interaction of ideas and interests as the main basis for ideological development. Compares the burning of an Ursuline Convent by a mob of poor, Protestant laborers on 11 August 1834 with the Massachusetts Anti-Slavery Society riot of 24 October 1835 (by "wealthier," establishment types). Contemporaries saw one as a danger to society, the latter as righteous action against society's disrupters. These two views represent society's bipartiality in developing ideological responses to events affecting it. Economics and class structure determine "rightness." 5 tables, 70 notes.
V. P. Rilee

188. Holt, Michael F. THE POLITICS OF IMPATIENCE: THE ORIGINS OF KNOW NOTHINGISM. *J. of Am. Hist. 1973 60(2): 309-331.* The Know-Nothing Party was the fastest growing political force in many parts of the United States, 1853-56, probably contributing to the disintegration of the Whig Party as much as did the slavery issue. Know-nothingism fed on a surge of anti-Catholic sentiment among workers and the middle class in several eastern and midwestern states. These support-ers were bewildered by rapid economic and social change and opposed political manipulators and the convention system. Voters previously identified with the traditional parties were impatient at their failure to take stands, especially on the issues of temperance and public schools. When the Know-Nothing Party nominated Millard Fillmore, many of its supporters turned to the Republicans who adopted the style and some issues of Know-Nothingism. 76 notes.
K. B. West

189. Keefe, Thomas M. THE CATHOLIC ISSUE IN THE CHICAGO TRIBUNE BEFORE THE CIVIL WAR. *Mid-America 1975 57(4): 227-245.* Blaming Chicago's troubles on Catholic immigrants, Henry Fowler's editorials began the Chicago *Tribune's* anti-Catholicism. However, he failed to defeat the Democrats in the 1854 municipal election. Editor Thomas Stewart followed Fowler's example, and with his editorial support the Know-Nothings won the next election. New owners of the *Tribune* Medill, Ray, and Vaughan carried on the Fowler-Stewart policy, which continued after the merger with the *Daily Democratic Press,* linking slavery and Catholicism, expressing sympathy for Italy's struggle for unity, and alleging that Stephen Douglas was a secret Catholic. Based on newspapers and secondary works; 83 notes.
T. H. Wendel

190. Kenny, William R. NATIVISM IN THE SOUTHERN MINING REGION OF CALIFORNIA. *J. of the West 1973 12(1): 126-138.* An account from contemporary newspapers of native American opposition to the employment of Mexicans, Chinese, Indians, Chileans, Australians, and Frenchmen in the southern mining region of California during 1850-60. "As early as July, 1850, the citizens of the town of Sonora had met and adopted a series of resolutions which they declared were for the preservation of lives and property. . . . All foreigners were ordered to leave Tuolumne County 15 days after the passage of these resolutions, unless they got a permit to the contrary." In 1851 the hatred and suspicion of Mexicans and South Americans expanded to include almost all foreigners. 39 notes.
D. D. Cameron

191. Kurtz, Henry I. RIOT AT ASTOR PLACE. *Am. Hist. Illus. 1974 9(7): 32-42.* The riot which took place on 10 May 1849 during a performance of *Macbeth* at the Astor Place Opera House, "which left in its wake some 30 persons dead and scores of others injured, was sparked by a petty rivalry between two vain actors—a rivalry, however, that brought to the surface the xenophobia of American nativists as well as simmering antagonism." The two actors involved in this dispute were the English actor William Charles Macready and Edwin Forrest, "the first truly outstanding native-born American actor . . ." 5 illus., 2 photos.
D. D. Cameron

192. McCrary, Royce C. JOHN MAC PHERSON BERRIEN AND THE KNOW-NOTHING MOVEMENT IN GEORGIA. *Georgia Hist. Q. 1977 61(1): 35-42.* Traces the influence of retired politician John M. Berrien (1781-1856) on the Know-Nothings in Georgia. Beginning with his letter "To the People of Georgia" of 4 September 1855, he encouraged a party emphasis on preserving the Union rather than on anti-Catholicism and nativism. He died before his ideas could take root, and the party reverted to its former views. Primary and secondary sources; 28 notes.
G. R. Schroeder

193. Neely, Mark E. RICHARD W. THOMPSON: THE PERSISTENT KNOW NOTHING. *Indiana Mag. of Hist. 1976 72(2): 95-122.* Discusses the anti-Catholic Know-Nothing Party, popular in the 1850's in American politics, and gives an in-depth view of the Party's leader and major speaker, Richard W. Thompson.

194. Renner, Richard Wilson. IN A PERFECT FERMENT: CHICAGO, THE KNOW-NOTHINGS, AND THE RIOT FOR LAGER BEER. *Chicago Hist. 1976 5(3): 161-169.* Discusses Chicago's Know-Nothing government of 1855 which alienated German supporters with a temperance law that provoked a major riot.

195. Rubin, Jay. BLACK NATIVISM: THE EUROPEAN IMMIGRANT IN NEGRO THOUGHT, 1830-1860. *Phylon 1978 39(3): 193-202.* During 1830-60, as wave after wave of European immigrants reached American shores—Irish fleeing the potato famine, Germans fleeing the suppression of the 1848 Revolution, and others leaving poverty and oppression—free American blacks in the North found themselves losing jobs and privileges to the newcomers. This—and not any fear of

Catholicism or "drunkenness" and "immorality"—explains the black dislike of the immigrants. The few black intellectuals who traveled to Europe found Europeans racially tolerant, and sympathized with the destitute people of Ireland. But in the United States, the immigrant was an economic and political threat, and this aroused black nativist feeling. 41 notes.

J. C. Billigmeier

196. Ryan, Thomas R. NEWMAN'S INVITATION TO ORESTES A. BROWNSON TO BE LECTURER EXTRAORDINARY AT THE CATHOLIC UNIVERSITY OF IRELAND. *Records of the Am. Catholic Hist. Soc. of Philadelphia 1974 85(1/2): 29-47.* The project to bring Orestes A. Brownson to the Catholic University of Ireland, a project which intrigued John Henry Newman, apparently was scuttled by the furor over Brownson's 1854 article on "Native Americanism" in his *Review.* 35 notes.

J. M. McCarthy

197. Schmandt, Raymond H. A PHILADELPHIA REACTION TO POPE PIUS IX IN 1848. *Records of the Am. Catholic Hist. Soc. of Philadelphia 1977 88(1-4): 63-87.* Reproduces a 24-page pamphlet recording the events of 6 January 1848, a day on which there was a huge, non-denominational public demonstration of enthusiasm for Pope Pius IX's efforts to establish constitutional reforms in the Papal States, a demonstration all the more significant because it came at a time of nativist tensions.

J. M. McCarthy

198. Schneider, John C. RIOT AND REACTION IN ST. LOUIS, 1854-1856. *Missouri Hist. R. 1974 68(2): 171-185.* Discusses the buildup, culmination, and aftermath of local political tension in St. Louis in the 1850's. Central to the conflict was a growing nativism and the emergence of the Know-Nothing Party which caused alarm among the Democrats. This resulted in rioting on election day, 7 August 1854, with a counterattack led by members of the Irish community. As a result of the conflict, the regular police force was reorganized and professionalized, the state passed a stronger riot law effective only in St. Louis County, and election procedures were restructured. The elections of 1855 and 1856 were again emotional races between the Know-Nothing Party and the Democrats, but order was kept during both, although the above changes were actually partisan in nature. Based on contemporary newspaper reports, St. Louis city documents, primary and secondary sources; 7 illus., 22 notes.

N. J. Street

199. Smith, Harold T. THE KNOW-NOTHINGS IN ARKANSAS. *Arkansas Hist. Q. 1975 34(4): 291-303.* The Arkansas Know-Nothing Party, organized in Little Rock by August 1855, was composed mainly of former Whigs with a sprinkling of Democrats opposed to the Kansas-Nebraska Act. Major ideological divisions in the campaign of 1856 were over Kansas-Nebraska and southern rights. After losing most elections within the state in 1856 the Know-Nothings made a poor showing in the national canvass and soon passed from existence. Based on primary and secondary sources; 28 notes.

T. L. Savitt

200. Soland, Martha Jordan. FAITH OF OUR FATHERS. *Daughters of the Am. Revolution Mag. 1975 109(9): 1012-1015, 1075.* Traces American religious history from the beliefs of the Revolutionary leaders to the anti-Catholic sentiments of the Know-Nothing Party during the mid-19th century.

S

201. Weinbaum, Paul O. TEMPERANCE, POLITICS, AND THE NEW YORK CITY RIOTS OF 1857. *New-York Hist. Soc. Q. 1975 59(3): 246-270.* During the 1850's there was much violence in urban areas of the United States. Investigates the connection between the New York City riots of 1857, ostensibly caused by the activities of temperance forces, and local politics, particularly of the Irish and German factions. Although the temperance campaign was the chief incitement to Irish and German rioting, it was only incidental to political violence with political action that led to larger participation in city politics. Primary sources; 7 illus., 45 notes.

C. L. Grant

202. Whitmore, Allan R. PORTRAIT OF A MAINE "KNOW-NOTHING": WILLIAM H. CHANEY (1821-1903); HIS EARLY YEARS AND HIS ROLE IN THE ELLSWORTH NATIVIST CONTROVERSY, 1853-1854. *Maine Hist. Soc. Q. 1974 14(1): 1-57.* On 14 October 1854, Jesuit priest John Bapst was tarred, feathered, and ridden on a rail by a nativist mob in Ellsworth, Maine, because of his militant

religious activities. Local newspaper editor William Henry Chaney largely created the charged atmosphere producing this riot. A harsh childhood and poverty had made Chaney a combative, defensive individual sensitive to criticism, obsessed with conspiracies, and constantly embroiled in controversies. He strongly denounced Bapst's activities as a Catholic conspiracy and soon inflamed the local citizenry to action. Primary and secondary sources; illus., 164 notes.

E. A. Churchill

Immigration Restriction and Nativism: 1890-1930

203. Abbey, Sue Wilson. THE KU KLUX KLAN IN ARIZONA, 1921-1925. *J. of Arizona Hist. 1973 14(1): 10-30.* Established in Phoenix and Tucson in 1921, the Ku Klux Klan soon spread to smaller towns and the rural and mining areas. It campaigned for better law enforcement through prohibition and the closing of brothels and gambling halls. The Klan, alarmed at the growth of the Mexican American population and the spread of Catholicism, preached the return to "higher" moral standards and the doctrine of white supremacy. Defeated in the November 1924 elections, the Klan became a victim of its own intolerance when its violence and excesses were widely publicized. 2 illus., 86 notes.

D. L. Smith

204. Baum, Dale. THE NEW DAY IN NORTH DAKOTA: THE NONPARTISAN LEAGUE AND THE POLITICS OF NEGATIVE REVOLUTION. *North Dakota Hist. 1973 40(2): 4-19.* Previous historians, particularly Robert Loren Morlan in his *Political Prairie Fire: The Nonpartisan League, 1915-1922* (Minneapolis: U. of Minnesota Press, 1955), have overlooked the shortcomings of the Nonpartisan League. The league is said to have been a part of the progressive and liberal American political tradition; instead, the league tended to view the world in terms of black and white. It contributed to Upper Midwest isolationism, nativism, and anti-Semitism. 15 illus., 41 notes.

D. L. Smith

205. Betten, Neil. NATIVISM AND THE KLAN IN TOWN AND CITY: VALPARAISO AND GARY, INDIANA. *Studies in Hist. and Soc. 1973 4(2): 3-16.* A study of the Ku Klux Klan during the 1920's in two urban centers. Indicates that "The Klan grew in Gary and Valparaiso by fashioning its appeal to the concerns of its white Protestant citizens . . ." and focused on such "myriad enemies" as corrupt politicians, bootleggers, prostitutes, imagined radicals, and immigrants who would not or could not instantly assimilate.

J. O. Baylen

206. Blankenship, Gary R. *THE COMMERCIAL APPEAL'*S ATTACK ON THE KU KLUX KLAN, 1921-1925. *West Tennessee Hist. Soc. Papers 1977 31: 44-58.* When the Ku Klux Klan revived itself in the 1920's, *The Commercial Appeal,* a leading Memphis newspaper, took a decided stand against it. The editorials of Charles Patrick Joseph Mooney and the cartoons of Jim Alley levelled a two-pronged attack of rationalism and ridicule against the Klan. The effort was so successful that in 1923 *The Commercial Appeal* received the Pulitzer Prize. In that same year it checked the political entrance of the Klan into the Memphis municipal election. From that time the Klan experienced rapid decline. Based on articles and editorials from *The Commercial Appeal;* illus., 59 notes.

H. M. Parker, Jr.

207. Boles, David C. EFFECT OF THE KU KLUX KLAN ON THE OKLAHOMA GUBERNATORIAL ELECTION OF 1926. *Chronicles of Oklahoma 1977-78 55(4): 424-432.* Despite Republican attempts to closely link Democratic gubernatorial candidate Henry S. Johnston to the Ku Klux Klan, Johnston won the 1926 Oklahoma election with a greater margin than any predecessor. Though affiliated with the Klan earlier and carrying its backing in this election, Johnston did not seek its support nor make Klan activity a political issue. Newspaper accounts; 2 photos, 46 notes.

M. L. Tate

208. Candeloro, Dominic. LOUIS F. POST AND THE RED SCARE OF 1920. *Prologue 1979 11(1): 41-55.* In 1920 as Assistant Secretary of Labor, 71-year-old Louis F. Post successfully thwarted the arbitrary and capricious enforcement of the Alien Anarchist Act (US, 1918), by

which scores of foreign-born radicals were deported under the aegis of Attorney General Mitchell Palmer and his assistant J. Edgar Hoover. Post, a long-time sympathizer with left-wing causes and a public admirer of the Russian Revolution, came under intensive Congressional scrutiny for his stand and an effort was made to remove him from office through impeachment proceedings. The effort failed, owing in large part to Post's own inspired defense of his position before Congressional committees. Post's insistence that due process and a rigid adherence to law mark governmental operations against foreign-born radicals did a great deal to stem the tide of wanton and arbitrary deportation of dissenters resident in the United States. Based mainly on research in the National Archives.
N. Lederer

209. Carter, L. Edward. RISE AND FALL OF THE INVISIBLE EMPIRE: KNIGHTS OF THE KU KLUX KLAN. *Great Plains J. 1977 16(2): 82-106.* Discusses the revived Ku Klux Klan of the early 1920's, especially in Lawton, Comanche County, Oklahoma. The Klan appeared in Lawton in 1921. Its parades, meetings, support of morality, religious overtones, and philanthropy "helped it gain widespread acceptance." In the later 1920's it fell apart, and by 1929 had lost virtually all influence. 4 illus., 62 notes.
O. H. Zabel

210. Cherry, Robert. RACIAL THOUGHT AND THE EARLY ECONOMICS PROFESSION IN THE USA. *Rev. of Social Econ. 1976 34(2): 147-162.* Examines the infiltration of racist sentiment and racial myth into economic theory, 1880's-1910's.

211. Coben, Stanley. THE ASSAULT ON VICTORIANISM IN THE TWENTIETH CENTURY. *Am. Q. 1975 27(5): 604-625.* During the 1920's confidence in Victorianism primarily declined because of academic and literary intellectual attacks on its conceptual foundations. Social scientists, historians, literary critics, ethnic minority representatives, and feminists attacked various aspects of Victorian culture. The Ku Klux Klan and its upper class counterparts tried unsuccessfully to protect it. They failed because of the strength of the opposition and their own lack of complete confidence in their beliefs. Based on primary and secondary sources.
N. Lederer

212. Cuddy, Edward. "ARE BOLSHEVIKS ANY WORSE THAN THE IRISH?" ETHNO-RELIGIOUS CONFLICT IN AMERICA DURING THE 1920'S. *Éire-Ireland 1976 11(3): 13-32.* Shattering effects of urbanization and fear of the loss of Anglo-Saxon hegemony in the United States resulted in much anti-Catholicism and anti-Irish sentiment during the 1920's.

213. Daugherty, Robert L. PROBLEMS IN PEACEKEEPING: THE 1924 NILES RIOT. *Ohio Hist. 1976 85(4): 280-292.* A riot on 1 November 1924 in Niles, Ohio, involved the Ohio Knights of the Ku Klux Klan and the Knights of the Flaming Circle. The riot, terminated by the Ohio National Guard, was a prime example of a state government's hesitation to become involved in local law enforcement problems. Based on archival, MS., contemporary comments, and secondary sources; 5 illus., 31 notes.
N. Summers

214. Dyer, Thomas G. THE KLAN ON CAMPUS: C. LEWIS FOWLER AND LANIER UNIVERSITY. *South Atlantic Q. 1978 77(4): 453-469.* In 1917 the doors of Lanier University opened, with Charles Lewis Fowler as its first President. The school was a Baptist-related college in the Druid Hills area of Atlanta. Fowler, who had considerable support from the Ku Klux Klan, aimed at making Lanier into an "All-Southern" Baptist university. The enterprise never lived up to Fowler's grandiose expectations nor up to the inflated figures he released regarding enrollment and physical assets. Finally, in 1921 the Klan took over the operation of the school, and a year later the school closed because of bankruptcy. Article chronicles the attempts of Fowler to achieve his goal, but the failure of the experiment as a regional, right-wing institution made it quite evident that enthusiasm for the principles of 100% Americanism extended well beyond the confines of the Klan. Based on the Lanier University file, University of Georgia, and contemporary newspaper accounts; 34 notes.
H. M. Parker, Jr.

215. Eisele, J. Christopher. JOHN DEWEY AND THE IMMIGRANTS. *Hist. of Educ. Q. 1975 15(1): 67-86.* Contrary to previous interpretations, John Dewey's writings on immigrants, 1902-27, show

that he sought to preserve ethnic differences within American society.

216. Flynt, Wayne, ed. WILLIAM V. KNOTT AND THE GUBERNATORIAL CAMPAIGN OF 1916. *Florida Hist. Q. 1973 51(4): 423-430.* William V. Knott was a candidate for governor of Florida in 1916 against Sidney J. Catts, preacher and alleged member of the Guardians of Liberty, a secret anti-Catholic organization. The highlight of the campaign was the "Sturkie Resolution," a Democratic Party resolution designed to prevent secret political club members from participating in primaries. The backlash to this resolution combined with anti-Catholic feeling in the state to bring about Catts' election. Based on 1958 manuscript of W. V. Knott; 14 notes.
J. E. Findling

217. Franzoni, Janet Brenner. TROUBLED TIRADER: A PSYCHOBIOGRAPHICAL STUDY OF TOM WATSON. *Georgia Hist. Q. 1973 57(4): 493-510.* Thomas E. Watson (1856-1922), prominent Georgia politician, legislator, congressman, and vice-presidential candidate, was an enigmatic figure. His colorful tirades and efforts ranged in extremes from pro- to anti-black, Catholic, and Jew. Psychological analysis may well hold the key to an understanding of his career. 79 notes.
D. L. Smith

218. Geiger, John O. THE EDGERTON BIBLE CASE: HUMPHREY DESMOND'S POLITICAL EDUCATION OF WISCONSIN CATHOLICS. *J. of Church and State 1979 20(1): 13-28.* Details the case of *State of Wisconsin ex rel. Frederick Weiss, et al.* vs. *District School Board of School District 8* (1890) concerning Bible reading in public schools, and Humphrey Desmond's (1852-1932) support of those who opposed the reading of only the King James version of the Bible by all students including Catholics. The case resulted in the elimination of Bible reading in Wisconsin schools. Covers 1888-90. 47 notes.
E. E. Eminhizer

219. Gerlach, Dominic B. ST. JOSEPH'S INDIAN NORMAL SCHOOL, 1888-1896. *Indiana Mag. of Hist. 1973 69(1): 1-42.* Racial and religious conflicts plagued St. Joseph's, and economic and political problems caused its demise. This Catholic school was supported by public, church, and private funds, but Protestant demands that federal support be withheld from parochial schools deprived the school of essential financing. The Indians resisted the kind of education offered by St. Joseph's; the average annual runaway rate was 50%. By 1895, the anti-Catholic American Protective Association had directed its attention to abolishing the contract schools, and in 1896 the school was closed. Its failure to meet its stated educational objectives was as important a factor as loss of government contracts.
N. E. Tutorow

220. Goldberg, Robert A. THE KU KLUX KLAN IN MADISON, 1922-1929. *Wisconsin Mag. of Hist. 1974 58(1): 31-44.* The stereotype of the Ku Klux Klan as violence-prone bigots who attacked blacks, Catholics, Jews, and immigrants is inaccurate for Madison Klansmen and for most Klans in the 1920's. Members were, instead, "ordinary men bewildered by changes that threatened to disrupt their lives and their city." Klan activity, aside from its similarity to other fraternal social organizations, concentrated on a law and order campaign and a drive to reassert American patriotism by stripping school textbooks of any negative remarks about American history or society. Internal dissension and the reform efforts of Dane County District Attorney Philip La Follette hastened their rapid decline. 7 illus., 58 notes.
N. C. Burckel

221. Goldstein, Robert J. THE ANARCHIST SCARE OF 1908: A SIGN OF TENSIONS IN THE PROGRESSIVE ERA. *Am. Studies (Lawrence, KS) 1974 15(2): 55-78.* Representative of the tensions in the Progressive era, the Anarchist Scare (1908) contradicts views of this period as one of optimism and social unity. The fear of radicals and particularly anarchists, the rapid spread of radicalism before 1908, and the social instability caused by labor unrest and the depression of 1907 precipitated conservative reaction. The federal government reacted sharply, and instituted a loyalty program for aliens. Based on primary and secondary sources; 3 illus., 42 notes.
J. Andrew

222. Hellwig, David J. BUILDING A BLACK NATION: THE ROLE OF IMMIGRANTS IN THE THOUGHT AND RHETORIC OF BOOKER T. WASHINGTON. *Mississippi Q. 1978 31(4): 529-550.* Discusses the subject of immigration in Booker T. Washington's Atlanta

Compromise speech at the Atlanta Exposition in 1895 in which he discusses immigration to the North from the South, foreign immigration to the South, and the effects of immigration on black America.

223. Holmes, William F. WHITECAPPING: ANTI-SEMITISM IN THE POPULIST ERA. *Am. Jewish Hist. Q. 1974 63(3): 244-261.* Whitecapping, a dirt farmer movement that became widespread in southwestern Mississippi during the early 1890's, espoused an anti-Semitic and anti-Negro ideology. It succeeded in driving black laborers off lands owned by merchants—mostly Jewish—and lumber companies, until forceful and courageous action by some local judges restored respect for law. In the counties wracked by whitecapping the Populist movement gained considerable support, but the two cannot be equated, even though some men may have belonged to both organizations. The two movements sprang from some of the same causes, however, and this study contributes an additional dimension to our knowledge of agrarian protest. 60 notes.

F. Rosenthal

224. Hux, Roger K. THE KU KLUX KLAN IN MACON 1919-1925. *Georgia Hist. Q. 1978 62(2): 155-168.* The Macon, Georgia, Ku Klux Klan of the 1920's, led by dentist C. A. Yarbrough, administered floggings primarily to punish moral offenders rather than to combat racial or foreign influences. Condemnation of violence, several trials of Klansmen, and political defeat brought about Klan decline. Newspapers and secondary sources; 30 notes.

G. R. Schroeder

225. Jenkins, William D. THE KU KLUX KLAN IN YOUNGSTOWN, OHIO: MORAL REFORM IN THE TWENTIES. *Historian 1978 41(1): 76-93.* The primary factor in the rapid growth of the Ku Klux Klan in Youngstown, Ohio, was not its white supremacy, anti-Catholicism, anti-Semitism, or nativism, but its desire to improve the morals of the community. An enforcement crusade, begun by the Mahoning County Dry Association, the Federal Council of Churches, and the Federation of Women's Clubs, soon fell under the control of the Klan and its leaders, who also met with surprising political success in local elections. Describes these leaders and Youngtown's attitudes toward other parts of the Klan platform. Speculates on causes of the decline of Klan influence in the area, and concludes that public confidence in the organization as the enforcer of community morals eroded as it proved unable to totally enforce the city's conservative moral code.

M. S. Legan

226. Jordan, Philip D. IMMIGRANTS, METHODISTS AND A "CONSERVATIVE" SOCIAL GOSPEL, 1865-1908. *Methodist Hist. 1978 17(1): 16-43.* While accepting a social creed in the name of Christian liberality in 1908 the Methodist Episcopal Church rejected an open door policy for immigrants. After the Civil War the church saw immigration as a danger to American civilization and to the wages of the laboring classes. At the same time Methodist missionaries saw China as a vast field for evangelism, and therefore the Methodist Episcopal Church opposed American mistreatment of Asians. By 1908, however, restriction of Oriental immigration was supported. Based on Methodist publications. 39 notes.

H. L. Calkin

227. Kamin, Leon J. THE SCIENCE AND POLITICS OF I.Q. *Social Res. 1974 41(3): 387-425.* Reviews history of intelligence testing and its use as an instrument of social and political discrimination, particularly with regard to immigrants in the 1920's.

S

228. Kostiainen, Auvo. MITEN MAA NORMALISOITIIN? YHDYSVALLAT 1910-JA 1920-LUKUJEN VAIHTEESSA [How was the country normalized? The United States at the turn of the decade, 1910-20]. *Hist. Aikakauskirja [Finland] 1979 77(1): 37-40.* After World War I a social crisis was created in the United States by economic depression and xenophobia. Both factors were successfully counteracted by the legislative restrictions placed on immigration in 1921 and 1924. Based on published English-language sources; 9 notes.

R. G. Selleck

229. Lane, A. T. AMERICAN LABOUR AND EUROPEAN IMMIGRANTS IN THE LATE NINETEENTH CENTURY. *J. of Am. Studies [Great Britain] 1977 11(2): 241-260.* During the 1890's, American labor unions argued about curbing immigration to America through alien contract labor laws, literacy test acts, and other exclusionary measures. In 1897, the national convention of the American Federation of Labor finally adopted a measure supporting literacy test legislation. That act, however, conflicted with rank and-file opinion and remained a minority view within the Federation for another decade. Federation leaders obtained approval of literacy tests in 1897 by persuasive campaigning, by maneuvering by the "literacy test lobby" at the 1897 convention, and by Samuel Gompers' artful use of personal influence over trade unionists. Based on labor union documents, government publications, and secondary sources; 44 notes.

H. T. Lovin

230. Marriner, Gerald Lynn. KLAN POLITICS IN COLORADO. *J. of the West 1976 15(1): 76-101.* The Ku Klux Klan came to Colorado in 1920 and soon had 50,000 members. In the elections of 1924 many Klan members and Klan-supported officials were elected, but in the elections of 1926 the Klan lost as part of a national decline of the Klan.

R. Alvis

231. McBride, Paul. PETER ROBERTS AND THE YMCA AMERICANIZATION PROGRAM, 1907-WORLD WAR I. *Pennsylvania Hist. 1977 44(2): 145-162.* As the YMCA's Special Secretary for Immigration Affairs, Dr. Peter Roberts developed the Roberts Method for teaching immigrants English. As a clergyman, Roberts had developed a respect for the Slavic immigrants in the Pennsylvania anthracite region. Although he used his texts to further Americanization, he preferred a subtle approach to the assimilationist theme in his elementary readers. The Daughters of the American Revolution and the North American Civic League for Immigrants, groups that were fearful and contemptuous of immigrants, screened the materials in his advanced readings. Consequently, these texts were more militantly nationalistic. During World War I, the assimilationist emphasis of the YMCA program for immigrants became strident. Primary sources; photo, 32 notes.

D. C. Swift

232. McCarty, Joey. THE RED SCARE IN ARKANSAS: A SOUTHERN STATE AND NATIONAL HYSTERIA. *Arkansas Hist. Q. 1978 37(3): 264-277.* Because Arkansas had a small proportion of immigrants, was largely rural, and had few problems with industrialization, the Red Scare was mostly confined to newspapers and a few orators like Governor Charles Brough. The average Arkansan was more interested in everyday problems such as inflation and influenza epidemics. Secondary sources and newspapers; 53 notes.

G. R. Schroeder

233. McClymer, John F. THE FEDERAL GOVERNMENT AND THE AMERICANIZATION MOVEMENT, 1915-24. *Prologue 1978 10(1): 23-41.* The World War I and postwar effort to convert aliens into politically conservative, homogeneous citizens was sponsored by federal agencies in addition to the plethora of state, local, and private bodies. The Bureau of Education, through its Committee of One Hundred, was one such agency in the Americanization movement. It was dominated by the National Americanization Committee whose membership was largely derived from the US Chamber of Commerce. The effort of the Education Bureau was implemented in direct and open conflict with the Americanization program of the Bureau of Naturalization in the Department of Labor; with other federal offices and agencies also participating in the overall Americanization effort. The confusion of effort during and after World War I, however, did not materially affect the common ideas on the necessity for Americanizing aliens and on the meaning of Americanization. Based on National Archives.

N. Lederer

234. Melching, Richard. THE ACTIVITIES OF THE KU KLUX KLAN IN ANAHEIM, CALIFORNIA, 1923-1925. *Southern California Q. 1974 56(2): 175-196.* The Ku Klux Klan in Anaheim was unlike the national organization in several respects; violence was at a minimum, Klan supporters endorsed prohibition, and their opponents were accused of favoring vice and gambling, thus presenting the Klan and their candidates as reformers. For a time, the Klan captured most of Anaheim's city offices, but a major blow against them occurred when the klavern's membership list was made public, revealing that the claimed membership of 1,400 did not match the reality of less than 300. Without its secrecy and with its true size revealed, the Klan went into decline, with the February, 1925 city election bringing about its complete defeat. For months afterwards resignations and firings purged the Klan from city hall, and despite a few subsequent attempts to resurrect it, the organization never regained its earlier power. Based chiefly on accounts in the Anaheim newspaper; 88 notes.

A. Hoffman

235. Meyer, Paul R.   THE FEAR OF CULTURAL DECLINE: JOSIAH STRONG'S THOUGHT ABOUT REFORM AND EXPANSION. *Church Hist. 1973 42(3): 396-405.* Contends that Josiah Strong's support for domestic reform and overseas expansion resulted from his religious preoccupation with the idea that the Protestant Anglo-Saxon was a major contributor to civilization's progress. Only a thoroughly Anglo-Saxonized population was capable of positive influence when it inevitably became a world ruler. Strong in his early works described Anglo-Saxon cultural superiority as justification for intervention into other nations' internal affairs. As increasing industrialization created social problems, Strong's writing revealed more pessimism, undermining his earlier confidence in an ultimate Anglo-Saxon cultural victory. His early emphasis upon expansion became overshadowed in later years by his fear of Anglo-Saxon cultural decline. Based on Strong's published works; 33 notes.   S. Kerens

236. Mohl, Raymond A.   *THE SATURDAY EVENING POST* AND THE "MEXICAN INVASION."   *J. of Mexican Am. Hist. 1973 3(1): 131-138.* World War I and the immigration laws of the 1920's severely restricted the flow of Europeans to the United States, but served to quicken the influx from countries such as Mexico, which were unaffected by the war and the quota system. The American press such as the *Post* and other periodicals, reflecting the intolerance and nativism of the decade, consistently portrayed Mexican immigrants as less desirable than European immigrants. 12 notes.   R. T. Fulton

237. Moseley, Clement Charlton.   THE POLITICAL INFLUENCE OF THE KU KLUX KLAN IN GEORGIA, 1915-1925. *Georgia Hist. Q. 1973 57(2): 235-255.* William Joseph Simmons revived the Ku Klux Klan in 1915. It barely survived its first six years but membership increased dramatically after two publicity agents were hired. Outbreaks of violence brought notoriety and a congressional investigation. Georgia became one of three major centers of KKK political strength in the country. Its influence was felt at all levels of government, including the congressional representation of the state. The KKK's power declined steadily after 1925. 48 notes.   D. L. Smith

238. Mugleston, William F.   JULIAN HARRIS, THE GEORGIA PRESS, AND THE KU KLUX KLAN. *Georgia Hist. Q. 1975 59(3): 284-295.* Chronicles a 1920's anti-Ku Klux Klan campaign waged by Columbus, Georgia, *Enquirer-Sun* editor Julian LaRose Harris in a traditionally pro-Klan area.

239. Piott, Steven L.   THE LESSON OF THE IMMIGRANT: VIEWS OF IMMIGRANTS IN MUCKRAKING MAGAZINES, 1900-1909. *Am. Studies (Lawrence, KS) 1978 19(1): 21-33.* Immigrants brought with them an undefiled sense of morality. Many early muckraking authors used this, and depicted innocent immigrants as victims of an industrial capitalism devoid of ethics or a sense of community. They argued for the reestablishment of a moral structure. A differentiated society had blinded citizens to corporate malefactors. Ordinary people could not perceive industrial patterns, and reform writers sought to implant a sense of guilt. Industrial capitalists, not the immigrants, were the true enemies. Primary and secondary sources; 36 notes.
                                                          J. Andrew

240. Satariano, William A.   IMMIGRATION AND THE POPULARIZATION OF SOCIAL SCIENCE, 1920 TO 1930. *J. of the Hist. of the Behavioral Sci. 1979 15(4): 310-320.* This article examines how social scientists presented their views on immigration to readers of popular magazines from 1920 to 1930, a period of public debate on the merits of immigration restriction. By comparing the content of these magazine articles with professional journal articles on immigration, the representativeness of the social scientific material presented to the public can be assessed. While similar issues were discussed in popular and professional articles, social scientists writing popular articles were more likely to support an outmoded racial interpretation of immigration. Their resulting support of immigration restriction was not representative of the dominant cultural perspective held by most social scientists. Thus, readers looking to social scientists for an "informed opinion" were not given an accurate impression of social scientific thought on immigration.   J

241. Shankman, Arnold.   JULIAN HARRIS AND THE KU KLUX KLAN. *Mississippi Q. 1975 28(2): 147-169.* Chronicles the efforts of Julian LaRose Harris, editor of the *Enquirer-Sun*, to expose the bigotry and racism of the Ku Klux Klan in Columbus, Georgia, during the 1920's.
                                                          S

242. Sloan, Charles William, Jr.   KANSAS BATTLES THE INVISIBLE EMPIRE: THE LEGAL OUSTER OF THE KKK FROM KANSAS, 1922-1927. *Kansas Hist. Q. 1974 40(3): 393-409.* Following a 1922 effort to recruit members for the Ku Klux Klan, William Allen White waged a campaign to oust the "fraternal order" from the state.

243. Thompson, James J., Jr.   SOUTHERN BAPTISTS AND ANTI-CATHOLICISM IN THE 1920'S. *Mississippi Q. 1979 32(4): 611-625.* Discusses the reasons for, and the nature of, anti-Catholicism among Southern Baptists who spearheaded the Protestant opposition to Roman Catholicism in the 1920's.

244. Traylor, Jack Wayne.   WILLIAM ALLEN WHITE'S 1924 GUBERNATORIAL CAMPAIGN. *Kansas Hist. Q. 1976 42(2): 180-191.* White was interested in politics, but usually was content to remain the semidetached editor, content to report and comment without being drawn into the battle himself. The rebirth of the Ku Klux Klan after World War I provided him with the incentive to become a combatant. Sporadic attacks on the Klan in Emporia after 1921 turned into a political struggle in 1924 when White's Republican Party supported Ben Paulsen, a man alleged to be subservient to the Klan. Whether White entered the race to win is open to debate, but he did undercut the Klan by speaking out against it. Primary and secondary sources; illus., 40 notes.
                                                          W. F. Zornow

245. Vittoz, Stan.   WORLD WAR I AND THE POLITICAL ACCOMMODATION OF TRANSITIONAL MARKET FORCES: THE CASE OF IMMIGRATION RESTRICTION. *Pol. and Soc. 1978 8(1): 49-78.* The assumption that continued labor migration would affect labor-capital power relationships in the American political economy, and was therefore partly responsible for the coming of restrictive immigration legislation in the post-World War I period, will not stand close scrutiny. Investigation of migration patterns, industrial growth, and capital's demands for labor from the 1870's to the 1920's shows that by the latter period, the structure of the economy was such that both labor and capital required changes that would enhance stability and predictability in both sectors of the economy. Any continued influx of foreign labor would not have altered the power structure. Primary and secondary sources; 75 notes.
                                                          D. G. Nielson

246. Walaskay, Paul William.   THE ENTERTAINMENT OF ANGELS: AMERICAN BAPTISTS AND AMERICANIZATION, 1890-1925. *Foundations 1976 19(4): 346-360.* Describes the efforts made by the American Baptists to assimilate and assist immigrants coming to America, 1890-1925. Describes the approaches used to reach those who did not have a Baptist group speaking their language. 51 notes.
                                                          E. E. Eminhizer

247. Wang, Peter H.   FARMERS AND THE IMMIGRATION ACT OF 1924. *Agric. Hist. 1975 49(4): 647-652.* In 1924 Midwestern farmers thought of southern Europeans as "un-American" and sought to prevent their entry, while Southerners wanted agricultural immigration for agricultural labor in the South. A compromise was reached in the National Origins Act (1924), which sharply reduced immigration but gave preference to immigrants who were farmers. 19 notes.   D. E. Bowers

248. Wang, Peter H.   THE IMMIGRATION ACT OF 1924 AND THE PROBLEM OF ASSIMILATION. *J. of Ethnic Studies 1974 2(3): 72-75.* Reviews the Americanization movement and the crusade for immigration restriction climaxing in the National Origins Act (1924). Contemporary quotations illustrate the major arguments of the restrictionists: fear of the undermining of American institutions by foreign radicalism, the linking of high levels of sin and vice with southern and eastern European newcomers, their disrespect "for the general social welfare," and the fear of a heterogeneous society, which was "probably the most potent force" behind the movement. Based on contemporary newspapers and periodicals, 17 notes.   G. J. Bobango

249. Weinberg, Daniel E.   THE ETHNIC TECHNICIAN AND THE FOREIGN-BORN: ANOTHER LOOK AT AMERICANIZATION

IDEOLOGY AND GOALS. *Societas 1977 7(3): 209-227.* The Foreign Language Information Service attempted to Americanize the foreign-born largely but not exclusively through news releases, 1918-39. Urban and highly educated, its leaders attempted to homogenize American society from a quite different perspective than the "reactionary nostalgia" suggested by other students of Americanization. Based upon the papers of the American Council for Nationalities Service, an interview with its former chairman, the papers of the American National Red Cross, and printed primary and secondary sources; 78 notes.   J. D. Hunley

250. Williams, David. SOWING THE WIND: THE DEPORTATION RAIDS OF 1920 IN NEW HAMPSHIRE. *Hist. New Hampshire 1979 34(1): 1-31.* During 1900-20, the population of eastern Europeans in New Hampshire grew to almost 10% of the state's foreign-born. On 2 January 1920, the US Justice Department arrested 260 New Hampshire residents as part of the nationwide "Palmer raids" directed against radicals. Removal of constitutional safeguards and denial of due process led to ill-treatment of the arrested, until critics of the arrests, and Judge Weston Anderson, originally from New Hampshire, brought about the release of the arrested. Based on Justice Department records and other primary and secondary sources. 60 notes.   D. F. Chard

The Twentieth-Century Response: Since 1930

251. Berger, Andrew. ALIEN VENUE: NEITHER NECESSARY NOR CONSTITUTIONAL. *New York U. J. of Int. Law and Pol. 1976 9(2): 155-176.* "Alien venue was born to fill a gap in venue caused by an alien's inability to satisfy the general venue statutes. That inability has ended in most cases.   E. P. Stickney

252. Bueler, William M. POPULATION AND AMERICA'S FUTURE. *Midwest Q. 1975 16(2): 135-149.* Discusses means by which the US birth rate can be controlled so as to achieve an optimum population. Examines the use of tax incentives, birth control, and immigration restriction as means to achieve this goal. Based on secondary sources.   H. S. Marks and S

253. Fragomen, Austin T., Jr. ALIEN EMPLOYMENT. *Int. Migration Rev. 1979 13(3): 527-531.* Discusses the implications of three Supreme Court decisions on citizen classification: *Graham* v. *Richardson* (US, 1971), *Foley* v. *Connelie* (US, 1978), and *Ambach* v. *Norwick* (US, 1979).

254. Fragomen, Austin T., Jr. PERMANENT RESIDENT STATUS REDEFINED. *Internat. Migration R. 1975 9(1): 63-68.* Analyzes the new definition of permanent resident status handed down by the United States Supreme Court on 25 November 1974.

255. Garza, E. (Kika) De La et al. SHOULD PEOPLE STAY HOME? REGULATION OF FREE MOVEMENT AND RIGHT OF ESTABLISHMENT BETWEEN THE U.S., CANADA, AND MEXICO. *Am. Soc. of Int. Law Pro. 1974 68: 38-58.* Discusses the public policies regulating immigration between the the United States, Canada, and Mexico from 1910 to 1974.

256. Goodenow, Ronald K. THE PROGRESSIVE EDUCATOR, RACE AND ETHNICITY IN THE DEPRESSION YEARS: AN OVERVIEW. *Hist. of Educ. Q. 1975 15(4): 365-394.* Focuses on the positions of progressive educators regarding race and ethnicity in the United States during the Depression and their subsequent influence on education and society.

257. Hohl, Donald G. and Wenk, Michael G. THE RODINO BILL AND THE ETHNIC HERITAGE STUDIES ACT. *Internat. Migration R. 1973 7(2): 191-194.*

258. Kramer, Jane M. DUE PROCESS RIGHTS FOR EXCLUDABLE ALIENS UNDER UNITED STATES IMMIGRATION LAW

AND THE UNITED NATIONS PROTOCOL RELATED TO THE STATUS OF REFUGEES: HAITIAN ALIENS, A CASE IN POINT; THE *PIERRE* AND *SANNON* DECISIONS. *New York U. J. of Int. Law and Pol. 1977 10(1): 203-240.* Examines connections among the 1977 cases *Pierre* v. *United States* and *Sannon* v. *United States* (which dealt with procedural rights accorded Haitians asking for US political asylum), the UN Protocol Relating to the Status of Aliens, and the Immigration and Nationality Act (US, 1952).

259. North, David S. THE GROWING IMPORTANCE OF IMMIGRATION TO POPULATION POLICY. *Policy Studies J. 1977 6(2): 200-207.* Approves of the current immigration rates, but asserts that a population policy must be formulated to avoid the creation of a lower class composed of aliens.

260. Parlin, Bradley W. IMMIGRANT, EMPLOYERS, AND EXCLUSION. *Society 1977 14(6): 23-26.* Discusses employment difficulties encountered by immigrants to the United States, especially their precarious legal standing, tendencies toward discrimination or exclusion, and their overall employability, 1960's-70's.

261. Pavlak, Thomas J. SOCIAL CLASS, ETHNICITY, AND RACIAL PREJUDICE. *Public Opinion Q. 1973 37(2): 225-231.* Results of a survey in 1969 of racial attitudes in Chicago among white ethnics (mostly lower-middle-class manual workers). Those tested showed a significant degree of hostility toward Negroes and especially toward interracial marriage. Hostility was weakest toward integrated work teams. Racial hostility may simply reflect economic and social competition and not inherent racial prejudice. 3 tables, 11 notes.   V. L. Human

262. Roof, Wade Clark. RELIGIOUS ORTHODOXY AND MINORITY PREJUDICE: CAUSAL RELATIONSHIP OR REFLECTION OF LOCALISTIC WORLD VIEW? *Am. J. of Sociol. 1974 80(3): 643-664.* Examines the relationship of religious orthodoxy to prejudice against minorities using a world-view perspective. Instead of regarding the two as causally related, argue[s] that both religious belief and intolerance toward minorities are reflections of a localistic world view formed by individuals with limited social perspectives. Data from a North Carolina survey sample support this explanation, showing that the orthodoxy-prejudice relationship is partially spurious when localism is controlled and that a portion of the influence of education upon prejudice is also expressed indirectly through localism as an intervening orientation. These findings, based upon a causal analysis of anti-Semitic, anti-black, and anti-Catholic attitudes, suggest the need for further attention to 'breadth of perspective' as a factor in theories concerning prejudice.   J

263. Schander, Edwin R. IMMIGRATION LAW AND PRACTICE IN THE UNITED STATES: A SELECTIVE BIBLIOGRAPHY. *Int. Migration Rev. 1978 12(1): 117-127.* This bibliography contains approximately 130 items and is limited to the review of the currently available legal literature of 1970-77.

264. Strange, Steven L. PRIVATE CONSENSUAL SEXUAL CONDUCT AND THE "GOOD MORAL CHARACTER" REQUIREMENT OF THE IMMIGRATION AND NATIONALITY ACT. *Columbia J. of Transnational Law 1975 14(2): 357-381.* Discusses the relationship between law, morality, and private sexual conduct in the McCarran-Walter Immigration Act (1952) and immigration and naturalization policy 1952-70's.

265. Weiss, Richard. ETHNICITY AND REFORM: MINORITIES AND THE AMBIENCE OF THE DEPRESSION YEARS. *J. of Am. Hist. 1979 66(3): 566-585.* Analyzes the changing attitudes of many Americans, especially intellectuals, regarding the relationship of ethnic groups to American culture during the 1930's. By the eve of World War II, many Americans had begun to view ethnic variety in American nationality not only as positive, but as essential. Racial and ethnic tolerance increased as a reaction to the racism of Nazi Germany. During the Depression years, immigrants and blacks were viewed as victims of the society, not as threats to it. 78 notes.   T. P. Linkfield

3. IMMIGRANTS AND ETHNICS: BY GROUPS

Austrian

266. Pennauer, Johann. JOHANN REISSNER—EIN BEITRAG AUS PAMHAGEN ZUM "JAHR DER AUSLANDSBURGEN-LÄNDER" [Johann Riessner: a contribution from Pamhagen to the "Year of the Burgenländer living abroad"]. *Burgenländische Heimatblätter [Austria] 1975 37(4): 145-162.* The Burgenlander Johann Riessner (1856-1939) who emigrated to the USA in 1882, dedicated many poems written in the United States, to his home country.

Baltic (Estonian, Latvian, Lithuanian)

267. Anicas, J. LIETUVIU KLERIKALINE EMIGRACIJA IR REAKCINIAI KAPITALISTINIU ŠALIU REŽIMAI 1945-1975 [The Lithuanian clerical emigration and reactionary regimes in the capitalist countries, 1945-1975]. *Lietuvos TSR Mokslu Akademijos. Darbai. Serija A: Visuomenes Mokslai [USSR] 1976 (4): 39-49.* The right wing of the emigration, the clergy, aligned itself with McCarthyism in the United States and with other antidemocratic regimes such as Franco's and Salazar's. 53 notes. A. E. Senn

268. Balys, J. P. THE AMERICAN LITHUANIAN PRESS. *Lituanus 1976 22(1): 42-53.* After 1875, as the number of Lithuanian immigrants in the United States grew, numerous Lithuanian newspapers and magazines were established to fill a need for news, information, opinion, and recreation. Many newspapers were shortlived; those with broad, middle of the road appeal were most successful. Approximately 12 of these newspapers are still being published. The journalists and intellectuals who emigrated to the United States after World War II are responsible for most of the Lithuanian journals and magazines now being published. Their chief interest is Lithuanian affairs, and the majority are anti-Soviet with strong ideological convictions. 5 notes.
K. N. T. Crowther

269. Baskauskas, Liucija. PLANNED INCORPORATION OF REFUGEES: THE BALTIC CLAUSE. *Int. Migration [Netherlands] 1976 14(3): 219-228.* Examines Lithuanian refugees relocated in Los Angeles as a result of the post-World War II Displaced Persons Act (US, 1948), focusing on their assimilation.

270. Borkovs'kyi, Roman. AKTUAL'NA PRYHADKA I PERE-STOROHA [A topical recollection and warning]. *Sučasnist [West Germany] 1975 (5): 92-97.* Discusses Soviet-American diplomacy in light of the Simas Kudirka affair, November 1970, when a Lithuanian defected from a Soviet vessel to an American Coast Guard vessel off Massachusetts but was recaptured by the Soviets aboard the US vessel, returned to the USSR, and sent to a prison camp; in 1974, after the United States granted Kudirka US citizenship on the basis of his mother's birth, the USSR allowed him to come to the United States with his family.

271. Dainauskas, J. LITHUANIAN FOLK ART MOTIFS AT ST. CASIMIR LITHUANIAN CEMETERY IN CHICAGO, ILLINOIS. *Lituanus 1975 21(3): 5-14.* Classifies and describes the folk art motifs found on monuments in St. Casimir Cemetery into six groups. The most distinctive motif of the six is the "Rūpintojelis" (The Worrier). Some individual works by J. Mulokas, Ramojus Mozoliauskas, and Feliksas Daukas are particularly distinctive. Illus. K. N. T. Crowther

272. Gavelis, Vytautus. A DESCRIPTIVE STUDY OF THE EDUCATIONAL ATTAINMENT, OCCUPATION, AND GEOGRAPHICAL LOCATION OF THE CHILDREN OF LITHUANIAN DISPLACED PERSONS AND OF AMERICAN BORN PARENTS WHO ATTENDED IMMACULATE CONCEPTION PRIMARY SCHOOL IN EAST ST. LOUIS FROM 1948 TO 1968. *Lituanus 1976 22(1): 72-75.* Discusses the summary results of a Ph.D. dissertation comparing the educational and occupational attainment of two groups of children of Lithuanian family background. The parents of one group were American born and English speaking, the other Lithuanian born and non-English speaking. Recommendations for further research based on the results of the study are made. K. N. T. Crowther

273. Paegelīte, Dz. and Ziemelis, S. LATVIEŠU REVOLUCIONĀRIE EMIGRANTI AMERIKĀ: LENINISMA PROPAGANDISTI (1904-1919) [Latvian revolutionary emigrés in America: propagators of Leninism (1904-19)]. *Latvijas PSR Zinātnu Akademijas Vestis [USSR] 1974 (4): 60-69.* Describes the political publications of Latvian Bolsheviks living in the United States, particularly the newspaper *Strādnieks* in which many Latvian translations of Lenin's work were published.

274. Senn, Alfred Erich. VINCAS KREVE'S JOURNEY TO AMERICA. *J. of Baltic Studies 1976 7(3): 255-263.* Prints 12 letters written in 1947 from a displaced persons camp in Austria by a refugee Lithuanian professor who awaited US government permission to accept a post at the University of Pennsylvania. 10 notes.
E. W. Jennison, Jr.

275. Sesplaukis, Alfonsas. LITHUANIANS IN UPTON SINCLAIR'S *THE JUNGLE.* *Lituanus 1977 23(2): 24-31.* Lithuanians were chosen as the main characters in *The Jungle* because they were the major ethnic group working in the Chicago stockyards at the time the novel was written. The characters do not embody the true Lithuanian character but represent stereotypes. Sinclair sought to bring about social justice and his Lithuanian characters were a means to that end.
K. N. T. Crowther

276. Võime, L. OKTOOBRIREVOLUTSIOON JA PÕHJA-AMEERIKA EESTLASTE AJALEHT "UUS ILM" [The October Revolution and the North-American Estonian Newspaper *Uus Ilm*]. *Eesti NSV Teaduste Akadeemia. Toimetised. Ühiskonnateadused [USSR] 1979 28(3): 199-209.* *Uus Ilm* (New World), a radical Estonian-language newspaper published in the United States since 1909, has invariably supported the Soviet cause. In October 1917, it hailed the Bolshevik victory over the provisional government and called for the end of World War I. In 1918, the paper rallied to support Estonian American workers and farmers against the US anti-Soviet intervention and campaigned for the recognition of the Soviet state. Because of its pro-Soviet leanings, the paper was censored by the federal government and nine of its 1918 issues were confiscated. Based on the newspaper *Uus Ilm* and secondary sources; 63 notes.
S. P. Forgus

277. Wolkovich-Valkavičius, William. THE IMPACT OF A CATHOLIC NEWSPAPER ON AN ETHNIC COMMUNITY: THE LITHUANIAN WEEKLY *RYTAS*, 1896-98, WATERBURY, CONNECTICUT. *Lituanus 1978 24(3): 42-53.* Father Joseph Zebris (d. 1915), editor and publisher of the Lithuanian weekly *Rytas,* used his newspaper to improve the welfare of his fellow countrymen in America. Zebris viewed preservation of the Catholic faith as his primary goal and did not hesitate to attack free thinkers in *Rytas.* He was also concerned with the immigrants' assimilation, commending citizenship, literacy, and voting. Through notices of available employment and encouragement of cooperative stores, Zebris aimed to improve the economic welfare of his readers. Health and social services were also a concern. Despite its brief life *Rytas* helped guide Lithuanian immigrants toward assimilation. 10 notes.
K. N. T. Crowther

Basque

278. Etulain, Richard W. BASQUE BEGINNINGS IN THE PACIFIC NORTHWEST. *Idaho Yesterdays 1974 18(1): 26-32.*

279. Munro, Sarah Baker. BASQUE FOLKLORE IN SOUTH-EASTERN OREGON. *Oregon Hist. Q. 1975 76(2): 153-174.* Presents aspects of the folklore of Basque immigrants in Jordan Valley, Oregon, near the Oregon-Idaho border. These settlers immigrated to Oregon in the early 20th century and established themselves as sheepherders. Their new experiences provided legends, jokes, and superstitions centered around immigration, herding, prohibition, disease, and ethnic prejudice. Details the problems experienced by the Basques in traveling to a new home and their confusion in establishing occupations in an alien environment. Based on interviews and collected folk stories; map, 18 photos, 37 notes.
J. D. Smith

280. Sheperson, Wilbur. AN ESSAY ON AMERIKANUAK. *Nevada Hist. Soc. Q. 1976 19(2): 139-144.* Review article prompted by *Amerikanuak: Basques in the New World* (Reno: U. of Nevada Pr., 1975), by William A. Douglass and Jon Bilbao, who analyzed Basque migratory patterns, sociological variables such as varied experiences and occupations of Basque immigrants, and distinctive Basque historical and cultural outlooks. Basque immigrants ranged from "the grandest grandee to the humblest sheepcamp drifter."
H. T. Lovin

British

General

281. Burchell, R. A. THE GATHERING OF A COMMUNITY: THE BRITISH-BORN OF SAN FRANCISCO IN 1852 AND 1872. *J. of Am. Studies [Great Britain] 1976 10(3): 279-312.* Analyzes census and other official statistical data about the in-migration and out-migration of British-born persons to and from San Francisco during 1852-72. San Francisco tended to attract transient British-born people who moved elsewhere shortly. The out-migration was partly that of persons who first entered the United States at San Francisco and then migrated to more eastward American cities. The available data disproves the view that out-migrants consisted chiefly of unskilled and poverty-ridden persons. Based on government documents and secondary sources; 12 tables, 29 notes.
H. T. Lovin

282. Burchell, Robert A. THE LOSS OF A REPUTATION; OR, THE IMAGE OF CALIFORNIA IN BRITAIN BEFORE 1875. *California Hist. Q. 1974 53(2): 115-130.* Before the gold rush period California enjoyed a reputation in Great Britain as a paradise which, though somewhat remote, offered a healthful climate and economic opportunities. Travelers' published narratives reported favorably on the harbor at San Francisco and the fertile soil. But with the gold rush came reports of a lawless society in which good people were outnumbered by vagrants, outlaws, and swindlers, and in which morality suffered in the face of the prevalent vice and crime. By 1857 California capitalists were attempting to counteract this negative image through dissemination of favorable propaganda and the formation of an Immigrant Aid Association. Unfortunately, the writings of travelers to California had created a new image of California which effectively counteracted the earlier favorable one. British citizens viewed California as a locale for vigilantes, criminals, and speculators; and British capitalists shied away from California as a place for possible investment. Not until the 1870's, when California society could put forth a more stable image, did the negative view of California in Britain change. Thus, while publicity about California in the gold rush period could prove attractive in some areas, in Britain it had a largely negative effect. Based on contemporary reports from Great Britain; 79 notes.
A. Hoffman

283. Dunlevy, J. A. and Gemery, H. A. BRITISH-IRISH SETTLEMENT PATTERNS IN THE U.S.: THE ROLE OF FAMILY AND FRIENDS. *Scottish J. of Pol. Econ. [Great Britain] 1977 24(3): 257-263.* Statistically examines Richard Vedder and Lowell Gallaway's study of British and Irish settlement patterns, using steerage passenger immi-grants for 1898. The exclusion of cabin passengers and those who entered via Canada may limit the study. British and Irish immigrants were attracted to densely populated areas of high income and high employment. Although the Scots and Welsh avoided the South, Irish and English immigrants did not. After 1880 friends and families who had settled outside the South encouraged English and Irish immigrants to do likewise. 8 notes, biblio.
J. D. Neville

284. Gottlieb, Amy Zahl. IMMIGRATION OF BRITISH COAL MINERS IN THE CIVIL WAR DECADE. *Int. Rev. of Social Hist. [Netherlands] 1978 23(3): 357-375.* Immigration of British coal miners to the United States was greatly accelerated during the Civil War decade and reached its peak in 1869. Profitable employment opportunities in the United States, punitive measures by mine owners against labor unions, encouragement from British unions to emigrate in order to reduce excess supply of miners, the rise of fatalities in mining explosions in Great Britain, and the prospect of earning a livelihood from inexpensive land in the United States all induced thousands of British miners to scrape their resources into a passage to the New World. Based on newspapers and other published sources; table, 112 notes.
G. P. Blum

285. Gottlieb, Amy Zahl. THE INFLUENCE OF BRITISH TRADE UNIONISTS ON THE REGULATION OF THE MINING INDUSTRY IN ILLINOIS, 1872. *Labor Hist. 1978 19(3): 397-415.* English and Scots immigrant miners settling in Illinois brought with them experience in political action and mining legislation. Their organizations supported legislation based on experience in Great Britain, and succeeded in 1872. Based on newspapers, periodicals, and legislative records; 36 notes.
L. L. Athey

286. Miller, Nyle H., ed. AN ENGLISH RUNNYMEDE IN KANSAS. *Kansas Hist. Q. 1975 41(1): 22-62, (2): 183-224.* Part I. After his arrival in Kansas, Francis J. S. Turnly of Drumnasole, Ireland, established thriving ranching operations in Kingman and Harper Counties. As a result of publicity and recruitment many English, Irish, and Scots were drawn to his town of Runnymede where they established such conventional enterprises as stores, churches, restaurants, hotels, livery stables, and a stage line. Nearby settlers notes that the "Runnymede boys" also had three race tracks, a billiard parlor, a polo field, a bowling alley, and tennis courts. After a brief existence during 1888-92, the town disappeared. By means of excerpts from the Norwich *News* and Harper *Sentinel*, the editor has attempted to separate fact from folklore in the town's history from 29 May 1886 to 9 May 1890. 2 illus., 12 photos, 2 maps, 8 notes. Part II. The story is continued by means of excerpts from the Harper *Sentinel*, Norwich *News*, Anthony *Weekly Journal*, and Wichita *Daily Eagle*, from 16 May 1890 to 29 July 1892. Opens with a lengthy report of the tragic death of Robert W. Watmough, who, under the name "The Bird of Freedom," contributed the earlier stories to the Harper *Sentinel*. Concludes with an epilogue detailing the location and relocation of post offices during 1879-1944 for Turnly's town as well as an earlier Runnymede and a later South Runnymede in Harper County. Provides a brief bibliographical note. Based on newspapers and the papers of Mary Constance Hooper, copies of which are in the Kansas State Historical Society. 5 photos, 29 notes.
W. F. Zornow

287. Wells, Ronald A. MIGRATION AND THE IMAGE OF AMERICA IN ENGLAND: A STUDY OF *THE TIMES* IN THE NINETEENTH CENTURY. *Indiana Soc. Studies Q. 1975 28(2): 35-62.* Discusses how the image of the United States, as portrayed by *The Times* of London during the 19th century, contributed to emigration from Great Britain.

288. Zambrano, Ana Laura. THE EXODUS TO AMERICA: 1820-1870. *Amerikastudien/Am. Studies [West Germany] 1975 20(1): 101-121.* In the 19th century the majority of people emigrating from Great Britain [and Ireland] settled in the United States. Women especially were termed "superfluous females" who burdened a kingdom already faced with overpopulation and starvation, and they were encouraged to emigrate. From 1820-1875 the United States had an open door policy accepting all immigrants, and these were often British paupers—men and women whose passage was paid by their parish, by charitable landlords, religious groups, or through their own savings. The rush to America gained impetus in 1846-50 through the Irish potato famine when people faced with starvation at home chose to try their luck abroad. Most emi-

grants came to America because they already had relatives there, the passage was shorter and cheaper than to Australia or New Zealand, the United States offered a fairly civilized land with a similar language and culture, and advertisements promised the emigrants land and good salaries. The voyage was filled with abuse and disease on-boardship, but once in America, the English and Scottish adapted easily to the new world, while the Irish encountered prejudice. Still, the United States offered most immigrants opportunity for work and land, and the freedom to rise above their social station.   J

English

289. Abbott, Collamer M. CORNISH MINERS IN APPALACHIAN COPPER CAMPS. *Rev. Int. d'Hist. de la Banque [Italy] 1973 (7): 199-219.* Although they did not constitute a majority, Cornish miners represented a significant part of the work force in the copper mines of Appalachia, 1830-90. Sources for development in the mining regions, especially those for Orange County in Vermont and Polk County in Tennessee, indicate that mine owners looked to the Cornishmen for the skills necessary for hardrock, underground mining. They also were sought out as foremen. Both the methods of working the mines and the systems of payment reflected the traditional practices of the Cornish miners in the old country. Based on US Census, mining company records, newspapers, and secondary sources; 51 notes.   D. McGinnis

290. Abbott, Collamer M. THOMAS POLLARD: CORNISH MINER. *Rev. Int. d'Hist. de la Banque [Italy] 1973 6: 169-178.* Thomas Pollard (1815-1900), a miner and farmer in the Appalachian Mountains, was a typical example of many Cornish miners who migrated to the United States in the 19th century.

291. Allen, James B. TO THE SAINTS IN ENGLAND: IMPRESSIONS OF A MORMON IMMIGRANT (THE 10 DECEMBER 1840 WILLIAM CLAYTON LETTER FROM NAUVOO TO MANCHESTER). *Brigham Young U. Studies 1978 18(3): 475-480.* William Clayton, a member of the first Mormon emigrant company of Englishmen to America, wrote (on his arrival in Nauvoo, Illinois) his reflections of the journey. Addressing his friends in Manchester, he describes the new country and the hardships and the faith of his fellow Mormons, and offers sage advice to those planning to emigrate. Most significant are Clayton's observations of Joseph Smith and his immediate attachment to him. He expresses deep feelings for those Saints he had left behind, but vows that he would undertake the same journey again.   M. S. Legan

292. Allen, James B. "WE HAD A VERY HARD VOYAGE FOR THE SEASON": JOHN MOON'S ACCOUNT OF THE FIRST EMIGRANT COMPANY OF BRITISH SAINTS. *Brigham Young U. Studies 1977 17(3): 339-341.* An introduction to, and the text of, a letter that John Moon, the leader of the first self-organized emigrant company of British Mormons, wrote to William Clayton, past president of the British Mission, who was preparing for his own emigration. The letter chronicles the experience, trials, testimony, and excitement of the 41 Saints who left Liverpool for America on 6 June 1840. Clayton later included Moon's descriptions in a letter that he wrote on 19 August 1840 to Brigham Young and Willard Richards who were in England on an important mission.   M. S. Legan

293. Berry, Virginia. WASHINGTON FRANK LYNN: ARTIST AND JOURNALIST. *Beaver [Canada] 1978 308(4): 24-31.* Washington Frank Lynn, an Englishman trained as an artist, came to the New World in the 1860's as a correspondent for the Toronto *Globe*. He covered the Civil War in the United States. He became interested in Canadian settlement, and after a few years in England returned to Canada and the United States to study the lives of the immigrants. During 1871-72, he traveled via Minnesota to the Red River country, making copious notes on the inhabitants and painting many scenes, including *The Dakota Boat*, *Pembina*, and *Flat-Boats on the Red River*. 5 illus.   D. Chaput

294. Evans, Max J. WILLIAM C. STAINES: "ENGLISH GENTLEMAN OF REFINEMENT AND CULTURE." *Utah Hist. Q. 1975 43(4): 410-420.* William C. Staines (1818-81) was born in England,

joined the Mormon church in 1841, and migrated to Utah in 1847. He occupied prominent positions as territorial librarian (for 12 years) and church emigration agent (for 20 years). He was a promoter, entrepreneur, and businessman in a variety of enterprises. Churchman, politician, horticulturist, amateur scientist, and socialite, he is an example of the diversity of interest and talents found in 19th-century Utah. Based on primary and secondary sources; 2 illus., 40 notes.   J. L. Hazelton

295. Folmar, J. Kent, ed. WHY A BRITISH PHYSICIAN SHOULD *NOT* EMIGRATE TO AMERICA: BROWNSVILLE IN 1830—TWO LETTERS. *Western Pennsylvania Hist. Mag. 1976 59(2): 240-243.* Reprints letters between John Crisp, a physician in Middlesex, England, and his cousin Robert W. Playford, a physician in Brownsville, Pennsylvania, in which the latter discourages the former from immigrating to the United States because of the crowded state of the medical profession as well as poor economic and social conditions.

296. Friggens, Paul. THE CURIOUS "COUSIN JACKS": CORNISH MINERS IN THE AMERICAN WEST. *Am. West 1978 15(6): 4-7, 62-63.* With tin and copper ores virtually exhausted, Cornish miners left their homeland and made "monumental contributions" to mining in other parts of the world. Thousands came to the United States to pioneer mining in several states from Pennsylvania to California, especially in the West. These "Cousin Jacks" ranked among the greatest hard-rock miners in the world. They have indelibly stamped the West with their curious language, culture, and customs. 3 illus., note, biblio.   D. L. Smith

297. Lohrl, Ann. LETTERS FROM "THE LAND OF GOLD." *Pacific Historian 1976 20(3): 252-264.* Presents letters from California written by Christopher and Charlotte Harrold in 1849 and 1851, first printed in Charles Dickens' periodical *Household Words*. Initial editorial comments are corrected and additional information supplied. Letters are significant as comments by working-class immigrants about the land to which they had come. Primary and secondary sources; illus., 31 notes.   G. L. Olson

298. MacPhail, Elizabeth C. ALLEN HUTCHINSON: BRITISH SCULPTOR (1855-1929): AN ARTIST'S CAREER: FROM ENGLAND, HAWAII AND THE SOUTH PACIFIC TO SAN DIEGO, CALIFORNIA. *J. of San Diego Hist. 1973 19(2): 21-38.*

299. Miller, Keith L. PLANNING, PROPER HYGIENE, AND A DOCTOR: THE GOOD HEALTH OF THE ENGLISH SETTLEMENT. *J. of the Illinois State Hist. Soc. 1978 71(1): 22-29.* The English settlement at Albion, Illinois was founded in 1818 by Morris Birkbeck and George Flower. By examining official town records for 1818-29, concludes that the healthfulness and fertility of the site, combined with the services of a trained physician, accounted for its success. Map, table, 47 notes.   J

300. Reese, Dora J. AN ENGLISH GIRL COMES TO CONNECTICUT. *New-England Galaxy 1974 15(4): 42-47.* An authentic account of Jane Hill, who immigrated to New England.   S

301. Salter, Mary Ann. GEORGE FLOWER COMES TO THE ILLINOIS COUNTRY: A NEW LOOK AT MOTIVATIONS. *J. of the Illinois State Hist. Soc. 1976 69(3): 213-223.* Flower's letters and journal of 1816-17 reveal the strong initiative of Morris Birkbeck in their joint venture, the English settlement in Illinois (Albion). Flower was drawn to the South and attempted to persuade his friend to stay in Virginia, where Flower had purchased a farm. Slavery seemed less oppressive than he had expected; frontier conditions could be formidable. His decision to accompany Birkbeck westward seems to have been influenced by the presence of Eliza Julia Andrews (later Flower's wife) in Birkbeck's party. Based on letters and diaries in the Illinois State Historical Library and the Chicago Historical Society; 4 illus., map, 38 notes.   J/S

302. Savage, William W., Jr. COWS AND ENGLISHMEN: OBSERVATIONS ON INVESTMENT BY BRITISH IMMIGRANTS IN THE WESTERN RANGE CATTLE INDUSTRY. *Red River Valley Hist. R. 1974 1(1): 37-45.*

303. Tyrrell, Charles W. PRIMITIVE METHODISM: THE MIDWESTERN STORY. *Methodist Hist. 1976 15(1): 22-42.* The English

brought Primitive Methodism to the eastern seaboard in 1829 and to the Midwest in 1842. In Illinois, Wisconsin, and Iowa the Primitive Methodist Church was considered to be a foreign group and was basically missionary in character. There was a constant struggle for survival, and it never consisted of more than a few small churches, with a total membership, in 1976, of 11,000 persons in 82 churches. 20 notes.

H. L. Calkin

304. Walker, Evalyn Capps. THE STRANGE STORY. *Colorado Mag. 1977 54(3): 294-311.* The author's grandparents, Henry and Susannah Strange, were married in 1850, migrated from England to America in 1855, probably under Mormon auspices, and in 1859 started for Salt Lake City. They got as far as Fort Bridger but returned to St. Joseph. From 1863 until their deaths in 1908 and 1912 they lived in various frontier Colorado communities. Describes the life of Walker's father, Samuel J. Capps, likewise an English immigrant. Reminiscences and secondary sources; 13 illus., 45 notes.   O. H. Zabel

305. Walker, Ronald W. THE WILLARD RICHARDS AND BRIGHAM YOUNG 5 SEPTEMBER 1840 LETTER FROM ENGLAND TO NAUVOO. *Brigham Young U. Studies 1978 18(3): 466-475.* Written by Richards and Young, this 1840 letter was sent to Joseph Smith with the first emigrant group they had officially organized in England. It provides a contemporary Mormon-American view of early Victorian England. Richards and Young examined English life with the objective of identifying English labor's receptivity to the Mormon message. In particular they pointed to the enclosure movement, industrialization, and religion, including the Anglicans and Methodists.

M. S. Legan

306. Watt, Ronald G. SAILING "THE OLD SHIP ZION": THE LIFE OF GEORGE D. WATT. *Brigham Young U. Studies 1977 18(1): 48-65.* George D. Watt (1815-81), the first Mormon convert to be baptized in Great Britain, served as a clerk in Brigham Young's office, as a founding editor of the *Journal of Discourses,* as one of the developers of the Deseret alphabet, and as an early proponent of silkworm culture in Utah. He made significant contributions to the Mormons' cause. His knowledge of stenography particularly aided in the compilation of a written record of the early theological teachings. However, Watt's personality, his questioning of many church doctrines, and his perennial financial straits engendered disputes with many of the Mormon elders and led eventually to his excommunication in 1874.   M. S. Legan

307. Wells, Ronald A. MIGRATION AND THE IMAGE OF NEBRASKA IN ENGLAND. *Nebraska Hist. 1973 54(3): 475-491.* A series of six letters appeared in *The London Times* in 1872 discussing the merits of Nebraska as a place to settle.   R. Lowitt

Scottish (including Scotch-Irish)

308. Chalker, Fussell M. HIGHLAND SCOTS IN THE GEORGIA LOWLANDS. *Georgia Hist. Q. 1976 60(1): 35-42.* Many Scots left Scotland following the Battle of Culloden in 1746, migrating to America and settling in the lowlands of Southeastern Georgia. They were primarily cattle raisers who maintained many of their original cultural customs for years. They were distinguised by their traditional dress, language, music and ways, tending to isolate themselves from mainstream society. They were successful in their dealings with the Creek Indians and acquired much land, and also remained deeply committed to the Presbyterian Church of Scotland. By Civil War times, these Scots had become more integrated into Georgia life and responded to the call to arms by wearing the Confederate gray. Primary and secondary sources. 53 notes.

M. R. Gillam

309. Harling, Frederick F. and Kaufman, Martin. THE SCOTS. *Hist. J. of Western Massachusetts Supplement 1976: 108-112.* Most Scots in the colonies were Loyalists during the American Revolution. There were some Scots on the patriot side, most notably Arthur St. Clair and John Paul Jones. References.   W. H. Mulligan, Jr.

310. Horne, Robert M. JAMES FERGUS IN THE COLORADO GOLD FIELDS. *Colorado Mag. 1973 50(1): 41-56.* James Fergus, a

Scottish immigrant, was a miner in Colorado 1860-61. Leaving his family in Minnesota, Fergus went to Colorado and found, as did so many others, hard work, poor food, and loneliness, but little gold. He returned eastward in 1861 "with an empty poke and a disappointed heart," but in 1862 he was off to the Montana gold mines and remained in that area after that, active in politics and successful in business. Based primarily on the James Fergus Collection, Montana Historical Society Library, Helena; 5 illus., 66 notes.   O. H. Zabel

311. Klein, Maury. [THE SCOTCH IRISH]. *Am. Hist. Illus. 1979 13(9): 30-38, (10): 32-39; 14(1): 8-12, 15-17.* Part I. A RACE IN UPHEAVAL. Discusses social, religious, and political conditions in Ulster during the 17th century and the economic sanctions which caused a great number of Scotch Irish to come to the United States. Parts II and III. THE NATION-BUILDERS. The Scotch Irish settled in Pennsylvania, New York, and Virginia's Shenandoah Valley, establishing agricultural settlements and proving a grim and resolute match for Indians on the western frontier, 1717-76. A general overview of daily life on the frontier focuses on education, religion, social organization, the duties of women, and leisure activities, 1770-76.

312. Leyburn, James G. PRESBYTERIAN IMMIGRANTS AND THE AMERICAN REVOLUTION. *J. of Presbyterian Hist. 1976 54(1): 9-32.* Focuses on the Scotch Irish and the Scots, because few English immigrants to the colonies came over as Presbyterians. Most migrants came because of unfavorable economic circumstances. The value of the immigrants to the revolution consisted in the fact that the Presbyterian Church was national in scope. More than in any other denomination, members were in touch with each other from Maine to Georgia. Moreover, their attachment was a patriotism for the cause of the nation as a whole, not the vindication of the rights of one colony alone. Based on primary and secondary sources; illus., 38 notes.

H. M. Parker, Jr.

313. McLeod, Dean L. JAMES ROSS: THE EXPERIENCES OF A SCOTTISH IMMIGRANT TO AMERICA. *Family Heritage 1978 1(6): 178-179, 182-183.* James Ross (1822-1900), who emigrated to America in the mid-19th century, was one of the first 600 Scots to join the Mormon Church in 1842, in Scotland.

314. Opie, John. A SENSE OF PLACE: THE WORLD WE HAVE LOST. *Appalachian J. 1977 4(4): 113-119.* The intimate relationship Appalachians feel with the land they live on, and the sense of belonging, is discussed in connection with the immigration of Lowland Scots into Appalachia during the 18th century.

315. Powell, Terese A. THE SCOTCH-IRISH. *Hist. J. of Western Massachusetts Supplement 1976: 85-93.* Discusses the origins of the Scotch Irish, how they came to America, and their role in the American Revolution. Prominent Scotch Irish were Patrick Henry, John Stark, and Henry Knox. The Scotch Irish were active in every phase of the Revolutionary struggle throughout the country. Notes.

W. H. Mulligan, Jr.

316. Voght, Martha. SCOTS IN HISPANIC CALIFORNIA. *Scottish Hist. R. [Great Britain] 1973 52(154): 137-148.* Hubert Howe Bancroft, author of *History of California,* seven vols. (San Francisco, 1884-90), compiled the Pioneer Register and Index which lists all non-Indians who came to California between 1542 and 1848. Fifty-five were native-born Scots. Gives an account of 14 who became influential. The list includes David Spence, James Scott, John Wilson, James McKinley, Hugo Reid, and John Gilroy. Based on Bancroft, the Larkin Papers, and articles from the California Historical Society *Quarterly;* 58 notes.

N. W. Moen

Welsh

317. Davies, Phillips G., ed. and transl. EARLY WELSH SETTLEMENTS IN ILLINOIS. *J. of the Illinois State Hist. Soc. 1977 70(4): 292-298.* Edits and translates the Illinois chapters of Robert D. Thomas's 1872 *Hanes Cymry America* (History of the Welsh in America). Thomas (1817-88), a minister and advocate of Welsh emigration to the United

States, emigrated to New York City. He describes Welsh churches in the United States as well as major industries employing Welshmen. 2 illus., 4 notes.   J

318. Davies, Phillips G., transl. REVEREND R. D. THOMAS'S "WELSH IN MISSOURI, 1872." *Missouri Hist. Rev. 1978 72(2): 154-175.* Reverend Thomas had congregations in New York, Pennsylvania, Ohio, and Tennessee. His religious duties did not keep him from writing poetry and prose. Translates chapter 6 of *Hanes Cymry America* (History of the Welsh in America) describing the life of Welsh communities in St. Louis and eight small towns in Missouri. 8 illus., 2 maps, note.
W. F. Zornow

319. Davies, Phillips G. THE WELSH IN OHIO: THOMAS'S *HANES CYMRY AMERICA.* Old Northwest 1977 3(3): 289-318. A translation from the Welsh of Chapter 5, Part 1, of *Hanes Cymry America* (History of the Welsh in America) by Robert D. Thomas (1872) which deals with the Welsh settlements in Ohio. Lists by name the Welsh settlers in 22 Ohio counties.   J

320. Davies, Phillips G., ed. WELSH SETTLEMENTS IN KANSAS. *Kansas Hist. Q. 1977 43(4): 448-469.* Translates a large portion of the seventh chapter of the second part of the Reverend Robert D. Thomas's (1817-88) *Hanes Cymry America* (History of the Welsh in America), published in Welsh at Utica, New York, in 1872. The chapter is of particular interest because it includes considerable firsthand information that Thomas gathered in 1869 in Kansas. Mentions the Congregational Church in Emporia, the Welsh churches in Arvonia, and in Lyon, Osage, Shawnee, Douglas, Leavenworth, and Atchison Counties, and other places where Welsh settlers gathered. Mentions several settlers, including Rowland Davies, who established a general store in Bala in 1870 and whose very high opinion of the Kansas prairie Thomas quoted. 80 notes.   A. W. Howell

321. Edwards, Jane Spencer. WILLS AND INVENTORIES OF THE FIRST PURCHASERS OF THE WELSH TRACT. *Pennsylvania Folklife 1973-74 23(2): 2-15.* Studies the material culture of a Welsh community near Philadelphia, 1650-1750.   S

322. Ellis, David Maldwyn. THE ASSIMILATION OF THE WELSH IN CENTRAL NEW YORK. *Welsh Hist. Rev. 1973 6(4): 424-447.* Examines the immigration of Welsh to central New York, particularly to Oneida County. Before the Civil War, most immigrants chose the countryside. After 1865, they tended to locate in cities like Utica. Discusses the life-styles, churches, political inclinations, and literature of the immigrants and their descendants. Traces the gradual disintegration of the Welsh as a separate community during the 20th century. Primary and secondary sources; 3 tables, 52 notes.   T. L. Auffenberg

323. Harling, Frederick F. and Kaufman, Martin. WELSH. *Hist. J. of Western Massachusetts 1976 (Supplement): 118-119.* Lists people of Welsh descent who were active politically or militarily in the American Revolution.   W. H. Mulligan, Jr.

324. Whitaker, James W., ed., and Davies, Phillips G., transl. WELSH SETTLEMENTS IN IOWA. *Palimpsest 1978 59(1): 24-32.* Presents an edited segment of *Hanes Cymry America*, published in 1872 and written by Welsh Congregational minister Robert D. Thomas, who served churches in Wales and the United States. Intended as an immigrants' guide, the book was often inaccurate and exaggerated. It did contain useful demographic and genealogical information, as well as information about individuals and social institutions. Photo, note.
D. W. Johnson

325. Williams, Gwyn A. WELSH INDIANS: THE MADOC LEGEND AND THE FIRST WELSH RADICALISM. *Hist. Workshop J. [Great Britain] 1976 1: 136-154.* A document signed by, among others, Sir Walter Raleigh, claimed a major part of the Americas for Queen Elizabeth I as the rightful heir of Madog ab Owain Gwynedd (1150?-1180), legendary Welsh prince, who supposedly discovered America ca. 1170. The 18th-century writings of Edward Thurlow, who visited Mexico, describe the natives as descendants of the Welsh. Additional evidence indicates that the Elizabethan court cultivated the Madog legend about America's discovery because it gave the English an older claim on the

Americas than had the Spanish. The extravagant English claims inspired by the Madog legend in turn inspired 18th-century Welsh missionaries in America, who can be seen as early Welsh radicals, looking for Welsh descendants among American Indian tribes.   A. J. Evans

Australian and New Zealand

326. Ricards, Sherman L. and Blackburn, George M. THE SYDNEY DUCKS: A DEMOGRAPHIC ANALYSIS. *Pacific Hist. Rev. 1973 42(1): 20-31.* Compares the legend and reputation of the mid-19th century immigrants from Australia to California with the facts as indicated by the California census of 1852 and other demographic statistics. These latter show that as a group they were more mature, family-oriented, and successful than other Californians. Some were undoubtedly criminals and gamblers, but as a total group they were unfairly maligned by the San Francisco citizens and their Committee of Vigilance. 4 tables, 23 notes.
E. C. Hyslop

327. Tanasoca, Steven and Sudduth, Susan. A JOURNAL KEPT BY GEORGE A. HARDING. *Oregon Hist. Q. 1978 79(2): 172-202.* After immigrating from Australia as boys in 1856, George A. Harding and his brother William worked in the Idaho mining fields during 1862. In 1877 George Harding married Margaret Barlow, daughter of the builder of the Barlow Road, and became a prominent citizen of Oregon City. Reproduces Harding's diary while in the mining fields from 7 May 1862 through 16 October 1862. Based on documents in the Oregon Historical Society, newspaper reports, and published secondary sources; map, 6 photos, 29 notes.   D. R. McDonald

Canadian

328. Brookes, Alan A. OUT-MIGRATION FROM THE MARITIME PROVINCES, 1860-1900: SOME PRELIMINARY CONSIDERATIONS. *Acadiensis [Canada] 1976 5(2): 26-56.* Emigration from the Maritime Provinces during 1860-1900 was largely because of persistent depressions and economic dislocation. By the 1880's the exodus had spread into rural areas not previously affected, and to industrializing urban centers. Beginning with young, single people, the movement later embraced older, more stable elements and whole families. Most went to New England, especially Boston, where they "assumed a wide range of better jobs." Transportation and communication links and commercial orientation favored Boston. 78 notes.   D. F. Chard

329. Kennedy, Albert J. "THE PROVINCIALS," WITH AN INTRODUCTION BY ALAN A. BROOKES. *Acadiensis [Canada] 1975 4(2): 85-101.* During the mid-1910's at Boston's South End settlement house, social worker Albert J. Kennedy wrote a description of Canadians who had fled to Boston from the Atlantic Provinces because of economic conditions. Titled "The Provincials," the description is opinionated and dated but still offers numerous insights. The provincials were largely unskilled or semi-skilled, fairly religious, and generally had high morals. Although the first generation was clannish and uninterested in politics or unions, the second generation soon became Americanized. Based on published secondary materials, United States and Canadian census reports; 9 notes.   E. A. Churchill

Dutch

330. Aiken, John R. NEW NETHERLANDS ARBITRATION IN THE 17TH CENTURY. *Arbitration J. 1974 29(3): 145-160.* Early mercantile arbitration on the American continent is usually assumed to have been derived from English common law and the experience of English merchants and guilds. But there were also Dutch colonies during the 17th century, and their tradition was traceable to Roman law, by way of the Netherlands. In the course of exhaustive research, the author may have found the earliest example of a woman serving as an arbitrator. In 1662, a dispute arose as to whether a woman had been paid properly for making linen caps. The issue turned on whether she had performed her job without excessive spoilage. A court appointed another women as an

expert arbitrator "to inspect the linen caps" and "settle the parties' case." The history of arbitration among Dutch colonies convinces the author that it was superior to that of the English common law.   J

331. Barone, Constance. THE DUTCH. *Hist. J. of Western Massachusetts 1976 (Supplement): 13-17.* Discusses the Dutch in New York and New Jersey. An individual's allegiance in the American Revolution was linked to his religious affiliation. Members of the Dutch Reformed Church were usually Whigs, and adherents of the Conferentie group were loyalists. Notes.   W. H. Mulligan, Jr.

332. Beardslee, John W., III. THE DUTCH REFORMED CHURCH AND THE AMERICAN REVOLUTION. *J. of Presbyterian Hist. 1976 54(1): 165-181.* Discusses the nature of the divisiveness which plagued the colonial Dutch church, and the relation that it bore to the division between Dutch Whig and Tory during the Revolution. For the Dutch churches, the Revolution was a bitter internal struggle, with lines of division which followed ecclesiastical patterns. A spirit of amnesty made possible the church's survival after the war. The divisiveness was also healed when the church immersed itself in an intensive foreign missions program in the early 18th century. Based on primary and secondary sources; illus., 41 notes.   H. M. Parker, Jr.

333. DeJong, Gerald. THE COMING OF THE DUTCH TO THE DAKOTAS. *South Dakota Hist. 1974 5(1): 20-51.* Dutch ethnic clustering was important in the Dakotas in certain places. Arriving first in the 1880's, they were never as many as the Scandinavians or Germans, but their culture marked a stamp of "Dutchness" on some landscapes. Leaving Holland for the traditional reasons, most Dutch did not go to the Dakotas. As free land became scarce in other midwestern states, Hollanders, like others, spread westward, often in small colonies. A large Dutch settlement in Northwest Iowa allowed nearby cultural contact. The Dutch in the Dakotas suffered all the hardships that settlers in that time experienced. Some left, but the number of Hollanders maintained itself with new arrivals. Their language, clothing and other personal articles, contact with other Dutch Americans, and especially religion continued their cultural traditions long after arrival. Based on primary and secondary sources; 10 illus., 63 notes.   A. J. Larson

334. DeJong, Gerald F. DUTCH IMMIGRANTS IN NEW JERSEY BEFORE WORLD WAR I. *New Jersey Hist. 1976 94(2-3): 69-88.* New Jersey was attractive to immigrants from the Netherlands because Dutch customs lingered from colonial times. Clergymen from the Reformed Dutch Church assisted immigrants financially and helped them find jobs. Dutch-language newspapers flourished, new churches were established, and organizations promoting Dutch camaraderie were founded. Dutch immigrants and their descendants developed a positive identity with American political and social ideals, and demonstrated their loyalty in World War I. Based on primary and secondary sources; 3 illus., 42 notes.   E. R. McKinstry

335. DeVries, George, Jr. THE DUTCH IN THE AMERICAN REVOLUTION: REFLECTIONS AND OBSERVATIONS. *Fides et Hist. 1977 10(1): 43-57.* The response of Dutch Americans and the Reformed Dutch Church to the American Revolution was varied, embracing Tory, Whig, and neutralist positions. The range of responses was dependent upon ecclesiastical, political, or economic considerations, never upon theological or scriptural considerations. Revolution is opposed to Scripture. Based on Biblical, secondary, and primary sources; 75 notes.   R.E. Butchart

336. Gehring, Charles. NEW YORK'S DUTCH RECORDS: A HISTORIOGRAPHICAL NOTE. *New York Hist. 1975 56(3): 347-354.* Describes the Dutch records of the history of New Netherland, preserved in the New York State Library, and tells the history of translations of the Dutch records during the 19th century. Cautions that 19th-century translations are unreliable and describes the current project for translation of all available Dutch records. 2 notes.   R. N. Lokken

337. Goodfriend, Joyce D. BURGHERS AND BLACKS: THE EVOLUTION OF A SLAVE SOCIETY AT NEW AMSTERDAM. *New York Hist. 1978 59(2): 125-144.* The development of a slave population in New Netherland was prompted by the Dutch West India Company to deal with the perpetual problem of underpopulation in the Dutch

settlements, and to assure prosperity by increasing agricultural production. At first slavery in New Netherland was institutionalized on a corporate basis, an unusual case in American colonial experience. By 1664, as the result of company practices, slavery had become a widespread mode of labor exploitation among the settlers in the colony. 4 illus., 44 notes.   R. N. Lokken

338. Hauptman, Laurence M. and Knapp, Ronald G. DUTCH-ABORIGINAL INTERACTION IN NEW NETHERLAND AND FORMOSA: AN HISTORICAL GEOGRAPHY OF EMPIRE. *Pro. of the Am. Phil. Soc. 1977 121(2): 166-182.* The 17th-century Dutch colonial empire depended on commerce and profit, not social interaction. Resulting policies towards nonwhites were neither uniform nor consistent. Religious conversion efforts and cultural diffusion in both colonies remained minimal. The Dutch imported Chinese laborers to supplant the native Formosans; the coastal Algonkins of New Netherland were simply eradicated by diseases, alcohol, and the ample weapons provided to their enemies, the Five Nations. 2 maps, table, 83 notes.   W. L. Olbrich

339. Hecht, Irene W. D. KINSHIP AND MIGRATION: THE MAKING OF AN OREGON ISOLATE COMMUNITY. *J. of Interdisciplinary Hist. 1977 8(1): 45-67.* Demonstrates how cooperative research between biomedicine and social history can be mutually productive by studying an isolate community of Dutch extraction in the Willamette Valley town of Verboort. Isolate communities are not necessarily obvious. Nuptial patterns, especially realliance and sibling exchange, can be identified as the basis of biological isolation or inbreeding. Based on parish registers, census returns, and printed sources; map, table, 4 figs., 15 notes.   R. Howell

340. Kenney, Alice P. LOST COLONISTS: THE DUTCH IN BERKSHIRE COUNTY. *New-England Galaxy 1977 19(1): 3-16.* Records the role played by Dutch settlers in Berkshire County, Massachusetts. Their contributions to the economic, political, and social life are stressed. Dutch family names included the Karners, Spoors, Van Schaacks, Van Deusens, Houcks, Freeses, and Van Tassels. 8 illus.   P. C. Marshall

341. Leder, Lawrence H. FUR: A REEVALUATION OF THE ALBANY DUTCH. *R. in Am. Hist. 1975 3(2): 183-186.* Thomas Elliot Norton's *The Fur Trade in Colonial New York, 1686-1776* (Madison: U. of Wisconsin Pr., 1974) examines "the interaction of war, politics, economics, and imperial policies upon the fur trade" and defends Dutch American merchants and traders "unjustly accused of shortsightedness in their attitudes toward the Indians and the fur trade."

342. Main, Gloria L. THE DUTCH "IN DUTCH" IN OLD NEW YORK. *Rev. in Am. Hist. 1976 4(3): 379-384.* Review article prompted by Thomas J. Archdeacon's *New York City, 1664-1710: Conquest and Change* (Ithaca, New York: Cornell U. Pr., 1976) which discusses the social structure of New York City, as well as ethnic tensions which arose over the British rule of Dutch inhabitants.

343. Nieuwenhuis, Nelson. A NEW COLONY IN NORTHWEST IOWA. *Palimpsest 1978 59(6): 182-193.* Under the direction of Henry Hospers, Dutch immigrants settled in northwest Iowa, 1860-72. Hospers was a surveyor and real estate agent and later was commissioned by the federal government to return to the Netherlands and promote immigration.

344. Nieuwenhuis, Nelson. ZWEMER HALL: A LANDMARK AT NORTHWESTERN COLLEGE. *Ann. of Iowa 1975 43(2): 103-112.* Erected in 1894, Zwemer Hall was the first building on the campus of Northwestern College in Orange City, Iowa. Today it houses the school's administrative offices and serves as the regional headquarters for the Dutch Reformed Church in America. Recounts the circumstances which led to the construction of the building, the selection of George Pass as architect, the cost of construction, and the dedication of the structure. In 1924, the Northwestern Board of Trustees voted to name the building "Zwemer Hall" in honor of the school's long-time principal, James F. Zwemer. Based largely on a local Dutch-language newspaper; photos, 9 notes.   P. L. Petersen

345. Prudon, Theodore M. THE DUTCH BARN IN AMERICA: SURVIVAL OF A MEDIEVAL STRUCTURAL FRAME. *New York Folklore 1976 2(3-4): 123-142.* Describes the prototypical 18th-century Dutch barn in the United States, tracing its frame construction to late medieval precedents.

346. Rhoads, William B. FRANKLIN D. ROOSEVELT AND DUTCH COLONIAL ARCHITECTURE. *New York Hist. 1978 59(4): 430-464.* President Franklin D. Roosevelt paralleled Thomas Jefferson in his interest in architecture. After his polio attack in 1921 FDR became active in preserving the historical and pictorial records of colonial Dutch houses, and he undertook the revival of Dutch fieldstone architecture in Dutchess County. As president he directed the architects of the Treasury Department to design new post offices in Dutchess and Ulster counties in conformity with local Dutch architectural traditions. Shows how involved FDR was in planning the architectural details of Hudson Valley buildings constructed during his presidency, including the Franklin D. Roosevelt Library at Hyde Park. 8 illus., 78 notes.
R. N. Lokken

347. Rink, Oliver A. COMPANY MANAGEMENT OR PRIVATE TRADE: THE TWO PATROONSHIP PLANS FOR NEW NETHERLAND. *New York Hist. 1978 59(1): 5-26.* Analyzes a recently discovered copy of the New Netherland patroonship plan of 1628 and the revised "Freedoms and Exceptions" adopted by the West India Company in 1629. What historians thought was a conflict between democracy and aristocracy in New Netherland was actually a struggle between patroons and company administration over questions of land and trade. The intent of the 1628 plan was to modify the company's trade monopoly so that private enterprise could bear the expense of the colony's settlement, and the 1629 plan gave the patroons greater privileges of trade and settlement. The patroons' victory came too late, however, as private merchants in Amsterdam successfully exploited the colony's trade. 5 illus., 63 notes.
R. N. Lokken

348. Ritchie, Robert C. GOD AND MAMMON IN NEW NETHERLAND. *R. in Am. Hist. 1974 2(3): 353-357.* George L. Smith's *Religion and Trade in New Netherland: Dutch Origins and American Development* (Ithaca, N.Y.: Cornell U. Pr., 1973) points out that Dutch Americans in New York increased their religious liberty during the 17th century due to "economic pressure, weak governments, schismatic movements, and secular influences."

349. Ritchie, Robert C. LONDON MERCHANTS, THE NEW YORK MARKET, AND THE RECALL OF SIR EDMUND ANDROS. *New York Hist. 1976 57(1): 5-29.* After conflict in 1674 between English mercantile interests in New York and the traditional governor's trade policies favoring the Dutch mercantile community resulted in Sir Edmund Andros's recall in 1680, and significant commercial and political changes in the province, including the Duke of York's grant of a representative assembly. 3 illus., 67 notes. R. N. Lokken

350. Stekelenburg, H. A. V. M. van. ROOMS-KATHOLIEKE LANDVERHUIZERS NAAR DE VEREENIGDE STATEN [Roman Catholic immigrants to the United States]. *Spiegel Hist. [Netherlands] 1977 12(12): 681-689.* Dutch immigration to the United States became rather substantial, 1845-75. Most of the immigrants who settled in Michigan, Iowa, and Illinois were secessionists of the Reformed Dutch Church. Less is known about a fairly large number of Catholics, most of whom came from the southern provinces of North Brabant and Limburg. The immigrants came primarily for economic reasons and settled in the Fox River Valley of Wisconsin. Much of the original impulse to immigrate came from T. J. van den Broek (1773-1851), the Dutch Catholic missionary among the Indians in Wisconsin. About 8,000 Catholic immigrants came between 1841 and 1875. Illus., biblio. G. D. Homan

351. Stern, Steve J. KNICKERBOCKERS WHO ASSERTED AND INSISTED: THE DUTCH INTEREST IN NEW YORK POLITICS, 1664-1691. *New-York Hist. Soc. Q. 1974 58(2): 112-138.* A study of New York politics indicates possible inaccuracy of the view in histories of early New York that the Dutch settlers accepted English rule after 1664 passively and were assimilated easily into the colonial society. Dutch politicians asserted themselves on many occasions, such as in retaining comparative freedom for the Dutch Reformed Church, and were able to

obtain a share of governmental power. Because English policy was designed to make the transition smooth, the Dutch were able to achieve compromises advantageous to them. Based largely on primary sources; 7 illus., 54 notes. C. L. Grant

352. Swierenga, Robert P. and Stout, Harry S. DUTCH IMMIGRATION IN THE NINETEENTH CENTURY, 1820-1877: A QUANTITATIVE OVERVIEW. *Indiana Soc. Studies Q. 1975 28(2): 7-34.* Discusses the pattern and extent of Dutch immigration to the United States during 1820-77, and the social, political, economic, and religious factors that prompted it.

353. Wacker, Peter O. DUTCH MATERIAL CULTURE IN NEW JERSEY. *J. of Popular Culture 1978 11(4): 948-958.* Examines the extent of Dutch influence in northern New Jersey and the cultural landscape there, 1740's-80's, according to the distribution of Dutch churches, Dutch-style houses and barns, and Dutch farming methods.

354. Wacker, Peter O. FOLK ARCHITECTURE AS AN INDICATOR OF CULTURE AREAS AND CULTURE DIFFUSION: DUTCH BARNS AND BARRACKS IN NEW JERSEY. *Pioneer Am. 1973 5(2): 37-47.* Investigates the Dutch barn and the barrack (a device used primarily for the storage of hay, straw, or grain), structures which were among the most distinctive features found on the cultural landscape of New Jersey during the 18th century. Both structures generally are considered to be of Dutch origin, and they may still be seen in their original forms in the Old World. Newspaper advertisements of property in New Jersey covering 1704-81 were utilized in compiling maps showing the distribution of the Dutch barn and barrack. This study contradicts the idea that acceptance of Dutch contributions by the non-Dutch has been minimal in this country. Based in part on secondary sources and primary sources found in New Jersey's Division of State Library, Bureau of Archives and History; illus., 2 photos, 4 maps, 28 notes. C. R. Gunter, Jr.

355. Whitridge, Arnold. PETER STUYVESANT: DIRECTOR GENERAL OF NEW NETHERLAND. *Hist. Today [Great Britain] 1960 10(5): 324-332.* Analyzes the significance of Peter Stuyvesant's (1592-1672) vision that New Amsterdam, now New York City, would be the most important city on the Atlantic seaboard.

356. Wright, Langdon G. LOCAL GOVERNMENT AND CENTRAL AUTHORITY IN NEW NETHERLAND. *New-York Hist. Soc. Q. 1973 57(1): 6-29.* A study of local government is the basis for comparison of popular participation and autonomy in Dutch and English colonial towns. Town patents were not identical, but all contained strict regulations concerning landowning and local government. The governor and council dominated, but even the autocratic Peter Stuyvesant gave the towns some freedom. Local government in New Netherland is best explained in terms of the "undefined and unstable balance" between the governor and local units. Based on colonial records; 2 illus., 45 notes.
C. L. Grant

357. Yzenbaard, John H. THE *KNICKERBOCKER*: A VESSEL OF UNFULFILLED HOPE. *Inland Seas 1973 29(1): 47-49.* In 1847 a group of Dutch settlers at Zeeland, Michigan, established a cooperative store and purchased the schooner *Knickerbocker* to bring it goods. The project failed in less than a year. Based on secondary sources; 6 notes.
K. J. Bauer

358. Yzenbaard, John H. SHATTERED DREAMS: THE BURNING OF THE *PHOENIX*. *Inland Seas 1974 30(3): 159-167.* The burning of the steamer *Phoenix* off Sheboygan, Wisconsin, 21 November 1847, killed at least 150 people, mostly Dutch immigrants. Although discussed in newspapers and known in the Netherlands, the catastrophe had little effect on the flow of Dutch settlers to Michigan, Wisconsin, and Illinois. Based on primary sources; 40 notes. K. J. Bauer

French (including French Canadians)

359. Allain, Mathé. L'IMMIGRATION FRANÇAISE EN LOUISIANE, 1718-1721 [French immigration into Louisiana, 1718-1721]. *Revue d'hist. de l'Amérique française [Canada] 1975 28(4): 555-564.* In 1715 there were no more than 215 French inhabitants in Louisiana, including military personnel. The colony was founded as a check on Spanish and English colonialism, and by 1715 was considered a buffer area of Canada. During 1718-21, a concerted attempt was made to populate Louisiana by exiling many undesirables from France. Not until mid-century would there be another attempt to stimulate emigration to Louisiana. Based on primary and secondary sources; 49 notes.
L. B. Chan

360. Allen, James P. FRANCO-AMERICANS IN MAINE: A GEOGRAPHICAL PERSPECTIVE. *Acadiensis [Canada] 1974 4(1): 32-66.* Depicts geographical and social characteristics of Maine's Franco-Americans, many of whom immigrated to the state during the later 19th and early 20th centuries. Major immigration included southward expansion of rural settlements along the upper St. John River and the migration of Canadians to textile and later pulp and paper manufacturing centers. Generally settling together and maintaining their language and Catholic faith, the Franco-Americans retained their ethnic identity surprisingly well, although there has been slippage in the last two decades due to changing conditions. Based on private and official census reports, published government materials, newspapers, and secondary sources; 3 maps, 7 tables, 85 notes.
E. A. Churchill

361. Auge, Thomas. THE LIFE AND TIMES OF JULIEN DUBUQUE. *Palimpsest 1976 57(1): 2-13.* Julien Dubuque, long acknowledged as one of the first white settlers in what is today Iowa, was an atypical frontiersman. Cultivated and accustomed to a lavish life-style, he was a cultural incongruity. But he was also shrewd and opportunistic in his business dealings, duplicitous in relationships with Indians, and constantly in debt. Illus., map, note.
D. W. Johnson

362. Barham, Mack E. LA MÉTHODOLOGIE DU DROIT CIVIL DE L'ÉTAT DE LOUISIANE [The methodology of the civil law in the state of Louisiana]. *Rev. Int. de Droit Comparé [France] 1975 27(4): 797-816.* In 1803 Louisiana adopted a civil law code based on the Napoleonic code. The procedure of the Louisiana courts resembled that of the common law courts of the other states more than that of the French courts, partly because of the greater availability of legal literature written in English. A struggle developed between those jurists who favored assimilation with the common law and those who sought to preserve the civil law tradition. Today the Louisiana State Law Institute is following the latter trend. Although some of the methods of Louisiana judges are derived from the common law, the Louisiana supreme court adheres to the civil law tradition because it serves the best interests of the people of the state. Primary and secondary sources; 99 notes.
J. S. Gassner

363. Beale, Georgia Robison. BOSC AND THE EXEQUATUR. *Prologue 1978 10(3): 133-151.* Louis Augustin Guillaume Bosc, a French nationalist and government employee under the Revolutionary regime, left France in 1796 for personal and political reasons, having been promised a diplomatic assignment in the United States by the administration of the Directory. While awaiting official word of his commission, Bosc resided in Charleston, South Carolina, where he made contact with French consul Victor de Nemours DuPont, botanist Andre Michaux, and French-speaking Huguenot refugees from the West Indies. He also studied the flora and fauna of the South Carolina coast. Eventually Bosc received appointment as French vice-consul at Wilmington, Delaware. Dupont became consul at Philadelphia. Both DuPont and Bosc returned to France in 1798, due to the worsening relations between France and the United States. Primary sources.
N. Lederer

364. Benoit, Virgil. GENTILLY: A FRENCH-CANADIAN COMMUNITY IN THE MINNESOTA RED RIVER VALLEY. *Minnesota Hist. 1975 44(8): 278-289.* Gentilly and its environs in northwestern Minnesota was heavily settled during the 1870's-80's by French Canadi-ans emigrating from Quebec. The French Catholic community has been held together by its religion, conservative family life, and the rural environment. Extensive ties with Canadian relatives still exist. Gentilly achieved a modicum of prosperity through the efforts to establish a cheese factory by the powerful Catholic priest Elie Theillon. Father Theillon was the spiritual and secular leader of Gentilly's French Canadians during 1888-1935. The Catholic Church has been a major factor in preserving the conservative social and economic world view of Gentilly's residents. Based on French and English language primary sources.
N. Lederer

365. Bezou, James F. HISTORIQUE DU JOURNALISME D'EXPRESSION FRANCAISE EN LOUISIANE [History of French-language journalism in Louisiana]. *Rev. de Louisiane 1977 6(1): 39-44.* Discusses the first French-language newspapers in Louisiana, including their popularity, growth, readership, publishers, and editors, 1794-1860.

366. Bilodeau, Therese. THE FRENCH IN HOLYOKE (1850-1900). *Hist. J. of Western Massachusetts 1974 3(1): 1-12.* Nicholas Proulx, one of the first French Canadians to migrate to Holyoke, recruited workers in Quebec. Management found them obedient, non-union workers whose life revolved around the Catholic Church. Primary and secondary sources; 3 illus., chart, 58 notes.
S. S. Sprague

367. Birbalsingh, Frank M. W. ADOLPHE ROBERTS: CREOLE ROMANTIC. *Caribbean Q. [Jamaica] 1973 19(2): 100-107.* W. Adolphe Roberts (1886-1962), a Creole born in Jamaica where he became a journalist, emigrated to the United States in 1906 and became a noted historian, journalist, editor, lecturer, novelist, scholar, and poet. His novels, 1929-49, cover a variety of New World areas and subjects, but the most famous is his trilogy on Louisiana—*Royal Street, Brave Mardi Gras,* and *Creole Dusk.* All emphasize his fondness for Creole culture and his sadness at its passing. 5 notes.
R. L. Woodward, Jr.

368. Blick, Boris and Grant, H. Roger. FRENCH ICARIANS IN ST. LOUIS. *Missouri Hist. Soc. Bull. 1973 30(1): 3-28.* Icarians, followers of Étienne Cabet (1788-1856), founded several utopian communities in the United States. Cabet came to America in 1849. Disputes among the Icarians erupted in 1852 and the faction that sided with Cabet moved to Missouri and established Cheltenham, six miles west of St. Louis. Cheltenham prospered until the residents quarreled and many withdrew. Financial problems finally destroyed the settlement, and the few stalwarts who had remained abandoned it in 1862. Describes Icarian industries, agriculture, and social practices. Reprints letters and documents. Based mainly on secondary sources; 7 photos, 24 notes.
H. T. Lovin

369. Blow, David J. THE ESTABLISHMENT AND EROSION OF FRENCH-CANADIAN CULTURE IN WINOOSKI, VERMONT, 1867-1900. *Vermont Hist. 1975 43(1): 59-74.* In 1867, French-speaking natives of Quebec and their children comprised 49% of the 1,745 people in Winooski village, Vermont, a woolen mill town with a machine shop and 10 other small industries. Bishop Louis de Goësbriand appointed a young Canadian priest, Jean Frédéric Audet, in 1868. Supported by three lay councillors in a "fabrique" organized in 1873, he enlarged a parochial school, built the church of St. Francis Xavier, 1870-84 (see table of its financial history), and presided over a francophone enclave with mutual aid societies and basically Democratic Party politics. The second generation gradually identified with anglophone Vermont rather than with Quebec. 41 notes.
T. D. S. Bassett

370. Bourne, Edward Gaylord. THE ROMANCE OF WESTERN HISTORY. *Missouri Hist. R. 1973 68(1): 55-73.* Discusses various aspects of western history, emphasizing the appreciation of French and Spanish influence on trans-Mississippi history and the value of the romantic element in history. Cites the expeditions of Hernando de Soto and Francisco Vásquez de Coronado and the sightings of the Rio Grande and the Grand Canyon as dramatic examples. Discusses the importance of the French quest for the "Western sea," and the designs and explorations of Father Jacques Marquette, La Motte Cadillac, Pierre LeMoyne, Nicholas de la Salle, and Father P. F. X. de Charlevoix. Credits an early prediction of the westward movement to Pierre LeMoyne d'Iberville, founder of Louisiana, and outlines the early history of the Missouri River area. First given as an address to the State Historical Society of Missouri in 1906. Primary and secondary sources; 6 illus., map, 35 notes.
N. J. Street

371. Brasseaux, Carl A. ACADIANS, CREOLES, AND THE 1787 LAFOURCHE SMALLPOX OUTBREAK. *Rev. de Louisiane 1979 8(1): 55-58.* Discusses the continuing animosity between Acadians and Creoles in Louisiana, particularly during 1766-90, and describes the smallpox outbreak of 1787 which maintained the cleavage between the two groups.

372. Brasseaux, Carl A. CONFUSION, CONFLICT, AND CURRENCY: AN INTRODUCTION TO THE REBELLION OF 1768? *Louisiana Hist. 1977 18(2): 161-169.* Confusion, dissension and economic instability were major problems in colonial Louisiana that grew in severity following the Seven Years' War. Illustrates the magnitude of these problems in the period 1762-68 by focusing on Denis-Nicolas Foucault, the *commissaire-ordonnateur.* Foucault's feuds with the director general, Charles Aubry, and with the New Spanish governor, Antonio de Ulloa, were sources of much of the dissension. Foucault also was at least partially responsible for much of the bureaucratic confusion and the currency problems of the colony. Foucault's feuding and poor administrative leadership created a situation which gave attorney-general Nicolas Chauvin de la Fresniere the opportunity and the motive to attempt a *coup d'état* in 1768. Based principally on materials in French Colonial Archives; 39 notes.   R. L. Woodward, Jr.

373. Broglie, Gabriel de. LOUISIANE BIEN-AIMÉE [Louisiana the well-loved]. *Nouvelle Rev. des Deux Mondes [France] 1976 (6): 619-627.* Presents a tribute to Louisiana, describing its historical ties to France, and current French social and cultural influences.

374. Burnett, Robert A. LOUISVILLE'S FRENCH PAST. *Filson Club Hist. Q. 1976 50(2): 5-27.* Concentrates on the contributions of individual French Americans in Louisville, Kentucky, in the 19th century. Special mention is made of Jean de Crevecoeur, John and Louis Tarascon, John J. Audubon, John Colmesnil, and Union General Lovell Harrison Rousseau. There is little analysis, but the author does note that the French were so well assimilated by 1850 that they were not targets of nativist hostility. Based on local histories and county records; 74 notes.   G. B. McKinney

375. Bush, Robert. CHARLES GAYARRÉ AND GRACE KING: LETTERS OF A LOUISIANA FRIENDSHIP. *Southern Literary J. 1974 7(1): 100-131.* Reprints 14 letters of Charles Gayarré, a Creole, and Grace King who learned a love of Louisiana history from him, and wrote several historical works on the subject.   S

376. Bush, Robert D. CIVILIAN VERSUS MILITARY PREROGATIVES IN NAPOLEONIC LOUISIANA: THE LAUSSAT-BURTHE AFFAIR, 1803. *Rev. de Louisiane 1977 6(1): 45-58.* Discusses the rivalry between two colonial officials in French Louisiana, an adjutant-commander, Charles André Burthe, and the prefect, Pierre Clément Laussat.

377. Bush, Robert D. COMMUNISM, COMMUNITY, AND CHARISMA: THE CRISIS IN ICARIA AT NAUVOO. *Old Northwest 1977 3(4): 409-428.* Describes the failure of the Icarian utopian community at Nauvoo, Illinois, under the leadership of the charismatic Etienne Cabet (1788-1865), a working-class organizer and propagandist. The community was never self-sufficient, and disputes over work sharing developed. Cabet became increasingly autocratic as criticism of his leadership mounted. He attempted to silence opponents by illegally amending the Icarian constitution. When the community divided into "Cabetists" and 'Dissidents," control over the membership, and with it voting rights, became an issue. Cabet was ousted in 1856, the year of his death; and the society was dissolved. Based on memoirs, the Icarian constitution, French-language newspapers, and secondary works; table, 54 notes.   J

378. Bush, Robert D. and Touchstone, Blake. A SURVEY OF MANUSCRIPT HOLDINGS IN THE HISTORIC NEW ORLEANS COLLECTION. *Louisiana Hist. 1975 16(1): 89-96.* Describes the principal manuscript holdings of the Historic New Orleans Collection, which includes many items of interest for New Orleans and Louisiana history from the colonial period to 1966. Especially notable holdings are 11 Spanish land grants and other Spanish colonial documents (particularly for the administration of Bernardo de Gálvez), numerous financial records of the early 19th century, records relating to slavery and the Civil War, papers relating to late 19th-century industrial expansion, and the papers of New Orleans composer and pianist Louis M. Gottschalk. Photo.   R. L. Woodward, Jr.

379. Carvalho, Joseph, III and Everett, Robert. STATISTICAL ANALYSIS OF SPRINGFIELD'S FRENCH CANADIANS (1870). *Hist. J. of Western Massachusetts 1974 3(1): 59-63.* Ninety-six percent of all Canadians in Ward 8, in Springfield, Massachusetts, worked in cotton mills. A majority were under the age of 21 and less than one-eighth of those over 21 were US citizens. They were a church centered group. Primary and secondary sources; 4 tables, 17 notes.   S. S. Sprague

380. Chandler, R. E. END OF AN ODYSSEY: ACADIANS ARRIVE IN ST. GABRIEL, LOUISIANA. *Louisiana Hist. 1973 14(1): 69-87.* Translated Spanish documents signed by Governor Antonio de Ulloa and detailing the settlement in St. Gabriel of more than 200 Acadians who arrived in New Orleans in 1767 contain instructions for settlement, distribution of lands, and a list of the families and their belongings. Original documents are in the Archivo General de Indias, Sevilla.   R. L. Woodward

381. Chandler, Richard E., ed. and transl. ODYSSEY CONTINUED: ACADIANS ARRIVE IN NATCHEZ. *Louisiana Hist. 1978 19(4): 446-463.* The second group of Acadians to reach New Orleans, in February 1768, consisted of 152 individuals. They were sent to Natchez. Four documents regarding their arrival are translated and published here, the originals being in the Archivo General de Indias in Sevilla, Spain, Audiencia de Santo Domingo, Legajo 2585. 1) Letter from Antonio de Ulloa to the Marqués de Grimaldi, New Orleans, 11 February 1768; 2) instructions for the settlement of the Acadians on land near the Fort at Natchez, and two lists of the colonists' names; 3) instructions for transporting the Acadians from New Orleans to Natchez; and 4) instructions for returning the boats to New Orleans and for a tour of the Acadian area for Jacob Walker. 17 notes.   R. L. Woodward

382. Chandler, R. E. A SHIPPING CONTRACT: SPAIN BRINGS ACADIANS TO LOUISIANA. *Rev. de Louisiane 1979 8(1): 73-81.* Traces the history of the Acadians from their exile from Canada in 1755 and their unwelcome arrival in England and France, to 1783 when Peyroux de la Coudreniere proposed to Spain that the Acadians in France be sent to Louisiana with expenses paid by Spain, until 1785 when the Acadians arrived in Louisiana.

383. Chaput, Donald. THE EARLY MISSOURI GRADUATES OF WEST POINT: OFFICERS OR MERCHANTS? *Missouri Hist. Rev. 1978 72(3): 262-270.* With the class of 1806 there was a slight shift from East to West when four of the 15 cadets came from Missouri. Auguste Pierre Chouteau, Charles Gratiot, Pascal Vincent Bouis, and Louis Loramier were members of prominent St. Louis business families. They owed their appointments to Meriwether Lewis who recommended them before starting his great trip to the Pacific because he believed they would be good cadets and because he was anxious to have good relations with powerful interests in St. Louis. Only Gratiot went on to have a military career. Primary and secondary sources; illus., 24 notes.   W. Zornow

384. Chaput, Donald. TREASON OR LOYALTY? FRONTIER FRENCH IN THE AMERICAN REVOLUTION. *J. of the Illinois State Hist. Soc. 1978 71(4): 242-251.* Considers the plight of the hundreds of French military officers who were driven from New France in 1763 but decided to return there as merchants, soldiers, or even British agents in the succeeding years. Some of the most prominent, including the families of Beaujeu, Joncaire, Hertel, Boucher, La Corne, and Celeron, created a second career as loyal, if not frequently suspect, allies of the British in the American Revolution. Documents in the Canadian Archives and Archives des Colonies; 7 illus., 34 notes.   J

385. Chartrand, René. THE TROOPS OF FRENCH LOUISIANA, 1699-1769. *Military Collector & Historian 1973 25(2): 58-65.* Emphasizes uniforms and armaments of the regiments.   S

386. Chassé, Paul P. THE OTHER YANKEE: THE FRANCO-AMERICAN. *Rev. de Louisiane 1977 6(2): 157-162.* Discusses the

presence and impact of persons of French ancestry in New England, 1524-1840's.

387. Comeaux, Malcolm. LES ACADIENS LOUISIANAIS: L'IMPACT DE L'ENVIRONNEMENT [Louisiana Acadians: Impact of the environment]. *Rev. de Louisiane 1977 6(2): 163-178*. Discusses the impact of the land in Louisiana on the daily life, folk culture, and occupations of Acadians there; discusses farming, river culture, and swamp life, 18th-19th centuries.

388. Conrad, Glenn R. LES ACADIENS: LA LEGENDE ET LA REALITE [Acadians: legend and reality]. *Rev. de Louisiane 1977 6(1): 5-17*. Chronicles the movements of the Acadians from France to, and in, the New World, 17th-20th centuries (including the Cajun culture in Louisiana), and discusses their daily life, customs, and religion, and myths about them; mentions Longfellow's *Evangeline*.

389. Conrad, Glenn R. L'IMMIGRATION ALSACIENNE EN LOUISIANE, 1753-1759 [Alsatian immigration into Louisiana, 1753-1759]. *Revue d'hist. de l'Amérique française [Canada] 1975 28(4): 565-577*. Revocation of the Edict of Nantes in 1685 by Louis XIV forced the exodus of many Protestants from France. When France was having difficulty maintaining its hold over Louisiana, 70 years later the government offered to pay the passage to Louisiana for those Protestants living in Alsace, if the immigrants would become Catholic. Many Alsatians accepted the offer and arrived in Louisiana in 1759. Based on primary and secondary sources; 48 notes.   L. B. Chan

390. Cool, Margaret. THE DUKE OF BURGUNDY. *Westways 1977 69(8): 43-45, 71*. Starting with little more than an education Paul Masson moved from Paris to the Santa Clara Valley of California and established a winemaking industry in 1878 which remains popular and world-renowned.

391. Crane, Robert. GALLIC ROOTS: OBSERVATIONS OF TWO NINETEENTH-CENTURY FRENCHMEN ON THE LOUISIANA OF THEIR DAY. *Rev. de Louisiane 1978 7(1): 65-78*. Excerpts from letters by François Ruelle, Sr. (1790-1855), and his son François (1821-77) offer insight into social organization, politics, daily life, and economic conditions of Louisiana, 1818-56.

392. D'Antoni, Blaise C. THE CHURCH RECORDS OF NORTH LOUISIANA. *Louisiana Hist. 1974 15(1): 59-67*. Outlines preservation efforts, 1930's-74, of colonial period Catholic records.

393. Davidson, Rondel V. VICTOR CONSIDERANT AND THE FAILURE OF LA RÉUNION. *Southwestern Hist. Q. 1973 76(3): 277-296*. Disillusioned with the corrupt monarchy and laissez-faire capitalism which spawned political and social injustices in France, Victor-Prosper Considerant (1808-93) was converted to the Fourierist movement. The European Society for the Colonization of Texas, a joint stock company, established La Réunion near Dallas. This short-lived communal experiment, 1854-59, faced insurmountable problems; the colonists did not follow the plans of Considerant; the culturally elite settlers were unsuited for life in frontier Texas; isolated and desirable land was too expensive; and the scheme was not financially viable. 52 notes.
                                                        D. L. Smith

394. Desroche, H. MÉMOIRE ET ESPÉRANCE DE LA "COMMUNAUTÉ" DANS LA RELIGION ICARIENNE [Memory and hope for the "community" in Icarian religion]. *Communautés [France] 1972 (31): 49-75*. Studies the religious intentions of the Icarians, especially in the writings of their founder, Étienne Cabet, and the implications of the quest for a utopian society as presented in his *Voyage to Icaria* (1840).

395. Din, Gilbert C. FRANCISCO BOULIGNY'S 1778 PLANS FOR SETTLEMENT IN LOUISIANA. *Southern Studies 1977 16(2): 211-224*. In November 1776, Captain Francisco Bouligny was appointed lieutenant governor of the province of Louisiana in charge of immigration, commerce, and Indian relations. Reprints the text of a letter Bouligny sent on 4 August 1778 to the Minister of the Indies in Seville. Bouligny requested discharged Spanish soldiers and their wives from Malaga to settle in purely Spanish towns in Louisiana, recommending

Ouachita. Loyal Spanish settlers would offset the French Creoles and prevent either the English or Americans from encroaching. The letter also provides information on conditions in Louisiana at the time of the American Revolution. Based on documents in Archivo General de Indias in Seville and secondary sources; 18 notes.   J. Buschen

396. Dormon, James H. ASPECTS OF ACADIAN PLANTATION LIFE IN THE MID-NINETEENTH CENTURY: A MICROCOSMIC VIEW. *Louisiana Hist. 1975 16(4): 361-370*. Provides a case study in southern Louisiana plantation life. Petite Anne was primarily a sugar plantation. The life is revealed by a diary kept in the 1850's by one of the inhabitants. Dormon focuses on the ways in which "the residents, black and white, related to their all-too-rare moments of leisure." 26 notes.
                                                        E. P. Stickney

397. Duffy, John. PHARMACY IN FRANCO-SPANISH LOUISIANA. Bender, George A. and Parascandola, John, eds. *American Pharmacy in the Colonial and Revolutionary Periods* (Madison, Wisconsin: American Inst. of the Hist. of Pharmacy, 1977): 15-26. Examines medical availability and the practice of pharmacy (including the legal aspects of it) during the French (1717-69), Spanish (1769-1803), and US (1803-52) jurisdictions in Louisiana; sketches individuals involved.

398. DuPasquier, Thierry. RAPPORTS ENTRE LES PROTESTANTS FRANCAIS ET L'AMÉRIQUE DU NORD [Connections between French Protestants and North America]. *Bull. de la Soc. de l'Hist. Protestantisme Français [France] 1976 122(3): 191-199*. Lists principal Huguenot settlements in North America, American Revolution leaders of French Protestant descent, some Protestant members of the French expeditionary force in America, Americans involved in the whaling industry in France in 1786-91 and 1817-30, and some contemporary French Huguenot societies in the United States and Canada. Summarized in English. Based on monographs; 16 notes.   O. T. Driggs

399. Early, Frances H. MOBILITY POTENTIAL AND THE QUALITY OF LIFE IN WORKING-CLASS LOWELL, MASSACHUSETTS: THE FRENCH CANADIANS CA. 1870. *Labour [Canada] 1977 2: 214-228*. Preliminary findings for a social history of French Canadians in Lowell (1870-1900) seem to indicate the "inaccuracy of the romantic portrayal of the French-Canadian experience" in New England. In 1870, at least, life for Lowell's French Canadians was "rather grim." Most were in working-class occupations; there was no Quebec-born lay *classe dirigeante;* the vast majority of children 10 and over held jobs outside the home. Evidence suggests French Canadians "would be slow to experience occupational mobility;" neither was it possible for most to accumulate savings for a return to Quebec. Census reports, other primary and secondary sources; 44 notes.   W. A. Kearns

400. Evans, William. CABLE, POQUELIN, AND MISS BURT: THE DIFFICULTIES OF A DIALECT WRITER. *Louisiana Studies 1976 15(1): 45-60*. In the short story "Jean-ah Poquelin" of 1875, George Washington Cable (1844-1925) used a French-flavored English dialect to create atmosphere and differentiation of character. Critics debate the credibility of writing in dialects. Cable's written expression of the dialect is probably correct, and the variants found subtly distinguish characters. In 1899 Cable revised the work for a secondary teacher, Mary E. Burt. This version shows that for dialectal creation, phonological problems are greater than grammatical variations for readers. Based on primary and secondary sources; 38 notes.   J. Buschen

401. Faucher, Albert. L'ÉMIGRATION DES CANADIENS FRANÇAIS AU XIX SIÈCLE: POSITION DU PROBLÈME ET PERSPECTIVES [French-Canadian emigration in the 19th century: situation and perspectives]. *Recherches Sociographiques [Canada] 1964 5(3): 277-317*. French-Canadian emigration from Quebec to the United States during 1850's-1900's was part of a Canadian phenomenon and can be attributed to accessible transportation, promising economic development, industrialization, and agriculture.

402. Foley, William E. and Rice, Charles David. COMPOUNDING THE RISKS: INTERNATIONAL POLITICS, WARTIME DISLOCATIONS AND AUGUSTE CHOUTEAU'S FUR TRADING OPERATIONS, 1792-1815. *Missouri Hist. Soc. Bull. 1978 34(3): 131-139*. A St. Louis founding father and leading fur merchant, Auguste Pierre

Chouteau (1786-1838) prospered while the region was under Spanish rule. Beginning in 1793, European wars immensely complicated Chouteau's business because much of his commerce was with English firms. But his acumen was so great that he readily overcame the hurdles that wars raised against commerce. American acquisition of the Louisiana Territory in 1803 and subsequent Anglo-American friction produced more commercial troubles for Chouteau. He weathered the new crises, but his commercial enterprises suffered major losses during the War of 1812. Based on the Chouteau archival collection at the Missouri Historical Society and on secondary works; 54 notes.

H. T. Lovin

403. Foley, William E. and Rice, Charles David. PIERRE CHOUTEAU: ENTREPRENEUR AS INDIAN AGENT. *Missouri Hist. Rev. 1978 72(4): 365-387.* Pierre Chouteau, a fur trader and first Indian agent in Upper Louisiana Territory during 1804-18, is portrayed as a man striving to handle complex Indian-White relations developing during the westward movement particularly among the Osage Indians. Primary and secondary sources; illus., 88 notes.

W. F. Zornow

404. Foner, Philip S. THE FRENCH TRADE UNION DELEGATION TO THE PHILADELPHIA CENTENNIAL EXPOSITION, 1876. *Sci. and Soc. 1976 40(3): 257-287.* The delegation of French workers, subsidized by public subscription and the Paris municipal government, reported that America was not a land of promise and opportunity for the worker compared with Europe. Workers from France would not benefit by emigrating to the United States. The French observers felt that American workers dissipated their efforts in futile strikes instead of concentrating on the more rewarding goals of building producer cooperatives. Based on French and American printed primary sources.

N. Lederer

405. Forbes-Robertson, Diana. ASYLUM IN AZILUM. *Am. Heritage 1976 27(3): 54-59, 98-101.* French aristocrats fleeing the French Revolution went to central Pennsylvania to build a community for their queen. For 10 years after her death the refugees hung on until amnesty was offered by Napoleon. 11 illus.

B. J. Paul

406. Grappe, Bernie. FRANÇOIS GRAPPE: UNIQUE NORTH LOUISIANA FRONTIERSMAN. *North Louisiana Hist. Assoc. J. 1978 9(2): 65-70.* Discusses the character, life, and career of François Grappe (1747-1825), whose contribution to North Louisiana history has been neglected. He served as Indian agent and interpreter for France, Spain, and the United States. His name is associated with the controversial "Grappe Reservation" of the Caddo Indian Treaty of 1835, but wrongly, because he had died a decade earlier. Colorful and gifted with an impressive knowledge of North Louisiana geography and Indian languages, he was held in high esteem. Based on the Grappe Collection, Centenary College, Shreveport, Louisiana, contemporary accounts, and secondary sources; 43 notes.

H. M. Parker, Jr.

407. Gray, John S. HONORE PICOTTE, FUR TRADER. *South Dakota Hist. 1976 6(2): 186-202.* Biography of Honore Picotte, a French fur trader on the Missouri River, 1820-65.

408. Griessman, B. Eugene and Henson, Curtis T., Jr. THE HISTORY AND SOCIAL TOPOGRAPHY OF AN ETHNIC ISLAND IN ALABAMA. *Phylon 1975 36(2): 97-112.* An "ethnic island" has emerged during the past century-and-a-half along the west bank of the Tombigbee River, 35 miles north of Mobile, in present-day Washington County. The inhabitants, who are often referred to as Cajans or Cajuns, are a mixture of red, black, and white. Probably the first settlers in the area were Daniel Reed and his wife Rose, who moved there early in the 19th century. The authors trace the background of the settlement, and its growth, and discuss how demographic and social topographic characteristics such as the roads and transportation networks, the schools, the churches, the land tenure, and economic conditions helped keep the settlement isolated. Recently, the members of the community have been merging with the society that surrounds them. Primary and secondary sources; 5 tables, 28 notes.

B. A. Glasrud

409. Haebler, Peter. HOLYOKE'S FRENCH-CANADIAN COMMUNITY IN TURMOIL: THE ROLE OF THE CHURCH IN ASSIMILATION 1869-1887. *Hist. J. of Western Massachusetts 1979 7(1): 5-21.* Examines the conflict between Fr. Andre B. Dufresne and his Catholic parishioners in the Holyoke, Massachusetts, French-Canadian parish over his continuation of traditional practices. The extent of the conflict over Dufresne's conduct is an example of the speed with which many French Canadians had changed their outlook on the role of the curé in their lives. 2 illus., 40 notes.

W. H. Mulligan, Jr.

410. Higginbotham, Jay. THE CHAUMONT CONCESSION: A FRENCH PLANTATION ON THE PASCAGOULA. *J. of Mississippi Hist. 1974 36(4): 353-362.* In 1717, Louis XV relinquished control of Louisiana to John Law's Company of the West. Antoine Chaumont, a wealthy Parisian bureaucrat, and his wife, Marie-Catherine Barre, invested extensively in the company and later secured a concession in Louisiana, where in 1721 their agents established a plantation on the Pascagoula River. Various problems apparently caused the Chaumonts to lose interest in the plantation within a few years, and it was entirely abandoned by 1732. Based on published French and primary sources; 39 notes.

J. W. Hillje

411. Higginbotham, Jay. PREPARATIONS FOR THE VOYAGE OF THE *PELICAN* TO LOUISIANA, 1703-1704. *Alabama Hist. Q. 1975 37(3): 165-175.* In 1703 Pierre Le Moyne d' Iberville suggested that the sending of marriageable girls to Mobile would provide a basis for natural population growth and encourage the Canadians there to become permanent settlers. Such a program was started, and girls of moral quality were secured in Paris. There were many delays in their sailing, and the number finally on the *Pelican* was only one-fourth the number d'Iberville hoped for. 25 notes.

E. E. Eminhizer

412. Hoese, H. Dickson. ON THE CORRECT LANDFALL OF LA SALLE IN TEXAS, 1685. *Louisiana Hist. 1978 19(1): 5-32.* Matagorda Bay, Texas, was not the site of Robert Cavelier, Sieur de La Salle's, Fort St. Louis colony. Based on contemporary and modern cartographic evidence, contemporary journals, and the theoretical track of the vessels in the La Salle expedition, concludes that La Salle landed at Aransas Bay and that Fort St. Louis was in that vicinity. 10 maps, 3 tables, 53 notes.

R. L. Woodward

413. Holli, Melvin G. FRENCH SEIGNIORIALISM AND THE SOCIAL STRUCTURE OF EARLY DETROIT. *Indiana Social Studies Q. 1975 28(2): 63-74.* Discusses the social, political, and cultural influence of French seignieurialism in the development of Detroit, Michigan, 1701-1837.

414. Horsman, Reginald. LAW AND EMPIRE IN LOUISIANA. *Rev. in Am. Hist. 1975 3(4): 448-451.* George Dargo's *Jefferson's Louisiana: Politics and the Clash of Legal Traditions* (Cambridge, Mass.: Harvard U. Pr., 1975) studies the effects of the French and Spanish minorities in politics from the cession of Louisiana to the United States in 1803, and records their demands to Thomas Jefferson and the territorial governor, William C. C. Claiborne, that their civil law be included with US common law in the Louisiana Digest of 1808.

415. Hulton, Paul. A HUGUENOT ARTIST: JACQUES LE MOYNE DE MORGUES. *Pro. of the Huguenot Soc. of London [Great Britain] 1979 23(3): 173-186.* An account of the ill-fated Huguenot colonists' expedition to Florida in 1564-65, as narrated and illustrated by naturalistic painter Jacques De Morgues Le Moyne of Dieppe (1533-88), who accompanied the expedition as its official artist, map-maker, topographical illustrator, and chronicler.

416. Jaenen, Cornelius J. FRENCH COLONIAL ATTITUDES AND THE EXPLORATION OF JOLLIET AND MARQUETTE. *Wisconsin Mag. of Hist. 1973 56(4): 300-310.* Discusses the explorations of Jolliet and Marquette in the context of French colonial and imperial administration of Louis XIV and Colbert. Although the two explorers had to finance their own expedition, they were expected to extend the French sphere of influence, act as diplomats and Indian negotiators, serve as consultants to the government, increase French geographical knowledge, and minister to the spiritual needs of Indians and colonists. After briefly discussing the separate careers of Jolliet and Marquette, the author traces their historic voyage and concludes with their activities following the exploration of the Mississippi River. Illus., 25 notes.

N. C. Burckel

417. Jaenen, Cornelius J. THE MEETING OF THE FRENCH AND AMERINDIANS IN THE SEVENTEENTH CENTURY. *R. de l'U. d'Ottawa [Canada] 1973 43(1): 128-144.* Reexamines the accepted theory, going back to Francis Parkman, that the French, unlike the Spaniards and English, " 'embraced and cherished' the Amerindians, and . . . that the French and Amerindians enjoyed a mutually satisfactory relationship . . . as equal partners in a great North American empire." This theory was based on a partial study of the evidence. A broader examination of French-Amerindian relations would indicate a complete lack of understanding in the meeting of the two cultures. The Amerindian was uniquely adapted to his habitat; any attempt at Frenchification was doomed to failure. "They had a will to survive, a strong sense of their own identity as a self-reliant, independent, self-sufficient, and well-adjusted people." The process was one of barbarization; the French trade and Catholic missions undermined the stabilizing factors, and "the concept of Amerindians as blood-thirsty, filthy and depraved barbarians" overshadowed the noble savage myth. Based on primary and secondary sources; 38 notes.   R. V. Ritter

418. Jammes, Jean-Marie. COMMENT ET POURQUOI NOUS POUVONS AND NOUS DEVONS SAUVER LE FRANCAIS EN ACADIANA [How and why we can and must save French in Acadiana]. *Rev. de Louisiane 1977 6(2): 101-134.* Relates the use of French in Acadiana (the southern sectors of Louisiana) and prescribes saving the French language in this area.

419. Jarrett, Walter. [NEW ORLEANS].
NEW ORLEANS: THE CITY THAT CARE FORGOT. PART I: UNDER FRENCH AND SPANISH FLAGS. *Mankind 1974 4(7): 16-23, 48-51.* Traces the early history of New Orleans until the Louisiana Purchase.
DOWN THE RIVER TO NEW ORLEANS, PART II: UNDER AMERICAN AND CONFEDERATE FLAGS. *Mankind 1974 4(8): 18-25, 58-59.* Describes New Orleans from 1803, when Louisianna was purchased from France by Thomas Jefferson, to about 1900.

420. Johnson, C. MISSOURI-FRENCH HOUSES: SOME RELICT FEATURES OF EARLY SETTLEMENT. *Pioneer Am. 1974 6(2): 1-11.* Traces the course of French settlement in the United States and, in particular, focuses on their building style. The largest concentration of French Colonial buildings may be found in Sainte Genevieve, Missouri; but some information may be gleaned from places as distant as Green Bay, Wisconsin, or Brown's Valley, Minnesota. The unique characteristic in French houses is wall structure; and according to the method used, wall construction may be divided into four main groups: 1) palisaded, the oldest type of construction practiced by the French in the Mississippi Valley, 2) timber-frame, 3) masonry, a type rarely found today in southern Missouri, and 4) horizontal log. Based on field observation and secondary sources; map, 9 photos, 16 notes, biblio.
                                         C. R. Gunter, Jr.

421. Jones, Russell M. VICTOR CONSIDÉRANT'S AMERICAN EXPERIENCE (1852-1869). *French-American Rev. 1976 1(1): 65-94.* Victor Prosper Considérant was a French disciple of Charles Fourier, the utopian socialist, who advocated communal organizations known as phalanxes. Considérant traveled in the United States during December 1852-July 1853. He concluded that an area in northern Texas would be ideal for establishing such a community. Returning to France, he wrote a travel book, *Au Texas,* which described the attractions of the United States to prospective emigrants and depicted the profits which could be made in investing in the western lands. Considérant would return to the United States to establish a colony in 1855. Based largely on primary sources; 118 notes. Article to be continued.   R. S. Barnard

422. Jordan, Terry G. ANTECEDENTS OF THE LONG-LOT IN TEXAS. *Ann. of the Assoc. of Am. Geographers 1974 64(1): 70-86.* The use of long-lots as a mode of land division in Texas during the 1730's-1880's diffused from central Europe through northern France, Quebec, and French colonies in Missouri and Louisiana.

423. Joyaux, Georges J. FRENCH PERIODICALS IN EARLY AMERICA. *French-American Rev. 1976 1(1): 96-98, (2): 163-165, (3): 249-251.* Part I. LE PETIT CENSEUR. This periodical was published irregularly for about six months in 1805, first in New York and then in Philadelphia. Its editor, Charles Alexis Daudet, was, with some few exceptions, the chief contributor to the paper. It concentrated initially on French literature, although Daudet's admiration for Napoleon was apparent, and then on French politics. It was designed to be useful to those who were learning the language and was abandoned when its editor launched a campaign for a Société Libre des Arts. Part II. L'HÉMISPHÈRE. This irregular weekly was published in Philadelphia from 7 October 1809 to 28 September 1811. It was printed and directed by Jean-Jacques Négrin. Négrin used the weekly to express his anti-Bonapartist sentiments. He concentrated his attack on Napoleon's financial policy, the invasion of Spain, and general veracity. The French colony in Philadelphia attacked Négrin for his views. The initial circulation of the publication soon dropped considerably. Part III. LE JOURNAL DES DAMES. This periodical, primarily intended for ladies, was published from New York City during January-December 1810. It concentrated on French Classical literature. Its issues were organized in two sections: the first commented on significant events of the past, while the second presented a general survey of literature. Its issues primarily were devoted to three authors of the French Classical period: Moliere, Corneille, and Racine. Inadequate support caused this publication to cease.
                                         R. S. Barnard

424. Keller, Allan. THE LONG MARCH TO TRIUMPH. *Am. Hist. Illus. 1978 13(4): 4-9, 44-47.* Describes the march of some 5,000 French troops under the Comte de Rochambeau, accompanied by elements of the American Army under Washington, from Newport, Rhode Island, to Yorktown, Virginia, in 1781, where they joined Lafayette in besieging Cornwallis. The allies were successful in convincing General Clinton on Staten Island, until the last possible moment, that his forces were the object of their march. The French soldiers were surprised to meet Huguenots and Acadians who spoke French. The citizens of Philadelphia were much impressed by the appearance, bearing, and discipline of the French, especially considering the difficult Connecticut roads over which they had passed. 9 illus., map.   L. W. Van Wyk

425. Kennedy, Michael. LA SOCIÉTÉ FRANÇAISE DES AMIS DE LA LIBERTÉ ET DE L'ÉGALITÉ DE PHILADELPHIE 1793-1794 [The French Society of the Friends of Liberty and Equality of Philadelphia]. *Ann. Hist. de la Revolution Française [France] 1976 48(4): 614-636.* Discusses those Frenchmen in Charleston, Alexandria, New York, Boston, and Philadelphia, whose sympathies with the French Revolution led them to establish Jacobin societies. Examines the vicissitudes of the Philadelphia society. This essentially middle class club, which soon admitted Americans to its membership, was greatly influenced by the participation of France's ambassador to Philadelphia: Edmond-Charles Genêt. On Genêt's resolution, the society officially forswore involvement in American politics; yet its tone was markedly anti-Federalist. Ultimately impaired by yellow fever, a schism, and Genêt's departure for New York, the society held its last recorded meeting on 4 June 1794. Based on archival, primary, and secondary sources; 44 notes.
                                         P. T. Newton

426. Kennedy, Michael. LE CLUB JACOBIN DE CHARLESTON EN CAROLINE DU SUD (1792-1795) [The Jacobin Club of Charleston, South Carolina (1792-95)]. *Rev. d'Hist. Moderne et Contemporaine [France] 1977 24: 420-438.* In Charleston, South Carolina, called by E. S. Thomas the "most aristocratic city in the Union," there was in the 1790's a Jacobin Club, devoted to defending the French Revolution and working for Franco-American friendship. Most members were French, but some were American, including several Jews. In American politics, these Jacobins supported the Democratic Republicans, but one, Robert Goodloe Harper, after being elected to Congress, became a Federalist and supported the Alien and Sedition Acts (his name was read out of the membership list). The Club persevered through the period of French-American hostility and Federalist ascendency in the 1790's until the coming of Republican dominance with Thomas Jefferson's election in 1800. Membership list, 60 notes.   J. C. Billigmeier

427. Kent, Donald H. THE MYTH OF ETIENNE BRULÉ. *Pennsylvania Hist. 1976 43(4): 291-308.* Finds insufficient evidence to support the claim that Etienne Brulé was the first white man to explore the interior of Pennsylvania. This claim rests upon Brulé's own narrative of a journey from the headwaters of the Susquehanna River to the sea in

the winter of 1615-16. This appeared in the 1619 edition of Samuel de Champlain's *Voyages*, but the narrative was not included in the 1632 edition. Uses a variety of primary sources to assess and ultimately reject Brulé's account. 2 maps, 48 notes.   D. C. Swift

428. Kilbourne, John D. FRENCH MANUSCRIPTS IN THE ARCHIVES OF THE SOCIETY OF THE CINCINNATI. *Manuscripts 1975 27(1): 65-68.* Discusses French memberships in the Society of the Cincinnati with a brief description of some of the French members' papers in the Society's Library. Illus.   D. A. Yanchisin

429. Konig, David T. A NEW LOOK AT THE ESSEX "FRENCH": ETHNIC FRICTIONS AND COMMUNITY TENSIONS IN SEVENTEENTH-CENTURY ESSEX COUNTY, MASSACHUSETTS. *Essex Inst. Hist. Collections 1974 110(3): 167-180.* Treats assimilation problems of Huguenots from France and French-speaking peoples from the Isle of Jersey, Great Britain.   S

430. Kosciusko-Morizet, Jacques. ALLOCUTION DE M. JACQUES KOSCIUSKO-MORIZET AMBASSADEUR DE FRANCE AUX ÉTATS-UNIS À FORT CAROLINE (JACKSONVILLE) LE 1er MAI 1976 [Address by M. Jacques Kosciusko-Morizet French Ambassador to the United States at Fort Caroline (Jacksonville) May 1st 1976]. *Bull. de la Soc. de l'Hist. Protestantisme français [France] 1976 122(3): 187-190.* Reprints a speech in honor of the 414th anniversary of the discovery of the River of May, in 1562, by a French expedition seeking New World treasure and a place for settlement. The following year a colony was formed at Fort Caroline by a second expedition. In fall 1565 Spaniards captured the fort, massacred many settlers, and enforced their claim to Florida. Admiral de Coligny had been instrumental in sending the French expeditions. Based on letters and memoirs.
                                                                O. T. Driggs

431. Lemieux, Donald J. THE MISSISSIPPI VALLEY, NEW FRANCE, AND FRENCH COLONIAL POLICY. *Southern Studies 1978 17(1): 39-56.* France had several purposes in holding the Louisiana Territory, 1683-1762: to prevent a foreign foothold at the mouth of the Mississippi, to realize commercial gains at Spain's expense, to prevent English expansion, and to increase the sale and consumption of French goods. However, Louisiana was a financial liability. This was caused by domestic problems and distractions in France and the nature of the goods produced in the colonies. The loss of the Louisiana Territory to Spain in 1762 was not a significant loss; the sugar production of the Antilles was of much greater value. Primary and secondary sources; 56 notes.
                                                                J. Buschen

432. Lemieux, Donald. SOME LEGAL AND PRACTICAL ASPECTS OF THE OFFICE OF *COMMISSAIRE ORDONNATEUR* OF FRENCH LOUISIANA. *Louisiana Studies 1975 14(4): 379-393.* The French developed a system of checks and balances to control the two officials—the governor and the commissaire ordonnateur—who were in charge of colonial administration in Louisiana 1712-69. They were invested with twin powers: the governor acted as the military leader and the chief administrator, the commissaire ordonnateur as the chief legal and financial officer. Constant bickering between the two officials, which resulted from a stalemate over duties, slow communication, and personal ambition, weakened the government of Louisiana and reflected the general condition of the bureaucracy. The commissaire ordonnateur was sent from France for an indefinite period of time with a salary that was not lucrative; the post was considered as a stepping-stone. Instructions for the post embraced five areas: religion, justice, police, military, and Indians. The commissaire ordonnateur often found himself in the predicament of defending his position because he manipulated large sums and directed an army of subordinates who often used their position to profit from commercial activities. Even the most able found their efforts subordinated to the demands of the Colonial System. Based on primary and secondary sources; 52 notes.   B. A. Glasrud

433. Lewis, Reid H. THREE HUNDRED YEARS LATER. *Historic Preservation 1974 26(3): 4-9.* Account of the reenactment of the 1673 exploratory voyage up the Mississippi River by Father Jacques Marquette and Louis Jolliet.

434. Loewenberg, Robert J. CREATING A PROVISIONAL GOVERNMENT IN OREGON: A REVISION. *Pacific Northwest Q. 1977 68(1): 13-24.* Questions the traditional thesis that the 1843 creation of a provisional government in Oregon Territory resulted from the work of a mysterious Committee of Twelve. Close scrutiny of the documents indicates that this story was fabricated by William Gray, a leader of the faction for independence, who contended that the French Canadians in Oregon joined missionary Jason Lee in traitorous opposition to a provisional government. Ethnic conflict was not a factor since French Canadians and Americans divided evenly over the issue. Lee's opposition was based on a fear of ultimate independence which would strip away home rule. Based on primary and secondary sources; 6 photos, 35 notes.
                                                                M. L. Tate

435. Matthews, Marcia M. RICHMOND BARTHÉ, SCULPTOR. *South Atlantic Q. 1975 74(3): 324-339.* American sculptor Richmond Barthé was born of Creole parents in an integrated district of the bayou country of Louisiana, and spent some years in a white household; he never had much to say against that race. Barthé originally intended to be a painter, but switched to sculpting; he primarily used the American Negro as his subject. His fame spread rapidly until his works graced the most prestigious museums. Barthé left the United States after World War II. He lived first in Switzerland and then in Italy, where he still resides. 3 notes.   V. L. Human

436. McDermott, John Francis. WILLIAM CLARK'S STRUGGLE WITH PLACE NAMES IN UPPER LOUISIANA. *Missouri Hist. Soc. Bull. 1978 34(3): 140-150.* William Clark (1770-1838), cartographer for the Lewis and Clark Expedition in 1804-06, frequently erred in identifying places along the Mississippi River and the Missouri River. Virtually unschooled, Clark was an abominable speller. Ignorant of the French language, he grossly misinterpreted many French place names. Based on Lewis and Clark expedition journals and secondary sources; 7 maps, 42 notes.   H. T. Lovin

437. Meyer, Larry L. THE FARTHEST WITH THE FEWEST. *Am. West 1975 12(4): 4-9, 61-63.* Discusses French explorers in the West during the 18th century: Louis Antoine Juchereau de St. Denis and Jean-Baptiste Bénard de la Harpe in Louisiana, Charles Claude du Tisne in the Indian country of Oklahoma, Etienne Veniard de Bourgmont in the Indian lands of the Missouri River, and Pierre Gaultier de Varennes, Sieur de la Verendrye, and sons in the western Canadian-American border fur territory. 2 illus., map.   D. L. Smith

438. Mills, Gary B. THE CHAUVIN BROTHERS: EARLY COLONISTS OF LOUISIANA. *Louisiana Hist. 1974 15(2): 117-132.* Examines the lives of pioneers in Louisiana 1699-1760, Jacques, Joseph, Nicolas, and Louis Chauvin.

439. Mills, Gary B. and Mills, Elizabeth Shown. THE FORGOTTEN PEOPLE. *Family Heritage 1979 2(3): 78-81.* Originating from the marriage of a black slave named Marie Thérèse Coincoin and a Frenchman named Claude Thomas Pierre Metoyer, ca. 1767, a free mixed-blood colony of Creoles developed in Natchitoches on Louisiana's Cane River, persisting as an integrated and self-sustained community until the Civil War; after that the land was gradually sold and the family's unique social status was greatly altered by changing race relations into the 20th century.

440. Mills, Gary B. and Mills, Elizabeth Shown. LOUISE MARGUERITE: ST. DENIS' *OTHER* DAUGHTER. *Southern Studies 1977 16(3): 321-328.* Louisiana historians have long been confused about the number and sequence of the children of Louis Antoine Juchereau de St. Denis (1676-1744), Louisiana's "Cavalier in the Wilderness." The first child was Louise Marguerite Juchereau de St. Denis, an illegitimate child probably born of a Natchitoches Indian woman ca. 1712. Church records indicate her first marriage in 1729 and her participation in various civic-religious functions. She was not included in the legitimate heirs of St. Denis, nor was she on good terms with St. Denis' wife. She had two children by her first marriage. She remarried in 1758. Based on Church records and court documents at Natchitoches and on secondary sources; 28 notes.   J. Buschen

441. Morris, James P.   AN AMERICAN FIRST: BLOOD TRANS-
FUSION IN NEW ORLEANS IN THE 1850'S.   *Louisiana Hist. 1975
16(4): 341-360.* The French-speaking group of New Orleans doctors reflected developments in Paris medicine. The first recorded transfusion of
blood into a human patient at Charity Hospital in New Orleans in 1854
was influenced by the work of French physicians. Dr. Samuel Choppin
soon after he returned from abroad decided to perform a transfusion
operation, using those instruments that he himself had seen successfully
employed there. Describes a successful transfusion in 1858 by Dr. N. B.
Benedict who noted that the experimental procedure had been tried in
Europe prior to 1853 only 21 times, all but two of which were successful.
Illus., 34 notes.   E. P. Stickney

442. Murdoch, Richard K.   CORRESPONDENCE OF FRENCH
CONSULS IN CHARLESTON, SOUTH CAROLINA, 1793-1797.
South Carolina Hist. Mag. 1973 74(1): 1-17, (2): 73-79. French minister
Edmond Genêt's mission to the United States was to bring the two
countries together, especially if England declared war on France. Two
1793 letters of Michel Angel Bernard de Mangourit, French consul in
Charleston, to his superiors, reproduced here in translation, cover Genêt
and Mangourit's plans and analyses. A 1797 letter of the new consul,
Victor DuPont de Nemours, deals with Spanish-English difficulties in
East Florida. 36 notes.   D. L. Smith

443. O'Neill, Charles E.   A HISTORY OF FRENCH LOUISIANA:
AN ESSAY REVIEW.   *Louisiana Hist. 1975 16(3): 303-306.* Reviews
Marcel Giraud's *A History of French Louisiana,* Vol. 1, *The Reign of
Louis XIV, 1698-1715* (Baton Rouge: Louisiana State U. Pr., 1974).
Basing his work on primary sources, Professor Giraud is the first to set
the colonial development in the context of detailed realism. In compari-
son with Giraud's work, others have fallen behind: Martin's was chroni-
cled, Gayarre's was romanticized, Lauvriere's was unevenly distributed.
Note.   E. P. Stickney

444. Orband, Edmond.   FACTEURS POLITICO-RELIGIEUX ET
ANGLICISATION DES FRANCO-AMERICAINS AU VERMONT:
INDICATEURS RECENTS [Political and religious factors and the
Anglicizing of Franco-Americans in Vermont: recent evidence]. *Can.
Ethnic Studies [Canada] 1976 8(2): 34-49.* The decision of the Catholic
Church in Vermont in 1960 to end encouragement of the use of the
French language has led to the decline of Franco-American institutions
in Vermont today.

445. Orband, Edmond.   FIN D'UN NATIONALISME: LE CAS RE-
CENT DES FRANCO-AMÉRICAINS DE LA NOUVELLE-
ANGLETERRE [End of a nationalism: the recent case of the New
England Franco-Americans]. *Can. Rev. of Studies in Nationalism [Can-
ada] 1976 4(1): 91-99.* Studies the nationalism of the Franco-Americans,
a group of unassimilated French Canadians in New England, who were
distinguished by the use of the French language and the practice of a rural
and conservative Catholic faith distinct from the Irish one. After 1940,
such nationalism gradually deteriorated and has disappeared today, because of Franco-Americans' exogamous marriages, their mobility due to
economic causes, their mixed parishes where priests officiate in English,
and a general decrease in their resistance to anglicization. Based on
primary and secondary sources; 2 tables, graph, 13 notes.
                                                      G. P. Cleyet

446. Ottoson, Dennis R.   TOUSSAINT CHARBONNEAU, A MOST
DURABLE MAN.   *South Dakota Hist. 1976 6(2): 152-185.* Biography
of Toussaint Charbonneau, best known as the husband of Sacagawea,
portraying him in a fair light as frontiersman.

447. Oukada, Larbi.   THE TERRITORY AND POPULATION OF
FRENCH-SPEAKING LOUISIANA.   *Rev. de Louisiane 1978 7(1):
5-34.* Twentieth-century studies of French-speakers in Louisiana contain
social, demographic, political, and linguistic biases; suggests criteria for
an interdisciplinary study of the extent of the French community in the
20th century.

448. Paquet, Gilles.   L'ÉMIGRATION DES CANADIENS FRAN-
ÇAIS VERS LA NOUVELLE-ANGLETERRE, 1870-1910: PRISES
DE VUE QUANTITATIVES [French-Canadian emigration into New
England, 1870-1910: taking a quantitative view]. *Recherches Sociogra-*

phiques [Canada] 1964 5(3): 319-370. Quantitative analysis of French-
Canadian emigration from Quebec to New England.

449. Parker, James H.   THE ASSIMILATION OF FRENCH
AMERICANS.   *Human Organization 1979 38(3): 309-312.* The
French-speaking population maintained a tight-knit enclave in Lewiston,
Maine, for five generations (1810's-1960's), but eventually upward social
mobility necessitated the use of the English language and cultural ties
began slowly to break down.

450. Plaisance, E. Charles, ed. and transl.   CHÉNIÈRE: THE DE-
STRUCTION OF A COMMUNITY.   *Louisiana Hist. 1973 14(2): 179-
193.* The hurricane of October 1893 devastated the Gulf Coast from
southern Louisiana to Pensacola, but was especially destructive at Chénière. Paroles de Jean Henriot, a resident of Chénière, wrote a narrative
poem describing the storm, "L'ouragon de la Chénière Caminada." Plaisance formerly possessed the original of this poem, which is now in the
Department of Archives of the Louisiana State University Library. The
manuscript is photoreproduced here, along with a transcription and
translation by Plaisance (pp. 184-193). Plaisance notes discrepancies in
the account published by Ormande Plater, "The Hurricane of Chénière
Caminada, A Narrative Poem in French," *Louisiana Folklore Miscellany*
1971 3: 1-9.   R. L. Woodward, Jr.

451. Plumstead, A. W.   CRÈVECOEUR: A "MAN OF SORROWS"
AND THE AMERICAN REVOLUTION.   *Massachusetts Rev. 1976
17(2): 286-301.* Michel Guillaume Jean de Crèvecoeur (1735-1813), born
in Caen, France, and best known for his *Letters from an American
Farmer,* emigrated to Canada in 1755, was wounded on the Plains of
Abraham, and left for New York in 1759. Here he became known as J.
Hector St. John, married Mehitabel Tippet, became a farmer, and wrote
his *Letters.* These extolled the happy valley syndrome. In 1779 Crèvecoeur left for Great Britain, where his *Letters* were published in 1782. He
finally moved to France. Not permitted to return to New York during the
French Revolution, he spent his final years in France.
                                                      E. R. Campbell

452. Pouyez, Christian.   LA POPULATION DE L'ILE ROYALE
EN 1752 [Population of Isle Royale in 1752]. *Hist. Sociale—Social Hist.
[Canada] 1973 6(12): 147-180.* Isle Royale in Lake Superior was a part
of New France in 1752. The royal surveyor La Roque performed a
geographical survey of the island, checked economic resources, investigated problems caused by concessions, and took a census. La Roque's
work described characteristics of the population, distribution by age,
profession, and sex, family structure, and the geographical origins of the
inhabitants. 3 maps, 13 tables, 36 notes.   G. E. Pergl

453. Price, W. J.   AUX ORIGINES D'UN SCHISME: LE CEN-
TENAIRE D'UNE RÉCONCILLIATION AVORTÉE [At the origins
of a schism: the centennial of an aborted reconciliation]. *Rev. d'Hist. de
l'Amérique Française [Canada] 1959 13(1): 45-78.* A biographical essay
of the work of Abbé Charles P. T. Chiniquy in Illinois with Canadian
immigrants from 1851 to 1856.

454. Rickels, Patricia.   LE FOLKLORE DES ACADIENS [The
Acadians' folklore]. *Rev. de Louisiane 1978 7(2): 101-115.* Studies
Acadian folklore in Louisiana since the 18th century and mentions social
customs still alive.

455. Robbins, Peggy.   THE "LITTLE ADVENTURES" OF MADE-
LEINE HACHARD.   *Am. Hist. Illus. 1977 12(4): 36-42.* A group of
Ursulines went from France to New Orleans in 1727 to teach female
settlers, Indians, and Negroes; focuses on Sister Marie Madeleine of St.
Stanislaus (d. 1760).

456. Robinson, Willard B.   MARITIME FRONTIER EN-
GINEERING: THE DEFENSE OF NEW ORLEANS. *Louisiana
Hist. 1977 18(1): 5-62.* Discusses the objectives, planning, and construction of fortifications protecting New Orleans during 1680-1896. Beginning with Fort Crèvecoeur (1680), depicts a large number of 18th-century
French and Spanish forts in the New Orleans area, including the fortifications of the city itself. The early federal period witnessed several new
fortifications, notably Forts Jackson, Pike, Philip, Macomb, and Living-
ston, and the Battery Bienvenue. These were expanded in midcentury as

part of a national system of forts. New forts were added during the Civil War at Proctor's Landing and Ship Island. Few fortifications were added until some improvements in coast artillery were made in the 1890's. The forts were abandoned in 1920 because they were obsolete. Some of the forts, examples of military architecture of the 18th and 19th centuries, have been made into state historical parks. Others are falling into ruin. Primary sources; 27 illus., 109 notes. R. L. Woodward, Jr.

457. Ross, Aileen. THE HUGUENOTS. *Pacific Hist. 1974 18(1): 52-65.* Many French Protestants immigrated to colonial America and contributed much to the society and culture. Discusses famous Americans who had Huguenot ancestors: George Washington, Jedediah Strong Smith, Elias Boudinot, John Jay, Pierre Harache, and Bernard Hubley. Biblio. S

458. Saloman, Ora Frishberg. VICTOR PELISSIER, COMPOSER IN FEDERAL NEW YORK AND PHILADELPHIA. *Pennsylvania Mag. of Hist. and Biog. 1978 102(1): 93-102.* French composer Victor Pelissier left France during the Revolution. He gave concerts in Philadelphia in 1792, when he arrived via the West Indies. The traveling Old American Company, finding in New York City a permanent home in 1798, engaged him as hornist and composer. In Philadelphia after 1811, he published *Pelissier's Columbian Melodies.* A leading composer, he spent his last years in or near New York. Based on published sources and secondary works; 24 notes. T. H. Wendel

459. Sansoucy, Debra P. THE FRENCH. *Hist. J. of Western Massachusetts 1976 (Supplement): 19-26.* Discusses French interest in exploiting American discontent with British rule before the Revolution, the negotiations leading to French assistance, and the role of French men, supplies, and money in the success of the American Revolution. Illus., notes. W. H. Mulligan, Jr.

460. Santos Hernández, Angel. PRESENCIA MISIONERA EN LA ANTIGUA LUISIANA [Missionary presence in old Louisiana]. *Missionalia Hispanica [Spain] 1975 32(94): 77-101.* Sketches the history of old Louisiana, dealing with its earliest exploration and evangelization connected with the Canadian Indian missions of the Jesuits. The Franciscan Recollects from Paris and the Capuchins were later entrusted with some areas. There were problems of ecclesiastical jurisdiction during the successive French, Spanish, and American periods. In the 20th century the evangelization of several Indian tribes has been the work chiefly of the Jesuits. Based on secondary sources; 29 notes.
J. Correia-Afonso

461. Schafer, Delbert F. FRENCH EXPLORERS IN OKLAHOMA. *Chronicles of Oklahoma 1977-78 55(4): 392-402.* Traces the history of approximately a dozen French expeditions through Oklahoma beginning with the 1719 exploration of Jean-Baptiste Bénard Sieur de la Harpe and concluding with the French and Indian War when France relinquished her Louisiana territory to Spain. The few Frenchmen in these expeditions did influence Indian trade and alliances and increased European knowledge of the vast interior regions of the southern Plains. Primary and secondary sources; 2 maps, 30 notes. M. L. Tate

462. Segura, Pearl Mary, ed. THE CAPTURE OF THE BLUFF OF BATON ROUGE. *Louisiana Hist. 1976 17(2): 203-209.* Discusses a translated poem by Julien Poydras de Lalande, a Frenchman who came to Louisiana about 1768 as a merchant. He became active in politics, being twice elected president of the new state court. He was known as a philanthropist, educator, and poet. In the poem he lavishly praised Governor Don Bernardo de Galvez for the capture of Baton Rouge from the English in 1779. Illus., 8 notes. E. P. Stickney

463. Silvia, Philip T., Jr. THE "FLINT AFFAIR": FRENCH-CANADIAN STRUGGLE FOR *SURVIVANCE. Catholic Hist. Rev. 1979 65(3): 414-435.* Examines ethnic tension in Fall River, Massachusetts, 1870's-85, between Irish Americans and French Canadians who, though coreligionists, were divided by cultural and economic differences. Central to this struggle was the militant French-Canadian determination to best preserve their "race," culture and religious heritage by establishing a national parish, Notre Dame de Lourdes, with a French-Canadian serving as pastor. Rome concurred, to the disappointment of Irish-born Thomas F. Hendricken, bishop of Providence, who, despite invoking the

spiritual weapon of interdiction, did not prevail in attempting to implement an assimilationist, Americanization approach to church governance. A

464. Smith, Ralph. ST. CROIX ISLAND. *Beaver [Canada] 1978 308(4): 36-40.* St. Croix Island, only a few hundred yards long, is in the St. Croix River, Maine, close to St. Andrews, New Brunswick. In 1604 this island was discovered by Pierre du Gua, Sieur de Monts, and Samuel de Champlain. The site was abandoned in 1605, but while it was in use the Frenchmen erected a fort accommodating 80 men. The US National Park Service has conducted excavations, and considerable pottery and other materials dating from the early 1600's have been located. 7 illus.
D. Chaput

465. Solano Costa, Fernando. LOS DESCUBRIMIENTOS DEL MISISIPI [Discoveries on the Mississippi]. *Estudios del Departamento de Hist. Moderna [Spain] 1975 (4): 7-18.* Discusses European exploration in the Mississippi River Valley by Spain in the 16th century and by France, beginning in the last third of the 17th century. Examines formation of the Louisiana territory and its boundaries with Canada and Mexico. P. M. (IHE 95071)

466. Sorrell, Richard S. FRANCO-AMERICANS IN NEW ENGLAND. *J. of Ethnic Studies 1977 5(1): 90-94.* Reiterates the distinction between French and French Canadian as ethnic backgrounds, two out of three Franco-Americans will be French Canadian in ancestry and nearly three-fourths are found in New England, mainly in New Hampshire. Majority of the article is a bibliographic essay on Franco-Americans, including unpublished dissertations and manuscripts. Focuses on the *survivance* idea, the realization of slow acculturation.
G. J. Bobango

467. Sorrell, Richard S. THE HISTORIOGRAPHY OF FRENCH CANADIANS IN THE UNITED STATES. *Immigration Hist. Newsletter 1979 11(1): 4-8.* Reviews historiographical essays written during the 1930's-70's, on the presence and activities of French Canadians in the United States, 19th-20th centuries.

468. Sorrell, Richard S. SENTINELLE AFFAIR (1924-1929)—RELIGION AND MILITANT SURVIVANCE IN WOONSOCKET, RHODE ISLAND. *Rhode Island Hist. 1977 36(3): 67-79.* Discusses French Canadians in Woonsocket; examines problems of assimilation, religion, and nationalism. Based on the author's doctoral dissertation; 8 illus., 14 notes. P. J. Coleman

469. Spitzer, Nicholas. CAJUNS AND CREOLES: THE FRENCH GULF COAST. *Southern Exposure 1977 5(2-3): 140-155.* Cajun and Creole cultural attributes persist among the white and black French-speaking residents of southern Louisiana and the Texas Gulf Coast. Cultural traditions from the 1600's are evident in celebrations such as Mardi Gras and All Saints' Day in many small French communities. Religious practices and rituals, black and white native popular music, and the use of the French Cajun dialect in everyday speech persist. The Council for the Development of French in Louisiana (CODOFIL) has been active in promoting the revival of the French language. Primary and secondary sources, interviews and personal observation. N. Lederer

470. Starr, J. Barton. CAMPBELL TOWN: FRENCH HUGUENOTS IN BRITISH WEST FLORIDA. *Florida Hist. Q. 1976 54(4): 532-547.* Located 20 miles north of Pensacola, Campbell Town was a French Huguenot colony led by Lieutenant Governor Montfort Browne. It was established in 1765 to promote the cultivation of grapes and the raising of silkworms. An example of the British government's eagerness to colonize West Florida, Campbell Town nonetheless was abandoned by 1770 due to internal friction, Indian problems, and unhealthy climate. Based mainly on sources in the Colonial Office. 50 notes.
P. A. Beaber

471. Stern, Madeleine B. JOSEPH NANCREDE, FRANCO-AMERICAN BOOKSELLER-PUBLISHER, 1761-1841. *Papers of the Biblio. Soc. of Am. 1976 70(1): 1-88.* Extensive biography of French-born bookseller and publisher, Joseph Nancrede.

472. Stopp, G. Harry, Jr. CULTURAL BROKERS AND SOCIAL CHANGE IN AN AMERICAN PEASANT COMMUNITY. *Peasant Studies Newsletter 1976 5(3): 18-22.* Discusses the cultural role of economic and political brokers among the Cajuns in south Alabama in the 1960's, emphasizing characteristics of rural settlements.

473. Taillemite, Etienne and Voorhies, Jacqueline K., transl. HISTORY OF FRENCH LOUISIANA: LOUISIANA AFTER LAW. *Louisiana Hist. 1976 17(3): 347-350.* Reviews Marcel Giraud's *Histoire de la Louisiane française*, tome IV, *La Louisiana après le système de Law (1721-1723)* (Paris: Presses Universitaires de France, 1974).
                                                    R. L. Woodward

474. Trotman, C. James. GEORGE W. CABLE AND TRADITION. *Texas Q. 1976 19(3): 51-58.* In 1879 the publication of *Old Creole Days* made George Washington Cable famous, though today few people read his work. Cable fit into the local color tradition, but he fit the romantic mold, too. In later years he dropped social criticism from his work, a price he paid for success. Based on primary and secondary sources; 8 notes.
                                                    R. H. Tomlinson

475. Walsh, Andrew S. and Wells, Robert V. POPULATION DYNAMICS IN THE EIGHTEENTH-CENTURY MISSISSIPPI RIVER VALLEY: ACADIANS IN LOUISIANA. *J. of Social Hist. 1978 11(4): 521-545.* Based on three censuses, those of 1766, 1769, and 1770. Discusses the general demographic patterns of Acadian immigrants, the social correlates of household size and composition, and a degree of change remarkable even for the frontier. The place is Cabanocey, on both banks of the Mississippi River; it grew from 252 in 1766 to 499 by 1769. Generally the Acadians had more children, more working age persons, and fewer slaves than their counterparts. Their fertility, mortality, and migration were high. 6 tables, 27 notes, appendix.
                                                    M. Hough

476. Wedel, Mildred Mott. THE BÉNARD DE LA HARPE HISTORIOGRAPHY ON FRENCH COLONIAL LOUISIANA. *Louisiana Studies 1974 13(1): 9-67.* A critical and analytical bibliography of the writings of Jean-Baptiste Bénard de la Harpe, colonial leader, trader, and explorer who arrived in Louisiana during August 1718 and spent three and one-half years there. Discusses the primary documents written by Bénard de La Harpe which are available in the United States, covering his travels and the Louisiana colony, with evaluations also of translations. Introduced by an outline of his activities in Louisiana and followed by a critical discussion of whether he or Jean de Beaurain wrote *Journal Historique de l'Establissement des Français a la Louisiana*. 96 notes.
                                                    R. V. Ritter

477. Wells, Carol. EARLIEST LOG CABINS OF NATCHITOCHES. *North Louisiana Hist. Assoc. J. 1975 6(3): 117-122.* Not until 1795 was a log cabin mentioned in the legal records of Natchitoches, although "judging by American names and English fences, log cabins probably were built about 10 years before their first mention in official records." The log cabins that were built "had already assumed a French character." In effect, "Natchitoches log cabins looked like Natchitoches *bousillage*-panelled framed houses. They were built in the same shape and size, had similar rooflines, galleries, chimneys, probable additions, and interior partition." Includes a table comparing three cabin contracts. 10 notes.
                                                    A. N. Garland

478. Wells, Carol. WHERE IS SAINT DENIS BURIED? *Louisiana Studies 1973 12(1): 391-395.* The remains of Louis Antoine Juchereau de Saint Denis (d. 1744), the founder of Natchitoches, are in the American Cemetery there, on the former site of a church. 10 notes.
                                                    S

479. Western, John. SOCIAL GROUPS AND ACTIVITY PATTERNS IN HOUMA, LOUISIANA. *Geographical R. 1973 63(3): 301-321.* The city of Houma, in the bayou country of southern Louisiana, was once a sequestered fishing, trapping, and sugarcane- and oyster-producing area where Cajun French was the dominant language. Since World War II, however, a surge in oilfield activity has almost tripled the population of Houma. The growth has brought the superimposition of a third social group, immigrant anglophone Texans, on the two principal local groups, the blacks and the Cajun whites. A simple model is constructed to describe the relationships of each group to the others, and the activitiy

patterns of each group on neighborhood, city, North American, and world scales are delineated. Cajuns are found to be acculturated into the exogenous white system more rapidly than blacks are, and several intermediate social groups emerge.
                                                    J

480. White, Stephen A. THE ARICHAT FRENCHMEN IN GLOUCESTER: PROBLEMS OF IDENTIFICATION AND IDENTITY. *New England Hist. and Genealogical Register 1977 131(April): 83-99.* Describes the settlement of the Acadians of the Arichat region of Nova Scotia in Gloucester, Massachusetts, in the late 19th century. Gloucester had always been dominated by the fishing industry, and the winter fishery of Georges Banks was just started when the Acadians, already skilled fishermen, began to arrive. Determining how many Acadians arrived and when is difficult, for a strong desire to "become American," as well as cultural and religious prejudice, caused the Frenchmen to change their names (LeBlanc to White, Fogeron to Smith) and to work diligently to banish any trace of a French accent. The high mortality on the seas encouraged intermarriage. In addition, the absence of French priests made interaction with other non-French—and later non-Catholic—groups almost inevitable, eventually contributing to the breakdown of a sense of community. Based on oral interviews and on primary and secondary sources; 3 charts, 80 notes.
                                                    S. L. Patterson

481. Wilson, Samuel, Jr. RELIGIOUS ARCHITECTURE IN FRENCH COLONIAL LOUISIANA. *Winterthur Portfolio 1973 (8): 63-106.* The original intent of French colonization in Louisiana was religious. That intention, however, was subordinated to France's military and political objectives. The building of religious structures was relegated to state officials and carried out by military engineers. Church construction was therefore subordinated to more worldly needs. Early missionaries were left to their own devices as the first churches were constructed inside forts. Early designs for New Orleans were attempts to translate the concepts of Sebastien Le Prestre, Marechal de Vauban (1633-1707), to New World conditions. Concepts of French architecture influenced Spanish design long after Spain took control of the territory. Based on primary and secondary sources; 39 illus., 122 notes.
                                                    N. A. Kuntz

482. Woods, Patricia D. THE FRENCH AND THE NATCHEZ INDIANS IN LOUISIANA: 1700-1731. *Louisiana Hist. 1978 19(4): 413-435.* Examines relationship between the French and the Natchez Indians, 1700-31, seeking an explanation for the massacre of more than 200 French settlers at Fort Rosalie (Natchez) in 1729. Unlike the more peaceful relations between French and Indians in Canada, a growing tension between the two had developed in Louisiana largely because of the French development of agriculture. As it became clear that the French were taking the Indians' land, the Indians struck back violently. Primary sources; 84 notes.
                                                    R. L. Woodward

483. Woolfson, Peter. THE HERITAGE AND CULTURE OF THE FRENCH-VERMONTER: RESEARCH NEEDS IN THE SOCIAL SCIENCES. *Vermont Hist. 1976 44(2): 103-109.* Reviews the limited historiography on an ethnic minority comprising nearly 10 percent of the population, and urges more study. 20 refs.
                                                    T. D. S. Bassett

484. Woolworth, Nancy L. GINGRAS, ST. JOSEPH AND THE MÉTIS IN THE NORTHERN RED RIVER VALLEY: 1845-1873. *North Dakota Hist. 1975 42(4): 17-27.* Discusses the role of Antoine Blanc Gingras in the fur trade, buffalo hunting, and settlement of the Northern Red River Valley of the Dakota Territory from 1845-73, including relations with Indians.

German (including Russian-Germans)

485. Achenbaum, W. Andrew. TOWARD PLURALISM AND ASSIMILATION: THE RELIGIOUS CRISIS OF ANN ARBOR'S WÜRTTEMBERG COMMUNITY. *Michigan Hist. 1974 58(3): 195-218.* The evolution of Ann Arbor's Württemberg community illustrates a point often obscured in the assimilationist-pluralist controversy among historians of American immigration: that in adjusting to American society, most ethnic groups have altered some cultural patterns while preserving others. Ann Arbor Württembergers quickly accommodated themselves politically and economically but maintained their social customs and religious traditions. Following a congregational schism in 1875, one faction endeavored to preserve the pietism and ethnic solidarity of the Württemberg heritage, while the other moved into the mainstream of American Protestantism. Primary and secondary sources; 2 illus., 8 photos, 54 notes.   D. W. Johnson

486. Amen, Ruth M. THE FIRST DECADE: FOR AHSGR IT IS ONLY THE BEGINNING. *J. of the Am. Hist. Soc. of Germans from Russia 1978 1(2): 1-3.* Provides an overview of the accomplishments of the American Historical Society of Germans from Russia on the occasion of the group's 10th anniversary, 1978.

487. Arndt, Karl J. R. BISMARCK'S SOCIALIST LAWS OF 1878 AND THE HARMONISTS. *Western Pennsylvania Hist. Mag. 1976 59(1): 55-70.* Following Otto von Bismarck's socialist laws of 1878, German socialist Clara Pittman applied for membership in George Rapp's Harmony Society (1879), an organization of Christian communists, headquartered in Economy, Pennsylvania.

488. Arndt, Karl J. R. DID FREDERICK RAPP CHEAT ROBERT OWEN? *Western Pennsylvania Hist. Mag. 1978 61(4): 358-365.* Questions the accusation that Harmonist Frederick Rapp cheated Robert Owen in the sale of New Harmony, Indiana, to Owen in 1825.

489. Arndt, Karl J. R. LUTHER'S GOLDEN ROSE AT NEW HARMONY, INDIANA. *Concordia Hist. Inst. Q. 1976 49(3): 112-122.* In 1822, in the archway over George Rapp's Lutheran Harmony Society, a golden rose was carved. Based on one of Luther's early translations of the Book of Micah, the *Güldene Rose* was a symbol of the struggle and strength of the church. Lutheran leaders, such as George Rapp who was a prominent leader in New Harmony, Indiana, and later in Economy, Pennsylvania, became involved in the development of utopian communities during the early decades of the 19th century. Primary sources; 18 notes.   W. T. Walker

490. Arndt, Karl J. R. THE STRANGE AND WONDERFUL NEW WORLD OF GEORGE RAPP AND HIS HARMONY SOCIETY. *Western Pennsylvania Hist. Mag. 1974 57(2): 141-166.* Examines the development of religious theory in George Rapp's collective religious settlement, the Harmony Society established in Economy, Pennsylvania.   S

491. Baade, Anne E. SLAVE INDEMNITIES: A GERMAN COAST RESPONSE, 1795. *Louisiana Hist. 1979 20(1): 102-109.* The abortive slave insurrection conspiracy in Pointe Coupee Parish in 1795 induced Spanish authorities to institute regulations to appoint sindics in the rural districts, levying a tax to finance slave indemnifications, and construct a new prison on the German Coast. Inhabitants of the German Coast petitioned Baron de Carondelet for relief from the tax, but Spanish authorities persuaded them to accept it. The petition is printed here in full, in German and English.   L. N. Powell

492. Barclay, Morgan J. IMAGES OF TOLEDO'S GERMAN COMMUNITY, 1850-1890. *Northwest Ohio Q. 1973 45(4): 133-143.* Studies reactions of the local press to Germans, the largest foreign-born element in Toledo until 1920. Because Germans "Americanized" rather quickly, the local newspapers usually regarded them as praiseworthy. Germans were criticized only when they joined radical political movements and when the temperance movement was strong in Toledo. On these occasions the Germans were accused of trying to "Germanize" America and of undercutting American morals. 72 notes.   W. F. Zornow

493. Barnett, James. WILLICH'S THIRTY-SECOND INDIANA VOLUNTEERS. *Cincinnati Hist. Soc. Bull. 1979 37(1): 48-70.* Describes German-American August Willich's command of the 32d Indiana Volunteers, the German regiment from Cincinnati, during the Civil War.

494. Barrick, Mac E. RURAL ECONOMICS IN CENTRAL PENNSYLVANIA, 1850-1867. *Pennsylvania Folklife 1972 22(1): 42-45.* Provides entries from the account book of Reverend Daniel Stock, a Lutheran minister living in central Pennsylvania around the 1860's, which is part of the Cumberland County Historical Society and Hamilton Library Association of Carlisle, Pennsylvania, collection of 18th- and 19th-century Pennsylvania folklife.

495. Batt, Ronald E. JOSEPH BATT AND THE CHAPEL: A BIOGRAPHICAL SKETCH OF AN ALSATIAN IMMIGRANT. *Niagara Frontier 1976 23(2): 49-55.* Discusses the role of Alsatian immigrant, Joseph Batt, in the building of the Chapel of Our Lady Help of Christians in Cheektowaga, in the Buffalo area, 1789-1872.

496. Bennett, James D. A TRIBUTE TO LOUIS H. HAST, LOUISVILLE MUSICIAN. *Filson Club Hist. Q. 1978 52(4): 323-329.* Louis H. Hast, an immigrant from Germany, was a dominant figure in establishing a strong musical tradition in Louisville, Kentucky. In 1878 Hast became organist and choir director for Christ Church Cathedral and introduced classical music to church functions. He also started the Philharmonic and *La Reunion* Musicale and contributed to the Public Library. Newspapers and secondary works; 24 notes.   G. B. McKinney

497. Blair, Virginia K. THE SINGING SOCIETIES AND PHILHARMONIC ORCHESTRA OF BELLEVILLE. *J. of the Illinois State Hist. Soc. 1975 68(5): 386-395.* The heavily German population of Belleville, Illinois, engaged in organized vocal and instrumental musical activities as early as the 1850's. The Philharmonic Society was founded in November 1867 and has maintained its existence as a symphony orchestra to the present day. Despite anti-German feeling during World War I and economic difficulties in the 1930's, the Philharmonic and other Belleville musical groups managed to survive and even to expand their activities.   N. Lederer

498. Brandau, Robert and Ward, Eleanor. STONE UPON STONE: THE CRAFT OF DRY STONE MASONRY. *Historic Preservation 1975 27(2): 26-29.* Brought by early English and German settlers, "dry walling" relies on tightly wedged stone instead of mortar or binding material. It has been used in "barn sidings, foundations, springhouses, terracing and bridges." Harvey Fite's "Opus 40" is a significant modern example. 8 photos.   R. M. Frame III

499. Brass, Maynard F. GERMAN PRESBYTERIANS AND THE SYNOD OF THE WEST. *J. of Presbyterian Hist. 1978 56(3): 237-251.* The Synod of the West was a German-ethnic ecclesiastical judicatory of the Presbyterian Church whose three presbyteries and 50 congregations overlapped seven synods of the Church. Organized in 1912, it shaped three aspects of its constituents' church life: their German usage, emphasis on mission activity, and publication. While the Synod thrived in its 47-year existence, its ethnic presence ran counter to the policy of the denomination's social concerns which focused on racial and cultural minority groups, and insisted on integration. The characteristic activities which had formerly bound the people together were gradually lost after the dissolution of the Synod was accomplished in 1959. The identity of German Presbyterians eroded. Based on ecclesiastical resources in the Archives of the University of Dubuque, oral interviews and secondary sources; map, 46 notes.   H. M. Parker, Jr.

500. Brister, Louis E. THE IMAGE OF ARKANSAS IN THE EARLY GERMAN EMIGRANT GUIDEBOOK: NOTES ON IMMIGRATION. *Arkansas Hist. Q. 1977 36(4): 338-345.* Discusses and elaborates on a three-part article by Jonathan James Wolfe entitled "Background of German Immigration," demonstrating with extracts from an early German guidebook why Germans immigrated to Texas in the 1840's but few came to Arkansas until the 1870's. Primary and secondary sources; 16 notes.   G. R. Schroeder

501. Brown, Waln K. CULTURAL LEARNING THROUGH GAME STRUCTURE: A STUDY OF PENNSYLVANIA GERMAN CHILDREN'S GAMES. *Pennsylvania Folklife 1974 23(4): 2-11.* Reviews several aspects of games scholarship, and uses a specific model— Pennsylvania German children's games—to yield new insights on group organization and social norms.   S

502. Cary, Lorin Lee. ADOLPH GERMER AND THE 1890'S DEPRESSION. *J. of the Illinois State Hist. Soc. 1975 68(4): 337-343.* Coal miners in a heavily German-populated area of southern Illinois, Adolph Germer and his father were active members of the early United Mine Workers of America. Germer was a participant in the strikes of 1894 and 1897. These strikes, culminating in the killing of seven miners by company guards at Virden, Illinois, in 1898, alonq with the depression of the 1890's, made Germer a staunch believer in unionism and Socialism. Based on primary and secondary sources.   N. Lederer

503. Cawthon, John Ardis. FREDERICK MILLER, THE FIRST WHITE MAN BURIED IN CLAIBORNE PARISH AND HIS DESCENDANTS. *North Louisiana Hist. Assoc. J. 1975 7(1): 27-30.* In 1820, the more prosperous colonizers of the old Murrell Settlement, some 12 miles northeast of Minden near the Claiborne-Webster line, took into their homes a group of impoverished German immigrants—Frederick Miller; his son, Frederick, Jr.; and his daughter, Maria, among them. John Murrell was the benefactor of the Miller family. Frederick Miller lived only two more years, dying in 1822. He was buried in Murrell's graveyard. While there is no known record of the name of the wife of Frederick Miller, Jr., it is known that she had at least eight children. Maria Miller married Judge Robert Lee Kilgore, and their descendants all have been through their daughters; none of the Kilgore boys married. "As late as the middle of the 20th century, several fourth-generation descendants of Frederick Miller were still living within a 25-mile radius of the old Murrell settlement sites." 20 notes.   A. N. Garland

504. Cazden, Robert E. THE GERMAN BOOK TRADE IN OHIO BEFORE 1848. *Ohio Hist. 1975 84(1&2): 57-77.* Not until 1807 did Ohio have its own German newspaper. Its first German books and almanacs were published about a decade later. The German population was in the orbit of the Pennsylvania-German book trade. Though there was a German bookseller in Canton ca. 1812, Cincinnati did not have one until 1834. The years 1834-35 were particularly significant as six Cincinnati German newspapers began publication. 4 illus., 64 notes.
                                                              S. S. Sprague

505. Conzen, Kathleen Neils. LOCAL HISTORY AS CASE STUDY. *Rev. in Am. Hist. 1978 6(1): 50-56.* Review article prompted by Stephanie Grauman Wolf's *Urban Village: Population, Community, and Family Structure in Germantown, Pennsylvania, 1683-1800* (Princeton, N. J.: Princeton U. Pr., 1976).

506. Cortinovis, Irene E. THE GOLDEN AGE OF GERMAN SONG. *Missouri Hist. R. 1974 68(4): 437-442.* Traces the history of singing societies in St. Louis, composed mostly of German-Americans, from the founding of the first club in 1846 to the present. Based on taped interviews, primary sources; 2 illus., photo, 13 notes.
                                                              N. J. Street

507. Costello, John R. CULTURAL VESTIGES AND CULTURAL BLENDS AMONG THE PENNSYLVANIA GERMANS. *New York Folklore 1977 3(1-4): 101-113.* Discusses "the development of three vestiges of German culture which have been maintained among the Pennsylvania Germans since colonial times": the charm, from the pre-Christian-to-*Macbeth* era; the sign of the pentagram, or witch's foot, from the medieval period, or earlier; and the literary character Till Eulenspiegel, from 1515 or earlier.

508. Cox, Richard W. ADOLF DEHN: THE MINNESOTA CONNECTION. *Minnesota Hist. 1977 45(5): 166-186.* Adolph Dehn increasingly drew on his Minnesota origins for his pictorial themes from the 1930's until his death in 1968. During 1916-36, Dehn specialized in social satire, which has led art critics to call Dehn one of the main social satirists of the "Jazz Age." During his years in Europe, he associated with such satirical artists as George Grosz, with whom Dehn was often compared. Born in Waterville, Minnesota, of German parents, Dehn imbibed a political radicalism from his elders which, along with his ethnicity, caused him considerable trouble during World War I. After spending most of the 1920's in Europe, Dehn returned to America in 1929. During the mid-1930's, Dehn, for aesthetic and monetary reasons, became immersed in American regionalistic art, using the rural and small town environment of Minnesota for many important works of his later career. Based on interviews with Dehn and his contemporaries.   N. Lederer

509. Cunningham, Barbara. AN EIGHTEENTH-CENTURY VIEW OF FEMININITY AS SEEN THROUGH THE JOURNALS OF HENRY MELCHIOR MUHLENBERG. *Pennsylvania Hist. 1976 43(3): 197-212.* In some respects, the journals of Henry Melchior Muhlenberg, an 18th-century Pennsylvania Lutheran clergyman, reflect attitudes toward women that historian Barbara Weltner has associated with the 19th-century "Cult of True Womanhood." For Muhlenberg, the ideal woman was religious, pure, submissive, and devoted to household duties. He thought that women were particularly vulnerable to a variety of physical, mental, and spiritual disorders. His views on sexuality prefigure Victorian prudery in some ways, but Muhlenberg did not think that one sex was more or less sensual than the other. "Muhlenberg placed the *female* center of mind, body, and soul very specifically in the uterus." 2 illus., 48 notes.   D. C. Swift

510. Diamond, Sander A. ZUR TYPOLOGIE DER AMERIKA-DEUTSCHEN NS-BEWEGUNG [On the typology of the German American National Socialist Movement]. *Vierteljahrshefte für Zeitgeschichte [West Germany] 1975 23(3): 271-296.* Analyzes four key German American Nazi organizations: Teutonia (1924-32), Gau USA (1931-36), adventurer Edmund Fürholzer's group around *Deutsche Zeitung* (1928-31), and the most notorious Bund (Bund der Freunde des neuen Deutschland, later Amerikandeutscher Volksbund, 1933-38). Composed largely of young, anti-Semitic, lower middle class, usually unemployed post-World War I immigrants, the groups eventually drew enough American mistrust upon themselves to be disowned even by their German Nazi supporters. Based on records primarily at the National Archives (Suitland); 68 notes.   D. Prowe

511. Dietz, Charlton. HENRY BEHNKE: NEW ULM'S PAUL REVERE. *Minnesota Hist. 1976 45(3): 111-115.* German-born Henry Behnke settled with the Behnke-Dietz family as part of the earliest contingent of Germans relocating in New Ulm under the auspices of the German Land Association of Minnesota. On the eve of the Sioux Uprising of 1862, 29-year-old Behnke was active in public service, holding a variety of appointed political positions. Behnke was assigned by the townspeople to contact Judge Charles E. Flandrau, a much respected man among the German-American community, to organize the resistance of New Ulm against the attacking Sioux Indians. Behnke did so on 19 August 1863, riding through hostile territory to accomplish his mission. Flandrau responded to the pleas of the townspeople and mounted a defense which prevented the taking of New Ulm by the Sioux. Based mainly on printed primary and secondary sources.   N. Lederer

512. Doerries, Reingard R. THE AMERICANIZING OF THE GERMAN IMMIGRANT: A CHAPTER FROM U.S. SOCIAL HISTORY. *Amerikastudien/Am. Studies [West Germany] 1978 23(1): 51-59.* While German historiography has produced a number of studies on the problem of emigration, the question of the absorption of German nationals in foreign societies has largley been neglected. Immigrants from Germany made up one of the largest contingents of the inflow to the United States throughout most of the nineteenth century. As was the case with other nationalities, they formed associations of social, economic, and cultural cooperation in the New World, often designed to maintain an ethnic cohesiveness but in many cases becoming in fact vehicles of Americanization. The social structure of the German-American community is not only of interest as an ethnic microcosm; the study of the ethnic minority and its interaction with the existing American social formations also reveals a number of valuable insights into the makings of American society. The interdisciplinary approach to American social history, drawing on findings in fields such as church history, sociology, applied sociolinguistics, and organizational history shows the multi-faceted Americanization to be a natural social process.   J

513. Dolan, Jay P. PHILADELPHIA AND THE GERMAN CATHOLIC COMMUNITY. Miller, Randall M. and Marzik, Thomas

D., ed. *Immigrants and Religion in Urban America* (Philadelphia: Temple U. Pr., 1977): 69-83. Ethnic consciousness of the German Catholic population, first evident in Philadelphia in the mid-1700's, led to a continuing battle with Church authorities who wanted a Catholic Church without national distinctions. With the heavy influx of German immigrants in the mid-19th century, the German Catholics became the largest subgroup of Catholics. As the wave of Irish emigration continued, the German Catholics lost control of the Church, and soon German Americans in Philadelphia were a social and religious minority. In reaction to the decline of devotion and practice, numerous national parishes appeared. The parish became the center of German Catholic life. The Mass was embellished with pageantry, music, and processions. Mutual benefit societies, hospitals, schools, and an orphan asylum were established to reinforce the "ethnic fortress." But these actions also created a separation from other German Americans. The early 1900's brought a decline in German culture and national parishes as American habits were adopted. Assimilation was further hastened by the anti-German hysteria of World War I and the stigma of the Nazis in World War II. 47 notes.

S. Robitaille

514. Dorfman, Mark H. THE EPHRATA CLOISTER. *Early Am. Life 1979 10(1): 38-41, 64-65.* The Ephrata Cloister in Pennsylvania's Conestoga Valley was a religious commune under the direction of founder Johann Conrad Beissel, Emmanuel Eckerlin, and Beissel once again, ca. 1732-68.

515. Dow, James R. and Roemig, Madeline. AMANA FOLK ART AND CRAFTSMANSHIP. *Palimpsest 1977 58(2): 54-63.* Colored photographs illustrate a commentary on Amana folk art and craftsmanship. Although the Amana Society valued tradition and utility, the articles illustrated show that Amanites also valued beauty, color, innovation, and creativity. 15 photos, note on sources.

D. W. Johnson

516. Dudek, Pauline and Dudek, Norman. RESEARCHING THE FIRST PEOPLE WHO CAME TO AMERICA FROM OUR ANCESTRAL VILLAGE. *J. of the Am. Hist. Soc. of Germans from Russia 1978 1(2): 9-15.* Discusses the background events leading up to the immigration of Russian Germans to the United States in the 1870's, and their experiences in America, based on letters and testimonials.

517. Dugan, Elaine K. and Kramer, Marilyn M. LANCASTER COUNTY IMPRINTS FROM THE GERMAN AMERICAN IMPRINT COLLECTION IN THE FRANKLIN AND MARSHALL COLLEGE LIBRARY. *J. of the Lancaster County Hist. Soc. 1975 79(4): 209-233.* Describes German American imprints from 1745 to 1888 in the collection of the Franklin and Marshall College Library.

518. Ehrlich, Clara Hilderman. MY CHILDHOOD ON THE PRAIRIE. *Colorado Mag. 1974 51(2): 115-140.* A descriptive autobiographical social history of the late 19th- and early 20th-century life of German-Russian immigrant farmers who settled in the South Platte Valley of northeastern Colorado. Described are sodhouses, sugar beet farming, kraut-making, butchering, hay-making, laundering, baking and shopping visits to the nearby village. Based upon reminiscences; 9 illus., 5 notes.

O. H. Zabel

519. Elder, Harris J. HENRY KAMP AND CULTURAL PLURALISM IN OKLAHOMA CITY. *Chronicles of Oklahoma 1977 55(1): 78-92.* In 1906, young Henry Kamp left Germany for St. Louis, Missouri, where his family had previously settled. Intent on setting up his own business, he found bustling Oklahoma City a promising location, and within a few years had established a lucrative grocery business. Kamp, a strong supporter of immigrants maintaining ties with their cultural heritage, helped found the Germania German Club and the German Evangelical and Reform Church in Oklahoma City. Anti-German sentiment during both world wars forced many German Americans to leave the area, but the Kamp family remained and helped strengthen the German American community. Based on primary and secondary sources; 4 photos, 49 notes.

M. L. Tate

520. Eng, Erling. LOOKING BACK ON KURT LEWIN: FROM FIELD THEORY TO ACTION RESEARCH. *J. of the Hist. of the Behavioral Sci. 1978 14(3): 228-232.* There is a remarkable consistency in the underlying current of Kurt Lewin's thought from his 1917 paper on "the landscape of war," through his post-World War II work in social conflict: namely, the effort to elucidate conflict situations by means of psychological field theory through a phenomenological perspective. The transplantation of Lewin from Germany to America posed a serious problem for the theoretical continuity of his work. The change from a culture placing a high value on theoretical science to one oriented to practical values diminished the meaningfulness of his phenomenological vision. However, it furnished him with opportunities to grapple with pressing human concerns, concerns to which he had always been sensitive. From the necessity of this shift emerged Lewin's notion of "action research" and "group dynamics." At the same time, these developments served to obscure his failure to develop a psychological counterpart to the physical type of field theory from which he had set out.

J

521. Everett, George A., Jr. THE HISTORY OF THE GERMAN-AMERICAN COMMUNITY OF GLUCKSTADT, MISSISSIPPI: A STUDY IN PERSISTENCE. *J. of Mississippi Hist. 1976 38(4): 361-369.* Describes the history of the small German American community of Gluckstadt, Mississippi, 9 miles north of Jackson, 1900-75. Based on primary sources; 24 notes.

J. W. Hillje

522. Everett, George A., Jr. 200 YEARS OF GERMAN INFLUENCE IN AMERICA. *Daughters of the Am. Revolution Mag. 1978 112(5): 427-433.* German Americans have contributed to the culture and growth of the American national character.

523. Fabian, Monroe H. JOHN DANIEL EISENBROWN, FRAKTURIST. *Pennsylvania Folklife 1974/75 24(2): 31-35.* Biographical sketch of John Daniel Eisenbrown (1795-1874), frakturist, providing more source material on the 19th-century Pennsylvania-German area.

S

524. Foner, Philip S. PROTESTE IN DEN VEREINIGTEN STAATEN GEGEN BISMARCKS SOZIALISTENGESETZ [Protests in the United States against Bismarck's antisocialist legislation]. *Zeitschrift für Geschichtswissenschaft [East Germany] 1975 23(1): 63-74.* Otto von Bismarck's antisocialist legislation of 1878 aroused considerable interest in the United States. Many German socialists had fled to the US after the 1848 revolutions. In 1879 the First International requested that its US comrades give special help to the refugees from the Bismarck program. Americans protesting the German legislation were those who feared similar laws in the US and social and labor reformers who found that their particular causes overlapped the protest against German antisocialist action. Based on primary and secondary sources; 64 notes.

G. H. Libbey

525. Foner, Philip S. PROTESTS IN THE UNITED STATES AGAINST BISMARCK'S ANTI-SOCIALIST LAW. *Internat. R. of Social Hist. [Netherlands] 1976 21(1): 30-50.* When Otto von Bismarck imposed the Anti-Socialist Law upon Germany in 1878, there were more protests in the United States than some historians have maintained. In addition to some non-Socialist newspapers and spokesmen in the United States who criticized Bismarck's suppressive acts, the recently established Socialist Labor Party, made up largely of Germans, organized protest meetings against the Anti-Socialist Law in Chicago, New York, and elsewhere during 1878-81. These meetings aroused considerable attention, because they were reported in leading American newspapers.

G. P. Blum

526. Foner, Philip S. "VATER DES MODERNEN SOZIALISMUS IN AMERIKA": FRIEDRICH ADOLPH SORGE ["Father of modern socialism in America": Friedrich Adolph Sorge]. *Beiträge Zur Geschichte Der Arbeiterbewegung [East Germany] 1978 20(1): 111-118.* Discusses the contributions of the German-born Marxist, Friedrich Adolph Sorge (1828-1906), to the early socialist movement in the United States. Sorge came to America in 1852 and was an active participant in the formation of the American section of the 1st International, the International Workingmen's Association (1869), which he served as secretary. Later Sorge helped form other Marxist organizations. After retirement from active politics Sorge served as an advisor and historian of the workers' movement. Secondary works; 27 notes.

J. B. Street

527. Ford, Larry and Fusch, Richard. NEIGHBORS VIEW GERMAN VILLAGE. *Hist. Preservation 1978 30(3): 37-41.* German Vil-

lage is a 19th-century German neighborhood near downtown Columbus, Ohio, which has undergone historic preservation since 1948. Surveys of surrounding neighborhood attitudes indicate that people "view preservation positively and believe that their own neighborhoods are better places because of it." Illus.   R. M. Frame, III

528. Frantz, John B. THE AWAKENING OF RELIGION AMONG THE GERMAN SETTLERS IN THE MIDDLE COLONIES. *William and Mary Q. 1976 33(2): 266-288.* Discusses German immigration and various German settlements in connection with the German Awakening, which began among German Baptists, particularly the Dunkards. Also evaluates the movement among the Reformed and the Lutheran Churches. Comments on clergymen and evangelists. Moravian missionaries were especially active in the German Awakening, and aided an interdenominationalism. Sectarians, ecumenists, and confessionalists all had pietism in common. German settlers responded enthusiastically to evangelism. As congregations increased, greater structural machinery resulted. The German Awakening was similar to that of other groups. Based on literature of the Great Awakening, church records, and German-language contemporary works. 81 notes.
                                                         H. M. Ward

529. Friesen, Gerhard K. AN ADDITIONAL SOURCE ON THE HARMONY SOCIETY OF ECONOMY, PENNSYLVANIA. *Western Pennsylvania Hist. Mag. 1978 61(4): 301-314.* Excerpts from a German book entitled *Scenes of Life in the United States of America and Texas,* collected by Friedrich Wilhelm von Wrede, describing the Harmony Society of Economy, Pennsylvania, based on von Wrede's experiences there on a visit in 1842.

530. Frizzell, Robert W. 'KILLED BY REBELS': A CIVIL WAR MASSACRE AND ITS AFTERMATH. *Missouri Hist. Rev. 1977 71(4): 369-395.* Of the several massacres in Missouri during the Civil War, the one on 10 October 1864 near Concordia was to have a deep influence on the Germans who had settled on the borders of Lafayette and Saline counties. Always aware of their different values, culture and religious beliefs, the Germans were driven by the violence inflicted on them to become even more isolated and conscious of their origins. The isolationism, which was reflected by their continued use of German and acceptance of the conservative Missouri Synod Lutheranism, lasted into the 20th century. Primary and secondary sources; illus., 93 notes.
                                                         W. F. Zornow

531. Gay, Peter. AT HOME IN AMERICA. *Am. Scholar 1976-77 46(1): 31-42.* Describes the background of the author's escape from Nazi Germany. His earliest feelings of America and Americans were those of acceptance and friendliness. Recollects early teachers who encouraged and inspired him. Despite the many problems and flaws in America, he still finds this nation of immigrants a rare and precious success.
                                                         F. F. Harling

532. Geldbach, Erich. THE BEGINNING OF GERMAN GYMNASTICS IN AMERICA. *J. of Sport Hist. 1976 3(3): 236-272.* In 1825, the first attempt to introduce physical education as a regular part of the daily school curricula was made at the Round Hill School, Northampton, Massachusetts. The experimental school had been established in the fall of 1823. In 1825 Karl Beck, who had studied under F. L. Jahn in Berlin, constructed a gymnasium at the school and began systematic training. Karl Follen, Beck's friend who had also studied in Berlin, introduced gymnastics into Harvard University in 1826, after the University's attempt to lure Jahn to America failed. Follen also was the superintendent of the first public gymnasium in America, begun in 1826 in Boston. Francis Lieber took over control of the gymnasium in 1827. Interest began to decline in 1827-28 because the exercises were too demanding for beginning students, and they were regimented and boring. In addition, Lieber's attention shifted to his *Encyclopedia Americana.* The gymnasium closed in 1828. 70 notes.   M. Kaufman

533. Geldbach, Erich. DIE VERPFLANZUNG DES DEUTSCHEN TURNENS NACH AMERIKA: BECK, FOLLEN, LIEBER [The transplantation of German gymnastics into America: Beck, Follen, Lieber]. *Stadion [West Germany] 1975 1(2): 331-376.* In the 1820's gymnastics became fashionable at some schools in New England, at Harvard, and among the citizens of Boston. Physical education was

encouraged by medical professors, educators, reform-oriented law professors, and theologians who felt that American education had to abandon its provincialism and puritanism. It was fostered by a reorientation of academic ideals toward European, particularly German, concepts. The American reformers found enthusiastic teachers among German political emigrés, followers of the gymnastic movement of Jahn. Accordingly, gymnastics followed the German pattern of Jahn who himself declined an offer from Harvard. It is not yet clear why the interest in gymnastics waned after a few years, though the emphasis on drill may have been one of the major reasons. Based on American archives and secondary sources; 107 notes.   M. Geyer

534. Goetsch, C. Carnahan. THE IMMIGRANT AND AMERICA: ASSIMILATION OF A GERMAN FAMILY. *Ann. of Iowa 1973 42(1): 17-27, (2): 114-125.* Part I. The story of the Goettsch family, who settled in Davenport, Iowa, after moving to the United States. Part II. Illustrates the importance of higher education to the five brothers and one sister; two have M.D.'s, three have Ph.D.'s, and one has a degree in engineering. Only through immigration to the United States would they have had this opportunity. Discusses also the anti-German feeling and its effect upon the family during World War I. The grandchildren did not share the strong bond of the Germanic background, while the great-grandchildren regarded themselves as completely American. 2 photos, 8 notes.   C. W. Olson

535. Gouger, James B. THE NORTHERN NECK OF VIRGINIA: A TIDEWATER GRAIN-FARMING REGION IN THE ANTEBELLUM SOUTH. *West Georgia Coll. Studies in the Social Sci. 1977 16: 73-90.* Although tobacco cultivation dominated antebellum Tidewater Virginia, the presence of knowledgable German immigrants and the availability of waterways had influenced a shift to grain production in the "Northern Neck" counties by 1790.

536. Grant, H. Roger, ed. THE AMANA SOCIETY OF IOWA: TWO VIEWS. *Ann. of Iowa 1975 43(1): 1-23.* Contains two accounts of the Amana Society of Iowa. The first, written by Bertha Horak Shambaugh, appeared in an Iowa state publication in 1901. It offers a view of Amana based on personal observation and research. Topics discussed include the agriculture, manufacturing, housing, education, religion, and government of the society. The other article, written in 1934 by Barthinius L. Wick, describes the Amana Society's demise in 1932 as a communal religious experiment. Editor's introduction, photos, 26 notes.
                                                         P. L. Petersen

537. Grant, H. Roger. HENRY OLERICH AND UTOPIA: THE IOWA YEARS, 1870-1902. *Ann. of Iowa 1976 43(5): 349-361.* Henry Olerich (1851-1927) was Iowa's only nationally prominent utopian author. Born of German immigrant stock, he eventually drifted from farming into education. Economic conditions of the 1890's prompted Olerich to write his best-known work, *A Cityless and Countryless World.* The novel brought Olerich little fame. He is remembered more for "a quasi-utopian" educational experiment in which he and his wife adopted a baby girl and sought to make her "the perfectly educated child." Primary and secondary sources; 2 illus., 2 photos, 21 notes.
                                                         P. L. Petersen

538. Grant, H. Roger. THE SOCIETY OF BETHEL: A VISITOR'S ACCOUNT. *Missouri Hist. R. 1974 68(2): 223-231.* Briefly outlines the background of the Society of Bethel, a German American religious communal experiment in Missouri and Oregon founded by William Keil. Presents a letter from Wilhelm Weitling to A. J. McDonald, which gives a visitor's report of the life within the society. Primary and secondary sources; 2 illus., 2 photos, 18 notes.   N. J. Street

539. Gwinn, Erna Ottl. THE LIEDERKRANZ IN LOUISVILLE, 1848-1877. *Filson Club Hist. Q. 1975 49(3): 276-290.* The Liederkranz, a German-American music society, played an important role in the integration of the German community into the life of Louisville, Kentucky. Started in 1848, the organization was strengthened by the arrival of German liberals after the failure of the revolution of that year. By the mid-1850's the Germans formed one-third of Louisville's population and faced nativist hostility organized in the Know-Nothing movement. Violent demonstrations forced the chorus to suppress publicity of its performances that included works by composer Richard Wagner. The Liederkranz suspended operations during the Civil War, but afterward

grew rapidly and was able to build a large auditorium by 1873. An audience of 8,000 that attended a performance in 1877 demonstrated that the Germans were an accepted part of Louisville life. Based on German language histories and Louisville newspapers; 71 notes.

G. B. McKinney

540. Hart, Kenneth Wayne. CINCINNATI ORGAN BUILDERS OF THE NINETEENTH CENTURY. *Cincinnati Hist. Soc. Bull. 1973 31(2): 79-98.* As Cincinnati quickly developed into a major community, that city experienced a remarkable expansion of churches. About 1850 a major influx of Germans made possible the development of organ building. Early organ builders were Adam Hurdus (the first), Luman Watson, and Israel Schooley. The premier early organ builder, however, was Matthias Schwab, who was succeeded by his principal apprentice, Johann Heinrich Koehnken. After Schwab retired, Koehnken and Gallus Grimm formed Koehnken and Company. In 1896 Koehnken retired and Grimm brought his son into the partnership and renamed it G. Grimm and Son, which lasted until 1900. Based on unpublished manuscripts, and on secondary sources; 8 photos, 65 notes.

H. S. Marks

541. Harwood, W. S. A BIT OF EUROPE IN DAKOTA: THE GERMAN RUSSIAN COLONY AT EUREKA. *J. of the Am. Hist. Soc. of Germans from Russia 1977 (25): 17-20.* This isolated colony was founded in 1889-90 on the border between South and North Dakota by Russian German peasants who had fled Russia.

542. Hays, Steele. BUTCHERTOWN. *Am. Preservation 1978 1(2): 58-63.* Butchertown, an older working-class German neighborhood in Louisville, Kentucky, is notable for its lively mixture of industrial, commercial, and residential buildings. Young, new residents attracted by low prices and community cohesiveness are purchasing the deteriorated "shotgun" houses and multistory brick townhouses. Since 1967, Butchertown Inc., a nonprofit community group, has been buying and renovating endangered structures for resale to local residents. Louisville government officials have been supportive of such efforts although social tensions exist within the community. Older residents oppose establishing a preservation district in Butchertown which would subject exterior changes to architectural review. Describes specific residential and commercial renovation projects. 11 photos.

S. C. Strom

543. Hirsch, Helmut. DIE TÄTIGKEIT DES EMIGRIERTEN DEUTSCHEN DEMOKRATEN KARL LUDWIG BERNAYS WÄHREND DES AMERIKANISCHEN BÜRGERKRIEGES [Activities of the emigrated German democrat Karl Ludwig Bernays during the American Civil War]. *Jahrbuch des Inst. für Deutsche Geschichte [Israel] 1976 5: 227-245.* Karl Ludwig Bernays, German-born US consul in Switzerland and Denmark, sought a similar post in Civil War America. Egotistic, he fabricated impossible schemes which he vainly urged on his superiors, sometimes before he secured the post he was seeking. He found his proper role in Missouri when he helped secure the loyalty of German Americans to the Union cause. After the war he devoted himself to strengthening the bonds between Germans in America and in Germany. 79 notes.

M. Faissler

544. Hirsch, Helmut. KARL LUDWIG BERNAYS: EIN EMIGRIERTER SCHRIFTSTELLER ALS US-KONSUL IN DER SCHWEIZ [Karl Ludwig Bernays: An emigrant writer as US Consul in Switzerland]. *Jahrbuch des Instituts für Deutsche Geschichte [Israel] 1975 4: 147-165.* Karl Ludwig Bernays was born in Mainz, Germany, on 16 November 1815 as Lazarus Bernays; he died in St. Louis, Missouri, in 1879. His family's conversion to Christianity caused him to change his name to Karl Ludwig. His journalistic jibes at the Bavarian nobles and even King Ludwig forced him to flee Germany for France. In France he received several diplomatic posts before finally immigrating to the United States where he continued his occupation as a journalist, especially for German-language newspapers. His writings against slavery in the St. Louis papers and his involvement with the Republican Party and Abraham Lincoln brought him into political prominence. After organizing 60 companies for the Union Army, he was appointed in 1861 as US Consul to Switzerland. His appointment was opposed by hundreds of Swiss Americans in Highland, Illinois, where he had once lived, and by the *Züricher Zeitung*. He was officially accepted by the Swiss government in September 1861. As consul he was instrumental in informing the Swiss and German exiles in Switzerland of the Union cause. He wrote in newspapers throughout

Switzerland and Germany about the US position in the Civil War. He developed lists of the capabilities of Swiss manufacturing. At his own request he was given a financially more lucrative post as Consul to Denmark in January 1862. Based on newspaper articles, published primary and secondary sources; 63 notes.

E. F. Stocker

545. Hoch, Paul. OLD SCHIMMEL. *Early Am. Life 1977 8(1): 44-47.* Wilhelm Schimmel became known for his wood carving in the Cumberland Valley of Pennsylvania, where he lived as an itinerant (1865-90) following immigration from Germany.

546. Holcomb, Grant. A PAINTER'S FIRST COMMISSION: THE PORTRAITS OF MR. AND MRS. GOTTLIEB STORZ OF OMAHA. *Nebraska Hist. 1976 57(3): 423-429.* Discusses the portraits painted by John Sloan in 1912 of an Omaha brewer and his wife.

R. Lowitt

547. Hopf, Carroll. CALLIGRAPHIC DRAWINGS AND PENNSYLVANIA GERMAN FRAKTUR. *Pennsylvania Folklife 1972 22(1): 2-9.* Gives the history of round hand flourishing, a type of calligraphy, particularly the acculturation of calligraphic flourishing among the Pennsylvania Germans in southeastern Pennsylvania in the late 19th century,

548. Ickstadt, Heinz and Keil, Hartmut. A FORGOTTEN PIECE OF WORKING-CLASS LITERATURE: GUSTAV LYSER'S SATIRE OF THE HEWITT HEARING OF 1878. *Labor Hist. 1979 20(1): 127-140.* Reviews and publishes the satire by Gustav Lyser of the Hewitt Committee hearing which was first issued in the Chicago *Vorbote*, 17 and 24 August 1878. The piece is an example of German working-class culture. 12 notes.

L. L. Athey

549. Ireland, Owen S. GERMANS AGAINST ABOLITION: A MINORITY'S VIEW OF SLAVERY IN REVOLUTIONARY PENNSYLVANIA. *J. of Interdisciplinary Hist. 1973 3(4): 685-706.* Analyzes ethnoreligious alignments over the abolition of slavery in Pennsylvania in 1779-88. Suggests that Germans from Lutheran and Reformed backgrounds were the most consistent opponents of abolition. This cannot be explained satisfactorily on the basis of economic self-interest, commitment to property rights, or worries about Negro poverty. Religious experience, political ideology, and cultural attitudes contributed to the Germans' opposition. A deep fear of social change intensified the impact of these considerations. 4 tables, 46 notes.

R. Howell

550. Jaehn, Klaus Juergen. THE FORMATION OF WALTER RAUSCHENBUSCH'S SOCIAL CONSCIOUSNESS AS REFLECTED IN HIS EARLY LIFE AND WRITINGS, PART II. *Foundations 1974 17(1): 68-85.* Expounds on Rauschenbusch's theories on Christian Socialism and the social gospel, written by the German American minister and theologian during 1891-1918. Continued from *Foundations* 1973 16(4).

551. Jaśkowski, Marian. EMIGRACJA NIEMIECKA DO STANÓW ZJEDNOCZONYCH [German emigration to the United States]. *Przegląd Zachodni [Poland] 1968 24(2): 250-269.* German immigration into the United States began as early as 1683; in the 19th century two great waves took place in the 1850's and the 1880's; in 1900 the Germans constituted more than 25% of all immigrants (this proportion continued for much of the century). The ethnically German population constitutes too large a community, and is too evenly distributed geographically, to have any united political front.

552. Jennings, Pauline. ELISA LEON: FIRST LADY OF THE GERMANTOWN COLONY. *North Louisiana Hist. Assoc. J. 1977 8(2): 43-51.* Although the self-styled "Count Leon" is more associated with the Germantown settlement from its beginnings than anyone else, he never actually reached Claiborne Parish (the settlement's area became a part of Webster Parish in 1871). He died in 1834 during a fever epidemic while his group was still near Natchitoches. His consort, Elisa Leon, was actually the leading figure in the Germantown community, "and the colony's 35-year experiment in communal sharing ended only when she grew old and moved away." 39 notes.

A. N. Garland

553. Jones, George Fenwick. TWO "SALZBURGER" LETTERS FROM GEORGE WHITEFIELD AND THEOBALD KIEFER II.

Georgia Hist. Q. 1978 62(1): 50-57. Reprints two letters of request (dating ca. 1738 and 1750) written to Gottfried Francke, director of the Francke Foundation orphanage at Halle, Germany, by George Whitefield, Anglican minister, and Theobald Kiefer, II, boat builder. These concern the settlement of Salzburgers at Ebenezer, Georgia, and their orphanage. The Kiefer letter is in the original German and in English translation. Based on primary sources; 18 notes. G. R. Schroeder

554. Jordan, Gilbert J. W. STEINERT'S VIEW OF TEXAS IN 1849. *Southwestern Hist. Q. 1976 80(1): 57-78, (2): 177-200, (3): 283-301, (4): 399-416; 1977 81(1): 45-72.* Part I. Letters of W. Steinert, a German traveler in Texas in 1849, describing the route from Galveston through Indianola to New Braunfels. He notes the activities of earlier German settlers, the state of agriculture, and the primitive conditions of life and travel. Covers 22 May-5 June. Map, 35 notes. Part II. Covers 6-18 June. Comments on German colonization schemes and the roughness of life in the area. Describes New Braunfels and a trip to San Antonio and Fredericksburg. 77 notes. Part III. Covers 20 June-20 July. Mentions traveling from Fredericksburg to New Braunfels. Describes the miserable circumstances of German settlers in central Texas. Mentions Indian raids, poor roads, and bad weather. 33 notes. Part IV. Covers 29 July-25 August. Describes life in San Antonio, Houston, and Galveston. Comments on travel difficulties, mosquito plagues, and news of German settlers in Texas. 19 notes. Part V. Provides Steinert's last advice (written 27 August) to Germans contemplating emigration to Texas. Steinert warned of the difficulties of farming, raising livestock, following a trade, and entering domestic service. He found considerable Anglo hostility to German settlers. His chief concern was to refute overly optimistic advice by earlier German commentators. 21 notes. J. H. Broussard

555. Jordan, Terry G. FOREST FOLK, PRAIRIE FOLK: RURAL RELIGIOUS CULTURE IN NORTH TEXAS. *Southwestern Hist. Q. 1976 80(2): 135-162.* In Cooke and Denton Counties, Texas, fundamentalists from the upper South settled the "Cross Timbers" oak forest and German Catholics settled the prairie land. Rural church architecture shows the cultural differences in the stern, one-room white frame "folk chapel" and the elaborate German "cathedral." Cemetery arrangements and customs also are quite different; German orderliness, attention to family history, and sense of community contrast with the southern Protestant simplicity and emphasis on family. Primary and secondary sources; 18 illus., 2 tables, 28 notes. J. H. Broussard

556. Kakuske, Louis F. PURSUIT THROUGH ARKANSAS. *Civil War Times Illus. 1975 13(10): 36-43.* The war experiences of Louis F. Kakuske, a German immigrant, who fought in Arkansas during the Civil War. S

557. Kamphoefner, Walter D. ST. LOUIS GERMANS AND THE REPUBLICAN PARTY, 1848-1860. *Mid-America 1975 57(2): 69-88.* German-American voting behavior, statistically analyzed, indicates that the Republican Party drew from Free Soil Democrats where Whig nativists were separate or subordinate. The influential Free Soil *Anzeiger des Westens*, edited by Forty-Eighter Heinrich Boernstein, reflected the interaction of European ideology with American society. Its anticlericalism did not hurt its cause. Based on published sources, newspapers, and secondary works; 5 tables, 41 notes. T. H. Wendel

558. Karlin, Athanasius. THE COMING OF THE FIRST VOLGA GERMAN CATHOLICS TO AMERICA: REWRITTEN FROM A DIARY STARTED FEBRUARY 8, 1887. *J. of the Am. Hist. Soc. of Germans from Russia 1978 1(3): 61-69.* Excerpts of a diary by Athanasius Karlin describing events leading up to his family's emigration from Russia to the United States in 1875, and their earliest experiences in the United States.

559. Kessler, Carol. TEN TULPEHOCKEN INVENTORIES: WHAT DO THEY REVEAL ABOUT A PENNSYLVANIA GERMAN COMMUNITY? *Pennsylvania Folklife 1973/74 23(2): 16-30.*

560. Keuchel, Edward F. A PURELY BUSINESS MOTIVE: GERMAN-AMERICAN LUMBER COMPANY, 1901-1918. *Florida Hist. Q. 1974 52(4): 381-395.* The German-American Lumber Company, organized in 1901 by Frederick Julius Schreyer, carried on lumber operations with considerable success in the Florida panhandle area in the years before World War I. After the beginning of the war and the closing of European markets, the company supplied lumber for US military camp construction. Upon the American entrance into the war, the company was seized by federal authorities, despite the lack of any evidence of disloyalty on the part of its German-American owners. The company was sold to American interests after the war's end, but no records exist of any financial settlement made with the former owners. Based on archival material from Florida State University and secondary sources; 2 illus., 38 notes. J. E. Findling

561. Kollman, Wolfgang; Marschalck, Peter; and Childers, Thomas C., transl. GERMAN EMIGRATION TO THE UNITED STATES. *Perspectives in Am. Hist. 1973 (7): 499-554.* Germans emigrated to the United States to remove the economic, social, and sometimes cultural disparities they experienced at home. Though the absolute overpopulation feared by Malthus was not the determining factor, relative overpopulation was still a problem. Germans fled to certain areas when they thought the capacity for subsistence could be improved by their arrival. 15 tables, 96 notes. W. A. Wiegand

562. Kondert, Reinhart. THE GERMANS OF ACADIA PARISH. *Rev. de Louisiane 1977 6(1): 19-37.* Chronicles the immigration of Germans into the mainly French Acadia Parish in Louisiana, 1870's-1917.

563. Kramer, Gerhardt. THE SAXON LUTHERAN MEMORIAL: A CASE HISTORY IN PRESERVATION. *Concordia Hist. Inst. Q. 1978 51(4): 155-167.* Since 1958 leaders of the Concordia Historical Institute had indicated an interest in acquiring the farm of the late Lina Bergt. Bergt was the last direct descendant of Saxon Lutherans who immigrated to Perry County, Missouri, in 1839. Initially the efforts to acquire the property met with failure; however, the farm was purchased in 1960 and restoration was inaugurated. The Saxon Lutheran Memorial was dedicated in 1964. Primary sources; 20 notes. W. T. Walker

564. Kramer, William A. LIFE IN PERRY COUNTY, MISSOURI, AT THE TURN OF THE CENTURY. *Concordia Hist. Inst. Q. 1975 48(1): 10-25.* There was a closer relationship between the society of Perry County and the Lutheran Church at the turn of the century than today. The people helped support the pastors and teachers of the church. A diversified agrarian system prevailed. Most children attended Lutheran parochial schools for the first six grades before transferring to the public schools. Weddings and funerals were major social events. Based on personal recollection. W. T. Walker

565. Krebs, Friedrich and Yoder, Don, transl. and ed. PALATINE EMIGRANTS TO AMERICA FROM THE OPPENHEIM AREA, 1742-1749. *Pennsylvania Folklore 1972 22(1): 46-48.* Official list of the Palatine emigrants to America from the Oppenheim area of Germany.

566. Krouse, Rita M. THE GERMANTOWN STORE. *North Louisiana Hist. Assoc. J. 1977 8(2): 53-64.* There must have been hundreds of country stores in the South before the Civil War, although little has been written about them. "Because of their isolation it is very probable that many of the country stores played a multiplicity of roles," and this was certainly true for the Germantown store which opened for business in 1851. Germantown was about seven miles north of Minden, and the surviving records from that store "provide a wealth of information apart from the names of customers and the prices which they paid for goods and services." Many of the store's customers were slaves, and quite a few products of the slaves' leisure-time labor were sold to the store. Contains extracts from a slave account; a list of the typical articles bought by the slaves; and a comparison of the prices charged at the store for certain products during the 1850's. 18 notes. A. N. Garland

567. Leverenz, David. REFLECTIONS ON TWO HENRIES— JAMES AND KISSINGER. *Soundings (Nashville, TN) 1976 59(4): 374-395.* Both Henry James and Henry A. Kissinger view the world in moral terms and perceive sharply differentiated forces of good and evil. Kissinger, as a German American, and James, as an American expatriate in England, are aliens in a particular nationalistic setting; and they have remarkably similar backgrounds and values. Both share basically European views on history, are especially sensitive to form, purpose and role, and have a passion for control and secrecy. They believe that life is a conflict between ambition and order. Kissinger especially is obsessed with

the role of the leader. They believe power is central to human motivation, and they tend to be insensitive to altruistic guides to action and behavior.

N. Lederer

568. Lich, Glen Ernest. BALTHASAR LICH, GERMAN RANCHER IN THE TEXAS HILLS. *Texana 1974 12(2): 101-123.* Biographical sketches of Balthasar Lich (1834-88) and his wife Elisabeth Scholl Lich (1842-1921). Balthasar, who came to Texas in 1857, lived in Fredericksburg and Kerrville before settling on Cypress Creek, 10 miles east of Kerrville and nine miles west of Comfort. He was a successful independent freighter during the Civil War and purchased a large amount of land to become a rancher after the war. After his death in 1888, his wife remained at Cypress Creek until she moved to Comfort in 1906 where she died in 1921. Primary and secondary sources; 81 notes.

B. D. Ledbetter

569. Lockyer, Timothy J. WALKING WITH THE LORD: RACHEL BAHN. *Pennsylvania Mag. of Hist. and Biog. 1979 103(4): 484-496.* A virtual paraplegic after 1849, Rachel Bahn (1829-1902), a Pennsylvania German born near York, is wrongly, if conventionally, recalled as "the happy cripple." Her poetry reflects her unique perspective—a synthesis of life, pain, and faith. Based on MS., Historical Society of York County; newspapers; and secondary works; 12 notes.

T. H. Wendel

570. Main, Elaine. THE FRAULEIN CHOOSES BACKWOODS IOWA. *Palimpsest 1978 59(6): 162-167.* Drawn by the work of Sigmund Fritschel who was soliciting funds among German Russian Lutherans, Auguste von Schwartz left Russia to move to Iowa where she worked at Wartburg College as a house mother, 1861-77.

571. Marten, William C., ed. "MY LONG AND SOMEWHAT EVENTFUL LIFE": FREDERICK G. HOLLMAN'S AUTOBIOGRAPHY. *Wisconsin Mag. of Hist. 1973 56(3): 202-233.* Five years before his death at age 85 in 1875, Hollman wrote his reminiscences. He traveled from Germany to Vandalia (the first state capital of Illinois) and then to the lead-mining area around Platteville, Wisconsin. His narrative mentions frontier conditions, Indian relations, establishment of law and order in Illinois and Wisconsin, his careers as justice of the peace, miner, rancher, farmer, builder, and town clerk, and several people prominent in early Wisconsin history. 7 illus., map, 36 notes.

N. C. Burckel

572. Mellon, Knox, Jr. CHRISTIAN PRIBER'S CHEROKEE "KINGDOM OF PARADISE." *Georgia Hist. Q. 1973 57(3): 319-331.* Christian Gottlieb Priber (1697-ca. 1744), a German lawyer, came to the American colonies in the early 1730's to establish a utopian colony, the "Kingdom of Paradise." His dream embodied elements of Cherokee tribal life, radical European political and social philosophy, and a general mixture of primitivism and fairly sophisticated ideas of government. The English were concerned about the effect of Priber's influence with the Cherokee with whom they had a trade monopoly. Priber was arrested and spent the rest of his days in prison. 50 notes.

D. L. Smith

573. Meyer, Judith W. ETHNICITY, THEOLOGY, AND IMMIGRANT CHURCH EXPANSION. *Geographical R. 1975 65(2): 180-197.* The Lutheran Church-Missouri Synod, like other immigrant churches in the United States, emphasized its ethnic character and conservative theology with resultant impact on its spatial distribution. Until after World War I, the Missouri Synod expanded primarily into midwestern communities with German-speaking people. Expansion has since taken place in the growing areas of the United States, but the conservative theological outlook of the denomination has concentrated dissemination in areas to which its members have migrated.

J

574. Moltmann, Günter. 200 JAHRE USA: EINE BILANZ DEUTSCH-AMERIKANISCHER BEZIEHUNGEN [200 years of the United States: a statement of German-American relations]. *Geschichte in Wissenschaft und Unterricht [West Germany] 1976 27(7): 393-408.* German liberals based their political orientation on the constitutional system of the United States. At the end of the 18th century, close economic relations were established between Germany and the United States. German immigration to the United States strengthened the ties, although conflicting ideologies and political power interests marred their

relations in the 20th century. The defeat of Germany and the polarization of the world after 1945 have again initiated very close cooperation between the United States and West Germany. Based on secondary sources; 31 notes.

R. Wagnleitner

575. Moore, Willard B. DOWN ON THE FARM: TRADITION IN THE LIFE OF AN AMERICAN FAMILY. *Family Heritage 1978 1(6): 164-169.* Traces the traditional Minnesota farm heritage of the Standke family, whose ancestors from Germany settled in Minnesota in 1873.

576. Morrow, Sara Sprott. ADOLPHUS HEIMAN'S LEGACY TO NASHVILLE. *Tennessee Hist. Q. 1974 33(1): 3-21.* Adolphus Heiman arrived in Nashville from his native Prussia in 1836 at the age of 27. Though first employed as a stone cutter, he was most successful in architecture, including college buildings, bridges, and churches. Traces the history of his most famous work, the College Building, originally designed for the University of Nashville in 1853 and subsequently used by several other colleges. Illus., 4 photos, 21 notes.

M. B. Lucas

577. Myers, Raymond E. THE STORY OF GERMANNA. *Filson Club Hist. Q. 1974 48(1): 27-42.* Virginia's colonial Governor Alexander Spotswood was the driving force behind the organization of the town of Germanna in 1714. Owning land that was rich in iron ore, Spotswood contracted with German Protestants to immigrate and work the land. At first the project was successful, but religious differences among the Germans and the desire of the immigrants to own their own land brought an end to the experiment. Documentation from secondary works; 84 notes.

G. B. McKinney

578. Naglack, James. GERMANS. *Hist. J. of Western Massachusetts 1976 (Supplement): 27-34.* Germans played many roles in the American Revolution. Baron von Steuben, Johann Kalb, and David Ziegler were important in the organization of the American army. Hessians initially fought on the side of the British but many deserted and joined the American army. Some had religious scruples, but most Germans supported the Whig position and served in the militia. Note.

W. H. Mulligan, Jr.

579. Nelsen, Frank C. THE GERMAN-AMERICAN IMMIGRANTS' STRUGGLE. *Int. Rev. of Hist. and Pol. Sci. [India] 1973 10(2): 37-49.* German immigrants to the United States, like other immigrant groups, came mainly for economic and political reasons. But, in general, the Germans viewed their own culture as superior. They intended to protect their culture by choosing isolated settlements, retaining their language, and controlling their own education. The force of external pressures, however, especially the international situation in the early 20th century, shattered their preservation of German culture. Based on secondary sources; 29 notes.

E. McCarthy

580. Newcomb, William W., Jr. GERMAN ARTIST ON THE PEDERNALES. *Southwestern Hist. Q. 1978 82(2): 149-172.* Treats primarily the life and artistic contributions of Richard Petri, brother-in-law of Hermann Lungkwitz, also a Texas immigrant artist. This family bought a small farm on the Pedernales River in Texas in 1852. Until his death in 1857, Petri produced industriously an invaluable record of the people and life in this frontier community. Archival and secondary material; 36 illus., 27 notes.

J. L. B. Atkinson

581. Obermann, Karl. BEZIEHUNGEN ZWISCHEN DEN EUROPÄISCHEN FORTSCHRITTSKRÄFTEN UND DEN USA IM 19. JAHRHUNDERT [Relations between the European forces of progress and the USA in the 19th century]. *Zeitschrift für Geschichtswissenschaft [East Germany] 1975 23(6): 651-665.* Throughout the 19th century progressive circles in the United States and Europe exchanged moral and often material support. German immigrants, especially those who left their homeland in 1848, supported abolitionists and the emerging workers' organizations. They also contributed to the Republican electoral triumph in 1860 and the victory of the Union in the Civil War. The formation of the Socialist Workers' Party in the United States and American leadership in the battle for the eight-hour day tightened the bonds between the progressive forces in America and Europe. Primary and secondary sources; 63 notes.

J. T. Walker

582. Obermann, Karl. ZUM ANTEIL DEUTSCHER EINWAN-DERER AN DER AMERIKANISCHEN REVOLUTION VON 1776 [On the participation of German immigrants in the American Revolution of 1776]. *Zeitschrift für Geschichtswissenschaft [East Germany] 1976 24(7): 761-775.* When the first 8,000 Hessian mercenaries landed in Staten Island, German immigrants tried to win them for the cause of the American Revolution. Benjamin Franklin ordered the translation into German of an address of the Continental Congress to the Hessian troops, in which deserters were promised land. Throughout the war more than 5,000 Hessians deserted and fought on the side of the revolutionaries. Secondary sources; 67 notes.　　　　　　　R. Wagnleitner

583. Oehling, Richard A. [GERMANS IN HOLLYWOOD FILMS]. GERMANS IN HOLLYWOOD FILMS: THE CHANGING IMAGE, 1914-1939. *Film & Hist. 1973 3(2): 1-10, 26.*
GERMANS IN HOLLYWOOD FILMS: THE CHANGING IMAGE, THE EARLY WAR YEARS, 1939-1942. *Film & Hist. 1974 4(2): 8-10.*
GERMANS IN HOLLYWOOD FILMS. *Film & Hist. 1974 4(3): 6-10.*

584. Oetgen, Jerome. OSWALD MOOSMÜLLER: MONK AND MISSIONARY. *Am. Benedictine R. 1976 27(1): 1-35.* Oswald Moos-müller exemplified the tension between 19th-century Benedictines' missionary zeal and the standards of traditional monastic observance. Moosmüller spent the first part of his monastic life as a missionary serving German Catholic immigrants. Later, he supported the contemplative ideal more vigorously, but his effort to exemplify that ideal at New Cluny in Southern Illinois was a failure. Based on primary and secondary sources; 71 notes.　　　　　　　J. H. Pragman

585. Olsen, Deborah M. and Clark, M. Will. MUSICAL HERITAGE OF THE AURORA COLONY. *Oregon Hist. Q. 1978 79(3): 233-268.* Established in 1844 by William Kiel, the Bethel Colony moved to Aurora, Oregon, in 1855 where it was known as the Aurora Colony. Well-known throughout Oregon for its members' musical talents, the Colony supported a brass band, known as the Aurora or Pioneer Band, an orchestra, and at least three choirs. The band's repertoire included both German and American tunes, many composed by the band members. The Pioneer Band continued into the 1920's long after the 1877 dissolution of the Colony. Many Aurora instruments have been restored; they were used in an October 1977 performance of Aurora Colony compositions by a re-created Pioneer Band. Based on documents in the Oregon Historical Society, Multnomah County Library, newspaper reports, and published secondary sources; 17 photos, illus., 61 notes.　　D. R. McDonald

586. O'Malley, J. Steven. THE OTTERBEINS: MEN OF TWO WORLDS. *Methodist Hist. 1976 15(1): 3-21.* The theology of Philip Wilhelm Otterbein (1726-1813) and his brothers was influenced by the teachings of the University of Herborn in Germany, which included the symbols of Protestant orthodoxy, the anti-Aristotelian logic of Peter Ramus, mysticism, and the new ideas which were the hallmark of Pietism and the Enlightenment. Otterbein was also influenced by his contacts with significant religious leaders of the 18th century in Europe and America. He served as pastor in Pennsylvania and Maryland. 68 notes.
　　　　　　　H. L. Calkin

587. Paraschos, Janet Nyberg. GRAND SURVIVOR. *Am. Preservation 1979 2(2): 53-61.* In 1907 Gottlieb Storz, the brewing magnate, built a mansion in Omaha's Gold Coast area. Despite an ill-conceived "modernization" in 1940, the house is maintained with all its original detail by grandson Arthur Storz, Jr. Fanciful details include hops motif stained glass windows, skylights, handmade fireplace tiles, gargoyles, and crystal chandeliers. However, with the rising cost of maintenance, the long-term future of the mansion is uncertain. 9 photos.
　　　　　　　S. C. Strom

588. Petersen, Albert J. GERMAN-RUSSIAN CATHOLIC SO-CIAL ORGANIZATION. *Plains Anthropologist 1973 18(59): 27-32.* The 18th century German agrarian village system has persisted on the plains of western Kansas as a consequence of a Roman Catholic centered social system. The acculturation process has been retarded by the centripetal forces of church, village, and kinship identities.　　J

589. Petersen, Albert J. THE GERMAN-RUSSIAN HOUSE IN KANSAS: A STUDY IN PERSISTENCE OF FORM. *Pioneer Am. 1976 8(1): 19-27.* Investigates an immigrant agrarian-village culture on the Great Plains utilizing Fred Kniffen's hypothesis that the form of traditional structure tends to persist even after construction materials change. The culture under consideration—the Russian Germans—originated in the German Rhine Palatinate, later replanted itself on the steppes along the Russian Volga during the reign of Catherine the Great, and eventually emigrated to the plains of western Kansas in 1876. The early village landscape was dominated by stone structures, but lumber was more popular. The architectural form of their houses was almost identical to that in Europe. The study supports Kniffen's conclusion that cultural heritage has been the dominant force for the preservation of the German-Russian house type. Based on the author's unpublished Ph.D. dissertation (Louisiana State University) and secondary sources; map, 9 photos, fig., 11 notes.　　　　　　　C. R. Gunter, Jr.

590. Pitzer, Donald E. THE HARMONIST HERITAGE OF THREE TOWNS. *Hist. Preservation 1977 29(4): 4-10.* Discusses the history, architecture, and historic preservation efforts of three communally oriented towns built by the followers of Lutheran dissenter (Johann) George Rapp (1757-1847), who came to the United States from the German province of Württemberg. Harmony, Pennsylvania (built 1804), New Harmony, Indiana (1814), and Economy (now Ambridge), Pennsylvania (1825), all face the problem of the restorations and interpretation of an entire town rather than a single building. 6 photos.
　　　　　　　R. M. Frame, III

591. Praschos, Janet Nyberg. 'THEY BUILT THEM SOLID.' *Am. Preservation 1978 1(6): 49-57.* Settled in the early 1800's by recent immigrants, German Village in Columbus, Ohio has survived years of neglect in the first half of the 20th century. In 1960 the area was declared an historic district and since 1963, the German Village Commission has coordinated and approved restoration projects. Today two-thirds of the 1,800 structures within the 233 acre Village have been restored. The small, sturdy, brick homes on tiny lots are reminiscent of 19th century Europe and the beauty of the community makes it a tourist attraction. Rising prices, noise, new residents, and inadequate parking have disenchanted many long time residents but the future of the German Village is tied to historic preservation. 9 photos.　　　S. C. Strom

592. Priestley, David T. DOCTRINAL STATEMENTS OF GER-MAN BAPTISTS IN NORTH AMERICA. *Foundations 1979 22(1): 51-71.* Traces the development of doctrinal statements of German Baptists in Germany and among German Americans. Comments on creedal statements, emphasizing Walter Rauschenbusch. His work among Germans at Rochester Seminary resulted in a definitely Baptist understanding of scripture, rather than a less denominational, generally pietistic and separatist view which had characterized German Baptists in America, 1800's-50's. German Baptists today are organized in the North American Baptist General Conference, with a seminary at Sioux Falls, South Dakota. Based on texts of confessions cited and other studies on Baptist creedal statements; 63 notes.　　　　H. M. Parker, Jr.

593. Prinz, Friedrich. DIE KULTURELLEN UND POLITISCHEN LEISTUNGEN DER SUDETENDEUTSCHEN FÜR DIE VEREI-NIGTEN STAATEN VON AMERIKA [Cultural and political contributions of the Sudeten Germans to the United States of America]. *Bohemia. Jahrbuch des Collegium Carolinum [West Germany] 1977 18: 144-154.* Emphasizes the contributions to Republican and anti-slavery policies of Hans Kudlich (1823-1917), the journalistic, civic and humanitarian work of Oswald Ottendorfer (1826-1900), the writings of Karl Postl (pseudonym Charles Sealsfield, 1793-1864), and the pastoral and missionary importance of [Saint] John Nepomucene Neumann, Bishop of Philadelphia (1811-60). These German emigrants from Bohemia and Moravia stood out among many of their countrymen who enriched American life; their fate and achievement foreshadowed aspects of the great Sudeten German migration of the mid-20th century.
　　　　　　　R. E. Weltsch

594. Purcell, L. Edward, et al. AN AMANA ALBUM. *Palimpsest 1977 58(2): 48-53.* Provides photographs of Amana from the Bertha M. Horack Shambaugh Collection. Ms. Shambaugh, a principal authority on the Inspirationists, took the pictures during the 1890's and the first decades of the 20th century. 9 photos.　　　D. W. Johnson

595. Randall, Stephen J. THE AMERICANIZATION OF HENRY KISSINGER. *Can. Rev. of Am. Studies [Canada] 1977 8(2): 221-228.* In *Kisssinger, The European Mind in American Policy* (New York: Basic Books, 1976), Bruce Mazlish ascribes to Secretary of State Henry A. Kissinger (1973-76) a unique position in the formulation and execution of US foreign policy. Mazlish believes that German antecedents and a conservatism derived from continental intellectuals such as Oswald Spengler (1880-1936) shaped Kissinger's views on international relations and caused him to apply balance of power concepts to produce order and detente in the world. 5 notes. H. T. Lovin

596. Rannalletta, Kathy. ILLINOIS COMMENTARY: "THE GREAT WAVE OF FIRE" AT CHICAGO: THE REMINISCENCES OF MARTIN STAMM. *J. of the Illinois State Hist. Soc. 1977 70(2): 149-160.* Based on the account of a United Evangelical minister whose church was in the vicinity hit hardest by the Chicago Fire of 1871. Translated from the German by Stamm's son Dante. 7 illus., 20 notes. J

597. Rauchle, Bob. REMINISCENCES FROM THE GERMAN-TOWN SETTLEMENT IN GIBSON COUNTY, TENNESSEE. *Tennessee Folklore Soc. Bull. 1979 45(2): 62-67.* Gives a brief history of Germantown in Gibson County, Tennessee, from 1880 to 1941, based on the oral reminiscences of Louise Theresa Rauchle Casey, born in 1888.

598. Rembe, Heinrich and Yoder, Don, trans. and ed. EMIGRATION MATERIALS FROM LAMBSHEIM IN THE PALATINATE. *Pennsylvania Folklife 1973/74 23(2): 40-48.* Genealogy of German families in Lambsheim in the Palatinate. S

599. Richard, L. C. PENNSYLVANIA DUTCH COUNTRY. *Indian R. [India] 1976 72(4): 19-22.* Examines the area as an enclave of religiosity, 18th century.

600. Richling, Barnett. THE AMANA SOCIETY: A HISTORY OF CHANGE. *Palimpsest 1977 58(2): 34-47.* Although the Iowa Amana colonies seem to represent stability in a changing world, they have gradually replaced their communal religious orientation with more secular values. More than 50 years before communalism formally ended in 1932, internal conflicts has begun to weaken the Amana Society. Among factors contributing to its spiritual decline were the deaths of the last Inspirationist prophets, a steady increase in wealth and population, tourism, the automobile, World War I, conversions to Christian Science, and the Great Depression. Primary and secondary sources; 4 illus., 5 photos, note on sources. D. W. Johnson

601. Rightmyer, Thomas Nelson. THE HOLY ORDERS OF PETER MUHLENBERG. *Hist. Mag. of the Protestant Episcopal Church 1961 30(3): 183-197.* Presents evidence that John Peter Gabriel Muhlenberg, a newly ordained priest in the Church of England, was priest and rector to the Beckford Parish in Dunmore County, Virginia, 1772-76.

602. Riley, Glenda, ed. THE MEMOIRS OF MATILDA PEITZKE PAUL. *Palimpsest 1976 57(2): 54-62.* Presents excerpts from the recorded recollections of Matilda Paul (1861-1938), who spent most of her life on a farm near Riceville in north-central Iowa. Matilda Paul "was the prototypal pioneer woman." 5 photos, note. D. W. Johnson

603. Riley, Jobie E. THE RHETORIC OF THE GERMAN-SPEAKING PULPIT IN EIGHTEENTH-CENTURY PENNSYLVANIA. *J. of the Lancaster County Hist. Soc. 1977 81(3): 138-159.* Discusses preaching in German-language churches in Pennsylvania during the 18th century, focusing on German Sectarians, Mennonites, the Church of the Brethren, Quakers, Schwenkfelders, and Separatists, and on some prominent church members.

604. Ritter, Christine C. LIFE IN EARLY AMERICA: FATHER RAPP AND THE HARMONY SOCIETY. *Early Am. Life 1978 9(2): 40-43, 71-72.* Under the leadership of George Rapp (1757-1847), German Protestant immigrants formed the Harmony Society in 1804 in Pennsylvania, and later in Indiana and then Pennsylvania again.

605. Rock, Kenneth W. THE COLORADO GERMANS FROM RUSSIA STUDY PROJECT. *Social Sci. J. 1976 13(2): 119-126.* Reports on previous research and proposes a new study project on the little-known and much misunderstood ethnic community of Russian Germans in Colorado, products of a double migration in the 18th and 19th centuries who made important social and economic contributions to the area.

606. Rock, Kenneth W. "UNSERE LEUTE": THE GERMANS FROM RUSSIA IN COLORADO. *Colorado Mag. 1977 54(2): 154-183.* Many Colorado immigrants were Russian Germans and most came to Colorado directly from Kansas and Nebraska. Except for Globeville and Pueblo, settlement, after 1900, was mainly in northeast Colorado which originally provided "stoop" labor for beet sugar production. Many prospered and the descendants are thoroughly Americanized. Primary and secondary sources; 12 illus., 83 notes. O. H. Zabel

607. Rodriguez, Janice Eichholtz. THE LANCASTER OF LEONARD EICHHOLTZ, 1750-1817. *J. of the Lancaster County Hist. Soc. 1975 79(4): 175-207.* Presents a biographical account of Lancaster, Pennsylvania, tavernkeeper, Leonard Eichholtz, his family, and their times.

608. Rose, Diane M. T. THE MAPS, PLANS, AND SKETCHES OF HERMAN EHRENBERG. *Prologue 1977 9(3): 162-170.* A German immigrant, Herman Ehrenberg was a surveyor, mining engineer, and cartographer in the 19th-century West. He fought for Texas in the war of independence from Mexico, and took part in the California gold rush, and the followup to the Gadsden Purchase. The first map drawing by Ehrenberg was a street plan of Honolulu; the last, charted while he was Indian Agent in Arizona Territory, outlined the northern portion of that Territory. His cartographical work in Arizona Territory was useful to land developers, transportation companies, and military strategists. Ehrenberg was killed, probably by Indians, in 1866. Primary sources. N. Lederer

609. Rutherford, Phillip. DEFYING THE STATE OF TEXAS. *Civil War Times Illus. 1979 18(1): 16-21.* On 10 August 1862, a Confederate force under Lieutenant C. D. McRae found and brutally defeated a contingent of pro-Union Texas Germans at their encampment along a bend in the Nueces River. 3 illus., 3 photos, map. D. P. Jordan

610. Rutledge, John. MADISON CAWEIN AS AN EXPONENT OF GERMAN CULTURE. *Filson Club Hist. Q. 1977 51(1): 5-16.* Madison Julius Cawein, a Kentucky regional poet, played a leading role in introducing German poetry into America. Cawein was able to win some personal recognition as an interpreter of mountain scenery and nature. In addition, he used his German family background to translate the works of Nicolas Lenau, Ludwig Uhland, Emmanuel Geibel, Friedrich Bodenstedt, Heinrich Heine, and Johann Wolfgang von Goethe. Primarily based on the Cawein Papers at the Filson Club, Louisville, Kentucky, and his published works; 43 notes. G. B. McKinney

611. Saul, Norman E. THE MIGRATION OF THE RUSSIAN-GERMANS TO KANSAS. *Kansas Hist. Q. 1974 40(1): 38-62.* 1974 is the centennial of the arrival in Kansas of Mennonites from the Tauride province of South Russia, as well as Roman Catholic, Lutheran and Baptist Russian-Germans from the Volga River region. The author explains why they left Russia; why they displayed so much interest in coming to Kansas; the distinguishing features of their settlements; the reception given to them by other Kansas residents; and their contributions to the history of Kansas. They may not have introduced hard winter wheat, as most writers have insisted, but they certainly increased the pace of adoption of wheat and helped make possible the rapid expansion of the Kansas wheat industry. Their most lasting contribution was their determination to stay. Unlike other immigrants who merely paused enroute to another frontier, the Russian-Germans stayed through good and bad times to develop the Great Plains. Primary and secondary sources; illus., 74 notes. W. F. Zornow

612. Schebera, Jürgen. HANNS EISLER IM VERHÖR [Hanns Eisler cross-examined]. *Beiträge zur Geschichte der Arbeiterbewegung [East Germany] 1975 17(4): 652-672.* Reprints (in German translation) selections from the cross-examination of Hanns Eisler before the House Committee on Un-American Activities in 1947. A progressive composer of socialist leanings, Eisler was forced to leave Germany in 1933. From that time he was active in antifascist circles of German emigrant writers.

By 1947 his socialist philosophy and the anti-Communist hysteria in the United States led to charges that he was a Soviet agent. 40 notes.

G. H. Libbey

613. Scheidt, David L. THE LUTHERANS IN REVOLUTIONARY PHILADELPHIA. *Concordia Hist. Inst. Q. 1976 49(4): 148-159.* Lutherans settled in the Delaware Valley prior to William Penn's arrival, but not until the 18th century did Lutherans come to Philadelphia in any great numbers. They adapted well and were absorbed by the expanding economic structure of the city; however, they maintained their ethnic identity by residing in the same areas and by speaking in their native German. When the American Revolution came, the Lutherans, as a group, did not demonstrate any enthusiasm for the patriot cause. Based on printed sources; 51 notes.

W. T. Walker

614. Schelbert, Leo. DIE STIMME EINES EINSAMEN IN ZION. EIN UNBEKANNTER BRIEF VON BRUDER JAEBEZ AUS EPHRATA, PENNSYLVANIEN, AUS DEM JAHRE 1743 [The voice of one of the solitary of Zion: an unknown letter of Brother Jabez from Ephrata, Pennsylvania, 1743]. *Zeitschrift für Kirchengeschichte [West Germany] 1974 85(1): 77-92.* Brother Jabez (Johan Peter Müller, 1709-96), abbot of the radical pietist (Seventh-Day Baptist) commune at Ephrata, Pennsylvania, wrote to the pietist preacher Jerome Annoni (1697-1770) in Basel, Switzerland describing living conditions in his community.

615. Schirmer, Jacob Frederick. THE SCHIRMER DIARY. *South Carolina Hist. Mag. 1975 76(1): 35-37, 76(2): 87-88, 76(3): 171-173, 76(4): 250-252.* Further installments of the Schirmer diary cover daily life in Charleston, South Carolina, 1 May 1845-31 March 1846.

616. Schirmer, Jacob Frederick. THE SCHIRMER DIARY. *South Carolina Hist. Mag. 1977 78(1): 71-73.* Reprints excerpts from the diary of Jacob Frederic Schirmer, January - April 1847.

617. Schirmer, Jacob Frederick. THE SCHIRMER DIARY. *South Carolina Hist. Mag. 1974 75(4): 249-251.* Entries from the diary of Schirmer, a German immigrant, depict life in Charleston, 1826-76. Traditionally, the entries have been precise enough to serve as evidence in South Carolina Courts. This journal has printed 25 installments intermittently between 1966 67(3) and 1974 75(4).

D. L. Smith and S

618. Schirmer, Jacob Frederick. THE SCHIRMER DIARY. *South Carolina Hist. Mag. 1976 77(1): 49-51, (2): 127-129, (3): 171-173.* Chronicles April-December 1846 in the continuing diary

619. Schlegel, Jacob. A TIME OF TERROR. *Am. Hist. Illus. 1976 11(2): 35-39.* Jacob Schlegel, a German emigrant in Civil War New York, wrote two letters to his family in Germany. They sketch general war events during 1861-63 in pro-Union terms. The second letter, dated 4 October 1863, also gives Schlegel's eyewitness account of the New York City Draft Riot of 1863, which he described as "a time of terror." 3 illus.

D. Dodd

620. Seaman, William M. THE GERMANS OF WHEELING. *Upper Ohio Valley Hist. Rev. 1979 8(2): 21-27; 9(1): 26-30.* Part I. Discusses German Americans of Wheeling, West Virginia, from the late 17th century, when the first wave of immigrants arrived from Europe, to 1917. Part II. Discusses beer brewing and families involved in that industry, 1840's-1910's.

621. Seaton, Beverly. HELEN REIMENSNYDER MARTIN'S "CARICATURES" OF THE PENNSYLVANIA GERMANS. *Pennsylvania Mag. of Hist. and Biog. 1980 104(1): 86-95.* Martin's short stories and 35 novels utilize ethnic and class stereotypes to convey her message of socialism and women's rights. Covers ca. 1904-39. Based on Martin's novels, secondary works and newspapers; 8 notes.

T. H. Wendel

622. Soper, Marley. "UNSER SEMINAR": THE STORY OF CLINTON GERMAN SEMINARY. *Adventist Heritage 1977 4(1): 44-55.* The Clinton German Seminary (later the Clinton Theological Seminary) in Clinton, Missouri, was for German-speaking Seventh-Day Adventists, 1910-25.

623. Sprunk, Larry J. ESTHER VAAGEN—WERNER. *North Dakota Hist. 1977 44(4): 14-16.* Interviews longtime school teacher Esther Vaagen. In 1915 North Dakota teachers made $50 per month teaching in schools that required them to build their own fires, clean the building, carry lunch and water to drink, and fumigate the building monthly with formaldehyde. Traveling to the rural school was often arduous, given the lack of roads and the necessity of lodging some distance from the schoolhouse. The schools were ungraded, so teachers taught all grades. Many of the students could not speak English. Although it was forbidden during World War I, teachers sometimes spoke German to students unable to understand English. In the early years Indians and Gypsies sometimes came by. During World War I there was much antagonism in Taylor, North Dakota, between the many German settlers and the native-born American supporters of the conflict against Germany.

N. Lederer

624. Stewart, Susan. SOCIOLOGICAL ASPECTS OF QUILTING IN THREE BRETHREN CHURCHES IN SOUTHEASTERN PENNSYLVANIA. *Pennsylvania Folklife 1974 23(3): 15-29.*

625. Swisher, Bob. GERMAN FOLK ART IN HARMONY CEMETERY. *Appalachian J. 1978 5(3): 313-317.* Photos of 11 tombstones found in Jane Lew, West Virginia, at the Harmony Methodist Church Cemetery show decorative folk symbols representative of local German settlers, 1827-55.

626. Thiele, Joachim. PAUL CARUS UND ERNST MACH: WECHSELBEZIEHUNGEN ZWISCHEN DEUTSCHER UND AMERIKANISCHER PHILOSOPHIE UM 1900 [Paul Carus and Ernst Mach: Interrelations between German and American philosophy around 1900]. *Isis 1971 62(2): 208-219.* The antimetaphysical ideas of Ernst Mach (1838-1916) reached American scholars primarily through the translations and publications of Paul Carus (1852-1919), German-born editor of *The Monist* (La Salle, Illinois). Carus was also a philosopher—Mach ultimately owned 20 of his books—and between the two men friendship and an extensive correspondence developed. Reproduces one of the early letters from Carus to Mach (1890). Its discussion of sensation and reality, which Carus was less willing to equate than Mach, and its comments on the related work of William Kingdon Clifford, whom Mach later studied and quoted, help to illustrate some of the similarities and differences in their thought. 33 notes.

H. S. Plendl and M. M. Vance

627. Tobler, Douglas F. KARL G. MAESER'S GERMAN BACKGROUND, 1828-1856: THE MAKING OF ZION'S TEACHER. *Brigham Young U. Studies 1977 17(2): 155-175.* In 1876, at Brigham Young's request, Karl G. Maeser, a convert to Mormonism in 1855, left Germany to come to Provo, Utah, to provide academic and religious direction to Brigham Young Academy. For a man who later exercised such a profound impact on Mormon education, little has been known concerning the European influences in the development of Maeser's character, world view, and educational philosophy. Illuminates the European background and preparation of this Mormon pedagogical reformer.

M. S. Legan

628. Tolzmann, Don Heinrich. MINNESOTA'S GERMAN-AMERICAN BOOK TRADE. *Am. Book Collector 1974 26(3): 20-22.*

629. Tolzmann, Don Heinrich. MUSENKLÄNGE AUS CINCINNATI [Sounds of the Muses from Cincinnati]. *Cincinnati Hist. Soc. Bull. 1977 35(2): 115-129.* Briefly examines the biographies and publications of the seven most prolific German American writers in Cincinnati: Heinrich A. Rattermann (1832-1923), Edwin Herman Zeydel (1893-1973), Heinrich H. Fick (1849-1945), Max Burghein (1848-1918), Gustav Bruehl (1829-1903), Hermann von Wahlde (1846-1917), and August H. Bode (1845-1918).

630. Tolzmann, Don Heinrich. THE ST. LOUIS FREE CONGREGATION LIBRARY: A STUDY OF GERMAN-AMERICAN READING INTERESTS. *Missouri Hist. Rev. 1976 70(2): 142-161.* The St. Louis Free Congregation was typical of most congregations of free thinkers. It was formed by immigrants who desired a free society without church and state interference. Many such congregations established schools, singing societies, and libraries. The circulation records of the

Free Congregation Library are still available at the Missouri Historical Society in St. Louis. These records provide a valuable guide for an understanding of German-American reading interests in the 19th century. They refute any notion that there was a cultural lag between Germans in America and Europe. Based on primary and secondary sources; illus., 40 notes.   W. F. Zornow

631. Tully, Alan. ENGLISHMEN AND GERMANS: NATIONAL-GROUP CONTACT IN COLONIAL PENNSYLVANIA, 1700-1755. *Pennsylvania Hist. 1978 45(3): 237-256.* Members of the proprietary faction in Pennsylvania were alarmed by the presence of a large number of Germans in the province and tended to exaggerate the political influence of these immigrants. Although the Quakers enjoyed the political support of the Germans, Philadelphia Quakers sometimes worried about a German threat to the dominance of English culture in the province. The Germans were less concerned with politics than other groups in Pennsylvania. Based on manuscript collections and secondary materials; photo, 43 notes.   D. C. Swift

632. Ward, Robert E. FINDING YOUR GERMAN ANCESTORS. *Family Heritage 1978 1(1): 13-17.* Provides basic guidelines and helpful hints for those tracing their German ancestors as far back as the 1600's.

633. Weaver, William Woys. PENNSYLVANIA GERMAN ARCHITECTURE: BIBLIOGRAPHY IN EUROPEAN BACKGROUNDS. *Pennsylvania Folklife 1975 24(3): 36-40.* Selected bibliography represents 150 years of German architectural studies, which provide a relevant background to Pennsylvania-German architecture.
S

634. Weigel, Lawrence A. THE CENTENNIAL CELEBRATION OF THE VOLGA GERMAN SETTLEMENTS IN ELLIS AND RUSH COUNTIES IN KANSAS. *J. of the Am. Hist. Soc. of Germans from Russia 1977 (23): 21-27.* Describes the centennial celebration held 25 July-1 August 1976 to commemorate the founding of Volga German settlements in Ellis and Rush Counties in Kansas, and provides a brief background of the villages.

635. Weiser, Frederick S. PIETY AND PROTOCOL IN FOLK ART: PENNSYLVANIA GERMAN *FRAKTUR* BIRTH AND BAPTISMAL CERTIFICATES. *Winterthur Portfolio 1973 (8): 19-43. Fraktur* describes a typeface dating back to 16th century Germany, but is now used to describe all Pennsylvania German primitive drawings. One of the more common forms of *Fraktur* is the baptismal certificate *Taufschein).* One basic fact must be remembered in studying the work of Pennsylvania German artists—"the illumination was auxiliary to the text." Analyzes birth and baptismal certificates issued to Pennsylvania German children. The wide variety of design on the certificates indicates that the certificate was an object of design for its own sake. Such designs were employed for their inherent beauty and popular appeal while the text contained religious meaning. Based on primary and secondary sources; 19 illus., 28 notes.   N. A. Kuntz

636. Weisert, John J. LEMCKE VISITS KENTUCKY'S GERMAN COLONIES IN 1885. *Register of the Kentucky Hist. Soc. 1977 75(3): 222-232.* Seeking to attract immigrants to Kentucky, Heinrich Lemcke was engaged to visit the state and record his impressions for those Germans and other Central Europeans contemplating emigration to the United States. Lemcke traveled in Kentucky in 1885. He published his observations later, proclaiming Kentucky a happy land, desirable as a place of settlement. 5 notes.   J. F. Paul

637. Wentz, Richard E. THE AMERICAN CHARACTER AND THE AMERICAN REVOLUTION: A PENNSYLVANIA GERMAN SAMPLER. *J. of the Am. Acad. of Religion 1976 44(1): 115-131.* Explains the influence of esoteric wisdom and folk religious, cultural, and intellectual history of the American people. These two elements, referred to as the complementary tradition, should be considered along with the more prominent elements of Enlightenment, Calvinism, and Puritanism. Pennsylvania Germans are used as an example of the complementary tradition and its influence. Secondary sources; 71 notes.
E. R. Lester

638. Wentz, Richard E. THE LILY AND THE TURTLEDOVE: THE SPIRITUALITY OF THE PENNSYLVANIA DUTCH. *Religion in Life 1977 46(2): 225-233.* Discusses the spirituality of the Pennsylvania Germans by examining the imagery and symbolism of their folk culture, particularly the representative images of the lily and the turtledove as expressions of their eschatological vision.

639. Bruntsch, Otto, ed.; and Wenzel, Otto, transl. A VOICE FROM THE PAST: THE AUTOBIOGRAPHY OF GOTTLIEB ISAAK. *J. of the Am. Hist. Soc. of Germans from Russia 1977 (25): 21-23.* Provides excerpts from the autobiography of Gottlieb Isaak (1834-1921), a Russian German who emigrated to South Dakota in the 1870's.

640. Wilhelm, Hubert G. H. and Miller, Michael. HALF-TIMBER CONSTRUCTION: A RELIC BUILDING METHOD IN OHIO. *Pioneer Am. 1974 6(2): 43-51.* Focuses on a specific building method, half-timbering, the presence of which in northeast Ohio can be related primarily to German settlers. These settlers, largely Amish, are identified with this method of construction. Half-timbering, consisting of a heavy frame of squared timbers and some form of filler, was a common method of construction in Western Europe until the 19th century. This method of construction was not as prevalent in the United States due to the abundance of timber and the early development of sawmills. The half-timbering building type, along with other diagnostic traits, helps in delineating a distinct settlement region in a five-county area of northeast Ohio. Based on interviews, field work, and secondary sources; 8 photos, map, 12 notes.   C. R. Gunter, Jr.

641. Winkler, Louis. PENNSYLVANIA GERMAN ASTRONOMY AND ASTROLOGY IX: JOHANN FRIEDERICH SCHMIDT. *Pennsylvania Folklife 1974 24(1): 45-48.* Describes the unique and highly sophisticated astronomical contributions of Pennsylvania-German Johann Friederich Schmidt (1746-1812).
S

642. Winkler, Louis. PENNSYLVANIA GERMAN ASTRONOMY AND ASTROLOGY III: COMETS AND METEORS. *Pennsylvania Folklife 1972 22(1): 35-41.* Discusses the reaction of Pennsylvania Germans toward the observation of several comets in the 18th century and the early 19th century, specifically their fear that comets precede disaster.

643. Winkler, Louis. PENNSYLVANIA GERMAN ASTRONOMY AND ASTROLOGY X: CHRISTOPHER WITT'S DEVICE. *Pennsylvania Folklife 1974/75 24(2): 36-39.* Speculates that a unique astronomical-astrological device, the *Horologium Achaz,* was primarily a religious relic of the Pietist sect.
S

644. Winkler, Louis. PENNSYLVANIA GERMAN ASTRONOMY AND ASTROLOGY VIII: DAVID RITTENHOUSE. *Pennsylvania Folklife 1974 23(3): 11-14.* Discusses the theoretical and mechanical accomplishments in astronomy and astrology of David Rittenhouse, a Pennsylvania German, 1750-96.
S

645. Wolf, Edward C. THE WHEELING *SAENGERFESTE* OF 1860 AND 1885. *Upper Ohio Valley Hist. Rev. 1978 8(1): 6-17.* Recounts the Saengerfest of 1860 and of 1885 in Wheeling, West Virginia; they hosted German singing societies from the Upper Ohio Valley.

646. Wolf, Stephanie G. ARTISANS AND THE OCCUPATIONAL STRUCTURE OF AN INDUSTRIAL TOWN: 18TH-CENTURY GERMANTOWN, PA. *Working Papers from the Regional Econ. Hist. Res. Center 1977 1(1): 33-56.* Through the case of Germantown, Pennsylvania, studies the basic economic conditions and occupational structure of the artisans of that community, 1767-91; manufacturing and preindustrial activity was greater than often suspected by historians, and required development of complex local production networks and economic infrastructures.

647. Yoder, Don. TWENTY FIVE YEARS OF THE FOLK FESTIVAL. *Pennsylvania Folklife 1974 23(Supplement): 2-7.* History of the largest regional folk festival in the United States, the Kutztown Folk Festival, founded in 1950.
S

648. —. AN APOLOGY TO EDWARD MENDEL: THE ORIGINAL OF LINCOLN'S LETTER FOUND IN CHICAGO. *Chicago*

Hist. 1979 8(2): 78-79. Provides a brief biography of Prussian-born lithographer Edward Mendel (1827-84), who established himself in business in Chicago as a lithographer, mapmaker, and engraver, and discusses in particular the letter from Abraham Lincoln thanking Mendel for the 1860 lithograph portrait of Lincoln.

649. —. AUGUSTUS KÖLLNER'S STATEN ISLAND DRAWINGS. *Staten Island Hist. 1971 31(6): 45-48.* Reproduces four 19th-century drawings of Staten Island from the W. C. Arnold Collection at the Metropolitan Museum of Art. Köllner was born in Dusseldorf in 1813, came to the United States in 1839 or 1840, and settled in Philadelphia. Additional Köllner drawings are believed to be extant, but as yet are undiscovered. Illus.
G. Kurland

650. —. GERMAN AMERICANS. Sowell, Thomas, ed. *Essays and Data on American Ethnic Groups* (Washington, D.C.: Urban Inst. Pr., 1978): 332-335. Statistics on German Americans by personal income distribution by sex; family income distribution; occupational distribution by sex; and education by age. From US Bureau of the Census, *Current Population Reports,* Series P-20, Nos. 221, 249; 3 tables.
K. A. Talley

651. —. [MENNONITE FRAKTUR]. *Mennonite Q. R. 1974 48(3): 305-342.*
Yoder, Don. FRAKTUR IN MENNONITE CULTURE, *pp. 305-311.* Fraktur is the generic name for the manuscript art of the Pennsylvania Germans, a religious word-oriented folk art which flourished during the 1740's-1860's.
Unsigned. COMMENTARY ON THE ILLUSTRATION, *pp. 311-342.* Explanation of 16 photographs of Mennonite frakturs.
S

Greek

652. Argyrakis, Panos. A TALK ON GREEK-AMERICANS DURING THE DICTATORSHIP. *J. of the Hellenic Diaspora 1976 3(1): 54, 55.* Discusses the reactions of Greek Americans to the dictatorship in Greece from 1967-75.

653. Banos, George C. A GREEK IMMIGRANT AND A WEALTHY BOSTONIAN. *New England Social Studies Bull. 1974 31(2): 8-11.* Explores the concept of oral history through two interviews, one with a Greek immigrant and the other with a wealthy Bostonian.
S

654. Eliopoulos, George T. GREEK IMMIGRANTS IN SPRINGFIELD, 1884-1944. *Hist. J. of Western Massachusetts 1977 5(2): 46-56.* Greeks began arriving to the Springfield, Massachusetts, area in 1884. Among the earliest arrivals was Eleftherios Pilalas, who went to work in the candy industry which was one of the earliest sources of employment for those who followed him to the area. During 1900-12, many Greek clubs and St. George's church were established. After 1912 factionalism related to Greek politics disrupted the unity of the community. Illus., notes.
W. H. Mulligan, Jr.

655. Eliopoulos, George T. THE GREEKS. *Hist. J. of Western Massachusetts Supplement 1976: 35-36.* Several small groups of Greeks came to fight in the American Revolution. Count Logothetis, an aide to Lafayette, led one group. Demetrios Ypsilante led another which fought in the Battle of Monmouth. The greatest Greek influence was the heritage of classical Greece and its impact on the founding fathers. Notes.
W. H. Mulligan, Jr.

656. Ellis, Ann W. THE GREEK COMMUNITY IN ATLANTA, 1900-1923. *Georgia Hist. Q. 1974 58(4): 400-408.* The Atlanta Greek community originated around the turn of the century when Greek immigrants came to the United States because of agricultural problems in Greece. They settled in northern cities primarily, but some came south to an existing small Greek community. They became involved in business and quickly became prosperous. They developed social clubs, churches, and schools. Their desire to preserve something of their cultural heritage was sometimes a source of conflict with others. Primary and secondary sources; 36 notes.
M. R. Gillam

657. Gizelis, Gregory. THE FUNCTION OF THE VISION IN GREEK-AMERICAN CULTURE. *Western Folklore 1974 33(1): 65-76.* Discusses both the background and nature of religious visions and their relation to folklife and folk religion. Basing his studies on the Greek Americans in Philadelphia, the author concludes that visions are "cultural phenomena with a recurrency which characterizes the folklore and folklife phenomena." Based on secondary sources and on oral interviews; 26 notes.
S. L. Myres

658. Humphrey, Craig R. and Louis, Helen Brock. ASSIMILATION AND VOTING BEHAVIOR: A STUDY OF GREEK-AMERICANS. *Int. Migration Rev. 1973 7(1): 34-45.* Discusses the roles of ethnicity and assimilation in the voting behavior and identification with the Republican Party of Greek Americans in the 1968 presidential election.

659. Kourvetaris, George A. GREEK-AMERICAN PROFESSIONALS: 1820'S-1970'S. *Balkan Studies [Greece] 1977 18(2): 285-323.* This study is a survey of Greek-American professionals focusing on the established professions, i.e., medical doctors, lawyers, and academics with emphasis on the latter. The analysis was based on qualitative (historical) and quantitative (survey-type) data. The former was used to assess the historical antecedents of the contemporary Greek-American professionals. The latter was used to analyze a selective number of socio-demographic and professional variables of 3,549 Greek-American professionals mostly academics, doctors, and lawyers. It was found that a Greek-American professional class is in the making which commenced before World War II. In addition, sources of professional recruitment, socio-demographic profiles, and social correlates of those born in the U.S. and/or Greece are examined.
J

660. Moskos, Charles C., Jr. GROWING UP GREEK AMERICAN. *Society 1977 14(2): 64-71.* Author reminisces about his life as a Greek American and offers insight into the assimilation of ethnic groups, as well as family history, 1898-1976.

661. Moskos, Charles C., Jr. SYMPOSIUM '76 OF THE MODERN GREEK STUDIES ASSOCIATION: THE GREEK EXPERIENCE IN AMERICA. *Balkan Studies [Greece] 1976 17(2): 391-393.* This symposium took place at the University of Chicago, 24-31 October 1976. Among the topics of papers presented were Greek immigration, beginning with the visit of one Don Teodoro to what is now the United States in 1528, the Greeks and Americanization, Greek-American attitudes on politics and the role of women, the Greek Orthodox Church in America including parochial education, and Greek-American journalism and literature—with particular reference to the Greek-language writer Theano Margaris, and the present-day English-language novelist Harry Petrakis, who attended the conference.
L. W. Van Wyk

662. P.T. and G.A. IMMIGRATION: A VIEW FROM THE GREEK CULTURAL ASSOCIATION. *J. of the Hellenic Diaspora: Critical Thoughts on Greek and World Issues 1975 2(2): 35-38.* Discusses the forces impelling emigration, especially economic considerations causing Greeks to emigrate to the United States after WWII.
S

663. Papacosma, Victor S. THE GREEK PRESS IN AMERICA. *J. of the Hellenic Diaspora 1979 5(4): 45-61.* Studies the Greek press in America, from its origins in 1892 to its nebulous future, based on the dwindling of strong Greek-language identification for many Greek Americans.

664. Papagiannis, Michael D. AMERICA: REFLECTIONS IN RED, WHITE, AND BLUE. *Greek Orthodox Theological Rev. 1976 21(4): 367-384.* Presents reminiscences of first impressions of the United States as an immigrant of Greek descent; discusses the Greek Orthodox Church, politics, education, and social life, 20th century.

665. Papanikolas, Helen. GREEK WORKERS IN THE INTERMOUNTAIN WEST: THE EARLY TWENTIETH CENTURY. *J. of the Hellenic Diaspora 1977 4(3): 4-13.* Greek Americans living in the western United States were among the groups agitating for labor organization on the railroads and in the mine, 1897-1924.

666. Patterson, G. James. GREEK MEN IN A COFFEE HOUSE IN DENVER: FIVE LIFE HISTORIES. *J. of the Hellenic Diaspora 1976*

3(2): 27-37. Presents life histories of five Greek Americans in Denver, Colorado, emphasizing problems in cultural assimilation in the 20th century.

667.   Petropoulos, Nikos.   GREEK-AMERICAN ATTITUDES TO-WARD AGNEW.   *J. of the Hellenic Diaspora 1975 2(3): 5-26.*

668.   Roucek, Joseph S.   CYPRUS IN THE MEDITERRANEAN GEOPOLITICS.   *Politico [Italy] 1976 41(4): 732-745.* Analyzes how Cyprus's strategic position has involved the United States in a conflict between two of its NATO allies. A Greek-American lobby helped persuade Congress to cut off military aid to Turkey in 1975, but Turkey was able to negotiate new arrangements with the United States in 1976. This Greco-Turkish hostility placed NATO and Washington in a no-win situation. Attempts to make the factions more flexible only made them more rigid. Based on government documents and on secondary sources; 15 notes.   W. R. Hively

669.   Saloutos, Theodore.   CAUSES AND PATTERNS OF GREEK EMIGRATION TO THE UNITED STATES.   *Perspectives in Am. Hist. 1973 (7): 381-437.* Greek emigration to the United States was primarily a 20th-century phenomenon. Reasons for emigration were numerous: a backward Greek economy, escape from military service, desire to make a fortune or to marry without dowry, encouraging correspondence from those who had emigrated, and escape from physical and social crises. Those who emigrated seldom returned. Waves of Greek emigration to the United States occurred between 1900 and 1914, immediately after World War I, and just after 1965; each was a reaction to domestic conditions in Greece. 158 notes.   W. A. Wiegand

670.   Saloutos, Theodore.   THE GREEK ORTHODOX CHURCH IN THE UNITED STATES AND ASSIMILATION.   *Internat. Migration R. 1973 7(4): 395-407.*

671.   Simon, Andrea J.   ETHNICITY AS A COGNITIVE MODEL: IDENTITY VARIATIONS IN A GREEK IMMIGRANT COMMUNITY.   *Ethnic Groups 1979 2(2): 133-154.* Studies Greek Americans in New York City, discerning types of adaptation to the question of ethnic identity versus assimilation. The orientations are organized around two Greek Orthodox churches, St. Demetrios, which has adopted modern architectural styles and dress patterns, and St. Markela, which clings to traditional and Old World ways. 5 notes, ref.   T. W. Smith

672.   Teske, Robert Thomas.   ON THE MAKING OF *BOBO-NIERES* AND *MARTURIA* IN GREEK-PHILADELPHIA: COMMERCIALISM IN FOLK RELIGION.   *J. of the Folklore Inst. 1977 14(3): 159-167.* *Bobonieres* and *marturia* are the small, ephemeral artifacts that are given as commemorative tokens at Greek American marriage and christening rites. Tells of one young couple who manufacture and sell these traditional artifacts from their shop in Upper Darby, Pennsylvania. Their experiences reveal the conflicts inherent when a traditional folk art is adapted to a commercial context. Based on personal interviews; 8 notes.   J. L. White

673.   Topping, Eva Catafygiotu.   JOHN ZACHOS: AMERICAN EDUCATOR.   *Greek Orthodox Theological Rev. 1976 21(4): 351-366.* John Zachos (1820-98), a Greek American, was sent from Cincinnati (Ohio) to Parris Island (South Carolina) as a teacher for blacks, 1862-63, and taught elsewhere until his death.

674.   Topping, Eva Catafygiotu.   JOHN ZACHOS: CINCINNATIAN FROM CONSTANTINOPLE.   *Cincinnati Hist. Soc. Bull. 1976 34(1): 46-69.* Chronicles the educational career of John Zachos, 1836-98.

Hungarian

675.   Congdon, Lee.   THE HUNGARIAN POCAHONTAS: *LAURA POLANYI STRIKER.*   *Virginia Mag. of Hist. and Biog. 1978 86(3): 275-280.* When historian Bradford Smith enlisted the aid of Hungarian-born Laura Polanyi Striker in determining the authenticity of Captain John Smith's account of his adventures in Hungary and Transylvania, Striker spent the rest of her life in a devoted and successful attempt to show that Smith had not been a liar. Based on English and Hungarian secondary sources; 21 notes.   R. F. Oaks

676.   Gunda, Béla.   AMERICA IN HUNGARIAN FOLKLORE.   *New Hungarian Q. [Hungary] 1974 15(55): 156-162.* Over a million Hungarians have migrated to the United States, mostly in the decades before the First World War; returning emigrants brought stories and customs such as the Christmas tree back with them to Hungary.

677.   Halász, Nicholas and Halász, Robert.   LEO SZILÁRD, THE RELUCTANT FATHER OF THE ATOM BOMB.   *New Hungarian Q. [Hungary] 1974 15(55): 163-173.* Leo Szilárd (1898-1964), a Hungarian émigré in the United States, was one of three Hungarian American scientists who induced Albert Einstein to sign the famous letter to President Franklin D. Roosevelt urging establishment of an American atomic weapons program during World War II; later he became a crusader for world peace and disarmament.

678.   Kardos, István.   A TALK WITH ALBERT SZENT-GYÖR-GYI.   *New Hungarian Q. [Hungary] 1975 16(57): 136-150.* Reprints the text of an interview with the Hungarian American biochemist Albert Szent-Györgyi in Hungary, 1974; discusses his youth, academic career, and work in biochemistry.

679.   Magocsi, Paul R.   IMMIGRANTS FROM EASTERN EUROPE: THE CARPATHO-RUSYN COMMUNITY OF PROCTOR, VERMONT.   *Vermont Hist. 1974 42(1): 48-52.* 20 families from Bereg, Hungary, attracted by the Vermont Marble Company, came to Proctor about 1914-19. Originally under a Uniate priest, they broke with him in 1917 and, shortly after, with a Greek Orthodox priest. Nine families organized an independent, Bible-reading, literalist congregation, influenced by the preaching of Charles Lee to nearby Swedes 1920-25. They also published a monthly, *Prorocheskoe Svietlo (The Prophetic Light)*. It will die with its founders since it does not attract the young.
                                                    T. D. S. Bassett

680.   Markowitz, Arthur A.   HUMANITARIANISM VERSUS RESTRICTIONISM: THE UNITED STATES AND THE HUNGARIAN REFUGEES.   *Int. Migration Rev. 1973 7(1): 46-59.* Discusses Congressional attempts to subvert the Eisenhower administration's humanitarian immigration policy toward refugees from Hungary in 1956-57; considers the role of US public opinion.

681.   McGinty, Brian.   THE LEGACY OF BUENA VISTA: AGOSTON HARASZTHY AND THE DEVELOPMENT OF CALIFORNIA VITICULTURE.   *Am. West 1973 10(3): 17-23.* After nearly a decade of pioneering in Wisconsin, Agoston Haraszthy de Mokcsa, a visionary aristocrat from the Austro-Hungarian Empire, set out for California in 1849. While holding public office in San Diego and San Francisco he experimented with vineyards, drawing upon his considerable experience in Hungary. In 1857, Haraszthy found suitable soil and climate conditions in the Sonoma area. Importing thousands of vines and roots from Europe, he made his vineyard estate of Buena Vista a laboratory for experimenting, demonstrating his theories, and perfecting practical techniques. With evangelical zeal Haraszthy spread the gospel of viticulture, won top honors for his products, produced valuable treatises, and studied European methods with which to perfect the industry. He also collected other products to introduce to California. In 1868 he established a large sugar cane plantation in Nicaragua where he drowned the next year. 13 illus.   D. L. Smith

682.   Nagy-Farkas, Peter.   HUNGARIANS.   *Hist. J. of Western Massachusetts 1976 (Supplement): 37-38.* Of the known 141 Hungarians who fought in the American Revolution, the most prominent was Colonel Michael Kovats, who was killed in the defense of Charleston, South Carolina. Ref.   W. H. Mulligan, Jr.

683. Quinn, David B. STEPHEN PARMENIUS OF BUDA: THE FIRST HUNGARIAN IN NORTH AMERICA. *New Hungarian Q. [Hungary] 1973 15(53): 152-157.* Stephen Parmenius, a native of Budapest, was among the crew who sailed to the New World in 1583; records some of the impressions which Parmenius, a poet, left of North America.

684. Rónai, Tamás. A NEW YORK-I MAGYAR TÁJÉKOZTATÓ KÖNYVTÁR TÖRTÉNETÉHEZ [On the history of the Hungarian Reference Library of New York]. *Magyar Könyvszemle [Hungary] 1978 94(1): 81-85.* Opened in 1938, the Hungarian Reference Library was based on the private collection of the bibliographer Károly Feleky (1865-1930). It was a cultural center for Hungarian Americans. As a propaganda organ of a hostile power, it was closed in 1942. 30 notes.
R. Hetzron

685. Sullivan, Charles L. A VITICULTURAL MYSTERY SOLVED: THE HISTORICAL ORIGINS OF ZINFANDEL IN CALIFORNIA. *California History 1978 57(2): 114-129.* Traces the origins of the Zinfandel grape, the basis for California's dry red table wine industry. Although its arrival in California resulted in widespread acceptance by knowledgeable winemakers, confusion about its origins occurred from misspellings, other grapes being mistaken for it, and its previous use as a table grape. Adding to the mystery were the assertions of winemaker Arpad Haraszthy who insisted in the 1880's that his father Agostín Haraszthy had imported the grape from Hungary in 1852. Contemporary evidence suggests four possible versions of Zinfandel's introduction into California, the most probable one being its importation from New England around 1855. No contemporary documentation exists to support the version propounded in the Haraszthy family tradition. Primary and secondary sources; photos, 54 notes.
A. Hoffman

686. Szilard, Leo. LEO SZILARD: HIS VERSION OF THE FACTS. *Bull. of the Atomic Scientists 1979 35(2): 37-40, (3): 55-59, (4): 28-32, (5): 34-35.* Part I. THE YOUNG SZILARD. Discusses Szilard's childhood in Budapest, Hungary, and his study of physics in Berlin, 1898-1922. Part II. Chronicles Leo Szilard's years of work in physics in Germany, 1928-33, his escape from Germany in 1933, and his further work in nuclear fission with Albert Einstein, 1933-39. Part III. Discusses the aftermath of a meeting with Washington officials in 1940 explaining the importance of uranium chain reactions and the beginning of nuclear research in the United States, 1940-42. Part IV. Describes Szilard's meeting with James F. Byrnes in 1945 in which Szilard opposed further nuclear testing.

687. Vazsonyi, Andrew. THE *CICISBEO* AND THE MAGNIFICENT CUCKOLD: BOARDINGHOUSE LIFE AND LORE IN IMMIGRANT COMMUNITIES. *J. of Am. Folklore 1978 91(360): 641-656.* The predominantly male boardinghouse life of Hungarian immigrants in the steel towns southeast of Chicago, Illinois, produced a special triangular relationship often resembling a sub rosa and unsanctioned form of polyandry among landlord, landlady, and the *föburdos* or starboarder. Covers 1899-1914. Primary and secondary sources; 51 notes.
W. D. Piersen

688. Weinberg, Daniel E. ETHNIC IDENTITY IN INDUSTRIAL CLEVELAND: THE HUNGARIANS 1900-1920. *Ohio Hist. 1977 86(3): 171-186.* Studies Hungarian immigrants in Cleveland, Ohio, in the early 20th century, the social and economic values, immediate and future goals, education, job selection, and behavior of the immigrants. Interviews 43 Hungarians who lived in the original Hungarian settlements in Cleveland, and supplements findings with traditional historical resources. Primary and secondary sources; illus., 38 notes, note on methodology.
N. Summers

689. Whitehead, James L. JOHN ALBOK'S RECORD OF THE PEOPLE OF NEW YORK: 1933-45. *Prologue 1974 6(2): 100-117.* Portfolio of Depression-era photographs by John Albok, Hungarian immigrant. Albok discovered success and happiness in America, but the Great Depression shocked him. A tailor by trade, he set out to record the people of New York through photography. 16 photos.
V. L. Human

Irish

690. Baker, B. Kimball. THE SAINT PATRICKS FOUGHT FOR THEIR SKINS, AND MEXICO. *Smithsonian 1978 8(12): 94-101.* During the Mexican War, the Mexican Army's San Patricios, or Saint Patrick Company, led by John Riley, consisted of US Army deserters enticed by Mexico's offers of citizenship and 320 acres of land, and prompted by the US Army's barbarous treatment, inhumane conditions, and anti-Catholic, anti-immigrant sentiments. Discusses the defense of the Franciscan convent of San Mateo in the battle of Churubusco in 1847. The unit fought desperately, but the US Army captured, tried, and eventually hanged 50 of the 72 survivors. 6 illus.
S. R. Quéripel

691. Bisceglia, Louis R. THE FENIAN FUNERAL OF TERENCE BELLEW MCMANUS. *Éire-Ireland 1979 14(3): 45-64.* Terence Bellew McManus (1811?-61) was arrested, tried, and exiled to Tasmania by the British in 1849 for his Young Ireland revolutionary activities of 1848. He escaped from Tasmania, and came to San Francisco in 1851. There, Irish Americans welcomed him as a hero. His strong disavowal of a move to seek pardon for him from the British in 1860 revealed his lasting, uncompromising opposition to British rule in Ireland. After his accidental death in January 1861, the Fenian Brotherhood, to advance their aims and encourage Irish nationalism, made plans to ship his remains back to Ireland. After Masses and huge processions in San Francisco and New York City in August and September-October respectively, the Fenians took McManus's remains to Ireland. McManus's funeral in Dublin in November 1861 was the largest in Ireland since that of Daniel O'Connell. It gave many thousands of Irish people the chance to demonstrate their reverence for McManus, and their anti-British sentiments, as the Fenians had hoped. Based on newspapers and secondary sources; 52 notes.
D. J. Engler

692. Brannigan, Colm J. THE LUKE DILLON CASE AND THE WELLAND CANAL EXPLOSION OF 1900: NON-EVENTS IN THE HISTORY OF THE NIAGARA FRONTIER REGION. *Niagara Frontier 1977 24(2): 36-44.* Luke Dillon (1848-1929), a member of the Clan-na-Gael, an Irish Republican group, was convicted "on very flimsy evidence" in the bombing of the Welland Canal, at Thorold, Ontario, in 1900; he was sentenced to life imprisonment in Kingston Penitentiary, and Irish American and Canadian groups did not obtain his release until 1914.

693. Brennan, Thomas A., Jr. BRENNANS AND BRANNANS IN AMERICAN MILITARY AND NAVAL LIFE, 1745-1918. *Irish Sword [Ireland] 1976 12(48): 239-245.* Provides an account of persons whose surnames were Brennan, Brannan, or similar, who participated in military and naval activities of the American colonies and the United States, 1745-1918. 9 notes.
H. L. Calkin

694. Brennan, Thomas A., Jr. BRENNANS AND BRANNANS IN WASHINGTON'S ARMY AND THE WAR OF 1812. *Irish Sword [Ireland] 1976 12(49): 310-312.* Information in addition to that in the article by Thomas A. Brennan, Jr., "Brennans and Brannans in American Military and Naval Life."
H. L. Calkin

695. Browne, Joseph. THE GREENING OF AMERICA: IRISH-AMERICAN WRITERS. *J. of Ethnic Studies 1975 2(4): 71-76.* Irish Americans, only eight percent of the population, have supplied America with a high number of significant and talented writers. Discusses the experiences and conditions that have created writers out of a large number of Irish Americans: first, because of the father-son relationship in the Irish family, and second, the "strong Manicheistic element in the Irish culture," combined with a large dose of Jansenism. The former produces a strong matriarchal tendency compensating for a world which has downtrodden and debased the Irish male, an Oedipal milieu attested to by the frequency and manner of the alienated son theme. The latter, the endless war between good and evil in which the forces of evil always prevail, results in one of two possible reactions to life: that of being "a stoical purveyor of doom," or one who can "laugh at it or blow it up into sudden drama." Thus the Irish "way of joking is to tell the truth." All this is further prompted by the *Seanachie* tradition, the love of words and storytelling carefully and deliberately cultivated for centuries. 11 notes.
G. J. Bobango

696. Browne, Joseph. JOHN O'HARA AND TOM MC HALE: HOW GREEN IS THEIR VALLEY? *J. of Ethnic Studies 1978 6(2): 57-64.* Analyzes the portrayal of Irish Americans in the novels of John O'Hara (d. 1970) and Tom McHale. O'Hara never seems to get beyond a contemptuous sniggering at his Irish characters, while McHale "has a delightfully irreverent sense of 'green' humor," and "doesn't insist that the Irish are more corrupt or corruptible than any other ethnic group. . . . For Tom McHale, the Irish simply are; for John O'Hara, they never should have been." When either writer departs from the scenes and people he knows best, his work deteriorates; thus O'Hara is at his finest in his Gibbsville novels and McHale the most sound when dealing with Philadelphia and Irish and Italians transplanted from his neighborhood in Scranton. Secondary sources; 10 notes. G. J. Bobango

697. Cadwalader, Mary H. CHARLES CARROLL OF CARROLLTON: A SIGNER'S STORY. *Smithsonian 1975 6(9): 64-71.* Presents a biography of Carroll, 1737-1832, a conservative, Catholic financier and Maryland state senator who signed the Declaration of Independence.

698. Callahan, Helen. A STUDY OF DUBLIN: THE IRISH IN AUGUSTA. *Richmond County Hist. 1973 5(2): 5-14.* Augusta had Irish residents before the Irish immigration which occurred nationally during and immediately after the potato famine of 1845-51. A number came during the early 1830's to work as railroad laborers. Historically Augusta's Irish took an active role in community affairs. Irishmen became important local politicians and prominent businessmen. One of six articles in this issue on Augusta. Based on newspapers, business directories, and secondary sources; 42 notes. H. R. Grant

699. Carey, Patrick. VOLUNTARYISM: AN IRISH CATHOLIC TRADITION. *Church Hist. 1979 48(1): 49-62.* Many American Irish Catholics saw voluntarism not as uniquely Protestant or American but as part of their Irish Catholic tradition. Focuses on the transition of the tradition from Ireland to the United States and concentrates on the efforts of Father (later Bishop) John England (1786-1842) to articulate and defend that tradition in Ireland and the United States. Outlines the historical context of the tradition and analyzes Father England's advocacy of the practices and principles involved. Family custom, hatred of the British, and other cultural and sociological factors influenced Irish Catholics' identification with the Catholic Church. The system of free will support, moreover, was voluntary in the sense that it had no legal basis of compulsion; custom, necessity, and community pressure insured that it had real sanction in fact as a sort of cultural Catholicism. M. Dibert

700. Carroll, Kenneth L. THE IRISH QUAKER COMMUNITY AT CAMDEN. *South Carolina Hist. Mag. 1976 77(2): 69-83.* In 1751, a group of Irish Quakers led by Robert Milhouse and Samuel Wyly came from Dublin and settled at Wateree (Camden), South Carolina. Indian raids troubled the community as did any military effort of the American colonies. Gradually migration to Bush River, Virginia, and North Carolina destroyed the Quaker's Wateree Monthly Meeting. Primary sources; 68 notes. R. H. Tomlinson

701. Casey, Daniel J. HERESY IN THE DIOCESE OF BROOKLYN: AN UNHOLY TRINITY. *New York Affairs 1978 4(4): 73-86.* Discusses three journalist-novelists, Jimmy Breslin, Pete Hamill, and Joe Flaherty, and their criticism of Catholic Irish Americans in Brooklyn, 1960's-70's.

702. Clark, Dennis. BABES IN BONDAGE: INDENTURED IRISH CHILDREN IN PHILADELPHIA IN THE NINETEENTH CENTURY. *Pennsylvania Mag. of Hist. and Biog. 1977 101(4): 475-486.* The Irish supplied most of the workers for the 18th-century's indentured labor system, an institution noted as late as the 1920's in some juvenile court cases. The system, rife with abuse, declined with population growth and mass production. Based on Philadelphia City Archives, Urban Archives, Temple University, official records, newspapers, and secondary works; 36 notes. T. H. Wendel

703. Clark, Dennis. ETHNIC ENTERPRISE AND URBAN DEVELOPMENT. *Ethnicity 1978 5(2): 108-118.* Examines the role of Irish general contractors in Philadelphia from the time of the potato famine (1846-47) to the 1960's. Construction of churches, parochial schools, and homes for Irish immigrants provided much of the impetus for Irish involvement in general contracting. In the early years, little capital was needed to start as a contractor and aspiring Irish entrepreneurs had access to fellow countrymen who had quickly acquired important construction skills. Irish participation in politics and in construction became closely linked. Discusses the individual careers of leading contractors, and the increasing legal and technological complexity of the business. Based on the Philadelphia *Evening Bulletin,* and secondary sources; 44 notes. L. W. Van Wyk

704. Clark, Dennis J. THE IRISH CATHOLICS: A POSTPONED PERSPECTIVE. Miller, Randall M. and Marzik, Thomas D., ed. *Immigrants and Religion in Urban America* (Philadelphia: Temple U. Pr., 1977): 48-68. Before 1850, Ireland was plagued by poverty, exploitation, and effects of the penal laws. After the Great Famine (1846-47) the country experienced a strengthening of religious energies. Irish emigrants, however, were met with adamant anti-Catholic sentiment in America. Too numerous to be coerced into conversion or dispersion, the Irish Catholics were denied assimilation into American society; in Philadelphia, especially, they were ostracized despite financial success. Responding to the situation, the immigrants constructed their own facilities and organizations. As the Church was the only "channel for the exercise of talent," bureaucratic management grew and "business bishops" gained control. From the original folk religion there emerged an ecclesiastical bureaucracy, an Irish American Church. 26 notes. S. Robitaille

705. Clark, Terry Nichols. THE IRISH ETHNIC AND THE SPIRIT OF PATRONAGE. *Ethnicity 1975 2(4): 305-359.* Irish Americans have been known for both political leaders and political machinery, 1880-1968. Under Irish ethic, or "nonideological particularism," individuals receive political payoffs according to their individual characteristics with the intention of accomplishing specific political aims; ideology is not important. The ethic emerged through Catholicism, trust, personal loyalty, sociability, localism, and basic social conservatism, and it was legitimized by the political patronage system in which it flourished. In the Irish American context, political patronage resulted in increased favors done for local regions, as an examination of expenditures for community-oriented programs—fire and police indicates. Such practices still occur in major cities among ethnic populations. 36 notes, biblio., appendix. G. A. Hewlett

706. Clayton, LaReine Warden. THE IRISH PEDDLER-BOY AND OLD DEERY INN. *Tennessee Hist. Q. 1977 36(2): 149-160.* After selling trinkets and notions in Ireland, William Deery (d. 1845) came to America where he purchased a trading post at Blountville, Tennessee in 1795. Deery made two additions to the building from hewn logs and chiseled stone, brought in stagecoaches, and backed steamboat ventures into the area. The building still stands and is a major landmark in East Tennessee. Primary and secondary sources; 2 illus., 8 notes. M. B. Lucas

707. Collins, C. W. ALEXANDER MACOMB. *York State Tradition 1974 28(3): 18-20.* Chronicles the life of Alexander Macomb, an Irish immigrant in New York. S

708. Cunningham, Patrick. IRISH CATHOLICS IN A YANKEE TOWN: A REPORT ABOUT BRATTLEBORO, 1847-1898. *Vermont Hist. 1976 44(4): 189-197.* Provides information from Patrick Cunningham about a Catholic parish in Brattleboro, Vermont, during 1847-98. The report was summarized in Bishop John Stephen Michaud's contribution to *The history of the Catholic Church in the New England States* (1899). Gives names, numbers, and dates for arrivals, pastors, places of worship, large contributors, baptisms, marriages, schools, and cemetery. Communicants worked mostly on the railroad or in the Estey organ factory. Notes "the intolerant spirit of a dominant party. . . . old prejudices now happily dead" which made nearly all Catholics Democrats. Based on the original report in Diocesan Archives. T. D. S. Bassett

709. Dolan, Jay P. THE IRISH DIASPORA. *Rev. in Am. Hist. 1977 5(2): 174-179.* Review article prompted by Lawrence J. McCaffrey's *The Irish Diaspora in America* (Bloomington: Indiana U. Pr., 1976).

710. Douglas, Ann. *STUDS LONIGAN* AND THE FAILURE OF HISTORY IN MASS SOCIETY: A STUDY IN CLAUSTROPHOBIA. *Am. Q. 1977 29(5): 487-505.* A study of James T. Farrell's fiction trilogy *Studs Lonigan* (New York: Signet Books, 1965; originally 1933-35) and its implications for society's sense of history, or loss of such a sense. Studs loses all sense of content in the forms of life he has been socialized to define as society; the Church, the family, the gang, have no substance. "His physical self had provided his only metaphor for hope." We can die without having lived, and our society has developed the mechanisms for insuring that very thing.   R. V. Ritter

711. Doyle, John E. CHICOPEE'S IRISH (1830-1875). *Hist. J. of Western Massachusetts 1974 3(1): 13-23.* Nineteenth-century Irish settlers came to the Chicopee mills via Canada and other parts of Massachusetts, and by 1848 Chicopee became a predominantly immigrant company town. Irish mores encouraged nativism among Protestants, but the record of Irish participation in the Civil War led to respectability. Primary and secondary sources; 2 illus., 34 notes.   S. S. Sprague and S

712. Dunleavy, Gareth W. and Dunleavy, Janet E. THE IRISH ABROAD: EVIDENCE FROM THE O'CONOR PAPERS. *Ethnicity 1975 2(3): 258-270.* The O'Conor Papers, a collection of letters and reports of members of the O'Conor family, represent accounts of Irish people in all parts of the world and serve to emphasize the role which the Irish played in international and economic circles. Notes discussions of the slave trade, Catholic disorder in Ireland, Cromwellian England, the French Revolution, Parliamentary politics, cultural and social life in continental Europe, and the sufferings of the Irish immigrants in America, 1690-1865. Based on the papers of Thady O'Rourke, Owen O'Conor, Charles O'Conor, and Charles Owen O'Conor; 2 notes.
                                    G. A. Hewlett

713. Edwards, Jerome E. PATRICK A. MC CARRAN: HIS YEARS ON THE NEVADA SUPREME COURT, 1913-1918. *Nevada Hist. Soc. Q. 1975 18(4): 185-205.* Discusses the tenure of Patrick A. McCarran (1876-1954) as an associate and later chief justice of the Nevada Supreme Court. Elected to the court in 1912, he soon grew displeased with the post. It impeded significantly the realization of his ambitions for winning higher public offices. McCarran's judicial decisions were primarily noteworthy for reflecting his view that the law was evolutionary rather than stationary and must take into account the elusive and ever-changing "components of human nature." Based on manuscript sources; photo, 71 notes.   H. T. Lovin

714. Eid, Leroy V. *PUCK* AND THE IRISH: "THE ONE AMERICAN IDEA." *Éire-Ireland 1976 11(2): 18-35.* During 1880-94 editorial cartoons in the American humor magazine *Puck* criticized Irish and Irish American society and politics.

715. Ellis, William E. PATRICK HENRY CALLAHAN: A KENTUCKY DEMOCRAT IN NATIONAL POLITICS. *Filson Club Hist. Q. 1977 51(1): 17-30.* Patrick Henry Callahan of Louisville, Kentucky, was an innovative businessman and a major spokesman for Catholics in the national Democratic Party. Callahan achieved fame by introducing a highly successful profit sharing plan in his Louisville Varnish Company. His strong commitment to prohibition was strengthened by his friendship with William Jennings Bryan and led Callahan to oppose Al Smith's presidential nomination in 1928. Callahan was an early supporter of Franklin D. Roosevelt and the New Deal. He defended the Roosevelt administration against attacks on its Mexican policy and from the challenge of Father Charles Coughlin. Based on the Callahan Papers at Catholic University and the Roosevelt, Bryan, and Woodrow Wilson Papers; 50 notes.   G. B. McKinney

716. Erie, Steven P. POLITICS, THE PUBLIC SECTOR AND IRISH SOCIAL MOBILITY: SAN FRANCISCO, 1870-1900. *Western Pol. Q. 1978 31(2): 274-289.* The argument that the Irish used political strategies and avenues to move from working-class to middle-class status in the nation's big cities is examined by (a) a case study of Irish political and economic progress in San Francisco, 1870-1900; and (b) a national comparison of Celtic political and economic development in urban versus non-urban settings for the same time period. The case study compares the Irish social mobility rate to rates for eight major ethnic groups; analyzes the magnitudes and ethnic distributions for three types

of "political" resources—public jobs, contracts and franchises, and "unofficial" patronage; and examines the relationships between "mass" and "elite" political mobilization, public job allocations, and aggregate mobility rates for the various ethnic groups. Findings: Only a small portion of the Irish used political resources and routes to move into the middle class. Public sector economic resources in the pre-New Deal era were too limited to more than marginally affect overall group economic progress.
                                    J

717. Everett, Barbara. JOHN BARRY: FIGHTING IRISHMAN. *Am. Hist. Illus. 1977 12(8): 18-25.* John Barry, a 30-year-old Philadelphian and senior captain of the landlocked navy during the winter of 1777-78, used seven barges to capture and destroy the transports *Mermaid* and *Kitty* and the schooner *Alert* in March 1778. Six months later Barry commanded the *Raleigh*, a 700-ton frigate with 36 guns and 235 crewmen. In late September 1778, the *Raleigh* engaged the *Unicorn*, a 22-gun ship, and the *Experiment,* a 50-gun ship-of-the-line. Barry lost the *Raleigh* and 135 men were captured, but he disabled the *Unicorn* and escaped with 86 men. Secondary sources; 8 illus.   D. Dodd

718. Fanning, Charles and Skerrett, Ellen. JAMES T. FARRELL AND WASHINGTON PARK: THE NOVEL AS SOCIAL HISTORY. *Chicago Hist. 1979 8(2): 80-91.* Gives a biography of author James T. Farrell, born in Chicago in 1904, and focuses on eight novels, of the 22 novels and 250 short stories he has written, set around Chicago's Washington Park and the people in its neighborhood, on the occasion of Farrell's 75th birthday in 1979.

719. Farwell, Byron. TAKING SIDES IN THE BOER WAR. *Am. Heritage 1976 27(3): 20-25, 92-97.* When Great Britain went to war against the Boers the official American view favored the British. However, many groups in the United States, including the Irish, thought the Boers were being wronged. American citizens went to South Africa to fight on both sides. 8 illus.   B. J. Paul

720. Foner, Eric. CLASS, ETHNICITY, AND RADICALISM IN THE GILDED AGE: THE LAND LEAGUE AND IRISH-AMERICA. *Marxist Perspectives 1978 1(2): 6-55.* During 1880-83 the American Land League introduced Irish Americans to modern reform and labor ideologies, helped integrate them into the broader context of reform, and shaped the traditions of the Irish working class.

721. Funchion, Michael F. IRISH NATIONALISTS AND CHICAGO POLITICS IN THE 1880'S. *Éire-Ireland 1975 10(2): 3-18.* The Chicago branch of the Clan na Gael, an American Irish nationalist organization, was "a highly effective local political machine." Those Clan members who were mavericks or Republican Party members, however, could not sway Irish Americans from voting Democratic, especially in presidential elections. Mentions Alexander Sullivan's pragmatic leadership of the Clan, a split in the Clan by followers of New York-based John Devoy in 1885, John Finerty's congressional campaigns in 1882 and 1884, and the presidential elections of 1884 and 1888. Based on newspapers, secondary sources, and the Devoy Papers in the National Library of Ireland; 39 notes.   D. J. Engler

722. George, Joseph, Jr. "A CATHOLIC FAMILY NEWSPAPER" VIEWS THE LINCOLN ADMINISTRATION: JOHN MULLALY'S COPPERHEAD WEEKLY. *Civil War Hist. 1978 24(2): 112-132.* In 1859 New York Archbishop John J. Hughes made John Mullaly's new *Metropolitan Record* his "official" organ, if there were no identification with party. Mullaly distrusted abolitionists but supported Lincoln and the Union until the January 1863 Emancipation Proclamation. Archbishop Hughes severed connections with the *Record* in March 1863. Mullaly joined the Copperhead press; he was bitterly anti-Lincoln and a "peace at any price" Democrat. He was arrested for resisting the 1864 draft. Supporting McClellan, he feared the worst. Racism seems to have been Mullaly's main motivation; added were religious fears of Know-Nothingism and Irish economic self-interest. Newqspaper and secondary sources; 57 notes.   R. E. Stack

723. George, Joseph, Jr. PHILADELPHIA'S CATHOLIC HERALD: THE CIVIL WAR YEARS. *Pennsylvania Mag. of Hist. and Biog. 1979 103(2): 196-221.* Largely aimed at the Irish, the *Catholic Herald and Visitor* (renamed after 1864, *The Universe: The Catholic*

Herald and Visitor) was suspicious of Republicans and unsympathetic to blacks, but always determined to support the war and avoid excessive partisanship. Based on Francis X. Reuss Papers, Ryan Memorial Library, Overbrook, Pennsylvania; "Cincinnati Papers, " University of Notre Dame Archives; other manuscripts, newspapers, printed sources, and secondary works; 58 notes. T. H. Wendel

724. Gitelman, H. M. NO IRISH NEED APPLY: PATTERNS OF AND RESPONSES TO ETHNIC DISCRIMINATION IN THE LABOR MARKET. *Labor Hist. 1973 14(1): 56-68.* Surveys ethnic discrimination against the Irish in the Waltham, Massachusetts, labor market 1850-90. With on-the-job training and formal education blocked, Irishmen received the lowest-paying, unskilled jobs, establishing a vicious cycle which tended to keep the Irish in unskilled positions. The experience in Waltham probably differs from large cities or one-industry towns, and generalizations are dangerous. Based on state and federal manuscript census returns, corporate records, public registers, and city directories; 2 tables, 19 notes. L. L. Athey

725. Goldberg, Joyce S. PATRICK EGAN: IRISH-AMERICAN MINISTER TO CHILE. *Éire-Ireland 1979 14(3): 83-95.* Discusses the political and diplomatic careers of Patrick Egan (1841-1919). Egan, a successful entrepreneur and an active Irish nationalist from at least 1860, left Ireland in the early 1880's to avoid imprisonment by the British. In Nebraska he rebuilt his finances. He became prominent in the national Republican Party and a good friend of James G. Blaine, who in 1889 arranged for Egan's appointment as US minister to Chile, possibly to oppose Great Britain's great commercial influence there. In Chile in 1891, Egan through his reports to Washington seemed to favor the elected president, José Manuel Balmaceda, against a revolution of the congress and the navy (with which Great Britain sympathized). After the revolution succeeded in August, anti-American sentiment was high. Eventually the Chileans tolerated Egan, who had defended US interests and growing hemispheric responsibility. Secondary sources and Egan correspondence; 33 notes. D. J. Engler

726. Good, Patricia K. IRISH ADJUSTMENT TO AMERICAN SOCIETY: INTEGRATION OR SEPARATION? *Records of the Am. Catholic Hist. Soc. of Philadelphia 1975 86(1-4): 7-23.* Offers insights concerning Irish adjustment to American society by analyzing a late 19th-century Irish Catholic immigrant community in a borough of Pittsburgh. Their St. Andrew Parish fulfilled two major adaptation functions: it operated as an enclosive society supplying the manifest functions of spiritual instruction, sustenance, and consolation as well as the latent functions of mate and friendship choice, and opportunities to express nationalistic and psychological needs. Because its parishioners were able to express basic value orientations of the dominant society, it also stood as a model and means of successful acculturation and adaptation to the American environment. 25 notes. J. M. McCarthy

727. Greco, Michael R. THE CRUCIBLE: ANTEBELLUM BOSTON'S IMPACT ON A "WAYWARD YOUTH." *Essex Inst. Hist. Collections 1975 111(3): 196-212.* Examines the early influence which Boston wielded over William Darrah "Pig-Iron" Kelley; discusses his early life and later political career (as a Congressman from Massachusetts) when he gained fame as a staunch supporter of protective tariffs and radical reform, 1830's.

728. Greeley, Andrew M. LOOKING BACKWARD: COMMODORE BARRY COUNTRY CLUB IN TWIN LAKES, WISCONSIN. *Chicago Hist. 1979 8(2): 112-119.* Describes the prestigious and exclusive Commodore Barry Country Club, founded in the 1920's by members of the Commodore Barry Council of the Knights of Columbus in Chicago to provide a place for Irish Catholics to socialize; also gives the history of the Knights of Columbus in Chicago, 1907-20's.

729. Greeley, Andrew M. MARGINAL BUT NOT ALIENATED: CONFESSIONS OF A LOUDMOUTHED IRISH PRIEST. *Social Policy 1974 5(1): 4-11.* The author discusses being a Catholic priest and an intellectual in contemporary society.

730. Greenhous, Brereton. 1814: AN IRISH GUNNER ON THE UPPER MISSISSIPPI. *Army Q. and Defence J. [Great Britain] 1974 104(4): 454-463.* A neglected aspect of the War of 1812 is the "ragged and irregular campaign" for control of the upper Mississippi Valley. The recapture of Michilimackinac by the British in July 1814 was largely the result of the efforts of Sergeant James Keating (1786-1849) of the Royal Artillery and his effective use of one three-pounder. Keating's artillery skill repulsed an American flotilla attempting relief. Regarded by his commanding officer as being entirely responsible for the British success, Keating then lapsed back into obscurity. D. H. Murdoch

731. Griffin, Richard T. BIG JIM O'LEARY: "GAMBLER BOSS IV TH' YARDS." *Chicago Hist. 1976-77 5(4): 213-222.* Discusses the gambling enterprises of Jim O'Leary in Chicago, Illinois, 1892-1925.

732. Groneman, Carol. WORKING-CLASS IMMIGRANT WOMEN IN MID-NINETEENTH-CENTURY NEW YORK: THE IRISH WOMAN'S EXPERIENCE. *J. of Urban Hist. 1978 4(3): 255-274.* Despite the disruption of immigration to the United States, kinship and cultural ties to the old country continued during 1840-60. As a result, the work, family, and leisure activities of the Irish immigrants were continuations or modifications of established Irish practices. 37 notes. T. W. Smith

733. Harling, Frederick F. and Kaufman, Martin. THE IRISH. *Hist. J. of Western Massachusetts 1976 (Supplement): 53-56.* Focuses on the political and military contributions of the Irish—especially John Carroll, Charles Thompson, George Read, John Sullivan, John Barry, and Hercules Mulligan—to the American cause. Also presents the negative attitude of the Irish Parliament toward the American Revolution, and the positive attitude of the Irish people. Illus., notes.

W. H. Mulligan, Jr.

734. Harper, Jared and Hudson, Charles. IRISH TRAVELER CANT IN ITS SOCIAL SETTING. *Southern Folklore Q. 1973 37(2): 101-114.*

735. Hellwig, David J. BLACK ATTITUDES TOWARD IRISH IMMIGRANTS. *Mid-Am. 1977 59(1): 39-49.* Surveys the interaction between blacks and Irish immigrants during the 19th century. Free blacks distrusted Irish immigrants and feared the loss of jobs to them, the Catholicism of the Irish, and apparent Irish support of slavery. With the Irish drifting into Democratic ranks and blacks into the Republican Party, there was also political animosity. Many violent confrontations occurred between the two groups, especially during the Civil War. Primary and secondary sources; 38 notes. J. M. Lee

736. James, Edward T. T. V. POWDERLY, A POLITICAL PROFILE. *Pennsylvania Mag. of Hist. and Biog. 1975 99(4): 443-459.* Traces the political life of Terence Vincent Powderly during 1876-1900. Originally a supporter of the Greenback-Labor party, Powderly's political impulses were largely shaped by local issues such as those he confronted while serving as mayor of Scranton. In 1879 Powderly became national head of the Knights of Labor. Its membership peaked around 1886, but shortly thereafter the Knights became more small-town and political-reform oriented rather than interested in trade unionism. Powderly flirted with both Democrats and Republicans, but in 1894 formally joined the Republicans. His political career ended as a federal officeholder in Washington when President McKinley appointed him Commissioner-General of Immigration. 65 notes. C. W. Olson

737. Jeffreys-Jones, Rhodri. MASSACHUSETTS LABOUR AND THE LEAGUE OF NATIONS CONTROVERSY IN 1919. *Irish Hist. Studies [Republic of Ireland] 1975 19(76): 396-416.* Criticizes the view that the Irish American vote was decisive in defeating Wilson's peace treaty. Taking Massachusetts as an example of Irish influence, shows that labor there generally favored the League in 1918, as likely to offer solutions to problems of high prices and high unemployment. In 1919 a militant faction pressed for rejection of any settlement which did not provide for Irish independence. Argues, however, that the eventual conversion of Massachusetts labor to opposition to the treaty rested not so much on ethnic factors as on apathy toward the League, generated by recent economic recovery, achievement of stable prices, and nearly full employment. Based on the Lodge Papers (Massachusetts Historical Society), League to Enforce Peace Papers (Harvard), and Walsh Papers (Holy Cross College); 65 notes. P. H. Hardacre

738. Kean, Kathleen Cochrane. GEORGE TIPPING, THE COR-CORAN IRISH LEGION, AND THE CIVIL WAR. *Niagara Frontier 1977 24(3): 53-65.* The letters of Sergeant George Tipping before he was killed in action describe the fierce fighting and heavy casualties, mainly in Virginia, of the Corcoran Irish Legion from New York state, 1862-64.

739. Kennelly, Karen. MARY MOLLOY: WOMEN'S COLLEGE FOUNDER. Stuhler, Barbara and Kreuter, Gretchen, ed. *Women of Minnesota: Selected Biographical Essays* (St. Paul: Minnesota Hist. Soc. Pr., 1977): 116-135. Born on 14 June 1880, in Sandusky, Ohio, Mary Aloysia Molloy grew up as the only child of Irish Catholic immigrant parents. In an age when few women attended college, Molloy earned her way through Ohio State University and graduated, in 1903, with more honors than anyone else up to that time. She went on to earn a master's degree and election to Phi Beta Kappa at Ohio State. In 1907 she earned her doctorate at Cornell. That same year, she began her career as a Catholic college educator in Winona, Minnesota, when she accepted a job with the Franciscan Sisters who, under the leadership of Sister Leo Tracy, were creating the liberal arts College of St. Teresa. The two women persevered and successfully established and administered the new collegiate institution for Catholic lay and religious women. Molloy was unique as the lay dean of a Catholic college, but in 1922 she became a nun, Sister Mary Aloysius Molloy, and in 1928 became the college president. As an educator, Molloy worked hard to improve the quality of women's education, wrestled with the unique problems of Catholic colleges, and carefully oversaw the development of her own school. By 1946, when she retired, the college was a firmly established institution producing outstanding graduate women. One of the last among the heroic generation of founders of Minnesota women's colleges, Molloy died on 27 September 1954. Primary and secondary sources; photo, 48 notes.

A. E. Wiederrecht

740. Ledbetter, Gordon T. APPEALING TO THE HEARTS OF MEN: JOHN MC CORMACK, 1884-1945. *Éire-Ireland 1978 13(4): 101-114.* Details and analyzes the career of the beloved Irish tenor John McCormack. An opera singer, a concert recitalist, and a recording artist, McCormack synthesized the classics and popular music in his repertoire and "remained, always, a vividly communicative artist." His opera career was distinguished, and he was "a master of German lieder [and] among the finest Mozartian and Handelian singers of this century." Describes his education and early training in Ireland, his opera studies in Italy, his becoming a US citizen, and his opera and concert performances in England, the United States, Australia, and Europe. D. J. Engler

741. Less, Lynn H. and Modell, John. THE IRISH COUNTRYMAN URBANIZED: A COMPARATIVE PERSPECTIVE ON THE FAMINE MIGRATION. *J. of Urban Hist. 1977 3(4): 391-408.* Urbanization for potato famine Irish people was more often than not international rather than internal. British and American cities rather than Dublin and other Irish centers drew the greatest share of Irish people who left the land. A macrolevel analysis of London and Philadelphia, two major centers of Irish emigration, shows that Irish people filled in the bottom of the urban economic and social systems. It also shows that these urban environments offered distinct advantages to Irish people, such as seasonal employment opportunities in British cities, employment for women, and better chances for marriage. 6 tables, 18 notes. T. W. Smith

742. Lummis, Keith. SOME OLD CALIFORNIA DOCUMENTS. *Masterkey 1978 52(3): 84-92.* Discusses recently discovered correspondence between John T. Doyle and his law partner Eugene Casserly on legal matters, 1851-71, and San Francisco life of the period, and several papers about Doyle's involvement in recovery of some of the Catholic Church's Pious Fund which had been seized after Mexican secularization.

743. MacDonagh, Oliver. THE IRISH FAMINE EMIGRATION TO THE UNITED STATES. *Perspectives in Am. Hist. 1976 10: 357-446.* In Ireland, overpopulation and the "new farming" combined to push one-third to one-half of the total work force out of agriculture. Although unemployed Irish found a scapegoat in British Protestants, they still exhibited a desire to "cling to country." Fortunately, however, an Atlantic passenger trade simultaneously developed so fast that by 1845 it was capable of transporting cheaply 75,000 people per season. Then came the potato famine during 1845-48, which weakened the peasant's desire to cling to Ireland. Once this attitude was broken, cheap passage to America

became a viable option. For many Irish, emigration was the only thing that saved them from almost certain death by starvation. In their new homeland they were for a generation the urban proletariat, but thereafter they stepped up the social ladder. They retained a distinctive identity because of their religion, Irish nationalism, and the development of their political base. Although this did not rid Anglo-Saxon Americans of their prejudice against the Irish, it did force the former to reckon with the Irish as political equals. W. A. Wiegand

744. Martin, Terry. THE RACE THAT GOD MADE MAD: A MEMOIR BY AN ARCHITECT'S GRANDDAUGHTER. *Kansas Q. 1974 6(2): 105-114.* Recounts the life of her grandfather Joseph Martin in the context of other Irish ancestors in 19th century Kansas. S

745. McCaffrey, Lawrence J. THE CONSERVATIVE IMAGE OF IRISH-AMERICA. *Ethnicity 1975 2(3): 271-280.* From their initial immigration to the United States, Irish Americans have been characterized as conservatives, as exemplified by their adherence to Catholicism, anti-intellectualism, sexual repression, political conservatism, and racist attitudes toward blacks. Irish immigrants became conservative through their avid and quick acculturation into the American system: though Catholicism was conservative and pietistic in practice, it represented a front for radical social change; political conservatism came about as a result of the political machine already in existence in urban ethnic ghettoes; abolitionism was rejected because of the fear of cheap black labor. Though outwardly not dedicated to cross cultural social reform, community social awareness was indicated through aid and welfare societies. 13 notes. G. A. Hewlett

746. McCullough, Laurence E. AN AMERICAN MAKER OF UIL-LEANN PIPES: PATRICK HENNELLY. *Éire-Ireland 1975 10(4): 109-115.* Chicago resident Patrick Hennelly is the sole manufactuere of uilleann pipes in the United States; covers 1928-75.

747. McCullough, Laurence E. MICHAEL COLEMAN, TRADITIONAL FIDDLER. *Éire-Ireland 1975 10(1): 90-94.* A 1912 immigrant from County Sligo, Ireland, Michael Coleman (1891-1945) became well-known for his Irish traditional fiddling in the 1920's and 30's.

748. McGinty, Brian. THE GREEN & THE GOLD. *Am. West 1978 15(2): 18-21, 65-69.* In the wake of the potato famine in Ireland and the gold discovery in California, thousands of impoverished farmers and artisans migrated to California. By 1860 Irish Americans constituted more than one-fifth of the foreign-born population. Their religious fervor, their passion for politics, and their involvement in the arts left indelible impressions on the history of the Far West. 9 illus., biblio. D. L. Smith

749. Melvin, Patrick. JOHN BARNWELL AND COLONIAL SOUTH CAROLINA. *Irish Sword [Ireland] 1973 11(42): 4-20, (43): 129-141.* Part I. John Barnwell went about 1701 from Ireland to South Carolina where he became a solider, frontiersman, colonial agent, and imperial expansionist. Details his best remembered military exploit, the command of an expedition against the Tuscarora Indians in 1711-12. Based largely on W. L. Saunders, ed., *The Colonial Records of North Carolina* (Raleigh, 1886-90); map, 104 notes. Part II. Barnwell was involved in the defense of South Carolina and in Indian trade, 1707-24. He participated in the Yamassee War (1715-16). Barnwell also was a storekeeper in Charleston, a superintendent of garrison, a special agent in London, and builder of a fort on the Altamaha River. 95 notes. H. L. Calkin

750. Michels, Eileen Manning. ALICE O'BRIEN: VOLUNTEER AND PHILANTHROPIST. Stuhler, Barbara and Kreuter, Gretchen, ed. *Women of Minnesota: Selected Biographical Essays* (St. Paul: Minnesota Hist. Soc. Pr., 1977): 136-154. Alice O'Brien was born on 1 September 1891 in the affluent Summit Hill area of St. Paul. The daughter of a wealthy lumberman, Alice attended private schools, traveled extensively, and became a prominent philanthropist and art collector. A curious, intelligent, and self-directed individual, Alice O'Brien was part of a large, affectionate, Irish Catholic family. She spent World War I as a volunteer mechanic, nurse, and canteen worker in Europe. She helped make a documentary film of Africa during the 1920's. Thereafter, she returned to St. Paul and participated in many social and political affairs, including

the National Prohibition Reform movement and Wendell Willkie's presidential campaign. Her two major interests were the Women's City Club and the Children's Hospital, to which she devoted much time, energy, and money. During her later years, O'Brien continued to financially help many civic organizations. She established the Alice M. O'Brien Foundation to support educational, scientific, religious, and charitable causes; and she became interested in conservation, especially in Florida where she spent many winters. She was on her way to Florida in November 1962 when she died. Primary sources; photo, 48 notes.

A. E. Wiederrecht

751. Monahan, Kathleen. THE IRISH HOUR: AN EXPRESSION OF THE MUSICAL TASTE AND THE CULTURAL VALUES OF THE PITTSBURGH IRISH COMMUNITY. *Ethnicity 1977 4(3): 201-215.* By monitoring the types of Irish music played and requested on a two-hour radio program of Irish music in Pittsburgh, assesses the elements of traditional culture, new culture, and external culture which combine to form present perceptions of Irishness and ethnicity in the Irish community. Though Irish music in America reflects influences from modern society and other ethnic types of music, adherence to and popularity of traditional modes and lyrics indicate a strong tie with traditional Irish culture. Further, though Irish music from 1900 to 1970 seemed to be blending into American music, recent trends show growing interest in ballads, anti-English lyrics, and learning Gaelic.

G. A. Hewlett

752. Morgan, John H. ETHNOCONSCIOUSNESS AND POLITICAL POWERLESSNESS: BOSTON'S IRISH. *Social Sci. 1978 53(3): 159-167.* A history of the city of Boston is in a real sense a history of ethnic enclaves and ethnic migratory patterns. As with the early English settlers, so with the later Irish, Italians, and Jews, each group entered at the bottom rung of the socioeconomic ladder gradually to climb up socioeconomically and out geographically into the suburbs. However, with each ethnic enclave, some did not middle-classify nor de-ethnicize. The Irish of South Boston are a living example of an intentional ethnic blue-collar community within the megalopolis.

J

753. Morgan, John H. THE IRISH OF SOUTH BOSTON. *Worldview 1975 18(6): 24-27.* Discusses the political and cultural factors since the late 19th century which led the Irish of South Boston, Massachusetts, to resort to civil disobedience against forced school busing in 1974.

754. Murray, Hugh T., Jr. THE GREEN AND THE RED UNBLENDING: THE NATIONAL ASSOCIATION FOR IRISH FREEDOM, 1972-1975. *J. of Ethnic Studies 1975 3(2): 1-21.* Covers the American movement on behalf of the nationalists of Northern Ireland. Focuses on the National Association for Irish Freedom formed in May 1972. Covers the NAIF's internal and external trials and tribulations in general, and the temporary cooperation and eventual schism between communist and noncommunist factions. Failure of the "popular front" collaboration is credited to personalities rather than ideologies. Based on personal observation and primary sources; 19 notes.

T. W. Smith

755. Neidhardt, W. S. THE FENIAN TRIALS IN THE PROVINCE OF CANADA, 1866-7: A CASE STUDY OF LAW AND POLITICS IN ACTION. *Ontario Hist. [Canada] 1974 66(1): 23-.* Discusses the trial of prisoners taken during the Fenian raids in the 1860's. Also discusses American reaction to the trials and international ramifications. Proves that the eventual commutation of the sentences was highly unwelcome to Fenian leaders in the United States. Primary and secondary sources; 85 notes.

W. B. Whitham and S

756. Neville, Mark K., Jr. THE IRELAND OF 1874: *JOURNAL OF CHARLES P. DALY* (1816-1899). *Éire-Ireland 1979 14(2): 44-51.* Provides excerpts from Judge Charles P. Daly's summary of his opinions about Ireland, from a journal he kept during a trip to his native Ireland in 1874. Daly, prominent in New York City and an example of the successful Irish immigrant, disliked not only Ireland's travel accommodations and damp climate, but also the conversation, appearance, economic habits, and political attitudes of the Irish people. Based on a journal in the Charles P. Daly Papers, MSS. Division of the New York Public Library; note.

D. J. Engler

757. Newton, Ada L. K. THE ANGLO-IRISH HOUSE OF THE RIO GRANDE. *Pioneer Am. 1973 5(1): 33-38.* Documents evidence of Irish settlement along the Rio Grande in both Texas and Mexico from distinctly North Irish house types. Colonization by northern Europeans, especially those who were cattle raisers by tradition, was encouraged by Mexico after 1821, and Texas after 1836. In their first state of development these houses were usually constructed of native rock, conglomerate, sandstone, or caliche, and consisted of one room (14 to 18 feet by 24 feet). No house type in either Mexico or Spain was its ancestor. Only further study will complete the story of diffusion. Presently, one can only speculate concerning related matters—how Mexican are the people? or how much did the Irish contribute to the southwestern cattle tradition? Based on interviews, secondary sources, and the author's unpublished master's thesis; 4 photos, map, 2 figs., 15 notes.

C. R. Gunter, Jr.

758. Oberley, Edith Toole. THE BARON C. C. O'KEEFFE: THE LEGEND AND THE LEGACY. *Montana 1973 23(3): 18-29.* "Baron" Cornelius C. O'Keeffe (d. 1883) was a Montana pioneer and ancestor of generations of civic leaders. Exiled from Ireland for rebellion, he escaped from a prison ship bound for Tasmania in 1853 and found refuge in California and Washington. He went to Montana with the Mullan Road party and took up a homestead northwest of Missoula. A legacy of anecdotes survives his turbulent career as rancher and politician. Based on family records; illus.

S. R. Davison

759. O'Connor, Thomas H. THE IRISH IN BOSTON. *Urban and Social Change Rev. 1979 12(2): 19-23.* Discusses the English military and political conquest of Ireland, and persecution of Irish Catholics, since the 16th century, and the Great Famine of 1845-49, as background to the immigration of many Irish people to the United States, particularly to the Boston area, and the subsequent involvement of Irish Americans in Boston politics and city government.

760. O'Donnell, L. A. THE GREENING OF A LIMERICK MAN: PATRICK HENRY MC CARTHY. *Éire-Ireland 1976 11(2): 119-128.* Offers a biographical sketch of the Irish youth, 1860-80, of Patrick Henry McCarthy, emphasizing influences on his later development as a powerful leader in the American labor movement.

761. O'Donnell, Seán. IRISH-AMERICAN SCIENTISTS. *Éire-Ireland 1979 14(2): 106-109.* Irish American scientists who were born in Ireland made notable contributions to science. Discusses the accomplishments of James Logan (1674-1751), economist Mathew Carey (1760-1839), mathematicians Robert Patterson (1743-1824), Robert Adrain (d. 1843), and Thomas Freeman (d. 1821), dentist Edward Hudson (1772-1833), physician Leslie Keeley (1834-1900), physiologist Henry R. Martin (1848-96), and inventors John Stephenson (1809-93), Patrick B. Delaney (1845-1924), John F. Kelly (1859-1922), and James J. Woods (1856-1928).

D. J. Engler

762. O'Fahey, Charles J. REFLECTIONS ON THE ST. PATRICK'S DAY ORATIONS OF JOHN IRELAND. *Ethnicity 1975 2(3): 244-257.* St. Patrick's Day Orations were a genre of public address which characterized St. Patrick's Day parades, 1840's-70's. Most dealt with a brief history of the country and the oppressions endured over the centuries, followed by descriptions of the life of St. Patrick, and ending with tales of the hardship endured in the United States. One particular Catholic priest, John Ireland, who spoke at New York St. Patrick's Day Parades, 1862-71, exemplified the genre with his mythic tales about St. Patrick and the pagan kings and discussion of the significance of the shamrock. Irish nationalism has enjoyed a resurgence among Irish Americans during the 1970's as evidenced by the popularity of such cultural entities as dance groups and choruses. 40 notes.

G. A. Hewlett

763. O'Flaherty, Patrick. JAMES HUSTON, A FORGOTTEN IRISH-AMERICAN PATRIOT. *Irish Sword [Ireland] 1973 11(42): 39-47.* Huston (1819-63), a Young Irelander, came to New York after the debacle of that organization in 1848. In New York City he participated in Irish-American political organizations and the New York militia before and during the Civil War. Based in large part on Irish-American newspapers in New York City; 52 notes.

H. L. Calkin

764. ÓSnodaigh, Pádraig. ÉIRENNAIGH SA CHOGADH CHA-THARTHA SNA STÁIT AONTAITHE [Irishmen in the Civil War in the United States]. *Studia Hibernica [Ireland] 1970 10: 95-107.* Irishmen fought on both sides in the Civil War. Mentions the names of the most famous Irishmen on both sides, lists the units which consisted of Irishmen or in which Irishmen were to be found and the most important engagements in the war in which Irishmen were involved. Points out that the reasons why Irishmen fought in the war were varied and complex. Concludes with some account of the part played by the Irish Brigade in the war and a brief assessment of the merits of the Irish as soldiers and of the work of the Irish nursing sisters during the war. 30 notes.
C. G. Ó Háinle

765. Osofsky, Gilbert. ABOLITIONISTS, IRISH IMMIGRANTS, AND THE DILEMMAS OF ROMANTIC NATIONALISM. *Am. Hist. R. 1975 80(4): 889-912.* The response of Garrisonian abolitionists to substantial immigration of Roman Catholic Irish was an attempt to reach beyond traditional Protestant and anti-foreign prejudice. They secured the support of reformers in Ireland, especially the Liberator Daniel O'Connell, identified Irish and black freedom, and defended the immigrants against American nativism. But the superpatriotism of first generation immigrants, suspected of divided loyalties in both politics and religion, rejected a radical minority movement. The first major Irish American movement, supporting repeal of the legislative union of England and Ireland, was disrupted by abolitionist pressure on the contradiction of Irish support for both slavery and repeal. Moreover, individualist values limited the abolitionists' response to Irish poverty to charity and preaching the work ethic. Events were violating the romantic nationalist tradition which viewed national independence as basis for individual liberty, for neither Irish nor nativist saw any need to extend personal freedom to all. The abolitionists' efforts to harmonize a universalist and egalitarian notion of personal freedom with national self-determination trace the decline of the romantic nationalist tradition and foreshadow the Civil War.
A

766. Ousley, Stanley. THE KENTUCKY IRISH AMERICAN. *Filson Club Hist. Q. 1979 53(2): 178-195.* The *Kentucky Irish American,* a Louisville newspaper, was founded in 1898. Until the end of World War I it centered its attention on ethnic and nationalist themes. After 1900 the paper increasingly was "Catholic in orientation and outlook." After 1930 the *Irish American* strongly supported the programs of the Democratic Party. The paper was forced to shut down in 1968. 69 notes.
G. M. McKinney

767. Owen, Polly. IS IT TRUE WHAT THEY SAY ABOUT THE IRISH? *West Tennessee Hist. Soc. Papers 1978 (32): 120-132.* Examines Irish-born men over age 20 in various occupations in the first three wards of Memphis in 1850, 1860, 1870, and 1880, and denies that Irish immigrants were less valuable, less sober, or less ingenious than their German counterparts. Points out positive qualities of the Irish-born as a group and as individuals to the economic development of Memphis and the South. Based largely on US Census statistics and Memphis histories; 4 charts, 52 notes.
H. M. Parker, Jr.

768. Packard, Hyland B. FROM KILKENNY: THE BACKGROUND OF AN INTELLECTUAL IMMIGRANT. *Éire-Ireland 1975 10(3): 106-125.* Biography of Francis Hackett, noted immigrant intellectual and literary critic covers his early years in Kilkenny and Clongowes Wood, Ireland, 1880's-1901, emphasizing the role of religion and education on his later career in the United States.

769. Reuter, William C. THE ANATOMY OF POLITICAL ANGLOPHOBIA IN THE UNITED STATES, 1865-1900. *Mid-America 1979 61(2): 117-132.* An examination of anti-British political attitudes in the last third of the 19th century. The three factors which are explored in detail are the appeal to Irish American voters, traditional dislike arising from the American Revolution and the War of 1812, and rivalry for economic and strategic advantages during this period. Anglo-American rivalry was the dominant reason for Anglophobia during this period. Secondary and some primary sources; 53 notes.
J. M. Lee

770. Riach, Douglas C. DANIEL O'CONNELL AND AMERICAN ANTI-SLAVERY. *Irish Hist. Studies [Ireland] 1976 20(77): 3-25.* Although Daniel O'Connell (1775-1847) was the most important European

ally of the abolitionists, expediency colored his stand and made it less than wholly consistent. Among factors which conditioned his support of anti-slavery were Irish American antipathy to the abolitionist movement, mutual suspicions among Irish abolitionists, hostility of the Irish American associations in the southern United States, and disillusion with his opposition to British recognition of Texas and its subsequent annexation. Based on printed and manuscript sources; 89 notes.
P. H. Hardacre

771. Ridgeway, Jacqueline. THE NECESSITY OF FORM TO THE POETRY OF LOUISE BOGAN. *Women's Studies 1977 5(2): 137-149.* Louise Bogan's (d. 1970) poetry is formal and objective and reflects such formal aspects of her upbringing as her Irishness, Catholicism, family, and classical education.

772. Roper, James E. PADDY MEAGHER, TOM HULING AND THE BELL TAVERN. *West Tennessee Hist. Soc. Papers 1977 31: 5-32.* Reassesses the roles of Paddy Meagher, the most colorful citizen of early Memphis, Tennessee, his son-in-law Tom Huling, and the Bell Tavern which Meagher operated for a short time. The article reconstructs the life of Meagher, traces the history of the Bell Tavern until it was torn down in 1918, and examines the various land transactions connected with Meagher. Based on the Thomas B. Huling Papers in the University of Texas Archives and the Shelby County, Tennessee, Register of Warranty Deeds; picture, 132 notes.
H. M. Parker, Jr.

773. Ryan, George E. SHANTIES AND SHIFTLESSNESS: THE IMMIGRANT IRISH OF HENRY THOREAU. *Éire-Ireland 1978 13(3): 54-78.* Some authors, especially Whitman and Whittier, championed Irish immigrants, but others, especially Emerson and Hawthorne, criticized them. Henry David Thoreau (1817-62) observed Irish immigrants in Concord from the early 1840's through the potato famine immigration of the late 1840's and the wreck of the immigrant vessel *Saint John* off Cohasset in 1849, and thereafter. At first he had trouble understanding the immigrants, but continued exposure to them improved his attitude. Two-thirds of his critical remarks about them were written during 1843-48, but 90% of his favorable comments were written during 1850-57. Though he criticized their poverty and what he saw as their faulty character and ignorance, he also befriended them, performed charitable acts for them, praised their honesty, industry, and cheerfulness, and learned that their plight was due to grasping Yankee employers. 70 notes.
D. J. Engler

774. Shumsky, Neil L. FRANK RONEY'S SAN FRANCISCO—HIS DIARY: APRIL, 1875-MARCH, 1876. *Labor Hist. 1976 17(2): 245-264.* Presents a diary of an Irish immigrant iron molder. Poverty, unemployment, money problems, and part-time labor dominated his life struggle. 30 notes.
L. L. Athey

775. Smith, Samuel Stelle. THE SEARCH FOR MOLLY PITCHER. *Daughters of the Am. Revolution Mag. 1975 109(4): 292-295.* Molly Pitcher, a heroine of the 1778 Battle of Monmouth in New Jersey, was an Irish American named Mary Hays McCauly; her maiden name is unknown.
S

776. Socolofsky, Homer E. WILLIAM SCULLY: HIS EARLY YEARS IN ILLINOIS, 1850-1865. *J. of the West 1965 4(1): 41-55.* Discusses Populist attacks on Irish landowner William Scully for being an absentee landlord, gives the background to his property investments beginning in 1843 in Ireland with property inherited from his mother, and follows his land purchases until the 1890's when he owned almost 220,000 acres in the Midwest.

777. Socolofsky, Homer E. WILLIAM SCULLY'S IRISH AND AMERICAN LANDS, 1843-1976. *Western Hist. Q. 1978 9(2): 149-161.* Irish landlord William Scully (1821-1906) began buying land in the United States in 1850. By the time of his death he had increased his holdings to some 225,000 acres in Illinois, Kansas, Nebraska, and Missouri. More than 1,200 tenants paid him cash rent for one year at a time. His reputation as "a strict, legalistic, even harsh landlord" inspired anti-landlord agitation against him in Ireland, where he owned thousands of acres, and in the United States. His estates are now managed by the third generation of Scullys, keeping pace with the latest changes in agriculture. Map, 15 notes.
D. L. Smith

778. Taylor, John M.   FENIAN RAIDS AGAINST CANADA. *Am. Hist. Illus. 1978 13(5): 32-39.* Military raids in 1866 from the United States into Canada by Irish American Fenians were undertaken to strike against British rule there and in Ireland—to "smite the tyrant where we can."

779. Tullos, Allen.   "THE DEAD BE BURIED HERE": IRISH JOKES OF TOMMIE BASS.   *Southern Folklore Q. 1977 41: 81-96.* Discusses "jokes" denigrating the Irish character which were fostered in Great Britain and the United States, 16th-19th centuries; reprints a series which the author collected from Tommie Bass, a herbalist in Leesburg, Alabama, 1973.

780. VanDyke, Mark A.   TIMOTHY MURPHY: THE MAN AND THE LEGEND.   *New York Folklore 1976 2(1-2): 87-110.* Attempts to separate fact from fiction surrounding Continental sharpshooter Timothy Murphy, a brilliant scout during the American Revolution.

781. Vinyard, Jo Ellen.   INLAND URBAN IMMIGRANTS: THE DETROIT IRISH, 1850.   *Michigan Hist. 1973 57(2): 121-139.* The Irish were the largest immigrant group in Detroit in 1850. With many opportunities and with negligible religious prejudice, the assets or liabilities of their background determined their economic and social roles in the city. They succeeded, encouraged more Irish to emigrate, and contributed to the growth of Detroit. 5 illus., 3 tables, 41 notes.   D. L. Smith

782. Walker, Samuel.   TERENCE V. POWDERLY, MACHINIST: 1866-1877.   *Labor Hist. 1978 19(2): 165-184.* An examination of Terence V. Powderly's early years in Carbondale and Scranton, Pennsylvania, reveals that he was well-acquainted with the realities of working-class life. His years as a machinist were successful, and they show that Powderly diligently practiced thrift, hard work, temperance, and self-improvement. Powderly's fundamental outlook on life was shaped in the essentially prebureaucratic age; he never changed that outlook. Based on the Powderly diaries in the Powderly Archives, Catholic University of America; 53 notes.   L. L. Athey

783. Walsh, James P. and Foley, Timothy.   FATHER PETER C. YORKE: IRISH-AMERICAN LEADER.   *Studia Hibernica [Ireland] 1974 14: 90-103.* Galway-born Father Peter Yorke (1864-1925) became champion of the Irish working class in San Francisco, advancing their unionization and education under Catholic auspices. He was ordained in 1887, became chancellor of the archdiocese of San Francisco and editor of the diocesan newspaper, *The Monitor*, where he fought the anti-Catholic American Protective Association. After losing editorship of that newspaper he established the Irish-American paper, *The Leader*, in 1902. During his defense of Father Richard Henebry he attacked the Catholic University of America as the preserve of Anglo-Irish-American Churchmen. During World War I he attacked Garret McEnerney, champion of the Home Rule Party and critic of Irish American supporters of Sinn Fein. After the war Yorke quarrelled bitterly with Mayor James Phelan. Though a bright, energetic defender of Irish Americans, he could only cooperate with subordinates, enjoyed excessively the glory attached to popular advocacy, and never accepted the legitimate differences of opponents. Based on Yorke's published writings and MSS at University of San Francisco, newspapers, and secondary sources; 40 notes.   T. F. Moriarty

784. Walsh, James P.   FATHER PETER YORKE OF SAN FRANCISCO.   *Studies [Ireland] 1973 62(245): 19-34.* Discusses the political attitudes of Father Peter Yorke, Catholic clergyman and Irish American, as a Regent of the University of California, 1900-12.

785. Walsh, James P.   PETER YORKE AND PROGRESSIVISM IN CALIFORNIA, 1908.   *Éire-Ireland 1975 10(2): 73-81.* Galway-born Father Peter C. Yorke championed the Catholic Church, Irish working people, and Irish nationalism in San Francisco from the 1880's until his death in 1925. Father Yorke, in his weekly newspaper *The Leader*, was a spokesman for Irish Americans who believed in political brokerage as a way to logically and democratically reconcile conflicting views. The Irish saw Progressive attempts at municipal charter revision in San Francisco in 1908 as the attempted removal of Irish political representation —by privileged, Protestant, University of California-oriented professional and business interests who thought themselves "disinterested" but did not accept cultural pluralism or political dissent. Based on *The Leader*, secondary sources, and correspondence; 28 notes.   D. J. Engler

786. Ward, Leo R.   THOSE PURITANIC AMERICAN IRISH! *Modern Age 1976 20(1): 94-100.* Records of a midwest Irish community from the late 19th century and the early 20th century show that the Irish left at sea any Puritanic attitudes toward liquor, women, and dance.   M. L. Lifka

787. Wilgus, D. K.   "ROSE CONNOLEY": AN IRISH BALLAD. *J. of Am. Folklore 1979 92(364): 172-195.* An analysis of the texts of the ballad *Rose Connoley* suggests that it originated in Ireland in the early 19th century but was popularized in the southern Appalachian region of the United States where the first examples were recorded. An index of 71 American performances is included. Based on song texts; 28 notes, index.   W. D. Piersen

788. Wilkinson, Dave.   "WRONG WAY" CORRIGAN.   *Am. Hist. Illus. 1978 12(9): 24-33.* On 16 July 1938, Douglas Corrigan flew out of New York City's Floyd Bennett Field in "Sunshine," a Curtis Robin with a 165 hp engine, apparently on a transcontinental flight to California. Supposedly he got turned around while passing through a cloud and flew 26 hours the wrong way, eventually landing in Dublin, Ireland. Government inspectors repeatedly had denied Corrigan's requests for a trans-Atlantic flight, so a hoax was suspected, but Corrigan stuck to his story. His autobiography, *That's My Story*, was made into a movie, *The Flying Irishman*, and he grossed $75,000 before his national fame faded. Primary and secondary sources; 6 illus.   D. Dodd

789. —.   IRISH AMERICANS.   Sowell, Thomas, ed. *Essays and Data on American Ethnic Groups* (Washington, D.C.: Urban Inst. Pr., 1978): 336-339. Statistics on Irish Americans' personal income distribution by sex; family income distribution; occupational distribution by sex; and education by age. From US Bureau of the Census, *Current Population Reports,* Series P-20, Nos. 221, 249; 3 tables.   K. A. Talley

790. —.   IRISH-BORN RECIPIENTS OF THE U.S. CONGRESSIONAL MEDAL OF HONOR.   *Irish Sword [Ireland] 1975 12(47): 149-151.* Lists 202 persons born in Ireland who received the United States Congressional Medal of Honor from the Civil War to World War I.   H. L. Calkin

Italian

791. Affron, Mirella Jona.   THE ITALIAN-AMERICAN IN AMERICAN FILMS, 1918-1971.   *Italian Americana 1977 3(2): 233-255.* A complete filmography of 68 films that feature an Italian American setting or an Italian American principal character during 1918-71.   M. T. Wilson

792. Aquino, Salvatore A.   THE THIRD OF TWELVE.   *Italian Americana 1978 4(1): 65-71.* Reminiscences of an Italian immigrant family's daily life in New York City in 1914, including the house, chores, and family relations.

793. Barbaro, Fred.   ETHNIC AFFIRMATION, AFFIRMATIVE ACTION AND THE ITALIAN-AMERICAN.   *Italian Americana 1974 1(1): 41-58.* Italian Americans are bringing charges against institutions of higher education for discriminatory employment practices.   S

794. Bardaglio, Peter W.   ITALIAN IMMIGRANTS AND THE CATHOLIC CHURCH IN PROVIDENCE, 1890-1930.   *Rhode Island Hist. 1975 34(2): 46-57.* The creation of national parishes was not always a success; animosities developed among Italian Americans in Providence, Rhode Island, 1890-1930, when the insensitivity of the Scalabrini order to the cultural traditions of southern Italians combined with their anticlericalism and propensity for disorder to form a rift between northern and southern Italian immigrants in the community.

795. Barone, Constance.   ITALIANS.   *Hist. J. of Western Massachusetts 1976 (Supplement): 57-60.* A few Italians fought in the American Revolution. The most prominent, Francesco Vigo, served with George

Rogers Clark. The most active was Philip Mazzei, a political philosopher and writer. Notes. W. H. Mulligan, Jr.

796. Belfiglio, Valentine J. THE CHRISTOPHER COLUMBUS OF AMERICAN STUDIES. *Italian Americana 1979 5(1): 37-46.* In 1924, Giovanni Schiavo wrote a history of Italian Americans in Chicago, which led to further histories of the American Revolution, the colonial period, individual Italians who contributed to American civilization, particular states, and the Mafia, 1924-62.

797. Belfiglio, Valentine J. ITALIANS AND THE AMERICAN REVOLUTION. *Italian Americana 1976 3(1): 1-18.* Discusses Italians who participated in the American Revolution (some under the French flag), highlighting three, Philip Mazzei, Carlo Bellini, and John Paca, 1773-83.

798. Belfiglio, Valentino J. ITALIANS AND THE AMERICAN CIVIL WAR. *Italian Americana 1978 4(2): 163-175.* Examines the contributions of Italians and Italian Americans to the American Civil War, especially Italians' sympathy for the Union effort.

799. Bergia, Thomas G. FORZA, RAGAZZI! 'HOLD EM,' YALE! *Italian Americana 1977 3(2): 193-204.* Italian ethnic heritage and the Yale football team are combined in order to examine the contributions and history of each. M. T. Wilson

800. Brown, Kenny L. PEACEFUL PROGRESS: AN ACCOUNT OF THE ITALIANS OF KREBS, OKLAHOMA. *Chronicles of Oklahoma 1975 53(3): 332-352.* During 1919, as the "Red Scare" gripped the nation, Governor J. B. A. Robertson of Oklahoma called for punitive action against a miner's strike. Because Italians represented the largest ethnic group in the strike, they received the bulk of criticism; yet throughout their 30 years of residence in the Krebs area, Italian miners had always demonstrated a moderate approach to reform, a revulsion toward violence, and a dedication to hard work. Even their association with the Socialist Party of Oklahoma and the United Mine Workers of America assumed a constructive and peaceful tone. Much maligned by xenophobic groups, their contributions to American society were positive and their assimilation into American society was rapid. Based on primary and secondary sources; 3 photos, 2 tables, 86 notes. M. L. Tate

801. Buhle, Paul and Celenza, James, eds. "BORN OUT OF STRIKES": AN INTERVIEW WITH LUIGI NARDELLA. *Radical Hist. Rev. 1978 (17): 153-160.* Luigi Nardella recounts his experiences in the textile strike of 1922 in Rhode Island.

802. Buhle, Paul. ITALIAN-AMERICAN RADICALS AND LABOR IN RHODE ISLAND, 1905-1930. *Radical Hist. Rev. 1978 (17): 121-151.*

803. Calascibetta, Pietro. DARIO PAPA E *L'ITALIA DEL POPOLO* (1890-1894) [Dario Papa and *L'Italia del Popolo,* 1890-94]. *Risorgimento [Italy] 1978 30(3): 125-150.* Dario Papa was a long-experienced journalist when in 1890 he became editor of a new paper, *L'Italia del Popolo.* Originally a moderate monarchist, Papa became convinced during his years in the United States (1881-84) that a federal republic would be best for Italy. American populism influenced him strongly, and *L'Italia del Popolo* was an attempt at an Italian populism. He ran articles on antimilitarism, the labor movement, the status of women, the condition of Italy's cities, and serialized novels of social significance by authors such as Émile Zola. The newspaper's main thrust, however, was political: Italy should be a federal republic. 70 notes. J. C. Billigmeier

804. Capeci, Dominic J. AL CAPONE: SYMBOL OF A BALLYHOO SOCIETY. *J. of Ethnic Studies 1975 2(4): 33-46.* In the late 1920's Al Capone, the "King of the gangsters, . . . Dictator of Chicago's underworld," was a folk hero and symbol for a multitude of Americans. His "public image was purified," just as those of Western heroes, to make it "acceptable to societal values . . . allowing many to identify with it." His image, bolstered by some sympathetic journalists and some writers, projected power, wealth, and infallibility, interwoven with the prestige these produced. Capone was seen to be an Horatio Alger protagonist, a defender of 100% American ideals, a family man, a philanthropist. Edito-

rialists viewed him as a product of circumstances, an effect of prohibition, an historic necessity of sorts; thus the public could rationalize its own violations of the Volstead Law. Finally, his exciting and dangerous lifestyle became the "surrogate self for thousands . . . providing the change and excitement they desired but were unable to achieve themselves." As Lindbergh was the actualization of the "spirit of America," so too, in a different vein, was Capone. Based on primary and secondary sources; 90 notes. G. J. Bobango

805. Capeci, Dominic J. FIORELLO H. LA GUARDIA AND THE AMERICAN DREAM: A DOCUMENT. *Italian Americana 1978 4(1): 1-21.* La Guardia's previously unpublished 1944 article, "Harlem: Homelike and Hopeful," which focuses on discrimination against blacks and compares their experience with other minorities, reflects his own marginalism and diverse ethnic origins.

806. Capozzola, Barbara. HIS CHILDREN'S CHILDREN. *Italian Americana 1978 4(2): 203-214.* Describes three generations of the Derrico family, immigrants to the United States in 1904 from Naples, Italy; shows the changing traditions, attitudes, and values of each generation as a result of assimilation and acculturation.

807. Caroli, Betty Boyd. ITALIAN WOMEN IN AMERICA: SOURCES FOR STUDY. *Italian Americana 1976 2(2): 242-254.* Examines information sources (including reference works, bibliographies, and first-hand accounts) for study of the immigration of Italians, primarily women, 1830-1920. 84 notes.

808. Caselli, Rob. MAKING IT IN AMERICA—THE ITALIAN EXPERIENCE. *Social Studies 1973 64(4): 147-153.* Discusses contributions of immigrant Italians in both eastern and western United States. Focuses on the place of Italians in California and Louisiana history. Explores the issue of assimilation versus pluralism in American culture. E. P. Stickney and S

809. Cavaioli, Frank J. ITALIAN AMERICANS SLAY THE IMMIGRATION DRAGON: THE NATIONAL ORIGINS QUOTA SYSTEM. *Italian Americana 1979 5(1): 71-100.* Political participation and strong lobbying efforts by the American Committee on Italian Migration, 1951-65, resulted in the Immigration Nationality Law (US, 1965).

810. Cerase, Francesco P. EXPECTATIONS AND REALITY: A CASE STUDY OF RETURN MIGRATION FROM THE UNITED STATES TO SOUTHERN ITALY. *Internat. Migration R. 1974 8(2): 245-262.* Studies the phenomenon of return migration to southern Italy from the United States 1964-68, detailing why these emigrants returned to Italy and what they felt about their American experience.

811. Conte, Stephen Gerald. A VISIT TO MY ANCESTORS' VILLAGE. *Family Heritage 1979 2(2): 36-39.* Recounts experiences in genealogy and visiting Andretta, Italy, 1971, the village from which his father's ancestors had originated.

812. Cordasco, Francesco. THE *RISORGIMENTO* OF ITALIAN-AMERICAN STUDIES. *J. of Ethnic Studies 1975 2(4): 104-112.* Presents a review essay dealing with Wayne Moquin, ed., *A Documentary History of the Italian-Americans* (1974) and Rose Basile Green's *The Italian-American Novel: A Document of the Interaction of Two Cultures* (1974). After some preliminary discussion as to how the wretchedness of the *contadini* experience long delayed serious study of the Italian-American past, the author calls Moquin's work "a disappointment," an undisciplined mass of materials lacking themes and conceptualizations and resorting to "grub street literary adventurism" and condescension to his subject. Green, however, has written "a significant milestone in American literary history," in this amplification of her dissertation on the ethnic novel. Despite some "baroque thematic panoply," Green's examination and summaries of some five dozen novels is an "incalculably significant" contribution to the new ethnic historiography. 13 notes. G. J. Bobango

813. D'Antonio, William V. CONFESSIONS OF A THIRD-GENERATION ITALIAN AMERICAN. *Society 1975 13(1): 57-63.* Describes the impact of the author's Italian American family life in Connecticut on his attitudes toward assimilation and ethnicity from approximately 1926-73.

814. DeRose, Christine A. INSIDE "LITTLE ITALY": ITALIAN IMMIGRANTS IN DENVER. *Colorado Mag. 1977 54(3): 277-293.* Italian immigrant history in Denver is characterized by economic difficulties, discrimination, and a lack of internal cohesiveness. Mentions the establishment of numerous societies, Catholic activities, the Angelo Noce-Columbus Day and the Father Mariano Lepore controversies, crime, poverty, business, labor, neighborhoods, and the entrance of several Italian Americans into influential positions in Denver society. Primary and secondary sources; 11 illus., 43 notes.   D. A. Hartford

815. Dumanoski, Dianne. BOSTON'S ITALIAN NORTH END. *Am. Preservation 1979 2(3): 42-49.* The North End, Boston's traditionally Italian blue collar neighborhood, is changing. Once an embarassment to the urban planners of the 1960's, this crowded neighborhood of three and four storey brick tenements was discovered by "outsiders" seeking low rent, convenient location, and ethnic vitality. With the renovation of the nearby waterfront and wholesale food district, North End has become fashionable. The facade of Italian shops remain but the blue collar jobs and residents are moving to the suburbs. Long time residents fear rising rents but little organized resistance to change has developed. 10 photos.
S. C. Strom

816. Falbo, Ernest S. ITALIAN-AMERICANS: STOCKTAKING. *Italian Q. 1974 17(68): 67-87.* Review-essay prompted by S. M. Tomasi and M. H. Engel's *The Italian Experience in the United States* (Staten Island, New York: Center for the Migration Studies, Inc., 1970), Humbert S. Nelli's *Italians in Chicago, 1880-1930: A Study in Ethnic Mobility* (New York: Oxford U. Press, 1970), Marie Hall Ets's *Roas—The Life of an Italian Immigrant* (Minneapolis: U. of Minnesota Pr., 1970), Joseph Lopreato's *Italian Americans* (New York: Random House, 1970), Irvin L. Child's *Italian or American? The Second Generation in Conflict* (New York: Russell and Russell, 1970), and Luciano J. Iorizzo and Salvatore Mondello's *The Italian-Americans* (New York: Twayne Publ., 1971). Discusses the American impact on immigrant Italians, and their processes of Americanization, transformation, and integration.
L. S. Frey and S

817. Feuerlicht, Roberta Strauss. VANZETTI'S FIRST TRIAL: AN ITALIAN GETS PURITAN JUSTICE. *Civil Liberties Rev. 1977 4(3): 53-67.* Excerpts a chapter from Roberta Strauss Feuerlicht's book *Justice Crucified: The Story of Sacco and Vanzetti* examining a trial in which Bartolomeo Vanzetti was convicted of a murder in 1920.

818. Franzina, Emilio. SUI PROFUGHI D'ITALIA: EMIGRANTI E IMMIGRATI NELLA STORIOGRAFIA PIÙ RECENTE (1975-1978) [Refugees from Italy: emigrants and those who immigrated in recent historiography (1975-78)]. *Movimento Operaio e Socialista [Italy] 1978 1(4): 413-425.* Surveys the literature on emigration from Italy in the 19th and 20th centuries, and on Italian immigrants in their new homes in North and South America, with emphasis on works which have appeared recently. Econometric and statistico-mathematical approaches have contributed enormously to the sociology and the historiography of migratory movements, allowing a clarity of perception without which our comprehension of the phenomena of immigration and emigration would be truncated and deformed. 51 notes.   J. C. Billigmeier

819. Fucilla, Joseph G. AN HISTORICAL COMMENTARY ON THE ITALIAN TEACHERS ASSOCIATION SUBSEQUENT TO THE RECENT PUBLICATION OF ITS ANNUAL REPORTS. *Italian Americana 1975 2(1): 101-107.* Traces the increase in the employment of Italian American teachers in US schools and the increase in the teaching of the Italian language since the founding of the Italian Teachers Association in 1912.

820. Gallani, Renato. A FRIEND OF THE AMERICAN REVOLUTION: PHILIP MAZZEI. *Italian Americana 1976 2(2): 213-227.* Philip Mazzei, an Italian immigrant, was a prorevolutionary and author during the American Revolution; presents summaries of two of his tracts, "Considerations of the Likely Outcome of the War" (1781) and "Reasons Why the American States Cannot Be Termed Rebels" (1781) and chronicles his life from 1773, when he came to America, until his death in Pisa in 1816. 35 notes.   G. A. Hewlett

821. Gisolfi, Anthony M. GIOVANNI PASCOLI'S "ITALIA RAMINGA" AND THE ITALIAN EMIGRANTS. *Italian Americana 1979 5(1): 25-36.* Discusses the poetry of Giovanni Pascoli, an Italian who in 1904 wrote an epic poem of the travails of poor Italians and "l'Italia raminga": Italian emigrants who found a better life in the United States.

822. Golden, Daniel. PASTA OR PARADIGM: THE PLACE OF ITALIAN-AMERICAN WOMEN IN POPULAR FILM. *Explorations in Ethnic Studies 1979 2(1): 3-10.* Examines the portrayal of Italian-American women via several post-war films including *Little Caesar, The Rose Tattoo, The Godfather (I&II), Lovers and Other Strangers,* and *Made for Each Other.*

823. Gould, Charles F. PORTLAND ITALIANS, 1880-1920. *Oregon Hist. Q. 1976 77(3): 239-260.* Discusses Italian immigration to Oregon in the late 19th and early 20th centuries. The process was gradual because the majority of immigrants settled in eastern cities. Still, a moderate trickle seeped into Oregon, especially Portland. Antiforeign feeling was high, but the Italians stayed and eventually left a mark on the communities in which they lived. They captured the truck farming and produce facets of the economy, then moved into other occupations as their means and education improved. World War I and a congressional law forbidding illiterate immigrants brought the flow to an abrupt end. 16 photos, 78 notes.   V. L. Human

824. Gullace, Giovanni. FIGURE DIMENTICATE DELL'INDIPENDENZA AMERICANA: FILIPPO MAZZEI E FRANCESCO VIGO [Forgotten figures of American independence: Philip Mazzei and Francis Vigo]. *Veltro [Italy] 1977 21(1-2): 37-68.* Mazzei (1730-1816), a historian, doctor, businessman, agricultural expert, counselor of princes, and revolutionary, influenced Thomas Jefferson, and Vigo (1747-1836), a protagonist of the conquest of the Midwest, contributed to American independence.

825. Gumina, Deanna Paoli. ANDREA SBARBORO, FOUNDER OF THE ITALIAN SWISS COLONY WINE COMPANY. *Italian Americana 1975 2(1): 1-17.* Details the founding of the Italian Swiss Agricultural Association in 1881 in San Francisco by immigrant Andrea Sbarboro (1839-1923) and its rise to become the Italian Swiss Colony Wine Company.

826. Gumina, Deanna Paoli. *CONNAZIONALI, STENTERELLO, AND FARFARIELLO*: ITALIAN VARIETY THEATER IN SAN FRANCISCO. *California Hist. Q. 1975 54(1): 27-36.* For two decades following 1905, San Francisco's Italian colony enjoyed the presentation of variety theater on a more or less regular basis. Antonietta Pisanelli, a theater impresario and noted singer herself, opened a succession of theaters which brought opera, comedy, arias, and character sketches to the Italian community at a reasonable price. Italian theater enjoyed its heyday in the years prior to World War I. Comic characters such as the *Stenterello,* an Italian provincial caricature, and the *Farfariello,* a caricature of the Italian immigrant, entertained the community. As assimilation increased, Italian variety theater could no longer be profitably sustained through regular performances. By 1925 the era of the Italian variety theater had ended, superseded several years later by a permanent opera house which owed its roots to the Italian community's devotion to opera. Primary and secondary sources; illus., 16 notes.   A. Hoffman

827. Gumina, Deanna Paoli. THE FISHERMEN OF SAN FRANCISCO BAY. *Pacific Historian 1976 20(1): 8-21.* Brief history of Italian fishermen of San Francisco Bay, 1850's-1940's. Presents Gaetano Tarantino, a 92-year-old fisherman who has seen major changes in the industry, including change from sail to motors, creation of "Fisherman's Wharf," organization of fishermen, development of restaurants along the wharf, and alien restrictions during World War II. Based on primary sources; 5 illus., 41 notes.   G. L. Olson

828. Haller, Herman. LINGUISTIC INTERFERENCE IN THE LANGUAGE OF "IL PROGRESSO ITALO-AMERICANO." *Italian Americana 1979 5(1): 55-68.* Examines the incidence of loan words in the form of translations, semantics, and adaptations and derivations which appear in Italian newspapers published in the United States for Italian Americans, 1976-78, especially *Il Progresso Italo-Americano.*

829. Harney, Robert F. THE COMMERCE OF MIGRATION. *Can. Ethnic Studies [Canada] 1977 9(1): 42-53.* Southern Italians who wished to come to Canada and the United States encountered bewildering emigration procedures in which cash payments were expected by middle-class "brokers," from the village mayor to loan financiers to travel and steamship agents. It was commercially advantageous to these "go-betweens" to allow and encourage emigration. Upon arrival in North America these immigrants once again found themselves indebted to similar bourgeois agents. The system continues today. The profit motive made and makes migration possible.   K. S. McDorman

830. Hartman, Peter and McIntosh, Karyl. EVIL EYE BELIEFS COLLECTED IN UTICA, NEW YORK. *New York Folklore 1978 4(1-4): 60-69.* Discusses evil eye, or malocchio, folklore collected among Italian Americans in Utica, New York, and describes perceptions of the power of the evil eye.

831. Henderson, Thomas M. IMMIGRANT POLITICIAN: SALVATORE COTILLO, PROGRESSIVE ETHNIC. *Int. Migration Rev. 1979 13(1): 81-102.* Describes the political career and attitudes of Salvatore Cotillo, an Italian American living in New York City during the rise of urban liberalism and reform in the early 20th century.

832. Hesse-Biber, Sharlene. THE ETHNIC GHETTO AS PRIVATE WELFARE: A CASE STUDY OF SOUTHERN ITALIAN IMMIGRATION TO THE UNITED STATES, 1880-1914. *Urban and Social Change Rev. 1979 12(2): 9-15.* Discusses the organization of immigrant communities in the United States, particularly the social and economic assistance networks, including the Padrone system, formed among southern Italian immigrants to the United States between 1880 and 1914.

833. Iorizzo, Luciano and Mondello, Salvatore. ORIGINS OF ITALIAN-AMERICAN CRIMINALITY: FROM NEW ORLEANS THROUGH PROHIBITION. *Italian Americana 1975 1(2): 217-236.* Discusses "the hostile, fanciful stereotypes" of Italian Americans as predisposed to crime and suggests ways in which the activities of the Mafia in the United States, particularly during the late 19th and early 20th centuries, has contributed to this false image.   S

834. Jacoby, Susan. THE ROOTS OF IMMIGRATION. *New York Affairs 1976 3(2): 54-67.* Unemployment and lack of opportunity at home force many young Italians to emigrate to the United States. More realistic and educated than their predecessors, these newcomers are providing New York City's neighborhoods with a steady flow of solid citizens.   J

835. Johnson, Cynthia Jean. A NEW LIFE: THE IOWA COAL MINES. *Palimpsest 1975 56(2): 56-64.* Reminiscences of John Corso, who arrived in New York City from Italy in 1914, journeyed to Iowa, and worked for 30 years in the coalfields of southeastern Iowa. Based on an interview conducted for the Iowa State University Coal Project. 7 photos.   D. W. Johnson

836. Juliani, Richard J. CHURCH RECORDS AS SOCIAL DATA: THE ITALIANS IN PHILADELPHIA IN THE NINETEENTH CENTURY. *Records of the Am. Catholic Hist. Soc. of Philadelphia 1974 85(1-2): 3-16.* Despite problems of completeness, coverage, and availability, church records can provide fragmentary information on the size and growth of the immigrant community, its duration in the place, occupations of individuals, and their origins in the home country and intentions in the new. They can also provide clues to infant mortality rates and to relations of immigrants with the larger society, and keys to the study of other materials. 24 notes.   J. M. McCarthy

837. Juliani, Richard N. AMERICAN VOICES, ITALIAN ACCENTS: THE PERCEPTION OF SOCIAL CONDITIONS AND PERSONAL MOTIVES BY IMMIGRANTS. *Italian Americana 1974 1(1): 1-25.* Examines how individual circumstances and changing social conditions in Italy have combined to provide motivation for immigration to the United States.   S

838. LaGumina, Salvatore J. REFLECTIONS OF AN ITALIAN-AMERICAN WORKER. *J. of Ethnic Studies 1975 3(2): 65-77.* Presents excerpts from the writings of Saverio Rizzo, an 87-year-old

Italian American worker who settled in the United States in 1903. Deals with the padrone system of labor recruitment, unionization, and the Triangle Waist Company fire of 1911. Based on primary and secondary sources; 7 notes.   T. W. Smith

839. Lentricchia, Frank. LUIGI VENTURA AND THE ORIGINS OF ITALIAN-AMERICAN FICTION. *Italian Americana 1975 1(2): 189-195.* Claims that Italian American author Luigi Ventura's (1845-1912) *Peppino* was first published in 1886, not in 1913 as is commonly believed.   S

840. López, Adalberto. VITO MARCANTONIO: AN ITALIAN-AMERICAN'S DEFENSE OF PUERTO RICO AND PUERTO RICANS. *Caribbean Rev. 1979 8(1): 16-21.* Recounts the political career of Vito Marcantonio (1902-54), Congressman from East Harlem, emphasizing those events that related to the radical Republican's interest in the well-being of his own Puerto Rican constituents in New York as well as to his support of independence for Puerto Rico.

841. Lotchin, Roger W. ETHNIC CONTINUITIES IN SICILIAN BUFFALO. *Rev. in Am. Hist. 1978 6(3): 373-378.* Review article prompted by Virginia Yans-McLaughlin's *Family and Community: Italian Immigrants in Buffalo, 1880-1930* (Ithaca, N.Y.: Cornell U. Pr., 1971, 1977).

842. Macnab, John B. BETHLEHEM CHAPEL: PRESBYTERIANS AND ITALIAN AMERICANS IN NEW YORK CITY. *J. of Presbyterian Hist. 1977 55(2): 145-160.* Presents the attempts of New York City Presbyterians, particularly the University Place Church, to minister to the needs of the mass numbers of Italian immigrants who moved into the Greenwich Village area at the turn of the century. The denomination as a whole was quite tardy in responding to the challenge which immigrants presented. Various kinds of programs, both religiously and secularly oriented, were undertaken to assist in Protestantizing and Americanizing the new immigrant. Though a couple of congregations were organized for the Italians, the formal ecclesiastical control remained in the hands of Anglo officials, in spite of a prediction that a strong ethnic church could result only if the people felt they were masters of their work. The hesitancy to turn complete control over to the Italians, coupled with the "caretaker paternalism" whereby the churches were supported by the Anglos, worked to hinder much Presbyterian growth among the Italians. Based on primary sources, including the archives of the First Presbyterian Church in the City of New York; illus., 47 notes.   H. M. Parker, Jr.

843. Mahevich, Nancy Viola. THE CASE FOR ETHNICITY: A PERSONAL VIEW. *Italian Americana 1979 5(1): 101-109.* Author analyzes ethnic attitudes of second- and third-generation Italian Americans concluding that the ethnic community has changed; however, certain strengths and traditions have been preserved, 1960's-70's.

844. Marchione, Margherita. PHILIP MAZZEI AND THE LAST KING OF POLAND. *Italian Americana 1978 4(2): 185-199.* Provides a biography of Philip Mazzei, an Italian who was appointed before and during the French Revolution as the political agent of the last king of Poland, Stanislaus II Poniatowski, 1764-95; Mazzei established an estate in Virginia in 1773 and corresponded with Thomas Jefferson until his death in 1795.

845. Margavio, Anthony V. THE REACTION OF THE PRESS TO THE ITALIAN AMERICAN IN NEW ORLEANS, 1880 TO 1920. *Italian Americana 1978 4(1): 72-83.* Mirroring the national pattern of discrimination, the New Orleans press tended to use stereotypes of Italian Americans as criminals.

846. Margavio, Anthony V. and Molyneaux, J. Lambert. RESIDENTIAL SEGREGATION OF ITALIANS IN NEW ORLEANS AND SELECTED AMERICAN CITIES. *Louisiana Studies 1973 12(4): 639-648.*

847. Marolla, Ed. HORICON, WISCONSIN, THE VENETO AND AOSTA. *Italian Americana 1978 4(1): 127-137.* The author discusses his Italian parents' immigration in 1893 to Wisconsin and his recent return to Pont Canavese, his ancestral home.

848. Martinelli, Phylis Cancilla. ITALY IN PHOENIX. *J. of Arizona Hist. 1977 18(3): 319-340.* Italians began to come to Phoenix in the 1880's. Their loosely knit community was small, and in many respects unlike Little Italies in other parts of the country. There were no Italian neighborhoods of stores, restaurants, churches, and newspapers. Yet practical concerns and their need to socialize with other Italians brought them together into clubs and other organizations. Uniquely, the Phoenix Italian American community has two distinguishable groups: one established by immigrants from Italy, and the other composed of migrants from within the United States. 4 illus., 61 notes.   D. L. Smith

849. Mathias, Elizabeth and Varesano, Angelamaria. THE DYNAMICS OF RELIGIOUS REACTIVATION: A STUDY OF A CHARISMATIC MISSIONARY TO SOUTHERN ITALIANS IN THE UNITED STATES. *Ethnicity 1978 5(4): 301-311.* Father Jesu began making an impact among Italian migrant workers in "Migrantville," Pennsylvania in the late 1920's and early 1930's. His approach to Catholicism struck a favorable chord in many Italian Americans not attracted by the dominant Irish and German forms of the faith. Father Jesu, a Spanish-born priest, espoused the traditional Italian manner of religious worship and behavior and stressed the figure of Christ as presented in the Gospels and described during the liturgical year. The priest wore humble clothing and eschewed appeals for money. Miracles were ascribed to him. The followers of Father Jesu eventually attained a foothold among the Italian community in Philadelphia and in other parts of Pennsylvania, New Jersey and New York. Based on field interviews July 1972-December 1973.   N. Lederer

850. Mathias, Elizabeth. THE GAME AS CREATOR OF THE GROUP IN AN ITALIAN-AMERICAN COMMUNITY. *Pennsylvania Folklife 1974 23(4): 22-31.* Discusses the locale and mechanics of the Italian game *bocce ball*, and reveals how it has preserved cultural identity through its formation of group ties among male Italian immigrants in Philadelphia.   S

851. Mathias, Elizabeth. THE ITALIAN-AMERICAN FUNERAL: PERSISTENCE THROUGH CHANGE. *Western Folklore 1974 33(1): 35-50.* Discusses retention and modification of the social and ritual elements in southern Italian funeral practices by Italian-American immigrants living in Philadelphia. Based on primary and secondary sources and on oral interviews; 11 illus., graph, 2 charts, 23 notes.   S. L. Myres

852. McBride, Paul. THE ITALIAN-AMERICANS AND THE CATHOLIC CHURCH: OLD AND NEW PERSPECTIVES. *Italian Americana 1975 1(2): 265-279.* Reviews Enrico C. Sartorio's *Social and Religious Life of Italians in America* (Clifton, New Jersey: Augustus M. Kelley, 1974) and Silvano Tomasi's *Piety and Power: The Role of the Italian Parishes in the New York Metropolitan Area* (New York: Center for Migration Studies, 1975), and discusses problems of historical objectivity.   S

853. Mitchell, John G. SAID CHICAGO'S AL CAPONE: "I GIVE THE PUBLIC WHAT THE PUBLIC WANTS . . . " *Am. Heritage 1979 30(2): 82-93.* Al Capone, who considered himself a pleasurable benefactor, arrived in Chicago in 1919 and gained control of most of that city's underworld prior to his demise in 1931 when found guilty of tax evasion. After eight years in prison, Capone was released. Syphillis had nearly destroyed his nervous system and he died in Miami in 1947. 18 illus.   J. F. Paul

854. Mondone, Mrs. Raymond. AN ITALIAN FAMILY IN PRINCETON. *Family Heritage 1978 1(4): 118-121.* Gives the history of the author's family since 1884, when her father, Achille "Charlie" Carnevale, came to America from Petronello di Molise, Italy, and settled in Princeton, New Jersey.

855. Monga, Luigi. PIER GIUSEPPE BERTARELLI: A MILANESE WAYFARER TO EL DORADO, 1849-1853. *Southern California Q. 1977 59(2): 129-138.* Describes the efforts of Pier Giuseppe Bertarelli (1819-69) to establish himself during the gold rush in California. A Milanese, Bertarelli decided to try California's commercial possibilities as soon as word came of the gold strike. He arrived in California on 12 May 1850. His ventures in merchandising, prospecting, livestock-selling, farming, and chicken raising all met with a variety of reverses. He gave up in late 1853 and returned to Italy, disillusioned at the elusive wealth offered by California. Based on Bertarelli's published letters and on other published contemporary and secondary works; 18 notes.   A. Hoffman

856. Morris, Jan. BARZINI'S AMERICA. *Encounter [Great Britain] 1978 50(1): 31-33.* Luigi Barzini's *O, America* (New York: Harper & Row, 1977) chronicles Barzini's belief in the "American way," his journalism career, and events during 1925-75.

857. Nelli, Humbert S. THE HENNESSY MURDER AND THE MAFIA IN NEW ORLEANS. *Italian Q. 1975 19(75-76): 77-95.* The assassination of police chief David C. Hennessy in October 1890 marked an important point in the development of Italian crime in the United States because of the national and worldwide publicity it received, the mob killings of 11 acquitted Italians, and the confrontation between the United States and Italy. The killers' actions "indicate either non-professional perpetrators or a carefully planned frameup." Italian immigrants would henceforth avoid New Orleans. One base of boss power in the city, namely the Italian immigrant vote, was not destroyed. "If the matrangas were responsible for Hennessy's murder, the killing was part of a vendetta involving the two feuding factions and did not represent an effort to establish *Mafia* control over the city." Nevertheless, the newspapers had disseminated the belief that acquittal of the accused "represented part of a *coup d'état* that necessitated a swift unequivocal response." 17 notes.   L. S. Frey

858. Nelli, Humbert S. THE PADRONE SYSTEM: AN EXCHANGE OF LETTERS. *Labor Hist. 1976 17(3): 406-412.* Reprints letters to the editor in a Chicago paper, *L'Italia*, November-December 1886, a complaint against a padrone and two replies. These letters represent two sides to the padrone system of using Italian immigrant labor in the United States.   L. L. Athey

859. Notarianni, Philip F. ITALIAN FRATERNAL ORGANIZATIONS IN UTAH, 1897-1934. *Utah Hist. Q. 1975 43(2): 172-187.* Italian immigrants in Utah organized lodges and societies for mutual aid during illness or misfortune and for protection against nativism. Fraternal organizations such as Stella D'America and the Christopher Columbus Lodge of Salt Lake City gave them a sense of security and continuity with the past, preventing demoralization. They were also vehicles for expressing Italian interests to the community. They promoted integration and eventual acculturation of immigrants into Utah society and American life. Based on primary and secondary sources; 5 illus., 50 notes.   J. L. Hazelton

860. O'Leary, Timothy and Schoenberg, Sandra. ETHNICITY AND SOCIAL CLASS CONVERGENCE IN AN ITALIAN COMMUNITY: THE HILL IN ST. LOUIS. *Missouri Hist. Soc. Bull. 1977 33(2): 77-86.* Describes the economic and cultural forces that created and maintained "The Hill" as a distinctive Italian community. Since 1950 residents of "The Hill" have stressed their ethnicity, tried to develop pride in their community, and battled to prevent their area from falling victim to commercial blight and economic deterioration. Based on secondary and newspaper sources; 2 illus., photo, 26 notes.   H. T. Lovin

861. Pane, Remigio U. DOCTORAL DISSERTATIONS ON THE ITALIAN-AMERICAN EXPERIENCE, 1921-1975. *Int. Migration Rev. 1976 10(3): 395-401.* A bibliography of 1921-75 doctoral dissertations dealing with the acculturation of Italian Americans.

862. Pane, Remigio U. SEVENTY YEARS OF AMERICAN UNIVERSITY STUDIES ON THE ITALIAN AMERICANS: BIBLIOGRAPHY OF 251 DOCTORAL DISSERTATIONS ACCEPTED FROM 1908 TO 1977. *Italian Americana 1978 4(2): 244-273.* A bibliography of doctoral dissertations accepted by American universities during 1908-77.

863. Pantaleone, Michele. MAFIA E VIOLENZA [The Mafia and violence]. *Problemi di Ulisse [Italy] 1978 14(86): 96-112.* Traces the Mafia from its roots in rural Sicily, through its suppression under the Fascist regime in Italy, to its spread to the United States, and today, to Europe, the Middle East, and other areas; blames it for the assassinations of John and Robert Kennedy, as well as Martin Luther King.

864. Parenti, Michael. THE MEDIA ARE THE MAFIA: ITALIAN-AMERICAN IMAGES AND THE ETHNIC STRUGGLE. *Monthly Rev. 1979 30(10): 20-26.* Discusses the mass media portrayal of Italian Americans since the early days of movies and radio, and the effects of stereotypes on the self-perception of Italian Americans.

865. Passi, Michael M. MYTH AS HISTORY, HISTORY AS MYTH: FAMILY AND CHURCH AMONG ITALO-AMERICANS. *J. of Ethnic Studies 1975 3(2): 97-103.* Reviews Silvano Tomasi's *Piety and Power: The Role of the Italian Parishes in the New York Metropolitan Area, 1880-1930* (1975), Richard Gambino's *Blood of My Blood: The Dilemma of the Italian Americans* (1974), and Carla Bianco's *The Two Rosetos* (1974). All three attempt to explain the nature of Italian-American society. Tomasi finds the core to be the Catholic Church and its ethnic parishes, Gambino sees the family system as the central element, and Bianco tackles the issue by comparing Rosetos, Italy, with its namesake in Pennsylvania. Of these three finds Bianco's to be the most illuminating and promising. 14 notes. T. W. Smith

866. Pernicone, Nunzio. CARLO TRESCA AND THE SACCO-VANZETTI CASE. *J. of Am. Hist. 1979 66(3): 535-547.* Reviews and analyzes a critical piece of evidence that has figured prominently in historian Francis Russell's revisionist interpretation of the Sacco-Vanzetti case. Russell posited the interpretation of Nicola Sacco's guilt and Bartolomeo Vanzetti's innocence based on declarations to that effect by Carlo Tresca, the prominent Italian anarchist and contemporary of Sacco and Vanzetti, 1941-43. Although Tresca definitely made such remarks, it is doubtful whether they shed new light on the South Braintree robbery and murder of 15 April 1920. 49 notes. T. P. Linkfield

867. Pietropaoli, Lydia Q. THE ITALIANS CAME UP WATERTOWN WAY. *New York Folklore Q. 1973 29(1): 58-79.*

868. Pozzetta, George E. ANOTHER LOOK AT THE PETROSINO AFFAIR. *Italian Americana 1974 1(1): 81-92.* The 1909 killing of New York City police lieutenant Joseph Petrosino in Palermo, Sicily, convinced many Americans that the crime rate in the United States could be reduced by restricting immigration from Italy. S

869. Pozzetta, George E. IMMIGRANTS AND RADICALS IN TAMPA, FLORIDA. *Florida Hist. Q. 1979 57(3): 337-348.* Reprints five articles from Italian-language newspapers revealing a rich cultural and intellectual life for Italian immigrants in Tampa, Florida. The immigrant workers were influenced in Sicily by "worker leagues." Such socialistic or anacharistic concepts were influencial in the development of Tampa. Primary and secondary sources; 14 notes. N. A. Kuntz

870. Pozzetta, George E. ITALIAN-AMERICANS AND THE NEW ETHNIC CONSCIOUSNESS: REVIEW ESSAY. *J. of Ethnic Studies 1976 3(4): 88-94.* Discusses the paucity of serious studies of Italian Americans as of the 1960's, commenting on five recent books dealing with this theme. Most attention is paid to Betty Caroli's *Italian Repatriation from the United States, 1900-1914* which estimates returnees as 50% of the total immigration. The book is "the fullest treatment available in English," despite its shortcomings. Francesco Cordasco's *The Italian-American Experience: An Annotated and Classified Bibliographical Guide* "must now be regarded as the standard in the field," while Andrew Rolle's *The Italian-Americans: Their History and Culture* is a readable introductory study for young people, relating the exploits of a host of Italian Americans from Columbus to LaGuardia. Eric Amfitheatrof, *The Children of Columbus*, is a biographical approach lacking any interpretive framework since it is an "avowedly popularized history." Concludes by citing historian Rudolph Vecoli's suggestions for further research and areas of inquiry. 7 notes. G. J. Bobango

871. Pozzetta, George E. A PADRONE LOOKS AT FLORIDA: LABOR RECRUITING AND THE FLORIDA EAST COAST RAILWAY. *Florida Hist. Q. 1975 54(1): 74-84.* Discusses the Florida East Coast Railway's use of the padrone, or labor boss, as a means of securing immigrant labor for railroad construction. Padroni were responsible for the recruiting and transporting of men to the job site, for which they collected a fee from the worker himself. On the job site, padroni ran the commissary and handled other financial matters for the workers, often doing so in a larcenous manner. However, the padrone system, with its faults, did provide a way for immigrants to make a living around the turn of the century. Reprints a letter written by a padrone, an advertisement from a New York Italian-language paper. Based on newspaper and secondary sources; 25 notes. J. E. Findling

872. Quart, Leonard and Rabinow, Paul. THE ETHOS OF *MEAN STREETS*. *Film and Hist. 1975 5(2): 11-15.* Examines the contributions of Martin Scorsese's film *Mean Streets* (1973) in portraying a deeper understanding of Italian Americans. S

873. Rizzo, A. Richard. INTERVIEWING ITALIAN-AMERICANS ABOUT THEIR LIFE HISTORY. *Italian Americana 1976 3(1): 99-109.* Offers suggestions on the collection of oral history from Italian immigrants in the 20th century.

874. Rosa, Alfred F. THE NOVELS OF MARI TOMASI. *Italian Americana 1975 2(1): 66-78.* Traces the life and works of Vermont novelist Mari Tomasi (1909-65), who wrote of Italian immigrant stonecutters.

875. Rosenwaike, Ira. TWO GENERATIONS OF ITALIANS IN AMERICA: THEIR FERTILITY EXPERIENCE. *Int. Migration Rev. 1973 7(3): 271-280.*

876. Rothenberg, Julius G. A GLANCE AT A 1911 SELF-HELP BOOK FOR ITALIAN IMMIGRANTS. *Italian Americana 1976 3(1): 45-53.* Alberto Pecorini's *La Grammatica—Enciclopedia italiana—inglese* served as a reference work for Italian immigrants in the second decade of the 20th century, including sections on immigrant regulations, domestic laws, customs, language, and hospitals.

877. Rusich, Luciano G. THE MARQUIS OF SANT'ANGELO, ITALIAN AMERICAN PATRIOT AND FRIEND OF TEXAS. *Italian Americana 1979 5(1): 1-22.* Originally fleeing Europe to avoid a revolution in Spain, Orazio Donato Gideon de Atellis, Marquis of Sant'Angelo came to the United States where he became interested in politics in Philadelphia, New York, and New Orleans, and where he published a newspaper, *El Correo Atlántico,* championing Texas's bid for independence, 1824-47.

878. Russell, Francis. SACCO AND VANZETTI: WAS THE TRIAL FAIR? *Modern Age 1975 19(1): 30-41.* Reviews events surrounding the famous Sacco-Vanzetti trial in 1921, concluding that it was fairer and more decorous than most court cases and relatively free from bias and prejudice. Based on primary and secondary sources; 27 notes. M. L. Lifka

879. Scarpaci, Jean Ann. IMMIGRANTS IN THE NEW SOUTH: ITALIANS IN LOUISIANA'S SUGAR PARISHES, 1880-1910. *Labor Hist. 1975 16(2): 165-183.* In the late 19th century the scarcity of labor during the sugar cane harvest in Louisiana attracted thousands of Italian immigrants to the sugar parishes. The immigrants were a temporary element in the state's population, yet the Italians were the largest immigrant group in Louisiana in 1900. Italians and Negroes apparently tolerated one another while on the same occupational level, but as Italians became more successful racial prejudice became more dominant. Based upon population censuses and government reports; 42 notes. L. L. Athey

880. Scarpaci, Jean. A TALE OF SELECTIVE ACCOMMODATION: SICILIANS AND NATIVE WHITES IN LOUISIANA. *J. of Ethnic Studies 1977 5(3): 37-50.* Narrates the harsh, unjust treatment of Sicilian immigrants in Louisiana parishes, and the gradual *modus vivendi* between them and southern native whites during 1871-1905. Whites stereotyped the Sicilians in the same categories as they did blacks, and attributed to them criminal involvement and intragroup violence. These suspicions produced episodes of lynching throughout the 1890's. Whites also were convinced that the "Dagoes" were primary carriers of yellow fever. Finally the Louisiana business community resented the large sums of money sent back to Italy by the immigrant laborers, funds which blacks would spend in the local economy. As Italians experienced upward economic mobility, however, behavioral changes forced by the desire for social acceptance took place, and they came to identify with the dominant white class attitudinally, yet retained strong group cohesiveness by ex-

tending *campanilismo* beyond their kinship groups. Primary and secondary sources; chart, 53 notes. G. J. Bobango

881. Scarzanella, Eugenia. L'EMIGRAZIONE ITALIANA NEGLI STATI UNITI NEI PRIMI DECENNI DEL NOVECENTO [Italian immigration in the United States in the first decades of the 1900's]. *Italia Contemporanea [Italy] 1975 26(121): 87-93.* Discusses the historiography of Italian immigration to the United States in the first decades of the 20th century. Primary and secondary souces; 26 notes. M. T. Wilson

882. Schnapper, Dominique. CENTRALISME ET FEDERALISME CULTURELS: LES EMIGRES ITALIENS EN FRANCE ET AUX ETATS-UNIS [Cultural centralism and federalism: Italian immigrants in France and the United States]. *Ann.: Econ., Soc., Civilisations [France] 1974 29(5): 1141-1159.* Studies the nature of Italian immigrant communities in the United States and France. The culture of the Italian immigrant is not dependent solely on the country of origin but is profoundly shaped by the attitudes and characteristics of the new home country. The marked cultural differences between Italian immigrants in the United States and in France is explicable in terms of the expectations and assumptions of the new home countries with respect to the pattern of assimilation. Primary and secondary sources; 60 notes. R. Howell

883. Shankman, Arnold. THE IMAGE OF THE ITALIAN IN THE AFRO-AMERICAN PRESS, 1886-1936. *Italian Americana 1978 4(1): 30-49.* Except in 1900-20, when Italian thriftiness and hard work was praised, the Afro-American press generally was suspicious and negative toward Italian Americans over such issues as immigration, Ethiopia, and competition for jobs, housing, and status.

884. Shankman, Arnold. THE MENACING INFLUX: AFRO-AMERICANS ON ITALIAN IMMIGRATION TO THE SOUTH, 1880-1915. *Mississippi Q. 1977-78 31(1): 67-88.* Belief in Darwinism gave Southern planters and landowners the idea of importing cheap European agricultural labor to replace black labor during 1880-1915. This unleashed fear and invective from Southern black newspapers, which proved unfounded, since most Italian Americans remained in urban areas to begin small mercantile operations.

885. Sinicropi, Giovanni. THE SAGA OF THE CORLEONES: PUZO, COPPOLA AND *THE GODFATHER*. *Italian Americana 1975 2(1): 79-90.* Writer Mario Puzo and moviemaker Francis Ford Coppola have hardly told the full story on Italian-American life and crime in their *Godfather* I and II of the 1970's.

886. Smith, Dwight C., Jr. MAFIA: THE PROTOTYPICAL ALIEN CONSPIRACY. *Ann. of the Am. Acad. of Pol. and Social Sci. 1976 (423): 75-88.* The attractiveness of alien conspiracy theories in American public opinion stretches back to the early days of the Republic. "Mafia" has been the name of one such theory. When placed in context with other conspiracy theories, such as the Bavarian Illuminati scare of 1798-1799 and the Red Scare of 1919-1920, the reasons for emergence of a "Mafia" theory in 1890-91, and again in 1946-63, become clear. Contemporary public opinion regarding crime is heavily influenced by the post-World War II resurgence of "Mafia" claims, though the evidence behind them is questionable. The role of "Mafia" as a force in public policy is clear, however, and the events of the last decade suggest that the consequent shifts in legal strategies, and an increasing sense of injustice generally, have been greater threats to American society than the presumed alien conspiracy behind the anti-Mafia policies. J

887. Smith, Dwight C., Jr. SONS OF THE GODFATHER: "MAFIA" IN CONTEMPORARY FICTION. *Italian Americana 1976 2(2): 190-207.* Discusses popular literature since Mario Puzo's *The Godfather* (1969) popularized Mafia-plot novels; discusses basic plot lines and the image of Italians in the works. Photo, 2 tables, 11 notes.

888. Soria, Regina. EARLY ITALIAN SCULPTORS IN THE UNITED STATES. *Italian Americana 1976 2(2): 170-189.* Chronicles the presence of Italian sculptors in the United States, 1776-1876, highlighting Giuseppe Ceracchi, Enrico Causici, Vittorio Alfieri, Antonio Capellano, Giuseppe Franzoni, and Giovanni Andrei. 6 photos, reproduction, 18 notes.

889. Stefanon, Gualtiero. LE FIGURE DELLA LEGGENDA [Legendary figure]. *Riv. Militare [Italy] 1976 99(4): 58-70.* John Martin (Giovanni Martini) (ca. 1850's-1900's), former soldier of Garibaldi, fought in the US Army under George A. Custer against Indians in the 1870's; details those wars.

890. Stout, Robert Joe. CAN'T YOU SEE THAT WE'RE HOME? *Westways 1977 69(11): 24-27.* Discusses the immigration of Italians to the San Francisco area of California, 1890-1977.

891. Traldi, Alberto. LA TEMATICA DELL'EMIGRAZIONE NELLA NARRATIVA ITALO-AMERICANA [The theme of emigration in Italian-American narrative]. *Comunità [Italy] 1976 30(176): 245-272.* Examines the major novels written by Italian Americans on Italian emigrants and their descendants in the 20th century, and analyzes the responses in the United States and Italy to this narrative.

892. Vecoli, Rudolph J. THE COMING OF AGE OF ITALIAN AMERICANS: 1945-1974. *Ethnicity 1978 5(2): 119-147.* About two thirds of America's Italian immigrants arrived during 1900-20. Having little education or training, most of them became unskilled laborers heavily concentrated in the cities. The 1970 census revealed, however, that of the second generation under 45 had achieved a level of education approaching the national average. Urban "Little Italies," strongholds of the Italian-American working class, have nonetheless shown exceptional vitality, although they have retreated in places before the advance of Blacks and Puerto Ricans. Italian Americans have tended strongly to emphasize the family at the expense of the Church, fraternal societies, and politics. Discusses anti-Italian prejudice and the prospects for the survival of Italian-American consciousness. Based on US census data and secondary sources; graph, 2 fig., 31 notes. L. W. Van Wyk

893. Vecoli, Rudolph J. CULT AND OCCULT IN ITALIAN-AMERICAN CULTURE: THE PERSISTENCE OF A RELIGIOUS HERITAGE. Miller, Randall M. and Marzik, Thomas D., ed. *Immigrants and Religion in Urban America* (Philadelphia: Temple U. Pr., 1977): 25-47. The *contadini* (peasants) of southern Italy constituted the majority of Italian immigrants to America in the late 19th century. Their folk religion of magical rituals and pagan beliefs comforted them in the New World but convinced many Protestants and Catholics alike that Italian Americans were not true Christians. Rising to their defense, Father Aurelio Palmieri and others called for assimilation through ethnic parishes and Italian priests. The Catholic Church became one of the major "Americanizing" agents by imposing the model of the "good American Catholic." But at the same time, through bureaucratization and rationalization, it created an irreparable secularization and scarred "man's capacity for religious faith." 44 notes. S. Robitaille

894. Vecoli, Rudolph J. EMIGRATI ITALIANI E MOVIMENTO OPERAIO NEGLI USA [Italian immigrants and the workers' movement in the United States]. *Movimento Operaio e Socialista [Italy] 1976 22(1-2): 153-167.* The history of Italian Americans in the American labor movement either has been ignored totally or has represented the Italian worker as a scab or the cause of salary reductions. Attracted by hopes of saving money, Italians from Central and Southern Italy flocked to America from about 1880. Many came only for brief periods and, because they did not speak English, understand American customs, or belong to the unions, found themselves isolated and often with the worst jobs. Without formal means to protest their situation, they often staged spontaneous strikes. These had no lasting effects, but definitely prove the fallacy of the stereotypical submissive Italian worker. After 1900, Italian radicals played organizational roles in the Industrial Workers of the World and the formation of the garment workers' unions. M. T. Wilson

895. Vecoli, Rudolph. THE ITALIAN AMERICANS. *Center Mag. 1974 7(4): 31-43.* Describes characteristics of Italian Americans: immigration, residence patterns, social mobility, organizations, discrimination, stereotypes, political power. One of six working papers presented at a joint conference of Center Fellows and leaders of the Immigration History Society on ethnicity today. S

896. Ventimiglia, Peter James. THROUGH OTHERS' EYES: THE IMAGE OF THE ITALIAN-AMERICAN IN MODERN DRAMA. *Italian Americana 1976 2(2): 228-239.* Examines the use of stereotypes

in American drama pertaining to the portrayal of Italian Americans, 1924-70's.

897. Wolfe, Margaret Ripley.   ALIENS IN SOUTHERN AP-PALACHIA, 1900-1920: THE ITALIAN EXPERIENCE IN WISE COUNTY, VIRGINIA.   *Virginia Mag. of Hist. and Biog. 1979 87(4): 455-472.* Discusses the padrone recruitment of immigrant labor for industrial activities in western Virginia, and the adjustment process of the workers to their new environment. The Stonega Company, and like northern financed coal and iron miners, brought in and paternalistically cared for many Italian laborers and their families. They could not retain them. Railroad construction was a similar livelihood, but short term and less humane. Ironically many operatives, alienated from their "native" neighbors, found themselves enmeshed in "backward" social situations similar to those in their former land. 36 notes.   P. J. Woehrmann

898. —. [FAMILY STRUCTURE IN CONFRONTATION WITH SOCIAL CHANGE].   *J. of Social Hist. 1974 7(4): 406-459.*
Yans-McLaughlin, Virginia.   A FLEXIBLE TRADITION: SOUTH ITALIAN IMMIGRANTS CONFRONT A NEW YORK EX-PERIENCE,   *pp. 429-445.* Examines the way in which Italian immigrants transformed canning factories into communities where Old World social attitudes and behavior could continue and where kinship ties operated to maintain them. "Modern economic institutions were quite capable of incorporating such traditional needs." 61 notes.
Harris, Alice Kessler.   COMMENTS ON THE YANS-MCLAUGH-LIN AND DAVIDOFF PAPERS,   *pp. 446-451.* The papers [including one by Leonore Davidoff on servants and wives in Victorian and Edwardian England, pp. 406-428] raise basic questions but do not go far enough in a number of questions or exploration of implications. 3 notes.
Tilly, Louise A.   COMMENTS ON THE YANS-MCLAUGHLIN AND DAVIDOFF PAPERS,   *pp. 452-459.* Familial rather than individualist values appear to be dominant. Consciousness of oppression did not come until individualist values replaced familial. We must view families in terms of their values, not ours. 18 notes.
                                                                    R. V. Ritter

899. —. ITALIAN AMERICANS.   Sowell, Thomas, ed. *Essays and Data on American Ethnic Groups* (Washington, D.C.: Urban Inst. Pr., 1978): 340-343. Statistics on Italian Americans' personal income distribution by sex; family income distribution; occupational distribution by sex; and education by age. From US Bureau of the Census, *Current Population Reports,* Series P-20, Nos. 221, 249; 3 tables.   K. A. Talley

Jewish

General

900. Alter, Robert.   MANNERS & THE JEWISH INTELLEC-TUAL.   *Commentary 1975 60(2): 58-64.* Reviews the revolutionary tradition in Jewish intellectual thought as examined by John Murray Cuddihy in *The Ordeal of Civility: Freud, Marx, Lévi-Strauss, and the Jewish Struggle with Modernity* (New York: Basic Books, 1974).   S

901. Alter, Robert.   WHAT JEWISH STUDIES CAN DO.   *Commentary 1974 58(4): 71-77.* Discusses the place of Jewish studies in American colleges and universities during the 1960's and 70's.   S

902. Aristides.   A LITERARY MAFIA?   *Am. Scholar 1975 44(2): 182-194.* Younger, less well-situated writers claim that there is a literary mafia, located in New York, predominantly Jewish, and largely comprised of older men and women, who control literature, divide up the spoils of fame, money, and power, and take care of their own. Its true seats of power are a handful of magazines. Discusses in detail *The End of Intelligent Writing*, by Richard Kostelanetz. Concludes that the notion of a literary mafia ignores all the difficult issues.
                                                                    E. P. Stickney

903. Asher, Robert.   JEWISH UNIONS AND THE AMERICAN FEDERATION OF LABOR POWER STRUCTURE 1903-1935.   *Am. Jewish Hist. Q. 1976 65(3): 215-227.* Jewish unions, those with a substantial number of Jewish members and led by Jewish officers, until the 1930's were largely in, but not of, the mainstream of the American labor movement. Recognizing their differences with the AFL, the Jewish unions cooperated with the AFL when they could, but went their own way politically in their attempt to build a welfare state through union institutions and trade agreements with employers. By the late 1920's the Jewish unions, especially the International Ladies' Garment Workers' Union, had drifted slowly to the right and the American Federation of Labor had moved toward the left, so that the Amalgamated Clothing Workers of America could be admitted into the AFL, and the ILGWU could be allowed into the AFL power structure (executive council and resolutions committee). The accomplishments of the New Deal Democratic Party accelerated this process. 23 notes.   F. Rosenthal

904. Auerbach, Jerold S.   FROM RAGS TO ROBES: THE LEGAL PROFESSION, SOCIAL MOBILITY AND THE AMERICAN JEW-ISH EXPERIENCE.   *Am. Jewish Hist. Q. 1976 65(2): 249-284.* The experiences of Jewish lawyers since 1900 illuminate the struggle for success within a profession whose elite members preferred to ostracize or exclude them. Retraces the route from "ghetto shyster and collection lawyer" to Wall Street partner, Federal and Supreme Court Justice, and government lawyer ever since the New Deal. As a result, in the 1970's Jewish lawyers have often become the spokesmen for the establishment against more recent "minorities" and the defenders of professionalism. At the same time, Jews still are overrepresented on local and national boards of civil rights organizations, to say nothing of the records of the four Jewish Supreme Court Justices. 79 notes.   F. Rosenthal

905. Baron, Salo W.   INTRODUCTION: REFLECTIONS ON THE ACHIEVEMENTS AND PROSPECTS OF *JEWISH SOCIAL STUD-IES.*   *Jewish Social Studies 1979 41(1): 1-8.* The first issue of *Jewish Social Studies* was published in January 1939 under Managing Editor Koppel S. Pinson, with the Conference on Jewish Relatins providing financial and scholarly support. The journal was issued to some extent to provide a forum for examination of contemporary and historical Jewish issues in a manner different from other Jewish scholarly journals, emphasizing ancient and medieval Biblical exegesis. Those connected with the journal and with the conference engaged in important bibliographical work on Jewish studies published in the journal and, after World War II, aided in the tracing and recovery of important Jewish artifacts lost during the Holocaust. Recently a monograph series has been started under the auspices of the journal. Based on personal observation and involvement.
                                                                    N. Lederer

906. Barron, Jerome A.   LIBERTY OR EQUALITY?   *Rhode Island Jewish Hist. Notes 1975 7(1): 5-11.* Discusses liberty and equality for Jews, centering on the court case which Marco De Funis brought against a Washington law school, charging that he had been discriminated against when less-qualified applicants were admitted because of their other-minority status.

907. Ben-Amos, Dan.   THE "MYTH" OF JEWISH HUMOR.   *Western Folklore 1973 32(2): 112-131.* Discusses current conceptions of Jewish humor as "self-critical" and attributes this attitude to Freud and other psychoanalysts. After examining Jewish humor, the author concludes that "joking in Jewish society does not involve mocking of self either directly or indirectly." Based on primary and secondary sources; 42 notes.   S. L. Myres

908. Benkin, Richard L.   ETHNICITY AND ORGANIZATION: JEWISH COMMUNITIES IN EASTERN EUROPE AND THE UNITED STATES.   *Sociol. Q. 1978 19(4): 614-625.* In most essential respects, the immigrant communities of American Jews (and the total American Jewish community) were a direct continuation of those which appeared in Eastern Europe prior to 1914. The author reconstructs the sociohistorical environment in which they appeared. The extensive communal organization which characterized both settings actually served the interests of societal demands. These institutions provided needed services to the community, but they also supported the out-group's status, as determined by the larger society. A clear picture emerges of the impact on the collective Jewish, and individual Jew's, adaptation to society

within a highly developed and organized community. Based on archives, government reports, and texts.   J

909. Berger, Graenum. AMERICAN JEWISH COMMUNAL SERVICE 1776-1976: FROM TRADITIONAL SELF-HELP TO INCREASING DEPENDENCE ON GOVERNMENT SUPPORT. *Jewish Social Studies 1976 38(3-4): 225-246.* The Jewish tradition of communal self-help was imported to America with the arrival of the first Jewish immigrants; it contributed to the rise of private, voluntary, sectarian social welfare agencies amid the American Jewish community. Jews assumed a responsibility to help their fellows in times of trouble in a way similar to that undertaken by various Christian denominations. With the necessity for increased governmental intervention in the social welfare area since the Depression of the 1930's, Jewish agencies have assumed a semiofficial, quasigovernmental status with increasingly nonsectarian emphases in their social services.   N. Lederer

910. Bergman, Elihu. THE AMERICAN JEWISH POPULATION EROSION. *Midstream 1977 23(8): 9-19.* Through a birth rate below replacement levels, assimilation (mainly through intermarriage), and lack of significant immigration, the Jewish population of the United States has declined since 1970, so that by the year 2076 this community, which once numbered six million, is likely to amount to no more than 944,000; such a drastic reduction would be, among other things, a disaster for Israel, which has received much support from American Jewry.

911. Best, Gary Dean. JACOB H. SCHIFF'S GALVESTON MOVEMENT: AN EXPERIMENT IN IMMIGRANT DEFLECTION, 1907-1914. *Am. Jewish Arch. 1978 30(1): 43-79.* Although the career of Jacob H. Schiff is usually associated with the world of high finance, he was also involved with a plan to send hundreds of thousands of immigrant Jews into the interior regions of the United States and Canada and away from the congested cities of America's east coast. The city of Galveston, Texas, would serve as the departure point for many of these Jews. The Galveston Plan, as it came to be known, necessitated complex political and financial maneuverings on the parts of Schiff, the American immigration authorities, and the English Territorialist, Israel Zangwill.   J

912. Blu, Karen I. VARIETIES OF ETHNIC IDENTITY: ANGLO-SAXONS, BLACKS, INDIANS, AND JEWS IN A SOUTHERN COUNTY. *Ethnicity 1977 4(3): 263-286.* Analyzes concepts of group identity in Robeson County, South Carolina, 1967-68, finding that each group studied (Negroes, Lumbee Indians, and Jews) identifies itself according to its relations to other minority-ethnic groups, the self-concept of each group, and stereotypes held by the greater Anglo-Saxon culture. Examines the bases for stereotypes and dimensions involved: concept of image, kind and depth of belief in the image, consensus on the image within outside social structure, and action related to the image.   G. A. Hewlett

913. Bluestein, Gene. *PORTNOY'S COMPLAINT*: THE JEW AS AMERICAN. *Can. R. of Am. Studies 1976 7(1): 66-76.* Cites reasons why a 1969 novel, *Portnoy's Complaint* by Philip Roth, is likely to attain critical recognition and high stature in the American literary tradition. Roth candidly treated themes and used language that long had been taboo in Jewish-American literature.   H. T. Lovin

914. Bradbury, Malcolm. SAUL BELLOW AND THE NOBEL PRIZE. *J. of Am. Studies [Great Britain] 1977 11(1): 3-12.* Analyzes the novels and ideas of Saul Bellow (b. 1915) that earned him the 1976 Nobel Prize in literature. Earlier American recipients of that prize usually experienced a decline in their work and reputations following its receipt. Bellow may escape these troubles because he clearly is "a novelist of an urban, alien, stressed world" who has never "shirked" that world's "mass and pressure." 12 notes.   H. T. Lovin

915. Brandes, Joseph. FROM SWEATSHOP TO STABILITY: JEWISH LABOR BETWEEN TWO WORLD WARS. *Yivo Ann. of Jewish Social Sci. 1976 (16): 1-149.* Traces the growth of the Jewish labor movement from its inception, with particular emphasis on the period between World War I and World War II. Stresses the uniqueness of the Jewish labor movement and puts particular emphasis on the growth of the Jewish labor movement within the garment industry. Describes the roles of such notable labor leaders as David Dubinsky and Sidney Hillquit. Particular

stress is put on the International Ladies' Garment Workers' and the United Hebrew Trades' role in the development of Jewish labor in the 1920's-30's.   R. J. Wechman

916. Busi, Frederick. THE DEFUNIS CASE REVEALS QUOTA PRACTICES IN U.S. HIGHER EDUCATION. *Patterns of Prejudice [Great Britain] 1974 8(4): 21-26.* Cites the legal case (1974) of Marco DeFunis, a Sephardic Jew who was denied admission to the graduate school of the University of Washington because he was not considered a member of a minority group.

917. Caditz, Judith. JEWISH LIBERALS IN TRANSITION: AMBIVALENCE TOWARD ETHNIC INTEGRATION. *Sociol. and Social Res. 1975 59(3): 274-287.* White liberals believing in ethnic integration were questioned on busing in schools, entrance of blacks into their occupations, blacks entering predominantly white neighborhoods, quotas in colleges, apartment rentals to blacks, and hiring blacks. The Jewish portion of the sample responded to questions on black anti-Semitism. These interracial situations thrust Jewish liberals more often than their non-Jewish counterparts into belief dilemmas and role conflicts that they resolved by mechanisms redefining liberal roles. Although the sample is representative of only the upper range of statuses among Jews and non-Jews, it permits rigorous test of an ethnic identification hypothesis among those most committed to racial liberalism.   J

918. Carmichael, Joel. A JEWISH DISEASE. *Midstream 1975 21(5): 52-57.* The disease referred to in this article is the Jews' tendency to self-alienation, which expresses itself for instance in Noam Chomsky's anti-Israel stance, which sacrifices Jewish identity for "humanity."

919. Chiel, Arthur A. GEORGE ALEXANDER KOHUT AND THE JUDAICA COLLECTION IN THE YALE LIBRARY. *Yale U. Lib. Gazette 1979 53(4): 202-210.* George Alexander Kohut's (1874-1933) love for books was inspired by the scholarship of his father, Rabbi Alexander Kohut. The Hebraic bibliophile's interest in Yale was first expressed in an editorial published in the *Jewish Exponent* in November 1901; it culminated in the Alexander Kohut Memorial Collection of Judaica donated to Yale in 1915 by George Alexander Kohut. The original Kohut gift to Yale was supplemented by the establishment of a fellowship in 1919 and a later gift of Heinrich Heine material in 1930. 8 notes.   D. A. Yanchisin

920. Chyet, Stanley F. AMERICAN JEWISH LITERARY PRODUCTIVITY: A SELECTED BICENTENNIAL BIBLIOGRAPHY. *Studies in Biblio. and Booklore 1976 11(1/2): 5-24.* Presents a bibliography of anthologies of literature dealing with the works of Jewish writers in the United States, published in the 1950's-70's.

921. Cohen, Naomi W. PIONEERS OF AMERICAN JEWISH DEFENSE. *Am. Jewish Arch. 1977 29(2): 116-150.* In antebellum America, Jews did not enjoy the services of an organized, institutional response to anti-Jewish outrages both at home and abroad. Instead, protests against anti-Semitism and other anti-Jewish activities were delivered by three American Jewish periodicals of the time—*The Occident, The Asmonean,* and *The Israelite.* Analyzes the methods employed by these pioneers of American Jewish defense.   J

922. Cohen, Naomi W. SCHOOLS, RELIGION, AND GOVERNMENT: RECENT AMERICAN JEWISH OPINIONS. *Michael: On the Hist. of the Jews in the Diaspora [Israel] 1975 3: 340-392.* Reproduces 11 documents reflecting American Jewish views on the principle of separation of church and state with regard to state-supported education. On the issue of keeping religion out of public schools, American Jewish organizations energetically supported separation, although Jews in smaller communities may have been inhibited in expressing such an opinion. But on the issue of public aid to church schools the American Jewish consensus broke down. Orthodox and even non-Orthodox circles began to support such aid, long demanded by Catholic groups, as the Jewish day-school movement grew. Primary and secondary sources; 24 notes.   T. Sassoon

923. Cox, Oliver C. JEWISH SELF-INTEREST IN "BLACK PLURALISM." *Sociol. Q. 1974 15(2): 183-198.* From time immemorial Jewish tribal exclusiveness among dominant societal groups has resulted

in various forms of conflict determined by the social situation. The critical force involved has been the group's peculiar resistance to social assimilation. Different social systems react differently to the persistence of this trait. The caste system of India, for example, would hardly notice it. But capitalist culture, which originated in the European medieval city, has constantly resisted it; that culture is basically assimilationist. American Negroes, in their opposition to racism have relied mainly on the ideology of assimilation. These two divergent tendencies have come into collision recently.   J

924. Cripps, Thomas. THE MOVIE JEW AS AN IMAGE OF AS-SIMILATIONISM. *J. of Popular Film 1975 4(3): 190-207.* Discusses ethnic stereotypes in early cinema (1900's-20's) dealing specifically with immigrants and Jews.

925. Davis, Moshe. FROM THE VANTAGE OF JERUSALEM. *Am. Jewish Hist. Q. 1974 63(4): 313-333.* Compares the Jewish studies program in Jerusalem to that which exists in the United States. One of nine related articles in this issue.   S

926. Davis, Perry. CORRUPTION IN JEWISH LIFE. *Present Tense 1978 5(2): 19-24.* Investigates the growth of "white-collar" crime within the Jewish community, and opposition to such crimes, 1969-78.

927. DeMartini, Joseph R. STUDENT ACTIVISTS OF THE 1930S AND 1960S: A COMPARISON OF THE SOCIAL BASE OF TWO STUDENT MOVEMENTS. *Youth and Soc. 1975 6(4): 395-422.* Student activists at the University of Illinois in the 1930's were generally from professional families, urban, Jewish, arts and sciences majors, and unlikely to belong to campus organizations. Thus their social background was very similar to that of student activists of the 1960's. However, they differ from those of the 1960's in having followed the lead of parent political groups, developed a greater conservatism during their life as students, and in lacking the type and degree of cultural alienation of their later counterparts. Based on University of Illinois archives; primary and secondary sources; 9 tables, 4 notes, biblio.   J. H. Sweetland

928. Dershowitz, Alan M.; Silverglate, Harvey A.; and Baker, Jeanne. THE JDL MURDER CASE: "THE INFORMER WAS OUR OWN CLIENT." *Civil Liberties R. 1976 3(1): 43-60.* Civil rights questions were raised by the trial of Sheldon Seigel. Seigel, along with other members of the Jewish Defense League, was indicted for murder in the bombing of Sol Hurok's office in New York City. The authors, Seigel's lawyers, learned that Seigel was a government informer after they accepted his case. Subsequently, their focus on the 1972-73 case changed to investigating the legal and moral limits "of governmental intervention to prevent and prosecute the most serious kinds of crime," and to protecting the civil rights of informers.   S

929. Dester, Chester McArthur. INTRODUCTION. *Am. Jewish Hist. Q. 1976 66(1): 3-9.* This Bicentennial issue explores different aspects of the role that American Jewish business enterprise has played in the economy of the United States. The eight monographs range from essays on colonial trade and mid-19th century financiers to Neiman-Marcus and Jewish businesswomen of the past and present.   F. Rosenthal

930. Dinnerstein, Leonard. SOUTHERN JEWRY AND THE DE-SEGREGATION CRISIS, 1954-1970. *Am. Jewish Hist. Q. 1973 62(3): 231-241.* Despite the participation of many Jews in the civil rights movement, the level of commitment varied widely. Southern Jews, many of them merchants dependent upon the goodwill of their neighbors, were circumspect in their allegiance to equal rights, except in a few areas like Atlanta and among some college groups. In the early 1960's, perhaps six to ten rabbis in the South worked for the cause, including Jacob Rothschild, Emmet Frank, Perry Nussbaum, and Charles Mantninband. Based on correspondence of southern rabbis at the American Jewish Archives; 32 notes.   F. Rosenthal

931. Dreier, Peter and Porter, Jack Nusan. JEWISH RADICALISM IN TRANSITION. *Society 1975 12(2): 34-43.* Chronicles the trend toward radical politics in theology, focusing on Jewish radicalism as a political and social indicator.   S

932. Dreier, Peter. POLITICAL PLURALISM AND JEWISH LIB-ERALISM: BEYOND THE CLICHES. *J. of Ethnic Studies 1976 4(3): 85-94.* Reviews Henry L. Feingold's *Zion in America: The Jewish Experience from Colonial Times to the Present*, and Stephen D. Isaacs' *Jews and American Politics*. The first is "solid social history, perhaps the most comprehensive and readable one-volume history of American Jewry to date," while Isaacs' work is an excellent documentation of political roles and behavior, but "weak on analysis and interpretation." The overall influence of the Jewish lobby and its control over American policy is overestimated. Assessing Jewish political behavior by focusing solely on cultural and psychological factors is of dubious merit. Jewish support for liberal politics and the Welfare State stems from the nature of their embourgeoisement: professional Jews rely on state spending to maintain occupational opportunities, while Jewish businessmen favor policies stimulating aggregate consumer demand. A cultural, or consensus, theory is an inadequate explanation which encourages "the myths of group pluralism and ethnic self-interest over class politics," and the current romanticization of the white ethnic obscures the dynamics of class society. Note.
G. J. Bobango

933. Eakin, Paul John. ALFRED KAZIN'S BRIDGE TO AMER-ICA. *South Atlantic Q. 1978 77(1): 39-53.* Alfred Kazin, Brooklyn-born Jew and author, has written three autobiographical works which underscore his belief in the continuities between private experience and a larger social reality. The rhythms of his Brooklyn experience found their way into *A Walker in the City* (1951), *On Native Grounds* (1956) and *Starting Out in the Thirties* (1965). All of his works have been devoted to the complex fate of the American artist, his problematical relation to his native land, and the working out of this common theme. Thus any account of Kazin's sense of America necessarily focuses on his autobiographies. Like Van Wyck Brooks, he believed that writers must be understood in relation to their native culture and its past. Based on Kazin's writings and criticism of his works; 18 notes.
H. M. Parker, Jr.

934. Edgar, Irving I. PRESIDENT'S ANNUAL REPORT, JUNE 14, 1973. *Michigan Jewish Hist. 1974 14(1): 3-6.* Report of the 14 Annual Meeting of the Jewish Historical Society of Michigan.   S

935. Eisendrath, Maurice N. THE UNION OF AMERICAN HE-BREW CONGREGATIONS: CENTENNIAL REFLECTIONS. *Am. Jewish Hist. Q. 1973 63(2): 138-159.* Evaluates the 100-year existence of the Union of American Hebrew Congregations. From a small nucleus of 28 congregations it grew to become the authoritative spokesman for American Reform Judaism and a vital participant in virtually all cooperative Jewish concerns. Describes some alternative modes for synagogues of the future.   F. Rosenthal

936. Elazar, Daniel J. CONTEMPORARY JEWISH CIVILIZA-TION ON THE AMERICAN CAMPUS: RESEARCH AND TEACHING: INTRODUCTION. *Am. Jewish Hist. Q. 1974 63(4): 311-312.* Introduces a colloquium on the teaching of contemporary Jewish civilization held at the annual meeting of the Association for Jewish Studies, 1972.   S

937. Elazar, Daniel J. THE PLACE OF JEWISH POLITICAL STUDIES ON THE CAMPUS. *Am. Jewish Hist. Q. 1974 63(4): 334-339.* Discusses the development of Jewish political studies as one facet of Jewish studies programs. One of nine related articles in this issue.   S

938. Ellman, Yisrael. THE ETHNIC AWAKENING IN THE UNITED STATES AND ITS INFLUENCE ON JEWS. *Ethnicity 1977 4(2): 133-155.* Ethnic consciousness, awakened largely by the emerging racial consciousness among American blacks, is examined as a largely economic force in social and occupational mobility among white ethnic groups. Statistics show a disproportionately high representation of Jews in high pay-high prestige positions in the United States. Statistics correspondingly show a greater fear among Jewish groups of affirmative action, which they view as a quota system against admission of Jews to elite positions in the social structure. Religiosity has been supplanted by ethnicity among Jewish groups as a result, and growing concern with poor Jews and Zionism is a reflection of Jewish response to possible exclusion.
G. A. Hewlett

939. Endelman, Judith E. JUDAICA AMERICANA. *Am. Jewish Hist. Q. 1974 64(1): 55-68.* Annotated bibliography of monographic and periodical literature published since 1960 and received in the library of the American Jewish Historical Society. Twelve topical headings are employed for this annotation (bibliography, biography, cultural life, etc.). F. Rosenthal

940. Endelman, Judith E. JUDAICA AMERICANA. *Am. Jewish Hist. Q. 1975 64(3): 245-257.* An annotated bibliography of monographic and periodical literature published since 1960 and received in the library of the American Jewish Historical Society. F. Rosenthal

941. Endelman, Judith E. JUDAICA AMERICANA. *Am. Jewish Hist. Q. 1975 64(4): 344-357.* An annotated bibliography of monographic and periodical literature published since 1960 and received in the library of the American Jewish Historical Society. F. Rosenthal

942. Erens, Patricia. GANGSTERS, VAMPIRES, AND J.A.P.'S: THE JEW SURFACES IN AMERICAN MOVIES. *J. of Popular Film 1975 4(3): 208-222.* Discusses the way Jews have been portrayed in recent American films which have done much to dispel earlier stereotypes (1970's).

943. Faur, José. INTRODUCING THE MATERIALS OF SEPHARDIC CULTURE TO CONTEMPORARY JEWISH STUDIES. *Am. Jewish Hist. Q. 1974 63(4): 340-349.* Discusses the teaching of Sephardic culture and intellectual tradition; one of nine related articles in this issue. S

944. Fein, Leonard J. LIBERALISM AND AMERICAN JEWS. *Midstream 1973 19(8): 3-18.*

945. Fein, Leonard J. THINKING ABOUT QUOTAS. *Midstream 1973 19(3): 13-17.* Jews should support quotas to end discrimination. S

946. Fine, David M. ABRAHAM CAHAN, STEPHEN CRANE AND THE ROMANTIC TENEMENT TALE OF THE NINETIES. *Am. Studies (Lawrence, KS) 1973 14(1): 95-108.* By the 1890's city slums had a proven marketability in American fiction. Reform journalism became fiction, which offered a radical departure from the genteel, Victorian drawing room. The result was a mixture of cynicism and sentimentality, with all the attention devoted to the moral implications of slum conditions. For Crane and Cahan, however, poverty was not ennobling —a defiance of the romantic tenement tale. This proved uncomfortable to genteel audiences. Based on primary and secondary sources; 21 notes. J. Andrew

947. Fine, David M. ATTITUDES TOWARD ACCULTURATION IN THE ENGLISH FICTION OF THE JEWISH IMMIGRANT, 1900-1917. *Am. Jewish Hist. Q. 1973 63(1): 45-56.* Most immigrant novelists, such as Elias Tobenkin, Ezra Brudno, and Edward Steiner, regarded assimilation and accommodation with the dominant culture as the true expression of "Americanization" or the melting pot. In their novels the immigrant protagonist achieves acceptance and fulfillment by marriage to a gentile girl. Sidney Nyburg's *The Chosen People* (1917) and Abraham Cahan's *The Rise of David Levinsky* (1917) probe the shallowness of that situation. In both books the hero meets loneliness, ennui, and guilt at the end of the American dream because outward success by denial of the past produces only emptiness. Old World values and New World experience did not yet produce a symbiosis of the kind suggested by Horace Kallen's philosophy of pluralism. F. Rosenthal

948. Fisher, Alan. CONTINUITY AND EROSION OF JEWISH LIBERALISM. *Am. Jewish Hist. Q. 1976 65(2): 322-348.* Attempts to document the attitudinal changes of American Jews by examining selected relevant voting studies and opinion polls over the last 20 years. Yet, if the data is trustworthy, continuity of Jewish liberalism is more deep-seated than its erosion. In attitudes toward integration, equal rights, welfare, and national health care, Jews are more liberal than they were in the 1950's; as to marijuana, abortion, and pollution, differences with non-Jews are considerable. 29 notes, 14 tables. F. Rosenthal

949. Fisher, Alan M. REALIGNMENT OF THE JEWISH VOTE? *Pol. Sci. Q. 1979 94(1): 97-116.* Tests some recent perceptions of party realignment among American Jews by examining different data sources for party affiliation and voting in national and local elections. He finds continued support among Jews for Democrats and a relatively constant difference with the non-Jewish vote for the last 30 years.

950. Fisher, Alan M. WHERE IS THE NEW JEWISH CONSERVATISM? *Society 1979 16(4): 5, 15-18.* Examines sociopolitical attitudes of US Jews, 1969-79, and concludes that their alleged growing conservatism is largely a myth.

951. Fishman, Joshua A.; Mosse, George L.; and Silberstein, Laurence J. DISCUSSANTS. *Am. Jewish Hist. Q. 1974 63(4): 369-378.* Discussion on the relationship between Jewish studies and existing academic departments. One of nine related articles in this issue. S

952. Foner, Philip S. BLACK-JEWISH RELATIONS IN THE OPENING YEARS OF THE TWENTIETH CENTURY. *Phylon 1975 36(4): 359-367.* Certain well-focused events in the early 20th century forced blacks to reconsider the view they had long entertained that Jews, who also had felt the sting of prejudice, were less antiblack than other Americans. The black press reacted bitterly to Jewish involvement in efforts to disenfranchise black voters in Maryland and to the indifference of the Jewish community toward racial discrimination once they had achieved greater acceptance for their own community. Based on newspaper accounts and secondary sources; 43 notes. K. C. Snow

953. Forster, Arnold. THE ANTI-DEFAMATION LEAGUE. *Wiener Lib. Bull. [Great Britain] 1975 28(33/34): 52-58.* Describes the aims and work of the American Jewish defense organization, the Anti-Defamation League of B'nai B'rith (ADL), established in 1913 to stop the defamation of the Jewish people and to work to end discrimination against all citizens. To the chief (and continuing) American concern of the ADL, the exposure of racism and bigotry, the energies of the ADL and of other Jewish service organizations now have to be marshalled to defend the validity of the Jewish claim to Israel against attacks from Arab and pro-Arab quarters. J. P. Fox

954. Fox, Marvin. PHILOSOPHY AND CONTEMPORARY JEWISH STUDIES. *Am. Jewish Hist. Q. 1974 63(4): 350-355.* Philosophy, as taught in the university, does not include Jewish philosophy; therefore Jewish studies should encompass it. One of nine related articles in this issue. S

955. Franck, Isaac. THE AMERICAN JEWISH EXPERIENCE. *Midstream 1976 22(3): 7-18.* Discusses the social history and culture of Jews in the United States from the 1950's-70's, emphasizing current Jewish concern about Israel, education, civil rights and ethnic intermarriage.

956. Frankel, Jonathan. THE JEWISH SOCIALISTS AND THE AMERICAN JEWISH CONGRESS MOVEMENT. *Yivo Ann. of Jewish Social Sci. 1976 (16): 202-341.* Studies the movement for an American Jewish Congress in the years 1914-18. Takes the position that this was essentially a movement of the nationalist forces in Jewish politics. Shows how it was initiated to a large extent by the nationalist wing of the socialist movement and how the American Jewish Committee with its philosophy of Americanization opposed the concept of a Jewish nationality and Jewish nationalism. R. J. Wechman

957. Friedmann, Thomas. BACK TO THE EDGES, THE CENTER WILL NOT HOLD: ONE REASON FOR THE EMERGENCE OF A NEW CONSCIOUSNESS IN AMERICAN JEWISH LITERATURE. *Am. Jewish Arch. 1978 30(2): 126-132.* American Jewish literature has usually been identified by its universalistic approach, where, according to the author, Jewish writers found it easier to write for all Americans "than to be Jewish writers for Jews." But the tide is turning with the current collapse of the "American [Jewish] dream." A new attitude has emerged within the discipline which reflects American Jewry's emphasis on self-protection and self-preservation. J

958. Gidwitz, Betsy. PROBLEMS OF ADJUSTMENT OF SOVIET JEWISH EMIGRES. *Soviet Jewish Affairs [Great Britain] 1976 6(1):*

27-42. Discusses problems of social and cultural assimilation of Soviet Jews emigrating to Israel and the United States, 1967-70's, including their difficulties in obtaining employment.

959. Gitelle, Tobey B. PRELIMINARY LIST AND SUBJECT INDEX OF *JEWISH SOCIAL STUDIES*, 1964 THROUGH 1978. *Jewish Social Studies 1979 41(1): 9-22.* Lists every article, conference report, review article, communication, and obituary published in *Jewish Social Studies* during 1964-78. Excludes reviews and book notes. A total of 276 entries are sequentially numbered and arranged according to last name of author or other identifier within each of the above indicated groups. A subject index with cross references is included.

N. Lederer

960. Gitelman, Zvi. SOVIET JEWISH EMIGRANTS: WHY ARE THEY CHOOSING AMERICA? *Soviet Jewish Affairs [Great Britain] 1977 7(1): 31-46.* Fewer Soviet Jews are emigrating to Israel, and those who are attracted by the democratic image of the United States also originate in areas such as the Ukraine and the Russian Republic, where Zionism is relatively weak.

961. Glanz, David. AN INTERPRETATION OF THE JEWISH COUNTERCULTURE. *Jewish Social Studies 1977 39(1-2): 117-128.* A recent development among American Jewry has been the activist role of a minority of Jewish students in support of the state of Israel, agitation for the rights of Soviet Jewry, the position of women in Judaism, and the search for a Jewish self-identity through an exploration of Jewish belief and ritual. The creation of this Jewish counterculture was based partially on the severance of Jewish involvement from the civil rights movement and a subsequent return to work within the Jewish community. The impact of the Six Day War and the tangible threat to the continued existence of Israel embodied in the conflict also was a factor in generating Jewish self-consciousness among the young. Within the Jewish community the counterculture has been spurred along by the successful work of the United Synagogue Youth and the Ramah camp movements of Conservative Judaism. To some extent this new thrust represents a return of third-generation Jews to their roots.   N. Lederer

962. Glanz, Rudolf. SOME REMARKS ON JEWISH LABOR AND AMERICAN PUBLIC OPINION IN THE PRE-WORLD WAR I ERA. *Yivo Ann. of Jewish Social Sci. 1976 (16): 178-202.* Shows how the Jewish labor movement influenced American and Jewish American public opinion about the popular conception of a Jew and how it influenced the entire American labor movement.   R. J. Wechman

963. Glanz, Rudolf. THE SPREAD OF JEWISH COMMUNITIES THROUGH AMERICA BEFORE THE CIVIL WAR. *Yivo Ann. of Jewish Social Sci. 1974 (15): 7-45.* Explores the spread of Jewish communities, especially the German-Jews, in the antebellum period. Studies the effects of American conditions on the founding of Jewish communities, quoting extensively from settlers' memoirs, and discussing the locations and economic determinants on the spread of the Jewish population. 239 notes.   R. J. Wechman

964. Glazer, Nathan. THE EXPOSED AMERICAN JEW. *Commentary 1975 59(6): 25-30.* "American Jews . . . are more vulnerable because they have been more fortunate than some other groups, and because they must ask from their fellow citizens heavy support for [Israel]."   S

965. Glickstein, Gary A. RELIGION AND THE JEWISH NEW LEFT: 1960 TO DATE. *Am. Jewish Arch. 1974 26(1): 23-30.* "A rising Jewish consciousness and an inability to adopt an anti-Israel stance have led many young Jewish radicals to break with the general New Left movement and form 'what could legitimately be called the Jewish New Left.' "   J

966. Golden, Harry. BICENTENNIAL OUTLOOK: JEWISH IMMIGRANT TODAY, AMERICAN TOMORROW. *Hist. Preservation 1976 28(4): 30-35.* Jews are, "at present, more middle-class American than middle-class America. . . . America gave the Jews political freedom and economic freedom of opportunity. The Jews gave America complete devotion, as well as intellectual achievement in science, commerce, medicine, and the arts." 3 illus., 2 photos.

R. M. Frame, III

967. Goldstein, Judith. ETHNIC POLITICS: THE AMERICAN JEWISH COMMITTEE AS LOBBYIST, 1915-1917. *Am. Jewish Hist. Q. 1975 65(1): 36-58.* During 1915-17 the American Jewish Committee engaged in extensive lobbying with the executive and legislative branches of the federal government with respect to foreign relations with Russia and the restrictive literacy test for immigrants. Concern for the persecuted Jews of Russia was the prime reason for these activities.

F. Rosenthal

968. Gordon, Leonard. THE FRAGMENTATION OF LITERARY STEREOTYPES OF JEWS AND OF NEGROES AMONG COLLEGE STUDENTS. *Pacific Sociol. Rev. 1973 16(4): 411-425.*

969. Greenberg, Gershon. A GERMAN-JEWISH IMMIGRANT'S PERCEPTION OF AMERICA, 1853-54. *Am. Jewish Hist. Q. 1978 67(4): 307-341.* In 1857 a German-Jewish literary society published this anonymous report in German of experiences of a German Jew. The identity of that writer remains a mystery, but he seems to have been well-educated, both yeshivah and university, and of the upper class. The report is extremely critical of the New York City Jewry, charging them with hypocrisy, lack of charity, and pride. The report ridicules the newly formed order of B'nai B'rith as the Jewish version of the American love for secret societies. 46 notes.   F. Rosenthal

970. Greenberg, Gershon. THE HISTORICAL ORIGINS OF GOD AND MAN: SAMUEL HIRSCH'S LUXEMBOURG WRITINGS. *Leo Baeck Inst. Year Book [Great Britain] 1975 20: 129-148.* Samuel Hirsch (1815-89) is significant in modern Jewish history for transplanting Reform Judaism to America. While his American publications are journalistic and pragmatic, concentrating on man and society, his writings during his stay in Luxembourg, 1843-66, concentrate on the theological problem of man and God in history. The contiguity between time and eternity unfolds in history out of which reason and revelation emerge. This refocusing of Hirsch's attention explains his ability to concentrate on the human aspects of religion in America and sublimate his philosophy into the pragmatic world of Reform Judaism's future. 81 notes.

F. Rosenthal

971. Greenberg, Gershon. SAMUEL HIRSCH'S AMERICAN JUDAISM. *Am. Jewish Hist. Q. 1973 62(4): 362-382.* Samuel Hirsch (1815-89), who served as rabbi in Philadelphia 1866-89, wrote extensively on the meaning of Reform Judaism in America. In the nonideological and essentially nontheological atmosphere of the New World, he emphasized the sociohistorical factors in the evolution of Scripture and religion. His articles appeared in *Der Zeitgeist, Die Deborah,* and *The Jewish Times.* 47 notes.   F. Rosenthal

972. Greenberg, Gershon. THE SIGNIFICANCE OF AMERICA IN DAVID EINHORN'S CONCEPTION OF HISTORY. *Am. Jewish Hist. Q. 1973 63(2): 160-184.* Einhorn (1809-79) served several congregations in America during his last 24 years. He was a prolific writer who described the role of Israel in the inevitable progress of history. His interpretation of America as the land where history would culminate and the messianic redemption would come is unique. Based on primary and secondary sources; 61 notes.   F. Rosenthal

973. Griessman, B. Eugene. PHILOSEMITISM AND PROTESTANT FUNDAMENTALISM: THE UNLIKELY ZIONISTS. *Phylon 1976 37(3): 197-211.* "Puritan respect for the Old Testament provided a basis for treating those few Jews who dwelt in the New England colonies in a humane manner." Several of the colonial leaders believed that the American Indians were the Ten Lost Tribes of Israel. This myth stirred missionary activity for converting Indians. A pro-Semitic interpretation of the Abrahamic covenant (Genesis 12) is standard fare in fundamentalist churches. Generally, the conservative and fundamentalist denominations have supported Zionism. The Jewish missions affirm that Jews eventually will accept the Messiah and that it is the duty of Christians to convert Jews to Christianity. 49 notes.

E. P. Stickney

974. Gross, Barry. WHAT SHYLOCK FORGOT, OR MAKING IT AND LOSING IT IN AMERICA. *J. of Ethnic Studies 1974 2(3): 50-57.* Surveys Jewish American writers and major works since 1917 when Abraham Cahan's *Rise of David Levinsky* began the tradition of

"warning American Jews against the dangers of assimilation," and the evils of materialistic American values, while equating Jewishness with spirituality. The incompatibility of these two values was preached also in the early works of Henry Roth, Budd Schulberg, and Michael Gold. After World War II the pattern changed and the "failed successes" gave way to the anti-heroes of Saul Bellow's *The Victim* and Bernard Malamud's *The Assistant*, wherein "suffering, failure, defeat represent a moral victory" and help atone for the American Jews' guilt for not having really suffered along with European Jewry. The pattern today is "thinning out," and may have climaxed, with works such as Philip Roth's *Goodbye Columbus* and *Portnoy's Complaint*, the latter being called "a satire on the Jewish-American novel itself." In essence, though, the old values have life yet, "as Jewish youth now turns its back on its parents' Americanness!"
G. J. Bobango

975. Grunwald, Kurt. THREE CHAPTERS OF GERMAN-JEW-ISH BANKING HISTORY. *Leo Baeck Inst. Year Book [Great Britain] 1977 22: 191-208*. The combination of a relative lack of anti-Jewish prejudice and presence of material self-interest formed the basis of economic collaboration between the many German rulers and the Jews after 1648. Jews' ability to procure goods and services, dispose of war booty advantageously, and provide necessary funds made them indispensable to their masters. The history of early 19th-century commercial banking in the United States shows the great contributions of immigrants, mostly from southwestern Germany. Summarizes the banking history of Abraham S. Joseph (1827-92) of Michelstadt and his descendants in Germany and England. 3 illus., 40 notes.
F. Rosenthal

976. Hadda, Janet. DI HASHPAOH FUN AMERICA OIF DER YIDDISHER LITERATUR [The influence of America on Yiddish literature]. *Yivo Bleter 1973 44: 248-255*. In analyzing the influence of America upon the Yiddish writers the author discusses the role of the writer's experiences, his place of residence, and the varied literary influences. The journal *Shriften*, published in New York City during 1912-26, was a bridge between the literature of the new arrivals and those who already went to college in this country. In their writings Yiddish writers reflected their experiences in America. Based on primary sources.
B. Klein

977. Halevy, Zvi. WERE THE JEWISH IMMIGRANTS TO THE UNITED STATES REPRESENTATIVE OF RUSSIAN JEWS? *Int. Migration [Netherlands] 1978 16(2): 60-73*. Considers whether the Jews who immigrated to the United States at the beginning of the 20th century were representative of the Jewish population in Russia. Despite their great social mobility and attainments, the Jewish immigrants were far from being representative, because for the most part they belonged to socially inferior classes. The middle classes were barely represented.
S/J

978. Halpern, Ben. THE "QUOTA" ISSUE. *Midstream 1973 19(3): 3-12*. Criticizes the use of quotas to end discrimination.
S

979. Halpern, Ben. THE ROOTS OF AMERICAN JEWISH LIB-ERALISM. *Am. Jewish Hist. Q. 1976 65(2): 190-214*. Examines the European and American antecedents that made a devout and conventional liberalism the most respectable Jewish position in the United States during the 20th century. Unites two disparate strands in the history of Jewish political attitudes: 1) the truly traditional policy of reliance on the constituted authorities (in America, constitutionally liberal) and 2) the more recent 19th-century Western European traditions of strongly stressed national patriotism. Since the Holocaust and the founding of Israel, the fact of ultimate Jewish isolation and therefore solidarity has modified the traditional Liberalism. 26 notes.
F. Rosenthal

980. Halpern, Sheldon. JEWISH FOLKLORE: A NEW IMAGE. *J. of Popular Culture 1974 8(2): 338-341*. Review article prompted by *The Folklore of the Jews*, originally published in 1937, by Angelo S. Rappoport (Detroit: Singing Tree Pr., 1972) and *In Praise of the Baal Shem Tov*, translated and edited by Dan Ben-Amos and Jerome R. Mintz (Indiana U. Pr., 1970). Places both books within the historical context of their publication dates. Discusses the books' importance to an understanding of Jewish folklore and its relevance for modern Westernized Jews in the United States and elsewhere.
A. E. Wiederrecht

981. Handlin, Oscar. A TWENTY YEAR RETROSPECT OF AMERICAN JEWISH HISTORIOGRAPHY. *Am. Jewish Hist. Q. 1976 65(4): 295-309*. Compares his 1948 evaluation of writing of the American Jewish past with the progress made since then. Greater abundance of material and its availability coupled with professionalization of authors and the elimination of an apologetic approach has contributed to greater scholarship. Setting the Jewish experience in America in a comparative, often sociological relationship to the contemporary trends in other immigrant religions and community organizations leads to a better understanding of the story, even though the extent of leakage through intermarriage, conversion, and apathy has not yet been assessed. The history of American anti-Semitism, 1900-40, also still remains to be written. Delivered at the 73rd annual meeting of the American Jewish Historical Society, 4 May 1975. 43 notes.
F. Rosenthal

982. Harap, Louis. IRVING HOWE AND JEWISH AMERICA. *J. of Ethnic Studies 1977 4(4): 95-104*. Review article prompted by Irving Howe's *World of Our Fathers* (New York: Harcourt Brace Jovanovich, 1976). The book was written so that the receding culture of Yiddish America would be adequately chronicled for future generations in a single, readable work. A central theme is the role of the socialist and labor movements on New York City's East Side. An avowed "democratic socialist," Howe's chief criticisms of contemporary society are against those he regards as a false left, rather than the right. His "abstract, perfectionist approach to socialism" occasionally brings him to tactics of omission and emphasis which he would condemn in totalitarians. Howe's qualifications for writing this work, his treatment of Yiddish scholarship, theater, literature, the European *shtetl*, and the social and mutual benefit organizations of the *landsmanshaften* are compelling and readable. The book is a comprehensive account of the origin and life-course of the massive Jewish immigration. 13 notes.
G. J. Bobango

983. Helmreich, William B. JEWISH MARGINALITY AND THE STRUGGLE FOR EQUALITY: SOME HISTORICAL CAUSES AND CONSEQUENCES. *J. of Intergroup Relations 1976 5(3): 37-40*. Jews, always prominent in social causes, should approach their participation in human rights movements with greater respect for themselves as Jews if they are to retain the respect of others.

984. Herscher, Uri D. HERMAN ROSENTHAL, *THE JEWISH FARMER*. *Michael: On the Hist. of the Jews in the Diaspora [Israel] 1975 3: 59-87*. Herman Rosenthal (1843-1917) came to the United States in 1881 from the Ukraine, as the agent of a group he had founded to transplant Russian Jews to other lands in socialist agricultural colonies. His efforts in southern New Jersey, Alliance (founded in 1882) and Woodbine (1891), were especially successful, largely due to their combination of agriculture and industry. Article reproduces seven excerpts, in Yiddish and English translation, from the Yiddish periodical Rosenthal edited in 1891-92, *Der Yudisher Farmer: Monatliche Isaytshrift fir Landvirtshaftliche Kolonizatsyan*, reporting on the colonies' progress. Biblio.
T. Sassoon

985. Hertz, Edwin. IDEOLOGICAL LIBERALS IN REFORM POLITICS: A NOTE ON THE BACKGROUND AND MOVEMENT OF POLITICAL OUTSIDERS INTO MAJOR PARTY POLITICS. *Int. J. of Contemporary Sociol. 1974 11(1): 1-11*. Discusses the political participation of working class Jews, Negroes, and Puerto Rican Americans as pressure groups in social reform and civil rights issues in New York City, 1963-70's.

986. Hertzberg, Arthur. THE AMERICAN JEWISH INTELLI-GENTSIA. *Midstream 1977 23(2): 45-47*. Considers the scope of characteristics of Jewish intellectuals and academics as a social class, 1945-70's.

987. Hertzberg, Arthur. GROWING UP JEWISH IN AMERICA. *Midstream 1979 25(2): 51-54*. Arthur Hertzberg, author of *Being Jewish in America*, discusses the evolution of his ideas concerning Judaism since the 1940's.

988. Howe, Irving. THE IMMIGRANT GLORY. *Midstream 1976 22(1): 16-26*. Studies the intellectual and cultural ferment of immigrant Jews in the US in the late 19th and early 20th centuries.

989. Howe, Irving. JEWISH IMMIGRANT ARTISTS. *Am. Scholar 1976 45(2): 241-252.* Since 1900 Jewish artists and sculptors have worked with devotion and success. With Jews who have become great artists, the qualities of individualism and universalism have predominated. Their art has lost its Jewishness and can be described under the inclusive category of modernism.   F. F. Harling

990. Hurvitz, Nathan. BLACKS AND JEWS IN AMERICAN FOLKLORE. *Western Folklore 1974 33(4): 301-325.* Examines "white Christian American" folklore about Negroes and Jews. Recounts jokes, stories, and folksayings to bear out the thesis that the two minority groups are frequently coupled together in folklore and "are deprecated and rejected individually and jointly by members of the dominant Christian society."   S. L. Myres

991. Inge, M. Thomas. THE ETHNIC EXPERIENCE AND AESTHETICS IN LITERATURE: MALAMUD'S *THE ASSISTANT* AND ROTH'S *CALL IT SLEEP. J. of Ethnic Studies 1974 1(4): 45-50.* Taking Bernard Malamud's *The Assistant* and Henry Roth's *Call it Sleep* as examples, argues for a greater place for "ethnic literature" in college curricula. There is a need to re-evaluate the traditional standards by which literature is judged, and as much can be gained from Roth's particularistic treatment of minority experience as can from Malamud's "very studied imitation of the majority-oriented classic American novel." 10 notes.   T. W. Smith

992. Jacoby, Susan. WORLD OF OUR MOTHERS: IMMIGRANT WOMEN, IMMIGRANT DAUGHTERS. *Present Tense 1979 6(3): 48-51.* Discusses the lack of literature on the accomplishments of women immigrants to the United States since the late 19th century, here examining Jewish women immigrants in particular, concluding that second generation immigrant daughters growing up with new attitudes, will be more successful in transcending women's traditional sex roles.

993. Jeser, Beth. THE JEWS. *Hist. J. of Western Massachusetts 1976 (Supplement): 61-66.* Jews participated in the American Revolution as soldiers and as politicians. Many Jews fought in the war with the militia and the Continental Army. Haym Solomon played a major role in financing the war effort. Notes.   W. H. Mulligan, Jr.

994. Jordan, Vernon E., Jr. TOGETHER! *Crisis 1974 81(8): 281-284.* Discusses the relations between Jews and Negroes during the 1960's-70's.   S

995. Joselit, Jenna Weissman. WITHOUT GHETTOISM: A HISTORY OF THE INTERCOLLEGIATE MENORAH ASSOCIATION, 1906-1930. *Am. Jewish Arch. 1978 30(2): 133-154.* The Intercollegiate Menorah Association was the first national organization which catered to the diversified needs of Jewish students at American colleges and universities. The author charts the rise, decline, and dissolution of this legendary institution which greatly influenced a whole generation of Jewish students in America with the genius of its aims and ideals.   J

996. Kabakov, Yaakov. MIKHTAVIM MI-YISRAEL ZINBERG LE-YISRAEL DAVIDZON [Letters from Israel Zinberg to Israel Davidson]. *Shvut [Israel] 1975 3: 128-130.* Reproduces four letters, 1925-37, from Israel Zinberg to Israel Davidson (1870-1939) concerning the American publication of the latter's *History of Jewish Literature.* Discusses five of the 12 volumes, published in English, 1972-74. Based on the Davidson Archive, Jewish Theological Seminary, New York; 23 notes.   T. Sassoon

997. Kaganoff, Nathan M. JUDAICA AMERICANA. *Am. Jewish Hist. Q. 1976 65(4): 353-367.* An annotated bibliography of monographical and periodical literature published since 1960 and received in the Library of the American Jewish Historical Society. The current section contains works published in 1974 and 1975.   F. Rosenthal

998. Kaganoff, Nathan M. and Katz-Hyman, Martha B. JUDAICA AMERICANA. *Am. Jewish Hist. Q. 1977 66(4): 513-537.* An annotated bibliography of monographic and periodical literature published since 1960 and received in the library of the American Jewish Historical Society.   F. Rosenthal

999. Kaganoff, Nathan M. and Katz-Hyman, Martha B. JUDAICA AMERICANA. *Am. Jewish Hist. Q. 1978 67(4): 363-377.* An annotated bibliography of monographic and periodical literature published since 1960 and received in the library of the American Jewish Historical Society.   F. Rosenthal

1000. Kaganoff, Nathan M. and Katz-Hyman, Martha B. JUDAICA AMERICANA. *Am. Jewish Hist. 1978 68(2): 213-230.* Annotated bibliography of new monographic and periodical literature published since 1960 as received in the Library of the American Jewish Historical Society.   F. Rosenthal

1001. Kaganoff, Nathan M. and Katz-Hyman, Martha B. JUDAICA AMERICANA. *Am. Jewish Hist. 1979 68(4): 534-551.* An annotated Bibliography of monographic and periodical literature published since 1960 and received in the Library of the American Jewish Historical Society. Covers general works and special studies.   S

1002. Kaplan, Lawrence J. THE DILEMMA OF CONSERVATIVE JUDAISM. *Commentary 1976 62(5): 44-47.* During the 20 years after World War II Conservative Judaism became the most popular religious movement among American Jews. There has been a crisis in Conservative Judaism in recent years, giving rise to a split between the right and left wings of the movement. The former tend toward Orthodoxy; the latter approach the Reform movement. The left wing argues for religious change through legislation rather than interpretation; the right wing contends that limits on change and liberalization must be maintained. The conflict reflects the most basic issue facing the modern Jewish community: how can Judaism exist in the modern world, while maintaining its distinct identity? Primary and secondary sources.

          S. R. Herstein

1003. Karp, Abraham J. FROM TERCENTENARY TO BICENTENNIAL. *Am. Jewish Hist. Q. 1974 64(1): 3-14.* Summarizes the changes in the developing self-image of the American Jewish community. Proposes a Center for the Study of Jewish Life and Institutions to achieve clarification and consistency. If, as sociologists suggest, America's new image is ethnic assimilation but religious differentiation, or "America as mosaic," the American Jew will need to know more about himself and his community, past and present, so that he can intelligently plan his future in response to his own personal need and in service to the nation. A Center would become an indispensable tool in the fashioning of this new community. 2 appendixes.   F. Rosenthal

1004. Karp, Abraham J. IDEOLOGY AND IDENTITY IN JEWISH GROUP SURVIVAL IN AMERICA. *Am. Jewish Hist. Q. 1976 65(4): 310-334.* As a result of enlightenment and emancipation in the early 19th century, the Jews of Western Europe adopted the thesis "Judaism qua Religion"; their brethren in Eastern Europe countered with the antithesis, "Judaism qua nationalism." The American Jews, comprised of and influenced by both communities and by the realities of America, were working out the synthesis of "Religion plus Nationalism." Only in such a way could the threat of the melting pot, total assimilation, be countered. The insight of Horace M. Kallen and of Mordecai Kaplan substantiated the dual image identity—both religious as well as ethnic community—and provides the most creatively viable response to the challenge of Jewish group survival today. 41 notes.   F. Rosenthal

1005. Katz, Jacob. EMANCIPATION AND JEWISH STUDIES. *Commentary 1974 57(4): 60-65.* Discusses assimilation and Jewish emancipation and Jewish studies since the 18th century.   S

1006. Keller, Allan. THOSE SHREWD YANKEE PEDDLERS. *Am. Hist. Illus. 1978 13(6): 8-16.* Selling goods from combs to stoves and later books and medicines, first in tinboxes, trunks, packs and later wagons, the Yankee peddlers were communication links from the east to the backcountry. Tycoons who started their businesses in this manner include: Moses Cone (textiles); Meyer Guggenheim (copper); Collis P. Huntington (railroads); Levi Strauss (levis); and B. T. Babbitt (soap).   D. Dodd

1007. Kessler-Harris, Alice. ORGANIZING THE UNORGANIZABLE: THREE JEWISH WOMEN AND THEIR UNION. *Labor Hist. 1976 17(1): 5-23.* Surveys the lives and work of Pauline Newman, Fannia

Cohn, and Rose Pesotta of the International Ladies' Garment Workers' Union. Their experience as women and their tasks as union officers persistently conflicted, but their class consciousness took precedence over their identification as women. Based upon the Pesotta, Schneiderman, and Cohn papers; 84 notes.   L. L. Athey

1008. Kessner, Carole S.   JEWISH-AMERICAN IMMIGRANT FICTION WRITTEN IN ENGLISH BETWEEN 1867 AND 1920: AN ANNOTATED BIBLIOGRAPHY. *Bull. of Res. in the Humanities 1978 81(4): 406-430.* Annotated bibliography of English-language works by Jewish Americans 1867-1920 covers bibliography, reference works, history, sociology, literary surveys and criticism, autobiography, and novels which relate the immigrant experience.

1009. Kislov, A. K.   "LIGA ZASHCHITY EVREEV"—ORUDIE KRAINEI REAKTSII [The Jewish Defense League: an instrument of extreme reaction]. *Sovetskoe Gosudarstvo i Pravo [USSR] 1975 (6): 97-104.* Discusses the creation, methods and main directions of the Jewish Defense League which stands on the extreme right flank of Zionism. The most essential part of the League's strategy is to aggravate in every possible way international tension and especially Soviet-American relations. As a rule special activity in this respect is displayed by the League on the eve of summit meetings. At the same time the League does not spare efforts to whip up nationalistic, chauvinistic feelings among Americans of the Jewish origin. The article gives characteristics of the leader of the League, Rabbi Meir Kahane, data on the organizational structure of the League, its membership and social structure. The author dwells on the League's relations with other Jewish and reactionary organizations in the United States, some of which take anti-Semitic positions and are openly gangster organizations.   J

1010. Kislov, A. K.   "LIGA ZASHCHITY EVREEV"—ORUDIE KRAINEI REAKTSII [The Jewish Defense League: an instrument of extreme reaction]. *Sovetskoe Gosudarstvo i Pravo [USSR] 1975 (6): 97-104.* Discusses the creation, methods and main directions of the Jewish Defense League which stands on the extreme right flank of Zionism. The most essential part of the league's strategy is to aggravate in every possible way international tension and especially Soviet-American relations. As a rule special activity in this respect is displayed by the league on the eve of summit meetings. At the same time the league does not spare efforts to whip up nationalistic, chauvinistic feelings among Americans of Jewish origin. The article gives characteristics of the leader of the league, Rabbi Meir Kahane, data on the organizational structure of the league, its membership and social structure. The author dwells on the league's relations with other Jewish and reactionary organizations in the United States, some of which take anti-Semitic positions and are openly gangster organizations.   J

1011. Klein, Jeffrey. ARMIES OF THE PLANET: A COMPARATIVE ANALYSIS OF NORMAN MAILER'S AND SAUL BELLOW'S POLITICAL VISIONS. *Soundings 1975 58(1): 69-83.* The politicized worlds created by Norman Mailer in *The Armies of the Night* and by Saul Bellow in *Mr. Sammler's Planet* reveal both authors to be essentially Jewish in their obsession with the moral meaning of events. Mailer's espousal of the idea that what feels good is good along with his anticipation of apocalyptic orgasm, attacks on corporate WASP authoritarianism, and hatred of familial bondage is juxtaposed to Bellow's Arthur Sammler, who fears the cominq holocaust because of the breakdown of civil order with youth as the leading edge of the problem.
                                    N. Lederer

1012. Korn, Bertram W.   AN AMERICAN JEWISH RELIGIOUS LEADER IN 1860 VOICES HIS FRUSTRATION. *Michael: On the Hist. of the Jews in the Diaspora [Israel] 1975 3: 42-47.* Though some American rabbis in the 1860's were men of stature who helped reorient Judaism and the Jew toward the conditions and demands of their new environment, most were minor religious functionaries who lacked any other specialized training. One such figure was Henry Loewenthal of Macon, Georgia, who reached the United States from England in 1854. Prints an 1860 letter he wrote to Rabbi Isaac Leeser of Philadelphia, complaining of ill treatment by members of his congregation and the poor Jewish example they present to their children. Primary and secondary sources; 12 notes.   T. Sassoon

1013. Kozłowski, Józef. "TKACZE" G. HAUPTMANNA NA SCENIE ŻYDOWSKIEJ NA PRZEŁOMIE XIX I XX W [G. Hauptmann's *The Weavers* on the Jewish stages at the turn of the century]. *Biuletyn Żydowskiego Inst. Hist. w Polsce [Poland] 1976 (4): 95-101.* The sociopolitical conflict expressed by Gerhart Hauptmann in his famous tragedy *The Weavers* aroused interest and vivid response among the Jewish working class in Poland. The first performance of *The Weavers* in Poland took place on the Jewish workers' stage and in Yiddish in Warsaw in 1899. In the Austrian Partition the tragedy was put on stage by the association Briderlichkeit in 1901. A year later the tragedy was put on stage in New York by a Jewish amateur troupe working at the Polish Socialist Party's Help Union. The drama of the 1840's deeply touched the spectators, and the revolutionary fight of the Silesian weavers was associated with actual working-class problems.   J

1014. Krausz, Ernest. THE RELIGIOUS FACTOR IN JEWISH IDENTIFICATION. *Int. Social Sci. J. [France] 1977 29(2): 250-260.* Examines the interconnections between religious and secular life for Jews, concluding that where religion is upheld, the ethnic factor is strong and that where shift in emphasis favors secularization, these will compensate for loss of religious identity; differentiates between Israeli and American Jews, 1957-77.

1015. Kriegel, Annie. JEWS AND BLACKS. *Jerusalem Q. [Israel] 1978 (7): 22-33.* Compares the American Negro and the Jewish experience of slavery, ghettos, and emancipation, 15th-20th centuries.

1016. Kuznets, Simon. IMMIGRATION OF RUSSIAN JEWS TO THE UNITED STATES: BACKGROUND AND STRUCTURE. *Perspectives in Am. Hist. 1975 9: 35-124.* From 1881 to 1914 1.5 million Russian Jews emigrated to the United States. Many of the forces motivating their emigration were common to most mass movements from Europe during the 19th century: the pressures of industrialization and new technology, and the dislocation of people from the land. Russian Jews, however, were also affected by factors not so common to other groups. Restrictions imposed by the Czarist Empire on Jews' residence, vocation, and education encouraged them to emigrate. Jewish immigrants were more likely to be family-oriented and to remain in their new homeland. 14 tables, 34 notes.   W. A. Wiegand

1017. Lacks, Roslyn. TRYING TO MAKE IT IN THE U.S.A.: NEW EMIGRES, NEW PROBLEMS. *Present Tense 1976 3(4): 45-49.* Of the more than 100,000 Jews who have left the USSR since 1971 (more than one half from the Ukraine, nearly a third from Moscow and Leningrad, and smaller groups from Georgia, Moldavia, Byelorussia, Latvia, Estonia, and Lithuania), at least one in 10 has settled in the United States (almost half in New York City). Groups such as the New York Association for New Americans and the Hebrew Immigrant Aid Society have been attempting to find employment for the new immigrants, who frequently are reluctant to take lower-level jobs because they are not accustomed to the American concept of upward mobility, while professionals such as physicians and dentists face formidable examinations before they can receive licenses to practice in the USA.   C. Moody

1018. Lavender, Abraham D. JEWISH COLLEGE WOMEN: FUTURE LEADERS OF THE JEWISH COMMUNITY? *J. of Ethnic Studies 1977 5(2): 81-90.* The American Jewish community deprives itself of needed talents by not encouraging participation of Jewish women in its leadership. Based on a questionnaire study of 488 Jewish undergraduate students at the University of Maryland during 1971, Jewish females are similar to Jewish males in their plans to obtain graduate degrees. They plan to combine their traditional mother-housewife role with that of a separate career. They have a higher degree of religious identity than their corresponding males, are more likely to date only Jews and oppose intermarriage, and have more concern than men on the vital issues of Israel and the treatment of Soviet Jews. Jewish women in America today have more opportunity than non-Jewish women for equality, though the situation is not as good as a few decades ago. Their religious position, although improving in non-Orthodox congregations, still remains far from one of equality. Primary and secondary sources; 7 tables, 11 notes.
                                    G. J. Bobango

1019. Lavender, Abraham D. THE SEPHARDIC REVIVAL IN THE UNITED STATES: A CASE OF ETHNIC REVIVAL IN A MI-

NORITY-WITHIN-A-MINORITY. *J. of Ethnic Studies 1975 3(3): 21-31*. The Sephardim number about 180,000 and comprise some 3% of the total US Jewish community, most of them in New York. Until now they have been neglected by laymen and social scientists as well, perhaps because they are non-Yiddish speakers and have "non-Jewish" names. Gives a brief background of the group and shows recent events of a scholarly and educational revival, such as the work of The American Society of Sephardic Studies, new journals, and programs at Yeshiva University. The Sephardi Federation raises funds for youth programs in Israel, now about 60% Sephardic itself. Sociological reasons for this more intense ethnicity might be the increased numbers migrating here since the 1950's, and the current Middle East situation which now has a "a power of arousal" to overcome previous apathy, as well as the increased ethnic consciousness of America in general. We must adopt a multidimensional view of Jews as is used in Spain and Islamic lands, rather than the one-dimensional portrait confined to Europe's Ashkenazim areas; few countries provide such a "living laboratory" of ethnic group relations as does Israel. Secondary materials; 46 notes.   G. J. Bobango

1020. Lavender, Abraham D. STUDIES OF JEWISH COLLEGE STUDENTS: A REVIEW AND A REPLICATION. *Jewish Social Studies 1977 39(1-2): 37-52*. A comparison of Jewish college students at the University of Maryland in 1971 with those surveyed at the same school by Irving Greenberg in 1949 indicates Jewish college students rank below their parents in overall observance of the Jewish religion, and in the preservation of their Jewish identity. However, the difference is not as great in 1971 as it had been in 1949. Specific findings show that the families of the 1971 freshmen students were economically better off than those of 1949; that synagogue attendance of the parents in both surveys was similar; that by 1971 observance of *kashruth* had declined; that Conservative Judaism had gained in strength at the expense of Orthodoxy; and that Reform Judaism made only minor percentile gains. Based on survey-questionnaires.   N. Lederer

1021. Ledeen, Michael. LIBERALS, NOT THE JEWS, HAVE CHANGED. *Society 1979 16(4): 5, 19*. Examines sociopolitical attitudes of US Jews, 1969-79, and observes that the Jewish community has actually remained quite faithful to its liberalism while many former liberal spokespersons have shifted to conservatism in foreign policy.

1022. Leventman, Paula Goldman and Leventman, Seymour. CONGRESSMAN DRINAN, S. J., AND HIS JEWISH CONSTITUENTS. *Am. Jewish Hist. Q. 1976 65(2): 215-248*. Robert Drinan in 1970 became the political representative of one of the largest areas of Jewish concentration outside of New York City. The importance of the "Jewish vote" for victory in this district encouraged a series of Jewish candidates to run against Father Drinan in subsequent elections. Nevertheless Drinan retained the active support of religious, communal, and political leaders and at least 50 percent of the Jewish voters, as is shown by analyses of the 1972 and 1974 returns. 28 notes.   F. Rosenthal

1023. Levinson, Robert E. AMERICAN JEWS IN THE WEST. *Western Hist. Q. 1974 5(3): 285-294*. Barred for centuries from farming and the professions, most Jews who participated in the settlement of the West used the occupational skills developed by their ancestors in merchandising. Some sold food, clothing, and hardware in the mining areas. Others concentrated on the farming regions where they frequently acted as agents for the shipping of farm produce. Many settled in urban communities as wholesale merchants. Much more research needs to be done to raise western Jewish history above the genealogical "begats" and the who's who of organization founders. 34 notes.   D. L. Smith

1024. Levinson, Robert E. KETUBOT FROM EARLY CALIFORNIA. *Michael: On the Hist. of the Jews in the Diaspora [Israel] 1975 3: 34-41*. During the first eight years of Californian statehood, no standardized state marriage certificate existed. County recorders usually simply copied statements from clergymen or judges who officiated at weddings. Two such certificates, dated 1855 and 1861, closely resemble the traditional Jewish marriage contract, the *ketubah*. They are printed here, as is an advertisement from the San Francisco *Weekly Gleaner* (6 Nov. 1857) for "kethuboth" in English and Hebrew at $3.00 per dozen. Primary sources; 16 notes.   T. Sassoon

1025. Levy, William. A JEW VIEWS BLACK EDUCATION: TEXAS 1890. *Western States Jewish Hist. Q. 1976 8(4): 351-360*. Reprints a speech given 6 August 1890 by William Levy at the cornerstone laying of the Northwest Texas Colored Citizens College in Sherman, Texas. Levy, the Mayor of Sherman, told his black audience that the way for Negroes to advance socially and economically was through the education of their children just like the Jews had done after their enslavement in Egypt. He told them that "Nothing upon earth elevates people more than learning and good moral conduct, nothing can civilize nations more than knowledge, progress and refinement." 4 notes.

R. A. Garfinkle

1026. Lewis, Stuart A. THE JEWISH AUTHOR LOOKS AT THE BLACK. *Colorado Q. 1973 21(3): 317-330*. Until recently Jewish-black antagonism was negligible. While Jewish authors saw blacks as members of another minority, there was still a feeling of uneasiness and lack of acceptance of the Jewish minority by the black minority. In recent years blacks have often singled out Jews as major antagonists. However, there exists a dream of love between the races which expresses itself symbolically in many Jewish authors' works.   B. A. Storey

1027. Lieberman, Samuel S. and Weinfeld, Morton. DEMOGRAPHIC TRENDS AND JEWISH SURVIVAL. *Midstream 1978 24(9): 9-19*. Discusses reasons for the decrease in the American Jewish population and speculates on the future of the Jewish community.

1028. Liebman, Arthur. THE TIES THAT BIND: THE JEWISH SUPPORT FOR THE LEFT IN THE UNITED STATES. *Am. Jewish Hist. Q. 1976 65(2): 285-321*. From the 1880's through the early 1920's a massive immigrant Yiddish-speaking working class led by indigenous radicals and attuned to Marxist-socialist values emerged in the United States. Post-World War II developments have eroded this basis of the Jewish left; nevertheless, in the 1950's and beyond, the middle-class college student, comfortably American and Jewish, became the cutting edge of social action and political activism. The story of the American Communist Party and its Jewish members illustrates these changing patterns. 45 notes.   F. Rosenthal

1029. Liebman, Charles S. ORTHODOX JUDAISM TODAY. *Midstream 1979 25(7): 19-26*. Discusses Orthodoxy in comparison to Conservative and Reform in terms of Jewish commitment, strength, and status in the Jewish community, distinguishing between the positions of strict and modern Orthodoxy.

1030. Lima, Robert. SEPHARDIC LEGACY. *Américas (Organization of Am. States) 1978 30(9): 2-8*. Discusses the Portuguese Sephardic Jews in the United States, beginning with their arrival in 1654 at the Dutch colony of New Amsterdam to escape persecution in Portugal.

1031. Lindberg-Seyersted, Brita. A READING OF BERNARD MALAMUD'S *THE TENANTS*. *J. of Am. Studies [Great Britain] 1975 9(1): 85-102*. Reviews Malamud's *The Tenants* (New York: Farrar, Straus and Giroux, 1971) in which Malamud emphasizes that minorities merit patience and understanding as they try to overcome social and cultural inequality. 11 notes.   H. T. Lovin

1032. Lobenthal, Richard H. FINDINGS OF THE COMMITTEE OF THE MICHIGAN DEPARTMENT OF EDUCATION ON REVIEWING HISTORY TEXTBOOKS. *Michigan Jewish Hist. 1973 13(2): 19-21*. Examines the report of the Michigan Department of Education on the portrayal of Jews in elementary and secondary social studies textbooks.   S

1033. Loewenberg, Robert. THE THEFT OF LIBERALISM—A JEWISH PROBLEM. *Midstream 1977 23(5): 19-33*. The contradictions of modern Jewish liberalism put Jews at odds with reality and force them to choose between particularism and universalism or, more specifically, between Judaism and liberalism.

1034. Maller, Allen S. CLASS FACTORS IN THE JEWISH VOTE. *Jewish Social Studies 1977 39(1-2): 159-162*. A study of the mayoral campaign in Los Angeles, California, in 1969 between liberal black candidate Tom Bradley and conservative Sam Yorty indicates the extent to which class factors amid the Jewish voting population are beginning to divide Jews into ascertainable subgroups. Reform rabbis and spokesmen supported Bradley in public meetings as part of their liberal commitment while Orthodox rabbis threw their allegiance to the far more conservative Yorty. Although a majority of Los Angeles Jewish voters supported Bradley, the percentage of Bradley supporters in the most highly affluent Jewish neighborhoods was significantly higher than that in less prosperous Jewish areas. The influence of changing neighborhoods and the school desegregation issue suggests that although Jewish voting patterns are still unique, various issues affecting the well-being and personal status of Jews are having their effect on voting behavior.   N. Lederer

1035. Marcus, Jacob Rader.   JEWS AND THE AMERICAN REVOLUTION: A BICENTENNIAL DOCUMENTARY.   *Am. Jewish Arch. 1975 27(2): 103-276.* When the civil war which we call the American Revolution entered its military phase in 1775, it proved impossible for British North America's tiny Jewish community of perhaps 2,500 souls to remain aloof from the conflict. Most of them, for political or socio-economic reasons or a combination of the two, abandoned their loyalty to the British crown and attached themselves to the Revolutionary cause. When the United States won its independence in 1783, it seemed to the Jews that the world had begun again.   J

1036. Masilamoni, E. H. Leelavathi.   THE FICTION OF JEWISH AMERICANS: AN INTERVIEW WITH LESLIE FIEDLER.   *Southwest Rev. 1979 64(1): 44-59.* Literary critic and novelist Leslie Fiedler discusses forces in American society—anti-Semitism, ethnic identification, and religious differences—as they affect Jews, especially Jewish writers, 1970's.

1037. Maslow, Will.   JEWISH POLITICAL POWER: AN ASSESSMENT.   *Am. Jewish Hist. Q. 1976 65(2): 349-362.* The proper assessment of Jewish political power or influence in the United States, aside from the voting pattern in areas of Jewish concentration, should include the following: a network of Jewish organizations, skilled professionals and dedicated laymen, an educated, affluent and committed membership, many political and governmental contracts, and concentration on three major issues (security of Israel, Arab boycott, and Soviet Jewry). 30 notes.   F. Rosenthal

1038. Maydell, Bodo von.   JUEDISCH-KABBALISTISCHE ELEMENTE IN DER RELIGIOESEN GESELLSCHAFT DER FREUNDE (QUAEKER) [Jewish-cabalistic elements in the religious Society of Friends (Quakers)].   *Judaica [Switzerland] 1973 29(3): 97-98.* Cabalistic Jews and Quakers share some basic beliefs, including the concept of the "inner light," the spark of the divine in every human being, and a distrust of hard and fast dogmas.

1039. Mayo, Louise Abbie.   HERMAN MELVILLE, THE JEW AND JUDAISM.   *Am. Jewish Arch. 1976 28(2): 172-179.* Melville is the only major American writer in the nineteenth century to include a serious consideration of Jews and Judaism in one of his works—*Clarel.*   J

1040. Mendelsohn, Ezra.   THE RUSSIAN ROOTS OF THE AMERICAN JEWISH LABOR MOVEMENT.   *Yivo Ann. of Jewish Social Sci. 1976 (16): 150-177.* The large emigration of Russian Jews to the United States following the pogroms of 1881-82 was mainly a movement of poor artisans and traders who came looking for an opportunity to work, grow prosperous, and live without fear. In addition, there were Russian Jewish intellectuals who felt themselves mentally superior to the masses. From the Russian Jewish intellectuals grew the Jewish US labor movement. 74 notes.   R. J. Wechman

1041. Mergen, Bernard.   "ANOTHER GREAT PRIZE": THE JEWISH LABOR MOVEMENT IN THE CONTEXT OF AMERICAN LABOR HISTORY.   *Yivo Ann. of Jewish Social Sci. 1976 (16): 394-423.* Emphasizes the uniqueness of the American Jewish labor movement within the context of American labor history. Shows the various relationships between the Jewish labor movement and the American labor movement, demonstrating similarities, differences, and influences.   R. J. Wechman

1042. Meyer, Michael A.   THE HEBREW UNION COLLEGE—ITS FIRST YEARS.   *Cincinnati Hist. Soc. Bull. 1975 33(1): 7-25.* Discusses the activities of Rabbi Isaac Mayer Wise as founder of the Hebrew Union College, America's first rabbinical seminary, in Cincinnati, Ohio, 1817-90's, including students' curricula in Jewish history.

1043. Meyer, Michael A.   LETTERS OF ISAAC MAYER WISE TO JOSEPH STOLZ.   *Michael: On the Hist. of the Jews in the Diaspora [Israel] 1975 3: 48-58.* Publishes 10 letters written during 1882-1900 by Rabbi Isaac Mayer Wise to Joseph Stolz, one of the early graduates of the rabbinical seminary Wise founded, Hebrew Union College. The letters reveal aspects of a poorly documented area of Wise's activities—the placement and advancement of HUC graduates in American congregations. The letters reflect Wise's fatherly concern for Stolz, as well as his hard-headed approach to rabbinical salaries and prerogatives, and relations with better-established rabbis. Primary and secondary sources; 28 notes.   T. Sassoon

1044. Mintz, Jacqueline A.   THE MYTH OF THE JEWISH MOTHER IN THREE JEWISH, AMERICAN, FEMALE WRITERS.   *Centennial Rev. 1978 22(3): 346-353.* Despite the prevalence of the "Molly Goldberg" caricature, the most damaging stereotype of the Jewish mother has been that of the source of ideal mother love. Tillie Olsen, Anzia Yezierska, and Susan Fromberg Schaeffer have dealt with this myth and the terrible burdens it placed on women who were expected to live up to its demands of total involvement with family and endless, selfless giving and nurturing. In showing the pernicious side of the myth, these writers contribute to its death, to the benefit of all caught up in it.   T. L. Powers

1045. Mongerman, Freda.   PIONEERS IN SOCIAL SERVICE: THE JEWISH COMMITTEE FOR PERSONAL SERVICE IN STATE INSTITUTIONS IN THE 1920'S.   *Western States Jewish Hist. Q. 1974 6(2): 83-99.* Studies the Jewish Committee for Personal Service in State Institutions founded in 1920 by Rabbi Martin A. Meyer. The purpose of this group was to help Jews who were in, or had been in, California mental hospitals and prisons. Elsie Shirpser, Executive Secretary of the JCPSSI for 24 years, pioneered the use of psychiatric social histories of the inmates. Primary and secondary sources; 32 notes.   R. A. Garfinkle

1046. Moonman, Jane; Buckley, Berenice; and Lacks, Roslyn.   "GUESS WHO'S COMING TO DINNER?"   *Present Tense 1974 1(2): 11-15.* Describes Jewish intermarriage in Great Britain, Australia and the United States.   S

1047. Morris, Jeffrey B.   THE AMERICAN JEWISH JUDGE: AN APPRAISAL ON THE OCCASION OF THE BICENTENNIAL.   *Jewish Social Studies 1976 38(3-4): 195-223.* Jews have played an interesting and important role as members of the judiciary in American history. As judges they have displayed significant differences in their behavior and legal attitudes but have also revealed certain similarities. Among the characteristics common to many Jewish members of the judiciary are a realization of the need for the law to conform to contemporary society, an awareness of the need to break away from mechanical jurisprudence, and a sensitivity to civil liberties and social justice. The marked Jewish affinity for the law as well as the concern for social justice may have its roots in Jewish practice and belief.   N. Lederer

1048. Mosk, Stanley.   A MAJORITY OF THE CALIFORNIA SUPREME COURT.   *Western States Jewish Hist. Q. 1976 8(3): 224-231.* For three months in 1852, the three-member California Supreme Court had two Jews on the bench. Henry A. Lyons (1809-72) was Chief Justice and Solomon Heydenfeldt (1816-90) was elected to the bench that year. Lyons was a poor justice who spent little time on court matters and wrote few opinions. Heydenfeldt was a brilliant legal scholar who wrote 45 opinions during his five years on the bench. Both men were from the South and were strong southern sympathizers during the Civil War. They both left large estates. 2 photos.   R. A. Garfinkle

1049. Neu, Irene D.   THE JEWISH BUSINESSWOMAN IN AMERICA.   *Am. Jewish Hist. Q. 1976 66(1): 137-154.* Provides thumbnail sketches of Jewish businesswomen in America from colonial days to the present. The scarcity of such individuals in the past is a reflection of the social mores of the 19th century which saw women as homemakers and at their best in communal and philanthropic activities. These patterns are now changing. 53 notes.   F. Rosenthal

1050. Neusner, Jacob. DEPARTMENTS OF RELIGIOUS STUD-IES AND CONTEMPORARY JEWISH STUDIES. *Am. Jewish Hist. Q. 1974 63(4): 356-360.* Although much material of contemporary Jewish studies is not religious in nature, it is often placed in religious studies departments. One of nine related articles in this issue.   S

1051. Neusner, Jacob. THE STUDY OF RELIGION AS THE STUDY OF TRADITION: JUDAISM. *Hist. of Religions 1975 14(3): 191-206.* Defines tradition as "something handed on from the past which is made contemporary and transmitted because of its intense contemporaneity." Stresses the importance of literary and legal sources for proper understanding of Jewish tradition. Draws distinctions between the aims and methods of historians of religion and regular historians. Contribution to a Symposium on Methodology and World Religions at the University of Iowa; 8 notes.   T. L. Auffenberg

1052. Newman, William M. and Halvorson, Peter L. AMERICAN JEWS: PATTERNS OF GEOGRAPHIC DISTRIBUTION AND CHANGE, 1952-1971. *J. for the Sci. Study of Religion 1979 18(2): 183-193.* Also discusses the effects of geographic change on patterns of American religious pluralism.

1053. Papanek, Miriam Lewin. PSYCHOLOGICAL ASPECTS OF MINORITY GROUP MEMBERSHIP: THE CONCEPTS OF KURT LEWIN. *Jewish Social Studies 1974 36(1): 72-79.* Lewin's conceptions about Jews as a minority group can be applied to other minority groups for social psychological study. Based on primary and secondary sources in English; 28 notes.   P. E. Schoenberg

1054. Passow, Isidore David. SHMUEL NIGER'S IDEAS ON BUILDING A JEWISH COMMUNITY IN THE UNITED STATES, 1920-1933. *Yivo Ann. of Jewish Social Sci. 1974 (15): 188-203.* Shmuel Niger was appalled by the East European Jewish immigrant's cultural stultification, urging Jews to retain their culture. The Jew in America should become more conscious of the heritage of East European Jewry.   R. J. Wechman

1055. Petuchowski, Jakob J. ABRAHAM GEIGER AND SAMUEL HOLDHEIM: THEIR DIFFERENCES IN GERMANY AND REPERCUSSIONS IN AMERICA. *Leo Baeck Inst. Year Book [Great Britain] 1977 22: 139-160.* In the emergence of a 19th-century German Reform Jewish ideology Abraham Geiger (1810-74) and Samuel Holdheim (1806-60) were dialectic opposites, with Geiger representing the right, traditionalist and Holdheim the left, modernist wing of the movement: evolutionary change versus a revolutionary break with the past. When translated to the United States by German-Jewish immigrants, this dichotomy was represented by Isaac Mayer Wise (1819-1900) and David Einhorn (1809-97). To this day the basic question remains: whether Reform Judaism is predicted on organic growth, i.e. on evolution, or whether it stands for revolution, a break with tradition. 79 notes.   F. Rosenthal

1056. Pinsker, Sanford. PIETY AS COMMUNITY: THE HASIDIC VIEW. *Social Res. 1975 42(2): 230-246.* Discusses the life, philosophy, and attitudes of Hasidic Jews in the United States, speculating on whether the traditional Jewish community is currently disintegrating.

1057. Pinsker, Sanford. SAUL BELLOW'S CRANKY HISTORI-ANS. *Hist. Reflections [Canada] 1976 3(2): 35-47.* Saul Bellow's most recent fiction is dominated by the protagonist-as-historian, rather than by the traditional concerns of "historical novels." History reflects individual sensibilities and mirrors that which must be synthesized for the culture's good, while, simultaneously, it transcends the heart's deepest needs. The embattled "historians" of *Herzog* (1964), *Mr. Sammler's Planet* (1970), and *Humboldt's Gift* (1975), suggest something of what a vision of history might mean to a contemporary novelist.   P. Travis

1058. Pinsky, Mark. ASSIMILATED IN MILLTOWN. *Present Tense 1978 5(3): 35-39.* Studies the socioeconomic patterns of several Jewish families in "Milltown" (not the real name), an average-sized city in the American South, from the 1890's to the present, as representative of the individual goals and attitudes of southern Jews.

1059. Popkin, Richard H. MOSES MENDELSSOHN AND FRAN-CISCO DE MIRANDA. *Jewish Social Studies 1978 40(1): 41-48.* Latin American revolutionary Francisco de Miranda visited Moses Mendelssohn and other prominent Jewish intellectuals in Berlin in 1785. *Journey to Prussia* records the events of this visit. Miranda wrote the Spanish passages in the book and Colonel William Stephens Smith, an aide-decamp to John Adams, then American envoy to London, almost certainly penned the English section. Unfortunately, the passage relating the conversation with Mendelssohn does not reveal the substance of the subjects discussed. Mendelssohn, a champion of the separation of church and state, would have been unhappy with Miranda's later espousal of Catholicism as the official religion for his Latin American constitution. The other Jewish intellectuals visited by the team expressed support for and interest in the United States, a republic founded on Enlightenment principles.   N. Lederer

1060. Porter, Jack Nusan. THE JEWISH INTELLECTUAL. *Midstream 1979 25(1): 18-25.* Discusses Jews within the American intellectual elite, 1945-78, assessing their divisions and intergroup conflicts as well as their role in modern American social circles.

1061. Porter, Jack Nusan. JEWISH SINGLES. *Midstream 1975 21(10): 35-43.* Proposes various Jewish community responses to the problems faced by adult singles in the 1970's.

1062. Porter, Jack Nusan; Rockovsky, Boris; and Agrillo, Anita Bach. THE JEWISH STUDENT: A COMPARATIVE ANALYSIS OF RE-LIGIOUS AND SECULAR ATTITUDES. *Yivo Ann. of Jewish Social Sci. 1974 (15): 297-338.* Gives the results of a study during April 1968-May 1969 of Jewish students at Yale and Northwestern Universities. The study surveyed attitudes of students on observance, attitudes toward Judaism and "Jewishness," Israel, intermarriage, assimilation, sex, God, and the Bible. 7 tables.   R. J. Wechman

1063. Porter, Jack Nusan. ROSA SONNENSCHEIN AND *THE AMERICAN JEWESS:* FIRST INDEPENDENT ENGLISH LAN-GUAGE JEWISH WOMEN'S JOURNAL IN THE UNITED STATES. *Am. Jewish Hist. 1978 68(1): 57-63.* Rosa Sonnenschein (1847-1932) published and edited the periodical *The American Jewess* during its short life, 1895-99. This "first English-language journal independently edited by women" addressed itself to upper-middle to upper class German and Sephardic Jewish women. Its articles reflected the tumultuous events of the period (Russian pogroms, Dreyfus affair, early Zionism, etc.) and reflected the women's suffrage movement and the noblesse oblige of the upper class to the poor. The magazine died in 1899, partly because of the strong assimilationist attitudes of so many Jews.   F. Rosenthal

1064. Pratt, Norma Fain. TRANSITIONS IN JUDAISM: THE JEWISH AMERICAN WOMAN THROUGH THE 1930S. *Am. Q. 1978 30(5): 681-702.* A study of the slow, but steady growth in the status of women in American Judaism, particularly during the 1920's-30's. Rapidity of status growth has depended partly on whether the country of origin was Eastern or Western Europe, but economic factors in the adopted country also had some influence. One can see very clear differences between Reform, Conservative, Orthodox, and secular Jews in their reaction to liberalizing tendencies and demands. A number of Jewish women's organizations have developed significant programs where women have found opportunity for making unique contributions. However, the fear of assimilation into Gentile culture patterns has been a strong inhibiting force among the women themselves. 60 notes.   R. V. Ritter

1065. Raab, Earl. BLACKS AND JEWS ASUNDER? *Midstream 1979 25(9): 3-9.* Discusses the political and social development of blacks and Jews in the United States since the 1930's, and views with alarm the disintegration of the traditional black-Jewish political coalition.

1066. Rabkin, Yakov M. SOVIET JEWS: THE BITTER AFTER-MATH OF EMIGRATION. *Bull. of the Atomic Scientists 1975 31(6): 35-38.* Focuses on the legal, social, and psychological adjustment and the resettlement of Jewish emigrant scientists in the United States and Israel. Contrasts the situation of Soviet immigrants with the more favorable situation of German Jewish scientists in the United States in the 1930's. Primary and secondary sources; 14 notes.   D. J. Trickey

1067. Rachleff, Owen. JEWISH COMICS. *Midstream 1976 22(4): 51-56.* Discusses humor themes and stereotypes of Jewish comedians in the United States in the 1960's and 70's, including Woody Allen, David Steinberg and Don Rickles.

1068. Rakeffet-Rothkoff, Aaron. THE ATTEMPT TO MERGE THE JEWISH THEOLOGICAL SEMINARY AND YESHIVA COLLEGE, 1926-1927. *Michael: On the Hist. of the Jews in the Diaspora [Israel] 1975 3: 254-280.* The merger attempt of the two leading American traditional rabbinical seminaries was prompted by the fund-raising campaigns launched by both institutions for new campuses in New York City. Some American Jewish lay leaders could not discern the differences between Jewish Theological Seminary and Yeshiva College, for many in the JTS administration and faculty were Orthodox in their theology and practice. Presents 26 documents relating to the attempted merger and serving as the basis for the description in the author's book, *Bernard Revel: Builder of American Jewish Orthodoxy* (Philadelphia, 1972), pp. 94-114. Primary and secondary sources; 40 notes.

1069. Raphael, Marc Lee. EUROPEAN JEWISH AND NON-JEWISH MARITAL PATTERNS IN LOS ANGELES, 1910-1913: A COMPARATIVE APPROACH. *Western States Jewish Hist. Q. 1974 6(2): 100-106.* Examines more than 25,000 marriage licenses for the years 1910-1913, and concludes that European national animosities persisted when immigrants moved to Los Angeles. There were few intermarriages between people of different nationalities. Jews tended to marry Jews from the same geographic homeland areas—for instance, East Europeans married East Europeans but did not marry Jews from other parts of Europe. 7 tables. R. A. Garfinkle

1070. Raphael, Marc Lee. THE JEWISH COMMUNITY AND ELLIS ISLAND, 1909. *Michael: On the Hist. of the Jews in the Diaspora [Israel] 1975 3: 172-187.* The Baron de Hirsch Fund, established in 1891, paid for an agent of the United Hebrew Charities of New York to meet Jewish immigrants at Ellis Island. Publishes condensed and edited document highlighting the activities of this agent, I. Irving Lipsitch (1884-1935) in 1909. Interviewed by David M. Bressler (1879-1942), general manager of the Industrial Removal Office, Lipsitch's testimony illuminates the plight of the immigrants and the complexity, frustration, and conflicts accompanying the self-help efforts of the American Jewish community in the early 20th century. T. Sassoon

1071. Raphael, Marc Lee. RABBI JACOB VOORSANGER OF SAN FRANCISCO ON JEWS AND JUDAISM: THE IMPLICATIONS OF THE PITTSBURGH PLATFORM. *Am. Jewish Hist. Q. 1973 63(2): 185-203.* Rabbi Voorsanger (1852-1908) utilized 19th-century Biblical criticism and current philosophies to support his interpretation of the Pittsburgh Platform, the 1885 statement of principles of American Reform Judaism. Strongly influenced by Darwin's studies, he rejected any notions of supernatural revelation and adjusted Jewish theology to the accepted scientific theories of the day. 41 notes. F. Rosenthal

1072. Rice, Dan. REINHOLD NIEBUHR AND JUDAISM. *J. of the Am. Acad. of Religion 1977 45(1): 72.* Identifies and investigates the main themes in the Jewish-Christian dialogue as Reinhold Niebuhr conceived them. Some attention is given to the history of this dialogue. Four major themes are discussed: Zionism and the state of Israel; anti-Semitism; theological issues dividing the two faiths; and the problem of missions. E. R. Lester

1073. Rockaway, Robert A. "WORTHY SIR . . . ": A COLLECTION OF IMMIGRANT LETTERS FROM THE INDUSTRIAL REMOVAL OFFICE. *Michael: On the Hist. of the Jews in the Diaspora [Israel] 1975 3: 152-171.* A hitherto untapped source of Jewish immigrant life in the United States in the early 20th century are the letters to the Industrial Removal Office (IRO). This correspondence is housed in the American Jewish Historical Society. The IRO's function was to disperse Jewish immigrants throughout the United States, persuading and assisting Jewish workers to leave the large cities on the East Coast for smaller cities where Jewish communities existed and jobs were available. Some 75,000 Jews were thus relocated in 1900-17. Publishes 11 immigrant letters from Detroit, most addressed to and answered by David Bressler (1879-1942) and Philip Seman (1881-1957). T. Sassoon

1074. Roditi, Edouard. NEO-KABBALISM IN THE AMERICAN JEWISH COUNTER-CULTURE. *Midstream 1979 25(8): 8-13.* In response to middle-class Jewish traditionalism and rationalism, young dissident Jews have turned to the mysticism of the Cabala for inspiration, 1940's-70's.

1075. Rodrigues, Eusebio L. SAUL BELLOW'S HENDERSON AS AMERICA. *Centennial R. 1976 20(2): 189-195.* Saul Bellow's novel *Henderson The Rain King* (1965) is a "daring parable about America and the American dream." Henderson, a man of gigantic size, symbolizes the size and potential of America; he combines technological achievement with the power of the human spirit. His voice is the voice of hope, which has always been present in the new world. Henderson restores to 20th-century America the ideals of brotherhood, love, and service, and represents Bellow's rejection of an America doomed to enslavement to the processes of technology. 7 notes. A. R. Stoesen

1076. Romanofsky, Peter. " . . . TO RID OURSELVES OF THE BURDEN . . ." NEW YORK JEWISH CHARITIES AND THE ORIGINS OF THE INDUSTRIAL REMOVAL OFFICE, 1890-1901. *Am. Jewish Hist. Q. 1975 64(4): 331-343.* Various motives combined to induce the primarily German-Jewish leadership of New York Jewish charities to actively support removal of new immigrants to other parts of the country. Overcrowding, the possibility of political radicalism, and the fear of renewed antisemitism led to various programs for job training, agricultural settlements, and resettlement outside New York. Both the Industrial Removal Office of 1901 and the Galveston Plan of 1907 were created to prevent limitation of Jewish immigration to the United States. By 1914 some 70,000 men and their families had been placed outside New York City, allowing Jewish charities to expand and develop their services to the children, widows, and the sick of the Jewish community. 31 notes. F. Rosenthal

1077. Rosenberg, Bernard and Howe, Irving. ARE AMERICAN JEWS TURNING TO THE RIGHT? *Dissent 1974 21(1): 30-45.* If there is a new Jewish conservatism, it is possibly the result of affluence, assimilation, decline in the Jewish labor movement, fear of Negroes, or reaction to Communist anti-Semitism. S

1078. Rosenblum, Herbert. IDEOLOGY AND COMPROMISE: THE EVOLUTION OF THE UNITED SYNAGOGUE CONSTITUTIONAL PREAMBLE. *Jewish Social Studies 1973 35(1): 18-31.* Traces the ideological and institutional development of the Conservative branch of American Judaism, 1910-13. The preambles of the articles of incorporation of the United Synagogue of America, the association for Conservative rabbis, indicate the ideological compromises among diverse groups to achieve unity. Based on primary and secondary sources, particularly letters and documents in the archives of the Jewish Theological Seminary of America; 45 notes. P. E. Schoenberg

1079. Rosenfeld, Alvin H. INVENTING THE JEW: NOTES ON JEWISH AUTOBIOGRAPHY. *Midstream 1974 20(4): 54-66.*

1080. Rosenthal, Marcus. THE JEWISH IMMIGRATION "PROBLEM." *Western States Jewish Hist. Q. 1974 6(4): 278-289.* On 27 January 1905, Rabbi Jacob Voorsanger, the editor of *Emanu-El*, published his feelings against the immigration of large numbers of East European Jews. The author's rebuttal attacks Rabbi Voorsanger's ideas, stating that if American Jews turn against the new arrivals the Christian community will use that as a sign to start a new round of anti-Semitism. Reprinted letter-to-the-editor from *Emanu-El*, San Francisco, 24 February 1905. R. A. Garfinkle

1081. Rosenwaike, Ira. ESTIMATING JEWISH POPULATION DISTRIBUTION IN U.S. METROPOLITAN AREAS IN 1970. *Jewish Social Studies 1974 36(2): 106-117.* Uses the Yiddish mother tongue data of the 1970 US census to determine the Jewish population and pattern of settlement in major metropolitan centers, concentrating on four Standard Metropolitan Statistical Areas: Baltimore, Cleveland, St. Louis, and Washington, D. C. The data implies that a high degree of geographical concentration still exists among Jews in most metropolitan areas, despite the transition to predominantly suburban residence. Yiddish mother tongue data of the 1970 US census is highly reliable and useful for similar studies of other cities. Primary and secondary sources are in English; 25 notes. P. E. Schoenberg

1082. Roth, Henry and Friedman, John S. ON BEING BLOCKED AND OTHER LITERARY MATTERS. *Commentary 1977 64(2): 27-38.* Discusses Roth's childhood in New York City, his student days at City College of New York, his authorship of *Call It Sleep,* his membership in the Communist Party, his growing sympathy for Israel, and his eventual reunion with Judaism.　　　　D. W. Johnson

1083. Rothchild, Sylvia. BRANDEIS UNIVERSITY: THE MAKING OF A FIRST CLASS INSTITUTION. *Present Tense 1979 7(1): 31-36.* Briefly discusses the history of Brandeis University from its founding in Waltham, Massachusetts, in 1948, to the present focusing on the diverse cultural backgrounds of the students and faculty.

1084. Rothchild, Sylvia. TRAVELING THROUGH MIDDLE AMERICA. *Present Tense 1975 2(2): 37-40.* Discusses patterns of assimilation in three generations of Jewish families in the United States, 1925-75, and how each generation has responded to the social and religious attitudes of its parents.

1085. Rothman, Sheila. THE LIMITS OF SISTERHOOD. *Rev. in Am. Hist. 1979 7(1): 92-97.* Review article prompted by *The Maimie Papers,* edited by Ruth Rosen and Sue Davidson (Old Westbury, N.Y.: The Feminist Pr., 1977), a record of the correspondence between Fanny Quincy Howe, the wife of a wealthy Boston writer, and Maimie Pinzer, a poor Jewish immigrant, during 1910-22, which represents the intimate friendships that transcend class boundaries.

1086. Rothman, Stanley. GROUP-FANTASIES AND JEWISH RADICALISM: A PSYCHODYNAMIC INTERPRETATION. *J. of Psychohistory 1978 6(2): 211-239.* In the last century, Jews have made up a significant proportion of members of radical movements in Western culture. The source of Jewish radicalism is both sociological and psychodynamic, stemming from the Jews' historical social marginality and childrearing patterns which produce paranoid masochistic personalities. The combination pushes many Jews toward radical action. Secondary historical and psychiatric sources and original research with student radicals in the United States; 105 notes.　　　R. E. Butchart

1087. Rubin, Steven J. CONTEMPORARY AMERICAN ETHNIC LITERATURE IN FRANCE. *J. of Ethnic Studies 1975 3(1): 95-98.* The French regard Jewish and Negro writings as representations of unique American experiences and not as important commentaries on universal themes. Argues that these ethnic writings lose much of their flavor and meaning when translated into French. 6 notes.　　T. W. Smith and S

1088. Rubinstein, Aryeh. ISAAC MAYER WISE: A NEW APPRAISAL. *Jewish Social Studies 1977 39(1-2): 53-74.* Traditional interpretations of the role of Isaac Mayer Wise as a leader of 19th-century American Judaism depict him as a proponent of moderate reform in Judaism and as a champion of religious unity in the Jewish community. In fact, he was a radical Reformist whose advocacy of reform led to religious disunity and the generation of enemies in the Jewish community. Wise was an opportunistic advocate of reform who craved popularity and a position at the head of American Jewry, and often tailored his pronouncements to suit the audience he was addressing at the moment. Basically, however, his conservative statements were a cover for his almost Deistic views, stressing the role of rationalist thought in Reform Judaism. Primary sources.　　　　N. Lederer

1089. Rubinstein, W. D. THE LEFT, THE RIGHT, AND THE JEWS. *Midstream 1979 25(8): 3-7.* Jews in the Western world are disproportionately represented among the elite, thanks to the inegalitarianism and plurality of power centers under capitalism; 20th century.

1090. Rudin, Marcia R. and Rudin, A. James. BLACK JEWS IN AMERICA. *Present Tense 1979 7(1): 37-41.* Interviews black Rabbi Moshe Paris from New York City about the problems of black Jews attempting integration into the white Jewish community in America.

1091. Rustin, Bayard. JEWS AND BLACKS: A RELATIONSHIP RE-EXAMINED. *Midstream 1974 20(1): 3-12.*

1092. Schappes, Morris U. EXCERPTS FROM ROBERT MORRIS' "DIARIES IN THE OFFICE OF FINANCE, 1781-1784," REFERRING TO HAYM SALOMON AND OTHER JEWS. *Am. Jewish Hist. Q. 1977 67(1): 9-49; (2): 140-161.* Part I. In his "Diaries" Robert Morris (1734-1806), then Superintendant of Finance, refers 162 times to seven Jewish businessmen and financial agents, of which 114 mentioned Haym Solomon. This relatively large number reflects great credit on the small Jewish communities of America. The allusions to Haym Solomon help to dispel some of the exaggerated myths that surround his career as well as reveal his contributions to the cause of the Republic. 71 notes. Part II. Concludes the reproduction and analysis of the diary entries. 114 notes.　　　　F. Rosenthal

1093. Schappes, Morris U. HOW AMERICAN WRITERS SAW THE JEWS: REVIEW ESSAY. *J. of Ethnic Studies 1978 6(2): 75-92.* Surveys and comments on Louis Harap, *The Image of the Jew in American Literature: From Early Republic to Mass Immigration* (1974), "a seminal work opening and defining new areas of perception and evaluation in American life and letters," and "exemplary in conception and execution." Harap examines not only belles lettres, but also popular forms from folklore to journalism and from the dime novel to mass-circulation popular fiction, and concludes that "the history of the Jewish character in American literature is also a chapter in the history of anti-Semitism." Schappes finds Harap even too mild in his criticisms in places, but calls his section on Emma Lazarus "the best single essay in print," and that on Abraham Cahan excellent. Still Harap is inadequate in his understanding of the Jewish transformation to a primarily ethnic rather than a religious entity.　　　　G. J. Bobango

1094. Schappes, Morris U. THE POLITICAL ORIGINS OF THE UNITED HEBREW TRADES, 1888. *J. of Ethnic Studies 1977 5(1): 13-44.* Details the origins, planning, and organizational meetings which produced the United Hebrew Trades (UHT) organization in New York City, a product of Branch 8 and Branch 17 of the Socialist Labor Party. The leaders were Yiddish-speaking workingmen such as Jacob Magidow, Lev Bandes, and Bernard Weinstein, who were products of the Jewish working class rather than the older middle-class composition of American Jewry. Demonstrates the close contacts and clearly imitative nature of the UHT and the older *Vereinigte Deutsche Gewerkschaften* (German Central Labor Union). The UHT faced opposition by Jewish middle class organs such as *The Jewish Messenger* and the *American Hebrew,* who called the Farein anarchistic. The opposition of Samuel Gompers, who objected to the socialist nature of the group's program and its religious basis, also took several years to overcome. Gompers' writings later falsely claimed him as one of the organizers of the UHT. For 25 years this union was a vital factor in organizing Jewish workers and bringing them into the American labor movement. Primary and secondary sources, 88 notes.　　　　G. J. Bobango

1095. Schatt, Stanley. THE GHETTO IN RECENT AMERICAN LITERATURE. *J. of Ethnic Studies 1973 1(1): 44-54.* Concludes from an extensive examination of recent black and Jewish literature, that an understanding of Jewish and black ghetto culture is necessary in order to understand ethnic literature. This literature can in turn provide deep insights into the nature of Jewish and black culture. Based on contemporary literature and related scholarship; 37 notes.　　　T. W. Smith

1096. Schneider, William; Berman, Michael D.; and Schilut, Mark. BLOC VOTING RECONSIDERED: "IS THERE A JEWISH VOTE?" *Ethnicity 1974 1(4): 345-392.* Analysis of voting behavior among Jews, 1952-72, indicates similar patterns to other "bloc voters" with tendencies toward liberalism, adherence to the Democratic Party, and the influence of "bloc forces."

1097. Schoenberg, Philip Ernest. THE AMERICAN REACTION TO THE KISHINEV POGROM OF 1903. *Am. Jewish Hist. Q. 1974 63(3): 262-283.* American reaction to the Kishinev pogrom (in which 47 Jews were killed, more than 400 injured, and 10,000 made homeless and dependent on relief) led first to the organization of financial help for the victims and then to plans for their orderly immigration. Perhaps most surprising was the strong protest which the Roosevelt administration tried to lodge in St. Petersburg. The events were, after all, an internal affair within Russia, persecution of minority groups was taking place in other parts of the world as well, and America's treatment of its own ethnic minorities left much to be desired. The formation of the American Jewish Committee was to permanently affect Jewish communal and organizational structure. 57 notes.   F. Rosenthal

1098. Schwartz, Henry. THE UNEASY ALLIANCE: JEWISH-ANGLO RELATIONS IN SAN DIEGO, 1850-1860. *J. of San Diego Hist. 1975 20(3): 53-60.* Describes the generally harmonious relations between Jewish and other settlers in San Diego during the 1850's.   S

1099. Schwartz, Lita Linzer and Isser, Natalie. FORGOTTEN MINORITIES, SELF-CONCEPT, AND THE SCHOOLS. *Social Studies 1978 69(5): 187-190.* Textbooks written about Chinese, Japanese, and Jewish children are biased because they show unrealistic views of their cultures and life-styles. Covers the periods 1880-1920 and 1945-65. Bias against minorities may lead to damage of their self-image. 15 notes.
                                                                   L. R. Raife

1100. Scult, Melvin. MORDECAI M. KAPLAN: CHALLENGES AND CONFLICTS IN THE TWENTIES. *Am. Jewish Hist. Q. 1977 66(3): 401-416.* Mordecai M. Kaplan was an immigrant who grew up on the lower East Side of New York City and who tried to reconcile his Orthodox Jewish upbringing with the new American culture. The struggle assumed both intellectual and spiritual aspects and was the basis for Kaplan's ambivalence toward the Jewish Theological Seminary where he served as head of its Teacher's Institute and as professor of Homiletics. Analyzes the gradual development of reconstructionist thoughts, clashes with Orthodoxy and seminary colleagues, relations with administrators and the lengthy negotiations with Stephen Wise and the Jewish Institute of Religion. 39 notes.   F. Rosenthal

1101. Segal, Sheila F. FEMINISTS FOR JUDAISM. *Midstream 1975 21(7): 59-65.* Discusses the compatibility of Judaism and feminism (1970's).   S

1102. Shankman, Arnold. THE PECULIAR PEOPLE AND THE JEWS. *Am. Jewish Hist. Q. 1975 64(3): 224-235.* During the last decades of the 19th century, when thousands of European Jews fled to the United States to escape religious persecution, Christian evangelical groups intensified their missionary efforts to convert Jews to Christianity. Among the religious periodicals founded to show the Jew "his need of repentance and of a saviour" was *The Peculiar People,* founded in New York City by the Reverend Herman Friedlaender as a weekly newspaper in 1888. On his sudden death four months later the magazine was taken over by the Reverend William C. Daland, backed by a group of Seventh Day Baptists. Daland served as editor until the paper's demise in 1898. Since Daland's efforts were primarily directed toward conversion of Jews, his interests in Palestinian colonization and his arguments against anti-Semitism were not effective in a wider sense.   F. Rosenthal

1103. Shapiro, Edward S. GERMAN AND RUSSIAN JEWS IN AMERICA. *Midstream 1979 25(4): 42-51.* Discusses the reactions of established German Jews in America to the mass immigration of Jews from Russia between 1880 and 1920, and their assimilation into American culture.

1104. Shapiro, Howard M. PERCEIVED FAMILY STRUCTURE AS AN EXPLANATION OF JEWISH INTELLECTUALITY. *Sociol. Q. 1977 18(4): 448-463.* Focuses on the perceived structure of parent-adolescent relations for its effect on intellectuality in young adulthood. In addition, position in the wider societal structure and integration into a supposed intellectually oriented subculture are considered for their effects on this personality characteristic. The data reported are based on a questionnaire survey of 181 Jewish men age 22-29 residing in metropolitan St. Paul. There is a clear association between the perception structure of parent-child relations and later intellectuality. On the other hand, integration into the Jewish subculture neither leads directly to intellectuality nor is associated with the relationship between perceived family structure, and intellectuality. Position in the wider social structure, however, is important in the development of intellectuality both directly and in terms of its effect on perceived family structure.   J

1105. Showalter, Dennis E. A RIVER OF BLOOD AND TIME: IMAGES OF JEWISH-GENTILE RELATIONS IN CONTEMPORARY PULP CULTURE. *South Atlantic Q. 1977 76(1): 12-31.* Tradi-

tional literary images of Jewish-Gentile relations define the Jew by the acts of his Christian oppressors. Until recently, the Jew was either physically brutalized or spiritually assimilated by the Christian world, whether he resisted or not. Post-World War II portrayals make the Jew into freedom fighters of a classically heroic mode, or into members of a matured, independent Israel. This shift has left the American Jew all the more self-conscious of his non-Israeli, nonoppressed, highly ambivalent cultural position. 25 notes.   W. L. Olbrich

1106. Shumsky, Neil Larry. ZANGWILL'S *THE MELTING POT:* ETHNIC TENSIONS ON STAGE. *Am. Q. 1975 27(1): 29-41.* The widely held interpretation of Israel Zangwill's play as a hymn to ethnic assimilation in America oversimplifies its contradictions and inconsistencies. Zangwill expresses ambivalence over the immigrant acceptance of Americanization at the expense of ethnic tradition. The hero, David Quixano, consciously tries to reject his Judaic heritage while other characters praise it. The play is a depiction of the tormented immigrant mind, including the dilemma of generational conflict.   N. Lederer

1107. Silberschlag, Eisig. THE THRUST OF HEBREW LETTERS IN AMERICA: A PANORAMIC VIEW. *Jewish Social Studies 1976 38(3-4): 277-288.* Hebrew literature in America has been a literature of immigrants and displays a concern with affairs of the homeland and a spiritual yearning for the *shtetl* as well as for the Holy Land. The literature, predominantly poetic in form, has been highly romantic and draws on Victorian and American models for some of its themes. Among the themes have been those concerned with blacks and the American Indian. Despite its foreign focus, Hebrew literature has been most cognizant of American ideals. Primary sources.   N. Lederer

1108. Silverberg, David. HILLEL ON THE CAMPUS. *Present Tense 1978 5(2): 53-59.* The Hillel Foundation is a Jewish association active in colleges and universities since 1923.

1109. Silverberg, David. JEWISH STUDIES ON THE AMERICAN CAMPUS. *Present Tense 1978 5(4): 52-56.* Both academic and community interest are reflected in the growth of Jewish studies programs in US colleges and universities, 1967-77; the movement resulted from growing ethnic consciousness and the Israeli victory in the 1967 Six-Day War.

1110. Silverberg, David. THE "OLD" POOR—AND THE "NEW": WHAT'S HAPPENING TO THEM? *Present Tense 1977 4(3): 59-64.* Examines the plight of American urban Jewish poor. Presents case studies, and quotes Ann G. Wolfe, Misha Avramoff, Yisroel Rosenfeld, Yaakov Tzimman, Rose Fefelman, Leonard Haber, Eugene Weiss, Jack Simcha Cohen, Max Friedson, Alfred P. Miller, and Steven Robbins. Cites official government, local community, and Hassidic sources. Primary and secondary sources; 4 photos.   R. B. Mendel

1111. Sinclair, Clive. A CONVERSATION WITH ISAAC BASHEVIS SINGER. *Encounter [Great Britain] 1979 52(2): 20-28.* Records a recent interview with Isaac Bashevis Singer, winner of the 1978 Nobel Prize for literature, in which he discusses his life in Poland and the United States, Jews, his writings, and the work of his brother, Israel Joshua Singer, author of *The Brothers Ashkenazi, Yoshe Kalb, East of Eden* and others.

1112. Singer, David. LIVING WITH INTERMARRIAGE. *Commentary 1979 68(1): 48-53.* Discusses the issue of marriage between Jews and Christians in the United States, which was discussed at a national symposium on intermarriage in 1963, and provides data on intermarriage from studies since 1962.

1113. Singer, David. A PROFILE OF THE JEWISH ACADEMIC: SOME RECENT STUDIES. *Midstream 1973 19(6): 57-64.*

1114. Singer, David. VOICES OF ORTHODOXY. *Commentary 1974 58(1): 54-60.* In view of the "Orthodox renaissance," describes ideological differences between modernist and sectarian branches of Orthodox Judaism.   S

1115. Singer, Isaac Bashevis and Howe, Irving. YIDDISH TRADITION VS. JEWISH TRADITION: A DIALOGUE. *Midstream 1973 19(6): 33-38.*

1116. Singerman, Robert. AMERICAN-JEWISH REACTIONS TO THE SPANISH CIVIL WAR. *J. of Church and State 1977 19(2): 261-278.* Considers the background of Jews in Spain and examines the America Jewish press's reaction to the treatment of Jews during the Spanish Civil War, 1936-39. 58 notes.   E. E. Eminhizer

1117. Sklare, Marshall. AMERICAN JEWRY—THE EVER-DYING PEOPLE. *Midstream 1976 22(6): 17-27.* Examines in the Bicentennial year the question of whether American Jewry will survive as a viable community in the United States in the next 100 years, and provides a brief history of the Jewish experience in America after 1880.

1118. Sklare, Marshall. THE GREENING OF JUDAISM. *Commentary 1974 58(6): 51-57.* Reviews *The Jewish Catalog: A Do-It Yourself Kit,* Richard Siegel, Michael Strassfeld, and Sharon Strassfeld, eds. (Jewish Publication Society of America, 1974).   S

1119. Sklare, Marshall. THE JEW IN AMERICAN SOCIOLOGICAL THOUGHT. *Ethnicity 1974 1(2): 151-173.* Jews in academia are more active professionally than non-Jews, but are quite often alienated from their own Jewish communities. Jewish sociologists involved in the study of Jews fall into three schools: assimilationists who see the Jewish community as a dying anachronism and advocate the right of assimilation, critical intellectuals who idealize the immigrant communities but are alienated from and critical of contemporary Jewry, and survivalists who see both continuity and assimilation, and are unsentimental about the old communities, but detect an ongoing liberalism. 28 notes.   E. Barkan

1120. Sklare, Marshall. JEWISH RELIGION AND ETHNICITY AT THE BICENTENNIAL. *Midstream 1975 21(9): 19-28.* The survival of the Jewish religion in the United States has been deeply dependent upon the Jews' sense of ethnic unity.

1121. Sklare, Marshall. PROBLEMS IN THE TEACHING OF CONTEMPORARY JEWISH STUDIES. *Am. Jewish Hist. Q. 1974 63(4): 361-368.* Contemporary Jewish studies is a newcomer in the academic world, and has several problems to resolve before it can become a fully developed discipline. One of nine related articles in this issue.   S

1122. Spetter, Allan. THE UNITED STATES THE RUSSIAN JEWS AND THE RUSSIAN FAMINE OF 1891-1892. *Am. Jewish Hist. Q. 1975 64(3): 236-244.* The United States, aware of its world power status, became involved in the internal affairs of the Russian Empire in the early 1890's because of Russia's persecution of the Jews and the great famine. Diplomatic representations made by American foreign service personnel are surveyed along with the evasive answers of Russian officials. Even though the Benjamin Harrison administration was not able to ameliorate the lot of the Russian Jews, it provided a haven for those who left. Russian policy led ultimately to the cancellation of the 1832 commercial treaty.   F. Rosenthal

1123. Sprenger, Bernice C. THE BURTON HISTORICAL COLLECTION AND ITS JEWISH ARCHIVES. *Michigan Jewish Hist. 1973 13(1): 5-7.* Covers items concerning Jews in Michigan from the Burton Historical Collection of the Detroit Public Library.   S

1124. Starr, Jerold M. RELIGIOUS PREFERENCE, RELIGIOSITY, AND OPPOSITION TO WAR. *Sociol. Analysis 1975 36(4): 323-334.* Discusses the high percentage of Jewish youth involved in the anti-Vietnam War protest movements of the 1960's.

1125. Stern, Malcolm H. REFORMING OF REFORM JUDAISM—PAST, PRESENT, AND FUTURE. *Am. Jewish Hist. Q. 1973 63(2): 111-137.* Summarizes the history of Reform Judaism from its beginnings in France and Germany during the time of the French Revolution to its flowering in America during the past 100 years. Includes an extensive bibliography of its history, institutions, biographies, sociological studies, rituals, periodicals, and congregational histories by states.   F. Rosenthal

1126. Stern, Norton B. and Kramer, William M. AN ISAAC MAYER WISE 1890 PLACEMENT LETTER TO SAN FRANCISCO.

Am. Jewish Hist. Q. 1973 63(2): 204-207. A recently discovered letter of Rabbi Isaac Mayer Wise to Abraham J. Prager, president of Congregation Sherith Israel of San Francisco, 28 April 1890, shows the role of Wise in rabbinic placement. As the patriarch of American Jewry he felt it his responsibility and moral duty to provide objective information when men of his close acquaintance, whether students or colleagues, applied for rabbinic positions. Reproduces the letter. 9 notes.   F. Rosenthal

1127. Stern, Norton B. and Kramer, William M. THE MAJOR ROLE OF POLISH JEWS IN THE PIONEER WEST. *Western States Jewish Hist. Q. 1976 8(4): 326-344.* In the West many Polish Jews hid their Polishness as an effort to expedite their social movement. Polish Jews were considered inferior to German Jews. The myth therefore developed that few Polish Jews settled in the West. This is now being repudiated by scholars studying voter records, tombstones, and other sources. Census records show that Polish Jews outnumbered German Jews in early California. Many so-called German synagogues were really established by Polish Jews and followed the Minhag Polem (Polish custom). Contemporary accounts credited Germans with starting the congregations. 70 notes.   R. A. Garfinkle

1128. Stern, Norton B. and Kramer, William M. THE POLISH JEW IN POSEN AND IN THE EARLY WEST. *Western States Jewish Hist. Q. 1978 10(4): 327-329.* Polish Jews came early and were the numerically dominant Jewish subethnic group in the West. Their Polish-Jewish culture was often disguised because they came from Prussian-occupied areas, carried Prussian passports, and frequently claimed to be Germans instead of Poles because of the prejudice of Americans. In America, they engaged in the same type of business they had known in the province of Posen—selling dry goods, hardware, farming implements, liquor, and so on. Covers the 1880's.   B. S. Porter

1129. Sultanik, Aaron. MOVE OVER, MARLOWE! *Midstream 1977 23(1): 81-84.* Discusses the influence of Jewish attitudes, wit, and characters in the detective novels of Roger Simon (*The Big Fix, Wild Turkey*) and Andrew Bergman (*The Big Kiss-Off of 1944, Hollywood and LeVine*), 1970's; the strain of cynicism in their work is a departure from the traditional detective fiction of Raymond Chandler, Ross Macdonald, and Dashiell Hammett.

1130. Szajkowski, Zosa. THE CONSUL AND THE IMMIGRANT: A CASE OF BUREAUCRATIC BIAS. *Jewish Social Studies 1974 36(1): 3-18.* Examines the tightening restrictions on immigration from Eastern Europe and Germany to the United States in the first few years after the end of World War I. Quotas enabled anti-Semitic diplomatic representatives to apply American immigration restrictions to Jews unequally. Based on primary and secondary sources in English, Yiddish, and Polish; 62 notes.   P. E. Schoenberg

1131. Szajkowski, Zosa. DEPORTATION OF JEWISH IMMIGRANTS AND RETURNEES BEFORE WORLD WAR I. *Am. Jewish Hist. Q. 1978 67(4): 291-306.* A series of acts during 1875-1907 effectively restricted free immigration to the United States, even though their confused wording allowed the most varied and contradictory interpretations by officials and the courts. Describes challenges to these interpretations, several by Simon Wolf and his associates. Mentions the plight of forced as well as voluntary returnees, who often were forced to work on cattle boats under the most inhumane conditions. The most unusual feature of Jewish immigration to America was its definitive character: the percentage of Jewish returnees was greatly below that of other ethnic groups. 43 notes.   F. Rosenthal

1132. Szajkowski, Zosa. THE *YAHUDI* AND THE IMMIGRANT: A REAPPRAISAL. *Am. Jewish Hist. Q. 1973 63(1): 13-44.* Recent research has shown that the American Jews of German origin—called the *yahudim* by their East-European brethren—undertook positive and meaningful action to assure mass immigration of Russian Jews into the United States in the period before World War I. Distribution of immigrants away from New York, care of women and children, appeals to prevent unjust deportations, and ultimately strenuous efforts to prevent limiting legislation were some of the efforts of the established Jewish organizations and of leaders such as Jacob Schiff, Abram I. Elkus, Max James Kohler, Louis Marschall, and Simon Wolf. Based on contemporary newspapers, archives, and collections of papers; 72 notes.   F. Rosenthal

1133. Tenenbaum, Marc H. HOLY YEAR 1975 AND THE JEWISH JUBILEE YEAR. *Lutheran Q. 1974 26(3): 258-268.* Describes the concept of the Jewish Jubilee Year as an aid to those Christians celebrating the holy year of 1975 proclaimed by Pope Paul VI. Derived from the God-given law on Mount Sinai, the Jubilee had four objectives: freeing the slaves with their families, restoring all purchased land to the original owner, releasing the land from cultivation, and educating the people in the knowledge of the Torah. For centuries, Jews observed the Jubilee every 50 years. It is estimated 1975 is the 20th year of the current Jubilee cycle. Based largely on the Torah; 4 notes.   J. A. Kicklighter

1134. Trunk, Isaiah. THE CULTURAL DIMENSION OF THE AMERICAN JEWISH LABOR MOVEMENT. *Yivo Ann. of Jewish Social Sci. 1976 (16): 342-393.* Divides the cultural history of the American Jewish labor movement into three periods. The first period, 1880's-90's, was characterized by socialism, a desire for educational achievement, and a tendency toward assimilation. The second period, 1900-20's, was caused by a new influx of immigrants coming after the Dreyfus trial and the Kishinev pogrom. As a result, they were disillusioned with socialism and tended toward cultural autonomy, radical nationalism, and Zionist socialism. A growth of the Hebrew and Yiddish press and literature characterized the Jewish labor movement during this period. The last period, extending from the 1930's to the end of World War II, saw a rise of national solidarity through such groups as the Workmen's Circle and the Jewish Labor Committee, which worked against anti-Semitism.   R. J. Wechman

1135. Urofsky, Melvin I. STEPHEN WISE: THE LAST OF THE SUPERSTARS. *Present Tense 1979 6(4): 21-26.* Recounts the deeds and achievements—especially those devoted to Zionism, ecumenism, charity, and efforts to persuade President Franklin Delano Roosevelt to assist in saving the European Jews during World War II—of the Hungarian-born American rabbi, Stephen Samuel Wise (1874-1949).

1136. Varon, Benno Weiser. THE HAUNTING OF MEYER LEVIN. *Midstream 1976 22(7): 7-23.* Discusses why the Jewish literary establishment has ignored the talented author Meyer Levin and gives a brief summary of his work, 1931-76.

1137. Wacker, R. Fred. AN AMERICAN DILEMMA: THE RACIAL THEORIES OF ROBERT E. PARK AND GUNNAR MYRDAL. *Phylon 1976 37(2): 117-125.* Many of Franz Boas's students were Jewish and helped popularize the idea that there were no biological races; by the 1940's the idea of race had become taboo in many quarters; social scientists preferred to talk about minority groups. In *An American Dilemma,* Gunnar Myrdal attacked the "overly pessimistic" race relations theory of Robert E. Park. Myrdal's major thesis was that "the Negro problem" was one of ideology. "His optimism . . . was based upon his belief that . . . white Americans felt a dissonance between their democratic ideals and their treatment of Negroes." Park did not believe that America was an idealistic nation. "For Park, California was a symbol of the "last frontier," a region and an environment where races and peoples would . . . intermingle." Park's vision was deeper than Myrdal's. 15 notes.   E. P. Stickney

1138. Wald, Alan M. THE MENORAH GROUP MOVES LEFT. *Jewish Social Studies 1976 38(3-4): 289-320.* A group of Jewish intellectuals clustered around Elliott Ettleson Cohen and worked on *The Menorah Journal* in the 1920's. They generated the development of a Jewish humanism that led to a Jewish cultural renaissance. In the early 1930's, Cohen, Lionel Trilling, George Novack, Herbert Solow and others in the group gravitated toward the Communists and became especially prominent in the National Committee for the Defense of Political Prisoners. By the mid-1930's, most of these individuals broke from the Communists and supported Trotskyist and other radical organizations. Tess Slesinger's novel, *The Unpossessed,* provides a vivid portrait of the attitudes and personality traits of some members of the Menorah Group.   N. Lederer

1139. Wald, Alan. MIKE GOLD AND THE RADICAL LITERARY MOVEMENT OF THE 1930'S. *Internat. Socialist R. 1973 34(3): 34-37.* Review essay on Michael Folsom's *Mike Gold: A Literary Anthology* (New York: Int. Publ., 1972).   S

1140. Weitz, Marvin. AFFIRMATIVE ACTION: A JEWISH DEATH WISH? *Midstream 1979 25(1): 9-17.* Assesses the outcome of affirmative action spawned by the Civil Rights Act of 1964 in light of the Bakke decision; discusses anti-Semitism in the black community and the need to reassess the workings of affirmative action.

1141. Weitz, Marvin. THE SHATTERED ALLIANCE BETWEEN THE US BLACKS AND JEWS. *Patterns of Prejudice [Great Britain] 1978 12(3): 11-18.* Economic and social competition during 1940's-70's has resulted in growing tension between American blacks and Jews, which may lead to violent conflict.

1142. Werner, Alfred. BEN-ZION, JEWISH PAINTER. *Midstream 1973 19(9): 24-35.* Discusses the career of the Expressionist painter Ben-Zion Weinman (b. 1897). Ben-Zion turned to the visual arts while living in New York in the 1930's. He exhibited as one of The Ten, with Adolph Gottlieb and Mark Rothko, 1936-42. 6 illus.   D. D. Cameron

1143. Werner, Alfred. GHETTO GRADUATES. *Am. Art J. 1973 5(2): 71-82.* For religious and political reasons, Jewish settlements in Eastern Europe were "devoid of anything artistic." But Jewish immigrants (1880's-1920's) settling in American urban ghettos were free from tradition, and ghetto artists involved themselves fully in revolutionary art trends. Secondary sources; 12 fig., 23 notes.   R. M. Frame III

1144. Werner, Alfred. THROUGH THE GOLDEN DOOR. *Am. Jewish Arch. 1977 29(2): 95-106.* Between 1905 and 1945, a "Jewish School" of artists and sculptors maintained a discernible presence in the world of American art and especially in New York City. Examines these individuals who shunned the stereotyped paths to Jewish success in America—as doctors or lawyers—and instead contributed their talents for the sake of beauty and expression.   J

1145. Williams, Oscar R., Jr. HISTORICAL IMPRESSIONS OF BLACK-JEWISH RELATIONS PRIOR TO WORLD WAR II. *Negro Hist. Bull. 1977 40(4): 728-731.* Prior to the 1920's, black and Jewish relations were limited to the South, where Jews reacted to blacks like other white southerners. Migration during World War I brought blacks into northern ghettos where they were exploited by Jewish landlords and merchants; this aroused "Black anti-Semitism" which was directed at the exploitation, not at Jewish religious beliefs. At the same time, blacks have held Jews as success models, identifying with their escape from bondage and their rise in status here. By 1940, black and Jewish relations had entered a new era of awareness from which developed cooperation in the area of civil rights. Based on secondary material; 22 notes.   R. E. Noble

1146. Wisse, Ruth R. *DI YUNGE* AND THE PROBLEM OF JEWISH AESTHETICISM. *Jewish Social Studies 1976 38(3-4): 265-276.* The group of working class Jewish immigrant writers known as *Di Yunge* emerged on the Yiddish literary scene, mainly in New York City, during 1902-13. Their goal of striving toward an aesthetic ideal by emphasizing mood and feeling was at variance with the dominant Yiddish literary tradition of homily, practicalism, and didacticism. To the young men of *Di Yunge,* beauty was the highest ideal; and the means to achieve its actuality were to be sought not only in the Jewish milieu but also within the literary traditions of other cultures.   N. Lederer

1147. Wolkinson, Benjamin W. LABOR AND THE JEWISH TRADITION—A REAPPRAISAL. *Jewish Social Studies 1978 40(3-4): 231-238.* Responds to Michael S. Kogan's "Liberty and Labor in the Jewish Tradition," *(Ideas, A Journal of Contemporary Jewish Thought,* Spring, 1975). Argues that union efforts to compel workers to join a union or to pay dues as a condition of employment do not conflict with biblical and talmudic principles concerning the rights of workers. Kogan, supported by Rabbi Jakob J. Petuchkowski, also stated that such union demands were opposed by leading Jewish figures in the trade union movement, including Samuel Gompers. Gompers supported voluntarism in the formulation of AFL policies, but he was very concerned about union security. Even Louis D. Brandeis, an opponent of the closed shop, favored preferential employment of union members. The thesis that union security is antagonistic to Jewish law and tradition regarding freedom of choice ignores the fact that throughout Jewish history freedom of choice has been subordinated to the well-being of the group.   N. Lederer

1148. Yellowitz, Irwin. AMERICAN JEWISH LABOR: HISTORIOGRAPHICAL PROBLEMS AND PROSPECTS. *Am. Jewish Hist. Q. 1976 65(3): 203-213.* Although the history of American Jewish labor has been a subject of inquiry for over half a century, the major problems in concept and method have not been resolved. The boundaries of American Jewish labor as distinguished from that of the American Jewish labor *movement* should be defined by the influence of Jewish identity and concerns upon leaders and institutions, and the impact of these major figures and their organizations upon the Jewish community. The complex interaction of Jewish, American, trade union, and socialist concerns deserves further study (e.g., Samuel Gompers or Meyer London as Jewish rather than American labor leaders) as well as considerations of events and persons outside New York City. 34 notes.　　　F. Rosenthal

1149. Yellowitz, Irwin. MORRIS HILLQUIT: AMERICAN SOCIALISM AND JEWISH CONCERNS. *Am. Jewish Hist. 1978 68(2): 163-188.* Morris Hillquit (1869-1933), an agnostic and an American socialist leader, posed antireligious appeals and worked to neutralize this issue because it tended to drive away potential supporters. Throughout his career Hillquit, often following the advice of his friend Abraham Cahan, had to accept the reality of his ethnic political base in the New York City Jewish ghetto. Evidence from his political campaigns illustrates this thesis. Ethnic identity and concerns were a stronger influence among socialists in the Jewish community in 1930 than in 1900, and Hillquit recognized this. 42 notes.　　　F. Rosenthal

1150. Yenish, Joseph. THE ASSOCIATION OF JEWISH LIBRARIES. *Special Lib. 1967 58(10): 707-709.* An offshoot of the Jewish Librarians Association (established in 1946), the Association of Jewish Libraries seeks to promote and improve Jewish libraries, the publication and dissemination of information of aid to Jewish libraries, and the establishment of more Jewish libraries; 1965-67.

1151. Zanger, Jules. ON NOT MAKING IT IN AMERICA. *Am. Studies (Lawrence, KS) 1976 17(1): 39-48.* The Jewish mother has become a standard literary stereotype, and a boy turning his back on his mother has symbolized the rejection of a cluster of religious and cultural values. This became a necessary reaction to the Americanization process. American Jewish literature also reveals that behind every Jewish mother is a failed Jewish father. To accept an Americanness, these immigrants frequently had to reject part of their Jewishness. Primary and secondary sources; 6 notes.　　　J. Andrew

1152. Zucker, Bat-Ami. RADICAL JEWISH INTELLECTUALS AND THE NEW DEAL. Artzi, Pinhas, ed. *Bar-Ilan Studies in History* (Ramat-Gan, Israel: Bar-Ilan U. Pr., 1978): 275-283. American socialists, communists and liberals of the 1930's were predominantly non-Jewish, but they contained small pockets of Jewish radicals, who had originated in the 1900's. Argues that the second generation Jews in the 1930's faced an "alienation" crisis because of their transition from poverty to wealth; therefore, many became radicals. But Franklin D. Roosevelt's election campaign of 1932 promised Jews greater social and economic freedom. This made it much easier for Jewish radicals to accept the new Establishment, which they saw as more unified than the Left. Based on newspapers and secondary works; 34 notes.　　　A. Alcock

1153. Unsigned. DATA ON DUTCH JEWRY IN AMERICA. *Michigan Jewish Hist. 1973 13(1): 30-31, (2) 22-31.* Gives the names, origins, occupation, age, and other information on Dutch Jews who immigrated to the United States during 1852-77.　　　S

1154. —. [ECONOMIC OPPORTUNITY AND EASTERN EUROPEAN JEWISH IMMIGRANTS]. *J. of Econ. Hist. 1978 38(1): 235-255.*
Kahan, Arcadius. ECONOMIC OPPORTUNITIES AND SOME PILGRIM'S PROGRESS: JEWISH IMMIGRANTS FROM EASTERN EUROPE IN THE U.S., 1880-1914, *pp. 235-251.* The Jewish immigrants from Eastern Europe during 1890-1914 can be distinguished as three successive cohorts which differed in terms of skills, education and degree of urbanization experienced in the countries of their origin. The Jewish immigrants were able to take advantage of the economic opportunities in the US for the following reasons: 1) To a large extent their skill endowment was congruent with the demand for labor of certain United States industries;

2) The high concentration of the immigrants in the large cities permitted development of various networks of communication which provided job information and facilitated search; 3) the immigrants' rate of literacy was high relative to other ethnic immigrant groups and their urban background made it easier to adjust to the conditions of an industrializing and urbanizing society. The Jewish immigrants from Eastern Europe were able after 10-15 years of residence in the United States to reach the income level of native-born workers of similar age, education and skill.
Hannon, Joan U. DISCUSSION, *pp. 252-255.*　　　J

1155. —. THE FIRST FUND-RAISERS FOR THE HEBREW UNION COLLEGE IN THE FAR EAST. *Western States Jewish Hist. Q. 1975 8(1): 55-58.* Founded in July 1873 by Rabbi Isaac Mayer Wise, the Union of American Hebrew Congregations set as one of its goals the establishment of a Hebrew college. Rabbi Wise used his Anglo-Hebrew weekly paper, *The Israelite,* to solicit funds for the school. Lists of principal Jews in many western communities were published in the paper. These men collected donations from their communities. Provides the lists for California, Nevada, New Mexico, Utah, and Washington Territory. On 4 October 1875 the first classes of the Hebrew Union College were held. 4 notes.　　　R. A. Garfinkle

1156. Unsigned. HEBREW UNION COLLEGE-JEWISH INSTITUTE OF RELIGION—A CENTENNIAL DOCUMENTARY. *Am. Jewish Arch. 1974 26(2): 103-244.* "Founded in Cincinnati in 1875 the Hebrew Union College was conjoined in later years with New York's Jewish Institute of Religion and subsequently added campuses in Los Angeles and Jerusalem. It is not only the Reform movement's leading seminary for the training of rabbis but also a major center of Jewish intellectual endeavor."　　　J

1158. —. AN INTIMATE PORTRAIT OF THE UNION OF AMERICAN HEBREW CONGREGATIONS—A CENTENNIAL DOCUMENTARY. *Am. Jewish Arch. 1973 25(1): 3-116.* The Union of American Hebrew Congregations is the national organization encompassing Reform Jewish congregations. Documents cover the founding in 1873, the famous "trefa" (nonkosher) banquet of 1883, Zionism, Jewish-Christian dialogues, Jewish chaplains for the armed forces, tradition and rituals, the exposure of anti-Semitism in the Soviet Union and racism in the United States, opposition to the Vietnam War and the Jewish Chautauqua Society. Based on the Union's archives; 7 photos, 46 notes.　　　E. S. Shapiro

1159. —. JEWISH AMERICANS. Sowell, Thomas, ed. *Essays and Data on American Ethnic Groups* (Washington, D.C.: Urban Inst. Pr., 1978): 362-373. Statistics on Jewish American family income distribution by number of income earners per family; family income by age, education, and sex of family head; family income by number of income earners, education, and sex of family head; and number of children in the household by woman's education and family income. From National Jewish Population Study, 1969; 3 tables.　　　K. A. Talley

1160. —. LIFE IN EARLY AMERICA: THE JEWS IN THE COLONIES. *Early Am. Life 1978 9(1): 20-25.* Throughout the colonies the reception of Jews varied greatly, but during the American Revolution Jews acted like other citizens: some were active revolutionaries, attracted to the Revolution by the Declaration of Independence, others remained loyal to Britain. It wasn't until 1876 however, that Jewish Americans achieved full protection of the law and legal equal opportunity.

1161. —. A WESTERN PICTURE PARADE. *Western States Jewish Hist. Q. 1976 8(4): 345-350.* Presents six photos with captions concerning early western Jewish history. Includes: cantor Josef (Yosele) Rosenblatt (1880-1933) with Yiddish actor Elia Tenenholtz (b. 1890) and Rabbi Solomon M. Neches (1893-1957); pioneer Tucson businessman Samuel H. Drachman (1837-1911); professional boxer Joe Choynski fighting Jeff Jeffries; San Bernardino County, California supervisor Isaac R. Brunn (1836-1917); Harris Newmark High School in Los Angeles; and Jewish owned tent stores in Candle City, Kotzebue Sound, Alaska. 6 photos.　　　R. A. Garfinkle

Specific Communities

1162. Angel, Marc D. NOTES ON THE EARLY HISTORY OF SEATTLE'S SEPHARDIC COMMUNITY. *Western States Jewish Hist. Q. 1974 7(1): 22-30.* The first Sephardic Jews arrived in Seattle in 1906 and by 1912 there were about 800 located there. They had many problems getting themselves organized as a religious group and locating a suitable rabbi. Their problems were similar to those faced by Sephardic Jews in other American cities who held onto the customs and traditions of their homelands. Few of the immigrants became American citizens. 15 notes.   R. A. Garfinkle

1163. Angel, Marc D. THE SEPHARDIC THEATER OF SEATTLE. *Am. Jewish Arch. 1973 25(2): 156-160.* "An account of how the Turkish immigrant Leon Behar and others developed a theater for the Seattle Sephardic community, particularly during the 1920's and 1930's."   J

1164. Applebaum, Phillip. THE JEWS OF IOSCO COUNTY, MICHIGAN. *Michigan Jewish Hist. 1976 16(1): 18-38.* Describes the settlement patterns of the Eastern European Jews, generally merchants and tailors, from 1866 to 1975.

1165. Applebaum, Phillip. THE JEWS OF KALKASKA COUNTY, MICHIGAN. *Michigan Jewish Hist. 1979 19(1): 4-10.* Discusses Jewish settlers during 1870-1900.

1166. Applebaum, Phillip. THE JEWS OF MONTMORENCY COUNTY, MICHIGAN. *Michigan Jewish Hist. 1978 18(1): 5-14.* Covers 1893-1970.

1167. Arden, Sylvia Ann. SAN DIEGO PURIM BALL IN 1888. *Western States Jewish Hist. Q. 1974 7(1): 39-43.* Reprints text of article from *The Jewish Progress*, San Francisco, 9 March 1888. Relates who served on the various Purim Ball committees with short biographies of the people mentioned in the original article. Primary and secondary sources; 20 notes.   R. A. Garfinkle

1168. Beck, Nelson R. THE USE OF LIBRARY AND EDUCATIONAL FACILITIES BY RUSSIAN-JEWISH IMMIGRANTS IN NEW YORK CITY, 1880-1914: THE IMPACT OF CULTURE. *J. of Lib. Hist. 1977 12(2): 129-149.* Discusses use of the public library and its services by Russian-Jewish immigrants in New York City between 1880 and 1914, and the historic and cultural influences which caused these particular immigrants not to fit Michael Harris's revisionist interpretation of American library history. Covers Hebrew educational associations and libraries, and Jewish newspapers of the period. Primary and secondary sources; 124 notes.   A. C. Dewees

1169. Berman, Myron, ed. JOSEPH JOEL: MY RECOLLECTIONS AND EXPERIENCES OF RICHMOND, VIRGINIA, U. S. A., 1884-1892. *Virginia Mag. of Hist. and Biog. 1979 87(3): 344-356.* Joel, a Jewish jewelry merchant of Richmond, looks back on his childhood from the perspective of the 1950's. Joel's family, headed by his father, a small-scale jewelry merchant, lived in Richmond to 1884 and returned to the Ukraine from whence it came. The younger Joel came back to the United States and ultimately Richmond in 1914. The bulk of the memoir deals with the social history of Richmond Jews. The editor provides translation of many Yiddish terms used by Joel. 70 notes.   P. J. Woehrmann

1170. Bernstein, Seth. THE ECONOMIC LIFE OF THE JEWS IN SAN FRANCISCO DURING THE 1860'S AS REFLECTED IN THE CITY DIRECTORIES. *Am. Jewish Arch. 1975 27(1): 70-77.*

1171. Berrol, Selma C. EDUCATION AND SOCIAL MOBILITY: THE JEWISH EXPERIENCE IN NEW YORK CITY, 1880-1920. *Am. Jewish Hist. Q. 1976 65(3): 257-271.* The New York City public schools were totally unprepared to accommodate the large number of immigrant children pouring into the Lower East Side. Because city schools held an educational philosophy unfriendly to non-English backgrounds, most Jews until 1910 or so did not move up the economic ladder by taking advantage of New York's educational opportunities. Widespread utilization of secondary and higher education followed improve-

ments in educational status, rather than the other way around. Primary and secondary sources; 33 notes.   F. Rosenthal

1172. Blumauer, Blanche. COUNCIL OF JEWISH WOMEN IN PORTLAND—1905. *Western States Jewish Hist. Q. 1976 9(1): 19-20.* Organized in 1895 for self-help and improvement, the Council of Jewish Women of Portland, Oregon, established a Neighborhood House in 1904. In 1905, 200 children took advantage of the various schools and activities provided by this project. Quoted from *The Jewish Times and Observer*, San Francisco, 17 February 1905.   B. S. Porter

1173. Braude, William G. *EZRA:* A JOURNAL OF OPINION. *Rhode Island Jewish Hist. Notes 1977 7(3): 432-436.* Short discussion on the aim, contents, and availability of a Jewish journal, *Ezra,* printed by the Order of Ezra, 1911-77, from Providence, Rhode Island.

1174. Breibart, Solomon. THE SYNAGOGUES OF KAHAL KADOSH BETH ELOHIM, CHARLESTON. *South Carolina Hist. Mag. 1979 80(3): 215-235.* Provides a brief history of Jews in South Carolina dating to 1695, and describes the synagogues of Kahal Kadosh Beth Elohim (Holy Congregation House of God), from 1749 until 1978, in Charleston; includes photographs and floor plans.

1175. Brener, David A. LANCASTER'S FIRST JEWISH COMMUNITY, 1715-1804: THE ERA OF JOSEPH SIMON. *J. of the Lancaster County Hist. Soc. 1976 80(4): 211-321.* Examines the Jewish community in Lancaster County, begun by the first Jewish resident, Joseph Simon.

1176. Broadbent, T. L. THE SUD-CALIFORNIA POST: A JEWISH EDITOR VIEWS THE NEWS. *Western States Jewish Hist. Q. 1973 6(1): 34-40.* Conrad Jacoby published the German-language newspaper *Die Sud-California Post* in Los Angeles, 1874-92. The paper ran until 1914 and served the large German-speaking population of southern California. 8 notes.   R. A. Garfinkle

1177. Burke, John C. THE BREAK IN. *Rhode Island Jewish Hist. Notes 1974 6(4): 532-541.* An account of the forcible reopening of the Touro Synagogue by the Jewish community of Newport, Rhode Island, as told by Judge John C. Burke, who aided in the 1902 struggle.   S

1178. Carosso, Vincent P. A FINANCIAL ELITE: NEW YORK'S GERMAN-JEWISH INVESTMENT BANKERS. *Am. Jewish Hist. Q. 1976 66(1): 67-88.* German Jewish bankers began to assume an important role in American finance in the 1830's when public and private borrowing to pay for internal improvement increased rapidly and significantly. Men such as August Belmont, Rothschild's agent, Philip Speyer, Jacob Schiff, the Seligmans, the Lehman brothers, Jules Bache, and Marcus Goldman are some of the people whose careers illustrate this financial elite. As was true of their non-Jewish counterparts, family, personal, and business connections, a reputation for honesty and integrity, ability, and a willingness to take calculated risks were essential to recruit capital from widely scattered sources. The contributions of these investment bankers to American and Jewish life and society have been continuous, many sided, and substantial for over a century. 55 notes.   F. Rosenthal

1179. Coffee, Rudolph I. JEWISH CONDITIONS IN SAN FRANCISCO. *Western States Jewish Hist. Q. 1976 8(3): 251-256.* In this reprint of an article published in *The Menorah*, New York, September 1906, the author details the condition of Jews in San Francisco after the earthquake. His report covers the destruction and repair of several synagogues. The Home for Aged and Disabled Hebrews was destroyed, the Old People's Home was damaged, and the buildings of the Eureka Benevolent Society and the Independent Order of B'nai B'rith were burned. Many Jews left the city and settled in Oakland. 11 notes.   R. A. Garfinkle

1180. Coiner, Miles W., Jr. THE GRAND OPERA HOUSE AND THE GOLDEN AGE OF THE LEGITIMATE THEATER IN KANSAS CITY. *Missouri Hist. R. 1973 67(3): 407-423.* Relates the history of the Grand Opera House in Kansas City, Missouri. Built in 1891 by Abraham Judah and a partner, the Grand earned a national reputation, attracted great stars, and maintained popular prices. In 1916 it was sold and became a movie house until 1926, when it was turned into a parking garage. Based on contemporary newspaper reports and secondary sources; 9 illus., 3 photos, 48 notes.   N. J. Street

1181. Cowan, Max P. MEMORIES OF THE JEWISH FARMERS AND RANCHERS OF COLORADO. *Western States Jewish Hist. Q. 1977 9(3): 218-225.* Two attempts to establish Jewish farm colonies in Colorado, in 1882 and 1884, failed, but many individual Jews were successful as farmers and ranchers. Young immigrants who came to Colorado as miners and railway laborers settled on the land and took up farming. Some who started out as cattle brokers acquired ranches and herds of their own. Most of the Jews who went into farming and ranching have passed away. Their children moved to the cities and their farms became part of large conglomerates. Based on personal recollection; 5 photos.   B. S. Porter

1182. Daniels, Doris Groshen. COLONIAL JEWRY: RELIGION, DOMESTIC AND SOCIAL RELATIONS. *Am. Jewish Hist. Q. 1977 66(3): 375-400.* Describes the activities of New York's colonial Jewry. Discusses social relations with Christian surroundings, the influx of Ashkenazi Jews until they outnumbered the Sephardim after 1720, inevitable intermarriages, the role of the synagogue, the nature of strong family bonds, and the problems of 18th-century schools. Abigail Franks, the best-known Jewish lady of the age, had much in common with Abigail Adams. 61 notes.   F. Rosenthal

1183. Dubrovsky, Gertrude. FARMDALE, NEW JERSEY: A JEWISH FARM COMMUNITY. *Am. Jewish Hist. Q. 1977 66(4): 485-497.* In 1919 the first Jewish farmer moved to Farmdale, New Jersey. He was aided by the Jewish Agricultural Society (JAS), which was helping immigrants to buy farms. Farming was supplemented by summer boarders. Within 10 years more than 50 Jewish families were attracted to the town. Most were assisted by the JAS, which also provided a loan for building a Jewish Community Center in 1930. A Yiddish school affiliated with the Sholem Aleichem Folk Institute provided instruction to the children. Acculturation and changing economic and social patterns at work gradually reduced the Jewish community to its present dwindling status.
F. Rosenthal

1184. Edgar, Irving I. BEGINNINGS OF DETROIT JEWISH WELFARE FEDERATION. *Michigan Jewish Hist. 1975 15(2): 6-8.* Minutes of the 5 May 1926 organization meeting of the Jewish Welfare Federation of Detroit.   S

1185. Edgar, Irving I. THE EARLY SITES AND BEGINNINGS OF CONGREGATION BETH EL: THE MICHIGAN GRAND AVENUE SYNAGOGUE, 1859-1861. *Michigan Jewish Hist. 1973 13(1): 13-20.* Discusses the beginnings of Congregation Beth El in Detroit.
S

1186. Engle, Paul. "THOSE DAMN JEWS . . . " *Am. Heritage 1978 30(1): 72-79.* The author tells of his introduction to Jews as a boy in Cedar Rapids, Iowa, and how his early fears changed to affection and sympathy for the plight of Jews, particularly in Germany. 5 illus.
J. F. Paul

1187. Eversole, Theodore W. THE CINCINNATI UNION BETHEL: THE COMING OF AGE OF THE SETTLEMENT IDEA IN CINCINNATI. *Cincinnati Hist. Soc. Bull. 1974 32(1-2): 47-59.* Outlines the history of social reform settlement houses in Cincinnati, Ohio, specifically the Jewish Cincinnati Union Bethel settlement house, 1838-1903.

1188. Faust, Ray. DI TSIRKULATSIE FUN YIDDISHE BICHER IN DI NEW YORKER SHTUTISHE BIBLIOTEKEN UN DI LEINERSHAFT [The circulation of Yiddish books in the New York public libraries, and the readership]. *Yivo Bleter 1973 44: 283-285.* The author visited several libraries in the Bronx, Manhattan, and Brooklyn to conduct a survey of the number of Yiddish books circulated over the last decade and to observe the people who read these books.   B. Klein

1189. Feuer, Lewis S. THE LEGEND OF THE SOCIALIST EAST SIDE. *Midstream 1978 24(2): 23-35.* The Jews of New York City during the early 20th century were primarily conservatives with traditional values of religion and property, not the radical socialists that myth has created.

1190. Fine, Henry and Fine, Lea. NORTH DAKOTA MEMORIES. *Western States Jewish Hist. Q. 1977 9(4): 331-340.* Like many other Jewish immigrants, the authors' grandparents came from eastern Europe in the 1870's. They homesteaded free farm land near Fargo, North Dakota, and later moved to town and opened a clothing store. Their children managed the first soda pop factory in North Dakota. Both subjects remember friendship and kindness from their neighbors in the gentile community. Edited from taped interviews with former North Dakota residents.   B. S. Porter

1191. Fisher, Minnie. THE YIDDISHE ARBEITEN UNIVERSITETT: AN ORAL HISTORY. *Urban Rev. 1976 9(3): 201-204.* Presents the narrative of a 76 year old former garment worker from the young immigrant Jewish community in New York City's Lower East Side during the 1920's. Through the Universitett the eager new citizens learned English, studied modern political and economic systems, debated, and developed socially.   D. L. Smith

1192. Franklin, Lewis A. and Levey, Samson H., ed. THE FIRST JEWISH SERMON IN THE WEST: YOM KIPPUR, 1850, SAN FRANCISCO. *Western States Jewish Hist. Q. 1977 10(1): 3-15.* Lewis Abraham Franklin (1820-79), an English Jew, arrived in San Francisco early in 1849. He opened a tent store in which religious services were conducted on High Holy Days. In 1851 Franklin moved to San Diego where he and his brother Maurice operated a general merchandise store and a hotel. He returned to England in 1860. The Yom Kippur sermon of 1850 centers on atonement and pleads for stricter observance of the Sabbath and a revival of religious (instead of monetary) goals. America provides a unique opportunity for spiritual freedom and self-identity for Jews. Quotes original text; 45 notes.   B. S. Porter

1193. Gastwirt, Zvi. KASHRUT AND THE LAW IN NEW YORK CITY. *Michael: On the Hist. of the Jews in the Diaspora [Israel] 1975 3: 281-301.* Reproduces and analyses document found among the personal papers of Lewis J. Gribetz, legal counsel to the Kashruth Association of Greater New York in its struggle to control *kashrut* supervision in New York City's kosher poultry industry during the 1930's. Scandals revealed in the *shohatim* (slaughterers) union prompted New York Jews to encourage Mayor James J. Walker to investigate the kosher poultry industry. The document represents the report issued in 1931 by Walker's committee. Despite the report's recommendations, the Department of Markets retained responsibility for the enforcement of New York State's 1915 "Kosher Bill" and licensing was never implemented. Primary and secondary sources; 31 notes.   T. Sassoon

1194. Geffen, M. David. DELAWARE JEWRY: THE FORMATIVE YEARS, 1872-1889. *Delaware Hist. 1975 16(4): 269-297.* Although the climate in Delaware was not hostile to Jews, few settled there until the great Jewish migrations from Russia and Eastern Europe in the late 19th century. The Jewish population remained small, concentrated in Wilmington, mercantile in character. The Wilmington Jews met with a favorable reception. They worked hard, earned the respect of the community, and invested their energies in establishing worship services in the city. The Moses Montefiore Mutual Aid Society took the lead in maintaining community life and in providing social and educational services. It also worked hard to bring Jews together for religious purposes, and by its fundraising efforts helped to underwrite the building of a synagogue staffed by a resident rabbi. The Wilmington Jewish community was largely of German origin and lived in a small area near the business district. By the end of the 1880's the Wilmington Jews were receiving an increasing number of Jewish families from Eastern Europe and feeling the cultural distance separating them. Based on contemporary newspapers; 2 illus., 84 notes.   R. M. Miller

1195. Gelfand, Mitchell B. JEWISH ECONOMIC AND RESIDENTIAL MOBILITY IN EARLY LOS ANGELES. *Western States Jewish Hist. Q. 1979 11(4): 332-347.* Jews settled in Los Angeles as early as the final Mexican years. By 1870 they were a stable part of the commercial, social, and political life of the city. The immigration boom of the 1880's increased their numbers but reduced their relative proportion of the population. They were primarily business and professional men with a large stake in the growth of the city, which explains their tendency to remain in the area. They resided in fashionable areas on the outskirts of the business district. Their economic mobility in excess of the general population is explained by their traditional (European) commercial background; business, social, and family ties that facilitated economic opportunities; and their possession of middle-class values that inspired recent immigrants—particularly the "low status" Polish Jews—to adopt German-Jewish and American culture. Based on census records, other primary and secondary sources; 32 notes.   B. S. Porter

1196. Gendler, Carol. THE FIRST SYNAGOGUE IN NEBRASKA: THE EARLY HISTORY OF THE CONGREGATION OF ISRAEL OF OMAHA. *Nebraska Hist. 1977 58(3): 323-341.* Examines the beginnings of a formal Jewish community in Omaha, from 1867 through the construction of Temple Israel, dedicated in 1908. Focuses on prominent members of the community, early rabbis who served it, and the tensions between reform and traditional groups.   R. Lowitt

1197. Gendler, Carol. THE JEWS OF OMAHA: THE FIRST SIXTY YEARS. *Western States Jewish Hist. Q. 1973 5(3): 205-224, (4): 288-305, 6(1): 58-71, 1974 6(2): 141-154, (3): 222-233, (4): 293-304.* Part I. Discusses the role of Jews in the settlement of Omaha, 1820's-30's. Part II. Chronicles the development of the Orthodox and Reform Jewish congregations, the tenures of rabbis, and the erection of synagogues, 1854-1904. Part III. The Jews in Omaha formed several charity and mutual aid societies in the late 1800's. The main social club, the Metropolitan Club, lasted until 1911. Several Jews became leaders in Omaha. Edward Rosewater (1841-1906) served in the state legislature and founded the Omaha *Bee.* He ran for the US Senate twice, but lost. Jonas L. Brandeis (1837-1903), a successful businessman, gave large sums of money to charities. Photo, 41 notes. Part IV. In the late 1880's, thousands of Jews fled from eastern Europe. Several Jewish organizations were set up to help the refugees find homes and jobs in America. The Jews in Omaha came to the aid of those Jews that came to Omaha and wanted to settle there. By 1880, enough Orthodox Jews had settled in Omaha to make it possible to hold orthodox prayer services. The congregations were organized according to the country of origin of the immigrants. A strong Jewish community developed in Omaha. Based on primary and secondary sources; 46 notes. Part V. Because of a depression that hit Omaha in 1890, many wealthy citizens lost their fortunes and had to move elsewhere. Although several wealthy Jews were hard hit by the bad economic conditions, the Jewish population of Omaha continued to grow. This growth necessitated the formation of new organizations to serve the community. The Jews set up their own charities, fraternal groups, and hospital. The Jewish community was a mixture of Orthodox and Reformed Jews working together to take care of their needs. Based on primary and secondary sources; 41 notes. Part VI. The Jews of Omaha became leaders in the professions and politics. Harry B. Zimman served on the city council and was acting mayor when the regular mayor died in 1906. In 1889, the first of many Jewish political groups was founded. A controversy developed over who controlled the "Hebrew vote." The Omaha Jews were planning on building a community center when in 1913 a tornado destroyed the center of the Jewish residential area. The Jewish Relief Committee was established to aid the victims. By 1915, the Jews in Omaha were well established within the larger community, and were taking an active part in its development. Based on primary and secondary sources; photo, 30 notes.   R. A. Garfinkle/S

1198. Gephart, Jerry C.; Siegel, Martin A.; and Fletcher, James E. A NOTE ON LIBERALISM AND ALIENATION IN JEWISH LIFE. *Jewish Social Studies 1974 36(3-4): 327-329.* A 1971 survey of the entire Jewish community of Salt Lake City indicated the willingness of the people to submerge their ideological differences in order to have one synagogue to serve the entire community instead of maintaining two separate synagogues, Reform and Conservative. Both groups saw a strengthening of a common Jewish identity but feared that the differences between Reform and Conservative Judaism would be lost through the union of the two synagogues. Primary and secondary sources; 5 notes.   P. E. Schoenberg

1199. Gilbert, Philip J. THE MEMORABLE SHOLEM ALEICHEM RECEPTION IN DETROIT, MICHIGAN, MAY 15, 1915. *Michigan Jewish Hist. 1977 17(1): 11-16.* The Detroit Progressive Literary and Dramatic Club held a reception in the Jewish community for Jewish author Sholem Aleichem in 1915.

1200. Gilson, Estelle. YIVO—WHERE YIDDISH SCHOLARSHIP LIVES: HISTORY AND MISSION ON FIFTH AVENUE. *Present Tense 1976 4(1): 57-65.* Traces the history of the Yidisher Visnshaftlekher Institut (YIVO) from its inception in Vilna, Lithuania to its present location in New York City. Describes the physical facilities of the Institute and discusses YIVO's historic purpose and goals. Primary and secondary sources; 5 photos.   R. B. Mendel

1201. Glanz, Rudolf. FROM FUR RUSH TO GOLD RUSHES: ALASKAN JEWRY FROM THE LATE NINETEENTH TO THE EARLY TWENTIETH CENTURIES. *Western States Jewish Hist. Q. 1975 7(2): 95-107.* The Jewish-owned Alaska Commercial Company, founded in 1868, obtained the fur trading concession from the federal government, giving the company a monopoly in Alaska. The company established 87 trading posts in the territory. When its concession expired in 1890, the company was able to survive because of its other activities. The gold rushes in Alaska attracted many Jews, many establishing small businesses in the gold areas. The first organized Jewish community was in Nome. The Nome Hebrew Benevolent Society was established in 1901. Rabbi Samuel Koch of Seattle conducted religious instruction by correspondence with Jewish children in Alaska, beginning in 1916. Primary and secondary sources; photo, 50 notes.   R. A. Garfinkle

1202. Glanz, Rudolf. THE JEWS IN THE SANDWICH ISLANDS. *Western States Jewish Hist. Q. 1974 6(3): 177-187.* During the 1850's-60's, many Jews left California to settle in the Sandwich Islands. Many set up prosperous businesses, and several became civic leaders. Some of the Jews mentioned in the article are; L. Cohen, Isaac Wormser, Paul Neumann, A. S. Grinbaum, Hirsch Rayman, Rabbi Rudolph Coffe, and Michael Phillips. Primary and secondary sources; 37 notes.   R. A. Garfinkle

1203. Glaser, Richard. THE GREEK JEWS IN BALTIMORE. *Jewish Social Studies 1976 38(3-4): 321-336.* A study of the 28 Greek Jews in Baltimore indicates that they constitute a unique entity in the Baltimore Jewish population. Some of their traditional holidays have been eliminated in order to conform with Ashkenazim customs of celebration, while others have been modified in their observance because of economic circumstances or a general lack of emphasis within the general Jewish community. Those holidays that have been retained from their Greek origins include a large amount of the traditional modes of celebration. The ethnic solidarity of the Baltimore Greek Jews is declining in strength because of the propensity of the young to marry within the Ashkenazim community and the exposure to other customs.   N. Lederer

1204. Goldberg, Arthur. THE JEW IN NORWICH, CONNECTICUT: A CENTURY OF JEWISH LIFE. *Rhode Island Jewish Hist. Notes 1975 7(1): 79-103.*

1205. Goldberg, Reuben. DER OFKUM UN DER UNTERGANG FUN GOLDFADEN'S NUYORKER YIDISHE ILUSTRIRTE TSAYTUNG (1887-1888) [The rise and decline of Goldfaden's *Nuyorker Yidishe Ilustrirte Tsaytung (1887-1888)*]. *Yivo Bleter 1973 44: 171-186.* Abraham Goldfaden's primary interest was always the theater. However, the cold reception given him in America compelled him to turn to journalism. Because he would not easily give up the idea of the theater he attempted to pursue both simultaneously. This was humanly impossible and the publication became the victim. There was also no room at the time for another newspaper in Yiddish; the competition, lack of funds, and a libel case contributed to cessation of publication. Primary and secondary sources; 40 notes.   B. Klein

1206. Goldowsky, Seebert J. LOCAL JEWISH HISTORY—THE RHODE ISLAND EXPERIENCE. *Rhode Island Jewish Hist. Notes 1974 6(4): 622-628.* Discusses the origin and activities of the Rhode Island Jewish Historical Association.   S

1207. Goldowsky, Seebert J. NEWPORT AS ARARAT. *Rhode Island Jewish Hist. Notes 1974 6(4): 604-609.* An account of the attempts by Mordecai Manuel Noah to establish a Jewish colony, Ararat, first in New York, then successfully in Newport, Rhode Island (1813-21).   S

1208. Goldstein, Sidney and Goldstein, Alice. THE DECLINING USE OF YIDDISH IN RHODE ISLAND. *Rhode Island Jewish Hist.*

Notes 1977 7(3): 401-409. The declining use of Yiddish as a mother tongue during 1910-70 is indicative of changing generational status and residential patterns among Jews in Rhode Island.

1209. Goren, Arthur A. MOTHER ROSIE HERTZ, THE SOCIAL EVIL, AND THE NEW YORK KEHILLAH. *Michael: On the Hist. of the Jews in the Diaspora [Israel] 1975 3: 188-210.* In 1912 the Jewish community of New York City launched its own anti-crime campaign, setting up a Bureau of Social Morals to gather eivdence and present it to the city's law-enforcement agencies for action. Presents documents written by the Bureau's chief investigator, 21-year-old Abe Shoenfeld, concerning a Hungarian Jewish immigrant family, headed by Mrs. Rosie Hertz, who owned and managed a string of brothels on the Lower East Side for more than 30 years. Convicted on 4 February 1913 of running a disorderly resort, Mrs. Hertz was committed to prison two months later. Primary and secondary sources; 15 notes.   T. Sassoon

1210. Gradwohl, Rebecca J. THE JEWESS IN SAN FRANCISCO —1896. *Western States Jewish Hist. Q. 1974 6(4): 273-276.* The Jewish woman of San Francisco in 1896 was not only concerned with running her household but was also active in charities and other societies. A few of the outstanding Jewish women in the city were: Dr. Adele Solomons Jaffa, Natalie Selling, and Amelia Levinson in medicine; writers Emma Wolf and her sister, Alice Wolf; teacher Mary Prag; Rabbi Ray Frank; and musicians Meta Asher and Mrs. Noah Brandt. Reprinted from *The American Jewess*, New York, October 1896.   R. A. Garfinkle

1211. Greene, Michael. THE HANNAH SCHLOSS OLD TIMERS. *Michigan Jewish Hist. 1975 15(2): 34-39.* History of the philanthropic group, the Hannah Schloss Old Timers, active in the United Jewish Charities, headquartered in Detroit, Michigan.   S

1212. Harris, Victor. THE BEGINNING OF LOS ANGELES' FIRST JEWISH HOSPITAL. *Western States Jewish Hist. Q. 1976 8(2): 136-138.* A Jewish hospital to treat people with tuberculosis was first proposed by Jacob Schlesinger, president of the Hebrew Benevolent Society. On 21 September 1902, the Kaspare Chon Hospital was dedicated at 1443 Carroll Avenue, Los Angeles. The house used as the hospital was donated to the society by Kaspare Chon. A memorial fund drive was started to supply the hospital with necessary equipment and supplies. In 1930 the name of the hospital was changed to Cedars of Lebanon Hospital. Reprints an article first published in *B'nai B'rith Messenger*, Los Angeles, 23 July 1909.   R. A. Garfinkle

1213. Harris, Victor. HONOLULU JEWRY IN 1919. *Western States Jewish Hist. Q. 1979 11(3): 279-282.* Honolulu's Jewish community in 1919 consisted of about 13 Jewish families and an equal number of mixed marriages. There was no congregation. The old Jewish cemetery had been abandoned. The active Jews on the island were the 100 or so Jews in the US Army. These men were interested in having a Jewish center where they could meet and offer mutual encouragement in this foreign place. Reprinted from *Emanu-El*, San Francisco, 25 July 1919; 4 notes.   B. S. Porter

1214. Hasson, Aron. THE SEPHARDIC JEWS OF RHODES IN LOS ANGELES. *Western States Jewish Hist. Q. 1974 6(4): 241-254.* During 1910-30, many Jews from Rhodes came to settle in Los Angeles. Rhodesli families have remained together and continue their unique Sephardic customs and life styles. In 1917 they formed their own congregation, the Peace and Progress Society, later changed to the Sephardic Hebrew Center. The immigrants spoke Ladino, and their language barrier forced them to take lower-paying jobs. Several immigrants went into the flower business, which became the most successful occupation of the Rhodeslis. Based on interviews and secondary sources; 4 photos, 21 notes.   R. A. Garfinkle

1215. Hentoff, Nat. NEIGHBORHOODS: A SHTETL IN THE NEW WORLD. *Social Policy 1979 10(2): 58-60.* The author recalls his childhood in the close-knit Jewish ghetto of Roxbury, a part of Boston, in the 1930's.

1216. Herscher, Uri D. THE METROPOLIS OF GHETTOS. *J. of Ethnic Studies 1976 4(2): 33-47.* Portrays the "classic" and stereotypical days of the Jewish ghetto from 1890 to 1920, with its sights, smells, tenements, habitual impoverishment and insecurity, and the all-consuming task of earning a living. Despite the hardship and ugliness of life, the ghetto was a world, complete and self-sustaining, with drama, humor, and romance as well. Fever for secular schooling was high, along with an innate distrust for the public, non-Jewish charities and their agencies. Intellectual life thrived in the cafes of Canal Street, prostitutes in Allen Street, and Jewish theaters in the Bowery. The Judaism of Europe grew progressively weaker, but still coexisted with the culture of the new land. World War I saw the garment manufacturers move to 14th Street, and non-Jews begin to move into the Lower East Side; they were willing to pay the higher rents traditionally levied on non-Jews. With these changes, the good old days of the ghetto were numbered. Based largely on personal conversations by the author in 1972 with individuals of immigrant stock who grew up on New York's Lower East Side; 25 notes.   G. J. Bobango

1217. Hershkowitz, Leo. SOME ASPECTS OF THE NEW YORK JEWISH MERCHANT AND COMMUNITY, 1654-1820. *Am. Jewish Hist. Q. 1976 66(1): 10-34.* The 160-year period under discussion saw New York City grow from a village to a community of 100,000 people, and its Jewish segment from 23 to some 2,000 people. Diversity of origin and of occupation, although trade remained preeminent, were characteristic traits of the Jewish community for the entire period. The right to trade, the acquisition of citizenship, the right to worship publicly, the right to vote and to be elected, resulted in court actions producing a wealth of statistical and legal data which are provided to illustrate these points. 68 notes, 3 appendixes.   F. Rosenthal

1218. Hertzberg, Steven. THE JEWISH COMMUNITY OF ATLANTA FROM THE END OF THE CIVIL WAR UNTIL THE END OF THE FRANK CASE. *Am. Jewish Hist. Q. 1973 62(3): 250-287.* Atlanta's Jewish community was by 1913 the largest in a South transformed by urbanization, industrialization, and Negro emancipation. There were more than 1,200 Jewish immigrants from Eastern Europe by 1910. Under the leadership of Rabbi David Marx (1872-1962) the established German Jews were led into classical Reform, while the East European and Levantine settlers maintained various forms of traditional Judaism. Thus two separate communities were created. Only in philanthropic activities did the two cooperate. In Atlanta and throughout the United States during this period, discrimination against even the established community of Western European Jews was increasing, setting the stage for the Leo M. Frank tragedy of 1913. 84 notes.   F. Rosenthal

1219. Hertzberg, Steven. MAKING IT IN ATLANTA: ECONOMIC MOBILITY IN A SOUTHERN JEWISH COMMUNITY, 1870-1911. *Ann. of Jewish Social Sci. 1978 17: 185-216.* Studies the mobility of Atlanta's Jewish population during 1870-1911. The Jews more than any other group viewed America as the Promised Land. Therefore, a study of their mobility within a major southern city is of special significance.   R. J. Wechman

1220. Hertzberg, Steven. UNSETTLED JEWS: GEOGRAPHIC MOBILITY IN A NINETEENTH CENTURY CITY. *Am. Jewish Hist. Q. 1977 67(2): 125-139.* Analyzes Jewish mobility in Atlanta, Georgia, between 1870 and 1896. Using institutional records, census schedules, city directories, and tax lists, seven tabulations are presented. Variables such as economic and marital status, and urban or rural background, are considered. It appears that Jews remained in Atlanta to a high degree (88% of Jewish immigrants v. 79% of gentile immigrants, or 71% vs. 50% as to upward social improvement) because of economic success, urban background, and advantages of living in an established center of Jewish activities. 7 tables, 16 notes.   F. Rosenthal

1221. Hindus, Milton. EDWARD SMITH KING AND THE OLD EAST SIDE. *Am. Jewish Hist. Q. 1975 64(4): 321-330.* American-born Edward Smith King (1848-96), author of the novel *Joseph Zalmonah*, and Scottish-born Edward Smith King (1846-1922), organizer of the Central Labor Union in New York in 1883, are often confused by later writers. This essay deals with the novelist and the background for his above-mentioned novel.   F. Rosenthal

1222. Horvitz, Eleanor F. THE JEWISH WOMAN LIBERATED: A HISTORY OF THE LADIES' HEBREW FREE LOAN ASSOCIA-

TION. *Rhode Island Jewish Hist. Notes 1978 7(4): 501-512.* The Ladies' Hebrew Free Loan Association (LHFLA), which was established in 1931 to provide a loan fund for Jewish women in Providence, Rhode Island, to match the Hebrew Free Loan Association established in 1903 for male Jews, enabled Jewish women to maintain some element of independence; the LHFLA, no longer needed, disbanded in 1965.

1223. Horvitz, Eleanor F. JEWS AND THE BOY SCOUT MOVEMENT IN RHODE ISLAND. *Rhode Island Jewish Hist. Notes 1977 7(3): 341-384.* Chronicles the participation of Rhode Island Jewish boys in the Boy Scouts of America, 1910-76.

1224. Horvitz, Eleanor F. OLD BOTTLES, RAGS, JUNK! THE STORY OF THE JEWS IN SOUTH PROVIDENCE. *Rhode Island Jewish Hist. Notes 1976 7(2): 189-257.* Discusses the settlement of southern Providence by large numbers of Jews, 1900-12; includes attention to famous local personalities, religion, and daily life.

1225. Horvitz, Eleanor F. THE OUTLET COMPANY STORY AND THE SAMUELS BROTHERS. *Rhode Island Jewish Hist. Notes 1974 6(4): 489-531.* Chronicles the establishment of the Outlet Company Store in Providence, Rhode Island.   S

1226. Horvitz, Eleanor F. THE YEARS OF THE JEWISH WOMAN. *Rhode Island Jewish Hist. Notes 1975 7(1): 152-170.* Discusses the various benevolent organizations in Rhode Island established by Jewish women, ca. 1877-1975.

1227. Jacobson, Daniel. LANSING'S JEWISH COMMUNITY: THE BEGINNINGS. *Michigan Jewish Hist. 1976 16(1): 5-17.* Traces the settlement of Jews from Henry Lederer in 1850 to the establishment of a formal community numbering 450 in 1918.

1228. Kaplan, Marilyn. THE JEWISH MERCHANTS OF NEWPORT, 1740-1790. *Rhode Island Jewish Hist. Notes 1975 7(1): 12-32.*

1229. Katz, Irving I. THE JEWISH PRESS IN DETROIT: AN HISTORICAL ACCOUNT ON THE OCCASION OF THE 150TH ANNIVERSARY OF THE JEWISH PRESS IN THE UNITED STATES. *Michigan Jewish Hist. 1974 14(1): 18-23.*

1230. Kinsey, Stephen D. THE DEVELOPMENT OF THE JEWISH COMMUNITY OF SAN JOSE, CALIFORNIA, 1850-1900. *Western States Jewish Hist. Q. 1974 7(1): 70-87, (2): 163-182, (3): 264-273.* Part I. Jews began to arrive in San Jose, California, in the 1850's. In 1861, they established Congregation Bickur Cholim, with Jacob Levy as the first president. There were 35 members in 1869 and the congregation purchased land to construct a synagogue. On 21 August 1870, the synagogue was dedicated. The first ordained rabbi to serve the congregation was Dr. Myer Sol Levy. By 1916 the congregation was a mixture of orthodox and reform Jews. Based on primary sources; 3 photos, 79 notes. Part II. The development of the Jewish community in San Jose depended upon merchants who could give their time and money for Jewish activities. Many of these individuals held offices in Jewish community organizations, Congregation Bickur Cholim, Ariel Lodge, B'nai B'rith, and other community groups. Short biographies are included in the article. Based on primary and secondary sources; 5 photos, 108 notes. Part III. Established in 1857, the Beth Olam Cemetery was the first Jewish communal organization in San Jose. Other Jewish community organizations were the Hebrew Ladies Benevolent Society (established 1869), the Hebrew Young Men's Benevolent Association of San Jose (established 1872), and Ariel Lodge No. 248 of B'nai B'rith (established 1875). Even with these few organizations, Congregation Bickur Cholim remained the center of the Jewish community in early San Jose. Based on primary sources; photo, 32 notes.   R. A. Garfinkle

1231. Klein, Walter E. THE JEWISH COMMUNITY COUNCIL OF METROPOLITAN DETROIT: THE ORGANIZING YEARS. *Michigan Jewish Hist. 1978 18(1): 20-32.* The Jewish Community Council of Metropolitan Detroit was founded in 1937 after several meetings of prominent Jewish groups, formation of an organizing committee in 1935, and aid from the American Jewish Congress.

1232. Kramer, William M. THE EMERGENCE OF OAKLAND JEWRY. *Western States Jewish Hist. Q. 1978 10(2): 99-125, (3): 238-259, (4): 353-373; 11(1): 69-86; 1979 11(2): 173-186, (3): 265-278.* Part I. Jewish families were among the pioneers of Oakland, California, in the 1850's. In the early years, the Oakland Hebrew Benevolent Society, founded in 1862, was the religious, social, and charitable center of the community. Later, the first synagogue, founded in 1875, took over religious and burial functions. Jews from Poland or Prussian-occupied Poland predominated in the community, and most of them worked in some aspect of the clothing industry. David Solis-Cohen, the noted author, was a leader in the Oakland Jewish community in the 1870's. Primary and secondary sources; 3 photos, 111 notes. Part II. In 1879 Oakland's growing Jewish community organized a second congregation, a strictly orthodox group, Poel Zedek. Women's religious organizations flourished, their charitable services extending to needy gentiles as well as Jews. Jewish participants in civic and political affairs included David S. Hirshberg, who served in several Alameda County offices, and Henry Levy, commander of the Oakland Guard militia organization. Oakland Jewry was part of the greater San Francisco community, yet maintained its own charm and character. Primary and secondary sources; 88 notes. Part III. On 6 July 1881 the First Hebrew Congregation of Oakland, California, elected Myer Solomon Levy as its rabbi. The London-born Levy practiced traditional Judaism. In 1884 the community faced the need of finding a larger, more fashionably located synagogue. The Israel Ladies Relief Society held a fair and raised $4,000 for the new building. On 17 June 1885 the First Hebrew's synagogue burned, increasing the urgency for a new building. Construction of the new synagogue began in May 1886 and was completed by September. Primary and secondary sources; 68 notes. Part IV. Oakland's Jews attended excellent schools, both secular and religious. Fannie Bernstein was the first Jewess to graduate from the University of California at Berkeley, in 1883. First Hebrew Congregation sponsored a Sabbath school which had 75 children in 1887. One of the pupils, Meyer Lissner, was a bright youngster whose letters were published in the Jewish press. The Jewish children of Oakland had an active social life with school events, birthday parties, and Bar Mitzvahs. The contract of the popular Rabbi Myer S. Levy was renewed for five years, from 1888 to 1893. Primary and secondary sources; 66 notes. Part V. Oakland Jewry was active in public affairs and charitable projects in the 1880's. Rabbi Myer S. Levy was chaplain to the state legislature in 1885, and was invited several times to speak to the congregation of the Unitarian Hamiltonian Church. The Daughters of Israel Relief Society continued its good works both inside and outside the Jewish community. Beth Jacob, the traditional congregation of Old World Polish Jews, continued its separate religious practices while it maintained friendly relations with the members of the first Hebrew Congregation. Primary and secondary sources; 44 notes. Part VI. Oakland's Jewish community had able social and political leadership in David Samuel Hirshberg. Until 1886 he was an officer in the Grand Lodge of B'nai B'rith. He served as Under Sheriff of Alameda County in 1883 and was active in Democratic Party political affairs. In 1885 he was appointed Chief Clerk of the US Mint in San Francisco. As a politician, he had detractors who accused him of using his position in B'nai B'rith to foster his political career. Primary and secondary sources; 56 notes. Part VII. In 1891 Rabbi Myer S. Levy moved to a new position in San Francisco's Congregation Beth Israel, bringing to a close this era of Oakland's Jewish history. Based on published sources; 21 notes.   B. S. Porter

1233. Kramer, William M. and Stern, Norton B. A JEWISH HISTORY OF OAKLAND: A REVIEW ESSAY. *Western States Jewish Hist. Q. 1977 9(4): 371-377.* Review article prompted by Fred Rosenbaum's book, *Free to Choose: The Making of a Jewish Community in the American West,* subtitled, "The Jews of Oakland, California, from the Gold Rush to the Present Day" (Berkeley: Judah L. Magnes Memorial Museum, 1976). The title is misleading as it mainly covers the 1920's to the present. The book has numerous errors and omissions, as Rosenbaum's research was confined primarily to personal interviews and not documented from primary sources. He selected subjects poorly, discussing several people who had little or no effect on Oakland Jewry, and one person who was a "bad example" to the community.

B. S. Porter

1234. Kramer, William M. and Stern, Norton B. A SEARCH FOR THE FIRST SYNAGOGUE IN THE GOLDEN WEST. *Western States Jewish Hist. Q. 1974 7(1): 3-20.* In 1851, the rivalry between

German and Polish Jews in San Francisco led to the founding of two separate synagogues within the city. The German synagogue is Temple Emanu-El and the Polish is Temple Sherith Israel. In 1900, Rabbi Jacob Voorsanger of Emanu-El tried to prove that his temple was the first, but he used a misdated lease as his main proof. Research shows that both congregations were founded on 6 April 1851. Primary and secondary sources; photo, 56 notes.   R. A. Garfinkle

1235. Kusinitz, Bernard and Kosch, Samuel. A HALF CENTURY OF JUDAH TOURO LODGE NO. 998 INDEPENDENT ORDER OF B'NAI B'RITH. *Rhode Island Jewish Hist. Notes 1975 7(1): 73-78.*

1236. Kusinitz, Bernard. THE 1902 SIT-IN AT TOURO SYNAGOGUE. *Rhode Island Jewish Hist. Notes 1975 7(1): 42-72.* Discusses a disagreement between members of the Newport, Rhode Island, Touro Synagogue and the congregation Shearith Israel in New York City (who, for legal reasons were official trustees of the Touro Synagogue) which led to the 1902 take-over of Touro Synagogue by the Newport members.

1237. Lamb, Blaine. JEWS IN EARLY PHOENIX, 1870-1920. *J. of Arizona Hist. 1977 18(3): 299-318.* Jews who came to Phoenix in the 1870's and 1880's were primarily of German and Polish extraction. By 1900 they were generally of Russian and East European origin. Though a small minority, Jews played a vital role in the maturing of Phoenix in its crucial 1870-1920 years. 5 illus., 50 notes.
                                                                     D. L. Smith

1238. Lapides, Abe. HISTORY OF THE JEWISH COMMUNITY OF PONTIAC, MICHIGAN. *Michigan Jewish Hist. 1977 17(1): 3-10.* Chronicles the presence of Jews and the growth of their community in Pontiac, Michigan, 1915-77.

1239. Leibo, Steven A. OUT THE ROAD: THE SAN BRUNO AVENUE JEWISH COMMUNITY OF SAN FRANCISCO, 1901-1968. *Western States Jewish Hist. Q. 1979 11(2): 99-110.* The first synagogue, Ahabat Achim, was formed in 1901, but the major growth of the San Bruno Avenue Jewish community took place after the 1906 earthquake. In its prime, the area comprised about 1200 Jewish residents, most of them poor, Eastern European immigrants. The Esther Hellman Settlement House, usually referred to as the "Clubhouse," was financed by wealthy "downtown" Jews, and provided educational and social needs of the community. San Bruno Avenue, the main thoroughfare, had numerous stores and businesses operated by the local Jewish residents. Beginning in the 1930's, as they became more affluent, the younger generations moved out of the old neighborhood. Based on interviews and published sources; 3 photos, 47 notes.   B. S. Porter

1240. Lerner, Samuel and Kaplan, Rose. A BRIEF HISTORY OF THE DETROIT JEWISH FAMILY AND CHILDREN'S SERVICE: AN OVERVIEW. *Michigan Jewish Hist. 1976 16(2): 22-26.* The Jewish Family and Children's Service is a community organization interested in the education and Americanization of Detroit's Jewish community, 1876-1976.

1241. Levitt, Abraham H. IMPRESSIONS OF THE SAN FRANCISCO EARTHQUAKE-FIRE OF 1906. *Western States Jewish Hist. Q. 1973 5(3): 191-197.* Recounts the confusion and destruction of this natural disaster, and the effect of the attitudes and edifices of the city's Jews.

1242. Levy, Abraham R. CENTRAL NORTH DAKOTA'S JEWISH FARMERS IN 1903. *Western States Jewish Hist. Q. 1978 11(1): 3-17.* The author was a founder of the Jewish Agriculturists' Aid Society of America (JAASA) which sponsored a "back to the soil" movement for Eastern European immigrants. In North Dakota, Jewish families had established homesteads on 160-acre plots where they raised flax, corn, oats, potatoes, and garden vegetables. Most of the settlers were from Russia, Rumania, and Galicia. They had worked in factories or small businesses in eastern American cities before obtaining loans from the JAASA and taking up homesteads on free government land. Reprinted from Charles S. Bernheimer, ed., *The Russian Jew in the United States* (Philadelphia, 1905). Photo, 22 notes.   B. S. Porter

1243. Lewis, Theodore. TOURO SYNAGOGUE, NEWPORT, R. I. *Newport Hist. 1975 48(3): 281-320.* Offers a history of the presence of Jews in Newport, Rhode Island, 1658-1963, and the synagogue built by them, eventuating in the construction of the Touro Synagogue, 1759. 3 reproductions, 19 photos, appendix.

1244. Losben, Andrea Finkelstein. NEWPORT'S JEWS AND THE AMERICAN REVOLUTION. *Rhode Island Jewish Hist. Notes 1976 7(2): 258-276.* Discusses activities of the Jews in Newport, Rhode Island, during the American Revolution, including political and economic support, as well as those who enlisted and fought, 1763-76.

1245. Magnes, Judah L. and Frenkel, Lee K. CONDITION OF SAN FRANCISCO JEWRY FOLLOWING THE 1906 EARTHQUAKE-FIRE. *Western States Jewish Hist. Q. 1979 11(3): 239-242.* The authors were sent to San Francisco by the National Conference of Jewish Charities to ascertain the needs of the Jewish community after the 1906 earthquake. They investigated refugee camps and found that about 1,000 Jews were housed in tents and shacks with the rest of the populace, and were adequately fed in the camps. Another 200 families were taken care of in Oakland. On the advice of the Jewish Relief Committee, they reported to their agency headquarters that no immediate appeal for funds in behalf of San Francisco's Jewish community was necessary. Reprinted from the Fourth Biennial Session of the National Conference of Jewish Charities (New York, 1907), pp. 262-265.   B. S. Porter

1246. Marshutz, Siegfried G. HISTORY OF THE MOVEMENT TO ESTABLISH A JEWISH ORPHANS' HOME IN LOS ANGELES. *Western States Jewish Hist. Q. 1977 9(2): 155-160.* Los Angeles Lodge No. 487, Independent Order of B'nai B'rith, determined in 1907 to organize and maintain a home for orphaned and half-orphaned Jewish children, and for the temporary maintenance of destitute and abandoned Jewish children. The Stern home on Mission Road was leased for this purpose. Jewish merchants and citizens subscribed to the home's annual support. The Jewish Orphans' Home of Southern California was informally opened on 4 January 1909 with a capacity of 50 children. This institution today (1977) is known as the Vista Del Mar Child Care Service. Reprints article published in the *B'nai B'rith Messenge*, Los Angeles, 29 January 1909; 5 notes.   B. S. Porter

1247. Mayer, Egon. GAPS BETWEEN GENERATIONS OF ORTHODOX JEWS IN BORO PARK, BROOKLYN, N.Y. *Jewish Social Studies 1977 39(1-2): 93-104.* The generation gap between Jewish parents and children takes on a unique form in the Orthodox Jewish neighborhood of Boro Park. The generations in Boro Park exhibit definite continuities in economic and cultural success from parents to children. However, while the children of Orthodox parents have continued the successful patterns of their parents and have been dependent in their success on that of their elders, tensions generated by status conflict have evolved. Children claim to be more Orthodox than their parents by asserting more sophisticated and deeper understanding of Orthodox ritual and practice. The economic successes of the parents are countered by their children's claims to academic and professional gains. Although both parents and children surround themselves with material evidences of success, the generations display different tastes in the acquisition of such objects. Largely based on survey research.   N. Lederer

1248. McKillop, Lucille. THE TOURO INFLUENCE—WASHINGTON'S SPIRIT PREVAILS. *Rhode Island Jewish Hist. Notes 1974 6(4): 614-628.* An address on religious liberty made at the Touro Synagogue, Newport, Rhode Island to commemorate an exchange of letters in 1790 between Moses Seixas, President of the Newport Congregation, and George Washington.   S

1249. Mesmer, Joseph. SOME OF MY LOS ANGELES JEWISH NEIGHBORS. *Western States Jewish Hist. Q. 1975 7(3): 191-199.* Personal accounts by the author (1855-1947), written in the 1930's about several of his close friends in Los Angeles. He wrote about his relationships with Maurice Kremer (1824-1907) and his wife Matilda, the daughter of Rabbi Joseph Newmark; Eugene Meyer (1842-1925) and his wife Harriet, youngest daughter of Rabbi Newmark; Ephraim Greenbaum; and Isaiah M. Hellman. In the 1870's, Rabbi and Mrs. Newmark lived next door to the author. 18 notes.   R. A. Garfinkle

1250. Michel, Sonya. CHILDREN, INSTITUTIONS, AND COMMUNITY: THE JEWISH ORPHANAGE OF RHODE ISLAND, 1909-1942. *Rhode Island Jewish Hist. Notes 1977 7(3): 385-400.* Although the community favored foster parents and one-to-one relations, Jews in Rhode Island founded an orphanage in 1909 which functioned well until 1942, when federal funds were made available to dependent children.

1251. Michel, Sonya. FAMILY AND COMMUNITY NETWORKS AMONG RHODE ISLAND JEWS: A STUDY BASED ON ORAL HISTORIES. *Rhode Island Jewish Hist. Notes 1978 7(4): 513-533.* These individual accounts of the lives of American Jews date as far back as 1882; based on interviews of residents of the Jewish Home for the Aged of Rhode Island, in Providence, in 1978.

1252. Moore, Deborah Dash. FROM KEHILLAH TO FEDERATION: THE COMMUNAL FUNCTIONS OF FEDERATED PHILANTHROPY IN NEW YORK CITY, 1917-1933. *Am. Jewish Hist. 1978 68(2): 131-146.* The Federation for the Support of Jewish Philanthropic Societies as an alternative communal structure to that of the Kehillah with its relgious and almost obligatory nuances began in New York City in 1917. A fund raising apparatus that recognized class differences but stressed mass participation and emphasized nonsectarianism remained the framework for a minimal community into the 1930's. Samson Benderly and other Federation leaders recognized early that potentially it could be transformed into a viable, broad, and truly Jewish community. 24 notes.   F. Rosenthal

1253. Morgan, David T. JUDAISM IN EIGHTEENTH-CENTURY GEORGIA. *Georgia Hist. Q. 1974 58(1): 41-54.* Traces the development of Judaism in Georgia until it achieved a permanent institutional form. The first group of Jewish immigrants met official opposition, but they freely observed their religion and remained until the War of Jenkins' Ear brought their departure. A second group arrived in 1762; they were forced out during the American Revolution. They returned after the peace. The state incorporated a Jewish congregation in 1790, evidence that religious freedom had become a reality. 34 notes.
                    D. L. Smith

1254. Mosbacker, George. PRESIDENT'S REPORT, FEDERATION OF JEWISH CHARITIES, LOS ANGELES, 1917. *Western States Jewish Hist. Q. 1978 11(1): 91-94.* Dora Berres, a social worker, was hired to coordinate the activities of charitable organizations of the Federation of Jewish Charities (FJC). Many families were made self-supporting by business concerns that hired applicants for employment. The Kaspare Cohn Hospital, the several orphans' homes, and the benevolent societies helped many in the community. The FJC began the year 1916 with a large funding deficit which was reduced; however, there was a continuing need for increased subscriptions. Reprinted from *B'nai B'rith Messenger,* Los Angeles, 16 February 1917.   B. S. Porter

1255. Newman, Phyllis. A SAN BERNARDINO CENTENNIAL. *Western States Jewish Hist. Q. 1975 7(4): 303-307.* On 2 May 1875, Paradise Lodge No. 237 of the Independent Order of B'nai B'rith was established in San Bernardino, California, and was granted its charter by Isidor N. Choynski, president of the Grand Lodge of B'nai B'rith, District No. 4. The Paradise Lodge was the first B'nai B'rith lodge in southern California. In 1883, it acquired a Jewish cemetery. The lodge is still active. 2 photos, 8 notes.   R. A. Garfinkle

1256. Nieto, Jacob. A 1906 SAN FRANCISCO PROTEST AND APPEAL. *Western States Jewish Hist. Q. 1977 9(3): 246-250.* Rabbi Jacob Nieto criticized the way relief money was distributed to casualties of the San Francisco earthquake of 18 April 1906. After the immediate needs for food, clothing, and shelter had been cared for, financial aid should have been given with a view to reestablishing commercial activities and religious institutions. Many who suffered great losses were too proud to seek aid, and these cases should have been sought out and ministered to in a way that would maintain their privacy and dignity. Reprint of article in *The Jewish Times and Observer,* San Francisco, 9 November 1906, pp. 8-9.   B. S. Porter

1257. Papermaster, Isadore. A HISTORY OF NORTH DAKOTA JEWRY AND THEIR PIONEER RABBI. *Western States Jewish*

Hist. Q. 1977 10(1): 74-89; 1978 10(2): 170-184, (3): 266-283. Part I. Rabbi Benjamin Papermaster was born in Lithuania in 1860. He agreed to come to America in 1890 to serve a party of immigrants as its religious leader and teacher. He settled in Grand Forks, North Dakota, amid a growing congregation of Jews from the Ukraine, Rumania, Poland, and Germany. Most of the Jews at that time were peddlers who mortgaged their houses and wagons to build the first synagogue. Rabbi Papermaster was enthusiastic about America; his letters to his family in Lithuania brought many relatives to join him. Grand Forks was considered a boom town because of the building of the Great Northern Railway. The influx of eastern capital helped the development of Jewish merchants. Based on personal experience and family records; 2 photos, 6 notes. Part II. Until the turn of the century, Rabbi Papermaster of Grand Forks was the only rabbi serving Jews in all of North Dakota and western Minnesota. Jewish families who started as peddlers became prosperous enough to move out to towns and villages where they opened small shops and stores. Other families followed the Great Northern Railway along its branch lines toward the Canadian border. In Grand Forks, the Jewish community established a modern Hebrew school, a Ladies' Aid Society, and a burial society. 2 photos, 11 notes. Part III. The city of Grand Forks, at the urging of Rabbi Papermaster, acquired a sanitary meat slaughtering facility with a special department for kosher beef. Rabbi Papermaster maintained an active interest in local politics, generally favoring the Republican Party but supporting Democrats when he knew them to be good men. Although a member of a Zionist organization, he worried about the antireligious character of the modern movement. During World War I he urged Jewish youths to their patriotic duty of joining the American armed forces. Rabbi Papermaster died on 24 September 1934. 3 photos, 14 notes.   B. S. Porter

1258. Petrusak, Frank and Steinert, Steven. THE JEWS OF CHARLESTON: SOME OLD WINE IN NEW BOTTLES. *Jewish Social Studies 1976 38(3-4): 337-346.* An analysis of survey data indicates that Jewry in Charleston, South Carolina, constitutes a well-defined, highly structured, nonassimilated ethnic group. The Jewish community retains its distinctiveness as a separate entity from the majority population despite great pressures to assimilate. The community has considerable self-identification, and the synagogue and the state of Israel play important roles as ethnic referents. Politically the Charleston Jews are strongly Democratic and have a social welfare and liberal orientation. Primary sources.   N. Lederer

1259. Pierce, Lorraine E. THE JEWISH SETTLEMENT ON ST. PAUL'S LOWER WEST SIDE. *Am. Jewish Arch. 1976 28(2): 143-161.* Much of what is known about life on the Lower West Side of St. Paul, Minn., between the late 1800's and 1920—when the neighborhood was for the most part, peopled by Jewish immigrants from Eastern Europe—"suggest[s] parallels with New York's Lower East Side."   J

1260. Raphael, Marc Lee. FEDERATED PHILANTHROPY IN AN AMERICAN JEWISH COMMUNITY: 1904-1948. *Am. Jewish Hist. 1978 68(2): 147-162.* The story and development of the Federation movement in one American Jewish community, that of Columbus, Ohio, illustrates the paths taken during those decades throughout the country. The shift from local to national and overseas allocations and the increase in contributors and contributions, especially after 1937-38, were accompanied by gradual democratization of the board, even though the bulk of the money continued to be contributed by a tiny minority. Yet the Federation, because of its control of philanthropy, brought secular and religious, traditional and non-traditional, Zionist and non-Zionist Jews together, the only true forum in the community. 28 notes.   F. Rosenthal

1261. Raphael, Marc Lee. THE GENESIS OF A COMMUNAL HISTORY: THE COLUMBUS JEWISH HISTORY PROJECT. *Am. Jewish Arch. 1977 29(1): 53-69.* Writes of the Columbus (Ohio) Jewish History Project as a joint undertaking of the Columbus Jewish Federation, the Ohio Historical Society, and the Ohio State University. Believes that "the writing of serious American Jewish communal history is still in its infancy," though "such studies are valuable for the insights they offer into particular historical processes, . . . the information they offer indirectly about a society, and . . . the questions they raise about similar cases."   J

1262. Raphael, Marc Lee. THE INDUSTRIAL REMOVAL OFFICE IN COLUMBUS: A LOCAL CASE STUDY. *Ohio Hist. 1976 85(2): 100-108.* Studies an organization responsible for relocating (in Columbus, Ohio) Jewish immigrants from the East Coast (1901-16). Based on archival sources; illus., 26 notes. T. H. Hartig

1263. Raphael, Marc Lee. ORAL HISTORY IN AN ETHNIC COMMUNITY: THE PROBLEMS AND THE PROMISE. *Ohio Hist. 1977 86(4): 248-257.* Discusses techniques in oral history interviews. Using brief excerpts from the tapes of the Jewish History Project of Columbus, Ohio, since 1920, the author touches on the strengths and weaknesses of recording and transcribing oral history. Secondary sources; 23 notes. N. Summers

1264. Raphael, Marc Lee. THE UTILIZATION OF PUBLIC LOCAL AND FEDERAL SOURCES FOR RECONSTRUCTING AMERICAN JEWISH LOCAL HISTORY: THE JEWS OF COLUMBUS, OHIO. *Am. Jewish Hist. Q. 1975 65(1): 10-35.* Using 19th-century and early 20th-century statistics from various sources, discusses the history of the majority of Jews in Columbus, Ohio, whose activities were not recorded by the local Jewish newspaper. Examines the validity of quantitative methods in history. 10 tables, 43 notes. F. Rosenthal

1265. Rapp, Michael G. SAMUEL N. DEINARD AND THE UNIFICATION OF JEWS IN MINNEAPOLIS. *Minnesota Hist. 1973 43(6): 213-221.* Rabbi Samuel N. Deinard (1873-1921), founder and editor of *The American Jewish World,* was the prime mover in bringing German and East European Jews together as a community in Minneapolis. His weekly newspaper is the principal source for this analysis. 5 illus., 28 notes. D. L. Smith

1266. Reutlinger, Andrew S. REFLECTIONS ON THE ANGLO-AMERICAN JEWISH EXPERIENCE: IMMIGRANTS, WORKERS AND ENTREPRENEURS IN NEW YORK AND LONDON, 1870-1914. *Am. Jewish Hist. Q. 1977 66(4): 473-484.* Many of the factors responsible for the divergent pattern of communal development among the East European Jewish immigrants in London and New York City lay in the process of migration itself and in the differences between British and American values and institutions. For example, financial difficulties or religious predilections of an orthodox nature might be determining factors in remaining in Great Britain. Even a temporary sojourn in London made possible changes in the factory method of garment manufacture and in the men working in it to humanize the consequences of this system. Also, the Jewish labor movement benefited from the experience of many of its leaders in London's sweat shops. English models made for communal paternalism exercised by the "Cousinhood" (Rothschilds, Montefiores, etc.), but American conditions precluded national institutions or the same degree of deference to the Jewish elite. F. Rosenthal

1267. Ripinsky, Sol. AN ALASKAN REPORT: 1909. *Western States Jewish Hist. Q. 1978 11(1): 56-59.* The author (1850-1927) came to Alaska in the early 1880's. He reported that there were about 300 Jews in Alaska in 1909. They were active in commercial, financial, educational, and political development. Rothschilds and Guggenheims had vast holdings of mineral claims of gold, copper, coal, and iron. The author operated a general store at Chilkat Peninsula—later known as Haines, Alaska. Reprinted from the *Jewish Tribune,* Portland, Oregon, 17 December 1909. 2 photos, 6 notes. B. S. Porter

1268. Rockaway, Robert A. THE EASTERN EUROPEAN JEWISH COMMUNITY OF DETROIT, 1881-1914. *Yivo Ann. of Jewish Social Sci. 1974 (15): 82-105.* Most East European Jews coming to Detroit in this period lived in the crowded downtown sections of the city. Author discusses the religious, economic, social and cultural life of the community, its religious identification, reaction to cultural change, and relations with non-Jews. "Although the Eastern European Jews made great strides in coming to terms with their American environment by 1914, they were still viewed with hostility and suspicion by native-born and foreign-born Detroiters." 83 notes. R. J. Wechman

1269. Rockaway, Robert A. THE PROGRESS OF REFORM JUDAISM IN LATE 19TH AND EARLY 20TH CENTURY DETROIT. *Michigan Jewish Hist. 1974 14(1): 8-17.*

1270. Rogers, Barbara. TO BE OR NOT TO BE A JEWISH HOSPITAL. *Western States Jewish Hist. Q. 1978 10(3): 195-201.* On 3 November 1887, a group of San Francisco citizens agreed to establish a charitable hospital for deserving and needy Israelites and others. Rabbi M. Friedlander of Oakland openly opposed the hospital's policy and urged that it accept only Jewish patients. San Francisco's prominent rabbis, Jacob Voorsanger, Jacob Nieto, and Myer S. Levy agreed with the hospital's board of directors that it should be nonsectarian in its admissions policy. Critics today claim the hospital is no longer Jewish because many patients and doctors are not Jewish; but supporters say that a high proportion of Bay area Jews are served by Mount Zion Hospital and it will continue to grow and develop with the San Francisco Bay area. Based on Board of Directors' minutes, secondary sources; 13 notes. B. S. Porter

1271. Romanofsky, Peter. "TO SAVE... THEIR SOULS": THE CARE OF DEPENDENT CHILDREN IN NEW YORK CITY, 1900-1905. *Jewish Social Studies 1974 36(3/4): 253-261.* During 1903-05 a small number of dependent children were placed in foster homes of working class families rather than families of middle class background. The program was initiated by the United Hebrew Charities of New York City in order to cope with the increasing number of orphans and other children that needed help as Jewish immigration from Eastern Europe increased. Ideological opposition and lack of financial support terminated the program but its pioneering prepared the way for a change in the general American approach. Primary and secondary sources; 27 notes. P. E. Schoenberg

1272. Rosen, Benton H. KING DAVID'S LODGE, A.F. & A.M., NO. 1 OF NEWPORT, RHODE ISLAND. *Rhode Island Jewish Hist. Notes 1974 6(4): 578-586.* A history of the King David's Masonic Lodge of Newport, Rhode Island (1780-90); includes copies of a letter from George Washington, ledger entries, and voting records. S

1273. Rosenshine, Jay. HISTORY OF THE SHOLOM ALEICHEM INSTITUTE OF DETROIT, 1926-1971. *Michigan Jewish Hist. 1974 14(2): 9-20.*

1274. Rosenwaike, Ira. THE FIRST JEWISH SETTLERS IN LOUISVILLE. *Filson Club Hist. Q. 1979 53(1): 37-44.* By 1832 the Jewish population of Louisville was large enough to support the establishment of the Israelite Benevolent Society. Most of the community was highly mobile at this time; few of the early Jewish settlers remained in the city for more than a decade. Based on local government records and the federal census. 38 notes. G. B. McKinney

1275. Rosenwaike, Ira. THE FOUNDING OF BALTIMORE'S FIRST JEWISH CONGREGATION: FACT VS. FICTION. *Am. Jewish Arch. 1976 28(2): 119-125.* Disputes the claim that Isaac Leeser's uncle Zalma Rehine was a founder of the Baltimore Hebrew Congregation. Writers of local history, he urges, "would do well not to rely on some of the hearsay evidence of their predecessors, who often lacked scholarly training." J

1276. Rosenwaike, Ira. THE JEWS OF BALTIMORE TO 1810. *Am. Jewish Hist. Q. 1975 64(4): 291-320.* The systematic examination of the Jewish population of Baltimore from 1770 to 1810 reveals that by 1810 a rough outline of the communal trends in the next stage of development had been shaped: differentiation had taken place between the relatively well-off older "American" Jews and the recent immigrant arrivals. Another two decades passed, however, before the first congregation was set up. Over 40 individuals and their families provide material for this study. 85 notes. F. Rosenthal and S

1277. Rosenwaike, Ira. THE JEWS OF BALTIMORE: 1820 TO 1830. *Am. Jewish Hist. Q. 1978 67(3): 246-259.* Provides biographical surveys of most of the 30 individuals whose families constituted the Jewish community of Baltimore, Maryland. One-fourth were native-born by 1830. Dutch Jews predominated among European newcomers. All but two of these heads of household practiced middle class occupations, and 10 of the 24 families contained one or more blacks. This small group of men founded the first congregations, led them for many years, and thus founded an enduring organizational structure. 26 notes. F. Rosenthal

1278. Rosenwaike, Ira. THE JEWS OF BALTIMORE: 1810 TO 1820. *Am. Jewish Hist. Q. 1977 67(2): 101-124.* The Jewish population of Baltimore during this period, although subject to considerable flux, remained small (less than 25 families). These individuals, nevertheless, seem to have been broadly representative of American Jewry; because of their mobility, they were also the Jews of Philadelphia and New York. Short biographical sketches are provided for both foreign-born and native-born heads of families. 2 tabulations, 74 notes.

F. Rosenthal

1279. Rothchild, Sylvia. A GREAT HAPPENING IN BOSTON: REVOLT OF THE YOUNG. *Present Tense 1976 3(3): 21-26.* Traces the development of the Jewish Student Movement, a renaissance born in 1960 radicalism, from Jewish Boston establishment antipathy to uneasy acceptance by urban and suburban Jewish and Gentile Boston. Describes the establishment and the impact of the student quarterlies *Response* and *Genesis 2*, the Jewish Student Projects, the communal Havurat Shalom, and the *Jewish Catalogue* on the educational and administrative policies of such religious and educational institutions as the Hillel Foundation(s), Boston University, Harvard-Radcliffe, and suburban synagogues. Quotes such movement notables as Alan Mintz, first editor of *Response*; writers Elie Wiesel and Bill Novak; activists Hillel Levine and Rav Kuk; rabbis Arthur Green, Zalman Schachter, Joseph Polak, Ben-Zion Gold, and Lawrence Kushner; professors Bernard Reisman and Leonard Fein. 4 photos.

R. B. Mendel

1280. Rothchild, Sylvia. RETURN TO "NORTHRUP," MASS. *Present Tense 1975 2(4): 36-41.* Author's comments on the community she once lived in, describing the social changes in the Jewish suburb.

S

1281. Rothschild, Janice. PRE-1867 ATLANTA JEWRY. *Am. Jewish Hist. Q. 1973 62(3): 242-249.* The first Jewish family—Jacob and Jeanetta Hirsch Haas with their four children—came to Atlanta in 1845, soon followed by Henry Levi, Herman Haas, David Mayer, and others, mostly from southern Germany. Sketches family, business, and social activities. Mayer was instrumental in organizing the Hebrew Benevolent Society and a Jewish cemetery, and led the small community during the Civil War. Based on contemporary newspaper data and family recollections; 26 notes.

F. Rosenthal

1282. Rudd, Hynda. CONGREGATION KOL AMI: RELIGIOUS MERGER IN SALT LAKE CITY. *Western States Jewish Hist. Q. 1978 10(4): 311-326.* Congregation Kol Ami was formed in 1972 by the merger of Congregations B'nai Israel (begun in 1873) and Montefiore (begun ca. 1880). Different opinions about ritual originally had divided Salt Lake City's Jewish community. Eventually grievances dissipated and new religious, social, and economic problems brought the people together. A consolidation committee was formed to discuss the issue, and members of both congregations voted in favor of the merger. The old synagogues were sold and a new synagogue was constructed in 1976. Based on archival, other primary, and secondary sources; 3 photos, 67 notes.

B. S. Porter

1283. Rudd, Hynda. SHAREY TZEDICK: SALT LAKE'S THIRD JEWISH CONGREGATION. *Western States Jewish Hist. Q. 1976 8(3): 203-208.* Sometime during 1916-19, Congregation Sharey Tzedick of Salt Lake City was formed. The founding members had belonged to the Montefiore synagogue but had become discouraged with the gradual movement away from Orthodox traditions. Sharey Tzedick was set up as an Orthodox temple and the congregation erected a synagogue. For reasons still unclear the congregation folded during the 1930's, and in 1948 its property was sold to the Veterans of Foreign Wars. Photo, 22 notes.

R. A. Garfinkle

1284. Ruxin, Robert H. THE JEWISH FARMER AND THE SMALL-TOWN JEWISH COMMUNITY: SCHOHARIE COUNTY, NEW YORK. *Am. Jewish Arch. 1977 29(1): 3-21.* A small percentage of American Jews maintain their existence in a rural environment. Examines the effort of one such group to remain a part of "country" life without sacrificing its Jewish identity.

J

1285. Schless, Nancy Halverson. PETER HARRISON, THE TOURO SYNAGOGUE, AND THE WREN CITY CHURCH. *Winterthur Portfolio 1973 (8): 187-200.* The Touro Synagogue, Newport, Rhode Island, 1759-63, demonstrates the reliance of Peter Harrison (1716-75) on English architectural books. In spite of brief mention by other authors, the existence of a specific architectural model for the Newport synagogue has been overlooked. The prototype was the Bevis Marks Synagogue in London. The London building was derived from two sources. First, the design recalls the first London synagogue of the Resettlement, the Creechurch Lane synagogue. Secondly, Bevis Marks is related to the most common type of Wren city church of the late 17th century. The Bevis Marks Synagogue marks a halfway point and a catalyst in the "amalgamation of aisled, galleried basilica into religious architecture on both sides of the Atlantic." Based on primary and secondary sources; 19 illus., 16 notes.

N. A. Kuntz

1286. Schmier, Louis. THE FIRST JEWS OF VALDOSTA. *Georgia Hist. Q. 1978 62(1): 32-49.* Valdosta's first Jews, Abraham Ehrlich and Bernard Kaul, arrived in 1866, closely followed by some of Ehrlich's relatives. Although the number of Jews in Valdosta, Georgia, during this period was never greater than 17, they were very involved with business and town affairs. Business ventures as well as acceptance by and involvement in the gentile community, particularly by the Ehrlichs and the Engels, are detailed. Based on primary sources, mainly newspapers, legal records, and interviews; 63 notes.

G. R. Schroeder

1287. Schwartz, Henry. THE FIRST TEMPLE BETH ISRAEL: SAN DIEGO. *Western States Jewish Hist. Q. 1979 11(2): 153-161.* A surge in population growth following rail connection with the east in 1885 helped the growth of San Diego's Jewish congregation and led to the construction of Temple Beth Israel in 1889. The facilities were expanded for another population increase after World War I, but continued growth demanded a new synagogue, built in 1926. The old building was sold at that time but was repurchased by congregation Beth Israel in 1978. The community now intends to restore the historic building and move it to Heritage Park in Old Town. Primary and secondary sources; photo, 45 notes.

B. S. Porter

1288. Segal, Beryl. JEWISH SCHOOLS AND TEACHERS IN METROPOLITAN PROVIDENCE: THE FIRST CENTURY. *Rhode Island Jewish Hist. Notes 1977 7(3): 410-419.* Covers 1854-1946.

1289. Selavan, Ida Cohen. THE EDUCATION OF JEWISH IMMIGRANTS IN PITTSBURGH, 1862-1932. *Yivo Ann. of Jewish Social Sci. 1974 (15): 126-144.* Looks at the education of the Jewish immigrants in public school, night school, and adult education. Jews flocked to the public education system and did well. Hebrew, religious, and Yiddish education are also briefly covered. 85 notes.

R. J. Wechman

1290. Selavan, Ida Cohen. THE FOUNDING OF COLUMBIAN COUNCIL. *Am. Jewish Arch. 1978 30(1): 24-42.* The Columbian Council of Pittsburgh was founded as a local section of the National Council of Jewish Women. Dr. Selavan examines the early years of the Council and highlights its most important contributions to the life of Pittsburgh Jewry.

J

1291. Selavan, Ida Cohen. JEWISH WAGE EARNERS IN PITTSBURGH, 1890-1930. *Am. Jewish Hist. Q. 1976 65(3): 272-285.* The formation of a Jewish proletariat in Pittsburgh began after the influx of a large number of Jews from Eastern Europe. During the 40 years under discussion Jewish wage earners were found in large numbers among stogy makers, the needle trades, and the bakery trade, which was unionized in 1906. These three industries, each different in conditions, wages, and work force, are described on the basis of oral interviews, contemporary journals, newspapers, etc. Attempts to unionize tailors and seamstresses were successful only in the larger shops before 1914. 39 notes.

F. Rosenthal.

1292. Shankman, Arnold. ATLANTA JEWRY—1900-1930. *Am. Jewish Arch. 1973 25(2): 131-155.* Though little research has been devoted to the subject, few ethnic groups have made as important a contribution to Atlanta history as have her Jewish citizens.

J

1293. Shankman, Arnold. HAPPYVILLE, THE FORGOTTEN COLONY. *Am. Jewish Arch. 1978 30(1): 3-19.* The name Happyville, South Carolina, has become a forgotten chapter in the history of the

American Jewish agricultural colonies. Yet Happyville needs to be remembered, more for the idealism and devotion of its colonists than for the failures which marked its short-lived existence. [Covers 1900-08].

J

1294. Stern, Norton B. AT THE SOUTHERN END OF THE MOTHER LODE. *Western States Jewish Hist. Q. 1976 8(2): 163-166.* Most of the Jews who lived in Mariposa County during the 1850's-60's resided in Mariposa and Hornitos, were foreign born, and were in business. By 1882 only two Jewish merchants were left in the county. The rest had left when the gold rush ended. No Jewish buildings, benevolent societies, or cemeteries were established in Mariposa County. 24 notes.

R. A. Garfinkle

1295. Stern, Norton B. BAD DAY AT SAN BERNARDINO. *Western States Jewish Hist. Q. 1974 7(1): 61-66.* On 2 January 1862, Wolff Cohn was killed in his own store by Dick Cole, while Cole was wounded by Wolff's brother Isaac. In August 1861, 35 citizens of San Bernardino signed a petition requesting the army to come and protect the merchants from attacks by desperadoes. Isaac Cohn was arrested but the grand jury refused to indict him for shooting Cole. 18 notes.

R. A. Garfinkle

1296. Stern, Norton B. CHOLERA IN SAN FRANCISCO IN 1850. *Western States Jewish Hist. Q. 1973 5(3): 200-204.* Notes the charity efforts of Jews led by Samuel I. Neustadt to ameliorate conditions during the cholera epidemic.

1297. Stern, Norton B. and Kramer, William M. THE FIRST JEWISH ORGANIZATION, THE FIRST JEWISH CEMETERY AND THE FIRST KNOWN JEWISH BURIAL IN THE FAR WEST. *Western States Jewish Hist. Q. 1979 11(4): 318-324.* The first Jewish burial in the West took place in San Francisco in December 1849. The deceased was Henry D. Johnson, religious rites were performed by Lewis A. Franklin, and burial was in the Yerba Buena public cemetery. Following this burial, the Jewish community organized the First Hebrew Benevolent Society and established a Jewish cemetery so that Jewish burials could take place in consecrated ground. The Benevolent Society was founded in January 1850, and the land for the cemetery was acquired in April 1950. Johnson's remains were moved to the new cemetery. The first funeral service in the Hart (Jewish) Cemetery was in the fall of 1850 when two victims of the Sacramento cholera epidemic were buried. Newspaper accounts and other published sources; photo, 22 notes.

B. S. Porter

1298. Stern, Norton B. THE FOUNDING OF THE JEWISH COMMUNITY IN UTAH. *Western States Jewish Hist. Q. 1975 8(1): 65-69.* Charges two authors, Leon L. Watters, *The Pioneer Jews of Utah* (New York: American Jewish Historical Society, 1952), and Juanita Brooks, *History of the Jews in Utah and Idaho* (Salt Lake City: Western Epics, 1973), with failing to research thoroughly for information about the founding of the Jewish community in Utah for their books on early Utah Jewish history. Cites a contemporary (1860's) report published in *The Hebrew* of San Francisco as the baisis for the facts. Watters and Brooks used other sources for their information. 16 notes.

R. A. Garfinkle

1299. Stern, Norton B. HELENA, MONTANA JEWRY RESPONDS TO A FRENCH APPEAL IN 1868. *Western States Jewish Hist. Q. 1979 11(2): 170-172.* Jews in France established the Alliance Israelite Universelle in 1860 to improve the living conditions of Jews in North Africa, the Near East, and Eastern Europe. The Alliance's appeal for aid, published in *The American Israelite* of Cincinnati on 17 January 1868, was met with a generous reponse from the Jewish population in Helena, Montana. Sixty-seven individuals were listed as donors, giving evidence of a large Jewish population in the pioneer Western town. Based on an article in *The American Israelite,* 17 January 1868; 9 notes.

B. S. Porter

1300. Stern, Norton B. and Kramer, William M. THE HISTORICAL RECOVERY OF THE PIONEER SEPHARDIC JEWS OF CALIFORNIA. *Western States Jewish Hist. Q. 1975 8(1): 3-25.* Virtually ignored by historians writing about Jews living in California in the 19th century, the Sephardic Jewish community has been rediscovered by historians. In

1853, the Sephardic Jews in San Francisco organized Congregation Shaar Hashamayim, but this group folded in less than a year. The members joined the two Ashkenazim congregations in the city. Because they were no longer an organized group, little was written about them. Discusses prominent California Sephardic Jews, including Abraham Cohen Labatt (and his sons), Joseph Rodriguez Brandon (1828-1916), Elcan Heydenfeldt, Solomon Heydenfeldt (1816-1890), Isaac Nunez Cardozo, California Governor Washington Bartlett (and his brothers Julian and Columbus), Joseph Simpson, Raphael Schoyer, Manuel Mordicai Noah, Elias De Sola, Seixas Solomons, Abraham H. L. Dias (1814-77), and Benjamin Franklin Davega. 3 photos, 78 notes.

R. A. Garfinkle

1301. Stern, Norton B. JEWS IN THE 1870 CENSUS OF LOS ANGELES. *Western States Jewish Hist. Q. 1976 9(1): 71-86.* The federal census taken in 1870 showed there were 330 Jews (5.76% of the population) in the city of Los Angeles. This high proportion of Jews was probably duplicated in other cities of the early West. Demographic analysis shows the Jewish population to be predominantly young, Polish or Prussian-Polish, and employed in the merchandizing of wearing apparel. Based on the Federal Census of 1870, city and county directories, cemetery records, register of voters, secondary publications, and demographic and name listings; 11 notes.

B. S. Porter

1302. Stern, Norton B. LOS ANGELES JEWRY AND THE CHICAGO FIRE. *Western States Jewish Hist. Q. 1974 6(4): 260-267.* Soon after the fire that destroyed most of Chicago in 1871, the Jews of Los Angeles collected $2,657 from several individuals and benevolent societies to send to the stricken city. 23 notes.

R. A. Garfinkle

1303. Stern, Norton B. MISSION TO SAN BERNARDINO IN 1879. *Western States Jewish Hist. Q. 1978 10(3): 227-233.* In the summer of 1879, Rabbi Aron J. Messing of San Francisco went to San Bernardino, California, for a "missionary visit." This unusual trip was undertaken to raise funds for construction of a synagogue for Messing's San Francisco Congregation Beth Israel. In San Bernardino Messing organized a Sabbath school and a Hebrew Association to promote the spiritual welfare of the community. Rabbi Messing undertook several fundraising journeys but was careful to avoid slander or suspicion by bringing along a trustee from his congregation to receive the collections. Primary and secondary sources; 25 notes.

B. S. Porter

1304. Stern, Norton B. THE NAME OF LOS ANGELES' FIRST JEWISH NEWSPAPER. *Western States Jewish Hist. Q. 1975 7(2): 153-157.* Lionel L. Edwards, publisher, and Victor Harris, editor, established the first Los Angeles Jewish newspaper, the *Emanu-El,* on 10 March 1897. Rabbi Jacob Voorsanger, publisher of the well-established Jewish newspaper *Emanu-El* in San Francisco, criticized the fact that the southern paper had copied his paper's name. In 1898, the southern paper was changed to the *B'nai B'rith Messenger,* and is still published under that title. 15 notes.

R. A. Garfinkle

1305. Stern, Norton B. A NEW CLUB FOR LOS ANGELES. *Western States Jewish Hist. Q. 1978 10(4): 374-376.* About 40 Jewish men met in Levy's Cafe in Los Angeles, California, on 9 December 1908 to organize the Jewish Progress Club. Its object was to read papers and discuss current literary and scientific topics, especially those pertaining to Judaism. Those who founded and joined the club were a homogeneous group of civic and business leaders.

B. S. Porter

1306. Stern, Norton B. THE ORANGEVALE AND PORTERVILLE, CALIFORNIA, JEWISH FARM COLONIES. *Western States Jewish Hist. Q. 1978 10(2): 159-167.* In 1891, David Lubin of Sacramento, California, helped organize The International Society for the Colonization of Russian Jews. Lubin and Harris Weinstock settled 10 families on land they owned at Orangevale, several miles northeast of Sacramento. Philip Nettre Lilienthal established the Porterville settlement in the southeastern San Joaquin Valley. Both colonies failed because of poor land, inadequate capital and equipment, and lack of experience and motivation on the part of the colonists, most of whom had backgrounds in commerce and small business. Based on interviews and published sources; photo, 37 notes.

B. S. Porter

1307.   Stern, Norton B. and Kramer, William M.   THE SAN BERNARDINO HEBREW AND ENGLISH ACADEMY 1868-1872. *Western States Jewish Hist. Q. 1976 8(2): 102-117.* The first Jewish day school in southern California was opened on 27 May 1868 by the Jewish community in San Bernardino. Siegmund Bergel served as the teacher for the San Bernardino Hebrew and English Academy during 1868-72. The subjects included English, Latin, Greek, Hebrew, and other branches of education. Theatrical productions were given each year for different Jewish holidays. Bergel was active in civic affairs. He helped establish the San Bernardino Literary Society and served as its first president. In 1872, he left for his homeland in Germany. He became internationally known for his work as a Jewish community leader. He died in 1912. Photo, 52 notes.
R. A. Garfinkle

1308.   Stern, Norton B.   A SAN FRANCISCO SYNAGOGUE SCANDAL IN 1893.   *Western States Jewish Hist. Q. 1974 6(3): 196-203.* A scandal developed at Temple Sherith Israel in 1893, when a new rabbi was being installed. The cantor, Max Rubin, did not want a new rabbi who would start receiving fees for weddings and funerals, as he had been filling in as reader for over a year and liked the large sum collected for officiating at various functions. In June, 1893, Rabbi Jacob Nieto was elected Rabbi of the congregation, and the scandal soon died down. Primary and secondary sources; 14 notes.   R. A. Garfinkle

1309.   Stern, Norton B.   WHEN THE FRANCO-PRUSSIAN WAR CAME TO LOS ANGELES.   *Western States Jewish Hist. Q. 1977 10(1): 68-73.* On 16 August 1868 a group of Los Angeles Jews formed a branch of the Universal Jewish Alliance (UJA), an international society whose objectives were the emancipation of all the Israelites, and the redress of all wrongs upon the race all over the globe. The officers of the Los Angeles branch included men of French, Polish, and German backgrounds. The UJA dissolved when several of the German- and French-born members became active in their respective war relief efforts. Bad feelings culminated in a fist fight in a saloon when Moritz Morris (Prussian) and Eugene Meyer (French), both naturalized American citizens, took sides with their former homelands in the Franco-Prussian War. Based on newspapers and other published sources; 19 notes.
B. S. Porter

1310.   Stern, Norton B. and Kramer, William M.   AN 1869 JEWISH STANDARD FOR GENTILE BEHAVIOR: A REVIEW ESSAY. *Western States Jewish Hist. Q. 1977 9(3): 282-285.* On 22 January 1869, the *Los Angeles Daily News* printed a lengthy essay describing the local Jewish community. Modern historians such as Esther Boulton Black in *Rancho Cucamonga and Dona Merced* (Redlands, Calif., 1975) and Leonard Pitt have revised the earlier interpretation of the article—that it was a defense of Jews under verbal attack—and have determined that it was a reproof of native Californios and immigrant Anglos for their shortcomings. The article praised Jews for their sobriety, literacy, charity, chastity, and decorous demeanor. By implication, their gentile neighbors were noted for intemperance, political corruption, financial extravagance, and criminal violence, among other faults. The article stated that the Jews were an example for the gentiles.   B. S. Porter

1311.   Swichkow, Louis J.   MEMOIRS OF A MILWAUKEE LABOR ZIONIST.   *Michael: On the Hist. of the Jews in the Diaspora [Israel] 1975 3: 125-151.* Summarizes the 159-page Yiddish memoir of Louis Perchonok (1889-1949), a founder and long-time secretary of the Poale Zion movement in Milwaukee, and includes an extract of the original. The memoir contains valuable information on the history of Jewish immigrant life in America and the role of Zionism. Milwaukee's Socialist Zionists, including Golda Meir in her youth, participated in all aspects of Jewish life and were especially influential during World War I in creating "Ezra Betzar" for the relief of Eastern European Jews, and in democratizing the community via popular elections to the American Jewish Congress. Primary and secondary sources; 32 notes.   T. Sassoon

1312.   Toll, William.   FRATERNALISM AND COMMUNITY STRUCTURE ON THE URBAN FRONTIER: THE JEWS OF PORTLAND, OREGON: A CASE STUDY.   *Pacific Hist. Rev. 1978 47(3): 369-403.* Portland's Jews were residentially dispersed according to class standing, but they clustered in occupations to which they had been confined in Germany and Russia. Extensive trading contacts with relatives and friends in San Francisco and elsewhere produced economic stability in the late 19th and early 20th centuries so that the community retained a higher proportion of its members than most ethnic enclaves and provided remunerative employment for most of its sons and many newcomers. In general, only Jews with capital, contacts, or skills migrated to Portland. Based on manuscript census, city directories, and B'nai B'rith lodge records; map, 11 tables, 51 notes.   W. K. Hobson

1313.   Toll, William.   VOLUNTARISM AND MODERNIZATION IN PORTLAND JEWRY: THE B'NAI B'RITH IN THE 1920'S. *Western Hist. Q. 1979 10(1): 21-38.* A case study of how ethnic groups and community development are related, addressing the issues raised by Moses Rischin, John Higham, and Kenneth Roseman. Examines the role of Jews in Portland, Oregon, in the 1920's in the local economy and their specific patterns of institutional adaptation to find out what their particular contributions were to the city's growth. Traces the effects of the particular region in which they settled on their internal patterns of change. Through its B'nai B'rith lodge, Portland Jewry "sorted out its social classes and allowed new spokesmen to coalesce." 3 tables, 37 notes.   D. L. Smith

1314.   Toury, Jacob.   M.E. LEVY'S PLAN FOR A JEWISH COLONY IN FLORIDA: 1825.   *Michael: On the Hist. of the Jews in the Diaspora [Israel] 1975 3: 23-33.* Publishes an 1825 letter addressed to Isaac L. Goldsmid of London by the American Jew, Moses Elias Levy, advocating the foundation of a Jewish colony in Florida, the nucleus of which was apparently to be a theological seminary. Levy was also an outspoken proponent of the abolition of Negro slavery and of Jewish political disabilities in Europe. His religious fervor inspired him to advocate a Bible-based socialism. Opposed to Jewish emancipation in Europe because of its ultimate threat to Jewish existence, Levy was a proud defender of the American "right to be different." Primary and secondary sources; 35 notes.   T. Sassoon

1315.   Twersky, Rebecca.   THE FOUNDING OF A JEWISH COMMUNITY: AHAVATH SHALOM OF WEST WARWICK.   *Rhode Island Jewish Hist. Notes 1977 7(3): 420-429.* History of the Congregation Ahavath Shalom of West Warwick, Rhode Island, from its inception in 1912 to around 1938.

1316.   Voorsanger, Jacob.   THE BEGINNING OF THE FIRST JEWISH HOSPITAL IN THE WEST.   *Western States Jewish Hist. Q. 1976 8(2): 99-101.* Reprint of an article first published in the *Emanu-El*, San Francisco, 1 January 1897, announcing the founding in San Francisco of Mount Zion Hospital. The hospital was to use the medical facilities of Julius Rosenstirn. There had been some concern about the necessity of a Jewish hospital, but a trial operation proved successful.
R. A. Garfinkle

1317.   Voorsanger, Jacob.   THE RELIEF WORK IN SAN FRANCISCO.   *Western States Jewish Hist. Q. 1976 8(3): 243-250.* In this reprint of an article published in *Out West*, June 1906, the author tells of his role in obtaining food for San Francisco after the earthquake of 1906. He was on Mayor Eugene Schmitz's Food Committee. His job was to locate food and to get it to relief centers. 2 notes.
R. A. Garfinkle

1318.   Warsen, Allen A.   THE DETROIT JEWISH DIRECTORY OF 1907 AS A RESEARCH SOURCE.   *Michigan Jewish Hist. 1978 18(2): 20-23.* The Detroit Jewish directory listed 2,470 people with their occupations and addresses, reflecting the demographic, vocational, and organizational history of Detroit Jewry.

1319.   Warsen, Allen A.   THE ODESSA PROGRESSIVE AID SOCIETY OF DETROIT, MICHIGAN.   *Michigan Jewish Hist. 1976 16(1): 39-42.* Reports on the operation, activities, and membership of the Odessa Progressive Aid Society, a charitable organization of Jews who assisted sick and disabled members and financially supported various associations, 1915-18.

1320.   Washburn, Emory.   THE JEWS IN LEICESTER, MASSACHUSETTS.   *Rhode Island Jewish Hist. Notes 1975 7(1): 34-41.* Discusses three Newport, Rhode Island Jewish families of Portuguese descent: those of Abraham Mendez, Jacob Rodriguez Rivera, and Aaron Lopez, who sought refuge from the invasion of British troops during the American Revolution, 1777-83.

1321. Wax, Bernard. "OUR TOURO SYNAGOGUE." *Rhode Island Jewish Hist. Notes 1977 7(3): 440-441.* Discusses the history and symbolism of the Touro Synagogue in Providence, Rhode Island; discusses Jews in Providence since 1654.

1322. Wax, Bernard. RHODE ISLAND MATERIALS IN THE AMERICAN JEWISH HISTORICAL SOCIETY COLLECTIONS. *Rhode Island Jewish Hist. Notes 1975 7(1): 171-174.*

1323. Whiteman, Maxwell. WESTERN IMPACT ON EAST EUROPEAN JEWS: A PHILADELPHIA FRAGMENT. Miller, Randall M. and Marzik, Thomas D., ed. *Immigrants and Religion in Urban America* (Philadelphia: Temple U. Pr., 1977): 117-137. Jewish clothiers from Eastern Europe who immigrated to the United States in the late 19th century were faced with impossible living and labor conditions. Long working hours, low pay, and especially the necessity of working on the Sabbath brought about the Jewish Tailors and Operators Association, in 1888. Lacking outside support, however, the organization saw its first wage-increase demand suppressed, and workers were warned they would be punished by God for their actions. Anarchists cited this to support their claim that religion was used to "subvert the labor movement." Their campaign became so strong that the union was reestablished in 1890 as the Cloakmakers Union No. 1 and another strike was called. The manufacturers formed the Philadelphia Cloak Manufacturers' Association. The most prominent Philadelphian rabbi, Sabato Morais, emerged as arbitrator. Negotiations progressed until the strikers demanded more and shattered all hopes for settlement. Manufacturers brought in Negro women to work. Three months later, Morais achieved settlement. His success in "rabbinical arbitration" reveals the force of religion in the immigrants' lives; their Judaic roots allowed Morais to build upon common religious concepts and sensibilities. 40 notes.
S. Robitaille

1324. Williams, John A. THE BOYS FROM SYRACUSE: BLACKS AND JEWS IN THE OLD NEIGHBORHOOD. *Present Tense 1977 4(3): 34-38.* Examines the historical and contemporary relationship between American Jews and Afro-Americans in Syracuse, New York. Cites author's experiences and those of other residents. Primary and secondary sources; photo, note.
R. B. Mendel

1325. Winn, Karyl. THE SEATTLE JEWISH COMMUNITY. *Pacific Northwest Q. 1979 70(2): 69-74.* Reproduces 10 photographs of Seattle's Jewish citizens and their businesses during the early 20th century. Though Jews constituted less than one percent of the city's population, their influence in civic and commercial affairs surpassed their numbers.
M. L. Tate

1326. Unsigned. CONGREGATIONAL POLITICS IN LOS ANGELES—1897. *Western States Jewish Hist. Q. 1974 6(2): 120-123.* There was much in-fighting in the B'nai B'rith Congregation in the 1890's over the type of rabbi for their temple, but no one was trying to solve the temple's financial problems. The wealthy members wanted to keep out the poor Jews by raising dues, but the increase in dues would not cover the temple's debts. Reprint of an article in *Emanu-El*, San Francisco, 9 July 1897.
R. A. Garfinkle

1327. —. FIRST SYNAGOGUE AT ALBUQUERQUE: 1900. *Western States Jewish Hist. Q. 1978 11(1): 46-48.* Temple Albert in Albuquerque, New Mexico, was dedicated on 14 September 1900. In a joint ceremony, Pizer Jacobs was installed as the new rabbi. Music and speeches preceded the solemn installation services which were presented to a large audience. Reprinted from *The American Israelite*, Cincinnati, 27 September 1900. Photo, 5 notes.
B. S. Porter

1328. Unsigned. IMPORTANT HISTORIC DOCUMENTS: REGARDING A STATE MARKER FOR THE LAFAYETTE STREET BETH EL CEMETERY. *Michigan Jewish Hist. 1973 13(1): 21-26.* Publishes letters on securing a historic marker for Beth El cemetery in Detroit, Michigan, the first Jewish cemetery owned and maintained by a Jewish congregation.
S

1329. —. JEWS IN EARLY SANTA MONICA: A CENTENNIAL REVIEW. *Western States Jewish Hist. Q. 1975 7(4): 327-350.* Many Los Angeles Jews spent their summers camping out at Santa Monica Canyon before the town was established in 1875. Many of these Jews were the first to purchase lots when the town was laid out by John P. Jones and R. S. Baker in 1875. The Jewish community consisted mostly of vacationers during the summer. The first Jewish religious services were held in 1912 by Los Angeles Rabbi Sigmund Hecht. In 1939, the first permanent Jewish congregation was formed. 16 photos, 56 notes.
R. A. Garfinkle

1330. —. LOS ANGELES B'NAI B'RITH LODGE NO. 487: A 1905 REPORT. *Western States Jewish Hist. Q. 1979 11(2): 167-169.* Los Angeles B'nai B'rith Lodge No. 487 was founded in 1899 with about 40 charter members. By 1905, it had approximately 170 members who enjoyed a new fraternal hall with a lodge room, billiard room, library, kitchen, and lockers. In addition to social events, the lodge devoted much money and energy to benevolent works. Reprinted from *The Jewish Times and Observer*, San Francisco, 17 February 1905.
B. S. Porter

1331. —. THE NEW JEWISH CEMETERY IN EAST LOS ANGELES, 1902. *Western States Jewish Hist. Q. 1978 11(1): 64-68.* Congregation B'nai B'rith (now the Wilshire Boulevard Temple) established the new Home of Peace Cemetery in East Los Angeles in 1902. Oscar Willenberg, the cemetery superintendent, kept a photograph album of scenes from the cemetery, which are presented here. 6 photos, 3 notes.
B. S. Porter

1332. —. NEWS FROM THE PORTLAND JEWISH COMMUNITY. *Western States Jewish Hist. Q. 1977 9(3): 235-237.* In 1885, Portland, Oregon, had 1,000 Jewish residents. Religious organizations included two B'nai B'rith lodges, the First Hebrew Benevolent Society, and the Judith Montefiore Society. Rabbi Jacob Bloch headed the Reform Congregation Beth Israel. The congregation, assisted by a leading merchant, Colonel L. Fleischner, undertook to raise funds for construction of a new temple, large enough for the needs of the active and growing Jewish community. Reprint of a report sent from Portland, Oregon, to *The American Israelite*, Cincinnati, Ohio, 8 January 1886; 4 notes.
B. S. Porter

1333. —. THE NEWS FROM WOODLAND AND OROVILLE, CALIFORNIA IN 1879. *Western States Jewish Hist. Q. 1979 11(2): 162-166.* Rabbi Aron J. Messing of Congregation Beth Israel in San Francisco traveled to scattered Jewish settlements in California encouraging fellow Jews to organize Hebrew societies and Sabbath schools. Following his visits to Woodland and Oroville, both communities established Hebrew associations and Sabbath schools for their children. Based on reports in *The American Israelite*, Cincinnati, 23 May 1879; photo, 23 notes.
B. S. Porter

1334. —. OAKLAND JEWRY AND THE EARTHQUAKE-FIRE OF 1906. *Western States Jewish Hist. Q. 1977 9(3): 251-252.* When refugees from the fire-stricken, poorer Jewish quarter of San Francisco came to Oakland, the synagogue provided immediate aid. Food and clothing were given to the needy and 350 people were given a place to sleep. For about a week the synagogue fed up to 500 people three times a day. A large part of the expenses were paid by the Jewish Ladies' organization of the synagogue. Reprint of article in *Emanu-El*, San Francisco, 4 May 1906.
B. S. Porter

1335. —. THE OLD JEWISH CEMETERY IN CHAVEZ RAVINE, LOS ANGELES: A PICTURE STORY. *Western States Jewish Hist. Q. 1977 9(2): 167-175.* The Hebrew Benevolent Society of Los Angeles established the Home of Peace Cemetery in 1855. A new cemetery was established in 1902. The remains and monuments were transferred to the new location during 1902-10. Based on photos collected by cemetery superintendent Oscar Willenberg, interviews, and published material; 8 photos, 3 notes.
B. S. Porter

1336. —. PORTLAND JEWRY COLLECTS FOR RUSSIAN REFUGEES. *Western States Jewish Hist. Q. 1978 10(4): 343-346.* On 4 January 1891 the International Society for the Colonization of Russian Jews was organized with the goal of settling Russian Jewish refugees on land in California or Mexico. A fund raising tour of Oregon and Washington included the city of Portland, Oregon. Meeting in Temple Beth Israel, the Jewish citizens of Portland subscribed $5,000. One of the fund raisers wrote a letter describing the Portland meeting and admonishing the Society's members to help check the influx of Jewish paupers and cheap labor in order to lessen the prejudice against the Russian Jews. Reprints the letter, which was first published in *The Jewish Voice* of St. Louis on 20 February 1891; 5 notes. B. S. Porter

1337. —. PROBLEMS OF A NEVADA JEWISH COMMUNITY IN 1875. *Western States Jewish Hist. Q. 1976 8(2): 160-162.* Reprints a letter to the editor of the *American Israelite*, 3 September 1875, in which an anonymous resident of Eureka, Nevada complained that his Jewish community could not afford a good rabbi for the High Holy Days. He complained that many of the men previously hired to be rabbis had been frauds. R. A. Garfinkle

1338. —. THE RISE AND FALL OF THE JEWISH COMMUNITY OF AUSTIN, NEVADA. *Western States Jewish Q. 1976 9(1): 87-90.* Reprints letters from Jewish correspondents to Jewish newspapers in San Francisco and New York. In 1864 there were 150 Jews, including three families, who kept the principles of the faith and maintained an active Hebrew Benevolent Association in Austin, Nevada. By 1882, silver mining had declined and so had the town's population. Jews numbered only 11. Religious observance was minimal among both Jews and Christians, although the town was remarkably law-abiding. B. S. Porter

1339. —. A SAN BERNARDINO CONFIRMAND'S REPORT: 1891. *Western States Jewish Hist. Q. 1979 11(2): 111-113.* The Henrietta Hebrew Benevolent Society sponsored the first Sunday School in San Bernardino, California, in 1891. Fourteen of the students were confirmed in their faith in a ceremony on 14 June 1891. Reverend Dr. Blum of Los Angeles officiated. Reprint of a letter from *The Sabbath Visitor*, Cincinatti, 31 July 1891; 6 notes. B. S. Porter

1340. —. TWO VIEWS OF AN INTERNATIONAL JEWISH COMMUNITY: BROWNSVILLE, TEXAS AND MATAMOROS, MEXICO. *Western States Jewish Hist. Q. 1978 10(4): 306-310.* Letters to editors of Jewish newspapers in 1876 and 1882 described the Jews of Brownsville (Texas) and Matamoros, (Tamaulipas, Mexico) as a unified religious community. Matamoros, having the greater number of Jewish families, was the location of religious ceremonies on feast and fast days. Some of the leading merchants in both towns were Jews; they were highly respected citizens who took an interest in civic affairs and contributed to every public and religious institution. Reprints letters to the *American Israelite*, Cincinnati, Ohio, 28 July 1876, and the *Jewish Messenger*, New York, 27 January 1882. 7 notes. B. S. Porter

1341. —. WORD FROM PORTLAND A CENTURY AGO. *Western States Jewish Hist. Q. 1979 11(3): 252-254.* Portland, Oregon's, Jewish community recently had received a lecture series by the Reverend Moses May, whose heavy German accent grated on the ears of the Congregation Beth Israel. Social visits between friends and relatives in San Francisco and Portland were frequent. The approaching state elections (3 June 1878) were of great interest because of the nominations of several excellent candidates, including Edward Hirsch, A. Noltner, and Solomon Hirsch. Reprinted from the *Jewish Progress*, San Francisco; 4 notes. B. S. Porter

Individuals

1342. Adler, Adam W. MY FATHER WAS BORN A JEW. *Western States Jewish Hist. Q. 1974 6(4): 255-259.* Lewis Adler (1820-96) was one of the first persons of Jewish descent to arrive in California. His father had converted to Christianity in Germany in 1829 but the family retained its ethnic identity. Adler worked as a journeyman cooper for William Heath Davis for eight months and then opened his own store in Sonoma in late 1847. By 1850, Lewis had acquired a small fortune and traveled to Germany to visit his mother. In 1855, he opened a wholesale business with Jacob Bloomingdale, and later expanded into the wholesale liquor business. Photo, 4 notes. R. A. Garfinkle

1343. Alpert, David B. THE MAN FROM KOVNO. *Am. Jewish Arch. 1977 29(2): 107-115.* Not all history is the history of the famous

or well-known. This is especially true for the story of American Jewry—where the poor and unlettered played a vital role in its development. Rabbi Abraham Alpert does not rank among the names that have become legend to most American Jews. But to a segment of Boston Jewry, his many efforts to improve the lot of immigrant life earned him a kind of love and respect that the rich and famous could indeed envy. J

1344. Alschuler, Al. THE COLMANS AND OTHERS OF DEADWOOD, SOUTH DAKOTA. *Western States Jewish Hist. Q. 1977 9(4): 291-298.* Nathan Colman, a German Jewish immigrant, came to Deadwood, South Dakota, in 1877 and opened a tobacco store. He was appointed postmaster in 1878, elected justice of the peace, and active in local Republican politics. In 1911 Colman's daughter Blanche became the first woman admitted to the South Dakota Bar. For more than 50 years she was a practicing attorney. Other Jews settled in frontier Deadwood in the 1870's and became prominent in businesses and industries. The Jewish community has diminished with the rest of Deadwood's population; Blanche Colman is the only remaining member of the pioneer Jewish community. Based on newspapers, family records and secondary sources; 4 photos, 20 notes. B. S. Porter

1345. Anderson, Elaine. WILLIAM KRAUS AND THE JEWISH COMMUNITY. *Northwest Ohio Q. 1977 49(4): 127-162.* Chronicles the demise of William Kraus, a leading member of the Jewish community in Toledo, Ohio, during 1869-76. A few unpopular acts during his administration as the city's mayor, compounded by the closing of his bank, and shady real estate dealings, led to his exile in Canada.

1346. Axe, Ruth Frey. SIGMUND FREY: LOS ANGELES JEWRY'S FIRST PROFESSIONAL SOCIAL WORKER. *Western States Jewish Hist. Q. 1976 8(4): 312-325.* Rabbi Sigmund Frey (1852-1930) came to Los Angeles to be the superintendent for the Jewish Orphan's Home then located at Mission and Macy streets. In 1910 a fire destroyed the home and in November 1912 the new Jewish Orphan's Home was dedicated in Huntington Park, California. Rabbi Frey became a well known author, scholar, journalist, bibliophile, and teacher. In 1921, he resigned as superintendent. Before his death in Los Angeles Rabbi Frey and his wife Hermine traveled several times to Europe. Primary and secondary sources; 4 photos, 5 notes. R. A. Garfinkle

1347. Bachmann, Lawrence P. JULIUS ROSENWALD. *Am. Jewish Hist. Q. 1976 66(1): 89-105.* Julius Rosenwald (1862-1932), vice president and treasurer of the world's largest retail company, Sears, Roebuck and Company, was at the same time one of the most generous philanthropists. Sketches his business career, emphasizing the business acumen which made his company a model organization, and details his philanthropic activities. From 1917-32 the Julius Rosenwald Foundation initiated the establishment of 5,357 public schools for blacks which raised the level of teaching and teaching instruction throughout the country. Contributions to the University of Chicago and to various Jewish philanthropies were on a similar scale. F. Rosenthal

1348. Barnes, Al. JULIUS H. STEINBERG, EARLY JEWISH PIONEER OF TRAVERSE CITY AND THE STEINBERG GRAND OPERA HOUSE. *Michigan Jewish Hist. 1974 14(2): 24-28.* Documents Julius H. Steinberg's activities in the 1890's in Michigan. S

1349. Barnett, Lincoln. HOW ALBERT EINSTEIN, A GENTLE, MODEST GENIUS BORN 100 YEARS AGO, FOUND SANCTUARY AND INSPIRATION IN PRINCETON. *Smithsonian 1979 9(11): 68-79.* Einstein decided to accept an appointment to the newly established Institute for Advanced Study in Princeton, New Jersey, in 1933 after observing with horror the Nazi assault on the intellect. He renounced his German citizenship while he was a visiting professor at Caltech, shortly after Hitler became chancellor of Germany. In 1939 he wrote President Roosevelt a prophetic letter warning about the atomic bomb. It was a prologue to the Manhattan Project and Hiroshima. Illus. E. P. Stickney

1350. Berry, Hannah Shwayder. A COLORADO FAMILY HISTORY. *Western States Jewish Hist. Q. 1973 5(3): 158-165.* Chronicles the history of the Isaac and Rachel Shwayder family, from their emigration from Poland in 1865, to their successful business activities in Denver in 1916.

1351. Boxerman, Burton Alan. THE EDISON BROTHERS, SHOE MERCHANTS: THEIR GEORGIA YEARS. *Georgia Hist. Q. 1973 57(4): 511-525.* Traces the history of the retail shoe store ventures of five sons of a Russian Jewish emigrant in Georgia and their merger into the Edison Brothers Company that became the largest chain of women's shoe stores in the nation.   D. L. Smith

1352. Boxerman, Burton Alan. KAHN OF CALIFORNIA. *California Hist. Q. 1976 55(4): 340-351.* Julius Kahn (1861-1924) was a 12 term Congressman from California whose career spanned the presidencies from Theodore Roosevelt to Calvin Coolidge. Born of German Jewish parents, Kahn came to California at age seven and grew up in San Francisco. After an initial career as an actor he became a lawyer. Elected to Congress in 1898, Kahn was continuously returned by his San Francisco constituents except for the 1902 election. Kahn generally followed the Republican Party position favoring free tolls for American ships through the Panama Canal, opposing Woodrow Wilson's Mexican policy and the League of Nations, and supporting the operation of Muscle Shoals by private enterprise. An advocate of military preparedness, Kahn crossed party lines to support Wilson's preparedness policy in 1917. He sponsored the first Selective Service Act and favored universal military training. While reflecting his constituents' opposition to Japanese immigration and naturalization, Kahn voted against laws designed to restrict European immigration. He died of a cerebral hemorrhage in 1924. Based on primary and secondary sources; photos, 48 notes.   A. Hoffman

1353. Boxerman, Burton A. LOUIS PATRICK ALOE. *Missouri Hist. Soc. Bull. 1974 31(1): 41-54.* Louis Patrick Aloe (1867-1929), a St. Louis businessman, served the city of St. Louis in many public capacities, always seeking to make St. Louis a "progressive, dynamic" city second to none in the United States. In 1925, Aloe ran for Mayor but lost the election. The embittered Aloe blamed his defeat upon anti-Semitism in the city. Based on newspaper sources; 43 notes.   H. T. Lovin

1354. Boxerman, Burton Alan. LUCIUS NATHAN LITTAUER. *Am. Jewish Hist. Q. 1977 66(4): 498-512.* Lucius Nathan Littauer (1859-1944) was the son of Nathan and Harriett Littauer of New York. After graduation from Harvard, he founded a flourishing glove factory and became a prominent businessman, active in Republican politics. He served 10 years in the House of Representatives and became one of the great philanthropists of the era. His gifts provided seed money for many educational, academic, medical, scientific, and civil activities. 41 notes.   F. Rosenthal

1355. Braude, William G. HARRY WOLFSON AS MENTOR. *Rhode Island Jewish Hist. Notes 1975 7(1): 140-148.* Author relates events of his academic and rabbinical career which was aided and influenced by a Brown University professor, Harry Wolfson.

1356. Braude, William G. SAMUEL BELKIN AT BROWN. *Rhode Island Jewish Hist. Notes 1974 6(4): 610-613.* Reminiscences about Samuel Belkin, President of Yeshiva University, by Rabbi William G. Braude, his friend during their years at Brown University (1932-35).   S

1357. Bronstein, Zelda and Kann, Kenneth. BASHA SINGERMAN, COMRADE OF PETALUMA. *California Hist. Q. 1977 56(1): 20-33.* Presents an interview with a resident of Petaluma, California, as part of an oral history project about the Petaluma Jewish chicken farmers. Names were changed to protect privacy. The interviewee, a socialist woman, left Minsk, Russia, to go to South Africa, Montreal, and finally California. In 1915 she and her husband bought land and began operating a chicken ranch. The work was hard but she preferred it to the big city sweatshops. Their neighbors were mainly Jewish socialists. In the 1920's, Petaluma's Jewish population grew to 100 families. The community prospered in the 1920's but suffered in the Depression. Eventually the subject had to sell her home. Now 83, she meets socially with a declining number of old friends, and the Socialist community is fading for a conservative suburban one. Photos.   A. Hoffman

1358. Choynski, Isidor N. and Eckman, Julius. TWO LETTERS TO HARRIET CHOYNSKI. *Western States Jewish Hist. Q. 1974 7(1): 44-48.* Two letters addressed to Harriet Choynski written in 1863 and 1872 give a glimpse of life in the West at that time. Mrs. Choynski had

five children, taught at a religious school in San Francisco for many years, and marched in San Francisco's first May Day parade. 19 notes.
                                                               R. A. Garfinkle

1359. Churgin, Gershon A. RAV TZAIR'S VIEWS ON THE CULTURAL UNITY OF THE JEWISH PEOPLE. *Bitzaron 1974 65(6): 277-281.*

1360. Chyet, Stanley F. MOSES JACOB EZEKIEL: A CHILDHOOD IN RICHMOND. *Am. Jewish Hist. Q. 1973 62(3): 286-294.* The sculptor Moses Ezekiel (1844-1917) spent most of his adult life in Europe but never concealed his American background or his Jewishness. His *Autobiography* describes his early interest in art. His maternal grandmother, Hannah Waterman, was a strong influence on him. 2 photos, 16 notes.   F. Rosenthal

1361. Clar, Reva. EARLY STOCKTON JEWRY AND ITS CANTOR RABBI HERMAN DAVIDSON. *Western States Jewish Hist. Q. 1973 5(2): 63-86, (3): 166-187.* Part I. A biography of Herman Davidson (1846-1911) emphasizes his operatic career in Russia, his family life, and his work with Jews in Stockton, 1876-91. Part II. Chronicles the relationship between Davidson and Stockton Jews, and efforts to reform the Jewish congregation, 1893-1911.

1362. Clar, Reva. PAVLOVA AND ME. *Western States Jewish Hist. Q. 1979 11(4): 350-353.* The author was a student at San Francisco's Hirsch-Arnold Ballet School in 1924 when Anna Pavlova (1885-1931) and her dance company came to the city to perform the ballet *Don Quixote.* The author and two or three other students volunteered to help as extras in the performance. Personal recollection; photo, 3 notes.
                                                               B. S. Porter

1363. Coerver, Don M. and Hall, Linda B. NEIMAN-MARCUS: INNOVATORS IN FASHION AND MERCHANDISING. *Am. Jewish Hist. Q. 1976 66(1): 123-136.* As innovative merchants and merchandizers Neiman-Marcus of Dallas, Texas, revolutionized the Southwestern approach to fashion. Relates the story of the store, its founders, and its progress until the present. 44 notes.   F. Rosenthal

1364. Cohen, Blanche Klasmer. BENJAMIN KLASMER'S CONTRIBUTION TO BALTIMORE'S MUSICAL HISTORY. *Maryland Hist. Mag. 1977 72(2): 272-276.* Records the important role played by Benjamin Klasmer in bringing music to Baltimore for over 30 years, first as a cofounder of the Baltimore Symphony Orchestra, in 1916, and then as conductor of the Jewish Educational Alliance Symphony Orchestra in the 1920's. Throughout his career, Klasmer was the "leading musical director of pit orchestras" furnishing accompaniment to silent movies and vaudeville acts at the New Theater, the Garden and Rivoli Theaters, and the Hippodrome until his death in 1949. The tradition which he began is continued today by the Jewish Community Center and other groups. Perhaps his most popular renown, however, comes from his coauthorship of the theme song of the Baltimore Colts. 3 illus.   G. J. Bobango

1365. Cohen, Robert, ed. BIBLIOTHECA ROSENTHALIANA TE KOOP ENIGE BRIEVEN VAN MEIJER ROEST MZN. EN GEORGE ROSENTHAL AAN DR. B. FELSENTHAL IN DE VERENIGDE STATEN [The Bibliotheca Rosenthaliana for sale: some letters from Meyer Roest and George Rosenthal to Dr. B. Felsenthal in the United States]. *Studia Rosenthaliana [Netherlands] 1975 9(1): 90-102.* Reprints letters 1868-96, from George Rosenthal and Meyer Roest in Amsterdam to Rabbi Bernard Felsenthal in Chicago, Illinois, concerning the purchase of the late Rabbi Leeser Rosenthal's library by US buyers.

1366. Cole, Sylvan. MEMORIES OF AN 1890'S POMONA BOYHOOD. *Western States Jewish Hist. Q. 1979 11(4): 327-331.* The author's father operated a dry goods and clothing store, known as the People's Store, in Pomona, California, 1886-1901. The author recalls working in his father's store, accepting cookies from the bakery next door, and playing with boys from a variety of ethnic and religious backgrounds. Personal recollections and published sources; 2 photos, 11 notes.
                                                               B. S. Porter

1367. Cronbach, Abraham. THE SPROUT THAT GREW. *Am. Jewish Arch. 1975 27(1): 51-60.* Points out the contributions of Isaac M. Wise to the Hebrew Union College in Cincinnati, 1870's-1900.   S

1368. Dawson, Nelson L. LOUIS D. BRANDEIS, FELIX FRANK-FURTER, AND FRANKLIN D. ROOSEVELT: THE ORIGINS OF A NEW DEAL RELATIONSHIP. *Am. Jewish Hist. 1978 68(1): 32-42.* The Brandeis-Frankfurter partnership influencing national political events began in 1917 (re the appointment of an economic "czar"). By the 1920's the extensive correspondence between them included politics, law, and Zionism. By 1933, Frankfurter acted as the intermediary between Brandeis and Roosevelt. The intellectual relation of these three men demonstrates the importance of personal contact as a source of political influence and the truth of their philosophy's central thesis: that the richest sources of a democracy are the individuals in public service.

F. Rosenthal

1369. Edgar, Irving I. DR. MAX BALLIN AND HARPER HOSPITAL OF DETROIT: PART III. *Michigan Jewish Hist. 1978 18(2): 3-6.* Concluded from a previous article (see *Michigan Jewish History,* January 1970 and July 1971). Discusses the association of Max Ballin, surgeon of international reputation, with Harper Hospital in 1906-24, noting his involvement in the development of teaching techniques and facilities and in fostering progressive change.

1370. Edgar, Irving I. RABBI LEO M. FRANKLIN: THE OMAHA YEARS (1892-1899). *Michigan Jewish Hist. 1976 16(2): 10-21.* Details the organizational abilities of Rabbi Leo M. Franklin in his work in Temple Israel in Omaha, Nebraska. 4 letters, 26 notes.

1371. Ellsworth, S. George, ed. SIMON BAMBERGER: GOVERNOR OF UTAH. *Western States Jewish Hist. Q. 1973 5(4): 231-242.* Simon Bamberger, a German, Jewish immigrant active in railroads and charity work, was elected the first non-Mormon, Democratic governor of Utah in 1916.

1372. Engelbourg, Saul. EDWARD A. FILENE: MERCHANT, CIVIC LEADER, AND JEW. *Am. Jewish Hist. Q. 1976 66(1): 106-122.* Edward A. Filene (1860-1937), American-born son of German Jewish immigrants, became a millionaire several times over, and because of his business success he was able to obtain fame as a philanthropist and a civic leader in Boston. He is credited with the "Automatic Bargain Basement" as his most distinctive business innovation. Describes the controversy with his associate Louis Kirstein (1867-1942), his cooperation with Louis Brandeis, his share in the development of the Credit Union movement, the influence of his Twentieth Century Fund, his marginal interest in Jewish philanthropy, and the fight against anti-Semitism. 49 notes.

F. Rosenthal

1373. Feld, Bernard T. EINSTEIN AND THE POLITICS OF NUCLEAR WEAPONS. *Bull. of the Atomic Scientists 1979 35(3): 5-16.* Chronicles Albert Einstein's work on the creation of nuclear arms, 1939-42, which he believed to be a necessary deterrent because of his Zionism and his fear of Nazi Germany, and his efforts to control and discourage the further use of the weaponry, which was rooted in his basic pacifism, 1943-55.

1374. Feuer, Lewis S. RECOLLECTIONS OF HARRY AUSTRYN WOLFSON. *Am. Jewish Arch. 1976 28(1): 25-50.* Presents a biography of the great Jewish scholar Harry Austryn Wolfson (1887-1974), including anecdotes about his teaching career, political philosophy, and religious beliefs.

1375. Fogelson, George J., ed. A CONVERSION AT SANTA CRUZ, CALIFORNIA, 1877. *Western States Jewish Hist. Q. 1979 11(2): 138-144.* In December 1877, Emma Schlutius was officially accepted as a convert to Judaism in a ceremony at the St. Charles Hotel in Santa Cruz. Schlutius correctly answered questions regarding her motives and tenets of the faith. On her admission to the covenant, her name was changed to Esther. She was shortly afterwards married to Abe Rothschild. Based on an article published in the *Santa Cruz Sentinel* on 8 December 1877; photo, 6 notes.

B. S. Porter

1376. Franklin, Harvey B. MEMORIES OF A CALIFORNIA RABBI: STOCKTON, SAN JOSE AND LONG BEACH. *Western States Jewish Hist. Q. 1977 9(2): 122-128.* Rabbi Harvey B. Franklin (1889-1976) spent his rabbinical career at Stockton, 1916-18; Oakland, 1918-20; San Jose, 1920-28; and Long Beach, 1928-57. Early in his career

he faced the necessity of developing a religious service that satisfied a mixed and mutually antagonistic congregation of Reform, Orthodox, and Conservative members. Relates several anecdotes, some humorous, of his experiences at each Jewish community.

B. S. Porter

1377. Freund, Paul A. JUSTICE BRANDEIS: A LAW CLERK'S REMEMBRANCE. *Am. Jewish Hist. 1978 68(1): 7-18.* The author who served as Supreme Court justice Louis D. Brandeis's law clerk in 1932-33, calls him a working justice, incisive moralist, observant host, and ardent Zionist. Brandeis' power derived from a harmonious fusion of biblical moral responsibility, classical restraint and proportion, and the common law tradition of rubbing against the hard face of experience.

F. Rosenthal

1378. Friedlander, Alice G. A PORTLAND GIRL ON WOMEN'S RIGHTS—1893. *Western States Jewish Hist. Q. 1978 10(2): 146-150.* In 1893 Alice G. Friedlander said there should be no question about the fundamental principal of women's equality. Any profession—such as journalism, law, medicine, education—requiring intellectual rather than manual force, is open to women. Soon they will vote and hold office, and, though lacking in parliamentary finesse, no matter how hard they try, they cannot be more ignorant and stupid than some gentleman legislators. These new skills and attainments do not conflict with women's duties in the home. Quoted from original speech at Portland (Oregon) Press Club; photo.

B. S. Porter

1379. Gartner, Lloyd P. NAPHTALI HERZ IMBER, POPULIST. *Michael: On the Hist. of the Jews in the Diaspora [Israel] 1975 3: 88-100.* Naphtali Herz Imber (1856-1909) was a minor Hebrew poet best known for his "Hatikvah" (The Hope), which became Israel's national anthem. Much less known is his pamphlet *The Fall of Jerusalem: Reflecting upon the Present Condition of America,* written shortly after his arrival in the United States in 1892 and reprinted here. It fabricates a myth of Biblical history paralleling the Populist myth of American history, exhorting Americans to heed the warning of Jewish experience and not allow their wealth to lead America to ruin. Primary and secondary sources; 5 notes.

T. Sassoon

1380. Gilson, Estelle. TRUDE'S A HOLY TERROR: SCHOLAR, CRITIC, REBEL, GADFLY. *Present Tense 1978 5(2): 33-37.* Chronicles the career of Trude Weiss-Rosmarin, editor of *The Jewish Spectator* but dedicated critic and adherent of the Jewish community, 1930's-78.

1381. Ginzberg, Eli. ROBERT SZOLD: AN AUTHENTIC AMERICAN. *Midstream 1979 25(9): 47-52.* Biographical sketch of Robert Szold, a New York City attorney and investor active in Zionism, 1920's-70's.

1382. Glazer, Michele. THE DURKHEIMERS OF OREGON: A PICTURE STORY. *Western States Jewish Hist. Q. 1978 10(3): 202-209.* Kaufman Durkheimer brought his family from Philadelphia to Portland, Oregon, in 1862, where he opened a second-hand furniture store. In 1874 his son Julius moved to Baker City, Oregon where he opened a general mechandise store. Julius sold the store in 1887 and opened a new store in Prairie City. The next year he opened another store in Canyon City. With the expansion of his merchandising businesses to a third site, in Burns, Oregon, Julius sent for his brothers Moses, Sam, and Sigmund to help run the firm. Julius's wife, Delia, was not happy in the primitive, isolated small towns of eastern Oregon, so the family moved to Portland. In 1896 Julius purchased an interest in the wholesale grocery firm of Wadham and Company, the northwest distributor of Olympia beer. Under the management of Julius's son and grandson, the company—now, Bevhold, Inc.—continues to market Olympia beer. Primary and secondary sources; 5 photos, 3 notes.

B. S. Porter

1383. Goldberg, Gordon J. MEYER LONDON AND THE NATIONAL SOCIAL INSURANCE MOVEMENT, 1914-1922. *Am. Jewish Hist. Q. 1975 65(1): 59-73.* Meyer London as legal counsel for the International Ladies' Garment Workers Union (ILGWU) and other unions became the principal spokesman for the labor movement and the urban immigrant. As the only Socialist representative in the 64th, 65th and 67th Congresses, London presented his party's social insurance program and waged a vigorous fight for its adoption. Although the plan was defeated, he helped educate colleagues and the public about labor reform, helping to pave the way for the New Deal.

F. Rosenthal

1384. Goldberg, Richard B. MICHAEL WORMSER, CAPITAL-IST. *Am. Jewish Arch. 1973 25(2): 161-206.* "French-born Wormser 'helped build Arizona. Above all, he embodied the spirit of frontier materialism.' When it came to business enterprise, 'his creative energy was unlimited.' "
                                                                      J

1385. Goldsmith, Steven R. SAM HAMBURG: WORLD'S FORE-MOST JEWISH FARMER. *Western States Jewish Hist. Q. 1978 10(4): 330-342.* Sam Hamburg (1898-1976) came to the United States from Palestine in 1920 to study modern agricultural techniques at the University of California at Berkeley and Davis. In 1932, after several years of tenant-farming, he bought land near Los Banos in the San Joaquin Valley. "Sam Hamburg Farms" became a showplace of modern agriculture, producing melons, cotton, vegetables, and seed alfalfa. In 1952 he returned to Israel where he used his own money and his knowledge of desert farming to develop cotton as an export crop that grossed $100 million a year by 1976. He commuted between California and Israel, bringing new agricultural ideas and materials to Israel, and developing strong bonds of friendship with Israeli leaders. In 1965 Hamburg developed Guillaume-Barre disease which left him deaf and partially paralyzed. When he died, he was mourned by great political leaders and small farmers from around the world. Based on personal interviews with friends and family; 4 photos, 11 notes.
                                                                      B. S. Porter

1386. Gordon, Dudley. CHARLES F. LUMMIS AND THE NEW-MARKS OF LOS ANGELES. *Western States Jewish Hist. Q. 1974 7(1): 32-38.* The friendship of author-editor Charles F. Lummis and the Newmark brothers, leading merchants in Los Angeles, led to the preservation of several historical sites and a crusade for culture in Los Angeles. Lummis founded the Southwest Museum and edited *Land of Sunshine* for many years. He also wrote the foreword to Harris Newmark's *Sixty Years in Southern California*.
                                                                      R. A. Garfinkle

1387. Greenberg, Gershon. THE DIMENSIONS OF SAMUEL ADLER'S RELIGIOUS VIEW OF THE WORLD. *Hebrew Union Coll. Ann. 1975 46: 377-412.* Samuel Adler (1809-91) was a German-born reform-rabbi who spent the last 35 years of his life as rabbi of Temple Emanuel of New York. For him Judaism is a significant level in the growth of moral consciousness where morality is amplified into an ontological realm, identical to the idealized world of creation. *Wissenschaft* becomes the God-given methodology for achieving insights into the moral possibilities of all literature and history. 100 notes.
                                                                      F. Rosenthal

1388. Greenwood, N. H. SOL BARTH: A JEWISH SETTLER ON THE ARIZONA FRONTIER. *J. of Arizona Hist. 1973 14(4): 363-378.* Solomon Barth (ca. 1843-1928) came to the United States from East Prussia in 1856 and crossed the plains that year with a Mormon handcart group. For 20 years he traveled in the Far West, dealing in cattle, farming, trading, and sometimes gambling. He specialized in the opportunity of the moment. In 1873 he won squatters' equities, water rights, thousands of head of sheep, and cash in a card game at a key point on the Little Colorado River, in east central Arizona, at the juncture of two developing trade routes. Consolidating his land titles, he established St. Johns. Barth's fortunes were enhanced when he permitted Mormon colonists to locate there. Mormon-Mexican conflicts, prominence in local politics and graft, and a prison term occupied Barth. His anti-Mormon inclinations were tempered by the years; in the end he requested his funeral to be conducted in the Mormon church. 3 illus., 30 notes.
                                                                      D. L. Smith

1389. Hall, Linda. NEIMAN-MARCUS: THE BEGINNING. *Western States Jewish Hist. Q. 1975 7(2): 138-150.* On 10 September 1907 in Dallas, Texas, Herbert Marcus and Al and Carrie Neiman opened their first store, which specialized in fine clothes for women. They had operated a store in Atlanta for two years, but sold it to open their new store in Dallas. They developed new methods of merchandising ready-to-wear clothing. In 1913, the store was destroyed by a fire, after which it moved to larger quarters and continued to grow. The Neiman-Marcus Co. contributed greatly to the development of Dallas as the major fashion market in the Southwest. 36 notes.
                                                                      R. A. Garfinkle

1390. Harris, Ira L. A LOS ANGELES POPULAR MUSIC DIRECTOR. *Western States Jewish Hist. Q. 1977 10(1): 62-67.* Abraham Frankum Frankenstein (1873-1934) began his musical career in Chicago,

came to Los Angeles in 1897 with the Grau Opera Company, and remained to form the first permanent theater orchestra. During the 1920's Frankenstein conducted the Orpheum Theater orchestra for such stars as Jack Benny, Fanny Brice, George Jessel, the Marx Brothers, and Sophie Tucker. He organized the bands of the Los Angeles Police and Fire Departments. He served on the Los Angeles Fire Commission for most of the 1913-27 period. In collaboration with F. B. Silverwood he wrote the song, "I Love You California," in 1913; it became the official state song in 1951. Based on personal knowledge and published sources; photo, 18 notes.
                                                                      B. S. Porter

1391. Hattem, Maurice I. I. M. HATTEM AND HIS LOS ANGELES SUPERMARKET. *Western States Jewish Hist. Q. 1979 11(3): 243-251.* Hattem's Day and Night Drive-In Market, established in 1927, was the first of its kind in Los Angeles. Its owner, Isadore M. Hattem (1894-1966), was a cosmopolitan merchant, born in Constantinople, Turkey, and a world traveler by the time he was 20. He came to Los Angeles in 1913, found a job at a fruit stand, and expanded the business. His flair for showmanship was apparent in the Spanish mission style of his famous Drive-In Market. Hattem's career in the grocery business encompassed both the wholesale and retail outlets until his retirement in 1949. 4 photos.
                                                                      B. S. Porter

1392. Henry, Henry Abraham. A SAN FRANCISCO RABBI REPORTS ON A VISIT TO SACRAMENTO IN 1858. *Western States Jewish Hist. Q. 1978 11(1): 60-63.* A letter from Rabbi Henry Abraham Henry to Rabbi Samuel Meyer Issacs on 17 August 1858 described Rabbi Henry's recent visit to Sacramento, California. Rabbi Henry was invited to preach in the synagogue, and participated in the ceremonial placement of a monument on the grave of Mr. Julius S. Winehill. The president and trustees of the synagogue offered a gratuity for Rabbi Henry's services. Reprinted from the *Jewish Messenger,* New York, 24 September 1858. 2 notes.
                                                                      B. S. Porter

1393. Henry, Marcus H. HENRY ABRAHAM HENRY: SAN FRANCISCO RABBI, 1857-1869. *Western States Jewish Hist. Q. 1977 10(1): 31-37.* Henry Abraham Henry (1806-79) came to the United States from England in 1849. He served congregations in Ohio and New York before coming to San Francisco in 1857. He was minister of San Francisco's Sherith Israel (Polish) synagogue, from 1857-69. A popular lecturer, he officiated at the consecration of many synagogues and the dedications of secular institutions. Rabbi Henry contributed many articles to American Jewish journals. He published his two-part *Synopsis of Jewish History* in 1859. In 1860 he started and edited the weekly *Pacific Messenger.* In 1864 he issued his volume of *Discourses on the Book of Genesis.* His religious views were conservative. He upheld the dignity of his profession to the admiration of both Jews and Christians. Photo.
                                                                      B. S. Porter

1394. Hexter, Maurice B. HISTORICAL REMINISCENCE. *Am. Jewish Hist. 1978 68(2): 122-130.* The author (b. 1871) entered Jewish communal work with the United Jewish Charities in Cincinnati, Ohio, in 1912. His reminiscences of the days before social work went academic and psychological deal with the real problems of illness, desertion, adjustments of immigrants, Hebrew free loans, etc. Then as now the relationship between the social service organizations and the synagogues might be categorized as "mutual distrust tinged with apprehension."
                                                                      F. Rosenthal

1395. Hicks, James L. and Vorspan, Albert. KIVIE KAPLAN: "AN INCREDIBLE MAN"—KIVIE KAPLAN: A BRIDGE BETWEEN BLACKS AND JEWS—HIS SMILE AND DEEDS WILL NEVER DIE. *Crisis 1975 82(7): 231-233.* Kivie Kaplan devoted his life to eliminating man's inhumanity to man. He was chairman of the committee for Life Membership of the NAACP. Even with a pacemaker he preached brotherhood all over the country and handed out cards that asked people to "Keep Smiling." He symbolized the cooperation between Jews and Negroes. He preferred to burn out rather than rust out, and died 5 May 1975 en route from one meeting to another.
                                                                      A. G. Belles

1396. Himmelfarb, Milton. ON LEO STRAUSS. *Commentary 1974 58(2): 60-67.*

1397. Hoffmann, Banesh. ALBERT EINSTEIN. *Leo Baeck Inst. Year Book [Great Britain] 1976 20: 279-288.* Reinterprets Albert Einstein's (1879-1955) life with emphasis on his religious and artistic sides. His writings and his major scientific achievements show the lucidity of his mind and his genius to see even the most complicated matters simply and artistically. The last 30 years of his life were devoted to furthering peace and strengthening human freedom. Einstein, the nonreligious Jew, shared the full burden of his Jewishness since he felt responsible for his people and their fate. 22 notes.
F. Rosenthal

1398. Hook, Sidney. MORRIS COHEN: FIFTY YEARS LATER. *Am. Scholar 1976 45(3): 426-436.* Discusses Morris R. Cohen of the College of the City of New York, as a philosophy teacher. He early resorted to the Socratic method with devastating and sometimes cruel effects, which he termed a "logical disinfectant." Although he might appear negative, his great wisdom overshadowed his often personal pettiness. His wisdom combined a basic liberalism with his philosophic pluralism and doctrine of polarity which made him a "dominant figure in the cultural life of New York City."
R. V. Ritter

1399. Hornbein, Marjorie. DR. CHARLES SPIVAK OF DENVER: PHYSICIAN, SOCIAL WORKER, YIDDISH AUTHOR. *Western States Jewish Hist. Q. 1979 11(3): 195-211.* Dr. Charles Spivak (1861-1927) was a founder of Denver, Colorado's, Jewish Consumptives' relief society sanatorium (J.C.R.S.) in 1904. The J.C.R.S., in contrast with the National Jewish Hospital, accepted patients in the advanced stages of tuberculosis. Rivalry between the hospitals was part of the schism in the city's Jewish community. A specialist in gastrointestinal diseases, Dr. Spivak taught at the Medical School of the University of Denver, and also found time to write essays on medicine and Judaism. His best known literary work was a Yiddish dictionary, published in 1911. In 1920 Dr. Spivak was part of a team of medical experts, sponsored by the US Army, sent to Europe to study and report on sanitary and medical conditions in Poland. Dr. Spivak was not actively religious until late in life, but his fortitude and serenity helped him accept his fate as a victim of cancer. One of his final requests was that his body be given to a medical school. Primary and secondary sources; 2 photos, 59 notes.
B. S. Porter

1400. Jaffe, Grace. FROM SAN JOSE TO HOLLYWOOD: THE RISE OF JESSE L. LASKY. *Western States Jewish Hist. Q. 1978 11(1): 20-24.* Jesse L. Lasky, vice-president of Paramount-Publix Corporation, started his career as a cornet player in San Francisco. He left the music business temporarily for newspaper reporting and gold mining in Alaska. On his return to San Francisco he performed in vaudeville. Later he formed a partnership with B. A. Rolfe to manage as many as 20 traveling vaudeville acts. Lasky met Cecil B. deMille and wrote several operettas with him, with great financial success. In 1912 Lasky opened a motion picture studio in Hollywood, a pioneer venture that eventually became Paramount enterprises. Reprinted from *Emanu-El*, San Francisco, 3 October 1930. 3 notes.
B. S. Porter

1401. Kaganoff, Nathan M. THE BUSINESS CAREER OF HAYM SALOMON AS REFLECTED IN HIS NEWSPAPER ADVERTISEMENTS. *Am. Jewish Hist. Q. 1976 66(1): 35-49.* Haym Salomon's career and importance as a businessman, apart from his role in financing the American Revolution, can be measured by the large number of advertisements he placed in the newspapers during 1777-85. Some 1,085 ads appearing in 14 papers (seven each in Philadelphia and New York) have been located which would indicate that Solomon was one of the first businessmen to exploit this potential fully (e.g., his use of French and German, or the meticulous enumeration of merchandise). 31 notes, 24 examples of ads, appendix.
F. Rosenthal

1402. Kaganoff, N. M. and Endelman, J. E. JUDAICA AMERICANA. *Am. Jewish Hist Q. 1973 62(4): 401-413.* An annotated bibliography of monographic and periodical literature published since 1960 and received in the library of the American Jewish Historical Society.
F. Rosenthal

1403. Kahane, Libby. MORDECAI MANUEL NOAH IN HEBREW PERIODICAL LITERATURE AND IN ISRAEL. *Am. Jewish Hist. Q. 1978 67(3): 260-265.* Tabulates 11 articles and six Mordecai Manuel Noah (1785-1851) manuscripts found in Israel. This listing is a supplement to the 1937 bibliographic essay by Jacob Kabakoff.
F. Rosenthal

1404. Kallison, Frances Rosenthal. WAS IT A DUEL OR A MURDER: A STUDY IN TEXAS ASSIMILATION. *Am. Jewish Hist. Q. 1973 62(3): 314-320.* In 1857, the merchant Siegmund Feinberg died after a quarrel with Benedict Schwartz, a Jewish immigrant from Russia. Whether he was murdered by Schwartz or was shot accidentally has never been established. A Hebrew poem on his tombstone implies that he was murdered. Schwartz was killed in his pawnshop in 1882. The incident indicates the rapidity with which immigrant Jews assimilated to the surrounding society. 20 notes.
F. Rosenthal

1405. Kaplan, Michael. THE JOKER IN THE REPUBLICAN DECK: THE POLITICAL CAREER OF OTTO MEARS 1881-1889. *Western States Jewish Hist. Q. 1975 7(4): 287-302.* Otto Mears was very influential in Colorado politics in the late 19th century. By 1876 he was an important Republican Party boss. He was elected to the state legislature in 1882 and served for one term. While a legislator he discovered that lobbyists held the real power to get laws passed. He began to lobby for laws that were favorable to his railroad business. In 1884 and 1886, he backed German-born William Meyer for governor. In 1889, Governor Job Cooper appointed Mears to the committee to build a state capitol building. 2 photos, 54 notes.
R. A. Garfinkle

1406. Kaplan, Michael D. THE TOLLROAD BUILDING CAREER OF OTTO MEARS. *Colorado Mag. 1975 52(2): 153-170.* Mostly during 1881-87 Mears built a network of approximately 450 miles of tollroads in the San Juan mining area of southwest Colorado. Cheap, efficient transportation was the basis for the growth of the area. Later he turned to railroads and automobile roads, but his tollroads remain the basis of the highway system in the San Juan. Mainly primary sources; 4 illus., 3 maps, table, 51 notes.
O. H. Zabel

1407. Karsh, Audrey R. MANNASSE CHICO: ENLIGHTENED MERCHANT OF SAN DIEGO. *Western States Jewish Hist. Q. 1975 8(1): 45-54.* In 1853, Joseph Samuel Mannasse (1831-97) moved to San Diego, California, from New York. He started in the merchandising business and then purchased several rancheros along with his partner and brother-in-law Marcus Schiller. They were very successful until an 1870 drought ruined the ranches and a fire in 1872 destroyed their store. The partnership soon broke up. Mannasse served on the San Diego city council and was very active in civic affairs until his death. 2 photos, 45 notes.
R. A. Garfinkle

1408. Katz, Irving I. RABBI KAUFMANN KOHLER BEGAN HIS DETROIT MINISTRY IN 1869. *Michigan Jewish Hist. 1979 19(1): 11-15.* Kaufmann Kohler (1843-1926) was a rabbi in Detroit; discusses his extensive influence in Reform Judaism in America, 1869-1926.

1409. Katz-Hyman, Martha B. A NOTE ON RABBI MOSES ZISKIND FINESILVER, 1847-1922. *Rhode Island Jewish Hist. Notes 1977 7(3): 430-431.* Note offers documentation of the fact that Moses Ziskind Finesilver was the Congregation Sons of Zion's (Providence, Rhode Island) first hazzan (cantor) and shohet (ritual slaughtering), not Eliasar Lipshitz as previously stated; covers 1880-83.

1410. Keenan, Jerry. MAX LITTMANN: IMMIGRANT SOLDIER IN THE WAGON BOX FIGHT. *Western States Jewish Hist. Q. 1974 6(2): 111-119.* Max Littmann was a German immigrant to the United States in the mid-1860's. He joined the US Army in 1866 and became a hero in the Wagon Box Fight in 1867. He saved the lives of several of his fellow soldiers and killed several Indians. He was discharged in 1869 and became a highly successful businessman in St. Louis. He died in 1921. Secondary sources; illus., photo, 4 notes.
R. A. Garfinkle

1411. Kerman, Julius C. ADVENTURES IN AMERICA AND THE HOLY LAND. *Am. Jewish Arch. 1976 28(2): 126-141.* "In my forty-three years in the rabbinate I served several communities, enjoying everywhere happy relationships with young and old. The thought that I have influenced some persons to think and live more Jewishly makes me happy." Byelorussian-born Rabbi Kerman also saw service in the Jewish Legion during World War I.
J

1412. Kramer, Will. BEANS TO BULLION. *Westways 1976 68(10): 18-21, 77.* Discusses the business career of Achille Levy (1853-1922), a native of France who immigrated to the United States in 1871 and moved in 1874 from San Francisco to Ventura County where he began raising beans, and eventually founded the Bank of A. Levy, 1905.
G. A. Hewlett

1413. Kramer, William M. DANIEL CAVE: SOUTHERN CALIFORNIA PIONEER DENTIST, CIVIC LEADER AND MASONIC DIGNITARY. *Western States Jewish Hist. Q. 1977 9(2): 99-121.* Daniel Cave (1841-1936) had practiced dentistry in Vienna, Austria, before coming to America in 1873 to improve his skills. He established a practice in San Diego, California, later moving to Los Angeles. As founder of the Dental Society of San Diego he emphasized that dentistry was a scientific medical profession. He was named a special clinician at the University of Southern California Dental School in 1897, attended every conference in his profession, and had a special interest in new equipment and techniques. Active participation in San Diego civic and political organizations was an important responsibility to Cave, who was a library trustee, president of the San Diego Water Company, an officer of the Society for the Prevention of Cruelty to Animals, and Republican candidate for alderman in 1889. Cave was also a leader of Masonic lodges in San Diego and Los Angeles. Based on interviews, personal correspondence and published material; 3 photos, 68 notes.
B. S. Porter

1414. Kramer, William M. and Clar, Reva. EMANUEL SCHREIBER: LOS ANGELES' FIRST REFORM RABBI, 1885-1889. *Western States Jewish Hist. Q. 1977 9(4): 354-370; 1977 10(1): 38-55.* Part I. Emanuel Schreiber left his native Germany in 1881. After serving synagogues in Mobile (Alabama) and Denver (Colorado) he was invited to Los Angeles' Congregation B'nai B'rith in 1885. Some of the traditionalists were offended by Schreiber's radical-Reform policies but the majority of the congregation supported him. He was active in community affairs; most significant was his role in the formation of the Associated Charities which developed into the present United Crusade. San Francisco journalist Isidore N. Choynski criticized Rabbi Schreiber's accumulation of wealth from astute land speculation. Based on newspapers and other published primary and secondary sources; 68 notes. Part II. Religious and social activities at Congregation B'nai B'rith were enhanced by the participation of the rabbi's wife. Reform-Orthodox tensions decreased as Rabbi Schreiber impressed the Jewish community with his considerable knowledge of religious phenomena. Schreiber's relations with the gentile community were excellent; Christian ministers appreciated his learning and invited him to speak to their congregations. Despite his esteemed position in Los Angeles, Schreiber's ambitions caused him to leave. He served at synagogues in Arkansas, Washington, Ohio, and Illinois, 1889-99. He was minister to Chicago's Congregation Emanu-El from 1899 to 1906 when he moved to the east coast. In 1920 he returned to Los Angeles, where he remained until his death in 1932. Based on newspapers and other published primary and secondary sources; illus., 65 notes.
B. S. Porter

1415. Kramer, William M. and Stern, Norton B. A. LEVY OF THE BANK: FROM BEANS TO BANKS IN VENTURA COUNTY. *Western States Jewish Hist. Q. 1975 7(2): 118-137.* Achille Levy (1853-1922) came to California in 1871 from France. In 1874, he settled in Hueneme, where he opened a general merchandise store. In 1881, he returned to France to visit his family and met Lucy Levy, a distant cousin. They were married in 1882, and returned to Hueneme. Levy went into business buying and selling farm products and supplies. By extending credit to the farmers he slowly became a banker, expanding his business ventures into many areas until he became a multimillionaire. Provides brief biographies of his children and his business partners. Primary and secondary sources; 3 photos, 76 notes.
R. A. Garfinkle

1416. Kramer, William M. LOS ANGELES JEWRY'S FIRST PRESIDENT. *Western States Jewish Hist. Q. 1975 7(2): 151-152.* Samuel K. Labatt served as the first president of the first Jewish organization in Los Angeles, the Hebrew Benevolent Society, which was formed in July 1854. Labatt had worked for Jewish organizations in his hometown of New Orleans before he came to California in 1853. His brother Henry J. Labatt was elected secretary of the First Hebrew Benevolent Society in San Francisco on 29 May 1853. 6 notes.
R. A. Garfinkle

1417. Kramer, William M. and Stern, Norton B. NATHAN NEWMARK: FIRST VALEDICTORIAN OF THE UNIVERSITY OF CALIFORNIA. *Western States Jewish Hist. Q. 1977 9(4): 341-349.* Nathan Newmark (3 June 1853-15 June 1928) was a poor but brilliant San Francisco schoolboy whose accomplishments brought him to the attention of Joseph P. Newmark (no relation). The elder Newmark helped Nathan attend the new University of California, and later, law school. After graduation Nathan opened a law office in San Francisco but was principally occupied as a journalist for the leading western Jewish weekly, *The Hebrew.* He was an active member and officer of the Young Men's Hebrew Association. Some friends and contemporaries viewed Newmark's career as a failure because he lacked the "combative spirit" required for financial success. Others claimed that his success was in legal scholarship and journalism although these pursuits were not financially rewarding. Based on recollections of contemporaries, private correspondence, published primary and secondary sources; photo, 32 notes.
B. S. Porter

1418. Kramer, William M. and Clar, Reva. RABBI SIGMUND HECHT: A MAN WHO BRIDGED THE CENTURIES. *Western States Jewish Hist. Q. 1975 7(4): 356-375, 8(1): 72-90.* Part I. Sigmund Hecht (b. 1849) emigrated to New York from Hungary with his parents. He completed his rabbinical studies at Temple Emanu-El's Theological School, New York. He soon became the leader of the temple's Sabbath school. In 1877, he became the Rabbi for Congregation Kahl Montgomery (Montgomery, Alabama). In 1885, he helped to establish and then served as the first treasurer of the Conference of Southern Rabbis. In 1888, he was appointed the Rabbi for Congregation Emanu-El, Milwaukee. He was active in many civic and religious groups. Based on primary and secondary sources; 2 photos, 68 notes. Part II. Rabbi Hecht left Milwaukee for Los Angeles in 1899 to become the rabbi at Temple B'nai B'rith. He found the congregation there very disunited. To reunite the congregation he started several new Jewish charitable organizations. In 1911, these separate groups united to form the Los Angeles Federation of Jewish Charities. He fought against movie censorship and anti-Semitism. Includes excerpts from several sermons. Photo, 65 notes. Article to be continued.
R. A. Garfinkle

1419. Kramer, William M. and Clar, Reva. RABBI SIGMUND HECHT: A MAN WHO BRIDGED THE CENTURIES (PART III). *Western States Jewish Hist. Q. 1976 8(2): 169-186.* Continued from a previous article. Rabbi Sigmund Hecht remained neutral toward Zionism. He was appointed to the board of directors of the Los Angeles public library by Mayor Meredith P. Snyder. He backed Mayor Snyder for reelection, but Snyder lost to Owen McAleer. Mayor McAleer appointed George N. Black, a Jewish friend of Hecht, to replace Hecht. Black refused the appointment so McAleer chose another Jew; patronage was strong in Los Angeles then. In 1914, Congregation B'nai B'rith hired Dr. Edgar Fogel Magnin to serve as an associate Rabbi for Rabbi Hecht. Rabbi Hecht died in 1925 after a long and distinguished career. He left many volumes of writings and had been active in many civic and Jewish community groups. 51 notes.
R. A. Garfinkle

1420. Kramer, William M. and Stern, Norton B. SAN FRANCISCO'S FIGHTING JEW. *California Hist. Q. 1974 53(4): 333-346.* Joe Choynski (1868-1943) was American Jewry's first international sports figure. A professional boxer from San Francisco, Choynski contradicted the stereotype which excluded Jews from competitive sports. He fought 77 bouts, winning 50 of them during his 20-year career. Six of his opponents were or later became world champions, including Jim Corbett, Jim Jeffries, John L. Sullivan, and Jack Johnson. Known as a "scientific" boxer, Choynski fought at a time when matches could be declared illegal and the participants arrested. Bouts lasted for dozens of rounds and fighters used bare fists or two-ounce gloves. The sports press of the period praised Choynski's abilities, and his opponents held him in high esteem. Based on interviews, newspapers, and published works; photos, 73 notes.
A. Hoffman

1421. Kramer, William M. THE STINGIEST MAN IN SAN FRANCISCO. *Western States Jewish Hist. Q. 1973 5(4): 257-269.* Humorous tales of the miserly attitudes and actions of one of the wealthiest Jews in San Francisco, Michael Reese, 1850-78.

1422. Krause, Allen. THE ENIGMATIC JUDAH BENJAMIN. *Midstream 1978 24(8): 17-20.* Although Judah Benjamin was an important civilian during the Confederacy and was tried with Jefferson Davis and Robert E. Lee in 1868, he has received little historical attention because of his Jewish background.

1423. Kreader, J. Lee. ISAAC MAX RUBINOW: PIONEERING SPECIALIST IN SOCIAL INSURANCE. *Social Service Rev. 1976 50(3): 402-425.* Provides a biography of Isaac Max Rubinow (1875-1936), a ground-breaking theorist and tireless fighter for American social insurance during the Progressive era.

1424. Landau, Francine. SOLOMON LAZARD OF LOS ANGELES. *Western States Jewish Hist. Q. 1973 5(3): 141-157.* Solomon Lazard (1826-1916) was an innovator in his work with charities, other Jews, and civic associations.

1425. Lawson, Michael L. FLORA LANGERMANN SPIEGELBERG: GRAND LADY OF SANTA FE. *Western States Jewish Hist. Q. 1976 8(4): 291-308.* In 1875 Flora Langermann Spiegelberg (1857-1943) and her husband Willi (1844-1929) moved to Santa Fe. Willi and his five brothers operated a wholesale business that, along with new family enterprises, dominated the economy of the Southwest for several years. In 1893, the now wealthy Spiegelberg family moved to New York City. "Garbage Can Flora" became involved in the movement to clean up the city and she campaigned for investigations of war profits in the munitions industry during World War I. In 1914, she helped organize the Metropolitan Protective Association to work for improved wages for the city street cleaners. After Willi died she donated many family items to the Museum of New Mexico. Based primarily on Flora's manuscripts; 3 photos, 33 notes.   R. A. Garfinkle

1426. Lease, Richard J. EUGENE J. STERN: MERCHANT, FARMER AND PHILANTHROPIST OF LAS CRUCES, NEW MEXICO. *Western States Jewish Hist. Q. 1977 9(2): 161-166.* Eugene J. Stern emigrated from Hungary in 1903. For several years he worked in the western states of Texas and Colorado before homesteading in New Mexico in 1914. In 1917 he moved to Las Cruces and opened a general store while continuing farming in the area of the Rio Grande Valley. Stern's philanthropies included contributing to the student loan fund at New Mexico State University and the building fund of every church in Las Cruces. He also helped establish a Salvation Army unit and a chapter of the Boys' Club of America. On the 50th anniversary of his affiliation with Masonry he gave a half million dollars for the construction of a new Scottish Rite Temple in Las Cruces. Based on interviews with the subject and his family; 2 photos, note.   B. S. Porter

1427. Levy, J. Leonard. A RABBI SAYS "NO." *Western States Jewish Hist. Q. 1973 5(4): 270-272.* J. Leonard Levy (1865-1917), the rabbi in Sacramento 1889-93, rejected an 1892 offer from San Franciscans to head their congregation.

1428. Lewis, Theodore. THE PLIGHT OF ISAAC TOURO. *Rhode Island Jewish Hist. Notes 1977 7(3): 442-443.* Reprints a 1782 document in which Rabbi Isaac Touro of Rhode Island petitions the British Commander-in-Chief for funds to take his family to Jamaica due to persecution by the British during their invasion of Rhode Island.

1429. Likhten, Iosyf L. ARNOL'D MARGOLIN: IOHO ZHYTTIA I PRATSIA [Arnold Margolin: his life and work]. *Sučasnist [West Germany] 1977 (5): 68-73.* Traces the life of Ukrainian American Jew Arnold Margolin, his participation in the Ukrainian struggle for independence, 1917-20, and his work on Ukrainian-Jewish relations.

1430. Lynch, Joseph D. THE BANKER OF THE SOUTHLAND IN 1885. *Western States Jewish Hist. Q. 1977 9(3): 226-228.* The Farmers' and Merchants' Bank of Los Angeles was founded in 1868 with $200,000 in paid up capital. Under Mr. Isaias W. Hellman, the president and major stockholder, it grew to be the sixth largest in the state in volume of business. By avoiding speculation and investing only where growth and natural development were certain, the bank gained the confidence and esteem of the business community. Reprint of article in the *Los Angeles Herald* "Annual" issue of January 1885; photo.   B. S. Porter

1431. Mark, Yudel. MENDEL ELKIN (ZU ZEIN ZENTEN YAHRZEIT) [Mendel Elkin (on the occasion of his 10th anniversary)]. *Yivo Bleter 1973 44: 292-295.* Presents, on the anniversary of his death, highlights of the life of one of the founders of the Yivo Library—his manifold activities, assistance and advice to writers, immigrants, and poor, and his love for the theater. Based on personal recollection.
                                                                                 B. Klein

1432. McQuaid, Kim. AN AMERICAN OWENITE: EDWARD A. FILENE AND THE PARAMETERS OF INDUSTRIAL REFORM, 1890-1937. *Am. J. of Econ. and Sociol. 1976 35(1): 77-94.* Edward A. Filene introduced industrial democracy in his Boston department store in 1891. He was deposed from the presidency of the store in 1928. His experiment ceased and thereafter he was denied any effective authority. He also directed his liberal energies to local, state, and national affairs such as his ambitious plan of urban reform, "Boston 1915." Such efforts were equally unsuccessful. He was a spokesman for the New Capitalism and a supporter of the New Deal, but in both movements his integrity isolated him from his peers. His enduring contributions were the cooperative and credit union movements.   P. Travis

1433. Merowitz, Morton J. MAX LILIENTHAL (1814-1882)—JEWISH EDUCATOR IN NINETEENTH CENTURY AMERICA. *Yivo Ann. of Jewish Social Sci. 1974 (15): 46-65.* Discusses Rabbi Max Lilienthal's educational endeavors, including his establishment of a boarding school, his directorship of the Noyoth Institute, and his work with the Mound St. Temple Sabbath School. Also stressed was Dr. Lilienthal's founding of the first Jewish children's magazine in America, *The Hebrew Sabbath School Visitor*, and his starting of the confirmation of boys and girls in America. 107 notes.   R. J. Wechman

1434. Meyer, Eugene and Stern, Norton B. MY EARLY YEARS. *Western States Jewish Hist. Q. 1973 5(2): 87-99.* Meyer (1842-1925), a leading Jew of Los Angeles, provides a personal account of his boyhood in France, and his stay in San Francisco in 1859-60.

1435. Michelman, Irving S. A BANKER IN THE NEW DEAL: JAMES P. WARBURG. *Rev. Int. d'Hist. de la Banque [Italy] 1974 8: 35-59.* James P. Warburg, scion of one of the great German Jewish banking houses in the United States, was one of the few Wall Streeters to become part of the FDR administration. Drawn into the frantic preparations to reopen the banks in March 1933, Warburg became a delegate to the World Economic Conference in London, only to resign shortly after his appointment. Roosevelt made it clear that domestic monetary policy could not be compromised by international agreements. Roosevelt's decision to take the United States off the gold standard and to accept legislation which gave him far-reaching power to increase the money supply led Warburg to break with the administration. A successful polemicist and writer, Warburg became associated with the anti-New Deal faction and the Liberty League. Secondary sources; 24 notes.
                                                                              D. McGinnis

1436. Miller, Sally M. FROM SWEATSHOP WORKER TO LABOR LEADER: THERESA MALKIEL, A CASE STUDY. *Am. Jewish Hist. 1978 68(2): 189-205.* Theresa Serber Malkiel (1874-1949) is an example of a female Jewish leader in the labor movement and in a minor political party (Socialist Labor Party, and later the Socialist Party of America). On the Women's National Committee of the Socialist Party in the decade before 1914 she gave her greatest attention to women and the party, unionization of women workers, foreign-born women, woman suffrage, and the party commitment to sexual equality. Her most lasting accomplishment was the establishment of the Brooklyn Adult Students Association. 20 notes.   F. Rosenthal

1437. Morgan, David T. THE SHEFTALLS OF SAVANNAH. *Am. Jewish Hist. Q. 1973 62(4): 348-361.* Benjamin Sheftall arrived in Savannah, Georgia, in 1733. The Sheftall Papers indicate that the family acquired real estate throughout the state before the Revolution. Mordecei and Levi Sheftall suffered imprisonment, banishment, and loss of livelihood for espousing the American cause when the British captured Savannah in 1778. Although the government did not reimburse the Sheftalls for losses suffered, they prospered again after 1790 and remained active in the affairs of Savannah's Jewish community. The Sheftall Papers, Keith Reid Collection, University of Georgia; 39 notes.   F. Rosenthal

1438. Myers, Carmel. FILM INDUSTRY RECOLLECTIONS. *Western States Jewish Hist. Q. 1976 8(2): 126-135.* An early movie star tells how she got started in films. Her father was Rabbi Isidore Myers (1856-1922). Rabbi Myers was asked by film director David Wark Griffith to be a consultant for his film *Intolerance.* As payment for his services, Rabbi Myers' daughter was allowed to try out for a movie part in Griffith's next film. She got a part and that started her career in which she played leading roles opposite such male stars as Rudolph Valentino, Douglas Fairbanks, Jr., John Gilbert, Lew Cody, and William Haines. She was also very active in Jewish community affairs in Los Angeles. Based on personal recollection; 4 photos, 12 notes.
R. A. Garfinkle

1439. Narell, Irena Penzil. BERNHARD MARKS: RETAILER, MINER, EDUCATOR, AND LAND DEVELOPER. *Western States Jewish Hist. Q. 1975 8(1): 26-38.* In 1852, Bernhard Marks (1832-1913) arrived in California from Providence, Rhode Island. He worked at various jobs and the got into gold mining. He became a partner in several mines, but met with little success. In 1859, he married Cornelia D. Barlow, a schoolteacher. In 1860, they opened a private school in Columbia. During 1862-72, he was principal of Lincoln Grammar School, San Francisco. In 1874, he established a raisin-growing colony in Fresno County. He failed at ranching, farming, and real estate development. 37 notes.
R. A. Garfinkle

1440. Newmark, Abraham. A ST. LOUIS VISITOR VIEWS SOUTHERN CALIFORNIA IN 1883. *Western States Jewish Hist. Q. 1978 10(3): 212-215.* Abraham Newmark visited Los Angeles on the occasion of the marriage of a close relative. Newmark wrote several letters to his wife and daughters about the beauty of the city, the mildness of the climate, and the lushness and variety of the agricultural products. Reprints two letters written in 1883; photo, 17 notes. B. S. Porter

1441. Newmark, Helen. A NINETEENTH CENTURY MEMOIR. *Western States Jewish Hist. Q. 1974 6(3): 204-218.* Autobiography of Helen Newmark (1840-1911), written in 1900. Immigrating in 1855 from Posen, Poland, Newmark gives a good account of life in San Francisco in the latter half of the 19th century. 3 photos, 15 notes.
R. A. Garfinkle

1442. Newmark, Rosa. A LETTER FROM MOTHER TO DAUGHTER—LOS ANGELES TO NEW YORK, 1867. *Western States Jewish Hist. Q. 1973 5(4): 274-284.* Mrs. Joseph Newmark, née Rosa Levy, describes the Jewish marriage celebration, and attendant social customs, of her daughter, Harriet, to Eugene Meyer in Los Angeles.

1443. Pitterman, Marvin and Schiavo, Bartholomew. HAKHAM RAPHAEL HAIM ISAAC CARIGAL: SHALIAH OF HEBRON AND RABBI OF NEWPORT, 5533 (1773). *Rhode Island Jewish Hist. Notes 1974 6(4): 587-603.* Biographical sketch of Hakham Raphael Haim Isaac Carigal's career as rabbi of Newport, Rhode Island (1773), and his contribution to the community's culture and history. S

1444. Quinn, Carin C. THE JEANING OF AMERICA—AND THE WORLD. *Am. Heritage 1978 29(3): 14-21.* A German immigrant, Levi Strauss (1829-1902), came to New York in 1848 and went to San Francisco in 1850, intent on selling canvas for tents. Finding a need for a sturdy material for men's pants, Strauss made a pair from some of his canvas. From then on, he was in business. Spreading to the eastern United States during the 1930's, today the market for jeans is worldwide. 16 illus.
J. F. Paul

1445. Rafael, Ruth. ERNEST BLOCH AT THE SAN FRANCISCO CONSERVATORY OF MUSIC. *Western States Jewish Hist. Q. 1977 9(3): 195-215.* Ada Clement and Lillian Hodghead, founders of the San Francisco Conservatory of Music, persuaded Ernest Bloch (1880-1959) to leave the Cleveland Institute of Music to become the director of their organization in 1925. Bloch contributed his prestige and administrative talents to acquire instruments and other equipment to aid in the school's expansion. He hired artists, established an orchestra and choir, and created a theory department after a survey of San Francisco's musical needs. On 6 June 1928, Bloch won first prize in a symphony contest for the score, "America, I Build for You." Bloch resigned as director of the Conservatory on 11 February 1930 due to financial considerations and his

desire to have more time for composing. Primary and secondary sources; 2 photos, 74 notes.
B. S. Porter

1446. Resnik, Bezalel Nathan. MEMOIR OF MY LIFE. *Rhode Island Jewish Hist. Notes 1978 7(4): 471-500.* The author (b. 1891) left his native Lithuania in 1933 for the United States, and became a businessman in Providence, Rhode Island.

1447. Reznick, Samuel. THE MARITIME ADVENTURES OF A JEWISH SEA CAPTAIN, JONAS P. LEVY, IN NINETEENTH-CENTURY AMERICA. *Am. Neptune 1977 37(4): 239-252.* Jonas Phillips Levy (1807-83) went to sea in 1823 as a cabin boy and eventually owned and commanded several sailing ships. Focuses on Levy's services as a sea captain in the Peruvian Revolution and the Mexican War. Based on Levy's unpublished memoirs; illus., 31 notes. G. H. Curtis

1448. Reznick, Samuel. A NOTE ON THE GENEALOGY OF AN EIGHTEENTH-CENTURY FAMILY OF JEWISH ORIGIN: THE NUNEZ FAMILY OF LEWES, DELAWARE. *Am. Jewish Arch. 1978 30(1): 20-23.* In colonial America, Jews occasionally left the security of the Jewish community to migrate into the hinterland. Often, deprived of essential contacts, they ceased to be Jewish. Reconstruction of three generations of one such family. J

1449. Reznick, Samuel. THE STRANGE ROLE OF A JEWISH SEA CAPTAIN IN THE CONFEDERATE SOUTH. *Am. Jewish Hist. 1978 68(1): 64-73.* Jonas Phillips Levy (1807-83), the younger brother of Commodore Uriah Levy, rose to the rank of captain in the American merchant marine. He was a participant in a Peruvian revolution in the 1830's and was made the harbor master of Vera Cruz during the Mexican War (1846-48). During the Civil War he conducted business activities for the Confederate government and frequently offered his advice and his services from Wilmington, North Carolina. His children became respected members of the Jewish and general community of New York. 22 notes.
F. Rosenthal

1450. Rogoff, Abraham S. HARRY T. MADISON, PAST NATIONAL COMMANDER OF THE JEWISH WAR VETERANS OF U.S.A. *Michigan Jewish Hist. 1974 14(2): 6-8.* Madison joined the Detroit, Michigan, chapter of this organization in 1938, and in 1953 was elected National Commander. S

1451. Roseman, Kenneth D. JONAS LEVI, A JEW. *Am. Jewish Arch. 1975 27(1): 67-69.* Presents a 1780 deposition of Jonas Levy, an American Jew, on the difficulties encountered in France.

1452. Rosen, Benton H. SAMUEL STARR, M.D., 1884-1950. *Rhode Island Jewish Hist. Notes 1976 7(2): 294-296.* Provides a short history of Samuel Starr, including his schooling and medical practice in Providence, Rhode Island, 1910-50.

1453. Rosenwaike, Ira. LEON DYER: BALTIMORE AND SAN FRANCISCO JEWISH LEADER. *Western States Jewish Hist. Q. 1977 9(2): 135-143.* Earlier accounts of the life of Leon Dyer (1807-83) have too often relied on legend instead of valid documentary sources. In fact, Dyer was a Baltimore butcher and real estate dealer who developed a business interest in California when his younger brother, Abraham, joined a group of immigrants to that state. Leon Dyer went to San Francisco in 1850 for business reasons and in the few months he spent there, he was chosen the religious leader of a temporary congregation of Jewish settlers. After his return to Baltimore he made several trips to Europe before settling in Louisville, Kentucky, in 1875. Based on documents in the National Archives, Baltimore Land Records, other primary, and secondary sources; 31 notes.
B. S. Porter

1454. Rosenwaike, Ira. LEVY L. LAURENS: AN EARLY TEXAN JOURNALIST. *Am. Jewish Arch. 1975 27(1): 61-66.* Discusses the death by duelling of Levy L. Laurens in 1837. S

1455. Rosenwaike, Ira. THE PARENTAGE AND EARLY YEARS OF M. H. DE YOUNG, LEGEND AND FACT. *Western States Jewish Hist. Q. 1975 7(3): 210-217.* A San Francisco publisher and civil leader in the late 1800's, Michael H. De Young dictated some autobiographical material which became the basis for a description of himself and his family in the *Encyclopedia of American Biography*. The author has disproved much of the information about his background that De Young passed on as fact. Primary and secondary sources; 25 notes.

R. A. Garfinkle

1456. Rozenstain, Yael. MEMOIRS OF AN ALASKAN MERCHANT. *Western States Jewish Hist. Q. 1977 9(3): 253-261.* The author left Russia as a boy of 12 in 1900. He worked as a cabin boy on an English ship, and as a peddler in Australia until 1906 when he came to the United States. Joining the gold rush to Alaska, he became an apprentice in a general store in Fairbanks, later opening his own business and following the placer miners from one mining camp to another. After World War I, he bought a lot and built a store in the mining town of Hyder in southern Alaska. The decline of the mining industry forced him to move to the big fishing camp at Dillingham in 1938. The fishing business proved too risky for Rozenstain. He sold his outfit in 1944 and retired to southern California. 5 photos, 7 notes.

B. S. Porter

1457. Rubenstein, Richard L. STUDYING AT HEBREW UNION COLLEGE: 1942-45. *Midstream 1974 20(6): 68-73.* From the author's *Power Struggle* (New York: Scribner's, 1974).

S

1458. Rubin, Lois. DISAPPOINTED EXPECTATIONS: AN IMMIGRANT ARRIVES IN WESTERN PENNSYLVANIA. *Western Pennsylvania Hist. Mag. 1976 59(4): 445-462.* Reprints excerpts from the unpublished memoir of a Jewish immigrant to western Pennsylvania, 1913-45, Harry Jackson.

1459. Rubinoff, Michael W. C. E. H. KAUVAR: A SKETCH OF A COLORADO RABBI'S LIFE. *Western States Jewish Hist. Q. 1978 10(4): 291-305.* Charles Eliezer Hillel Kauvar (1879-1971) was elected rabbi of Denver's Beth Ha Medrosh Hagodol Synagogue in 1902. Kauvar's devotion to Zionism caused friction between him and Rabbi William S. Friedman of Denver's Temple Emmanuel. The schism between the two rabbis affected the community at large when, in 1903, Rabbi Kauvar helped found the Jewish Consumptives' Relief Society (later the American Medical Center), open to Jews and non-Jews alike. In 1899 Temple Emmanuel had helped start the Jewish Hospital for Consumptives, an institution with a restricted admission policy. In 1920 Rabbi Kauvar was invited to the chair of rabbinic literature at the Methodist-sponsored University of Denver; he held this post for 45 years. Rabbi Kauvar became rabbi emeritus of his synagogue in 1952. In his later years he received many civic and religious awards and honors. Based on archival and published sources; 2 photos, 39 notes.

B. S. Porter

1460. Rubinoff, Michael W. RABBI IN A PROGRESSIVE ERA: C.E.H. KAUVAR OF DENVER. *Colorado Mag. 1977 54(3): 220-239.* Russian-born (1879) and New York-educated, Rabbi Charles Eliezer Hillel Kauvar served Denver's orthodox Beth Ha Medrosh Hagodol synagogue during 1902-71. A leading progressive reformer, Kauvar founded the Jewish Consumptives' Relief Society and an orphanage, worked closely with Judge Banjamin Barr Lindsey in attacking juvenile delinquency, and was a long-time leader of Denver's Community Chest. He was a Zionist, urged ecumenism, and vigorously opposed the Ku Klux Klan in the 1920's. Primary and secondary sources; 10 illus., 51 notes.

O. H. Zabel

1461. Rudd, Hynda. AUERBACH'S: ONE OF THE WEST'S OLDEST DEPARTMENT STORES. *Western States Jewish Hist. Q. 1979 11(3): 234-238.* Auerbach's Department Store was founded in Salt Lake City, Utah, in 1864. The Auerbach brothers had earlier stores in the mining camps of California. In the 1860's the Auerbachs operated tent stores along the route of the transcontinental railroad while it was under construction. The main store in Salt Lake City remained in the family from 1864 to 1977, although it had many changes of location. Published and archival sources; 7 photos, 3 notes.

B. S. Porter

1462. Rudd, Hynda. SAMUEL NEWHOUSE: UTAH MINING MAGNATE AND LAND DEVELOPER. *Western States Jewish Hist. Q. 1979 11(4): 291-307.* Samuel Newhouse (18554-1930) had a freighting business to mining camps in Colorado, 1879-86, when he made several successful mining investments. He moved to Utah in 1896 as a millionaire investor and developer of mining properties. Newhouse, and his partner Thomas Weir, developed rich copper mines in Bingham Canyon, near

Salt Lake City. British investors backed Newhouse and Weir in the 1898 establishment of the Boston Consolidated Copper and Gold Mining Company, Ltd. Fluctuations in the copper market prompted the merger of Boston Consolidated with the Utah Copper Company in 1910. At the same time, Newhouse financed the construction of many large commercial buildings, including a luxury hotel, in Salt Lake City. These investments overextended Newhouse financially, leading to bankruptcy in 1915. Newhouse moved to France to live with his sister in 1920. He died in 1930. Interviews and published sources; 5 photos, 58 notes.

B. S. Porter

1463. Rudd, Hynda. THE UNSINKABLE ANNA MARKS. *Western States Jewish Hist. Q. 1978 10(3): 234-237.* Anna Marks (1847-1912) and her husband Wolff Marks (1842-1918) operated a store in Eureka City, Utah during the 1880's and 90's. They made a fortune in real estate and mining investments. Anna earned a reputation as a feisty character, especially concerning disputed property boundaries. She was handy with a gun and had a full vocabulary of cuss words. Secondary sources; 3 photos, 5 notes.

B. S. Porter

1464. Ryan, Frances B. SIG STEINER: FATHER OF ESCONDIDO'S GRAPE DAY. *Western States Jewish Hist. Q. 1976 8(4): 361-369.* In 1886 Sigmund Steiner arrived in Escondido, California and in 1886 opened the town's first store with P. A. Graham. The store served the rural community until 1912 when Steiner retired to Los Angeles. He was very active in Escondido's community affairs and served as mayor for twelve years (1894-1906). In 1908, he organized the first Grape Day which became an annual event there. 3 photos, 42 notes.

R. A. Garfinkle

1465. Salomon, H. P. JOSEPH JESURUN PINTO (1729-1782): A DUTCH HAZAN IN COLONIAL NEW YORK. *Studia Rosenthaliana [Netherlands] 1979 13(1): 18-29.* Recounts the scholarly, professional, and personal activities of a Sephardic cantor who traveled from Amsterdam to London and New York, where he lived, 1759-66, while serving at the Congregation Shearith Israel, whence he returned to London and to Amsterdam, where he died in 1782.

1466. Sarna, Jonathan D. A GERMAN-JEWISH IMMIGRANT'S PERCEPTION OF AMERICA, 1853-54: SOME FURTHER NOTES ON MORDECAI M. NOAH, A JEWEL ROBBERY, AND ISAAC M. WISE. *Am. Jewish Hist. 1978 68(2): 206-212.* Prompted by Gershon Greenberg's translation of *Deutsch-Amerikanische Skizzen . . . .* Greenburg and the 1854 author of *D.A.S.* erred regarding Mordecai Manuel Noah's Ararat colony, Noah's role in the Polari jewel theft case, and the lack of comment on *D.A.S.* (as disproved by Isaac Mayer Wise's denunciation of it). Reprints Noah's "The Crown Jewels" in his *Sunday Times and Noah's Weekly Messenger* of 27 January 1850. 18 notes.

1467. Schwartz, Henry. THE LEVI SAGA: TEMECULA, JULIAN, SAN DIEGO. *Western States Jewish Hist. Q. 1974 6(3): 161-176.* A biography of Simon Levi (1850-1918) and his brother Adolph Levi (1858-1943), who came to San Diego from Bohemia, set up stores in several locations, and became successful businessmen. Examines their many years of public service. Primary and secondary sources; 5 photos, 53 notes.

R. A. Garfinkle

1468. Segal, Beryl. THE EDUCATION OF AN IMMIGRANT. *Rhode Island Jewish Hist. Notes 1976 7(2): 277-293.* Reminiscences of Russia before World War I and of the immigration of a Jewish family to Canada and the United States, 1900-70's.

1469. Segal, Beryl and Goldowsky, Seebert J. JAMES JACOBS, EARLY JEWISH MERCHANT OF PROVIDENCE, RHODE ISLAND. *Rhode Island Jewish Hist. Notes 1978 7(4): 461-470.* James Jacobs, possibly the first Jew to settle in Providence, was successful and prominent there, 1820's-30's and 1850's.

1470. Seretan, L. Glen. DANIEL DE LEON, "WANDERING JEW" OF AMERICAN SOCIALISM: AN INTERPRETIVE ANALYSIS. *Am. Jewish Hist. Q. 1976 65(3): 245-256.* A psychohistorical analysis of the life of Daniel DeLeon (1850-1914), socialist leader and theoretician, and American labor radical and organizer, is provided in this essay, using Eugene Sue's literary concept of the Wandering Jew as a frame of reference. 19 notes.

F. Rosenthal

1471. Shain, Samson Aaron. ODE TO THE UNITED STATES ON ITS BICENTENNIAL AND TO THE REDEDICATION OF ITS PEOPLE TO THE PRINCIPLES OF THE DECLARATION OF INDEPENDENCE. *J. of the Lancaster County Hist. Soc. 1976 80(2): 109-112.* The late author (1906-76), a contributor to this journal, was Rabbi to Congregation Shaarai Shomayim in Lancaster 1956-76; presents Hebrew and English versions of his Bicentennial poem.

1472. Shechner, Mark. ISAAC ROSENFELD'S WORLD. *Partisan Rev. 1976 43(4): 524-543.* Isaac Rosenfeld was a literary journalist who wrote book reviews, critical essays and occasional fiction. He wrote during and after World War II for such publications as *New Republic, Nation, Commentary* and *Partisan Review.* As a Jewish intellectual, Rosenfeld's theme was alienation. He often used the ideas of Whilhelm Reich in his cultural analysis. While a minor figure in his own life-time, Rosenfeld's work demonstrated the continuing and significant contribution of Jewish intellectuals to America's moral and cultural life. Undocumented.
                                                          D. K. Pickens

1473. Shook, Robert W. ABRAHAM LEVI: FATHER OF VICTORIA JEWRY. *Western States Jewish Hist. Q. 1977 9(2): 144-154.* Victoria, Texas, was a trade and cattle center serving Texas and northern Mexico since before the Civil War. Abraham Levi (1822-1902) was among the earliest Jewish settlers in Victoria, arriving in 1848 or 1849. By the 1870's the Jewish community included 15 families and had organized a reform congregation. Levi operated a retail store, and engaged in land transactions and private banking. The Levi Bank and Trust Company (now the Victoria Bank and Trust) was franchised in 1910. Levi's activities in the community included serving as president of the Jewish congregation and as a city alderman. Primary and secondary sources; 3 photos, 26 notes.
                                                          B. S. Porter

1474. Sichel, Carolyn Meyberg. LOS ANGELES MEMORIES. *Western States Jewish Hist. Q. 1974 7(1): 49-58.* The author relates her experiences growing up in Los Angeles at the turn of the century. Relatives and close family friends included civic, business, and religious leaders in Los Angeles. As a second generation Jewish family, their goal was Americanization. Yiddish was not spoken in her home, but the family was very religious. 2 photos, 6 notes.
                                                          R. A. Garfinkle

1475. Simons, Leonard N. MY YEARS OF COMMUNAL ACTIVITIES IN THE DETROIT JEWISH COMMUNITY: SOME PERSONAL MEMOIRS. *Michigan Jewish Hist. 1975 15(2): 9-33.* Short autobiographical sketch of the author (1901-75) and his community involvement, including work with the Detroit Jewish Welfare Federation, the Jewish Home for the Aged, and the Sinai Hospital in Detroit, Michigan.
                                                          S

1476. Singerman, Robert and Grumet, Elinor, eds. WAYWARD ETCHINGS: I. N. CHOYNSKI VISITS SOUTHERN CALIFORNIA, 1881. *Western States Jewish Hist. Q. 1979 11(2): 119-135.* Isidor Nathan Choynski (1834-99) was the West's foremost Jewish journalist of the 19th century. Choynski set out from his home in San Francisco in 1881 to visit several cities in southern, California. His reports on San Luis Obispo, Santa Barbara, Los Angeles, San Gabriel, San Bernardino, Riverside, and San Diego mention the numbers of Jews in these cities, praise their commercial success, and criticize their religious indifference. Based on articles published in *The American Isralite* on 8, 15, and 29 July 1881; 2 photos, 19 notes.
                                                          B. S. Porter

1477. Sokolov, Raymond A. HARRY SALTZSTEIN, M.D. (1890-): A PERSONAL MEMOIR. *Michigan Jewish Hist. 1976 16(2): 5-9.* Reminisces about Harry Saltzstein, a fellow surgeon and leader in the Jewish community in Chicago, 1935-75.

1478. Solomon, Joseph. AUTOBIOGRAPHY. *Am. Jewish Arch. 1976 28(1): 51-58.* Provides an autobiographical sketch of Joseph Solomon (b. 1905), from his birth until his admission to the bar in December 1928, including his education and his fascination with the law.

1479. Steiner, Ruth Heller. "THE GIRLS" IN CHICAGO. *Am. Jewish Arch. 1974 26(1): 5-22.* Aunt Ernestine and Aunt Louise would have summed up their lives as "a combination of luck and nerve," but their niece, Mrs. Steiner, reflected that the word she would have chosen "would have been character."
                                                          J

1480. Stern, Malcolm H. GROWING UP IN PIONEER SAVANNAH: THE UNFINISHED MEMOIR OF LEVI SHEFTALL (1739-1809). *Michael: On the Hist. of the Jews in the Diaspora [Israel] 1975 3: 15-22.* Levi Sheftall was a son of Benjamin Sheftall (1692-1765), a native of Prussia and one of the first Jews to settle in Georgia; he was half-brother to Mordecai Sheftall. Reprints the oldest known memoir of an American Jew and possibly the earliest description of life in pioneer Savannah. Starting from scratch, Levi Sheftall accumulated a large fortune, including many slaves, but eventually lost most of it. Imprisoned as a rebel during the American Revolution, he denied entertaining such sentiments. He was active in Jewish community life. 10 notes.
                                                          T. Sassoon

1481. Stern, Norton B. and Kramer, William M. ARIZONA'S MINING WIZARD: BLACK JACK NEWMAN. *Western States Jewish Hist. Q. 1979 11(3): 255-264.* John B. (Black Jack) Newman (1862-1928) seemed to have an uncanny ability to locate rich copper ore deposits near Globe, Arizona, in the 1880's through 1910. With the money earned in the mining business, Newman invested real estate both in Arizona and in his new home in southern California (1910-28). His pet project in his later years was a cattle ranch and orchard in the San Joaquin Valley. Beginning as a penniless, illiterate miner, he developed a fortune estimated at $12 million at the time of his death. Primary and secondary sources; 2 photos, 23 notes.
                                                          B. S. Porter

1482. Stern, Norton B. THE BERNSTEINS OF BAJA CALIFORNIA. *Western States Jewish Hist. Q. 1975 7(2): 108-115.* Max Bernstein (1854-1914) went to Baja California during the gold rush of 1881. He became the resident agent of the International Company of Mexico, working to develop Ensenada for the company. He married Governor Teodoro Riveroll's daughter, Guadalupe, and had seven children. Includes information about their descendants living mainly in California. 9 photos, 5 notes.
                                                          R. A. Garfinkle

1483. Stern, Norton B. CALIFORNIA'S JEWISH GOVERNOR. *Western States Jewish Hist. Q. 1973 5(4): 285-287.* Discusses Washington Bartlett (1824-87), journalist and politician in San Francisco and governor of the state in 1886.

1484. Stern, Norton B. DENOUEMENT ON SAN DIEGO IN 1888. *Western States Jewish Hist. Q. 1978 11(1): 49-55.* David and Fannie Green, married in Ripin, Poland, in 1863, had a stormy marriage with a pattern of desertion and reconciliation until 1888 when Fannie decided to divorce her husband. By this time Fannie operated a boarding house in San Diego, California. David, who opposed the divorce, came to the house on the evening of 31 August 1888, and during an argument with his wife and her lawyer's clerk, wounded Fannie with a revolver and fatally shot himself. The Jewish press viewed the incident and the Green family as a disgrace to Judaism. Based on primary sources; 34 notes.
                                                          B. S. Porter

1485. Stern, Norton B. THE FRANKLIN BROTHERS OF SAN DIEGO. *J. of San Diego Hist. 1975 21(3): 32-42.* Describes the lives of Lewis Abraham Franklin (1820-79) and his brother Maurice Abraham Franklin (1817-74), pioneer merchants of San Diego during the 1850's.
                                                          S

1486. Stern, Norton B. THE KING OF TEMECULA: LOUIS WOLF. *Southern California Q. 1976 58(1): 63-74.* Provides a profile of Louis Wolf (1833-87), merchant and rancher in the Temecula Valley, 60 miles north of San Diego. Born in France of Jewish parentage, Wolf arrived in San Francisco in 1852. By the late 1850's he had constructed a general store and hostelry in the Temecula Valley. For 30 years he dominated the economic life of the valley. His enterprises included livestock, hotel, retail sales, and real estate. Wolf and his wife, who was of Indian blood, met Helen Hunt Jackson in 1882. Jackson based characters on them in her novel *Ramona*, which she named after Wolf's wife. Known for his sympathy for the Indians in the region, he was called by them "King of Temecula." At his death in 1887 his estate was worth more than $100,000. Not an observant Jew, Wolf shared many characteristics of his coreligionists in his economic activities, participation in civic affairs, and friendship for Indians and Californios. Based on primary and secondary sources; 52 notes.
                                                          A. Hoffman

1487.   Stern, Norton B. and Kramer, William M.   THE LILIENTHAL FAMILY PACT.   *Western States Jewish Hist. Q. 1975 7(3): 220-224.* The pact of seven families surnamed Lilienthal created on 20 August 1880 established a family corporation whereby the signers pooled their assets and their abilities to aid each other and "the furtherance of the common interest." "In this document the age-old Jewish ideal of family solidarity was formalized by a contractual agreement under the laws of the State of New York." Included are short biographies of the Lilienthals, the text of the pact, and the individual roles of the signers within the agreements of the pact. 5 notes.   R. A. Garfinkle

1488.   Stern, Norton B.   THE MASONIC CAREER OF BENJAMIN D. HYAM, CALIFORNIA'S THIRD GRAND MASTER.   *Western States Jewish Hist. Q. 1975 7(3): 251-263.* Benjamin Daniel Hyam came to California in 1850. He organized the Benecia Lodge and held several offices within the Masonic order. In 1850 he attended a convention to form a Grand Lodge of California, and in 1852 was elected Grand Master. After trying to help a Jewish friend be reinstalled into the order, he was attacked by his fellow Masons and suffered their prejudice for many years. Hyam served as a quartermaster clerk during the Civil War and practiced law in Washington, D.C., until his death. Based on primary and secondary sources; photo, 46 notes.   R. A. Garfinkle

1489.   Stern, Norton B.   A "MURDER" TO BE FORGOTTEN.   *Western States Jewish Hist. Q. 1977 9(2): 176-185.* On 20 May 1875 in the settlement of Rincon, California, in today's Riverside County, Simon Goldsmith fatally shot his business partner George Kallman. The dispute concerned Goldsmith's handling of a large sum of the firm's money. A popular and respected man in his community and in Los Angeles, Goldsmith was tried and found innocent. The general feeling in the community was that the universal practice of carrying concealed weapons was a large cause of the tragedy. Goldsmith continued to operate his store in Rincon until 1883 when he joined his brothers in a general merchandise business in Santa Ana, and later retired to San Francisco in 1902 or 1903. The reaction of the Jewish community was to repress the memory of the killing to the extent that none of the direct or collateral descendants has ever heard of it. Based on newspaper reports, court records, interviews and published sources; 2 photos, 40 notes.   B. S. Porter

1490.   Stern, Norton B. and Kramer, William M.   THE SINSHEIMERS OF SAN LUIS OBISPO.   *Western States Jewish Hist. Q. 1973 6(1): 3-32.* Traces Aaron Sinsheimer's family from his German ancestors to his children who reside in California. Aaron Zachary Sinsheimer came to America in 1845, settled in Vicksburg, Mississippi, and then moved to San Luis Obispo, California, in 1878. In 1884 the Sinsheimers built an iron front store that is considered one of the best-preserved structures of its style. Aaron took over the store in 1898 and was a leading citizen in his day. Includes short biographies of the 10 Sinsheimer children. 2 illus., 4 photos, 90 notes.   R. A. Garfinkle

1491.   Stern, Norton B. and Kramer, William M.   THE WINE TYCOON OF ANAHEIM.   *Western States Jewish Hist. Q. 1977 9(3): 262-278.* Benjamin Dreyfus (1824-1886) came to America from Bavaria in the late 1840's, moving to Los Angeles, California in 1854. He immediately became involved in several businesses, including a general store, a brewery, and an oil refinery manufacturing kerosene. In 1858 he moved to Anaheim where he established vineyards and produced sweet and dry wines. By 1880, he owned vineyards and wineries in Anaheim, San Gabriel, Cucamonga, and Napa, California. Much of the wine was shipped to San Francisco and eastern cities. Dreyfus was an active Democratic Party member, and was elected to the posts of city councilman and mayor in Anaheim. Primary and secondary sources; 3 photos, 68 notes.   B. S. Porter

1492.   Stuhler, Barbara.   FANNY BRIN: WOMAN OF PEACE. Stuhler, Barbara and Kreuter, Gretchen, ed. *Women of Minnesota: Selected Biographical Essays* (St. Paul: Minnesota Historical Society Press, 1977): 284-300. In 1884, three-month-old Fanny Fligelman came to Minneapolis with her Romanian Jewish parents. A serious student in high school and at the University of Minnesota, Fanny was active in the Minerva Literature Society and was elected to Phi Beta Kappa. She became a teacher, and in 1913 wed Arthur Brin, a successful businessman. Fanny raised a family, became a prominent volunteer activist, and worked for woman suffrage, world peace, democracy, and Jewish heritage. Dur-

ing the 1920's and 30's, she was especially active in the National Council of Jewish Women and served as director of the Minneapolis Woman's Committee for World Disarmament. Stimulated by the Nazi attack on Jews, Fanny became a strong Zionist. As the alternate delegate for the Women's Action Committee for Lasting Peace, Fanny attended the 1945 San Francisco meetings which gave birth to the United Nations. An excellent speaker, Fanny served in many organizations, promoted many causes, took civic responsibilities as serious duties, and worked to better use women and their contributions to improve world affairs. Primary and secondary sources; photo, 44 notes.   A. E. Wiederrecht

1493.   Stuppy, Laurence J.   HENRY H. LISSNER, M.D., LOS ANGELES PHYSICIAN.   *Western States Jewish Hist. Q. 1976 8(3): 209-216.* Dr. Henry H. Lissner (1875-1968), San Francisco-born and Oakland-raised, took over his father's pawnshop in Oakland in 1886 along with his two brothers. In 1895, Henry and his brother Meyer moved to Los Angeles to open a branch of the pawnshop. They soon closed the new store when Meyer entered law school and Henry started medical school. Henry opened his medical practice in Los Angeles and became a prominent doctor. He was a pioneer in electrocardiography. He served on the staff of several hospitals and was the chief of staff at Cedars of Lebanon Hospital. Photo, 19 notes.   R. A. Garfinkle

1494.   Stutz, George M.   FIFTY YEARS OF DETROIT JEWISH COMMUNAL ACTIVITY: A PERSONAL BIOGRAPHICAL MEMOIR.   *Michigan Jewish Hist. 1975 15(1): 5-25.*

1495.   Sutherland, John F.   RABBI JOSEPH KRAUSKOPF OF PHILADELPHIA: THE URBAN REFORMER RETURNS TO THE LAND.   *Am. Jewish Hist. Q. 1978 67(4): 342-362.* Joseph Krauskopf (1858-1923) came to the United States as a 14-year-old. He graduated with the first class of four at Hebrew Union College in 1883 and was Philadelphia's foremost reform rabbi during 1887-1922. He introduced English into both services and the religious school, popularized the Jewish Sundry Services, and drafted the Pittsburgh Platform of 1885. His great concern with social reform led him into close cooperation with Jacob Riis. After a visit with Leo Tolstoy at Yasnaya Polyana, Krauskopf became the driving spirit of the Jewish "back-to-the land" movement and of the National Farm School, today known as the Delaware Valley College of Science and Agriculture, the only private agricultural school in the country. Thoroughly part of America's urban milieu, Krauskopf nevertheless sought to modify it with the agrarian myth, an urban-agrarian ambivalence which still influences American thought and action.

F. Rosenthal

1496.   Trilling, Diana.   LIONEL TRILLING, A JEW AT COLUMBIA.   *Commentary 1979 67(3): 40-46.* Describes the difficulties Lionel Trilling had to face as a Jew in the early 1930's establishing himself as an English professor at Columbia University.

1497.   Unrau, William E.   JUSTICE AT FORT LARAMIE: THE TRIAL AND TRIBULATIONS OF A GALVANIZED YANKEE.   *Arizona and the West 1973 15(2): 107-132.* By 1864, when the manpower needs of the Union Army became critical, Confederate prisoners ("Galvanized Yankees") were enrolled and deployed to Indian country. The monotony, inhospitable environment, low morale, arbitrary military justice, and indecisive Indian policy debilitated the average western soldier. Emanuel H. Saltiel, alias Sergeant Joseph Isaacs, a British citizen and military officer and an ambitious Galvanized Yankee, was court-martialed on trumped-up charges of mutiny, sedition, and encouraging desertion and disloyalty. He was convicted of "entertaining and promulgating disloyal sentiments." Though he was drummed out of the service at Fort Laramie, Dakota Territory, in May 1866, Saltiel's subsequent business ventures left a spectacular mark on the economy of Colorado Territory. He was recognized as a leading citizen and benefactor of the Jewish community of Denver. 4 illus., 47 notes.   D. L. Smith

1498.   Vanger, Max.   MEMOIRS OF A RUSSIAN IMMIGRANT. *Am. Jewish Hist. Q. 1973 63(1): 57-88.* The author, a retired businessman, recounts his experiences since his arrival in Canada before World War I. He worked as a shoemaker, junk peddler, cloth cutter, fish merchant, cattle buyer, lumber dealer, shoe store operator, millinery and sweater manufacturer, and finally garage operator and owner in New York City.   F. Rosenthal

1499. Viener, Saul. ROSENA HUTZLER LEVY RECALLS THE CIVIL WAR. *Am. Jewish Hist. Q. 1973 62(3): 306-313.* A letter written in 1907 by Rosena Hutzler Levy (1840-1914) to her children recalled the Civil War service of their father, Richard Levy (1828-97). The hitherto unpublished letter is a telling record of the catastrophe which altered so many southern families.   F. Rosenthal

1500. Voorsanger, Jacob and Stern, Malcolm H., ed. LEON MENDEZ SOLOMONS, 1873-1900. *Western States Jewish Hist. Q. 1978 10(2): 138-145.* Leon Mendez Solomons was born in San Francisco, California. He graduated from the University of California in 1893 with degrees in mathematics and physics, but found his interest turning to the new science of psychology. After earning his Ph.D. in psychology at Harvard University, he accepted a teaching post at the University of Wisconsin. Publication of several research reports enhanced his reputation and led to the offer of a permanent chair at the University of Nebraska. After one semester he became ill and died at the age of 26 from complications following surgery. Quoted from eulogy; 7 notes.
B. S. Porter

1501. Wall, Bennett H. LEON GODCHAUX AND THE GODCHAUX BUSINESS ENTERPRISES. *Am. Jewish Hist. Q. 1976 66(1): 50-66.* Reconstructs the life and influence of Leon Godchaux (1824-99), New Orleans merchant, plantation owner, sugar refiner, real estate developer, and financier, who proved that hard work, canny business judgment and ingenuity made it possible for a poor immigrant boy to rise rapidly to wealth and importance. Based on papers and clippings of the Godchaux family. 29 notes.   F. Rosenthal

1502. Walton, Clyde C. PHILIP DAVID SANG, 1902-1975. *J. of the Illinois State Hist. Soc. 1975 68(5): 429-434.* Despite his extensive business involvement, Philip David Sang found time to demonstrate his life-long interest in the cause of human freedom, and his concerns for education, for the Jewish religion and for the importance of history. He avidly collected manuscripts and other historical materials and donated them to historical societies and libraries. Sang devoted considerable time, effort and money to the growth of the Illinois State Historical Society.
N. Lederer

1503. Ward, Dana. KISSINGER: A PSYCHOHISTORY. *Hist. of Childhood Q. 1975 2(3): 287-348.* Basic tensions in Henry A. Kissinger's psyche, traceable to traumatic childhood and adolescent experiences, influence his world view and hence his actions as Secretary of State. Notable among those events were his Jewish childhood near Hitler's Nuremberg and subsequent need to flee to the United States, his father's loss of economic status and importance in the family, and the presence of favored siblings or quasi-siblings. Examines development of the "depressive personality" resulting from these factors. Explains Kissinger's relationships with business and political leaders, his first wife, and other women in terms of ego fulfillment, and relates his decisions of state to his personality development. Based on interviews, newspapers and magazines, and other primary and secondary sources; 187 notes.
R. E. Butchart

1504. Warsen, Allen A. MORRIS GARVETT—A GREAT COMMUNITY LEADER, 1893-1971. *Michigan Jewish Hist. 1973 13(1): 8-11.* An obituary of Morris Garvett, active in the Detroit Jewish community.   S

1505. Watters, Gary. THE RUSSIAN JEW IN OKLAHOMA: THE MAY BROTHERS. *Chronicles of Oklahoma 1975-76 53(4): 479-491.* Facing increased persecution in tsarist Russia, Hyman Madanic and his son Ben emigrated to the United States in 1889. After leaving Ellis Island, where their name was changed to Madansky, they took jobs in the sweatshop system of St. Louis' clothing industry. Hard work and frugality brought enough money to bring the rest of the family from Russia in 1893. Soon the family was Americanized and opened its own clothing store in Fairfield, Illinois. In 1908 they moved to the boomtown of Tulsa, Oklahoma, where their business proved successful enough to open branches in nearby towns. Following World War I, they changed their name to the May brothers and their business became widely known. The Great Depression undercut the family fortunes and closed the Tulsa store, but the branches survived. Primary and secondary sources; 3 photos, 21 notes.
M. L. Tate

1506. Weyne, Arthur. THE FIRST JEWISH GOVERNOR: MOSES ALEXANDER OF IDAHO. *Western States Jewish Hist. Q. 1976 9(1): 21-42.* Moses Alexander (1853-1932), a Bavarian immigrant to the United States, first entered politics in Chillicothe, Missouri, where he was elected as city councilman and mayor. Stagnant business conditions prompted him to move his dry goods business to Boise, Idaho. After two terms as Boise's mayor, the Democratic Party persuaded him to run for governor in 1914. As a two-term governor (1915-18) Alexander's chief accomplishment was to cut back expenditures. He was also credited with passage of a prohibition law, enactment of a workman's compensation act, creation of a state highway system, and construction of the Arrowrock Dam and the Dalles-Celilo Canal. Critics charged that he used his veto power too frequently. After his second term of office Alexander became an informal elder statesman while remaining active in his merchandizing business. Based on family records and published material; 3 photos, 27 notes.   B. S. Porter

1507. Wieseltier, Leon. PHILOSOPHY, RELIGION AND HARRY WOLFSON. *Commentary 1976 61(4): 57-64.* Harry Austryn Wolfson (1887-1974) occupied the chair in Hebrew Literature and Philosophy at Harvard for more than 30 years and published prodigiously. His works include *The Philosophy of Spinoza* (1934), *Philo: Foundations of Religious Philosophy in Judaism, Christianity, and Islam* (1947), *The Philosophy of the Church Fathers* (1956), and others. His philosophy of history premised the deepest meaning for philosophy in its encounter with religion. The paganism of the ancients and the skepticism of the moderns pales for Wolfson before the marriage of philosophy and religion exemplified by the medievals. For Wolfson, the Jews held central place in medieval culture. Based on Wolfson's works.   S. R. Herstein

1508. Wildavsky, Aaron. THE RICHEST BOY IN POLTAVA. *Society 1975 13(1): 48-56.* The author primarily discusses his Jewish father, Sender Wildavsky, who immigrated to Brooklyn, New York, from the USSR about 1921.

1509. Winchevsky, Morris. ZIHRONOTH [Memoirs]. *Asupoth [Israel] 1965 (9): 71-84.* Memoirs on Jewish personalities, culture, and Hebrew works by Morris Winchevsky (1856-1932), known as the grandfather of Jewish socialism.   B. Lubelski

1510. —. A COLLECTION OF CALIFORNIA JEWISH HOMES. *Western States Jewish Hist. Q. 1973 6(1): 43-47.* Photographs of the homes of five prominent California Jews: Jacob Leow, David and Jacob Neustader, Jacob Stern, Edward R. Levy, and Max Meyberg. Includes short biographies of each family. 5 photos.   R. A. Garfinkle

1511. —. THE MARKS BROTHERS OF LOS ANGELES, A PICTURE STORY. *Western States Jewish Hist. Q. 1979 11(4): 311-317.* Joshua H. Marks (1884-1965) and David X. Marks (1891-1977) were brought to Los Angeles by their parents in 1902. Joshua entered their father's brick business and became a building designer and contractor. Among his better known works are Grauman's Chinese and Egyptian theaters, and the Santa Anita Race Track. He also built several shopping centers, churches, business offices, and movie studios. David entered the insurance business and was active in civic affairs. He helped establish the Los Angeles Civic Light Opera Association, and contributed financially to developments at the University of Southern California, and other educational institutions. Family records and published sources; 7 photos, 8 notes.   B. S. Porter

1512. —. MEN OF DISTINCTION IN EARLY LOS ANGELES. *Western States Jewish Hist. Q. 1975 7(3): 225-233.* Contains brief biographies of Samuel Norton (1834-1902), Charles Gerson (1839-1907), Isaiah M. Hellman (1831-90), Abraham Baer (1814-82), Samuel Prager (1831-1907), Wolf Kalisher (1826-89), Leopold Harris (1836-1910), David Solomon (1824-?), and Joseph Newmark (1799-1881), 9 photos.
R. A. Garfinkle

1513. —. [MYER MYERS, SILVERSMITH]. *Am. Art and Antiques 1979 2(3): 50-59.*
Werner, Alfred. MYER MYERS: SILVERSMITH OF DISTINCTION, *pp. 50-57.* Gives the biography of American silversmith Myer Myers (1723-1795), one of a few Jews among 3,000,000 American colonists in the 18th century, a prominent member of the

New York Jewish community and a colleague of Paul Revere whose fine work was largely unappreciated until the beginning of the 20th century.

Feigenbaum, Rita. CRAFTSMAN OF MANY STYLES, pp. 58-59. Describes the varied styles of silversmith Myer Myers who designed pieces for households and churches, and most notably for Jewish rituals in the 18th century.

1514. —. NELLIE NEWMARK OF LINCOLN, NEBRASKA: A PICTURE STORY. *Western States Jewish Hist. Q. 1979 11(2): 114-118.* Nellie Newmark (1888-1978) was the clerk of the District Court at Lincoln, Nebraska, during 1907-56. She gained a reputation for assisting judges and new attorneys assigned to the court. Primary sources; 5 photos, 3 notes.   B. S. Porter

1515. —. NOTES ON SOL RIPINSKY OF ALASKA IN 1905. *Western States Jewish Hist. Q. 1976 8(4): 370-374.* Reprints a 28 September 1905 article from Cincinnati's *The American Israelite*. Discusses Sol Ripinsky (1850-1927), a merchant, doctor, political advisor, and teacher who lived in the township of Haines Mission in southeastern Alaska for many years. He worked as the United States Commissioner to Alaska and as a teacher for the native Alaskans. He was a character and loved to pull practical jokes. 2 photos, 4 notes.   R. A. Garfinkle

1516. —. THE SHAFSKY BROTHERS OF FORT BRAGG: A MENDOCINO COUNTY VIGNETTE. *Western States Jewish Hist. Q. 1976 9(1): 49-54.* The Shafsky family, Russian emigrants, came to the United States by way of Canada. Starting as pack peddlers in the lumber camps of northern California, two of the brothers, Abraham Harry and Samuel, opened a general merchandise store in Fort Bragg. The business prospered and is still operated by a son and grandson of Abraham Harry Shafsky. Based on interviews, family records, and published works; 3 photos, 13 notes.   B. S. Porter

1517. Unsigned. SIGMUND ROTHSCHILD. *Michigan Jewish Hist. 1973 13(2): 16-18.* Gives a biography of Sigmund Rothschild (1838-1907), founder of the Detroit leaf-tobacco house Rothschild & Brother.
S

1518. —. TWO LETTERS FROM THE JEWISH PATRIARCH OF LOS ANGELES. *Western States Jewish Hist. Q. 1979 11(3): 231-233.* Joseph Newmark (1799-1881), was one of the principal founders of Los Angeles's Congregation B'nai B'rith (1862). In 1881, several months before his death, he wrote these letters to his granddaughter, Caroline, who lived in St. Louis, Missouri. The letters contain news of family members' health and activities. They are published through the courtesy of the addressee's granddaughter; 17 notes.   B. S. Porter

Zionism and the State of Israel

1519. Adler, Frank J. REVIEW ESSAY: *HARRY S. TRUMAN. Am. Jewish Hist. Q. 1973 62(4): 414-425.* Criticizes Margaret Truman's description of the Palestine issue in her biography of her father. The review focuses on the partition question (1946-47) and on the part played by Truman's Jewish friend Eddie Jacobson. Margaret Truman mentions only one White House interview with Jacobson but the presidential records show 24 appointments during this period. Margaret Truman's picture of her father's dispassionate stance on these issues is inaccurate. 47 notes.   F. Rosenthal

1520. Barberis, Mary A. THE ARAB-ISRAELI BATTLE ON CAPITOL HILL. *Virginia Q. R. 1976 52(2): 203-223.* Insists that in the struggle for US support in the Middle East the Jewish lobby in Washington has been far more influential than Arab supporters. Pro-Israel lobbying, aimed at Congress, has "acted to strengthen pre-existing attitudes." Most influential has been the American Israel Public Affairs Committee (AIPAC). Fewer Arabs in the US, less well-organized lobbying, and American public opinion have weakened the Arab position, but that may be changing now.   O. H. Zabel

1521. Belakoui, Janice Monti. IMAGES OF ARABS AND ISRAELIS IN THE PRESTIGE PRESS, 1966-74. *Journalism Q. 1978 55(4):* 732-738, 799. Compares US public opinion toward Israel and the Arab states from 1967 to 1975 and press coverage, 1966-74, by three US news magazines and two New York newspapers. The press presented a more generally favorable image of Arab leaders and spokesmen in 1973 than it had six years before, just as Gallup opinion polls showed a slight increase in the percentage of respondents who expressed sympathy for the Arabs. 11 notes.   R. P. Sindermann, Jr.

1522. Berger, Elmer. MEMOIRS OF AN ANTI-ZIONIST JEW. *J. of Palestine Studies [Lebanon] 1975-76 5(1-2): 3-55.* Publishes the memoirs of Rabbi Elmer Berger, an American anti-Zionist, who for over 30 years has led an active opposition to Zionism, racism toward the Arabs, and US support for such policies.

1523. Berman, Myron. RABBI EDWARD NATHAN CALISH AND THE DEBATE OVER ZIONISM IN RICHMOND, VIRGINIA. *Am. Jewish Hist. Q. 1973 62(3): 295-305.* Rabbi Calish, who served the Richmond Jewish community 1891-1945, was a consistent foe of the Zionist movement, and thus shared the position of many southern Jews of his time and generation. He was one of the original founders of the American Council for Judaism.   F. Rosenthal

1524. Bronstein, Phil. ELDRIDGE CLEAVER—REBORN. *Midstream 1977 23(1): 57-63.* Examines the hesitancy of Jews to support black activist Eldridge Cleaver because of his anti-Israeli stand as a member of the Black Panther Party in the 1960's; considers Cleaver's discovery of racism and the servitude of blacks in Arab States as the reason for his changing attitudes toward Jews and Zionism, 1968-70's.

1525. Clifford, Clark M. RECOGNIZING ISRAEL: THE 1948 STORY. *Am. Heritage 1977 28(3): 4-11.* Admitting that political considerations are a part of every major policy decision, the author defends Harry S. Truman against revisionist charges on the Palestine question. Suggests that Truman's position was consistent with his long-standing position of favoring the underdog. Serious internal opposition, spearheaded by the Office of Near Eastern and African Affairs in the State Department, hampered the formulation of US policies. 3 illus.
J. F. Paul

1526. Cohen, Michael J. AMERICAN INFLUENCE ON BRITISH POLICY IN THE MIDDLE EAST DURING WORLD WAR TWO: FIRST ATTEMPTS AT COORDINATING ALLIED POLICY ON PALESTINE. *Am. Jewish Hist. Q. 1977 67(1): 50-70.* US entry into Middle Eastern politics during World War II inevitably led to friction with Great Britain. The British feared a US challenge to their political, military, and economic hegemony. The United States suspected British imperialism would exploit American resources. The author examines problems blocking an Anglo-American consensus on the Palestine question, such as attitudes toward Zionism, immigration quotas, and the formation of a Jewish Army. Franklin D. Roosevelt's attempts to placate the British on these issues highlight the dilemma American policymakers faced. 63 notes.   F. Rosenthal

1527. Eris, Alfred. ONE MAN'S WARS: AN ECHO OF 1967. *Midstream 1977 23(5): 56-65.* Personal account of the hysteria of New York City Jews and the near-nonchalance and courage of Israelis actually faced with the outbreak of the 1967 Six-Day War.

1528. Feingold, Henry. AMERICAN ZIONISM. *Midstream 1975 21(8): 70-72.* Reviews Melvin I. Urofsky's *American Zionism from Herzl to the Holocaust* (New York: Doubleday, 1975).   S

1529. Feuer, Leon I. THE BIRTH OF THE JEWISH LOBBY: A REMINISCENCE. *Am. Jewish Arch. 1976 28(2): 107-118.* Rabbi Feuer "was in at the beginning of [the] so-called Jewish Lobby" in Washington, D.C., "and in fact was the first lobbyist." His efforts on behalf of Zionism during the early 1940's contributed toward "building a substantial base of support for Israel in American public opinion."   J

1530. Fram, Harry. WRITINGS OF A FOUNDER OF ZIONISM IN LOS ANGELES. *Western States Jewish Hist. Q. 1977 9(3): 238-245.* Harry Fram (1877-1960), owner of a retail stationery store, was one of the founders of Zionism in Los Angeles. He helped establish the Nathan Straus Palestine Advancement Society (later known as the Nathan Straus

Israel Society) and the Young Zionist Association of Los Angeles. Fram published two pamphlets in 1905 and 1944 which explained the reason for creating a homeland for Jews, and advocated the establishment of a national financial institution to administrate this great project. Reprints excerpts from Fram's speeches and writings. Primary and secondary sources; photo, 13 notes.
                                                                    B. S. Porter

1531.   Gal, Allon.   IN SEARCH OF A NEW ZION: NEW LIGHT ON BRANDEIS' ROAD TO ZIONISM.   *Am. Jewish Hist. 1978 68(1): 19-31.* Louis D. Brandeis's conversion both to a more positive Judaism as well as Zionism had taken place by the end of 1910 after he had sought support for his progressive position from the Boston Jewish community and after his contacts with Jewish workers and employers in the New York garment strike. Another factor was his association with Aaron Aronsohn of the Jewish Agricultural Experiment Station in Palestine. He was deeply impressed by the morality of the pioneer Zionists. 32 notes.
                                                                    F. Rosenthal

1532.   Ganin, Zvi.   THE LIMITS OF AMERICAN JEWISH POLITICAL POWER: AMERICA'S RETREAT FROM PARTITION, NOVEMBER 1947-MARCH 1948.   *Jewish Social Studies 1977 39(1-2): 1-36.* Forces within the Truman administration sought to undo the US commitment to the United Nations' Partition of Palestine resolution of 29 November 1947. These oppositionists included important members of the State Department, Secretary of Defense James Forrestal and members of the National Security Council and Central Intelligence Agency. Outside the government important sources of opposition were represented by James Reston of the *New York Times* and Kermit Roosevelt. President Truman was irritated by the interference of the American Jewish community into foreign policy matters by injecting the issue into domestic politics. Domestic Jewish groups and individuals failed to stem the retreat from supporting partition because they were unable to persuade the American foreign policy elite that the creation of a Jewish state was in the national interest. The foreign policy elite was able to effectively counter the presumed great strength of domestic Jewish political pressure.
                                                                    N. Lederer

1533.   Garnham, David.   FACTORS INFLUENCING CONGRESSIONAL SUPPORT FOR ISRAEL DURING THE 93RD CONGRESS.   *Jerusalem J. of Int. Relations [Israel] 1977 2(3): 23-45.* Presents a model designed to assess dependent and independent factors affecting attitudes of Congress toward foreign aid to Israel, 1973-74, concluding that because of economic and political ties, Arab-US relations have a great bearing on Israeli-US relations and that the executive branch tended to support the Arabs while the Congress tended to support Israel.

1534.   Geller, Stuart.   WHY DID LOUIS BRANDEIS CHOOSE ZIONISM?   *Am. Jewish Hist. Q. 1973 62(4): 383-400.* Opposes the thesis advanced by Yonathan Shapiro that Louis Dembitz Brandeis (1856-1941) became a Zionist in order to secure political advancement during the administration of Woodrow Wilson. That Brandeis in 1912 joined the small and then unpopular group of Zionists rather than the American Jewish Committee is proof that he acted out of convictions rather than opportunism. Brandeis had learned to accept the new Jewish immigrant who, he thought, could be Americanized by Zionism, which he identified with an oppressed minority. 35 notes.
                                                                    F. Rosenthal

1535.   Geoll, Yohai.   ALIYA IN THE ZIONISM OF AN AMERICAN OLEH: JUDAH L. MAGNES.   *Am. Jewish Hist. Q. 1975 65(2): 99-120.* Judah L. Magnes (1877-1948) was one of the native-born and American-educated Jews who formed a significant element of the leadership during the first two decades of American Zionism. Once Magnes had gone to Palestine, he assumed vital responsibilities there too, culminating in his service as president of the newly founded Hebrew University. Magnes' attitudes and his development as a Zionist are described on the basis of letters, diary entries, and excerpts from his many publications. 50 notes.
                                                                    F. Rosenthal

1536.   Ghosh, Partha Sarathy.   PRESENT STATE OF AMERICAN ZIONISM AND THE MIDDLE EAST CRISES OF 1967.   *Q. Rev. of Hist. Studies [India] 1975-76 15(3): 151-157.* Zionist-organized activities exert a great influence on American government policy. This results from the scores of Jewish legislative and legal assistants serving in government, and the threat of the Jewish vote. Although fewer American Jews claim

to be Zionists, they believe Israel must be preserved because it gives American Jews a sense of ethnic identity, and as a moral matter. 38 notes.
                                                                    J. C. Holsinger

1537.   Gorni, Yosef.   THE JEWISHNESS AND ZIONISM OF HAROLD LASKI.   *Midstream 1977 23(9): 72-77.* Follows Harold Laski's career during 1910-46 and concludes that, despite his early claims to the contrary, Laski was always a Zionist at heart and always felt himself a part of the Jewish nation, although he viewed traditional Jewish religion as restrictive.

1538.   Gotlieb, Yosef.   EINSTEIN THE ZIONIST.   *Midstream 1979 25(6): 43-48.* Albert Einstein (1879-1955) had little sense of Jewish identity during his early years, but about 1911 he became acquainted with Zionism in Prague, although he tended toward internationalism and pacifism until 1919, a date which marked the beginning of his strong belief in Zionism and his association with Hebrew University in Tel Aviv.

1539.   Hudson, Michael C.   POLITIQUE INTÉRIEURE ET POLITIQUE EXTÉRIEURE AMÉRICAINE DANS SES RAPPORTS AVEC LE CONFLIT ISRAÉLO-ARABE [American foreign and domestic policy as affected by the Israeli-Arab conflict].   *Pol. Étrangère [France] 1974 39(6): 641-658.* As a result of the Israeli-Arab conflict of the 1970's, various pressure groups act on the Congress and American public opinion, thereby limiting the kind of foreign policy initiatives a president is able to take.

1540.   Ibrahim, Saad.   AMERICAN DOMESTIC FACTORS AND THE OCTOBER WAR.   *J. of Palestine Studies [Lebanon] 1974 4(1): 55-81.* Examines the impact of economic conditions, traditional loyalties, the mass media, the oil embargo, and pro-Zionist lobbies on the formation of US public opinion toward Arab-Israeli relations and the Six-Day War and the October War, 1967 and 1973.

1541.   Isaacs, Stephen D.   SO WHO HAS THE POWER?: HOW HARD DARE YOU PUSH IN FOREIGN POLICY?   *Present Tense 1974 1(4): 24-28.* Jewish influence in United States politics and foreign policy.
                                                                    S

1542.   Kabakoff, Jacob.   TE'UDOT MITOKH "OSEF DEINARD" [Documents from the Deinard Collection].   *Michael: On the Hist. of the Jews in the Diaspora [Israel] 1975 3: 15-40.* Ephraim Deinard (1846-1930) immigrated from Eastern Europe to the United States in 1888, despite his conviction that Jews should immigrate to Palestine rather than America. He authored some 50 works, including bibliographies, and edited several newspapers, including the short-lived Hebrew weekly *Haleumi* (1889). Later he collaborated in Ze'ev Shur's weekly, *Hapisgah*. Active in the Hibbat Zion movement, he dreamt of establishing a center of Hebrew literature and culture in America, which would strengthen American Jewry's ties with Palestine. Important American libraries acquired Hebrew books which Deinard collected on his European and Middle Eastern travels. Presents five documents from his extensive archive, including a letter to Moshe Leib Lillienblum. Primary and secondary sources; 73 notes.
                                                                    T. Sassoon

1543.   Kislov, A. K.   BELYI DOM I SIONISTSKOE LOBBI [The White House and the Zionist lobby].   *Voprosy Istorii [USSR] 1973 (1): 48-61.* The author discloses the interrelations between the White House and the Zionist lobby over the past fifty years, tracing the influence exerted by the Zionists on the political life of the United States. Considerable attention is devoted in the article to the causes of this influence which becomes especially pronounced during election campaigns, as well as to the methods employed by the Zionists. The Zionists' ability to gain their objectives is limited. In the final analysis the decision to further one or another concrete course of action remains the prerogative of the US authorities which express the interests of the capitalist class as a whole. Consequently international Zionism has been forced to adapt itself to American interests.
                                                                    J/S

1544.   Knee, Stuart E.   [ETHNIC ANTI-ZIONISM, 1917-41].
ETHNIC ANTI-ZIONISM IN U.S.A., 1917-1941.   *Patterns of Prejudice [Great Britain] 1977 11(5): 30-33.* Greek, Irish, Polish, Negro, and Arab groups expressed varying degrees of anti-Zionism during the interwar period.

AMERICAN ARABS AND PALESTINE. *Patterns of Prejudice [Great Britain] 1977 11(6): 25-31, 34.* Reviews Arab American anti-Zionist movements and organizations (e.g., Dr. E. G. Tabet's Syria-Mt. Lebanon League of Liberation, Dr. Fuad Shatara's Palestine Anti-Zionism Society, etc.) during 1912-41, and finds that some groups became not only anti-Zionist but anti-Jewish and Fascist.

1545. Knee, Stuart E. FROM CONTROVERSY TO CONVERSION: LIBERAL JUDAISM IN AMERICA AND THE ZIONIST MOVEMENT, 1917-1941. *Ann. of Jewish Social Sci. 1978 17: 260-289.* Deals with the gradual change within US Reform Judaism from firm anti-Zionism to reluctant acceptance of Zionism and gradually to pro-Zionism. The chief catalyst in this change was the advent to power of Adolf Hitler in Germany and the spread of Nazism.

R. J. Wechman

1546. Knee, Stuart E. THE IMPACT OF ZIONISM ON BLACK AND ARAB AMERICANS. *Patterns of Prejudice [Great Britain] 1976 10(2): 21-28.* Discusses the impact of Zionism on black and Arab Americans from 1941 to the present, showing the Six-Day War (1967) as a turning point in the formation of the Third World.

1547. Knee, Stuart E. JEWISH NON-ZIONISM IN AMERICA AND PALESTINE COMMITMENT 1917-1941. *Jewish Social Studies 1977 39(3): 209-226.* The non-Zionist element within American Jewry played a major role in shaping the destiny of Zionism; a role in fact equal to that exerted on the movement by American Zionists and anti-Zionists. Non-Zionists opposed the creation of a Jewish state but supported Jewish immigration to Palestine, economic development of the region, and a revival of religiocultural Judaism. The American Jewish Committee was the principal non-Zionist gathering place. Louis Marshall and, following his death, Felix Warburg and Cyrus Adler, were prominent in non-Zionist leadership. The involved efforts of these men and their adherents to follow a middle path in regard to Palestine and its future led to their participation in a series of conferences in the interwar period resulting in the bankruptcy of non-Zionism as a viable philosophy of action. By 1941 non-Zionism had been absorbed into the Zionist camp, largely through the medium of the Jewish Agency and its increasing commitment to a Jewish Palestine.

N. Lederer

1548. Knee, Stuart E. JEWISH SOCIALISTS IN AMERICA: THE DEBATE ON ZIONISM. *Wiener Lib. Bull. [Great Britain] 1975 28(33-34): 13-24.* Surveys the changing nature of the debate on Zionism among American Jewish socialists from World War I to World War II with particular reference to the issue of Jewish nationalism in Palestine. Emphasizes the influence of Jewish European immigrants and through them the views of the *Bund*, the European Jewish labor organization. Bundists emphasized revisionist socialism; the Zionists the establishment of a Jewish national home in Palestine. Despite periods of apparent modification, Jewish socialists remained opposed to the pro-capitalist and anti-Palestinian Arab views of the Zionists. Also discusses the anti-Zionist views of the American Communists in the 1930's against the background of international developments and Comintern directives. Based on private papers, interviews, and published sources; 62 notes.

J. P. Fox

1549. Knee, Stuart E. THE KING-CRANE COMMISSION OF 1919: THE ARTICULATION OF POLITICAL ANTI-ZIONISM. *Am. Jewish Arch. 1977 29(1): 22-52.* The [US] anti-Zionist King-Crane Report of 1919 [on Palestine] owed much to the Christian missionary goals of its authors. It did not reflect the wishes of the Middle East's Moslem majority, but deserves to be recalled as a pro-Christian document.

J

1550. Lapomarda, Vincent A., S. J. MAURICE JOSEPH TOBIN AND THE BOSTON JEWISH COMMUNITY: THE MOVEMENT FOR THE STATE OF ISRAEL, 1926-1948. *Am. Benedictine Rev. 1973 24(1): 59-73.* Maurice Joseph Tobin, the sixth Secretary of Labor (1948-53), supported the establishment of a Jewish state in Palestine. Reviews Tobin's firm support of Zionist objectives in relationship to his career as Boston's Mayor, Massachusetts' Governor, and President Truman's Secretary of Labor. Based on primary and secondary sources; 57 notes.

J. H. Pragman

1551. Levin, N. Gordon, Jr. ZIONISM IN AMERICA. *Rev. in Am. Hist. 1975 3(4): 511-515.* Melvin I. Urofsky's *American Zionism from Herzl to the Holocaust* (Garden City, New York: Anchor Pr., 1975) considers primarily the years 1880-1930, the efforts to adapt European Zionism to liberal American society, and the "major domestic and diplomatic events impinging on Jews in America and in Palestine."

1552. Lubin, David. A LETTER ON ZIONISM. *Western States Jewish Hist. Q. 1973 5(2): 100-109.* David Lubin (1849-1920), a Sacramento Jewish merchant, in a 1918 letter, advocated the establishment of an industrial state for Jews in Palestine.

1553. Luttwak, Edward N. THE DEFENSE BUDGET AND ISRAEL. *Commentary 1975 59(2): 27-35.* Discusses the dilemma of Jewish liberals and liberal Senators who support the existence of Israel but oppose defense spending in the United States.

1554. Maslow, Will. THE STRUGGLE AGAINST THE ARAB BOYCOTT: A CASE HISTORY. *Midstream 1977 23(7): 11-26.* The American Jewish Committee, the American Jewish Congress, and the Anti-Defamation League of B'nai B'rith have tried during 1975-77 to effect legislation against the Arab boycott of Israel.

1555. Maurer, Marvin. QUAKERS IN POLITICS: ISRAEL, P.L.O. AND SOCIAL REVOLUTION. *Midstream 1977 23(9): 36-44.* The American Friends Service Committee sponsored a conference in Chevy Chase, Maryland, in February 1977 on "New Imperatives for Israeli-Palestinian Peace" at which the Religious Society of Friends showed a definite bias toward the Palestinians, comparing today's Palestinians to holocaust victims and criticizing Israel for alleged behavior of a kind which the Society has apparently ignored among groups and nations whom it considers its "clients."

1556. Meshcheryakov, V. AT THE SERVICE OF US REACTION. *Internat. Affairs [USSR] 1975 (2): 90-95.* Zionism is an integral aspect of American reactional foreign policy. Zionists have a broad network of influential organizations in the United States with strong ties to government and the news media. These organizations actively spread Zionist propaganda. 24 notes.

D. K. McQuilkin

1557. Moshe, Meir. THE YOM KIPPUR WAR IN MIDDLE AMERICA. *Midstream 1974 20(6): 74-79.* Comments on public opinion about the 1973 Arab-Israeli War in a Middle American university town, where the majority of Jews are assimilated.

S

1558. Osipova, N. V. PROIZRAIL'SKAIA KOALITSIIA V AMERIKANSKOM KONGRESSE, [The pro-Israeli lobby in the American Congress]. *Voprosy Istorii [USSR] 1974 (6): 78-86.* Taking the activity of US Congress as an example, the author examines the influence exerted by American Zionists on the Administration's Middle East policy. The article describes in detail the forms and methods employed by the Zionists to exert pressure on congressmen. Analyzing the composition of this coalition, the author makes a point of stressing that it consists in the main of the representatives of military-industrial circles which are resolutely opposed to any relaxation of international tension.

J

1559. Panitz, Esther. LOUIS DEMBITZ BRANDEIS AND THE CLEVELAND CONFERENCE. *Am. Jewish Hist. Q. 1975 65(2): 140-162.* The culmination of a prolonged controversy between European and American Zionist leaders occurred at the 1921 Cleveland Conference of the Zionist Organization of America. This contest of wills and personalities over attitudes and techniques to adopt in the achievement of a common goal ultimately pitted Louis Brandeis against Chaim Weizmann. Since the final vote went against him, Brandeis and Judge Julian Mack of Chicago resigned from their Zionist offices but continued to work for the economic development of Palestine's Jewish colonists.

T. Rosenthal

1560. Parzen, Herbert. THE ENLARGEMENT OF THE JEWISH AGENCY FOR PALESTINE: 1923-1929 A HOPE—HAMSTRUNG. *Jewish Social Studies 1977 39(1-2): 129-158.* The confirmation of the World Zionist Organization as the Jewish Agency for Palestine created serious dissension in Jewish ranks, especially with regard to the positions of European Zionists led by Chaim Weizmann and the governing board of the Zionist Organization of America headed by Louis D. Brandeis. Distrust between these two groups was exacerbated by the distrust of Zionists in general exhibited by the non-Zionist American Jews, perhaps best represented by the position of Louis Marshall, president of the American Jewish Committee, who felt that the Zionists desired complete control over Palestine developments through the use of monetary contributions by non-Zionists. The terrific infighting of these various groups colored the deliberations of various international convocations held during the 1920's to discuss approaches to the Palestine situation. The creation in 1929 of an enlarged Jewish Agency including non-Zionists did not fulfill expectations for any group.   N. Lederer

1561. Parzen, Herbert. LOUIS MARSHALL, THE ZIONIST ORGANIZATION IN AMERICA, AND THE FOUNDING OF THE JEWISH AGENCY. *Michael: On the Hist. of the Jews in the Diaspora [Israel] 1975 3: 226-253.* In 1920 the Zionist movement split over the launching of the Keren Hayesod fund for the development of Jewish Palestine. Louis D. Brandeis and his supporters withdrew from Zionist leadership, while Louis Lipsky (1876-1963) led the US Zionists who backed Chaim Weizmann's alliance with prominent non-Zionist American Jews such as Louis Marshall (1856-1929). In 1924 a strengthened Jewish agency for Palestine assumed control of the fund, and had to deal with "Palestine Securities", a rival investment scheme, and the Crimea colonization program, then being advocated for Russian Jews. A memorandum prepared by Meyer W. Weisgal in 1925 concerning the "Understanding between Mr. Marshall and the Zionist Organization" is reproduced. 22 notes, appendix.   T. Sassoon/S

1562. Parzen, Herbert. THE PURGE OF THE DISSIDENTS, HEBREW UNION COLLEGE AND ZIONISM, 1903-1907. *Jewish Social Studies 1975 37(3-4): 291-322.* The assumption of the presidency of this Reform Judaism college in Cincinnati by Dr. Kaufmann Kohler in the fall of 1903 led to the expulsion of its Zionist faculty. Kaufmann, a vehement assimilationist and anti-Zionist, paid only lip service to academic freedom as he moved to curb pro-Zionist utterances and writings by Caspar Levias, Max L. Margolis, and Max Schloessinger. His success in purging the faculty of these individuals met with the general approval of the Reform Judaism constituency. Includes a letter from Max L. Margolis explaining his position to Rabbi Clarke S. Levi. Primary and secondary sources.   N. Lederer

1563. Podet, Allen H. ANTI-ZIONISM IN A KEY U.S. DIPLOMAT: LOY HENDERSON AT THE END OF WORLD WAR II. *Am. Jewish Arch. 1978 30(2): 155-187.* Describes Loy Henderson as the "single diplomat most centrally involved in questions of Zionism, of Palestine, and of the world Jewish movement that centered on these issues," at the end of World War II. The case of Loy Henderson must be seen as central to any understanding and evaluation of State Department policy during this important and controversial period leading to the creation of Israel.   J

1564. Polishook, Sheila Stern. THE AMERICAN FEDERATION OF LABOR, ZIONISM, AND THE FIRST WORLD WAR. *Am. Jewish Hist. Q. 1976 65(3): 228-244.* The period of World War I brought with it recognition of organized labor as an essential element in the nation's development, whose support the Wilson administration sought and needed. Thus, even though the AFL leadership readily accepted the principle of national self-determination, its endorsement of a Jewish national state in Palestine came as a surprise which Samuel Gompers was able to push through against vociferous opposition by the pacifist and socialist spokesmen of the ILGWU. Labor's commitment to a Jewish homeland has strengthened over the years. 39 notes.   F. Rosenthal

1565. Raab, Earl. IS ISRAEL LOSING POPULAR SUPPORT? THE EVIDENCE OF THE POLLS. *Commentary 1974 57(1): 26-29.* Discusses public opinion in the United States about US foreign policy toward Israel.   S

1566. Rausch, David A. ARNO C. GAEBELEIN (1861-1945): FUNDAMENTALIST PROTESTANT ZIONIST. *Am. Jewish Hist. 1978 68(1): 43-56.* Arno C. Gaebelein (1861-1945), originally of the Methodist Episcopal Church, was a central figure in the formulation of Fundamentalism in America. He became a student of Hebrew and Yiddish and a

missionary to Jews of New York. In 1893 he began publishing, in Yiddish, *Tiqweth Israel,* or *The Hope of Israel Monthly,* on the pages of which he actively encouraged Jewish settlement of Palestine. This strong Zionist concern was to characterize his work as an evangelist and a teacher at the Dallas Theological Seminary. 28 notes.   F. Rosenthal

1567. Rausch, David A. OUR HOPE: PROTOFUNDAMENTALISM'S ATTITUDE TOWARD ZIONISM, 1894-1897. *Jewish Social Studies 1978 40(3-4): 239-250. Our Hope,* founded by Arno C. Gaebelein and edited for its first three years by Dr. Ernst F. Stroeter, was an English-language Christian publication designed to further Fundamentalism in the United States and emphasizing the importance of the Jews and their place in biblical prophecy. Original articles and those taken from Jewish publications were pro-Zionist and stressed the everlasting quality of the nation of Israel. Other pieces discussed Christian missions to the Jews and the Jewish colonization of Palestine. In 1897 the periodical changed from its original purpose to a popular Bible study publication. Attitudes similar to those in the early years of *Our Hope* regarding the restoration of the Jews to Palestine were expressed in the international prophetic conference movement and the Christian missions to the Jews in the 19th century.   N. Lederer

1568. Rivlin, Helen Anne B. THE HOLY LAND: THE AMERICAN EXPERIENCE: AMERICAN JEWS AND THE STATE OF ISRAEL. *Middle East J. 1976 30(3): 369-389.* The authenticity of the American commitment to Israel derives from the nature of American society, "while the American Jewish consensus regarding Israel has arisen out of the exceptional circumstances of the Jewish experience in this country." No group benefited more from the American Revolution than the Jews. Assistance to the Jews of Palestine began as early as the 18th century. Covers American-Jewish relations up to the present. 58 notes.   E. P. Stickney

1569. Romanofsky, Peter. "AN ATMOSPHERE OF SUCCESS": THE KEREN HAYESOD IN MISSOURI, 1921-1922. *Jewish Social Studies 1978 40(1): 73-84.* The World Zionist Organization (WZO) founded the Keren Hayesod organization in the United States in 1921 to provide an umbrella organization for the receipt of all funds, donations, and investments designed to implement the creation of a Jewish national homeland in Palestine. Opposed by the American group led by cultural Zionists Louis D. Brandeis and Julian W. Mack, the Keren Hayesod and the Brandeis group competed for the allegiance and funds of American Jews. The Missouri situation, especially in Kansas City and St. Louis, revealed that the Keren Hayesod gained the full support of the majority of American-born leaders as well as European-born, American-educated Jews. These persons not only supported but led the campaign to provide backing for the instrument of the WZO. The overwhelming majority of Missouri Zionists supported Keren Hayesod owing to its "atmosphere of success," based on efficient and speedy organization and the skillful employment of attention gaining publicity.   N. Lederer

1570. Ruchames, Louis. MORDECAI MANUEL NOAH AND EARLY AMERICAN ZIONISM. *Am. Jewish Hist. Q. 1975 64(3): 196-223.* Discusses the intellectual history of Mordecai Manuel Noah (1785-1847), for many years America's most prominent Jew, a man devoted to alleviating the sufferings of his people by advocating a return to Palestine. Noah's adherence to Zionism grew from his family background and the strong influence exerted upon him by Gershom Mendes Seixas (1743-1816). 51 notes.   F. Rosenthal

1571. Rudavsky, David. LOUIS D. BRANDEIS AT THE LONDON INTERNATIONAL ZIONIST CONFERENCE OF 1920. *Yivo Ann. of Jewish Social Sci. 1974 (15): 145-165.* Delves into Louis D. Brandeis's conflicts with Chaim Weizmann at the London Conference on the questions of including the National Jewish Councils, and over Dubnow's doctrine of diaspora nationalism which Brandeis was against. Brandeis complained that the Zionist confederations in English-speaking countries were carrying too much of the financial burden, and wanted the World Zionist Executive to be moved to Jerusalem. 76 notes.   R. J. Wechman

1572. Sandler, Bernard I. HOACHOOZO—ZIONISM IN AMERICA AND THE COLONIZATION OF PALESTINE. *Am. Jewish Hist. Q. 1974 64(2): 137-148.* At the beginning of the 20th century, many of the East European Jewish immigrants to America had succeeded in improving their economic position. Some, however, still aspired to live in a totally Jewish environment in Palestine and were imbued with the spirit of Jewish nationalism. An ingenious program for land acquisition in Palestine eventually led to the establishment of colonies. Simon Goldman of St. Louis and Dr. Arthur Ruppin were leading members of these early undertakings. Herzlia, Afule, Raanana, and Gan Yavne were among the colonies founded by these Achoosa-Zionists between 1908 and 1934, settlements which continue to thrive and develop in modern Israel. 21 notes.   F. Rosenthal

1573. Schmidt, Sarah. HORACE M. KALLEN AND THE "AMERICANIZATION" OF ZIONISM—IN MEMORIAM. *Am. Jewish Arch. 1976 28(1): 59-73.* Discusses the life of Horace M. Kallen (1882-1974), especially detailing Kallen's beliefs about Zionism and American Jews.

1574. Schmidt, Sarah. HORACE M. KALLEN AND THE "PROGRESSIVE" REFORM OF AMERICAN ZIONISM. *Midstream 1976 22(10): 14-23.* Examines the efforts of Horace M. Kallen to bring about progressive reform within American Zionism during the early 20th century.

1575. Schmidt, Sarah. THE *PARUSHIM*: A SECRET EPISODE IN AMERICAN ZIONIST HISTORY. *Am. Jewish Hist. Q. 1975 65(2): 121-139.* Horace M. Kallen, best known in American intellectual history for his theory of cultural pluralism, became a Zionist in 1903 as a means to retain Jewish identity. Ten years later he founded a secret Zionist society which he called *Parushim* (separate ones) to realize his ideas on Zionism and to bring about statehood in Palestine. Even though the *Parushim* failed in these endeavors, their activities stirred and directed an unwieldy organizational structure, bedevilled by clashes of strong personalities, such as Rabbi Wise, Justice Brandeis, and Henrietta Szold. Contains excerpts of letters written in 1914.   F. Rosenthal

1576. Schmidt, Sarah. THE ZIONIST CONVERSION OF LOUIS D. BRANDEIS. *Jewish Social Studies 1975 37(1): 18-34.* Brandeis's change in attitude from a long-held, deeply felt belief in Jewish assimilation to that of an espousal of a Zionist state was based to a considerable extent on his contacts with and the influence of Horace Kallen, ca. 1912-15. Kallen's papers reveal that before Brandeis's agreement to take over leadership of the American Zionism movement, he and Kallen met on various occasions for the exchange of ideas on the subject. Brandeis's Zionist speeches are quite similar to Kallen's recorded thought. Based on primary and secondary sources, and the author's interviews with Kallen.
N. Lederer

1577. Schoenbaum, David. THE UNITED STATES AND THE BIRTH OF ISRAEL. *Wiener Lib. Bull. [Great Britain] 1978 31(45-46): 87-100.* In 1946-47, three possibilities existed for US policy toward Palestine: support partition, oppose it, or adopt neutrality. The first one raised the possibility of military responsibility for the protection of the Jews; neutrality would open the area to the Russians. What remained was a cantonized federal Palestine under some kind of trusteeship. However, Jewish successes led US foreign policy to recognize a de facto partition. Shows variety of pressures on Harry S. Truman, from domestic political concerns to the exigencies of the Cold War, and concludes that his policy was "neither an opportunistic nor an incompetent one." It helped create Israel while maintaining the Anglo-American alliance, keeping up the ties with the Arab states, and avoiding being pulled into a major war. Summarizes contemporary opinions, for example, Secretary Forrestal's note in his diary in 1948 that unless the United States had access to Middle Eastern oil, American motorcar companies would have to design a four-cylinder motorcar. 77 notes.   R. V. Layton

1578. Sergeyev, S. NEKOTORYE OSOBENNOSTI RAZVITIIA SIONIZM V SSHA [Certain peculiarities attending the development of Zionism in the United States]. *Voprosy Istorii [USSR] 1973 11: 66-80.* Analysis of the development of American Zionism as the ideology and practice of the Jewish bourgeoisie, focussing on the close connection between the objectives of Zionism and the interests of America's ruling class as a whole, which is one of the principal factors determining the specific features of the development of Zionism in the United States. The article highlights the multi-various forms and methods of Zionism's activ-

ity on the US political scene and gives a careful appraisal of the Zionist potential to exert influence on America's home and foreign policies. The author also examines the question concerning the role of America's Zionist movement in the over-all system of international Zionism.   J/S

1579. Shapiro, Edward S. AMERICAN JEWRY AND THE STATE OF ISRAEL. *J. of Ecumenical Studies 1977 14(1): 1-16.* Changing attitudes of American Jews toward Israel, especially the increasing pro-Israel sentiment created by the wars of 1967 and 1973, helped to develop a uniquely American Zionism that makes criticism or indifference toward Israel within the United States seem anti-Semitic.

1580. Siskin, Edgar E. CHAIM WEIZMANN AND JAMES H. BECKER: THE STORY OF A FRIENDSHIP. *Am. Jewish Arch. 1975 27(1): 32-50.* Chaim Weizmann sought the aid of successful businessman James H. Becker in furthering the cause of Zionism in the 1920's.
S

1581. Stern, Norton B. and Kramer, William M. A PRE-ISRAELI DIPLOMAT ON AN AMERICAN MISSION, 1869-1870. *Western States Jewish Hist. Q. 1976 8(3): 232-242.* Rabbi Hayyim Zevi Sneersohn (1834-82) spent several years traveling the world lecturing about the Holy Land with the goal of gaining support for the establishment of a Jewish homeland in Palestine. In 1869 he succeeded in having President Grant send a Jew to work in the American consulate in Jerusalem. In 1870 President Grant sent another Jew as US consul in Rumania. Rabbi Sneersohn wanted Jews in these posts because he believed they would be able to help their fellow Jews in areas of oppression. His lectures were well attended. 29 notes.   R. A. Garfinkle

1582. Stork, Joe and Rose, Sharon. ZIONISM AND AMERICAN JEWRY. *J. of Palestine Studies [Lebanon] 1974 3(3): 39-57.* Discusses the attitudes of American Jews toward Zionism and the development of those attitudes since the 1920's; Zionism today is accepted by most Americans as equal to Judaism itself.

1583. Strober, Gerald S. AMERICAN JEWS AND THE PROTESTANT COMMUNITY. *Midstream 1974 20(7): 47-66.* The 1972 Dallas-based General Assembly of the National Council of Churches illustrates the problem of the Jewish community in presenting its agenda and forestalling anti-Jewish or anti-Israeli actions.   S

1584. Tabory, Ephraim and Lazerwitz, Bernard. MOTIVATION FOR MIGRATION: A COMPARATIVE STUDY OF AMERICAN AND SOVIET ACADEMIC IMMIGRANTS TO ISRAEL. *Ethnicity 1977 4(2): 91-102.* Comparative analysis of academic Jews migrating to Israel from the United States and the USSR shows that both groups are prompted by negative factors in the larger society. American Jews, however, are measurably more religious and find that pursuit of a truly Jewish lifestyle is easier in Israel. Soviet Jews, because of subtle yet constant discrimination and harassment, are less religious but cling to their Jewish heritage as a form of nationalism. This pattern may also hold true for Jews outside academe, and Soviet Jews may be as willing to migrate to other economically advanced countries as to Israel.   G. A. Hewlett

1585. Toren, Nina. RETURN TO ZION: CHARACTERISTICS AND MOTIVATIONS OF RETURNING EMIGRANTS. *Social Forces 1976 54(3): 546-558.* Examines the relationships between certain characteristics and motivations of return migrants from the United States to Israel. Characteristics are those bearing on "success" as measured by level of education and occupation. Motivations are classified by using a push-pull model to explain migratory selection and movement. The data show that return migration from the United States to Israel is nonselective and that remigrants are motivated mainly by the attraction of the country of destination. A subclassification of the push-pull dichotomy reveals that: (1) the decision of the more successful return migrants is primarily influenced by occupational opportunities back home; (2) the less successful are motivated chiefly by patriotic attachment and loyalty to the home country. The predictive value and policy implications of the results of this analysis are indicated.   J

1586. Trice, Robert H. FOREIGN POLICY INTEREST GROUPS, MASS PUBLIC OPINION AND THE ARAB-ISRAELI DISPUTE. *Western Pol. Q. 1978 31(2): 238-252.* Considers the roles played by domestic groups and mass public opinion in the American foreign policy process. Interest groups use both direct and indirect strategies in attempts to influence decisions. Earlier studies have concluded that domestic groups generally have very little impact on foreign policy decisions. An essential part of an indirect strategy is to rally mass public support behind the group's policy position. A comparative analysis of the behavior and indirect impact of pro-Israel and pro-Arab groups on American Middle East policy suggests that public opinion may be relatively insensitive to interest group activities on foreign policy issues. These findings raise serious questions concerning the general ability of nongovernmental forces to have any meaningful impact on American foreign policy.   J

1587. Tuchman, Barbara W. THE ASSIMILATIONIST DILEMMA: AMBASSADOR MORGENTHAU'S STORY. *Commentary 1977 63(5): 58-62.* In 1914 Henry Morgenthau, Sr., then US Ambassador to Turkey, arranged for financial aid to the Jewish colony in Palestine, enabling it to survive and preserving it for eventual Jewish statehood. Yet in 1918 he resigned as president of the Free Synagogue, when its Rabbi, Stephen S. Wise, led a delegation to the White House to support the Zionist homeland, and in 1921 he wrote an article stating his strong opposition to Zionism. Not until after the Holocaust, when he was in his 80's, did Morgenthau acknowledge that he had misread history. Assimilation into American life was his ideal, assimilation meaning acceptance as Jews, not absorption into Christianity. The Western Democracies did not function according to his ideal and the horrors of the Holocaust turned many assimilationists into supporters of the Jewish State. Based on primary and secondary sources as well as personal recollections.   S. R. Herstein

1588. Urofsky, Melvin I. AMERICA AND ISRAEL: TRYING TO FIND THE STRAIGHT PATH. *Reviews in Am. Hist. 1975 3(3): 383-388.* Discusses the evolution, 1945-48, of President Truman's policy on Israel, analyzes the importance of the Zionist cause in the 1948 presidential election, and summarizes the social and theological responses of American Protestantism since the Puritans in this review of Hertzel Fishman's *American Protestantism and a Jewish State* (Detroit, Mich.: Wayne State U. Pr., 1973) and John Snetsinger's *Truman, the Jewish Vote, and the Creation of Israel* (Hoover Institution Studies 39. Stanford, Calif.: Hoover Institution Pr., 1974).

1589. Urofsky, Melvin I. AMERICAN ZIONISTS AND THE BALFOUR DECLARATION. *Midstream 1978 24(10): 28-34.* The declaration stated that the British government favored and would work for a Jewish homeland in Palestine that would not prejudice the rights of non-Jews; Arthur James Balfour's letter to Lord Rothschild in 1917 confirmed President Woodrow Wilson's approval for the establishment of a Jewish homeland in Palestine.

1590. Urofsky, Melvin I. THE EMERGENCE OF BRANDEIS AS A ZIONIST. *Midstream 1975 21(1): 42-58.* Describes the work of Louis D. Brandeis (1856-1941) in the American Zionist movement and his efforts to aid Jewish settlements in Palestine during World War I.   S

1591. Urofsky, Melvin I. FIFTY YEARS OF THE JEWISH AGENCY. *Midstream 1979 25(9): 42-46.* Reviews the history of the Jewish Agency for Palestine in Western Europe and the United States since its creation by Chaim Weizmann and Louis Marshall in Zurich in 1929.

1592. Voss, Carl Hermann. THE AMERICAN CHRISTIAN PALESTINE COMMITTEE: THE MID-1940S IN RETROSPECT. *Midstream 1979 25(6): 49-53.* Reviews the efforts of American Christian groups to influence world opinion, and in particular the British government, to establish a homeland for the Jews in what is now Israel.

1593. Waldinger, Albert. ABRAHAM CAHAN AND PALESTINE. *Jewish Social Studies 1977 39(1-2): 75-92.* As a result of Abraham Cahan's (1860-1951) trip to Palestine in the fall of 1925 he became an ardent advocate of the creation of a Jewish state. Influential in the American Jewish community as the founder and editor of the *Jewish Daily Forward,* a Yiddish-language, Socialist daily newspaper, Cahan sought the support of the American Jewish labor establishment for the creation of a Jewish Palestine after 1925. Based on firsthand observations, his newspaper articles reported favorably on the religious, commer-

cial, and industrial aspects of the Jewish settlements in Palestine, especially emphasizing the contributions of the agricultural communes and the various institutions created by the Histadrut. In revising his attitude toward a Jewish homeland, Cahan proved more flexible than many of his Jewish Socialist colleagues, including members of his editorial board.   N. Lederer

1594. Watters, William R., Jr. THE LONELINESS OF BEING JEWISH: THE CHRISTIAN'S UNDERSTANDING OF ISRAEL. *Religion in Life 1975 44(2): 212-221.*

1595. Waxman, Chaim I. and Helmreich, William B. RELIGIOUS AND COMMUNAL ELEMENTS OF ETHNICITY: AMERICAN JEWISH COLLEGE STUDENTS AND ISRAEL. *Ethnicity 1977 4(2): 122-132.* Surveys of attitudes among Jewish students in the Northeast show that attitudes on Zionism, Jewishness, and Israel were part of strong and complex self-images based on combinations of Americanism, religiosity, and belief in communalism. Most expressed positive identification with Israel, but few expressed desire to live there. Extent of support of Zionism was based upon its compatibility with their self-professed Americanism (which seemed to consistently outweigh identification with Jewishness). Covers 1973-76.   G. A. Hewlett

1596. —. LETTERS FROM JACOB H. SCHIFF AND DAVID WOLFFSON TO BERNARD SCHIRESON, EL CENTRO, CALIFORNIA, 1914. *Western States Jewish Hist. Q. 1977 9(4): 350-353.* Bernard Schireson was a Zionist who operated a wholesale general merchandise business in El Centro, California. Jacob Schiff was a New York philanthropist and major contributor to the Technion, Israel Institute of Technology. In his letter, he offers more money to the project on condition that it be completed. David Wolffson was a pioneer Zionist leader in Germany. His letter tells of ill health and his hopes to recover and return to his home. Reprint of private correspondence; 2 photos, 5 notes.   B. S. Porter

1597. —. [ZIONISM]. *Am. Jewish Hist. Q. 1974 63(3): 215-243.*
Urofsky, Melvin I. ZIONISM: AN AMERICAN EXPERIENCE, pp. 215-230. Zionism in America, as it was structured by such men as Louis Brandeis, developed along unique American lines. Brandeis' assertion that Zionism and Americanism shared similar values, and his insistence on a pragmatic, nonideological approach to all problems, were responsible for the success and acceptance of Zionism by ever larger numbers of Jews.
Feingold, Henry L. DISCUSSANT, pp. 230-238. Disputes Urofsky's thesis and maintains that concern with matters of organization and fund raising and the Provisional Executive Committee for General Zionist Affairs' insistence on migration to Palestine, was shared by all west European countries.
Sachar, Howard Morley. DISCUSSANT, pp. 238-243. Supports Urofsky, but reiterates the watershed significance of the Balfour Declaration which galvanized positive Jewish support. The east European background of most American Jews since 1900 should also be weighed properly.   F. Rosenthal

1598. —. A ZIONIST DISCUSSION IN 1904. *Western States Jewish Hist. Q. 1977 9(4): 315-318.* Israel Zangwill (1864-1926) was an English Zionist who advocated settlement in East Africa as a Jewish homeland instead of the apparently unattainable Palestine. Colonel Henry I. Kowalsky (1858-1914), a former US Army officer and prominent San Francisco lawyer, stated that a good Jew ought to aid the fulfillment of the Lord's promise by working for a Jewish state. Kowalsky argued that America should be the Jews' homeland, and that Jews were equal and integral members of the American community and owed loyalty and patriotism. Based on a report in the *Jewish Times and Observer,* San Francisco; 3 notes.   B. S. Porter

Anti-Semitism

1599. Alter, Robert. DEFAMING THE JEWS. *Commentary 1973 55(1): 77-82.* Examines the negative image of Jews in the film *Portnoy's Complaint* and other Jewish and non-Jewish fiction and humor since the late 1960's; contrasts useful satire with destructive stereotypes.

1600. Appelbaum, Paul S. U.S. JEWS' REACTION TO SOVIET "ANTI-ZIONISM." *Patterns of Prejudice [Great Britain] 1978 12(2): 21-32.* Examines attitudes toward anti-Semitism and anti-Zionism in the USSR by Jews in the United States, 1948-78.

1601. Ashton, Dore. NO MORE THAN AN ACCIDENT? *Critical Inquiry 1976 3(2): 235-249.* Examples ever since the Franco-Prussian War demonstrate how in Europe and in the United States vulgar associations of Jews with art have persisted.

1602. Berman, Hyman. POLITICAL ANTISEMITISM IN MIN-NESOTA DURING THE GREAT DEPRESSION. *Jewish Social Studies 1976 38(3-4): 247-264.* Anti-Semitism was successfully used as a political weapon to unseat Minnesota Farmer-Labor Governor Elmer A. Benson in the campaign of 1938. Many of Benson's liberal political aides and associates were Jewish. They were libeled as radical Jewish elements seeking to import Marxism into the state by political opponents such as Hjalmar Petersen and Raymond Chase. Political anti-Semitism in Minnesota proved a valuable tool in the conservative effort to thwart further government intervention to assist the unemployed, the unions, and producer-cooperative farmer elements. Primary sources.   N. Lederer

1603. Bingham, Richard D.; Frendreis, John P.; and Rhodes, James M. THE NOMINATING PROCESS IN NONPARTISAN ELECTIONS: PETITION SIGNING AS AN ACT OF SUPPORT. *J. of Pol. 1978 40(4): 1044-1053.* Arthur Jones was the candidate of the (Nazi) National Socialist White People's Party in the nonpartisan Milwaukee mayoral primary of 17 February 1976. Under the conditions of "minimal information" elections, interviews with registered voters who signed Jones' nominating petition indicated that most: were unaware of Jones' party affiliation, neither supported the Nazi party's principles nor shared Nazi millenarian views, and did not vote for Jones in the election. Primary and secondary sources, especially interviews; 3 tables, 8 notes.
                                                                A. W. Novitsky

1604. Brokhin, Yuri. FATHOMING THE FREE WORLD: OR: ADVENTURES OF SOVIET JEWISH EMIGRANTS. *Dissent 1974 21(4): 542-548.* Discusses conditions of Soviet Jews inside the USSR and the United States.

1605. Carson, Herbert L. and Carson, Ada Lou. THE JEWS, ROY-ALL TYLER, AND AMERICA'S DIVIDED MIND. *Am. Jewish Arch. 1976 28(1): 79-84.* Discusses early American playwright and novelist Royall Tyler (1757-1826) as an example of America's divided attitudes of toleration and prejudice towards Jews.

1606. D'Ancona, David Arnold. AN ANSWER TO ANTI-SEMITISM: SAN FRANCISCO 1883. *Western States Jewish Hist. Q. 1975 8(1): 59-64.* Reprint of a letter to the editor of the *San Francisco Call*, 26 January 1883, in response to anti-Semitic statements published in the San Francisco *Argonaut* by its editor, Frank M. Pixley. Pixley's remarks contained many untruths and misconceptions concerning Jewish religious ceremonies and life-styles. D'Ancona (1827-1908) clearly rebutted Pixley's statements. Pixley recognized his mistakes and ceased his anti-Semitic writings.   R. A. Garfinkle

1607. Dobkowski, Michael N. ACCEPTANCE OR REJECTION: THE IMAGE OF THE JEW IN AMERICAN SOCIETY. *Studies in Hist. and Soc. 1974 5(2): 61-65.* A review essay on the role of American Jews in American society, prompted by Leslie H. Carlson and George A. Colburn, eds., *In Their Place: White America Defines her Minorities* (New York: John Wiley and Sons, Inc., 1972), Rudolf Glanz's *The Jew in Early American Wit and Graphic Humor* (New York: KTAV Publishing House, 1973), Arthur A. Goren's *New York Jews and the Quest for Community* (New York: Columbia U. Pr., 1970), Michael Selzer's *"Kike!": A Documentary History of Anti-Semitism in America* (New York: World Publishing Co., 1972), and Robert G. Weisbrod and Arthur Stein's *Bitter-Sweet Encounter: The Afro American and the American Jew* (New York: Schrocken Books, 1972). These diverse works generally dispute the theory that American anti-Semitism has had economic rather than stereotypic causes. 7 notes.   V. L. Human

1608. Dobkowski, Michael N. AMERICAN ANTISEMITISM: A REINTERPRETATION. *Am. Q. 1977 29(2): 166-181.* Popular American literature and drama of the 19th and early 20th centuries presented unfavorable stereotypes of the Jews which contributed to a generation of anti-Semitism. Religious novels depicted Jews as bigots. Plays and popular novels included Jewish representations who were greedy and mercenary in business, amoral in social behavior, and generally unscrupulous. By the early 20th century, Jews were associated with radicalism and politically revolutionary movements in popular literature. Primary sources; 59 notes.   N. Lederer

1609. Dobkowski, Michael N. POPULIST ANTISEMITISM IN U.S. LITERATURE. *Patterns of Prejudice [Great Britain] 1976 10(3): 19-27.* Discusses anti-Semitism and racial stereotypes of Jews in US literature during the Populist era, including the influence of the Rothschild image and the theory of Jewish world conspiracy.

1610. Dobkowski, Michael N. WHERE THE NEW WORLD ISN'T NEW: ROOTS OF U.S. ANTISEMITISM. *Patterns of Prejudice [Great Britain] 1975 9(4): 21-30.* Discusses the historiography of anti-Semitism in the United States from 1855 to the turn of the century, emphasizing ethnic stereotypes in popular novels and in Populism.

1611. Ellerin, Milton. AMERICAN NAZI FACTIONS. *Patterns of Prejudice [Great Britain] 1978 12(2): 16-20.* Delineates eight political factions established in the United States, 1950's-77, which have been associated with Nazism.

1612. Eris, Alfred. PORTRAIT OF THE ARTIST AS A MASS-MURDERER. *Midstream 1976 22(2): 50-60.* Reviews anti-Semitism in 20th-century literature, including gentiles such as T. S. Eliot and Ezra Pound and Jews such as Philip Roth.

1613. Feldman, Egal. AMERICAN EDITORIAL REACTION TO THE DREYFUS CASE. *Michael: On the Hist. of the Jews in the Diaspora [Israel] 1975 3: 101-124.* The court-martial and public degradation in 1895 of Captain Alfred Dreyfus in France aroused little interest in the United States, but events in 1898 including Émile Zola's trial, conviction, and flight to England, made Dreyfus's retrial a conspicuous issue in the US press. Reproduces 11 US editorials, 1898-99, reflecting a cross section of public opinion on the case. Anti-Semitism was but one of the themes evoked by this affair, which forced the United States to consider the possibility of an American Dreyfus case. A 12th editorial, dated 1906, reflects the renewed if brief interest aroused by Dreyfus's exoneration. 13 notes.   T. Sassoon

1614. Forrey, Robert. THE "JEW" IN NORRIS' *THE OCTOPUS*. *Western States Jewish Hist. Q. 1975 7(3): 201-209.* An analysis of the character S. Behrman in Frank Norris' (1870-1902) book *The Octopus* (1901) and the real life Jewish financier and possible secret railroad agent Marcus Pollasky. Pollasky helped establish a branch railroad line in the San Joaquin Valley in California and then turned it over to the hated Southern Pacific Railroad. The fictional character Behrman is a banker who squeezes the local farmers for every cent they have. There are many similarities in the lives of these two men, and Norris capitalized on the anti-Semitism of his time to create hatred for his character, S. Behrman. 14 notes.   R. A. Garfinkle

1615. Fried, Lewis. JACOB RIIS AND THE JEWS: THE AMBIVA-LENT QUEST FOR COMMUNITY. *Am. Studies (Lawrence, KS) 1979 20(1): 5-24.* Examines Jacob Riis's treatment of Jews against his general beliefs in civil liberties and social freedom. His thought expressed the tensions between the promise of egalitarianism and the realities of American society, and to him the downtown Jews highlighted this disparity. Their attachment to European cultural traditions confused Riis's impulse for cultural unity and Christian endeavor. Primary and secondary sources; 2 illus., 59 notes.   J. A. Andrew

1616. Friedman, Murray. BLACK ANTI-SEMITISM ON THE RISE. *Commentary 1979 68(4): 31-35.* Discusses the rise of political anti-Semitism among well-educated black leaders, including Jesse Jackson and Reverend Joseph Lowery, and in the black middle class as a whole in the United States since the mid-1960's.

1617. Gutfeld, Arnon. "A RUSSIAN JEW NAMED LEVINE". *Michael: On the Hist. of the Jews in the Diaspora [Israel] 1975 3: 211-225.*

On 7 February 1919, Chancellor Edward C. Elliott suspended Prof. Louis Levine (later Lewis Lorwin, d. 1971) from the faculty of Montana State University for insubordination and unprofessional conduct prejudicial to the welfare of the university. Levine had published a monograph entitled *The Taxation of Mines in Montana*, questioning the tax exemptions enjoyed by the state's omnipotent mining interests and thus incurring the wrath of the Anaconda Copper Mining Co. Reconstructs the affair, connecting it with the "red scare" of the time and with anti-Semitism. Primary and secondary sources; 20 notes, 3 appendixes.   T. Sassoon

1618. Hamlin, David M. SWASTIKAS AND SURVIVORS: IN-SIDE THE SKOKIE-NAZI FREE SPEECH CASE. *Civil Liberties Rev. 1978 4(6): 8-33.* Denial of the right to peaceably assemble, enforced by the village of Skokie, Illinois, in 1977 against an attempted assembly of the National Socialist Party of America, brought the American Civil Liberties Union into the fight to guarantee freedom of speech and freedom of assembly to the Nazi group in that primarily Jewish Chicago suburb.

1619. Henig, Gerald S. CALIFORNIA JEWRY AND THE MENDEL BEILISS AFFAIR, 1911-1913. *Western States Jewish Hist. Q. 1979 11(3): 220-230.* Mendel Beiliss was a Jewish laborer in a Russian brick factory, charged with murdering a Christian boy for religious purposes. The nature of the charges, with their anti-Semitic overtones, aroused worldwide protest. California Jews, and especially the Jewish newspapers, recognized that the prosecution of Beiliss was an attempt to justify pogroms. Public rallies attended by Jews and Christians in San Francisco and Oakland condemned the Russian government's action. Beiliss was acquitted, but the jury ruled that the boy was murdered as a ritual victim, and the Jews, as a group, were blamed for his death. Secondary sources; 55 notes.   B. S. Porter

1620. Henig, Gerald S. "HE DID NOT HAVE A FAIR TRIAL": CALIFORNIA PROGRESSIVES REACT TO THE LEO FRANK CASE. *California History 1979 58(2): 166-178.* Analyzes the reaction of California progressives to the Leo Frank case, 1913-15. Frank, a Jew, was convicted of the murder of a 13-year-old factory girl in Georgia in 1913. Evident violations of due process of law provoked criticism of the verdict, especially in California where progressives actively protested. Progressive newspapers and spokesmen commented on aspects of social injustice involved in the affair. On the other hand, except for California Jewish leaders, few progressives discussed the problems of capital punishment and anti-Semitism evoked by the trial. When the death sentence was commuted to life imprisonment in 1915, Californians praised the courage of Georgia's governor. Soon after, however, Frank was lynched by a mob. Progressives and conservatives alike united in condemning that act. California stood as a leader in the fight for justice for Frank, though its leadership failed to confront the deeper issues brought forth by the Frank case. Photo, 91 notes.   A. Hoffman

1621. Hentoff, Nat. THE ACLU'S TRIAL BY SWASTIKA. *Social Policy 1978 8(4): 50-52.* The American Civil Liberties Union's defense of the right of Chicago-based Nazis to demonstrate in a mainly Jewish suburb, Skokie, stirred up controversy among ACLU members and supporters, 1977-78.

1622. Hook, Sidney. ANTI-SEMITISM IN THE ACADEMY: SOME PAGES OF THE PAST. *Midstream 1979 25(1): 49-54.* Personal account chronicling the growth of Jewish faculty members, including Lionel Trilling, and the anti-Semitism they encountered at Columbia University, New York City, 1920's-70's.

1623. Lavender, Abraham D. DISADVANTAGES OF MINORITY GROUP MEMBERSHIP: THE PERSPECTIVE OF A "NONDE-PRIVED" MINORITY GROUP. *Ethnicity 1975 2(1): 99-119.* Though perceived by outside society to be nondeprived, minorities such as Jews actually feel cultural or social disadvantages because of stereotyping, anti-Semitism, discrimination, exclusion, prejudice, separatism, and marginality.

1624. Levy, Eugene. "IS THE JEW A WHITE MAN?": PRESS REACTION TO THE LEO FRANK CASE, 1913-1915. *Phylon 1974 35(2): 212-222.* An analysis of white, black, and Jewish press reactions to the trial, conviction, and appeal of Leo Frank, a Jew, for the murder of a young Gentile girl in Atlanta, Georgia, in 1913. Frank's conviction

depended on the testimony of James Conley, a black. The big city, white newspapers questioned the character of Conley, an ex-convict. The Jewish press perceived a shift in prejudices from Negroes to Jews. During the appeals processes, the black newspapers decried the attempt to substitute a black man for the Jew as perpetrator of the crime. 50 notes.   V. L. Human

1625. Lifshitz, Yehezkel. SHNEI MIKHTAVIM AMERIKANIIM 'AL ZEKHUYOT-HAMI'UTIM SHEL HAYEHUDIM BEMIZRAH-EIROPA [Two American letters on Jewish minority rights in Eastern Europe]. *Gal-Ed: On the Hist. of the Jews in Poland [Israel] 1975 (2): 340-352.* A 1927 exchange of letters between Morton W. Royse, a young sociologist, and Isaiah Bowman, director of the American Geographical Society, illuminated American attitudes toward the League of Nations' responsibilities regarding Jewish minority rights in Eastern Europe.

1626. Littell, Franklin H. UPROOTING ANTISEMITISM: A CALL TO CHRISTIANS. *J. of Church and State 1975 17(1): 15-24.* Christian anti-Semitism, rooted in the theological teaching that Jews are guilty of the crucifixion of Christ, has had social and political implications, exhibited notably in the Holocaust of World War II, as well as in the theology and historiography of such anti-Semitic liberals as Arnold Toynbee.

1627. Maibaum, Matthew. THE ENERGY CRISIS IN THE U.S.A.: FUEL TO PREJUDICE. *Patterns of Prejudice [Great Britain] 1974 8(1): 1-4.* Discusses the possible role the oil shortage may play in changing public opinion toward Jews in the United States in the 1970's, emphasizing the dangers of anti-Semitism.

1628. Mann, Peggy. THE DENTIST AND THE BISHOP: "I KNEW THE MAN WAS A SATAN . . ." *Present Tense 1974 1(4): 29-35.* Charles H. Kremer has tried to expose Rumanian (now US-based) Bishop Valerian Trifa's role in the murder of Jews during World War II.

1629. Moltmann, Günter. DIE AMBIVALENZ DES AMERIKA-NISCH-SCHWEIZERISCHEN VERTRAGES VON 1850/1855 [The ambivalence of the American-Swiss treaty of 1850-55]. *Schweizerische Zeitschrift für Geschichte [Switzerland] 1976 26(1-2): 100-133.* In 1850 the United States and Switzerland signed a "Convention of Friendship, Commerce and Extradition." It was not ratified until 1855. The treaty came under attack because it contained a clause that made the treatment of citizens subject to existing laws. Because some Swiss cantons still discriminated against non-Christians, US Jews were hostile to the treaty and remained so even after its ratification. The motives of the originator of the treaty, A. Dudley Mann, nonetheless had been truly liberal. Inspired by the French General Louis Cavaignac, Special Agent Mann prevailed upon Washington to make a treaty with the Helvetic sister republic to demonstrate to the reactionary powers of Europe that America supported republican ideals. Sheds new light on the Cavaignac-Mann role. 62 notes.   H. K. Meier

1630. Oxman, Daniel K. CALIFORNIA REACTIONS TO THE LEO FRANK CASE. *Western States Jewish Hist. Q. 1978 10(3): 216-224.* In August 1913, Leo Frank, a Jewish factory superintendent in Atlanta, Georgia, was tried and convicted of murdering a 14-year-old girl. Despite some indication of improper legal procedures, the verdict was upheld after several appeals. The case received nationwide publicity, resulting in thousands of letters and petitions to Georgia's governor. In June 1915, the governor commuted the death sentence to life imprisonment, but on 17 August 1915, a vigilante group removed Frank from prison and lynched him. Throughout the trial and period of appeals, and after the lynching, California newspapers accused Georgia officials and common citizens of moral injustice. Contemporary newspapers and secondary works; 34 notes.   B. S. Porter

1631. Polos, Nicholas C. BLACK ANTI-SEMITISM IN TWENTIETH-CENTURY AMERICA: HISTORICAL MYTH OR REALITY? *Am. Jewish Arch. 1975 27(1): 8-31.*

1632. Porter, Jack Nusan. A NAZI RUNS FOR MAYOR: DANGEROUS BROWNSHIRTS OR MEDIA FREAKS? *Present Tense 1977 4(4): 27-31.* Discusses the resurgence of Matt Koehl's National Socialist White People's Party. Traces the Party's activities during

1974-76 in Milwaukee, Wisconsin. Examines the political repercussions and the split in the Jewish community. Analyzes Jewish reactions: the activist-confrontationists vs. the minimalists. Primary and secondary sources; 4 photos. R. B. Mendel

1633. Rausch, David. AMERICAN EVANGELICALS AND THE JEWS. *Midstream 1977 23(2): 38-41.* Discusses American Jews' fears of anti-Semitism by Protestant Fundamentalists and Evangelicals; considers trends in Fundamentalists' Messianic beliefs, 1970's.

1634. Rockaway, Robert A. ANTISEMITISM IN AN AMERICAN CITY: DETROIT, 1850-1914. *Am. Jewish Hist. Q. 1974 64(1): 42-54.* Detroit, headquarters of the anti-Semitic activities of Henry Ford and Charles E. Coughlin in the 1920's and 1930's, was the site of many earlier instances produced by party politics in the 1850's and the emotionalism of the Civil War. After the great migration of Jews from eastern Europe to the city anti-Semitism became increasingly apparent and led to the formation of the Jewish Peddlers Protective Association in 1892. This decade also witnessed the first explicit act of social discrimination involving the Detroit Athletic Club. Overt anti-Semitism in the city created anxiety and apprehension among Detroit's Jewish citizens and led some of them to reevaluate their position as Americans and as Jews. 36 notes. F. Rosenthal

1635. Rockaway, Robert A. "CAUSE FOR RICHUS"; MAGNUS BUTZEL OF DETROIT TO MEYER SAMUEL ISAACS OF NEW YORK: AN EXAMPLE OF NINETEENTH CENTURY AMERICAN JEWISH INSECURITY. *Michigan Jewish Hist. 1974 14(2): 3-5.* Discusses Jewish reluctance in the 19th century to join Jewish organizations which were "international in scope," fearing that it would lead to a questioning of "Jewish loyalty," and possibly be used as a pretext for anti-Semitism. S

1636. Rockaway, Robert A. LOUIS BRANDEIS ON DETROIT. *Michigan Jewish Hist. 1977 17(1): 17-19.* Reprints a letter from Louis Brandeis to his brother Alfred about anti-Semitism in Detroit, 1914.

1637. Rosenfeld, Stephen S. THE POLITICS OF THE JACKSON AMENDMENT: "A PIECE OF POLITICAL BAGGAGE WITH MANY DIFFERENT HANDLES." *Present Tense 1974 1(4): 17-23.* Details the efforts of Senator Henry M. Jackson, supported by American Jews, to attach a free emigration condition to the Nixon administration's bill granting the USSR "most favored nation" status in international trade. S

1638. Silverberg, David. "HEAVENLY DECEPTION": REV. MOON'S HARD SELL. *Present Tense 1976 4(1): 49-56.* Describes the growth and decline of Reverend Sun Myung Moon's Unification Church. Discusses the Moonie experience, deprogramming, the Divine Principle, anti-Semitism, Jewish involvement and reaction. Primary and secondary sources; 5 photos. R. B. Mendel

1639. Simms, Adam. A BATTLE IN THE AIR: DETROIT'S JEWS ANSWER FATHER COUGHLIN. *Michigan Jewish Hist. 1978 18(2): 7-13.* A memorandum written in 1939 by executive director William I. Boxerman outlines the initial stages of the Jewish Community Council's radio campaign against Charles Edward Coughlin's anti-Semitism.

1640. Steinberg, Jacob. THE MOSCOW BOOK FAIR—REVISITED. *Freedom at Issue 1978 (46): 27-30.* Discusses a vitriolic attack made on the Association of Jewish Book Publishers by a Soviet journal following a display of AJBP books at a Moscow book fair, 1977.

1641. Stern, Norton B. and Kramer, William M. ANTI-SEMITISM AND THE JEWISH IMAGE IN THE EARLY WEST. *Western States Jewish Hist. Q. 1974 6(2): 129-140.* A study of California newspapers in the gold rush period; centers on anti-Semitic articles and stories, and Jewish responses to those articles. Primary sources; 21 notes. R. A. Garfinkle

1642. Thurlow, Richard C. THE POWERS OF DARKNESS: CONSPIRACY BELIEF AND POLITICAL STRATEGY. *Patterns of Prejudice [Great Britain] 1978 12(6): 1-12, 23.* The Jewish conspiracy theory, a theme in 20th-century intellectual history, was developed in the

"notorious" document *Protocols of the Elders of Zion,* and was embraced by neofascist and rightist political groups in Great Britain and the United States.

1643. Tsukashima, Ronald Tadao and Montero, Darrel. THE CONTACT HYPOTHESIS: SOCIAL AND ECONOMIC CONTACT AND GENERATIONAL CHANGES IN THE STUDY OF BLACK ANTISEMITISM. *Social Forces 1976 55(1): 149-165.* Studies indicate that respondents experiencing equal-status contact across ethnic lines are more likely to hold tolerant attitudes toward minorities than those not having been exposed to such interaction. The authors build on the thesis by examining (1) responses of blacks reporting equal-status contact with Jews; (2) effects of equal-status contact compared with other types of reported associations with Jews such as perceived economic mistreatment; and (3) possible trends in the shifting effects of both types of reported contact over time. The findings indicate strong support for the contact hypothesis, particularly when equal-status contact is intimate and occurs in a noninstitutional setting. On the other hand, they show that perceived economic mistreatment is strongly related to heightened antipathy towards Jews. Examines trends in the changing effects of these two types of reported contact on anti-Semitism. The younger generation of blacks exhibits a weaker inverse relationship between intimate, equal-status contact and anti-Semitism than do older cohorts. The positive association between perceived economic mistreatment and the dependent variable increases with each younger generation. These findings suggest that there are generational changes taking place in black-white relations. J

1644. Tuerk, Richard. JACOB RIIS AND THE JEWS. *New-York Hist. Soc. Q. 1979 63(3): 178-201.* The great influx of immigrants during 1875-1920's increased opposition in the United States to immigrants in general and Jews in particular. A result was the post-World War I nativism and the restrictive immigration act of 1924. For some, however, the opposite reaction took place; Jacob Riis, an immigrant himself, was one of these. His most famous work, *How the Other Half Lives,* published in 1890, contained much anti-Semitism, for he believed that Jews from Eastern Europe would never be assimilated. Within a decade he was changing his mind and, after another ten years, much of his prejudice had disappeared. He had begun to accept the idea that people could be different but live in harmony and be "good Americans." Primary sources; illus., 5 photos, 42 notes. C. L. Grant

1645. Walker, Sheila S. THE BLACK-JEWISH PARADOX: AMBIVALENCE OF U.S. RACE FEELING. *Patterns of Prejudice [Great Britain] 1973 7(3): 19-24.* Black intellectuals identify closely with Biblical Hebrews and accept Jewish nationalism as a model. Blacks respond to the economically dominant Jews in the ghettos with an anti-Semitism which is really an antiwhite feeling directed at area whites who happen to be mainly Jewish. Based on personal observation and on secondary sources; 11 notes. M. W. Szewczyk

1646. Wiegand, Wayne A. THE LAUCHHEIMER CONTROVERSY: A CASE OF GROUP POLITICAL PRESSURE DURING THE TAFT ADMINISTRATION. *Military Affairs 1976 40(2): 54-59.* Demonstrates the effectiveness of political pressure on the Taft administration in the case of the transfer of Colonel Charles Lauchheimer, a Jewish Marine Corps officer, from Washington, D.C. in 1910. After a dispute between the colonel and the Marine Corps Commandant, a court of inquiry concluded that he had been in Washington too long. Lauchheimer was returned in 1912, a victory for his friends, but there is no concrete evidence to prove that he was the victim of anti-Semitism. Based on primary and secondary sources; 11 notes. A. M. Osur

1647. —. [ANTI-SEMITISM AND CHRISTIAN BELIEFS]. *Am. Sociol. R. 1973 38(1): 33-61.*
Middleton, Russell. DO CHRISTIAN BELIEFS CAUSE ANTISEMITISM?, *pp. 33-52.*
Glock, Charles Y. and Stark, Rodney. DO CHRISTIAN BELIEFS CAUSE ANTI-SEMITISM?—A COMMENT, *pp. 53-59.*
Middleton, Russell. RESPONSE, *pp, 59-61.*
Middleton examines Glock and Stark's contention that certain Christian religious beliefs are causally related to anti-Semitism, using data from a 1964 national survey. Religious orthodoxy proves to be uncorrelated with anti-Semitism at the zero-order. A path analysis reveals that the relation-

ships in the causal sequence hypothesized by Glock and Stark are weak. Furthermore, the influence of religious orthodoxy, religious libertarianism, religious particularism, and religious hostility to the historic Jew is not expressed solely through the intervening step of religious hostility to modern Jews; the coefficents for the direct paths to anti-Semitism are in some cases sizable. The five religious belief variables taken together in a simple additive model account for approximately 15 percent of the variance in anti-Semitism. When socio-economic status, a number of other social attributes, and a number of social psychological traits are held constant, however, the five religious belief variables account uniquely for only 2 percent of the variance in anti-Semitism. Even here one must be cautious in inferring a causal relationship, particularly since some of the religious measures may simply reflect a more general anti-Semitic ideology. A revised model is presented which includes socioeconomic status and social psychological variables.   J

1648.   —.   A GENTILE REPROVES AN ANTI-SEMITE: FRESNO —1893.   *Western States Jewish Hist. Q. 1977 9(4): 299-300.* During a murder trial in Fresno, California, defense lawyer William D. Foote attempted to undermine the testimony of a Jewish prosecution witness by abusing Jews generally. Grove L. Johnson, prosecuting attorney, in offering a rejoinder to Foote's anti-Semitic views, emphasized traditional American religious tolerance and Constitutional rights and privileges. Johnson's speech is quoted at length. 9 notes.   B. S. Porter

1649.   —.   [STOW AND ANTI-SEMITISM].   *Western States Jewish Hist. Q. 1975 7(4): 312-322.*
Stern, Norton B.   LOS ANGELES JEWRY AND STOW'S ANTI-SEMITISM,   *pp. 312-320.* Speaker of the California State Assembly William W. Stow (1824-95) made anti-Semitic remarks during a debate on a Sunday closing law before the legislature. During this debate on 16 March 1855 he showed that he had no sympathy for Jews and that he was ignorant of their role within the state. Within a few days many newspapers throughout the state carried editorials denouncing Stow's remarks.
Shumate, Albert.   OTHER SAN FRANCISCO REACTIONS TO STOW'S REMARKS,   *pp. 321-322.* "This early criticism of the Jewish community in California was quickly refuted. . . ."
                                                                  R. A. Garfinkle and S

1650.   —.   50 YEARS OF THE *AMERICAN MERCURY*.   *Patterns of Prejudice [Great Britain] 1974 8(2): 27-29.* Discusses anti-Semitism and the doctrine of white supremacy in *American Mercury* magazine, 1924-74, and the attitudes of founder Henry Louis Mencken.

Portuguese

1651.   Fontes, Manuel da Costa.   A NEW PORTUGUESE BALLAD COLLECTION FROM CALIFORNIA.   *Western Folklore 1975 34(4): 299-310.* The author describes his work and that of Joanne B. Purcell in collecting traditional ballads among Portuguese immigrants to southern California. He urges more research in this area since the materials immigrants remember are quickly disappearing and "the oral tradition in Portugal itself is weakening." Partial texts of several ballads and a list of 56 ballad variations are included. Based on personal interviews and primary and secondary sources; 24 notes.   S. L. Myres

1652.   Greenfield, Sidney M.   IN SEARCH OF SOCIAL IDENTITY: STRATEGIES OF ETHNIC IDENTITY MANAGEMENT AMONG CAPE VERDEANS IN SOUTHEASTERN MASSACHUSETTS.   *Luso-Brazilian Rev. 1976 13(1): 3-18.* Delineates the major ethnic identity strategies employed by Cape Verdean immigrants to New England. Although immigration began in the mid-19th century, assimilation was delayed until World War II. Maritime occupations allowed continued involvement in Cape Verdean rather than American social life. A part-African and part-Portuguese heritage created racial diversity which influenced the manner in which the larger society viewed the Cape Verdeans. In response, four fluid strategies have developed: Cape Verdean-Portuguese, Cape Verdean-Black, Cape Verdean-African and Cape Verdean-American. Based on secondary sources; 7 notes, biblio.
                                                                  J. M. Walsh

1653.   Monteiro, Lois A.   IMMIGRANTS WITHOUT CARE.   *Society 1977 14(6): 38-43.* Examines perceptions of illness and medical care facilities used by Portuguese immigrants in the Rhode Island area, 1960-75.

1654.   Rogers, Francis M.   THE PORTUGUESE OF SOUTHEASTERN NEW ENGLAND: SUGGESTIONS FOR RESEARCH.   *Luso-Brazilian Rev. 1974 11(1): 3-18.* Suggests potential research topics in Portuguese history and culture as well as immigration, acculturation, and political, social, and cultural contributions of Portuguese immigrants in America, 18th-20th centuries.

1655.   Ussach, Steven Samuel.   THE NEW ENGLAND PORTUGUESE: A PLURAL SOCIETY WITHIN A PLURAL SOCIETY.   *Plural Societies [Netherlands] 1975 6(2): 47-57.* Studies the attitudes of Portuguese immigrants and Portuguese Americans living in southeastern New England toward assimilation and pluralism, 1840-1975.

Rumanian

1656.   Bobango, Gerald J.   THE UNION AND LEAGUE OF ROMANIAN SOCIETIES: AN "ASSIMILATING FORCE" REVIEWED.   *East European Q. 1978 12(1): 85-92.* The Union and League of Romanian Societies was not particularly significant in helping Rumanians assimilate into American society. Most Rumanians did not join, and many returned to the homeland. Covers ca. 1900-39. Based on records of the Union and on published works; 32 notes.   C. R. Lovin

1657.   Netea, Vasile.   ROMANIANS IN AMERICA UP TO 1918. Comité National des Historiens de la République Socialiste de Roumanie. *Nouvelles Études d'Hist.* (Bucharest: Editura Academiei Republicii Socialiste România, 1975): pp. 259-267. Rumanian emigration to the United States became significant ca. 1900. Not until 1903 do the records show the country from which each Rumanian emigrant came; after 1905 there is further breakdown by sex, profession, and cultural background. Rumanians settled in Chicago, Detroit, Pittsburgh, Philadelphia, and especially in new towns in Indiana and Ohio. By World War I they numbered almost 150,000. There were more than 100 economic and cultural societies (the most important ones are listed in order of establishment). The first periodicals were founded in 1904 and the main newspaper, *Românul*, in 1905. By 1916 there were more than 20 publications. During World War I Rumania undertook a number of activities to encourage Rumanian Americans to support its claims on Transylvania and to influence US policy in its interest. 8 notes.   J. D. Falk

Scandinavian

General

1658.   Anderson, Harry H.   SCANDINAVIAN IMMIGRATION IN MILWAUKEE NATURALIZATION RECORDS.   *Milwaukee Hist. 1978 1(1-2): 25-37.* Presents a recent survey of naturalization records of Norwegians, Swedes, and Danes in Milwaukee during 1837-1941 in a discussion of Scandinavian political involvement and community development in Milwaukee.

1659.   Askey, Donald E.; Gage, Gene G.; and Rovinsky, Robert T. NORDIC AREA STUDIES IN NORTH AMERICA: A SURVEY AND DIRECTORY OF THE HUMAN AND MATERIAL RESOURCES.   *Scandinavian Studies 1975 47(2): 109-256.* In separate subsections the authors define their methodology in compiling the data and defend the validity of their results. The first area covered in this survey is the Humanities. Enrollment in the Nordic languages apparently is down but enrollment in non-language courses such as culture, history, and social sciences has risen. There is a slight increase in enrollment in Scandinavian studies majors at all levels. The second area covered is Social Studies. Enrollment in Scandinavian social studies increased by nearly 50% during 1970-73. Includes a directory of scholars and a section on Nordic Library resources in North America. 20 tables, 20 notes.
                                                                  O. W. Ohrvall

1660. Bjarnson, Donald Einer. SWEDISH-FINNISH SETTLE-MENT IN NEW JERSEY IN THE SEVENTEENTH CENTURY. *Swedish Pioneer Hist. Q. 1976 27(4): 238-246.* Swedes and Finns were among the first colonizers of America, settling primarily in the Delaware River Valley during the mid-17th century. The settlement venture seemed doomed from the beginning because of dissension among the promoters over the objectives of the settlement. Another problem was to find people willing to become colonists. During the 17 years of the colony, the usual population was 50-100 inhabitants, and included soldiers and criminals. Incoming colonists often returned home. The final blow was the conflict with the Dutch who had settled the area earlier. Several of the Scandinavian settlers and Scandinavian settlements are discussed. Secondary sources.   C. W. Ohrvall

1661. Bjork, Kenneth O. A PLAN FOR THE FUTURE. *Swedish Pioneer Hist. Q. 1974 25(3/4): 264-270.* The Norwegian-American Historical Association and the Swedish Pioneer Historical Society face problems similar to those of the Danish and Finnish societies. Many projects await research and publication, such as biographies, the roles of institutions, and translations. Future accomplishment will require cooperation.   K. J. Puffer

1662. Coffey, James D. SCANDINAVIANS. *Hist. J. of Western Massachusetts Supplement 1976: 80-83.* Swedes and Norwegians participated in the American Revolution as sailors and with the French army. They also had several notable political leaders, including John Morton and John Hanson. Notes.   W. H. Mulligan, Jr.

1663. Dunlevy, James A. and Gemery, Henry A. SOME ADDITIONAL EVIDENCE ON SETTLEMENT PATTERNS OF SCANDINAVIAN MIGRANTS TO THE UNITED STATES: DYNAMICS AND THE ROLE OF FAMILY AND FRIENDS. *Scandinavian Econ. Hist. Rev. [Denmark] 1976 24(2): 143-152.* Scandinavian settlement patterns were discussed by Richard K. Vedder and Lowell E. Gallaway in *Scandinavian Economic History Review* 1970 18(2): 159-176. Through the use of the declaration of destination, clearer evidence of the influence of family and friends can be discerned. Varieties of tests are available and these show results that parallel and complement the Vedder-Gallaway model. Friends and family influenced settlement location.   R. E. Lindgren

1664. Ekman, Ernst. WETTERMAN AND THE SCANDINAVIAN SOCIETY OF SAN FRANCISCO. *Swedish Pioneer Hist. Q. 1974 25(2): 87-102.* August Wetterman (1828-1917) came to California during the Gold Rush. His history of the Scandinavian Society now is in the state library. Karl Wilhelm Lübeck was the leader in forming *Det Scandinaviska Sällskapet i San Francisco*, a social and benevolent organization. Based on Wetterman's *History and Review of the Scandinavian Society of San Francisco* (San Francisco: 1970) and on primary and secondary sources; 34 notes.   K. J. Puffer

1665. Farr, William E. SOLLID WANTS TO SEE YOU: GEORGE SOLLID, HOMESTEAD LOCATOR. *Montana 1979 29(2): 16-27.* During 1909-28, George Sollid was a homestead locator at Dutton, Montana. His activities were part of the homestead rush which swept Montana during 1909-17. For $25, Sollid helped prospective homesteaders locate a 320-acre parcel of public land and complete all the necessary forms to claim it under provisions of the Enlarged Homestead Act of 1909. In partnership with his brother Samuel, George Sollid formed the Sollid Land Company, purchased the Dutton Townsite, and began promoting the region. Sollid had particular success recruiting Scandinavian homesteaders. During his career, Sollid settled approximately 80% of the farmers in the Dutton region. Based on interviews with George Sollid, newspapers, and secondary sources; 14 illus., biblio.   R. C. Myers

1666. Hale, Frederick. NORDIC IMMIGRATION: THE NEW PURITANS? *Swedish Pioneer Hist. Q. 1977 28(1): 27-44.* Examines the relations between the established American churches and the Nordic immigrant churches, and the impact of the former on the development and integration of the latter during the second half of the 19th century. Uses the Congregationalist press and the eastern Lutheran press as a basis for examination. The reception of Nordic immigrants was generally favorable, in part due to the similarity of Protestant beliefs. 56 notes.   C. W. Ohrvall

1667. Krontoft, Torben. FACTORS IN ASSIMILATION: A COMPARATIVE STUDY. *Norwegian-American Studies 1974 26: 184-205.* Compares the Danes' and Norwegians' speed of assimilation, comparing factors including the use of English, dress, church attendance, eating and drinking habits, organization of farms, schools, ethnic associations, family traditions, national consciousness, and change in social status (especially among second and later generations), 19th and 20th centuries. Both groups assimilated with a fair amount of ease, but the Norwegians maintained a stronger ethnic identity because of their tendency to settle in communities composed primarily of their own ethnic stock. 9 tables, 61 notes.   G. A. Hewlett

1668. Nelson, Edward O. RECOLLECTIONS OF THE SALVATION ARMY'S SCANDINAVIAN CORPS. *Swedish Pioneer Hist. Q. 1978 29(4): 257-276.* The author came to America from Sweden in 1928. He served in the Salvation Army from 1929 until he retired as a Lieutenant Colonel in 1975. Based on his own experiences, on the experiences of his friends who were also in the "wheel within a wheel" which was the *Frälsningsarmén* or Scandinavia Corps of the Salvation Army, and on books and articles written on the Corps. The Corps, begun in Brooklyn in 1877, at its height had 80 corps wherever Scandinavians, especially Swedes, were located. 4 photos.   C. W. Ohrvall

1669. Nicpon, Philip. SCANDINAVIAN-AMERICANS IN ALASKA. *Am. Scandinavian Rev. 1974 62(3): 271-284.* Surveys the contributions of several Alaskan leaders of Scandinavian descent in the development of Alaska, with brief biographical sketches. Illus., 10 photos.   J. G. Smoot

1670. Poulson, Richard C. FOLK MATERIAL CULTURE OF THE SANPETE-SEVIER AREA: TODAY'S REFLECTIONS OF A REGION'S PAST. *Utah Hist. Q. 1979 47(2): 130-147.* Symbolic artifacts represent more than houses, barns, gravestones, or wagons. They represent latent desires, aspirations, and hostilities which are constantly changing according to societal pressures, family wants and needs, religion, and other influences that change our basic perception of reality. In the Sanpete-Sevier region of Utah, severe acculturation of Scandinavians led to a highly structured loss of symbols (vernacular regression) in material folk culture. Symbols used in burial and housing are those of the dominant English-Mormon culture. 24 illus., 34 notes.   J. L. Hazelton

1671. Rice, Cindy. SPRING CITY: A LOOK AT A NINE-TEENTH-CENTURY MORMON VILLAGE. *Utah Hist. Q. 1975 43(3): 260-277.* Spring City, Utah, is a prototype of the Mormon village, with large lots, broad streets in a typical grid system oriented to the compass points, and its use of local building materials. It is unique in having so many original structures unchanged, its Scandinavian building traditions, and the absence of large commercial establishments. It has all the ingredients needed for an insight into rural life in a 19th-century Mormon village. It merits preservation. Based on primary and secondary sources; 10 illus., 40 notes.   J. L. Hazelton

1672. Skårdal, Dorothy Burton. SCANDINAVIAN-AMERICAN LITERATURE: A FRONTIER FOR RESEARCH. *Swedish Pioneer Hist. Q. 1977 28(4): 237-251.* Scandinavian-American literature was primarily written by immigrants for fellow immigrants. Only occasionally were authors published in their home country. Points out that there are relatively few writers, but the volume and diversity of their work was amazing. The hundreds of Scandinavian-American newspapers and magazines of the 1800's provided a market for these writers and their products. Book publishers began in the 1870's and groups founded their own publishing houses. Describes the literary products as a source of material for social history research and suggests the cooperation of immigration historians and specialists in Scandinavian studies to prepare a literary history. Photo, 22 notes.   C. W. Ohrvall

1673. Strong, C. Peter. THE FOUNDATION'S STORY. *Scandinavian Rev. 1976 64(2): 38-45.* Gives an account of the American-Scandinavian Foundation. Founded in 1911, the foundation is a major Scandinavian cultural force in the United States. It publishes the *Scandinavian Review*, has printed some 150 books, has regional chapters of members, and supports exchange students. Illus.   J. G. Smoot

1674. Tiblin, Mariann and Welsch, Erwin K., ed. AMERICAN-SCANDINAVIAN BIBLIOGRAPHY FOR 1972. *Scandinavian Studies 1973 45(4): 324-375.* Classifications include: General Bibliography, Language, Literature, Social Sciences, History, and a subdivision, Scandinavians in the US. Arrangement within each class is by country. Mostly unannotated references are provided for books published in Scandinavia. Includes books, parts of books, periodical articles, book reviews, and dissertations published in the United States and Canada, and a few English publications published abroad.   E. P. Stickney

1675. Varg, Paul A., ed. REPORT OF COUNT CARL LEWENHAUPT ON SWEDISH-NORWEGIAN IMMIGRATION IN 1870. *Swedish Pioneer Hist. Q. 1979 30(1): 5-24.* Count Carl Lewenhaupt was acting chargé d'affaires in the Swedish legation in Washington in 1870. This report was made from information he collected on a trip to Minnesota and from correspondence with consuls and vice-consuls. In addition, he carried on an extensive correspondence with American authorities. The report was sent to the Foreign Ministry in Stockholm and came to the attention of General C. C. Andrews, American minister to Sweden and Norway, who was favorably impressed and forwarded a translation to Washington. It was published in the Executive Documents of the House of Representatives, 42nd Congress, 2nd Session (vol. 1502, pp. 794-802). The report, reprinted here, contains a wealth of factual detail concerning the problems facing the immigrant.   C. W. Ohrvall

1676. Webster, Janice Reiff. DOMESTICATION AND AMERICANIZATION: SCANDINAVIAN WOMEN IN SEATTLE, 1888 TO 1900. *J. of Urban Hist. 1978 4(3): 275-290.* Two major processes affected Scandinavian women in Seattle, domestication and Americanization. These changes were stimulated by the fact that Seattle during this period was a boom town and that most Scandinavians had already been partly acculturated during earlier eastern residences. Table, 51 notes.   T. W. Smith

1677. Westerberg, Wesley M. ETHNICITY AND THE FREE CHURCHES. *Swedish Pioneer Hist. Q. 1973 24(4): 231-237.* All the groups in the free church movement in the Scandinavian population of America have undergone the same transitions. Swedish Methodism was never independent of the parent church. The Swedish Baptist Church became an avowedly American denomination. The Evangelical Free Church of America developed out of two groups which merged in 1950 to become an American denomination. The Salvation Army and the Pentecostal churches are now the only segments of the free church movement carrying on a deliberate ministry to Scandinavians. The Evangelical Covenant Church of America remains reasonably loyal to their ethnic origin and desirous of maintaining it. The newspapers serving the memberships of these churches were one of the great influences in terms of ethnicity. There is nothing comparable for the present generation. Based on personal experience.   K. J. Puffer

1678. Wilson, William A. FOLKLORE OF UTAH'S LITTLE SCANDINAVIA. *Utah Hist. Q. 1979 47(2): 148-166.* The Sanpete-Sevier region of Utah has produced a distinctive body of folklore, almost all growing out of the Mormon experience. Four main themes (settlement, temple building, polygamy, and Scandinavian immigrant tales) reflect dominant attitudes, values, and concerns. 8 illus., 50 notes.   J. L. Hazelton

Danish

1679. Anderson, C. LeRoy. THE SCATTERED MORRISITES. *Montana 1976 26(4): 52-69.* A fragment of the Morrisite group fled Utah in 1862 and settled in Montana's Deer Lodge Valley. The small membership dwindled as rival leaders struggled for supremacy. By 1954, at the death of aged President George Johnson, the Montana Morrisite community had disappeared. Some descendants live in the area, and the church building still stands. Based on contemporary letters and accounts. Illus.   S. R. Davison

1680. Collier, Malcolm. JENS JENSEN AND COLUMBUS PARK. *Chicago Hist. 1975-76 4(4): 225-234.* Retraces the life and career as park designer and superintendent of West Parks, Chicago, of Danish immigrant Jens Jensen, who designed Columbus Park.

1681. Friedman, Philip S. A DANISH-AMERICAN BIBLIOGRAPHY. *Scandinavian Studies 1976 48(4): 441-444.* A listing (alphabetical by author) of articles, pamphlets, books, etc., on Danish Americans. These include material written and/or published in Denmark and America, in English and Danish.   C. W. Ohrvall

1682. Howard, G. M. MEN, MOTIVES, AND MISUNDERSTANDINGS: A NEW LOOK AT THE MORRISITE WAR OF 1862. *Utah Hist. Q. 1976 44(2): 112-132.* Ostensibly, the issue was law enforcement in the Morrisite War of 1862, but politics and religion were involved. At stake was the unity and leadership of Utah territory. Joseph Morris's (1824-62) predominantly Danish followers were unfamiliar with American law and disenchanted with Mormon orthodoxy. When Robert T. Burton marched a federal posse on Kingston Fort, Morrisites mistakenly thought Mormons were attacking in a religious war. Needless anguish, bloodshed, and lasting scars resulted. Primary and secondary sources; 7 illus., 32 notes.   J. L. Hazelton

1683. Marzolf, Marion. THE PIONEER DANISH PRESS IN MIDWEST AMERICA 1870-1900. *Scandinavian Studies 1976 48(4): 426-440.* Some 360,039 Danes settled in the United States after 1820. Immigrant newspapers tell the story of their assimilation. The papers at first balanced news from the homeland with news of the new land. Gradually the papers emphasized news of Danish American affairs. As language skills declined, so did the newspapers; after World War II only two remained. Describes some of the most famous early papers and printers. These include *Den Danske Pioneer,* published in Omaha, Nebraska, by Sophus F. Neble, and the publishing empire of Christian Rasmussen in Minneapolis. Because the Danish imigrants rapidly assimilated, it is surprising that the Danish press survived. Based on the author's dissertation, "The Danish-Language Press in America" (U. of Michigan, 1972). 47 notes.   C. W. Ohrvall

1684. Neal, Harry Edward. DANISH LEGACY IN AMERICA. *Scandinavian Rev. 1976 64(1): 55-63.* Reviews Danish immigration to and settlement in the United States, especially in Wisconsin. Refers to Dana College, founded by Danish Americans, and describes the achievements of outstanding immigrants, including those of journalist Jacob Riis (1849-1914) and sculptor Gutzon Borglum (1871-1941).   J. G. Smoot

1685. Nelson, Frank G. A DANISH ACCOUNT OF MISSOURI IN 1839. *Missouri Hist. Soc. Bull. 1977 33(4): 265-268.* Reprints, in English translation, a letter published in the 30 September 1839 issue of *Christianssandsposten,* a provincial Norwegian newspaper. The writer, an unidentified Danish immigrant to America, described his travels to Florida and then to Missouri where he acquired a farm. The clues in the letter suggest that the author settled in Ste. Genevieve County. Sketch, 7 notes.   H. T. Lovin

1686. Norseng, Mary Kay. CLEMENS PETERSEN IN AMERICA. *Scandinavian Studies 1976 48(4): 384-404.* Clemens Petersen (1834-1918) was the "feared dictator" of cultural and intellectual life of Denmark and Norway during the 1860's, as the leading critic for Copenhagen's newspaper, *Faedrelandet.* In his zeal to revitalize literature he was often ruthless, arrogant, and intolerant. After an incident he left Copenhagen in 1869, stayed in Vienna, and then spent the next 34 years in the United States. He moved back and forth between New York City and Chicago, writing for Scandinavian newspapers. His life in America was plagued by rootlessness, lack of recognition, and poverty. He returned to Denmark in 1904. Petersen's contribution to Danish literary criticism is still not fully understood. Based in part on correspondence with Bjørnstjerne Bjørnson; 62 notes.   C. W. Ohrvall

1687. Reagh, Jean. THEY CAME TO SOLVANG. *Westways 1975 67(3): 30-33.* The dream of a western educational center motivated the settlement of the Danish American community and the founding of Atterdag College in Solvang, California, in the early 20th century.   S

1688. Rinehart, Robert. DENMARK GETS THE NEWS OF '76. *Scandinavian Rev. 1976 64(2): 5-14.* Tells of the early printing of the Declaration of Independence in Denmark and Danish reaction to American independence. There was much popular support for the colonies but the king's ministers were divided. Count Andreas Peter von Bernstorff, foreign minister, felt that American independence would threaten the Virgin Islands, Danish trade in Europe, disrupt the commercial credit system, and challenge Denmark's collection of Sound Dues. During the war Danish trade greatly increased. Describes Danish diplomacy related to Great Britain and the treaty of 1780, the League of Armed Neutrality, the three Bergen prizes taken by one of John Paul Jones's ships, and efforts to negotiate a treaty with the United States. Includes a sketch of Christian Febiger, the most prominent Dane in the American Army, and mentions John Paul Jones's efforts after the war to gain compensation for the Bergen prizes. Illus.

J. G. Smoot

1689. Skårdal, Dorothy Burton. DANISH AMERICAN LITERATURE: A CALL TO ACTION. *Scandinavian Studies 1976 48(4): 405-425.* Regrets that no broad survey of Danish American literature is available for study, and calls for action in this area with such rich, varied, and extensive research sources. This material is in three main archives: at Grand View College, Des Moines, Iowa; Dana College, Blair, Nebraska; and Udvandrerarkivet in Aalborg, Denmark, the oldest emigrant archive in Scandinavia. Examines the forms of literature and the sources and problems of research. Discusses several famous Danish American authors and their principal works. 30 notes.

C. W. Ohrvall

1690. Skarsten, Trygve R. DANISH CONTRIBUTIONS TO RELIGION IN AMERICA. *Lutheran Q. 1973 25(1): 42-53.* History of Danish Lutherans in the United States, 1619-1973, emphasizing the ministries of Vilhelm Beck (1829-1901) of the Inner Mission Movement and N. F. S. Grundtvig (d. 1872).

S

Finnish (including Swedish Finns)

1691. Gedicks, Al. ETHNICITY, CLASS SOLIDARITY, AND LABOR RADICALISM AMONG FINNISH IMMIGRANTS IN MICHIGAN COPPER COUNTRY. *Pol. and Soc. 1977 7(2): 127-156.* Case study of the growth of class consciousness among Finnish immigrants to the Michigan copper region. Examines the antecedents of labor radicalism among the Finnish miners during 1890-1920 and the strategies of the mining companies for the maintenance of a stable labor force. Primary and secondary sources; map, 106 notes.

D. G. Nielson

1692. Gedicks, Al. THE SOCIAL ORIGINS OF RADICALISM AMONG FINNISH IMMIGRANTS IN MIDWEST MINING COMMUNITIES. *Rev. of Radical Pol. Econ. 1976 8(3): 1-31.* Examines the reactions of Finnish and Swedish immigrants to the mining areas of Michigan, Wisconsin, and Minnesota, 1865-1920.

1693. Hoglund, A. William. FINNISH IMMIGRANT FICTION AND ITS EVOLUTION FROM ROMANTICISM TO REALISM IN THE UNITED STATES, 1885-1925. *U. of Turku, Inst. of General Hist. Publ. [Finland] 1977 9: 15-30.* Finnish American publishers distributed at first mainly romantic fiction, "wooing young adult readers who represented the majority of immigrants." Though most novelists defended moral values, their aim was to entertain rather than to inculcate morality. After the turn of the century novels portrayed farmers as well as agricultural laborers among the victims of class exploitation by the bourgeoisie. During 1885-1925 the theme of the novelists was the concern of immigrants seeking better economic opportunities in America. 48 notes.

E. P. Stickney

1694. Kaups, Matti. A FINNISH SAVUSAUNA IN MINNESOTA. *Minnesota Hist. 1976 45(1): 11-20.* The Finnish Savusauna was a cultural transplant with several different traditions. Its chief purpose was to bathe and perspire, but it also served as summer sleeping quarters, a place for wet cupping, a maternity ward, and a laundry. Construction techniques are described in detail. Based on interviews, inspections of the remains of savusauna, and published sources; 12 illus., 26 notes.

S. S. Sprague

1695. Kero, Reino. SUOMALAISTEN SIIRTOLAISTEN "VAPAA AMERIKKA" ["Free America" and the Finnish immigrants]. *Turun Hist. Arkisto [Finland] 1975 30: 71-81.* In the educated circles of Finland, the social conditions in the United States in the 1850's appeared, in comparison with those in Finland, exemplary. Editorials in Finnish newspapers for the following two decades exalted the social conditions of the United States and spoke in glowing terms of free America, but failed to specify what their idolized American freedom consisted of. When Finnish emigration to the United States reached mass proportions in the 1870's, the authorities began to fear that it would never be possible to complete the settlement of Finland. This appears to be one of the reasons for the attitude toward the United States becoming more negative; newspaper editorials continued along these lines into the beginning of the 20th century. Among prospective emigrants, however, the term 'free America' continued to be used, and may have spurred those who were discontented with the social conditions in Finland to leave the country. However, American society did not embrace newly-arriving immigrants, and the disillusioned Finnish-American immigrants were now using the term in a new sense, to express their sarcasm at American society.

J

1696. Kostiainen, Auvo. AINO KUUSINEN KOMINTERNIN ASIAMIEHENÄ AMERIKASSA [Aino Kuusinen as a Comintern agent in America]. *Turun Hist. Arkisto [Finland] 1975 30: 234-256.* Aino Kuusinen, the second wife of the international Communist leader Otto Wille Kuusinen, spent the period from spring 1930 to summer 1933 in the United States. The reason for her coming to the United States appears to have been differences of opinion between the Communist Party of the United States and the Finnish-American Communists, which had been going on for several years. In her capacity as a Comintern emissary, Aino Kuusinen-Morton soon took over a leading position in the communist Finnish Workers' Federation. Under the name of A. Morton, she began to write articles for the theoretical journal *Viesti*, and became its editor. It would appear that Aino Kuusinen-Morton was not a fully-authorized agent of the Comintern, but that she acquired considerable authority among the Finnish-American Communists. She gradually took over control of the Finnish Workers' Federation, and thus came into conflict with both Henry Puro and the American Communist leaders. These differences of opinion received considerable publicity in the press of the Finnish-American labor movement. Eventually the Finnish-American Communists and the Party leadership appealed to the Comintern to have Aino Kuusinen withdrawn, and she was soon afterwards ordered back to Moscow.

J

1697. Kostiainen, Auvo. AMERIKANSUOMALAISTEN KUVA: TYÖTTÖMYYSTYÖNÄ Ą TALLENNETTUA MINNESOTAN SUOMALAISTEN HISTORIAA [The portrait of Finnish Americans: Materials on the Minnesota Finns collected by the WPA Writers' Project]. *Turun Hist. Arkisto [Finland] 1976 31: 414-431.* Deals with the materials on the Finns preserved at the Minnesota Historical Society, St. Paul, Minnesota. The workers of the Writers' Project interviewed 143 Finnish-Americans, of whom 28 were second generation Finnish-Americans born in the United States. The Finnish-Americans were asked their place and date of birth, the time of arrival in America, the reasons for emigrating, their movements inside the United States, occupation, education, social activities and so on. A few as yet unstudied topics could be researched with the help of these interviews; namely the mobility of Finnish-Americans and occupational changes of the immigrants during these recent decades. The Minnesota Finns seem to have been relatively mobile, because half of them had previously lived in other parts of the United States. The occupational changes are also well described: many immigrants came to work in the mines and lumbering industry, but when interviewed in the late 1930's only a few of them still worked in the mines, there occurred a great diversification of occupations in benefit of services, business, and farming.

J

1698. Kostiainen, Auvo. FEATURES OF FINNISH-AMERICAN PUBLISHING. *U. of Turku, Inst. of General Hist. Publ. [Finland] 1977 9: 54-70.* The only bibliographical work on Finnish American publishing to appear so far in the United States is John I. Kolehmainen's *The Finns in America—A Bibliographical Guide to Their History* (Hancock, Michigan, 1947) based on two collections, those in the Emigration History Research Center of the University of Turku and in the Immigration History Research Center of the University of Minnesota in St. Paul. Publishing activity was mainly concentrated on newspapers. The Finnish-American publishers dealt either in religious, temperance, labor, or other literature. Hancock, Michigan, the seat of the Suomi Synod in 1890 was the seat of publication of 111 books and pamphlets. In Duluth several publishers produced largely for labor and the Industrial Workers of the

World (IWW). The small number of Finnish-speaking people in the United States (300,000) caused publishers in the labor field to collaborate and rationalize their business operations and costs. Table, 45 notes.

E. P. Stickney

1699. Kukkonen, Walter J. THE MINISTRY OF ENABLING: THE FINNISH TRADITION IN THE LUTHERAN CHURCH IN AMERICA. *Lutheran Q. 1976 28(4): 331-351.* Describes the importance of the Finnish tradition of spiritual faith to the contemporary Lutheran Church. The tradition has several characteristics: close relationship between the institutional church and spiritual movements among the people; the Bible as the sole repository of the word of God; the nature of faith as inward knowledge of Jesus Christ; and the existence of small groups containing those who love Christ. This tradition can be extremely valuable to the Lutheran Church in America in reaching those outside the denomination and helping people to understand the importance of repentance and self-discovery. Based on secondary sources; 11 notes.

J. A. Kicklighter

1700. Lockwood, Yvonne R. THE SAUNA: AN EXPRESSION OF FINNISH-AMERICAN IDENTITY. *Western Folklore 1977 36(1): 71-84.* Examines the traditional and present use of the sauna as an element of Finnish-American culture. Despite changes in its ritual use, "the sauna is one of the most viable expressions of Finnish-American identity [and] . . . a ritualized enactment of cultural expression." Based on primary and secondary sources and on interviews; 33 notes.

S. L. Myres

1701. Luodesmeri, Varpu. AMERIKANSUOMALAISTEN TYÖVÄENJÄRJESTÖJEN SUHTAUTUMINEN SUOMESTA VUODEN 1918 SODAN JÄLKEEN TULLEISIIN SIIRTOLAISIIN: "HILJAN SUOMESTA TULLEITTEN TUTKIJAKOMITEAT" [The attitudes of the Finnish American workers' movement toward immigrants coming from Finland after the 1918 war: the "Committees of examination of recent arrivals from Finland"]. *Turun Hist. Arkisto [Finland] 1974 29: 63-113.* Describes radical labor organizations of Finnish immigrants in the United States and Canada. Recent immigrants were screened to determine their roles in the 1918 Finnish civil war before that person was allowed to join the local organization. At least 68 local committees were established, ceasing in the United States after 1924, but continuing longer in Canada. Based on newspapers, manuscripts and interviews collected at Turku University, Finland; map, 195 notes, English summary.

R. G. Selleck

1702. McLean, Mildred Evans. RECOLLECTIONS OF DEEP RIVER. *Pacific Northwest Q. 1979 70(3): 98-109.* Records the reminiscences of a young Nebraska woman who in 1913 accepted a one year teaching job in a one room schoolhouse in southwestern Washington state. She recalls both the problems and pleasures found in this remote Finnish logging settlement which lacked electricity, shopping facilities, and easy access to the outside world. She also describes brief trips to the larger towns of Astoria and South Bend where movies and window browsing marked important diversions from the isolated life. 10 photos, 2 maps.

M. L. Tate

1703. Moyne, Ernest J. CHARLES LINN, FINNISH-SWEDISH BUSINESSMAN, BANKER, AND INDUSTRIALIST IN NINETEENTH-CENTURY ALABAMA. *Swedish Pioneer Hist. Q. 1977 28(1): 97-105.* In *The Land of Thor* (New York, 1867), J. Ross Browne tells of meeting a Finnish supporter of the South in Finland during the Civil War. He turned out to be a Finnish American who had lived in Montgomery, Alabama, for 25 years and was visiting his homeland. Describes this Finn, Charles Linn, as a "nice old gentleman" who did not advocate slavery but was interested in the economic advancement of his adopted state and the South. 38 notes.

C. W. Ohrvall

1704. Myhrman, Anders. SELMA JOSEFINA BORG: FINLAND: SWEDISH MUSICIAN, LECTURER, AND CHAMPION OF WOMEN'S RIGHTS. *Swedish Pioneer Hist. Q. 1979 30(1): 25-34.* Selma Josefina Borg was born in Gamlarkarleby, Finland, in 1838, the youngest of nine children in an apparently well-to-do middle-class family. She studied music in Finland, Sweden, and Switzerland. She taught music in Helsinki for some years before coming in 1864 to Philadelphia, where she established herself as a private music and language teacher. In collabora-

tion with Marie A. Brown, she began translating current Swedish works into English. Borg joined a women's committee formed to promote the Centennial Exposition of 1876 in Philadelphia and returned to Finland in 1875 to arouse interest and possibly participation in the celebration. She had, by this time, become a champion of the rights of women and most of her lectures dealt with developments and conditions in America. Describes her lecture tour. Returning to America, she became well known as a musician and speaker on women's rights.

C. W. Ohrvall

1705. Ollila, Douglas J., Jr. A TIME OF GLORY: FINNISH-AMERICAN RADICAL INDUSTRIAL UNIONISM, 1914-1917. *U. of Turku, Inst. of General Hist. Publ. [Finland] 1977 9: 31-53.* The industrial unionists in 1916 became heavily involved in the great Mesabi Iron Range strikes in Minnesota which Finnish radicals viewed as "a time of glory." But instead of ushering in the destruction of American capitalism, it was short-lived. Describes the stabilization of the Finnish-American radical industrial union movement, the evolution of its political-economic Marxist orientation to pure economic Marxism, and "an analysis of the ethnic factors related to the Mesabi strike and the ensuing challenge to the lumber industry which precipitated the eventual downfall of the IWW." Primary sources; 87 notes.

E. P. Stickney

1706. Paananen, Eloise Engle. FINNS FROM ALASKA TO FLORIDA. *Scandinavian Rev. 1976 64(1): 16-26.* Reviews the immigration history of Finns to the United States. In colonial Delaware and Pennsylvania they showed settlers how to build the notched log cabin. In Michigan they were miners. In the Great Lakes states they were farmers. They also settled in Alaska and Florida. Mentions contributions of Finns in art, architecture, and engineering, including those of sculptor Kalervo Kallio (1909-60) and architect Eero Saarinen (1910-61). Illus.

J. G. Smoot

1707. Pedersen, Elsa and Pierce, Richard A. PORT AXEL. *Alaska J. 1976 6(2): 113-117.* Port Axel was a paper town to be developed by the Alaska Colonization and Development Company headed by Axel Gustaf Hornborg (d. 1905). Describes the plans for the town, which was to house Finnish immigrants, and the activities of Adam Widenius, the company's agent at the town site. Discusses Widenius's suggestions for development of coal, oil, fishing, guano, and farming.

E. E. Eminhizer

1708. Virtanen, Keijo. THE INFLUENCE OF THE AUTOMOTIVE INDUSTRY ON THE ETHNIC PICTURE OF DETROIT, MICHIGAN, 1900-1940. *U. of Turku, Inst. of General Hist. Publ. [Finland] 1977 9: 71-88.* During 1910-30 the automotive industry drew the labor it needed largely from outside areas rather than from the immigrant communities already established in Detroit. The foreign-born population underwent its most vigorous increase at this time. Social activity among the Finns living in Detroit, despite its late start, developed fairly vigorously; its inception was clearly bound up with the progress of the automotive industry. Statistics show that half of the Finns who had arrived in the United States after 1916 and resided in Detroit had made the journey from Finland straight to Detroit, the others having first lived in some other locality in the United States. Map, fig., 5 tables, 36 notes.

E. P. Stickney

1709. Virtanen, Keijo. THE MIGRATION OF FINNISH-AMERICANS TO FLORIDA AFTER WORLD WAR II. *Turun Hist. Arkisto [Finland] 1976 31: 432-445.* Examines the growth of Finnish American settlement in Florida from the 1940's to the present. Most migrants have been older people of retirement age. Based on church records, US Census data, and data collected at the University of Turku, Finland; map, 3 tables, 29 notes.

R. G. Selleck

1710. Virtanen, Reino. THE FINNISH LANGUAGE IN AMERICA. *Scandinavian Studies 1979 51(2): 146-161.* The author, a second-generation Finnish American, discusses the new awareness of the treasures contained in preserving languages spoken by immigrants to America, especially Finnish. He relates the dispersion pattern of Finnish immigrants and compares English and Finnish phonology. 31 notes.

C. W. Ohrvall

1711. Wargelin, Raymond W. CONFRONTATION OF MARXIST RADICALISM WITH THE FINNISH LUTHERAN CHURCH IN FINLAND AND ON THE NORTH AMERICAN CONTINENT. *Lutheran Q. 1976 28(4): 361-377.* Both at home in Finland and in North America where they have immigrated, Finns have been divided by their adherence to Lutheranism and Marxist socialism. As early as the late nineteenth century, the division became overt as Finnish Marxists attacked the Lutheran Church and its hierarchy in Finland. This situation is now critical because many Finnish governmental officials today are either avowed Marxists or sympathetic to the ideology. In North America, Finns found themselves separated by the same issue with each side competing for adherents and using whatever methods possible to gain them. Today, however, both in Finland and North America, Finnish Lutherans are attempting to maintain a realistic dialogue with the Marxists, while appreciating the common concern of both for human well-being. The Church's concern for human economic improvement may serve to end the traditional alienation of working people from religion. Secondary sources; 53 notes.
J. A. Kicklighter

Icelandic

1712. Bjornson, Valdimar. ICELANDERS IN THE UNITED STATES. *Scandinavian Rev. 1976 64(3): 39-41.* Briefly surveys the Icelandic settlements in Utah, Wisconsin, Minnesota, and South Dakota. Mentions some leading Icelandic people in the United States. In the 1960 census, there were 9,023 people of Icelandic descent widely dispersed in the United States. Illus.
J. G. Smoot

1713. Tate, George A. HALLDÓR LAXNESS, THE MORMONS AND THE PROMISED LAND. *Dialogue 1978 11(2): 25-37.* Halldór Laxness, the Icelandic novelist who won the Nobel Prize in 1955 for fiction based on his native literary heritage, completed *Paradise Reclaimed* in 1960, a novel based on the experiences of Eiríkur á Brúnum (1832-1900). Brúnum, an Icelander, converted to Mormonism and spent eight years in Utah before he rejected it and returned to Iceland. Laxness chooses to ignore the renunciation of the church, focusing instead on his fictional hero's ideological odyssey in search of utopia. The mood of the novel is a mixture of melancholy over lost innocence and ironic humor. A paper read at the second annual meeting of the Association for Mormon Letters, 8 October 1977. Based on the novel, literary criticism, and correspondence with Laxness; 51 notes.
C. B. Schulz

Norwegian

1714. Anderson, Avis R., ed. PASTOR ON THE PRAIRIE. *Montana 1974 24(1): 36-54.* Biography of Christian Scriver Thorpe (1883-1968), a pastor of the Norwegian Lutheran Church in eastern Montana. His letters 1906-08 reveal many hardships of life on that frontier.
S. R. Davison

1715. Anderson, Harry H. NORWEGIAN SHIPBUILDING IN EARLY MILWAUKEE. *Milwaukee Hist. 1978 1(3-4): 81-104.* Traces the participation of Norwegian Americans in shipbuilding, ship ownership, and related industry during the 19th century in Milwaukee.

1716. Arndt, Karl J. R. GEORGE RAPP'S HARMONISTS AND THE BEGINNINGS OF NORWEGIAN MIGRATION TO AMERICA. *Western Pennsylvania Hist. Mag. 1977 60(3): 241-264.* Describes George Rapp's settlements of Norwegian immigrants in Harmony, Pennsylvania, and New Harmony, Indiana, 1816-26, and their letters home to relatives, friends, and interested parties in Norway whom they encouraged to emigrate.

1717. Bern, Enid, ed. THEY HAD A WONDERFUL TIME: THE HOMESTEADING LETTERS OF ANN AND ETHEL ERICKSON. *North Dakota Hist. 1978 45(4): 4-31.* The Erickson sisters homesteaded in Hettinger County, North Dakota, in 1910 and 1911. Their correspondence with their parents in Iowa reveals the details of daily life on the treeless prairie, including life in a shack, problems with raising poultry, the vagaries of the weather, depredations on garden crops by wandering animals and the self-sufficiency necessitated by being located at the end of the route of supply. Their letters also indicate instances of neighborliness, holiday festivities, dances, socials, etc., and the popularity of single women of marriageable age in a region containing many young bachelors. Based on Erickson family correspondence.
N. Lederer

1718. Bloch-Hoell, Nils E. NORWEGIAN IDEAS OF AMERICAN CHRISTIANITY. *Norwegian Contributions to Am. Studies 1973 4: 69-88.* Norwegian opinions of American Christianity are not homogeneous and generally are vague. "On the whole the school text books of church history have dealt almost exclusively with Europe. Most text books of general history and geography do not even mention the division in the United States between state and church. American Christianity has not been static. Religious life in the U.S. of the 1830s was very different from what it is in 1972. I can see in the present Norwegian ideas of American Christianity the willingness in the Church of Norway to learn from practical church life in the United States." 57 notes.
D. D. Cameron

1719. Canuteson, Richard L. THE KENDALL SETTLEMENT SURVIVED. *Norwegian-American Studies 1977 27: 243-254.* Refutes previous information concerning the demise of the Kendall colony in New York. The colony, the first Norwegian American oasis in America, was not totally depleted by emigration to Illinois in 1834. Census reports of 1820-1925 document the continual (though at times unstable) presence of Norwegian Americans in Kendall. Kendall served both as a place of settlement for newly arrived Norwegians, as well as a stopping off place on the way to points further inland, primarily the Midwest. Based on New York state census reports; 7 notes.
G. A. Hewlett

1720. Chrislock, Carl H. INTRODUCTION: THE HISTORICAL CONTEXT. Lovoll, Odd S., ed. *Cultural Pluralism versus Assimilation: The Views of Waldemar Ager* (Northfield, Minn.: The Norwegian-American Historical Assoc., 1977): 3-37. The first organized emigration from Norway to America was in 1825. Anticipated assimilation into the "melting pot" did not soon occur, as the quickly established church and press promoted a kind of ethnic insulation. By 1900, several Norwegian American societies were operating, Norwegian language was introduced into the educational system, and families, desiring familiarity of their homeland, banded in closely-knit communities. Another reinforcement to thriving ethnicity was the continuing influx of Norwegian immigrants at the turn of the century. But by 1914, assimilation began to take hold. Proclamations by Woodrow Wilson and Theodore Roosevelt that victory in World War I would require "thorough Americans" led to antihyphenism thought. The 1925 centennial celebration commemorating the first organized migration of Norwegians was both a nostalgic look at the past and a proclamation of "full emergence as '100 percent Americans.' " Primary and secondary sources; 53 notes.
S. Robitaille

1721. Chrislock, Carl H. NAME CHANGE AND THE CHURCH, 1918-1920. *Norwegian-American Studies 1977 27: 194-223.* In 1918 the first biennial convention of the Norwegian Lutheran Church of America voted to delete Norwegian from its name due to America's war against Germany and rampant nationalism. Fear of foreigners led Iowa's governor to restrict the use of any foreign language in public or conversation, as well as in education and church services. For many Norwegian Americans, however, the church was their sole connection with their original culture. Since a name change for the church required the approval of two successive conventions, a campaign was begun to deny approval in 1920. While the appendage "Norwegian" indicated to some exclusive membership, the majority argued that it indicated place of origin and further, that the insane wave of nativism sweeping the country should not be allowed to influence pride in ancestry nor to imbue the belief that such recognition necessarily negated support of the adopted country. Hence, the subsequent convention maintained Norwegian and it remained until reorganization of the entire synod in 1946. 56 notes.
G. A. Hewlett

1722. Christianson, J. R. THE GOLDEN AGE OF LUREN. *Palimpsest 1975 56(5): 141-149.* The Luren Quartet, founded in Decorah, Iowa, in 1868, was the first Norwegian-American choral society. Reorganized in 1874, it has had a continuous history since that date. Concerts, travels, contacts with other singing societies, and some Republican political involvement characterized its early activities. Luren was an integral part of the self-conscious Norwegian nationalism which developed after 1905. 4 photos, note.
D. W. Johnson

1723. Christianson, J. R. VESTERHEIM. *Palimpsest 1975 56(5): 131-140.* Norwegian pioneers and energetic young individuals brought the Norwegian-American Museum (Vesterheim) into being in the 1890's in Decorah, Iowa. First established as a repository for relics, books, and manuscripts, the museum has from its inception focused upon the life and material culture of common people rather than upon the art and treasures of the rich. "The idea of a folk museum dedicated to the accomplishments of a single ethnic group was unusual" in the late 19th century. Although the museum was almost left behind by the times during and immediately after World War II, growth has been steady and significant since 1964, when it became a non-profit corporation. Illus., 14 photos.
D. W. Johnson

1724. DeQuille, Dan. SNOWSHOE THOMPSON. *Nevada Hist. Rev. 1974 2(2): 44-73.* Reprint of an 1886 article on the life and times of John A. "Snowshoe" Thompson (1827-76), famous mail carrier of the High Sierras, who crossed the mountains to deliver mail in winter on a pair of home-made skis for over 20 years. S

1725. Gaster, Patricia, ed. HOGAN OUREN IN NEBRASKA AND COLORADO, 1861-1866. *Nebraska Hist. 1977 58(2): 219-249.* Hogan Ouren left Norway for Canada in 1853. After working briefly on railraod construction in Quebec he crossed the border into the United States. During the 1860's he sometimes freighted across the Nebraska plains to Colorado. Reminiscences of these early years mention Indian affairs, mining, freighting, cattle driving, and military operations.
R. Lowitt

1726. Gildner, Judith. IOWANS IN THE ARTS: JOSEPH LANGLAND. *Ann. of Iowa 1977 43(7): 515-533.* Poet Joseph Langland (b. 1917) often uses as a background for his writings the Midwest, especially the farmlands of northeastern Iowa where he spent his youth. In answer to a series of questions submitted to him by Judith Gildner, editor of the *Annals of Iowa,* Langland reflects upon his origins and the "shaping form" of his boyhood during the 1920's and 30's. He describes the impact upon his poetry of his Norwegian ancestry, Lutheran upbringing, early reading, and the sense of being "rooted" which accompanied rural life. Reprints four Langland poems. 2 illus.
P. L. Petersen

1727. Hale, Frederick. MARCUS HANSEN, PURITANISM, AND SCANDINAVIAN IMMIGRANT TEMPERANCE MOVEMENTS. *Norwegian-American Studies 1977 27: 18-40.* Discusses the historiographical work done by Marcus Lee Hansen, a historian of the 1920's-30's who dealt with Norwegian American immigrants. Examines one of his lectures on immigrant Scandinavians and temperance movements. According to Hansen, immigrants upon reaching the United States joined the movement because of a Puritanism comparable to that of colonial New England. Further, the temperance movement came about as a result of the immigrants' reaction to frontier life. Through study of temperance movements both in Europe and the United States, the author refutes Hansen's arguments, contending that immigrant objection to alcohol use was an old one stemming from preimmigration times. 45 notes.
G. A. Hewlett

1728. Hamre, James S. GEORG SVERDRUP AND THE AUGSBURG PLAN OF EDUCATION. *Norwegian-American Studies 1974 26: 160-183.* Discusses the foundation of Augsburg Seminary, 1869-1907, with special attention given to the contributions of Georg Sverdrup, its president, 1877-1907, and his educational philosophy. Sverdrup helped to set up the various parts of the eight-year institution to include the "Greek School," practical education, college preparatory, and the theological school in order to emphasize the practical rather than the classical side of education, so that its graduates might be better prepared for America's evolving society. Political upheaval within the Lutheran Church produced a split between the Free Lutheran Church and the United Lutherans, resulting in the founding of another religious school, St. Olaf College. Discusses the competition between the two schools in recruiting faculty and students, as well as the differences in educational philosophy followed at both institutions. 37 notes.
G. A. Hewlett

1729. Haugen, Einar. OPDALSLAGET I AMERIKA OG DETS ÅRBØKER [The Opdal settlement in America and its annals]. *Heimen [Norway] 1977 17(8): 453-459.* Discusses settlements, founded ca. 1865, mainly in Iowa and South Dakota of immigrants from Opdal, Norway,

and describes the life and works of the editors of the annal of the Opdal settlement, published 1922-41. They were Eric H. Loe (1856-1929), P. P. Hagen (1873-1927), Kristine Haugen (1878-1965), and Halvor B. Reese. Based on personal experiences and secondary literature; note.
U. G. Jeyes

1730. Haugen, Einor. SMYRA: A MEMOIR. *Norwegian-American Studies 1977 27: 101-110.* In 1905 Kristian Prestgard and Johannes B. Wist, two Norwegian immigrants began the literary magazine *Smyra* in Decorah, Iowa. It stressed the Norwegian heritage of its readership and printed literary and theater criticism of Norwegian origin, as well as literary pieces from Norway's strong nationalistic period, 1814-1905. The greatest percentage of its articles were written by Norwegian Americans, however. Though it remained in publication only 10 years, it served the Norwegian American community as a link to their cultural history as a Norwegian-language organ of their ethnicity, culture, and language.
G. A. Hewlett

1731. Haugen, Eva L. and Semmingsen, Ingrid. PEDER ANDERSON OF BERGEN AND LOWELL: ARTIST AND AMBASSADOR OF CULTURE. *Norwegian Contributions to Am. Studies 1973 4: 1-29.* Anderson (originally Andersen), who was born in Bergen, Norway, in 1811, emigrated at age 19 to America and resided in Massachusetts until his death in 1874. Anderson was instrumental in broadening the scientific and cultural contact between Norway and America. He succeeded in establishing exchanges between the Museum of Bergen and the Smithsonian Institution as early as 1849. He was also one of the first to stimulate the interest of Norwegian doctors in the study of leprosy in America. "In his later years he seems to have become more of a realistic observer of emigration and was more concerned about explaining Norwegian conditions to an American audience. But he always wanted to effect contact between his old and his new country." 6 photos, 75 notes.
D. D. Cameron

1732. Haugen, Eva L. THE STORY OF PEDER ANDERSON. *Norwegian-American Studies 1974 26: 31-48.* Autobiography and a personal letter of Peder Anderson, a Norwegian American immigrant, 1824-73; discusses his life and offers his impressions of America. 39 notes.

1733. Haugrud, Raychel A. ROLVAAG'S SEARCH FOR SORIA MORIA. *Norwegian-American Studies 1974 26: 103-117.* Maintains that rather than trying to enumerate every good thing which Norwegian Americans have done for the United States, as some critics have argued, the literature of Ole Edvart Rølvaag deals with a more universal theme; that of man's search for happiness, symbolized in Norwegian folklore by the castle of Soria Moria. 37 notes.

1734. Helgeland, John. BERET'S PROBLEM: AN ESSAY ON IMMIGRANT PIONEER RELIGION. *Lutheran Q. 1976 28(1): 45-53.* In the novel *Giants in the Earth* (1927), Ole Edvart Rolvaag considers the problems of cultural adjustment a Norwegian immigrant family faces in life on the South Dakota prairies. Particularly significant is the question of religion. Norwegians, like many other immigrants, were accustomed to an environment in which their religion was part of their essential culture, bounded by space and time. The emigration to the frontier necessitated a massive transformation of religious thinking and brought great problems for some like the heroine, Beret, who finds the unbounded space of her new home extremely difficult to fit into her old religion (adherent versus conversion style of religion). A sermon on God's love unbounded by time and space results in Beret's acceptance of her new situation, while she gradually develops a view based on the division of people into the saved and the unregenerate. Thus the frontier experience was a major factor in the development of a unique Protestant tradition in America. Based on secondary sources; 28 notes.
J. A. Kicklighter

1735. Herseth, Lorna B., ed. A PIONEER'S LETTER. *South Dakota Hist. 1976 6(3): 306-315.* Reprints an 1882 letter from Walborg Strom Holth to her step-daughter in Norway describing her trip to visit her two sons—Christian in South Dakota and Severin in Chicago.

1736. Jenson, Carol. THE LARSON SISTERS: THREE CAREERS IN CONTRAST. Stuhler, Barbara and Kreuter, Gretchen, ed. *Women of Minnesota: Selected Biographical Essays* (St. Paul: Minnesota Hist. Soc. Pr., 1977): 301-324. Agnes, Henrietta, and Nora Larson grew up in

Minnesota. Daughters of a successful farmer-businessman and a gentle mother, they were raised in an environment of Norwegian American traditions and the Lutheran Church. They all attended St. Olaf College in Northfield, pursued graduate studies, and became teachers. Agnes Larson became a historian, taught at St. Olaf, and wrote the meticulously researched and well-written monograph, *History of the White Pine Industry in Minnesota*. Henrietta Larson became a prominent pioneer in business history. She taught at colleges and universities. She became a noted editor and writer while working as a research associate at Harvard, where she became the first woman named as an associate professor by the business school despite that university's tradition of sex discrimination. Nora Larson became a bacteriologist. She did research at the Mayo Foundation, the Lakey Clinic, and the Takamine Laboratories before finally settling back in Minnesota in 1950, where she became the only woman among the principal scientists at the University of Minnesota's Hormel Institute. She studied swine diseases and was active in professional and community organizations. In 1960, Nora joined the faculty of St. Olaf where she taught until her retirement in 1972. Primary sources; 3 photos, 50 notes. A. E. Wiederrecht

1737. Leiren, Terje I. AMERICAN PRESS OPINION AND NORWEGIAN INDEPENDENCE, 1905. *Norwegian-American Studies 1977 27: 224-242*. Discusses American press reaction to dissolution of ties between Norway and Sweden, 1905. While opinion ran both pro and con, many newspapers expressed disdain and pessimism at the possibility of future progressive government for Norway with the election of Haakon VII and the decision to remain a monarchy. Regardless, American public opinion ran in favor of Norwegian independence, and hearty congratulations were extended both because of Norway's new found independence and because of the importance played by Norwegian Americans in the settlement and foundation of the United States. Based on newspaper accounts; 30 notes. G. A. Hewlett

1738. Leirfall, Jon and Clausen, C. A., ed. and transl. HEGRA BEFORE AND AFTER THE EMIGRATION ERA. *Norwegian-American Studies 1977 27: 3-17*. Discusses the effects of emigration on Hegra, Norway. Prior to emigration, conditions were crowded, often to the point where families lacked sufficient means of subsistence. Land was divided and redivided among successive generations, causing some to leave agriculture and causing those who remained to farm land at higher elevations. A great migration to the United States occurred during 1865-90. Following the loss of some 1,200 young persons, the birth rate fell and the death rate seemed to increase. Though many young people left, conditions improved; farms expanded and the young who remained in Norway developed a stronger community and country attachment which eventually led to independence from Sweden, 1905. G. A. Hewlett

1739. Lovoll, Odd S. *DECORAH-POSTEN*: THE STORY OF AN IMMIGRANT NEWSPAPER. *Norwegian-American Studies 1977 27: 77-100*. Chronicles the history of the *Decorah-Posten*, a Norwegian-language newspaper from Decorah, Iowa, 1874-1972. Founded by B. Anundsen in 1872 after a number of other unsuccessful printing ventures, the *Decorah-Posten* gained subscription strength until 1885 on the platform of local news (both from home and abroad) and lack of political opinion. It was the most popular of the three newspapers in the county and soon spread throughout the Midwest after it began in 1889 to serialize novels, primarily by Norwegians and Norwegian Americans; nearly all novels pertained to immigrants and their lives or to Norway and the folklore of that country. Discusses editors Johannes B. Wist, Erik S. Gjellum, and Kristian Prestgard and the editorial policy adopted in the 20th century. The circulation remained high through the 1940's, but dwindling subscriptions forced the editors to end publication in 1972. 35 notes. G. A. Hewlett

1740. McQuaid, Kim. THE BUSINESSMAN AS REFORMER: NELSON O. NELSON AND THE LATE 19TH CENTURY SOCIAL MOVEMENTS IN AMERICA. *Am. J. of Econ. and Sociol. 1974 33(4): 423-435*. Nelson O. Nelson's efforts at profit-sharing and cooperatives are traced with reference to the times in which they were tried. His interest in communitarian cooperative ventures is explored. Secondary sources; 28 notes. W. L. Marr

1741. Morstad, A. E. ERIK MORSTAD'S WORK AMONG THE WISCONSIN INDIANS. *Norwegian-American Studies 1977 27: 111-*

150. Discusses the missionary work of Norwegian immigrant Eric O. Morstad among the Indians of Wisconsin. Included in his missionary endeavors were the Ojibwa, Ottawa, and Pottawatomie Indians. The greatest amount of Morstad's work was done from 1895 to his death in 1920, though throughout this period he was called on by the Lutheran Church to carry out other church-related tasks. Despite the interruptions, Morstad served beyond his original missionary intent as a teacher. He became an advocate for the Indians in the face of land claims and minor legal skirmishes. G. A. Hewlett

1742. Naess, Harald S. YGDRASIL LITERARY SOCIETY 1896-1971. *Norwegian Contributions to Am. Studies 1973 4: 31-45*. Ygdrasil Literary Society of Madison, Wisconsin, was founded 4 December 1896. The society's aim was "the promotion of good fellowship, and mutual benefit and advancement in knowledge, particularly in Scandinavian literature and history." Only male Norwegians by birth or parentage who were college graduates were eligible. In 1897 the Gudrid Reading Circle was founded for members' wives. More than 600 papers have been presented dealing with numerous subjects. Its members are mainly university professors, lawyers, doctors, and businessmen who "have retained their knowledge of and interest in the old country." 24 notes.

D. D. Cameron

1743. Nelsen, Frank C. THE SCHOOL CONTROVERSY AMONG NORWEGIAN IMMIGRANTS. *Norwegian-American Studies 1974 26: 206-219*. Discusses the feelings of the Norwegian Evangelical Lutheran Synod toward the educational system of the United States. Though a majority of Norwegian immigrants accepted the educational system, a small but powerful minority, represented by the Lutheran clergy, labelled the system as heathen, religionless, and antithetical to a continued appreciation of Norwegian culture. As a result attempts were made to force schools to accept Lutheran culture classes in areas dominated by Norwegians. The controversy fostered bitter rivalries between members of the Norwegian American communities throughout the Midwest and finally came to an end in 1880 when an argument over elections caused a split in the clergy and laity of the Synod. 25 notes. G. A. Hewlett

1744. Nelson, Bersven and Clausen, C. A., ed. and transl. NOTES OF A CIVIL WAR SOLDIER. *Norwegian-American Studies 1974 26: 118-145*. Notes from the diary of Bersven Nelson, a Norwegian American member of the 15th Wisconsin Regiment, 1861-63. Contains one short excerpt describing his trip from Norway, but concentrates on his military service from training through fighting, and ending with his return home on sick leave. Discusses aspects of camp life and daily operations during the Civil War. 14 notes. G. A. Hewlett

1745. Nelson, David T. KNUT GJERSET. *Norwegian-American Studies 1972 25: 27-53*. Chronicles the life and career of Knut Gjerset, an immigrant from Norway who was instrumental in beginning organizations and publications relating to Norwegian Americans, as well as writing immigrant histories, 1873-1935.

1746. Nelson, Frank G. FOLLOWING THE PATHFINDER: A NORWEGIAN'S ACCOUNT OF WESTERN MISSOURI IN 1848. *Missouri Hist. Soc. Bull. 1976 32(2): 110-116*. Reprints a lengthy letter written by Peder Nielsen Kalehaven (1794-1884) in 1848. The writer described the emigration of the Kalehaven family from Norway to Buchanan County, Missouri, and the troubles encountered by the Kalehavens in establishing a new home and in adjusting to American agricultural products and practices. H. T. Lovin

1747. Odegard, Ethel J. FAREWELL TO AN OLD HOMESTEAD. *Norwegian-American Studies 1974 26: 146-159*. Reminiscences of Ethel J. Odegard concerning her home town, Merrill, Wisconsin. Discusses the earliest division of the land into townships, businesses in the town, neighbors, friends, and family with whom she grew up. Also mentions the Norwegian Americans in the community, 1874-1974.

G. A. Hewlett

1748. Paulson, Kristoffer F. BERDAHL FAMILY HISTORY AND RØLVAAG'S IMMIGRANT TRILOGY. *Norwegian-American Studies 1977 27: 55-76*. Examines sources for events in Ole Edvart Rølvaag's *Giants in the Earth*, 1873-1900. His marriage to Jennie Berdahl in 1908 introduced him to extensive information on Norwegian Americans in the South Dakota region since her family had migrated from Minnesota to South Dakota in 1873. Reprints portions of interviews Rølvaag conducted with residents of Sioux Falls and other small towns in South Dakota, many of whom were relatives of his wife, in preparation for his novel. Reprints portions of the autobiographies of two of his wife's uncles, Erick Berdahl and Andrew Berdahl, which give family history from preimmigration days. 22 notes.   G. A. Hewlett

1749. Petersen, Peter L. A NEW OSLO ON THE PLAINS: THE ANDERS L. MORDT LAND COMPANY AND NORWEGIAN MIGRATION TO THE TEXAS PANHANDLE. *Panhandle-Plains Hist. Rev. 1976 49(1): 25-54.* Anders L. Mordt's 1907 establishment of Oslo in Hansford County, Texas marked the first Norwegian town in the Texas Panhandle. Rather than seeking immigrants directly from Norway, Mordt aimed his promotional literature at Norwegian communities throughout the Midwest. A small but steady stream of settlers took up sites during the initial years, but after 1912 the migration slowed. A sustained drought and a bitter dispute with the editor of its chief promotional newspaper undercut confidence in the scheme which went bankrupt by 1914. Despite this, about 30 families remained and built a stable community. Based on primary and secondary sources; 4 photos, table, 57 notes.   M. L. Tate

1750. Pryser, Tore. UTVANDRINGEN TIL AMERIKA [The emigration to America]. *Heimen [Norway] 1977 17(8): 463-468.* A review article prompted by Inge Semmingsen's *Drøm og dåd: Utvandringen til Amerika* (Oslo: H. Aschehoug og Co., 1975), which describes the reasons for the emigration to America and the social conditions of the average immigrant family.

1751. Qualey, Carlton C., transl. and ed. THREE AMERICAN LETTERS TO LESJA. *Norwegian-American Studies 1977 27: 41-54.* Reprints three letters from Norwegian Americans, immigrants who left Lesja and Rana to move to various places in the United States. Describes life for the immigrants and the conditions which they met when they arrived. Among the three, written 1867-96, only one expresses disappointment and disparagement at conditions found there.
G. A. Hewlett

1752. Rosholt, Malcolm. THE BROTHERS WEEK. *Norwegian-American Studies 1974 26: 75-102.* Biographies of two Norwegian American immigrants, Andrew Week, who went to California to seek his fortune in the goldfields and John Week, who started a lumbering enterprise in Wisconsin, 1838-60.

1753. Sandaker, Arvid and Clausen, C. A., transl. EMIGRATION FROM LAND PARISH TO AMERICA, 1866-1875. *Norwegian-American Studies 1974 26: 49-75.* Examines emigration which occurred from Land Parish, Norway, 1866-75. Several factors in Norway, among them a high birth rate, unfavorable agricultural conditions, a constricted labor market, increased taxes, overall poor living conditions, and a high percentage of people on relief led a great number of Norwegians to immigrate to the United States where conditions seemed brighter with the end of the Civil War, passage of the Homestead Act of 1862, suppression of Indian uprisings, and the economic boom of 1865. Details the place of destination, social and familial connections, and general job descriptions as well as age, sex, and social status of Land Parish emigrants. 30 notes.
G. A. Hewlett

1754. Sandnes, Jørn. DE NORSKE BYGDELAG I AMERIKA [The Norwegian settlements in America]. *Heimen [Norway] 1977 17(8): 460-463.* A review article prompted by Odd Sverre Lovoll's, *A Folk Epic: The Bygdelag in America* (Boston: Twayne Publ., 1975), which emphasizes the efforts by the Norwegian immigrants to retain their language and culture and the characteristics of the Norwegian settlements (bygdelag) in America.   U. G. Jeyes

1755. Seljaas, Helge. NORWEGIANS IN "ZION" TEACH THEMSELVES ENGLISH. *Norwegian-American Studies 1974 26: 220-228.* Discusses the quick assimilation by Mormon Norwegian immigrants after they learned to speak English, 1853-1974.

1756. Seljaas, Helge. POLYGAMY AMONG THE NORWEGIAN MORMONS. *Norwegian-American Studies 1977 27: 151-162.* While not strictly subscribing to polygamy, many Norwegian Americans (an equal percentage of men and women) migrated to America after having been converted to Mormonism. The incidence of women marrying the men who had converted them aided in making Mormonism synonymous with polygamy in the Scandinavian mind. Through church sanction, members were forced to practice polygamy, many taking one additional wife in order to appease church authorities. Polygamy had a slightly lesser incidence among Norwegian converts than among other Mormons, and when, in 1904, under pressure from the American government, the Mormons dropped polygamy as official church dogma, most Norwegian converts were relieved. 24 notes.   G. A. Hewlett

1757. Semmingsen, Ingrid and Barton, H. Arnold, trans. A SHIPLOAD OF GERMAN EMIGRANTS AND THEIR SIGNIFICANCE FOR THE NORWEGIAN EMIGRATION OF 1825. *Swedish Pioneer Hist. Q. 1974 25(3-4): 183-192.* A ship with 500 German religious separatists, bound for America, was forced into Bergen, Norway, in 1817. The emigrants were stranded through the winter. Consequences included rumors of America and emigration in politically discontented eastern Norway. In 1821, Norwegian religious dissenters sent Cleng Peerson to America. Primary and secondary sources; 6 notes.
K. J. Puffer

1758. Skrien, Sandra H. OLE JOHNSON SKRIEN: A NORWEGIAN IMMIGRANT IN THE 1870'S. *North Dakota Hist. 1976 43(1): 32-35.* Johnson Skrien emigrated from Norway to the United States in 1874, primarily for economic reasons. Taking up a tract of land in the Sheyenne River Valley of Dakota Territory in 1879, Skrien and his family subsequently moved to various sites in Minnesota. Describes Norwegian American domestic life, recreation, food, religious beliefs, farming practices, and attitudes toward education. Discusses taking up land under the Homestead Act. Based on primary and secondary sources, and family reminiscences.   N. Lederer

1759. Sletten, Harvey M. GROWING UP ON BALD HILL CREEK. *North Dakota Hist. 1978 45(1): 14-20.* The experiences of boyhood in a small North Dakota town during the 1920's often revolved around recreation at and in the local river or creek. Bald Hill Creek served that function for Sletten and his contemporaries. The creek was the center for summer swimming and for fishing expeditions using primitive equipment. Wild berry picking was a frequent activity along its banks, including the picking of juneberries, wild strawberries, and chokeberries at different points of the growing season. Automobile driving was a challenging enterprise in the period owing to the rudimentary or nonexistent roads of rural North Dakota. The settlement of Norwegians in the area brought with them an interest in skiing, which resulted in the erection of a ski jump used for regional contests and by the local youth. Based on personal recollections.   N. Lederer

1760. Thorson, Gerald. TINSEL AND DUST: DISENCHANTMENT IN TWO MINNEAPOLIS NOVELS FROM THE 1880'S. *Minnesota Hist. 1977 45(6): 210-222.* The Norwegian-language novels by immigrants Kristofer Janson and his wife, Drude Krog Janson, reveal the dissatisfaction with America and Minnesota of two highly intelligent, social reform-minded individuals. The narrowness of both Norwegian ethnic society and of the greater American culture unfavorably impressed these observers, who eventually returned to Europe. Drude Janson's romance novel, *A saloonkeeper's daughter,* first published in 1887, is colored by socially realistic prose emphasizing alcoholic intemperance in America, crude behavior in the New World, and the low position of women in a male-dominated society. Kristofer Janson's *Behind the Curtain,* issued in 1889, is a social satire which attacks American materialism, class cleavages, and the victimization of women.   N. Lederer

1761. Torres, Luis. CONVERSATIONS WITH THE RECENT PAST. *Ann. of Iowa 1976 43(3): 192-221.* Contains six short articles based on interviews conducted by Luther College faculty and students with elderly residents of the Decorah, Iowa, area, as a part of the Northeast Iowa Oral History Project, a program inspired by the Foxfire Project in Raburn Gap, Georgia. Describes the cohesion of Norwegian American families; harvesting oats in the precombine era (1900-1925); the use of horses on a farm; the role of neighbors in rural society; the operation of the mill at Line Springs, Iowa; and the musical experiences of a 78 year-old fiddler. 8 photos.   P. L. Petersen

1762. Veblen, Andrew A. AT LUTHER COLLEGE, 1877-1881. *Palimpsest 1975 56(5): 150-160.* A lively chronicle of events and personalities, written many years after Andrew A. Veblen had left Luther College in Decorah, Iowa. Andrew, who was Thorstein's brother, paid particular attention in his reminiscence to his constant difficulties with Thrond Bothne, a "professional Norwegian" and, like Veblen, an instructor of Latin. Veblen's precise and pensive style provides a clear view of academic activity among Norwegian Americans in pioneer days. Based on Andrew Veblen's manuscript in the Minnesota Historical Society, 4 photos, note.   D. W. Johnson

1763. Wallace, Gladys Tjossem. MY GRANDFATHER: PIONEER IN RECLAIMING LAND. *Pacific Northwesterner 1979 23(3): 33-40.* Rasmus Peder Tjossem (1841-1922) was born in Norway, immigrated to America, and eventually settled near the Yakima River in Ellensburg, Washington, to build and operate five grist mills, harvest ice, and design an irrigation system.

Swedish

1764. Adolfsson, Sven. MAGNUS JONASSON LINNELL: A REAL KARL OSKAR. *Swedish Pioneer Hist. Q. 1978 29(1): 34-42.* The story of the first emigrant from Kronsberg *lan*, Sweden, to the Chicago Lake area of Minnesota in the 19th century. This is an area made famous in the novels of Vilhelm Moberg. Compares Linnell's experiences to those of the character in Moberg's novels. Describes Linnell's first years in the new world. Photo, 26 notes.   C. W. Ohrvall

1765. Almqvist, Sten. THE KNAVE OF FALLEBO. *Swedish Pioneer Hist. Q. 1976 27(1): 6-25.* Carl Johan Nilsson (1811-69) changed his name to Fallenius to go into business and later emigrated to the United States to escape creditors. He set himself up as the magician and physician, Dr. C. W. Roback. He was successful in Philadelphia, and then settled in Boston, where he was a celebrity in the 1850's, and very rich in the 1860's. Based on secondary sources; 6 illus., biblio.   K. J. Puffer

1766. Anderson, B. Frank and Smith, Roberta Anderson, ed. BY COVERED WAGON FROM ILLINOIS TO IOWA, 1868. *Swedish Pioneer Hist. Q. 1979 30(4): 240-244.* The author recalls the overland trek made by his family from Geneseo, Illinois, to central Iowa. His parents had come from Sweden in 1854 with four children. They farmed in Illinois for 14 years before moving to Iowa. They settled near Swede Point, now called Madrid. The original of this article first appeared in the *Des Moines Register* for 25 August 1968. Photo.   C. W. Ohrvall

1767. Anderson, Harry H., ed. REMEMBRANCES OF NASHOTAH DAYS: TWO LETTERS OF GUSTAF UNONIUS. *Swedish Pioneer Hist. Q. 1976 27(2): 111-115.* Reprints two letters of Gustaf Unonius originally published in the *Nashotah Scholast* in 1884. Unonius was very busy; he feels he should have accomplished more in life. He fondly remembers those he knew at Nashotah House, the Protestant Episcopal seminary. Based on primary sources; 4 notes.   K. J. Puffer

1768. Andresen, Grant W. THE AMERICAN REVOLUTION AND THE SWEDISH CHURCH IN THE DELAWARE VALLEY. *Swedish Pioneer Hist. Q. 1976 27(4): 261-269.* Four congregations of the Swedish Lutheran Church in the Delaware River Valley were the last vestiges of Swedish colonization in America at the beginning of the American Revolution. Ecclesiastically the churches were drawing further away from the mother Church because of the anglicization of the congregations and their dissatisfaction over the policy of transferring ministers without considering the parish sentiment. During the Revolution the congregations were divided in loyalty. The clergymen suffered when they attempted to remain neutral, professing loyalty to the King of Sweden. Recounts the many problems of the congregations and the ministers during the Revolution. By the end of the war the churches had become independent of Swedish control and eventually became Episcopalian. Primary sources; 18 notes.   C. W. Ohrvall

1769. Atwood, Evangeline. PIONEER BANKER. *Alaska J. 1978 8(1): 26-30.* Edward Anton Rasmuson (1882-1949) was president of the National Bank of Alaska during 1917-43. He was born in Copenhagen and raised in Sweden. He came to America at age 18. He arrived in Alaska as a missionary in 1904. He married fellow missionary Jenny Olson in 1905. He studied law in his spare time, passed the Alaska bar in 1916, was hired as legal counsel of the newly formed Bank of Alaska, and soon became its president. This bank, with headquarters at Skagway and branches in several other towns, the largest at Anchorage, financed most of these towns' commercial enterprises. Rasmuson was knighted by King Gustaf of Sweden in 1938. He was an active Republican. Based on newspapers; 10 notes.   L. W. Van Wyk

1770. Barton, H. Arnold. [E. GUSTAV JOHNSON]. *Swedish Pioneer Hist. Q. 1975 26(2): 117-118; 120-127.*

E. GUSTAV JOHNSON: IN MEMORIAM, *pp. 117-118.* Born in Sweden, E. Gustav Johnson (1893-1974) resumed his education after the age of 30. He devoted long service to North Park College in Chicago and to the Swedish Pioneer Historical Society. Illus.

E. GUSTAV JOHNSON: A SCHOLARLY TESTAMENT, *pp. 120-127.* A letter by E. Gustav Johnson to Franklin D. Scott concerning publishing by the Swedish Pioneer Historical Society. 13 notes.   K. J. Puffer

1771. Barton, H. Arnold. THE EDITOR'S CORNER: SWEDISH CRAFTSMANSHIP AND FOLK ARTS ON AMERICAN SOIL. *Swedish Pioneer Hist. Q. 1976 27(4): 235-237.* Explains that this issue of the *Quarterly* is devoted to Swedes in America during the colonial and revolutionary periods. Only fragments of the old Swedish material culture have survived the sea change of the ocean crossing. The demands of survival in the frontier left little time or opportunity for the practice of ancient decorative arts and crafts. Modern day descendants have rediscovered the old crafts and learned traditional folk dances.
                                        C. W. Ohrvall

1772. Barton, H. Arnold. SCANDINAVIAN IMMIGRANT WOMEN'S ENCOUNTER WITH AMERICA. *Swedish Pioneer Hist. Q. 1974 25(1): 37-42.* The Swedish immigrants' response to the position of women in America (ca. 1850-90) depended upon social background, age, and marital status. Young, unmarried women adopted American conventions of gentility. Men were impressed by the consideration shown women, whom they found spoiled and pretentious. Only a few upper-class women found a "Woman Problem" in America. Originally a paper for the Society for the Advancement of Scandinavian Study in May 1973. Based on primary and secondary sources; 8 notes.   K. J. Puffer

1773. Beijbom, Ulf. "THE FUTURE BRIGHTENS BEFORE US!" REPORT ON THE VÄXJÖ SYMPOSIUM ON THE PRESERVATION OF SOURCES FOR SWEDISH IMMIGRATION HISTORY IN NORTH AMERICA, AUGUST 1977. *Swedish Pioneer Hist. Q. 1978 29(1): 3-8.* Report of a symposium held by the Society and the Swedish Institute of Stockholm. The 40 participants included researchers, museum and institution directors, and Swedish diplomats in America. Their aim was to find ways to improve the field research in America's Swedish immigration districts. The opening remarks called for cooperation between agencies and increased American initiative. Among the items discussed were projects involving handwritten and printed source materials and museums and collections of objects. The participants recommended continuing microfilming of Swedish-American church records and newspapers and magazines, indexing Swedish-American historical manuscripts, preparing a complete Swedish-American bibliography, and supporting preservation efforts.   C. W. Ohrvall

1774. Beijbom, Ulf. THE PRINTED WORD IN A NINETEENTH-CENTURY IMMIGRANT COLONY: THE ROLE OF THE ETHNIC PRESS IN CHICAGO'S SWEDE TOWN. *Swedish Pioneer Hist. Q. 1977 28(2): 82-96.* By 1870 Swede Town, on Chicago's north side, was the largest Swedish urban settlement and a cultural capital of Swedish Americans. Outlines the character of the Swedish-language press in Chicago and its intellectual function. The press was instrumental in the creation of Swedish America. Based in part on the author's *Swedes in Chicago* . . . 34 notes.   C. W. Ohrvall

1775. Bergendoff, Conrad. AN ANCIENT CULTURE IN A NEW LAND. *Swedish Pioneer Hist. Q. 1976 27(2): 127-134.* Swedish immigrants brought with them the traditions of Swedish Lutheran Church. Augustana College in Rock Island was formed to train clergy. The college and the synod formed a point of contact for cultural transmission and communication within the Swedish community. Based on secondary sources; 5 notes.   K. J. Puffer

1776. Bergendoff, Conrad. AUGUSTANA IN AMERICA AND IN SWEDEN. *Swedish Pioneer Hist. Q. 1973 24(4): 238-241.* The Augustana Synod, organized in 1860, is the largest single organization of the Swedish immigrants in the United States. It preserved the immigrants' form of worship and culture but gradually integrated with American society. In 1962 it joined a merger to form the Lutheran Church of America. The Augustana church lives on in the memories of those who still associate themselves with Sweden, and in its influence on the larger church. Paper presented at the conference "The Scandinavian Presence in America," Minneapolis, May 1973.   K. J. Puffer

1777. Bergendoff, Conrad. IN SEARCH OF SELF. *Swedish Pioneer Hist. Q. 1979 30(2): 87-93.* An account of the founding of the organization in 1948, with the celebration of the Swedish Pioneer Centennial. Based on the personal experiences of the author. The keynote address at the Society's 30th anniversary banquet in Chicago, Illinois, 14 October 1978.   C. W. Ohrvall

1778. Berry, Mildred Freburg. MEMORIES OF A SWEDISH CHRISTMAS. *Palimpsest 1978 59(1): 20-23.* Describes the Swedish Christmas celebrations on a farm near Pomeroy, Iowa, early in the 20th century. Photo.   D. W. Johnson

1779. Bingham, Robert D. SWEDISH-AMERICANS IN UTAH: A BIBLIOGRAPHY. *Swedish Pioneer Hist. Q. 1979 30(3): 205-210.*

1780. Bingham, Robert D. SWEDISH-AMERICANS IN WASHINGTON STATE: A BIBLIOGRAPHY OF PUBLICATIONS. *Swedish Pioneer Hist. Q. 1974 25(2): 133-140.* This bibliography of material on Swedish Americans and their culture in Washington state is annotated with location symbols for the three libraries surveyed. Lists books, articles, Swedish newspapers, periodicals, and annuals, with dates of publication.   K. J. Puffer

1781. Carlsson, Olle. THE SEARCH FOR VERNER LINDBÄCK. *Swedish Pioneer Hist. Q. 1977 28(1): 62-67.* Discusses the efforts of an engineer from Umea, Sweden, Ola Lindbäck, to find his grandfather who emigrated to the United States in 1906. He traced him to Minneapolis in 1934. 2 photos.   C. W. Ohrvall

1782. Carlsson, Sten and Barton, H. Arnold, transl. FROM MID-SWEDEN TO THE MIDWEST. *Swedish Pioneer Hist. Q. 1974 25(3-4): 193-207.* Describes rural-urban patterns of immigration by Swedes, 1850-1930. About 35% of the emigrants moved from Swedish to American farms, about one-third from rural Sweden to American cities, and another third from urban Sweden to urban America. The majority emigrated for economic reasons. Primary and secondary sources; 38 notes.   K. J. Puffer

1783. Carlsson, Sten and Nordstrom, Byron J., transl. JOHN HANSON'S SWEDISH BACKGROUND. *Swedish Pioneer Hist. Q. 1978 29(1): 9-20.* A genealogical study based on work in 1876 by George A. Hanson, a Maryland lawyer. John Hanson was one of Maryland's two great forefathers and a political activist during the American Revolution. He was President of Congress in Philadelphia in 1781-82. He was born in either 1715 or 1721 and died in 1783. In 1903 a statue was erected over his grave in Statuary Hall in the Capitol in Washington, D.C. Concludes that George Hanson established a clear set of traditions which do include genealogical links with Sweden. Photo, chart, 46 notes.
C. W. Ohrvall

1784. Carlsson, Sten. SWEDEN AND AMERICA AFTER 1860: A RESEARCH PROJECT. *Swedish Pioneer Hist. Q. 1976 27(3): 204-214.* In 1962 the American Council of Learned Societies gave a five-year grant to fund research in American Studies in a Swedish university. Uppsala was selected as the site and a professorship in American literature and a research assistant in history were supported. These activities were continued at the end of the five years by the Swedish government. In addition a special section for American History was founded in 1962 in the Department of History. The project was called "Sweden and America After 1860." As a result, about 30 postgraduate students and many undergraduates worked on the project and produced papers. Describes the project.   C. W. Ohrvall

1785. Danielson, Larry. PUBLIC SWEDISH-AMERICAN ETHNICITY IN CENTRAL KANSAS: A FESTIVAL AND ITS FUNCTIONS. *Swedish Pioneer Hist. Q. 1974 25(1): 13-36.* Lindsborg expresses its Swedish ethnic identification in four community observances. Recently introduced, and created by imaginative residents, the most important is the *Svensk Hyllnings Fest.* Describes the 1969 observance. It is representative of American ethnic festivals. The social and economic consequences are important, as well as the cultural identification. Based on research for a doctoral dissertation and on primary sources; 3 photos, 16 notes.   K. J. Puffer

1786. Dowie, James I. UNGE MAN, GÅ WESTERHUT [Young Man, Go Westward]. *Nebraska Hist. 1973 54(1): 47-63.* Discusses Swedish pioneers and settlements in Nebraska. Between 1870 and 1890, the number of Scandinavians in the state rose from 2,352 to 28,634.
R. Lowitt

1787. Duncan, Marie-Louise. FROM WOODSTOCK TO POTOMAC: ACCULTURATION THEN AND NOW. *Swedish Pioneer Hist. Q. 1977 28(1): 45-56.* Reveals the daily life of a Swedish family in Woodstock, Connecticut, as seen by their eight-year-old child in 1906. The emphasis at home and school was on assimilation. Describes a 1970 day at the Swedish School of Washington, D.C., founded to expose children to their heritage as Swedes and Americans. 2 photos.
C. W. Ohrvall

1788. Ekman, Ernst. A SWEDISH VIEW OF CHICAGO IN THE 1890'S: HENNING BERGER. *Swedish Pioneer Hist. Q. 1974 25(3/4): 230-240.* Discusses account of Chicago in the 1890's by Swedish author Henning Berger (1872-1924), who established his literary reputation with writings based on his experiences there. He viewed Chicago as the essence of America, and Chicago fascinated and dismayed him. He criticized Swedish immigrants who adjusted too well to America. Based on primary sources; 31 notes.   K. J. Puffer

1789. Elmen, Paul. BISHOP HILL: UTOPIA ON THE PRAIRIE. *Chicago Hist. 1976 5(1): 45-52.* Chronicles the progress of a group of Swedish immigrants known as Janssonists, who established a religious utopian colony in Bishop Hill, Illinois, 1846-60. ishop Hill Colony.

1790. Elmen, Paul. UNONIUS AND THE SWOPE AFFAIR. *Swedish Pioneer Hist. Q. 1976 27(2): 101-107.* In 1851, the vestry of Trinity Church, Chicago, sought the removal of Cornelius E. Swope as rector. Bishop Philander Chase supported the removal and issued a pamphlet to the diocese on the controversy. Gustaf Unonius felt the removal was unjust and issued a pamphlet supporting Swope. Then an anonymous pamphlet was issued defending the bishop. None of the pamphlets dealt with the real issue, the controversy over ritual. Based on primary sources; 16 notes.   K. J. Puffer

1791. Elovson, Harald. AUGUST STRINDBERG AND EMIGRATION TO THE UNITED STATES 1890-1912. *Norwegian Contributions to Am. Studies 1973 4: 47-67.* Analyzes Strindberg's (1849-1912) opinions and comments about Swedish emigration to the United States 1890-1912. In his reading Strindberg "had looked first and foremost for an answer to the question as to why the country had been depopulated through emigration, the question which had been with him from his early youth and which had occupied him when he wrote *Götiska rummen* [Gothic Rooms] and *Svarta Fanor* [Black Banners] in 1904. Now, when he was once more looking for an answer, he seems mainly to have benefited from his reading of the Emigration Inquiry Committee's Appendix No. 7: *Ultvandrarnas egna uppgifter* [Statement by the Emigrants Themselves]." Strindberg then wrote a rather subjective and personal summary of the emigrant biographies, in which he stressed that depopulation was considerably influenced by the labor conflict of 1909, followed by the general strike, which ended in the capitulation of the workers. 17 notes.
D. D. Cameron

1792. Erickson, E. W. JOHAN G. R. BANER: MICHIGAN'S VIKING POET. *Swedish Pioneer Hist. Q. 1973 24(2): 73-93.* Johan Gustav Runeskeold Banér (1861-1938) was recognized in Swedish American literary circles as an outstanding poet. He came to America in 1884 after his discharge from the army. In Ashland, Wisconsin, he helped publish a newspaper for a year, and his work was widely reprinted. He moved to Ironwood, Michigan, where he married, published a newspaper for a decade, and engaged in business. In his writing he attempted to be all things to all people. He published poems in English as early as 1911 under many pen names, but was never accepted by literary circles in Sweden. He corresponded with numerous prominent persons, was a free thinker, and became interested in Norse and Indian mythology. Based on letters, autobiographical material, and secondary sources; 58 notes.
K. J. Puffer

1793. Erickson, George F. and Johnson, Martha G., ed. and transl. LETTERS TO LINUS. *Swedish Pioneer Hist. Q. 1975 26(4): 231-246.* George F. Erickson (1891-1950) corresponded for 40 years with Linus Paulin, who lived in Sweden. Erickson came to Michigan in 1909. His letters, herein excerpted, tell of working in the mines and learning English. He became a citizen, married, and raised a family. He observed the depression and both World Wars, and commented on American politics. He began looking toward old age. Primary sources; illus.
K. J. Puffer

1794. Ericson, C. George. SWEDISH RADIO SERVICES IN CHICAGO. *Swedish Pioneer Hist. Q. 1973 24(3): 157-162.* Station WIBO in Chicago broadcast Swedish services each Sunday from 1926 to 1933. Professor Gustav Edwards' Swedish broadcast over WHFC continued for almost 15 years. Interdenominational services were broadcast over various stations from 1933 to 1962. Visiting ministers and singers from Sweden participated in the broadcasts. Lists ministers who served as committee members and announcers. A Swedish service sponsored by the Salvation Army started in 1964. 2 photos.
K. J. Puffer

1795. Friman, Axel. GUSTAF UNONIUS AND PINE LAKE: JOINING THE EPISCOPAL CHURCH. *Swedish Pioneer Hist. Q. 1978 29(1): 21-33.* Based on the journal of Gustaf Unonius, who with his family and three friends emigrated from Sweden in 1841 to settle in Pine Lake, Wisconsin. Without an evangelical Lutheran church in the area they attempted, through daily household worship, to preserve the teachings of the church. The friendship of the Scandinavians with missionaries of the Protestant Episcopal Church led to a "stabilization" of religion in the area by 1843. Gustaf Unonius was selected to be ordained as the religious leader of the Scandinavian settlers, under the Episcopalian Church. His ordination took place in 1845. He served several congregations in the area until he left in 1848. Discusses Lutheran and Episcopalian churches in the area during 1845-75. Unonius and his family returned to Sweden in 1858 after living for a while in Chicago. 2 photos, 18 notes.
C. W. Ohrvall

1796. Friman, Axel. GUSTAF UNONIUS IN MANITOWOC 1848-1849. *Swedish Pioneer Hist. Q. 1976 27(2): 87-100.* The discovery of a journal and letters sheds light on the work of Gustaf Unonius with St. James Church, a newly organized Episcopal parish in Manitowoc, Wisconsin. He preached in English and occasionally in Norwegian at both Manitowoc and Manitowoc Rapids. He left when invited to go to Chicago by Scandinavians. Based on primary sources; illus., 7 notes.
K. J. Puffer

1797. Goranson, Greta K. IN SEARCH OF MY HERITAGE. *Swedish Pioneer Hist. Q. 1976 27(1): 26-43.* The author had a genealogical account left by her great-great-grandfather, Gustaf Göransson (b. 1832), and wanted to discover why and how he had left Sweden. She went to Sweden as a student and discovered relatives at a house near the parish church of her ancestor. She visited the isolated and enclosed farm her ancestor had owned. They had been the only family to emigrate from the parish. 5 photos.
K. J. Puffer

1798. Guelzo, Allen C. GLORIA DEI: OLD SWEDES' CHURCH. *Early Am. Life. 1977 8(3): 18, 64-66.* The Gloria Dei Congregation was a group of Swedish immigrants who built Old Swedes' Church in Philadelphia, Pennsylvania during 1638-98.

1799. Hasselmo, Nils. LANGUAGE AND THE SWEDISH IMMIGRANT WRITER: FROM A CASE STUDY OF G. N. MALM. *Swedish Pioneer Hist. Q. 1974 25(3/4): 241-253.* The Swedish-American author G. N. Malm deals with language acculturation in his novel *Charli Johnson, Svensk-Amerikan* (1909) and in his play *Härute* (1919). He was very familiar with immigrant speech which he tried to record accurately. Differences in the use of loan words and of English distinguish types of characters and different generations. Based on primary sources.
K. J. Puffer

1800. Hesslink, George K. KIMBALL YOUNG: SEMINAL AMERICAN SOCIOLOGIST, SWEDISH DESCENDANT, AND GRANDSON OF MORMON LEADER BRIGHAM YOUNG. *Swedish Pioneer Hist. Q. 1974 25(2): 115-132.* Kimball Young (1893-1972), whose mother was Swedish, was a direct descendant of Brigham Young. Summarizes Kimball Young's career, accomplishments, and ancestry. Scandinavian converts to Mormonism experienced a great cultural break. Unfulfilled expectations of the Mormon settlements and perceptions of the Mormon establishment led to disillusionment. Based on primary and secondary sources; photo, table, 34 notes.
K. J. Puffer

1801. Isaacson, John A. AMERICAN-SWEDISH HISTORY OF MANY, ILLUSTRATED BY EXPERIENCE. *Swedish Pioneer Hist. Q. 1975 26(4): 247-259.* Autobiography of John A. Isaacson (1892-1974), who emigrated from Sweden to Canada in 1911. He worked at laboring jobs, he tried investing in real estate, attended Minnesota College in Minneapolis (at the end of his second year he was offered a bank position), volunteered for World War I and became a US citizen, studied banking, and went to Chicago in 1927. 2 illus.
K. J. Puffer

1802. Johansson, Anders. AN EMIGRANT LETTER FROM QUEBEC, 1854. *Swedish Pioneer Hist. Q. 1979 30(4): 234-239.* This letter, erroneously dated 1853, is believed to be the oldest one preserved by an emigrant from Kronoberg's *län.* Anders Johansson (or Jaensson), the writer of the letter, was born in Tävelsås parish, Kronoberg's *län* (Småland), in 1822. He emigrated with his family to America in 1854. They settled in Chisago county, Minnesota, where he bought a farm and assumed its former owner's name, Porter, after the latter died. Johansson and his family subsequently did well. The letter is to his brother-in-law and "other relatives" back in Sweden. It was written in the Quebec quarantine station and describes the sea voyage. Photo.
C. W. Ohrvall

1803. Johnson, Emeroy. JONAS JONSSON—JOHN JOHNSON: PAGES FROM A DIARY, 1864-1895. *Swedish Pioneer Hist. Q. 1977 28(1): 7-26.* Excerpts from the diary of Swedish-born Jonas Jonsson (1814-97), who emigrated to Minnesota in 1882 and took the name John Johnson. Shows his transition from Swede to American. 3 photos.
C. W. Ohrvall

1804. Johnson, Emeroy. PER ANDERSSON'S LETTERS FROM CHISAGO LAKE. *Swedish Pioneer Hist. Q. 1973 24(1): 3-31.* The letter of Joris Per Andersson (1817-81), written at Chisago Lake, Minnesota, and mentioned by Helmer Lång in "Moberg, the Emigrant Saga and Reality" *Swedish Pioneer Historical Quarterly,* 1972 23(1): 3-24, is not lost. It is one of 12 letters of 1851-53 in the Gustavus Adolphus College archives with the papers of Eric Norelius, a good friend. Andersson came to Minnesota in 1851 and left in 1856 or 1857. He believed that Chisago Lake was ideal for Swedish settlement and encouraged others to come. Prices for food were high, but a worker made $20 to $30 per month. He gave news about other Swedish settlers, and expressed concern about religion. Letters are translated in full. Based on primary sources; 3 photos, 36 notes.
K. J. Puffer

1805. Johnson, Emeroy. SWEDISH ELEMENTARY SCHOOLS IN MINNESOTA LUTHERAN CONGREGATIONS. *Swedish Pioneer Hist. Q. 1979 30(3): 172-182.* After a brief history of the Swedish school program established by the several Lutheran churches in America during the late 19th century, the author describes his experiences as a student and as a teacher. 2 photos, reproduction of a page from *Barnens andra bok* (1890).
C. W. Ohrvall

1806. Johnson, Sherman E.   A MINNESOTA IMMIGRANT AT AGE SEVENTY.   *Swedish Pioneer Hist. Q. 1978 29(4): 240-256.* Johan Persson (1804-85) was an unusual immigrant from Sweden because he and his wife lived a full and active life in Sweden and did not come to America until he was 70 years old. Describes the life of Persson and his family—three sons and two daughters. Based on a brief autobiography and letters written to relatives. The author is the great-grandson of Johan on his mother's side. 4 photos, 9 notes.   C. W. Ohrvall

1807. Johnson, Sherman E.   "WOOD-JOHN": A SWEDISH PIONEER IN MINNESOTA.   *Swedish Pioneer Hist. Q. 1977 28(4): 274-282.* Nils Johan Johnson was born in Sweden in 1828 and received his nickname because of his dealings in cordwood and charcoal. He left no written records, so his grandson has written this article with the aid of church records in Sweden and in Scandia, Minnesota, and other archives and records. 7 notes.   C. W. Ohrvall

1808. Jönsson, Peter Johan.   "SOME CRIED AND SOME SANG . . .": THE EMIGRANT JOURNAL OF PETER JOHAN JÖNSSON, 1866.   *Swedish Pioneer Hist. Q. 1975 26(3): 157-183.* Traces the 1866 journey of Swedish immigrant Peter Johan Jönsson from his homeland to Chicago, Illinois. His journal vividly describes the ocean voyages from Liverpool, England, to New York, including an outbreak of cholera.   S

1809. Keller, Allan.   LITTLE SWEDEN ON THE DELAWARE.   *Am. Hist. Illus. 1979 13(9): 10-17.* Sweden's half-hearted attempt to establish an empire in the New World on the Delaware River, 1637-53, ended in the colony's absorption by William Penn's Pennsylvania colony.

1810. Kero, Reino.   RUOTSISTA AMERIKKAAN [From Sweden to America].   *Historiallinen Aikakauskirja [Finland] 1976 74(4): 326-330.* Surveys the research project on 19th- and 20th-century Swedish emigration conducted at Uppsala University, Sweden, since 1962. Major results are published in Harald Runblom and Hans Norman, eds., *From Sweden to America, a History of the Migration* (Minneapolis and Uppsala, 1976). The comparable Finnish project is located at Turku University, Finland. Due to modest finances, the Finnish research results have been much more limited so far.   R. G. Selleck

1811. Lahikainen, Dean.   THE FOLK SCULPTURE AND VIOLINS OF GUSTAF NYMAN.   *Swedish Pioneer Hist. Q. 1976 27(4): 270-285.* Gustaf Nyman (1864-1954) was born in Ramsberg, Sweden and trained as a farmer and craftsman. He learned the basic art of constructing violins from his father but taught himself woodcarving skills. He immigrated to the United States in 1887 and settled in Gardner, Massachusetts. Describes several of the products of Nyman's creativity in statuary, sculptures, and violins. Based in part on oral history interviews with Nyman's children and relatives; 16 photos, 11 notes.   C. W. Ohrvall

1812. Landfors, Arthur and Hasselmo, Nils.   ON THE SWEDISH-AMERICAN LANGUAGE.   *Swedish Pioneer Hist. Q. 1974 25(1): 3-12.* American Swedish is a mixed language, and is not highly regarded. However, it was used by more than one million Swedes; it is shaped by the influence of English and is bound by linguistic laws; Malm and Anna Olsson have preserved it in their books; and it is important in cultural history.   K. J. Puffer

1813. Langguth, Ellen Peterson.   CHARLES OF LÅNGEMÅLA AND MATHILDA OF GLIMÅKRA.   *Swedish Pioneer Hist. Q. 1977 28(1): 118-125.* Discusses the courtship and married life of Charles and Mathilda Peterson. Based on conversations with their children; 4 photos.   C. W. Ohrvall

1814. Larson, Bruce L.   THE EARLY LIFE OF CHARLES A. LINDBERGH, SR., 1859-1883.   *Swedish Pioneer Hist. Q. 1973 24(4): 203-222.* Charles Augustus Lindbergh, Sr., of Swedish immigrant farmer stock, played a significant role in the development of Minnesota and national reform politics. His father, August Lindbergh (b. 1809), a reformist member of the Riksdag, was forced by political enemies to emigrate in 1859. The initial years in Minnesota were not easy, but August became a local leader and held official positions. Charles financed his law study at the University of Michigan in 1881-83 with profits from marketing game birds. The first chapter of *Lindbergh of Minnesota: A Political Biography* (New York: Harcourt, Brace, Jovanovich, 1973). Based on primary and secondary sources; 4 photos, 35 notes.   K. J. Puffer

1815. Leamon, James S.   MAINE'S SWEDISH PIONEERS.   *Swedish Pioneer Hist. Q. 1975 26(2): 73-91.* In July 1880, New Sweden, Maine, celebrated its 10th anniversary. Maine had made deliberate efforts to attract Swedish immigrants, who were believed to be the most suitable. To prevent migration westward, William Widgery Thomas proposed a colony of picked settlers. He recruited immigrants in Sweden and accompanied them to Maine, making sure his letters home were published in Maine newspapers to insure a warm welcome. Secondary sources; 2 illus., map, 72 notes.   K. J. Puffer

1816. Lindquist, Emory.   REFLECTIONS ON THE LIFE OF HENRY BENGSTON.   *Swedish Pioneer Hist. Q. 1975 26(4): 261-264.* Henry Bengston (1887-1974) emigrated from Sweden in 1907. He came to Chicago in 1909, where his career in editing and publishing covered more than 40 years. He actively supported Swedish organizations, and published books and articles in Swedish and English. He was a true Christian, always ready to help others. In 1968 he moved to Northfield, Minnesota, where he died. Based on the eulogy at Henry Bengston's funeral; illus.   K. J. Puffer

1817. Linton, S. J.   THE SWEDISH ELEMENT IN WISCONSIN: THE TRADE LAKE SETTLEMENT.   *Swedish Pioneer Hist. Q. 1979 30(4): 254-261.* Burnett County, Wisconsin, was settled by Swedes during the mid-19th century. By 1890 this county was 35% Swedish. Trade Lake was the first settled, largest, and most influential Swedish community in the county. The first Swedes arrived in 1865. 51 notes.   C. W. Ohrvall

1818. Ljungmark, Lars.   HANS MATTSON'S *MINNEN*: A SWEDISH-AMERICAN MONUMENT.   *Swedish Pioneer Hist. Q. 1978 29(1): 57-68.* Hans Mattson was one of 13 Swedish-born colonels in the Union Army during the Civil War. Uses incidents in Mattson's life to show that *Minnen,* the only book he wrote, was in great part autobiographical. Mattson also was a journalist who actively tried to get Swedes to populate Minnesota. He served that state twice as elected Secretary of State and was consul general in Calcutta, India. Illus., 20 notes.   C. W. Ohrvall

1819. Lonaeus, Gunnar.   STAND UP AND BE COUNTED; THE SWEDISH STOCK IN AMERICA AND THE UNITED STATES BICENTENNIAL 1976.   *Swedish Pioneer Hist. Q. 1973 24(4): 223-230.* The 1970 census shows a decrease in the number of Swedish-born Americans. There is continuing urbanization; New York is now the leading Swedish city in America. For the first time in this century the total Swedish stock is less than one million.   K. J. Puffer

1820. Lorentzon, Betsy.   AN IMMIGRANT'S INNER CONFLICT.   *Swedish Pioneer Hist. Q. 1978 29(2): 137-142.* Lars Erickson was born in 1865. He came from Sweden to the United States in 1882. This article is based on correspondence between Lars and his family in Sweden. In his letters Lars seemed to dream of his life in Sweden—he was homesick. In 1927, when he returned to Sweden for a visit, he was homesick for his home in America. He died on 5 December 1929 in the United States.   C. W. Ohrvall

1821. Lund, Dennis W.   THE STONE AND THE STATUE.   *Swedish Pioneer Hist. Q. 1977 28(4): 283-292.* Oscar Sjoquist immigrated to the United States from Sweden in 1901. His grandson visited Sweden, and the small rural community where his grandfather grew up to record his grandfather's life story. The stone in the title refers to a stone in the farm yard on which Oscar carved his initials and birthdate "so that his brothers and sisters would always remember him." The statue refers to a wooden statue of Oscar leaving for America which his brother, Sven, carved. It is located in his home yard. Based on personal memories and talks with family members. 3 photos.   C. W. Ohrvall

1822. Lund, Eric R.   THE SWEDISH PIONEER HISTORICAL SOCIETY'S FIRST THIRTY YEARS.   *Swedish Pioneer Hist. Q. 1978 29(4): 235-239.* Discusses the founding of the society and its first 30 years.

Better and larger quarters for the archives, increased membership and financial support, and expanded programs are the goals of the society. Reprinted from the Norwegian-American newspaper, *Vinland* (Evanston, IL), of 13 April 1978. Based on annual meeting reports and other articles in the past issues of the *Quarterly;* 16 notes.

C. W. Ohrvall

1823. Magnusson, Gustav A. THE HOUSE THAT PROCLAIMED THE GOSPEL WITH TYPE AND PRESSES. *Swedish Pioneer Hist. Q. 1979 30(2): 117-128.* The Augustana (Lutheran) Book Concern of Rock Island, Illinois, began as a small print shop in a basement in Galesburg, Illinois, in 1855. It closed in 1967 due to the merger of three national Lutheran church bodies. Based on secondary sources published by the Concern; 6 photos.

C. W. Ohrvall

1824. McIntosh, Hugh E. HOW THE SWEDES CAME TO PAXTON. *Swedish Pioneer Hist. Q. 1979 30(1): 35-52.* The removal of Augustana College and Theological Seminary from Chicago to Paxton, Illinois, in 1863 brought about the formation of a Swedish community in the prairie town. Follows the course of events which drew so many Swedes to Paxton so that it attained significance as a community. By 1860 more than half of the 18,625 Swedes in the United States were living in Illinois and Minnesota. At this time the Scandinavians, who had at first joined with other Lutherans, separated and formed the Augustana Synod and the Augustana Seminary in Chicago. This was to be temporary until the Synod could found a colony. Several Midwestern sites were examined. William H. Osborn of the Illinois Central Railroad convinced the group to found its colony along the route of the railroad. Paxton was chosen because of the attractive offers made by the townspeople. Although the school prospered it never became a permanent part of the Paxton community and it moved to Rock Island in 1873. 4 photos, 95 notes.

C. W. Ohrvall

1825. McKnight, Roger. ANDREW PETERSON'S JOURNALS: AN ANALYSIS. *Swedish Pioneer Hist. Q. 1977 28(3): 153-172.* Discusses the diary of Andrew Peterson of Minnesota. Born in Sweden, he emigrated to America in 1849 and began keeping a journal in Swedish in 1854. (Quoted entries are also translated into English). Analyzes the diary as literature and as history. The diary was used by other writers, especially Vilhelm Moberg. Compares Peterson and his journals with other early Swedish writers. 16 notes.

C. W. Ohrvall

1826. Melloh, Ardith K. NEW SWEDEN, IOWA. *Palimpsest 1978 59(1): 2-19.* A small group of Swedish immigrants led by Peter Cassel founded one of the first lasting Swedish settlements in the United States in Jefferson County, Iowa, in 1845. For 10 years northern European immigrants came directly to Iowa. Thereafter, the Homestead Act stimulated internal migration. A third phase of New Sweden's history began with the organization of the English Lutheran Church in Lockridge in 1912. 4 illus., 10 photos, note.

D. W. Johnson

1827. Metcalf, Michael F. DR. CARL MAGNUS WRANGEL AND PREREVOLUTIONARY PENNSYLVANIA POLITICS. *Swedish Pioneer Hist. Q. 1976 27(4): 247-260.* Carl Magnus Wrangel was provost of the Swedish Lutheran Churches in America from 1757 until his recall to Sweden in 1768. Sheds new light on his controversial ministry and political activities. He arrived from Sweden with broad powers which, combined with his youthfulness, his lack of experience, and his noble origins, contributed to dissension within the ministerial ranks. Wrangel and Henry Melchior Muhlenberg, the renowned German Lutheran minister, strived to reinvigorate Lutheranism. In 1763, Pontiac's Rebellion started a struggle which culminated in an attempt to change Pennsylvania from a proprietary to a royal colony. Both sides worked to persuade the Swedish Lutherans to accept their point of view. Wrangel ultimately supported the proprietary cause. His actions in church and state matters reflect the central problem of the descendants of the original Swedish settlers, their assimilation into the emerging American population and the disintegration of their religious and cultural ties with Sweden. Based in part on original manuscripts; 65 notes.

C. W. Ohrvall

1828. Millgård, Per-Olaf. LETTERS FROM NEW SWEDEN, MAINE. *Swedish Pioneer Hist. Q. 1975 26(2): 104-111.* Selections from the letters of Swedish immigrant families in Maine, 1873-88. Things went badly at first, the new settlers felt homesick, and many household items

were hard to find. By 1879, food became plentiful and work for wages available. The selection from 1888 is by a widow informing her mother-in-law of her husband's death from pneumonia. Primary sources; illus.

K. J. Puffer

1829. Millgård, Per-Olaf, ed., transl. MORE LETTERS FROM NEW SWEDEN, MAINE. *Swedish Pioneer Hist. Q. 1979 30(4): 245-253.* Continued from a previous article. The writers were John Södergren (1820-1902), father, Paul (b. 1849), his son, and Brita (b. 1859), his daughter. There are four letters translated and edited. All are to relatives remaining in Sweden. Photo, 4 notes.

C. W. Ohrvall

1830. Moyne, Ernest J. RICHARD HENRY DANA, JR., AND MATHIAS LILLJEQUIST, THE CARPENTER OF THE SHIP "ALERT." *Swedish Pioneer Hist. Q. 1973 24(1): 49-54.* In *Two Years Before the Mast,* Richard Henry Dana, Jr. (1815-82), reported a great deal of information about the carpenter of the ship *Alert,* a Swede who had left his wife in Boston. According to the crew lists prepared for the 1911 edition, the carpenter was M. Lilljequist, 35 years old. The Boston *Directory* for 1835-36 lists Mary Lilljequist, dressmaker. Perhaps she then returned to Sweden, because the name is not seen again until 1844 when "Mathias Lilliequies, mariner," appears. With variant spellings the two names continue until 1860 when the *Directory* lists Mrs. Matthew Lillgequist, widow. The name continues sporadically until the 1878 *Directory,* which contains the notice "Lillgequist M., died Sept. 23, 1877." Based on primary sources; 13 notes.

K. J. Puffer

1831. Nelson, Charles H. TOWARD A MORE ACCURATE APPROXIMATION OF CLASS COMPOSITION OF THE ERIK JANSSONISTS. *Swedish Pioneer Hist. Q. 1975 26(1): 3-15.* The occupations of Janssonist emigrants can be identified from ship manifests for the period 1845-47, when the majority emigrated to Illinois. The class distribution of the emigrants was found to be similar to the county they were from, with about two-thirds coming from impoverished classes. Based on a chapter of the author's doctoral dissertation, "Erik Janssonism: A Socio-Cultural Interpretation of the Emergence and Development of a Religious Sect in Sweden in the 1840's." 4 tables, 21 notes.

K. J. Puffer

1832. Nelson, David P. RYSSBY: FIRST SWEDISH SETTLEMENT IN COLORADO. *Colorado Mag. 1977 54(2): 184-199.* In 1869, the first seven Swedish Americans settled at Ryssby. In spite of the Panic of 1873 and grasshoppers, others came and built a schoolhouse and Lutheran church. But, by 1914, economic problems caused Swedish families to desert Ryssby. Descendants completed restoration of the church in 1976. Primary and secondary sources; 12 illus., 30 notes.

O. H. Zabel

1833. Nelson, Ronald E. BISHOP HILL: SWEDISH DEVELOPMENT OF THE WESTERN ILLINOIS FRONTIER. *Western Illinois Regional Studies 1978 1(2): 109-120.* Bishop Hill Colony, Illinois, a small frontier settlement of Swedish immigrants warrants study as a communalistic experiment, as an area of concentrated Swedish immigration (virtually the first of frontier America), and as a remarkable example of quick economic growth through cooperation, 1846-59.

1834. Norelius, Theodore A. MEMORIES OF VILHELM MOBERG AT CHISAGO LAKES. *Swedish Pioneer Hist. Q. 1979 30(1): 53-59.* Perhaps no rural community in the United States has more visitors directly from Sweden than the Chisago Lakes area in Minnesota, made famous by the novels of Vilhelm Moberg. After a brief history of the area recounts the visit of the Swedish author, Vilhelm Moberg, to the lakes in 1948. 4 photos.

C. W. Ohrvall

1835. Norton, John, transl. and ed. ANDERS WIBERG'S ACCOUNT OF A TRIP TO THE UNITED STATES IN 1852-1853. *Swedish Pioneer Hist. Q. 1978 29(2): 89-116, (3): 162-179.* Part I. When he left for the United States, 16 July 1852, Anders Wiberg had been a Swedish Lutheran pastor of pietist leanings. On the ship Wiberg broke completely with the state church of Sweden. He was baptized in Copenhagen by the banished Swedish seaman-lay preacher F. O. Nilsson, father of the Swedish Baptist movement. From New York Wiberg journeyed to the western frontier as a colporteur in the service of the American Baptist Publication Society. His letters home were serialized in the liberal Stockholm newspaper, *Aftonbladet,* and must have profoundly influenced prospective emigrants. They also helped fuel the debate on religious freedom. He remained in America for two years and then returned in 1863 for three more years. The original of the Wiberg manuscript diary is in the archives of Bethelseminariet in Stockholm. 19 notes. Part II. Wiberg describes the conditions of Swedish immigrants in Illinois and their problems in getting there. His return to New York was via St. Louis and the Ohio River to Columbus, Ohio. He comments about Swedes he had met, the country, and other people. He especially was taken with Niagara Falls. 9 notes.

C. W. Ohrvall

1836. Norton, John E., ed. "FOR IT FLOWS WITH MILK AND HONEY"; TWO IMMIGRANT LETTERS ABOUT BISHOP HILL. *Swedish Pioneer Hist. Q. 1973 24(3): 163-179.* Translates letters by Anders Andersson and Anders Larsson about the colony of Bishop Hill in 1847, which were published in *Aftonbladet.* Andersson, a devoted Janssonist, reported that all arrived in good health. Larsson reported that the Janssonists were laying out their new city, including communal mills, shops, and farms. Erik Jansson was accepted as the Prophet and Bishop Hill as the new spiritual Israel. Illus., notes.   K. J. Puffer

1837. Norton, John E. "...WE HAVE SUCH GREAT NEED OF A TEACHER": OLOF BÄCK, BISHOP HILL, AND THE ANDOVER SETTLEMENT OF LARS PAUL ESBJÖRN. *Swedish Pioneer Hist. Q. 1975 26(4): 215-220.* One of the America-letters of Olof Bäck was written to Pastor Lars Paul Esbjörn of the Swedish State Church. Esbjörn had it published in *Norrlandsposten* in 1849. Bäck had been converted to Methodism. His wife had remained with the Janssonists. The letter tells of Bäck's life in America and expresses the great need for clergymen. Esbjörn, sympathetic to the "Reader" movement, emigrated with many of his congregation. Primary sources; illus., 4 notes.

K. J. Puffer

1838. Olson, Olof. A LETTER FROM ONE GENERATION TO ANOTHER. *Swedish Pioneer Hist. Q. 1973 24(4): 242-258.* The author's family emigrated to Minnesota in 1869, when he was six. Four families obtained homesteads in Maple Ridge township, and built a small cabin in which 19 people lived until spring. They traded with Indians and befriended the Shingwaw family, their nearest Indian neighbors. They collected and sold ginseng and slowly cleared the land. In 1871 a school district was organized. 4 photos.   K. J. Puffer

1839. Olsson, Nils William. PETER ARVEDSON: EARLY SWEDISH IMMIGRANT EPISCOPALIAN MISSIONARY IN ILLINOIS. *Swedish Pioneer Hist. Q. 1976 27(2): 116-126.* Peter Arvedson or Pehr Arvidsson (1822-80), a Swedish immigrant to Algonquin, Illinois, devoted years of labor to the Protestant Episcopal Church. First as a lay reader and finally as an ordained priest, he held services in a variety of places, including his own farm home. Occasionally he preached in Swedish. Based on primary sources.   K. J. Puffer

1840. Olsson, Nils William. THE SWEDISH BROTHERS: AN EXPERIMENT IN IMMIGRANT MUTUAL AID. *Swedish Pioneer Hist. Q. 1974 25(3-4): 220-229.* Swedish immigrants to the United States formed mutual aid societies in the 19th century. In Minneapolis, *Svenska Bröderna* was formed in 1876; its early history was recorded by Alfred Söderström, who is quoted. Recently the membership roster for 1876 to 1888 was discovered, with statistical analyses of the information given in the entries producing valuable insights. Based on primary sources; 3 tables, 2 notes.   K. J. Puffer

1841. Osberg, Edward E. ENGLEWOOD MEMORIES: SWEDISH BUSINESSMEN ON CHICAGO'S 59TH STREET. *Swedish Pioneer Hist. Q. 1977 28(1): 57-61.* Edward E. Osberg recalls the Swedish businessmen on Chicago's 59th street, 50 years ago.   C. W. Ohrvall

1842. Ostergren, Robert C. A COMMUNITY TRANSPLANTED: THE FORMATIVE EXPERIENCE OF A SWEDISH IMMIGRANT COMMUNITY IN THE UPPER MIDDLE WEST. *J. of Hist. Geography 1979 5(2): 189-212.* Compares the physical and cultural background of Dalarna Province, Sweden, with Isantic County, Minnesota, to which Swedish migration took place. The answers to the establishment of the migrants' old world in the new are mixed. The group's focal point continued to be the Lutheran Church and many of their social customs and ties

continued as before, but the economic conditions of frontier Minnesota caused a switch to crops more characteristic of the American frontier. 7 maps, 6 tables, graph, 31 notes.   A. J. Larson

1843. Ostergren, Robert C. CULTURAL HOMOGENEITY AND POPULATION STABILITY AMONG SWEDISH IMMIGRANTS IN CHISAGO COUNTY. *Minnesota Hist. 1973 43(7): 255-269.* Ethnic group spatial concentration was common among immigrants in 19th-century America. Within that concentration there was further ethnic or cultural segregation, even within national groups, of identification of common customs, dialect, and historical experience. Mobility was also becoming a hallmark of the American people. Analyzes ethnic concentration and population mobility in several rural Swedish immigrant communities in eastern Minnesota 1885-1905, finding a positive correlation between population stability and cultural homogeneity. Illus., 11 maps, 5 tables.   D. L. Smith

1844. Palmquist, Peter E. FRONTIER IN TRANSITION: CALIFORNIA'S REDWOOD COAST AS PHOTOGRAPHED BY A. W. ERICSON. *Am. West 1975 12(4): 30-39.* Photographic essay from the works of Swedish immigrant Augustus William Ericson (1848-1927) documents the social change and economic growth of northern California from the frontier conditions of the 1880's to 20th-century modernity. 16 photos.   D. L. Smith

1845. Pearson, Daniel M. THE TWO WORLDS OF CARL A. SWENSSON, 1873-1888. *Swedish Pioneer Hist. Q. 1977 28(4): 259-273.* Carl Aaron Swensson was the founder of Bethany College, Lindsborg, Kansas. Several biographical sketches have been written since his death in 1904 but few have analyzed his life and his importance, both in American society and in Midwest Swedish immigrant communities. Swensson's father, Jonas, was a Lutheran minister who despised many aspects of American culture, so he did not allow his children to attend public schools or find American friends. Thus Carl grew up a Swede. He attended Augustana College and Seminary during 1873-79 which further enhanced his Swedish orientation. But he realized that the promise of America was not only that it was Christian, but that it was energetic, strong, and educated. After he graduated, he added Swedish immigrant colonization projects, politics, and railroad promotion to his active concern for religious education. Describes his efforts in these areas. Based on the writings of Swensson; photo, 23 notes.   C. W. Ohrvall

1846. Peterson, Martin. THE SWEDES OF YAMHILL. *Oregon Hist. Q. 1975 76(1): 5-27.* Presents the history and personal memoirs of the Swedish American community in the vicinity of Carlton, Oregon, and the Yamhill River Valley. In the late 19th century John Wennerberg helped many of his fellow Swedes to settle in western Oregon. The immigrants labored as farmhands and housekeepers, and purchased farms with the aid of Wennerberg. Describes the Swedish folkways, expressions, agricultural methods, and recreational activities established in the immigrants' new environment. Based on remembrances of 14 persons and letters to the author; 14 photos, 5 notes.   J. D. Smith

1847. Pettersson, Carl-Werner. FROM BRINKELID TO SUNRISE —A MODERN SAGA OF DISCOVERY. *Swedish Pioneer Hist. Q. 1974 25(1): 42-61.* With only a document mentioning Sunrise, Minnesota, and an unidentified photograph, the author visited Minnesota to find Sunrise and search for relatives who had come to America around 1890. He found many relatives and many people interested in Sweden. 6 photos.   K. J. Puffer

1848. Rice, Gwen and Howard, Robert M. PETER GIBSON: ADVENTURER, BLACKSMITH, AND PROSPEROUS FARMER. *Swedish Pioneer Hist. Q. 1976 27(1): 44-60.* Peter Gibson (1836-1924) was born in Sweden as Per Jeppesson. He emigrated to England where he met young men who were planning to search for gold in California. At the gold fields he worked as a blacksmith. In Knoxville, Illinois, he again worked as a blacksmith, and married. Under the leadership of Reverend S. G. Larson he homesteaded in Saunders County, Nebraska, where the family became important. From *Swedish Pioneers in Saunders County, Nebraska: A Collection of Family Histories of Early Settlers in Nebraska,* ed. and privately published by Albert P. Strom (Pittsburgh, 1972). 2 photos.   K. J. Puffer

1849. Roosa, Alma Carlson and Hamilton, Henry W. HOMESTEADING IN THE 1880'S: THE ANDERSON-CARLSON FAMILIES OF CHERRY COUNTY. *Nebraska Hist. 1977 58(3): 371-394.* Alma Carlson Roosa was five years old when her parents and grandparents homesteaded in Cherry County, Nebraska, in the 1880's. Her uncle, photographer John A. Anderson (1869-1948), lived in 1879 in the home of a married sister, Amanda Anderson Carlson. Her daughter, Alma Carlson Roosa, contributed valuable reminiscences to the editor and his wife as they prepared their biography of Anderson. R. Lowitt

1850. Runblom, Harald and Tederbrand, Lars-Göran. FUTURE RESEARCH IN SWEDISH-AMERICAN HISTORY: SOME PROSPECTIVES. *Swedish Pioneer Hist. Q. 1979 30(2): 129-140.* The authors were associated with the Uppsala Migration History Project, 1962-76. THey discuss several areas in which the Swedish background of the emigration to North America still has not been adequately investigated. These areas include the sociological study of pioneer emigrant groups; emigration in the 1920's; emigration from America in the Depression years; and the migration of craftsmen. Other areas are also recommended. They argue for a "highly interdisciplinary study in a broadly comparative perspective of the Swedish immigrants and their descendants," to gain an understanding of "the transformation from Swedish immigration to American society." Chart, 26 notes. C. W. Ohrvall

1851. Runeby, Nils and Barton, H. Arnold, transl. GUSTAV UNONIUS AND PROPAGANDA AGAINST EMIGRATION. *Swedish Pioneer Hist. Q. 1973 24(2): 94-107.* In the struggles between Swedish religious factions in the United States, Gustav Unonius became greatly disillusioned, and a zealous opponent of emigration. He left America in 1858. He was opposed to religious freedom and the American school system. In 1858 he distributed a questionnaire to clergymen concerning Scandinavian settlement. The replies did not agree with his beliefs: the immigrants were generally well off and content. Unonius' efforts to discourage emigration met with positive interest in Sweden. The Riksdag of 1859-60 awarded him a gratuity and the Riksdag of 1862-63 discussed emigration. In 1861 Unonius began to bring out his memoirs, perhaps the most cited writing of the earlier emigration. His activity was supported in the Riksdag by individuals of differing political views, but he attained no results. Excerpted from *Den nye världen och den gamla* (Uppsala, 1969). Based on primary and secondary sources; 28 notes. K. J. Puffer

1852. Salisbury, Robert S. SWEDISH-AMERICAN HISTORIOGRAPHY AND THE QUESTION OF AMERICANIZATION. *Swedish Pioneer Hist. Q. 1978 29(2): 117-136.* Compares early 20th-century and current historiography. The earliest work on Swedish American assimilation discussed is Kendric C. Babcock's *The Scandinavian Element in the United States* (Urbana: U. of Illinois, 1914). In it Babcock extols the putative virtues of the Scandinavian race as more nearly approaching the American type than any other immigrants except those from Great Britain. As with other authors, Babcock states that the Swedes assimilate easily into American life. The author finds an increased emphasis on "ethnicity" and "maintenance phenomena" in the historiography of the late 1960's and 70's. Using new analytical techniques on new types of source material, these studies cast doubt upon the assumption that Swedes fused quickly and quietly into the melting pot. Concludes that the humanistic approach of the earlier works and the social science approach of the later works both contribute to better understanding, are complementary, and offer the broadest insight. 55 notes. C. W. Ohrvall

1853. Scott, Franklin D. THE SAGA OF NELS M. HOKANSON: IMMIGRANT AND IMMIGRANT HISTORIAN. *Swedish Pioneer Hist. 1978 29(3): 198-208.* Nels M. Hokanson was born in Copenhagen of Swedish parents in 1885. In 1887 the family came to America and settled in St. Paul, Minnesota. After four or five years the family moved to Aitkin, Minnesota, where Nels lived until he joined a circus band at age 16. Discusses his life and times, based on his published writings and especially on autobiographical notes which he prepared in 1977-78. Hokanson's concern with his Swedish compatriots began in childhood and continued throughout his life. He is best known for his book, *Swedish Immigrants in Lincoln's Time.* It was first published in 1942 and is now being reprinted. He has written many articles for Swedish American journals. Photo, 11 notes. C. W. Ohrvall

1854. Setterdahl, Lilly. EMIGRANT LETTERS BY BISHOP HILL COLONISTS FROM NORA PARISH. *Western Illinois Regional Studies 1978 1(2): 121-175.* Reprints a series of letters from Bishop Hill Colony, Illinois, by Swedish immigrants who settled in the commune led by Erik Jansson. The letters, dated 1847-56, are directed to relatives and friends still in Sweden and describe the sea voyage, building operations, and daily life in the community.

1855. Setterdahl, Lilly and Wilson, J. Hiram. HOTEL ACCOMMODATIONS IN THE BISHOP HILL COLONY. *Swedish Pioneer Hist. Q. 1978 29(3): 180-197.* Although the Janssonists of the Bishop Hill Colony in Illinois largely were isolated from neighboring communities by rules and circumstances, the leaders did travel and realized the importance of contact with the outside world. To accommodate visitors, hotels were constructed. Describes the founding of the Colony, the building of the hotels, and the visitors who came out of curiosity and to trade. The hotels currently are undergoing restoration. Based in part on information found in letters written by colonists and on interviews with original colonists in 1907; 4 photos, 41 notes. C. W. Ohrvall

1856. Setterdahl, Lilly. A VISIT TO NEW SWEDEN, MAINE: REMINISCENCES OF AN ERA. *Swedish Pioneer Hist. Q. 1975 26(2): 92-103.* Swedish settlers first came to Aroostook County, Maine, at the invitation of the state in 1870. Early years were difficult, with severe winters and a stony soil to contend with. State aid ceased in 1873 when the settlement had made impressive progress. Although many young people have left the area, the population has remained primarily Swedish. Primary sources; 22 notes. K. J. Puffer

1857. Sjöberg, Leif. ARTHUR LANDFORS IN RETROSPECT. *Swedish Pioneer Hist. Q. 1974 25(2): 141-144.* Arthur Landfors (1888-1973) was one of the most important American-Swedish poets. He was a gentle man who made his living as a painter. His poetry articulated the experience of the immigrant. K. J. Puffer

1858. Sjöborg, Sofia Charlotta and Westerberg, Wesley M., transl. JOURNEY TO FLORIDA, 1871. *Swedish Pioneer Hist. Q. 1975 26(1): 24-45.* Reprints Sofia Charlotta Sjöborg's diary of her journey from Sweden to New York, then south to central Florida. The company was friendly and happy during the ocean crossing, the time being spent with sermons, religious texts, and singing. Impressions of cities, people, and the countryside are given. Based on primary sources; 14 notes. K. J. Puffer

1859. Smith, Roberta Anderson. THE DALANDER COLONY AT SWEDE POINT, IOWA. *Swedish Pioneer Hist. Q. 1979 30(3): 162-171.* The history of the colony at Swede Point (now Madrid), Iowa, founded in 1846 by the widow Anna Dalander and her party from Sweden. The author was born and raised there and is a descendent of the Cassels and the Dalanders, two of the first families. Based in great part on the writings of the author's father and on stories heard as she was growing up; 2 photos. C. W. Ohrvall

1860. Strombeck, Rita. SUCCESS AND THE SWEDISH-AMERICAN IDEOLOGY. *Swedish Pioneer Hist. Q. 1977 28(3): 182-191.* In the America of ca. 1870-1910, the hero was the self-made man who succeeded from humble origins by right moral living and in spite of difficulties. Swedish American journalists and clergymen espoused this doctrine and it became the goal for many Swedish Americans. An example was John A. Johnson, who rose from backwoods cabin to become governor of Minnesota in 1908. Cites articles in Swedish American literature which extol the self-made man doctrine. (Swedish language passages are also translated into English). 12 notes. C. W. Ohrvall

1861. Telleen, Jane. "YOURS IN THE MASTER'S SERVICE": EMMY EVALD AND THE WOMAN'S MISSIONARY SOCIETY OF THE AUGUSTANA LUTHERAN CHURCH, 1892-1942. *Swedish Pioneer Hist. Q. 1979 30(3): 183-195.* Emmy Evald founded the society in 1892. By 1907 the society was in control of its own finances but not its mission efforts. They petitioned and gained this authority. They kept it until 1939 when the Synod mission board took back the authority. this time women were represented on all of the church boards. The The society was an active force in the church and nation but was not an overly feminist or radical organization. It gave the church strength and the

women confidence and provided younger generations of church women with a tradition. This paper was first presented at the 1977 Woman Historians of the Midwest conference. Based on interviews and the papers of Emmy Evald and secondary sources; 3 photos, 26 notes.
C. W. Ohrvall

1862. Tolzmann, Don Heinrich. COLONEL HANS MATTSON AND AXEL LUNDEBERG: MINNEN/REMINISCENCES. *Swedish Pioneer Hist. Q. 1975 26(4): 221-230.* The unpublished autobiography of Axel Lundeberg, "I Amerika," suggests that Lundeberg had a considerable role in writing the memoir of Colonel Hans Mattson, *Minnen af Öfverste Hans Mattson* (Lund: 1890, 1891), *Reminiscences: the Story of an Emigrant* (St. Paul: D. D. Merrill Company, 1892). Lundeberg states that he translated and reworked English diary notations. The memoir reflects the scholarship and literary ability of Lundeberg. Primary sources; illus., 36 notes.
K. J. Puffer

1863. Tolzmann, Don Heinrich. DR. AXEL LUNDEBERG, SWEDISH AMERICAN SCHOLAR. *Swedish Pioneer Hist. Q. 1973 24(1): 33-48.* Axel Johan Sigurd Mauritz Lundeberg (1852-1940) was born into an influential Swedish family. He was well educated and traveled through Europe reporting on various social systems for Swedish newspapers. In 1888 he arrived in America. From 1890, when he settled in Minneapolis, until his death he was a leading Swede in the Midwest. In 1910 he established a Swedenborgian church; he was its minister until 1919. He was a pacifist during World War I. He collected over 10,000 books and wrote prolifically. Primarily a theologian strongly influenced by Swedish philosophy, he can be characterized as an ethnic intellectual. Reprints one of his poems. Based on primary and secondary sources; 2 photos, 29 notes, biblio.
K. J. Puffer

1864. Trotzig, E. G. EARLY SWEDISH SETTLEMENTS IN THE DAKOTA TERRITORY. *Swedish Pioneer Hist. Q. 1977 28(1): 106-117.* The Dakota Territory was opened to white settlement in 1859. The first Swedish settlers arrived seven years later to found the Ahlsborg settlement near Fort Randall. Completion of the railroad to Sioux City, Iowa, in 1868 brought more settlers, including Swedes, to Clay and Union Counties. Describes the homesteading procedure followed by a typical immigrant and the Swedish communities, including the 106th annual *"Midsommar Fest"* held in Dalesburg in 1976. Based on Centenary booklets published by churches in the area; 2 photos, map, 6 notes.
C. W. Ohrvall

1865. Trotzig, E. G. THURE KUMLIEN, PIONEER NATURALIST. *Swedish Pioneer Hist. Q. 1979 30(3): 196-204.* Thure Kumlien was born in Sweden in 1819, where he received a good education, majoring in botany. In 1843 he emigrated to America with his bride-to-be, Christina Wallberg. They settled near Lake Koshkonong, Wisconsin, where they married. Never a farmer-in-earnest, Thure spent much time in his pursuits as a naturalist. In 1850 this came to the attention of Thomas M. Brewer, a Boston naturalist. Brewer financed and publicized Thure as a naturalist and brought him world-wide recognition. In 1867 he was appointed to teach natural history, at Albion Academy and later accepted a commission from the state to prepare natural history exhibits for the University at Madison and act as conservator at the museum of the Wisconsin Natural History Society. He died in 1888. Based on the works of Angie Kumlien Main, his granddaughter; 3 photos, 8 notes.
C. W. Ohrvall

1866. Vontver, May. EMIGRATION: AN AUTOBIOGRAPHICAL STORY. *Swedish Pioneer Hist. Q. 1977 28(3): 205-214.* The story of one Swedish family as the sons and daughters emigrated to America, ca. 1900. The mother grieves at her loss, especially when the oldest son is killed on a railroad construction project. The return of the other son for a visit causes anguish as the parents try to keep him on the farm.
C. W. Ohrvall

1867. Westerberg, Wesley M. THE SWEDISH CONNECTION. *Scandinavian Rev. 1976 64(2): 15-20.* Traces emigration from Sweden to the United States from the first settlement at New Sweden in the 17th century through the great exodus beginning about 1840 but increasing heavily in the second half of the 19th century. When the floodtide stopped in the 1920's, some 1,240,000 Swedish immigrants had settled in the United States. Describes Swedish reaction to the emigration. Illus.
J. G. Smoot

1868. White, Joyce L. THE AFFILIATION OF SEVEN SWEDISH LUTHERAN CHURCHES WITH THE EPISCOPAL CHURCH. *Hist. Mag. of the Protestant Episcopal Church 1977 46(2): 171-186.* By 1650 the Church of Sweden had established seven mission congregations along the Delaware River. In 1831 the Church left these congregations to go their separate ways. For years they had been largely supplied by Episcopal clergy and the services had long been conducted in English rather than Swedish. The formal steps by which these Swedish Lutheran congregations assimilated into the structure of the Protestant Episcopal Church is presented. Discusses each congregation from its founding through its assimilation into the Episcopal Church. Based on church records and histories. 53 notes.
H. M. Parker, Jr.

1869. Whyman, Henry C. PETER BERGNER, PIONEER MISSIONARY TO SWEDISH SEAMEN AND IMMIGRANTS. *Swedish Pioneer Hist. Q. 1979 30(2): 103-116.* Peter Bergner (1797-1866) and his family arrived in New York City in 1832 to settle there after Peter had led the sailor's life. He was converted to active Christianity in 1844 and began to preach to immigrant Swedes and Swedish sailors in their own language. These services were held on ships, or floating Bethels, under the auspices of the Methodist Church. This article is the story of Peter Bergner and also of these Bethel Ships. Peter Bergner died in 1866, having worked for the Lord for 17 years. Based on records of the *New York City Tract Society* and several autobiographs and articles in Methodist journals; 3 photos, 25 notes.
C. W. Ohrvall

1870. Wiren, Agnes. EARLY EMIGRATION FROM BLEKINGE. *Swedish Pioneer Hist. Q. 1978 29(1): 43-56.* Discusses initial emigration to America, 1851-70, from Blekinge, a province on the southern coast of Sweden. Concludes that "many problems remain to be solved before the first Blekinge emigrant's routes in the new land can be fully determined." Photo.
C. W. Ohrvall

1871. Wright, Rochelle. STUART ENGSTRAND AND BISHOP HILL. *Swedish Pioneer Hist. Q. 1977 28(3): 192-204.* Describes the book, *They Sought for Paradise,* by Stuart Engstrand and compares its plot and characters with historic facts concerning the Bishop Hill Colony. Although a novel, the book does stick close to history. Bishop Hill was a community founded in Illinois in 1846 by Swedish immigrant followers of the religious prophet, Erik Jansson. The novel is a "fascinating fictionalized study of a particular historical figure" and a "commentary on the conflict between individualism and social consciousness." 29 notes.
C. W. Ohrvall

1872. Unsigned. THE DREAM OF AMERICA: PICTURES FROM AN EXHIBITION. *Swedish Pioneer Hist. Q. 1975 26(3): 145-156.* Photographs and illustrations from the 19th century showing life in Sweden, and Swedish immigration and life in the United States. Materials from Stockholm Stadsmuseum and the Emigrant Institute in Växjö. Primary sources; 12 illus.
K. J. Puffer

Slavic

General

1873. Beal, Stephen. FIGHT FOR SURVIVAL. *Am. Preservation 1978 1(2): 42-47.* Chicago's Pilsen neighborhood once was newly reclaimed swampland inhabited by Czechs and Poles in the 1850's. Today Pilsen is 85% Mexican-American and contains the oldest housing stock in Chicago. With badly deteriorating buildings and low-income residents, Pilsen Neighbors and the Eighteenth Street Development Corporation are attempting to renovate buildings without displacing tenants. CETA funds and federal loans have made possible the Pilsen Rehab Project, which renovates homes with local labor and sells them to area residents. However, the nearby South Loop New Town project may bring rising land values, displacements, and demolition. The future is uncertain despite impressive community solidarity and recent gains. 20 photos.
S. C. Strom

1874. Bodnar, John E. IMMIGRATION AND MODERNIZATION: THE CASE OF SLAVIC PEASANTS IN INDUSTRIAL

AMERICA. *J. of Social Hist.* 1976 10(1): 44-71. Studies the impact of modernization on immigrant peasants from southern Poland, eastern Slovakia, the Ukraine, Croatia, Bosnia, Slovenia, and Serbia. Urban, industrial society can elicit behavioral patterns similar to peasant culture. "The dialectical process of modernization involves the interplay between tradition and working class necessity, producing a new working-class consciousness." This consciousness was a synthesis forged by immigrants within the structural context of a new socioeconomic milieu. "Modernization involved a clash of peasant culture and working-class pragmatism which resulted in a reinforcement of traditional behavior and perceptions." 6 tables, 88 notes. R. V. Ritter

1875. Bodnar, John E. MATERIALISM AND MORALITY: SLAVIC-AMERICAN IMMIGRANTS AND EDUCATION. *J. of Ethnic Studies* 1976 3(4): 1-19. Analyzes attitudes of Poles, Ukrainians, Croats, and Slovaks in America who saw education primarily as trade and occupation oriented, and necessary for linguistic, religious, and cultural preservation. Groups such as the Slovaks especially feared the moral degeneracy and materialism associated with American secular schools. These beliefs are demonstrated in the pages of Joseph Husek's Slovak paper *Jednota*, Frank Petrich's Slovenian news *Proletarec*, and the Polish *Dziennik Chicagoski*. Illustrates the low percentages of public school attendance and the median years of schooling among Slavic immigrants. Slavs did not immediately assimilate and embrace American notions of upward success and acquisitiveness. Based on primary materials of the IHRC, University of Minnesota, and personal interviews; tables, 61 notes. G. J. Bobango

1876. Cincura, Andrew. SLOVAK AND RUTHENIAN EASTER EGGS IN AMERICA: THE IMPACT OF CULTURE CONTACT ON IMMIGRANT ART AND CUSTOM. *Slovakia* 1976 26(49): 40-68. Discusses the cultural transmission of the Easter egg decorative tradition from Europe to America among Slovak Americans and Ukrainian (Ruthenian) Americans in Cleveland, Ohio, in the 1970's; considers folk art techniques.

1877. Fenchak, Paul. ARTFUL DODGERS: THE DIRECTORS OF ETHNIC STUDIES PROGRAMS. *Ukrainian Q.* 1974 30(1): 55-60. Ethnic studies programs and various governmental tabulators of minorities fail to include East Europeans. S

1878. Fenchak, Paul. CURRENT STATUS OF SLAVIC STUDIES IN THE PUBLIC SCHOOLS OF MARYLAND. *Jednota Ann. Furdek* 1977 16: 211-221. Examines current efforts in Maryland schools to include courses on the language, history, and culture of Slavic Americans as an important ethnic minority.

1879. Kamenets'kyi, Ihor. DRUHYI NATSIONAL'NYI KONGRES AMERYKANS'KYKH SLAVISTIV [The second national congress of American Slavists]. *Ukrainskyi Istoryk* 1967 4(1-2): 87-90. Describes proceedings at the second national congress of the American Association for the Advancement of Slavic Studies, held in Washington, 30 March-1 April 1967.

1880. Kedro, Milan James. COLORADO'S SLAVIC IMMIGRANTS. *Family Heritage* 1979 2(2): 46-49. Relates the experiences of two immigrant families in the mining town of Pueblo, Colorado, 1900's-10's: that of George Olyejar, Slovenes from present-day Yugoslavia, and that of Mary and Florian Krasovich, Slovaks from present-day Czechoslovakia.

1881. Kimball, Stanley B. SOUTH SLAVIC SOCIETIES IN UTAH. *East European Q.* 1977 11(3): 365-370. Discusses the immigration of South Slavs to Utah and describes the lodges which they established. Since 1904, they have set up 39 lodges and societies of which 20 are still active. They are primarily social clubs. The Slovenes are the dominant South Slavic group in Utah. C. R. Lovin

1882. March, Richard. THE TAMBURITZA TRADITION IN THE CALUMET REGION. *Indiana Folklore* 1977 10(2): 127-138. Relates findings of a 1976 folklore project pertaining to oral tradition, customs, ceremonies, music, and dance among Slavic Americans (Croats, Serbs, and Macedonians) in urban northwestern Indiana.

1883. Procko, Bohdan P. SOTER ORTYNSKY: FIRST RUTHENIAN BISHOP IN THE UNITED STATES, 1907-1916. *Catholic Hist. R.* 1973 58(4): 513-533. "Describes the jurisdictional problems that Bishop Soter Ortynsky (1866-1916) faced in his attempt to build an effective administrative system for the Byzantine-Slavic rite of the Catholic Church in the United States. Pope Pius X's appointment of a bishop for the Eastern Rite Catholics, who were then generally known as Ruthenians (primarily Ukrainian and Rusin immigrants from Austria-Hungary), altered a traditional administrative principle of the Roman Catholic Church in the West. This principle constituted an important element in the persistent conflicts between the Ruthenian priests and the Latin hierarchy." J

1884. Roucek, Joseph S. NEGLECTED ASPECTS OF THE SLAVS IN AMERICAN HISTORIOGRAPHY. *Ukrainian Q.* 1976 32(1): 58-71. Examines attitudes toward the Slavs in American history. Initial opinion characterized them as socialists and anarchists. The waves of immigrants from Slavic Europe after 1880 were considered unskilled, poorly educated, morally corrupt, and racially inferior compared to earlier immigrants from Western Europe. The Immigration Commission report of 1911 (Dillingham Report) gave official support to these opinions and influenced the restrictive immigration laws of 1921 and 1924. These laws, based on national quotas, were not abolished until 1965. Soviet domination of Eastern Europe after 1945 aroused American sympathy for certain Slavic nationalities. Such feelings were also fostered by a growing interest in ethnicity in the 1960's and by the objective reporting of such periodicals as the *Ukrainian Quarterly*. K. N. T. Crowther

1885. Stipanovich, Joseph. SOUTH SLAV SETTLEMENTS IN UTAH, 1890-1935. *Utah Hist. Q.* 1975 43(2): 155-171. A reconstruction of the settlement of South Slav labor immigrants in Utah. Midvale, Highland Boy, and Helper reflect the industries (metal and coal mining, smelting, and railroads) which drew immigrant labor. These industries affected the lives of the immigrants and patterns of settlement. Institutions such as lodges pulled together the disparate strands of nationalism and culture into a group ethos. Thus many records were preserved which show the role immigrants played in the industrialization of the West. Based on primary and secondary sources; 5 illus., 58 notes. J. L. Hazelton

Czechoslovakian

1886. Barton, Joseph J. RELIGION AND CULTURAL CHANGE IN CZECH IMMIGRANT COMMUNITIES, 1850-1920. Miller, Randall M. and Marzik, Thomas D., ed. *Immigrants and Religion in Urban America* (Philadelphia: Temple U. Pr., 1977): 3-24. With the growing imbalance of household needs and nonagricultural employment, Czech peasant families migrated from their small communities to areas of industry, even to the United States. The resultant breakdown of traditional communal ceremonies created a new system of voluntary associations which protected Czech Americans against the strange new world. Religious associations grew to "maintain increasingly fragmented religious observance." As parish life developed, the Catholic Church emerged "to find some middle way between the opposing perils of self-isolation and total absorption." Secondary sources; 51 notes. S. Robitaille

1887. Berko, John F. THOMAS BELL: SLOVAK-AMERICAN NOVELIST. *Jednota Ann. Furdek* 1977 16: 147-162. Discusses the novels and labor organizing of Thomas Bell (Belejčák), a Slovak American, 1920's-63.

1888. Bodnar, John. MATERIALISM AND MORALITY: SLAVIC-AMERICAN IMMIGRANTS AND EDUCATION, 1890-1940. *Slovakia* 1976 26(49): 21-39. Discusses Slovak Americans' attitudes toward public education 1890-1940; examines how their working-class pragmatism was often at variance with American values and materialism.

1889. Boxerman, Burton Alan. ADOLPH JOACHIM SABATH IN CONGRESS: THE ROOSEVELT AND TRUMAN YEARS. *J. of the Illinois State Hist. Soc.* 1973 66(4): 428-443. Continued from a previous article. Congressman Sabath of Illinois became increasingly critical of

President Herbert Hoover's Republican Party policies between 1930 and 1931. As a liberal who championed the cause of immigrants he was also a key defender of the rights of labor. As an unfailing supporter of Presidents Franklin D. Roosevelt and Harry S. Truman, Sabath particularly backed legislation to improve health, housing, and welfare. He had a limited knowledge of parliamentary procedure despite his seniority and chairmanship of the Rules Committee. However, Sabath helped guide significant legislation of the New Deal and Fair Deal through the Rules Committee. Based on the *Congressional Record,* interviews, and contemporary newspapers; 2 photos, 56 notes.   A. C. Aimone

1890. Boxerman, Burton Alan. ADOLPH JOACHIM SABATH IN CONGRESS: THE EARLY YEARS, 1907-1932. *J. of the Illinois State Hist. Soc. 1973 66(3) : 327-340.* Sabath, a progressive reformer, represented the Fifth Congressional District of Illinois under eight presidents. A Bohemian, Sabath became an ethnic Democratic politician popular with Chicago's immigrant populations. Sabath's ardent support of the League of Nations resulted in his closest election victory (in 1920). His loyalty to presidents Franklin Delano Roosevelt and Harry S. Truman was unswerving and he became one of the most effective men in the House. Based on secondary sources and the *Congressional Record;* illus., 32 notes. Article to be continued.   A. C. Aimone

1891. Corzine, Jay and Dabrowski, Irene. THE ETHNIC FACTOR AND NEIGHBORHOOD STABILITY: THE CZECHS IN SOULARD AND SOUTH ST. LOUIS. *Missouri Hist. Soc. Bull. 1977 33(2): 87-93.* Surveys the migration of Czechs to St. Louis since 1848 and traces their dispersion to various parts of the city since 1930. Although geographically dispersed, they continued to value their "ethnic identity" and have maintained it through social organizations which focused on social affairs, gymnastics, and studying European languages. Based on secondary sources; photo, 2 illus., 13 notes.   H. T. Lovin

1892. Čulen, Konštantín. THE LATTIMER MASSACRE. *Slovakia 1977 27(50): 44-61.* Examines press reactions, foreign and domestic, to the murder of two dozen Slovak American coal miners in the Lattimer area of Pennsylvania during a strike, September 1897; the event fostered unity within the Slovak American press.

1893. Durica, Milan S. AMERICKÍ SLOVÁCI A SNAHY O SAMOBYTHNOST NÁRODA NA 60.VYROČIE PODEPSANIA PITTSBURGHSKEJ DOHODY [American Slovaks and the endeavor for Slovak national independence: 60 years since the signing of the Pittsburgh Agreement]. *Kalendár Jednota 1979 (82): 96-110.* Explains the historical background of this important Czech-Slovak agreement of May 1918 and the participation of Slovak Americans in the struggle for Slovak national independence.   G. E. Pergl

1894. Gosiorovský, Miloš. AMERICKÍ KRAJANIA A 30. VÝROČIE OSLOBODENIA ČSSR [Czechs and Slovaks in the USA and the 30th anniversary of the liberation of Czechoslovakia]. *Slovanský Přehled [Czechoslovakia] 1975 61(2): 124-131.* Examines the participation of a million Czechs and Slovaks in the United States in 1940 in the liberation of Czechoslovakia and in securing aid to the anti-German coalition during World War II. 36 notes.   G. E. Pergl

1895. Harling, Frederick F. and Kaufman, Martin. CZECHS AND SLOVAKS. *Hist. J. of Western Massachusetts 1976 (supplement): 11-12.* Discusses the 17th- and 18th-century migration of Czechs and Moravians to America and the role in the American Revolution of Alexander Barta, William Paca, and several Slovaks who came with the French army. References.   W. H. Mulligan, Jr.

1896. Hricko, M. Gabriel. DR. JOSEPH PAUČO: HIS LIFE'S GOAL. *Jednota Ann. Furdek 1977 16: 119-123.* Dr. Joseph Paučo (d. 1975), a leading scholar and a publicist for the Slovak cause in America and Slovakia, "mortgaged his very life on the altar of freedom for Slovakia."

1897. Johnson, Anna. ROUGH WAS THE ROAD THEY JOURNEYED. *Palimpsest 1977 58(3): 66-83.* Excerpts from Anna Dockal Johnson's account of Czech family life in Pocahontas, Iowa, during the first two decades of the 20th century. 10 photos.   D. W. Johnson

1898. Kalvoda, Josef. MASARYK IN AMERICA IN 1918. *Jahrbücher für Geschichte Osteuropas [West Germany] 1979 27(1): 85-99.* Examines the visit of Tomaš Masaryk to the United States in 1918 to dispute the widely accepted theory that he almost single-handedly achieved the national liberation of the Czechs and Slovaks. Other factors played a greater role in the establishment of Czechoslovakia than did the propaganda of Masaryk and his followers-in-exile. The Czech Legion's uprising against the Bolsheviks created a favorable climate for the Czech cause in American circles, while Austria-Hungary's renewed military commitments to Germany after the Sixtus Affair convinced the Allies of the need to dismember the Dual Monarchy. Moreover, home politicians led by Karel Kramář, and not by Masaryk, carried out the revolution within the Empire, thus realizing Czech independence. Based on memoir materials and on documents from the Foreign Office in London and the National Archives in Washington; 56 notes.   S. A. Welisch

1899. Kedro, M. James. CZECHS AND SLOVAKS IN COLORADO, 1860-1920. *Colorado Mag. 1977 54(2): 92-125.* Czech Americans and Slovak Americans in Colorado were never numerous and most came from other midwestern states rather than directly from Europe to work in mines, smelters, or agriculture. Uses specific immigrants to illustrate "a complicated network of religious, lodge and family interaction . . ." which created close-knit ethnic communities. However, upward mobility and Americanization also occurred. Secondary sources; 20 illus., 61 notes.   O. H. Zabel

1900. Kirschbaum, J. M. DR. PAUČO'S WRITINGS. *Jednota Ann. Furdek 1976 15: 203-213.* Discusses the works of Slovak nationalist and scholar Joseph Paučo (1914-75).

1901. Krahsa, Joseph C. PAUČO: THE FRATERNALIST. *Jednota Ann. Furdek 1976 15: 188-194.* Discusses the literary, political, and journalistic career and the activities, in Slovakia and the United States, of Slovak nationalist and scholar Dr. Joseph Paučo (1914-75).

1902. Kral, Tonka. GROWING UP SLOVAK IN A YANKEE TOWN. *Jednota Ann. Furdek 1977 16: 167-173.* Personal account; town and period are not given.

1903. Matus, Margaret. SLOVAKIA ON MY MAP. *Slovakia 1976 26(49): 106-110.* Discusses the author's research into her Slovak American background, covering the period since her grandfather's emigration to the United States in 1910.

1904. Matus, Margaret. SLOVAKIA ON MY MAP. *Jednota Ann. Furdek 1978 17: 95-100.* The author recounts her findings after she was assigned to do a genealogy of her Slovakian family, which had immigrated to the United States after World War I.

1905. Paučo, Joseph. CULTURAL REVIVAL OF AMERICAN AND CANADIAN SLOVAKS. *Slovakia 1973 23(46): 72-81.* During the past decade there has been a revival of interest by Slovak Americans and Slovak Canadians in their cultural heritage, strengthened by Slovaks who migrated after the Second World War. This revival has resulted in an increase in books, pamphlets, periodicals, and newspapers that are devoted to the history and culture of Slovakia. Slovak organizations are placing increasing emphasis on Slovak achievements in art, music, and literature.   J. Williams

1906. Paučo, Joseph. FRANCIS HRUŠOVSKÝ, PH.D. *Jednota Ann. Furdek 1977 16: 16-19.* Outlines the career and achievements of Francis Hrušovský (1903-56), who devoted himself to literary and cultural pursuits, made outstanding contributions to Slovak research and scholarship, and was a great source of strength and encouragement to the Slovak League of America.

1907. Paučo, Joseph. FURDEK AND HLINKA. *Jednota Ann. Furdek 1977 16: 31-35.* Examines the action of Father Stephen Furdek in defense of Andrew Hlinka who in 1906 was sentenced to prison as a dangerous Pan-Slavist, an incident which "rallied the American Slovaks to a common cause" and brought about "a strong awareness of their obligation on behalf of their Slovak national interests."

1908. Paučo, Joseph. FURDEK CONFOUNDS THE MAGYA-RONES. *Jednota Ann. Furdek 1977 16: 27-31.* Discusses pre-World War I efforts of the ruling Magyars in Slovakia to oppress Slovaks in their homeland, examining the actions of Slovak Americans, including Father Stephen Furdek, in connection with this problem.

1909. Paučo, Joseph. JOHN SABOL—"MR. JEDNOTA." *Jednota Ann. Furdek 1977 16: 23-27.* John Sabol was elected supreme secretary of the First Catholic Slovak Union (Jednota) in Pennsylvania in 1926 and made important contributions to Slovak American life.

1910. Paučo, Joseph. THE NATIONAL SLOVAK SOCIETY. *Jednota Ann. Furdek 1977 16: 3-6.* Briefly examines individuals, programs, and objectives of the National Slovak Society (founded 16 February 1890 in Pittsburgh, Pennsylvania), the parent of all Slovak fraternal organizations in the United States.

1911. Paučo, Joseph. THE SISTERS OF SS. CYRIL AND METHODIUS. *Jednota Ann. Furdek 1977 16: 7-15.* In Philadelphia, Pennsylvania, on 10 October 1903 Father Matthew Jankola founded the Sisters of SS. Cyril and Methodius, the first and only community of Sisters in the world founded by a Slovak, which became an effective force for cultivating the Slovak language and preserving and promoting Slovak culture in the United States.

1912. Paučo, Joseph. SLOVAK PIONEERS IN AMERICA. *Slovakia 1974 24(47): 67-79.* Recounts the religious accomplishments of Reverend Gregory Vaniščák, O.S.B., and of Reverend Joseph J. Dulík during the first part of the 20th century.   S

1913. Paučo, Joseph. SLOVAKS AND THEIR LIFE: GEORGE A. HRICKO. *Jednota Ann. Furdek 1977 16: 19-22.* George A. Hricko (1883-1963) was a Slovak American interested in state politics in Pennsylvania and in immigrants' organizations such as the Jednota Society.

1914. Paučo, Joseph. TWENTY YEARS OF THE SLOVAK INSTITUTE IN CLEVELAND. *Slovakia 1973 23(46): 16-23.* Traces the history of the Slovak Institute of Cleveland during 1952-72. Founded at St. Andrew Svorad Abbey in Cleveland, Ohio, 15 September 1952, the purpose of the Institute was to give support to Slovak writers and artists. The Institute publishes the Slovak cultural quarterly *Most*, has a library of 70,000 items, and has established a branch in Rome.

J. Williams

1915. Pier, Andrew V. A HISTORY OF SLOVAKS IN CLEVELAND, OHIO. *Jednota Ann. Furdek 1978 17: 32-36.* Discusses the assimilation of Slovak Americans in Cleveland, Ohio, 1930's-50's.

1916. Pier, Andrew V. IN RETROSPECT: SLOVAK AMERICAN BICENTENNIAL. *Jednota Ann. Furdek 1977 16: 261-263.* On the occasion of its 200th birthday, Slovak Americans pay tribute to the United States as a nation which has "provided the opportunity for them to work and live as free men and women" since their arrival in the late 19th century.

1917. Pier, Andrew V. SLOVAK COLLECTIVE FARMS IN FLORIDA. *Jednota Ann. Furdek 1978 17: 25-28.* Begun in 1912 by Lutherans of Slovak ancestry, the agricultural cooperative of A. Duda and Sons Corporation in Slavia, Florida, grew from 40 to more than 100,000 acres in Florida, as well as much acreage elsewhere in the United States and three million acres in Australia.

1918. Pier, Andrew V. VISIBLE SIGNS OF SLOVAK CULTURE IN CLEVELAND, OHIO. *Slovakia 1975 25(48): 73-79.*

1919. Pier, Andrew V. THE 70TH ANNIVERSARY OF THE SLOVAK LEAGUE OF AMERICA. *Jednota Ann. Furdek 1978 17: 17-19.* Originally intended as a material and moral support organization for the Slovak nation in Europe, the Slovak League of America also has encouraged and promoted Slovak cultural programs since 1907.

1920. Pír, A. V. POMNÍK GENERÁLA M.R.ŠTEFÁNIKA V CLEVELANDE: 55.VÝROČIE ODHALENIA PRIPADÁ NA 29.JÚNA 1979 [General M.R.Štefánik's monument in Cleveland: the

55th anniversary of its unveiling, 29 June 1979]. *Kalendár Jednota 1979 (82): 111-115.* Follows the history of the Cleveland monument to Slovak national hero M. R. Stefánik from the birth of the idea until the monument's festive unveiling by American Slovak community, 1920-24.

G. E. Pergl

1921. Regis, Sister M. THE HISTORY OF OUR LADY OF LEVOČA. *Jednota Ann. Furdek 1975 14: 25-33.* Traces Slovak devotion to Our Lady of Levoča from the 13th century in the town of Levoča in Spiš county, Slovakia; a replica of the Levoča statue was carved in Slovakia and shipped in 1930 to Bedford, Ohio.

1922. Rudinsky, Alexander J. A SLOVAK-AMERICAN PERSPECTIVE IN A CHANGING SOCIETY. *Slovakia 1977 27(50): 136-143.* Examines the importance of recognizing, retaining, and incorporating ancestral roots into contemporary Slovak Americans' lifestyles and values in order to retain ethnicity and respect for Old World values and immigrant heritage.

1923. Sapak, Theresa. GROWING UP SLOVAK IN AMERICA. *Jednota Ann. Furdek 1977 16: 67-71.* Personal account of the trials of growing up as a Slovak in a small town in Pennsylvania.

1924. Schooley, Harry B., III. THE LATTIMER MASSACRE AND TRIAL. *Slovakia 1977 27(50): 62-79.* Discusses a trial which led to the acquittal of Sheriff James Martin and his deputies for the murder of two dozen Slovak American coal miners during a strike in the Lattimer area of Pennsylvania, 1897.

1925. Simko, Michael. ETHNIC OBLIVION THREATENS SLAVIC MINORITIES. *Jednota Ann. Furdek 1977 16: 241-247.* Pleads for more Slovak studies courses; intermarriage and apathy of youth due to lack of education about their native land account for the current ethnic dissolution of Slovak Americans.

1926. Stolarik, M. Mark. DOCUMENTATION—FROM FIELD TO FACTORY: THE HISTORIOGRAPHY OF SLOVAK IMMIGRATION TO THE UNITED STATES. *Internat. Migration R. 1976 10(1): 81-102.* Discusses the historiography of the immigration and assimilation of Slovaks to the United States, 1880's-1940's.

1927. Stolarik, M. Mark. IMMIGRATION AND EASTERN SLOVAK NATIONALISM. *Slovakia 1976 26(49): 13-20.* Discusses the rise of nationalist sentiments among Slovaks in northern Hungary, their resistance to Magyar cultural assimilation, and the efforts of Slovak American immigrants to preserve their native language, 1780-1903.

1928. Stolarik, M. Mark. IMMIGRATION, EDUCATION, AND THE SOCIAL MOBILITY OF SLOVAKS, 1870-1930. *Slovakia 1977 27(50): 80-89.* Examines the influence of Old World values and religion on Slovak immigrants in the United States; discusses the effect of Magyarization on the Slovaks and the resultant dedication to education and tendencies toward upward mobility, 1890's-1930's.

1929. Stolarik, M. Mark. IMMIGRATION, EDUCATION, AND THE SOCIAL MOBILITY OF SLOVAKS, 1870-1930. Miller, Randall M. and Marzik, Thomas D., ed. *Immigrants and Religion in Urban America* (Philadelphia: Temple U. Pr., 1977): 103-116. Lay leaders of the Old World advocated education for social mobility. Slovaks responded by building and supporting educational institutions. The Hungarian government, however, saw these efforts as a threat to official Magyarization policy and shut down or nationalized Slovak schools. Teachers were instructed to use only Magyar texts and language. By the late 19th century, large numbers of Slovaks began emigrating to the United States. With them, they took their contempt for public schools which they believed denationalized children. Slovak Americans stressed the moral and ethnic value of education. Because 80% of the Slovaks were Catholic, parochial schools were built. Few Slovak students continued their education after learning the catechism; only 20% graduated from high school during 1910-40. Slovak men retained strong ethnic identity, became skilled, blue collar laborers, had large families, and lived in the same neighborhood all their lives. Success was measured not by social mobility but by social stability. 42 notes.   S. Robitaille

1930. Tanzone, Daniel F. BISHOP ANDREW GRUTKA. *Jednota Ann. Furdek 1978 17: 81-86*. Discusses the life of Bishop Andrew G. Grutka (b. 1908), a Catholic parish priest in and eventually Bishop of the Diocese of Gary, Indiana; covers 1933-78.

1931. Tanzone, Daniel F. JOHN C. SCIRANKA: OUTSTANDING SLOVAK AMERICAN FRATERNALIST. *Jednota Ann. Furdek 1978 17: 151-160*. Discusses John Coleman Sciranka (b. 1902), a historian and journalist, and his involvement with Slovak American organizations since 1924.

1932. Tanzone, Daniel F. JOHN J. KUBAŠEK, PRIEST AND PATRIOT. *Slovakia 1976 26(49): 69-75*. Discusses the life and career of Slovak American Catholic priest John J. Kubašek in Yonkers, New York, 1902-50; emphasizes his work for Slovakian independence from Hungary.

1933. Tanzone, Daniel F. SLOVAK CONTRIBUTIONS TO THE AMERICAN CULTURAL MOSAIC. *Slovakia 1975 25(48): 119-127*.

1934. Tanzone, Daniel F. SLOVAK FRATERNAL ORGANIZATIONS. *Slovakia 1975 25(48): 68-70*.

1935. Turner, George A. THE LATTIMER MASSACRE AND ITS SOURCES. *Slovakia 1977 27(50): 9-43*. Chronicles antecedents of a massacre of two dozen Slovak American coal miners in the Lattimer area of Pennsylvania, 1897; hiring discrimination, low wages, and exclusionary practices toward Slovak Americans led to a strike and the massacre.

1936. Tybor, M. Martina. ETHNICITY AND AMERICAN SLOVAKS. *Jednota Ann. Furdek 1978 17: 119-124*. Delineates the achievements of Slovak Americans in America's economic growth, war efforts, politics, and culture during the 20th century.

1937. Tybor, M. Martina. SLOVAK AMERICAN CATHOLICS. *Jednota Ann. Furdek 1977 16: 53-66*. Examines the immigration of Catholic Slovaks to America, their problems upon arrival, and their activities to ensure their cohesiveness and their spiritual, cultural, economic, political, and intellectual development in a new environment.

1938. Unterberger, Betty M. THE ARREST OF ALICE MASARYK. *Slavic Rev. 1974 33(1): 91-106*. A study of the impact of the arrest of Alice Masaryk, older daughter of Thomas G. Masaryk who was imprisoned by Austria-Hungary on charges of high treason on 28 October 1915. Examines the way it affected US and British interests in Slovakian affairs and their opposition to the Austro-Hungarian regime. The publicity given to the affair resulted from three factors: 1) the efforts of Charles R. Crane, businessman and philanthropist, 2) the support of leaders in the women's movement in Chicago, New York, Boston, and Washington, D.C., and 3) the work of the Bohemian National Alliance. These people were effective in arousing popular antagonism to the Habsburg Empire and in promoting sympathy for the Czechoslovak independence movement. 64 notes.   R. V. Ritter

1939. Vnuk, F. IN MEMORIAM . . . DR. JOZEF PAUČO: EDITOR OF *SLOVAKIA* FROM 1964 TO 1975. *Slovakia 1976 26(49): 6-8*. Discusses the life, career, and journalism of *Slovakia* editor Dr. Paučo 1939-75; emphasizes his work on behalf of Slovakian independence.

1940. Wagner, William. THE SISTERS OF SS. CYRIL AND METHODIUS AND THE PRESERVATION OF SLOVAK CULTURE IN AMERICA. *Slovakia 1974 24(47): 132-155*. Discusses the work of the sisters of St. Cyril Academy (1909-73) to preserve Slovak culture in Danville, Pennsylvania.   S

1941. Zubek, Theodoric. REMINISCENCES AND REFLECTIONS OF A SLOVAK REFUGEE PRIEST IN AMERICA. *Jednota Ann. Furdek 1978 17: 259-267*. The author, a Franciscan, recounts Communist persecution of religion in Czechoslovakia, his escape in 1951, his arrival in the United States in 1952, and his ministry in America. Discusses social and spiritual occurrences affecting religious thought in the United States, 1960's-78.

1942. —. MILESTONES IN THE LIFE OF SAINT JOHN NEUMANN. *Jednota Ann. Furdek 1978 17: 133-136*. Lists significant events in the life of Bohemia-born Saint John Nepomucene Neumann (1811-60), a Redemptorist and the fourth Bishop of Philadelphia; he was canonized in 1977.

Slovakian (Pre-WWI identity)

1943. —. JOHN A. SABOL, K.G.G. *Jednota Ann. Furdek 1978 17: 65-67*. This biographical sketch of John A. Sabol focuses on his contributions to Slovakian ethnic associations in his native Pennsylvania and on his nationwide participation in associations established to further Slovak culture and ethnic identity, 1922-78.

Polish

1944. Ainsworth, Catherine Harris. POLISH-AMERICAN CHURCH LEGENDS. *New York Folklore Q. 1974 30(4): 286-294*. Church motifs are numerous in tales of immigrants from Poland who settled in Buffalo, New York.   S

1945. Baker, T. Lindsay. THE EARLY YEARS OF REV. WINCENTY BARZYNSKI. *Polish Am. Studies 1975 32(1): 29-52*. A colorful account of a dedicated, hardworking pioneer who travelled through the early Polish-American communities from Texas to Chicago. Provides an account of American social history, following the Reverend Barzynski's career as a Polish insurrectionist in 1863, a missionary in Texas in 1866, and after 1874 a builder of St. Stanislaus Kortka Church in Chicago, which was to become the largest Catholic parish in the United States. Adding to his many accomplishments Father Barzynski is also credited with starting a printing house, a newspaper, orphanages, and a college, and was one of the cofounders of the Polish Roman Catholic Union, one of the two largest Polish-American associations in the United States.   S. R. Pliska

1946. Baker, T. Lindsay, ed. and trans. FOUR LETTERS FROM TEXAS TO POLAND IN 1855. *Southwestern Hist. Q. 1974 77(3): 381-389*. Panna Marya, Texas, established 1854, is the oldest Polish colony in America. It was the focal point for the first organized Polish peasant immigrants. Reproduces in translation four 1855 letters of Father Leopold Moczygemba and relatives, prime movers in the venture, lauding their new homes and encouraging others to follow. 33 notes.   D. L. Smith

1947. Baran, Alina. DISTRIBUTION OF THE POLISH ORIGIN POPULATION IN THE USA. *Polish Western Affairs [Poland] 1976 17(1-2): 139-144*. According to US census data, Polish Americans are one of the seven largest ethnic groups. First-generation Poles still live in central cities, but second-generation Poles live in suburbs and enjoy a higher socioeconomic status. Polish immigrants during 1950-70 settled principally in New York, New Jersey, and Illinois; their children usually remained in these states.   M. Swiecicka-Ziemianek

1948. Beeten, Neil. POLISH AMERICAN STEELWORKERS: AMERICANIZATION THROUGH INDUSTRY AND LABOR. *Polish Am. Studies 1976 33(2): 31-42*. The United States Steel Corporation in Gary, Indiana, manipulated immigrant workers under the guise of Americanization. In a final analysis, both immigrants and the employers profited from the corporation programs. Unplanned and unnoticed during the process, however, was a steady exposure of the immigrant workers to the merits of unionization, the potential benefits of organized strikes, and the necessary techniques of survival in a hard economic world. Covers ca. 1906-20. Based primarily on English newspaper accounts; 21 notes.   S. R. Pliska

1949. Blejwas, Stanislaus A. A POLISH COMMUNITY IN TRANSITION: THE EVOLUTION OF HOLY CROSS PARISH, NEW BRITAIN, CONNECTICUT. *Polish Am. Studies 1978 35(1-2): 23-53*. Discusses a Polish American parish in relation to assimilation and the pressure to Americanize. Since its beginnings in 1928, this parish has become Polish American and no longer strictly Polish. Polish and English primary and secondary sources; 69 notes.   S. R. Pliska

1950. Blejwas, Stanislaus A. A POLISH COMMUNITY IN TRANSITION. *Polish Am. Studies 1977 34(1): 26-69.* This account of two parishes in New Britain, Connecticut, mirrors the development of hundreds of Polish parishes throughout the United States during 1890-1955, especially the acculturation and Americanization of the immigrant. Based on sources in English and Polish; 114 notes. S. R. Pliska

1951. Bodnar, John; Weber, Michael P.; and Simon, Roger D. MIGRATION, KINSHIP, AND URBAN ADJUSTMENT: BLACKS AND POLES IN PITTSBURGH, 1900-1930. *J. of Am. Hist. 1979 66(3): 548-565.* Analyzes the adaptation of Poles and blacks to Pittsburgh, 1900-30, by comparing their migration experiences, socialization practices, and occupational mobility patterns. The analysis relies heavily on 94 oral history interviews of Polish immigrants and black migrants. For both groups, adaptation involved strategic reactions to specific conditions in Pittsburgh. Adjustment to the new urban setting was a product of the interaction of premigration culture and urban racism. 4 tables, 42 notes.. T. P. Linkfield

1952. Brożek, Andrzej. FOUR LETTERS FROM TEXAS TO POLAND IN 1855. *Acta Poloniae Hist. [Poland] 1976 33: 177-178.* Four letters from Texas to Poland, edited and translated by T. Lindsay Baker, appeared in *Southwestern Historical Quarterly* in 1974. These letters were already published previously in Polish. The author, who contributed to their Polish publication, finds the translation inaccurate, some omissions of text, and misleading editorship. He is, however, glad that an important source concerning Polish immigration to Texas has appeared in America in print. H. Heitzman-Wojcicka

1953. Brożek, Andrzej. THE NATIONAL CONSCIOUSNESS OF THE POLISH ETHNIC GROUP IN THE UNITED STATES, 1854-1939: PROPOSED MODEL. *Acta Poloniae Hist. [Poland] 1978 37: 95-127.* Interpolates from the selected characteristic sources the feelings and experiences with which the Polish-American community identified itself in the sphere of national consciousness. Proposes a dynamic model of the sense of national identification of this community. Traces the stages through which the predominantly peasant Polish group became conscious of their Polishness in confrontation with the American melting pot, then gradually through a "hyphenated americanism" became Americans of Polish descent. The political situation of Poland played a considerable role in this process. 70 notes. H. Heitzman-Wojcicka

1954. Brożek, Andrzej. THE ROOTS OF POLISH MIGRATION TO TEXAS. *Polish Am. Studies 1973 30(1): 20-35.* Describes the first Polish settlements in Texas in the early 1850's. The causes of this movement from Silesia and Prussia are the traditional ones: unhappy conditions at home and the promise of a better life in distant lands. This small wave of immigration subsided quickly. By the end of the 1850's it disappeared, for these reasons: 1) improved rural economy in Germany, 2) the growth of modern industry and its demand for labor, and 3) the Civil War in the United States which temporarily closed the gates of immigration. Based on English, Polish, and German sources; 61 notes. S. R. Pliska

1955. Brożek, Andrzej. ŚWIADOMOŚĆ POLSKIEJ GRUPY ETNICZNEJ W STANACH ZJEDNOCZONYCH W LATACH 1854-1939 [The national consciousness of the Polish ethnic group in the United States, 1854-1939]. *Kwartalnik Hist. [Poland] 1977 84(2): 333-353.* Traces the stages by which the Poles who started a mass emigration to the United States after 1854 gradually lost their Polish national consciousness and became Americans of Polish origin. After World War I the inflow of Poles ended and it became clear that Polish Americans did not intend to return to newly independent Poland. Their attitude toward Poland and any attempt by the Polish government to interfere in Polonia affairs made it clear that they considered themselves a part of America. 89 notes. H. Heitzman-Wojcicka

1956. Buczek, Daniel S. POLISH AMERICAN PRIESTS AND THE AMERICAN CATHOLIC HIERARCHY: A VIEW FROM THE TWENTIES. *Polish Am. Studies 1976 33(1): 34-43.* Discusses the conflict between Catholic Irish American bishops and the Polish American clergy during the 1920's. Treats only the dioceses of Buffalo, Brooklyn, and Pittsburgh, but states that a revolutionary attitude pervaded the minds of Polish Americans in other dioceses as well. The bishops ad-

vocated Americanization in the Polish parishes, but the Poles called this "Irishism." Irish bishops insisted upon English as the language of instruction in all parochial schools, and the Poles fought for bilingualism. The Poles won the battle during the 1920's only to lose the campaign during the 1940's because of the gradual disappearance of the Polish language among the second and third generations. Based on primary and secondary sources; 24 notes. S. R. Pliska

1957. Buczek, Daniel S. POLISH AMERICANS AND THE ROMAN CATHOLIC CHURCH. *Polish Rev. 1976 21(3): 39-62.* Examines the role which the Catholic Church played in the Americanization of Polish immigrants and the "benign neglect" of the Poles so the hierarchy could hold onto other more renegade ethnic groups who found themselves in a new country, 1860's-1930's.

1958. Buczkowski, Claudia. SEVENTY YEARS OF THE PITASS DYNASTY. *Niagara Frontier 1977 24(3): 66-75.* John Pitass, a Catholic priest of Polish descent, was largely responsible for the success of Polonization in Buffalo's east side during 1890-1934.

1959. Cable, John N. VANDENBERG: THE POLISH QUESTION AND POLISH AMERICANS, 1944-1948. *Michigan Hist. 1973 57(4): 296-310.* Michigan's Republican Senator Arthur H. Vandenberg, best remembered for his strong bipartisanship as World War II ended and the Cold War began, was only moderately bipartisan on the Polish issue. Responding sympathetically to his staunchly anti-Communist, heavily Polish American constituency, Vandenberg articulated and championed the Polish cause at the national level. While critical of alleged diplomatic errors committed during the war and after, he realistically understood the impossibility of repudiating the East European agreements made at the Yalta Conference. Based largely upon primary sources; 2 photos, 43 notes. D. W. Johnson

1960. Chałasiński, Józef. EMIGRACJA I INSTYTUCJE POLONIJNE W STANACH ZJEDNOCZONYCH A.P. A PRZEOBRAŻENIE SPOŁECZNO-KULTUROWE W KRAJU [Emigration and Polish institutions in the United States of America and sociocultural changes in Poland]. *Kultura i Społeczeństwo [Poland] 1976 20(1): 41-60.* *The Polish Peasant in Europe and America* (1918-20) by W. Thomas and Florian Znaniecki and the *Prace niesyzyfowe* [Non-Sisyphean labors] (1974) by the Rzeszowskie Towarzystwo Przyjaciół Nauk, are very important works for the history of Polish peasants and of the American Poles. Many peasants returned to Poland from America, invested their money in land and contributed to the development of Polish villages. But the educated Polish emigrant lacked any ties with the worker and peasant groups of the American Poles. Recently, this has changed; a new generation of educated Polish Americans has received a link with its ethnic heritage through such organizations as the Polish Institute of Arts and Sciences in America. M. Swiecicka-Ziemianek

1961. Chojnacki, Władysław and Drzewieniecki, Walter M. TOWARDS A BIBLIOGRAPHY OF AMERICAN POLONIA. *Polish Am. Studies 1978 35(1-2): 54-77.* Discusses several bibliographies of books and articles on Polish America, published in both Poland and the United States. Mentions studies of the Polish press in America. The bibliographies mentioned are repositories of more than 3,000 titles, but the authors feel that this is but a modest beginning in any attempt to cover the approximately 20,000 titles extant somewhere. The authors challenge historians to compile a comprehensive bibliography. Polish and English primary and secondary sources; 90 notes. S. R. Pliska

1962. Chrobot, Leonard. THE ELUSIVE POLISH AMERICAN. *Polish Am. Studies 1973 30(1): 54-59.* The Census Bureau's "Characteristics of the Population by Ethnic Origin" (GPO, 1969) 4.02 million figure for Polish America is too low. From this inaccurate base, the author yet attempts to present a composite picture of Polish America in true proportion though on a reduced scale, emphasizing these features: 1) age and sex percentages, 2) language used at home now and in childhood, 3) origin of the head of the household, 4) highest grade of school completed, and 5) family income. The typical Polish American is a "male born in the U.S. [who] spoke Polish in his home when he was a child, but speaks English now, is 38.7 years old (female: 40.9), and is married to a Polish wife. If he is between 25 and 34 years of age, he completed 12.7 years of school, and if he is over 35, he completed 10.9 years. His median family income is $8,849. The male works as a craftsman, foreman, or kindred occupation, and his wife is employed as a clerical worker."

S. R. Pliska

1963. Copson-Niećko, Maria J. E. ORTHOGRAPHY AND THE POLISH EMIGRANTS FROM TRIESTE 1834-1835. *Polish Am. Studies 1974 31(2): 20-29.* A plea for absolute accuracy in historical research so that future historians will not be compelled to generalize for lack of specific information. Criticizes two sources which listed and spelled, or misspelled, the names of the 233-234 Polish exiles who came from Trieste to New York City and Boston 1834-35.

S. R. Pliska

1964. Copson-Niećko, Maria J. E. THE POLISH POLITICAL EMIGRATION TO THE UNITED STATES 1831-1864. *Polish R. 1974 19(3-4): 45-82.* Examines Florian Stasik's *Polska emigracja polityczna w Stanach Zjednoczonych Ameryki 1831-1864* (Warsaw, 1973), claiming that basic questions of this emigration will remain unanswered until a scientific approach and archival materials are utilized.

1965. Copson-Niećko, Maria J. E. POLSKA EMIGRACJA POLITYCZNA W STANACH ZJEDNOCZONYCH W XIX WIEKU [Polish political emigration to the United States in the 19th century]. *Przegląd Hist. [Poland] 1975 66(1): 93-103.* Review article prompted by Florian Stasik's *Polska emigracja polityczna w Stanach Zjednoczonych Ameryki 1831-1864* (Warsaw: PWN, 1976), the first scholarly work on the subject of Polish emigration to the United States.

1966. Cuba, Stanley L. POLES IN THE EARLY MUSICAL AND THEATRICAL LIFE OF COLORADO. *Colorado Mag. 1977 54(3): 240-276.* Many internationally known actors and musicians who performed in Denver and other Colorado cities during the 19th and early 20th centuries were of Polish background, such as Helena Modjeska, Ignace Paderewski, and Marcella Sembrich. Coloradans' enthusiasm for the arts was demonstrated by creation of local societies and patronage of grand theaters. Mainly primary sources; 14 illus., 93 notes.

D. A. Hartford

1967. Davis, Susan G. OLD-FASHIONED POLISH WEDDINGS IN UTICA, NEW YORK. *New York Folklore 1978 4(1-4): 89-102.* The traditional folk rites surrounding an old-fashioned Polish wedding in Utica, New York, would last for days; describes antecedents of the wedding, the actual ceremony, and the subsequent festivities, 1900-40's.

1968. Davis, Susan G. UTICA'S POLKA MUSIC TRADITION. *New York Folklore 1978 4(1-4): 103-124.* The tradition of Polish dance, or polka music, of Polish Americans in Utica, New York, 1900-78, comes from the polka which was popular throughout Europe during the 19th century and which is now found in some form in North, Central, and South America; briefly discusses festivities surrounding the polka, based on reflections of Utica residents.

1969. Davis, Susan G. WOMEN'S ROLES IN A COMPANY TOWN: NEW YORK MILLS, 1900-1951. *New York Folklore 1978 4(1-4): 35-47.* Traces the roles of the women (predominantly Polish) in New York Mills, New York, 1900-51, based on their personal reflections, including their roles as wives, mothers, millworkers, union members, landladies, etc.

1970. Dietrich, R. Krystyna Tołczyńska. ALEXANDER ORŁOWSKI IN AMERICA. *Polish Rev. 1976 21(3): 203-206.* A short bibliography of articles and books about Polish painter Alexander Orłowski (1777-1832).

1971. Drzewieniecki, Walter M. and Drzewieniecki-Abugattas, Joanna E. PUBLIC LIBRARY SERVICE TO AMERICAN ETHNICS: THE POLISH COMMUNITY ON THE NIAGARA FRONTIER, NEW YORK. *J. of Lib. Hist., Phil. and Comparative Librarianship 1974 9(2): 120-137.* Chronicles the development of the Polish community around Buffalo, New York, from the latter half of the 19th century to 1974, and the parallel specific service of the Buffalo Public Library to Polish-Americans following 1901. Largely the story of the William Ives Branch (renamed for Francis E. Fronczak in 1965), the record shows that the "public libraries in Buffalo and the surrounding area have done an excel-

lent job of responding to the needs of the Polish ethnic community and in several cases have gone out of their way to arouse interest and educate." Based on primary sources; 2 illus., 69 notes.

D. G. Davis, Jr.

1972. Froncek, Thomas. KOSCIUSKO. *Am. Heritage 1975 26(4): 4-11, 78-81.* Born in Poland and educated in military engineering in France, Thaddeus Kosciusko came to the United States in 1776 to offer his services to the colonial revolutionaries. His brilliant engineering ability helped win the American Revolution. After an unsuccessful attempt to lead Poland's defense against Russia in 1794, Kosciusko lived in exile for the rest of his life. 9 illus.

B. J. Paul

1973. Galush, William J. AMERICAN POLES AND THE NEW POLAND. AN EXAMPLE OF CHANGE IN ETHNIC ORIENTATION. *Ethnicity 1974 1(3): 209-222.* During 1870-1910 Catholic, anti-Catholic, and secular organizations appeared in the American Polish community. Friction arose among them at a series of conventions over policies involving the reestablishment of a Polish state and relations with Russia. While few American Poles returned after 1918, many were actively involved in Polish affairs, supporting various factions there. In the 1920's interest shifted with the second generation to American issues and to the preservation of Polish ethnicity in the United States. 65 notes.

E. Barkan

1974. Galush, William J. FAITH AND FATHERLAND: DIMENSIONS OF POLISH-AMERICAN ETHNORELIGION, 1875-1975. Miller, Randall M. and Marzik, Thomas D., ed. *Immigrants and Religion in Urban America* (Philadelphia: Temple U. Pr., 1977): 84-102. Polish immigrants to the United States in the 1860's encountered a strong, Irish-dominated Church. Their need for an "ethnically enclosed place of worship" led to the development of Polish national parishes under the initiative of lay voluntary associations. In the 1900's, growing religious dissent caused the coalescence of several congregations and a demand for administrative change within the Church. Denial of the demands led to creation of the Polish National Catholic Church under Father Francis Hodur which stressed a "mystical and specific ethnoreligion"; less than 5% of Polish American Catholics joined it before 1914. Parish schools quickly spread because immigrants regarded them as nurturers of ethnoreligion, but several factors, such as antiforeign thought during the world wars, limited the effectiveness of the schools. Polish Catholic descendants still possess a "lingering commitment" to the immigrants' ethnoreligion. 65 notes.

S. Robitaille

1975. Goldstein, Elizabeth and Green, Gail. PIEROGI- AND BABKA-MAKING AT ST. MARY'S. *New York Folklore 1978 4(1-4): 71-79.* The cooking and selling of pierogi (filled dumplings) and babka (sweet bread) by Catholic Polish American women of New York Mills, New York, for three weeks during Advent and three weeks during Lent (to raise money for St. Mary's Church through the Rosary Society) represents an important folk and cultural tradition from the early 1900's in America.

1976. Greene, Victor. THE POLISH AMERICAN WORKER TO 1930: THE "HUNKY" IMAGE IN TRANSITION. *Polish Rev. 1976 21(3): 63-78.* Examines the evolution in thought, 1920's-60, among historians and intellectuals studying the image of Polish immigrant labor, 1860-1930, from one in which the laborer was portrayed as a naive illiterate bumbler to a more widely accepted contemporary image of the Polish American worker as one who was able to socially, psychologically, and intellectually adjust to the new socioeconomic system encountered in the United States.

1977. Greenstone, J. David. ETHNICITY, CLASS, AND DISCONTENT: THE CASE OF THE POLISH PEASANT IMMIGRANTS. *Ethnicity 1975 2(1): 1-9.* Examines the interaction between ethnicity, social class, and discontent of Polish Americans, 1920-39.

1978. Groniowski, Krzysztof. SOCJALISTYCZNA EMIGRACJA POLSKA W STANACH ZJEDNOCZONYCH (1883-1914) [Polish socialist emigrants in the United States of America 1883-1914]. *Z Pola Walki [Poland] 1977 20(1): 3-35.* Polish Socialist activity in New York City in 1883 was contemporaneous with the first Marxist working-class party, Proletariat, in Poland. In 1886 the Association Równość [Equality] was founded in New York. In that same year the first Polish groups in the Knights of Labor were founded; their center was in Milwaukee. By 1890 the first Polish section of the American Socialist Labor Party was established; Polish centers developed in major cities and established contacts with the Socialist movement in the Prussian sector of Poland. Leadership conflicts developed within the American party over the national question. During the Revolution of 1905, a Polish Revolutionary Committee was established in the United States. It collected funds for the Polish Socialist Party. The influx of Poles after the revolution increased the splintering of the Polish Socialist movement over the issue of the home parties. The closest collaboration with the US movement took place in Milwaukee where in 1910 Socialists won the municipal elections.

J/S

1979. Gross, Feliks. NOTES ON THE ETHNIC REVOLUTION AND THE POLISH IMMIGRATION IN THE USA. *Polish Rev. 1976 21(3): 149-176.* Examines the effects of internal migration, 1946-76, changes in this pattern 1965-75, and enactment of various civil rights laws which are aiming the United States toward a pluralistic society of many well-defined ethnic groups.

1980. Grzeloński, Bogdan. POLACY W WOJNIE O NIEPODLEG-ŁOŚĆ ZJEDNOCZONYCH AMERYKI [Poles in the American War of Independence]. *Kwartalnik Hist. [Poland] 1976 83(2): 338-352.* Discusses attempts to add new data based on American publications on the Revolutionary War, George Washington's papers, and the journals of the Continental Congress. Adds more details to the American period of the biographies of Kościuszko and Pulaski, and mentions several names of other Poles who fought either on the side of the Revolution or on the British side. 84 notes.

H. Heitzman-Wojcicka

1981. Hammersmith, Jack L. FRANKLIN ROOSEVELT, THE POLISH QUESTION, AND THE ELECTION OF 1944. *Mid-Am. 1977 59(1): 5-17.* Examines Democratic Party strategies to retain Polish American voters in 1944. The Republicans made major gains in the 1942 congressional elections and concentrated on winning ethnic minorities, especially Polish Americans, in 1944. Roosevelt and the Democrats took special care to retain and woo the Polish Americans by keeping the Polish-Russian question at arm's length and appealing to the special interests of Poles. Although Roosevelt won by the narrowest margin ever, it was perhaps the Polish-American vote which contributed the most to his victory. Primary and secondary sources; 66 notes.

J. M. Lee

1982. Hartman, Peter and Tull, Marc. PHOTOGRAPHIC DOCU-MENTATION OF A POLISH-AMERICAN COMMUNITY. *New York Folklore 1978 4(1-4): 21-34.* Discusses a study of Polish Americans in East and West Utica and New York Mills, New York, based on their discussion of photographs by the article authors to evoke memories of growing up in an ethnic community.

1983. Irons, Peter H. "THE TEST IS POLAND": POLISH AMERI-CANS AND THE ORIGINS OF THE COLD WAR. *Polish Am. Studies 1973 30(2): 5-63.* Documents Polish American efforts to influence U.S. policy toward Poland and the Soviet Union during and shortly after World War II. The Polish Americans failed to exert any lasting influence, even though the Roosevelt and Truman administrations rendered some rhetorical support. 169 notes.

S. R. Pliska

1984. Janta, Alexander. CONRAD'S "FAMOUS CABLEGRAM" IN SUPPORT OF A POLISH LOAN. *Polish Rev. 1972 17(2): 69-77.* Discusses a 1920 cablegram from Joseph Conrad to the US National Campaign Committee, Polish Government Loan in support of a proposed loan to Poland to aid the Poles against Soviet intervention, 1919-23.

1985. Janta, Alexander. TWO DOCUMENTS ON POLISH-AMERICAN ETHNIC HISTORY. *Polish R. 1974 19(2): 3-23.* THE VIRGINIA VENTURE: A PROPOSED POLISH COLONY WHICH WENT WRONG, *pp. 3-19.* Gives documents and biographical data on Joseph Smolinski, who initiated the short-lived Polish Emigration Land Company in the 1860's.
THE PHILADELPHIA INQUIRY: A CHAPTER IN EARLY STUD-IES OF THE POLISH IMMIGRANT IN THE USA, *pp. 20-23.* Describes a field study on Polish assimilation in Philadelphia, from a John Dewey seminar at Columbia University, 1917-18.   S

1986. Jedlicki, Jerzy. LAND OF HOPE, LAND OF DESPAIR: POLISH SCHOLARSHIP AND AMERICAN IMMIGRATION. *Rev. in Am. Hist. 1975 3(1): 87-94.* Review article prompted by Andrzej Brozek's *Slazacy w Teksasie: Relacje o najstarszych osadach polskich w Ameryce* [Silesians in Texas: accounts of the oldest Polish settlements in America] (Warsaw-Wrocław: Panstwowe Wydawnictwo Naukowe, 1972), *Listy emicrantow z Brazylii i Stanow Zjednoczonych 1890-1891* [Emigrants' letters from Brazil and the United States, 1890-1891], edited by Witold Kula, Nina Assorodobraj-Kula, and Marcin Kula (Warsaw: Ludowa Spoldzieinia Wydawnicza, 1973), and Florian Stasik's *Polska emicracja polityczna w Stanach Zjednoczonych Ameryki 1831-1864* [Polish political emigration in the United States, 1831-1864] (Warsaw: Panstwowe Wydawnictwo Naukowe, 1973).

1987. Kennon, Peg Korsmo; Mahoney, Libby; and Wolter, Marcia Britton. TEACHING AND COLLECTING FOLKLORE AT ST. MARY'S SCHOOL. *New York Folklore 1978 4(1-4): 125-137.* The authors describe their experiment in teaching and collecting Polish American folklore from seventh graders at St. Mary's School in New York Mills, New York in 1978.

1988. Keuchel, Edward F. THE POLISH AMERICAN MIGRANT WORKER: THE NEW YORK CANNING INDUSTRY 1900-1935. *Polish Am. Studies 1976 33(2): 43-51.* In New York state the early canning industry was primarily rural. By 1900, when local sources could no longer meet the expanding labor demands, migrant workers, including many Polish Americans, were introduced. An investigation by the New York State Factory Investigating Commission in 1912 described jobs, wages, and living conditions. Polish Americans continued in canning through World War II, but by then in the canneries, blacks and Puerto Ricans succeeded them in the field. Based chiefly on the 1912 report and on other secondary sources, all in English; 21 notes.

S. R. Pliska

1989. Knawa, Anne Marie. JANE ADDAMS AND JOSEPHINE DUDZIK: SOCIAL SERVICE PIONEERS. *Polish Am. Studies 1978 35(1-2): 13-22.* Compares the life and work of Sister Mary Theresa (Josephine Dudzik), the founder of the Franciscan Sisters of Chicago, with that of the internationally renowned Jane Addams (1860-1935). Sister Mary Theresa (1860-1918) was an indefatigable worker. Official steps are being taken for her beatification and possible canonization. Polish and English primary and secondary sources; 23 notes.

S. R. Pliska

1990. Kolyszko, Edward V. PRESERVING THE POLISH HERI-TAGE IN AMERICA: THE POLISH MICROFILM PROJECT. *Polish Am. Studies 1975 32(1): 59-63.* Presents the Polish Microfilm Project and its director, the Advisory Committee, and the cooperating societies and universities, particularly the Immigration History Research Center of the University of Minnesota. Provides an updated list of Polish American newspapers and publications which have been microfilmed to date.

S. R. Pliska

1991. Kubiak, Hieronim. THE PROCESS OF THE POLISH EMI-GRANTS' SOCIAL ADAPTATION TO THE CULTURAL CONDI-TIONS IN THE COUNTRIES OF IMMIGRATION (FUNDAMENTAL PREMISES AND THEORETICAL CONCLU-SIONS). *Polish Western Affairs [Poland] 1976 17(1-2): 44-58.* Sees three distinct stages in the assimilation process of Polish emigrants, each embracing a different generation: those immigrants from the same region, who are gradually transformed into a social group; the continued existence of an ethnic group as a substitute for the whole society; and a reduction in the scope of functions performed by an immigrant group. Polish immigrants are neither more nor less assimilated than the immigrants from other national groups who arrived in a given territory at the same time.

M. Swiecicka-Ziemianek

1992. Kucharski, Jerzy S. *HALKA*—WISCONSIN'S FIRST MO-TION PICTURE. *Polish Am. Studies 1976 33(1): 44-47.* Details production of the first motion picture filmed in Wisconsin. The place was Milwaukee and the year 1925. The production was called *Halka*, an adaptation from a Polish national opera, and was first presented on stage by the Milwaukee Polish Opera Club. Provides the names of the chief actors and of the directors of the American Motion Picture Company of Detroit which did the filming. Mentions humorous incidents and one near-tragedy. After a three-week showing in Milwaukee the film was shown in Chicago, Detroit, Buffalo, Cleveland, Toledo, New York City, and Poland. Based on Milwaukee newspapers, both English and Polish; 15 notes.   S. R. Pliska

1993. Kuniczak, W. S. POLONIA: THE FACE OF POLAND IN AMERICA. *Am. Heritage 1978 29(3): 34-44.* Adapted from a forth-coming book, *My Name is Million: An Illustrated History of the Poles in America.* Arriving in the 1870's and after, most Poles were illiterate, unskilled, and Catholic. The early years were tough and the creation of Polonia was a triumph of endurance and determination; yet, it resulted often in ghetto-like restrictiveness, from which the Polish peasant class long sought to escape. 6 illus.   J. F. Paul

1994. Kuznicki, Ellen Marie. A HISTORICAL PERSPECTIVE ON THE POLISH AMERICAN PAROCHIAL SCHOOL. *Polish Am. Studies 1978 35(1-2): 5-12.* Covers this school system from its beginning in the 1870's to the phasing-out era in the 1960's. Lists successes and failures of the system and concludes that, above all, ". . . it was an effective Americanizer easing its pupils into English without depriving them of their ethnic heritage. . . ." Polish and English sources; 16 notes.   S. R. Pliska

1995. Kuzniewski, Anthony J. BOOT STRAPS AND BOOK LEARNING: REFLECTIONS ON THE EDUCATION OF POLISH AMERICANS. *Polish Am. Studies 1975 32(2): 5-26.* Reviews Józef Miąso's *Dzieje oświaty polonijnej w Stanach Zjednoczonych [The History of the Education of Polish Immigrants in the United States* (Warsaw, 1970)]. Argues that Miąso is overcritical of those involved with Polish parochial school education ca. 1870-1970 and contends that despite over-crowded conditions, less-than-professional teachers, and lack of proper instructional media, the parochial schools served a worthy purpose. 43 notes.   S. R. Pliska

1996. Kuzniewski, Anthony J. MILWAUKEE'S POLES, 1866-1918: THE RISE AND FALL OF A MODEL COMMUNITY. *Milwaukee Hist. 1978 1(1-2): 13-24.* Discusses the Polish immigrant community in Milwaukee during 1866-1918, including economic and political successes, community pride, and optimism.

1997. Kuzniewski, Anthony J. THE POLISH NATIONAL CATHO-LIC CHURCH—THE VIEW FROM PEOPLE'S POLAND. *Polish Am. Studies 1974 31(1): 30-34.* Hieronim Kubiak's [*The Polish National Church in the United States of America—1897-1965*] (Cracow: Polish Academy of Science, 1970), "the first good work on the subject," traces the history of the church through three generations of Polish Americans. Marxist in orientation and Polish in viewpoint, the book refers to the origin of the church as a revolutionary plebian movement among the immigrants. During three generations the church passed from a Polish institution to an American institution "only minimally colored by its Polish past." The reviewer sees more ethnicity there than Kubiak does.   S. R. Pliska

1998. Lee, Ellen K. THE CATHOLIC MODJESKA. *Polish Am. Studies 1974 31(1): 20-27.* Describes the great Shakesperean actress, Helena Modrzejewska [or Modjeska, as she anglicized the name]. She came to San Francisco in 1876, at the age of 36, with her husband, son, and a small group of friends hoping to establish a Polish colony near Los Angeles. Though she was recognized in Russian Poland through her association with the Imperial Theater of Warsaw, the language barrier delayed her rise to fame in the United States. Deals mostly with services rendered for the small Catholic churches which she attended. Includes an account of a confrontation in Santa Ana, California in 1897 between Madame Modjeska and the American Protective Association. 23 notes.   S. R. Pliska

1999. Lerski, George J. POLISH EXILES IN MID-NINETEENTH CENTURY AMERICA. *Polish Am. Studies 1974 31(2): 30-42.* A criti-cal review of Dr. Florian Stasik's *Polska Emigracja Polityczna w Stanach Zjednoczonych Ameryki, 1831-1864* [Polish Political Emigration in the United States of America, 1831-1864].   S. R. Pliska

2000. Lopata, Helena Znaniecki. FLORIAN ZNANIECKI: CRE-ATIVE EVOLUTION OF A SOCIOLOGIST. *J. of the Hist. of the Behavioral Sci. 1976 12(3): 203-215.* Florian Znaniecki (1882-1958), Pol-ish sociologist, taught and studied in the United States from 1939. Defin-ing sociology as the study of social systems, Znaniecki indicated four classes of study: social relations, social roles, social groups, and societies. He maintained that sociology could be used as a means of studying the dynamism of social systems and the advantages of a cooperative world society. This field is one form of scientific thinking in which peoples can be studied through their culture and values, and it always retains the humanistic coefficient. 47 notes.   R. I. Vexler

2001. Lopata, Helena Znaniecki. A LIFE RECORD OF AN IMMI-GRANT. *Society 1975 13(1): 64-74.* Discusses her family in Poland from 1882 to their escape to the United States in 1940, describing the impact of the subsequent clash between desire for assimilation and ethnic identity on her role as a woman.

2002. Lopata, Helena Znaniecki. POLISH IMMIGRATION TO THE UNITED STATES OF AMERICA: PROBLEMS OF ESTIMA-TION AND PARAMETERS. *Polish Rev. 1976 21(4): 85-108.* Exam-ines Polish immigration to the United States, 1820-1970, and the effects which transplantation of a national ethnic culture undergo when placed into a new national culture peopled by several smaller ethnic groups.

2003. Lopata, Helena Znaniecki. WIDOWHOOD IN POLONIA. *Polish Am. Studies 1977 34(2): 7-23.* Describes the lot of widows of city workers, 1880-1977.   S. R. Pliska

2004. Madaj, M. J. THE MEANING OF THE BICENTENNIAL TO THE POLISH AMERICAN COMMUNITY. *Polish Am. Studies 1976 33(1): 53-59.* Dwells on the kindred spirit of the people in Poland and those in America. To emphasize the love of freedom and individual-ism among both peoples the author reviews Polish American participa-tion in the country's most significant developments from the Revolution through World War II, and the overdue emergence of Polish names in American politics, business, and above all, education. Reprints a revised version of a presidential address delivered at the Atlanta meeting of the Polish American History Association on 28 January 1975.   S. R. Pliska

2005. Madaj, M. J. OBITUARIES. *Catholic Hist. Rev. 1978 64(1): 138.* A remembrance of Father Joseph Vincent Swastek (1913-77), who died unexpectedly on 5 September 1977. Swastek was ordained in 1940, and thereupon began graduate work at the University of Notre Dame, Catholic University, Ottawa University, and the University of Michigan. He specialized in Polish American history, in which discipline he was both a pioneer and a leader. He was a charter member of the Polish American Historical Association and very active in its affairs for a quarter century. He published extensively.   V. L. Human

2006. Małecka, Teresa. KAPITAŁ STANÓW ZJEDNOCZONYCH W POLSKIEJ BANKOWOSCI OKRESU MIĘDZYWOJENNEGO [American capital in interwar Polish banking]. *Przegląd Hist. [Poland] 1976 67(1): 39-54.* Interwar Poland had trouble attracting long-term American investment. Immediately after World War I, Polish Americans bought Polish bonds and stock in a Poznan bank, but were severely hurt by Polish inflation. Currency reform did not ease foreign skepticism based on the earlier inflation. In 1927 William Averell Harriman took a seat on the board of Warsaw's Bank Handlowy after investing in the Upper Silesian zinc industry. With the Depression's onset he withdrew his stake in Polish industry and banking. American investment, which in 1927 had reached its apex, totaling 14.7% of all foreign credits, declined through-out the 1930's. Based on archival sources; table, 90 notes. Summaries in French and Russian.   J. T. Hapak

2007. Markiewicz, Władysław. PRINCIPAL TRENDS AND CIR-CUMSTANCES OF CHANGES IN POLISH COMMUNITIES ABROAD. *Polish Western Affairs [Poland] 1976 17(1-2): 26-36.* Each successive generation of Polish immigrants has achieved obvious eco-nomic progress in the adapted countries. The growing interest, especially of the third generation, in the country of their forefathers applies also to the Polish immigrants in America.   M. Swiecicka-Ziemianek

2008. Mars, Anna M. "AMERICANA" IN THE ARCHIVES OF THE JOZEF PILSUDSKI INSTITUTE IN NEW YORK. *Polish Rev.*

1977 22(4): 65-75. Lists chronologically the contents of archives in the Americana section of the Jozef Pilsudski Institute and its library, dealing with the life of American Polonia, beginning with the 19th century. Other materials cover the two World Wars and interwar period. 3 notes.
J. Tull

2009. Miller, Eugene. LEO KRZYCKI: POLISH AMERICAN LABOR LEADER. *Polish Am. Studies 1976 33(2): 52-64.* Leo Krzycki (1881-1966) contributed in no small measure to the history of political radicalism in the United States. He was vice-president of the Amalgamated Clothing Workers for 25 years. At one time he was national chairman of the executive committee of the Socialist Party. He was also active in the early organizing drives of the CIO. His fiery speeches resounded throughout Pennsylvania's Schuylkill Valley during the Depression. As a Polish American leader he dared support the Yalta agreement and the pro-Soviet regime following the end of World War II. Based on Polish and English sources; 46 notes.
S. R. Pliska

2010. Mostwin, Danuta. THE PROFILE OF A TRANSPLANTED FAMILY. *Polish R. 1974 19(1): 77-89.* Studies the families of immigrants from Poland to the United States after World War II.

2011. Napierkowski, Thomas J. REYMONT AFTER FIFTY YEARS. *Polish Am. Studies 1974 31(2): 48-54.* Review of Jerzy Krzyzanowski's *Wladyslaw Reymont* (New York: Twayne, 1972). Admires both the author and the subject. Summarizes vividly and encourages Polish Americans to imitate the achievements of Nobel Prize-winner Wladyslaw Reymont.
S. R. Pliska

2012. Obidiński, Eugene. AMERICAN POLONIA: SACRED AND PROFANE ASPECTS. *Polish Am. Studies 1975 32(1): 5-18.* Interprets the dualistic aspects, the sacred and the profane, of Polish American ethnicity. In the former the author lodges traditional subjective values (language, history, literature), and in the latter he places materialistic objective values (membership in a Polish bowling team, costumes, dances, Polish sausages). He is apprehensive that with time and the lack of new immigrants the second aspect will prevail. The profane aspect is visible and acts as a reenforcing agent, but by itself does not add body to ethnicity. The author admits that there still are strong, well-knit enclaves which nourish the sacred aspect, but they represent a small number of the 6,000,000 Americans of Polish descent. Based on secondary sources.
S. R. Pliska

2013. Obidiński, Eugene. THE LOS ANGELES POLONIA. *Polish Am. Studies 1974 31(2): 43-47.* Reviews Neil C. Sandberg's *Ethnic Identity and Assimilation: The Polish-American Community Case Study of Metropolitan Los Angeles* (New York: Praeger, 1974). Discusses the use of "survey research rather than content analysis of documents and symbols," and the delineation of ethnicity in terms of cultural, religious, and national aspects. However, the detailed analysis of methodology with emphasis on the group cohesiveness scale will interest only the sociologist.
S. R. Pliska

2014. Obidiński, Eugene. POLISH AMERICAN SOCIAL STANDING: STATUS AND STEREOTYPE. *Polish Rev. 1976 21(3): 79-102.* Discusses stereotyped views of Polish American life, studies various Polish American communities, examines objective and subjective indexes of their social status, and observes the patterns of social mobility developed; covers 1930's-70.

2015. Obidiński, Eugene. THE POLISH AMERICAN PRESS: SURVIVAL THROUGH ADAPTATION. *Polish Am. Studies 1977 34(2): 38-55.* Covers 1863-1977. Tables, 29 notes.
S. R. Pliska

2016. O'Connell, Lucille. TRAVELERS' AID FOR POLISH IMMIGRANT WOMEN. *Polish Am. Studies 1974 31(1): 15-19.* The Travelers' Aid Society was formed in 1907 to protect rural American and immigrant girls who came to New York City alone. After immigration had peaked, and during the depression of the 1930's, the Society took care primarily of native American girls, eventually evolving into an organization to help all travelers in all major cities of the United States. Gives examples of assistance rendered Polish immigrant girls. 15 notes.
S. R. Pliska

2017. Pacyga, Dominic A. CRISIS AND COMMUNITY: THE BACK OF THE YARDS, 1921. *Chicago Hist. 1977 6(3): 167-176.* Polish Americans living in the Back of the Yards district of Chicago, Illinois, though Catholic and conservative working class, were instrumental in labor organization and especially in organizing and carrying out a strike of the meat packing workers in 1921.

2018. Parot, Joseph. THE RACIAL DILEMMA IN CHICAGO'S POLISH NEIGHBORHOODS, 1920-1970. *Polish Am. Studies 1975 32(2): 27-37.* Analyzes the continuing conflict in the minds of Chicago's Polonia: the ideology of neighborhood maintenance versus the ideology of escape. Because the Poles are the last ethnics to be moving into the suburbs they find themselves in the area into which blacks are steadily moving. The Poles persist in the racial frontier because of a cultural concentration. They saturate their original areas of settlement with churches, schools, hospitals, clubs, and then find it difficult to disassociate themselves from this heavy economic, social, and religious investment.
S. R. Pliska

2019. Pasturiak, Longin. POLES AND THE AMERICAN REVOLUTION. *Polish Perspectives [Poland] 1976 19(7-8): 29-37.* Discusses Thaddeus Kosciusko and Casimir Pulaski in the American Revolution; explores Polish public opinion in support of US independence.

2020. Pasturiak, Longin. W ZWIAZKU Z DWOCHSETLECIEM AMERYKANSKIEF WOJNY O NIEPODLEGLOSC [In connection with the Bicentennial of the American War of Independence]. *Nowe Drogi [Poland] 1976 322(3): 168-175.* The emergence of the young, independent American Republic was regarded by Lenin as a progressive event. Since then, however, other, more progressive revolutions have taken place while the Bicentennial of the American Revolution is often exploited in that country for the political needs of the present day. Marxist historiography of the American Revolution is modest but mature in such writers as Herbert Aptheker, William Z. Foster, and Herbert M. Morais. Its main emphasis is on the participation in the revolution of the broad masses of farmers and workers and on the significance of the economic factor leading to the outbreak of the war of national liberation. More than 100 Poles took part in the revolutionary war in America, among them Tadeusz Kosciuszko and Kazimierz Pulaski. American bourgeois historiography tends to diminish the role Poles played in that revolution. 9 notes.
W. J. Lukaszewski

2021. Pienkos, Angela. A BICENTENNIAL LOOK AT CASIMIR PULASKI: POLISH, AMERICAN AND ETHNIC FOLK HERO. *Polish Am. Studies 1976 33(1): 5-17.* Describes Casimir Pulaski as a Polish, an American, and a Polish American hero. Both Poland and the United States have been honoring him since his death in Savannah in 1779 during the American Revolution. Lists counties, cities, streets, parks, and schools named in his memory. Presents a concise history of 18th-century Poland and Pulaski's role in the American Revolutionary Army. 35 notes.
S. R. Pliska

2022. Pienkos, Donald. DIMENSIONS OF ETHNICITY: A PRELIMINARY REPORT ON THE MILWAUKEE POLISH AMERICAN POPULATION. *Polish Am. Studies 1973 30(1): 5-19.* There still is a strong contemporary ethnicity among the descendents of the 20th-century immigrants. In an in-person study based on interviews with 1) leading members of Milwaukee's Polish population, 2) randomly selected individuals, 3) students of Polish ancestry, and 4) non-Polish college students, the author concludes that ethnic conscience will be bolstered only with an energetic effort by the Polish government itself to present a more positive image of contemporary Poland among the Polish descendants in this country. 12 notes.
S. R. Pliska

2023. Pienkos, Donald E. ETHNIC ORIENTATIONS AMONG POLISH AMERICANS. *Int. Migration Rev. 1977 11(3): 350-362.* Ethnicity is "a significant psychological factor in American society"; Polish Americans in the 1970's have been enriched by an awareness of their ancestry and cultural heritage.

2024. Pienkos, Donald E. FOREIGN AFFAIRS PERCEPTIONS OF ETHNICS. THE POLISH AMERICANS OF MILWAUKEE. *Ethnicity 1974 1(3): 223-236.* Concerns attitudes toward homeland, related American foreign policies, and the continuing interest in homeland problems of American-born ethnic group members. A study of Milwaukee Poles reveals ideological and generational differences; active Polish Americans retain a stronger sense of ethnic identification, family ties in Poland, and language usage than other Polish Americans. They know more about Polish organizations and issues related to Poland. Analysis also controlled for occupational, educational, age, residential, and ideological variables. 4 tables, 23 notes.   E. Barkan

2025. Pienkos, Donald E. RESEARCH ON ETHNIC POLITICAL BEHAVIOR AMONG THE POLISH AMERICANS: A REVIEW OF THE LITERATURE. *Polish Rev. 1976 21(3): 123-148.* Examines major works in political science dealing specifically with the political and voting behavior of Polish Americans as well as other ethnic groups; attempts to determine the impact ethnic groups have had on national political trends in the 20th century.

2026. Platt, Warren C. THE POLISH NATIONAL CATHOLIC CHURCH: AN INQUIRY INTO ITS ORIGINS. *Church Hist. 1977 46(4): 474-489.* In the United States, the Polish immigrant deprived of old social institutions acquired the capacity to satisfy religious and social particularity. Schisms resulted and parochial life was recognized as an instrument of social cohesion and religious tradition. True to these concerns, the Polish National Catholic Church focused on ethnic nationalism, a force defined by language which would outline the Polish character of the affiliated and the nationalism that accentuated Polish liberation and its coupling with a theology of national religions. The emergence of the Polish National Catholic Church is a testament to the ethnic parish as an effective voluntary association for the preservation of linguistic, cultural, and religious traditions. At the same time, it was a product of the American experience whose traditions of voluntarism and free association allowed its creation and whose religious structure of denominationalism provided the necessary organizational framework. 43 notes.
M. D. Dibert

2027. Polzin, Theresita. THE POLISH AMERICAN FAMILY: PART I, THE SOCIOLOGICAL ASPECTS OF THE FAMILIES OF POLISH IMMIGRANTS TO AMERICA BEFORE WORLD WAR II, AND THEIR DESCENDANTS. *Polish Rev. 1976 21(3): 103-122.* Examines families in terms of structure (type, size, ascribed roles, and division of labor), value orientations (social, religious, and cultural), and social control (from other family members, church, and community) in the 20th century. To be continued.

2028. Pomian, Krzysztof. PROFILE: FLORIAN ZNANIECKI. *Polish Perspectives [Poland] 1973 16(7-8): 47-58.* Reviews the life and theories of the philosopher-sociologist, Florian Znaniecki (1882-1958) in Western Europe, the United States, and Poland.

2029. Pula, James S. THE AMERICAN WILL OF THADDEUS KOSCIUSZKO. *Polish Am. Studies 1977 34(1): 16-25.* Discusses Thaddeus Kosciuszko's will from its drawing in 1798 to its invalidation by the US Supreme Court in 1852, when the estate was worth close to $60,000. Polish American historians maintain, with some convincing documentation, that it was Kosciuszko's intent to free slaves with the money, but the wish was never realized. Despite the influence of Thomas Jefferson who was first executor, the matter became entangled in the other European wills of Kosciuszko. To settle the will it was first necessary to establish Kosciuszko's true citizenship, and with no Polish state this was no easy matter. Based primarily on *Cases Argued and Decided in the Supreme Court of the U.S.;* 19 notes.   S. R. Pliska

2030. Radzialowski, Thaddeus. THE VIEW FROM A POLISH GHETTO. SOME OBSERVATIONS ON THE FIRST ONE HUNDRED YEARS IN DETROIT. *Ethnicity 1974 1(2): 125-150.* In the 1870's Polish immigrants built St. Albertus Church on the east side of Detroit and later St. Casimir to the west. The parishes have each been socially self-contained and much feeling exists for them. The Poles see black advancements as threatening their jobs, homes, communities, and churches, while a symbiotic relationship exists with the Jews. Political competition with blacks has been great, but a new Polish pride and determination to fight discrimination and exclusion has recently arisen. 15 notes.   E. Barkan

2031. Radzialowski, Thaddeus C. THE COMPETITION FOR JOBS AND RACIAL STEREOTYPE: POLES AND BLACKS IN CHICAGO. *Polish Am. Studies 1976 33(2): 5-18.* The struggle for jobs, not hunger for status, produced Polish prejudice against blacks in Chicago, ca. 1890-1919. Blacks from the South threatened the jobs of the settled Polish immigrants. In no time, blacks found themselves serving as strikebreakers and even killing Polish workers. For these prejudices and racial antagonisms much blame rests with American industry. Based on newspaper accounts and Polish and English secondary sources; 28 notes.
S. R. Pliska

2032. Radzialowski, Thaddeus C. REFLECTIONS ON THE HISTORY OF THE FELICIANS IN AMERICA. *Polish Am. Studies 1975 32(1): 19-28.* Stresses the importance of this sisterhood in Polish-American history. Though originating in Poland in 1855, the order spread to the United States in 1874 and soon became a predominantly American order, with 82 percent of its membership residing on this side of the Atlantic. Throughout its history it provided social mobility for immigrant women. Although the congregation was involved in the care of orphans, the aged, and the sick, teaching remained its primary concern. Only after the decline and almost total disappearance of the Polish language from parochial schools did the order accept other responsibilities. As a result of their dedication and hard work, the Felicians were able to draw capital and invest it in schools, orphanages, hospitals, and retirement homes. Based on primary and secondary sources; 21 notes.
S. R. Pliska

2033. Renkiewicz, Frank. THE USES OF THE POLISH PAST IN AMERICA. *Polish Am. Studies 1977 34(1): 70-79.* Discusses changes in Polish American historiography, from the edifying and flattering accounts about the Polish elite to a sociological and psychological study of Polish American institutions. As of 1976, "Polish Americans have been unable to restore a past which offers a base for a satisfying present and a promising future." The search should continue, with accruing benefits to Polish American historiography. 16 notes. Revised presidential address to the PAHA meeting in Washington, D.C., 28 December 1976.
S. R. Pliska

2034. Rusinowa, Izabela. THE UNITED STATES. *Acta Poloniae Historica [Poland] 1975 (32): 191-204.* Provides writings by Polish historians on US history. Reviews the existing publications of the 18th and 19th centuries. Notes a shortage of information on the United States in Poland during the late 19th and early 20th centuries, which was peculiar since that was a period of heavy Polish emigration to the United States. Divides the principal direction of Polish historians' research to date into five categories: 1) syntheses and textbooks, 2) internal history, 3) foreign relations, 4) the evolution of the sociopolitical system, and 5) ethnic relations in the United States, particularly Polish immigrant groups.

2035. Sadler, Charles. "POLITICAL DYNAMITE": THE CHICAGO POLONIA AND PRESIDENT ROOSEVELT IN 1944. *J. of the Illinois State Hist. Soc. 1978 71(2): 119-132.* Considers the creation and operation of the Polish-American Congress, founded by moderate groups in Buffalo, New York, to rally support for an independent Poland. National in membership and headquartered in Chicago, the Congress was treated deferentially by Franklin D. Roosevelt and some ethnic-minded officials in industrial states, but failed in the end to influence foreign policy. Based on Congress documents, State Department files, and Polish-American newspapers; 3 illus., map, 63 notes.   J

2036. Sadler, Charles. 'PRO-SOVIET POLISH-AMERICANS': OSKAR LANGE AND RUSSIA'S FRIENDS IN THE POLONIA, 1941-1945. *Polish Rev. 1977 22(4): 25-39.* Describes Oscar Lange's (1904-65) role in furthering the American public's acceptance of Soviet occupation of eastern Poland. Lange emerged from the pro-Soviet faction of American Poles to become an articulate statesman of its beliefs. He conferred with US, Soviet, and Polish exile government leaders. Later, after Stalin's suggestion, he renounced the US citizenship he had received in 1943, and became the first ambassador to the United States from the postwar Polish government. Mentions the roles of President Franklin D. Roosevelt and others in ceding eastern Poland. 65 notes.   J. Tull

2037. Sandberg, Neil C. THE CHANGING POLISH AMERICAN. *Polish Am. Studies 1974 31(1): 5-14.* Attempts to measure the viability of ethnicity among the different generations of Polish Americans in California. Concludes that the later generations, third and fourth, are less ethnic than the earlier generations even though ethnicity still continues to have meaning in the lives of large numbers. Ethnicity also diminishes among the upwardly mobile and the more affluent. The article also touches upon the early Polish immigrants to California and discusses activities of the Los Angeles Poles. Biblio.   S. R. Pliska

2038. Sarna, Jan. MARCHE, ARKANSAS: A PERSONAL REMINISCENCE OF LIFE AND CUSTOMS. *Arkansas Hist. Q. 1977 36(1): 31-49.* Marche, Arkansas, ten miles north of Little Rock, was for many years a thriving community consisting primarily of Polish immigrants and their descendants. Originally called Warren, in 1877 the town began to be a place for Poles to settle if they were dissatisfied with life in large cities like Chicago. They were also able to maintain their old country customs and heritage among friends. The author's family provides a typical history of an immigrant family. Primary and secondary sources; 7 illus., 23 notes.   T. L. Savitt

2039. Siemankowski, Francis T. THE MAKING OF THE POLISH AMERICAN COMMUNITY: SLOAN, NEW YORK AS A CASE STUDY. *Polish Am. Studies 1977 34(2): 56-67.* Discusses a small Polish community on the outskirts of Buffalo, 1873-1977. Mentions immigrant adjustment, promotion of homogeneity, the declining influence of the parish school, and inability to perpetuate the Polish language. Concludes that Polish Americans will continue to survive as an ethnic group because of a "pride in family, church, community and country." 10 notes.   S. R. Pliska

2040. Simon, Roger D. HOUSING AND SERVICES IN AN IMMIGRANT NEIGHBORHOOD: MILWAUKEE'S WARD 14. *J. of Urban Hist. 1976 2(4): 435-458.* The 14th ward in the southwest corner of Milwaukee was the center of the city's Polish Americans at the turn of the century. Although populated by immigrants employed in unskilled and factory jobs, the ward was a neighborhood not of tenements or decayed dwellings, but of small, recently constructed, single unit dwellings. More than half of the houses were owned by their occupants. This was not achieved without sacrifices. Boarders were a frequent source of added income (and added crowding), and municipal services such as water and sewers were often delayed until residents could afford their installation. Based on the Wisconsin state census of 1905 and other primary and secondary sources; 4 tables, 6 fig., 35 notes.   T. W. Smith

2041. Stasik, Florian. ADAM GUROWSKI'S ROAD TO ABOLITIONISM. *Acta Poloniae Hist. [Poland] 1977 35: 87-112.* Discusses Gurowski's social and political activities and their philosophical background. He fought in the November uprising, travelled in western Europe and wrote articles for radical causes. Disillusioned with the West he turned to Tsarist Russia—which also rejected his political ideas. He left for the United States in 1849 and took up Negro emancipation, writing prolifically in journals and newspapers. His radicalism intensified, antagonizing even his political partners, including President Lincoln. He died in 1866 in poor circumstances, failing to draw recognition even among the protagonists of the abolition of slavery. 90 notes.   H. Heitzman-Wojcicka

2042. Symmons-Symonolewicz, Konstantin. IMMIGRANT PASTOR: ACHIEVEMENTS AND PROFILE. *Polish Rev. 1974 19(3/4): 204-208.* Reviews Daniel Stephen Buczek's *Immigrant Pastor: The Life of the Right Reverend Monsignor Lucyan Bójnowski of New Britain, Connecticut* (Waterbury, Conn: Heminway Corp., 1974).   S

2043. Symmons-Symonolewicz, Konstantin. A SOCIOLOGICAL ANALYSIS OF POLISH-AMERICANS. *Polish Rev. 1978 23(2): 76-79.* Review article. William I. Thomas and Florian Znaniecki's *Chlop polski w Europie i Ameryce* (The Polish Peasant in Europe and America), Vol. I-V (Warsaw: Ludowa Spoldzielnia Wydawnicza, 1976), a Polish translation of an early-20th-century work in English, is a classic which has influenced several generations of sociologists. Jozef Miaso's *The History of the Education of Polish Immigrants in the United States,* Ludwik Krzyzanowski, transl. (New York: Kościuszko Foundation, 1977), is a basic, well-documented reference work on Polish education in America. Grzegorz Babinski's *Lokalna społeczność polonijna w Stanach Zjedno-*

zonych Ameryki w procesie przemian (The local Polonia community in the USA in the process of transformation) (Wroclaw: Ossolineum, Polska Akademia Nauk, Komitet Badania Polonii Zagranicznej, 1977) is a carefully researched monograph on social changes in local Polish communities as exemplified by Wallington, New Jersey.   R. V. Ritter

2044. Thuma, Linnie H. IMAGE AND IMAGINATION: HOW AN ETHNIC COMMUNITY SEES ITSELF. *New York Folklore 1978 4(1-4): 7-19.* Discusses the perceptions of the 4,000 Polish Americans in the former textile milling village, New York Mills, toward their ethnicity, history, and important traditions, based on a three-month study. Traces the town's beginnings, 1800's-40's, when it was predominantly Scottish and Welsh, through the time it became mostly Polish in the early 20th century, until the closure of the mills in 1951.

2045. Treppa, Allan R. JOHN A. LEMKE: AMERICA'S FIRST NATIVE-BORN POLISH AMERICAN PRIEST? *Polish Am. Studies 1978 35(1-2): 78-83.* This Polish American (1866-90) was ordained to the priesthood in Detroit in 1889. Monographs and newspapers in English; 17 notes.   S. R. Pliska

2046. Walicki, Andrzej. ADAM GUROWSKI: POLISH NATIONALISM, RUSSIAN PANSLAVISM AND AMERICAN MANIFEST DESTINY. *Russian Rev. 1979 38(1): 1-26.* Frequent shifts and reversals punctuated the life and thought of Adam Gurowski (1805-66). Originally a leading exponent of Polish nationalism, he renounced that cause and took up residence in Russia. Though Gurowski continued to believe that only Russia could unite all Slavonic nations, he became disillusioned with the Tsar and emigrated to the United States where he assumed an editorial position at the *New York Tribune.* For the rest of his life, Gurowski was, simultaneously, a persuasive advocate of Russian Pan-Slavism and American Manifest Destiny. 96 notes.

M. R. Yerburgh

2047. Wardziński, Zygmunt. THE OLDEST SLAVIC MAGAZINE IN THE UNITED STATES: *POLAND: HISTORICAL, LITERARY, MONUMENTAL, PICTURESQUE* AND ITS ARTICLE ON *COPERNICUS* (1842). *Polish Rev. 1974 19(3-4): 83-98.* Gives information on the early years of Polish emigré Paul Sobolewski, publisher and editor of the first paper of the Polish-American press *Poland: Historical, Literary, Monumental, Picturesque* and discusses his article on the life and achievement of Nicolaus Copernicus.   S

2048. Wells, Miriam J. ETHNICITY, SOCIAL STIGMA, AND RESOURCE MOBILIZATION IN RURAL AMERICA: REEXAMINATION OF A MIDWESTERN EXPERIENCE. *Ethnohistory 1975 22(4): 319-343.* Examines the interconnection of ethnicity, social stigma, and resource mobilization in order to improve understanding of the historical development of Euro-American communities. It explores the process through which an economically dependent and ethnically stigmatized Polish immigrant population became incorporated into a small midwestern town. Contrary to assimilationist assumptions, ethnic incorporation entailed little homogenization of cultural and associational structures. Although ethnic differences were negatively viewed by powerholders, they did not invariably constitute a liability in minority resource mobilization. The rate of assimilation and role of ethnicity vary sharply with historical period and context of activity considered.   J

2049. Wieczerzak, Joseph. PRE- AND PROTO-ETHNICS: POLES IN THE UNITED STATES BEFORE IMMIGRATION "AFTER BREAD." *Polish Rev. 1976 21(3): 7-38.* Examines the immigration from Poland to the United States, 1608-1860's, events in Europe which led to emigration, the differences between those "after bread" ("real ethnics") and the political exiles ("proto-ethnics"), and the influence of the "after breads" on the exiles.

2050. Wojniusz, Helen K. ETHNICITY AND OTHER VARIABLES IN THE ANALYSIS OF POLISH AMERICAN WOMEN. *Polish Am. Studies 1977 34(2): 26-37.* Discusses preliminary research, hypothesis, and methodology of previous research on ethnicity and the variables that affect it, 1940-77. 31 notes.   S. R. Pliska

2051. Zamachaj, Stanley E. POLISH. *Hist. J. of Western Massachusetts 1976 (Supplement): 75-79.* Discusses the activities of Polish settlers

at Jamestown and in other colonies before the American Revolution and the activities of Poles in the Revolution with particular attention given to Thaddeus Kosciuszko, Casimir Pulaski, and Haym Salomon. Notes.
W. H. Mulligan, Jr.

2052. Zerby, Charles L. JOHN DEWEY AND THE POLISH QUESTION: A RESPONSE TO THE REVISIONIST HISTORIANS. *Hist. of Educ. Q. 1975 15(2): 17-30.* A 1918 summer project designed to ascertain forces within American society oppressing immigrant Poles living in Philadelphia led John Dewey to a broader study of American foreign policy toward Poland; it also led him to point out rhetorical and administrative discrepancies in Woodrow Wilson's Polish policy which Dewey labeled as anti-Semitic and antidemocratic methods of economic control benefiting a minority of conservatives.

2053. —. [POLAND AND AMERICA: THE ECONOMIC CONNECTION 1918-1939]. *Polish Am. Studies 1975 32(2): 38-54.*
Landau, Zbigniew. POLAND AND AMERICA: THE ECONOMIC CONNECTION 1918-1939, *pp. 38-50.* American investments and loans contributed substantially to Poland's recovery between the wars despite the fact that most of the money went into existing firms. Perhaps Polish American families provided Poland with more dollars than the expensive industrial loans contracted during 1924-29. 58 notes.
Blejwas, Stanislaus A. "POLAND AND AMERICA: THE ECONOMIC CONNECTION"—A COMMENT, *pp. 51-54.* Considers the study a first in the exploration of an unknown area in Polish-American relations. Those American investments which went into so-called existing firms only liberated Polish capital for other new ventures. Note.
S. R. Pliska/S

2054. —. POLISH AMERICANS. Sowell, Thomas, ed. *Essays and Data on American Ethnic Groups* (Washington, D.C.: Urban Inst. Pr., 1978): 376-379. Statistics on Polish Americans' personal income distribution by sex; family income distribution; occupational distribution by sex; and educational distribution by age. From US Bureau of the Census *Current Population Reports,* Series P-20, Nos. 221, 249.
K. A. Talley

Russian and Ukrainian

2055. Allen, Robert V. PETER DEMENS, THE REDOUBTABLE HUSTLER. *Q. J. of the Lib. of Congress 1977 34(3): 208-236.* A colorful figure in Russian-American relations during the late 19th and early 20th centuries, Petr Alekseevich Dement'ev was a sawmill owner, railroad promoter, contractor, banker, grower of citrus fruit in Florida and California, and secretary of a firm which manufactured shaving soap. For more than 20 years he contributed articles on American affairs to a Russian journal. He was a controversialist with Tolstoi. He came to the United States in 1881, and was naturalized as Peter Demens. He died in 1919 at age 69. Illus., 53 notes.
E. P. Stickney

2056. Barratt, Glynn R. THE RUSSIAN INTEREST IN ARCTIC NORTH AMERICA: THE KRUZENSHTERN-ROMANOV PROJECTS, 1819-1823. *Slavonic and East European R. [Great Britain] 1975 53(130): 27-43.* Captain-Commodore Ivan Fedorovich Kruzenshtern and Lieutenant Vladmir Pavlovich Romanov belonged to a group of naval officers who promoted scientific exploration of Arctic America between the Bering Strait and Hudson's Bay. In the early 1820's Romanov prepared for a voyage that would promise material benefits to the struggling Russian American Company. By 1825 political conditions had minimized any expansionist potential in the project, and it remained abortive. Based on Moscow naval archives; map, 45 notes.
R. E. Weltsch

2057. Beliajeff, Anton S. THE OLD BELIEVERS IN THE UNITED STATES. *Russian Rev. 1977 36(1): 76-80.* Old Believers are those individuals who cling to the traditional customs of the Russian Orthodox Church as it existed prior to the ecclesiastical reforms of the 17th century. Since the 1890's, small groups of these believers periodically have immigrated to the United States. They became known for their industrious, self-reliant ways. Today, 8,000 Old Believers live primarily in Oregon, Pennsylvania, Michigan, New Jersey, and Alaska. 10 notes.
M. R. Yerburgh

2058. Bergquist, Harold E. THE RUSSIAN UKASE OF SEPTEMBER 16, 1821: THE NONCOLONIZATION PRINCIPLE, AND THE RUSSO-AMERICAN CONVENTION OF 1824. *Can. J. of Hist. [Canada] 1975 10(2): 165-184.* Examines foreign relations between the United States and Russia pertaining to the Northwest Coast area, 1821-25; examines the role of Great Britain, trade relations among the three, and the ukase issued by Tsar Alexander I in 1821.

2059. Buryk, Michael. AGAPIUS HONCHARENKO: PORTRAIT OF A UKRAINIAN AMERICAN KOZAK. *Ukrainian Q. 1976 32(1): 16-36.* Outlines the life of Agapius Honcharenko (1832-1916), first Ukrainian priest in the United States. Threatened and pursued by Russian authorities for his anti-tsarist writings in radical periodicals published abroad, Honcharenko emigrated to the United States in 1865. The first issue of his newspaper *The Alaska Herald* in 1868 marked the realization of his dream of establishing a Russian publishing house in America. However, Honcharenko's attacks on the monopolistic practices of American companies in Alaska and his criticism of anti-Chinese feeling in the West provoked slander and physical threats which forced his resignation as editor in 1872. Following this Honcharenko hoped to found a cooperative Ukrainian community in California, but this plan also failed. His remaining life was spent on his farm "Ukraina."
K. N. T. Crowther

2060. Chirovsky, Nicholas L. THE CONTRIBUTION OF THE SHEVCHENKO SCIENTIFIC SOCIETY TO AMERICAN SCHOLARSHIP. *Ukrainian Rev. [Great Britain] 1977 24(1): 25-42.* Catalogs scholarship in the social sciences, the arts, and the natural sciences, by members of the Shevchenko Scientific Society in the United States (incorporated 1950) following their departure from the Ukraine in 1947.

2061. Croskey, Robert, transl. THE RUSSIAN ORTHODOX CHURCH IN ALASKA: INNOKENTII VENIAMINOV'S SUPPLEMENTARY ACCOUNT (1858). *Pacific Northwest Q. 1975 66(1): 26-29.* Reprints the translation of an 1858 account of the standing of the Russian Orthodox Church in Alaska written by Metropolitan Innokentii Veniaminov, which includes the size and extent of the Church, its relations with the Russian-American Company, sources for its financial support, and its educational activities.

2062. Dobriansky, Lev E. IN THE MAINSTREAM OF BASIC ISSUES. *Ukrainian Q. 1974 30(3): 370-378.* In its 30-year history, the *Ukrainian Quarterly* has been concerned with basic issues of Ukrainian history.

2063. Dunn, Ethel and Dunn, Stephen P. RELIGION AND ETHNICITY: THE CASE OF THE AMERICAN MOLOKANS. *Ethnicity 1977 4(4): 370-379.* An analysis of the nature and activities of the Molokans in California, a small group of religious dissidents who emigrated from Russia around the turn of the century. The San Francisco colony remains, though it has grown but little and has not successfully protected its neighborhood from outside penetration. Certainly the Molokans are no longer peasants, but they can hardly be called an ethnic group. Rather they are simply an offshoot religious sect, whose efforts to develop an ethnicity have largely failed.
V. L. Human

2064. Dushnyck, Walter. METROPOLITAN SENYSHYN—GREAT CHURCHMAN AND LEADER. *Ukrainian Q. 1977 33(1): 57-66.* Describes the life and work of Metropolitan Ambrose Senyshyn (1903-1976) of the Philadelphia Archeparchy. Born in the Ukraine and educated there and in Poland, Metropolitan Senyshyn came to the United States in 1933. Here he distinguished himself as a builder and organizer of churches and as a leader of the Ukrainian Catholic order in the United States.
K. N. T. Crowther

2065. Dushnyck, Walter. *THE UKRAINIAN QUARTERLY*: A CONTINUING SCHOLARLY QUEST FOR FREEDOM. *Ukrainian Q. 1974 30(4): 348-369.* Presents a history of this 30-year-old journal and its contribution to an understanding of the Ukraine.

2066. Fechin, Eya. FECHIN'S HOME IN TAOS. *Southwestern Art 1978 7(1): 4-13.* During 1926-33 Nicolai Fechin, a landscape painter from Russia, moved from New York City to Taos, New Mexico, where he built a house which architecturally combined indigenous and Russian styles, and resumed his career in landscape painting.

2067. Gardner, Thomas. THE LIFE AND TIMES OF MADAME VERA STRAVINSKY. *Horizon 1979 22(4): 46-49.* Biographical sketch of Madame Vera Stravinsky (b. 1888) focuses on her youth in Russia, her life with composer Igor Stravinsky, and her lifelong pursuit of painting, 1917-79.

2068. Gibson, James R. CALIFORNIA IN 1824 BY DMITRY ZAVALISHIN. *Southern California Q. 1973 55(4): 369-412.* Dmitry Zavalishin (1804-92) was a young naval officer who visited Alta California during 1823-24. He suggested in a report to Tsar Alexander I that Russia pursue an aggressive policy in California, but his proposals were rejected. Zavalishin describes mission life, social habits of the Californians, incorporation and exploitation of the Indians into Spanish-Mexican society, trade and economy, and the possibilities for California's future if the region accepted annexation by Russia. Zavalishin credited Russian fur trappers with the first discovery of gold in California, suppressing the find in the belief that higher authorities would prevent them from profiting by it. Translation of an article originally published in 1865 in a Russian periodical; photo, 25 notes. A. Hoffman

2069. Gibson, James R. RUSSIAN AMERICA IN 1821. *Oregon Hist. Q. 1976 77(2): 174-188.* Sketches the life and activities of Kirill Khlebnikov (1785-1838), Russian agent in the North American colonies. Translates one of Khlebnikov's accounts of the Russian-American Company's colonies. Khlebnikov wanted travel and adventure and got both. He became a highly respected agent who always found time to make valuable contributions to natural history. His account of the colonies on the Pacific coast is primarily commercial in nature and emphasizes the colonies' products and their quantities and values. 3 photos, 9 notes. V. L. Human

2070. Giffin, Frederick C. THE DEATH OF WALTER KRIVITSKY. *Social Sci. 1979 54(3): 139-146.* Walter Krivitsky, an important figure in the Soviet Military Intelligence service, defected to the West in 1937. During the next several years, while residing in the United States, he not only published a series of magazine articles and a book which were highly critical of Stalinist Russia, but his well-publicized testimony before the Dies Committee did much to discredit those who argued that American Communists were independent of Moscow and posed no threat to this country's security. His death in Washington, D.C., early in 1941 provoked considerable controversy. Although the police issued a verdict of suicide, Krivitsky's wife and others familiar with the workings of the Soviet espionage establishment charged that he was a victim of foul play. J

2071. Glushankov, I. V.; Sadouski, Mary; and Pierce, Richard A., transl. THE ALEUTIAN EXPEDITION OF KRENITSYN AND LEVASHOV. *Alaska J. 1973 3(4): 204-210.* Discusses the expedition to Alaska's Aleutian Islands by Russian explorers Petr Kuz'mich Krenitsyn and Mikhail Dmitrievich Levashov in 1769, including their observations on the culture of the Aleut Eskimos.

2072. Grauman, Melody W. WOMEN AND CULTURE IN RUSSIAN AMERICA. *Am. West 1974 11(3): 24-31.* When the *promyshlenniki*, Russian fur hunters, began to arrive in the Aleutians about 1755, they seized female Aleut hostages demanding ransom in sea otter furs. This introduced the Russians to the native adaptive survival techniques. A Russian-native settlement was established that was more "nativized" than Russian. Russian wives of Russian merchants and officials in Alaska sought "to transplant the superficialities of Russian culture" on the promyshlenniki-native hybrid culture. When the Russian women finally departed in 1867, the "cultural shell" they had established crumbled. Remnants of the promyshlenniki cultural influence persisted. 8 illus., biblio. D. L. Smith

2073. Hanable, William S. NEW RUSSIA. *Alaska J. 1973 3(2): 77-80.* Discusses the history of the Russian-American colony New Russia, Alaska, 1788-1807, emphasizing the revolt of the Tlingit Indians in 1805.

2074. Heckrotte, Warren. THE DISCOVERY OF HUMBOLDT BAY: A NEW LOOK AT AN OLD STORY. *Terrae Incognitae [Netherlands] 1973 5: 27-41.* Before development, the natural entrance to California's Humboldt Bay was virtually invisible to ships, so it remained

undiscovered until 1806-07. The American Captain Jonathan Winship and the Russian Commander Slobodchikon of the Russian American Company, in a joint fur-hunting venture, anchored offshore and led Aleut canoemen in to explore the "Bay of Indians" or "Bay of Rezanov." The entrance was treacherous for large ships, so the bay remained unknown and unsettled for years, despite the desire of the Russians for a base in the area. Humboldt Bay was "rediscovered" (by land) by Americans in 1849. Based on scientific reports, atlases, and secondary sources; 4 maps, 50 notes. C. B. Fitzgerald

2075. Jacoby, Susan. JOSEPH BRODSKY IN EXILE. *Change 1973 5(6): 58-63.* One of the Soviet Union's leading poets now teaches at an American university. His views on culture and American students provide a fascinating portrait of an important intercultural encounter. J

2076. Jellico, John. NICOLAI FECHIN. *Southwestern Art 1976 5(2): 19-31.* Describes the life and work of Nicolai Fechin (1881-1955), a Russian artist who did his most noted work, usually paintings of Indians, following a move to Taos, New Mexico, in 1927.

2077. John, Fred and John, Katie. THE KILLING OF THE RUSSIANS AT BATZULNETAS VILLAGE. *Alaska J. 1973 3(3): 147-148.* Discusses the killing of an expedition of Russian explorers and fur traders by Copper River Indians at Batzulnetas Village, Alaska, in 1847-48.

2078. Koropets'kyi, Ivan S. VSEVOLOD HOLUBNYCHYI (1928-1977) [Vsevolod Holubnychyi (1928-77)]. *Sučasnist [West Germany] 1977 (7-8): 154-161.* Describes the life and publications of Vsevolod Holubnychyi (1928-77), a Ukrainian American economist, historian, and politician.

2079. Kushner, Howard I. "SEWARD'S FOLLY"? AMERICAN COMMERCE IN RUSSIAN AMERICA AND THE ALASKA PURCHASE. *California Hist. Q. 1975 54(1): 4-26.* A reassessment of the US purchase of Alaska from Russia in 1867 for $7,200,000. Far from being the desolate "ice box" usually depicted by historians, Alaska possessed many resources and potential industries that had attracted American entrepreneurs as far back as the early 1850s. The American-Russian Commercial Company carried on a profitable trade in ice from 1851 on; fur traders, whalers, and fishermen successfully operated in the Russian American region; and the Russian colony obtained supplies from American merchants. Aggressive American entrepreneurs pressed for contracts with Russia providing for commercial enterprises. Tsarist Russia quickly recognized that American aggressiveness in business and colonization would inevitably place Russia in a position similar to the one that Spain and Britain had faced with American expansion. Russia was therefore amenable to the sale of Alaska, a move that went even beyond the maneuverings of some of the American businessmen. Further investigation and reappraisal of American-Russian relations in the Pacific Northwest is called for. Primary and secondary sources; illus., maps, 85 notes. A. Hoffman

2080. Lain, B. D. THE DECLINE OF RUSSIAN AMERICA'S COLONIAL SOCIETY. *Western Hist. Q. 1976 7(2): 143-153.* The Russian colonial society of Alaska was only a pale image of Russian society. After the 1867 Alaskan purchase and removal of the Russian American Company, the Russian colonial society declined gradually. Today, it has been almost completely absorbed by the native population. The Russian Orthodox Church, Russian place-names, and Slavic surnames are all that remain. 29 notes. D. L. Smith

2081. Luts'ka, Svitliana. ZHINOCHA PRESA V URSR [Women's press in the Ukrainian Soviet republic]. *Sučasnist [West Germany] 1974 (7-8): 128-132.* Compares women's publications in Soviet Ukraine with those produced by Ukrainian women emigrés, 1924-74.

2082. McElligott, Mary Ellen, ed. "A MONOTONY FULL OF SADNESS": THE DIARY OF NADINE TURCHIN, MAY, 1863-APRIL, 1864. *J. of the Illinois State Hist. Soc. 1977 70(1): 27-89.* An annotated version of the unpublished diary of the wife of Union General John Basil Turchin. The diary was written in French and translated by unknown persons. Liberal aristocrats, the pair fled Russia in search of political freedom in 1856. They were strong abolitionists but were frankly disgusted by what they considered the temerity, inexperience, and lack of conviction of the Union Army. Mrs. Turchin accompanied her husband on the field with the Army of the Cumberland; her reports reveal her own military-background expertise and private political sentiments. 19 illus., 2 maps, 132 notes.   J/S

2083. Mull, Gil and Plafker, George. THE FIRST RUSSIAN LANDING IN ALASKA. *Alaska J. 1976 6(3): 134-145.* The Russians first explored Alaska under Vitus Bering in 1741 in two shipes, *St. Peter* and *St. Paul.* In 1917 F. A. Golder discovered a number of documents related to the voyage, including official reports, ships' logs and the journal of naturalist Georg Wilhelm Steller. Presents an account of a recent revisitation of the areas described in the documents and discusses changes in the geological features since the first landings. 12 photos, map, graph, 12 notes.   E. E. Eminhizer

2084. Odarchenko, Petro. OLEKSA POVSTENKO: ARK-HITEKTO I MYSTETSTVOZNAVETS' [Oleksa Povstenko: architect and connoisseur of art]. *Sučasnist [West Germany] 1973 (9): 61-75.* Traces the life and activities of Oleksa Povstenko in America from 1949-68 including his work on designs for American government buildings.

2085. Odarchenko, Petro. PSUVANNIA I ZAMICHENNIA UK-RAINS'KOI MOVY V AMERYTSI [The deterioration and imposi-tions into the Ukrainian language in America]. *Sučasnist [West Germany] 1977 (7-8): 185-194.* Discusses the development and influences on the Ukrainian language in the Ukrainian American emigré society, 1920's-77.

2086. Oliner, Samuel P. SOROKIN'S CONTRIBUTION TO AMERICAN SOCIOLOGY. *Nationalities Papers 1976 4(2): 125-151.* Pitirim A. Sorokin was a founder of modern sociology and one of the best minds of the 20th century.

2087. Orfalea, Greg. HEART OF THE OLD BELIEVERS. *Westways 1976 68(4): 34-37, 68-69.* Leaving their native Russia in order to practice freedom of religion, several members of the Old Believers sect of the Russian Orthodox Church settled in small towns on Alaska's Kenai Peninsula, 1920's.

2088. Peterson, Dale E. SOLZHENITSYN'S IMAGE OF AMER-ICA: THE SURVIVAL OF A SLAVOPHILE IDEA. *Massachusetts Rev. 1978 19(1): 141-166.* The Soviet government has successfully dis-placed Alexander Solzhenitsyn from east to west. Americans were shocked to discover that he would attack their beliefs, and that he was a reborn orthodox "Slavophile," a philosophy which advocated a return to the virtues and traditions of old Russia. Ivan Vasilevich Kireevsky (1808-56) and Prince Vladimir Fedorovich Odoevsky (1803-69) were early Slavophiles. Next came the Pan-Slavs. Today Slavophilism is pro-mulgated by Solzhenitsyn. The intellectual traditions of American and Russian nationalism have encouraged each nation to embrace its own distinctive mission. Americans can expect sibling rivalry in their contacts with the USSR. Recognition of each culture's "otherness" must be ob-served. Letters, speeches, interviews, and secondary works; 42 notes.
                                                            E. R. Campbell

2089. Petrov, G. D. ALEKSANDRA KOLLONTAI V SSHA [Aleksandra Kollontai in the USA]. *Novaia i Noveishaia Istoriia [USSR] 1972 (3): 128-142.* A revolutionary from early years, Kollontai (1872-1952) fled Russia in 1908. She settled, eventually, in Norway. Invited by the American Socialist Party, she departed for the USA in 1915. Throughout America she promoted Marxism-Leninism, denounced the imperialist war, and, in her meetings with Russian emigres, fostered international solidarity. At Lenin's behest she arranged the publication of Bolshevik literature. On 21 February 1916 she returned to Norway, only to leave again for the USA in August 1916 with her son. This essentially private visit she turned to political use by establishing close contact with the Socialist labor party. She tirelessly denounced the imperialist war. She left America on 27 January 1917, and news of America's joining the war reached her on the ship. She was a true internationalist, and in the USA did much useful propaganda work. Based on Lenin's work, Istoricheskii arkhiv and Inostrannaia literature; 94 notes.   A. J. Evans

2090. Pierce, Richard A. ALASKA'S RUSSIAN GOVERNORS. *Alaska J. 1973 3(1): 20-30.* Concluded from a previous article. Part VII. PRINCE D. P. MAKSUTOV. Dmitri Petrovich Maksutov was the last chief manager of the Russian-American Company in Alaska, 1859-67.

2091. Pierce, Richard A. THE RUSSIAN COAL MINE ON THE KENAI. *Alaska J. 1975 5(2): 104-108.* Russians became interested in coal mining in Alaska as the fur trade declined in value. Discusses the Russian interest in coal, and gives a biographical sketch of Enoch Hjal-mar Fvrvhjelm. Reproduces a long letter from Fvrvhjelm to an uncle dated 22 January 1863 which contains a detailed description of the mine at Kenai and its development. Map, 4 photos, 4 notes.
                                                            E. E. Eminhizer

2092. Pierce, Richard A. VOZNESENSKII: SCIENTIST IN ALASKA. *Alaska J. 1975 5(1): 11-15.* Between 1839 and 1849 Il'ia Voznesenski traveled in Russian America, gathering specimens and ar-tifacts (now located in the Museum of Anthropology and Ethnology, Leningrad). Describes his travels and the details of seven of his drawings of the Alaskan landscape and people. 7 illus., biblio.
                                                            E. E. Eminhizer

2093. Pirenne, J.-H. LA COMPAGNIE RUSSO-AMÉRICAINE ET LA POLITIQUE MONDIALE D'ALEXANDRE I^e [The Russian-American Company and Alexander I's world policy]. *Bull. des Séances de l'Acad. Royale des Sci. d'Outre-Mer [Belgium] 1976 (3): 316-342.* Examines the origins, development, and decline of the Russian-American Company, a Russian mixed-economy company founded in 1799 to pro-mote the expansion of Siberian merchants' commerce along the American Northwest coast. It momentarily affected Russian maritime ascendancy in the Northern Pacific at the apogee of Alexander I's international influence. The company's rise and decline were due to changes in his foreign policy. 46 notes, biblio.   R. O. Khan

2094. Procko, Bohdan P. THE ESTABLISHMENT OF THE RU-THENIAN CHURCH IN THE UNITED STATES, 1884-1907. *Pennsylvania Hist. 1975 42(2): 137-154.* In 1884 the first priest of the Byzantine-Slavonic Rite of the Roman Catholic Church came to the United States to minister to Ruthenian Catholics. He established a church in Shenandoah, Pennsylvania. Efforts to provide for the spiritual needs of these people were impeded by divisions between Ukrainians and Rusins and by jurisdictional disputes with the American bishops, who were unwilling to accept married priests of the Byzantine Rite. The appoint-ment of an administrator and, later, an "Apostolic Visitor," did little to improve the situation. Some Ruthenians left the Church of Rome and joined the Greek Orthodox Church. In 1907 Pope Pius X named a bishop for Ruthenian Catholics in the United States, and a new phase of develop-ment began. Illus., 71 notes.   D. C. Swift

2095. Rokitiansky, Nicholas John. FORT ROSS. *Voprosy Istorii [USSR] 1977 (7): 213-217.* Describes Russian colonial and commercial expansion in North America by the Russian-American Company and its expeditions to northern California in 1808 and 1811 under Ivan A. Kus-kov (1765-1823). Fort Ross was established in 1812 and developed into an important agricultural and sea-mammal hunting base. In 1841, it was sold to the American frontiersman John Augustus Sutter. Lecture deliv-ered at the Institute of History of the Academy of Sciences, USSR, 2 September 1976. 6 notes.   N. Frenkley

2096. Rokitiansky, Nicholas John. RUSSKOE SELENIE V AMERIKE: FORT ROSS [A Russian settlement in America: Fort Ross]. *Vestnik Moskovskogo U., Seriia 8: Istoriia [USSR] 1977 32(2): 84-88.* Ivan A. Kuskov's Russian-American Company expedition came to northern California in December 1808. Fort Ross was completed in 1812. A wharf was built and the interior was explored. The "Russian River" was discovered and named the "Slavianka." With the help of the Spanish, trade was established with the King of the Sandwich Islands. Kuskov died in Russia. Fort Ross was then under the command of A. G. Rotchev. The Fort was sold in 1841.   D. Balmuth

2097. Rudenko, Oleks. RUSSIA IN THE PACIFIC BASIN. *J. of the West 1976 15(2): 49-64.* Discusses the rise and fall of the Russian Pacific Basin Empire. Based on the fur trade, exploitative rather than developmental, with poor military backing, the expansionist effort lasted only as long as it was not seriously challenged. The movement into Alaska was a logical extension of the fur trade in Siberia which had begun in 1581. Population constantly compounded the difficulty of supply. The Russians were never able to field a Pacific fleet of sufficient size to protect their possessions. And so, with the sale of Alaska to the United States in 1867, Russia withdrew to Asia.   R. Alvis

2098. Samedov, V. Yu.   RUSSKAIA RABOCHAIA GAZETTA V AMERIKE [Russian workers' newspaper in America]. *Istoriia SSSR [USSR] 1973 (5): 172-179.* In 1889 a Russian group of socialists published the first issue of *Znamia* (Banner) and called it a workers' newspaper. It criticized the capitalist system, pointed out the shortcomings of the bourgeoisie, and called on the workers to liberate themselves. It published K. Marx's "Civil War in France" and some articles by the members of the group "Liberation of Labor." Its own writers published "Ownership, Religion and Family," based on Engels' work on the same topics. Other interesting articles were "March Anniversary," which celebrated the 18th anniversary of the Paris commune; "Paris Congress," which informed its readers of the International Workers' Congress which was being held in Paris in the summer of 1889; and "Russian Review," which told about uprisings and difficult conditions in Russia. This newspaper came to a halt in June 1889 and was not published for half a year. When it again started to come out, it was somewhat different—it had lost its vitality, and by its content and dry style it resembled a periodical or a literary journal. In its sixth issue, the editors informed their readers that *Znamia* was being changed from a weekly newspaper into a monthly periodical. However, the periodical *Znamia* was never published. Primary and secondary sources; 23 notes.   L. Kalinowski

2099. Sarafian, Winston L.   ALASKA'S FIRST RUSSIAN SETTLERS. *Alaska J. 1977 7(3): 174-177.* The first Russian settlers in Alaska were serfs owned by the Shelekhov-Golikov Company and later the Russian-American Company. These people, 51 in all, arrived in 1794. A brief description of their treatment by the company is given here. 3 illus., 47 notes.   E. E. Eminhizer

2100. Sarafian, Winston L.   SMALLPOX STRIKES THE ALEUTS. *Alaska J. 1977 7(1): 46-49.* The treatment afforded the Aleut Indians by the white man has reduced their population from 20,000 in 1741 to about 2,000 today. Most of this attrition results from ill treatment by the Russians and diseases introduced by Europeans. The smallpox epidemic of 1837-38 killed thousands of Aleuts in a matter of weeks. 4 illus., 26 notes.   E. E. Eminhizer

2101. Savyts'kii, Roman.   DO ISTORII UKRAINS'KOHO MUZYCHNOHO INSTYTUTU [On the history of the Ukrainian Institute of Music]. *Sučasnist [West Germany] 1973 (4): 111-113.* Describes the founding of the Ukrainian Institute of Music in New York in 1952, its aims and some founder members.

2102. Schuhmacher, W. Wilfried.   AFTERMATH OF THE SITKA MASSACRE OF 1802. *Alaska J. 1979 9(1): 58-61.* A Russian-American Company redoubt was established about seven miles from present-day Sitka in 1799 and named Redoubt St. Archangel Michael. The settlement, with a skeleton crew and still not completed, in June 1802 was attacked by the Tlingit Indians and burned to the ground. Excerpts some reports on this disaster and its punitive aftermath in Alaska's waters. 2 illus.   G. E. Pergl

2103. Schur, Leon Avelevich and Pierce, Richard A.   ARTISTS IN RUSSIAN AMERICA: MIKHAIL TIKHANOV (1818). *Alaska Hist. 1976 6(1): 40-49.* Describes and traces the history of Tikhanov's portrait of Alexander Baranov, Russian manager of Alaska for 28 years. Provides 17 illustrations of Baranov's portrait and paintings of native Alaskans by Russian artists.   E. E. Eminhizer

2104. Schwartz, Harvey.   FORT ROSS, CALIFORNIA: IMPERIAL RUSSIAN OUTPOST ON AMERICA'S WESTERN FRONTIER, 1812-1841. *J. of the West 1979 18(2): 35-48.* The Russian settlement at Fort Ross was a fur-trading, agricultural, trade, and shipbuilding base established during the height of the sea otter exploitation. The site was selected for it promising agricultural and timber resources and for its defensible position a safe distance from Spanish settlements. After the decline in the sea otter population made hunting unprofitable, Fort Ross

became a financial liability to the Russian-American Company. Swissborn pioneer John Augustus Sutter bought the settlement in 1841. Based on published sources; 8 photos, 2 maps, 17 notes.   B. S. Porter

2105. Shackop, Antoinette.   STEPAN USHIN, CITIZEN BY PURCHASE. *Alaska J. 1977 7(2): 103-108.* Russians who stayed following the purchase of the Alaska territory by the United States were given citizenship by the treaty of purchase. Details the life of Stepan M. Ushin (1853-95) and his problems under the new government. Describes Sitka, where he lived in the 1860's and early 1870's. Based in part on Ushin's diary; 7 photos, 10 notes.   E. E. Eminhizer

2106. Shalkop, Antoinette.   THE TRAVEL JOURNAL OF VASILII ORLOV. *Pacific Northwest Q. 1977 68(3): 131-140.* Discusses the Alaska Church Collection of Russian Orthodox ecclesiastical documents in the Library of Congress. Presents excerpts from the diary of missionary Vasilii Orlov during his 1886 stay in Alaska. He berated the lack of successful conversions among native peoples and the disrespect shown to missionaries by settlers. A final note discusses the fate of the priest Juvenal who allegedly was murdered by Indians. Photo, map, 22 notes.
M. L. Tate

2107. Shtohryn, D. M.   PROFESSOR E. RADZIMOVSKY, UKRAINIAN ENGINEER. *Ukrainian Q. 1973 29(1): 60-65.* A biographical sketch of Dr. Eugene Radzimovsky, an outstanding Ukrainian engineer, who lived until 1944 in the Ukraine and since 1950 in the United States at the University of Illinois.   Y. Slavutych

2108. Shur, Leonid A. and Pierce, Richard A.   PAVEL MIKHAILOV: ARTIST IN RUSSIAN AMERICA. *Alaska J. 1978 8(4): 360-363.* Pavel Mikhailov (1786-1840), during his trip on the *Moller* (1826-29) as the M. N. Staniokovich expedition artist, painted and sketched scenes and natives. Describes his life and gives some history of the pictures. 7 illus., 3 notes.   E. E. Eminhizer

2109. Shur, Leonid A. and Gibson, James R., transl.   RUSSIAN TRAVEL NOTES AND JOURNALS AS SOURCES FOR THE HISTORY OF CALIFORNIA, 1800-1850. *California Hist. Q. 1973 52(1): 37-63.* The Russian point of view has been neglected in the study of the California of the first half of the 19th century. A survey of Russian archival sources reveals an immense amount of hitherto unknown or little-used material, only a fraction of which is in English. Sources include correspondence, journals, travel notes, and unpublished reports by sailors, employees of the Russian American Company, natural scientists, and missionaries, and contain observations of the Spanish-Mexican political scene, mission life, the Indians, the towns, and other foreign visitors and settlers. Cites Russian archives plus a few important American archives. Originally published in a Russian journal in 1971. Illus., 113 notes.
A. Hoffman

2110. Sorokin, Elena.   MY LIFE WITH PITIRIM SOROKIN. *Int. J. of Contemporary Sociol. 1975 12(1/2): 1-27.* Presents the author's memoirs of the life of revolutionary and teacher Pitirim Sorokin (1889-1968) in Russia and the United States, 1889-1959, including his career at the University of Minnesota (1924-30) and Harvard University.

2111. Sosnovs'kyi, Mykhailo.   UKRAINS'KA DIASPORA I POLITYCHNYI SEKTOR [The Ukrainian diaspora and the political sector]. *Sučasnist [West Germany] 1975 (10): 53-72.* An historical analysis of Ukrainian emigration to various parts of the world, mainly to the United States and Canada, and the political climate in the various emigré communities.

2112. Stachiw, Matthew.   UKRAINIAN RELIGIOUS, SOCIAL AND POLITICAL ORGANIZATION IN U.S.A. PRIOR TO WORLD WAR II. *Ukrainian Q. 1976 32(4): 385-392.* Until the 1850's emigration from the Ukraine was sporadic and depended on the degree of serfdom imposed and the opportunity to flee to free lands outside of Russian control. After serfdom was abolished in 1861, migration to the Urals and Central Asia was encouraged by the tsarist government. However, US industrial growth in the 1870's produced a demand for labor and enticing offers to immigrants. An estimated 500,000 persons of Ukrainian birth came to the United States prior to 1914. 17 notes.
K. N. T. Crowther

2113. Starr, S. Frederick. SCHOLARS FROM THE SOVIET UNION AND AMERICA MEET AT SITKA TO REHASH THE OLD QUESTION OF WHY RUSSIA SOLD ALASKA. *Smithsonian 1979 10(9): 129-144.* A 1979 conference of Soviet, US, and Canadian historians, anthropologists, and geographers, discussed Russia's sale of Alaska to the United States in 1867.

2114. Startsev, A. I. I. V. TURCHANINOV I GRAZHDANSKAIA VOINA V SSHA [I. V. Turchaninov and the Civil War in the United States]. *Novaia i Noveĭshaia Istoriia [USSR] 1974 (6): 96-110.* Ivan V. Turchaninov (1822-1901), once a colonel in the Russian General Staff, went to live in the United States after the end of the Crimean War. His reports from there reveal his disenchantment with the bourgeois republic: Turchaninov was an enemy of tsarist despotism, but also of the despotism of capital. He failed to establish himself as a farmer on Long Island, or to obtain a government position, or be appointed a topographer on Isaac Hayes's projected second Arctic voyage. Having moved to Chicago and changed his name to John Basil Turchin he became the leader of the 19th Illinois Volunteer Regiment in the northern army. After the Civil War he pubished an antislavery magazine *Military Rambles.* Later he became a topographic engineer for the railways, and finally settled with a group of Polish emigrés at Radom to become a farmer. Based on documents, those for his career in Russia being from the Central State Military Historical Archive in Moscow, memoirs and contemporary accounts; 54 notes.   D. N. Collins

2115. Stercho, Peter G. MATTHEW STACHIW: SCHOLAR AND OUTSTANDING UKRAINIAN CIVIC AND POLITICAL LEADER. *Ukrainian Q. 1979 35(1): 31-42.* Matthew Stachiw (1895-1978), active in the Ukrainian Radical Party in the 1920's and 1930's, arrived in Germany after World War II and emigrated to the United States in 1949. A scholar also, Stachiw wrote, edited, and translated many works on Ukraine. He was, in addition, active in Ukrainian community affairs in America. 9 notes.   K. N. T. Crowther

2116. Townsend, Joan B. MERCANTILISM AND SOCIETAL CHANGE: AN ETHNOHISTORIC EXAMINATION OF SOME ESSENTIAL VARIABLES. *Ethnohistory 1975 22(1): 21-32.* Ethnohistoric data are used to examine aspects of Russian-American Company mercantilism in Alaska and implications for socio-cultural change studies. For example, use of numbers of trade goods in contact archaeological sites as an index of the degree of contact change is questioned. Trade goods data and information involving relationships of the Company, middlemen, and Indians, derived from ethnohistorical sources, are applied to a nineteenth century Athapaskan village site for broader interpretations. Four propositions are suggested of more general applicability for interpretations of contact, archaeologically and ethnohistorically, in both Alaskan and non-Alaskan situations.   J

2117. Vávra, Jaroslav. RUSKÁ AMERIKA A RUSKO-AMERICKÉ STYKY V 18. STOLETÍ [Russian America and Russian-American relations in the 18th century]. *Slovanský Přehled [Czechoslovakia] 1974 60(6): 463-472.* Discusses the history of Russian-American contacts which started in the last years of Peter the Great's reign. Focuses on important discoveries during Russian expeditions in the North Pacific and changes in foreign relations caused by the American and French Revolutions. 27 notes.   G. E. Pergl

2118. Volynets', Liubov. UKRAINS'KA ZHINOCHA PRESA V MYNULOMU [Ukrainian women's press in the past]. *Sučasnist [West Germany] 1974 (7-8): 113-127.* Text of a speech at the jubilee meeting of the *Nashe Zhyttia* women's magazine in New York, February 1974, looking at the origins of the Ukrainian women's press in the Ukraine and in the USA.

2119. Wood, Raymund F. EAST AND WEST MEET IN CALIFORNIA IN 1806. *Pacific Historian 1976 20(1): 22-33.* Recounts meeting of Catholicism and Orthodoxy in California, after each set out in opposite directions from Jerusalem several centuries earlier. The first meeting was at San Francisco when Russian Nikolai Rezanov arrived in 1806 seeking to trade for foodstuffs. His betrothal to the daughter of the Spanish Comandante, Maria de la Concepcion Arguello, marked the formal meeting of the two branches of the Church. Based on secondary sources; biblio.   G. L. Olson

Yugoslavian

2120. Andonov-Poljanski, Hristo. ECHOES OF THE ILLINDEN UPRISING IN EUROPE AND AMERICA. *Macedonian Rev. [Yugoslavia] 1973 3(1): 30-33.* Examines the effect of the Illinden Uprising of 1903 on public opinion in America and Europe, in particular through the press and the establishment of Macedonian committees.

2121. Čizmić, Ivan. DOBROVOLJAČKI POKRET JUGOSLOVENSKIH ISELJENIKA U SAD U PRVOM SVJETSKOM RATU [The volunteer movement of Yugoslav emigrants in the United States during World War I]. *Historijski Zbornik [Yugoslavia] 1970-71 23-24: 21-43.* Habsburg propaganda attempts were unsuccessful in the United States in securing Slav emigrant recruits for the empire's armies, though by 1916 a modest number had enlisted in the Serbian and Montenegrin armies. The efforts of the Yugoslav Committee in London and the Serbian government succeeded after 1916, though not politically, and the total number of wartime volunteers was only 10,000 rather than the anticipated 30,000. The efforts of the US government to recruit Slav legions for the war was also unsuccessful because they began too late. The military recruitment drive, however, did familiarize the American public with the nationalities problems of the Habsburg Empire.   A. C. Niven/S

2122. Gasinski, T. Z. CAPTAIN JOHN DOMINIS AND HIS SON, GOVERNOR JOHN OWEN DOMINIS: HAWAII'S CROATIAN CONNECTION. *J. of Croatian Studies 1976 17: 14-46.* A Croatian immigrant from Dalmatia, Captain John (Ivan) Dominis, and his American-born son, John Owen Dominis, have had a significant place in the history of Hawaii. The son became Governnor of Oahu and Prince Consort of the last Hawaiian Queen, Liliuokalani. In 1838, Captain Dominis moved his center of business from the Pacific Northwest to Honolulu, taking his family with him. Details of his life in Honolulu, including his commercial exploits and importance in official governmental circles. After the father lost his life in the South Seas in 1846, his son turned from commerce to government and had an important place in the last years of the native Polynesian kingdom as an adviser of state policy based on a deep love for the Hawaiian people. After his death in 1891 his royal wife's attempt to trace rumored noble connections in her husband's ancestry were without positive results. His influence was continued through his natural son, John Dominis Aimoku. 5 photos, 41 notes.
R. V. Ritter

2123. Gobetz, Giles Edward. SLOVENIAN ETHNIC STUDIES. *Nationalities Papers 1974 2(1): 19-23.* Traces the development of work by Slovenian writers and researchers in America which originated in the 17th century and grew to warrant the establishment of the Slovenian Research Institute in the 1950's.

2124. Gobetz, Giles E. SLOVENIAN ETHNIC STUDIES. *J. of Ethnic Studies 1975 2(4): 99-103.* Surveys outstanding Slovenians in America from the settlements in Georgia of the 1730's to "the most thoroughly studied Slovenian immigrant," the bishop and scholar Frederick Baraga, to 20th-century notables such as Louis Adamic and Marie Prisland. Lists the major annual Slovenian almanacs and newspapers and notes the work of the Slovenian Research Center of America, Inc. 31 notes.   G. J. Bobango

2125. Ivanovski, Ordé. GEORGI DIMITROV'S LETTER TO THE MACEDONIANS IN AMERICA: 1934. *Macedonian Rev. [Yugoslavia] 1975 5(2): 160-166.* Reproduces, together with the reply, a letter sent by Georgi Dimitrov to the fourth congress of the Macedonian National Association in the United States in 1934 in which he outlines the aims and tasks of the Macedonian revolution.

2126. Kovačević, Ante. ON THE DESCENT OF JOHN OWEN DOMINIS, PRINCE CONSORT OF QUEEN LILIUOKALANI. *Hawaiian J. of Hist. 1976 10: 3-24.* Researches the origins of the Consort of the Queen of Hawaii. These origins appear to have been Croatian and more particularly Dalmatian. A family tree and photographs are included.   R. Alvis

2127. McAdams, C. Michael. THE CROATIANS OF CALIFORNIA AND NEVADA. *Pacific Hist. 1977 21(4): 333-350.* Summarizes

Croatian contributions to California and Nevada history, from earliest Catholic missionaries to gold-seekers, subsequent migrations in 1880's and 1890's, and after each world war. In addition to mining, Croatians were fishermen, sailors, and fruitgrowers. Today the 125,000 Croatian Americans in California and Nevada quietly contribute to the states and the nation. 4 illus., 36 notes.

G. L. Olson

2128. Samardžić, Dragana. ZASTAVE DOBROVOLJACA IZ SE-VERNE AMERIKE 1917-1918 GOD [Flags of the volunteers from North America, 1917-1918]. *Vesnik Vojnog Muzeja-Beograd [Yugoslavia] 1974 (19-20): 101-120.* The military museum in Belgrade contains World War I flags carried by volunteer fighters consisting of Yugoslav emigrants in the United States and Canada. The flags can be divided into three groups: 1) military flags carried by combatants from North America, 2) flags of different societies (mainly *Sokols*) which organized the recruiting and expeditions of the volunteers, and 3) American flags which were carried beside the flags belonging to the volunteers and various societies. Describes all the flags and insignias carried and worn by Yugoslav volunteers. 14 photos, 35 notes.

A. C. Niven

2129. Stanonik, Janez. AMERICAN STUDIES IN YUGOSLAVIA. *Am. Studies (Washington, DC) 1973 11(3): 22-27.* Reviews the major studies of America in Yugoslavia before the application of the Fulbright lectureships there in 1966. The major interest has been literature; there is need for research in the history of emigration and foreign relations.

L. L. Athey

2130. Susel, Rudolph M. ASPECTS OF THE SLOVENE COMMUNITY IN CLEVELAND, OHIO. *Papers in Slovene Studies 1977: 64-72.* Slovene immigrants who settled in the Cleveland area during 1880-1924 were mostly of agrarian background, albeit with some degree of literacy in Slovene. By the end of the 1890's these immigrants were numerous enough to be able to support specifically Slovene economic, cultural, and religious organizations, instrumental in easing the transitional and cultural shock problems. Eventually a hybrid culture emerged which was enormously satisfying to most of its members, although American-born descendants accepted Slovene cultural traits and attitudes only to a limited degree.

T. Hočevar

2131. Winner, Irene Portis. ETHNICITY AMONG URBAN SLOVENE VILLAGERS IN CLEVELAND, OHIO. *Papers in Slovene Studies 1977: 51-63.* Examines social networks and informal groups that link immigrants who came to the Cleveland area from a traditional Slovene village (Zerovnica) with other Slovene Americans. Their relations to the nation of origin, Slovenia, are also discussed. Based on oral histories and written sources. Ref.

T. Hočevar

2132. Winner, Irene Portis. THE QUESTION OF CULTURAL POINT OF VIEW IN DETERMINING THE BOUNDARIES OF ETHNIC UNITS: SLOVENE VILLAGERS IN THE CLEVELAND, OHIO AREA. *Papers in Slovene Studies 1977: 73-82.* Research among Slovene Americans in Cleveland shows evidence of regional identification based on Slovene regions (e.g., Lower, Upper, Inner Carniola) or even smaller units (e.g., Lož Valley). Another approach in defining a significant minimal ethnic unit hinges on identification with distinct regions and micro-regions in the United States. There may be considerable correspondence between these units because immigrants from the same area tended to settle near each other. Based on oral history and written sources; ref.

T. Hočevar

2133. Zellick, Anna. THE MEN FROM BRIBIR. *Montana 1978 28(1): 44-55.* Stonemasons from Bribir, Croatia, came to Lewistown, Montana, in the early 1900's to construct buildings in the growing community. The Croatian population in Lewistown grew to more than 373 by 1915, as the masons and their families became part of the community. Labor problems and ethnic prejudice occasionally marred working conditions. Major construction projects on which Croatians worked included schools, a town reservoir, the Carnegie Library, the Masonic temple, and St. Joseph's Hospital. Workmen quarried the stone locally, made mortar, operated lime kilns, and handled all facets of construction. Families which followed the first stonemasons formed the basis for an active Croatian community, unified by religious beliefs and language. The former Bribir residents adopted many American customs while retaining native traditions; most became naturalized citizens and their descendants

remain in the Lewistown area. Based on secondary sources, interviews, Lewistown city records, and personal reminiscences; 7 illus., biblio.

R. C. Myers

Swiss

2134. Aerni, Mary Jean. JEAN JACQUES VIOGET: THE FORGOTTEN SWISS OF EARLY CALIFORNIA. *Swiss Amer. Hist. Soc. Newsletter 1977 13(3): 4-22.* Jean Jacques Vioget, sea captain, musician, hotel keeper, engineer, surveyor, and entrepreneur, was a 19th-century Swiss American hero.

2135. Arlettaz, Gérald. L'INTÉGRATION DES ÉMIGRANTS SUISSES AUX ÉTATS-UNIS 1850-1939 [The integration of Swiss emigrants into the United States, 1850-1939]. *Relations Int. [France] 1977 (12): 307-325.* Some 300,000 Swiss migrated to the United States during 1881-1939. Seventy-five percent of all Swiss emigration was to the United States with the peak about 1885. Except during 1850-80 Swiss were welcomed as almost model immigrants. Integration was easier for the more affluent, the typical emigrant after 1890. Gives distribution patterns of Swiss in the United States and patterns of integration.

R. Stromberg

2136. Brooks, Juanita, ed., and Butler, Janet G., ed. UTAH'S PEACE ADVOCATE, THE "MORMONA": ELISE FURER MUSSER. *Utah Hist. Q. 1978 46(2): 151-166.* Excerpts the writings, diaries, and letters of Elise Furer Musser (1877-1967), who was born in Switzerland, migrated to Utah in 1897, and married Burton Musser in 1911. Her social service and political career began with work in Neighborhood House. She became influential in Utah's Democratic Women's Club, serving as state senator (1933-34), and was the only woman delegate to the Buenos Aires Peace Conference in 1936. Her life puts the current women's liberation movement into perspective as a continuum rather than a new, spontaneous phenomenon. Primary sources; 5 illus., 18 notes.

J. L. Hazelton

2137. Cromwell, James, ed. JOURNAL OF A TRADING VOYAGE AROUND THE WORLD, 1805-1808. *New-York Hist. Soc. Q. 1978 62(2): 86-137.* A journal of a two and a half year voyage around the world, taken from the diary of Isaac Iselin, a young Swiss who had come to the United States only four years before. Despite his youth, Iselin was put in charge of commercial activities on the brig *Maryland*, sailing for a Swiss-American company. Iselin narrated the problems, tragedies, and high points of the voyage in a vessel largely at the mercy of the elements. Iselin was taken into the company upon his return and later became a partner. A keen observer, his journal is a valuable source of information for such voyages in the days of the sailing vessel. 7 illus.

C. L. Grant

2138. Durrer, Margot Ammann. MEMORIES OF MY FATHER. *Swiss Am. Hist. Soc. 1979 15(2): 26-35.* Personal portraits of Othmar Hermann Ammann (1879-1965) by his daughter.

2139. Grueningen, John Paul von. BIOGRAPHY OF J. J. VON GRUENINGEN. *Swiss Am. Hist. Soc. Newsletter 1978 14(1): 12-21.* Discusses Johann Jakob von Grueningen's (1845-1911) youth in Switzerland, schooling, immigration to America, and his life career as pastor in a strongly Swiss Reformed Church in Sauk City, Wisconsin, 1876-1911.

2140. Harling, Frederick F. and Kaufman, Martin. THE SWISS. *Hist. J. of Western Massachusetts 1976 (Supplement): 116-117.* Discusses three Swiss Americans who played a role in the American Revolution. Emannuel Zimmerman was a member of the Pennsylvania Committee of Safety. John Joachim Zubly, a Georgia delegate to the Continental Congress, opposed independence. Henry Wisener operated a gunpowder mill near Phillipsburg, N.Y., and was a member of the Second Continental Congress. Biblio.

W. H. Mulligan, Jr.

2141. Hockings, Paul. ALBERT STAUB: THE STORY OF A WAYWARD IMMIGRANT. *Swiss Am. Hist. Soc. Newsletter 1978 14(3): 17-21.* Details the short criminal life of Albert Staub, a 19-year-old Swiss immigrant to America, who committed theft and murder in Blue Island, a village south of Chicago, in 1857 and was hanged in Chicago in 1858.

2142. Kuhn, W. Ernst. RECENT SWISS IMMIGRATION INTO NEBRASKA: AN EMPIRICAL STUDY. *Swiss Am. Hist. Soc. Newsletter 1976 12(3): 12-20.* A survey in 1975 of Swiss immigrants residing in Nebraska indicated that a majority of questionnaire respondents did not encounter undue difficulties in their assimilation into American life.

2143. Lewis, Brian A. SWISS GERMAN IN WISCONSIN—THE IMPACT OF ENGLISH. *Am. Speech 1973 48(3/4): 211-228.* English is rapidly replacing the Swiss German of New Glarus, Wisconsin, the major Swiss settlement in the state. Urges a comparative analysis of German spoken throughout North America. 3 tables, 26 notes.
P. A. Beaber

2144. Martin, Roger A. JOHN J. ZUBLY COMES TO AMERICA. *Georgia Hist. Q. 1977 61(2): 125-139.* Describes the early career of John Joachim Zubly, a Swiss immigrant who became an influential Presbyterian minister in the Savannah area during the colonial period. Primary and secondary sources; 62 notes.
G. R. Schroeder

2145. Meier, Heinz K. EMIGRATION: A NEW BEGINNING OR PREMATURE END? *Swiss Am. Hist. Soc. Newsletter 1979 15(1): 20-25.* Review article prompted by *Die grossartige Auswanderrung des Andreas Dietsch und seiner Gesellschaft nach Amerika* (Zurich: Limmat Verlag Genossenschaft, 1978) and Max Schweizer's *Bilder aus Neu-Schweizerland* (Zug: Verlag Zürcher AG, 1978) discussing comparative results of planned immigration of Swiss to the United States, 1844-50's.

2146. Morier, Claude. LETTRES INÉDITES D'AUGUSTE GOUF-FON (1848-1861) [Unpublished letters by Auguste Gouffon (1848-61)]. *Schweizerische Zeitschrift für Geschichte [Switzerland] 1977 27(3): 324-339.* Auguste and Henriette Gouffon emigrated to the United States in spring 1848. Together with other families from Canton Vaud, they settled at Beverly near Knoxville, Tennessee, where they formed one of the rare French-Swiss colonies in the New World. Excerpts of six letters written by Gouffon between 1848 and 1861 are published here. The Gouffons made the transition from Vaud to Tennessee without mishap and with apparent ease; the letters, of a generally descriptive nature, are full of praise for the new surroundings. 19 notes.
H. K. Meier

2147. Parsons, William T. "DER GLARNER": ABRAHAM BLUMER OF ZION REFORMED CHURCH, ALLENTOWN. *Swiss Am. Hist. Soc. Newsletter 1977 13(2): 7-22.* Chronicles the ministerial career of Abraham Blumer (1736-1822), a pastor ordained in Switzerland in the German Reformed Church, highlighting his tenure with Pennsylvania parishes, 1771-1801, especially Zion Reformed Church in Allentown.

2148. Pauley, William E., Jr. TRAGIC HERO: LOYALIST JOHN J. ZUBLY. *J. of Presbyterian Hist. 1976 54(1): 61-81.* The Swiss-born Reverend John J. Zubly (1724-81), pastor of the Independent Presbyterian Church, Savannah, Georgia, heroically articulated the principles upon which the colonies sought redress of grievances from the crown government. He could not or would not, however, alter his principles to include the possibility of political separation from the mother country. He was an independent thinker who analyzed the Anglo-American relationship in ways that closely paralleled the major voices of patriotic thinking in other colonies, but he arrived at different conclusions concerning the wisdom and justice of seeking political separation. Consistent in his thinking to the end, he died a broken man. Based largely on Zubly's writings and sermons; illus., 59 notes.
H. M. Parker, Jr.

2149. Rikoon, J. Sanford. THE REUSSER HOUSE: A LOG STRUCTURE IN IOWA'S "LITTLE SWITZERLAND." *Ann. of*

Iowa 1979 45(1): 3-43. A study of the Reusser house, built in 1891 with additions in 1895 and 1905, by Christian Reusser (1863-1909), a Swiss-German immigrant. An analysis of Reusser's construction techniques reveals certain patterns of living that suggest accommodations made by Swiss-German immigrants in northeastern Iowa. Based on examination of the house and secondary sources; drawing, 16 photos, 19 notes.
P. L. Petersen

2150. Schelbert, Leo. THE AMERICAN REVOLUTION: A LESSON IN DISSENT: THE CASE OF JOHN JOACHIM ZUBLY. *Swiss Am. Hist. Soc. Newsletter 1976 12(3): 3-11.* The Reverend John Joachim Zubly of Savannah, Georgia, a Presbyterian, denounced British prerevolutionary theories and practices as unconstitutional and advocated armed resistance; however, his conscientious adherence to the concept of a sacred and inviolable union between England and the colonies led to his subsequent incarceration and sociopolitical ostracism.

2151. Schelbert, Leo. PIERRE-FRÉDÉRIC DROZ: THE 'AMERICAN': THE STORY OF AN ITINERANT WATCHMAKER. *Swiss Am. Hist. Soc. Newsletter 1977 13(1): 11-20.* Pierre-Frédéric Droz, a Swiss watchmaker, journeyed through Europe and British North America, 1768-70.

2152. Schweizer, Niklaus R. THE SWISS IN HAWAII. *Swiss Am. Hist. Soc. Newsletter 1976 12(2): 14-19.* Discusses the settlement of notable Swiss immigrants John Sutter and Paul Emmert in Hawaii, and the Swiss contribution to Hawaii's culture and polyglot society.

2153. Steiguer, J. E. de. THE SWISS-AMERICAN FAMILY DE STEIGUER. *Swiss Am. Hist. Soc. Newsletter 1978 14(3): 4-16.* Outlines the history of the Swiss Steiguer family, including its 16th-century settlement in Bern, rise to the governing aristocracy in the 18th century, decline after the French Revolution, emigration to Athens County, Ohio, in 1819, and gradual resettlement in California, Texas, and Oklahoma.

2154. Widmer, Urs C. BIBLIOGRAPHY: PUBLICATIONS BY AND ABOUT O. H. AMMANN. *Swiss Am. Hist. Soc. 1979 15(2): 34-41.* A bibliography of publications by and about bridge engineer Othmar Hermann Ammann (1879-1965).

2155. Widmer, Urs C. OTHMAR HERMANN AMMANN, 1879-1965: HIS WAY TO GREAT BRIDGES. *Swiss Am. Hist. Soc. 1979 15(2): 4-25.* A biography of Othmar Hermann Ammann (1879-1965), including notes, diagrams, and photographs of all the major bridges he built through 1954.

Other

2156. Jansen, Norbert. NACH AMERIKA!: GESCHICHTE DER LIECHTENSTEINISCHEN AUSWANDERUNG NACH DEN VEREINIGTEN STAATEN VON AMERIKA [To America!: the history of emigration from Liechtenstein to the United States of America]. *Jahrbuch des Hist. Vereins für das Fürstentum Liechtenstein [Liechtenstein] 1976 76: 1-222.* Explains the periods of heavy emigration and the fate of individual immigrants. During the 19th century most of the immigrants from Liechtenstein settled in Dubuque and Gutenberg, Iowa, in Wabash, Indiana, and in Freeport, Illinois. In the 20th century they settled in Chicago, Cincinnati, and Milwaukee. Includes a very comprehensive list of all emigrants from Liechtenstein to the United States with biographical information. Based on documents in the Liechtensteinischen Regierungsarchiv, court records, interviews, and secondary sources; 38 illus., 2 maps, 267 notes, biblio.
A. K. Oser

2157. Sutherland, Anne. GYPSIES, THE HIDDEN AMERICANS. *Society 1975 12(2): 27-33.* Studies the customs, social life, and increasing political and financial difficulties of American Gypsies.
S

4. IMMIGRANTS AND ETHNICS: BY TOPICS

Religion

General

2158. Abramson, Harold J. THE RELIGIOETHNIC FACTOR AND THE AMERICAN EXPERIENCE: ANOTHER LOOK AT THE THREE-GENERATIONS HYPOTHESIS. *Ethnicity 1975 2(2): 163-177.* Examines the hypotheses of Marcus Hansen ("principle of third-generation interest" in cultural realms) and Will Herberg (rise-decline-rise of religious association) in an effort to study the religious behavior of different generations of ethnic groups. Examination of three generations—grandparents, their children, and grandchildren—does not sustain these hypotheses. Rather, it is found that ethnic variation over generational time is the case, depending not on the fact of American residence but on the religioethnic nature of the individual culture. Differences in the perception of the exact length of a generation, as well as variation in the perception of the "American experience," make it difficult to draw any firm conclusion about the influence of the latter on religious behavior among ethnic groups. 3 tables, 5 notes, biblio.
G. A. Hewlett

2159. Ahlstrom, Sydney E. *E PLURIBUS UNUM:* RELIGIOUS PLURALISM AND THE AMERICAN IDEAL. *Soundings 1978 61(3): 328-338.* Examines Puritanism, patriotism, unlimited immigration (1620's-1920's), and slavery as each affected religious pluralism, American idealism, and national characteristics, through World War II.

2160. Alston, Jon P. and McIntosh, William Alex. AN ASSESSMENT OF THE DETERMINANTS OF RELIGIOUS PARTICIPATION. *Sociol. Q. 1979 20(1): 49-62.* Assesses patterns of religious participation and church attendance based on a 1974 study of American Protestants and Catholics.

2161. Alston, Jon P.; McIntosh, William A.; and Wright, Louise M. EXTENT OF INTERFAITH MARRIAGES AMONG WHITE AMERICANS. *Sociol. Analysis 1976 37(3): 261-264.* The General Social Survey Program makes available data dealing with the religious preferences of respondents and their spouses from national samples of the American population. Seventeen percent of the white population have spouses with different religious preferences. Interfaith marriage is associated with lower church participation and with lower levels of perceived family satisfaction.
J

2162. Blumin, Stuart M. CHURCH AND COMMUNITY: A CASE STUDY OF LAY LEADERSHIP IN NINETEENTH-CENTURY AMERICA. *New York Hist. 1975 56(4): 393-408.* A statistical study of the socioeconomic status, residential tenure, and family background of the leaders of 19th-century Kingston (New York) Protestant and Jewish churches, and their secular leadership in the Kingston community. Although church leaders "comprised a significant minority of the community's secular leadership," the underlying characteristic of community leadership was "membership in a fairly wide and fairly diverse commercial class." Illus., 7 tables, 9 notes.
R. N. Lokken

2163. Faia, Michael A. SECULARIZATION AND SCHOLARSHIP AMONG AMERICAN PROFESSORS. *Sociol. Analysis 1976 37(1): 63-73.* In 1969, a large majority of American professors subscribed to a religion, while only one in five had no religion at all. Given the persistence of religious commitment among academicians, it is important to assess the popular notion that religious involvement is incompatible with high scholarly productivity. Recent studies comparing Catholics with Protestants, and secularized Jewish academicians with their non-secularized Jewish colleagues, have led to contradictory conclusions about the impact of secularization on scholarship. A multiple regression analysis indicates that neither 'secularism' nor 'secularization' has any appreciable, direct effect on scholarly productivity, except among those disciplines with a high degree of 'scholarly distance' from religion. In conclusion, there appears to be little incompatibility between scholarly productivity and the typical form of religious commitment found among academicians, and the lack of incompatibility may be an emergent phenomenon related to increased academic specialization.
J

2164. Goodman, Paul. A GUIDE TO AMERICAN CHURCH MEMBERSHIP DATA BEFORE THE CIVIL WAR. *Hist. Methods Newsletter 1977 10(2): 85-89; 1978 10(4): 183-190.* Part I. Reviews the limitations of census returns for finding relationships between religion and voting, then discusses the advantages of town-level membership data from the archives and historical societies of the various denominations. The main advantage of this material is that it begins earlier and is more systematic; therefore, more judicious generalizations can be made. 3 tables. Part II. Includes the guide to the church data previously omitted. 3 tables, 2 fig.
D. K. Pickens

2165. Himmelfarb, Harold S. THE INTERACTION EFFECTS OF PARENTS, SPOUSE AND SCHOOLING: COMPARING THE IMPACT OF JEWISH AND CATHOLIC SCHOOLS. *Sociol. Q. 1977 18(4): 468-477.* Discusses the literature on the long-range impact of schooling and the types of effects that schools have shown. It compares data on the impact of Jewish schooling on adult religiosity with similar data from a study of Catholic schooling. Like previous studies on other types of schools, the main effect of Jewish schooling seems to be an accentuation of parental influences. This effect is diminished substantially if not supported by marriage to a religious spouse. However, on some types of religiosity, extensive Jewish schooling produces "conversion" effects which persisted even when pre-school and post-school supports were lacking.
J

2166. Himmelfarb, Milton. PLURAL ESTABLISHMENT. *Commentary 1974 58(6): 69-73.* Discusses the effect of the New Ethnicity on religion, drawing on Matthew Arnold's formulation of the theory of plural establishment in the 19th century.
S

2167. Hutchinson, William R. AMERICAN RELIGIOUS HISTORY: FROM DIVERSITY TO PLURALISM. *J. of Interdisciplinary Hist. 1974 5(2): 313-318.* Reviews the work of Sydney E. Ahlstrom with special reference to his *A Religious History of the American People* (New Haven, 1972). Focuses on the theme of the failure of pluralism. Suggests several criticisms, but argues that the book "will be lastingly recognized as a *tour de force*." 2 notes.
R. Howell

2168. James, Janet Wilson. WOMEN AND RELIGION: AN INTRODUCTION. *Am. Q. 1978 30(5): 579-581.* The series of essays in this issue explores various facets and expressions of the place of women in religion as seen in Protestantism, Catholicism, and Judaism. The whole is set against two constants: women usually outnumber men and men exercise the authority. The paradox revealed is one of a religious heritage imparting hopes of freedom, but at the same time blocking women's way.
R. V. Ritter

2169. Janis, Ralph. ETHNIC MIXTURE AND THE PERSISTENCE OF CULTURAL PLURALISM IN THE CHURCH COMMUNITIES OF DETROIT, 1880-1940. *Mid-America 1979 61(2): 99-115.* In 1880 all church officers were male and tended to come from the middle and upper classes. Church membership was homogeneous ethnically (86% to 98%). The economic growth of Detroit changed this considerably by 1940. For example, while Lutheran parishes were uniformly German in 1880, they were less than 70% German in 1940. Other social factors involved in Detroit during this period, though, did not lead to the "melting pot" that might be expected. The cultural and social changes were silent, and other melting pot barriers arose when older ones dropped. 45 notes.
J. M. Lee

2170. Lazerwitz, Bernard. RELIGIOUS IDENTIFICATION AND ITS ETHNIC CORRELATES: A MULTIVARIATE MODEL. *Social Forces 1973 52(2): 204-220.* Studies the religious and ethnic identifications of white Protestants and Jews in Chicago, using eight identification dimensions. There is a mainstream of identification that runs from childhood home religious background to religious education to religious behavior to activity in ethnic organizations and to concern over one's children's religious education. Lenski's findings that ethnic community life and religious institutions were somewhat separated is supported for Protestants, but not for Jews. The findings for high-moderate status Jews show weak or negative relations between identification measures and liberalness. Low-status Jews show positive relations between five dimensions and liberalness. Protestants display weak relations between their identity dimensions and liberalness with no evidence of an interaction with social status.   J

2171. McCutcheon, William J. THEOLOGICAL ETHNICITY. *Methodist Hist. 1974 12(3): 40-56.* Ethnicity denotes a measurable social, religious, and theological identity not necessarily restricted to previous linguistic or geographical pasts. Theological ethnicity is reflective thought about God that comes from a denomination as it acts within its own society. In the Methodist Episcopal Church the period from 1919 to 1939 was the "golden age" in its theology. 51 notes.   H. L. Calkin

2172. Miller, Randall M. INTRODUCTION. Miller, Randall M. and Marzik, Thomas D., ed. *Immigrants and Religion in Urban America* (Philadelphia: Temple U. Pr., 1977): xi-xxii. The misleading belief that European immigrants to America in the early 19th century quickly assimilated into the "melting pot" suggests that the immigrants were transformed into a set "American mold." But there was no set mold; transplanted Old World religion helped them establish order and became their refuge from assimilation. Ethnic groups within the religious institutions battled for power. In American Catholicism, in the 1850's, Irish bishops gained control and used Church resources to promote Irish welfare. Religious institutions became "battlegrounds of ethnicity and nationalism," most intensely on local levels. Thus, ethnic and religious rivalry became an important factor in defining ethnic character in America.   S. Robitaille

2173. Monahan, Thomas P. SOME DIMENSIONS OF INTER-RELIGIOUS MARRIAGES IN INDIANA, 1962-67. *Social Forces 1973 52(2): 195-203.* Data were selected from Indiana computer tapes, 1962-67, for detailed analysis of intrafaith as compared to interfaith marriages for four religious groups—Protestant, Catholic, Jewish, Other. The influence of age, previous marital status, and occupational class was examined, along with other factors such as age difference and type of ceremony. Although the proportion of mixed marriages among non-Protestants was found to be high and increasing somewhat, a comparison of actual with possible random matings disclosed considerable selectivity, with Jewish persons being by far the most endogamous and Catholics the most intermarried of the minority groups.   J

2174. Nelsen, Hart M. and Allen, H. David. ETHNICITY, AMERICANIZATION, AND RELIGIOUS ATTENDANCE. *Am. J. of Sociol. 1974 79(4): 906-922.* Two trends in the pattern of Americanization of immigrant groups are noted, one involving decreased second-generation religious interest due to alienation from the ethnic tradition and the other showing an increase in attendance at worship services from first to second generation due to the prominence of religion in American culture. The pattern of second-generation attendance depends on the extent of difference between the ethnic culture and the dominant American culture. In a secondary analysis of data on New York City Catholics, the respondents are grouped into western, eastern, and southern European categories based on country of origin. There are no meaningful differences in religious attendance among first-generation Catholics; among second-generation respondents there are substantial differences. Western Europeans show an increase in attendance from first to second generation, while southern Europeans show a decrease. The meltingpot concept of assimilation fails to take into account interethnic variations in patterns of Americanization.   J

2175. Norton, Wesley. "LIKE A THOUSAND PREACHERS FLYING": RELIGIOUS NEWSPAPERS ON THE PACIFIC COAST TO 1865. *California Hist. Q. 1977 56(3): 194-209.* Surveys religious newspapers on the Pacific Coast from the gold rush era through the Civil War. Religious newspapers included secular news as well as religious topics, were generally ambitious, underfinanced, and enjoyed varying runs. They included dailies, weeklies, semimonthlies, monthlies, and

other schedules. Most were short-lived, but some lasted to the 20th century. In an era of nativism these papers exercised a moderating influence. For the most part they were antislavery and called for toleration of the Chinese. Denominations included Catholic, Jewish, and numerous Protestant sects. With increasing urbanization and the growth of general-readership newspapers, the religious newspapers turned more to coverage of religious affairs and less to worldly matters. Primary and secondary sources; illus., 66 notes, bibliography of West Coast religious newspapers to 1865.   A. Hoffman

2176. Redekop, Calvin. A NEW LOOK AT SECT DEVELOPMENT. *J. for the Sci. Study of Religion 1974 13(3): 345-352.* Discusses the relationship between society and the development of religious sects, such as the Mormons and Mennonites, during the 19th and 20th centuries.

2177. Redekop, Calvin. RELIGIOUS INTENTIONAL COMMUNITIES. *Indiana Social Studies Q. 1976 29(1): 52-65.* Discusses sociological and cultural factors in the development of Christian communes and utopias in the United States from 1790-1970.

2178. Romo, Oscar I. LANGUAGE MISSIONS IN THE NORTHEAST. *Baptist Hist. and Heritage 1975 10(1): 57-62.* One phase of the work of the Home Missions Board of the Southern Baptist Convention is language missions. Discusses their development in the northeast United States, and provides historical background for the 1975 Home Mission Graded Study of the Southern Baptist Convention. Sixty-eight languages and over 100 dialects are spoken in this region. In several urban areas the language mission of a particular group forms the largest, and frequently the only, Southern Baptist congregation. Southern Baptists have one missionary for every 500,000 language persons.

H. M. Parker, Jr.

2179. Shipps, Howard Fenimore. THE REVIVAL OF 1858 IN MID-AMERICA. *Methodist Hist. 1978 16(3): 128-151.* The Revival of 1858 was brought about by worldliness, a materialistic attitude which threatened to engulf the church. The revival, originating with the laity, seemed to have little if any limitation. It extended to all racial, social, national, and ethnic groups, and to many denominations and cultural divisions. It emphasized the leadership of the Holy Spirit, the prominence of prayer and its ecumenical nature, and the important role of laymen. The revival resulted in an extensive renewal of the church. 43 notes.

H. L. Calkin

2180. Singleton, Gregory H. "MERE MIDDLE-CLASS INSTITUTIONS": URBAN PROTESTANTISM IN 19TH-CENTURY AMERICA. *J. of Social Hist. 1973 6(4): 489-504.* Review article prompted by Nathan Irvin Higgins' *Protestants Against Poverty: Boston's Charities, 1870-1900* (Westport, Conn.: Greenwood, 1971), Richard J. Jensen's *The Winning of the Midwest: Social and Political Conflict, 1888-1896* (Chicago: U. of Chicago Pr., 1971), Carroll Smith Rosenberg's *Religion and the Rise of the American City: The New York City Mission Movement, 1812-1870* (Ithaca: Cornell U. Pr., 1971), and Alvin W. Skardon's *Church Leader in the City: Augustus Muhlenberg* (Philadelphia: U. of Pennsylvania Pr., 1971).

2181. Smith, Timothy Lawrence. RELIGION AND ETHNICITY IN AMERICA. *Am. Hist. Rev. 1978 83(5): 1155-1185.* The ethnic mobilization of what became America's immigrant peoples whose origins lay in Europe or the Near East began in most instances in their homelands, amidst a complex rivalry for economic and cultural advantage. Even in the Old World, the developing sense of peoplehood depended heavily upon religious identification. Migration to America, both before and after it became a largely urban and industrial society, produced three important alterations in the relationship of faith to ethnic identity: 1) the redefinition, usually in religious terms, of the boundaries of peoplehood, through a broadening of geographic and linguistic expectations and frequently a decisive narrowing of religious ones; 2) an intensification of the psychic basis of theological reflection and ethno-religious commitment, due to the emotional consequences of uprooting and repeated resettlement; and 3) a revitalization of the conviction, deeply rooted in Judaism and Christianity, that the goal of history is the millennialist or messianic one of a common humanity, a brotherhood of faith and faithfulness. The last two developments made the relationship between religion and ethnicity dialectical, faith commitments helping on the one hand to define more sharply the boundaries among subcultures and communities, while the other affirming the hoped-for unity of all humankind. All three developments demonstrate the dynamic relationship between religion and ethnicity which has recently begun to replace the state model which long prevailed in studies of ethnology.

2182. Snyder, Eldon E. and Spreitzer, Elmer. PATTERNS OF VARIATION WITHIN AND BETWEEN ETHNORELIGIOUS GROUPINGS. *Ethnicity 1975 2(2): 124-133*. Examines recent studies concerning variation among ethnic groups within Catholicism and Protestantism and compares the two. Ethnicity is contingent on a number of characteristics, including geography, social status, generations within a country, and cultural background. Examines four ethnic groups within Catholicism: Germans, Irish, Italians, and Poles; four within Protestantism: English, German, Scottish, and Scandinavian; and five Protestant denominations: Baptists, Methodists, Lutherans, Presbyterians, and Episcopalians. There is considerably more ethnic variation within Catholicism, and inter- and intra-group comparisons are of little relative value because of the degree of variation. 5 tables, biblio.

G. A. Hewlett

2183. Stout, Harry S. ETHNICITY: THE VITAL CENTER OF RELIGION IN AMERICA. *Ethnicity 1975 2(2): 204-224*. In variant forms religion and ethnicity have realized nearly identical forms of expression. Development of ethnoreligion has gone through three stages: immigration to preserve the religious totality of a particular group, with ethnicity being the primary factor and the religion a stabilizer for that culture; extroversion of the ethnicity of the group (in an effort to "Americanize" and become a part of the main stream while still maintaining their basic ethnicity); and a cultural or civic religion in which religious associations expand until they are associated with the nation as a whole. America is fast moving toward a cultural religion—a blending of Protestantism, Catholicism, and Judaism where plurality and consensus form the "American Way." 80 notes.

G. A. Hewlett

2184. Toney, Michael B. RELIGIOUS PREFERENCE AND MIGRATION. *Int. Migration Rev. 1973 7(3): 281-288*.

2185. Walker, Charles O. GEORGIA'S RELIGION IN THE COLONIAL ERA, 1733-1790. *Viewpoints: Georgia Baptist Hist. 1976 5: 17-44*. Examines Anglicans, Jews, Lutherans, Presbyterians, Congregationalists, Quakers, and Baptists in Georgia, 1733-90, taking into account the American Revolution and its effect on religious practices in the state.

2186. Ward, W. R. WILL HERBERG: AN AMERICAN HYPOTHESIS SEEN FROM EUROPE. *Durham U. J. [Great Britain] 1973 65(3): 260-270*. Discusses religion and religiosity in the United States; prompted by Will Herberg's (b. 1909) *Protestant-Catholic-Jew: An Essay in American Religious Sociology* (Gloucester, Massachusetts: Peter Smith, 1955). Examines Herberg's hypothesis that the relatively high religiosity professed in the United States, coupled with vapidness of the religiousness expressed, is the result of generations of immigrants identifying in religion "the one element in their past which they had not been asked to change." Conflict theory modifications suggested by recent sociologists and historians dealing with U.S. religion are not wholly adequate as explanations of current trends. "Renewed economic growth may make possible the development of a quadripartite Herberg religion of Protestant-Catholic-Jew-Black . . . . Consensus history is after all a correlate of conflict history and it may be that in another decade a fresh wave of religious historians may find the Herberg thesis worth examining." 23 notes.

D. H. Murdoch

2187. Williams, Preston N. RELIGION AND THE MAKING OF COMMUNITY IN AMERICA. *J. of the Am. Acad. of Religion 1976 44(4): 603-611*. Ethnicity, or group formation based on ties of race, nationality, culture, or religion, is the process by which assimilation has occurred in American life, and the future will see this assimilation producing further consciousness of ethnicity. The role and responsibility of religion in this continuing process is to test and evaluate ethnicity in terms of fundamental human values and to mediate the knowledge of God who unifies across ethnic boundaries. Secondary sources; 9 notes.

E. R. Lester

Amish, Hutterite, and Mennonite

2188. Baer, Hans A. THE EFFECT OF TECHNOLOGICAL INNOVATION ON HUTTERITE CULTURE. *Plains Anthropologist 1976 21(73, pt. 1): 187-198*. The Hutterites of North America are often envied by their rural neighbors as being efficient and productive agriculturalists who combine twentieth century technology with a life style reminiscent of an earlier age. A closer examination of Hutterite culture reveals that a tension exists between these two elements.   J

2189. Belk, Fred R. THE FINAL REFUGE: KANSAS AND NEBRASKA MIGRATION OF MENNONITES FROM CENTRAL ASIA AFTER 1884. *Kansas Hist. Q. 1974 40(3): 379-392*. Discusses a nonmilitant group of Mennonites who migrated to the American Middle West from Asia following intrasect disunity.

2190. Belk, Fred R. TO MEET THE LORD AND ESCAPE THE DRAFT. *Mennonite Life 1974 29(1-2): 38-41*. Reprints a chapter from Fred R. Belk's *The Great Trek of the Russian Mennonites to Central Asia, 1880-1884* (1973) describing the Mennonites' flight from Russia to avoid the draft and to meet the Lord; chronicles their eventual immigration to the Great Plains of the United States.

2191. Bender, Elizabeth, transl. and Kadelbach, Ada. HYMNS WRITTEN BY AMERICAN MENNONITES. *Mennonite Q. R. 1974 48(3): 343-370*. Discusses the 50 hymns composed by Mennonites in America before 1860, and includes biographical data on the composers.
S

2192. Bennett, John W. SOCIAL THEORY AND THE SOCIAL ORDER OF THE HUTTERIAN COMMUNITY. *Mennonite Q. Rev. 1977 51(4): 292-307*. An analysis of the social underpinnings of Hutterian society. The cement that holds the society together is belief: the concept that they are living the way Christ meant men to live, whereas the remainder of the world is living in sin. Commitment simply results in controls, not causes. Certainly the Hutterites pay a price for their way: aggression is internalized, later to show up in the forms of stomach trouble and alcoholism. Hutterite society is indeed strict, though change is both possible and continuous, but the internal structure of genuine belief is by far the most significant controlling force. The system has succeeded admirably; Hutterite society is indeed Utopian, probably because its members have succeeded in welding together religion and practicality. 3 notes.

V. L. Human

2193. Brunk, Ivan W. BRUNK ANCESTORS. *Mennonite Hist. Bull. 1975 36(4): 5-6; 1976 37(3): 5-7*. Part I. Traces the genealogy of the Brunk family which probably goes back to immigrants from the Palatinate area of Europe, but can only be established for certain with Mennonite families in Pennsylvania in the 1750's. Part II. Examines the Brunk family genealogy, 1750-1850, their affiliation with the Mennonite Church, their spread throughout Maryland, Virginia, and Pennsylvania, and their military service.

2194. Buck, Roy C. BLOODLESS THEATRE: IMAGES OF THE OLD ORDER AMISH IN TOURISM LITERATURE. *Pennsylvania Mennonite Heritage 1979 2(3): 2-11*. Provides a survey of popular views of the Old Order Amish in tourist literature in Lancaster County, Pennsylvania, from 1910 to 1978.

2195. Burnbaugh, Donald F. RELIGION AND REVOLUTION: OPTIONS IN 1776. *Pennsylvania Mennonite Heritage 1978 1(3): 2-9*. The German Dunkards and Mennonites remained neutral due to their basic nonresistant positions, but had pro-British sympathies, as is evidenced in the Pennsylvania and Maryland loyalist movements and an attempt by European Mennonites in 1784 to secure land for settlement.

2196. Charles, Daniel E.; Espenshade, Kevin R.; and Kraybill, Donald B. CHANGES IN MENNONITE YOUTH ATTITUDES, 1974-1978. *Pennsylvania Mennonite Heritage 1979 2(4): 20-25*. A study of Lancaster Mennonite High School students reveals a continuing positive identification with the Mennonite Church, but a decreasing acceptance of rituals and practices.

2197. Crowley, William K. OLD ORDER AMISH SETTLEMENT: DIFFUSION AND GROWTH. *Ann. of the Assoc. of Am. Geographers 1978 68(2): 249-264.* Discusses the spread of Amish communities in the United States, 1717-1977.

2198. deFehr, Art. DEVELOPMENT FROM AN ANABAPTIST PERSPECTIVE. *Mennonite Life 1976 31(2): 17-20.* International aid usually falls into three categories; investment approach, institution-building approach, and the people approach. The first two consist of the affluent elite donating technology and information without regard to the needs of Third World peoples. The people approach, which Mennonites have used, ideally speaks of equality, mutual concern and assistance. Mennonites, with their history of rural life, migration, minority status, and belief in the dignity of work, have a unique perspective on what is needed in international development. B. Burnett

2199. Denlinger, A. Martha. KATIE HESS REMINISCES. *Pennsylvania Mennonite Heritage 1978 1(4): 2-9.* Discusses Katie Charles Hess's (b. 1883) reminiscences about her childhood in a Mennonite community near Lancaster, Pennsylvania, including her daily life, involvement with the church, and early married years.

2200. Doyle, James. MENNONITES AND MOHAWKS: THE UNIVERSALIST FICTION OF J. L. E. W. SHECUT. *Mennonite Q. Rev. 1977 51(1): 22-30.* John Linnaeus Edward Whitredge Shecut (1770-1836) wrote a novel, *The Eagle of the Mohawks,* which states that the Mennonites were universalists who made up the majority of the Dutch in New Amsterdam. Investigates how Shecut acquired these ideas and why he put them in his work. 15 notes. E. E. Eminhizer

2201. Driedger, Leo. THE ANABAPTIST IDENTIFICATION LADDER: PLAIN-URBANE CONTINUITY IN DIVERSITY. *Mennonite Q. Rev. 1977 51(4): 278-291.* A study of social change in Plain People communities. The geographical propinquity of the larger technological society forces changes in the communities whether they want them or not. Not all respond to these changes, but some members have long since moved to urban centers, and conservatism is not uniform within all rural communities. The Hutterites are the most conservative and rural, followed by the Old Order Amish, Old Colony Mennonites, and Urban Mennonites. This "identification ladder" permits variation in individual belief and behavior. If rural communities become untenable, as now seems likely, the Plain People no doubt will be able to maintain their distinctive image in urban areas, much as the Jews have done. Table, 2 notes. V. L. Human

2202. Driedger, Leo; Fretz, J. Winfield; and Smucker, Donovan E. A TALE OF TWO STRATEGIES: MENNONITES IN CHICAGO AND WINNIPEG. *Mennonite Q. Rev. 1978 52(4): 294-311.* Mennonites do not seem to survive in the large urban areas, but do well in rural settings. Studies the mission strategies used in Chicago and Winnipeg with an analysis of the results of each and a comparison of the two in detail. 20 notes. E. E. Eminhizer

2203. Dyck, Cornelius J. and Kreider, Robert. MENNONITE WORLD CONFERENCES IN REVIEW: A PHOTOGRAPHIC ESSAY. *Mennonite Life 1978 33(2): 4-23.* The Mennonite World Conference formed in response to a plea for unity. In 1925 the First World Conference, held in Switzerland under the leadership of Christian Neff (d. 1946), established an office, a treasury, and a registry of churches. The second conference in Danzig, 1930, concentrated on resettlement problems of immigrants. The prime concern of the third conference in Amsterdam, 1936, was Russian Mennonite refugees. Attendance increased at the next six conferences, which had spiritual themes. 48 photos. B. Burnett

2204. Easton, Carol. A TOUCH OF INNOCENCE. *Westways 1976 68(12): 27-29, 60.* Discusses the life of German American Hutterites in agricultural cooperatives in northwestern states in the 20th century, emphasizing their pacifism and education.

2205. Ediger, Marlow. OTHER MINORITIES: OLD ORDER AMISH AND HUTTERITES. *Social Studies 1977 68(4): 172-174.* Presents information on Old Order Amish and Hutterites and calls for extension of study of ethnic groups and minorities beyond those commonly associated with those terms.

2206. Esh, Levi A. THE AMISH PAROCHIAL SCHOOL MOVEMENT. *Mennonite Q. Rev. 1977 51(1): 69-75.* Examines Old Order Amish church schools started after 1937 in Lancaster County, Pennsylvania. E. E. Eminhizer

2207. Eshleman, Wilmer J. OLD WEST LAMPETER TOWNSHIP CEMETERIES. *Pennsylvania Mennonite Heritage 1978 1(3): 10-12.* Lists the names found on graves located in Mennonite cemeteries near Lampeter in Lancaster County, Pennsylvania, dating from the 18th century.

2208. Friesen, Steven. MENNONITE SOCIAL CONSCIOUSNESS, 1899-1905. *Mennonite Life 1975 30(2): 19-25.*

2209. Gingerich, Melvin. MENNONITE FAMILY NAMES IN IOWA. *Ann. of Iowa 1974 42(5): 397-403.* Describes the settlement of Mennonites in Iowa from 1839 by tracing family names. Mennonite genealogy in the United States has its origins in Dutch and ethnic Swiss names, both of which are present in Iowa. 4 notes. C. W. Olson

2210. Gingrich, J. Lloyd and Zimmerman, Noah L. SNYDER COUNTY MENNONITES OF LANCASTER CONFERENCE. *Pennsylvania Mennonite Heritage 1979 2(2): 2-16.* Overview of Mennonites in Snyder County, Pennsylvania, 1780's-1970's, includes local history and a listing of clergy serving the parishes.

2211. Gizycki, Horst von. ALTERNATIVE LEBENSFORMEN [Alternative life-styles]. *Frankfurter Hefte [West Germany] 1975 30(10): 45-54.* In his search for alternative life-styles, the author visited the Hutterites of Canada and South Dakota, a religious, communalistic group formed in central Europe centuries ago, which fled persecution by Habsburgs and Tsars, coming to the new world during 1874-79.

2212. Goering, Jacob D. and Williams, Robert. GENERATIONAL DRIFT ON FOUR VARIABLES AMONG THE SWISS-VOLHYNIAN MENNONITES IN KANSAS. *Mennonite Q. Rev. 1976 50(4): 290-297.* Studies cultural changes among a group of Russian Mennonites who settled in McPherson County, Kansas, in 1874. The study is concerned with four variables: 1) location, 2) occupation, 3) religious affiliations, and 4) educational level. The findings, which follow a brief historical sketch of the group and a statement on the procedures followed, suggest the following: 1) the group dispersed in the past 100 years to 30 states, 2) farming dropped to less than 50 percent as the chief occupation, 3) unless there was no Mennonite church in the area of relocation, the group remained Mennonites, and 4) about 30 percent of the third generation received some college training. 5 notes. E. E. Eminhizer

2213. Gross, Leonard, ed. and Bender, Elizabeth, trans. THE COMING OF THE RUSSIAN MENNONITES TO AMERICA: ANALYSIS OF JOHANN EPP, MENNONITE MINISTER IN RUSSIA 1875. *Mennonite Q. R. 1974 48(4): 460-475.* Introduces and reprints Johann Epp's letter of 1875 arguing against Mennonites' emigration from Russia to North America.

2214. Gross, Leonard, ed. THE MENNONITE GENERAL CONFERENCE SECRETARY BOOK. *Mennonite Hist. Bull. 1973 34(3): 1-8.* Through excerpts from the 1921 Mennonite General Conference Secretary Book, the editor "traces . . . the development of the general conference or assembly idea within the Mennonite Church. Bishop John F. Funk . . . figured prominently in the story, at first enthusiastically furthering the Conference movement, then taking a more cautious stance, and finally, when Mennonite General Conference did actually emerge in 1898, deciding that the idea was being realized all too rapidly." S

2215. Gross, Leonard, ed. MENNONITES AND THE REVOLUTIONARY ERA. *Mennonite Hist. Bull. 1974 35(1): 3-11.* Original documents by and about Christian Funk of Indian Field, Pennsylvania, who "was excommunicated from the brotherhood, and formed his own short-lived Mennonite branch called the 'Funkites.' " Discord arose between Funk and other Mennonites in 1760, and again in 1774-76 when Funk was called a rebel for urging support for the new revolutionary government in Pennsylvania. The discord continued at least through 1809. S

2216. Habegger, David.   A STORY RECORDED IN STONE. *Mennonite Life 1978 33(3): 19-21.* An analysis of the Mennonite community cemetery in Lyon County, Kansas, shows that six women, three men, and 14 children were buried there during 1870-1917. The names include: Stoltfuz, Umble, Miller, Stutzman, Stuckey, Steckley, Riehl, Kaufman, Bender, Sutter, Musselman, Rediger, Rich and Schlegel.
B. Burnett

2217. Harms, Marianne.   THE MENNONITE RESPONSE TO THE BICENTENNIAL 1975-76. *Mennonite Life 1977 32(2): 28-31.* Provides a compilation of books, leaflets and periodicals published during 1975-76 relating to the Mennonites and the American Bicentennial. The bibliography is divided into four sections: articles, books and leaflets, letters, and news. Over 500 items are listed.
B. Burnett

2218. Haury, David A.   BERNHARD WARKENTIN: A MENNONITE BENEFACTOR. *Mennonite Q. R. 1975 49(3): 179-202.* Describes Bernhard Warkentin's early life in Russia, his relationship to Russian Mennonites' immigration to Kansas, and his involvement with the railroads in the West. Warkentin influenced several thousand people to settle in Kansas, where he served on the Board of Guardians and the Kansas Local Relief Committee. Some problems occurred when he married a Methodist. He became a miller for several years, sold out to his father-in-law in 1885, but returned to milling in 1887, and expanded his business several times. He was instrumental in the founding of Bethel College. By 1896, he was a member of the Presbyterian Church. 116 notes.
E. E. Eminhizer

2219. Haury, David A.   BERNHARD WARKENTIN AND THE KANSAS MENNONITE PIONEERS. *Mennonite Life 1974 29(4): 70-75.* Discusses the life of Bernhard Warkentin, 1872-1908, his immigration from the Ukraine to Kansas and the influence he had in a large migration of Russian Mennonites in 1873; also highlights his interests in agriculture and milling in Kansas.

2220. Haury, Samuel S.; Rediger, Beatrice and Juhnke, James, transl. LETTERS ABOUT THE SPREAD OF THE GOSPEL IN THE HEATHEN WORLD. *Mennonite Life 1979 34(2): 4-7.* Samuel S. Haury, the first conference-sponsored Mennonite missionary in North America, began work among Arapaho Indians in Indian Territory in 1880. Trained in Ohio and Germany, Haury explained in *Briefe ueber die Ausbreitung des Evangeliums in der Heidenwelt* (1876) that mission, or the spread of the gospel among the heathen, is a work of inner necessity based on the theology that Jesus is the owner of all lost souls. It is the obligation of evangelical Christians to reclaim them. Photo.
B. Burnett

2221. Hershberger, Guy F.   IN TRIBUTE TO MELVIN GINGERICH. *Mennonite Hist. Bull. 1975 36(4): 2-4.* Obituary for Melvin Gingerich, a Mennonite educator, historian, and churchman, 1902-75.

2222. Hostetler, Beulah S.   THE CHARTER AS A BASIS FOR RESISTING THE IMPACT OF AMERICAN PROTESTANT MOVEMENTS. *Mennonite Q. Rev. 1978 52(2): 127-140.* A study of the influence of American Protestant movements on the structure and beliefs of Mennonite society. American Protestantism went through waves of change during the last half of the 19th century, including institutionalization, but the Mennonite Church, not without a few defections, clung to its time-honored beliefs. The records of the Franconia Conference during the period 1840-1940, scattered though they are, reveal that the unwritten charter continued to be adhered to. There were calls for institutionalization, the keeping of written records, and creation of a written charter, but to follow the Protestant churches would dangerously suggest equality and that the outside churches were really not very different. 42 notes.
V. L. Human

2223. Hostetler, Beulah S.   AN OLD ORDER RIVER BRETHREN LOVE FEAST. *Pennsylvania Folklife 1974-75 24(2): 8-20.* Details a contemporary (1973) love feast given by the Old Order River Brethren, and presents the sect's historical and theological background.   S

2224. Hostetler, John A.   OLD ORDER AMISH SURVIVAL. *Mennonite Q. Rev. 1977 51(4): 352-361.* An attempt to explain why the Old Order Amish not only survive, but prosper. Conventional theories about revitalization are not relevant, nor are those relating to social cohesiveness and in-group protectionism. The Amish violate all of these, but still their numbers double every 23 years. Their secret is to keep everything on a human level, including schools, industry, and farms. Forces that can, and inevitably would, become bureaucratic and impersonal if existing for their own sake, are prevented from gaining a foothold. American society is dynamic and changing; the Amish must and do change also, but they change as they wish to change, always keeping the human element in mind.
V. L. Human

2225. Huenemann, Mark W.   HUTTERITE EDUCATION AS A THREAT TO SURVIVAL. *South Dakota Hist. 1976 7(1): 15-27.* Currently Hutterite culture is endangered by new legislation in South Dakota which would require secondary education, outside educators using modern audiovisual techniques, the closing of Hutterite attendance centers, and the refusal of school districts to allow new centers for new colonies. Hutterite culture stresses only basic skills, because more education and knowledge are considered dangerous and unnecessary. The basic aim of the Hutterites is to pass on the conservative, thrifty, hard-working doctrines of their ancestors. Primary and secondary sources; 5 photos, 26 notes.
A. J. Larson

2226. Israel, Jerry.   MIDWESTERN SMALL CITIES: BUILDING AN INTEGRATED SOCIAL SCIENCE CURRICULUM. *AHA Newsletter 1979 17(4): 4, 6.* Development of an integrated social science curriculum at Illinois Wesleyan University focused on community and local history, the Amish community of Arthur, Illinois, and the community development of Pontiac, Illinois, 19th-20th centuries.

2227. Janzen, Heinz.   FROM BATUM TO NEW YORK. *Mennonite Life 1974 29(4): 82-84.* Discusses immigration of Russian Mennonites from the Ukraine to the United States in 1923.

2228. Jentsch, Theodore W.   CHANGE AND THE SCHOOL IN AN OLD ORDER MENNONITE COMMUNITY. *Mennonite Q. Rev. 1976 50(2): 132-135.* The question of how the Old Order Mennonites have successfully avoided social changes is discussed. The conclusion is that the educational system of this group has preserved them from outside influences. 6 notes.
E. E. Eminhizer

2229. Jentsch, Theodore W.   EDUCATION, OCCUPATION, AND ECONOMICS AMONG OLD ORDER MENNONITES OF THE EAST PENN VALLEY. *Pennsylvania Folklife 1975 24(3): 24-35.* Describes educational, occupational, and economic conditions in an old order Mennonite commune (1949-75) in the East Penn Valley of Pennsylvania.   S

2230. Jentsch, Theodore W.   OLD ORDER MENNONITE FAMILY LIFE IN THE EAST PENN VALLEY. *Pennsylvania Folklife 1974 24(1): 18-27.* Surveys present-day aspects of Old Order Mennonite family life: courtship and marriage, the home, recreation, sickness and death.   S

2231. Johnson, David R.   THE EARLY EAST PETERSBURG AREA HERSHEY FAMILY. *Pennsylvania Mennonite Heritage 1978 1(1): 6-16.* Chronicles land patents and genealogy of various members of the Hershey family residing in Lancaster County, Pennsylvania, 1730's-1870's.

2232. Jones, Clifton H.   "THE HUTERISCH PEOPLE": A VIEW FROM THE 1920'S. *South Dakota Hist. 1976 7(1): 1-14.* Two manuscripts written in 1921 by Bertha W. Clark, not published then because of anti-German sentiment after World War I, include a brief history of the Hutterites and how they came to be located in South Dakota. The attitudes and social and religious life of the Hutterites in the 1920's showed them to be antiwar but not anti-American. The sect was no threat to its neighbors. The Hutterites were described as having Swiss origin and using English, although German was the religious language. Organized baseball, automobiles, and greater knowledge of the outside world were breaking down their isolation. Primary source; 5 photos.
A. J. Larson

2233. Joseph, Ted.   THE *BUDGET* OF SUGARCREEK, OHIO, SINCE 1920. *Mennonite Hist. Bull. 1978 39(2): 3-5.* Discusses the history of The Weekly Budget, a newspaper from Sugarcreek, Ohio, and national newsletter for the Mennonite Church, 1920's-78.

2234. Juhnke, James et al. EAST WEST AND HOME. *Mennonite Life 1975 30(1): 10-14.* Testimonials from Russian Mennonites, some of whom remained in Russia, others of whom immigrated to the United States, and still others who moved into central Asia hoping to find religious and economic freedom, 1870's-1920's.

2235. Kauffman, Earl H. ANABAPTIST INFLUENCE ON UNITED METHODISM IN CENTRAL PENNSYLVANIA. *Mennonite Hist. Bull. 1977 38(3): 4-5.* Discusses Anabaptist thought and the influence which it had, 1815-1942, on the mainstream of Methodist thought in central Pennsylvania.

2236. Kauffman, J. Howard. BOUNDARY MAINTENANCE AND CULTURAL ASSIMILATION OF CONTEMPORARY MENNONITES. *Mennonite Q. Rev. 1977 51(3): 227-240.* Discusses Mennonite assimilation into the larger society and Mennonite reaction to it. Strategies, such as parochial schools, are used to avoid assimilation. This aricle is based on a study done between 1972-75. Boundary maintenance seems important, but systemic linkage to other groups seems to be openly increasing. Describes the problems of evaluating the changes wrought on the Mennonite norms. Boundary maintenance is positively associated with the maintenance of the norms. 21 notes. E. E. Eminhizer

2237. Kauffman, S. Duane. MISCELLANEOUS AMISH MENNONITE DOCUMENTS. *Pennsylvania Mennonite Heritage 1979 2(3): 12-16.* Provides excerpts from notes and letters found among the papers of the late Doctor D. Heber Plank of Morgantown, Pennsylvania, which offer glimpses of American Amish history, 1668-1790's.

2238. Kehler, Larry. THE ARTISTIC PILGRIMAGE OF JOHN P. KLASSEN. *Mennonite Life 1973 28(4): 114-118, 125-127.* Discusses John P. Klassen's life 1909-33; he emigrated to the United States from Chortitza in the Ukraine and established himself as an artist and an instructor of art.

2239. Kerstan, Reinhold J. THE HUTTERITES: A RADICAL CHRISTIAN ALTERNATIVE. *Fides et Hist. 1973 5(1-2): 62-67.* The Hutterite sect was founded in 1528 in Moravia. They have maintained an agricultural communal form of society and culture. Caught often in the European wars at grave threat to their existence, they migrated to Canada and the United States in the 1870's. They are highly innovative and invariably successful farmers, but cling tenaciously to their original cultural and social patterns. Based on secondary sources; 6 notes. R. Butchart

2240. Klaassen, Walter. MENNONITES AND WAR TAXES. *Pennsylvania Mennonite Heritage 1978 1(2): 17-22.* Traces traditional views of government and taxation held by Anabaptists in Switzerland and Germany during the 16th century; examines Anabaptists' refusal to pay taxes connected with war in the United States from the American Revolution to the Vietnam War.

2241. Klingelsmith, Sharon, comp. and Springer, Kenneth, comp. BIBLIOGRAPHY OF THE WRITINGS OF MELVIN GINGERICH. *Mennonite Q. Rev. 1978 52(2): 170-182.* A bibliography of all published writings of Mennonite scholar Melvin Gingerich, except several hundred book reviews which he wrote while an editor. All published works are arranged by year, 1921-75. V. L. Human

2242. Krahn, Cornelius. RADICAL REFORMATION AND MENNONITE BIBLIOGRAPHY 1975-1976. *Mennonite Life 1977 32(1): 26-30.* Contains all significant books, doctoral dissertations, and masters' theses dealing with Anabaptist-Mennonite related subjects published during 1975-76. Topical headings include: 1) radical reformation and Anabaptism, 2) Muenster and Muentzer, reformation and revolution, war and peace, 3) Mennonites and related movements and denominations, 4) service, outreach, family, education, fine arts, and 5) dissertations and theses. B. Burnett

2243. Kraybill, Donald B. RELIGIOUS AND ETHNIC SOCIALIZATION IN A MENNONITE HIGH SCHOOL. *Mennonite Q. Rev. 1977 51(4): 329-351.* A study of the effects of ethnic schools on ethnicity in the Mennonite community of Lancaster, Pennsylvania. A comparative study of Mennonites in ethnic and public schools, as well as transfers, with allowance for sex and parental attitudinal changes, suggests that the prime function of the ethnic school, i.e., to solidify members in the precepts of the faith, is hardly fulfilled. The ethnic school does not change student attitudes toward orthodoxy, ethnicity, and ethnic ritual, although the ethnic school students did develop a higher avoidance pattern than their public school counterparts and a greater compatibility with their parents. All results are based on attitudinal changes over a three-year period, with testing both at the beginning and at the end of this period. 8 tables, 4 appendixes. V. L. Human

2244. Kreider, Rachel. A MENNONITE COLLEGE THROUGH TOWN EYES. *Mennonite Life 1977 32(2): 4-13.* During the 1860's in the large Mennonite settlement in Median County, Ohio, the Reverend Ephraim Hunsberger (1814-1904) and the General Conference began plans for the first Mennonite college in America. Completed in May 1866, the large brick building cost about $14,000, considerably more than expected. After difficulty in finding a faculty, Wadsworth Institute opened to students in January 1868 with a course of study in English and one in German. A conflict developed between professors Carl Justus van der Smissen and Christian Showalter over educational standards just as Mennonite attention turned from education to immigration problems. The General Conference opened the college to non-Mennonites in 1875, then abruptly closed it in 1879. Based on contemporary newspaper accounts; 8 photos. B. Burnett

2245. Kreider, Robert. THE HISTORIC PEACE CHURCHES' MEETING IN 1935. *Mennonite Life 1976 31(2): 21-24.* In the fall of 1935 representatives of the Mennonites, Dunkards (Church of the Brethren), and Quakers met in Newton, Kansas, to discuss the possibilities for peace in a world threatened by war. Mennonite leader H. P. Krehbiel convened the meeting and was instrumental in changing the name of the group from Conference of Pacifist Churches to Historic Peace Churches in response to fundamentalist criticism of "pacifism" as a "secular" word. The conference drafted a message to the Methodist General Conference of 1936 (reprinted) and planned future meetings. 2 photos. R. Burnett

2246. Kreider, Robert. WINDOWS TO THE MENNONITE EXPERIENCE IN AMERICA: A PHOTOGRAPHIC ESSAY. *Mennonite Life 1978 33(2): 24-47.* Fifty-six photographs covering 1880-1940 emphasize social customs, the Mennonite mission to the Cheyenne, and the beginning of Mennonite institutions on the prairie. From the Mennonite Library and Archives, North Newton, Kansas. B. Burnett

2247. Lehman, James O. THE MENNONITES OF MARYLAND DURING THE REVOLUTIONARY WAR. *Mennonite Q. Rev. 1976 50(3): 200-229.* Discusses conditions in colonial Maryland, emphasizing problems faced by the Mennonites. The Mennonites centered around Elizabethtown and their relationship with the Committee of Observation which was their point of contact with the pro-American revolutionary government. Being conscientious objectors, they generally paid high fines to avoid military service. Details the treatment of Loyalists and neutrals, and the involvement of Mennonites in the American Revolution. 93 notes. E. E. Eminhizer

2248. Lehman, Thomas L. THE PLAIN PEOPLE: RELUCTANT PARTIES IN LITIGATION TO PRESERVE A LIFE STYLE. *J. of Church and State 1974 16(2): 287-300.* Discusses legal cases involving the Amish people of Pennsylvania and Wisconsin from as early as 1755, showing their reluctance to participate in the military practices and school religion of the dominant society.

2249. Leisy, Bruce R. THE LAST OF THE MENNONITE BREWERS. *Mennonite Life 1976 31(1): 4-9.* Chronicles the beer brewing industry started by the Leisy family in Peoria, Illinois, 1884-1950.

2250. Loewen, Esko. NOT A DUTCH BUT A GERMAN CABINET ORGAN—A TESCHEMACHER. *Mennonite Life 1976 31(2): 8-12.* Recounts the probable history of the cabinet pipe organ housed at the Kauffman Museum, Bethel College, Newton, Kansas. First owned by Dutch Mennonite pastor Johannes Deknatel (1720-59), the organ was built by Jacob Teschemacher of Elberfeld, Germany, in about 1740—a fact determined by its similarity with other known Teschemacher organs. Inherited by the van der Smissin family of Germany, the organ traveled

with them from Europe to Ohio in 1868, to Illinois in the 1890's, then to Kansas where it was donated to Bethel College in 1910. 9 photos.
B. Burnett

2251. Loomis, Charles P. A FARMHAND'S DIARY. *Mennonite Q. Rev. 1979 53(3): 235-256.* The diary is part of Walter M. Kollmorgen's *Culture of a Contemporary Rural Community: The Old Order Amish of Lancaster County, Pennsylvania,* a study for the Agriculture Department done in 1940. Discusses the Amish family of Christian King, for whom the author worked during May 1940. Describes agricultural labor, particularly caring for livestock. Also describes meals and how the women prepared them. Gives examples of the Amish rejection of modern conveniences and of how they ran their farms. The Amish believed in self-help and criticized some New Deal programs. 3 diagrams, 8 notes.
D. L. Schermerhorn

2252. Markle, G. E. and Pasco, Sharon. FAMILY LIMITATION AMONG THE OLD ORDER AMISH. *Population Studies [Great Britain] 1977 31(2): 267-280.* The Indiana Amish, a high-fertility Anabaptist population, regulate their marital fertility according to their family finances. We linked demographic data from the Indiana Amish Directory with personal property tax records at 5, 15 and 25 years after marriage and found fertility differences by occupation and wealth. Correlations between family size and wealth at the beginning, middle and end of childbearing years were positive. Wealthier women exhibited higher marital fertility, had longer first birth intervals, were older at the birth of their last child, and had larger families than poorer women. Over the past 30 years, marital fertility has remained constant among older women; but birth rates among younger women have been rising rapidly.
J

2253. Martineau, William H. and MacQueen, Rhoda Sayres. OCCUPATIONAL DIFFERENTIATION AMONG THE OLD ORDER AMISH. *Rural Sociol. 1977 42(3): 383-397.* Examines occupational differentiation among the Old Order Amish living in Lancaster County, Pennsylvania, in terms of their resistance to social change and internal sources of change and stability, 1970's.

2254. Miller, David L. DANIEL E. MAST (1848-1930): A BIOGRAPHICAL SKETCH. *Mennonite Hist. Bull. 1978 39(1): 2-6.* Gives a biography of Daniel E. Mast, 1886-1930, an Amish deacon and minister who wrote for a German-language newspaper, *Herald der Wahrheit* in Reno County, Kansas.

2255. Miller, J. Virgil. AMISH-MENNONITES IN NORTHERN ALSACE AND THE PALATINATE IN THE EIGHTEENTH CENTURY AND THEIR CONNECTION WITH IMMIGRANTS TO PENNSYLVANIA. *Mennonite Q. Rev. 1976 50(4): 272-280.* To date, there has been no attempt to locate the residences of Amish-Mennonites in Alsace and the Palatinate. These people originally settled in this area as early as 1700. In the early days, there were probably no formally organized congregations. The congregations are identified and the names of the families are given. The history of the churches is traced to about 1800. Provides a list of immigrants from these churches to America, with the years they came. 44 notes.
E. E. Eminhizer

2256. Mumaw, George Shaum. A COUNTRY SINGING SCHOOL TEACHER OF THE 19TH CENTURY: AN AUTOBIOGRAPHY. *Mennonite Hist. Bull. 1975 36(2): 1-3.* An account of George Mumaw's activities as a Mennonite Singing School conductor in Indiana and Ohio, 1900-53.
S

2257. Musselman, Howard Y. THE MARSH CREEK SETTLEMENT OF ADAMS COUNTY, 1769-1823. *Pennsylvania Mennonite Heritage 1979 2(4): 2-12.* Discusses settlement in Franklin and Cumberland townships, Pennsylvania, by Mennonite individuals and families.

2258. Overholser, J. Spencer. THE TERRE HILL OBERHOLTZER FAMILY. *Pennsylvania Mennonite Heritage 1978 1(2): 2-8.* Offers a genealogy of several members of the Oberholtzer family who originated in Switzerland, immigrated to Pennsylvania, and established farms in the community of Terre Hill, 1720's-1850's.

2259. Oyer, John S. MELVIN GINGERICH, 1902-1975. *Mennonite Q. Rev. 1978 52(2): 91-112.* Melvin Gingerich, a Mennonite scholar, early developed a flair for learning, probably because he came from a long line of churchmen. His books and articles were numerous, the most famous being a history of the Mennonites in Iowa. He also edited several periodicals, acted as research counselor and archivist, and was an active churchman until his death. Never radical or at the forefront of new movements, Gingerich managed to soothe the more ardent spirits at both ends of the political spectrum. 92 notes.
V. L. Human

2260. Pinsker, Sanford. THE MENNONITE AS ETHNIC WRITER: A CONVERSATION WITH MERLE GOOD. *J. of Ethnic Studies 1975 3(2): 57-64.* Interview with Merle Good, author of *Happy as the Grass Was Green* (1971) and folk writer of the Pennsylvania Dutch. Discusses the problem of ethnic survival, the Mennonites, and ethnic writing as exploitation.
T. W. Smith

2261. Raitz, Karl B. THEOLOGY OF THE LANDSCAPE: A COMPARISON OF MORMON AND AMISH-MENNONITE LAND USE. *Utah Hist. Q. 1973 41(1): 23-34.* A comparative study of land use by two closely knit subcultures, using the Mormon village of Escalante, Utah, and the village of Intercourse, Lancaster County, Pennsylvania, as typical examples. Both cases demonstrate that the underlying motivational theological doctrine of a group provides "parameters for behavior which have shaped religious ideals and have also had a pronounced effect on the way each group utilizes its land resources . . . Each subculture has created a distinctive landscape—a landscape born out of theological edict." Two completely different landscape patterns have resulted. 2 photos, 2 maps, 24 notes.
R. V. Ritter

2262. Redekop, Calvin and Hostetler, John A. THE PLAIN PEOPLE: AN INTERPRETATION. *Mennonite Q. Rev. 1977 51(4): 266-277.* An analysis of the nature and causes of the Plain People, who include Amish, Hutterites, Mennonites, Molokans, and Dukhobors. The Plain People perceive that religion has failed to integrate larger communities, but have faith that it can integrate small communities. Plain People are not interested in joining the larger majority, a policy which separates them from so-called minority groups. They simply want to be left alone to deal with people on a person-to-person basis. Their major concerns at present are perpetuation of their society in the face of technological change and the acquisition of new lands to support expanding communities. 4 notes.
V. L. Human

2263. Reinford, Wilmer. INDEX TO THE JACOB B. MENSCH COLLECTION OF LETTERS, 1861-1912. *Mennonite Q. Rev. 1978 52(1): 77-85.* Lists letters of Jacob B. Mensch (d. 1912), a Mennonite minister from Pennsylvania, who is best remembered for his library of rare books, his many records and diaries, and his Franconia Conference minutes. Lists libraries and archives having microfilm copies of the Mensch Collection.
A. W. Howell

2264. Rempel, David G. C. B. SCHMIDT, HISTORIAN: FACT OR FICTION? *Mennonite Life 1974 29(1/2): 33-37.* Corrects misconceptions brought out in the historical writings of C. B. Schmidt, who wrote a history of the Mennonites from their beginnings in Germany and Russia through their immigration to the New World; attempts to clear up misstatement of fact and outright fallacies perpetrated by Schmidt.

2265. Ressler, Martin E. A SONG OF PRAISE. *Pennsylvania Mennonite Heritage 1978 1(4): 10-13.* Traces the history since 1590 of the "Lob Lied," Song of Praise, the most widely sung hymn of Mennonite authorship, citing its appearances and variations in 19th- and 20th-century hymnals and giving tune and verses.

2266. Ringenberg, William C. DEVELOPMENT AND DIVISION IN THE MENNONITE COMMUNITY IN ALLEN COUNTY, INDIANA. *Mennonite Q. Rev. 1976 50(2): 114-131.* The Allen County Mennonites' background is traced into Europe, with a discussion of the controversy leading to the division by the Amish. The reasons for the settlement in Allen County by the Amish are listed. Local divisions are discussed indicating their effect on marriage and resultant genetic problems. The general development of the Mennonite-Amish community is detailed. 52 notes.
E. E. Eminhizer

2267. Rushby, William F. THE OLD GERMAN BAPTIST BRETHREN: AN INTIMATE CHRISTIAN COMMUNITY IN URBAN-INDUSTRIAL SOCIETY. *Mennonite Q. Rev. 1977 51(4): 362-376.* A consideration of the culture, life-style, and chances for survival of The Old German Baptist Brethren, an ultra-conservative offshoot of a larger church. The Brethren hardly qualify as Plain People, for they accept a lot of modern gadgets and conveniences. They are not nearly so introversionist as some Plain Peoples, but they still survive and maintain their separate identity, though internal numerical growth has been slow. Strict adherence to Church doctrine, rather than differences in clothes or customs, marks off the Brethren. Although this religious emphasis is seen by some sociologists to spell their doom, others argue that it may be the very thing which saves the Brethren from eventual assimilation, for religion is no longer considered important enough to fight over in the larger society. Table, note.   V. L. Human

2268. Ruth, John. MENNONITE IDENTITY AND LITERARY ART. *Mennonite Life 1977 32(1): 4-25.* Story-tellers, those who value and transmit the traditions of any culture, give meaning and a spiritual sense to life. Mennonites have lost much of their sense of tradition in their desire to be acculturated. Sentimental nostalgia and ridicule do not touch the souls of people and are not stories. The scruples that Mennonites traditionally have held and which some consider antithetical to art can spur creativity rather than paralyze it by using one's imagination. The artistic challenge today lies in penetrating and articulating the unique values of the Mennonite ethos rather than in betraying them, in transcending social pressures and finding what is true and lasting.
B. Burnett

2269. Sauder, David L. METZLER MENNONITE CONGREGATION, 1728-1978. *Pennsylvania Mennonite Heritage 1978 1(2): 9-16.* Established in 1728 in the town of Groffdale, the Metzler Mennonite congregation got its name from the family of Jacob and Maria Metzler who settled in West Earl Township in 1786. Offers a history of the church and lists its bishops, ministers, and deacons, 1728-1978.

2270. Schelbert, Leo and Leubking, Sandra. SWISS MENNONITE FAMILY NAMES: AN ANNOTATED CHECKLIST. *Swiss Am. Hist. Soc. Newsletter 1978 14(2): 2-32.* Lists the major family names of the Swiss Brethren, a body of Mennonites who migrated to North America, 1680-1880; gives variant names, Swiss origins, and names of successive first migrated family members.

2271. Schlabach, Theron F. THE HUMBLE BECOME "AGGRESSIVE WORKERS": MENNONITES ORGANIZE FOR MISSION, 1880-1910. *Mennonite Q. Rev. 1978 52(2): 113-126.* For a time the traditionally humble Mennonites became much more aggressive in the United States and Canada, having missions, Sunday Schools, revivalism, etc. Conflicts arose at once; it was not easy to reconcile the old doctrine of defenselessness with the new aggressiveness. The extent of aggressiveness may be questioned: perhaps it was more apparent than real. Many of the institutional changes seem to have been intended to support the much older and traditional Mennonite value system. 47 notes.
V. L. Human

2272. Schlabach, Theron F. PARADOXES OF MENNONITE SEPARATISM. *Pennsylvania Mennonite Heritage 1979 2(1): 12-17.* Discusses attitudes toward separatism, political activism, and social reform among Mennonites, 1840's-1930's.

2273. Schlabach, Theron F. REVEILLE FON *DIE STILLEN IM LANDE!* A STIR AMONG MENNONITES IN THE LATE NINETEENTH CENTURY. *Mennonite Q. Rev. 1977 51(3): 213-226.* In the period between 1860-90, the North American Mennonites and Amish underwent a notable religious revival. This movement has been stereotyped as an "awakening" in Mennonite history. Examines this stereotype by offering alternative explanations and descriptions. It was more a quickening than an awakening; an acculturation rather than a revival (many shifted to English as their language); and a move from Anabaptist avoidance of personal pride to an individual being allowed to be somebody within the church and society in general. 48 notes.
E. E. Eminhizer

2274. Schmidt, Dennis. J. E. ENTZ (1875-1969): SHEPHERD TO HIS FLOCK. *Mennonite Life 1976 31(3): 14-17.* A minister of the First Mennonite Church in Newton, Kansas, John Edward Entz (1875-1969) was committed to pacificism, nonresistance, and evangelical Christianity. He supported the Deaconness movement, worked for high quality music in the church, and produced the *Church Letter* during World War II to keep up morale of men in Civilian Public Service Camps. Because his preaching was monotonous and his message very conservative, he was unseated as an active minister in 1946 and given the title Elder Emeritus. He continued visitation work and other church work until his death. In 1960 he received a Distinguished Alumnus award from Bethel College. Photo.   B. Burnett

2275. Schmidt, John F., comp. ACROSS THE ATLANTIC BY STEAM AND SAIL. *Mennonite Life 1973 28(2): 48-52.* Pictorial essay of vessels, both steam and sail, which transported Mennonite immigrants to America in the 19th century.

2276. Schmidt, John F. THE HORSE AND BUGGY DOCTOR AND HIS FRIENDS. *Mennonite Life 1976 31(2): 4-7.* Highlights the correspondence between Kansas doctor A. E. Hertzler, author of the popular autobiography *Horse and Buggy Doctor* (ca. 1938), and Mennonites J. H. Lagenwalter, C. E. Krehbiel, E. G. Kaufman, and Walter H. Hohmann. (The latter two were associated with Bethel College). 2 photos, note.   B. Burnett

2277. Schmidt, John F. THE IMMIGRANTS AND THE RAILROADS. *Mennonite Life 1974 29(1/2): 14-16.* Discusses travel within the United States by Mennonites recently immigrated; details typical traveling cases and attire, and some of the frontier settlements visited, 1870-74.

2278. Schmidt, John F. "THREE YEARS AFTER DATE..." *Mennonite Life 1973 28(2): 35-39.* Chronicles events within a Mennonite congregation in Kansas, 1873-80.

2279. Schmidt, John F. TURKEY WHEAT: A MENNONITE CONTRIBUTION TO GREAT PLAINS AGRICULTURE. *Mennonite Life 1974 29(4): 67-69.* Discusses the introduction of a particularly hardy strain of wheat, Turkey wheat, by immigrant Mennonites in the Great Plains, 1880-1922.

2280. Schrag, Martin H. THE BRETHREN IN CHRIST CONCEPT OF THE CHURCH IN TRANSITION, 1870-1910. *Mennonite Q. Rev. 1978 52(4): 312-327.* During 1870-1910 the Brethren in Christ brought into their organization a change in basic outlook which moved toward individualizing the faith. They were influenced by individualistic, perfectionistic, and conservative American Christianity. These influences and the changes they brought about are discussed under the headings: "The New Birth Individualized," "The Christian Life Individualized," and "The Concept of the Church Individualized." Each of these areas is reflected through the adoption of Sunday schools, revivalism, holiness, a periodical, a church school, and centrally organized mission program. 45 notes.   E. E. Eminhizer

2281. Schrag, Martin H. THE BRETHREN IN CHRIST ATTITUDE TOWARD THE "WORLD": A HISTORICAL STUDY OF THE MOVEMENT FROM SEPARATION TO AN INCREASING ACCEPTANCE OF AMERICAN SOCIETY. *Mennonite Q. R. 1974 48(1): 112-113.* Originally nonconformists, the Brethren in Christ have moved closer to American Protestantism, and have begun to accept economic individualism, higher education, and politics.   S

2282. Schrag, Orpha and Schrag, Stella. LIFE, LEISURE AND WORK IN PIONEER DAYS. *Mennonite Life 1974 29(1-2): 18-23.* Describes life on a farm in South Dakota through the eyes of a young Mennonite, 1944.

2283. Schwieder, Dorothy and Schwieder, Elmer. THE BEACHY AMISH IN IOWA: A CASE STUDY. *Mennonite Q. Rev. 1977 51(1): 41-51.* Briefly discusses the history of the Beachy Amish, with emphasis on two colonies in Iowa which have grown rapidly. Notes differences between them and the Old Order Amish. Lists their characteristics, indicating unique features. 33 notes.   E. E. Eminhizer

2284. Schwieder, Dorothy A. FRONTIER BRETHREN. *Montana 1978 28(1): 2-15.* Hutterites found in the American West land and isolation, which persecution as European Anabaptists had denied them during the 16th-19th centuries. Communal colonies were first established during 1874-77 near Yankton, South Dakota, spreading during the next century to North Dakota, Montana, Washington, Alberta, Saskatchewan, and Manitoba. Training and education in each colony perpetuated traditions, strengthened communal goals, and reinforced male/female roles in adult life. Colonies are led by an elected minister and a council of 5 to 7 men. When the population reaches 130, a colony seeks to establish a new unit. Intercolonial marriages and religious traditions strengthen group ties. Hutterites were not a product of the American frontier, nor were they shaped by it. Thus Frederick Jackson Turner's frontier thesis and the Great Plains hypothesis of Walter Prescott Webb do not apply to the Hutterite colonies' experiences. Accompanying photographs by Kyrn Taconis are central to the article. Based on secondary sources and author's M.A. thesis; 12 illus., map, biblio. R. C. Myers

2285. Scott, Stephen E. THE OLD ORDER RIVER BRETHREN CHURCH. *Pennsylvania Mennonite Heritage 1978 1(3): 13-22.* Describes the Old Order River Brethren communities, their membership and leaders since 1855, their schisms, contrasts between the groups, and the 1977 merger between the Musser and Keller-Strickler groups.

2286. Sharp, John E. SOLOMON ZOOK SHARP: EDUCATOR AND OPTIMIST. *Pennsylvania Mennonite Heritage 1979 2(1): 8-11.* Solomon Zook Sharp worked in Mennonite education in Pennsylvania, Tennessee, Kansas, Missouri, California, and Colorado; covers 1860-1931.

2287. Sprunger, Milton F. COURTSHIP AND MARRIAGE. *Mennonite Life 1976 31(2): 13-16.* Contains the diary account of Indiana Mennonite farmer and widower David Sprunger (1857-1933) in his search for a second wife and mother for his seven children. He married Caroline Tschantz (d. 1939) of Sonneberg, Ohio, 4 April 1895. 2 photos. B. Burnett

2288. Stoltzfus, Victor. AMISH AGRICULTURE: ADAPTIVE STRATEGIES FOR ECONOMIC SURVIVAL OF COMMUNITY LIFE. *Rural Sociol. 1973 38(2): 196-206.* Examines Amish adaptive responses in Coles, Douglas, and Moultrie counties in Illinois to changes in social organization and economic conditions of the outside community and how these aid in securing community cohesiveness, covering 1960-72.

2289. Stoltzfus, Victor. REWARD AND SANCTION: THE ADAPTIVE CONTINUITY OF AMISH LIFE. *Mennonite Q. Rev. 1977 51(4): 308-318.* Analyzes the forces operating to keep Amish society from flying apart in the presence of the larger society. A system of rewards and punishments is in effect: the rewards, though very different from those of the outside world, are seen as being at least equally attractive. Deviants are faced with a number of punishments, running the gamut from simple neighborly admonishment to excommunication. Seldom is the latter necessary, nor is voluntary defection common, for the difficulties of starting all over again in the outside world are a powerful inducement to put up with whatever shortcomings the individual perceives in the society. Fig. V. L. Human

2290. Suderman, Elmer F. THE MENNONITE COMMUNITY AND THE PACIFIST CHARACTER IN AMERICAN LITERATURE. *Mennonite Life 1979 34(1): 8-15.* A comparison of four novels —*Erloesung* by Peter Epp, *Peace Shall Destroy Many* by Rudy Wiebe, *Mennonite Soldier* by Kenneth Reed, and *The Long Tomorrow* by Lee Brackett—and two plays—*The Blowing and the Bending* by James Juhnke and Harold Moyer, and *The Berserkers* by Warren Kliewer—shows the reactions of Mennonite pacifist communities and characters to a violent world. These worlds lack the radical pacifism that demands a commitment to love and forgiveness and do not present an admirable hero who refuses to fight nor a serious alternative to war. In most, a sense of community strength and church leadership are lacking. 2 photos, 9 notes. B. Burnett

2291. Sutter, Sem C. MENNONITES AND THE PENNSYLVANIA GERMAN REVIVAL. *Mennonite Q. Rev. 1976 50(1): 37-57.* The view of most church historians is that Mennonites were nearly unaffected by the revivals of the 18th and 19th centuries. Discusses active Mennonite revivalists and their influence on the movement. Those discussed include Martin Boehm (1725-1812) and Christian Newcomer (1750-1830). Groups other than Mennonite, but important to them, are the Baptists in Virginia, the United Brethren in Christ, and the Evangelical Association. Also discusses Mennonite opposition to revivalism. 116 notes. E. E. Eminhizer

2292. Teichroew, Allan. AS FAR AS THE EYE CAN SEE: SOME DEPRESSION PHOTOGRAPHS OF MENNONITE FARMERS. *Mennonite Life 1978 33(3): 4-15.* During the 1930's Depression and Dust Bowl, the Farm Security Administration intended to provide welfare services to displaced farmers and to furnish loans for those still working the land. A side effect of the investigation into farm conditions was the accumulation of thousands of striking photographs of rural poverty. In 1937 Russell Lee photographed the 15-member John Harshenberger family of Montana, Mennonites who lived in grim deprivation yet maintained a strong integrity. Dorthea Lange photographed the more prosperous 5-member John Unruf (Unruh) family of Boundary County, Idaho in 1939, pioneers determined to build a new farm. From the Farm Security Administration collection, Library of Congress; 12 photos, 8 notes. B. Burnett

2293. Ulle, Robert F. PACIFISTS, PAXTON, AND POLITICS: COLONIAL PENNSYLVANIA, 1763-1768. *Pennsylvania Mennonite Heritage 1978 1(4): 18-21.* Discusses the effect on political behavior of the religious convictions of Mennonites and nonresistants versus Presbyterians after the Paxton Massacre, a massacre of peaceful Indians by frontiersmen in 1763.

2294. Unruh, John D. and Unruh, John D., Jr. DANIEL UNRUH AND THE MENNONITE SETTLEMENT IN DAKOTA TERRITORY. *Mennonite Q. R. 1975 49(3): 203-216.* By 1870, it was clear that Russian Mennonites were going to lose their place in Russia and immigration began. About 10,000 settled in the western United States. Although South Dakota was not recommended by the investigating committee, over 2,000 settled in the area because of Daniel Unruh. Describes his life in Russia. He brought 100 Mennonites to America in 1873. Details their trip across the country and describes their investigation of available lands and final settlement in Dakota. Unruh was successful and relatively wealthy. He devoted some time to the community needs. A negative report on Oregon land by him in 1882 prevented a move there. 49 notes. E. E. Eminhizer

2295. Wagoner, Gerald C. WENGERITES: PENTECOSTAL BRETHREN IN CHRIST. *Pennsylvania Mennonite Heritage 1978 1(4): 14-17.* Traces the origin and development of this holiness branch of the Brethren in Christ in Ohio and Indiana during 1836-1924, discussing doctrine and leaders.

2296. Wiebe, Menno. TO BE OR NOT TO BE MENNONITE PEOPLE? *Mennonite Life 1973 28(3): 67-71.* Discusses 20th-century Mennonites and the solidarity which they must express, in terms of spiritual ends and community relations, in order to retain their religious beliefs.

2297. Wittlinger, Carlton O. THE ADVANCE OF WESLEYAN HOLINESS AMONG THE BRETHREN IN CHRIST SINCE 1910. *Mennonite Q. Rev. 1976 50(1): 21-36.* In 1910 the Brethren in Christ, located mainly in Canada and the North Central States, adopted in their general conference a statement embodying the Wesleyan perfectionism. Charles Baker, Bishop of Nottawa District, Ontario, objected to the view that the sanctified no longer had inner desire to sin. No one challenged his view until 1916. In that year, the perfectionists gained control of the *Visitor* and controversy followed. By 1930 the perfectionists were seeking change in the 1910 statement to say "second work of grace." Following this there developed holiness camp meetings. 75 notes. E. E. Eminhizer

2298. Wittlinger, Carlton O. THE IMPACT OF WESLEYAN HOLINESS ON THE BRETHREN IN CHRIST TO 1910. *Mennonite Q. R. 1975 49(4): 259-283.* The Brethren in Christ, a branch of the Mennonites, developed divergent views as they came in contact with other Protestant ideas at the end of the 19th century. The Wesleyan influence was important in this change of direction, as can be seen by the number of Charles Wesley's hymns in their hymnal of 1874. Traces the development of Wesley's influence particularly on the Brethren in Kansas. Contact with the American Holiness Movement also caused changes in the doctrinal values held by the Brethren.　　　　　　E. E. Eminhizer

2299. Wittlinger, Carlton O. THE ORIGIN OF THE BRETHREN IN CHRIST. *Mennonite Q. R. 1974 48(1): 55-72.* Discusses the 1775-80 founding of the Brethren in Christ in Lancaster County, Pennsylvania, by Jacob Engel (1753-83), the nature of their belief, and disputes between the United States and Canadian branches over the organization's name.　　　　　S

2300. Yoder, Eleanor. NICKNAMING IN AN AMISH-MENNONITE COMMUNITY. *Pennsylvania Folklife 1974 23(3): 30-37.*

2301. Yoder, Paton. "TENNESSEE" JOHN STOLTZFUS AND THE GREAT SCHISM IN THE AMISH CHURCH, 1850-1877. *Pennsylvania Mennonite Heritage 1979 2(3): 17-23.* Discusses John Stoltzfus (1805-1887), particularly his role in the Great Schism between the liberals and the conservatives in the Amish Church between the 1870's and the turn of the century, in Lancaster County, Pennsylvania.

2302. Zook, Lois Ann. BISHOP JOHN N. DURR AND HIS TIMES. *Pennsylvania Mennonite Heritage 1978 1(1): 18-21.* John N. Durr (1853-1934) served as a bishop in the Mennonite Church in Pennsylvania and was largely responsible for establishing the Southwestern Pennsylvania Mennonite Conference, 1872-1934.

2303. Zook, Lois Ann. MORITZ ZUG, AMISH MENNONITE IMMIGRANT. *Pennsylvania Mennonite Heritage 1979 2(1): 2-7.* Genealogy of the family of Moritz Zug, Pennsylvania Amish, 1742-1886.

2304. —. AMERICAN MENNONITE SCENE IN THE 1860'S. *Mennonite Hist. Bull. 1973 34(2): 2-6.*
Funk, John F. MORE BORDER RUFFIANISM, pp. 2-3.
Funk, John F. CHICAGO IN 1861, pp. 3-4.
Lehman, James O., ed. THE BUILDING OF SONNENBERG'S SECOND CHURCH HOUSE IN THE 1860'S, pp. 3, 5.
Yoder, Eli L. WAYNE CO., OHIO, IN 1861, pp. 4-5.
—. CIVIL WAR C.O. DOCUMENTS, p. 6. Original letters and documents by Mennonites.　　　　　S

2305. —. MENNONITES AND THE POLITICAL ELECTIONS OF 1856: JOHANNES RISSER ON POLITICS AND THE SLAVERY ISSUE. *Mennonite Hist. Bull. 1976 37(4): 1-3.* Reprints three letters from Johannes Risser to his sister and brother-in-law in 1857 discussing the slavery issue, the Democratic Party, and the general state of politics at the time.

2306. —. [MENNONITES AND THE CIVIL WAR]. *Mennonite Hist. Bull. 1973 34(4): 1-3.*
Gross, Leonard, ed. JOHN M. BRENNEMAN AND THE CIVIL WAR, pp. 1-3. Two wartime documents by Brenneman—a draft of a petition to President Abraham Lincoln on behalf of the Mennonites, and a covering letter for the petition, sent to Bishop Jacob Nold.
Swope, Wilmer D. DISCOVERY, 1973, p. 3. Relates the discovery of a collection of Mennonites letters in which the above documents were found.　　　　　S

2307. —. [MENNONITES BEFORE THE REVOLUTION]. *Mennonite Hist. Bull. 1974 35(3): 1-7.*
Gross, Leonard, ed. MENNONITE PETITION TO THE PENNSYLVANIA ASSEMBLY, 1775, p. 1. Prints the German text of "A Short and Sincere Declaration . . . " presented by Mennonites and German Baptists on 7 November 1775 to the Pennsylvania House of Assembly.
Ulle, Robert F., ed. PREPARING FOR REVOLUTION, pp. 2-7. "The following set of [16] documents [now at the Historical Society of Pennsylvania], beginning with the Lancaster 'Association' Resolution of May 1, 1775, footnotes the tension caused when nonresistant Mennonites refused to serve in the military units being established."　　　　　S

2308. —. PIONEERS, WHEAT, AND FAITH. *Mennonite Life 1974 29(1-2): 24-29.* Pictorial essay showing scenes from pioneer life on the Great Plains among Mennonites who farmed the land, 1870-1974.

2309. —. SCHOWALTER ORAL HISTORY EYEWITNESS ACCOUNTS. *Mennonite Life 1975 30(3): 19-25.* Accounts taken as oral history transcripts from Mennonites discussing their experiences during World War I, 1917-18.

2310. —. [SPEAK SCHOOLS]. *Mennonite Hist. Bull. 1975 36(2): 3-6.*
Hollenbach, Raymond E. "SPEAK SCHOOLS" OF THE 19TH CENTURY, pp. 3-4.
Gehman, John B. SPEAK SCHOOL ACCOUNT, HEREFORD, [18]-53, pp. 4-6.
Presents an introduction to John B. Gehman, a Pennsylvania Mennonite, and an excerpt from his diary dealing with Speak Schools.　　　　　S

Catholic

2311. Agonito, Joseph. THE JOHN CARROLL PAPERS. *Catholic Hist. Rev. 1977 63(4): 537-572.* Father Thomas O'Brien Hanley, who edited the John Carroll Papers, has brought together the large and diversified body of Archbishop Carroll's writings, scattered in over thirty North American and European archives. Excellent translations of Carroll's numerous Latin, French, and Italian letters have been provided. Carroll's letters, sermons, and theological writings are fully and accurately presented, with explanatory notes attached to each piece. Hanley provides a brief, though historically rich introduction to each volume, and a fine Index. The JCP reveal, in rich detail, the portrait of a remarkable prelate who established a Church that was American in spirit and yet, at the same time, faithful in essentials to its Roman heritage.　　　　　A

2312. Aspinwall, Bernard. ORESTES A. BROWNSON AND FATHER WILLIAM CUMMING. *Innes Rev. [Great Britain] 1976 27(1): 35-41.* Publishes a letter from Father Cumming to Orestes A. Brownson in 1857 and describes their lives and the history of Scottish Catholics in America in the 1850's.

2313. Baerwald, Friedrich. DER EINFLUSS DER KATHOLIKEN AUF DIE POLITISCHE MORAL DER USA [The influence of Catholics on the political morality of the USA]. *Frankfurter Hefte [West Germany] 1973 28(6): 392-399.* Catholics, especially intellectuals, have played an important role in attempting to lift the public morality of American politics; yet, judging from the support given the Vietnam War and other Nixon policies by rank-and-file Catholics, it seems doubtful whether protests on moral grounds ever move the masses.

2314. Barrett, Joseph. A HISTORY OF SAINT DENIS PARISH. *Records of the Am. Catholic Hist. Soc. of Philadelphia 1975 86(1-4): 33-42.* Dennis Kelly, who immigrated to the United States in 1806 and died a wealthy man in 1864, founded St. Denis Parish, the oldest Catholic church in Delaware County. Presents a sketch based on the author's *Sesquicentennial History of Saint Denis Parish.* 11 notes.　　　　　J. M. McCarthy

2315. Barry, Colman J. THE BICENTENNIAL REVISITED. *Catholic Hist. Rev. 1977 63(3): 369-391.* The essay is an evaluation of American Catholic religious phenomena during the United States Bicentennial of 1976. Historical comparisons drawn from the history of the Roman Catholic community and other Christian religious experiences in the New World are made and analyzed. The thesis is advanced and defended that, despite current confusion and dissension in the American Catholic community following Vatican Council II, a vibrant and challenging religious renewal is developing that has both ancient roots and major ecumenical associations among divided Christians.　　　　　A

2316. Barry, Colman J. THE FIRST HURRAH: BONIFACE WIMMER, O.S.B. *Am. Benedictine Rev. 1977 28(1): 30-40.* Reviews *An American Abbot: Boniface Wimmer, O.S.B., 1809-1887* by Jerome Oetgen (Latrobe, Pa.: The Archabbey Press, 1976). Wimmer was responsible for establishing the Benedictine Order on the American frontier. 3 notes.　　　　　J. H. Pragman

2317. Bernardin, Joseph L. A BICENTENNIAL REFLECTION UPON AMERICAN CATHOLIC HISTORY. *Jednota Ann. Furdek 1977 16: 185-188.* Discusses the problems of Catholics from all ethnic groups in the United States since colonial times.

2318. Bouvy, Jane Faulkner. FOLK CATHOLICISM IN INDIANA. *Indiana Folklore 1976 9(2): 147-164.*

2319. Brady, James E. FATHER GEORGE ZURCHER: PROHIBITIONIST PRIEST. *Catholic Hist. Rev. 1976 62(3): 424-433.* In 1884 the Third Plenary Council of the American Catholic Church issued a strong condemnation of the liquor trade. It encouraged Catholics to remove themselves from all aspects of this trade and also forbade the sale of alcoholic beverages at church functions. Father George Zurcher became increasingly unhappy with the widespread disregard with which this proclamation was treated. Zurcher regarded the control of alcohol as a vehicle for both assimilation and social reform. He thus turned to the state to accomplish his goal because the Church would not, he felt, follow its own teaching.   A

2320. Broderick, Francis L. DEFINING THE AMERICAN CATHOLIC CHURCH. *Rev. in Am. Hist. 1979 7(1): 37-42.* Review article prompted by Neil Betten's *Catholic Activism and the Industrial Worker* (Gainesville: U. Pr. of Florida, 1976) and Jay P. Dolan's *Catholic Revivalism: The American Experience, 1830-1900* (Notre Dame, Ind.: U. of Notre Dame Pr., 1978).

2321. Carey, Patrick. THE LAITY'S UNDERSTANDING OF THE TRUSTEE SYSTEM, 1785-1855. *Catholic Hist. Rev. 1978 64(3): 357-376.* American Catholic trusteeism has usually been interpreted as lay insubordination. The author argues that many of the American Catholic laity who were elected trustees for their congregations during the national period tried to adapt the European Catholic Church to American culture by identifying that Church with American republican experiences. Trusteeism, therefore, was not simply a matter of insubordination, but rather a manifestation of the all-pervasive democratic spirit of the times, an implementation of European Catholic practices which were adapted to new republican experiences, and a result of the laity's changing theological perceptions of the Church and their role in it. The trustees were trying to create a republican Catholic Church in America.   A

2322. Carey, Patrick. TWO EPISCOPAL VIEWS OF LAY-CLERICAL CONFLICTS, 1785-1860. *Records of the Am. Catholic Hist. Soc. of Philadelphia 1976 87(1-4): 85-98.* Episcopal responses to trusteeism in the 19th century show two divergent kinds of opposition. Republican opposition believed that the Catholic Church should appropriate elements of American democracy in its administration while retaining the centrality of episcopal authority. Monarchical opposition was based on attempts of some bishops to establish the Catholic structures of the ancien régime in this country. 42 notes.   J. M. McCarthy

2323. Curran, Robert Emmett. PRELUDE TO "AMERICANISM": THE NEW YORK ACCADEMIA AND CLERICAL RADICALISM IN THE LATE NINETEENTH CENTURY. *Church Hist. 1978 47(1): 48-65.* Recent discovery of a New York priests' association, The Accademia, started in 1865, shows another facet of the Americanist controversy which attempted to adapt Roman Catholicism to democratic institutions and values. For more than 20 years, the Accademia was regarded as the epitome of unrest fomenting against the established order of American Catholicism. 55 notes.   M. D. Dibert

2324. Curry, Thomas J. ETHNIC PAROCHIAL SCHOOLS: DIVERSITY OF ISOLATION? *Rev. in Am. Hist. 1977 5(3): 354-359.* Review article prompted by James W. Sanders's *The Education of an Urban Minority: Catholics in Chicago, 1833-1965* (New York: Oxford U. Pr., 1977).

2325. Dexter, Lorraine Le H. STEPS FROM THE TRINITY CHURCH TO THE POINT: ZABRISKIE MEMORIAL CHURCH OF ST. JOHN. *Newport Hist. 1975 48(4): 329-347.* History of the construction of the (Catholic) Church of St. John the Evangelist, 1883-1934. 7 photos, reproduction, biblio.

2326. Duchschere, Kevin A. JOHN SHANLEY: NORTH DAKOTA'S FIRST CATHOLIC BISHOP. *North Dakota Hist. 1979 46(2): 4-13.* John Shanley, a New York-born priest of Irish descent, became the first Catholic bishop of North Dakota in January 1890, for Jamestown, North Dakota. His earlier clerical career had been mainly spent in St. Paul, Minnesota, where he championed the cause of his black and Italian parishioners and exhibited a pronounced Irish ethnicity and affinity for other ethnics. Throughout his career, Bishop Shanley was an ardent advocate of temperance. In North Dakota the bishop proved to be an indefatigable worker in uniting his far-flung coreligionists through the erection of a network of churches and schools. He displayed considerable sympathy for Indians. He was instrumental in bringing an end to North Dakota's law allowing a 90-day residency for people seeking divorce.
N. Lederer

2327. Dwyer, Robert J. CATHOLIC EDUCATION IN UTAH: 1875-1975. *Utah Hist. Q. 1975 43(4): 362-378.* The Bishops of Utah Territory, Father Lawrence Scanlan, the Most Reverends Joseph Sarsfield Glass, John J. Mitty, and James E. Kearney, Monsignor Duane G. Hunt, and the Most Reverend Joseph Lennox Federal encouraged the development of Catholic education. Noteworthy schools were Saint Mary's Academy (later Saint Mary-of-the-Wasatch College and Academy for Women), All Hallows College, Judge Memorial High School, and Saint Joseph's High School. A century of educational effort by a religious minority is a tribute to the Catholic Church. Based on primary and secondary sources; 5 illus.   J. L. Hazelton

2328. Edward, C. ELIZABETH ANN SETON: MOTHER, FOUNDER, SAINT. *Am. Hist. Illus. 1975 10(8): 12-21.* Describes the life of Elizabeth Ann Seton (1774-1821), founder of The White House, the first Catholic parochial school in the United States.

2329. Ellis, John Tracy. AUSTRALIAN CATHOLICISM: AN AMERICAN PERSPECTIVE. *J. of Religious Hist. [Australia] 1979 10(3): 313-321.* Review article prompted by Patrick O'Farrell's *The Catholic Church and Community in Australia: A History* (West Melbourne: Thomas Nelson, 1977). The strengths of the work—thorough research, lucid writing, mature interpretations—recommend it to the professional community. The development of Catholicism in Australia is similar in many respects to the development of Catholicism in the United States. In both cases, the Church emerged from direct contact with English Catholicism. Comparisons, such as the rather slow development of a Catholic intellectual community, are developed with frequent reference to the social and economic origins of Catholic immigrants.
W. T. Walker

2330. Faherty, William Barnaby. IN THE FOOTSTEPS OF BISHOP JOSEPH ROSATI. *Italian Americana 1975 1(2): 281-291.* Reviews several works on the life of Bishop Joseph Rosati (1789-1843), focusing on his work for the Catholic Church in the Midwest (including Louisiana) during the first half of the 19th century.   S

2331. Fish, Lydia Marie. ROMAN CATHOLICISM AS FOLK RELIGION IN BUFFALO. *Indiana Folklore 1976 9(2): 165-174.* Folk religion practiced by ethnic groups within the Catholic Church in Buffalo, New York, stems from its import from tradition-oriented rural Europe and basic ignorance of Church tenets.

2332. Fogarty, Gerald P. THE AMERICAN HIERARCHY AND ORIENTAL RITE CATHOLICS, 1890-1907. *Records of the Am. Catholic Hist. Soc. of Philadelphia 1974 85(1-2): 17-28.* Focuses on the role of the American archbishops, who in almost all of their annual meetings from 1890 to 1907 discussed the problem of Oriental rite Catholics coming to this country. They obtained restrictive Church legislation prohibiting retention by these groups of married clergy. 33 notes.
J. M. McCarthy

2333. Fox, Richard W. RELIGION, POLITICS, AND ETHNICITY: TWO REVIEW ESSAYS. *J. of Ethnic Studies 1974 2(2): 76-82.* In his first essay the author commends Harold J. Abramson's *Ethnic Diversity in Catholic America* (1973) for tabulating and crosstabulating a large body of data showing the precise dimensions of ethnic diversity among Catholics. The results show the need to revise the claims of sociologists Will Herberg and Ruby Jo Kennedy on the "triple-meltingpot" theory. Abramson shows that "the structural assimilation of Catholic-American sub-groups has not yet occurred, and shows no signs of doing so in the near future." Also, differences among Catholics in religious involvement are not generational, as assumed to now, but ethnic. In his second essay the author examines the "New Political History" of ethnicity and politics, praising Samuel Hays and his students for uncovering "The *local* basis of political commitment." National leaders, indeed, may run on "issues" which are anything but "real" ones, "real" meaning local, ethnocultural issues. Fox discusses other works relevant to this new approach, which stress that commitment to ethnic institutions may retard political "activity" but not political "identification," and point to the need for more research. 3 notes.   G. J. Bobango

2334. Gavigan, Kathleen. THE RISE AND FALL OF PARISH COHESIVENESS IN PHILADELPHIA. *Records of the Am. Catholic Hist. Soc. of Philadelphia 1975 86(1-4): 107-131.* A special characteristic of the Catholic Church in Philadelphia, Pennsylvania, traditionally has been a strong identification with parish communities. This came about as a response to fear and insecurity, and the separation it provided created both strength and weakness for the Catholic community. Because, for many Catholics, the fears and insecurities have dissipated, the result is more vigorous participation in the community at large. 62 notes.
                                                J. M. McCarthy

2335. Hemmen, Alcuin. THE POST-VATICAN II THRUST OF AMERICAN BENEDICTINES. *Am. Benedictine Rev. 1976 27(4): 379-399.* Review article prompted by *Mönchtum und kirchlicher Heilsdienst, Entstehung und Entwicklung des nordamerikanischen Benediktinertums in 19. Jahrhundert* (1974) by Basil Doppelfeld, who presents and evaluates the history of the founding of St. Vincent Abbey and other abbeys by Abbot Boniface Wimmer and the founding of St. Meinrad Abbey and other abbeys by Benedictine monks from Switzerland. The reviewer concludes on the basis of Doppelfeld's study that American Benedictines must maintain the cenobitical tradition even as they exercise pastoral roles and missionary work in individual congregations. Primary and secondary sources; table, 41 notes.   J. H. Pragman

2336. Hennesey, James. SQUARE PEG IN A ROUND HOLE: ON BEING ROMAN CATHOLIC IN AMERICA. *Records of the Am. Catholic Hist. Soc. of Philadelphia 1973 84(4): 167-195.* Roman Catholicism is the largest single religious group in the United States, claiming over 48 million members in 1972. Against the background of the notion that the United States is a Protestant nation, the article seeks to clarify who Roman Catholics are, where they come from, and whether they do or have ever belonged. 143 notes.   J. M. McCarthy

2337. Hitchcock, James. SECULAR CLERGY IN 19TH CENTURY AMERICA: A DIOCESAN PROFILE. *Records of the Am. Catholic Hist. Soc. of Philadelphia 1977 88(1-4): 31-62.* The history of the St. Louis archdiocesan clergy during 1841-99 provides a model by which comparative studies of other dioceses can be made, with a view to achieving a historical-sociological understanding of the American priesthood during the critical decades of immigration and gradual Americanization. 15 tables, 136 notes.   J. M. McCarthy

2338. Kindermann, A. BÖHMERWALDSOHN UND BISCHOF VON PHILADELPHIA JOHANN NEP. NEUMANN SELIGGESPROCHEN [John Neumann, born in the Bohemian Forest, Bishop of Philadelphia, beatified]. *Sudetenland [West Germany] 1964 6(1): 49-66.* Presents a biography of John Neumann, a Sudeten German, born 28 March 1811 in Prachatitz (now Prachatice, Czechoslovakia), Bohemian Forest. He emigrated to America, joined the order of Redemptorists in 1840 and died 5 January 1860 in Philadelphia, Pennsylvania. Describes his missionary work in America since 1836, posthumous miraculous healings through his intercession, and beatification in March 1963. English summary; illus., 12 notes.   N. Frenkley

2339. Lazerson, Marvin. UNDERSTANDING AMERICAN CATHOLIC EDUCATIONAL HISTORY. *Hist. of Educ. Q. 1977 17(3): 297-317.* The development of the American Catholic parochial school system can be divided into three phases. During the first (1750-1870), parochial schools appeared as ad hoc efforts by parishes, and most Catholic children attended public schools. During the second period (1870-1910), the Catholic hierarhcy made a basic commitment to a sepa-

rate Catholic school system. These parochial schools, like the big-city parishes around them, tended to be ethnically homogeneous; a German child would not be sent to an Irish school, nor vice-versa, nor a Lithuanian pupil to either. Instruction in the language of the old country was common. In the third period (1910-1945), Catholic education was modernized and modelled after the public school systems, and ethnicity was deemphasized in many areas. In cities with large Catholic populations (such as Chicago and Boston) there was a flow of teachers, administrators, and students from one system to the other. 46 notes.
                                                J. C. Billigmeier

2340. Leonard, Henry B. ETHNIC CONFLICT AND EPISCOPAL POWER: THE DIOCESE OF CLEVELAND, 1847-1870. *Catholic Hist. Rev. 1976 62(3): 388-407.* In the Diocese of Cleveland the competing socioreligious desires of immigrant groups were frequently divisive. Louis Amadeus Rappe, Cleveland's first bishop, was a staunch Americanizer and an authoritarian administrator who resisted the demands of German and Irish Catholics for separate parishes and schools served by priests of their own nationality, stirred ethnic antagonisms, and raised a fundamental question concerning the proper limits to episcopal authority. By 1870 the diocese had become so disrupted by the issues of ethnicity and authority that Bishop Rappe was forced to resign his office.   A

2341. Luebke, Frederick C. CHURCH HISTORY FROM THE BOTTOM UP. *Rev. in Am. Hist. 1976 4(1): 68-72.* Review article prompted by Jay P. Dolan's *The Immigrant Church: New York's Irish and German Catholics, 1815-1865* (Baltimore, Maryland: Johns Hopkins U. Pr., 1975) which discusses the social aspects of religious establishment among ethnic groups.

2342. McDonough, Madrienne C. MEMORIES OF A CATHOLIC CONVENT. *Hist. New Hampshire 1978 33(3): 233-245.* In 1902, the author, then six years old, entered the Mount St. Mary Convent school in Manchester for a seven-year stay. Particularly well-remembered was a visit by Bishop Denis M. Bradley, Mass, Benediction, and the Angelus, ghost stories told by an older girl on Sunday evenings, music practice, and morning walks, including walks on special feast days to the old covered bridge over the Merrimack River. Each year of study culminated in Distribution Day, in June, when prizes were awarded with appropriate ceremonies and entertainments. 5 illus., 3 notes.   D. F. Chard

2343. McGreal, Mary Nona. SAMUEL MAZZUCHELLI, PARTICIPANT IN FRONTIER DEMOCRACY. *Records of the Am. Catholic Hist. Soc. of Philadelphia 1976 87(1-4): 99-116.* In his *Memoirs,* Father Samuel Mazzuchelli, a Dominican missionary to the Old Northwest, formulated his views on American democracy, concluding that church and state in the United States are mutually supportive of their respective independence and freedom, that Catholicism is not incompatible with the republican government, that liberty of worship is expedient, and that legal recognition of religious institutions is beneficial. 28 notes.
                                                J. M. McCarthy

2344. McKevitt, Gerald. THE JESUIT ARRIVAL IN CALIFORNIA AND THE FOUNDING OF SANTA CLARA COLLEGE. *Records of the Am. Catholic Hist. Soc. of Philadelphia 1974 85(3-4): 185-197.* Father Michael Accolti, a Jesuit priest, arrived in San Francisco in 1849. By 1851 he had opened Santa Clara College, the first permanent school in American California, the oldest institution of higher education in the state, and the foundation of the Jesuits' educational apostolate in California. 57 notes.   J. M. McCarthy

2345. Melville, Annabelle M. JOHN CARROLL AND LOUISIANA, 1803-1815. *Catholic Hist. Rev. 1978 64(3): 398-440.* Investigates the relations between John Carroll, Bishop of Baltimore, and his flock in Louisiana, which suddenly became an American possession in 1803. Primary sources are few, the issues involved were peripheral, and the various personalities in the new territory were contradictory to the extreme. Essentially, Bishop Carroll was concerned to put religious affairs in Louisiana in order, but the various ethnic and political forces each wanted effective power. Bishop Carroll could do little but issue orders which on the wild frontier were ignored more often than not. Curiously, the eventual settlement of the prime issue of ecclesiastical control did not evolve until the year of Bishop Carroll's death, and history does not reveal whether he lived to know of it. 176 notes.   V. L. Human

2346. Moberg, David O. and McEnery, Jean N. CHANGES IN CHURCH-RELATED BEHAVIOR AND ATTITUDES OF CATHOLIC STUDENTS, 1961-1971. *Sociol. Analysis 1976 37(1): 53-62.* The Marquette Study of Student Values analyzes religious practices, moral values, and attitudes among Catholic college students. From 1961 to 1971 decreasing frequency of student attendance at Mass and Confession together with attitudinal changes toward religious practices are evident. Changes in attitudes about dating, decreased scrupulosity in areas of personal honesty and responsibility, looser attitudes toward selected items of personal morality, and increased consideration for others also were revealed. Most changes may be interpreted as reflecting decreased compliance with traditional Church norms, increased conformity to values of American society, and conflicting values related to both cultural pluralism and pluralism within the Catholic Church.   J

2347. Molson, Francis J. FRANCIS J. FINN., S.J.: PIONEERING AUTHOR OF JUVENILES FOR CATHOLIC AMERICANS. *J. of Popular Culture 1977 11(1): 28-41.* Father Francis J. Finn (1859-1928) was a prolific and the first popular author of novels and short stories for American Catholic youths. Examination of Fr. Finn's works reveals three primary goals in his stories: to show the compatibility of Americanism and Catholicism, to display the good Catholic boy and girl, and to provide moral and religious instruction. To attain these he employed the conventions of juvenile fiction, changing it as need be to meet changes on the American scene. Primary and secondary sources; 13 notes.
D. G. Nielson

2348. Odermann, Valerian J. ABBOT PLACID HOENERBACH AND THE BANKRUPTCY OF ST. MARY'S ABBEY, RICHARDTON. *Am. Benedictine Rev. 1978 29(2): 101-133.* Reviews the history of Benedictine monasticism in North Dakota in the late 19th and early 20th centuries. Analyzes the financial plight of St. Mary's Abbey in Richardton, and the role of Placid Hoenerbach, the abbey's second abbot, in the abbey's bankruptcy. The abbey's plight reflects the agricultural and financial collapse of the 1920's. Primary and secondary sources; 64 notes.
J. H. Pragman

2349. Pfaller, Louis L. FORT KEOGH'S CHAPLAIN IN BUCKSKIN. *Montana 1977 27(1): 14-25.* Eli Washington John Lindesmith served as Catholic Chaplain at Fort Keogh near Miles City, Montana, from 1881 until he retired in 1891. Born in 1827, he became a priest in 1855, serving in Ohio before and after his duty at Fort Keogh. Lindesmith was the only clergyman within a radius of 800 miles for many years and provided religious services for military and non-military residents of the area. Entries in Lindesmith's diary mention ministry to outlaws, prostitutes, soldiers, and prominent settlers like Pierre Wibaux. Lindesmith also built a chapel at Fort Keogh and founded a church in Forsyth. Between his retirement and his death in 1922, he lectured about his experiences, wearing a buckskin suit he acquired in Montana. Based on Lindesmith writings in the Catholic University of America; 9 illus., biblio.
R. C. Myers

2350. Rahill, Peter J. NEW LANGUAGE FOR ST. LOUIS CATHEDRAL. *Missouri Hist. R. 1975 69(4): 449-460.* At St. Louis Cathedral in 1818 Bishop Louis William Du Bourg prescribed that the sermons after Vespers should be in English. The practice was soon discontinued to avoid a conflict between older settlers who favored French, and the rapidly increasing number of American settlers who knew only English. Eventually in 1842 Bishop Richard Kenrick complained that French services decreased attendance and collections. He then had English sermons at all the Sunday Masses and restricted French to the talk following Sunday evening vespers. Based on primary and secondary sources; illus., 18 notes.
W. F. Zornow

2351. Ralph, Raymond M. THE CITY AND THE CHURCH: CATHOLIC BEGINNINGS IN NEWARK, 1840-1870. *New Jersey Hist. 1978 96(3-4): 105-118.* By the mid-19th century, reflecting the presence of Irish and German immigrants, Newark, New Jersey's Catholics constituted one of the city's largest religious groups. The church hierarchy had to contend with tensions between these two groups as parishes were established and churches constructed. Raising sufficient money to operate, confronting hostilities from the Protestant community, and dealing with problems involving the public schools were other concerns. The typical Catholic in Newark during the mid-19th century was

a blue-collar worker who consciously retained his national characteristics. Based on the archives of the Archdiocese of Newark, church records, and directories and secondary sources; 9 illus., 32 notes.
E. R. McKinstry

2352. Real, Michael R. TRENDS IN STRUCTURE AND POLICY IN THE AMERICAN CATHOLIC PRESS. *Journalism Q. 1975 52(2): 265-271.* Immigrants started the American Catholic press in the 19th century and by World War II several large chains had developed, largely under the control of various dioceses and supported by saturation subscription plans. The Second Vatican Council brought a new atmosphere of freedom, so that certain Catholic papers became prestigious and editorially independent, and discussed controversial issues. However, Pope Paul VI's reiteration of the Church's rejection of birth control in 1968 marked a reversal of the trend. Based on interviews, a monitoring of Catholic publications, and study of historical data. Based on primary sources; table, 21 notes.
K. J. Puffer

2353. Renggli, M. Beatrice and Voth, M. Agnes, transl. FROM RICKENBACH TO MARYVILLE: AN ACCOUNT OF THE JOURNEY (1874). *Am. Benedictine Rev. 1976 27(3): 247-269.* Translates Mother M. Beatrice Renggli's record of the trip she and four other Benedictine sisters made from Maria Rickenbach Convent in Switzerland to Conception (outside Maryville), Missouri, in 1874. Later, Mother Renggli was the superior of the group of sisters who founded what became Holy Angels Convent in Jonesboro, Arkansas. Based on original and secondary sources; 22 notes.
J. H. Pragman

2354. Rippinger, Joel. SOME HISTORICAL DETERMINANTS OF AMERICAN BENEDICTINE MONASTICISM, 1846-1900. *Am. Benedictine R. 1976 27(1): 63-84.* Investigates significant elements in the development of American Benedictine life. Notes the similarities and the dissimilarities between American and European—specifically German and Swiss—Benedictine life. Stresses the activist character of American life in reshaping the Benedictines' experience in America. Based on primary and secondary sources; 63 notes.
J. H. Pragman

2355. Rusk, Alfred C. THE SECOND VATICAN COUNCIL, 1962-1965, AND BISHOP NEUMANN. *Records of the Am. Catholic Hist. Soc. of Philadelphia 1974 85(3-4): 123-128.* The *Acta* of Vatican Council II in paragraph 50 of the Constitution on the Church refers to the decree of the Congregation of Rites on the heroicity of Bishop John Nepomucene Neumann (1811-60), a decree which clarified the norms for judging heroic virtue in canonization processes. 17 notes.
J. M. McCarthy

2356. Rybolt, John E. KENRICK'S FIRST SEMINARY. *Missouri Hist. Rev. 1977 71(2): 139-155.* St. Mary's of the Barrens was a school for secular and diocesan clergy students until Bishop Joseph Rosati decided to use land obtained from the Antoine Soulard family to build a seminary, Trinity Church, and some rental property. Peter Richard Kenrick, his successor in 1841, later moved the project. Between 1844 and 1848 the seminarians moved from St. Mary's to the city, thereby fulfilling Rosati's and Kenrick's dream to have the school in the city. For some unknown reason the school relocated at Carondelet in 1848 and did not return to St. Louis until 1893. Primary and secondary sources; illus., 56 notes.
W. F. Zornow

2357. Rybolt, John E. MISSOURI IN 1847: THE PASTORAL VISIT OF ARCHBISHOP KENRICK. *Missouri Hist. Soc. Bull. 1979 35(4): 202-209.* Publishes here for the first time a 3 December 1847 letter written by Peter Richard Kenrick, the Archbishop of St. Louis from 1841 to 1895. Kenrick reviewed his work during 1847, much of which required him to travel extensively in the Missouri diocese that was still predominantly a frontier area. This frontier diocese, Kenrick noted, mainly lacked sufficient priests and financial support for implementing the improvements Kenrick prescribed for the diocese. Photo, 44 notes.
H. T. Lovin

2358. Sauer, Walter. UNPUBLISHED VIENNESE LETTERS OF BENEDICTINE MISSIONARIES: BONIFACE WIMMER AND JOHN BEDE POLDING. *Am. Benedictine R. 1975 26(4): 369-380.* Analyzes and publishes four letters relating to the work of Boniface Wimmer in establishing Benedictine monasticism in North America and one letter relating to the work of John Bede Polding, O.S.B., as the first archbishop of Sydney, Australia. The originals (1847-55) are in the archives of the Benedictine Abbey of Our Blessed Mother of Schotten in Vienna. Original and secondary sources; 40 notes.

J. H. Pragman

2359. Schmandt, Raymond H.   THE FRIENDSHIP BETWEEN BISHOP REGIS CANEVIN OF PITTSBURGH AND DR. LAWRENCE FLICK OF PHILADELPHIA.   *Western Pennsylvania Hist. Mag. 1978 61(4): 283-300.* Describes the 40 year relationship between two prominent Pennsylvania Catholics, Bishop Regis Canevin (1853-1927) and Dr. Lawrence Flick (1856-1938).

2360. Schmandt, Raymond H.   SOME FINANCIAL RECORDS OF BISHOP MICHAEL O'CONNOR OF PITTSBURGH.   *Western Pennsylvania Hist. Mag. 1979 62(4): 369-376.* Introduces and reprints correspondence, 1843-49, between Mark Anthony Frenaye, financial advisor to Catholic clerics, and Michael O'Connor, first bishop of Pittsburgh.

2361. Schmidt, Thomas V.   EARLY CATHOLIC AMERICANA: SOME ADDITIONS TO PARSONS.   *Records of the Am. Catholic Hist. Soc. of Philadelphia 1975 86(1-4): 24-32.* This checklist of early Catholic titles is made up of copies located at Catholic University which were not reported in Wilfrid Parsons' *Early Catholic Americana.* The list is particularly strong in titles dealing with the Hogan Schism in Philadelphia. 3 notes, biblio.

J. M. McCarthy

2362. Schnell, R. L. and Rooke, Patricia T.   INTELLECTUALISM, EDUCATIONAL ACHIEVEMENT, AND AMERICAN CATHOLICISM: A RECONSIDERATION OF A CONTROVERSY, 1955-1975.   *Can. Rev. of Am. Studies [Canada] 1977 8(1): 66-76.* Reviews controversies since 1955 among American Catholics about the causes for lesser scholastic achievements and upward social mobility of Catholics in American intellectual affairs. Clearly, American Catholics have, since the 1960's, increasingly succeeded academically and professionally. However, Catholic educational institutions have not progressed comparably toward excellence. Based on materials published by participants in the debates and secondary sources; 24 notes.

H. T. Lovin

2363. Shaw, Richard.   JAMES GORDON BENNETT: IMPROBABLE HERALD OF THE KINGDOM.   *Records of the Am. Catholic Hist. Soc. of Philadelphia 1977 88(1-4): 88-100.* From 1835 until after the Civil War, James Gordon Bennett's *New York Herald* far outstripped its rivals in circulation and influence. A Roman Catholic who bore some ill-will to the Church, Bennett was a valuable asset to the cause of immigrant Catholicism by reason of his independent stance and honest criticism of the Church. He gave Catholicism a strong secular voice and his independence refuted nativist slurs. 49 notes.

J. M. McCarthy

2364. Sihelvik, LaVerne.   DIAMOND JUBILEE OF THE VINCENTIAN SISTERS OF CHARITY.   *Jednota Ann. Furdek 1978 17: 197-200.* Established in Pittsburgh, Pennsylvania, in 1902 after coming from what is now Czechoslovakia, the Vincentian Sisters of Charity have provided nursing services for the poor, the incurable, and the aged in the United States and Canada.

2365. Stritch, Thomas.   AFTER FORTY YEARS: NOTRE DAME AND *THE REVIEW OF POLITICS.*   *Rev. of Pol. 1978 40(4): 437-446.* Under the leadership of Waldemar Gurian and aided by such colleagues as Father Leo Ward, Frank O'Malley, and M. A. Fitzsimons, *The Review of Politics* was founded 40 years ago at the University of Notre Dame in Indiana. The composition of the editorial staff was a "fusion of the Old World and the New, and a symbol of the Church universal as well as Notre Dame."

L. Ziewacz

2366. Stritch, Thomas J.   THREE CATHOLIC BISHOPS FROM TENNESSEE.   *Tennessee Hist. Q. 1978 37(1): 3-35.* Much of the material about these three Catholic, Irish American bishops is reproduced from the author's memory. The three bishops, John Morris (1866-1946), John P. Farrelly (1856-1921), and Samuel A. Stritch (1887-1958), were all southerners whose lives were intertwined. They were wise, possibly great men who exhibited a tremendous influence on the South. Primary and secondary sources; 2 illus., 70 notes.

M. B. Lucas

2367. Swan, George Steven.   THE OUT-CASTE CATHOLICS: REPULSED FROM THE VERGE OF SUCCESS?   *J. of Intergroup Relations 1975 4(4): 4-20.* Continued underrepresentation of Catholics in intellectual circles and higher education staffs may be due to their unfashionable ethnic backgrounds, and the solution for this and other discrimination may be the formation of a Catholic-based ethnic rights lobby.

S

2368. Thomas, Samuel J.   THE AMERICAN PERIODICAL PRESS AND THE APOSTOLIC LETTER *TESTEM BENEVOLENTIAE.*   *Catholic Hist. Rev. 1976 62(3): 408-423.* American periodicals reacted sharply to Pope Leo XIII's letter *On Americanism* (1899). Catholic and non-Catholic journals noted the division in the American hierarchy and seemed to intensify it by their impassioned reporting. Protestant writers revealed a self-righteous understanding of liberal Catholicism by their assertion that although certain bishops did adhere to the theological Americanism condemned by Leo, such Americanism was perfectly Christian (i.e., Protestant). Collectively, non-Catholic periodicals expressed or implied that the letter not only confirmed Leo's ultramontanism and the reintrenchment of the conservative bishops, but also would hinder the process of getting Catholicism accepted into the mainstream of American life.

A

2369. Vogeler, Ingolf.   THE ROMAN CATHOLIC CULTURE REGION OF CENTRAL MINNESOTA.   *Pioneer Am. 1976 8(2): 71-83.* Selects for a geographical study of religion, the Roman Catholic Diocese of St. Cloud, Minnesota, which represents the largest percentage of Catholics, by diocese and archdiocese, in Minnesota and the second largest in the Midwest. Three major themes—the genesis and geographical distribution of religions, the spatial organization of religions, and the landscape expression of religious groups—were utilized in analyzing the subject area. Microanalysis of other Catholic regions in North America could verify or modify the findings of this study. Based on handbooks preserved in the Immigrant Archives, University of Minnesota, Minneapolis, personal interviews, field work, and secondary sources; 7 maps, 5 photos, 25 notes.

C. R. Gunter, Jr.

2370. Walch, Timothy.   CATHOLIC EDUCATION IN CHICAGO: THE FORMATIVE YEARS, 1840-1890.   *Chicago Hist. 1978 7(2): 87-97.* Unable to secure state tax funds for parochial education, Chicago's Catholic community sustained itself on donations and fund raising, an enterprise led by Father Arnold Damen, 1840-90.

2371. Walsh, James P.   A NON-IRISH CATHOLIC AND THE INTELLECTUAL LIFE: MSGR. CHARLES A. RAMM.   *Southern California Q. 1973 55(1): 49-58.* Sketches the biography of Msgr. Charles A. Ramm (1863-1951), who devoted his career to brotherhood and public service. He was born in California to German immigrants and attended the University of California, graduating with honors. He converted from Lutheranism, was ordained in 1892, and served 21 years on the State Board of Charities and 32 years on the Board of Regents. In Catholic intellectual life Ramm served by quiet example rather than active advocacy, a tactic made necessary by the dominance of Irish Americans in the American Catholic hierarchy. Based on unpublished sources and secondary works; photos, 50 notes.

A. Hoffman

2372. Wangler, Thomas E.   A BIBLIOGRAPHY OF THE WRITINGS OF ARCHBISHOP JOHN J. KEANE.   *Records of the Am. Catholic Hist. Soc. of Philadelphia 1978 89(1-4): 60-73.* Lists almost all of the surviving articles, pastorals, sermons, discourses, books, and important administrative documents written or spoken by Keane, to be used in conjunction with Patrick Ahern's *The Life of John J. Keane: Educator and Archbishop, 1838-1918* (Bruce, 1955).

J. M. McCarthy

2373. Weber, Francis J.   CATHOLICISM AMONG THE MORMONS, 1875-79.   *Utah Hist. Q. 1976 44(2): 141-148.* In 1873, Father Laurence Scanlan (1843-1915) became pastor of Salt Lake parish and the anchor-chain of Catholicism in Utah. He found 800 Catholics in the territory, 100 in the Salt Lake area. His letters to the Società de la Propagation de la Foi for financial assistance are historically pivotal, revealing both his own personality and the complex status of the nascent Catholic community in Mormon territory. Two letters reproduced here are dated 16 November 1875 and 31 October 1879. Primary and secondary sources; illus., 3 notes.

J. L. Hazelton

2374. —. A HISTORY OF BENEDICTINE HIGH SCHOOL. *Jednota Ann. Furdek 1978 17: 165-176.* Benedictine High School has educated boys in Cleveland, Ohio, since 1928.

Evangelical and Reformed

2375. Beal, William C., Jr. THE PLANTING OF THE EVANGELICAL ASSOCIATION IN WESTERN PENNSYLVANIA, 1800-1833. *Methodist Hist. 1978 16(4): 218-229.* The planting of the Evangelical Association in western Pennsylvania occurred in waves during the first, second, and fourth decades of the 19th century. The Association started with a single class and regular preaching appointments under Jacob Albright and John Walter. Under John Dreisbach the work of the Association began to accelerate in 1813 until it had expanded throughout western Pennsylvania in 1833. 2 photos, 13 notes.   H. L. Calkin

2376. Gorrell, Donald K. OHIO ORIGINS OF THE UNITED BRETHREN IN CHRIST AND THE EVANGELICAL ASSOCIATION. *Methodist Hist. 1977 15(2): 95-106.* During 1806-39, the United Brethren in Christ and the Evangelical Association evolved in Ohio from simple and informal origins to well developed and expanding denominations. Both became identifiable as German-speaking religious groups. Recruitment of itinerant preachers was a constant problem. Other problems were the need for more financial support to build churches, inability to move into the cities, and competition by both groups in the same areas of Ohio. 31 notes.   H. L. Calkin

2377. Hood, Fred J. THE AMERICAN REFORMED TRADITION IN AFRICAN COLONIZATION AND MISSIONS. *J. of Church and State 1977 19(3): 539-555.* The interest in African missions came about in the reformed churches (Congregational, Presbyterian, and Dutch and German Reformed) through their concern over a growing free black population in America. Reviews the sources for this concern and then discusses the influence of the "millennial vision" on this concern. Discusses how they approached the practical implementation of this concern through the form of mission societies, the sending of missionaries, and their relation to the colonization society. 55 notes.   E. E. Eminhizer

2378. Spotts, Charles D. BRICKERVILLE OLD ZION REFORMED CHURCH. *J. of the Lancaster County Hist. Soc. 1973 77(2): 61-87.*

2379. Stein, K. James. WITH PARALLEL STEPS: THE EVANGELICAL BRETHREN AND THE AMERICAN SCENE. *Methodist Hist. 1974 12(3): 16-39.* The Evangelical United Brethren Church was a definite part of the American scene with which it interacted. This relationship was shaped by theological factors—German pietism, Arminianism and evangelical revivalism—and non-theological factors—the frontier and rural ethos of the denomination, the ethnological character of the church, the lower class stratification from which it drew members, and its small size. Specific areas of interaction were slavery, war and peace, capital and labor, and church-and-state relations. 68 notes.   H. L. Calkin

2380. Warman, John B. FRANCIS ASBURY AND JACOB ALBRIGHT. *Methodist Hist. 1978 16(2): 75-81.* Compares Francis Asbury (1745-1816), Bishop of the Methodist Episcopal Church, and Jacob Albright (1759-1808), founder of the Evangelical Association, and their work in the early years of their respective churches in America. 8 notes.   H. L. Calkin

2381. Yrigoyen, Charles, Jr. EMANUEL V. GERHARDT: CHURCHMAN, THEOLOGIAN, AND FIRST PRESIDENT OF FRANKLIN AND MARSHALL COLLEGE. *J. of the Lancaster County Hist. Soc. 1974 78(1): 1-28.* Biography of German Reformed Church clergyman Emanuel V. Gerhardt (1817-1904), touching on his career as a minister and missionary and his writings on theological and philosophical subjects, and finally, his 36 years as professor and President at Franklin and Marshall College in Lancaster, Pennsylvania. 2 photos, 127 notes.

Lutheran

2382. Baur, John C. FOR CHRIST AND HIS KINGDOM, 1923. *Concordia Hist. Inst. Q. 1977 50(3): 99-105.* Confronted by overcrowded and obsolete facilities at Jefferson Avenue and Miami Street, St. Louis, the leadership of the Concordia Seminary launched a major fund raising project in 1923 to erect a new seminary in Clayton, Missouri. A synodical committee, which consisted of Dr. John H. C. Fritz, Theodore Eckhardt, and Dr. John C. Baur, confronted numerous and complex difficulties in raising the necessary funds during the 1920's. This memoir records the success of the committee in overcoming those problems. Dedication of the new campus occurred in 1926. Based on personal recollections.
W. T. Walker

2383. Buettner, George L. CONCORDIA PUBLISHING HOUSE AS I KNEW IT (1888-1955). *Concordia Hist. Inst. Q. 1974 47(2): 62-69.* Discusses his experiences as part of the Concordia Publishing House (1888-1955) in St. Louis, Missouri.   S

2384. Dallmann, Roger Howard. SPRINGFIELD SEMINARY. *Concordia Hist. Inst. Q. 1977 50(3): 106-130.* During the mid-19th century the spiritual needs of German Lutherans in the Midwest were not being tended. As a result of the efforts of such missionaries as Friedrich Wynecken, Wilhelm Loehe, and Wilhelm Sihler, this situation was remedied by the deployment of additional Lutheran ministers, the opening of Lutheran schools, and the creation in Ft. Wayne of the Concordia Seminary in 1846. The Seminary moved to St. Louis, Missouri, in 1861, and its practical division moved to Springfield, Illinois, in 1874. Through this seminary, during the last half of the 19th century and the first half of the 20th, the Lutheran Church (Missouri Synod) succeeded in serving the spiritual needs of midwestern congregations by establishing additional seminaries, and by developing a viable synodical tradition. Primary sources; 99 notes.   W. T. Walker

2385. Delaney, E. Theo. EPHPHATHA CONFERENCE: A HISTORICAL OVERVIEW. *Concordia Hist. Inst. Q. 1977 50(2): 71-83.* Traces the history of the Ephphatha Conference, a vehicle of Lutheran missionary activity directed toward the deaf during the 1890's-1976. Examines the roles of prominent contributors such as H. A. Bentrup, Augustus H. Reinke, and Enno A. Duemling as well as the relationships that developed between the Conference and other Lutheran institutions. Primary sources; 23 notes.   W. T. Walker

2386. Elbert, Gotthold, transl. THE TRAIN ACCIDENT. *Concordia Hist. Inst. Q. 1975 48(2): 51-57.* Translates an article published in *Bericht ueber das deutsche Ev. Luth. Waisenhaus zu Addison, IL. Fuer das Jahr 1890-'91.* Describes a train accident in Chicago, Illinois which resulted in the deaths of six young people and the serious injury of 15 others who were going to an Orphan Festival of the Lutheran Church. A brief account of each of the deceased is provided, with comments on their funerals; the seriously injured are also listed.   W. T. Walker

2387. Erickson, Gary Lee. LINCOLN'S CIVIL RELIGION AND THE LUTHERAN HERITAGE. *Lincoln Herald 1973 75(4): 158-171.* In 1862 various social resolutions concerning the nation were adopted by the General Synod Convention of the Evangelical Lutheran Church, held in Lancaster, Pennsylvania. They were presented to President Lincoln on 13 May 1862. Discusses the background of the social resolutions, the resolutions themselves, and Lincoln's response. Lincoln believed it mandatory to have dialogue with theologians; he cordially received church representatives. Based on the Minutes of the General Synod Convention, 6 May 1864, Baser's *Collected Works of Abraham Lincoln,* and secondary sources; 72 notes.   A. C. Aimone

2388. Feucht, Oscar E. ST. PAUL'S LUTHERAN CHURCH, WARTBURG, TENNESSEE. *Concordia Hist. Inst. Q. 1975 48(3): 67-86.* The history of St. Paul's Lutheran Church in Wartburg, Tennessee, dates from 1844 when George F. Gerding founded the town and donated land for the church. The church has steadily developed from the pastorates of John F. Wilkes, John L. Hirschmann, Carl A. Bruegemann, Otto Carl Praetorius, and others. The mission churches which developed out of St. Paul's were located in Deermont, Deer Lodge, and Oakdale, Tennessee. 27 photos, biblio.   W. T. Walker

2389. Gockel, Herman W. AUTOBIOGRAPHY FOR MY GRANDCHILDREN. *Concordia Hist. Inst. Q.* 1978 51(1): 9-22. The author recalls his varied experiences in the service of the Lutheran Church (Missouri Synod) from the 1920's to his retirement in 1971. The author was pastor, editor, writer, and television producer of *This Is The Life.*   W. T. Walker

2390. Grimm, A. Ira. SYNODICAL LOYALTY 1910 STYLE. *Concordia Hist. Inst. Q.* 1975 48(3): 99-109. Translates a paper presented in German by the Rev. A. Grimm at some time between 1905 and 1917. The paper was translated and introduced by Grimm's son, A. Ira Grimm. In the paper, Rev. Grimm attempted to point out the advantages of synodical membership (Lutheran Church, Missouri Synod). Grimm attempted to correct the images or ideas of the synod which he thought had developed in the minds of many people.   W. T. Walker

2391. Hahn, Stephen S. LEXINGTON'S THEOLOGICAL LIBRARY, 1832-1859. *South Carolina Hist. Mag.* 1979 80(1): 36-49. Chronicles the growth of the Lutheran Theological Seminary Library of Lexington, South Carolina, 1832-59.

2392. Hamre, James S. JOHN O. EVJEN: TEACHER, THEOLOGIAN, BIOGRAPHER. *Concordia Hist. Inst. Q.* 1974 47(2): 52-61. Discusses the achievements of John O. Evjen, Lutheran theologian in Minnesota (1874-1942).   S

2393. Hansel, William H. 50 YEARS IN THE MINISTRY. *Concordia Hist. Inst. Q.* 1975 48(1): 4-9. A brief survey of the author's ministry in the Lutheran Church. Centered in Colorado, Nebraska, and Oklahoma, the author's ministry was involved with the establishment of churches and schools related to the Lutheran Church (Missouri Synod). The German language was a barrier between the Lutheran Church and other denominations in this area.   W. T. Walker

2394. Helmreich, Ernst C., ed. and trans. LETTERS OF PASTOR CHRISTIAN HELMREICH: ESTABLISHING A LUTHERAN CONGREGATION IN WEYERTS, NEBRASKA, 1887-1888. *Nebraska Hist.* 1977 58(2): 175-192. Reprints two letters written by Helmreich during 1887-88. They were to his parents in Bavaria about his ordination, and his journey from Illinois to Nebraska where he was called to establish a congregation.   R. Lowitt

2395. Holt, Benjamin M. AND SO THEY GAVE ME A 36-INCH BIRTHDAY CARD: A REMEMBRANCE OF 90 EVENTFUL YEARS. *Concordia Hist. Inst. Q.* 1974 47(1): 24-38. Discusses Benjamin M. Holt's activities, especially in the Lutheran Church in Minnesota, 1882-1974.   S

2396. Knudsen, Johannes. ONE HUNDRED YEARS LATER— THE GRUNDTVIGIAN HERITAGE. *Lutheran Q.* 1973 25(1): 71-77. Nikolai Frederik Severin Grundtvig (1783-1872) revitalized the corporate body of the Lutheran Church and healed the dichotomy between religious and secular life.   S

2397. Kramer, William A. WHY CONCORDIA HISTORICAL INSTITUTE? *Concordia Hist. Inst. Q.* 1978 51(2): 70-75. The Concordia Historical Institute is a depository of Lutheran history in the United States (with a special emphasis on the Missouri Synod) and provides resources in order to encourage and stimulate Christian, especially Lutheran, values and ideas.   W. T. Walker

2398. Kuhnle, Howard A. THE WORK OF THE CHURCH NECROLOGIST. *Concordia Hist. Inst. Q.* 1973 46(4): 158-163.

2399. Lee, Knute. ESTABLISHING LUTHERAN COLLEGES IN THE UNITED STATES. *Concordia Hist. Inst. Q.* 1973 46(1): 18-27. Reviews the history of church-related institutions in the United States and focuses on the history of Valparaiso University. Based on manuscript and secondary sources; 3 photos, table, 19 notes.   B. W. Henry

2400. Lemke, Lloyd H. THE HISTORICAL BACKGROUND OF J. P. KOEHLER'S "GESETZLICH WESEN UNTER UNS." *Concordia Hist. Inst. Q.* 1976 49(4): 172-177. Koehler's "Gesetzlich Wesen Unter Uns" first appeared in the *Wisconsin Lutheran Quarterly* during

October 1914 and July 1915. The series was motivated by the doctrinal strife which had characterized the Lutheran synods since the election controversy of the 1880's. Primary sources; 7 notes.   W. T. Walker

2401. Meyer, Carl S. A VIEW OF THE LUTHERAN CHURCH— MISSOURI SYNOD: 1866. *Concordia Hist. Inst. Q.* 1974 47(3): 99-102. Reprints a letter to the editor from an 1866 edition of the *Evangelische Kirchen-Zeitung,* a German-based Lutheran Church newsletter, from W. Fister, describing the Missouri Synod.   S

2402. Miller, H. Earl. THE OLD SEM AND THE NEW. *Concordia Hist. Inst. Q.* 1976 49(2): 52-63. A comparison of student lifestyles in the old and new Lutheran seminaries in St. Louis. The author took six years to complete a three year course of studies and came to know numerous members of the faculty and a significant number of students. Includes brief biographical sketches of faculty members.   W. T. Walker

2403. Mueller, Peter Dietrich. KANSAS VICARAGE. *Concordia Hist. Inst. Q.* 1976 49(2): 72-87. An excerpt from Peter Mueller's *Lebensgeschichte* which was written "after 1930" on the development of Concordia Seminary in Missouri as well as Mueller's student career. Recounts the problems of student life, the memorable teachers and friendships which were developed, and his experiences during his first vicarage at Clay Center, Kansas.   W. T. Walker

2404. Norlin, Dennis A. THE RESPONSE IN RELIGIOUS JOURNALS TO SAMUEL SCHMUCKER'S FRATERNAL APPEAL. *Lutheran Q.* 1973 25(1): 78-90. Discusses response to an article by Samuel Simon Schmucker in 1838 on Christian unity.   S

2405. Rehmer, Rudolph F. OLD DUTCH CHURCH. *Concordia Hist. Inst. Q.* 1976 49(3): 98-111. Discusses the establishment of the Old Dutch Church on the outskirts of Elletsville, Indiana. Examines the building of this Lutheran church, the earliest church constitution, and the church's early development. The constitution described procedures, doctrinal views, and other church matters. Covers 1830-1956. Primary sources; 16 notes.   W. T. Walker

2406. Rehmer, R. F., ed. SHEEP WITHOUT SHEPHERDS: LETTERS OF TWO LUTHERAN TRAVELING MISSIONARIES, 1835-1837. *Indiana Mag. of Hist.* 1975 71(1): 21-84. As missionaries for two Pennsylvania-based Lutheran bodies, John Christian Frederick Heyer and Ezra Keller each conducted six-month tours of the states of Illinois, Indiana, and Missouri during the 1830's. These 12 letters, together with the editor's introductory essay, reveal a church suffering from cultural, social, and geographical isolation, a serious shortage of trained ministers, synodical differences between "confessional" and "American" Lutheran bodies, and the suspicions of nativists who viewed "foreign" churches with distrust. Despite these and other hardships, Heyer and Keller succeeded in laying the groundwork for the future growth of Lutheranism in these states. Primary and secondary sources; 94 notes.   K. F. Svengalis

2407. Reith, Ferdinand. A SWEDISH PASTOR AMONG GERMANS: NIELS ALBERT WIHLBORG, 1848-1928. *Concordia Hist. Inst. Q.* 1978 51(4): 168-178. This account of the career of Niels Albert Wihlborg was originally written by his daughter, Ingrid Schroeder; it has been rewritten by Ferdinand Reith, his grandson. Wihlborg was a successful representative of the Lutheran Church (Missouri Synod); he was assigned to Lutheran churches in Minnesota and Missouri during 1893-1918. Previously Wihlborg held a variety of positions including teacher and shopkeeper. Based on personal recollections.   W. T. Walker

2408. Repp, Arthur C. A STUDY OF THE AUTHORSHIP OF SCHWAN'S CATECHISM. *Concordia Hist. Inst. Q.* 1973 46(3): 106-111. Surveys the editorship and contributions of others (1893-1912) to Henry C. Schwan's exposition of Luther's Small Catechism.   S

2409. Scharlemann, E. K. and Scharlemann, M. H. [AN INTERVIEW WITH ERNST SCHARLEMANN]. A "HOSPITANT" TO THE SEMINARY. *Concordia Hist. Inst. Q.* 1976 49(1): 23-28. Transcript of a taped interview of Ernst K.

Scharlemann, a retired Lutheran pastor, by his son, Martin H. Scharlemann. E. K. Scharlemann arrived in St. Louis during the first decade of this century and attended Concordia Seminary as a "hospitant," one who attended classes but did not write examinations. He later changed his status and graduated in 1909. A FOREIGNER GOES NATIVE. *Concordia Hist. Inst. Q. 1976 49(2): 64-71.* E. K. Scharlemann reflects upon his pastorate in Hahlen, Illinois from 1909-18. This period witnessed the development of St. Peter's Lutheran Church under his direction and the further extension of Lutheran influence in the Hahlen-Nashville, Illinois area.
W. T. Walker

2410. Schiotz, Fredrik A. OBSERVATIONS ON PARTS OF DR. NELSON'S LUTHERANISM IN NORTH AMERICA, 1914-1970. *Lutheran Q. 1977 29(2): 150-166.* Comments on the parts of E. Clifford Nelson's *Lutheranism in North America, 1914-1970* that deal with efforts toward Lutheran unification in America during 1950-70. Schiotz, who represented the American Lutheran Church (ALC) in its conversations with other Lutheran bodies, believes that Nelson's subjective treatment of the topic has brought about an erroneous, sinister view of his church's work toward unification. Although the work is both useful and important, its failure to credit the ALC with honest purpose, and its obvious prejudices against that body, mean that the story of Lutheran unification in the two decades needs to be considered in greater perspective. 2 notes.
J. A. Kicklighter

2411. Schlegel, Ronald J. "DADDY" HERZBERGER'S LEGACY. *Concordia Hist. Inst. Q. 1974 47(3): 139-143.* The work of Pastor F. W. Herzberger, missionary to St. Louis, Missouri, for the Lutheran Church.
S

2412. Schmidt, George P. CONCORDIA-FORT WAYNE IN THE TWENTIETH CENTURY. *Concordia Hist. Inst. Q. 1974 47(3): 103-109.* Author's reminiscences of the first years of the 20th century at Concordia (Junior) College.
S

2413. Scholz, Robert F. WAS MUHLENBERG A PIETIST? *Concordia Hist. Inst. Q. 1979 52(2): 50-65.* Denies that Lutheran minister Henry Melchior Muhlenberg, who preached in colonial Pennsylvania during the mid-18th century, was a pietist.

2414. Schreiber, Clara Seuel. MISSION FESTIVAL IN FREISTADT. *Concordia Hist. Inst. Q. 1977 50(4): 148-151.* At the turn of the 20th century, Mission Festival Sunday was the occasion of a major celebration in Freistadt, Wisconsin. The entire town became involved in the necessary preparations which centered on the arrival of Lutheran missionaries. Based on personal recollections.
W. T. Walker

2415. Schreiber, Clara Seuel. PALM SUNDAY IN FREISTADT, 1898. *Concordia Hist. Inst. Q. 1977 50(1): 32-36.* Reminisces about a Lutheran observation of Palm Sunday in Freistadt, Wisconsin, in 1898. 3 photos.
W. T. Walker

2416. Schulze, Eldor P. E. C. L. SCHULZE AND H. C. STEUP. *Concordia Hist. Inst. Q. 1973 46(1): 28-34.* Presents brief biographies of his two grandfathers, Pastors Ernst Carl Ludwig Schulze (1854-1918) and Henry Christian Steup (1852-1931?). Illus., 2 photos.
B. W. Henry

2417. Smith, John Abernathy. THE SCHMUCKER MYTH AND THE EVANGELICAL ALLIANCE. *Concordia Hist. Inst. Q. 1974 47(1): 7-23.* Argues that Samuel Simon Schmucker, leader of the American party in the Lutheran General Synod, was himself largely responsible for the myth that he instigated the Evangelical Alliance during the latter half of the 19th century.
S

2418. Steege, Martin. CHRONICLE OF A MINISTER. *Concordia Hist. Inst. Q. 1976 49(1): 4-22.* An autobiographical review of a career in the Lutheran ministry from induction in the Concordia Collegiate Institute in 1921 to retirement in 1973. Steege's career included pastorates in Trenton and East Rutherford, New Jersey, and Brooklyn, New York. These pastorates witnessed building programs and expansion of Lutheran educational programs.
W. T. Walker

2419. Suelflow, August R. MICROFILM AND PHOTODUPLICATION. *Concordia Hist. Inst. Q. 1974 47(3): 131-136.* A report to the Lutheran Laymen's League on the microfilm activities of Concordia Historical Institute, 1973.
S

2420. Suelflow, August R. MICROFILM AND PHOTODUPLICATION: A REPORT TO THE LUTHERAN LAYMEN'S LEAGUE ON THE MICROFILM ACTIVITIES OF THE CONCORDIA HISTORICAL INSTITUTE FOR 1971. *Concordia Hist. Inst. Q. 1973 46(1): 35-39.* Discusses research uses of microfilm and prospects for the future, and lists acquisitions between 1 October 1970 and 30 September 1971.
B. W. Henry

2421. Svengalis, Kendall F. THEOLOGICAL CONTROVERSY AMONG INDIANA LUTHERANS 1835-1870. *Concordia Hist. Inst. Q. 1973 46(2): 70-90.* Analyzes religious and political viewpoints. S

2422. Thode, Frieda Oehlschlaeger. THE REV. E. L. ARNDT. *Concordia Hist. Inst. Q. 1974 47(2): 90-95.* Chronicles the work of Reverend E. L. Arndt, father of the China mission of the Lutheran Church, 1913-29.
S

2423. Waltmann, Henry G. THE STRUGGLE TO ESTABLISH LUTHERANISM IN TIPPECANOE COUNTY, INDIANA, 1826-1850. *Indiana Mag. of Hist. 1979 75(1): 28-52.* Lutheranism scored striking successes in Tippecanoe County between 1826 and 1850. The initial growth of Lutheranism was inhibited by a small German immigrant population, the existence of previously established denominations, and a shortage of clergymen. The latter development was affected by interdenominational disharmony, because four separate schools of Lutheranism were established in Tippecanoe County. 72 notes.
J. Moore

2424. Wartluft, David J. THE PASTOR AS HISTORIAN. *Concordia Hist. Inst. Q. 1978 51(2): 76-78.* The Lutheran Church pastor can and should be viewed as a historian in three ways. First, the pastor must record and maintain the daily business of his congregation; in this way, he accumulates primary source material. Second, the pastor's own sense of history has an important bearing on how he leads his congregation. Finally, a pastor should preserve materials about himself so that others who follow him will have an opportunity to understand his conception of history.
W. T. Walker

2425. Wolf, Edward C. AMERICA'S FIRST LUTHERAN CHORALE BOOK. *Concordia Hist. Inst. Q. 1973 46(1): 5-17.* Lutheran German immigrants were troubled by the absence of a standard hymnal with four-part harmonies for each hymn text. Pastor Justus Henry Christian Helmuth (1745-1825) of Philadelphia strongly supported the publication in 1786 of *Erbauliche Lieder-Sammlung,* a standardized book of hymn texts. Helmuth, with the aid and support of his congregation, produced in 1813 the complementary *Choral-Buch fuer die Erbauliche Lieder-Sammlung der deutschen Evangelisch-Lutherischen Gemeinden in Nord Amerika,* containing 266 different tunes and an index relating each hymn text of the *Erbauliche Lieder-Sammlung* to an appropriate tune. Based on primary and secondary sources; 12 notes.
B. W. Henry

2426. Wulff, O. H. AUTOBIOGRAPHY. *Concordia Hist. Inst. Q. 1975 48(3): 87-98.* An account of O. H. Wulff's career as a professional Lutheran educator. The chronicle starts in Glenview, Illinois, where Wulff was born, moves on to Concordia-River Forest College, and then on to Bristol, Connecticut, where Wulff became an instructor, and later principal of the Immanuel Lutheran School.
W. T. Walker

2427. Wyneken, Frederick G. and Wyneken, Chet A., transl. CONCISE HISTORY OF EMANUEL LUTHERAN CONGREGATION, CORONA, QUEENS BOROUGH, NEW YORK, 1887-1907. *Concordia Hist. Inst. Q. 1978 51(2): 62-69.* Translation of a church history written in 1967 by Pastor Frederick G. Wyneken in German. Emanuel Lutheran Church was established in 1887 and within 20 years a new facility was in operation. During that 20-year period the church witnessed both triumph and setbacks. Sees divine intervention and guidance in the developing years of the congregation.
W. T. Walker

2428. —. ACADEMIC FREEDOM AND TENURE: CON-CORDIA SEMINARY. *AAUP Bull. 1975 61(1): 49-59.*

2429. Unsigned. ERNST LUDWIG HERMANN KUEHN: FRAN-CONIAN PIONEER. *Concordia Hist. Inst. Q. 1974 47(3): 123-130.* Describes the missionary work of German-born Kuehn and his immigra-tion in 1850 to the United States where he settled in Michigan and became a minister of the Lutheran Church.   S

2430. —. GROWING IN THE LORD: 75 YEARS OF LU-THERAN SECONDARY EDUCATION IN MILWAUKEE. *Concordia Hist. Inst. Q. 1978 51(1): 3-8.* From its founding in 1903, the Immanuel Lutheran School had the support of Lutherans in Milwaukee. Established through the efforts of Pastors J. F. G. Harders and Otto Hagedorn who were assisted by Emil Sampe, the Immanuel Lutheran School was the first Lutheran high school in Milwaukee. During the 75 years since its founding the school has grown from 18 to more than 1,000 students. This article is a committee report.   W. T. Walker

Moravian

2431. Africa, Philip. SLAVEHOLDING IN THE SALEM COM-MUNITY, 1771-1851. *North Carolina Hist. Rev. 1977 54(3): 271-307.* Between the founding of Salem in 1771 as a congregation town and the outbreak of Civil War, Moravians altered their attitudes toward slave-holding. The communal sense of *gemeinschaft* slowly changed during the 19th century to a more business-like attitude of *gesellschaft*. Moravians came to regard slaves not as persons but as property. Secular pressures eroded opposition to slavery on religious and moral grounds, and by the 1850's slaves were used in a variety of pursuits. Based on papers in the Moravian Archives and on published primary sources; 8 illus., map, 101 notes.   T. L. Savitt

2432. Bolhouse, G. E. THE MORAVIAN CHURCH IN NEW-PORT. *Newport Hist. 1979 52(1): 10-16.* History of the Moravian Church in Newport, Rhode Island, 1767-1835; mentions church artifacts now in the Newport Historical Society.

2433. Gilbert, Daniel R. BETHLEHEM AND THE AMERICAN REVOLUTION. *Tr. of the Moravian Hist. Soc. 1977 23(1): 17-40.* The Moravians in Bethlehem, Pennsylvania, rendered considerable voluntary and semicoerced support to the American Revolution through the provi-sion of foodstuffs and supplies to the armies, prisoners of war, and the wounded, shelter to troops, and the extension of high quality medical services. Some damage to the town resulted from undisciplined troops, especially in the militia, although the community was never the scene of actual fighting. The prewar isolation of the town was only temporarily affected by the war. Following the shifting of combat to the South, Bethlehem rapidly returned to its prewar state, with the Moravian leaders reestablishing "rigid community control of thought and behavior." Pri-mary and secondary sources.   N. Lederer

2434. Goodwin, Grethe. MORAVIANS IN MAINE: 1762-1770. *New England Q. 1979 52(2): 250-258.* Sketches the history of the Moravian mission at Broad Bay (now Waldoboro, Maine) from the ar-rival of pastor Georg Soelle (1709-1773) until the settlers moved to Wa-chovia, North Carolina. The harsh climate, hostile attitude of other German settlers, and especially a lack of leadership led to the communi-ty's failure. Soelle was a good preacher but unable to help to solve the practical problems of the farmers. Based on Soelle's letters in the Moravian Archives, Bethlehem, Pa.; 14 notes.   J. C. Bradford

2435. Jordan, Albert F. SOME EARLY MORAVIAN BUILDERS IN AMERICA. *Pennsylvania Folklife 1974 24(1): 2-18.* Discusses the early architecture of Moravian builders (1740-68) in Bethlehem and Nazareth, Pennsylvania.   S

2436. Lineback, Donald J. JOHANN HEINRICH MULLER: PRINTER, MORAVIAN, REVOLUTIONARY. *Tr. of the Moravian Hist. Soc. 1977 23(1): 61-76.* Born in northern Germany in 1702, Johann Heinrich Muller joined the Moravians on their voyage to America and eventually became a member of the denomination. His contacts with the founder of the Moravian Church, Count Ludwig von Zinzendorf, resulted in Muller's keeping the group's travel journal and later returning to Germany under Moravian auspices to establish a printing press. Zinzen-dorf arranged a marriage between Muller and Johanna Dorothea Blaun-der, a wealthy widow. Muller used his wife's money to create a publication outlet in America. The marriage was an unhappy one, with Muller evidently unwilling to abide by the dictates of the Moravian faith. After various travels to and from Europe, Muller, in 1762, began publish-ing *Heinrich Mullers Pennsylvanischer Staatsbote* in German in Phila-delphia. This newspaper became a leading champion of the American cause and printed the first German edition of the Declaration of Indepen-dence. Primary sources.   N. Lederer

2437. Nelson, Vernon H. LIFE IN EARLY AMERICA: THE MORAVIANS AT BETHLEHEM. *Early Am. Life 1978 9(4): 26-29, 62-63.* Examines the influence of the Moravian religious sect on the establishment, growth, religion, art, and social organization of Bethle-hem, Pennsylvania, 1741-1865.

2438. Surratt, Jerry L. THE ROLE OF DISSENT IN COMMU-NITY EVOLUTION AMONG MORAVIANS IN SALEM, 1772-1860. *North Carolina Hist. R. 1975 52(3): 235-255.* Alterations in the nature of the Salem Moravian theocracy, from *gemeinschaft* to *gesellschaft*, can be traced through the effects of rising dissent on military involvement, relationships between the sexes, and the rise of economic individualism. Salem Brethren were forced, between 1820 and 1850, to permit residents to join the militia, ease the strict rules regarding courting and marriage, abandon the community landholding system, and allow residents to en-gage in the slave trade. Based primarily on manuscript and printed records at the Moravian Archives, as well as on secondary materials; 7 illus., 74 notes.   T. L. Savitt

2439. Weinlick, John R. THE MORAVIANS AND THE AMERI-CAN REVOLUTION: AN OVERVIEW. *Tr. of the Moravian Hist. Soc. 1977 23(1): 1-16.* The Moravians were pacifists and nonjurors, but there was considerable division on these issues within their ranks during the American Revolution. Although divided, the overwhelming majority of Moravians came to favor American victory. Given the location of the battle, the Moravians rendered more service of a noncombatant nature to the Americans than to the British. Bethlehem, Nazareth, Litiz, Hope, Bethabara, and Salem, Pennsylvania were centers of war production and providers of medical service. In this manner the Moravians aided the Americans far more than if they had merely supplied troops. The war generated the breakdown of the Moravian Indian missionary enterprises and disrupted communication with the Moravian headquarters in Eu-rope. Primary and secondary sources.   N. Lederer

2440. Yates, W. Ross. THE PERIOD OF QUESTIONING, BETH-LEHEM, 1850-1876. *Tr. of the Moravian Hist. Soc. 1975 22(3): 193-212.* The Period of Questioning for the Moravian community in Bethlehem ensued for several decades following the ending of the lease system and the incorporation of the borough in 1844-45. The moral crisis within the community was reflected in the newly established weekly newspaper, *The Moravian*. The editorials challenged the materialistic nature of American society, insisted on the need for the United States to live as a Christian nation, and wrestled with the problem of slavery. By the aftermath of the Civil War the community had regained its inner stability. Documentation based largely on *The Moravian*.   N. Lederer

Politics

Responses to Specific Events and Political Leaders

2441. Archdeacon, Thomas J. NEW YORK MIGHT BE AMER-ICA. *R. in Am. Hist. 1975 3(2): 187-191.* Patricia U. Bonomi's *A Factious People: Politics and Society in Colonial New York* (New York: Columbia U. Pr., 1971) and Milton M. Klein's *The Politics of Diversity: Essays in the History of Colonial New York* (Port Washington, N.Y.: Kennikat Pr., 1974) discuss the effect of ethnic and religious diversity on

New York's political institutions in the 1690's-1770's, and the importance of this experience for the political development of the nation after the Revolution.

2442. Arnold, Joseph L. THE LAST OF THE GOOD OLD DAYS: POLITICS IN BALTIMORE, 1920-1950. *Maryland Hist. Mag. 1976 71(3): 443-448.* While Progressive-era reforms in Maryland did end classic-style bossism as embodied in the famous Rasin-Gorman machine, still the heirs of this machine continued to monopolize Baltimore city and county politics for 35 years, since "individual leaders and their relationships, not the total organizational structure, determine the continuing strength of machine control." Democrats successfully identified the Republicans with the voters' fear of black control during the 1920's, and both European and rural white immigrants registered heavily Democratic. Personal conflicts between Democratic bosses John J. (Sonny) Mahon and Frank Kelly, heirs of the two major machine factions, weakened their party's control at the center, and 15 years of battling between the forces led by William Curran and perennial mayor Howard Jackson splintered the party further. Local ward bosses were thus able to develop independent neighborhood machines, and control of city council and the mayoralty depended on shifting and temporary alliances of such local groups. Republicans, however, were never able to take advantage of such Democratic in-fighting. Primary and secondary sources; 13 notes.
G. J. Bobango

2443. Bockelman, Wayne L. and Ireland, Owen S. THE INTERNAL REVOLUTION IN PENNSYLVANIA: AN ETHNIC-RELIGIOUS INTERPRETATION. *Pennsylvania Hist. 1974 41(2): 125-159.* Surveys the ethnic and religious composition of the legislative, executive, and judicial branches of Pennsylvania government, 1755-80. During 1756-76, the Quakers remained the largest group in the legislature, but they had lost their overwhelming numerical dominance. Subsequent assemblies saw the emergence of a Presbyterian majority and the decline of Quaker and Anglican strength. Concludes that religious and ethnic conflict was more important than sectional and class conflict. Portrait, 12 charts and graphs, 46 notes.
D. C. Swift

2444. Bradford, Richard H. RELIGION AND POLITICS: ALFRED E. SMITH AND THE ELECTION OF 1928 IN WEST VIRGINIA. *West Virginia Hist. 1975 36(3) 213-221.* In the 1928 Democratic presidential primary, New York Governor Alfred E. Smith faced Missouri Senator James A. Reed in West Virginia. Although Smith never set foot in the state while Reed campaigned vigorously, and although Smith was a Catholic running in a 95% Protestant state, he won the primary, 82,000 to 76,000. In November, Hoover won; but West Virginia had been a Republican state for some time, and Smith did better than previous Democratic candidates. Based on newspapers and secondary sources; 50 notes.
J. H. Broussard

2445. Bukowski, Douglas. WILLIAM DEVER AND PROHIBITION: THE MAYORAL ELECTIONS OF 1923 AND 1927. *Chicago Hist. 1978 7(2): 109-118.* Efforts of Chicago mayor William Dever to impose a reform-minded and prohibitionist city government following his election in 1923 led to discontent within the electorate, erosion of support from ethnic groups and blacks, and his defeat in 1927.

2446. Bulkley, Peter B. TOWNSENDISM AS AN EASTERN AND URBAN PHENOMENON: CHAUTAUQUA COUNTY, NEW YORK, AS A CASE STUDY. *New York Hist. 1974 55(2): 179-198.* Challenges the standard view that the Townsend Movement was primarily rural and Western, and supported by "Grant Wood type" native-born Americans. In New York's 43rd Congressional District (Chautauqua, Cattaraugus, and Allegany Counties), the Townsendites, in alliance with the minority Democratic party, came close to defeating the conservative Republican incumbent, Daniel A. Reed, in the 1936 elections. The pro-Townsend vote was strongest in Jamestown (the chief city of the district), which had a large immigrant population, and was weakest in the native American rural areas of the district. Townsendism, in this Eastern and highly industrialized region, had its greatest strength in urban areas with large immigrant populations. Based on primary and secondary works; 3 illus., map, table, 50 notes.
G. Kurland

2447. Clark, Cal; Clark, Janet; and Karnig, Albert K. VOTING BEHAVIOR OF CHICAGO DEMOCRATS AT THE ILLINOIS CON-STITUTIONAL CONVENTION: MACHINE UNITY AND DISUNITY. *Am. Pol. Q. 1978 6(3): 325-344.* Most urban political machines have run aground due to improved economic conditions, reduced immigration, expansion of state-federal welfare programs, and the adoption of municipal reforms. One model of urban machine is the retention of power by a fairly small group of politicians; this model pictures the relationship between machine politician and city dweller as one more of manipulation than of representation. In contrast a second model "argues that the representation role of machine has generally been understated." These competing models are tested by data from the 1970 Illinois Constitutional Convention. The Chicago machine constituted a distinct voting group at the Convention. The Chicago delegation exhibited the highest degree of roll-call voting solidarity, but was marked by the greatest heterogeneity in ethnic composition. 3 tables, 6 notes, ref.
E. P. Stickney

2448. Daniels, Doris. BUILDING A WINNING COALITION: THE SUFFRAGE FIGHT IN NEW YORK STATE. *New York Hist. 1979 60(1): 59-80.* In the 1917 New York state referendum, the urban population provided the majority of votes for the extension of the suffrage to women. Shows how the suffragist victory in New York City resulted from a coalition of traditional suffragists, industrial workers, Eastern European immigrants, and settlement house women led by Lillian D. Wald. 6 illus., 2 tables, 53 notes.
R. N. Lokken

2449. Eisinger, Peter K. ETHNIC POLITICAL TRANSITION IN BOSTON, 1884-1933: SOME LESSONS FOR CONTEMPORARY CITIES. *Pol. Sci. Q. 1978 93(2): 217-239.* Defines and describes (as an example for today's Detroit, Atlanta, Newark, and New Orleans) how Boston Yankees were forced into a political minority due to the consolidation of Irish political power.

2450. Ford, Trowbridge H. THE POLITICAL CRUSADE AGAINST BLAINE IN 1884. *Mid-America 1975 57(1): 38-55.* James G. Blaine's defeat was a matter of neither ideology nor sociology, but of his unknowningly becoming a pawn in a plot by Edwin L. Godkin and A. V. Dicey to bring American pressure to bear on Great Britain to grant Ireland home rule. Included were important Englishmen and Irish Americans. But the Irish were divided, and Blaine failed to respond, and ultimately Godkin utilized the British and Irish press to achieve Grover Cleveland's narrow victory. Based on the Godkin Papers, Houghton Library, and secondary sources; 72 notes.
T. H. Wendel

2451. Galvin, John T. THE DARK AGES OF BOSTON POLITICS. *Massachusetts Hist. Soc. Pro. 1977 89: 88-111.* During the 1880's women emerged as a political force, questions of corruption emerged, the park system developed, the parochial school system was debated, and Irish Americans became a force in local politics. Many of these issues' effects are still felt. Primary and secondary sources; 109 notes.
G. W. R. Ward

2452. Issel, William. CLASS AND ETHNIC CONFLICT IN SAN FRANCISCO POLITICAL HISTORY: THE REFORM CHARTER OF 1898. *Labor Hist. 1977 18(3): 341-359.* The passage of the Reform Charter of 1898 in San Francisco revealed a political struggle divided by class and ethnic tensions that resulted in centralization of city government. The "business and professional elite" were victorious over labor and ethnic interests in city reform. Based on San Francisco newspapers; 51 notes.
L. L. Athey

2453. McCarthy, G. Michael. THE BROWN DERBY CAMPAIGN IN WEST TENNESSEE: SMITH, HOOVER, AND THE POLITICS OF RACE. *West Tennessee Hist. Soc. Papers 1973 (27): 81-98.* The hard-fought political campaign between Alfred E. Smith and Herbert C. Hoover in Tennessee dredged up racial, religious, ethical, and political issues and ultimately resulted in Hoover's breaking the solid South for the first time since the end of Reconstruction.

2454. McCarthy, G. Michael. SMITH VS. HOOVER: THE POLITICS OF RACE IN WEST TENNESSEE. *Phylon 1978 39(2): 154-168.* When the Democrats in 1928 nominated for President of the United States Al Smith of New York, a big-city, Catholic, anti-prohibition, pro-immigration, professional politician, there were wide defections in parts of the South, which was overwhelmingly rural and small-town, Protestant, prohibitionist, and anti-immigration. Herbert Hoover won over many southern Democrats because he was from a rural background, was a Protestant, a prohibitionist, and an old stock American. West Tennessee resisted this anti-Smith trend for racial reasons. Blacks were one-third the population in West Tennessee, and the whites feared that they might become politically powerful. The Republican Party had always been the party of the blacks, and in 1928 it reinforced this image by including in its platform a strong anti-lynching plank. The result was white, Democratic solidarity behind Al Smith. Of the 19 counties west of the Tennessee River, only 4 went for Hoover. 71 notes.

J. C. Billigmeier

2455. Miller, Zane L. THE ETHNIC REVIVAL AND URBAN LIBERALISM. *R. in Am. Hist. 1974 2(3): 418-424.* John D. Buenker's *Urban Liberalism and Progressive Reform* (New York: Charles Scribner's Sons, 1973) studies the coalition of ethnic groups and middle-class reformers of the Progressive Movement who attempted political reform in metropolitan areas in the 1910's.

2456. Obermann, Karl. BEZIEHUNGEN ZWISCHEN DEN EUROPÄISCHEN FORTSCHRITTSKRÄFTEN UND DEN USA IM 19. JAHRHUNDERT [Connections between European progressive forces and the United States in the 19th century]. *Jahrbuch für Geschichte [East Germany] 1975 13: 71-108.* Ever since the American War of Independence, 1775-83, European progressives had looked to the United States for inspiration, hope, and refuge. Many fought for the American Revolution; while some then stayed, others returned to fight for the same ideals in Europe. After 1815, and again after the failure of the 1848 revolutions, many Europeans, especially Germans, fled to America. There, led by such figures as Carl Schurz, they became active in the struggle against slavery, supported Abraham Lincoln in 1860, and flocked to the Union standard when the Civil War broke out. After that war, European immigrants, including large numbers of Germans, played important parts in the beginnings of the American labor movement. 134 notes.

J. C. Billigmeier

2457. Petersen, Peter L. STOPPING AL SMITH: THE 1928 DEMOCRATIC PRIMARY IN SOUTH DAKOTA. *South Dakota Hist. 1974 4(4): 439-454.* Rural "dry" Democrats failed to defeat Al Smith's nomination in 1928 in the first primary of the year. Although Smith won by less than 2,000 votes, opposition among Democrats nationwide melted away after the attempt in South Dakota. The attempt failed owing to the well-established Smith campaign, the reluctance of Thomas Walsh of Montana to announce his candidacy, and the ascendency of the urban East. Internally, South Dakota Democrats patched up differences to reelect the state's first Democratic governor. 3 photos.

A. J. Larson

2458. Qualls, J. Winfield. THE 1928 PRESIDENTIAL ELECTION IN WEST TENNESSEE: WAS RACE A CHIEF FACTOR? *West Tennessee Hist. Soc. Papers 1973 (27): 99-107.* Statistical analysis of the impact of black voting in Tennessee indicates that lack of organization and split political party affiliation demoted the black vote to a relatively innocuous position in the list of factors affecting the presidential election outcome in 1928.

2459. Reese, William J. THE CONTROL OF URBAN SCHOOL BOARDS DURING THE PROGRESSIVE ERA: A RECONSIDERATION. *Pacific Northwest Q. 1977 68(4): 164-174.* Traces the history of educational reform in Toledo, Ohio during the Progressive Era. The Niles Bill of 1898 reduced the city's school board to five members, nominated on nonpartisan ballots and elected on a city-wide basis rather than by wards. This produced a wave of progressive victories during 1898, but the victors were just as elitist as the group they replaced. Suggests that future studies should focus on members who dominated school boards and on outside forces which influenced policy. Primary and secondary sources; 3 photos, 32 notes.

M. L. Tate

2460. Roff, Kenneth L. BROOKLYN'S REACTION TO BLACK SUFFRAGE IN 1860. *Afro-Americans in New York Life and Hist. 1978 2(1): 29-40.* New York City businessmen spread anti-black propaganda among poor and immigrant laborers to negate black suffrage and secure a Democratic Party victory in Brooklyn in the 1860 elections.

2461. Rorabaugh, William J. RISING DEMOCRATIC SPIRITS: IMMIGRANTS, TEMPERANCE, AND TAMMANY HALL, 1854-1860. *Civil War Hist. 1976 22(2): 131-157.* Discusses the emergence of a political coalition among the Irish, Germans, and Anglos in New York City during 1840's-50's. It turned the metropolis into a Democratic stronghold, while the rest of the North was becoming largely Republicanized. Although these groups differed on other matters, hostility to prohibition united immigrant Irish and German Catholics with enough native-born Protestants to control New York City. The corner saloon evolved from an unimportant neighborhood shop to a highly structured nerve center. It became the needed power base from which the coalition could effectively function.

E. C. Murdock

2462. Silverman, Robert A. NATHAN MATTHEWS: POLITICS OF REFORM IN BOSTON, 1890-1910. *New England Q. 1977 50(4): 626-643.* Traces Nathan Matthews's (1853-1927) role in forming the Yankee-Irish alliance in the Democratic Party and his chairmanship of the Boston Finance Commission during 1907-09. Focuses on his four terms as the reform mayor of Boston during 1891-95 when he achieved his main goal of cutting expenditures through better management and established the Board of Survey which provided Boston with its first coordinated planning. Based on Matthews' correspondence and secondary sources; 42 notes.

J. C. Bradford

2463. Thelen, David P. URBAN POLITICS: BEYOND BOSSES AND REFORMERS. *Rev. in Am. Hist. 1979 7(3): 406-412.* Reviews John M. Allswang's *Bosses, Machines and Urban Voters: An American Symbiosis* (Port Washington, New York: Kennikat Pr., 1977), Lyle W. Dorsett's *Franklin D. Roosevelt and the City Bosses* (Port Washington, New York: Kennikat Pr., 1977), Michael H. Ebner and Eugene M. Tobin's (eds.) *The Age of Urban Reform: New Perspectives on the Progressive Era* (Port Washington, New York: Kennikat Pr., 1977), and Kenneth Fox's *Better City Government: Innovation in American Urban Politics, 1850-1937* (Philadelphia: Temple U. Pr., 1977).

2464. Walsh, James P. JAMES PHELAN'S MONTALVO: MANY ACCEPTED, ONE DECLINED. *Southern California Q. 1976 58(1): 95-111.* Presents a profile of James D. Phelan, successful businessman and politician, and his home near San Jose, which he named Montalvo. Montalvo became a center for the region's literary and cultural elite; guests included novelist Gertrude Atherton, poets Edwin Markham and George Sterling, and political and celebrity figures ranging from Democratic politicians to the Boy Scouts. In marked contrast to the image of hospitality and genteelness offered by Phelan, one notable figure declined to attend Montalvo affairs. Father Peter C. Yorke, spokesman for San Francisco's ethnic and working classes and a sponsor of Phelan's entry into politics in 1896, repudiated his earlier support of Phelan. He condemned Phelan for his failure to expand his political views to include concrete reforms for workingmen rather than civic and cultural matters. Thus Phelan's Montalvo contained the rarefied air of genteel refinement, and not a more enduring union with the masses who had supported Phelan. Based on primary and secondary sources; photo, 42 notes.

A. Hoffman

2465. Wingo, Barbara C. THE 1928 PRESIDENTIAL ELECTION IN LOUISIANA. *Louisiana Hist. 1977 18(4): 405-415.* Although Alfred E. Smith's majority in Louisiana in 1928 (76.3%) was very similar to Democratic majorities in that state in the 1920 and 1924 elections, the composition of his support was markedly different. Reviews and analyzes the election, showing that his strength was in the "wet," Catholic, southern part of the state rather than in the "dry," Protestant north. Black participation remained a factor in the state's Republican Party. Notes some similarities in the support for Smith and Huey P. Long. Primary sources; 3 tables, 66 notes.

R. L. Woodward, Jr.

2466. Zink, Steven D. CULTURAL CONFLICT AND THE 1928 PRESIDENTIAL CAMPAIGN IN LOUISIANA. *Southern Studies 1978 17(2): 175-197.* Religious differences had played an accepted but subordinate role in Louisiana politics until 1928. Al Smith (1873-1944), the Democratic nominee for president, represented for many an East Coast, Catholic, urban supporter of alcoholic beverages. The typical Southern solidarity in voting based on race was broken as patterns show a clear difference between Catholic and Protestant parishes in Louisiana. Strong anti-Catholic bias is reflected in the newspapers. The division was not based on religion itself, but on issues such as prohibition that reflected religious attitudes. Primary and secondary sources; 2 tables, 84 notes.

J. Buschen

Political Elites

2468. Brown, Richard D. THE FOUNDING FATHERS OF 1776 AND 1787: A COLLECTIVE VIEW. *William and Mary Q. 1976 33(3): 465-473.* Discusses the status and other factors related to the 99 men who either signed the Declaration of Independence or the Constitution. Various quantitative data are given as to a profile of collective identity. Similarities noted: for example, concerning birth, region, ethnic background, family, occupation, climatic conditions, and longevity. Includes a list of personnel examined, background information, occupations, cohort groups, family size, and factors relating to deaths. Based on secondary sources, including population studies; 9 tables, 33 notes.

H. M. Ward

2469. Busch, Ronald J. and Abravanel, Martin D. THE URBAN PARTY ORGANIZATION AS AN OPPORTUNITY STRUCTURE: RACE AND PARTY DIFFERENCES AMONG CLEVELAND WARD LEADERS. *Western Pol. Q. 1976 29(1): 59-85.* Viewing the political party as an opportunity structure, this study examines race and party differences among ward leaders in a major American city. When communications patterns, recruitment incentives, and retention incentives are examined, race and party differences in basic political orientations emerge. The findings suggest that Black ward leaders tend to be more constituency oriented while White ward leaders tend to be more leader oriented. Moreover, the party differences indicate that minority party durability may be influenced by incentives originating in other political jurisdictions. These findings further suggest that Black ward leaders, like their White ethnic predecessors, may use the party as a vehicle for upward mobility, especially when the opportunities in the private sector are limited. In addition to the party differences, so often identified in this genre of literature, then, race of the ward leader furthers our understanding of the incentives underlying partisan involvement in an urban setting.

J

2470. Clubb, Jerome M. and Allen, Howard W. COLLECTIVE BIOGRAPHY AND THE PROGRESSIVE MOVEMENT: THE "STATUS REVOLUTION" REVISITED. *Social Sci. Hist. 1977 1(4): 518-534.* Assesses the possibilities for the use of collective biography or prosopography in the quantitative assessment of history, especially as displayed by George E. Mowry in his 1963 study, *The California Progressives* and Alfred C. Chandler, Jr.'s "The Origins of Progressive Leadership" in Elting E. Morison's (ed.) *The Letters of Theodore Roosevelt* (Cambridge, 1954).

2471. Elbert, E. Duane. SOUTHERN INDIANA IN THE ELECTION OF 1860: THE LEADERSHIP AND THE ELECTORATE. *Indiana Mag. of Hist. 1974 70(1): 1-23.* A statistical study of a cross-section of the electorate and party leaders in six select Indiana counties. Examines Republicans, Democrats, and Constitutional Unionists from the perspectives of place of birth, average age, occupation, and wealth. The existing correlations are evident. There was no positive correlation between foreign birth and political party; age was not a distinction among the parties; there were definite occupation correlations; and wealth was about the same with Democrats and Republicans, while Constitutional Unionists were on the whole better off than the leaders and members of the other two parties. Concludes that party leadership in all three parties in the six counties studied was strongly southern and midwestern in origin. Based on secondary sources; 12 tables, 23 notes.

N. E. Tutorow

2472. Feinstein, Estelle F. TOWARD A MEANING FOR MUGWUMPERY. *R. in Am. Hist. 1975 3(4): 467-471.* Gerald W. McFarland's *Mugwumps, Morals & Politics, 1884-1920* (Amherst: U. of Massachusetts Pr., 1975) outlines the profile, values, and subsequent political history of 420 Mugwumps in New York City who left the Republican Party in 1884 over a matter of principle.

2473. Folsom, Burton W., II. THE POLITICS OF ELITES: PROMINENCE AND PARTY IN DAVIDSON COUNTY, TENNESSEE, 1835-1861. *J. of Southern Hist. 1973 39(3): 359-378.* Examines the prominent men of Davidson County, Tennessee, during 1835-61 in terms of political attitudes, affiliation, education, occupation, interrelations, religion, ethnic background, and Unionist sentiment. No clear socioeconomic differences appear between Whig and Democratic party members. Secondary sources; 45 notes.

N. J. Street

2474. Garrard, John A. THE HISTORY OF LOCAL POLITICAL POWER: SOME SUGGESTIONS FOR ANALYSIS. *Pol. Studies [Great Britain] 1977 25(2): 252-269.* Studies local politics by comparing the author's own work on Salford, England since 1830 with the study of New Haven by Robert A. Dahl *Who Governs?* (New Haven: Yale U. Pr., 1961). Generalizations about the location of power in the past need to go beyond analysis of the background of office holders and the identifications of socioeconomic elites. The author's work on Salford suggests a framework for the comparative study of the political context within which the political leadership of 19th century cities operated. Graph, 36 notes.

R. Howell

2475. Janick, Herbert. AN INSTRUCTIVE FAILURE: THE CONNECTICUT PEACE MOVEMENT, 1919-1939. *Peace and Change 1978 5(1): 12-22.* The peace movement in Connecticut failed, because its local hierarchy reflected upper middle class values and found it difficult to incorporate the ethnic and minority ideologies of most residents.

2476. Julien, Stephen W. THE UTAH STATE SUPREME COURT AND ITS JUSTICES, 1896-1976. *Utah Hist. Q. 1976 44(3): 267-285.* Utah State Supreme Court justices have similar backgrounds—western European ancestry, American birth, most from small communities, humble parentage. Most began their public careers as city or county attorneys. Generally outsiders and non-Mormons served on the court before 1926, and later Utah-born Mormons, with better legal educations and more judicial experience. The creation of nonpartisan ballots in 1961 and recent judicial legislation may take politics out of the court and provide more qualified candidates. Based on primary and secondary sources; 31 illus., 2 charts, 13 notes.

J. L. Hazelton

2477. Marger, Martin. ETHNIC SUCCESSION IN DETROIT POLITICS, 1900-1950. *Polity 1979 11(3): 343-361.* In tracing the changing ethnic patterns in the composition of the highest elective offices in Detroit from 1900 to 1950, the author distinguished three eras in the ethnic makeup of the city's political elite directly related to shifts in the economic and industrial structure. The relative ethnic balance during the first two decades of the century was displaced by Anglo-Saxon domination after the automotive industrialists, Detroit's new economic elite, had succeeded in instituting an electoral reform. The alliance of the Democratic party with the United Automobile Workers restored the predominance of the non-Anglo-Saxon ethnics in the 1930's.

J

2478. Ryerson, R. A. POLITICAL MOBILIZATION AND THE AMERICAN REVOLUTION: THE RESISTANCE MOVEMENT IN PHILADELPHIA, 1765 TO 1776. *William and Mary Q. 1974 31(4): 565-588.* Calls for de-emphasis of ideological origins of the Revolution and more study of the translation of beliefs and anxieties into revolutionary action. Deals with one aspect of the mobilization of popular sentiment, leadership recruitment, attempting to identify patterns and impact. Examines the personnel who sat on the Philadelphia Resistance Committee, their persistence and continuity, age, wealth, occupation, ethnic origins, place of birth, and religion. Because of a new and more broadly-based elite, the resistance movement succeeded. Based on the author's unpublished Ph.D. dissertation, newspapers, and secondary sources; 2 tables, 3 figs., 42 notes.

H. M. Ward

2479. Swidorski, Carl L. NEW YORK COURT OF APPEALS: WHO ARE THE JUDGES? *Natl. Civic Rev. 1977 66(11): 558-561, 571.* Descriptive data on place of birth, residence, education, career patterns, religion, ethnicity, age, sex, party affiliation and bar association activity were gathered for the 23 judges who sat on the court from 1950 through 1976, to determine routes of access, how the judges reflect and/or represent the general population, and what factors affect recruitment.

J

2480. Tobin, Eugene M. THE PROGRESSIVE AS HUMANITARIAN: JERSEY CITY'S SEARCH FOR SOCIAL JUSTICE, 1890-1917. *New Jersey Hist. 1975 93(3-4): 77-98.* Social reformers in Jersey City are classified into three groups: private, religious, and public. The Whittier House social settlement tackled problems associated with tenement slums, crime, infant mortality, and juvenile delinquency. Protestants campaigned for broad social welfare reform, while less affluent Catholics opted for assistance on an individual basis for its immigrant communicants. A separate juvenile court was established. World War I changed the priorities of reformers. A typical Jersey City reformer was "a native-stock, middle-class Protestant who resided in the Eighth or Ninth Ward and had some college training." Based on primary and secondary sources; 7 illus., 44 notes.
E. R. McKinstry

2481. Ulmer, S. Sidney. SOCIAL BACKGROUND AS AN INDICATOR TO THE VOTES OF SUPREME COURT JUSTICES IN CRIMINAL CASES: 1947-1956 TERMS. *Am. J. of Pol. Sci. 1973 17(3): 622-630.* Considers the role of social background as an influencing factor in Supreme Court criminal decisions. Twelve social background variables were selected which explained over 91% of all decisions during the period 1947-56. Researchers who have reached opposite conclusions probably erred in variable selection, had different objectives, or worked with different courts. Nevertheless, the justices' decisionmaking process is complicated; an intimate knowledge of the social backgrounds of justices probably will never permit precise prediction of decisions. 3 tables, 14 notes.
V. L. Human

2482. Zimmerman, James A. WHO WERE THE ANTI-IMPERIALISTS AND THE EXPANSIONISTS OF 1898 AND 1899? A CHICAGO PERSPECTIVE. *Pacific Hist. Rev. 1977 46(4): 589-601.* Local study of the public debate concerning American expansionism during 1898-99 shows that anti-imperialists were a more diverse group than previous scholarship has assumed. Chicago anti-imperialist leaders were not of an older generation than the expansionists, but were younger. The anti-imperialists were newer to the city and of lower social status. Their occupations and religious and political affiliations were more diverse. The anti-imperialists were more involved in domestic reform activity and may well have seen imperialist adventures as a threat to the continuation of the reform impulse. Based on Chicago newspapers and biographical directories; 22 notes.
W. K. Hobson

Voting Behavior

2483. Acock, Alan C. and Halley, Robert. ETHNIC POLITICS AND RACIAL ISSUES RECONSIDERED: COMMENTS ON AN EARLIER STUDY. *Western Pol. Q. 1975 28(4): 737-738.* Reevaluates Harlan Hahn and Timothy Almy's "Ethnic Politics and Racial Issues: Voting in Los Angeles" (see abstract 13A:2513), which concluded America was moving from ethnic politics to class politics. Due to a mistake in calculations Hahn and Almy drew the wrong conclusions. A second look at the statistics proved: first, ethnicity is a good predictor of voting for a liberal black mayor. Second, socioeconomic status measured by median income or education is not highly related to voting for a liberal black mayor when there are no controls. Third, socioeconomic status is moderately related when ethnicity is controlled, but the relationship is the opposite direction from the report by Hahn-Almy study, thus discrediting a class coalition transcending ethnicity. 3 notes.
K. McElroy

2484. Alvarez, David J. and True, Edmond J. CRITICAL ELECTIONS AND PARTISAN REALIGNMENT: AN URBAN TEST-CASE. *Polity 1973 5(4): 563-576.* Ward-by-ward voting behavior in Hartford, Connecticut, during 1896-1940 indicates that support for the Democrats came from established middle-class, Protestant sectors of society, rather than from realignment of pro-Democratic Party ethnic groups in 1928.

2485. Benjamin, Gerald. PATTERNS IN NEW YORK STATE POLITICS. *Pro. of the Acad. of Pol. Sci. 1974 31(3): 31-44.* Examines the party system in the state of New York, with special emphasis on voting behavior within the Democratic Party and the Republican Party since World War II.
S

2486. Blocker, Jack S., Jr. THE PERILS OF PLURALISM. *Can. R. of Am. Studies 1973 4(2): 201-205.* Review article of: Paul Kleppner's *The Cross of Culture: A Social Analysis of Midwestern Politics, 1850-1900* (New York: Free Press, 1970), and Richard Jensen's *The Winning of the Midwest: Social and Political Conflict, 1888-1896* (Chicago: U. of Chicago Press, 1971), analyses of midwestern political behavior in the late 19th century. Unlike earlier histories which emphasized political institutions, debates between political groups, and midwestern power elites, Kleppner and Jensen focus on religion and other cultural forces and conclude these forces were determinative factors in shaping midwestern political activities. Kleppner studied Ohio, Michigan, and Wisconsin. Jensen included Indiana, Iowa, and Illinois in his work.
H. T. Lovin

2487. Bohmer, David A. STABILITY AND CHANGE IN EARLY NATIONAL POLITICS: THE MARYLAND VOTER AND THE ELECTION OF 1800. *William and Mary Q. 1979 36(1): 27-50.* Contends, from examination of electoral and population data from all of Maryland's counties for the presidential election of 1800, that there was no substantial realignment. Nor was there any significant increase in voter participation. Voting patterns were similar in elections during 1796-1816. Most persons, however, who switched their voting preference in 1800 from that of the off-year election in 1798 voted for Jefferson. Evaluates ethnic voting patterns. Federalist strength still remained in Maryland after the election of 1800. Consults poll lists and federal and local records; 39 notes.
H. M. Ward

2488. Borowiec, Walter A. PERCEPTIONS OF ETHNIC VOTERS BY ETHNIC POLITICIANS. *Ethnicity 1974 1(3): 267-278.* Investigates attitudes of ethnic political leaders, their perception of the responsiveness of group members to ethnic stimuli, and the effect of class and generation on those perceptions. Employed a sample of 83 in Buffalo, New York. Findings revealed their stress on a candidate's nationality and party label. Controlling for education and generation still showed that the assimilation of political leaders did not lead them to view voters in non-ethnic terms, thus affecting the political choices presented to voters. 4 tables, 21 notes.
E. Barkan

2489. Bozeman, Barry and James, Thomas E. TOWARD A COMPREHENSIVE MODEL OF FOREIGN POLICY VOTING IN THE U.S. SENATE. *Western Pol. Q. 1975 28(3): 477-495.* Three explanations of foreign policy voting in the Senate have been especially prominent, the "Constituency Model," the "Idiosyncratic/Roll Model," and the "Military-Industrial Complex Model." In this study of Senate foreign policy voting the significance of these models is investigated in an effort to formulate a more comprehensive empirically based explanation. A factor analysis of the variables selected to perationalize the three models indicated that only the Military-Industrial Complex Model was cohesive. Other factor dimensions that emerged were named "Tenure," "Bigness," "Urban-Ethnic," "Dissensions," "Ideology," and "Cohesiveness." The factor scores for foreign policy voting dimensions were regressed on those factors in order to test the predictive importance of each. The best explanation of foreign policy voting was in terms of the senators' ideology and support for the administration. The military-industrial complex explanation was not generally useful.
J

2490. Brye, David L. WISCONSIN SCANDINAVIANS AND PROGRESSIVISM, 1900-1950. *Norwegian-American Studies 1977 27: 163-193.* Examines voting behavior among Scandinavian Americans in Wisconsin, 1900-50, concentrating on their support for the Progressive Movement. Through careful examination of precinct voting records, the author shows categorical breakdowns of each ethnic component (Norwegian, Dane, Swede, and Finn) according to political preference. While all Scandinavian immigrants were members of the Republican Party initially (1840's-90's), they overwhelmingly supported Progressive candidates and reforms, 1900-14. Slowly, support began to drift from Republican to Democrat with the highest overall percentage occurring in 1932. By mid-century, support among Finnish Americans and Norwegian Americans in Wisconsin was largely for the Democrats, while Swedish Americans split fairly evenly between the two parties, and Danish Americans preferred moderate Republicans to conservative Republicans. 8 tables, 46 notes, appendix.
G. A. Hewlett

2491. Buenker, John D. CHICAGO'S ETHNICS AND THE POLI-
TICS OF ACCOMMODATION. *Chicago Hist. 1974 3(2): 92-100.*

2492. Buenker, John D. DYNAMICS OF CHICAGO ETHNIC
POLITICS, 1900-1930. *J. of the Illinois State Hist. Soc. 1974 67(2):
175-199.* Reviews Chicago's Italian, Irish, Swedish, Bohemian, German,
Polish, and black city wards and why they supported the more effective
Democratic Party. Native-stock politicians were to lose out to ethnic-
orienated politicians despite financial, educational, and social advantages.
The Chicago Irish took particular advantage of their numbers and group
cohesiveness, and were successful on such issues as the repeal of Prohibition. Based on political biographies and recent political studies; 37 notes.
                                                                    A. C. Aimone

2493. Byrne, Gary C. and Pueschel, J. Kristian. BUT WHO
SHOULD I VOTE FOR FOR COUNTY CORONER? *J. of Pol. 1974
36(3): 778-784.* Voters faced with a ballot containing unknown candidates for obscure offices resort to cues found on the ballot in making
decisions. This study based on a series of California elections, 1948-70
concludes that "seemingly irrelevant facts about candidates, such as sex,
place on the ballot, possession or lack of a nickname, and ethnic background of the last name are important indicators of chances for electoral
success." 4 tables, 2 fig., 4 notes.   A. R. Stoesen

2494. Campbell, Ballard C. ETHNICITY AND THE 1893 WIS-
CONSIN ASSEMBLY. *J. of Am. Hist. 1975 62(1): 74-94.* Analyzes the
relationship of ethnicity, party affiliation, and roll-call voting in the Wisconsin assembly of 1893. Establishes a functional definition of ethnicity,
formulates indices of disagreement and cohesion, and tentatively concludes that, in this case, cultural background probably affected each
legislator's response to public policy questions, particularly social legislation. Based on published legislative proceedings, the Blue Book of the
State of Wisconsin for 1893, correspondence with descendants of legislators, and secondary works; 6 tables, 30 notes.   J. B. Street

2495. Campbell, Ballard. THE STATE LEGISLATURE IN
AMERICAN HISTORY: A REVIEW ESSAY. *Hist. Methods News-
letter 1976 9(4): 185-195.* Reviews the following books: John D. Buenker,
Urban Liberalism and Progressive Reform (N.Y.: Charles Scribner's
Sons, 1973); Don S. Kirschner, *City and Country: Rural Responses to
Urbanization in the 1920's* (Westport, Conn.: Greenwood Pr., 1970); J.
Morgan Kousser, *The Shaping of Southern Politics: Suffrage Restrictions
and the Establishment of the One-Party South, 1880-1910* (New Haven:
Yale U. Pr., 1974); Stanley B. Parsons, *The Populist Context: Rural
Versus Urban Power On A Great Plains Frontier* (Westport, Conn.:
Greenwood Pr., 1973); James Edward Wright, *The Politics of Populism:
Dissent in Colorado* (New Haven: Yale U. Pr., 1973). Acknowledges
their methodological contributions as statistical analysis of roll-call vot-
ing in going beyond the traditional rural-urban thesis. 2 tables, 17 notes.
                                                                    D. K. Pickens

2496. Cohen, Steven Martin and Kapsis, Robert E. RELIGION,
ETHNICITY, AND PARTY AFFILIATION IN THE U.S.: EVI-
DENCE FROM POOLED ELECTORAL SURVEYS, 1968-72.
Social Forces 1977 56(2): 637-653. Analyzes a white Christian subsample
of pooled national survey data collected in 1968, 1970, and 1972 to
determine whether ethnicity has a direct effect on party identification net
of parental party identification and raises subsidiary issues: (1) how best
to measure ethnicity, (2) the need to distinguish between ethnically identified and ethnically assimilated respondents, and (3) possible regional variation in the impact of ethnicity. Religion alone (Protestant versus
Catholic) is an adequate measure of ethnicity for this analysis, there being
little intrareligious variation in party identification by national origin.
Second, religion's effect is largely limited to the ethnically identified.
Third, its effect holds up when controlling for parental party identification and SES. Fourth, regional variation in the impact of religion is
understood as largely flowing from regional variations in the distribution
of Catholics.   J

2497. Cole, Leonard A. BLACKS & ETHNIC POLITICAL TOL-
ERANCE. *Polity 1977 9(3): 302-320.* Survey of 16 New Jersey municipalities with substantial black populations to determine the degree of
political tolerance shown by white voters toward black candidates for
political office. The increasing support given to black candidates follows
the pattern of political success evident among white ethnic groups.
                                                                         J/S

2498. Cummings, Tom J. AN EXAMINATION OF THE LUBELL
THESIS: MCINTOSH COUNTY, NORTH DAKOTA, 1936-1940.
North Dakota Q. 1974 42(4): 26-41. Applies Samuel Lubell's thesis on
the role of isolationism in foreign relations to a Russian German population in North Dakota.   S

2499. Cunningham, Robert B. and Winham, Gilbert R. COMPARA-
TIVE URBAN VOTING BEHAVIOR: CANADA AND THE
UNITED STATES. *Am. Rev. of Can. Studies 1973 3(2): 76-100.* Com-
pares the roles of social classes, ethnicity, religion, and political party
identification in the voting behavior of urban residents of Canada and the
United States in elections 1952-68.

2500. Dannenbaum, Jed. IMMIGRANTS AND TEMPERANCE:
ETHNOCULTURAL CONFLICT IN CINCINNATI, 1845-1860.
Ohio Hist. 1978 87(2): 125-139. Ethnocultural issues, primarily anti-
Catholicism, nativism, and temperance, sparked the breakdown of electoral politics and the realignment of contemporary cultural mores during
the 1850's in Cincinnati, Ohio. As German and Irish immigrants grew in
political power, native-born Cincinnatians increasingly associated them
with rapidly worsening social problems. The issues severely disrupted the
local party system and led to the virtual demise of the Whig Party in
Cincinnati. Based on newspapers, contemporary comments, and secondary sources; illus., 47 notes.   N. Summers

2501. Engelmann, Larry. DRY RENAISSANCE: THE LOCAL OP-
TION YEARS, 1889-1917. *Michigan Hist. 1975 59(1-2): 69-90.* Passage
of a local option law by the Michigan legislature in 1887 ushered in twenty
difficult years for prohibitionists. In 1907 only one county remained
under local option, but dry forces enjoyed a renaissance thereafter, and
in 1916 Michigan approved statewide prohibition by a sizable majority.
Ethnicity and class, rather than a rural-urban dichotomy, best explain this
transformation. After 1907, counties with a relatively high percentage of
native-born residents united into a single dry bloc. Prohibition was popularly accepted as a social experiment rather than a moral imperative
during the local option years. Primary and secondary sources; 2 illus., 2
photos, 3 tables, graph, 26 notes.   D. W. Johnson

2502. Fainstein, Norman I. and Martin, Mark. SUPPORT FOR
COMMUNITY CONTROL AMONG LOCAL URBAN ELITES.
Urban Affairs Q. 1978 13(4): 443-468. Several distinctive, even contradictory motivations are used to justify administrative decentralization. Because of its political structure and ethnic characteristics New York City
is an ideal locale for the study of local elites' community control attitudes.
Based on surveys and intensive interviews with 201 individuals in 1974,
of whom 151 had been analyzed in 1972, the authors conclude that local
elites favor administrative devolution. Furthermore, decentralization has
become increasingly popular among both minority groups and whites.
The data suggest that the minority group liberation motivation for community control is waning while the conservative desire to protect the
community from outside intrusion, including racial, is growing. 2 tables,
2 notes, biblio., appendix.   L. N. Beecher

2503. Fee, Joan L. PARTY IDENTIFICATION AMONG AMERI-
CAN CATHOLICS, 1972, 1973. *Ethnicity 1976 3(1): 53-69.* Examines
the relationship between the Catholic Church and the Democratic Party,
comparing social and vital statistics to determine culturally what type of
Catholic is a Democrat and what the personal perceptions of Catholic
Democrats are.

2504. Gerson, Louis L. ETHNICS IN AMERICAN POLITICS.
J. of Pol. 1976 38(3): 336-346. Studies the directions and goals of the
resurgent ethnic groups. More research is needed on the role of ethnicity
in American politics and diplomacy, but it is evident that the ethnic
nationalism of hyphenated Americans is less related to winning political
power, championing the old country, and exalting culture and religion
than it is to achieving dignity, equality, respectability, and unhampered
access to American values and benefits.   R. V. Ritter

2505. Greeley, Andrew M. HOW CONSERVATIVE ARE AMERI-
CAN CATHOLICS? *Pol. Sci. Q. 1977 92(2): 199-218.* The conventional wisdom about Catholic ethnics is false. They have not been more
racist, less likely to support civil liberties, more antagonistic toward the
counter culture, stronger supporters of the Vietnam War, or heavier

supporters of George Wallace than other Americans. Catholics are in fact less conservative than the average, and they have not abandoned the Democratic Party as they have become more affluent and moved to the suburbs. Their conservative image may be based not on substantial issues, but rather on political style; Catholics are more likely to call their precinct captains than to join civic organizations. Based on NORC General Social Surveys, Gallup polls, voting records, and secondary sources; 9 tables, 5 figs., 13 notes.

W. R. Hively

2506. Greeley, Andrew M. A MODEL FOR ETHNIC POLITICAL SOCIALIZATION. *Am. J. of Pol. Sci. 1975 19(2): 187-206.* A model is presented to analyze the transmission of political values across generational lines. The variables within the model are social class, parental values, family structure, and ethnic heritage. Political values differ among ethnic groups in both parental and adolescent generations. Ethnicity is a stronger predictor of adolescent values than is parental teaching. 2 fig., 8 tables.

S. P. Carr

2507. Greeley, Andrew M. POLITICAL PARTICIPATION AMONG ETHNIC GROUPS IN THE UNITED STATES: A PRELIMINARY RECONNAISSANCE. *Am. J. of Sociol. 1974 80(1): 170-204.* Religioethnic background is a meaningful predictor of political participation in American society. Its impact does not go away when social class is held constant, and it has an independent explanatory power that compares favorably with social class. Different causal models for political participation seem to apply for different ethnic collectivities, and the diversity among such collectivities is of similar magnitude to the diversity found in various nations in cross-national studies. Irish Catholics and Jews are the most active groups; Irish Protestants and blacks, the least active. The importance of ethnicity as a predictor variable can no longer be ignored by American social research.

J

2508. Hackett, D. L. A. SLAVERY, ETHNICITY, AND SUGAR: AN ANALYSIS OF VOTING BEHAVIOUR IN LOUISIANA, 1828-1844. *Louisiana Studies 1974 13(2): 73-118.* Analyzes voting behavior in Louisiana by parishes, examining the votes given to the National Republicans/Whigs and Democrats in the presidential elections, and the Creole/Whigs and American/Democrats in the gubernatorial elections. These votes are examined in relation to the possible influence of ethnicity, nativity, slavery, sugar, cotton, wealth, and population change on voting patterns. Concludes that ethnicity and sugar production were the variables showing the greatest impact on voting behavior. Slavery is much less significant. Thus it appears that ethnocultural conflict, not class conflict, was more important in influencing voting behavior. 53 tables, 9 notes.

R. V. Ritter

2509. Halley, Robert M.; Acock, Alan C.; and Greene, Thomas H. ETHNICITY AND SOCIAL CLASS: VOTING IN THE 1973 LOS ANGELES ELECTIONS. *Western Pol. Q. 1976 29(4): 521-530.* Discusses how race and social status affect voting in city elections. Confirms the importance of race in biracial elections and suggests the importance of distinguishing between ethnic groups in theories of acculturation.

J/S

2510. Hammond, John L. REVIVAL RELIGION AND ANTISLAVERY POLITICS. *Am. Sociol. R. 1974 39(2): 175-186.* Tests the proposition that religious belief directly affects political attitudes and behavior with respect to revivals and antislavery voting in 19th-century Ohio. It has been claimed that revivals preached a new doctrine which demanded active opposition to slavery. The claim that revivalism had a direct, nonspurious effect on antislavery voting is tested in a multiple regression model which incorporates variables representing social structure, ethnicity, denominational membership, and prior political tradition. The effect of revivalism is strong despite all controls; the revivals transformed the religious orientations of those who experienced them, and this transformation affected their voting behavior.

J

2511. Hansen, Stephen L. THE ILLUSION OF OBJECTIVISM: A REVIEW OF RECENT TRENDS IN THE NEW POLITICAL HISTORY. *Hist. Methods 1979 12(3): 105-110.* In the New Political History, a combination of political science and history, there is presently an imbalance toward political science. Traditional historical evidence has come to be excluded entirely and only evidence that is objective and measurable is considered valid in research. Such a restricted notion of

reality trivializes and obscures history. Of the three books examined, only Kleppner's uses both traditional historical evidence and neutral data: Melvyn Hammarberg, *The Indiana Voter: The Historical Dynamics of Party Allegiance During the 1870s* (1977); Joel Silbey, Allan G. Bogue, and William H. Flanigan, eds., *The History of American Electoral Behavior* (1978); and Paul Kleppner, *The Third Electoral System, 1853-1892: Parties, Voters and Political Cultures* (1979). Based on these books and additional secondary literature; 22 notes.

J. D. Falk

2512. Harmond, Richard. TROUBLES OF MASSACHUSETTS REPUBLICANS DURING THE 1880'S. *Mid-America 1974 56(2): 85-99.* The historians Carl Degler and H. Wayne Morgan argue that the Republican Party's appeal to urban dwellers made it better able to deal with new urban and industrial problems than the Democratic Party. Other historians, like Paul Kleppner and Richard Jensen, discern no trend toward urban power in the Republican Party, and suggest that local, ethnic-cultural commitments are a better gauge of party success or failure than national political ideology. A case study of Massachusetts Republicans' mismanagement of local liquor and school issues suggests support for the Kleppner-Jensen hypothesis. Based on primary and secondary sources; 42 notes.

T. D. Schoonover

2513. House, James S. and Mason, William M. POLITICAL ALIENATION IN AMERICA, 1952-1968. *Am. Sociol. R. 1975 40(2): 123-147.* Social scientists and journalistic social commentators have viewed the 1950s as a period of political de-alienation and the 1960s as a period of re-alienation, and have designated a variety of groups as especially alienated in the 1960s—an impatient black population, restive Middle Americans and white ethnics, rebellious youth, etc. Converse (1972) showed that agreement with three of four survey items measuring political alienation declined in the 1950s and rose in the 1960s, and contended that the rise in the 1960s was fairly uniform across the whole population. This paper finds little change in the alienation items across demographically defined social aggregates. It analyzes attitudinal correlates of alienation in 1968, and shows that for two of the items alienation is higher among those whose attitude preferences deviate from the perceived status quo in *either* a right-wing *or*, left-wing direction. The rise in political alienation of the 1960s resulted from increasing discontent with policies and events, but this discontent cut across traditional demographic aggregates.

J

2514. Ireland, Owen S. THE ETHNIC-RELIGIOUS DIMENSION OF PENNSYLVANIA POLITICS, 1778-1779. *William and Mary Q. 1973 30(3): 423-448.* Discusses ethnic-religious antagonisms in Pennsylvania politics. Presbyterians were prominent in the Independence movement, and they captured political power. Much of the religious division erupted over the Test Acts, the state constitution, and the Anglican-dominated College of Philadelphia. Quakers were the most vociferous dissenters. Investigates voting patterns in the legislature and counties. Based on ethnic and county histories and on legislative and local records; 9 tables, 43 notes.

H. M. Ward

2515. Jensen, Richard. HISTORY FROM A DECK OF IBM CARDS. *Rev. in Am. Hist. 1978 6(2): 229-234.* Review article prompted by Melvyn Hammarberg's *The Indiana Voter: The Historical Dynamics of Party Allegiance During the 1870s* (Chicago: U. of Chicago Pr., 1977), a study of Indiana voting behavior which is more sociological than social psychological.

2516. Kelley, Bruce Gunn. ETHNOCULTURAL VOTING TRENDS IN RURAL IOWA, 1890-1898. *Ann. of Iowa 1978 44(6): 441-461.* Tests the ethnocultural model of midwestern voting patterns in the late 19th century developed by historians Paul Kleppner and Richard Jensen by examining the voting behavior of Irish, German, and Bohemian Catholics; German, Danish, Norwegian, and Swedish Lutherans; and Reform Dutch in rural Iowa during the 1890's. Concludes that the shift of "rural Iowa ethnics" to the Republican Party confirms the ethnocultural model as an explanation of voting patterns. Based on primary sources; 6 tables, 2 maps, 42 notes.

P. L. Petersen

2517. Kelley, Robert Lloyd. IDEOLOGY AND POLITICAL CULTURE FROM JEFFERSON TO NIXON. *Am. Hist. Rev. 1977 82(3): 531-562.* A revolution has occurred in the way historians look at American politics. We no longer consider just economic influences, but cultural

ones; ethnic identity, religious attitudes and memberships, styles of life; influences emotional as well as rational, cultural and ideological as well as economic and pragmatic. American politics begins in the British Isles, where the Anglican English served as the dominant host culture, the Scots, Irish, Welsh, and Dissenting English as the outgroups. Centuries of warfare and mutual hatred helped align peoples on either side in the two parties which formed in the United States: the Federalist-Whig-Republican line of descent being rooted in those of English (Yankee, New England) descent, aggressively moralistic in the older state-church tradition; the Jeffersonian Republican-Jacksonian Democratic line of descent being derived from a coalition of out-groups (Southern whites, Scotch-Irish, Dutch and German in the Middle States) with the secularistic, libertarian and equalitarian groups who were anti-Yankee, and devoted to laissez-faire not only in economics (designed to prevent capitalists from getting undue privileges and power over others through use of government) but in cultural affairs as well. Article traces progression of this fundamental alignment through the five party systems to the 1970's, relating party ideologies to their cultural membership. [Includes comments by Geoffrey Blodgett, Ronald P. Formisano, and Willie Lee Rose].
A

2518. Kellstedt, Lyman A. ETHNICITY AND POLITICAL BE-HAVIOR: INTER-GROUP AND INTERGENERATIONAL DIF-FERENCES. *Ethnicity 1974 1(4): 393-415.* Study of voting behavior and political participation in Buffalo, New York, 1967-68, indicates greater tendency toward participation among ethnic groups.

2519. Kleppner, Paul. IMMIGRANT GROUPS AND PARTISAN POLITICS. *Immigration Hist. Newsletter 1978 10(1): 1-5.* Examines the historiography (1940's-70's) of the effects of immigrant groups on the political system; calls for further study, specifically of immigrant voting during 1896-1928, attitudinal bases of group partisanship, and party activist and candidate recruitment.

2520. Knoke, David and Felson, Richard B. ETHNIC STRATIFI-CATION AND POLITICAL CLEAVAGE IN THE UNITED STATES, 1952-68. *Am. J. of Sociol. 1974 80(3): 630-642.* Data from five national survey samples show a small and declining covariation of ethnic prestige and party identification. Controls for socioeconomic stratification fail to eliminate the relationship, but controls for father's party or respondent's religion reduce the net effect of ethnic prestige to insignificance. The findings support a model of cultural lag in which the effects of ethnicity on politics persist via an intergenerational socialization of traditional ethnic group loyalties.
J

2521. Kolbe, Richard L. CULTURE, POLITICAL PARTIES AND VOTING BEHAVIOR: SCHUYLKILL COUNTY. *Polity 1975 8(2): 241-268.* In Schuylkill County, Pennsylvania, the Republican party has dominated in the 20th century, where the ethnic (Catholic majority) and economic (low income) composition of the population might lead to expectations of Democratic strength. In explaining the paradox of Republican success (after a strong 19th-century tendency to division on ethnic lines) with a population whose economic interests might reasonably have led them to support Democrats, the individualistic culture of the voters and the consonant laissez-faire ideology of the Republicans emerge as significant. One-party politics is the consequence, and the effect of an ineffective opposition is considered.
J

2522. Kousser, J. Morgan. THE "NEW POLITICAL HISTORY": A METHODOLOGICAL CRITIQUE. *Rev. in Am. Hist. 1976 4(1): 1-14.* Review article prompted by Ronald Formisano's *The Birth of Mass Political Parties: Michigan, 1827-1861* (1971), F. Sheldon Hackney's *Populism to Progressivism in Alabama* (1969), and Paul Kleppner's *The Cross of Culture: A Social Analysis of Midwestern Politics, 1850-1900* (1970); discusses the use of mass voting behavior in the writing and interpretation of political history.

2523. Kremm, Thomas W. CLEVELAND AND THE FIRST LIN-COLN ELECTION: THE ETHNIC RESPONSE TO NATIVISM. *J. of Interdisciplinary Hist. 1977 8(1): 69-86.* Politics in Cleveland, Ohio, on the eve of the Civil War did not revolve exclusively around the question of slavery extension. Accepted theories on the election do not adequately explain ethnic voting patterns in the city. The major division within the electorate was one of Catholics versus non-Catholics. The

Republican Party was as much an anti-Catholic coalition as it was an anti-slavery extension organization and non-Catholic voters, ethnic and native-American, voted accordingly. Newspapers and printed sources; 8 tables, 19 notes.
R. Howell

2524. Latner, Richard B. and Levine, Peter. PERSPECTIVES ON ANTEBELLUM PIETISTIC POLITICS. *Rev. in Am. Hist. 1976 4(1): 15-24.* Review article prompted by Ronald P. Formisano's *The Birth of Mass Political Parties: Michigan, 1827-1861* (1971), William G. Shade's *Banks or No Banks: The Money Issue in Western Politics, 1832-1865* (1972), and Michael F. Holt's *Forging a Majority: The Formation of the Republican Party in Pittsburgh, 1848-1860* (1969); discusses recent reinterpretations of US political history.

2525. Leventman, Seymour. POLITICS, ETHNICITY AND CLASS. *Urban and Social Change Rev. 1979 12(2): 32-34.* Discusses the response of ethnic groups to their participation in the political process for achieving social and economic goals in the 1960's and 1970's.

2526. Lorinskas, Robert A. THE POLITICAL IMPACT OF AN-GLO-SAXON ETHNICITY. *Ethnicity 1974 1(4): 417-421.* Fictitious election ballots using Polish and Anglo-Saxon surnames indicate that ethnicity is more powerful than political affiliation in electoral choice, 1970.

2527. McCormick, Richard L. ETHNO-CULTURAL INTERPRE-TATIONS OF NINETEENTH-CENTURY AMERICAN VOTING BEHAVIOR. *Pol. Sci. Q. 1974 89(2): 351-378.* Gives a critical overview of the findings of American political historians who have tried to explain late 19th-century party alignments in terms of ethnic and religious identifications of voters.
J

2528. McSeveney, Samuel T. ETHNIC GROUPS, ETHNIC CON-FLICTS, AND RECENT QUANTITATIVE RESEARCH IN AMERICAN POLITICAL HISTORY. *Int. Migration Rev. 1973 7(1): 14-33.* Discusses recent quantitative historiography about the role of ethnic groups in American politics 1850's-1960's; considers the impact of racial attitudes on the voting behavior of immigrants and minorities.

2529. Miller, Abraham H. ETHNICITY AND PARTY IDENTIFI-CATION: CONTINUATION OF A THEORETICAL DIALOGUE. *Western Pol. Q. 1974 27(3): 479-490.* In terms of party identification in the national political universe, ethnic-based political loyalties have converged under the umbrella of religion.
S

2530. Monroe, Alan D. OPERATIONALIZING POLITICAL CULTURE: THE ILLINOIS CASE. *Publius 1977 7(1): 107-120.* Systematically and quantitatively measures the historical sources of cultural variation in Illinois's 102 counties. Historical data reveal three distinct migratory streams into the state during the 19th century: native, Anglo-Saxon immigrant, and southern European immigrant. Election data suggest that these were characterized, in turn, by the moralistic, traditional, and individualistic traits set forth by Daniel Elazar in *Cities of the Prairie: The Metropolitan Frontier and American Politics* (New York: Basic Books, Inc., 1970). 3 tables, 7 notes.
A. Clive

2531. Nicholas, H. G. THE 1972 ELECTIONS. *J. of Am. Studies [Great Britain] 1973 7(1): 1-15.* An analysis, heavily emphasizing the presidential election, of the 1972 U.S. elections. In 1972, only 55% of the eligible voters cast ballots in the presidential election, indicating a significant distaste for politics among the American electorate. Speculates about probable reasons for the voter apathy. Examines the campaign issues, the tactics employed by the forces of Richard Milhous Nixon and George Stanley McGovern, and the "enigmatic" ethnic vote. Widespread "ticket-splitting" in the 1972 elections sharply differentiates this election from earlier electoral contests.
H. T. Lovin

2532. Nie, Norman H.; Curtis, Barbara; and Greeley, Andrew M. POLITICAL ATTITUDES AMONG AMERICAN ETHNICS: A STUDY OF PERCEPTUAL DISTORTION. *Ethnicity 1974 1(4): 317-344.* Empirical data on political and social attitudes and voting behavior among white ethnic groups, 1960's-74, indicates they are neither predominately liberal, nor wholly conservative.

2533. Plax, Martin. TOWARDS A REDEFINITION OF ETHNIC POLITICS. *Ethnicity 1976 3(1): 19-33.* Political decisionmaking, participation, and voting among ethnic groups show that consensus rather than conflict earmarks ethnic participation in politics during the 1960's.

2534. Polakoff, Keith Ian. DEMOCRATIC FACTIONALISM IN CALIFORNIA AND TEXAS, 1880-1920. *Rev. in Am. Hist. 1974 2(4): 535-540.* Review essay which describes the contents and major conclusions of R. Hal Williams' *The Democratic Party and California Politics, 1880-1896* (Stanford, Calif.: Stanford U. Pr., 1973) and Lewis L. Gould's *Progressives and Prohibitionists: Texas Democrats in the Wilson Era* (Austin: U. of Texas Pr., 1973), and assesses the books' contributions to understanding some of the political and ethnocultural issues during 1880-1919.

2535. Ratcliffe, Donald J. THE ROLE OF VOTERS AND ISSUES IN PARTY FORMATION: OHIO 1824. *J. of Am. Hist. 1973 59(4): 847-870.* The presidential election of 1824 in Ohio was a race among three candidates: Henry Clay, Andrew Jackson, and John Quincy Adams. Historians have traditionally viewed that election, narrowly won by Clay, as one in which ambitious politicians created catch-all party organizations designed to attract voters who were insensitive to political issues or ideology. In fact, issues were of predominant importance, and political organizations were built around constituency interests. Clay attracted votes from counties hoping to benefit from his "American system" of federally-supported internal improvements, Adams got support from New Englanders repelled by Clay's involvement in slavery, and Jackson gathered support from depression-ridden Cincinnati, Scotch Irish and German voters, and a general antipolitical animus. These alignments continued into the Whig Democrat era. 4 tables, 69 notes.
K. B. West

2536. Reynolds, John F. PIETY AND POLITICS: EVANGELISM IN THE MICHIGAN LEGISLATURE, 1837-1861. *Michigan Hist. 1977 61(4): 322-351.* Statistical analysis of roll-call votes in the Michigan House of Representatives during 1837-60 confirms the complexity of political motive during the Jacksonian Era. Neither the class conflict theory nor the ethnocultural, or "evangelical," approach fully explains voting on such issues as slavery, temperance, adultery, and public prayer. Although non-Democrats supported evangelical legislation in greater number, the major political parties were generally similar in their stands regarding such measures. Bills and resolutions regarding slavery were the most divisive partisan issues. Although there was a degree of evangelical cleavage, neither the Democrats nor the Whigs capitalized on it. Primary sources; 30 notes, 8 illus., 2 photos, 4 tables.
D. W. Johnson

2537. Rojek, Dean G. THE PROTESTANT ETHIC AND POLITICAL PREFERENCE. *Social Forces 1973 52(2): 168-177.* In a series of articles, Benton Johnson has investigated the effects of ascetic Protestantism on political party preference. His findings indicate that among laymen exposed to fundamentalist teachings, religious involvement would vary directly with Republican party preference. However, among laymen exposed to liberal teachings, religious involvement would vary inversely with Republican identification. This present study shows that church involvement and political party identification are not significantly related. A refinement of Johnson's liberal-fundamentalist dichotomy and his church interaction index again resulted in non-significant findings. Finally, a weighted least-squares procedure was employed yielding a set of linear estimation equations that again showed no significant effect. Results such as these should make the social scientist wary of the dangers associated with the measurement of religion and the contemporary relevance of Weber's Protestant ethic.
J

2538. Ryan, Thomas G. ETHNICITY IN THE 1940 PRESIDENTIAL ELECTION IN IOWA: A QUANTITATIVE APPROACH. *Ann. of Iowa 1977 43(8): 615-635.* After a statistical analysis of voting patterns in selected Iowa counties in 1936 and 1940, supports the traditional assumption of a large-scale defection of German American voters from Franklin D. Roosevelt. The data do not support, however, interpretations such as those of Robert E. Burke or Malcolm Moos which attribute Democratic losses between 1936 and 1940 to farm dissatisfaction, or the interpretations of Harold F. Gosnell or Warren Moscow which emphasize the general defection of Catholics from the Roosevelt coalition. Primary and secondary sources; 10 tables, 27 notes.
P. L. Petersen

2539. Schneider, Mark. MIGRATION, ETHNICITY AND POLITICS: A COMPARATIVE STATE ANALYSIS. *J. of Pol. 1976 38(4): 938-962.* To make possible a more accurate evaluation of ethnic identification as a basis of political organization, defines four dimensions of ethnicity important in US politics that have been used by social scientists as analytic foci; presents empirical evidence from six states documenting the relative political importance of the different dimensions of ethnicity; and identifies the characteristics of the states that appear to account for the observed variations in the relative impact of each form of ethnicity. 8 tables, 32 notes.
R. V. Ritter

2540. Shortridge, Ray M. THE VOTER REALIGNMENT IN THE MIDWEST DURING THE 1850'S. *Am. Pol. Q. 1976 4(2): 193-222.* Focuses on the shift of party loyalties in the 1850's which created the Republican Party. The Whigs, Free Soilers, and American Party faded from the political scene by 1860 and were superseded by the Republicans. The vote-flow among the political parties of the Midwest in the 1850's is examined. The realignment process varied among the most populous midwestern states. The 1850's realignment involved the 1856 fusion of Free Soilers and Whigs into a core of Republican voters, and the movement of many 1856 nativist voters and some 1856 innovators into the Republican ranks in 1860.
P. Travis

2541. Shover, John L. THE EMERGENCE OF A TWO-PARTY SYSTEM IN REPUBLICAN PHILADELPHIA, 1924-1936. *J. of Am. Hist. 1974 60(4): 985-1002.* Samuel Lubell has popularized the thesis that Al Smith's ethnic appeal in the 1928 election foreshadowed the urban, ethnic, "New Deal coalition" that Franklin D. Roosevelt put together so effectively after 1932. The evidence for Philadelphia voting patterns demonstrates that 1928 was *not* a critical election. Some major ethnic groups did vote Democratic in that year, but Jews, blacks, and Germans were not a part of the coalition till much later, and the Irish and Italian vote, heavily Democratic for Smith in 1928, did not persist in 1930 or even 1932. Furthermore, there was no great surge of voter protest against the Depression in 1932. Casts doubt upon the concept of a "critical election," emphasizing rather the importance of a critical, fluctuating period when new voter patterns start to crystallize. 4 tables, 43 notes.
K. B. West

2542. Shover, John L. ETHNICITY AND RELIGION IN PHILADELPHIA POLITICS, 1924-40. *Am. Q. 1973 25(5): 499-515.* When Philadelphia's ethnic and religious groups confronted vital political choices in 1928, they responded as blacks, Jews, Germans, or Catholics, not as assimilated Americans grouped cross-culturally by occupation, class, or neighborhood. Ethno-religious political consciousness continued to flourish in the 1930's leaving sparse evidence to sustain interpretations of voting behavior predicated on social classes. Based on primary and secondary sources; 6 tables, 40 notes.
W. D. Piersen

2543. Smith, W. Wayne. INVOLVING STUDENTS IN THE HISTORICAL PROCESS: AN ANALYSIS OF JACKSONIAN POLITICS. *Teaching Hist.: A J. of Methods 1978 3(1): 20-22.* Describes a laboratory exercise that historians can use in American political history to demonstrate how history can change. The basic question with which the students deal is this: what is the basis of American electoral behavior? Using the Jacksonian Era in American history, students can trace the historical debate over politics. Initially students examine the perspective of the "class-conflict" school of historians and draw conclusions about electoral behavior. Then by comparing socio-economic data with voting patterns, students test the class-conflict thesis. This exercise results in a general discussion about interpretations of American electoral behavior. 3 notes.
J

2544. Stave, Bruce M. A CONVERSATION WITH SAMUEL P. HAYS. *J. of Urban Hist. 1975 2(1): 88-123.* A transcription of a taped interview tracing the background, education, and works of Hays as well as the people and sources that had the most impact upon him. Biblio, 12 notes.
S. S. Sprague

2545. Vandermeer, Philip R. THE NEW POLITICAL HISTORY: PROGRESS AND PROSPECTS. *Computers and the Humanities 1977 11(5): 265-278.* Provides guidelines for research in areas of political history that require the use of quantitative methods, such as voting behavior, legislative roll-call analysis, prosopography, and analysis of institutions and organizations. 96 notes.
S

2546. Venecko, James J. and Kronenfeld, Jennie. PREFERENCES FOR PUBLIC EXPENDITURES AND ETHNO-RACIAL GROUP MEMBERSHIP: A TEST OF THE THEORY OF POLITICAL ETHOS. *Ethnicity 1977 4(4): 311-336.* A case study of the question of whether Anglo-Saxon Americans are more public-oriented than immigrant groups, and if these preferences persist despite changes in socioeconomic status. A test of the theory by means of interviews of 4,266 persons in 10 cities revealed that neither proponents nor opponents are entirely correct. Anglo-Saxons are not more public-conscious, nor are other groups necessarily more oriented to personal greed. The same mixed results prevail when socioeconomic conditions are analyzed. Certainly the theory holds in regard to some distinct issues, but no overall pattern could be discerned. 5 tables, 6 fig., 29 notes.					V. L. Human

2547. Weissman, Stephen R. WHITE ETHNICS & URBAN POLITICS IN THE SEVENTIES: THE CASE OF JERSEY CITY. *Polity 1976 9(2): 182-207.* Although the social rise of the "white ethnic" working class and the concomitant decline of the urban political machine has long been common knowledge, there is little systematic knowledge of the emerging patterns of urban politics. To provide a better understanding of contemporary white ethnic politics and policy, the author provides a case study of "reform" in Jersey City.					J

2548. Wyman, Roger E. AGRARIAN OR WORKING-CLASS RADICALISM? THE ELECTORAL BASIS OF POPULISM IN WISCONSIN. *Pol. Sci. Q. 1974-75 89(4): 825-848.* Demonstrates that Populism in Wisconsin arose out of socialist-oriented labor radicalism rather than from agricultural distress and that urban workers, not agrarians, provided the largest component of Populist supporters. His findings thus challenge the commonly held belief that Wisconsin had a long tradition of agrarian radicalism in the late nineteenth century.					J

2549. Wyman, Roger E. MIDDLE-CLASS VOTERS AND PROGRESSIVE REFORM: THE CONFLICT OF CLASS AND CULTURE. *Am. Pol. Sci. Rev. 1974 68(2): 488-504.* The middle-class character of the leadership of Progressivism has been well established for early 20th-century America, but the nature of the voting base of support for progressivism has not yet been established. The author examines whether or not middle-class voters supported progressive candidates at the polls and tests the relative strength of cultural factors (i.e., ethnicity and religion) versus class considerations as determinants of voting behavior. At least in the key progressive state of Wisconsin, middle-class voters failed to support progressive candidates in either general or primary elections; to the contrary, they provided the bulwark of support for conservative opponents of reform. Ethnocultural factors remained as the most powerful determinant of voter choice among urban voters in general elections, but class considerations often proved more influential in motivating voters in primary election contests.					J

Labor, Unions, and Radicalism

2550. Andersen, Arlow W. AMERICAN LABOR UNREST IN NORWAY'S PRESS: THE HAYMARKET AFFAIR AND THE PULLMAN STRIKE. *Swedish Pioneer Hist. Q. 1974 25(3-4): 208-219.* The labor movement in 19th-century America was paralleled in Norway, where it was sparked by Marcus Thrane. The Norwegian press closely followed the Haymarket affair and the Pullman strike. The reaction was generally antisocialist. The Norwegian press lacked the anti-alien prejudice and the emotionalism of the American press. Primary and secondary sources; 12 notes.					K. J. Puffer

2551. Andrews, Clarence A. "BIG ANNIE" AND THE 1913 MICHIGAN COPPER STRIKE. *Michigan Hist. 1973 57(1): 53-68.* The first large-scale mining operations in North America were in copper on the Keweenaw Peninsula of Upper Michigan. In 1913 when the Western Miners' Federation refused to call a strike over the introduction of labor-saving drills, Finn, Slovenian, Croatian, and Italian immigrant laborers called their own strike. Anna "Big Annie" Clemenc carried a flag at the head of the daily parade. The paraders wished to intimidate nonstrikers but to avoid violence. The tragedy-marked strike lasted nearly a year. "Big Annie" was jailed and never heard from again. 5 illus., 30 notes.					D. L. Smith

2552. Bailey, Kenneth R. A JUDICIOUS MIXTURE: NEGROES AND IMMIGRANTS IN THE WEST VIRGINIA MINES, 1880-1917. *West Virginia Hist. 1973 34(2): 141-161.* Ethnic and racial changes in West Virginia from the 1870's to the 1920's resulted from the expansion of the coal mining industry. Until 1890 few foreigners came to the mines, but by 1915 they constituted more than half of the work force. Recruitment by mining interests largely accounts for the influx. The introduction of Negroes, generally as an effort to check unionism, was only partly successful, as ties of common economic problems often overcame racial and ethnic differences. Based on newspapers; 81 notes.					C. A. Newton

2553. Birenbaum, Arnold and Greer, Edward. TOWARD A STRUCTURAL THEORY OF CONTEMPORARY WORKING CLASS CULTURE. *Ethnicity 1976 3(1): 4-18.* Explores historical features of the working class to assess relations with the ruling elites which failed to generate class consciousness. Immigrant ethnic and minority elements failed to unite due to extensive ethnic diversity, duality in forming the labor aristocracy, and race relations in developing working class culture during the 19th-20th centuries.					G. A. Hewlett

2554. Bo, Daniele. SUL PROCESSO DI FORMAZIONE DEL PARTITO COMUNISTA NEGLI STATI UNITI [On the formation process of the American Communist Party]. *Movimento Operaio e Socialista [Italy] 1976 22(1-2): 51-86.* The Communist Party of America began with the formation of the Socialist Party of America in 1901, then characterized by enormous geographical, ethnic, and ideological diversities. Within this context, the left wing slowly crystallized around issues such as the strike in 1912 in Lawrence by the workers of the American Woolen Company. The outbreak of war in 1914 also led to the further differentiation of positions. It was not until January 1921 that some of these dissenting groups merged to form the Communist Party. Its first few years were dedicated primarily to the "Americanization" of its political orientation. Part of this reorientation around national issues was an attempt to redefine the relationship between the Communist movement and the Negro movement. Primary and secondary sources; 153 notes.					M. T. Wilson

2555. Bodnar, John E. THE IMPACT OF THE "NEW IMMIGRATION" ON THE BLACK WORKER: STEELTON, PENNSYLVANIA, 1880-1920. *Labor Hist. 1976 17(2): 214-229.* Black workers in Steelton entered unskilled and semiskilled trades during 1880-1905, but with the rapid influx of Slavic and Italian immigrants Negroes suffered a devastating decline in occupational mobility until after World War I. Based on interviews and local records; 8 tables, 16 notes.					L. L. Athey

2556. Bodnar, John E. THE PROCUREMENT OF IMMIGRANT LABOR: SELECTED DOCUMENTS. *Pennsylvania Hist. 1974 41(2): 189-206.* Presents 23 letters during 1915-23 dealing with the Robesonia Iron Company's efforts to recruit immigrant and black laborers. The greatest efforts were made to obtain Italian and Slavic laborers, and company officials corresponded with a Russian lawyer in Philadelphia that specialized in the recruitment of foreign laborers. Efforts to recruit Negroes were made through a labor agent in Tennessee. The Robesonia Iron Company was located near Reading and operated a quarry, furnace, and mines. The company correspondence is part of the Colemen Collection held by the Pennsylvania Historical and Museum Commission; 9 notes.					D. C. Swift

2557. Bongiovanni, Bruno. LA TRADIZIONE RIVOLUZIONARIA AMERICANA E I COMMUNISTI DEI CONSIGLI EUROPEI [The American revolutionary tradition and the "Council Communists" of Europe]. *Movimento Operaio e Socialista [Italy] 1977 23(4): 457-474.* For Marx and his socialist contemporaries, the United States was a great laboratory. They hoped that unbridled capitalism and rapid industrial growth would bring with them a rise in proletarian consciousness and power. In America, in contrast to Europe outside the Iberian peninsula, the anarchist strains represented by the Industrial Workers of the World (IWW) often were stronger than Marxist elements (and both were outweighted in the United States by reformism). The IWW was in decline and the Stalinist US Communist Party in the ascendancy on the Left, when German exiles such as Paul Mattick arrived in the United States (he in 1926, more after 1933). He represented Left or

Council Communism, carrying on the traditions of Rosa Luxemburg, standing for decentralization, and for the sovereignty of the working class itself, without need for a Leninist vanguard, and for the inevitability of the revolution. His influence, and that of his allies, was strongly felt on the left of American Marxism in the 1930's. 31 notes.

J. C. Billigmeier

2558. Buhle, Mari Jo. SOCIALIST WOMEN AND THE "GIRL STRIKERS," CHICAGO, 1910. *Signs 1976 1(4): 1039-1051.* The 1910 Chicago garment workers' strike showed a new determined spirit in the American labor movement. The "new immigrants," especially young women, militantly opposed the United Garment Workers' conciliations with factory owners. Contemporary newspaper articles by Nellie M. Zeh and Mary O'Reilly represented Socialist women's responses to the strike and their efforts to publicize the implications of the struggle. Their perspective was rooted in their interpretation of the historic position of women workers. They themselves had given their girlhood to commodity production and felt a sisterhood with the young strikers. They saw the actions of the "girl strikers" as a symbol of the larger tendency in the industrial working class to determine their own destiny. Based on newspaper articles; 11 notes.

J. Gammage

2559. Cotkin, George B. STRIKEBREAKERS, EVICTIONS AND VIOLENCE: INDUSTRIAL CONFLICT IN THE HOCKING VALLEY, 1884-1885. *Ohio Hist. 1978 87(2): 140-150.* Examines the absence of violence toward strikebreakers in the Hocking Valley coal strike of 1884-85 in Ohio. Immigrant strikebreakers were brought to the coal mines by the operators and armed guards were posted on the properties, but violence against the strikebreakers was rare. When violence did appear, it was directed against the coal companies' property. Lasting over nine months, the strike ended in defeat for the miners. The strikers clearly had imposed limitations on the forms and objects of their violence. Based on manuscripts, archives, newspapers, and secondary sources; 2 illus., 43 notes.

N. Summers

2560. Dancis, Bruce. SOCIAL MOBILITY AND CLASS CONSCIOUSNESS: SAN FRANCISCO'S INTERNATIONAL WORKMEN'S ASSOCIATION IN THE 1880'S. *J. of Social Hist. 1977 11(1): 75-98.* Examines the social characteristics of the class conscious members of the International Workmen's Association revealing that they differ from the general working population of San Francisco because they were "both more stable and prosperous." This is because they were older and were more skilled workers which enabled them "to overcome ethnic differences within their own ranks." More research needs to be done, however, in regard to marital status and background of descent. 16 tables, 52 notes.

L. E. Ziewacz

2561. Dubofsky, Melvyn. THE "NEW" LABOR HISTORY: ACHIEVEMENTS AND FAILURES. *Rev. in Am. Hist. 1977 5(2): 249-254.* Review article prompted by Herbert G. Gutman's *Work, Culture, and Society in Industrializing America: Essays in American Working-Class and Social History* (New York: Alfred A. Knopf, 1976).

2562. Dye, Ira. EARLY AMERICAN MERCHANT SEAFARERS. *Pro. of the Am. Phil. Soc. 1976 120(5): 331-360.* Analyzes 2,388 American Seaman's Protection Certificates dated 1796 to 1818 "to build a quantitative, statistical description of [American seafarers] and to provide some initial analyses and inferences [about them]." The results were then compared with similar studies for 1940-45 and 1962-63. British prisoner-of-war data from the War of 1812 will be added in the future to complete the study of an important segment of early American society. Based on primary and secondary sources; 7 tables, 7 figs., 101 notes, biblio.

W. L. Olbrich

2563. Ehrlich, Richard L. IMMIGRANT STRIKE BREAKING ACTIVITY: A SAMPLING OF OPINION EXPRESSED IN THE NATIONAL LABOR TRIBUNE, 1878-1885. *Labor Hist. 1974 15(4): 529-542.* Investigates the question of the strikebreaking activity of immigrants as found in the *National Labor Tribune* from 1878-85. The lack of evidence for widespread use of immigrants to break strikes suggests that the traditional interpretation of unskilled immigrants relationship to the strike needs severe modification. 23 notes.

L. L. Athey

2564. Gerstle, Gary. THE MOBILIZATION OF THE WORKING CLASS COMMUNITY: THE INDEPENDENT TEXTILE UNION IN WOONSOCKET, 1931-1946. *Radical Hist. Rev. 1978 (17): 161-172.* Gives the history and purpose of the Independent Textile Workers, an industrial trade union founded in 1931 by Belgians in Woonsocket, Rhode Island; during 1934-43 they organized Woonsocket's French-Canadian workers.

2565. Gersuny, Carl. ELEANOR MARX IN PROVIDENCE. *Rhode Island Hist. 1978 37(3): 85-87.* Karl Marx's daughter Eleanor, with her companion Edward Aveling and Wilhelm Liebknecht, a Socialist deputy in the Reichstag, toured the United States at the invitation of the Labor Party. She spoke in Providence under the sponsorship of the Rhode Island Central Labor Union on 22 October 1886 as part of the effort to expand American socialism beyond the confines of German-speaking groups. Based on newspapers and secondary accounts; illus., 17 notes.

P. J. Coleman

2566. Gordon, Michael A. THE LABOR BOYCOTT IN NEW YORK CITY, 1880-1886. *Labor Hist. 1975 16(2): 184-229.* The labor boycotts in New York City originated primarily in the previous agricultural experiences of Irish immigrants in their struggle for land reforms. Thus, the labor boycott was a pre-industrial mode of protection adapted to industrial conditions. The mass arrests and trials of immigrants who advocated boycotts during 1880-86 are examined. Based upon newspapers, reports of the New York Bureau of Labor Statistics and secondary sources; 79 notes.

L. L. Athey

2567. Hareven, Tamara K. THE LABORERS OF MANCHESTER, NEW HAMPSHIRE, 1912-1922: THE ROLE OF FAMILY AND ETHNICITY IN ADJUSTMENT TO INDUSTRIAL LIFE. *Labor Hist. 1975 16(2): 249-265.* A case study of the Amoskeag Mills in Manchester, New Hampshire, which demonstrates the effect of ethnocentrism and family ties upon the modernization process. When the corporation introduced an efficiency and welfare system, the workers responded with attempts to control job mobility and hiring through their own ethnic and family affiliations. This was largely successful until the nine-month strike of 1922. Based on statistical family research, government reports and the *Amoskeag Bulletin*. Table; 25 notes.

L. L. Athey

2568. Hareven, Tamara and Langenbach, Randolph. VOICES OF A VANISHED AMOSKEAG. *Am. Heritage 1978 29(6): 14-25.* Excerpted from the authors' book *Amoskeag: Life and Work in an American Factory-City.* Selections are illustrative of the varied reactions of workers in the Amoskeag textile mills in Manchester, New Hampshire, to life in such an environment, 1920's-30's. 11 illus.

J. F. Paul

2569. Harney, Robert F. THE PADRONE AND THE IMMIGRANT. *Can. R. of Am. Studies 1974 5(2): 101-118.* Reexamines traditional conceptions of the padrone system, in which immigrants are viewed as "slaves without volition and powerless before the padrone." In reality, padrones were both exploiters and patrons of the immigrants. They provided jobs for immigrants and simultaneously were the cultural link to the European homelands to which most immigrants planned to return after brief sojourns in America. Based on government documents and secondary sources; 80 notes.

H. T. Lovin

2570. Holt, James. TRADE UNIONISM IN THE BRITISH AND U.S. STEEL INDUSTRIES, 1888-1912: A COMPARATIVE STUDY. *Labor Hist. 1977 18(1): 5-35.* Compares the development of labor unions in the steel industry in the United States and Great Britain. The weakness of US industrial and political labor organizations is found in the structure and policies of the steel industry's business organizations and not in a lack of class solidarity, new immigration, etc. Based on union membership rolls, government reports, and newspapers; 64 notes.

L. L. Athey

2571. Jeffreys-Jones, Rhodri. THEORIES OF AMERICAN LABOUR VIOLENCE. *J. of Am. Studies [Great Britain] 1979 13(2): 245-264.* Historians disagree when attempting to explain those outbreaks of labor violence plaguing America during the Gilded Age and early 20th century. Some emphasized environmental forces; others stressed the impacts of race and heredity. A third group focused on clashing cultural elements, while another attributed the violence to "biological-instinctual imperatives." A fifth group claimed that ideology had insured such turmoil. 49 notes.   H. T. Lovin

2572. Klehr, Harvey. THE BRIDGMAN DELEGATES. *Survey [Great Britain] 1976 22(2): 87-95.* In August 1922 the third convention of the Communist Party USA met secretly near Bridgman, Michigan. The convention, which was attended by nearly all the leading party figures, was raided by the FBI and the police, who acted on information provided by an informant posing as a conventioneer. Seized dossiers provided biographical information about each of the delegates and indicated that they came largely from Eastern and Central Europe, only two failed to list English as a language they spoke or as their main language, most were Americanized, the most popular former party of affiliation was the Socialist Party and the second was the IWW, most had been radicals prior to the Russian Revolution of 1917, the vast majority did not hold official trade union positions, very few worked in heavy industry, and a substantial number had been arrested at least once. Primary and secondary sources; table, 4 notes, appendix.   R. G. Neville

2573. Klehr, Harvey. FEMALE LEADERSHIP IN THE COMMUNIST PARTY OF THE UNITED STATES OF AMERICA. *Studies in Comparative Communism 1977 10(4): 394-402.* In 1921 representation of women on the Central Committee was small; in the 1930's it rose and in 1959 and 1961, 10 women were in the party leadership, the largest number ever. Women took an average of 15.4 years from admission to the party to membership in the Central Committee while men took 11.6 years. Jews constituted the single largest ethnic group among Party leaders but took the longest time to reach Central Committee membership, presumably because of a Party effort to present a less Jewish image. Few women were members of the many committees connected with the Central Committee. On some committees however, the percentage of women reflected the female percentage of the Party. The fact that the Party was heavily foreign-born may have affected the careers of women since many of the foreign cultures placed women in a subordinate position. Communists were not notably more successful than other associations in bringing women into leadership positions despite an ideological commitment. 3 tables, fig., 6 notes.   D. Balmuth

2574. Leinenweber, Charles. SOCIALISTS IN THE STREETS: THE NEW YORK CITY SOCIALIST PARTY IN WORKING CLASS NEIGHBORHOODS, 1908-1918. *Sci. and Soc. 1977 41(2): 152-171.* Socialism in New York City before World War I not only was politically oriented as part of an international radical movement but also was an integral part of the manifestation of working class culture, revealing cultural influences derived from ethnic and class traditions still vitally extant in urban neighborhoods. Socialism took to the streets through organized and spontaneous parades held to indicate neighborhood working class solidarity with striking employees, many of whom were residents of the areas of the parades. Socialist election campaigns were demonstrations of working class self-confidence and provided opportunities for neighborhood entertainment as well as being appeals for votes for radical candidates. The socialist street corner speaker provided a colorful addition to neighborhood street culture.   N. Lederer

2575. Licht, Walter and Barron, Hal Seth. LABOR'S MEN: A COLLECTIVE BIOGRAPHY OF UNION OFFICIALDOM DURING THE NEW DEAL YEARS. *Labor Hist. 1978 19(4): 532-545.* Analyzes labor leadership during the New Deal years from the 1940 edition of *Who's Who in Labor.* A sample of 400 officials reveals that labor leaders were predominantly male, white, and middle-aged. Ideological factors were more important to the labor movement. 7 tables, 19 notes.   L. L. Athey

2576. Lynd, Staughton. WHY IS THERE NO SOCIALIST MOVEMENT IN THE UNITED STATES? *Rev. in Am. Hist. 1974 2(1): 115-120.* Reviews Gerald Roseblum's *Immigrant Workers: Their Impact on American Labor Radicalism* (New York: Basic Books, 1973) and suggests that the failure of American socialism resulted from immigrant labor's narrow economic motivation and ethnic fragmentation, while Harold V. Aurant, *From the Molly Maguires to the United Mine Workers: The Social Ecology of an Industrial Union, 1869-1897* (Philadelphia: Temple U. Pr., 1973) argues that union membership transformed ethnic consciousness to worker consciousness. 3 notes.   W. D. Piersen

2577. McCormack, John F., Jr. HELL ON SATURDAY AFTERNOON. *Mankind 1976 5(5): 21-27.* A devastating fire which claimed the lives of 146 factory workers in the Asch Building in New York City's garment district, 1911, made public the dangerous working conditions in the city's factories.

2578. McGouldrick, Paul F. and Tannen, Michael B. DID AMERICAN MANUFACTURERS DISCRIMINATE AGAINST IMMIGRANTS BEFORE 1914? *J. of Econ. Hist. 1977 37(3): 723-746.* Fits wage functions to two distinct data sources: US Immigration Commission surveys of 1908-10, supplemented by the 1909 Census of Manufactures, and a Department of Labor survey of production costs in nine protected industries, directed by the US Commissioner of Labor, Carroll D. Wright. Regression analysis applied to both sets of data concludes that there was moderate discrimination against southern and eastern European immigrants. Based on census data, Department of Labor statistics, and secondary sources; 3 tables, 34 notes.   D. J. Trickey

2579. Monteleone, Renato. SAM GOMPERS: PROFILO DI UN JINGO AMERICANO [Sam Gompers: profile of an American jingo]. *Movimento Operaio e Socialista [Italy] 1976 22(1-2): 133-152.* Defines "jingo" in its American context and says it accurately describes Samuel Gompers, founder of the American Federation of Labor. Gompers openly supported and initiated racist policies; AFL exclusion of nonqualified workers coincided with an influx of immigrant workers. Gompers fought hard to stop immigration, particularly of Orientals, because he feared for American independence and security. Along with the industrialists and financiers of his day, Gompers refused to acknowledge a connection between capitalism and imperialism and failed to recognize what was occurring in international politics. Protesting Bolshevism, he failed to comprehend the threat of a reactionary crisis of the democratic bourgeoisie and thus later suggested to American workers that fascism was a model for the reconciliation of the classes. Primary and secondary sources.   M. T. Wilson

2580. Montgomery, David. GUTMAN'S NINETEENTH-CENTURY AMERICA. *Labor Hist. 1978 19(3): 416-429.* Review article prompted by Herbert G. Gutman's *Work, Culture, and Society in Industrializing America* (1976). 27 notes.   L. L. Athey

2581. Musselman, Barbara L. WORKING CLASS UNITY AND ETHNIC DIVISION: CINCINNATI TRADE UNIONISTS AND CULTURAL PLURALISM. *Cincinnati Hist. Soc. Bull. 1976 34(1): 121-143.* Chronicles attempts of working classes, 1893-1920, in Cincinnati to unify along class rather than ethnic lines; discusses the labor union movement in Cincinnati, its pre-World War I domination by German and Irish Americans, and postwar ascendancy of Russian Jews, Orientals, and Blacks.

2582. Myers, George C. MIGRATION AND THE LABOR FORCE. *Monthly Labor Rev. 1974 97(9): 12-16.* A review article prompted by five books dealing with migration of labor in the United States and western Europe: Ellen M. Bussey, *The Flight from Rural Poverty—How Nations Cope* (Lexington, Mass.: D. C. Heath, 1973), Stephen Castles and Godula Kosack, *Immigrant Workers and Class Structure in Western Europe* (London: Oxford U. Pr., 1973), Gerald Rosenblum, *Immigrant Workers: Their Impact on American Labor Radicalism* (New York: Basic Books, 1973), Lyle and Magdaline Shannon, *Minority Migrants in the Urban Community: Mexican-American and Negro Adjustments to Industrial Society* (Beverly Hills, Calif.: Sage Publications, 1973), and Michael Mann, *Workers on the Move: The Sociology of Relocation* (New York: Cambridge U. Pr., 1973).

2583. Papanikolas, Helen Z. UNIONISM, COMMUNISM, AND THE GREAT DEPRESSION: THE CARBON COUNTY COAL STRIKE OF 1933. *Utah Hist. Q. 1973 41(3): 254-300.* In 1933 the United Mine Workers of America and the National Miners Union attempted to unionize the bituminous coal fields of Carbon County. Immigrant laborers were attracted to the NMU. A strike set for Labor Day spread unrest, protests, and violence throughout the county. Mine operators called for the National Guard, maintaining that strikers were anarchists and communists. Many strikers were arrested and placed in bullpens at a ball park. While the NMU was involved with the strike the UMWA negotiated with operators on a coal code, which was adopted in

October. The NMU declined in importance thereafter. Significant gains for labor did occur in Carbon County in 1933. Map, illus., 147 notes.
H. S. Marks

2584. Papanikolas, Helen Z. UTAH'S COAL LANDS: A VITAL EXAMPLE OF HOW AMERICA BECAME A GREAT NATION. *Utah Hist. Q. 1975 43(2): 104-124.* The discovery of vast coal fields in eastern Utah in 1875 and the resulting railroad competition ended pioneer Utah's fuel problems. Mines also brought immigrants. Each major immigrant group came as strike-breakers during Utah's struggling labor movement. Each group contributed its own nationalism, folk culture, and animosities. The coal fields brought together pioneer hardiness, American individualism, immigrant brawn, and bountiful resources to form a unique blend of cultures. Based on primary and secondary sources; 10 illus., 34 notes.
J. L. Hazelton

2585. Pollnac, Ricard B.; Gersuny, Carl; and Poggie, John J., Jr. ECONOMIC GRATIFICATION PATTERNS OF FISHERMEN AND MILLWORKERS IN NEW ENGLAND. *Human Organization 1975 34(1): 1-7.* Describes a 1972 study of economic gratification orientations, concluding that they "are related to occupation, temporal perspective, and ethnicity."
S

2586. Powell, Allan Kent. THE "FOREIGN ELEMENT" AND THE 1903-4 CARBON COUNTY COAL MINERS' STRIKE. *Utah Hist. Q. 1975 43(2): 125-154.* Finnish, Slavic, and Italian miners provided the strength behind a serious labor confrontation in Carbon County, Utah, in 1903. The Utah Fuel Company refused union recognition. The Utah National Guard was called out. Charles DeMolli, Con Kelliner, Mother Mary Jones, and Samuel H. Gilson involved themselves in the strike. The strike failed because the union lacked internal and external support and the company played on antiforeign sentiments in defending its position. Based on primary and secondary sources; 9 illus., 65 notes.
J. L. Hazelton

2587. Roediger, David. RACISM, RECONSTRUCTION, AND THE LABOR PRESS: THE RISE AND FALL OF THE *ST. LOUIS DAILY PRESS,* 1864-1866. *Sci. and Soc. 1978 42(2): 156-177.* The *Daily Press* originated during a period of class struggle in St. Louis, Missouri, as striking printers established the organ either as a means of winning their strike or as a beginning towards a permanent major labor voice in the city. The newspaper continued its existence after the strike as a medium for exploited white labor and was supported on an international basis. It endeavored to attract Irish workers through its espousal of the cause of Fenianism. It also tried to advocate the cause of female labor equality. It failed to become a permanent part of the St. Louis newspaper scene owing to fragmentation in labor's political ranks between the conservative Johnsonian Democrats exhibiting racism and the adherents of Radical Republicanism, many of whom were German workers. During its last days, it tried to reverse its field on racism and Radical Republicanism by championing black rights and the Republican cause, but to no avail. Its history illustrated the corroding influence of racism on labor.
N. Lederer

2588. Scott, Joan W. L'HISTOIRE DU MONDE OUVRIER AUX ÉTATS-UNIS DEPUIS 1960 [The history of the labor world in the United States since 1960]. *Mouvement Social [France] 1977 July-Sept.(100): 121-131.* Studies information in historical research orientation in the United States after 1960. Historians have reversed their perspective on the labor movement, from a previous emphasis on economic history to an emphasis on social history. The change in methodology which resulted from this reversal was evident in research published in the early 1970's. The new methodology is influenced by three factors: 1) the New Left trend of local militant groups which express class conflict outside established organizations, calling for reinterpretation of class struggle and class consciousness concepts, 2) the influence of the social sciences and especially sociology on labor history, calling for research into the causes of social agitation and instability, such as urban violence and labor unrest, and 3) the new availability of statistical analysis and scientific method in research, permitting the historian to take into account certain quantitative data never before considered. The new research orientation also considers aspects of culture rather than ideology in the labor movement, leading to studies on ethnic background, family life, professional mobility, and cultural political movements, such as those led by blacks and women. Based on published works; 12 notes.
S. Sevilla

2589. Silvia, Philip T., Jr. THE POSITION OF "NEW" IMMIGRANTS IN THE FALL RIVER TEXTILE INDUSTRY. *Internat. Migration Rev. 1976 10(2): 221-232.* Discusses the reception of Portuguese and Polish immigrants by French Canadians in textile industries and trade unions in Fall River, Massachusetts, 1890-1905.

2590. Smith, Duane A. THE SAN JUANER: A COMPUTERIZED PORTRAIT. *Colorado Mag. 1975 52(2): 137-152.* Using the questionnaires of the federal census of 1880 and the state census of 1885, the author presents a computerized portrait of San Juan miners of southwestern Colorado. Analyzes origins, nationality, age, marital status, profession, sex, and the like. Based mainly on primary sources; 5 illus., 17 notes.
O. H. Zabel

2591. Sturmthal, Adolf. WERNER SOMBART UND DER AMERIKANISCHE SOZIALISMUS [Werner Sombart and American socialism]. Botz, Gerhard; Hautmann, Hans; and Konrad, Helmut, eds. *Geschichte und Gesellschaft. Festschrift für Karl R. Stadler zum 60. Geburtstag* (Linz-Wien: Europa Verlag, 1974): 281-295. At the turn of the century Werner Sombart (1863-1941) analyzed phenomena in American industrial society, which lacked a strong socialist movement. Sombart's studies proved that the high living standard of American workers and the continuous threat of unemployment as a result of the never-ending supply of workers through immigration caused a lack of solidarity and class consciousness among the American working class. Based on Sombart's works and secondary literature; 8 notes.
R. Wagnleitner

2592. Thompson, Agnes L. NEW ENGLAND MILL GIRLS. *New-England Galaxy 1974 16(2): 43-49.* Describes life in the woolen and cotton mills of Lowell, Massachusetts, in the 1840's and 1850's. Farm girls gained economic independence by working for a few years before marriage, but were closely supervised in the mill, boarding house, and community, and had to cope with long hours, low wages, and limited social and educational opportunities. By 1857 competition forced their replacement by a permanent industrial working class of Irish and French Canadians. 6 illus.
P. C. Marshall

2593. Walkowitz, Daniel J. STATISTICS AND THE WRITING OF WORKINGCLASS CULTURE: A STATISTICAL PORTRAIT OF THE IRON WORKERS IN TROY, NEW YORK, 1860-1880. *Labor Hist. 1974 15(3): 416-460.* Provides a statistical profile of the iron workers of Troy, New York, as a vehicle for examining the relationship between class and culture. Census data can illuminate cultural and class configurations which shape working-class behavior, but it is necessary to integrate statistics with more traditional sources to encompass all dimensions of culture. Based on census schedules for 1860 and 1880 and secondary sources; 11 statistical tables, 66 notes.
L. L. Athey

2594. Zieger, Robert H. OLDTIMERS & NEWCOMERS: CHANGE AND CONTINUITY IN THE PULP, SULPHITE UNION IN THE 1930'S. *J. of Forest Hist. 1977 21(4): 188-201.* The International Brotherhood of Pulp, Sulphite, and Paper Mill Workers was organized in 1909, but it failed to expand as rapidly as did the paper industry. In the mid-1930's, however, it did expand rapidly to include urban workers, many of whom were European immigrants and women. When it expanded into the South, it had to establish separate charters for black and white workers at the paper mills. Its new locals in the Pacific Northwest "exhibited a remarkable degree of suspicion and even contempt for the international union." Based on the IBPSPMW Papers and on primary and secondary sources; 12 illus., 27 notes.
F. N. Egerton

Foreign Policy Involvement

2595. Bryson, Thomas A. A BICENTENNIAL REASSESSMENT OF AMERICAN-MIDDLE EASTERN RELATIONS. *Australian J. of Pol. and Hist. [Australia] 1978 24(2): 174-183.* A consideration of the ethnic factor in American relations with the Middle East, concentrating on the efforts of Greeks, Armenians, and Zionists. Appeals by the small US Greek community in the 1820's were met by official neutrality but private goodwill. The 52,000-strong Armenian community got some influential support for the abortive plan for a US Mandate in Armenia 1919. Zionists proved the most successful lobbyists: President Harry S. Truman endorsed partition and de facto recognition of Israel in 1948, against State Department advice, to secure electoral advantage. Criticizes the recent "special relationship" with Israel in the context of wider Middle East interests. Documented from monographs and articles; 65 notes.
W. D. McIntyre

2596. Dobriansky, Lev E. THE UNFORGETTABLE FORD GAFFE. *Ukrainian Q. 1977 33(4): 366-377.* Examines the effect on President Gerald R. Ford's election campaign of his statement on Soviet domination of Eastern Europe during the second campaign debate. Presents evidence to show that this was the deciding mistake in Ford's loss of the presidential election, particularly when viewed with other statements and actions emanating from the Kissinger policy of detente. The Carter administration also has demonstrated a lack of true understanding for the position of Eastern Europe and the other captive nations. 27 notes.
K. N. T. Crowther

2597. Garrett, Stephen A. EASTERN EUROPEAN ETHNIC GROUPS AND AMERICAN FOREIGN POLICY. *Pol. Sci. Q. 1978 93(2): 301-323.* Discusses the significance of Eastern European Americans in US politics and US foreign policy regarding Eastern Europe and the USSR.

2598. Hansen, Niels. DER EINFLUSS ETHNISCHER MINDERHEITEN AUF DIE AUSSENPOLITIK DER VEREINIGTEN STAATEN [The influence of ethnic minorities on the foreign policy of the United States]. *Europa-Archiv [West Germany] 1977 32(17): 551-560.* The influence of ethnic groups, most notably Poles, Jews, and Greeks, on American foreign policy (to the benefit of the homeland) has grown stronger since World War II.

2599. Miller, James E. A QUESTION OF LOYALTY: AMERICAN LIBERALS, PROPAGANDA, AND THE ITALIAN-AMERICAN COMMUNITY, 1939-1940. *Maryland Hist. 1978 9(1): 49-71.* Examines the extensive effort of the Roosevelt administration to counter Fascist support among the Italian Americans. Despite massive efforts by the Office of War Information, conservative Italians remained in control of media and Italian fraternal organizations. The fear of fifth column activity was baseless. The entire campaign was led by liberals and illustrates the increasing tendency of liberals to turn to the government to achieve their ends. Based on US archives and secondary sources; 3 illus., 59 notes.
G. O. Gagnon

2600. Weil, Martin. CAN THE BLACKS DO FOR AFRICA WHAT THE JEWS DID FOR ISRAEL? *Foreign Policy 1974 (15): 109-129.* Compares the influence of black Americans on US foreign policy with that of American Jews and Poles.
S

Wars and Responses to Wars

The Civil War

2601. Cook, Adrian. "ASHES AND BLOOD." *Am. Hist. Illus. 1977 12(5): 30-35, 38-40.* Chronicles the riots in New York City July 1863, sparked by anti-draft sentiment during the Civil War.

2602. Gallman, Robert E. HUMAN CAPITAL IN THE 80 YEARS OF THE REPUBLIC: HOW MUCH DID AMERICA OWE THE REST OF THE WORLD? *Am. Econ. Rev. 1977 67(1): 27-31.* Suggests two sets of immigrants contributed to American history far beyond what any conventional or statistical analysis has indicated. The condition of immigrant slaves contributed to the advent of the Civil War while later Irish and German immigrants determined the war's outcome. 9 refs.
D. K. Pickens

2603. Horowitz, Murray M. ETHNICITY AND COMMAND: THE CIVIL WAR EXPERIENCE. *Military Affairs 1978 42(4): 182-189.* Ethnic considerations in appointments to leadership positions in the North were evident during the American Civil War, especially so in the case of the Germans, less so with the Irish, and only to a negligible extent with other groups. Republicans vied for the German vote, and Carl Schurz, a spokesman for the Germans, recruited and attained general rank. While many Germans were moving into the Republican ranks, the Irish were not. They were recruited but sensitivity toward them never matched the administration's concern for the Germans. Other ethnic groups, smaller in number, did not warrant special attention nor present significant problems. Primary and secondary sources; 47 notes.
A. M. Osur

2604. Klement, Frank L. SOUND AND FURY: CIVIL WAR DISSENT IN THE CINCINNATI AREA. *Cincinnati Hist. Soc. Bull. 1977 35(2): 99-114.* Gives reasons for Civil War dissent in the Cincinnati area, particularly among the Irish Americans and German American Catholics, and includes the political portraits of six prominent Democrats who represented dissenting views.

2605. Lerski, George J. JEWISH-POLISH AMITY IN LINCOLN'S AMERICA. *Polish Rev. 1973 18(4): 34-51.* Describes the participation of Polish Americans and Polish Jews in the Civil War, their social organizations, and cooperation in reacting to the 1863 Polish insurrection.
S

2606. Mills, Gary B. ALIEN NEUTRALITY AND THE RED RIVER CAMPAIGN: A STUDY OF CASES HEARD BEFORE THE INTERNATIONAL CLAIMS COMMISSIONS. *Southern Studies 1977 16(2): 181-200.* In Louisiana during the Civil War there were 81,000 aliens, primarily British and French. Although enjoined by their own and the American national government to remain neutral, many found it difficult. Compulsory conscription, confiscation of possessions, and destruction of property frequently occurred. When Union troops entered the South, they followed the same practices. Recovery of losses suffered by aliens was neither prompt nor easy after the war. Two international claims commissions sat, 1871-73 and 1880-84. Of 53 claims, 15 were ruled valid. Based on Records of Boundary and Claims Commissions in the National Archives and on secondary sources; 43 notes, 4 appendixes.
J. Buschen

World War I

2607. Alexander, Ronald. HENRY WATTERSON AND WORLD WAR I. *J. of the West Virginia Hist. Assoc. 1977 1(1): 15-25.* Reviews the stinging anti-German sentiment expressed by Henry Watterson in the Louisville *Courier-Journal*'s editorials during 1914-17.

2608. Alexander, Ronald R. HENRY WATTERSON AND WORLD WAR I. *Filson Club Hist. Q. 1978 52(3): 251-262.* Covers the period before America entered World War I. Henry Watterson, editor of the Louisville *Courier-Journal*, was a rabid anti-German propagandist who advocated war with the Central Powers despite his personal isolationism. His crude attacks on German Americans, particularly those living in Louisville, drew protests from that community, but these editorials were the forerunner of later government policy. Documentation from the Louisville *Courier-Journal*. 52 Notes.
G. B. McKinney

2609. Allen, Leola. ANTI-GERMAN SENTIMENT IN IOWA DURING WORLD WAR I. *Ann. of Iowa 1974 42(6): 418-429.* Because of the presence of a large number of German Americans in Iowa at the time of World War I, concern for their loyalty and persecution were serious problems during the governorship of William Lloyd Harding. German Americans who did not meet their county quota under the Liberty Loan bond campaigns often faced "slacker courts." The governor's ban on the public use of foreign languages in the state, coupled with

Woodrow Wilson's request that foreign-born citizens plan Fourth of July celebrations, were only part of the contradictory and confusing scenario which developed. Germans were accused of sedition and even espionage, and humiliating tactics used against them did not cease with the signing of the Armistice. 33 notes.

C. W. Olson

2610. Bigham, Darrel E. CHARLES LEICH AND COMPANY OF EVANSVILLE: A NOTE ON THE DILEMMA OF GERMAN AMERICANS DURING WORLD WAR I. *Indiana Mag. of Hist. 1974 70(2): 95-121.* German immigrant Charles Leich, a naturalized American citizen and resident (for nearly 70 years) of Evansville, Indiana, was stranded in Germany just when the United States entered World War I. For years, his sons tried to get money to him and to protect his Indiana business, which was threatened with confiscation by the Alien Property Custodian and Mitchell Palmer's Bureau of Investigation. Time and again Leich's sons had to prove his American citizenship and that he had remained an American citizen after the outbreak of hostilities. Finally, in 1922, the government dropped claims against the business of the now-deceased Leich. Based on primary sources; illus., photo, 61 notes.

N. E. Tutorow

2611. Bilger, Edda. THE *OKLAHOMA VORWÄRTS*: THE VOICE OF GERMAN-AMERICANS IN OKLAHOMA DURING WORLD WAR I. *Chronicles of Oklahoma 1976 54(2): 245-260.* Discusses the wartime editorial stance taken by the *Oklahoma Vorwärts,* a German-language newspaper edited by John Hüssy; examines public opinion about "anti-loyal" statements in the newspaper and about German Americans, 1914-18.

2612. Chern, Kenneth S. THE POLITICS OF PATRIOTISM: WAR, ETHNICITY, AND THE NEW YORK MAYORAL CAMPAIGN, 1917. *New-York Hist. Soc. Q. 1979 63(4): 290-313.* The mayoral election in New York City in 1917 reflected the tensions, ethnic-aroused passions, and uncertainties in American life as the nation geared for war. The incumbent, John Purroy Mitchell, hoped for reelection on a Fusion ticket; instead he was opposed by a Tammany Democrat, a Republican, and a Socialist. In the bitter campaign which followed, Mitchell stressed patriotism and the cause of the Allies and thus alienated a large segment of the city's voting population, heavily weighted with second generation Irish and Germans. The result was a plurality for Tammany-backed John F. Hylan; Mitchell ran a poor second, barely beating the Socialist candidate, Morris Hillquit. Hylan's victory seemed to indicate that the American voter, in time of high tension or stress, tended to turn to a conservative leader who promised political security. It would happen again in 1952 on the national level. 7 illus., 40 notes.

C. L. Grant

2613. Chrystal, William G. REINHOLD NIEBUHR AND THE FIRST WORLD WAR. *J. of Presbyterian Hist. 1977 55(3): 285-298.* Reinhold Niebuhr (1892-1970) was recently ordained in the German Evangelical Synod of North America and had just become pastor of a congregation in Detroit when America became involved in World War I. During the war he repeatedly stressed the need to be loyal to the nation of one's birth or adoption. Theologically, however, he went beyond the issue of national loyalty as he endeavored to fashion a realistic ethical perspective of patriotism and pacifism. He endeavored to work out a realistic approach to the moral danger posed by aggressive powers which many idealists and pacifists failed to recognize. During the war he also served his denomination as Executive Secretary of the War Welfare Commission while maintaining his pastorate in Detroit. A pacifist at heart, he saw compromise as a necessity and was willing to support war in order to find peace—"compromising for the sake of righteousness." Based largely on Niebuhr's papers and publications; 41 notes.

H. M. Parker, Jr.

2614. Clary, David A., ed. "DIFFERENT MEN FROM WHAT WE WERE": POSTWAR LETTERS OF CARL A. SCHENCK AND AUSTIN F. CARY. *J. of Forest Hist. 1978 22(4): 228-234.* Carl A. Schenck (1868-1955) and Austin F. Cary (1865-1936) were pioneer foresters of similar outlook who had much impact on forestry in America. But German-born Schenck returned home to fight with the Imperial Army during World War I. In a letter to Cary (1921), Schenck revealed the anguish of postwar Germany and decried the revenge taken by the Allies. In a rather cool letter several years later (1924), Cary noted his distaste for

Schenck's political position ("We . . . are considerably different men from what we were a dozen years ago, . . ."), but offered cooperation on the basis of the "old professional sympathy between us." Biographical and bibliographical sketches of both men are included in this article, which is part of a theme issue on forestry and the World War I era. Primary and secondary sources; 4 illus., 14 notes.

R. J. Fahl

2615. Dorsett, Lyle W. THE ORDEAL OF COLORADO'S GERMANS DURING WORLD WAR I. *Colorado Mag. 1974 51(4): 277-293.* Discusses the indignities suffered by German nationals in Colorado, 1917-18.

2616. Dwyer, James A. *DER CHRISTLICHE APOLIGETE:* GERMAN PROPHET TO AMERICA: 1914-1918. *Methodist Hist. 1977 15(2): 75-94. Der Christliche Apologete* was the official organ of German Methodists in the United States. At the outbreak of World War I in 1914 it took a stand against militarism and resolution of international disputes by warfare. It called for neutrality on the part of the United States, arguing against American entry into the war. As the war progressed in 1917 and 1918, changes were made both in the editorial content of *Apologete* and the administration at Baldwin-Wallace College, both of which were in disfavor with English-speaking Methodists. 48 notes.

H. L. Calkin

2617. Edwards, John Carver. AMERICA'S VIGILANTES AND THE GREAT WAR, 1916-1918. *Army Q. and Defence J. [Great Britain] 1976 106(3): 277-286.* Discusses the prowar sentiments, propaganda, and extreme patriotism of vigilantes and civilian preparedness organizations before and during US participation in World War I, 1916-18.

2618. Edwards, John Carver. PRINCETON'S PASSIONATE PATRIOT: MC ELROY'S COMMITTEE ON PATRIOTISM THROUGH EDUCATION. *New Jersey Hist. 1977 95(4): 207-226.* The National Security League's Committee on Patriotism through Education was founded in April 1917. Shortly thereafter Prof. Robert M. McElroy of Princeton University succeeded Albert Bushnell Hart as its director. McElroy soon organized an extremely active speakers program to prepare Americans for a prolonged war and to awaken their patriotism. An understaffed, overworked, and poorly funded McElroy quit in the summer of 1919. The committee was ultimately involved in programs of cultural and intellectual oppression against minorities because of an underlying hostility to the US transnational society. Based on McElroy's papers and secondary sources; 5 illus., 38 notes.

E. R. McKinstry

2619. Entz, Margaret. WAR BOND DRIVES AND THE KANSAS MENNONITE RESPONSE. *Mennonite Life 1975 30(3): 4-9.* Discusses bonds bought during World War I, 1917-18, by Mennonites living in Kansas.

2620. Fowler, James H., II. TAR AND FEATHER PATRIOTISM: THE SUPPRESSION OF DISSENT IN OKLAHOMA DURING WORLD WAR I. *Chronicles of Oklahoma 1978-79 56(4): 409-430.* On both organized and unorganized levels, Oklahomans attempted to enforce loyalty to the United States during World War I. They brought pressure against German Americans, antiwar groups, and radical labor unions such as the Industrial Workers of the World. Chief among these organizations was the Oklahoma State Council of Defense (under the federally created Council of National Defense) which worked to outlaw teaching of the German language in schools, organized economic boycotts against suspect businessmen, forced loyalty oaths on citizens, and in some cases encouraged violence against dissenters. Oklahoma newspapers furthered the suppression of civil liberties by praising such actions. Primary and secondary sources; 5 photos, 83 notes.

M. L. Tate

2621. Gibbs, Christopher C. THE LEAD BELT RIOT AND WORLD WAR ONE. *Missouri Hist. Rev. 1977 71(4): 396-418.* The riot of 13-14 July 1917 in St. Francois County was one of many disturbances in the United States at the outbreak of World War I. Historians have described these outbreaks as manifestations of the prowar, antiforeign sentiment that swept America in 1917. The Missouri riot, however, resulted more from opposition to industrial modernization, to corporate arrogance, and to involvement in a foreign war. Primary and secondary sources; illus., 67 notes.

W. F. Zornow

2622. Glidden, William B. INTERNMENT CAMPS IN AMERICA, 1917-1920. *Military Affairs 1973 37(4): 137-141.* About 6,000 enemy aliens were interned in the United States during World War I in camps at Fort Douglas (Utah), Fort Oglethorpe (Georgia), Fort McPherson (Georgia), and Hot Springs (North Carolina). All camps came to be operated by the Army. Although the treatment was good, the internees were not allowed much communication with the outside. This worked a hardship on those with families and also induced some mental problems. As the war continued the order and morale of the camps deteriorated; nevertheless, only about 500 of the civilian internees chose to return to Germany before the camps closed in April 1920. Based on Army records; 17 notes. K. J. Bauer

2623. Hachey, Thomas E. BRITISH WAR PROPAGANDA AND AMERICAN CATHOLICS, 1918. *Catholic Hist. R. 1975 61(1): 48-66.* Examines the British strategy and deliberations concerning propaganda in the United States in January 1918. With the outcome of World War I still in doubt, the British wished to combat anti-British propaganda and to influence American Catholic opinion. They were concerned that this important and influential constituency not be offended by crude British counterpropaganda. The highly divisive Irish problem was especially serious. Based on documents made available for the first time under the provisions of The British Public Record Act of 1967. S

2624. Hokanson, Nels M. THE FOREIGN LANGUAGE DIVISION OF THE CHICAGO LIBERTY LOAN CAMPAIGN. *J. of the Illinois State Hist. Soc. 1974 67(4): 429-439.* The author reminisces about his involvement as an organizer with the Foreign Language Division of the Chicago Liberty Loan Campaign during World War I. 3 illus., photo, 3 notes.

2625. Hummasti, P. George. WORLD WAR I AND THE FINNS OF ASTORIA, OREGON: THE EFFECTS OF THE WAR ON AN IMMIGRANT COMMUNITY. *Int. Migration Rev. 1977 11(3): 334-349.* Studies the influences of World War I on communities of European immigrants in America; focuses on Finnish socialists in Astoria and attempts by Americans (1917-20) to suppress their radicalism.

2626. Jemnitz, János. AZ AMERIKAI EGYESÜLT ÁLLAMOK MUNKÁSMOZGALMA AZ ELSŐ VILÁGHÁBORÚ ÉVEIBEN (1914-1917) [The labor movement in the United States of America during the years of the First World War (1914-1917)]. *Pártörténeti Közlemények [Hungary] 1974 20(2): 88-128.* The outbreak of the war took the American Socialist Party by surprise. They went on the wrong track by addressing the US Government to mediate for peace. The anarchists also agitated against the war. Tne small Socialist Labor Party (SLP) attempted to coordinate action with radicals and pacifists. The left wing of the SP, Hillquit and Lee, remained pacifist even after the sinking of the *Lusitania*, while the right wing, Upton Sinclair, Herron and A. M. Simmons, turned vehemently anti-German. Many immigrants and political exiles took active parts in these propaganda campaigns. The AFL, led by Gompers, isolated itself from the pacifists and drifted closer to the Wilson administration. When the USA entered the War in 1917 the AFL joined the National Defense Council and worked out a *modus vivendi* with Washington. The leftist union, the IWW, refused to suspend the labor struggle for the duration of the war. This union opposed the war, but allowed its members to enlist. The SP demanded that the President organize a referendum on US participation in the war. Meanwhile, the government turned on the antiwar agitators with the newly passed Espionage Law. Many SP and IWW leaders were jailed. The courts dealt severely with the anarchists who encouraged draft dodging. 146 notes. P. I. Hidas

2627. Johnson, Niel M. THE MISSOURI SYNOD LUTHERANS AND THE WAR AGAINST THE GERMAN LANGUAGE. *Nebraska Hist. 1975 56(1): 137-156.* Examines the attack on the Missouri Synod Lutherans for teaching German in church schools. The Nebraska Council of Defense charged them with disloyalty, but in 1923, the US Supreme Court overturned a decision by the Nebraska Supreme Court, and held that laws designed to make English the mother tongue of all children reared in the state were unconstitutional. R. Lowitt

2628. Joseph, Ted. THE UNITED STATES VS. S. H. MILLER: THE STRANGE CASE OF A MENNONITE EDITOR BEING CON-

VICTED OF VIOLATING THE 1917 ESPIONAGE ACT. *Mennonite Life 1975 30(3): 14-18.* Examines the trial and conviction of Samuel H. Miller, editor of a Mennonite newspaper, for publishing a letter allegedly containing pro-German sentiments, 1917-18.

2629. Juhnke, James C. MOB VIOLENCE AND KANSAS MENNONITES IN 1918. *Kansas Hist. Q. 1977 43(3): 334-350.* Discusses mob violence in central Kansas during 1918 against certain local Mennonites, some of them German-speaking, who refused on account of their pacifist convictions to buy Liberty bonds and to otherwise support the World War I effort. No legal action was ever taken against the vigilantes. Based on archival materials, interviews, contemporary newspaper accounts, and secondary sources; 5 illus., 56 notes. L. W. Van Wyk

2630. Juhnke, James C. THE VICTORIES OF NONRESISTANCE: MENNONITE ORAL TRADITION AND WORLD WAR I. *Fides et Hist. 1974 7(1): 19-25.* The nonresistant Mennonites suffered harsh treatment in America during World War I from civilians and the military. Their oral tradition preserves the memory of that period as personal and group victories over their persecutors. Based on taped interviews in the Schowalter Oral History Collection, Bethel College, and on secondary sources; 19 notes. R. E. Butchart

2631. Lovin, Hugh T. MOSES ALEXANDER AND THE IDAHO LUMBER STRIKE OF 1917: THE WARTIME ORDEAL OF A PROGRESSIVE. *Pacific Northwest Q. 1975 66(3): 115-122.* Representing the reformist impulse of the Progressive Era, Moses Alexander won the governorship of Idaho in 1914 and was reelected two years later. World War I disrupted his legislative programs and placed him in the arena of conflict between "patriotic" groups and the Industrial Workers of the World. The State Council of Defense, supported by Idaho industrial interests, chided Alexander for protecting the IWW and other alleged pro-German interests, but he remained steadfast in their defense. Yet when the IWW threatened violence, he cracked down on their activities and promoted compromise at the conference table. Violence was averted and some of the barriers to labor reform were gradually overcome. Based on primary sources; photo, 34 notes. M. L. Tate

2632. Lovin, Hugh T. WORLD WAR VIGILANTES IN IDAHO, 1917-1918. *Idaho Yesterdays 1974 18(3): 2-11.* Describes anti-German and anti-Austro-Hungarian vigilante activity in Idaho during 1917-18. S

2633. Mason, Julian. OWEN WISTER AND WORLD WAR I: APPEAL FOR PENTECOST. *Pennsylvania Mag. of Hist. and Biog. 1977 101(1): 89-102.* Reviews Owen Wister's attitude toward President Woodrow Wilson and World War I. Wister, a Republican, had been fond of Wilson in the early years but rebelled against the latter's reluctance to get involved in World War I and his neutrality in word but not in deed. Wister composed a scorching sonnet, blasting the President, which evoked strong, though mixed, reviews. Himself a German, Wister published a booklet which compared peaceful prewar Germany with the monster nation that had evolved. Wister simply could not understand why America did not rise in defense of the small states of Europe. 44 notes. V. L. Human

2634. Mitchell, Charles Reed. NEW MESSAGE TO AMERICA: JAMES W. GERARD'S *BEWARE* AND WORLD WAR I PROPAGANDA. *J. of Popular Film 1975 4(5): 275-295.* Examines various films of 1918 and 1919 with anti-German and anti-Kaiser Wilhelm themes, particularly the last in that genre, Gerard's *Beware* (1919).

2635. Moore, William Haas. PRISONERS IN THE PROMISED LAND: THE MOLOKANS IN WORLD WAR I. *J. of Arizona Hist. 1973 14(4): 281-302.* The Molokans, a Russian religious sect, left Russia because they opposed military service and war itself. They came to the United States and settled in the Phoenix, Arizona, area. Though originally the United States had no draft law, the federal draft law of 1917 posed some difficulties. Since they were emigrés, the Molokans had to register as such, but no amount of explanation convinced them that registration was not equivalent to a draft. Though the state had many draft dodgers and Spanish-speaking Mexican nationals who were unaware of the registration requirement, an example was made of the Molokans and those who refused to register were jailed. Twenty-eight of the

34 jailed were released 10 months later upon agreement to register. On a technicality, the other six were regarded as deserters and transferred to a guardhouse on a military post in the state, but were released in 1919 as part of an amnesty program for religious conscientious objectors. 68 notes.

D. L. Smith

2636. Mormino, Gary Ross. OVER HERE: ST. LOUIS ITALO-AMERICANS AND THE FIRST WORLD WAR. *Missouri Hist. Soc. Bull.* 1973 30(1): 44-53. At the onset of World War I Italo-Americans in St. Louis mostly lived in tight ethnic pockets and adhered closely to Old World practices. Wartime seemed to demand that "hyphenate" groups accept 100% Americanization; Italo-Americans responded favorably. Wartime pressures speeded the processes of assimilation and acculturation to American society. However, Italo-Americans suffered an unascertained degree of "psychological damage" as a result of pressure to "reject the culture and values of one's parents." Based on newspaper sources and documents in the Woodrow Wilson and George Creel papers; 32 notes.

H. T. Lovin

2637. Noer, Thomas J. THE AMERICAN GOVERNMENT AND THE IRISH QUESTION DURING WORLD WAR I. *South Atlantic Q.* 1973 72(1): 95-114. Irish American leaders such as John Devoy and Daniel Cohalan hoped for a German victory in World War I to ensure Irish independence. With America's entry they fought to include Ireland in Wilson's principle of self-determination. When British propaganda branded the Easter Rising and the whole independence movement as German plots, American sympathy for Ireland weakened. Wilson's failure to force an Irish settlement ultimately cost him Irish American support of the war effort, the Versailles treaty, and the League of Nations. Primary and secondary sources; 90 notes.

W. L. Olbrich

2638. Ollila, Douglas J., Jr. DEFECTS IN THE MELTING POT: FINNISH-AMERICAN RESPONSE TO THE LOYALTY ISSUE 1917-1920. *Turun Hist. Arkisto [Finland]* 1976 31: 397-413. Describes prosecution of left-wing Finnish American syndicalists and socialists by the State of Minnesota and by the US government during 1917-20. These events helped polarize left- and right-wing factions among Finnish-Americans. Based on Finnish American newspapers and polemical literature; 60 notes.

R. G. Selleck

2639. Pankratz, Herbert L. THE SUPPRESSION OF ALLEGED DISLOYALTY IN KANSAS DURING WORLD WAR I. *Kansas Hist. Q.* 1976 42(3): 277-307. Superpatriots in Kansas during World War I vilified those who did not seem to contribute to the war effort and those suspected of disloyalty. They criticized Germans and other alien minorities, conscientious objectors, religious sects that preached against war, organized labor, socialists, and members of the Non-Partisan League and the Industrial Workers of the World. The Kansas press and public leaders created an atmosphere of intolerance and mass hysteria by mid-1918. Based on primary and secondary sources; illus., 121 notes.

W. F. Zornow

2640. Petersen, Peter L. LANGUAGE AND LOYALTY: GOVERNOR HARDING AND IOWA'S DANISH-AMERICANS DURING WORLD WAR I. *Ann. of Iowa* 1974 42(6): 405-417. Discusses the governorship of Republican William Lloyd Harding in Iowa during World War I, and the ban on the public use of foreign languages proclaimed 23 May 1918. While there was little protest concerning the German language, other ethnic groups protested strongly, especially the Danish Americans, under the leadership of Peder Sorensen Vig, a Lutheran pastor. Their religious and community cohesiveness, their anti-Prussian sentiments, and their enthusiastic support for US entry into the war were reasons why Danish Americans resented Harding's proclamation. Although he was re-elected, Harding's poor showing in the 1918 gubernatorial election can be traced in part to the language issue. Photo; 26 notes.

C. W. Olson

2641. Reid, Bill G. JOHN MILLER BAER: NONPARTISAN LEAGUE CARTOONIST AND CONGRESSMAN. *North Dakota Hist.* 1977 44(1): 4-13. John M. Baer became a fulltime cartoonist for the *Nonpartisan Leader* in 1916. He graphically depicted the struggle of the North Dakota Nonpartisan League's reform movement against the opposition of the Democratic and Republican Parties. Baer's cartoons provided simplistic images of the honest, stalwart, democratic farmer in

battle with "Big Biz" and "Crafty" in the fight to control state government and make it truly responsive to the needs of the people. Baer served a term and a half in Congress, under the League's banner, during and immediately after World War I. During his tenure, he was unfairly accused of pro-German sentiments. He later became a cartoonist for *Labor*, a publication of the railroad unions.

N. Lederer

2642. Rippley, La Vern. AMERICAN MILK COWS FOR GERMANY: A SEQUEL. *North Dakota Hist.* 1977 44(3): 15-23. After World War I German-American farmers contributed desperately needed milk cows to Germany. Local organizations sprang up to receive dairy cattle donations and facilitate shipment. In April 1921 the Lebanon-Ixonia, Wisconsin, *Committee zur Hilfeleistung der Notleidenden in Deutschland und Osterreich* shipped two carloads of cattle to German orphanages and hospitals. Many German American farmers from South Dakota and Wisconsin went along. The venture was successful, but no more shipments took place. Based largely on a diary by Vilas Behl, a participant, and on interviews.

N. Lederer

2643. Rippley, La Vern J. GIFT COWS FOR GERMANY. *North Dakota Hist.* 1973 40(3): 4-15, 39. There were a number of private American relief efforts to alleviate the post-World War I suffering in Germany. Russian Germans in North and South Dakota were especially concerned with Germany's milk shortage, to which increased tuberculosis and child mortality were attributed. Mercy cattle shipments were organized. Although they met with violent resistance from ex-soldiers and members of the American Legion, three shiploads were successfully delivered. However, the currency problem, resulting from inflation, stalled further deliveries. By 1922 only clothing the shipping cost of which was prepaid by the donor could be sent. Based on newspapers; 54 notes.

2644. Sale, Roger. SEATTLE'S CRISIS, 1914-1919. *Am. Studies (Lawrence, KS)* 1973 14(1): 29-48. Discusses Seattle in World War I and the General Strike of 1919. Local events reflected national developments, and Seattle newspapers developed strong support for President Wilson and Americanism. Organizing activity by the Industrial Workers of the World was cast as foreign subversion and German plots. The war (and productivity) gave Seattle labor leaders false hopes. These hopes collapsed with the failure of the General Strike in 1919. Based on primary and secondary sources; 13 notes.

J. Andrew

2645. Schlabach, Theron, ed.; Reist, Ilse; and Bender, Elizabeth, trans. *AN ACCOUNT* BY JAKOB WALDNER: DIARY OF A CONSCIENTIOUS OBJECTOR IN WORLD WAR I. *Mennonite Q. R.* 1974 48(1): 73-111. Young Hutterite Jakob Waldner (b. 1891) describes his life in Camp Funston in Kansas from 1917-18.

S

2646. Teichroew, Allan. MENNONITES AND THE CONSCRIPTION TRAP. *Mennonite Life* 1975 30(3): 10-13. Discusses Mennonite feelings surrounding World War I both from the angle of pro-German feelings (many of them having recently immigrated from Germany) and from the vantage point of antidraft sentiment (most being staunch believers in pacifism), 1914-18.

2647. Ventresco, Fiorella B. LOYALTY AND DISSENT: ITALIAN RESERVISTS IN AMERICA DURING WORLD WAR I. *Italian Americana* 1978 4(1): 93-122. Examines the diplomatic friction and economic repercussions of the return to Italy of reservists, whom Italy considered subject to military duty, the Italian American radical press which argued against their return, and the problems of primary loyalty which arose with US entry into the war.

2648. Waldenrath, Alexander. THE GERMAN LANGUAGE NEWSPRESS IN PENNSYLVANIA DURING WORLD WAR I. *Pennsylvania Hist.* 1975 42(1): 25-41. The decline of German-American newspapers began in the late 19th century; however, the outbreak of World War I stimulated greater interest. Prior to American entry into the war, the Pennsylvania German-American papers attempted to counterbalance pro-British arguments and urged strict neutrality, however, their satisfaction with early German successes was obvious. US involvement in the war destroyed the German-American press in Pennsylvania. Although these papers supported the US war effort, advertising revenues declined as anti-German sentiment increased. A few papers, located in Pittsburgh and Philadelphia managed to survive. Based on Pennsylvania German-language newspapers; illus., 16 notes.

D. C. Swift

2649. Wrede, Steven. THE AMERICANIZATION OF SCOTT COUNTY. *Ann. of Iowa 1979 44(8): 627-638.* During World War I, a Council of National Defense attempted to assure the loyalty of the large German-American population in Scott County, Iowa, through public hearings and investigations. The Council's activities created an atmosphere of fear among many German Americans and forced them to support the American war effort to prove their loyalty. Special efforts were made to eliminate the use of the German language. The war worked to increase the assimilation of German Americans in Scott County.
P. L. Petersen

2650. —. COURT MARTIAL 1918: PVT. URA V. ASCHLIMAN (420382). *Mennonite Life 1976 31(3): 18-21.* Provides excerpts from the transcipts of the 1918 court martial of Pvt. Ura V. Aschliman, Mennonite conscientious objector to World War I. Aschliman, sentenced to a five-year term at Ft. Leavenworth, joined the Amish Mennonites only two weeks before he was drafted. Based on the Mennonite Archives and Schowalter Oral History Collection at Bethel College.   B. Burnett

World War II

2651. Abrahams, Edward. THE PAST FAILURE OF FASCISM IN THE U.S.A. *Patterns of Prejudice [Great Britain] 1974 8(2): 23-27.* Discusses fascist organizations and leaders in the United States in the 1930's, emphasizing anti-Semitism.

2652. Adler, Selig. THE UNITED STATES AND THE HOLOCAUST. *Am. Jewish Hist. Q. 1974 64(1): 14-23.* The US government did less to mitigate the catastrophe that befell European Jews than it could have because 1) Washington initially made incorrect assumptions concerning the extent and possible alleviation of the holocaust, 2) measures taken lacked a sense of urgency because of low priority on the war timetable and the end of war political maneuvers, and 3) measures taken came too late to save any considerable number of Jews. Proofs for these points constitute a new approach to the entire question. 23 notes.
F. Rosenthal

2653. Arndt, Karl J. R. MISSOURI AND THE BAD BOLL, 1948. *Concordia Hist. Inst. Q. 1979 52(1): 2-31.* Discussions held between American and German synodic leaders of the Lutheran Church at the Bad Boll Conferences, 1948, were sessions intended to repair torn church affiliations and provide a positive note in the gloom of post-World War II Germany.

2654. Banks, Dean. H. L. MENCKEN AND "HITLERISM," 1933-1941: A PATRICIAN LIBERTARIAN BESIEGED. *Maryland Hist. Mag. 1976 71(4): 498-515.* Charles Angoff's *H. L. Mencken: A Portrait from Memory* (1956) was a chief source of the charges of "Hitlerism" leveled at H. L. Mencken after 1933. The book "marshalled selected data" and stressed Mencken's insensitivity to anti-Semitism. In reality, Mencken had an attachment to liberty and freedom of speech which also carried with it the "right to refrain from expression, the right to judicious restraint or silence." Mencken's elitist distrust of public opinion and mass emotionalism restrained him from actively joining the anti-Hitler militants. While scorning political radicalism, he consistently championed the right of free speech for all American extremists. Mencken's growing anti-New Deal sentiments would have spurred much resentment among intellectuals after early 1933 anyway; but his consistent scorn for chauvinism and emotional group behavior of all sorts, his basic belief that Nazism was most akin to Ku Klux Klanism, and the memory of his World War I attitude toward the "dangerous hysterias of democracy," made him equally oppose Jewish nationalism, 100 percent Americanism, and German racialism during the 1930's. Primary and secondary materials; 89 notes.
G. J. Bobango

2655. Bauer, Yehuda. "ONKEL SALY": DIE VERHANDLUNGEN DES SALY MAYER ZUR RETTUNG DER JUDEN 1944/45 ["Uncle Saly": the negotiations of Saly Mayer to save Jews, 1944-45]. *Vierteljahrshefte für Zeitgeschichte [West Germany] 1977 25(2): 188-219.* Describes the negotiations of Saly Mayer (1882-1950), Swiss industrialist and chairman of the Union of Jewish Communities in Switzerland, with representatives of SS Chief Heinrich Himmler. The American Jewish

Joint Distribution Committee and the US government authorized negotiations in order to gain time, but did not authorize the offer of dollars and goods desired by the Nazis. With very limited means Mayer was able to delay and finally to prevent the deaths of many thousands of Jews. Based on records at the Roosevelt Library and in British, Israeli, and US archives, published documents, memoirs, and secondary sources; 64 notes.
D. Prowe

2656. Blayney, Michael S. HERBERT PELL, WAR CRIMES, AND THE JEWS. *Am. Jewish Hist. Q. 1976 65(4): 335-352.* Herbert Claiborne Pell, a Harvard classmate of Franklin D. Roosevelt, was one of Roosevelt's political appointees in various foreign service posts. Pell was an early and vigorous denouncer of Nazi policies; his letters to the President stand in marked contrast to the restrained style and attitude of the State Department. His 1943 appointment to the UN War Crimes Commission led almost from the beginning to increased conflict with the State Department, which did not agree with his definition of war crimes and atrocities. The question whether crimes against Jews, regardless of location and nationality, came within the jurisdiction of the commission was another issue that divided Pell and the Department. All of this led to his abrupt dismissal in 1945. 45 notes.
F. Rosenthal

2657. Cannistraro, Philip V. FASCISM AND AMERICANS IN DETROIT, 1933-1935. *Int. Migration Rev. 1975 9(1): 29-40.* Explores the impact of Italian Fascism on Italian Americans in Detroit during 1933-35, including the specific questions of Fascism and anti-Fascism within the community and the more general internal dynamics of the community's sociopolitical integration.

2658. Cannistraro, Philip V. GLI ITALO-AMERICANI DI FRONTE ALL'INGRESSO DELL'ITALIA NELLA SECONDA GUERRA MONDIALE [Italian Americans and the entry of Italy into World War II]. *Storia Contemporanea [Italy] 1976 7(4): 855-864.* During the 1920's and 1930's, most Italian Americans had a favorable attitude toward Fascist Italy. The strong nationalism and alleged (by massive propaganda directed by Rome) accomplishments of Mussolini's regime attracted Italian Americans to whom Italy was an important psychological support in the often hostile American environment. Italy's entry into World War II on the Axis side—the famous "stab in the back"—caused an abrupt change in Italian American opinion, so that by the time Italy declared war on the United States in the wake of Pearl Harbor, the vast majority of Italian Americans were firmly in the anti-Fascist camp. Includes as an appendix a memorandum of 5 July 1940 on Italian American public opinion by A. Colonna of the Italian Embassy in Washington. 27 notes, appendix.
J. C. Billigmeier

2659. Diamond, Sander A. *HOLOCAUST* FILM'S IMPACT ON AMERICANS. *Patterns of Prejudice [Great Britain] 1978 12(4): 1-9, 19.* Discusses American public opinion about the television miniseries, *Holocaust,* which appeared in 1978.

2660. Dinnerstein, Leonard. ANTI-SEMITISM IN THE EIGHTIETH CONGRESS: THE DISPLACED PERSONS ACT OF 1948. *Capitol Studies 1978 6(2): 11-26.* The Displaced Persons Act (US, 1948), enacted to aid homeless victims of World War II, discriminated against Jews in favor of ethnic Germans who fled Eastern Europe.

2661. Dinnerstein, Leonard. THE U.S. ARMY AND THE JEWS: POLICIES TOWARD THE DISPLACED PERSONS AFTER WORLD WAR II. *Am. Jewish Hist. 1979 68(3): 353-366.* Forced to deal with the care and supervision of millions of displaced persons, the US Army did a generally creditable job. Unfortunately, subordinate military personnel often showed little awareness of the particular difficulties of Jewish DP's, the remnants of the final solution. Earl G. Harrison's inspection of conditions in July 1945 led to orders by President Truman and General Eisenhower which abolished some of the worst abuses and provided better facilities and treatment for the survivors of the death camps. 28 notes.
F. Rosenthal

2662. Drier, John A. KENTON COUNTY, KENTUCKY: RE-EVALUATING THE ETHNIC ORIGINS OF ISOLATIONISM. *Filson Club Hist. Q. 1977 51(3): 262-275.* Kenton County, Kentucky, a suburban area south of Cincinnati, was not a stronghold of isolationist sentiment in 1940 despite the presence of a large German population. A strong attachment to the Democratic Party may have been a significant cause for the absence of isolationist feeling. Statistical data are presented. Based on Cincinnati newspapers and federal census reports; 8 tables, 41 notes.   G. B. McKinney

2663. Eckardt, Alice L. THE HOLOCAUST: CHRISTIAN AND JEWISH RESPONSES. *J. of the Am. Acad. of Religion 1974 42(3): 453-469.* Surveys, with some analysis and evaluation, the writings of leading Jewish and Christian scholars who have offered responses to the slaughter of six million Jews by Hitler. While most agree that no solution can be considered adequate, some explanation must be attempted. Stresses the nature of this theological problem for Jews and Christians. 68 notes.   E. R. Lester

2664. Epstein, Helen. CHILDREN OF THE HOLOCAUST: SEARCHING FOR A PAST—AND A FUTURE. *Present Tense 1976 3(4): 21-25.* Children of Holocaust survivors possess a legacy that Jews everywhere have sworn never to forget; some of the children have refused to cooperate in that effort, others have joined it, and still others have not decided how to assimilate these events into their own lives.

2665. Etzold, Thomas H. THE (F)UTILITY FACTOR: GERMAN INFORMATION GATHERING IN THE UNITED STATES, 1933-1941. *Military Affairs 1975 39(2): 77-82.* German intelligence service operations in the United States 1933-41, in spite of their volume and scope, were not particularly effective, and they contributed little to the formulation and conduct of an operative policy. Internal failings doomed German intelligence work from the outset. Primary and secondary sources; 26 notes.   A. M. Osur

2666. Fein, Helen. ATTITUDES IN THE U.S.A., 1933-1945: TOLERATION OF GENOCIDE. *Patterns of Prejudice [Great Britain] 1973 7(5): 22-28.* Alleges toleration of genocide by the Roosevelt administration in its refusal to aid Jewish refugees from Germany by amending US immigration laws, 1933-45.

2667. Feingold, Henry L. THE LIMITS OF HYPHENATE POWER: NAZISM IN AMERICA. *Rev. in Am. Hist. 1974 2(4): 563-568.* Review article prompted by Sander A. Diamond's *The Nazi Movement in the United States, 1924-1941* (Ithaca, N. Y.: Cornell U. Pr., 1974), depicting the relation between Nazism, German efforts to form ties with German Americans, and responses in the United States to these efforts.

2668. Feingold, Henry L. RESCUE THROUGH MASS RESETTLEMENT: SOME NEW DOCUMENTS, 1938-1943. *Michael: On the Hist. of the Jews in the Diaspora [Israel] 1975 3: 302-335.* Presents 12 documents from the James G. McDonald papers relating primarily to ideas for the resettlement of European Jews under Nazi control. McDonald (1886-1959) headed the President's Advisory Committee on Political Refugees. The documents reflect the unwillingness and inability of the United States and the other major powers to confront the Jewish refugee problem directly, and include plans for diverting the Jews to places like Brazilian rubber plantations (Henry Ford's scheme), Surinam, Angola, the Dominican Republic, the Philippines, British Guiana, and Alaska. Also included is a proto-Zionist scheme by an American Christian woman, and a letter from Valdimir Jabotinsky, leader of the Zionist Revisionists. 28 notes.   T. Sassoon

2669. Feingold, Henry L. WHO SHALL BEAR GUILT FOR THE HOLOCAUST: THE HUMAN DILEMMA. *Am. Jewish Hist. 1979 68(3): 261-282.* Analyzes the inability to save Jewish lives during the Holocaust and indicts the Roosevelt administration, the Vatican, the British government, other governments, and American Jewry's leadership. Political and military priorities were compounded by the sheer impossibility for most Americans, including Jews, to absorb what was happening, even as late as December 1944.   F. Rosenthal

2670. Fram, Leon. DETROIT JEWRY'S FINEST HOUR. *Michigan Jewish Hist. 1978 18(2): 14-19.* The author reminisces about his leadership role in Detroit's League for Human Rights during 1930's-40's, boycotting Nazi goods and services, and organizing a campaign of resistance to Nazism.

2671. Genizi, Haim. AMERICAN NON-SECTARIAN REFUGEE RELIEF ORGANIZATIONS (1933-1945). *Yad Vashem Studies on the European Jewish Catastrophe and Resistance [Israel] 1976 11: 164-220.* Examines the activities and role of the American nonsectarian organizations in the general field of aid and relief to refugees from Nazi Germany. The creation of nonsectarian committees comprising Jews and Christians was designed to ensure the greatest possible public support for a task which also involved the fight against the rising wave of anti-Semitism in the United States. The establishment of nonsectarian committees also stemmed from the need to care for professional groups with specific problems. Based on archival and published sources; 185 notes.   J. P. Fox

2672. Genizi, Haim. JAMES G. MCDONALD: HIGH COMMISSIONER FOR REFUGEES, 1933-1935. *Wiener Lib. Bull. [Great Britain] 1977 30(43-44): 40-52.* The League of Nations instituted a High Commission for Refugees in response to the Nazi-created refugee problem. Headed by an American, James G. McDonald, the commission had to contend with American and world apathy toward refugees interned in camps and without a permanent haven. After two years of frustration McDonald resigned. His letter of resignation called on the League to confront the refugee problem at its source in Nazi Germany. His letter aroused a great but short-lived response. The member states of the League and the United States must share most of the responsibility for McDonald's failure, though a stronger man as high commissioner might have negotiated more successfully with the Germans, or might have obtained better access to foreign governments. 61 notes.   R. V. Layton

2673. Genizi, Haim. JAMES MCDONALD AND THE ROOSEVELT ADMINISTRATION. Artzi, Pinhas, ed. *Bar-Ilan Studies in History* (Ramat-Gan, Israel: Bar-Ilan U. Pr., 1978): 285-306. Assesses the career of James G. McDonald (1886-1964) and his assistance to Jewish refugees in the 1930's. In 1933, the League of Nations set up a High Commission for Refugees; America put McDonald forward as a candidate, although it wanted to remain isolationist. As High Commissioner, McDonald found little support in America; he resigned after the Nuremberg decrees in 1935. Franklin D. Roosevelt became more helpful to the Jews after the German annexation of Austria in 1938. He set up the President's Advisory Committee, with McDonald as chairman and as liaison between the State Department and the social services. Various countries were suggested for the Jewish national home, but many European consuls and the State Department objected. For his strenuous efforts on the Jews' behalf, he was awarded the Gottheil Medal for Services to American Jewry. Based on archive sources and secondary works; 114 notes.   A. Alcock

2674. Glaser, Martha. THE GERMAN-AMERICAN BUND IN NEW JERSEY. *New Jersey Hist. 1974 92(1): 33-49.* Discusses the German-American Bund in New Jersey, centering on the state's attempt, 1933-42, to expel the group because of its pro-Nazi sentiment and the American Civil Liberties Union's defense of the group on the basis of their civil rights.

2675. Goldman, Martin S. TEACHING THE HOLOCAUST: SOME SUGGESTIONS FOR COMPARATIVE ANALYSIS. *J. of Intergroup Relations 1977 6(2): 23-30.* Comparing historiography of the Nazi treatment of Jews and the discrimination against Negroes and Indians in the United States would increase cultural understanding and cure prejudice.

2676. Gottlieb, Moshe. BOYCOTT, RESCUE, AND RANSOM: THE THREEFOLD DILEMMA OF AMERICAN JEWRY IN 1938-1939. *Yivo Ann. of Jewish Social Sci. 1974 (15): 235-279.* Studies attempts to deal with the Jewish refugee problem and the work of American Jews in organizing boycott, rescue, and ransom procedures. 95 notes.   R. J. Wechman

2677. Grobman, Alex. THE WARSAW GHETTO UPRISING IN THE AMERICAN JEWISH PRESS. *Wiener Lib. Bull. [Great Britain] 1976 29(37-38): 53-61.* To establish the response of American Jewry to the Warsaw Ghetto revolt (1943), suggests that it is necessary to determine if American Jewry knew what was happening in Poland and in the Warsaw Ghetto prior to the revolt, and their reaction. It is also essential to examine and critically analyze the type of information received about the uprising and investigate the response of the American Jewish community. Finds that there was a steady stream of accurate information about the deteriorating plight of the Jews in the Warsaw Ghetto long before the rebellion. Furthermore, there was little response to the news of the uprising. Based on primary sources; 56 notes.   J. P. Fox

2678. Grobman, Alex. WHAT DID THEY KNOW? THE AMERICAN JEWISH PRESS AND THE HOLOCAUST, 1 SEPTEMBER 1939-17 DECEMBER 1942. *Am. Jewish Hist. 1979 68(3): 327-352.* Examination of more than 20 periodicals and newspapers for the period in question shows that, while details often were inaccurate or incomplete, a general idea of the Nazi concentration camps was available. By 1942, the full horror story was known and was continuously being published in the general American press and the Yiddish press. American Jews reacted with protest meetings, memorial services, and days of fasting. 142 notes.   F. Rosenthal

2679. Johnson, Ronald W. THE GERMAN-AMERICAN BUND AND NAZI GERMANY, 1936-1941. *Studies in Hist. and Soc. 1975 6(2): 31-45.* The German-American Bund was directed by Fritz Kuhn, a fervent pro-Nazi who attempted to organize US support for Adolf Hitler's government. Two visits to Germany led to a brief interview with Hitler in 1936 and to rejection by one of Hitler's aides in 1938. Kuhn's leadership was an embarrassment to the German foreign ministry and to German Americans who opposed the Nazi regime. The Bund achieved none of its intended goals of aiding the German fascist empire. Primary sources; 75 notes.   G. H. Libbey

2680. Kaufman, Menachem. 'ATIDAH SHEL SHE'ERIT HAP-LEIṬAH BESHE'ELAT ERETS YIŚRAEL BE'EINEI HA-IRGUNIM HALO-TSIYONIIM BE-ARTSOT HABRIT BISHNAT 1945 [The future of the Holocaust survivors and the Palestine problem in the eyes of the non-Zionist Jewish organizations in the US]. *Yalkut Moreshet Periodical [Israel] 1976 21: 181-198.* Non-Zionist Jewish organizations in the US began to link the need for a home for the survivors of the Nazi Holocaust with the creation of a Jewish state in Palestine only when the US Government did so in late 1945.

2681. Keim, Albert N. SERVICE OR RESISTANCE? THE MENNONITE RESPONSE TO CONSCRIPTION IN WORLD WAR II. *Mennonite Q. Rev. 1978 52(2): 141-155.* Mennonites' experiences during World War I caused them to seek an alternative military conscription in the event of another war, an impulse which quickened as World War II approached during the 1930's. Representatives of the Peace Churches approached the federal government with a plan for alternative service in the United States. Neither Congress nor President Roosevelt was enthusiastic about it, but eventually it was adopted. The Mennonites were satisfied with this solution, because they opposed not conscription but war. Some Quakers were more reserved. Ironically, the civilian service units operated under military control, although the individual churches acted as "camp managers." 52 notes.   V. L. Human

2682. Klaidman, Stephen. THE NAZI HUNTERS: JUSTICE, NOT VENGEANCE. *Present Tense 1977 4(2): 21-26.* Examines the motivations and activities of Nazi hunters (1947-77), including Shirley Korman, Vincent A. Schiano, Anthony DeVito, Wayne Perlmutter, Bessy Pupko, Charles R. Allen, Jr. Discusses litigation against suspected Nazi war criminals. Reviews the policies and actions of the US Immigration and Naturalization Service, US Department of Justice, US Congress, National Council of Churches, World Jewish Congress, Concerned Jewish Youth, Yad Vashem (Israel), etc. Primary and secondary sources; 5 photos.   R. B. Mendel

2683. Kruger, Arnd. "FAIR PLAY FOR AMERICAN ATHLETES": A STUDY IN ANTI-SEMITISM. *Can. J. of Hist. of Sport and Physical Educ. [Canada] 1978 9(1): 42-57.* In his 1935 pamphlet "Fair Play for American Athletes" and elsewhere, American Olympic Committee President Avery Brundage, in opposing the proposed boycott of the 1936 Olympic Games to be held in Berlin, indulged in anti-Semitism.

2684. Laqueur, Walter. JEWISH DENIAL AND THE HOLOCAUST. *Commentary 1979 68(6): 44-55.* Describes the dissemination of information about Hitler's Final Solution during the 1940's and Jews' reluctance to believe the extent of Nazi genocide.

2685. Mashberg, Michael. AMERICAN DIPLOMACY AND THE JEWISH REFUGEE, 1938-1939. *Yivo Ann. of Jewish Social Sci. 1974 (15): 339-365.* Discusses the American planning and participation in the Évian Conference dealing with the resettlement of German-Jewish refugees. The conference made it clear that the "Jew was a universal minority having no national representation or protection. Once a state revoked the protection of a hyphenated Jew, be he a German-Jew or an Austrian-Jew, he was isolated from the nation state system.... The Jewish refugee became a legal freak in the diplomacy of the nation-state." 52 notes.   R. J. Wechman

2686. Mashberg, Michael. DOCUMENTS CONCERNING THE AMERICAN STATE DEPARTMENT AND THE STATELESS EUROPEAN JEWS, 1942-1944. *Jewish Social Studies 1977 39(1-2): 163-182.* A collection of documents from the papers of Franklin D. Roosevelt's wartime Secretary of the Treasury, Henry M. Morgenthau, Jr., indicates the efforts of the Treasury Department to investigate and bring to the attention of the President the role of State Department officials in preventing any tangible efforts to rescue European Jewry from extermination at the hands of the Nazis. Treasury Department investigators, especially general counsel Randolph E. Paul, believed that the State Department prevented Jewish rescue through procrastination and failure to act, that it refused to work with private rescue agencies, that it prevented public disclosure of news about the exterminations, and that it covered up its role in regard to the Jewish situation. The actions of Morgenthau and his staff finally resulted in the creation of the War Refugee Board and efforts to retrieve refugees from the hands of the Nazis. Based on documents in the Franklin D. Roosevelt Library.   N. Lederer

2687. Mashberg, Michael. PREJUDICE THAT MEANT DEATH: THE WEST AND THE HOLOCAUST. *Patterns of Prejudice [Great Britain] 1978 12(3): 19-32.* Examines social and scientific attitudes toward Jews, 1880's-1900's, and their effects on US immigration quotas in the 20th century and later, during World War II, on the lethargy displayed by the US government and other Allied governments as well as other Allied nations in organizing the rescue of European Jews.

2688. Miller, James E. CARLO SFORZA E L'EVOLUZIONE DELLA POLITICA AMERICANA VERSO L'ITALIA: 1940-1943 [Carlo Sforza and the evolution of American policy toward Italy: 1940-43]. *Storia Contemporanea [Italy] 1976 7(4): 825-853.* Count Carlo Sforza, in the United States after 1940, galvanized Italian American public opinion against Fascism, and helped make clear to other Americans the distinction between Fascists and the Italian people. He tried to win recognition of a free Italian government-in-exile similar to DeGaulle's Free French, but the effort was unsuccessful, due in part to British opposition. After the fall of Fascism, Sforza soon returned to Italy. He sought to drive a wedge between King Victor Emmanuel and General Pietro Badoglio, and was so successful that only the intervention of Churchill and Eisenhower saved Victor Emmanuel's throne. He also succeeded in blocking an Allied effort to deal with moderate Fascists like Dino Grandi. By their successes and their failures the exiles led by Sforza contributed to the moderate solution of Allied-Italian relations and to the relative postwar stability. 95 notes.   J. C. Billigmeier

2689. Moore, John Hammond. ITALIAN POWS IN AMERICA: WAR IS NOT ALWAYS HELL. *Prologue 1976 8(3): 141-151.* Italy's switch from the ranks of the Axis to that of the Allies in 1943 generated plans to utilize Italian Prisoners of War (POWS) in the United States as a source of labor and reflected an unwillingness to release large numbers of former enemy soldiers while the conflict was still going on. The Italian Service Units were an uneasy compromise to achieve these goals, in which Americans were called upon to view as equals recent POWS. Contacts with the Italian American community helped to make these men feel at home and also led to a considerable number of escapes. The scheme was accompanied by broken promises to the Italians, inefficient work utilization, and a general embarrassment on the part of all concerned. Primarily based on archival materials in the National Archives.   N. Lederer

2690. Naske, Claus-M. JEWISH IMMIGRATION AND ALASKAN ECONOMIC DEVELOPMENT: A STUDY IN FUTILITY. *Western States Jewish Hist. Q. 1976 8(2): 139-157.* During the 1930's when Nazi Germany was persecuting Jews, the United States provided little aid to help the Jews to emigrate. No area in the United States wanted a large group of Jewish immigrants. It was proposed that they be settled in Alaska, but the leaders in Alaska fought all efforts to enact special federal legislation to allow the refugees to settle there, stating that Alaska could not support a mass immigration at that time. The 1940 King-Havenner bill proposed that public purpose corporations be set up to establish colonies in Alaska for the refugees if Congress passed the necessary laws, but the bill never passed and by then it was too late to save the Jews. Based on primary sources; 46 notes.　　　　　　R. A. Garfinkle

2691. Poliakov, Léon. RÉFLEXIONS SUR "HOLOCAUSTE" [Reflections on "Holocaust"]. *Études [France] 1979 350(6): 759-765.* Analyzes the factors in present day Western society which contributed to the overwhelming emotional effect of the television film "Holocaust" on its viewers.

2692. Priebe, Paul M. and Rubinoff, Michael W. HITLER'S GIFT TO THE UNIVERSITY OF DENVER. *Western States Jewish Hist. Q. 1976 9(1): 55-62.* On 23 November 1936, the German consul in Denver, Colorado, donated 450 books to the University of Denver. The city's *Rocky Mountain News* and the *Intermountain Jewish News* charged that the books were propagandistic. The *Denver Clarion* and University officials maintained that most of the books were classics, printed in German, and that the University's acceptance of the gift did not imply approval of the Nazi government. Despite the controversy, the books were available to the students and the public. Based on documents in University of Denver Archives and contemporary newspaper articles; 17 notes.
　　　　　　B. S. Porter

2693. Ribuffo, Leo. FASCISTS, NAZIS AND AMERICAN MINDS: PERCEPTIONS AND PRECONCEPTIONS. *Am. Q. 1974 26(4): 417-432.* Review essay of several monographs on the American reaction during the New Deal era to Italian Fascism, German Nazism and the German-American Bund, Father Charles Coughlin's homegrown brand of extremism, and the United States and countersubversives on the eve of World War II: John P. Diggins, *Mussolini and Fascism: The View from America* (Princeton: Princeton U. Pr., 1972); Sander A. Diamond, *The Nazi Movement in the United States 1924-1941* (Ithaca, N.Y.: Cornell U. Pr., 1973); Leland V. Bell, *In Hitler's Shadow: The Anatomy of American Nazism* (Port Washington: N.Y.: Kennikat Pr., 1973); Sheldon Marcus, *Father Coughlin: The Tumultuous Life of the Priest of the Little Flower* (Boston: Little, Brown, 1973); Geoffrey S. Smith, *To Save a Nation: American Countersubversives, the New Deal, and the Coming of World War II* (New York: Basic Books, 1972). 12 notes.
　　　　　　C. W. Olson

2694. Rockaway, Robert A. THE ROOSEVELT ADMINISTRATION, THE HOLOCAUST, AND THE JEWISH REFUGEES. *Rev. in Am. Hist. 1975 3(1): 113-118.* Review article prompted by Saul S. Friedman's *No Haven for the Oppressed: United States Policy toward Jewish Refugees, 1938-1945* (Detroit, Mich.: Wayne State U. Pr., 1973).

2695. Rosen, Norma. THE HOLOCAUST AND THE AMERICAN-JEWISH NOVELIST. *Midstream 1974 20(8): 54-62.*

2696. Rubinoff, Michael W. THE REACTION TO HITLER BY THE INTERMOUNTAIN JEWISH NEWS OF DENVER. *Western States Jewish Hist. Q. 1977 9(4): 301-314.* Between 1932 and 1935 the *Intermountain Jewish News* (IJN) of Denver, under editor Carl Mandel, encouraged its readers to respond to Nazi anti-Semitism by raising funds for refugees, boycotting German products, and protesting US participation in the 1936 Olympics in Germany. Early in this period the IJN was optimistic about the overthrow of Hitler and the future of German Jews. After 1935 the IJN muted its call for positive action to aid German Jews and overthrow Hitler. The apparent reasons for this were: 1) fear of latent anti-Semitism in the U.S. and 2) financial hardship caused by the Depression. Despite the failure of many Jews to take militant action against Nazi Germany, they were by no means "disinterested bystanders" to Hitler's persecution of the Jews. Based on the *Intermountain Jewish News* and other primary and secondary sources; 51 notes.　　　　　　B. S. Porter

2697. Shafir, Shlomo. TAYLOR AND MCDONALD: TWO DIVERGING VIEWS ON ZIONISM AND THE EMERGING JEWISH STATE. *Jewish Social Studies 1977 39(4): 323-346.* Myron Taylor and

James G. McDonald were public-spirited citizens involved in President Roosevelt's pre-World War II effort to ameliorate the condition of European Jews persecuted by Nazism. Taylor, head of the intergovernmental committee on refugees and later presidential emissary to the Vatican, was anti-Zionist; he felt that Jews should be absorbed by various countries rather than be allowed to migrate in large numbers to a newly created Israel. McDonald, one of the few Americans early aware during the 1930's of the Nazi threat to European Jews, became deeply involved in refugee activities and eventually, under President Truman, became the first US ambassador to Israel. McDonald understood the central position of Palestine as a place of refuge and rehabilitation for Jewish survivors of the Holocaust and consequently strongly supported unrestricted Jewish immigration to Palestine and the creation of Israel.
　　　　　　N. Lederer

2698. Singer, David. THE PRELUDE TO NAZISM: THE GERMAN-AMERICAN PRESS AND THE JEWS 1919-1933. *Am. Jewish Hist. Q. 1977 66(3): 417-431.* Analyzes editorial and news materials which appeared in the German-American presses, particularly those of the Midwest during 1919-33. Shows that attitudes toward Jews changed from support to strong unfriendliness. Newspapers, such as the Illinois *Staats-Zeitung*, the Milwaukee *Herald*, and the St. Louis *Weltiche Post*, reflected the rise of anti-Semitism, racism and xenophobia in America and Western Europe. 35 notes.　　　　　　F. Rosenthal

2699. Ullmann, Walter. AMERICAN AND VATICAN REACTIONS TO THE TISO TRIAL. *Bohemia. Jahrbuch des Collegium Carolinum [West Germany] 1977 18: (1887-1314.* Msgr. Jozef Tiso (1887-1947), former president of Slovakia, was tried, convicted, and executed by the Communist Czechoslovak government as a traitor and war criminal. The proceedings took from December 1946 to April 1947, but even before their onset Slovak American organizations petitioned the US State Department in Msgr. Tiso's behalf, making use of interested congressmen. The US government refused to intervene and implicitly recognized the justice in the indictment. No encouragement of intervention came from the Holy See, which saw Tiso as a political prelate who had cooperated with Nazi Germany against Rome's advice. Published and archival documents; 38 notes.　　　　　　R. E. Weltsch

2700. Wilson, E. Raymond. EVOLUTION OF THE C. O. PROVISIONS IN THE 1940 CONSCRIPTION BILL. *Quaker Hist. 1975 64(1): 3-15.* At the Burke-Wadsworth bill hearings in the summer of 1940, the author and Paul C. French, representing Friends, combined with Mennonites and Brethren to urge legalizing conscientious objection based on personal conviction, civilian control of drafted C.O.'s, and complete exemption for absolutists (nonregistrants). They failed to achieve most of their objectives, experiencing unfavorable discrimination in the hearings. Selective Service control cost the government millions and did injustice to the C.O., and the peace churches should have refused to operate C.O. camps. 14 notes.　　　　　　T. D. S. Bassett

2701. Winograd, Leonard. DOUBLE JEOPARDY: WHAT AN AMERICAN ARMY OFFICER, A JEW, REMEMBERS OF PRISON LIFE IN GERMANY. *Am. Jewish Arch. 1976 28(1): 3-17.* The author, who was a prisoner of war held by the Germans 1944-45, emphasizes the treatment of Jewish prisoners of war.

2702. Wyman, David S. WHY AUSCHWITZ WAS NEVER BOMBED. *Commentary 1978 65(5): 37-46.* Chronicles the numerous requests to the War Department to bomb the rail lines evacuating Hungarian Jews to Auschwitz and the camp itself in 1944. The War Department replied that such air strikes required diversion of air support from more strategic targets and were of doubtful efficacy. The Allies controlled the skies of Europe at the time and, on several occasions, the Air Force bombed installations very near Auschwitz with considerable success, so that it could have struck the camp and its gas chambers.　　　　　　J. Tull

2703. Young, Michael. FACING A TEST OF FAITH: JEWISH PACIFISTS DURING THE SECOND WORLD WAR. *Peace and Change 1975 3(2-3): 34-40.* Pacifist convictions and the necessity to fight the Nazis created a dilemma for the Jews of the Jewish Peace Fellowship in 1943.

2704. Zuroff, Efraim. RESCUE PRIORITY AND FUND RAISING AS ISSUES DURING THE HOLOCAUST: A CASE STUDY OF THE RELATIONS BETWEEN THE VA'AD HA-HATZALA AND THE JOINT, 1939-1941. *Am. Jewish Hist. 1979 68(3): 305-326.* The rescue of a group of East European rabbis and students by the Orthodox Jews of America through the Yeshiva Aid Committee (Va'ad Ha-Hatzala) was organized by Rabbi Eliezer Silver of the Union of Orthodox Rabbis. In complex dealings with the Joint Distribution Committee (JDC) the Va'ad, even though it needed the funds contributed by the JDC, maintained its independent stance and engaged in some separate fund raising. By December 1941, approximately 625 rabbis, students, and members of their families had been rescued via Japan and Shanghai. 4 illus., 3 photos, 27 notes. F. Rosenthal

2705. —. ATTITUDES OF YOUTH TO THE HOLOCAUST. *Yad Vashem News [Israel] 1973 4: 19-22.* Reports on the research of Dr. Hillel Klein and Uriel Last, "Conscious and Emotional Aspects in Attitudes to the Holocaust and its Victims among Jewish Youth in Israel and in the U.S.A." which tested the hypothesis that the experience of the European Holocaust is a basic component of contemporary Jewish and Israeli experience. The differences in responses between US and Israeli youth was attributed to the subject's emphasis in Israel's educational system and the Israeli youths' closer link with Holocaust survivors. J. P. Fox

Social Organization

Family

2706. Bean, Lee L.; May, Dean L.; and Skolnick, Mark. THE MORMON HISTORICAL DEMOGRAPHY PROJECT. *Hist. Methods Newsletter 1978 11(1): 45-53.* Describes the creation of a common data base of Mormon families which experienced a single demographic event on the Mormon pioneer trail or in Utah. The final plan is to achieve 12 analytical goals: demographic structure and change, nuptiality, polygamy, fertility, natural fertility, mortality, migration, community studies, inheritance, familial correlations, genetic demography, and sex ratios. The authors briefly cite some results of the project. 2 tables, graph, 2 fig., 16 notes. D. K. Pickens

2707. Bodnar, John E. SOCIALIZATION AND ADAPTATION: IMMIGRANT FAMILIES IN SCRANTON, 1880-1890. *Pennsylvania Hist. 1976 43(2): 147-162.* Studies the social mobility of the Irish and Welsh in Scranton during 1880-90 in order to test hypotheses advanced by Talcott Parsons, Philippe Aries, and Richard Sennett regarding the role of family structure in preparing children for adulthood in industrial society. Children from Irish and Welsh nuclear families enjoyed greater economic success than those reared in extended families. The sons of Welsh parents were more successful than those of Irish background because they were exposed to industrial life at an earlier age. The Welsh were somewhat more inclined to live in nuclear families than were the Irish. Based on census data and other sources; illus., 7 tables, 30 notes. D. C. Swift

2708. Chudacoff, Howard P. NEW BRANCHES ON THE TREE: HOUSEHOLD STRUCTURE IN EARLY STAGES OF THE FAMILY CYCLE IN WORCESTER, MASSACHUSETTS, 1860-1880. *Pro. of the Am. Antiquarian Soc. 1976 86(2): 303-320.* Links family history and urban history by examining family adjustment to change in a growing city. The nuclear family prevailed here, but living arrangements varied among families in different stages of development. Contextual factors, such as housing supplies, physical growth of the city, and economic change, caused household structures to fluctuate. Primary and secondary sources; 35 notes. J. Andrew

2709. Dowdall, Jean A. WOMEN'S ATTITUDES TOWARD EMPLOYMENT AND FAMILY ROLES. *Sociol. Analysis 1974 35(4): 251-262.* Greeley has argued that not enough is known about American ethnic group differences but that such differences exist primarily in the 'common core of assumptions' about familial role expectations. A measure of women's attitudes toward questions of female employment and family responsibilities is taken as an index of such expectations. Using a sample of 673 white, native born, married Rhode Island women, nationality, religious affiliation and social class are explored in relation to attitudes. Significant nationality-linked differences in attitudes were found. Religion was not significantly associated with attitudes, but among Catholic respondents there were significant differences associated with nationality. Taking social class into consideration, nationality group differences in attitudes were significant only among non-high school graduates and among those from non-white collar families. As Greeley predicted, there is considerable nationality-linked attitudinal variation among working class women; the reasons for it require further research. J

2710. Dubovik, Paul N. HOUSING IN HOLYOKE AND ITS EFFECTS ON FAMILY LIFE 1860-1910. *Hist. J. of Western Massachusetts 1975 4(1): 40-50.* The poverty of the "Shanty Irish" of "The Patch," the financial difficulties of the Hadley Falls Company, inadequate transportation, and expensive land led to barracks-like tenements. High rental company housing was a method of exploiting the workers. Based on the Holyoke *Transcript*, Green's *Holyoke*, and state and local documents; 3 illus., 62 notes. S. S. Sprague

2711. Easterlin, Richard A. FACTORS IN THE DECLINE OF FARM FAMILY FERTILITY IN THE UNITED STATES: SOME PRELIMINARY RESERACH RESULTS. *J. of Am. Hist. 1976 63(3): 600-614.* After contolling for age and marital differences, statistical tests indicate an average 25% fertility difference (woman/child ratio) between old and newly settled rural areas in 1860. Average frontier fertility was 5-10% lower than in newly settled areas slightly behind the frontier. Fertility differences cannot be attributed to a variable proportion of immigrants or to possible statistical biases. Declining land availability in older areas created pressures to reduce fertility. More research is needed to determine how this pressure operated through cost, taste, or income considerations. Based on Fred Bateman and James D. Foust's sampling of the 1860 federal manuscript census; table, 31 notes. W. R. Hively

2712. Elder, Glen H., Jr. and Rockwell, Richard C. MARITAL TIMING IN WOMEN'S LIFE PATTERNS. *J. of Family Hist. 1976 1(1): 34-53.* Studies the average age of first marriage for white women born in 1925-29, using data from the 1965 and 1970 National Fertility Surveys. Age at marriage is divided into early (under 19), on time (19-22), and late (23 and after). These groups differ greatly in their socioeconomic background, religion, other background variables, and subsequent life styles and fertility patterns. 7 tables, 10 notes, biblio. T. W. Smith

2713. Embry, Jessie L. MISSIONARIES FOR THE DEAD: THE STORY OF THE GENEALOGICAL MISSIONARIES OF THE NINETEENTH CENTURY. *Brigham Young U. Studies 1977 17(3): 355-360.* Since Mormons believe in salvation after death, a significant part of their missionary outreach during the late 19th century included genealogical missions. Immigrating saints were encouraged to bring genealogies of persons, living and dead, who might not ever come to Utah or accept the gospel while alive. Records unavailable in Utah were sought by genealogical missionaries returning to their ancestral homelands. Some 178 saints engaged in such missions between 1885 and 1900. Their efforts led to the organization of the Genealogical Society of Utah in 1894. The Church's genealogical library subsequently became the largest in the world with more than 100 branches. M. S. Legan

2714. Fairbanks, Carol. LIVES OF GIRLS AND WOMEN ON THE CANADIAN AND AMERICAN PRAIRIES. *Int. J. of Women's Studies [Canada] 1979 2(5): 452-472.* Uses two autobiographies: Hamlin Garland's *Son of the Middle Border* and Fredelle Bruser Maynard's *Raisins and Almonds;* seven novels: James Fenimore Cooper's *The Prairie*, O. E. Rolvaag's *Giants in the Earth,* and others; plus Nancy Stockwell's short fiction, *Out Somewhere and Back Again* to analyze the vision of prairie settlers in Canada and America and the effects of that vision on the lives of their wives and daughters.

2715. Glasco, Laurence A. THE LIFE CYCLES AND HOUSEHOLD STRUCTURE OF AMERICAN ETHNIC GROUPS: IRISH, GERMANS, AND NATIVE-BORN WHITES IN BUFFALO, NEW YORK 1855. *J. of Urban Hist. 1975 1(3): 339-364.* A study of the household structure of different ethnic groups produced evidence that the following trends existed: foreign-born women often became domestics, thus reducing the size of the family living at home; German girls remained domestics for shorter periods of time and married earlier; native-born women were the last to leave home, and German males left home earliest; the Irish were the least apt to be homeowners; and the native-born population most frequently boarded with family. 6 figs., 11 notes.

S. S. Sprague

2716. Goldin, Claudia. FAMILY STRATEGIES IN LATE NINETEENTH-CENTURY PHILADELPHIA. *Working Papers from the Regional Econ. Hist. Res. Center 1979 2(3): 60-106.* Analyzes the family decisionmaking process regarding economics in late 19th century Philadelphia households, based on a study of urban families from 1870 to 1880 United States Federal Population Censuses.

2717. Goldin, Claudia. HOUSEHOLD AND MARKET PRODUCTION OF FAMILIES IN A LATE NINETEENTH CENTURY AMERICAN CITY. *Explorations in Econ. Hist. 1979 16(2): 111-131.* Apart from the male head of household, urban families relied upon children as an important source of labor income. An examination of Philadelphia, Pennsylvania, in 1880 shows substitution between mothers and their daughters and the role of comparative advantage in family decisions concerning the allocation of their members' time. Ethnic differences were important only for daughters. Based on published documents and secondary accounts; 4 tables, 29 notes, 23 ref.

P. J. Coleman

2718. Griswold del Castillo, Richard. A PRELIMINARY COMPARISON OF CHICANO, IMMIGRANT AND NATIVE BORN FAMILY STRUCTURES 1850-1880. *Aztlan 1975 6(1): 87-95.* Compares European immigrants and native born Anglo Americans in Detroit, Michigan, with Mexican Americans in Los Angeles during 1850-80. The urban Chicano family was more drastically affected by economic changes and economic opportunities were more restricted for Chicano household heads. Chicano family structure resembled that of the native born Anglo American. 14 notes.

A

2719. Hareven, Tamara K. CYCLES, COURSES AND COHORTS: REFLECTIONS ON THEORETICAL AND METHODOLOGICAL APPROACHES TO THE HISTORICAL STUDY OF FAMILY DEVELOPMENT. *J. of Social Hist. 1978 12(1): 97-109.* The historical study of the family has undergone significant methodological shifts in the past decade, but a basic objective remains the same, to "explore the interactions between individual time, family time, and historical time." Identifies and analyzes approaches in the study of the family, in particular "family cycle" and "life course." Shifts position from an earlier advocacy of the use of family cycle to a support for the life course concept which offers new perspectives, new questions, and new beneficial methodologies, one of which is age cohorts. Secondary sources; 26 notes.

R. S. Sliwoski

2720. Hareven, Tamara K. and Vinovskis, Maris A. ETHNICITY, AND OCCUPATION IN URBAN FAMILIES: AN ANALYSIS OF SOUTH BOSTON MARITAL FERTILITY, AND THE SOUTH END IN 1880. *J. of Social Hist. 1975 8(3): 69-93.* Quantitative study of fertility in South Boston and the South End in 1880 "suggest that ethnicity was a major determinant of fertility differentials at the household levels." Occupation and location in the city also had an impact on fertility ratios. More work is needed on the relationship of fertility and women's work and also on evaluating the importance of the "level of education, religion, and income." 7 tables, 6 graphs, 29 notes, appendix.

L. Ziewacz

2721. Hareven, Tamara K. THE FAMILY PROCESS: THE HISTORICAL STUDY OF THE FAMILY CYCLE. *J. of Social Hist. 1974 7(3): 322-329.* Proposes a new mode of analysis of family patterns in 19th-century society. The family is viewed as a process over time rather than as a static unit within certain time periods. This model "assumes fluidity, change and transition in family structure . . . that individuals live through a variety of patterns of family structure and household organization during different stages of their life cycle, and that families and households evolve different types of organization, structure and relationships which are generally obscured in cross-sectional analysis." Supports the validity of this approach by data from a study of family structure in 19th-century Boston. 15 notes.

R. V. Ritter

2722. Hareven, Tamara K. FAMILY TIME AND HISTORICAL TIME. *Daedalus 1977 106(2): 57-70.* The family did not "break down" under the impact of industrialization and urbanization, but rather it contributed to both processes. Families aided in adapting their members to industrial work and to living in large urban settings. It is inaccurate to hold that the timing of family transitions was once more orderly than it is now. In fact, families are now less subject to sudden change. Some of the major problems facing the contemporary family arise from the demands placed on it by those who require that it be a haven and retreat from the outside world, which it has never been. Secondary sources; 27 notes.

E. McCarthy

2723. Hareven, Tamara K. FAMILY TIME AND INDUSTRIAL TIME: FAMILY AND WORK IN A PLANNED CORPORATION TOWN 1900-1924. *J. of Urban Hist. 1975 1(3): 365-389.* Cumulative individual employee files 1910-36 of the Amoskeag Manufacturing Company of Manchester, New Hampshire, coupled with marriage and insurance records and oral histories, reveal a pervasive family influence in working. Vacancies were discovered via word-of-mouth, family members substituted for each other, family finances postponed marriages and caused babies to be dropped off so women could return to work. Young children found summer jobs in the mills, and many met their future spouses there. 45 notes.

S. S. Sprague

2724. Hareven, Tamara K. INTRODUCTION: THE HISTORICAL STUDY OF THE FAMILY IN URBAN SOCIETY. *J. of Urban Hist. 1975 1(3): 259-267.* Considers "the family . . . a critical variable" shedding "light on . . . migration . . . patterns which determine population change." This overview covers ca. 1750-1975 and introduces five papers in the same issue. 17 notes.

S. S. Sprague

2725. Hareven, Tamara K. MODERNIZATION AND FAMILY HISTORY: PERSPECTIVES ON SOCIAL CHANGE. *Signs: J. of Women in Culture and Soc. 1976 2(1): 190-206.* The concept of modernization can be a valuable framework in which to study society and particularly the history of the family. It is often assumed in modernization theory that traditional values and patterns of behavior are replaced by modern ones in a continuous and consistent way. However, historical reality is always more complex and illustrates the uneven changes in individual and societal patterns of behavior. Family history must acknowledge diverse patterns of change from pre- to post-modern behavior within families as well as taking into account differences in class and ethnicity. An attempt must be made to evaluate the means by which families balance traditional and modern attitudes and it must be remembered that families did not modernize as units, but that men and women modernized at different rates within the family structure. 38 notes.

S. R. Herstein

2726. Hareven, Tamara K. THE SEARCH FOR GENERATIONAL MEMORY: TRIBAL RITES IN INDUSTRIAL SOCIETY. *Daedalus 1978 107(4): 137-149.* Describes the interest in tracing one's ancestors, providing examples of methods for tracing earlier generations since the founding of the Daughters of the American Revolution (DAR) in 1890.

2727. Harris, Barbara J. RECENT WORK ON THE HISTORY OF THE FAMILY: A REVIEW ARTICLE. *Feminist Studies 1976 3(3/4): 159-172.* Gerda Lerner has recently warned against equating family history and women's history. However, family history is certainly an important element in the history of women. Only when changes in the modern family are understood will we have an accurate picture of women's role in the transition to modern society. Christopher Lasch attacked the "modernization theory" and supported much current work on family history in a series of articles in the *New York Times Review of Books* in 1975. The theory assumes that the change from an extended to a nuclear family marks the transition from traditional to industrial society. Lasch is mistaken in questioning the importance of current research on family structure, in that structure in itself is vital because of its connection with demography. The question of the relation of family history to women's history remains. The changing role of women in modern family structures is a study vitally needed to complete our understanding of the total history of modern women. 51 notes.

S. R. Herstein

2728. Hastings, Donald W. and Harrison, Jerry N. A NOTE ON THE USE OF SPSS CONTROL CARDS TO CREATE SELECTED ALGORITHMS FOR MANIPULATION OF DATA OBTAINED

FROM FAMILY RECONSTRUCTION FORMS. *Hist. Methods 1979 12(3): 129-136.* Discusses the Statistical Package for the Social Sciences (SPSS) control cards, the construction of a sample file, and the use of algorithms in analysis. Based on Mormon birth, death, and marriage records from Manti, Utah, 1849-1948; 2 appendixes.

2729. Hays, Samuel P. HISTORY AND GENEALOGY: PATTERNS OF CHANGE AND PROSPECTS FOR COOPERATION. *Prologue 1975 7(2): 81-84, (3): 187-191.* Part II. There has been a reorientation in genealogy "from tracing one's family back to some point [or important ancestor] in the past to tracing it forward through history" to determine the sequence of descendants. This shift in perspective focuses on two problems of interest to the historian: migration and community development. Census data and local and family histories help reveal "the differentiating processes of migration between individuals and institutions of movement and those of community development." 7 notes. Part III. "The new social history is simply the new genealogy writ large . . ." Both require a new archival perspective, one that shifts from classifying records in terms of the agencies that created them to considering individuals as they move through life and come into contact with government. Archivists, social historians, and genealogists should cooperate to preserve local records, compile biographical material, and make individualized data more accessible. Specifically, manuscript census data should be computerized in a universal format useful to both historians and genealogists. Veterans' service and pension records should also have a high priority. "The possibilities are enormous and eminently worthwhile." 4 notes.
T. Simmerman/W. R. Hively

2730. Jeffrey, Kirk. VARIETIES OF FAMILY HISTORY. *Am. Archivist 1975 38(4): 521-532.* Describes current trends in research in American family history, and discusses current interpretations in the field. 36 notes.
J. A. Benson

2731. Kessner, Thomas and Caroli, Betty Boyd. NEW IMMIGRANT WOMEN AT WORK: ITALIANS AND JEWS IN NEW YORK CITY, 1880-1905. *J. of Ethnic Studies 1978 5(4): 19-31.* Statistical analysis of first and second generation Italian and Jewish women shows that "gender proved less significant than ethnicity in shaping the occupational distribution of wives" in lower Manhattan, Brooklyn, and Harlem. Upward mobility is demonstrable from unskilled blue-collar to skilled blue-collar jobs outside the home for Italian daughters, but none reached professional status. Jewish women started at higher status levels and continued to move up rapidly. Attitudes toward education among the two groups, willingness to defer to brothers, familial values as to suitable work for women, and Italian girls' acceptance of homework on garments and artificial flowers, which Jewish girls by 1905 had abandoned, explain the divergent occupational priorities and objectives flowing from different cultural and historical perspectives. Primary and secondary data; 4 tables, 23 notes.
G. J. Bobango

2732. Klaczynska, Barbara. WHY WOMEN WORK: A COMPARISON OF VARIOUS GROUPS—PHILADELPHIA, 1910-1930. *Labor Hist. 1976 17(1): 73-87.* Analyzes the reasons for women working by comparing patterns of Italian, Polish, Irish, Jewish, black, and native-born white women. Central determinants were strong ethnic familial traditions, the lack of strong familial ties, and class consciousness. Italian and Polish women worked least often, and blacks, native-born whites, and Irish most often. Jewish women tended to move from a work tradition to a nonwork position as they moved into the middle class. Based on government publications and periodicals; 20 notes.
L. L. Athey

2733. Kleinberg, Susan J. TECHNOLOGY AND WOMEN'S WORK: THE LIVES OF WORKING CLASS WOMEN IN PITTSBURGH, 1870-1900. *Labor Hist. 1976 17(1): 58-72.* Pittsburgh's economic structure relied primarily on male labor which prevented working-class women from an industrial role, thus reinforcing the traditional segregation of men and women. Working-class women continued time-consuming housework without technological advantages well into the 20th century, because of the political priorities of the city. For example, the decision to lay only small water pipes in working-class neighborhoods meant that only the middle and upper classes and heavy industry got enough water and sewage facilities. Working-class women were forced to perform all their household cleaning chores without adequate water. Domestic, technological inventions such as washing machines and gas stoves were also beyond the means of the working class. Based upon Pittsburgh government publications and secondary sources; 35 notes.
L. L. Athey

2734. Kleinberg, S. J. DEATH AND THE WORKING CLASS. *J. of Popular Culture 1977 11(1): 193-209.* Explores attitudes toward death in their social and economic context among working-class residents of Pittsburgh during the 1890's. Use of both quantitative and qualitative approaches in studies of popular culture overcomes in part the possibility of placing too much emphasis on the unusual or unrepresentative, as is the case where conventional sources alone are employed. Primary and secondary sources; 3 tables, 50 notes.
D. G. Nielson

2735. Krause, Corinne Azen. ITALIAN, JEWISH, AND SLAVIC GRANDMOTHERS IN PITTSBURGH: THEIR ECONOMIC ROLES. *Frontiers 1977 2(2): 18-27.* Interview 75 women in the Pittsburgh area challenging the notion that immigrants' wives rarely worked outside the home during the early 1900's; part of a special issue on women's oral history.

2736. Krause, Corinne Azen. URBANIZATION WITHOUT BREAKDOWN: ITALIAN, JEWISH, AND SLAVIC IMMIGRANT WOMEN IN PITTSBURGH, 1900-1945. *J. of Urban Hist. 1978 4(3): 291-306.* Most immigrant women adjusted to the cultural shock of immigration without serious or lasting problems. In part this was due to general human resiliency, but in Pittsburgh it was also due to the existence of immigrant neighborhoods and other bridges to the old world. Based on oral histories; fig., 41 notes.
T. W. Smith

2737. Lackey, Richard S. GENEALOGICAL RESEARCH: AN ASSESSMENT OF POTENTIAL VALUE. *Prologue 1975 7(4): 221-225.* Genealogists should accept a mutually beneficial partnership with researchers in all related fields. Too often, genealogists fail to make their discoveries available. Although historians and genealogists possess separate areas of expertise, each can serve the other by suggesting the potential value of records which one or the other may discover. Uses several primary sources uncovered by genealogists to illustrate the potential benefits to historians, and suggests published aids that could be usefully consulted. Based on documents in the National Archives and on secondary sources; illus., 28 notes.
W. R. Hively

2738. Laslett, Barbara. FAMILY MEMBERSHIP, PAST AND PRESENT. *Social Problems 1978 25(5): 476-490.* Summarizes contemporary attitudes toward the US family. Factors affecting the family include lower mortality rates, younger marriage age, declining fertility rates, urbanization, and migration. The contemporary family represents the contradiction between its traditional and nontraditional forms. Questions whether it can sustain and satisfy the search for meaning and the weight of expectation. Primary and secondary sources; 12 notes; refs.
A. M. Osur

2739. Laslett, Barbara. SOCIAL CHANGE AND THE FAMILY: LOS ANGELES, CALIFORNIA, 1850-1870. *Am. Sociol. Rev. 1977 42(2): 268-291.* Explores the impact on the family of changes in the individual's access to actual and potential wealth. A multivariate analysis, based on the individual census schedules for the city of Los Angeles in 1850 and 1870, is used to explore the changing relationships between economic, demographic and other structural variables on household structure. The findings suggest that a dynamic, Marxian model can help explain the effects of social change on the family.
J

2740. Leet, Don R. THE DETERMINANTS OF THE FERTILITY TRANSITION IN ANTEBELLUM OHIO. *J. of Econ. Hist. 1976 36(2): 359-378.* The cross-sectional and secular variations in the fertility of the white population in pre-Civil War Ohio are analyzed with special regard to the role of population pressure in conditioning these patterns and trends. Other factors, such as urbanization, education, cultural heritage, and the sex ratio, all of which are often cited as major explanatory variables during the demographic transition are also introduced. Although each of these variables is shown to have some impact, none can account for more than a minor proportion of the variance in human fertility. It appears that the major force affecting both inter-county fertility and the secular trend for the state was the variation in the degree of population pressure as measured by the average assessed value of an acre of non-urban land.
J

2741. Modell, John; Furstenberg, Frank F.; and Hershberg, Theodore. SOCIAL CHANGE AND TRANSITIONS TO ADULTHOOD IN HISTORICAL PERSPECTIVE. *J. of Family Hist. 1976 1(1): 7-32.* It has been generally assumed that the industrial revolution changed the transition process from childhood to adulthood. Yet there is virtually no empirical data on what the maturation processes were in the 19th century, or how they have changed over the last 100 years. Drawing on evidence from the Philadelphia Social History project, the authors analyze the prevalence, timing, spread, age-congruity, and integration of the transition process. They find that over the last century the prevalence of the usual transition has increased somewhat, that the spread has narrowed, that there is much greater age-congruity, and that transitions are more contingent and integrated since formal institutions play a larger role. 2 tables, 6 graphs, 19 notes, biblio.   T. W. Smith

2742. Morgan, Myfanwy and Golden, Hilda H. IMMIGRANT FAMILIES IN AN INDUSTRIAL CITY: A STUDY OF HOUSEHOLDS IN HOLYOKE, 1880. *J. of Family Hist. 1979 4(1): 59-68.* From a sample of the census manuscript for 1880 studies the relationship between ethnicity and 1) household size, 2) household composition, and 3) family type in Holyoke, Massachusetts. Important differences are found among the major ethnic groups (native born whites, Irish, and Canadians). The native born had small household size, but included more non-relatives and non-immediate kin than the immigrant groups. As a result the native households were more frequently extended families than the immigrant households were. 6 tables, 8 notes, biblio.
                                                          T. W. Smith

2743. Moynihan, Daniel Patrick. THE STATE, THE CHURCH, AND THE FAMILY. *Urban and Social Change Rev. 1977 10(1): 7-9.* Religious institutions have forsaken their traditional societal role as a moral force in favor of the government in the 1960's and 70's; examines the implications for the family unit and ethnic groups.

2744. Novak, Michael. THE FAMILY OUT OF FAVOR. *Urban and Social Change Rev. 1977 10(1): 3-6.* Discusses the role of capitalism in diminishing the moral and economic importance of the family in social organization, particularly among ethnic groups, in the 1970's.

2745. O'Connor, Peter. NUCLEAR VERSUS EXTENDED HOUSEHOLDS, STOCKTON, CALIFORNIA 1880: AN EMPIRICAL INVESTIGATION OF VARIATION. *Australian and New Zealand J. of Sociol. [Australia] 1976 12(1): 68-72.* Considers the question of hypothesized differences between extended and nuclear families, and attempts to test empirically the effectiveness of five predictor variables (age, marital status, birthplace, sex, and SES position as measured by occupation—all referring to household head) on type of family in Stockton, California, in 1880. Confirms previous studies indicating the absence of extended family households in the 19th century. The view that in the past extended families predominated is a function of "western nostalgia." Primary sources; 2 tables, note, biblio.   R. G. Neville

2746. Reiff, Janice. DOCUMENTING THE AMERICAN FAMILY. *Midwestern Archivist 1978 3(1): 39-46.* Describes sources used by historians today.

2747. Rozen, Frieda Shoenberg. THE PERMANENT FIRST-FLOOR TENANT: WOMEN AND *GEMEINSCHAFT. Mennonite Q. Rev. 1977 51(4): 319-328.* Discusses the role of women in Amish and Hutterite communities, based on written materials, and includes a comparison with the Jewish Chassidim of Brooklyn and the kibbutzim of Israel. In all such societies the women are subordinate to the men. Structures have been built to maintain this position even in the face of avowed equality. This much is known, but otherwise a number of questions remain unanswered. Studies are needed to determine whether women are in inferior positions or merely subordinate ones, and to determine how satisfied and happy they are in comparison with their liberated sisters of the larger society. 6 notes.   V. L. Human

2748. Seller, Maxine S. BEYOND THE STEREOTYPE: A NEW LOOK AT THE IMMIGRANT WOMAN, 1880-1924. *J. of Ethnic Studies 1975 3(1): 59-70.* Questions the standard stereotypes of immigrant women as ignorant seamstresses or subservient, simplistic wives and mothers. Studies of Antonietta Pisanelli Alessandro (founder of professional Italian theater in the United States), Josephine Humpel Zeman (Bohemian journalist), and Rose Pesotta (Russian Jewish trade unionist), show that immigrant women often led movements for cultural, intellectual, and economic improvement. Sources exist to further examine the contributions of the neglected half of the immigrant population. Secondary and autobiographical sources; 38 notes.   T. W. Smith

2749. Skolnick, Mark L.; Bean, Lee L.; Dintelman, Sue M.; and Mineau, Geraldine. A COMPUTERIZED FAMILY HISTORY DATA BASE SYSTEM. *Sociol. and Social Res. 1979 63(3): 506-523.* Describes the development of a unique, computer-based, data management system designed to increase the ability of scholars in social history and historical demography to collate and analyze large bodies of historical data. This system extends efforts, largely mounted in Europe, to develop computerized systems for data manipulation and record linkage. Describes the Mormon historical demography research project, for which this system was developed, and the system's file structure, input systems, and data access facilities. Includes an illustration of the possible types of analysis.
                                                                    J/S

2750. Smith, Daniel Scott. A COMMUNITY-BASED SAMPLE OF THE OLDER POPULATION FROM THE 1880 AND 1900 UNITED STATES MANUSCRIPT CENSUS. *Hist. Methods 1978 11(2): 67-74.* After a lenghty discussion of methodology and sampling techniques, this study concludes that the subject of old age needs reliable historical data which, within discussed limits, the census provides and secondly, that only in recent decades has the family status of the older population begun to change. In this study "old age" is not just being 65 but it is rather a process in which individual variations, marital status, sex, and ethnicity contribute to a stage of life concept. Table, 30 notes.
                                                          D. K. Pickens

2751. Smith, Judith E. OUR OWN KIND: FAMILY AND COMMUNITY NETWORKS. *Radical Hist. Rev. 1978 (17): 99-120.* Provides a study of immigrant family ties and traditions, particularly among southern Italian and eastern European Jewish immigrants as they experienced the urban industrial environment of Rhode Island during 1880-1940.

2752. Stoloff, Carolyn. WHO JOINS WOMEN'S LIBERATION? *Psychiatry 1973 36(3): 325-340.* Responses to questionnaires sent to female graduate students at the University of Michigan in order to determine the differences between members of the women's liberation movement and others who remained out of the movement indicate that there were distinct differences in socioeconomic, religious, intellectual and political background, and the political attitudes of the students' parents. Those who join the movement are most typically from middle- or upper-middle-class urban or suburban families, with a Jewish or "nonformalistically religious" Protestant background, and from homes in which religion was not strongly emphasized. Parents of those who joined the movement are most likely college graduates or employed in professional or intellectual occupations, and they are more politically liberal than parents of the nonjoiners. Most of those in each group reported that they had a close relationship with their mothers, but the participants reported that their mothers were considerably more competitive than mothers of nonparticipants, and somewhat more competitive than their husbands. The women's liberationists tend to be more sexually experienced, and they tended to be participants in the earlier Civil Rights movement and the recent Peace Movement. Subjects in each group, however, subscribed to the women's liberation view of women's rights, roles, and responsibilities. 6 notes, biblio.   M. Kaufman

2753. Thavenat, Dennis. A SEARCH FOR ALL THE PEOPLE: FAMILY HISTORY COMES OF AGE. *Family Heritage 1978 1(2): 58-62.* Collaboration of genealogists and historians in the 1970's has resulted in renewed interest in history of the masses through family history, adding perspectives on the general population's effect of national affairs, social structure, kinship patterns, and value formation.

2754. Vinovskis, Maris A. MARRIAGE PATTERNS IN MID-NINETEENTH-CENTURY NEW YORK STATE: A MULTIVARIATE ANALYSIS. *J. of Family Hist. 1978 3(1): 51-61.* Uses the New York state censuses of 1845, 1855, 1865, and 1875, and the federal census of 1850, to carry out an ecological analysis of the demographic and socioeconomic determinants of the marriage pattern. Finds that the sex ratio was the single best predictor of the proportion married. Two measures of agricultural opportunity also were strong predictors. The foreign-native distribution was a moderate predictor. Urbanness, industrialization, and economic development were not good predictors. 3 tables, 16 notes, biblio., appendix.   T. W. Smith

2755. Wright, Raymond S. AN INTERNATIONAL CENTER FOR THE STUDY OF THE FAMILY. *J. of Family Hist. 1977 2(2): 169-171.* The archives of the Genealogical Society of Utah, supported by the Church of Jesus Christ of Latter-Day Saints, are unparalleled in the fields of genealogy, family history, and many related areas. The Mormon archives should be consulted as a source of primary data about much of American history. It also covers many other countries. Table.
                    T. W. Smith

Organizations

2756. Blouin, Francis X., Jr. "FOR OUR MUTUAL BENEFIT": A LOOK AT ETHNIC ASSOCIATIONS IN MICHIGAN. *Chronicle 1979 15(2): 12-15.* Mutual aid societies for Italian, Polish, Scandinavian, and German ethnic groups in Michigan provided spiritual, monetary, and cultural support and eased the traumas of acculturation, 1850's-1950's.

2757. Cochran, Robert. FOLK ELEMENTS IN A NON-FOLK GAME: THE EXAMPLE OF BASKETBALL. *J. of Popular Culture 1976 10(2): 398-403.* "Playground" basketball, with its regional rules of play, has its own styles of play as well. These styles, which often vary between ethnic groups and which should be regarded as the folk elements of the game, have significantly affected professional and scholastic play over the years. Secondary sources; 18 notes.   D. G. Nielson

2758. Galey, Margaret E. ETHNICITY, FRATERNALISM, SOCIAL AND MENTAL HEALTH. *Ethnicity 1977 4(1): 19-53.* Examines 14 ethnic groups' fraternal organizations formed in Pittsburgh, Pennsylvania, 1900-70, in order to investigate the services offered, the alleviation of pains of assimilation, and implications of these health- and social-minded organizations for contemporary health care. Fraternal organizations helped immigrants from southern and eastern Europe assimilate early in this century, giving benefits for sickness, death, and disability, and helping socioculturally. The associations cemented ethnic feeling. They shared a lack of provision for mental health (due primarily to the stigma attached to mental illness), extensive self-help programs, focus on community benefit, and reinforcement of ethnic insularity through health care administered within ethnic communities.   G. A. Hewlett

2759. Luckingham, Bradford. BENEVOLENCE IN EMERGENT SAN FRANCISCO: A NOTE ON IMMIGRANT LIFE IN THE URBAN FAR WEST. *Southern California Q. 1973 55(4): 431-443.* From almost the inception of San Francisco as a booming urban center of gold rush California, various groups banded together for mutual assistance. Organized along national, religious, or occupational lines, these benevolent associations advised newcomers, provided information about friends and relatives, gave immediate financial aid, maintained clinics, obtained jobs for the unemployed, and provided transportation to the mines or back home. Typical organizations included the French Benevolent Society, Masons, Odd Fellows, Young Men's Christian Association, and the San Francisco Ladies' Protection and Relief Society. The benevolent associations resembled the efforts of groups in older American cities, with the groups attempting to provide for the welfare of their members. Based on primary and secondary sources; 21 notes.   A. Hoffman

2760. McCaghy, Charles H. and Neal, Arthur G. THE FRATERNITY OF COCKFIGHTERS: ETHNICAL EMBELLISHMENTS OF AN ILLEGAL SPORT. *J. of Popular Culture 1974 8(3): 557-569.* Gives the history of cockfighting, 3000 BC-1975 and centers on the ethnic groups which are most frequently associated with the illegal sport, principally in the United States.

2761. Rader, Benjamin G. THE QUEST FOR SUBCOMMUNITIES AND THE RISE OF AMERICAN SPORT. *Am. Q. 1977 29(4): 355-369.* Sports clubs were an important form of voluntary association during

the 19th century through which subcommunities of the American population established groupings based on ethnicity and social status. The sport club assumed some of the traditional functions of the church and the geographical community and also laid the groundwork for organized sports activities of more recent times. Ethnic groups such as the Scottish Caledonians and the German Turners, emphasized their ethnicity through sports. Upper class native Americans founded private sports clubs in such areas of activity as yachting and baseball, as well as establishing urban athletic clubs which combined recreation with status exclusivity. Primary and secondary sources.   N. Lederer

Social Mobility and Social Status

2762. Alcorn, Richard S. LEADERSHIP AND STABILITY IN MID-NINETEENTH CENTURY AMERICA: A CASE STUDY OF AN ILLINOIS TOWN. *J. of Am. Hist. 1974 61(3): 685-702.* American 19th-century communities were, according to some historians, stable "island communities," while according to others massive population mobility made such stability impossible. A demographic study of Paris, Illinois, reveals the existence of a stable, older, wealthy elite maintaining control of the community through a period of rapid population change involving non-leader residents. A significantly high proportion of leaders in politics, boosterism, and temperance reform persisted as residents from 1840-60, lending an image of stable leadership flexible enough to meet local needs and to reflect local values. 8 tables, 23 notes.   K. B. West

2763. Chiswick, Barry R. THE EFFECT OF AMERICANIZATION ON THE EARNINGS OF FOREIGN-BORN MEN. *J. of Pol. Econ. 1978 86(5): 897-922.* Analyzes the earnings of immigrant men compared with native born and among foreign born according to their country of origin, years in the United States, and citizenship; uses 1970 census data.

2764. Chiswick, Barry R. SONS OF IMMIGRANTS: ARE THEY AT AN EARNINGS DISADVANTAGE? *Am. Econ. Rev. 1977 67(1): 376-380.* Native-born white males have a small income advantage over second-generation male Americans. Income disadvantages appear to result from other factors such as class, intelligence, and motivation. 3 tables, 4 references.   D. K. Pickens

2765. Conk, Margo A. SOCIAL MOBILITY IN HISTORICAL PERSPECTIVE. *Marxist Perspectives 1978 1(3): 52-69.* That social mobility studies often employ binary or dichotomous rather than linear occupations classifications results in disparate beliefs on ranking between survey takers and participants.

2766. Dietrick, Barbara A. SOCIAL MOBILITY: 1969-1973. *Ann. of the Am. Acad. of Pol. and Social Sci. 1974 (414): 138-147.* A selective survey of social mobility research published in English over a five-year period. Much work was devoted to "extending and elaborating" the Blau-Duncan model, but "the largest increase in the volume of research on mobility has been in the area of individual career mobility." Studies concerning political behavior, mobility and ascribed status, and culture are also considered. 56 notes.   S

2767. Engerman, Stanley L. UP OR OUT: SOCIAL AND GEOGRAPHICAL MOBILITY IN THE UNITED STATES. *J. of Interdisciplinary Hist. 1975 5(3): 469-489.* Analysis of "the new social history" in the United States with particular respect to Stephan Thernstrom, *The Other Bostonians: Poverty and Progress in the American Metropolis* (Cambridge, Mass., 1973). Although there are reservations about both procedures and conclusions, the critical point is that Thernstrom and others "have clearly shown the basic usefulness of their methods and have greatly advanced our knowledge of what happened among the non-elite." 2 tables, 40 notes.   R. Howell

2768. Fraundorf, Martha Norby. RELATIVE EARNINGS OF NATIVE- AND FOREIGN-BORN WOMEN. *Explorations in Econ. Hist. 1978 15(2): 211-220.* Sees little difference in wages in the United States between native- and foreign-born women during 1890-1911, though there were some differences between single and married women. If anything, foreign-born women encountered the same or less discrimination than their husbands. Based on published documents and secondary accounts; 6 tables, 37 notes, biblio.   P. J. Coleman

2769. Frisch, Michael. LADDERS, RACING, AND FOREST TRAILS. *Labor Hist. 1974 15(3): 461-466.* Reviews Stephan Thernstrom's *The Other Bostonians: Poverty and Progress in the American Metropolis, 1880-1970* (Cambridge: Harvard, 1973), praising the logic and precision of analysis in the work, but questioning its relationship to broader problems of meaning for the individuals involved, and the character of economic development and social-structural change.
          L. L. Athey

2770. Garofalo, Charles. BLACK-WHITE OCCUPATIONAL DISTRIBUTION IN MIAMI DURING WORLD WAR I. *Prologue 1973 5(2): 98-101.* Selective Service registration records for the three registrations of 1917-18 provide data on white and black registrants with each group further divided into categories of native and foreign-born. The 6,429 subjects are grouped in the four classes by seven occupational categories from "unskilled" to "professional." Perceived patterns may be compared with other urban center records. Based on primary sources; 2 tables, 14 notes.   D. G. Davis, Jr.

2771. Ghent, Joyce Maynard and Jaher, Frederic Cople. THE CHICAGO BUSINESS ELITE, 1830-1930: A COLLECTIVE BIOGRAPHY. *Business Hist. Rev. 1976 50(3): 288-328.* Attempts to determine whether the profile of a business elite, that of Chicago during 1830-1930, conformed to the national pattern found in previous investigations of this subject. Concludes that in education, religion, geography of birth, vintage of wealth, and family background, the commercial elite "had more privileged characteristics than did the national population." It became even less "Algeristic" with each succeeding generation. 32 tables, 19 notes.   C. J. Pusateri

2772. Glassberg, Eudice. WORK, WAGES, AND THE COST OF LIVING, ETHNIC DIFFERENCES AND THE POVERTY LINE, PHILADELPHIA, 1880. *Pennsylvania Hist. 1979 46(1): 17-58.* A family of five in Philadelphia in 1880 needed $643 per year for an adequate income. Even workers in most skilled trades could not earn that much, and unskilled laborers were far worse off. Children had to work and wives had to earn money, often through "home work." Male white Americans had the best prospects of earning nearly enough money. Germans held more skilled jobs than did Irishmen. Blacks encountered the most occupational difficulties. Based on Philadelphia Social History Project data and other materials; 2 photos, 10 tables, 87 notes.   D. C. Swift

2773. Goyder, John C. and Pineo, Peter C. MINORITY GROUP STATUS AND SELF-EVALUATED CLASS. *Sociol. Q. 1974 15(2): 199-211.* Self-evaluated class status is shown to vary among white Protestants, Catholics, Jews, and black Protestants. Holding economic status constant, Jews are most likely to select the middle- (or upper-) class label, followed by white Protestants, white Catholics, and black Protestants. Thus, the independent effect of minority status on self-evaluated class status reinforces the ranking directly attributable to the economic levels of each of the four groups. Also, the congruence between self-identified class and objective economic status is closer among Jews and white Protestants than among white Catholics or black Protestants. The hypothesis that affiliation with a minority necessarily reduces class consciousness was, therefore, not supported.   J

2774. Greeley, Andrew M. THE ETHNIC MIRACLE. *Public Interest 1976 (45): 20-36.* The "ethnic miracle" refers to the economic and educational success of southern and eastern European immigrants who came to the United States before World War I. Special attention is given to the Poles of Chicago and to the Italians. Evidence is based on an analysis of a composite file assembled from 12 National Opinion Research Center (NORC) national sample surveys. The immigrants improved their lot during the three decades since World War II because of ambition, hard work, saving, sacrifice, and close and intense parental attention. Italians are now the third richest religio-ethnic group in America. Poles earn nearly $1,000 a year more than the average white in the metropolitan north. By the 1960's people from both groups were more likely to attend college than the national average for white Americans. However, Polish and Italian college graduates find it difficult to enter prestigious occupations. Discrimination seems to be the reason. 2 tables.   S. Harrow

2775. Greeley, Andrew M. THE "RELIGIOUS FACTOR" AND ACADEMIC CAREERS: ANOTHER COMMUNICATION. *Am. J. of Sociol. 1973 78(5): 1247-1255.* Strong evidence indicates that, despite social, economic, historical, cultural, and perhaps religious obstacles, many more Catholics are electing academic careers. Little is known about either the facts or the dynamics of this change, and there seems to be little interest among sociologists or the funding agencies to inquire about it. While these changes occur, the long-standing assumption that the absence of Catholics in scholarly careers is a proof of Catholic intellectual inferiority remains essentially unchallenged.   J

2776. Greer, Edward. SOCIAL MOBILITY IN THE U.S. WORKING CLASS. *Monthly R. 1975 26(9): 51-57.* Discusses Stephan Thernstrom's *The Other Bostonians: Poverty and Progress in the American Metropolis, 1880-1970* (Harvard U. Pr., 1973) in the context of social mobility in the United States.

2777. Hanushek, Eric. ETHNIC INCOME VARIATIONS: MAGNITUDES AND EXPLANATIONS. Sowell, Thomas, ed. *Essays and Data on American Ethnic Groups* (Washington, D.C.: Urban Inst. Pr., 1978): 139-166. Discusses income determination as influenced by factors of ethnic background, divided by Standard Metropolitan Statistical Areas (SMSA). For example, blacks who, on the whole, earn less than whites, have less schooling and are concentrated in the South. Uses a variation of the human capital model which views education and training as an investment and concludes that there is a high return on postsecondary education, decreasing by ethnic group and economic region. Primary sources; 13 tables, 23 notes.   K. A. Talley

2778. Hardy, Melissa A. OCCUPATIONAL MOBILITY AND NATIVITY-ETHNICITY IN INDIANAPOLIS, 1850-60. *Social Forces 1978 57(1): 205-221.* Rates and patterns of occupational mobility in Indianapolis during the 1850's are analyzed using data from manuscript federal census schedules. Between 1850 and 1860, nearly half the working males who remained in the city were mobile, most of them within the nonmanual or manual categories. Analysis by age cohorts revealed that the young were more likely to be upwardly mobile and less likely to be downwardly mobile than older cohorts of workers. This differential mobility was almost totally a result of the different origin distributions of the cohorts. An analysis of nativity-ethnicity indicated that immigrant males occupied favorable positions in the occupational hierarchy in 1850, which led to considerable upward mobility. Once structural conditions were taken into account, however, differences between the mobility rates of native-born and foreign-born were small, with the native-born somewhat more likely to cross the manual-nonmanual boundary. Basic findings from this study are compared with those from studies of Boston, Philadelphia, and Houston.   J

2779. Hart, Jack R. HORATIO ALGER IN THE NEWSROOM: SOCIAL ORIGINS OF AMERICAN EDITORS. *Journalism Q. 1976 53(1): 14-20.* The editors of the major daily newspapers of 1875 and 1900 were compared with the characteristics of industrial executives of that period. Both were primarily from the business and professional classes. The editors often had fathers who were editors. Career patterns were increasingly bureaucratized during the period studied. Both groups were typically well educated and born in the Northeastern or Mid-Atlantic states. Based on primary sources; 4 tables, 12 notes.
          K. J. Puffer

2780. Hazelrigg, Lawrence E. OCCUPATIONAL MOBILITY IN NINETEENTH-CENTURY U.S. CITIES: A REVIEW OF SOME EVIDENCE. *Social Forces 1974 53(1): 21-32.* Reviews intracity trends in occupational status change among adult males from four studies of three cities—Boston, Philadelphia, and Poughkeepsie, New York—for the mid-nineteenth century. The quality of the data and problems of cross-study comparability are discussed. Rates of grossly defined vertical mobility and the transmission of status through adults' careers were stable among the nonmigrant male populations of the three cities for the periods of time in question. Data available for Boston indicate that the level of son's career beginnings had a substantial impact on his subsequent attainments and that the effect of father's occupation was largely interpreted by son's career-entry level.   J

2781. Henretta, James A. THE STUDY OF SOCIAL MOBILITY: IDEOLOGICAL ASSUMPTIONS AND CONCEPTUAL BIAS. *Labor Hist. 1977 18(2): 165-178.* The study of mobility embodies assumptions about the nature of human motivation and social reality. Striving and success are valued and there is the presupposition of social inequality. A cautious use of these ideas is necessary since they may cause historians to overlook subcultural perceptions of reality not in accord with social mobility. 27 notes.   L. L. Athey

2782. Hershberg, Theodore, et al. OCCUPATION AND ETHNICITY IN FIVE NINETEENTH-CENTURY CITIES: A COLLABORATIVE INQUIRY. *Hist. Methods Newsletter 1974 7(3): 174-216.* Examines employment and ethnicity in Philadelphia, Pennsylvania; Hamilton, Ontario; Kingston, New York; Buffalo, New York; and Poughkeepsie, New York, and concludes that property ownership was related to class considerations, but was substantially modified by ethnicity and culture. Based on primary and secondary sources; tables, graphs, and charts.   D. K. Pickens

2783. Hershberg, Theodore and Dockhorn, Robert. OCCUPATIONAL CLASSIFICATION. *Hist. Methods Newsletter 1976 9(2-3): 59-99.* After a brief historiographic background discusses the nature of the Occupation Dictionary Codebook for The Philadelphia Social History Project and its contributions to various research projects. The Codebook is included in this article.   D. K. Pickens

2784. Hershberg, Theodore. THE PHILADELPHIA SOCIAL HISTORY PROJECT: AN INTRODUCTION. *Hist. Methods Newsletter 1976 9(2-3): 43-58.* The author, Director of the Projects, describes the Philadelphia Social History Project in terms of trying to find the specific workings and consequences of industrialization and urbanization. Many research programs are underway. The main thrust of the parent project is in four areas; the nature of work, the uses of urban space, life course developments, and special group experiences.   D. K. Pickens

2785. Hershberg, Theodore; Burstein, Alan; and Dockhorn, Robert. RECORD LINKAGE. *Hist. Methods Newsletter 1976 9(2-3): 137-164.* Deals with various problems of record linkage (tracing individuals and groups from census to city directories, etc.) in the Philadelphia Social History Project. As in the study of social mobility, the major problem is the lack of a common methodology, though one is quite possible in the near future.   D. K. Pickens

2786. Higgs, Robert. PARTICIPATION OF BLACKS AND IMMIGRANTS IN THE AMERICAN MERCHANT CLASS, 1890-1910: SOME DEMOGRAPHIC RELATIONS. *Explorations in Econ. Hist. 1976 13(2): 153-164.* Using quantitative evidence, confirms the generally held assumptions that urbanization promoted a group's participation in retailing, that minority groups participated more commonly in southern locations, and that participation was lowest for blacks, five times as great for native-born whites, and 10 times as great for foreign-born whites. Further research on a broad range of social differentials is required to explain these patterns. Based on published census data and secondary sources.   P. J. Coleman

2787. Hill, Peter J. RELATIVE SKILL AND INCOME LEVELS OF NATIVE AND FOREIGN BORN WORKERS IN THE UNITED STATES. *Explorations in Econ. Hist. 1975 12(1): 47-60.* Challenges the widely held view that immigrants were overwhelmingly unskilled, that they almost always entered the job market at the bottom, and that their economic position was generally much lower than that of the native-born. In the period 1870-1920, native- and foreign-born were comparable in economic status, annual earnings and savings were nearly equal, the foreign-born had a higher rate of home ownership than the native-born, and there were no very significant differences between the two groups in job skills. Based on published statistics and secondary accounts.   P. J. Coleman

2788. Ingham, John N. RAGS TO RICHES REVISITED: THE EFFECT OF CITY SIZE AND RELATED FACTORS ON THE RECRUITMENT OF BUSINESS LEADERS. *J. of Am. Hist. 1976 63(3): 615-637.* Analyzes the backgrounds of 696 iron and steel manufacturers in six US cities, ca. 1874-1900. The pattern of social continuity presented by Frances W. Gregory and Irene D. Neu seems more applicable to this

data than the "new elite" thesis of Matthew Josephson or Herbert G. Gutman. The typical manufactuer does not conform to the rags and riches stereotype. In the larger, established cities, industrialists belonged to antebellum upper social classes that had controlled the preindustrial economy. In smaller, more recently established cities, however, origins and social status were more complex. Primary and secondary sources; 9 tables, 12 notes.   W. R. Hively

2789. Jackson, Susan. MOVIN' ON: MOBILITY THROUGH HOUSTON IN THE 1850'S. *Southwestern Hist. Q. 1978 81(3): 251-282.* Less than 1/6 of the free adults living in Houston, Texas, in 1860 had been there in 1850. The median age, male-female sex ratio, and percentage of unmarried men, foreign-born, unskilled workers, and adults without real property, all increased during the 1850's. Single young men, manual workers, and the propertyless, and the foreign-born left Houston at a greater than average rate after 1850. Most stayed within 200 miles of town, but increased their occupational status and amount of real property less than men who continued to live inside Houston. Primary sources; 13 illus., 4 tables, 35 notes.   J. H. Broussard

2790. Kirk, Gordon W. and Kirk, Carolyn Tyirin. THE IMMIGRANT, ECONOMIC OPPORTUNITY, AND TYPE OF SETTLEMENT IN NINETEENTH-CENTURY AMERICA. *J. of Econ. Hist. 1978 38(1): 226-234.* The historical literature on economic opportunity implicitly suggests that community characteristics affect patterns of opportunity. Employing a secondary analysis of existing community studies of 19th-century occupational mobility, the research reported here measures systematically the impact of community characteristics on levels of male foreign-born occupational mobility in an attempt to build an explicit model. Community characteristics clearly affected the amount of immigrant opportunity in 19th-century America; collectively, the region involved, changes in the occupational structure and population change explain 46% of the variance in foreign-born mobility.   J

2791. Kirk, Gordon W., Jr. and Kirk, Carolyn Tyirin. MIGRATION, MOBILITY AND THE TRANSFORMATION OF THE OCCUPATIONAL STRUCTURE IN AN IMMIGRANT COMMUNITY: HOLLAND, MICHIGAN, 1850-80. *J. of Social Hist. 1974 7(2): 142-164.* A statistical study of three factors which alter the size and composition of a community's labor force—migration, natural or vital processes, and vertical social mobility. Explores especially the relationship among these three factors in meeting the occupational needs of a community and thus transforming its structure. Questions whether persistence or migration was the more viable avenue for upward mobility in the 19th century. At the same time the study becomes a check on varying methodologies in determining actual rates of vertical mobility. Concludes that "while certain relationships hold both in the nineteenth and twentieth centuries, others vary—implying that the relationships among structure and size of labor force, vertical mobility, migration, persistence and natural processes may depend on the historical period or period of economic development involved." 6 tables, 21 notes.   R. V. Ritter

2792. Laurie, Bruce; Hershberg, Theodore; and Alter, George. IMMIGRANTS AND INDUSTRY: THE PHILADELPHIA EXPERIENCE, 1850-1880. *J. of Social Hist. 1975 9(2): 219-248.* Attempts to provide more secure categories of occupational status for 19th-century activities beyond the ahistorical reach of sociological studies in this century. Examines 14 manufacturing industries in Philadelphia, 1850-80, and attempts to explain changes in the job status, and how the changes affected the distribution to different ethnic groups. Little change is seen in the ethnic distribution because of disadvantages different groups brought with them, and because industrialization did not necessarily equal mechanization. 11 tables, 5 figs., 30 notes.   M. Hough

2793. Liebermann, Richard K. A MEASURE FOR THE QUALITY OF LIFE: HOUSING. *Hist. Methods 1978 11(3): 129-134.* Housing is a more dynamic measure of social class than occupation. Drawing on his research on the East Village of New York City in 1899, the author demonstrates that housing data provides significant insight into social structure and the gradations of social class. The areas of religion and mobility can also be analyzed in the context of housing. 2 tables, 8 notes.   D. K. Pickens

2794. Luria, Daniel D. TRENDS IN THE DETERMINANTS UN-DERLYING THE PROCESS OF SOCIAL STRATIFICATION: BOSTON 1880-1920. *Rev. of Radical Pol. Econ. 1974 6(2): 174-193.* Both descriptive history and statistical analysis suggest that individual economic attainment became more significant in the process of Boston's social stratification after 1890; conversely the importance of ascriptive nativity and religious traits, which had increased during 1870-90, declined. By 1920 economic differences surpassed national origin and religion in determining stratified social outcomes within the city. Based on primary and secondary sources; table, 82 notes.   P. R. Shergold

2795. Lynn, Kenneth S. THE REBELS OF GREENWICH VILLAGE. *Perspectives in Am. Hist. 1974 8: 335-378.* A biographical analysis of approximately 125 residents of New York's Greenwich Village during the Progressive era, challenging accepted beliefs concerning this "rebel" population. Their average age in 1912 was 31, and most were from established urban location in the East and Europe. Though all professed an aesthetic love of poverty, the majority were from middle to upper class backgrounds. 48 notes, appendix.   W. A. Wiegand

2796. Martin, Walter T. and Poston, Dudley L., Jr. DIFFERENTIALS IN THE ABILITY TO CONVERT EDUCATION INTO INCOME: THE CASE OF THE EUROPEAN ETHNICS. *Int. Migration Rev. 1977 11(2): 215-231.* Based on the 1970 census, investigates ability to convert college education into income increase, drawing differentials between first and second generations and finding that second generation male offspring with foreign-born fathers and native-born mothers and European ethnic groups are most apt to increase income.

2797. Matthews, Glenna. THE COMMUNITY STUDY: ETHNICITY AND SUCCESS IN SAN JOSÉ. *J. of Interdisciplinary Hist. 1976 7(2): 305-318.* A community study of social structure and social mobility in relation to ethnicity in San Jose, California, between 1860 and 1870. San Jose differed markedly from eastern cities in that there was a roughly equal mobility of Europeans and native-born Americans. There have been important regional variations in immigrant experience. 8 tables; 25 notes.   R. V. Ritter

2798. Nash, Gary B. UP FROM THE BOTTOM IN FRANKLIN'S PHILADELPHIA. *Past and Present [Great Britain] 1977 (77): 57-83.* From 1681 to about 1750 there was remarkable opportunity for new immigrants in Philadelphia. Marriage choices, business connections, and personal attributes determined who did well. In the 18th century, however, population growth was rapid (from 2,404 to 34,297). By mid-century, wealth had been redistributed to create a wealthy elite and an indigent poor. The moneyed elite of the early 18th century controlled shipping and urban real estate. This fact and the economic fluctuations and recessions of the late colonial period made it nearly impossible to emerge from poverty after the 1740's, and under these conditions militant radical artisan-laborer movements gained a major place in Philadelphian politics. Based on published works, documents, and manuscripts at the Historical Society of Pennsylvania, the Department of Wills, City Hall Annex, Philadelphia, City Archives, City Hall, and the Pennsylvania State Archives, Harrisburg; 6 tables, graph, 63 notes.   D. N. Levy

2799. Pessen, Edward. SOCIAL MOBILITY IN AMERICAN HISTORY: SOME BRIEF REFLECTIONS. *J. of Southern Hist. 1979 45(2): 165-184.* Critical analysis of important questions raised by social mobility research is of greater interest than a report of recent research. Some imbalances are obvious. The professions and slavery have been studied, but rural and even political occupations have not been examined for social mobility. Little attention has been paid to downward mobility. Most important, however, the students of social mobility must try to make their writing less boring, less technical, and directed more at the intelligent general reader. Printed secondary sources; 57 notes.   T. D. Schoonover

2800. Pessen, Edward. THE SOCIAL NETWORK WOVEN BY AN ENTREPRENEURIAL ELITE IN THE INDUSTRIAL CENTURY. *Rev. in Am. Hist. 1979 7(3): 394-400.* Reviews John N. Ingraham's *The Iron Barons: A Social Analysis of an American Urban Elite, 1874-1965* (Westport, Connecticut: Greenwood, 1978) and discusses the myth of the self-made man as evidenced by the upper class social networks in the iron industry in Pittsburgh and Philadelphia (Pennsylvania), Youngstown, (Ohio), and Wheeling (West Virginia).

2801. Peterson, Richard H. THE FRONTIER THESIS AND SOCIAL MOBILITY ON THE MINING FRONTIER. *Pacific Hist. R. 1975 44(1): 52-67.* Collective biography of 50 leading entrepreneurs in the western mining industry, 1870-1900, reveals the mining frontier to have been more democratic than the eastern business world for aspiring businessmen. Mining entrepreneurs in the West were more likely than eastern businessmen to have experienced poverty in their youths, to have come from outside the region, to have begun work at a young age and have had little education, to be foreign-born, and to have had fathers who were farmers or who were lower class. Based on biographical directories, personal papers, and unpublished biographies; 7 tables, 25 notes.   W. K. Hobson

2802. Ridgway, Whitman. MEASURING WEALTH AND POWER IN ANTE-BELLUM AMERICA: A REVIEW ESSAY. *Hist. Methods Newsletter 1975 8(2): 74-78.* A discussion prompted by Edward Pessen's *Riches, Class, and Power Before the Civil War* (Lexington, Mass.: D.C. Heath & Co., 1973). The author praises Pessen's discussion of research abuses and uses of tax records, but believes that unsystematic aggregation, imprecise conceptualization, and inadequate measurement tragically injure his data and conclusions. Notes.   D. K. Pickens

2803. Riess, Steven A. RACE AND ETHNICITY IN AMERICAN BASEBALL, 1900-1919. *J. of Ethnic Studies 1977 4(4): 39-55.* Professional baseball was an excellent source of upward social mobility for Irish and German working-class sons, but only a handful of Jews, Italians, or Slavic players can be found in the first third of the 20th century. The most successful new immigrant group was the Czechs, and several Bohemians entered the major leagues in the 1910's. Underrepresentation of the post-1880 migrations resulted from parental attitudes, discrimination by team owners and fans alike, the low status and salary originally associated with baseball, and more attractive role models for immigrant sons, such as policemen, criminals, or boxers. American Indians were far more prominent and successful in professional baseball than new immigrants down to 1920. Blacks were completely excluded and organized their own semi-professional teams and leagues. Baseball's democratic ideology extended to them not at all, and their talent went unused as late as 1946. Primary and secondary sources; 52 notes.   G. J. Bobango

2804. Rolle, Andrew. UPROOTED OR UPRAISED? IMMIGRANTS IN AMERICA. *Rev. in Am. Hist. 1978 6(1): 95-98.* Review article prompted by Thomas Kessner's *The Golden Door: Italian and Jewish Immigrant Mobility in New York City, 1880-1915* (New York: Oxford U. Pr., 1977).

2805. Rosenwaike, Ira. INTERETHNIC COMPARISONS OF EDUCATIONAL ATTAINMENT: AN ANALYSIS BASED ON CENSUS DATA FOR NEW YORK CITY. *Am. J. of Sociol. 1973 79(1): 68-77.* Further studies of educational attainment among white ethnic groups are necessary to deemphasize studies about white-nonwhite differences; 1960-73.

2806. Schlozman, Kay Lehman. COPING WITH THE AMERICAN DREAM: MAINTAINING SELF-RESPECT IN AN ACHIEVING SOCIETY. *Pol. and Soc. 1976 6(2): 241-263.* Case study (1972) of an inner-city working class neighborhood in Chicago. Explores how the residents of this ethnic neighborhood resolve the discrepancies between the realities of inequality and the equal opportunity message of the American Dream. The roles of work and assumed responsibilities, and the security and satisfaction derived from them, play significant parts in the maintenance of self-respect. Based on primary and secondary sources; tables, 30 notes.   D. G. Nielson

2807. Shade, William G. CLASS AND SOCIAL MOBILITY IN AMERICAN HISTORY: A REVIEW ESSAY. *Pennsylvania Hist. 1975 42(3): 248-251.* A review essay discussing Edward Pessen's *Riches, Class and Power Before the Civil War* (1973), Stow Persons's *The Decline of American Gentility* (1973), Stephan Thernstrom's *The Other Bostonians: Poverty and Progress in the American Metropolis, 1880-1970* (1973), and Frederick C. Jaher, ed., *The Rich, Well Born, and the Powerful: Elites and Upper Classes in History* (1973).   D. C. Swift

2808. Shergold, Peter R. RELATIVE SKILL AND INCOME LEVELS OF NATIVE AND FOREIGN BORN WORKERS: A REEXAM-

INATION. *Explorations in Econ. Hist. 1976 13(4): 451-461.* Reexamines the methodology and data used by Peter J. Hill in 1975 and supplies additional data. Generally confirms Hill's findings, but suggests that there are more important questions. Asks to what extent were immigrant workers subject ca. 1840-1920 to discrimination in employment security, housing, education, and entry into trade unions? Based on published reports and secondary sources.   P. J. Coleman

2809. Soltow, Lee. THE ECONOMIC HERITAGE OF AN IOWA COUNTY. *Ann. of Iowa 1975 43(1): 24-38.* By examining census wealth declarations of each individual resident in 1860 and 1870, the author concludes that Sac County, Iowa, had little wealth inequality and that there was a pattern of strong wealth accumulation throughout an individual's normal working years. Several hypotheses are subject to empirical testing. Speculates that the economic environment was a stimulus to creative activity. Based on census information; 3 statistical tables, 8 notes.   P. L. Petersen

2810. Stephenson, Charles. DETERMINANTS OF AMERICAN MIGRATION: METHODS AND MODELS IN MOBILITY RESEARCH. *J. of Am. Studies [Great Britain] 1975 9(2): 189-197.* Describes research at the Newberry Library to trace the migration of peoples in the United States and to explain the reasons for the geographic mobility of Americans. The studies depend upon Soundex indexes to the United States Censuses of 1880-1900 as their basic tool. The research design calls for the use of a sophisticated system of variables in explaining the data. Secondary sources; 27 notes.   H. T. Lovin

2811. Stephenson, Charles. TRACING THOSE WHO LEFT: MOBILITY STUDIES AND THE SOUNDEX INDEXES TO THE UNITED STATES CENSUS. *J. of Urban Hist. 1974 1(1): 73-84.* With soundex indexes for 1880 and 1900, historians have a tool with which they can trace individuals who move from cities.   S. S. Sprague

2812. Story, Ronald. CLASS AND CULTURE IN BOSTON: THE ATHENAEUM, 1807-1860. *Am. Q. 1975 27(2): 178-199.* The founding of the library, The Athenaeum, provided a private gathering place for the Bostonian elite patterned after the British (especially the Liverpool) model. Business and cultural influences were combined in its exclusive, hereditary membership, shaping a durable elite within the capitalist order in Boston. The Athenaeum assisted in building civic pride, fostering learning, and providing stability, consolidation, and career enhancement for the Bostonian upper class.   N. Lederer

2813. Tank, Robert M. MOBILITY AND OCCUPATIONAL STRUCTURE ON THE LATE NINETEENTH-CENTURY URBAN FRONTIER: THE CASE OF DENVER, COLORADO. *Pacific Hist. Rev. 1978 47(2): 189-216.* Quantitative study of occupational and geographic mobility in Denver, 1870-92, finds that Denver resembled long-established urban communities in some ways and frontier communities in others. Like urban communities, Denver's occupational structure in 1870 favored native whites over immigrants and blacks and between 1870 and 1890 blacks and immigrants without skills were less likely to advance than similarly low skilled native whites. However, unlike urban communities, but like frontier communities, skilled and white-collar immigrants were able to experience considerable upward mobility. Geographical mobility was high in Denver and varied inversely with social status. Based on census manuscript schedules and city directories; 7 tables, 29 notes.   W. K. Hobson

2814. Walsh, Margaret. INDUSTRIAL OPPORTUNITY OF THE URBAN FRONTIER: "RAGS TO RICHES" AND MILWAUKEE CLOTHING MANUFACTURERS, 1840-1880. *Wisconsin Mag. of Hist. 1974 57(3): 174-194.* Challenges the persistence of the "rags to riches" idea in American culture by looking at the business careers of Milwaukee's leading clothing manufacturers for a 40 year period. Emphasizes that, rather than any single factor, Jewish connections, German origins, technological innovation, previous business experience, substantial capital and credit, and good local market conditions, when combined in varying degrees, were the ingredients of a successful company. Instead of a spectacular leap from rags to riches, the Milwaukee clothing manufacturers' experience suggests that vertical mobility was possible, but "it was generally modest in both its claims and its end results." 12 illus., 5 tables, 51 notes.   N. C. Burckel

2815. Weber, Michael P. and Boardman, Anthony E. ECONOMIC GROWTH AND OCCUPATIONAL MOBILITY IN NINETEENTH CENTURY URBAN AMERICA. *J. of Social Hist. 1977 11(1): 52-74.* An analysis of the horizontal and vertical mobility of one Pennsylvania community in the 19th century reveals that "individual success was determined more by the structure of the city than by individual ethnic and cultural background." More importantly the "time one entered a city, the skill level of one's occupation at that time, one's industrial occupation and whether one switched occupations were crucial determinants of one's success in America." 5 tables, 29 notes, appendix.   L. E. Ziewacz

2816. Weber, Michael P. QUANTIFICATION AND THE TEACHING OF AMERICAN URBAN HISTORY. *Hist. Teacher 1975 8(3): 391-402.* Discusses the course, "Opportunity in 19th Century America: A Quantitative View," taught at Carnegie-Mellon University. Students read and discuss the literature relating to opportunity and social mobility in 19th-century America, then test hypotheses using quantitative data from selected communities. Data is recorded, tabulated, compared, and discussed in oral reports. Primary and secondary sources; 5 notes, biblio.   P. W. Kennedy

2817. Weber, Michael P. RESIDENTIAL AND OCCUPATIONAL PATTERNS OF ETHNIC MINORITIES IN NINETEENTH CENTURY PITTSBURGH. *Pennsylvania Hist. 1977 44(4): 317-334.* Focuses on occupational and residential patterns of ethnic groups in four Pittsburgh industrial wards during 1880-1920. In comparison to native-born workers, Irish and German immigrants were not disadvantaged in occupational mobility. Blue-collar workers who remained in Pittsburgh experienced considerable upward mobility. Age had little influence on transiency or persistence, but place of birth and occupation did influence residential persistence. Based on census data; 3 illus., map, 3 tables, 16 notes.   D. C. Swift

2818. Weber, R. David. SOCIOECONOMIC CHANGE IN RACINE, 1850-1880. *J. of the West 1974 13(3): 98-108.* Explores upward mobility in Racine, Wisconsin, in the 19th century. Considers studies of other cities in terms of Frederick Jackson Turner's thesis on the levelling effect of the frontier. Measures socioeconomic mobility by occupation and property ownership. Confirms Turner's thesis that greater egalitarianism and social change occurred in the rural West and adds to it the dimension of urban areas. Based on contemporary newspaper reports and secondary sources; 8 tables, 16 notes.   N. J. Street

2819. White, Martha M. FACTORS OF NATIONALITY IN FRONTIER MOBILITY IN SAN DIEGO COUNTY. *J. of San Diego Hist. 1975 20(2): 44-53.* Studies the mobility of different nationalities in San Diego County during the 1850's, comparing the migratory habits of Anglo-Americans to Mexican-Americans.   S

2820. Wilkie, Janet Riblett. SOCIAL STATUS, ACCULTURATION AND SCHOOL ATTENDANCE IN 1850 BOSTON. *J. of Social Hist. 1977 11(2): 179-192.* An examination of race, origin, and class differences in Boston in 1850 indicates that the "equal access to educational opportunity" appears to have preceded class mobility for much of the white immigrant population. For northern blacks, however, "formal schooling had no counter effect on the deterioration of their economic position." 6 tables, 33 notes.   L. E. Ziewacz

2821. —. [THE HISTORICAL STUDY OF SOCIAL MOBILITY] *Hist. Methods Newsletter 1975 8(3): 92-120.*
Miller, Roberta Balstad. THE HISTORICAL STUDY OF SOCIAL MOBILITY: A NEW PERSPECTIVE, *pp. 92-97.* Criticizes Stephan Thernstrom's *The Other Bostonians and Progress in the American Metropolis, 1880-1970* (Cambridge: Harvard U. Press, 1973) for being too narrowly focused and for having several conceptual problems such as overestimating occupational mobility. Further, the real poor do not appear in Thernstrom's figures.
Alcorn, Richard S. and Knights, Peter R. MOST UNCOMMON BOSTONIANS, *pp. 98-114.* The authors charge that Thernstrom used biased material. They find errors in six of the book's nine chapters to be based on bad methodology.
Thernstrom, Stephan T. REJOINDER TO ALCORN AND KNIGHTS, *pp. 115-120.* Provides a general defense of his work and acknowledges some minor errors.   D. K. Pickens

2822. —. INCOME, MEDIAN AGE, OCCUPATION AND FERTILITY BY ETHNIC GROUPS. Sowell, Thomas, ed. *Essays and Data on American Ethnic Groups* (Washington, D.C.: Urban Inst. Pr., 1978): 257-259. A table dividing statistics on income, median age, occupation and fertility in 13 different ethnic groups in the United States. Statistics are from the 1970 Census Public Use Sample and from *Current Population Reports*, Series P-20.   K. A. Talley

2823. —. [INTELLECTUAL AUTONOMY AMONG PROTESTANTS AND CATHOLICS]. *Am. J. of Sociol. 1974 80 (1): 218-220.*
Humphreys, Claire. THE RELIGIOUS FACTOR: COMMENT ON GREELEY'S CONCLUSION, *pp. 217-219.*
Greeley, Andrew M. GREELEY REPLIES TO HUMPHREYS, *pp. 219-220.*
The authors debate the extent of intellectual autonomy among Protestants and Catholics in the 1960's and 70's—in response to Greeley's earlier article on growing Catholic representation in the academy, and reasons for previous underrepresentation.

Health and Social Welfare

2824. Ellis, John H. THE NEW ORLEANS YELLOW FEVER EPIDEMIC IN 1878: A NOTE ON THE AFFECTIVE HISTORY OF SOCIETIES AND COMMUNITIES. *Clio Medica [Netherlands] 1977 12(2-3): 189-216.* During 1830-60 many epidemics in New Orleans ravaged primarily the immigrant communities, and provoked mainly local interest. In 1878 a yellow fever epidemic killed the rich as well as the poor. In the early days 40,000 of the 211,000 inhabitants fled the city. That the federal government took notice led in 1879 to the establishment of the National Board of Health and the Quarantine Act. This legislation was enacted before the study of the Yellow Fever Commission was completed. 82 notes.   A. J. Papalas

2825. Fox, Richard W. THE INTOLERABLE DEFIANCE OF THE INSANE: CIVIL COMMITMENT IN SAN FRANCISCO, 1906-1929. *Am. J. of Legal Hist. 1976 20(2): 136-154.* Analyzes the cases of more than 12,000 persons charged, convicted, and committed for insanity in San Francisco 1906-29, based on the Records of Commitment for Insanity of the Superior Court of the City and County of San Francisco. Doctors and judges convicted and committed thousands of persons to Bastille-like, state hospitals with little regard for whether the accused were insane. The cases ranged from ones involving common strangers arrested on the streets for vagrancy to those of immigrants who were arrested and refused to talk. Examiners reported nearly one-third of the people as being quiet and retiring individuals and almost two-thirds as being residual deviants who had no organic or functional disabilities and no violent or destructive tendencies. Causes of arrest, physical and mental characteristics, patterns of behavior, race and ethnic origins, and social, economic, and religious background are discussed. Primary sources; 23 notes.   L. A. Knafla

2826. Grob, Gerald N. CLASS, ETHNICITY, AND RACE IN AMERICAN MENTAL HOSPITALS, 1830-75. *J. of the Hist. of Medicine and Allied Sci. 1973 28(3): 207-229.* Discusses the difference between the theory of equality of treatment for patients in mental institutions and the practice, which often was dependent upon the patient's class, ethnic origin, and color. Private patients got the best care, followed by native poor and indigent patients, ethnic poor, especially in most urban areas with large immigrant populations, and black patients. "The evolution of the mental hospital offers an unusually good illustration of how a social institution, established with the best and most honorable of intentions, was inadvertently transformed by the behavior of many individuals and groups." Based on primary sources; 51 notes.   J. L. Susskind

2827. Heale, M. J. PATTERNS OF BENEVOLENCE: ASSOCIATED PHILANTHROPY IN THE CITIES OF NEW YORK, 1830-1860. *New York Hist. 1976 57(1): 53-79.* The growth of associated philanthropy in New York during 1830-60 was a response to urbanization, immigration, increasing social distance between rich and poor, and mounting urban social problems. Describes the work of philanthropic associations in New York City, Albany, Brooklyn, Buffalo, and Rochester. 6 illus., 30 notes.   R. N. Lokken

2828. Kahana, Eva and Felton, Barbara J. SOCIAL CONTEXT AND PERSONAL NEED: A STUDY OF POLISH AND JEWISH AGED. *J. of Social Issues 1977 33(4): 56-74.* The material history of a study of ethnic aged in their neighborhood context is described. As part of a larger study on service needs of older persons in a predominantly Polish and in a predominantly Jewish neighborhood, interviews were conducted with 402 older persons. Special problems and pitfalls to be dealt with in studying ethnic aged are discussed in terms of gaining access to respondents, instrumentation, and in terms of interpretation of data. Ethical issues in studying disadvantaged groups without providing services to them were of special concern. Findings indicated major service needs of urban aged in areas of housing, health, and financial needs. Similarities in service needs emerged despite cultural and lifestyle differences in the two communities. Personal correlates of vulnerability among ethnic aged are reported.   J

2829. Katz, Robert S. INFLUENZA 1918: A FURTHER STUDY IN MORTALITY. *Bull. of the Hist. of Medicine 1977 51(4): 617-619.* Examination of considerable statistical evidence finds the unusual mortality from influenza in 1918-19 to be a product of the sociological, political, and geographical considerations of the period. Italians, Russians, and Poles arrived in America after the last wave of influenza, and moved from rural areas where they were not exposed to the disease, to congested tenement areas where they were targets for the disease. The "unusual mortality from influenza would appear to be related to the immigration patterns of various ethnic groups in early twentieth century America." 10 notes.   M. Kaufman

2830. Kusmer, Kenneth L. THE FUNCTIONS OF ORGANIZED CHARITY IN THE PROGRESSIVE ERA: CHICAGO AS A CASE STUDY. *J. of Am. Hist. 1973 60(3): 657-678.* A study of the Charities Organization Society Movement in Chicago in the 1880's and 1890's demonstrates that in the beginning the society was concerned with transmitting the values of small-town rural America to the urban context. Values of community, country life, and the middle class were stressed by upwardly mobile charity workers from small midwestern towns whose cultural values were threatened by the many immigrant poor. The movement employed as "friendly visitors" middle-class women who applied values of the "home" to the city, and was financed by wealthy merchants, bankers, and lawyers who thought broadly of the need to avoid growing social conflict. Increasing economic dislocation and unemployment after 1890 led toward a more modern welfare system. Table, 90 notes.   K. B. West

2831. Leavitt, Judith W. POLITICS AND PUBLIC HEALTH: SMALLPOX IN MILWAUKEE, 1894-1895. *Bull. of the Hist. of Medicine 1976 50(4): 553-568.* A smallpox epidemic hit Milwaukee during summer-fall 1894 and reduced the reputation and powers of the city's health department. The episode dramatizes the relationship between politics and public health, and reminds historians that medical factors "do not alone determine the course of public health events." The epidemic had a retrogressive effect on the public health movement in Milwaukee. Health Commissioner Walter Kempster reacted to the epidemic by launching a widespread vaccination campaign, moved to isolate patients by removal to the Isolation Hospital, enforced a strict quarantine on those allowed to remain at home, and carried on education campaigns. Citizens, especially in German and Polish areas, resisted. Kempster was seen as symbolizing governmental authority which was subverting immigrant culture and threatening personal rights. The Common Council voted to dismiss the health commissioner after a lengthy investigation of charges made against him. "Patronage, class and ethnic divisions were responsible" for much of the opposition to him. Illus., 4 figs., 44 notes.   M. Kaufman

2832. McIntosh, Karyl. FOLK OBSTETRICS, GYNECOLOGY, AND PEDIATRICS IN UTICA, NEW YORK. *New York Folklore 1978 4(1-4): 49-59.* Discusses a study (in 1978) of Italian and Polish women in Utica, New York, regarding folk beliefs and practices concerning childbirth, pregnancy, and early childhood which are transmitted by the family and the group.

2833. Mohl, Raymond and Betten, Neil. PATERNALISM AND PLURALISM: IMMIGRANTS AND SOCIAL WELFARE IN GARY, INDIANA, 1906-1940. *Am. Studies (Lawrence, KS) 1974*

15(1): 5-30. Examines social welfare in Gary and substantiates the theme that public welfare programs manipulate the poor, keep them under social control, and drive them into low income, menial jobs. Settlement house work served "the interests of American society more than those of the immigrants themselves." The houses exhibited a nativist paternalism, and tried to Americanize all immigrants. A few exceptions, such as the International Institute, fostered a sense of ethnic identification. Based on primary and secondary sources; 56 notes.   J. Andrew

2834. Nash, Gary B. POVERTY AND POOR RELIEF IN PRE-REVOLUTIONARY PHILADELPHIA. *William and Mary Q. 1976 33(1): 3-30.* Discusses the growth of private and public responsibility for the care of the increasing poor in Philadelphia in the 18th century. Emphasizes the role of the Pennsylvania Hospital for the Sick Poor. The relocation of Acadian neutrals in Philadelphia during the French and Indian War and the revival of Irish and German immigration in the 1760's added to the burden of poor relief. Quakers contributed much private philanthrophy. Also notes the new ideology regarding the poor, with some comparison to ideas in England. Based on manuscript records and secondary sources; 3 tables, 79 notes.   H. M. Ward

2835. Rosen, George. SOCIAL SCIENCE AND HEALTH IN THE UNITED STATES IN THE TWENTIETH CENTURY. *Clio Medica [Netherlands] 1976 11(4): 245-268.* During 1860-1910 the urban population of America rose from 19 to 45 percent of the total population. The influx of European immigrants and southern blacks to industrial centers caused serious health problems. Henry W. Farnam, a Yale professor (1881-1918), urged Congress to investigate industrial diseases. In 1909 the Pittsburgh survey revealed that tuberculosis and typhoid were more likely to hit the poor living in squalid tenements. Newly established sociology departments in universities studied crime, ethnic groups, prostitution, and other urban problems. Most of these studies had chapters on public health, and in the 1930's specific works on urban health appeared. This interaction between social science and the health field has led to improvements in public health. 62 notes.   A. J. Papalas

2836. Smith, Billy G. DEATH AND LIFE IN A COLONIAL IMMIGRANT CITY: A DEMOGRAPHIC ANALYSIS OF PHILADELPHIA. *J. of Econ. Hist. 1977 37(4): 863-889.* This study analyzes the demographic characteristics of a previously neglected area in colonial America—the urban center. Growth, birth, and death rates in Philadelphia between 1720 and 1775 are estimated using a variety of sources. Immigration, smallpox, economic vacillations, and a skewed age structure are attributed primary responsibility in determining the level of and changes in Philadelphia's vital rates. The elevated level of these rates is evident in a comparison with vital rates in Andover and Boston, Massachusetts, and Nottingham, England.   J

2837. Spector, Rachel. ETHNICITY AND HEALTH: A STUDY OF HEALTH CARE BELIEFS AND PRACTICES. *Urban and Social Change Rev. 1979 12(2): 34-37.* Members of ethnic groups often fail to seek modern health care due to internal factors (including cultural background and belief in folk remedies) and to external barriers in the US medical care system.

2838. Stam, A. THE PSYCHIATRIC IMPLICATIONS OF ETHNIC STRATIFICATION IN THE USA: A HISTORICAL REVIEW. *Plural Societies [Netherlands] 1975 6(2): 31-46.* Analyzes psychiatric interpretations of mental illness among ethnic groups in the United States, 1840-1975.

2839. Thompson, Kenneth. EARLY CALIFORNIA AND THE CAUSES OF INSANITY. *Southern California Q. 1976 58(1): 45-62.* Examines the belief, widely held in the 1860's and 1870's, that California had a higher rate of insanity than other states. Prominent physicians searched for the reasons behind this belief and found a number of factors that contributed to mental instability. These included discontent, homesickness, ambition, reverses of fortune, passion, self-abuse, and other possibilities. Also under suspicion was the climate (though others defended it), manual labor, and the foreign-born, who seemed to have a higher incidence of insanity. Such theories confused environmental causes of disease with social problems and indicate attitudes toward morality as well as medicine in the 19th century. Based on primary and secondary sources; 53 notes.   A. Hoffman

Education

2840. Banks, James A. EVALUATING THE MULTIETHNIC COMPONENTS OF THE SOCIAL STUDIES. *Social Educ. 1976 40(7): 538-541.* Discusses guidelines for the teaching of the concept of ethnicity in social studies programs in the 1970's, including testing procedures.

2841. Banks, James A. MULTIETHNIC EDUCATION ACROSS CULTURES: UNITED STATES, MEXICO, PUERTO RICO, FRANCE AND GREAT BRITAIN. *Social Educ. 1978 42(3): 177-185.* Examines the problems of ethnic groups, race relations, and immigrants, and how each country's educational policy deals with ethnicity.

2842. Banks, James A. PLURALISM, IDEOLOGY AND CURRICULUM REFORM. *Social Studies 1976 67(3): 99-106.* Advocates curriculum reform which can provide experiences that would reflect the multicultured patterns of American students, in addition to those experiences and values determined by the dominant Anglo culture. 27 notes.
                                                        L. R. Raife

2843. Banks, James A. TEACHING ETHNIC STUDIES: KEY ISSUES AND CONCEPTS. *Social Studies 1975 66(3): 107-113.* Provides insight into the teaching of ethnic concepts and regards such factors as key aspects in the social studies curriculum. 26 notes.
                                                        L. R. Raife

2844. Banks, Samuel L. THE NEED FOR A MULTIETHNIC CURRICULUM. *Crisis 1974 81(4): 125-128.*

2845. Berrol, Selma C. SCHOOL DAYS ON THE OLD EAST SIDE: THE ITALIAN AND JEWISH EXPERIENCE. *New York Hist. 1976 57(2): 201-213.* Compares the educational progress of Italian and Jewish immigrant children in New York City's Lower East Side during the early 1900's. Old world backgrounds and traditional attitudes explain why Jewish immigrant children were more successful academically than Italian children. In later generations the academic performance of Italian and Jewish children approached equality. 3 illus., 19 notes.
                                                        R. N. Lokken

2846. Butts, R. Freeman. PUBLIC EDUCATION AND POLITICAL COMMUNITY. *Hist. of Educ. Q. 1974 14(2): 165-183.* Discusses conflicting revisionist theories in the historiography of American education. Urges attention to the role of organized public education in building a political community in a society divided along religious, linguistic, racial, ethnic, economic, cultural, and social class lines. Historians should analyze the successes and failures of public education in developing a sense of citizenship appropriate to the goals of a libertarian political community. Based on primary and secondary sources; 45 notes.
                                                        L. C. Smith

2847. Cordasco, Francesco. SOCIAL REFORM AND AMERICAN EDUCATION: A BIBLIOGRAPHY OF SELECTED REFERENCES. *Bull. of Biblio. and Mag. Notes 1976 33(3): 105-110.* Presents a bibliography of writings from the 1960's and '70's about the relationship among ethnic minorities, social reform, and education in the United States.

2848. Crouchett, Lawrence P. THE DEVELOPMENT OF THE SENTIMENT FOR ETHNIC STUDIES IN AMERICAN EDUCATION. *J. of Ethnic Studies 1975 2(4): 77-85.* "We are wrong if we assume that sentiment for ethnic studies emerged only recently," or that it is a new phenomenon peculiar to the present minorities. Bilingualism, biculturalism, and ethnic subjects were a fact of American education long before "ethnic studies" became defined in the 1960's. Cites examples as early as the 1660's showing white minority groups insisting on their own schools as a means of preserving their languages, religions, and cultures against the assimilative influences of the school systems of the dominant classes. The 19th century especially saw the Irish and Germans creating curricula in their parochial schools to combat the prevailing Protestant nativism. "Black studies" courses were offered as early as 1919 and the 100%-ism of the WWI era brought renewed stress on ethnic subjects. Surveys the efforts of W. E. B. Du Bois and Carter G. Woodson for national programs of ethnic education, and the current "revival" of white ethnic topics as a result of the civil rights movement. Based on primary and secondary sources; 23 notes.   G. J. Bobango

2849. Fenchak, Paul. THE ARTFUL DODGERS: DIRECTORS OF ETHNIC STUDIES PROGRAMS. *Slovakia 1974 24(47): 112-119.* Ethnic studies dealing with Eastern Europeans are nonexistent in American high schools.   S

2850. Field, Alexander James. ECONOMIC AND DEMOGRAPHIC DETERMINANTS OF EDUCATIONAL COMMITMENT: MASSACHUSETTS, 1855. *J. of Econ. Hist. 1979 39(2): 439-459.* More than half the variance in length of school session in a cross section of 329 localities in Massachusetts in 1855 can be explained by the share of Irish in the town's population, the family per dwelling ratio, and a proxy for the share of male merchants over 15 in the population, all of which enter regression equations with strong positive coefficients. This paper considers what these results may tell us about a number of hypotheses that link industrialization and educational revitalization in antebellum Massachusetts, discusses independent confirmation of these basic relationships, and concludes with a more general discussion of the implications of this Massachusetts evidence.   J

2851. Finkelman, Paul. CLASS AND CULTURE IN LATE NINETEENTH-CENTURY CHICAGO: THE FOUNDING OF THE NEWBERRY LIBRARY. *Am. Studies (Lawrence, KS) 1975 16(1): 5-22.* The Newberry Library was founded in the 1880's. Nominally public, the library remained a bastion for upper class values in the genteel tradition. Its collections reflected these interests and largely ignored the city's ethnic minorities. Primary and secondary sources; 64 notes.   J. Andrew

2852. Glazer, Nathan. ETHNICITY AND THE SCHOOLS. *Commentary 1974 58(3): 55-59.*

2853. Greeley, Andrew M. ANTI-CATHOLICISM IN THE ACADEMY. *Change 1977 9(6): 40-43.* A prominent Catholic educator says American academics discriminate against white ethnics, labeling them culturally inferior and socially deficient.   J

2854. Hogan, David. EDUCATION AND THE MAKING OF THE CHICAGO WORKING CLASS, 1880-1930. *Hist. of Educ. Q. 1978 18(3): 227-270.* Examines why children enrolled in Chicago schools between 1880 and 1930 stayed in school for a longer time, particularly those over the age of 14, regardless of ethnic background.

2855. Horlick, Allan Stanley. RADICAL SCHOOL LEGENDS. *Hist. of Educ. Q. 1974 14(2): 251-258.* Reviews Colin Greer's, *The Great School Legend: A Revisionist Interpretation of American Public Education* (New York: Basic Books, 1972). Recognizes as valid Greer's criticism of the "legend" that public schooling leads to social and economic success, despite the high rate of school failure of the urban poor, but criticizes Greer's plea for social change by invigorating classroom teaching as not facing up to the practical monetary and physical difficulties. 33 notes.   L. C. Smith

2856. Hunt, Thomas C. PUBLIC SCHOOLS, "AMERICANISM," AND THE IMMIGRANT AT THE TURN OF THE CENTURY. *J. of General Educ. 1974 26(2): 147-155.* Examines both sides of the assimilation problems of the many immigrant children in urban schools and city life circa 1890's-1920.   S

2857. Hunt, Thomas C. THE SCHOOLING OF IMMIGRANTS AND BLACK AMERICANS: SOME SIMILARITIES AND DIFFERENCES. *J. of Negro Educ. 1976 45(4): 423-431.* Lists similarities and differences between the effects of education on the eastern and southern European immigrant children of 1890-1920 who successfully assimilated into the American middle class, and the black children who migrated to northern cities during 1940-66 and were not upwardly mobile. The major difference is that education cannot easily offset the long history of oppression and frustration experience by blacks, who, unlike European immigrants, did not come willingly to this country in the hope of a better future. 26 notes.   B. D. Johnson

2858. Inglehart, Babette. THE IMMIGRANT CHILD AND THE AMERICAN SCHOOL: A LITERARY VIEW. *Ethnicity 1976 3(1): 34-52.* Discusses the immigrant experience in American public schools in 19th and 20th century literature, asserting that today, as historically, immigrants and migrants face problems with English, enforced assimilation, and general ignorance of traditions and cultural differences.

2859. Issel, William. AMERICANIZATION, ACCULTURATION AND SOCIAL CONTROL: SCHOOL REFORM IDEOLOGY IN INDUSTRIAL PENNSYLVANIA, 1880-1910. *J. of Social Hist. 1979 12(4): 569-590.* Analyzes school reform efforts as a consequence of dislocations caused by industrialization in Pennsylvania. It is true that elites initiated reform efforts, however, Marxists and revisionists are incorrect in asserting that economics was the motivating force. Strikes, riots, and hordes of immigrants had to be dealt with. Reformers acted to unite state, school, and community, arguing that what was good for one was good for all. The schools, therefore, stressed social control themes. Some allowance was made for the new values of immigrants as well as for those of poor native laborers. Control was designed to benefit state and society rather than industry or the individual. 54 notes.   V. L. Human

2860. Issel, William. THE POLITICS OF PUBLIC SCHOOL REFORM IN PENNSYLVANIA, 1880-1911. *Pennsylvania Mag. of Hist. and Biog. 1978 102(1): 59-92.* The impulse for educational reform serving conservative purposes emerged in industrial areas with a high proportion of non-English-speaking population, strikes, and class and ethnic conflict. Legitimacy-seeking interest groups desired concentration of authority over education. Their compulsory education campaign paralleled the push for child labor legislation and ultimately a comprehensive school code. Based on official records and secondary works; 61 notes.   T. H. Wendel

2861. Ives, Richard. COMPULSORY EDUCATION AND THE ST. LOUIS PUBLIC SCHOOL SYSTEM: 1905-1907. *Missouri Hist. Rev. 1977 71(3): 315-329.* Missouri enacted compulsory education laws in 1905 and 1907. Discusses what groups supported or opposed the laws, whether the laws were equally enforced or immigrants were discriminated against, and whether the laws attracted new students. Newspapers, legislative voting records, and state publications reveal that the laws enjoyed wide support. Most truancy cases were settled out of court, but school administrators often were influenced by an ethnic racism. Truancy was not a serious problem. Immigrants left school at a lower percentage rate than natives because they were aware of educational values. Illus., 42 notes.   W. F. Zornow

2862. Kamin, Leon J. SIBLING I.Q. CORRELATION AMONG ETHNIC GROUPS. Sowell, Thomas, ed. *Essays and Data on American Ethnic Groups* (Washington, D.C.: Urban Inst. Pr., 1978): 239-249. Investigating similarities between sibling IQ's provides clues to the nature-nurture controversy and a background to the magnitude of IQ variance in five ethnic groups, differentiating between elder and younger members of a sibling pair. Only among blacks did the younger sibling have a higher mean IQ. Concludes that there is a variety of ways for the data to be interpreted and that either environmental or genetic factors will have to be isolated to determine conclusively which is the greater influence. Secondary sources; biblio.   K. A. Talley

2863. Katz, Michael B. THE ORIGINS OF URBAN EDUCATION. *Rev. in Am. Hist. 1974 2(2): 186-192.* Review article prompted by Carl F. Kaestle's *The Education of An Urban School System: New York City, 1750-1850* (Cambridge: Harvard U. Pr., 1973) and Stanley K. Schultz's *The Culture Factory: Boston Public Schools, 1789-1860* (New York: Oxford U. Pr., 1973). Boston and New York City schools shifted from instructing the elite to moral "enculturation" of the unassimilated masses.   W. D. Piersen

2864. Lazerson, Marvin. CONFLICT AND CONSENSUS IN URBAN EDUCATION. *Rev. in Am. Hist. 1976 4(3): 421-427.* Review article prompted by Selwyn K. Troen's *The Public Schools: Shaping the St. Louis System, 1838-1920* (Columbia: U. of Missouri Pr., 1975); takes into account conflict and consensus in the religious, political, educational, ethnic, and economic ideologies of those in the public schools of St. Louis.

2865. Lazerson, Marvin. CONSENSUS AND CONFLICT IN AMERICAN EDUCATION: HISTORICAL PERSPECTIVES. *Hist. of Educ. [Great Britain] 1978 7(3): 197-205.* Suggests that American beliefs about schools are best understood as an expression of the American philosophy of life in general. Argues that the quest for national cultural homogeneity since the mid-19th century caused public education to resist ethnic pluralism. This attitude led to the extensive bureaucratization of America's school administration structure by the late 19th century. 20 notes.　　　S

2866. Lazerson, Marvin. REVISIONISM AND AMERICAN EDUCATIONAL HISTORY. *Harvard Educ. Rev. 1973 43(2): 269-283.* Review article prompted by Michael B. Katz's *Class, Bureaucracy and Schools: The Illusion of Educational Change in America* (New York: Praeger, 1971), Colin Greer's *The Great School Legend: A Revisionist Interpretation of American Public Education* (New York: Basic Books, 1972), and Joel H. Spring's *Education and the Rise of the Corporate State* (Boston: Beacon Pr., 1972). These books criticize the failures of American schools. Katz focuses on institutional structures and the emergence of educational bureaucracy. Greer discusses the failure of educators to use the schools to aid immigrants' adjustment to America. Spring argues that the schools defined their task as fitting the young for cooperative tasks in modern life, introducing vocational and extracurricular programs in accordance with progressive and liberal ideology. All three books are marred by a one-dimensional approach which is unconvincing. The revisionist approach of these books is a timely corrective to the traditional celebratory histories of education.　　　J. Herbst

2867. Liggio, Leonard P. and Peden, Joseph R. SOCIAL SCIENTISTS, SCHOOLING, AND THE ACCULTURATION OF IMMIGRANTS IN 19TH CENTURY AMERICA. *J. of Libertarian Studies 1978 2(1): 69-84.* Fear of ethnic, cultural, and religious diversity expressed in the writings of Benjamin Rush, Benjamin Franklin, and Thomas Jefferson spawned ideas of public education designed to school immigrants in republicanism and citizenship carried out by educational reformers such as Lyman Beecher, Samuel F. B. Morse, William Torrey Harris, and Herbert Spencer 1840's-1910's.

2868. Luckingham, Bradford. AGENTS OF CULTURE IN THE URBAN WEST: MERCHANTS AND MERCANTILE LIBRARIES IN MID-NINETEENTH CENTURY ST. LOUIS AND SAN FRANCISCO. *J. of the West 1978 17(2): 28-35.* A desire for the moral and intellectual development of their profession prompted western merchants to establish libraries in St. Louis, Missouri, (1846) and in San Francisco, California, (1853) modeled on the mercantile libraries of eastern cities. Members of the Mercantile Library Association were also concerned about the cultural and educational development of immigrant and rural youth; teachers at the libraries provided training in business skills and the liberal arts. To counter the temptations of city life, the libraries provided chess, draughts, and backgammon games, lectures, art galleries, and natural history exhibits. Primary sources; 4 photos, 22 notes.　　　B. S. Porter

2869. McLachlan, James. THE AMERICAN COLLEGE IN THE NINETEENTH CENTURY: TOWARD A REAPPRAISAL. *Teachers Coll. Record 1978 80(2): 288-306.* American historians of higher education have assumed about 19th-century colleges that: they were essentially elitist, their numbers declined after the Civil War, they were narrow and dogmatically Protestant, and they gave way suddenly to universities after 1870. Recent, admittedly fragmentary historical evidence suggests that these schools were far less elitist than formerly believed, that their numbers increased steadily throughout the century, that they were ethnically pluralistic, and they they coexisted with universities. Secondary sources; 48 notes.　　　E. Bailey

2870. Menatian, Steve and Lynch, Patrick D. ETHNIC POLITICS IN A NORTHEASTERN URBAN SCHOOL SYSTEM. *Educ. and Urban Soc. 1974 6(3): 318-332.*

2871. Mills, Nicolaus. COMMUNITY SCHOOLS: IRISH, ITALIANS AND JEWS. *Society 1974 11(3): 76-84.* Reviews the long-standing issue of community-controlled schools in New York City's ethnic neighborhoods.　　　S

2872. Moravcevich, Nicholas. THE FUTURE OF SMALLER LANGUAGES AND CULTURES IN HUMANISTIC PROGRAMS OF AMERICAN INSTITUTIONS OF HIGHER LEARNING. *J. of Bal-*

tic Studies 1974 5(3): 205-210. Proposes ways to increase funding, academic regard, student interest, and language training essential to programs on smaller cultures, which are still inadequate despite the vogue for ethnicity.　　　E. W. Jennison, Jr.

2873. Ornstein, Allan C. SOME TRENDS CONCERNING ETHNIC EDUCATION. *Social Sci. 1976 51(4): 195-199.* Examines reasons for the rise of ethnicity and ethnic education in schools. Three broad areas of ethnicity and education are detailed: curriculum development, in-service training, and interpersonal relations. Emerging state ethnic educational trends are discussed; there is emphasis on unequal interest and treatment of white ethnics, in context with current interest for traditional minority groups.　　　J

2874. Paulston, Rolland G. and LeRoy, Gregory. STRATEGIES FOR NONFORMAL EDUCATION. *Teachers Coll. Record 1975 76(4): 569-596.* Discusses types of nonformal education (NFE) and their role in achieving more equitable income distribution and greater personal growth. NFE, that is "organized systematic educational activity outside . . . the formal school system," seems more capable than does formal education of achieving such goals. Most scholars, particularly Frederick H. Harbison and Philip H. Coombs, see NFE's goals as primarily imposed upon target groups from outside and aimed at national economic development. However, successful but rarely studied programs developed by various economic and ethnic groups and aimed at greater self-realization have been initiated in Scandinavia, Canada, and the United States. These programs offer hope of expanding the scope of NFE. Based on primary and secondary sources; diagram, 59 notes.　　　E. C. Bailey

2875. Perlmutter, Philip. ETHNICITY AND THE PUBLIC SCHOOLS. *J. of Intergroup Relations 1975 4(4): 28-38.* Discusses possible cases of covert racism against ethnic groups in US public schools in the 20th century, emphasizing the positive value of ethnic identification in the 1970's.

2876. Peters, Charles. WINNING BACK THE ETHNICS: PUBLIC HELP FOR PRIVATE SCHOOLS. *Washington Monthly 1973 4(11): 57-61.*

2877. Ravitch, Diane. ON THE HISTORY OF MINORITY GROUP EDUCATION IN THE UNITED STATES. *Teachers Coll. Record 1976 78(2): 213-228.* The cynicism of contemporary students of minority group education who see the American educational system as oppressively assimilationist is no more justified than the optimism of earlier theorists who extolled the system's perfect democracy. Different minority groups have had different educational experiences; but most, with the exception of Indians and blacks, have been able to take what they needed from the system without sacrificing group integrity. Secondary sources; 29 notes.　　　E. Bailey

2878. Record, Jane Cassels and Record, Wilson. ETHNIC STUDIES AND AFFIRMATIVE ACTION: IDEOLOGICAL ROOTS AND IMPLICATIONS FOR THE QUALITY OF AMERICAN LIFE. *Social Sci. Q. 1974 55(2): 502-519.* The separatist-particularist orientation of current ethnic studies movements and the integrationist-universalistic roots of affirmative action are inherently conflicting. Attempts by federal agencies to accommodate both ideological perspectives have implications for the quality of American society. The essay discusses the emergence of 'vertical ghetto corridors,' the justifiability of black colleges, questions of individual equity, the role of schools in the socialization process, and responsibilities of the state for shaping egalitarian attitudes.　　　J

2879. Ritterband, Paul. ETHNIC POWER AND THE PUBLIC SCHOOLS: THE NEW YORK CITY SCHOOL STRIKE OF 1968. *Sociol. of Educ. 1974 47(2): 251-267.* The 1968 New York City school strike was more a struggle between ethnic communities than a labor-management dispute.　　　S

2880. Scarpaci, Jean A. CULTURAL PLURALISM: AN EMERGING FORCE IN SOCIAL STUDIES. *Social Studies 1975 66(5): 225-230.* Asserts that public schools' social studies curriculum should emphasize cultural pluralism for greater effectiveness of instruction, since the United States has great cultural diversity. Each person should have the right to be respected in his own cultural orientation. 23 notes.　　　L. R. Raife

2881. Seller, Maxine. THE EDUCATION OF IMMIGRANT CHILDREN IN BUFFALO, NEW YORK 1890-1916. *New York Hist. 1976 57(2): 183-199.* Examines the efforts to reform the public school education of immigrant children in Buffalo, New York during 1890-1916. School reformers, mostly of old Protestant Anglo-Saxon stock, understood little about immigrants, and thought of educational reform as part of municipal reform, and as a method of Americanizing immigrant workers and discouraging radicalism. Illus., 36 notes.
R. N. Lokken

2882. Seller, Maxine. THE EDUCATION OF THE IMMIGRANT WOMAN, 1900-1935. *J. of Urban Hist. 1978 4(3): 307-330.* Progressive educational reformers at the turn of the century underestimated the extent of the immigrant woman's interest in education. Heavy use was made of educational facilities maintained by the ethnic communities themselves. While learning English and improving homemaking skills were the most common goals, the educational interests of immigrant women went far beyond those basic areas. 81 notes.
T. W. Smith

2883. Soltow, Lee and Stevens, Edward. ECONOMIC ASPECTS OF SCHOOL PARTICIPATION IN MID-NINETEENTH-CENTURY UNITED STATES. *J. of Interdisciplinary Hist. 1977 8(2): 221-243.* Economic conditions in the Northeast and Northwest, in both rural and urban sectors, were significant in determining school enrollment for adolescents. The relation between enrollment and literacy is not clear. It is unlikely the common school served as a vehicle for social mobility; "the impact of common school expansion was differential, with the wealth of parents being a critical factor." The common school did not alter patterns of economic inequality; instead, it tended to perpetuate them. Printed sources; 11 tables, 44 notes.
R. Howell

2884. Sowell, Thomas. RACE AND I.Q. RECONSIDERED. Sowell, Thomas, ed. *Essays and Data on American Ethnic Groups* (Washington, D.C.: Urban Inst. Pr., 1978): 203-238. Examining more than 70,000 IQ records from more than a dozen ethnic groups going back to 1915, the author explores three fundamental questions regarding IQ and race: 1) Do the IQ scores of racially distinct minorities differ in pattern or level from European groups at a similar socioeconomic stage? 2) Have IQ's of European ethnic minorities changed as their socioeconomic position has changed? 3) Have the scores for close-knit groups such as Orientals and Jews changed less than those that have intermarried freely? Lists results from IQ tests given in 1921 and compares them to more recent scores by ethnic group and concludes that IQ patterns are very often similar for groups sharing the same socioeconomic level. Primary sources; 15 tables, fig., 99 notes, appendix.
K. A. Talley

Law, Crime, and the Courts

2885. Enloe, Cynthia H. POLICE AND MILITARY IN THE RESOLUTION OF CONFLICT. *Ann. of the Am. Acad. of Pol. and Social Sci. 1977 433: 137-149.* Militaries and police forces are rarely neutral actors in ethnic conflicts. They are typically ethnically imbalanced as a result both of historical socioeconomic maldistributions of opportunities and of deliberate recruitment strategies pursued by central government elites. The modernization and professionalization of security forces is no guarantee of their communal or political neutrality. Lasting resolution of inter-ethnic and ethnic-state conflicts require a reorganization of police and militaries thorough enough that vulnerable communities' security is substantially enhanced.
J

2886. Feldberg, Michael. THE CROWD IN PHILADELPHIA HISTORY: A COMPARATIVE PERSPECTIVE. *Labor Hist. 1974 15(3): 323-336.* Assesses Philadelphia history during 1830-50 in the context of the model of crowd behavior advanced by European historians and sociologists to explain pre-industrial collective violence. Philadelphia violence was clearly goal-oriented and dominated by economic and political power objectives. American exceptions to the model constituted collective violence against both Negroes and abolitionists. Local government forces tended to stand aside in ethnic and racial conflicts while violence became a part of politics, utilized to win jobs and political power and enforce an ideology. Based on the Philadelphia *Public Ledger* and unpublished doctoral dissertations; 30 notes.
L. L. Athey

2887. Johnston, A. Montgomery. GENEALOGY: AN APPROACH TO HISTORY. *Hist. Teacher 1978 11(2): 193-200.* Using personal genealogies in history teaching makes history relevant to students, and introduces them to historical method. Includes basic types of genealogical charts. Primary and secondary sources; 4 fig.
P. W. Kennedy

2888. Miller, W. R. POLICE AUTHORITY IN LONDON AND NEW YORK CITY, 1830-1870. *J. of Social Hist. 1976 8(2): 81-101.* "The London policeman represented the 'public good' as defined by the governing classes' concern to maintain an unequal social order with a minimum of violence and oppression. The result was impersonal authority. The New York policeman represented a 'self-governing people' as a product of that self-government's conceptions of power and the ethnic conflicts which divided that people. The result was personal authority." 95 notes.
L. Ziewacz

2889. Mogey, John. RESIDENCE, FAMILY, KINSHIP: SOME RECENT RESEARCH. *J. of Family Hist. 1976 1(1): 95-105.* With family reconstitution techniques and household level analysis of census lists, historians have begun to devise precise and sophisticated means to examine the form, organization, and function of households and residential family units. Drawing on work from sociology and anthropology, the author argues that for a fuller understanding of the family it is necessary to examine the kinship system and related extra-household networks as well. Advances no concrete method to accomplish this, but strongly supports the need for such study. Biblio.
T. W. Smith

2890. O'Kane, James M. THE ETHNIC FACTOR IN AMERICAN URBAN CIVIL DISORDERS. *Ethnicity 1975 2(3): 230-243.* Throughout the 19th and 20th centuries, civil disorders have occurred among minorities in urban areas. The riots take two basic forms: nativistic, where a specific ethnic group is attacked by members of socially dominant groups, and ethnic-reactive situations in which the ethnic group reacted against a perceived socially substandard living situation. While most minorities in America—Germans, Italians, Chinese, Mexicans, Irish, and blacks—were involved in the former, the latter is usually limited to Irish Americans and blacks. Nativistic riots are declining in incidence and importance, most having occurred prior to World War II, whereas the relative incidence of ethnic-reactive riots has been on the increase following World War II. Examines several samples of both riot types and draws parallels between the tactics of Irish and blacks. The similarities pertain to historical antecedents. Both groups were subjected to colonial domination and oppression, both had relatively weak family structures when compared to other ethnic or minority groups, both have been characterized by high incidences of alcoholism, and clerical as well as lay leaders were important to both groups. 21 notes, biblio.
G. A. Hewlett

2891. Schneider, John C. COMMUNITY AND ORDER IN PHILADELPHIA, 1834-1844. *Maryland Historian 1974 5(1): 15-26.* Examines Philadelphia's resistance to the creation of a professional police force despite riots and violence during the 1830's-40's. Concludes that Philadelphia's sense of community tolerated violence against and by outsiders but as violence was directed against the community itself professional police were soon to follow. Based on primary and secondary sources; illus., 33 notes.
G. O. Gagnon

2892. Shapiro, Edward S. PROGRESSIVISM AND VIOLENCE. *North Dakota Q. 1978 46(2): 47-54.* The Progressives believed that the establishment of new institutions fostering social solidarity in the 1880's-1910's would prevent the urban violence which derived from economic, class, and ethnic rivalries.

2893. Turnbaugh, Roy. ETHNICITY, CIVIC PRIDE, AND COMMITMENT: THE EVOLUTION OF THE CHICAGO MILITIA. *J. of the Illinois State Hist. Soc. 1979 72(2): 111-127.* By the early 1870's, only a few militia companies remained in Illinois. They received no state funds. Under Adjutant General Edwin L. Higgins's measures, the condition of the Illinois militia improved. In 1877, in fear of the radical labor movement, the general assembly enacted a comprehensive military code and the militia was renamed the Illinois National Guard. The guardsmen were exempt during service from jury duty and from road and poll taxes. In 1877 a railroad strike occurred. The success of the First Brigade in dealing with the strike differed from the Second Regiment. The strike proved the need of a permanent Chicago militia. Official reports; illus., 51 notes. — E. P. Stickney

2894. Walker, Samuel. THE POLICE AND THE COMMUNITY: SCRANTON, PENNSYLVANIA, 1866-1884: A TEST CASE. *Am. Studies (Lawrence, KS) 1978 19(1): 79-90.* Seeks to explain police operations "in the midst of extreme industrial conflict and ethnic tensions" and uses Scranton, Pennsylvania, as a microcosm of American society. Development of the anthracite coal fields, economic uncertainty, and ethnic immigration frequently produced mob violence after the Civil War, and led to insurgent working-class political activity. These events led Scranton to create a police department. Surveys the development and problems of this department, focusing on political activism and public concern with curbing the cost of government. Primary and secondary sources; 12 notes. — J. Andrew

Economic and Business Activities

2895. Amerine, Maynard A. THE NAPA VALLEY GRAPE AND WINE INDUSTRY. *Agric. Hist. 1975 49(1): 289-291.* During 1840-1900 the Napa Valley became a prime center for American wine production as major vineyards were established by Easterners and Europeans. — D. E. Bowers

2896. Bairati, Piero. LA TECNICA EUROPEA E LE ORIGINI DELLA MANIFATTURA AMERICANA: 1750-1820. [European technique and the origins of American manufacture: 1750-1820]. *Ann. della Fondazione Luigi Einaudi [Italy] 1977 11: 203-234.* During the late colonial period, the importation of techniques assumed importance. The transfer of technologies became an instrument of emancipation from the colonial power's tutelage and afterwards laid the bases of the American industrial revolution. Already by 1775 the colonial production of unrefined iron exceeded that of England and Wales and was one-seventh of world production. In the field of military technique French chemistry provided an important contribution to the American war of independence. From 1695 to 1799 the British Parliament approved a great number of bills to prevent the emigration of skilled craftsmen and the export of machinery, but these were not enforced. Examines different examples of importation of technologies from Europe and concludes that historians are now revising the concept of "yankee ingenuity," according to which the technological development of the United States was considered home grown. Based on published sources; 65 notes. — M. de Leonardis

2897. Bartosik, Jerzy. EMIGRACJA EUROPEJSKA WYSOKO KWALIFIKOWANEJ SIŁY ROBOCZEJ DO USA [The European emigration of a highly qualified labor force to the USA]. *Przegląd Zachodni [Poland] 1968 24(4): 455-458.* Discusses the "brain drain", particularly from Western Europe to America which reached such alarming proportions during 1963-66. It is estimated that annually 10,000 specialists (40% of those from Europe) emigrate to the United States.

2898. Boyd, Monica. OCCUPATIONS OF FEMALE IMMIGRANTS AND NORTH AMERICAN IMMIGRATION STATISTICS. *Int. Migration Rev. 1976 10(1): 73-80.* Discusses labor force potential and occupations of women immigrants to the United States and Canada, 1964-71.

2899. Hancock, Harold B. DELAWARE FURNITUREMAKING, 1850-1870: TRANSITION TO THE MACHINE AGE. *Delaware Hist. 1977 17(4): 250-294.* Describes the lives and products of Delaware furnituremakers in the 19th century. Furniture craftsmen suffered from inflation, an increase in the number of immigrant craftsmen, strikes, and the transition to machine production which gradually eroded the craftsmen's prominence. Wilmington remained the center of production in the state. Many workers worked in small shops even to 1870. Change was gradual, and the quality of craftsmanship did not decline dramatically, despite the changes in tastes to heavier Victorian pieces. Lists almost 350 cabinetmakers and 70 apprentices in Delaware in the mid-19th century. 4 illus., 18 notes. — R. M. Miller

2900. Hancock, Harold B. THE INDENTURE SYSTEM IN DELAWARE, 1681-1921. *Delaware Hist. 1974 16(1): 47-59.* Dutch, Swedish,

and English colonists practiced indenture to repay transportation costs to America (or other debts), and later used it "to provide for poor children and to see that they learned a trade." Debtors found indenture "a convenient means by which to work off their obligations," and the British used it to dump "undesirables" in the colony. Terms of indenture became fixed and formalized and gave overwhelming supervisory and disciplinary powers to the master. Negroes found that apprenticeship laws discriminated against them, but in time indenture enabled beneficent masters to manumit their slaves. In the 19th century apprenticeship generally served to introduce youths to useful trades and especially to provide workers for industry. Indenture declined after the Civil War but was not formally abolished until 1921. Based largely on court records; 39 notes. — R. M. Miller

2901. Jacobs, Julius L. CALIFORNIA'S PIONEER WINE FAMILIES. *California Hist. Q. 1975 54(2): 139-174.* A survey of viticulture and enology in California. Of the more than 240 bonded wineries in the state, only four which trace their origins back to the 19th century—Biane, Mirassou, Wente, and Concannon—are still under family operation. The history of these four and other pioneering wine families are described. California proved ideal for the production of fine red and white wines. Although the industry received a setback during Prohibition, it has expanded greatly since the law's repeal, with more than 325 million gallons being produced. Both tiny producers and giant companies have contributed to making wine production a major California industry. Primary sources, including oral history interviews and secondary studies; 5 illus., 19 photos, 37 notes. — A. Hoffman

2902. McGowan, James T. PLANTERS WITHOUT SLAVES: ORIGINS OF A NEW WORLD LABOR SYSTEM. *Southern Studies 1977 16(1): 5-26.* The institutionalization of African slavery as the dominant form of labor organization in Louisiana arose in response to class conflict during 1790-1820. The unrelenting refusal of craftsmen, hunters, and soldiers, the men recruited in Europe, to be tied to the land paved the way for the rejection of white labor on staple-producing plantations. These men had neither the experience nor the inclination for the responsibilities of farming or marriage, preferring adventure and Indian mistresses. Their life style brought about the failure to create agricultural communities based on white labor in Louisiana, and led, after 1717, to the importation of African slaves. Based on Archives of the Ministry of Colonies in Paris, other primary and secondary sources; 56 notes. — J. Buschen

2903. Morrissey, Charles T. ORAL HISTORY AND THE CALIFORNIA WINE INDUSTRY: AN ESSAY REVIEW. *Agric. Hist. 1977 51(3): 590-596.* Ruth Teiser, Director of the California Wine Industry Oral History Project, has recorded 24 interviews bound in 20 volumes (19 of which are open to research). The interviewees include Martini (both father and son), Petri, Wente, Gallo, Perelli-Minette, Rossi, and Brother Timothy of Christian Brothers. The other 15 interviews are with viticulturalists and enologists at the University of California as well as two bankers, a wine merchant, an attorney, and a publicist. — R. T. Fulton

2904. Orton, Eliot S. CHANGES IN THE SKILL DIFFERENTIAL: UNION WAGES IN CONSTRUCTION, 1907-1972. *Industrial and Labor Relations Rev. 1976 30(1): 16-24.* This study examines the year-to-year movement in the wage differential between skilled and unskilled workers, 1907-72, using union contract rates in the construction industry. The author examines a number of hypotheses that have been suggested as explanations for changes in the skill differential. He finds that changes in the price level (a demand factor) best explain cyclical changes and that the level of foreign immigration (a supply factor) best explains secular changes. Although the author's model predicts a narrowing of the skill differential since the early 1960's, the differential has remained essentially unchanged in recent years, leading the author to conclude that the increasing level of illegal immigrants, not recorded in official statistics, has served to retard the expected decrease in the premium paid to skilled workers. — J

2905. Shergold, Peter R. WAGE RATES IN PITTSBURGH DURING THE DEPRESSION OF 1908. *J. of Am. Studies [Great Britain] 1975 9(2): 163-188.* Assesses statistical and qualitative evidences to explain the phenomenon of wage rates declining less drastically in Pittsburgh during the depression of 1908 than in earlier recessions of considerably less severity. The depression of 1908 encouraged emigration from Pittsburgh, discouraged immigration from Europe to the United States, and produced "relative tightness" in the Pittsburgh labor market. Hence, wage rates remained higher than depression conditions otherwise warranted. Based on newspaper and secondary sources; 75 notes.

H. T. Lovin

2906. Sprunk, Larry J. AL J. VOHS—WILLISTON. *North Dakota Hist. 1977 44(4): 41-44.* Interviews Al J. Vohs. Techniques of butchering meat for sale by a Williston, North Dakota, meat market were primitive, but effective. Meat would be butchered at night for sale early the next morning. The Williston area was initially settled by large numbers of Germans followed by equally large numbers of Norwegians. During the 1930's, Vohs, as a member of the City Commission, founded a municipal soup kitchen based on donations of food and city funds which fed many individuals and families for some years. The relief enterprise was a successful venture of its type and attracted considerable attention from outside the community.

N. Lederer

2907. Stewart, James B. and Hyclak, Thomas. ETHNICITY AND ECONOMIC OPPORTUNITY. *Am. J. of Econ. and Sociol. 1979 38(3): 319-335.* In this analysis, data from the 1970 Census of Population are used to determine whether ethnic discrimination has been an important factor contributing to differential economic performance among immigrant groups. The measures of economic performance employed in this investigation are mean family income and the extent of poverty among cohorts of immigrants. Discrimination against particular groups has been a major contributing factor to differential economic performance among groups. As a consequence, we are led to reject the competing explanation of differential economic performance advanced by some analysts that differentials in economic performance merely reflect skill differentials among groups.

J

2908. Trnka, Pavel. EVROPSKÁ IMIGRACE A INDUSTRIALIZACE USA (1870-1910) [European immigration and US industrialization, 1870-1910]. *Sborník Hist. [Czechoslovakia] 1976 24: 187-230.* The Atlantic economy was characterized by a unidirectional flow of capital, mainly from Great Britain, and of labor, from all of Europe, and by American demand for labor. The prevalence of males and adults among the new immigration influenced the American demographic profile and accelerated the growth of the available labor force. It also facilitated emigration in response to recessions. Mining, metallurgy, processing industries, and transportation absorbed most of the newcomers, some of whom brought useful skills acquired at the expense of their home countries. 12 tables, 3 diags., 104 notes.

R. E. Weltsch

2909. Uselding, Paul J. PEDDLING IN THE ANTEBELLUM ECONOMY. *Am. J. of Econ. and Sociol. 1975 34(1): 55-66.* Peddling in the United States during 1790-1860 provided opportunities for economic and occupational mobility. The interaction of peddlers with other forms of marketing institutions are investigated. Secondary sources; table, 25 notes.

W. L. Marr

Culture, the Arts, and Ideas (including Popular Culture)

2910. Barshay, Robert. ETHNIC STEREOTYPES IN FLASH GORDON. *J. of Popular Film 1974 3(1): 15-30.*

2911. Bauman, Richard; Abrahams, Roger D.; and Kalčik, Susan. AMERICAN FOLKLORE AND AMERICAN STUDIES. *Am. Q. 1976 28(3): 360-377.* Early investigators in the field of American folklore shared the belief that America was fundamentally a pluralistic society. A review of the practical and conceptual organizing principles of the study of American folklore reveals that regionalism has played an important, but not completely defined role in definition, while collections organized by states and regions, have, except for compilations, been arranged by genre as well. In recent years scholars have turned their attention towards the analysis of folk performers, urban folklore, contemporary occupational folklore, etc.

N. Lederer

2912. Callahan, John M. FRITZ EMMET: ST. LOUIS'S FAVORITE GERMAN. *Missouri Hist. Soc. Bull. 1979 35(2): 69-82.* Joseph Kline Emmet (1841-91), an Irish American actor born in St. Louis, started his theatrical career in 1858. Before 1869 he achieved only limited recognition, first as an Irish comedian and later as vocalist and actor in minstrel shows. In 1869, Emmet and Charles Gaylor created for German dialect dramas a character named Fritz Van Vonderblinkenstoffenheisen. Playing the role of Fritz first in *Fritz, Our Cousin German* and subsequently in many other plays, Emmet won national fame. Archival material, newspapers, and secondary sources; photo, 80 notes.

H. T. Lovin

2913. Daley, Mary. ETHNIC CRAFTS IN CLEVELAND. *Historic Preservation 1974 26(1): 19-23.* Peoples and Cultures, Inc. was formed in 1971 to celebrate the diverse heritage of the approximately 90 ethnic groups in Cleveland, Ohio. A major project is the preservation of ethnic craft traditions and skills, and the selling of local craft products. 4 photos.

R. M. Frame III

2914. David, John R. JOSEPH K. EMMET AS *FRITZ, OUR COUSIN GERMAN:* THE STAGE IMMIGRANT AND THE AMERICAN DREAM. *Missouri Hist. Rev. 1979 73(2): 198-217.* Joseph K. Emmet (1841-91) began his acting career in 1858. It was still an age when most actors came from Europe. *Fritz, Our Cousin German* by Charles Gayler opened the way for this variety house actor from St. Louis to move to New York in 1869 to become one of the first American-born stars. Fritz was more than a burlesque figure of a German immigrant struggling with American customs and English syntax; he was designed to show how America and the immigrant could benefit from each other's talents and dreams. While Fritz put his faith in migrating to America, Emmet was no less an immigrant pinning his hopes for success on migration to the East. Illus., 103 notes.

W. F. Zornow

2915. Dorson, Richard M. AMERICAN FOLKLORE BIBLIOGRAPHY. *Am. Studies Int. 1977 16(1): 23-37.* A selective list, emphasizing "interpretive works which relate folklore to American civilization" and eschewing "collections of tales or songs or other genres, unless they help establish that relationship in a special way." Covers general studies, historical, regional, heroes, occupational, literature, ballad, folk song, folk music, folklife and material culture, oral history, urban, Afro-American, immigrant-ethnic, and Indian.

R. V. Ritter

2916. Dorson, Richard M. FOLKLORE IN AMERICA VS. AMERICAN FOLKLORE. *J. of the Folklore Inst. 1978 15(2): 97-111.* Analyzes folklore studies in the United States. Distinguishes between a distinctly American folklore, which has influenced American social, political, and economic institutions and actions, and has been influenced by them; and folklore in America, which treats folklore as discrete, isolated functions of the past. The failure to consider the uniqueness of the United States, the immigrants, the westward movement, and sectional tensions, unlike the lengthy classical and medieval-based folklore systems of Europe, seriously weakens, or at least biases, the majority of folklore studies in America. 20 notes.

V. L. Human

2917. Dorson, Richard M. HUNTING FOLKLORE IN THE ARMPIT OF AMERICA. *Indiana Folklore 1977 10(2): 97-106.* Results of a folklore project in northwestern Indiana, an area of heavy industrialization and urbanization, yielded local geographical and cultural, steelworker, ethnic, black, and crime folklore, 1976.

2918. Downey, Patricia Kemerer. CURRENT TRENDS IN DECORATIVE EMBROIDERY: FOLKLORE OR FAKELORE? *Tennessee Folklore Soc. Bull. 1976 42(3): 108-124.* Compares current designs, stitches, and materials used by young women in decorative embroidery with those of immigrants in the late 19th and early 20th centuries.

2919. Gordon, Bertram M. FOOD AND HISTORY: TEACHING SOCIAL HISTORY THROUGH THE STUDY OF CUISINE PATTERNS. *Social Studies 1974 65(5): 204-207.* Emphasis is shifting toward an interest in social history, and accurate study of the cuisine patterns of cultures and ethnic groups is an effective approach. 14 notes.

L. R. Raife

2920. Horowitz, Robert F. BETWEEN A HEARTACHE AND A LAUGH: TWO RECENT FILMS ON IMMIGRATION. *Film and Hist. 1976 6(4): 73-78.* Discusses two recent films, *Hester Street* (1975) and *Lies My Father Told Me* (1974), dealing with immigration of white ethnic groups to the United States, 1896-1920's.

2921. Kirby, Jack Temple. D. W. GRIFFITH'S RACIAL POR-TRAITURE. *Phylon 1978 39(2): 118-127.* In his more than 400 films, David Wark Griffith treated racial themes frequently. He used stereo-types constantly: Jews were ingratiating and parsimonious, Italians and Hispanics passionate and often violent; American Indians noble savages; Orientals inscrutable and tradition-bound. Yet all of these ethnic types could be either good or bad, depending on the film. Griffith makes Indi-ans heroes more often than villains, and sympathizes with the struggle against the encroaching whites. *Ramona* (1910) depicts white persecution of the *mestiza* Ramona and her Indian lover. Blacks, however, were either wicked or docile retainers; in *Birth of a Nation* (1915) Griffith enshrines these racial stereotypes in one of the greatest films ever made. In *Intolerance,* he chronicles many instances of that vice in history, but never racial prejudice as a form thereof. Griffith's racism, however, should not be singled out for condemnation; it was typical of the time, and many made films more viciously racist than did Griffith. 33 notes.
J. C. Billigmeier

2922. Lewis, Jo Ann. IMMIGRANT ARTISTS: WHO THEY WERE AND WHAT THEY DID. *Smithsonian 1976 7(2): 92-101.* Reports on the immigrants during 1876-1976 who helped introduce the modern art movement to America, the problems they faced in gaining acceptance, and the 1976 exhibit of their art at the Hirshhorn Museum and Sculpture Garden in Washington, D.C.

2923. Lieberson, Stanley; Dalto, Guy; and Johnston, Mary Ellen. THE COURSE OF MOTHER-TONGUE DIVERSITY IN NATIONS. *Am. J. of Sociol. 1975 81(1): 34-61.* The course of mother-tongue diver-sity is abstracted from longitudinal data gathered for 35 nations. Diversity declines over time in the majority of cases, but there is considerable variation between nations and in 14 cases diversity has increased. Accord-ingly, various national characteristics are considered to see whether they help account for the magnitude and direction of change observed among nations. Two factors, the spatial isolation of language groups and official educational policies, have fairly high correlations with changes in diver-sity. In addition, several geopolitical factors have affected diversity change in the past: age of nation, boundary changes, forced population movements, and World War II. Two specially puzzling results are the comparatively rapid rate of mother-tongue change in the United States and the failure of national development to have much bearing on the course of mother-tongue diversity.
J

2924. MacDonald, J. Frederick. "THE FOREIGNER" IN JUVE-NILE SERIES FICTION, 1900-1945. *J. of Popular Culture 1974 8(3): 534-548.* Discusses the portrayal of foreigners and the stereotypes of various ethnic groups in juvenile fiction.

2925. Mercier, Denis; Brown, Waln K.; and Varesano, Angela. "NIPSY": THE ETHNOGRAPHY OF A TRADITIONAL GAME OF PENNSYLVANIA'S ANTHRACITE REGION. *Pennsylvania Folk-life 1974 23(4): 12-21.* An ethnographic study in 1972 of the Pennsylvania village of Eckley yielded new insights on the game of nipsy, including its popularity, strategy, and the physical prowess necessary to master it.
S

2926. Nickerson, Bruce E. IS THERE A FOLK IN THE FAC-TORY? *J. of Am. Folklore 1974 87(344): 133-139.* Blue-collar workers are a "folk-like" group possessing verbal materials, traditional customs, crafts, and cultural attitudes of interest to folklorists. Further studies are required to evaluate the importance of specific genres of folklore in vary-ing industrial contexts. Based on fieldwork in two large Boston industrial plants and a smaller Midwest facility, and secondary sources; 11 notes.
W. D. Piersen

2927. Nicolaisen, W. F. H. FOLKLORE AND GEOGRAPHY: TO-WARDS AN ATLAS OF AMERICAN FOLKLORE CULTURE. *New York Folklore Q. 1973 29(1): 3-20.*

2928. Paymans, H. PROPAGANDISTIC ASPECTS OF MODERN COMIC-BOOKS. *Gazette [Netherlands] 1976 22(4): 219-229.* Comic books can provide propaganda as well as entertainment; the American comic *Buck Danny,* 1941-47, chronicled the triumph of American impe-rialism; *Barcus* divided good and bad characters according to sex, racial or ethnic origin, and political belief. Discusses European, American, and Middle Eastern comics during the 20th century.
G. A. Hewlett

2929. Pillsbury, Richard. PATTERNS IN THE FOLK AND VER-NACULAR HOUSE FORMS OF THE PENNSYLVANIA CUL-TURE REGION. *Pioneer Am. 1977 9(1): 12-31.* Surveys the Pennsylvania culture area to determine if previous microstudies have valid geographical analyses of traditional vernacular and folk housing distribution. Both housing types, traditionally classified by the arrange-ment of rooms, reveal two broad categories—one-room-deep and two-room-deep housing. Based on field research, two unpublished Ph.D. dissertations, and secondary sources; 11 photos, 2 maps, 3 figs., 15 notes.
C. R. Gunter, Jr.

2930. Stoner, Paula. EARLY FOLK ARCHITECTURE OF WASH-INGTON COUNTY. *Maryland Hist. Mag. 1977 72(4): 512-522.* Ex-amines the adaptation of German, Scotch-Irish, and English building traditions to the environmental materials in Washington County, Mary-land, during the latter 18th and early 19th centuries, as seen in houses, arch bridges, farm walls, barns, and gristmills. The abundance of wood and limestone strongly influenced durability and styles, which ranged from log cabins to weatherboarded log houses to formal Georgian-style stone mansions. The number of these buildings still standing testifies to the harmony possible between people and nature. Based on the "Conogo-chegue Manor" Survey of 1767 and the 1798 Pennsylvania tax lists for nearby Franklin County; 13 illus.
G. J. Bobango

2931. Wander, Philip. COUNTERS IN THE SOCIAL DRAMA: SOME NOTES ON *ALL IN THE FAMILY. J. of Popular Culture 1974 8(3): 602-607.* Examines the characters and plot of *All in the Family* and inspects the character of the program as it both reflects and belies American society during the 1970's.

2932. Willett, Ralph. NATIVISM AND ASSIMILATION: THE HOLLYWOOD ASPECT. *J. of Am. Studies [Great Britain] 1973 7(2): 191-194.* Reviews the meager scholarly literature about the American motion picture industry and its handling of nativist concerns. American cinema has featured considerable material offensive to ethnic groups in the United States. World War I and the Bolshevik Revolution encouraged the production of movies which prolonged the ethnocentric prejudices of nativists. Recent films focus sympathetically on assimilation of minorities into American society. 8 notes.
H. T. Lovin

5. CONTEMPORARY ETHNICITY

Ethnicity and Assimilation

2933. Alba, Richard D. ETHNIC NETWORKS AND TOLERANT ATTITUDES. *Public Opinion Q. 1978 42(1): 1-16.* This study describes an empirical association between the ethnic homogeneity or heterogeneity of an individual's network of primary relations and his or her attitudes toward free speech and child rearing. J

2934. Alba, Richard D. SOCIAL ASSIMILATION AMONG AMERICAN CATHOLIC NATIONAL-ORIGIN GROUPS. *Am. Sociol. Rev. 1976 41(6): 1030-1046.* The current resurgence of interest in white ethnicity largely has taken the form of asserting the continued vitality of ethnic communities. Current scholars, following Gordon's (1964) well-known distinction between acculturation and social or structural assimilation, acknowledge the great extent of acculturation but maintain that, nonetheless, social assimilation has not taken place. They claim, in other words, that primary relationships are generally between individuals of like ethnicity. This paper, using data about Catholic national-origin groups in the early 1960s, finds little support for these present assertions of ethnic vitality. J

2935. Banks, James A. and Gay, Geneva. ETHNICITY IN CONTEMPORARY AMERICAN SOCIETY: TOWARD THE DEVELOPMENT OF A TYPOLOGY. *Ethnicity 1978 5(3): 238-251.* The nature of ethnic groups and relationships between them have undergone considerable change since earlier definitions of ethnicity were devised. New definitions must be formulated. A typology of ethnic groups can be posited in which an ethnic group is defined as "an involuntary group whose members share a sense of peoplehood and an interdependence of fate." The types of ethnic groups can be particularistic in emphasis, clustering around culture, economics, or political themes, or holistic in which all of the above themes are incorporated into the group's reason for being. The interrelationships existing between ethnic identification, ethnic heritage, and ethnic culture must be recognized along with the fact that the degree of ethnicity varies according to various social, economic, and political conditions operative in society at different times. N. Lederer

2936. Bell, Wendell. COMPARATIVE RESEARCH ON ETHNICITY: A CONFERENCE REPORT. *Social Sci. Res. Council Items 1974 28(4): 61-64.* Reports on the conference convened by the Social Science Research Council in April 1974 to discuss the current state of methodology and theory in research on ethnicity and the opportunities for facilitating cross-cultural research. S

2937. Bellow, Saul. STARTING OUT IN CHICAGO. *Am. Scholar 1974-75 44(1): 71-77.* Analyzes the social and cultural environment in Chicago during the late 1930's and the efforts of immigrants and their children to be "American," and discusses the way "being American" has developed since then. Our biggest enemy is "the Great Noise," the terrible excitement and distraction generated by the crises of modern life." Based on a commencement address delivered at Brandeis University, Spring 1974. R. V. Ritter

2938. Blake, J. Herman. AFTER THE ETHNIC EXPERIENCE. *Center Mag. 1974 7(4): 44-50.* Paper presented at a joint conference of the Center for the Study of Democratic Institutions and the Immigration History Society on ethnicity today. Describes Americans' inability to incorporate ethnic dreams into political life, with illustrations of the evolution of the Black Panther Party from a militant organization to a political machine. S

2939. Bogina, Sh. A.; Kozlov, V. I.; Nitoburg, E. L.; and Fursova, L. N. NATSIONAL'NYE PROTSESSY I NATSIONAL'NYE OTNOSHENIIA V STRANAKH ZAPADNOI EVROPY I SEVERNOI AMERIKI [National processes and ethnic relations in developed capitalist countries of Europe and North America]. *Sovetskaia Etnografiia [USSR] 1975 5: 3-16.* In a number of developed European countries ethnic consolidation may be regarded as completed but in some of them

acute inter-ethnic situations are developing both between their long established peoples (e.g. in Belgium and Spain), and through the rise of a considerable immigrant population (e.g. in France and England). The aggravation of inter-ethnic situations is due to economic causes called forth by the revolution in science and technology. In North America inter-ethnic consolidation is not as yet complete. The American nation, a young ethnic formation, comprises a number of structural elements formed by immigrant ethnic groups in different stages of assimilation. While inter-ethnic integration in the various aspects of human activity is far advanced, the ethnic components of the U.S. population have of late shown more active ethnocentrism, stimulated by the Negro movement. Canada owes the aggravation of its national contradictions mainly to the French Canadian problem but also to the presence of a large number of immigrant groups and to the discrimination against the Indian and Eskimo population. An all-Canadian problem is the drive towards liberation from US monopolies. This aggravation of the nationalities problem may in part be explained by: the influence of colonial liberation movements; the increasing inequalities between different nationalities due to the technological revolution; a reaction against the monotony of mass culture. J

2940. Boguina, C. A. MEZHETNICHESKIE OTNOSHENIYA V SSHA (XIX VEK) [Interethnic relations in the United States (19th century)]. *Sovetskaia Etnografiia [USSR] 1974 (4): 63-72.* "An attempt is made at a theoretical analysis of the problem. Migrations in the course of which the multi-ethnic population of the United States (as of many other countries) was formed are viewed as intersections of space and historic time, immigrant life depending on the relation of the degree of development of the country of emigration to that of the receiving country. The processes of assimilation are analyzed with special stress on linguistic developments. Ethnic discrimination is regarded as the principal phenomenon of the system of interethnic relations, the whole system formed by a hierarchy of ethnic groups and expressed by a set of stereotypes and, conversely, autostereotypes. The role of confessional divisions for the system is considered. The absence of an ethno-territorial division of the country is emphasized as an important condition of the US ethnic structure. The interplay of tendencies toward cultural uniformity and ethnic isolation throughout American history has produced a sort of dual ethnic consciousness—that of belonging to the American nation as a whole and that of belonging to one of the ethnic groups forming part of its structure, the first tendency having apparently proved the stronger." J

2941. Chrobot, Leonard F. THE NEW ETHNICITY IN AMERICA: TOWARD CULTURAL AND HUMAN RESOURCES. *Indiana Hist. Bull. 1978 55(5): 62-68.* Examines the concept of integrated pluralism, the idea of recognizing one's ethnicity and observing customs of folk culture while participating actively in whatever urban culture one may find oneself without regard to ethnic origin.

2942. Clecak, Peter. NOTES ON WORK. *Antioch Rev. 1978 36(4): 397-421.* Reminiscences of a third-generation immigrant seeking assimilation as an academic within the context of the changing character of and assumptions about work in 19th- and 20th-century America.

2943. D'Antonio, William V. TOWARD A MORE PERFECT UNION. *Jednota Ann. Furdek 1978 17: 241-246.* Through ethnic pride and racial pride, American social organization can be directed toward cultural pluralism, thus forming a more perfect union.

2944. Dashefsky, Arnold. THEORETICAL FRAMEWORKS IN THE STUDY OF ETHNIC IDENTITY: TOWARD A SOCIAL PSYCHOLOGY OF ETHNICITY. *Ethnicity 1975 2(1): 10-18.* Examines four theoretical frameworks used in assessing ethnicity: sociocultural, interactionist, group dynamicist, and psychoanalytic.

2945. Gambino, Richard. PUBLIC POLICIES AND THE RISE OF ETHNICITY: BASIC CONSIDERATIONS AND PRACTICAL SUGGESTIONS. *Freedom At Issue 1974 (25): 11-19.* "Comprehensive recommendations for countering the ethnic chauvinism of 'affirmative action' . . . by stressing fairness and merit as basic to the preservation of individual rights."   S

2946. Glazer, Nathan.   THE UNIVERSALISATION OF ETHNICITY: PEOPLES IN THE BOILING POT. *Encounter [Great Britain] 1975 44(2): 8-17.* Discusses cultural assimilation and ethnic conflicts in multi-ethnic societies in Europe, Africa, and the United States in the 20th century.

2947. Glazer, Nathan and Moynihan, Daniel P.   WHY ETHNICITY? *Commentary 1974 58(4): 33-39.* The ethnic group has become the basis of social identification and conflict in modern societies.   S

2948. Gottlieb, David and Sibbison, Virginia.   ETHNICITY AND RELIGIOSITY: SOME SELECTIVE EXPLORATIONS AMONG COLLEGE STUDENTS. *Int. Migration Rev. 1974 8(1): 43-58.* A study of ethnic-religious factors as an integral part of the socialization process.   S

2949. Grabosky, Peter N. and Rosenbloom, David H.   RACIAL AND ETHNIC INTEGRATION IN THE FEDERAL SERVICE. *Social Sci. Q. 1975 56(1): 71-84.* Analyzes integration in the general schedule positions of 19 major cities, and evaluates these positions.   S

2950. Greeley, Andrew M. and McCready, William C.   DOES ETHNICITY MATTER? *Ethnicity 1974 1(1): 91-108.* Discusses the continuing impact of Old World heritages on the personalities and behavior patterns of American ethnic groups. Based on studies of Ireland and southern Italy, the authors predicted patterns of responses of Italian and Irish Americans in comparison with Anglo Americans in terms of seven personality variables, political participation, drinking habits, and sexual attitudes. Twenty-two of 45 hypotheses were validated, and the conclusions held when controlling for region, education, and generation. 6 tables, 6 notes, biblio., appendix.   E. R. Barkan

2951. Greenbaum, William.   AMERICA IN SEARCH OF A NEW IDEAL: AN ESSAY ON THE RISE OF PLURALISM. *Harvard Educ. Rev. 1974 44(3): 411-440.* Demands by cultural and ethnic groups for equal power and political leverage in society have increased steadily between 1950 and 1970.   S

2952. Greene, Victor.   OLD ETHNIC STEREOTYPES AND THE NEW ETHNIC STUDIES. *Ethnicity 1978 5(4): 328-350.* The constant change in ethnic relationships is not reflected in the stereotypes of ethnics held by the majority population or by descendants of the immigrants. Immigrants, especially southern and eastern Europeans, are held to have been an undifferentiated mass, ill-educated and abysmally poor. These were characteristics of most of the immigrants, but not all. Immigrant groups contained group elites of businessmen, editors, politicians, clericals, etc., who mightily labored to create viable ethnic entities. The stereotypes derive in some instances from photographs remaining from the period of mass immigration, which were employed for purposes of social reform and therefore present an unrelieved, dismal view of the ethnic groups. Contemporary ethnic studies, to be valid, must concern themselves with the complexity and diversity of ethnic groups.
                                                                     N. Lederer

2953. Higham, John.   HANGING TOGETHER: DIVERGENT UNITIES IN AMERICAN HISTORY. *J. of Am. Hist. 1974 61(1): 5-28.* The 1974 annual presidential address before the Organization of American Historians, devotes attention to three "adhesive forces" characteristic of the development of modernizing societies. "Primordial" unity binds kinsmen and neighbors and has been intense among American Indians, immigrant groups, and American whites of the Southeast. Ideological unity stems from a Puritan, and later a generalized Protestant ideology, which was fused with ideas of nationalism into an emphasis on collective mission, dispersal of power, and individual responsibility and opportunity. Since the Civil War the primary unifying force has been technology, exemplified in the engineer, inventor, and scientific manager with emphasis on efficiency and power over nature. For a time technology was considered a servant of a democratic, rational collectivity, but recently technology has been considered specialized, undemocratic in its implications, and contrary or irrelevant to idealism. 56 notes.
                                                                     K. B. West

2954. Higham, John.   INTEGRATION VS. PLURALISM: ANOTHER AMERICAN DILEMMA. *Center Mag. 1974 7(4): 67-73.* Paper presented at a joint conference of the Center for the Study of Democratic Institutions and the Immigration History Society on ethnicity today, exploring two opposing views of ethnicity: integration and pluralism.   S

2955. Hijiya, James A.   ROOTS: FAMILY AND ETHNICITY IN THE 1970S. *Am. Q. 1978 30(4): 548-556.* A bibliographic essay reviewing a variety of titles that reflect a common preoccupation with human heritage whether family or ethnic as an obvious and significant phenomenon of this decade. Explores what this significance might be and its effect on our society. The interest in family is accompanied by a complementary interest in ethnic groups. Some see relatively little influence of the family or ethnic group on the character of an individual. Others strongly disagree. The idea of the self-made man will no doubt surface again shortly, rising from its temporary overshadowing before the power of family and ethnicity.   R. V. Ritter

2956. Hollinger, David A.   ETHNIC DIVERSITY, COSMOPOLITANISM AND THE EMERGENCE OF THE AMERICAN LIBERAL INTELLIGENTSIA. *Am. Q. 1975 27(2): 133-151.* The American intelligentsia of the 1930's and 40's was composed of white Anglo-Saxon Protestants such as Edmund Wilson and Dwight MacDonald and ethnic, especially Jewish, thinkers including Morris R. Cohen, Lionel Trilling, Alfred Kazin, and Philip Rahv. These intellectuals transcended their native and imported parochialisms to formulate a cosmopolitan attitude based on total human experience and the understanding of that experience, while stressing the culturally pluralistic, rather than the "melting pot," context of American society.
                                                                     N. Lederer

2957. Irby, Charles C.   A DEVELOPMENTAL DESIGN FOR UNDERSTANDING ETHNICITY. *Explorations in Ethnic Studies 1978 1(1): 3-15.* Suggests a framework for studying ethnicity and ethnic mechanisms in American social organization including examination of accessibility and isolation, race, culture, demography, family, ideology, and cultural transmission.

2958. Isaacs, Harold R.   BASIC GROUP IDENTITY: THE IDOLS OF THE TRIBE. *Ethnicity 1974 1(1): 15-41.* Relying on the ideas of Sigmund Freud, Erik Erikson, and Erich Fromm, the author defines Basic Group Identity as endowments and identifications acquired by birth or at the time of birth. B.G.I. represents "man's essential tribalism" and is rooted in the need for security, belonging, and self-esteem. Individual and ethnic group identities are complementary. Qualities of B.G.I. include physical characteristics, names, status, language, religion. The author then focuses on the role of body images and names. 19 notes.
                                                                     E. R. Barkan

2959. Isajiw, Wsevolod W.   DEFINITIONS OF ETHNICITY. *Ethnicity 1974 1(2): 111-124.* Based on an analysis of 27 definitions of ethnicity, a list of features ranked by frequency was compiled. A definition applicable specifically to North America was sought. Concluded by defining ethnicity as referring to an involuntary group of people (one is born into such a group), sharing a common culture, ancestry, peoplehood, *Gemeinschaft*-type relations, and immigrant background. They identify themselves and/or are identified by others as belonging to that group. They possess either a majority or minority status. Biblio.
                                                                     E. Barkan

2960. Isajiw, Wsevolod W.   OLGA IN WONDERLAND: ETHNICITY IN TECHNOLOGICAL SOCIETY. *Can. Ethnic Studies [Canada] 1977 9(1): 77-85.* Not the marketplace but technological culture most affects immigrant assimilation. Componential, materialistic technology creates a yearning for the maintenance of holistic, natural ethnicity. Impersonal technological culture "heightens the need for identity and creates the search for identity." The revival of ethnic identities in modern society promises a real pluralism which accepts and affirms all human differences. Discusses Canada and the United States.
                                                                     K. S. McDorman

2961. Jarolimek, John.   BORN AGAIN ETHNICS: PLURALISM IN MODERN AMERICA. *Social Educ. 1979 43(3): 204-209.* Describes the author's 1975-76 study of pluralism, ethnicity, bilingualism, and multicultural and ethnic heritage, based on immigration statistics and legislation since the late 1880's.

2962. Jeffres, Leo W. and Hur, K. Kyoon. WHITE ETHNICS AND THEIR MEDIA IMAGE. *J. of Communication 1979 29(1): 116-122.* Discusses the results of a 1976 study of ethnics in the Cleveland metropolitan area culled from the 1974 Ethnic Directory of Greater Cleveland, on ethnic groups' attitudes toward their media image, which indicates that attitudes depend on ethnic orientation, and the education level and affluence of ethnic respondents.

2963. Keller, Edward and Roël, Ronald. FOREIGN LANGUAGES AND U.S. CULTURAL POLICY: AN INSTITUTIONAL PERSPECTIVE. *J. of Communication 1979 29(2): 102-111.* Insensitivity to foreign languages and cultures is not ameliorated by disunited government policies and lack of attention by the mass media.

2964. Kitch, Laura W. and Mayer, Egon. THE NEW PLURALISM: FROM TOLERANCE TO NEGLECT. *Ethnicity 1976 3(4): 378-387.* Examines societal attitudes and perceptions of pluralism, 1850's-1970's, taking into account historical, cultural, and structural trends, focusing on post-World War II social structure. Relates these trends to the proliferation of new religious movements, asserting that structural conditions have caused individuals to express minority world views not necessarily accepted by the larger social atmosphere, and have fostered a new form of pluralism based on neglect rather than on traditional tolerance.
G. A. Hewlett

2965. Klobus, Patricia A. and Edwards, John N. THE SOCIAL PARTICIPATION OF MINORITIES: A CRITICAL EXAMINATION OF CURRENT THEORIES. *Phylon 1976 37(2): 150-158.* Analyzes four explanations of minority participation: 1) isolationism: the undermotivated; 2) compensation: the overmotivated; 3) ethnic community: the drive for structural assimilation; and 4) cultural inhibition: resistance to cultural assimilation. Finds these explanations too simplistic. It is "necessary to give careful consideration to the sub-populations studies and to display some restraint in trying to apply a global explanation where sub-population variations are evident." 31 notes.
E. P. Stickney

2966. Kolm, Richard. ETHNICITY AND ETHNIC GROUPS: RESEARCH NEEDS. *Int. Migration Rev. 1974 8(1): 59-67.*

2967. Lewis, Herbert S. EUROPEAN ETHNICITY IN WISCONSIN: AN EXPLORATORY FORMULATION. *Ethnicity 1978 5(2): 174-188.* Two overlapping groups, Americans of Northwest European origin and rural Americans, have yet to be studied extensively in terms of their specific ethnicities. Focuses on Wisconsin, where both groups are heavily represented, with this problem in mind. Examines the extent to which people identify with a given European country or even a given locale, the survival of languages and other aspects of each national heritage, the extent (often extremely limited) to which different groups interact, and the survival of distinctive national attitudes on a variety of subjects. Four ethnically distinctive localities (one German, one Norwegian, one Dutch, and one Polish) are studied in detail. Based on the published and unpublished results of field work by other researchers, plus secondary sources; note, 41 ref.
L. W. Van Wyk

2968. Magner, Thomas F. THE RISE AND FALL OF THE ETHNICS. *J. of General Educ. 1974 25(4): 253-264.* Argues that although some social commentators foresee a new surge of ethnic revivalism, "much of the ethnic activity of recent years has been a kind of death spasm and that ethnic groups . . . are now subsiding and disappearing."
S

2969. Morawska, Ewa. KLASOWE CZY ETNICZNE DETERMINANTY ZRÓŻNICOWANIA SPOŁECZEŃSTWA STANÓW ZJEDNOCZONYCH [Class or ethnic determinants of differentiation of society in the United States]. *Kultura i Społeczeństwo [Poland] 1977 21(3): 143-156.* It is impossible to reach any final conclusions of such a young discipline as ethnic studies in the United States at the present time. The great interest in the sources and characteristics of differentiation of sociocultural nature in the United States may bring about a common

theoretical denominator of ethnicity and standardize research materials and the varied methods of analysis.
M. Swiecicka-Ziemianek

2970. Morsell, John A. ETHNIC RELATIONS OF THE FUTURE. *Ann. of the Am. Acad. of Pol. and Social Sci. 1973 408: 83-93.* One of the significant developments of recent years in American life is the birth, or re-birth, of interest in ethnicity. Although the melting pot model of ethnic relations never really implied the disappearance of all traces of ethnic identity, the interests of ethnicity were expected to remain subordinated to those of the community, represented by the nation. Under the stimulus of the Negro revolution of the 1960's, with its accompanying emphasis on racial identity, other ethnic groupings in America have shown signs of increasing discontent with what they regard as the submergence of their ethnic interests. These developments have not only paralleled those in the black community, they are intricately related to them in a complex of interethnic competition for recognition, public attention, and social and economic benefits. The new ethnicity is a source of social tension.
J

2971. Myrdal, Gunnar. THE CASE AGAINST ROMANTIC ETHNICITY. *Center Mag. 1974 7(4): 26-30.* The new ethnicity is a movement of upper-class intellectual romantics whose abstract craving for historical identity avoids the problems of poverty and passivity among ethnic poor. One of six working papers presented at a joint conference of Center Fellows and leaders of the Immigration History Society on ethnicity today.
S

2972. Novak, Michael. ETHNICITY FOR INDIVIDUALS. *Jednota Ann. Furdek 1977 16: 75-84.* One can be an American and maintain the culture and consciousness of an ethnic minority; discusses topics such as cultural pluralism, shared social history, and acculturation without assimilation.

2973. Novak, Michael. HOW AMERICAN ARE YOU IF YOUR GRANDPARENTS CAME FROM SERBIA IN 1888? *Soundings 1973 56(1): 1-20.* Discusses the recent rediscovery of white ethnicity and its societal results.
S

2974. Novak, Michael. THE NEW ETHNICITY. *Center Mag. 1974 7(4): 18-25.* Discusses the political consequences of the new ethnicity, which is defined as the renewed self-consciousness of third- and fourth-generation immigrants. One of six working papers presented at a joint conference of Center Fellows and leaders of the Immigration History Society on ethnicity today.
S

2975. Parente, William J. THE REDISCOVERY OF ETHNICITY BY AMERICAN RADICALISM. *Soundings 1973 56(1): 59-67.* Maintains the so-called "new ethnicity" is not new, but merely rediscovered; pursues political results of white ethnicity such as ethnic voting blocks and Nixonian tactics of the "silent majority" in the 1972 election, and the New Left's use of ethnicity.
S

2976. Parot, Joseph J. UNTHINKABLE THOUGHTS ABOUT UNMELTABLE ETHNICS. *Polish Am. Studies 1974 31(1): 35-42.* Reviews Michael Novak's *The Rise of the Unmeltable Ethnics: Politics and Culture in the Seventies* (New York: Macmillan, 1972). Recognizes the book's place in the historiography of minorities during the 1960's and 1970's, but disagrees with many of its principles and questions the purpose of its publication. Holds a "healthy distrust of any theologian . . . who tackles knotty social questions in the absence of any exacting and rigorous historical analysis." Novak indulges in constant WASP-baiting and favoritism toward the blue-collar, lower-middle-class, white ethnic; according to Novak, WASPs are to give way to the Catholic PIGS (Poles, Italians, Greeks, Slavs). 5 notes.
S. R. Pliska

2977. Pier, Andrew V. THE VANISHING ETHNICS. *Jednota Ann. Furdek 1978 17: 21-23.* Discusses dealing with ethnicity in a pluralistic society; other ethnic groups, if they wish to participate in the national life, should not emulate Indians.

2978. Rubin, Israel. ETHNICITY AND CULTURAL PLURALISM. *Phylon 1975 36(2): 140-148.* Considers whether cultural pluralism is desirable, and whether the actual trend in the United States is toward an ethnically pluralistic society. Concludes that cultural pluralism is desirable, but that it is unlikely that the nation will witness a far-reaching multiple ethnocentric basis for community life. Small pockets of ethnicity will continue. Based on secondary sources; 10 notes.

B. A. Glasrud

2979. Sarna, Jonathan D. FROM IMMIGRANTS TO ETHNICS: TOWARD A NEW THEORY OF "ETHNICIZATION." *Ethnicity 1978 5(4): 370-378.* The American experience created rather than allowed ethnicity among some immigrant groups. When they arrived in America, such groups as the Italians, Jews, and Chinese were sharply divided along national, regional, and even village lines. The American experience tended to meld local and parochial trends into a single unifying ethnicity. In part this emergence of ethnicity was caused by the fact that the majority society labeled all immigrants coming from a particular cultural area in Europe with the same name, e.g. Italians for Sicilians, Calabrians, Neopolitans, etc. The unification into ethnic entities was also caused by immigrant needs to unite against outside antagonism toward them.

N. Lederer

2980. Saxton, Alexander. NATHAN GLAZER, DANIEL MOYNIHAN, AND THE CULT OF ETHNICITY. *Amerasia J. 1977 4(2): 141-150.* Scholarly critics of affirmative action programs, such as Nathan Glazer and Daniel P. Moynihan, are using liberal principles to hinder the exposure and reversal of institutionalized collective racial discrimination. In using the successes of white ethnic groups in middle-class America as models for today's nonwhite minorities, they ignore the pervasive effects of white racism and blame its victims for their own plight. They bypass contrary evidence, slight the works of scholars whose conclusions do not support their own, base their views on "historical misunderstandings," and turn their own pseudo-scholarship to polemic and political purposes. 2 notes.

T. L. Powers

2981. Schermerhorn, R. A. ETHNICITY IN THE PERSPECTIVE OF THE SOCIOLOGY OF KNOWLEDGE. *Ethnicity 1974 1(1): 1-14.* Defines the components of ethnicity and how they vary with time and place. The riots during 1965-67 were a watershed in 20th-century American history. The crisis generated a new ethnicity, a new pluralism, and the nation soon will move toward either polarization or a pluralist alliance. Biblio.

E. R. Barkan

2982. Schooler, Carmi. SERFDOM'S LEGACY: AN ETHNIC CONTINUUM. *Am. J. of Sociol. 1976 81(6): 1265-1286.* The effects of ethnicity appear to occur along a historically determined continuum which reflects the social, legal, economic, and occupational conditions of the European countries from which American ethnic groups emigrated. Ethnic groups with a recent history of serfdom show the intellectual inflexibility, authoritarianism, and pragmatic legalistic morality previously found characteristic of American men working under occupational conditions limiting the individual's opportunity for self-direction. A model emphasizing the effects on ethnic groups' culture of historical conditions restricting the individual's autonomy seems a probable explanation of contemporary ethnic differences.

J

2983. Shostak, Arthur B. ETHNIC REVIVALISM, BLUE-COLLARITES, AND BUNKER'S LAST STAND. *Soundings 1973 56(1): 68-82.* Blue-collar members of the working class may not be assumed to be at the base of the white ethnicity movement, despite the image portrayed by Archie Bunker.

S

2984. Siemieńska, Renata. ZRÓDŁA "BIAŁEGO RUCHU ETNICZNEGO" W STANACH ZJEDNOCZONYCH [The sources of the "White Ethnic Movement" in the United States]. *Kultura i Społeczeństwo [Poland] 1976 20(2): 89-107.* The white ethnic movement of the South, Central and East European groups in the United States in the 1970's is not a movement against the existing socioeconomic system, but a movement supported by the central government as a counterbalance to the growing stronger movements of the colored masses, especially the Negro. The government displays an increasing interest in these white groups which still are characterized by vast differences despite significant changes in their social structure and economic status in the last three decades.

M. Swiecicka-Ziemianek

2985. Smith, Page. FROM MASSES TO PEOPLEHOOD. *Hist. Reflections [Canada] 1974 1(1): 113-138.* Subordinate groups in a society

"assert their humanity" or move from the "masses" to the "people" through self-definition and self-consciousness, not through any efforts of members of the dominant culture. Women and Negroes, the primary examples of this process, are compared to various immigrant and ethnic groups. Subordinate groups seeking to escape from the "masses" have common traits: passionate speech, eccentric and symbolic costume, discipline, violence, and pronounced sexual elements. Secondary sources; 20 notes, French summary.

C. G. Eiel

2986. Stein, Howard F. and Hill, Robert F. THE NEW ETHNICITY AND THE WHITE ETHNIC IN THE UNITED STATES. *Can. Rev. of Studies in Nationalism [Canada] 1973 1(1): 81-105.* In the late 1960's the specific term "ethnic" was adopted by American journalists and intellectuals to denote a particular socioeconomic segment of white America: blue-collar workers, working class people, "the silent majority," "the forgotten Americans," and so on. Within the "new ethnicity," three aspects complement each other: the socioeconomic common denominator, panethnicity as a common cultural denominator, and interethnic separatism and rivalry. A major symptom of the "new ethnicity" is "identity foreclosure," or a defensive rigidification and self-deprecation of ego identity. Emphasizes the behavior, role, and function of blue-collar Slovaks in Pennsylvania. Based on secondary literature and interviews; table, 42 notes.

T. Spira

2987. Stein, Howard F. THE WHITE ETHNIC MOVEMENT, PANISM, AND THE RESTORATION OF EARLY SYMBIOSIS: THE PSYCHOHISTORY OF A GROUP FANTASY. *J. of Psychohistory 1979 6(3): 319-359.* Analyzes the "new ethnicity" movement—the search for ethnic identity among white Americans—from a psychological or "psychohistorical" perspective, arguing that the movement is a regressive process seeking "symbolic fusion with the pregenital mother." The white ethnic movement embraces a disillusionment with the American dream, and an attempt to resurrect an idealized past based on supposed ethnic heritages. That process is interpreted as a group-fantasy of flight from adult responsibility through regression to an earlier world. Based on recent primary sources, personal correspondence, and secondary sources; 71 notes.

R. E. Butchart

2988. Strauss, Herbert A. CHANGING IMAGES OF THE IMMIGRANT IN THE U.S.A. *Amerikastudien/American Studies [West Germany] 1976 21(1): 119-137.* Ethnicity, as a model of identity and social structure and a guide to social policy, is tested as to its potential persistence as an image and model of group behavior by projecting it onto the background of American immigration history since 1740. Examines the concept of acculturation and its aspects in the context of sociological and anthropological research. In contrast to recent trends the author discounts the future relevance of ethnicity as a cultural and social fact of American immigrant life. The traditional push for integration and the social changes supporting it outweigh the social forces favoring ethnicity as a central phenomenon in American society. 29 notes.

G. Bassler

2989. Swierenga, Robert P. ETHNICITY IN HISTORICAL PERSPECTIVE. *Social Sci. 1977 52(1): 31-45.* In the 1960's the long-entrenched, melting-pot ideology in America began to retreat before a new ideal—ethnic pluralism. The lack of historical studies of ethnic diversity, however, hampered social scientists in their efforts to develop theoretical structural models of the nation's institutional system. This article traces assimilationist (majority) and pluralist (minority) ideologies and surveys the significant findings of the new "ethnocultural historians" who have studied change and continuity in ethnic group structure from early colonial times.

J

2990. Valentine, C. A. CLASS AND ETHNICITY, MARXISM AND LUMPENISM: NOTES IN RESPONSE TO A CRITIQUE OF "VOLUNTARY ETHNICITY." *J. of Ethnic Studies 1976 4(3): 53-68.* Emphasizes the Marxian teaching that class and ethnicity are closely intertwined in capitalist societies, and therefore "battles for minority interests should be consistent with rather than opposed to the class struggle." Analyzes the importance of studying the many interethnic revolutions and national liberation struggles of our times and urges that attention to ethnic, national, and racial issues not divert Marxists from working for interethnic unity against oppression. Discusses the implications of the lumpen ideology, outlined by Eldridge Cleaver and others, for today's class struggle. Earlier Marxist definitions of the lumpen "are too narrow and restricted for the realities of our time." The growth of the welfare-bourgeois state, increasing technological unemployment, and the reactionary and racist nature of the organized labor movement point to significantly increasing the size of the lumpen element in humanity. Since socialism is tied to the interests and needs of the organized working class, the rising demands of the lumpenproletariat may require the struggle to advance beyond socialist goals to communist ones. Secondary sources; 25 notes.

G. J. Bobango

2991. Yancey, William L.; Ericksen, Eugene P.; and Juliani, Richard N. EMERGENT ETHNICITY: A REVIEW AND REFORMULATION. *Am. Sociol. Rev. 1976 41(3): 391-403.* This paper is a review and partial reformulation of the sociological literature on the persistence of ethnicity in American society. In contrast to the traditional emphasis on the transplanted cultural heritage as the principal antecedent and defining characteristic of ethnic groups, the development and persistence of ethnicity is dependent upon structural conditions characterizing American cities and position of groups in American social structure. Attention is focused on the question: under what conditions does ethnic culture emerge? Specifically, what social forces promote the crystallization and development of ethnic solidarity and identification? As an emergent phenomenon, ethnicity continues to develop with the changing positions of groups and individuals within society. As society changes, old forms of ethnic culture may die out but new forms may be generated.

J

2992. —. [ETHNICITY AND EDUCATION: PLURALISM AND TRADITION]. *Am. Scholar 1973-74 43(1): 113-132.*
Novak, Michael. ONE SPECIES, MANY CULTURES, *pp. 113-121.* Suggests that "our common culture" is a glib expression and needs reflection. Difficulties arise over a misperception of class and culture, and there is a need for public and popular humanities, a high culture, and professional skills.
Patterson, Orlando. ON GUILT, RELATIVISM AND BLACK-WHITE RELATIONS, *pp. 122-132.* The American Negro is only partly responsible for "creating a viable moral community on the national level, in which he meets other Americans in equal moral terms, and in which he shares equally the obligations and rewards of a great industrial society." White Americans must not act directly on behalf of blacks, but reject ethnicity and return to the cosmopolitan ideal.

C. W. Olson

2993. —. [THE NEW ETHNICITY]. *Foundations 1976 19(3): 223-237.*
Shapiro, Deanne Ruth. THE NEW ETHNICITY: MYTH OR REALITY?, *pp. 223-234.* Divides the treatment of ethnic groups into three areas, 1) the "melting pot," 2) cultural pluralism, and 3) the New Ethnicity. In the present period, the ethnic individual is able to look beyond America for identity. Exponents of the New Ethnicity fail to explore fully the theological influence the new views have on the identities of American ethnics. Suggests several areas where further consideration is necessary by those supporting the new ethnic pluralism. 35 notes.
Handy, Robert T. RESPONSE TO DEANNE RUTH SHAPIRO, *pp. 235-237.* Holds that Baptists support the cultural pluralism suggested. Offenses against ethnic minorities did not come in terms of size or percentages, but rather from considering one's own tradition as being the one to which conformity is expected. Note.

E. E. Eminhizer

Group and Race Relations

2994. Allen, Irving Lewis. WASP—FROM SOCIOLOGICAL CONCEPT TO EPITHET. *Ethnicity 1975 2(2): 153-162.* Examines the etymology of the acronym WASP, standing for White Anglo-Saxon Protestant. The term apparently first came into use during the civil rights movement of the 1960's when minority groups began referring to a nebulous group of persons, perceived as the originators and maintainers of an oppressive society, as WASP's. WASP, however, is a counterproductive term, since within the white race there are so many smaller ethnic groups, that there is neither cultural, economic, nor ethnic homogeneity. Although stereotypes usually originate in some bit of truth, use of the term

WASP to indicate the large ethnic group is meaningless because of the social, economic, and cultural diversity which characterizes it. 6 notes, biblio.

G. A. Hewlett

2995. Barbaro, Fred. ETHNIC RESENTMENT. *Society 1974 11(3): 67-75.* Discusses other minorities' resentment of the blacks' disproportionate share of Kennedy-Johnson antipoverty program money. S

2996. Caditz, Judith. ETHNIC IDENTIFICATION, INTERETHNIC CONTACT, AND BELIEF IN INTEGRATION. *Social Forces 1976 54(3): 632-645.* Analyzes some factors related to ambivalence toward ethnic integration among a segment of white liberals. Drawing from the sociological literature on ethnic identification, interethnic contact, ethnocentrism, and the cosmopolitan-local typology, we test and find support for several hypotheses. Tests are based on interviews with members of an organization which supports civil rights and whose members, Protestants and Jews, are well above national mean ranks in education, occupation, and income. When status concerns and central values of ethnic groups are threatened, people become ambivalent about integration. "Localistic embeddedness" is a major correlate of ambivalence.

J

2997. Cummings, Scott. RACIAL PREJUDICE AND POLITICAL ORIENTATIONS AMONG BLUE-COLLAR WORKERS. *Social Sci. Q. 1977 57(4): 907-920.* Under certain economic conditions and contrary to neo-Marxist theory, racial prejudice is a manifestation of, rather than an obstacle to, white working class militancy. Analyzes recent survey data that measure prejudice toward blacks and three types of political orientation. Union affiliation, region of the country, and craft versus noncraft occupations were control variables. Historical evidence from early industrial development in the United States supports the conclusions drawn from these data and suggests several reasons why there is no systematic connection between racial prejudice, class militancy, and efforts to organize. Based on data from the 1972 Survey Research Center's national election survey and secondary sources; 2 tables, 6 notes, biblio.

W. R. Hively

2998. Glazer, Nathan. LIBERTY, EQUALITY, FRATERNITY AND ETHNICITY. *Daedalus 1976 105(4): 115-127.* The achievement of equality in a multiethnic society has proved more difficult than the civil rights legislation of the 1960's or public opinion anticipated. Equality of opportunity and treatment do not automatically lead to an equal outcome for all. Moreover, differences tolerated within a specific racial or ethnic group are inadmissible when used to suggest why one group may be doing better than another. There is a danger of Balkanization if groups demand special treatment on the basis of present or past alleged discrimination. Secondary sources; 12 notes.

E. McCarthy

2999. Greeley, Andrew M. ETHNICITY AND RACIAL ATTITUDES: THE CASE OF THE JEWS AND THE POLES. *Am. J. of Sociol. 1975 80(4): 909-933.* Data from a 1968 survey drawn from the population of 15 US cities that had experienced racial unrest revealed that Polish Americans were the least sympathetic to black militancy, the Jews the most sympathetic.

S

3000. Handlin, Oscar. NATIONHOOD AND ETHNICITY: AN AMERICAN DILEMMA. *Cultures [France] 1978 5(2): 151-164.* Discusses the dichotomy between nationhood and ethnicity in the United States and the resultant tensions and divisions in American society, by citing developments in intergroup relations since 1957.

3001. Horowitz, Irving Louis. RACE, CLASS AND THE NEW ETHNICITY. *Worldview 1975 18(1): 46-53.* Analyzes attitudes of working class ethnic groups toward blacks, religion, Jews, and the class structure, and discusses their increasing conservativism and potential for political power, 1974.

3002. Jackson, Agnes Moreland. TO SEE THE "ME" IN "THEE": CHALLENGE TO ALL WHITE AMERICANS; OR, WHITE ETHNICITY FROM A BLACK PERSPECTIVE AND A SOMETIMES RESPONSE TO MICHAEL NOVAK. *Soundings 1973 56(1): 21-44.* A black view of white ethnicity during the 1970's maintains that it is based on racism.

S

3003. Lavender, Abraham D. and Forsyth, John M. THE SOCIO-LOGICAL STUDY OF MINORITY GROUPS AS REFLECTED BY LEADING SOCIOLOGICAL JOURNALS: WHO GETS STUDIED AND WHO GETS NEGLECTED? *Ethnicity 1976 3(4): 388-398.* Sociologists' tendency to equate ethnic studies with minority studies has emphasized race relations but not intergroup relations, resulting in little coverage and understanding of interethnic relations. Interethnic studies are needed because ethnics comprise much of the populace, much black-white interaction is often black-ethnic white, and many conflicts within the United States have been interethnic. There is dominant society-ethnic group conflict currently, and ethnics are often the oppressed. Ethnicity needs to be discussed as a positive force, and scholarly work must transcend the descriptive and enter the analytic. G. A. Hewlett

3004. Lichten, Joseph L. POLISH AMERICANS AND AMERI-CAN JEWS: SOME ISSUES WHICH UNITE AND DIVIDE. *Polish Rev. 1973 18(4): 52-62.* Read at a conference (in Chicago, 1970) on Polish American-Jewish community relations. S

3005. Perlmutter, Philip. INTERGROUP RELATIONS TODAY: NO CASE FOR THE PESSIMIST. *J. of Intergroup Relations 1973 2(4): 21-26.* Argues that current relations among racial, religious, and ethnic groups are improving. S

3006. Ravitch, Diane. THE EVOLUTION OF SCHOOL DESEG-REGATION POLICY: 1964-1978. *Hist. of Educ. [Great Britain] 1978 7(3): 229-236.* Examines the changing nature of school desegregation in America since the early 1960's, noting the remarkable advances made, but also pointing out emerging complications. Black consciousness and resulting social transformations have strengthened other kinds of ethnic consciousness, thereby creating a new impediment to the realization of a culturally and ethnically integrated America. 10 notes. S

3007. Schlozman, Kay Lehman. HARD HATS AND ETHNICS HAVE TAKEN A BUM RAP: PUBLIC OPINION AND YOUTH DISSENT. *Ethnicity 1977 4(1): 71-89.* Exploration of attitudes of skilled laborers ("hard-hats") and ethnic groups shows that no actual correlation can be found to support stereotypes that these groups are any more against youth protest (both political and cultural) than other groups. Statistics point out that no visible differences may be found between blue- and white-collar workers or between southern and eastern European ethnic groups and WASPs. Some indication is made for rural persons, those of limited education, whites, and aged persons being

against youth protest. Ethnic groups and hard-hats are no more bigoted than any other white Americans. Covers the 1960's.
G. A. Hewlett

3008. Tate, Eugene D. and Surlin, Stuart H. AGREEMENT WITH OPINIONATED TV CHARACTERS ACROSS CULTURES. *Journalism Q. 1976 53(2): 199-203.* Uses survey research techniques to show that Canadian adults find less humor and realism in the television show *All in the Family* than US adults. Both American and Canadian adults exhibiting high levels of dogmatism agree significantly more with the views of Archie Bunker. Concludes that people in a foreign culture identify more with an opinionated TV character when they possess the same social and psychological characteristics. The results are based on surveys of 276 adults each in Athens, Georgia, and in Saskatoon, Saskatchewan. 2 tables, 14 notes. E. Gibson

3009. Van Dyke, Vernon. HUMAN RIGHTS AND THE RIGHTS OF GROUPS. *Am. J. of Pol. Sci. 1974 18(4): 725-742.* Discusses the possibility for discrimination and denial of equality when human (individual) rights are subsumed below those accorded to particular ethnic, linguistic, and religious groups.

3010. Vidmar, Neil and Rokeach, Milton. ARCHIE BUNKER'S BIGOTRY: A STUDY IN SELECTIVE PERCEPTION AND EXPO-SURE. *J. of Communication 1974 24(1): 36-47.* Questions whether television's "All in the Family" reinforces or reduces racial and ethnic prejudice. S

3011. Vincent, Joan. THE STRUCTURING OF ETHNICITY. *Human Organization 1974 33(4): 375-379.* Examines the need for precise term definitions for minorities and ethnic groups in sociological studies of intergroup relations. S

3012. —. [CONFERENCE ISSUE]. *J. of Intergroup Relations 1973 2(3): 3-141.* Includes papers written for the conference of the National Association of Intergroup Relations Officials by a distinguished group of authors representing several social groups, including American Indians, Asians, Jews, the poor, women, Spanish-speaking peoples, citizens' lobbies, and blue collar workers. The papers deal with the issues of mass media, government relations, coalitions, group differences, ethnic renaissance, and social revolution. F. F. Harling

CANADA

6. HISTORIOGRAPHY, SOURCES, AND GENERAL STUDIES

3013. Artibise, Alan F. J. PATTERNS OF POPULATION GROWTH AND ETHNIC RELATIONSHIPS IN WINNIPEG, 1874-1974. *Social Hist. [Canada] 1976 9(18): 297-335.* Winnipeg's population growth can be divided into five major periods during 1874-1974. During the formative years, 1874-99, Anglo-Canadian migration set the enduring character and tone of Winnipeg society. During 1900-13, the population more than tripled because of an influx of Slavic and Jewish immigrants. Anglo-Canadians expressed bigotry toward the immigrants and used the schools in an attempt to Anglicize them. During 1914-20, ethnic conflict escalated and left social scars that took decades to heal. After 1921 the growth rate slowed and Winnipegers searched for ways to create more harmonious relationships between ethnic groups. After 1960, a period of stability and maintenance of earlier trends can be identified. Based on newspapers, other primary sources, and secondary sources; 2 maps, 12 tables, 96 notes. W. K. Hobson

3014. Breton, Raymond; Burnet, Jean; Hartmann, Norbert; Isajiw, Wsevolod; and Lennards, Jos. RESEARCH ISSUES ON CANADIAN CULTURES AND ETHNIC GROUPS: AN ANALYSIS OF A CONFERENCE. *Can. Rev. of Sociol. and Anthrop. 1975 12(1): 81-94.* Synopsis of discussions on Canadian ethnic groups at the National Conference on Canadian Culture and Ethnic Groups in Canada, October 1973, including ethnicity and stratification, prestige, social class, pluralism, ethnic boundaries, immigration, and generational differences.

3015. Driedger, Leo. IN SEARCH OF CULTURAL IDENTITY FACTORS: A COMPARISON OF ETHNIC STUDENTS. *Can. R. of Sociol. and Anthrop. 1975 12(2): 150-162.* Factor analysis of Likert-type items administered to undergraduate students suggests that modes of ethnic identification can be described in terms of six factors: religion, endogamy, language use, ethnic organizations, parochial education, and choice of ingroup friends. A comparison of the factor profiles of seven ethnic groups revealed considerable variations. For example, the Jewish students identified strongly with endogamy and ingroup choice of friends but ranked low on the importance of religion and the use of their ethnic language. The French students' identification with their language and religion was high. Both the French and the Jewish students valued parochial education. Scandinavian and Polish ethnic ingroup identification was the lowest of all seven groups compared. The modes of identification tended to vary with the historically important experiences of ethnic groups. Therefore the measures of the modes exhibited a multifactor structure. J

3016. Ervin, Linda and Bogusis, Ruth. COLLECTIONS OF ETHNIC CANADIANA AT THE NATIONAL LIBRARY OF CANADA: THE ETHNIC SERIALS PROJECT. *Serials Librarian 1977 1(4): 331-336.* The Ethnic Serials Project was undertaken by the National Library of Canada to preserve and make available all ethnic newspapers and to promote national appreciation and knowledge of ethnic groups in Canada, 18c-20c.

3017. Frideres, J. S. and Goldenberg, Sheldon. HYPHENATED CANADIANS: COMPARATIVE ANALYSIS OF ETHNIC, REGIONAL AND NATIONAL IDENTIFICATION OF WESTERN CANADIAN UNIVERSITY STUDENTS. *J. of Ethnic Studies 1977 5(2): 91-100.* Notes the problematic nature of the concept of identity and its systematic relationship to other structural and contextual features. Relates this to the upsurge of interest in ethnic identity in Canada in recent years and the official policy of multiculturalism. Urges social scientists to pay greater attention to these phenomena. Reports the results of a questionnaire survey of 213 native born and naturalized Canadian students as to their levels of ethnic, regional, and national identity consciousness. Results display high national identification, slightly lower regional identity, and very low ethnic identity. Possible social and psychological factors such as age, sex, father's occupation, residential mobility seem to have no significant bearing on the intensity or salience patterns of the three dimensions of identity. Some sense of unified Canadian

history is therefore emerging, although in the West it must compete with a high regional identity; or, perhaps, ethnic oriented youths do not attend universities. Primary sources; 2 tables, fig., 3 notes.
G. J. Bobango

3018. Hanham, H. J. CANADIAN HISTORY IN THE 1970'S. *Can. Hist. Rev. [Canada] 1977 58(1): 1-22.* Surveys recent literature about the history of Canada, especially major works published during 1970-76 in French or English. Emphasizes the growing preoccupation with economic and social history, and the special strengths of French-Canadian historiography. Suggests areas for further research in Canadian-American relations, the history of the Catholic Church in Quebec, economic, labor, and urban history. A

3019. Jackson, Robin. DEVELOPMENT OF THE MULTICULTURAL POLICY IN CANADA, A BIBLIOGRAPHY. *Can. Lib. J. [Canada] 1976 33(3): 237-243.* This annotated bibliography lists works published during 1967-76 that trace the development of Canadian multicultural policy, government programs, provincial initiatives, and non-governmental evaluations of the policy. L. F. Johnson

3020. Jenness, R. A. CANADIAN MIGRATION AND IMMIGRATION PATTERNS AND GOVERNMENT POLICY. *Internat. Migration Rev. 1974 8(1): 5-22.*

3021. Jones, Frank E. CURRENT SOCIOLOGICAL RESEARCH IN CANADA: VIEWS OF A JOURNAL EDITOR. *J. of the Hist. of the Behavioral Sci. 1977 13(2): 160-172.* Sociology in Canada, 1960's-70's, has focused on studies of social problems in an empirical and a theoretical context; discusses ethnic studies and immigrant adjustment.

3022. Kelly, John J. ALTERNATIVE ESTIMATES OF THE VOLUME OF EMIGRATION FROM CANADA, 1961-1971. *Can. Rev. of Sociol. and Anthrop. [Canada] 1977 14(1): 57-67.* The contribution of immigration to Canada's population growth has received considerable analytical attention. However, much less is known about the impact which emigration has had on the nation's population growth, particularly since actual data are not available on the number of persons emigrating from Canada. This paper presents three different emigration estimates for Canada for the 1961-71 intercensal period derived from different estimation procedures, endeavors to determine which estimate is the most reliable one, and demonstrates the importance of considering emigration in the continuing reformulation of Canada's immigration policies. J

3023. Laforce, Ernest. IMMIGRATION ET IMMIGRANTS [Immigration and immigrants]. *Action Natl. [Canada] 1978 67(7): 547-558.* Canadian immigration policy has continued as an instrument of repression against French Canadian society. To counter the possible French majority in the province of Manitoba, John A. MacDonald actively recruited immigrants from Europe, Asia, and Africa who would become part of a dominant British culture, ensuring its preponderance in western Canada. After the election of 1896, with the appointment of Clifford Sifton as minister of immigration, the rate of new arrivals passed 500,000 per year. Thus, despite a strong birthrate, French Canadians remained a perpetual minority. A. W. Novitsky

3024. Landy, Sarah. THE CULTURAL MOSAIC: SOME PSYCHOLOGICAL IMPLICATIONS. *Can. Lib. J. [Canada] 1976 33(3): 245-247.* Urges more psychological analyses of relations between immigrants and receiving societies. Aspects of the relations include alienation, ambiguity, loss of status, and residential alienation; at the same time, attachment and amalgamation with the new society occur. In societies demanding too early or too thorough assimilation, migrants exhibit psychological regression, behavioral breakdown, and psychopathological difficulties. Multiculturalism attempts to allow the individual to integrate at his own pace, to retain his uniqueness, and to appreciate his own and other cultures. Implications are drawn for libraries serving multicultural groups. 11 notes. L. F. Johnson

3025. LaRose, André. BIBLIOGRAPHIE COURANTE SUR L'HISTOIRE DE LA POPULATION CANADIENNE ET LA DÉMOGRAPHIE HISTORIQUE AU CANADA, 1977 [A current bibliography on the history of Canadian population and historical demography in Canada, 1977]. *Social Hist. [Canada] 1979 12(23): 192-197.* An annotated bibliography, compiled on behalf of the International Union for the Scientific Study of Population (Lieges), and the Society of Historical Demography (Paris). Lists 1977 publications on the history of Canadian population.   D. F. Chard

3026. Neutell, Walter. NATIONAL ETHNIC ARCHIVES. *Can. Lib. J. [Canada] 1976 33(5): 435-436.* Canada's archival repositories have largely neglected ethnic records. The 1971 multiculturalism policy placed increased emphasis on ethnic archives and initiated a project to collect records and papers from organizations and persons of other than English or French backgrounds who have had broad impact on their communities or on Canadian society.   L. F. Johnson

3027. Parenteau, Roland. L'INFLUENCE DE L'ESPACE SUR LA VIE CANADIENNE [The influence of space on Canadian life]. *Tr. of the Royal Soc. of Can. [Canada] 1976 14: 123-125.* Canada's large size and small population has greatly influenced Canadian life. It has encouraged the development of regional peculiarities which probably needed no extra incentives since Canada's multitude of ethnic groups had already given the provinces a plethora of peculiarities. Although Canada has cut its umbilical cord with Great Britain, British influence is still great in Canada. Many postwar actions of the Canadian government reflected policies of the British government. American influence has increased largely because of geographical influences. Although Canada is a horizontal country, East-West, its lines of communication are vertical, North-South. New York and Boston are as close to Montreal as is Toronto, and closer than Winnipeg, Vancouver, or Halifax.   J. D. Neville

3028. Prang, Margaret. NATIONAL UNITY AND THE USES OF HISTORY. *Can. Hist. Assoc. Hist. Papers [Canada] 1977: 2-12.* Reassesses the historian's function in relation to the national culture and the sense of community. There has been a tendency to turn away from national themes and to reflect the "contemporary realities" which highlight "fragmentation, dissension, and the growth of regional consciousness," exploring regional and local history. A review of contemporary Canadian studies, however, helps us to realize that even the specialized and limited can in the long run be "compatible with the central traditions of Canadian historiography" and can contribute to a much broader, yet genuine national spirit. 21 notes.   R. V. Ritter

3029. Rakhmanny, Roman. THE CANADIAN OPTION FOR 1975 AND BEYOND: UNITY THROUGH DIVERSITY. *Ukrainian Q. 1974 30(2): 151-165.* Discusses the role of minorities in Canada, particularly French Canadians and Ukrainians.   S

3030. Rawlyk, G. A. J. B. BREBNER AND *THE WRITING OF CANADIAN HISTORY. J. of Can. Studies [Canada] 1978 13(3): 84-93.* Review article prompted by Carl Berger, *The Writing of Canadian History: Aspects of English-Canadian Historical Writing: 1900-1970* (Toronto, 1976). Berger's tends to ignore the Maritime Provinces, and in particular to underestimate the stature of J. B. Brebner, who wrote two highly influential works on the history of Nova Scotia, covering the 150 years up to 1783. Disagrees with some of Brebner's ideas, such as that New England influence was largely responsible for the expulsion (1755) of the Acadians, but describes him as one of the few with a genuine international reputation. 37 notes.   L. W. Van Wyk

3031. Richmond, Anthony H. and Verma, Ravi P. THE ECONOMIC ADAPTATION OF IMMIGRANTS: A NEW THEORETICAL PERSPECTIVE. *Int. Migration Rev. 1978 12(1): 3-38.* Compares classical "functionalist" migration theories with neo-Marxian models, and finds both inadequate to explain international trends in migration and the Canadian experience of immigration since World War II. Advances an alternative "global systems model" of international and internal migration which takes into account the movements within and between industrial and postindustrial societies, as well as movements from less developed to more developed areas. The most mobile sections of the population will continue to be those with higher education, professional and technical skills, or managerial experience.   C. Moody

3032. Richmond, Anthony H. LANGUAGE, ETHNICITY, AND THE PROBLEM OF IDENTITY IN A CANADIAN METROPOLIS. *Ethnicity 1974 1(2): 175-206.* Discusses a central Canadian problem, cultural diversity and national identity, and determines types of self-identification among a Toronto sample from 1970. The analysis focuses on competing identifications, the influence of age at time of arrival and length of residence in Canada, the effects of status and mobility, attitudes toward Canadian society, and the relationship of language to identification. Age, language, mobility, and length of residence are critical factors. 20 tables, biblio.   E. Barkan

3033. Rubinoff, Lionel. NATIONALISM AND CELEBRATION: REFLECTIONS ON THE SOURCES OF CANADIAN IDENTITY. *Queen's Q. [Canada] 1975 82(1): 1-13.* Examines nationalism in a Canadian context from the viewpoint that it is intimately connected with economic and political interests. Because nationalism is already becoming an outdated concept, argues that the diversity of the Canadian cultural traditions which has led to the development of a Canadian consciousness should be a cause for celebration. 13 notes.   J. A. Casada

3034. Schroeter, Gerd. IN SEARCH OF ETHNICITY: MULTICULTURALISM IN CANADA. *J. of Ethnic Studies 1978 6(1): 98-107.* Discusses the historiography of the "new ethnicity' and problems of definition, while viewing the "policy" of multiculturalism in Canada today as fraught with contradictions. Reviews the first three volumes of the federally commissioned *Generations: A History of Canada's Peoples,* viz., Anderson and Higgs's *A Future to Inherit: The Portuguese Communities of Canada,* Radecki's *A Member of a Distinguished Family: The Polish Group in Canada,* and W. Stanford Reid, ed., *The Scottish Tradition in Canada.* All are valuable contributions which will remain standard sources, and all point to the conclusion, "there is no indication that a neo-ethnicity, of the sort described by Novak or Glazer and Moynihan, is developing in Canada." Schroeter suggests ethnicity may be largely a statistical artifact arising from censuses, or merely the exploitation of government support for "cultural" programs. Secondary sources; 30 notes.   G. J. Bobango

3035. Simeon, Richard. REGIONALISM AND CANADIAN POLITICAL INSTITUTIONS. *Queen's Q. [Canada] 1975 82(4): 499-511.* "The regionalized character of Canadian politics . . . is not only a function of the territorial character of our underlying ethnic, economic and cultural diversity, but also, perhaps more important, a result of the operation of three major institutional characteristics of Canadian Government: the federal system, the electoral system and British-style cabinet." These political institutions reinforce the territorial dimensions of politics and minimize nonregional, national cleavages. 6 notes.   T. Simmerman

3036. Stegner, Wallace. LETTER FROM CANADA. *Am. West 1974 11(1): 28-30.* Finds that the current search for Canadian national identity is similar to past preoccupations with regionalism south of the border, particularly in the American West. The parallels are striking and numerous. The common effort to define Canadian identity is fraught, however, with the basic contradictions posed by regionalism and ethnicity —the intractable French Canada-English Canada division, and the ethnic "vertical mosaic" instead of the melting pot.   D. L. Smith

3037. Stokesbury, James L. HISTORY OF CANADA. *British Heritage [Great Britain] 1979-80 1(1): 11-22, (2): 24-37, (3): 32-41, 44-46.* Part I. Discusses Canadian history as initially shaped in spite of geography, from prehistory to the Vikings' landings to French and British exploration, colonization, and war during the 16th and 17th centuries. Part II. Traces the French and British contest for control of Canada, 1715-59. Part III. Discusses Canada as part of the British Empire, 1763-1817. Article to be continued.

3038. Tishkov, V. A. OSNOVNYE NAPRAVLENIIA SOVREMENNOI KANADSKOI ISTORIOGRAFII (OBZOR NOVEISHIKH ISSLEDOVANII) [Basic tendencies of contemporary Canadian historiography: a survey of the latest researches]. *Novaia i Noveishaia Istoriia [USSR] 1977 (2): 166-180.* A summary of the vast increase in research, publishing, and government funding for history leads into a discussion of English and French Canadian historiography. Works from the 1930's through the 1970's are included. Political, economic, social, and international aspects are covered, with indications as to new trends in interpretation. The present crisis in Canadian historiography reflects the crisis of bourgeois-monopolistic capitalism and the critical state of race relations. Stemming from neopositivist conceptions and philosophical idealism, Canadian historiography suffers from the lack of an overall basic conception which would enable it to treat the material and spiritual sides of history and the role of class relationships in an adequate manner. However, there are trends toward seeing history as a law-determined process. 73 notes.   D. N. Collins

3039.   Tremblay, Marc-Adelard.   ESPACES GÉOGRAPHIQUES ET DISTANCE CULTURELLE: ESSAI DE DEFINITION DU FONDEMENT DES MENTALITÉS REGIONALES AU QUEBEC   [Geographical space and cultural distance: essay on the definition of the cause of regionalism in Quebec]. *Tr. of the Royal Soc. of Can. [Canada] 1976 14: 131-147.* Questions the influence of space on the Canadian and Quebecois mentalities. Canada is made up of many diverse ethnic groups each settled in its own region. The railroad changed Canadians' view of space and brought more cultural interaction. Canada is multicultural with four main geographical regions: the west coast, the Prairies, the central region, and the Atlantic region. Notes Alfred Kroeber's studies concerning ethnic groups. The spaces are too vast and culture too heterogeneous to make valid studies in all cases. Studies the effect of space on French Canadians and discusses the impact of urbanization on areas such as Quebec. 4 notes, biblio.   J. D. Neville

3040.   Wertheimer, Leonard.   MULTICULTURALISM AND PUBLIC LIBRARIES.   *Can. Lib. J. 1973 30(3): 243-245.*

3041.   Yuzyk, Paul.   THE NEW CANADIAN CONSTITUTION AND THE RIGHTS OF ETHNIC GROUPS.   *Ukrainian Rev. [Great Britain] 1973 20(1): 85-94.* Discusses the need for a new Constitution for Canada and the importance of insuring the rights of non-English, non-French ethnic groups (1972).   S

3042.   Zielinska, Marie F.   MULTICULTURALISM: THE IDEA BEHIND THE POLICY.   *Can. Lib. J. [Canada] 1976 33(3): 223-225.* A selection of quotations providing definitions of multiculturalism and insights into Canadian multiculturalism policy. 10 notes.
                                    L. F. Johnson

3043.   —.   CANADA.   *Américas (Organization of Am. States) 1974 26(11-12): Supplement 1-32.* Overview of the history, geography, cities, customs, agriculture, industry, ethnic groups, and government of Canada, prehistory-1974.

7. SETTLEMENT AND COMMUNITY STUDIES

3044. Driedger, Leo and Church, Glenn. RESIDENTIAL SEGRE-GATION AND INSTITUTIONAL COMPLETENESS: A COMPARISON OF ETHNIC MINORITIES. *Can. R. of Sociol. and Anthrop.* 1974 11(1): 30-52. The importance of residential segregation for the maintenance of institutional completeness is clearly demonstrated by this study of six ethnic groups in Winnipeg. The French community maintainers follow Joy's Quebec core area pattern in St. Boniface with extensions of their ethnic belt adjacent to the ore and extensive intra-area mobility. On the other hand, the Scandinavians were never able to establish a very complete ethnic institutional base in a segregated ecological area, so they scattered as assimilationists would predict. Contrary to Joy's prediction, extensive Jewish mobility into their West Kildonan and River Heights suburban extended belt areas resulted in the establishment of two new segregated Jewish communities where they have created new complexes of ethnic institutions, leaving the original North End Jewish core area almost entirely. J

3045. England, Robert. ETHNIC SETTLERS IN WESTERN CANADA: REMINISCENCES OF A PIONEER. *Can. Ethnic Studies [Canada]* 1976 8(2): 18-33. A personal account by a Canadian businessman, teacher, and government official, of 50 years of involvement in ethnic settlement in Western Canada, starting in the early 1920's.

3046. Harney, Robert F. and Troper, Harold. INTRODUCTION [TO AN ISSUE ON IMMIGRANTS IN THE CITY]. *Can. Ethnic Studies [Canada]* 1977 9(1): 1-5. Seeking to offer broader perspectives than the Anglo-Celtic political historian's approach to urban studies, this issue analyzes 19th- and 20th-century Toronto through its immigrant communities. The eight contributors, using a variety of nontraditional sources (demotic and oral), examine tensions along ethnic boundaries. They conclude that immigrants who encountered overt hostility to their urban settlement reluctantly identified themselves, personally and economically, by their Canadian "caretakers' " stereotypes. This ethnocultural research provides a new and "more honest" dimension in urban history. K. S. McDorman

3047. Harney, R. F. THE NEW CANADIANS AND THEIR LIFE IN TORONTO. *Can. Geographical J. [Canada]* 1978 96(2): 20-27. Discusses the influx of immigrants from Spain, Portugal, Hungary, Germany, Greece, Yugoslavia, Korea, France, and the United Kingdom, 1950's-70's and their acculturation in Toronto.

3048. Inglis, R. E. LOCHABER: A TYPICAL RURAL COMMUNITY. *Nova Scotia Hist. Soc. Collections [Canada]* 1977 39: 89-106. History of Lochaber, Nova Scotia, 1830-1972, including immigration, churches, schools, and industries.

3049. Landry, Dollard. LA NATURE ET LES CAUSES DES DISPARITES SOCIO-ECONOMIQUES SUR LE TERRITOIRE ACADIEN [The nature and the causes of socioeconomic disparities in the Acadian territory]. *Tr. of the Royal Soc. of Can. [Canada]* 1977 15: 169-195. Discusses the economy of Acadia noting the difficulties in making such a study. Explains economic circumstances of the area, i.e. a largely rural, undeveloped area with a stagnant economy. Emigration has been great. Notes the different types of employment in the area and discusses the distribution of English-speaking and French-speaking elements of the population. Makes several hypotheses concerning degrees of urbanization, population, employment, women, and ethnicity. 25 tables. J. D. Neville

3050. Larouche, Fernand. L'IMMIGRANT DANS UNE VILLE MINIÈRE: UNE ÉTUDE DE L'INTERACTION [The immigrant in a mining city: A study of interaction]. *Recherches Sociographiques [Canada]* 1973 14(2): 203-228. Three descriptive portraits of workers in a northern Quebec mining community. The immigrant worker prefers to assimilate himself into the English-speaking milieu rather than the French-speaking, because the former appears to offer greater consistency and stability. Secondary sources augmented with on-site field work. A. E. LeBlanc

3051. Little, J. I. THE SOCIAL AND ECONOMIC DEVELOPMENT OF SETTLERS IN TWO QUEBEC TOWNSHIPS, 1851-1870. *Can. Papers in Rural Hist.* 1978 1: 89-113. During 1851-70 there were many changes in Quebec's agriculture, as can be seen in a study of Compton Township and the more rural Winslow Township. In this period the English-speaking farmers prospered primarily because they tended to consolidate landholdings in one branch of the family, while the French Canadians tended to divide lands among the family members. French Canadians were much more reluctant to emigrate to the more productive lands of the West than were the English Canadians. The English and Scots accepted changing patterns of agricultural production more readily, while the French settlers identified their particular and, as it turned out, inefficient agricultural systems with their cultural identity, thereby forcing themselves to adhere to outdated techniques. 28 notes, 6 appendixes. J. W. Leedom

3052. McCracken, Jane. YORKTON DURING THE TERRITORIAL PERIOD, 1882-1905. *Saskatchewan Hist. [Canada]* 1975 28(3): 95-110. Discusses the importance of Canadian national policy in the settlement and economic growth of Yorkton, Saskatchewan, and specifically the effects of colonization companies and the extension of the Manitoba and North Western Railways lines. Map, 3 photos, 25 notes.

3053. Melnyk, George. WINNIPEG REVISITED: NOTES OF AN IMMIGRANT SON. *Can. Dimension [Canada]* 1977 12(4-5): 31, 34-35. The author discusses his impressions of Winnipeg, Manitoba; he moved there as an immigrant in 1949.

3054. Norton, William. THE PROCESS OF RURAL LAND OCCUPATION IN UPPER CANADA. *Scottish Geographical Mag. [Great Britain]* 1975 91(3): 145-152. The location decisions of settlers to Upper Canada, 1782-1851, are related to several factors. Initial settlement cores resulted from the previous pattern of French occupation and the need to strengthen the border with the United States. The availability of surveyed land influenced location decisions throughout the period. Of less significance were the land-granting procedure and the various official policies which prompted land speculation and resulted in areas of reserved land. J

3055. Richtik, James M. THE POLICY FRAMEWORK FOR SETTLING THE CANADIAN WEST, 1870-1880. *Agric. Hist.* 1975 49(4): 613-628. To compete with the free land for homesteading available on the American frontier, Canada implemented government policy decisions designed to make settlement on the Prairie Provinces more desirable than settlement further to the south. More generous to the railroad, the Canadian government withheld land for large groups of immigrants and revised the grid system of settlement to make land in Canada more attractive than land in the United States. Based on primary and secondary sources; 48 notes. R. T. Fulton

3056. Troper, Harold. IMAGES OF THE "FOREIGNER" IN TORONTO, 1900-1930: A REPORT. *Urban Hist. Rev. [Canada]* 1975 (2): 1-8. Describes a 1974 archival project to assemble photographs of early immigrants in Ontario, 1900-30.

3057. Walker, Gerald. HOW HOLLAND MARSH COMMUNITY DEVELOPED. *Can. Geographical J.* 1976 93(1): 42-49. Discusses the settlement of Holland Marsh by foreign ethnic groups, 1930's-76, which remains one of the true rural settlements in southern Ontario.

8. THE RESPONSE TO IMMIGRATION

3058. Appleblatt, Anthony. THE SCHOOL QUESTION IN THE 1929 SASKATCHEWAN ELECTION. *Study Sessions: Can. Catholic Hist. Assoc. [Canada] 1976 43: 75-90.* Summarizes the historical background of the school question in the 1929 provincial election, examines the impact and implications of separate school legislation in Saskatchewan, and outlines and analyzes the issues, especially heated Ku Klux Klan anti-Catholicism and campaigning.

3059. Baker, William M. SQUELCHING THE DISLOYAL, FENIAN-SYMPATHIZING BROOD: T. W. ANGLIN AND CONFEDERATION IN NEW BRUNSWICK, 1865-6. *Can. Hist. Rev. 1974 55(2): 141-158.* Examines the nature of the "loyalty" issue which was a major contributor to the victory of the pro-Confederation forces in New Brunswick in 1866. Concludes that the loyalty issue involved an anti-Catholic campaign which utilized the Fenian scare and directed itself against the prominent anti-Confederate and lay leader of New Brunswick Catholics, Timothy W. Anglin. S

3060. Calderwood, William. RELIGIOUS REACTIONS TO THE KU KLUX KLAN IN SASKATCHEWAN. *Saskatchewan Hist. 1973 26(3): 103-114.* By 1926 the Ku Klux Klan was organized in most of the Canadian provinces. It fed on long-standing prejudices, but never had spectacular success. Its greatest impact was felt in Saskatchewan in 1927-30 where the prominent political issues of language, sectarianism, immigration, and control of natural resources could all be associated with a "Catholic plot." Evidence is strong that many conservative Protestants embraced and supported the principles of the KKK. 57 notes.
D. L. Smith

3061. Chapman, Terry L. EARLY EUGENICS MOVEMENT IN WESTERN CANADA. *Alberta Hist. [Canada] 1977 25(4): 9-17.* Following the impact of heavy immigration from southern and eastern Europe in the early 1900's, Canadian officials and the press began to examine the possibility of eugenics. Traces immigration history, as well as forces for control. James S. Woodsworth, prominent mission official of Winnipeg, pushed for popular acceptance of eugenics policies. Convinced that recent immigrants had more than a reasonable share of vices, the Alberta legislature in 1928 passed an Act of Sexual Sterilization, the first such law in western Canada. 61 notes.
D. Chaput

3062. Corbet, Elise A. WOMAN'S CANADIAN CLUB OF CALGARY. *Alberta Hist. [Canada] 1977 25(3): 29-36.* The Woman's Canadian Club of Calgary was founded in 1911 as part of the elitism prominent at the turn of the century. Prior to World War I, the group was active in community affairs and patriotic activities. During the war, the club's efforts supported defense efforts. In postwar years, the group emphasized nationalism, integrating immigrants, and encouraging music and the arts. By the end of the 1920's, the group primarily was concerned with fostering a Canadian identity. Based on executive minutes and other organizational sources; 2 illus., 43 notes.
D. Chaput

3063. Decarie, M. G. PAVED WITH GOOD INTENTIONS: THE PROHIBITIONISTS' ROAD TO RACISM IN ONTARIO. *Ontario Hist. [Canada] 1974 66(1): 15-.* Examines the prohibition movement in the late 19th century in Ontario and its effect on other aspects of reform. Traces the logic of prohibition (as distinct from temperance) from stereotyping users of alcohol to racism. 20 notes.
W. B. Whitham/S

3064. Dobell, Peter and d'Aquino, Susan. THE SPECIAL JOINT COMMITTEE ON IMMIGRATION POLICY 1975: AN EXERCISE IN PARTICIPATORY DEMOCRACY. *Behind the Headlines [Canada] 1976 34(6): 1-24.* Evaluates the steps taken by Martin O'Connell, chairman, and the special committee to discover public opinion about the "green paper," or suggested changes in the immigration law.
S. G. Yntema

3065. Frideres, J. S. BRITISH CANADIAN ATTITUDES TOWARD MINORITY ETHNIC GROUPS IN CANADA. *Ethnicity 1978 5(1): 20-32.* 184 adults of British (and Irish) background in Calgary,

Alberta, were questioned to measure prejudice against North American Indians, French Canadians, and Asians. Very little prejudice against Indians was found, while French Canadians were often regarded unfavorably and Asians far more so. Quebecois were almost unanimously chosen as the most disliked group among French Canadians, while Métis were the most popular subgroup among Indians. Youth, education, and contact with the group in question all tended to minimize prejudice. Interestingly, while fears of future competition seemed to arouse prejudice, actual competition did not. 3 tables, 12 notes, 41 ref.
L. W. Van Wyk

3066. Godler, Zlata. DOCTORS AND THE NEW IMMIGRANTS. *Can. Ethnic Studies [Canada] 1977 9(1): 6-17.* Expands upon H. E. MacDermot's thesis that the Canadian medical profession was politically active both before and after the Department of Health's establishment in 1919. This is especially noticeable in immigrant legislation. Revealing in their journals that their opinions were based more often on racial fears than on scientific fact, Canada's physicians helped inhibit the infusion of Southern and Eastern Europeans. Such prejudice and its legislation peaked in the 1920's when the United States imposed an immigration quota system.
K. S. McDorman

3067. Hawkins, Freda. CANADA'S GREEN PAPER ON IMMIGRATION POLICY. *Int. Migration Rev. 1975 9(2): 237-249.* Discusses Canada's current Green Paper on immigration policy, focusing on its implications for future immigration and development policies.

3068. Hawkins, Freda. CANADIAN IMMIGRATION: PRESENT POLICIES, FUTURE OPTIONS. *Round Table [Great Britain] 1977 (265): 50-64.* Traces Canada's immigration policy since 1945. Discusses the 1962 immigration regulations, the Department of Manpower and Immigration, and the problems of settlement and assimilation. Because the fertility rate is below the replacement level, the Canadian government has adopted the Australian idea of planned population growth through immigration.
C. Anstey

3069. Hawkins, Freda. CANADIAN IMMIGRATION POLICY AND MANAGEMENT. *Internat. Migration Rev. 1974 8(2): 141-153.* Discusses present immigration policy and management in Canada, including major features of the Canadian immigration situation since the end of World War II.

3070. Hawkins, Freda. CANADIAN IMMIGRATION: A NEW LAW AND A NEW APPROACH TO MANAGEMENT. *Int. Migration Rev. 1977 11(1): 77-94.* The 1976 Immigration Bill before the House of Commons would institute an integrated method of management of employment problems and immigration policy.

3071. Hawkins, Freda. DEMOGRAPHIC STUDIES NEEDED TO SUPPLEMENT GREEN PAPER. *Int. Perspectives [Canada] 1975 (5): 3-9.* Discusses the need for demographic research in Canada's immigration policy in the 1970's, emphasizing the implications for federal and local government.

3072. Hawkins, Freda. PUBLIC AFFAIRS: DIFFICULT DECISIONS IN IMMIGRATION POLICY. *Queen's Q. [Canada] 1975 82(4): 589-599.* In 1975 the Canadian Liberal government published a Green Paper on Immigration Policy to elicit the attitudes of citizens on immigration, to amend 1967 and 1972 immigration acts, and to develop long-term national goals. Since 1967 international pressure has resulted in increased rates of immigration, yet by 1975 internal pressure from overcrowded metropolitan areas and labor shortages has shown a need to limit these rates.
T. Simmerman

3073. Henson, Tom M. KU KLUX KLAN IN WESTERN CANADA. *Alberta Hist. [Canada] 1977 25(4): 1-8.* The Ku Klux Klan began in British Columbia in 1921, then moved into Alberta and Saskatchewan. Primarily anti-French at first, the Klan soon advocated immigration restriction, especially of Orientals and Eastern Europeans. The Klan also became antiunion, as most of the recent immigrants were union affiliated. The Klan was influential in several local elections, but overall lasting impact of the organization in western Canada was slight. By the early 1930's, the Klan was practically dead, due to local scandals (embezzlement) and to effective opposition from the Communist and working-class parties. 49 notes.   D. Chaput

3074. Hill, Daniel G. RACISM IN ONTARIO. *Can. Labour 1977 22(2): 24-26, 36.* Examines methods sought by Ontario officials and human rights agencies to deal with racism toward ethnic groups, minorities, and native peoples during 1973-77.

3075. Horn, Michiel. KEEPING CANADA "CANADIAN": ANTI-COMMUNISM AND CANADIANISM IN TORONTO, 1928-29. *Canada 1975 3(1): 34-47.* Discusses the role of immigration and national self-image in anti-Communist movements and anti-Semitism in Toronto, Ontario, in 1928-29, emphasizing freedom of speech issues.

3076. Jones, H. R. CANADA REVIEWS IMMIGRATION POLICY. *Geography [Great Britain] 1978 63(3): 217-219.* The passage of a new Immigration Act by Canada's Parliament in 1977 marks the culmination of a long debate over immigration. Until recently few industrial nations besides Canada had an expansionist immigration law, yet that policy seems destined to change. From the 1950's to the present Canada has changed from a quota system giving preference to certain nationalities to a system giving preference to immigrants with qualification of education, experience, and skill. But throughout these decades, the constant in her policy towards immigration has been the state of unemployment among Canadians: there is an inverse relationship between unemployment and immigration. Table, fig.   J. W. Leedom

3077. Labovitz, Sanford. SOME EVIDENCE OF CANADIAN ETHNIC, RACIAL, AND SEXUAL ANTAGONISM. *Can. Rev. of Sociol. and Anthrop. 1974 11(3): 247-254.* Examined the nature of ethnic, racial, and sexual antagonism in mid-western Canada in 1972 and 1973 by using the evaluation of name types that represented selected ethnic groups. Respondents differentially evaluated the names of Edward Blake (English Canadian male), Edith Blake (English Canadian female), Joseph Walking Bear (Canadian Indian male), and Marcel Fournier (French Canadian male). The rank ordering of names on an evaluational scale ranging from highly favorable to highly unfavorable was: (1) Edward Blake, (2) Edith Blake, (3) Joseph Walking Bear, (4) Marcel Fournier. The Indian and the French names were ranked well below the two names representing English Canadians.   J

3078. Miller, James R. THE JESUITS' ESTATES ACT CRISIS: "AN INCIDENT IN A CONSPIRACY OF SEVERAL YEARS' STANDING." *J. of Can. Studies 1974 9(3): 36-50.* Rejects Orange bigotry and general Protestant opposition as a satisfactory explanation for the furor over the Jesuits' Estates Act. Slow economic growth brought pre-Confederation conflicts to the surface of politics, and the Jesuit Estates agitation was in the mainstream of English Canadian life. Based on personal papers, House of Commons debates, newspapers, periodicals, theses, secondary works; 71 notes.   G. E. Panting

3079. Monk, Janice. RACE AND RESTRICTIVE IMMIGRATION: A REVIEW ARTICLE. *J. of Hist. Geography 1978 4(2): 192-196.* Review article prompted by R. A. Huttenback's *Racism and Empire: White Settlers and Colored Immigrants in the British Self-Governing Colonies, 1830-1910* (Cornell U. Pr., 1976); C. A. Price's *The Great White Walls are Built: Restrictive Immigration to North America and Australia 1836-1888* (Canberra: Australian Inst. of Int. Affairs and

Australian Natl. U. Pr., 1974); and C. Y. Choi's *Chinese Migration and Settlement in Australia* (Sydney U. Pr., 1975). Compares recent changes of immigration policies in some English-speaking countries. In the past 20 years greater emphasis has been given to familial ties and occupational skills. Huttenback and Price stress restrictive policies, while Choi's book shows effects of policies on migration and settlement. All three emphasize the importance of perceptions, myths, and ideologies in shaping policy.
                                                        A. J. Larson

3080. Palmer, Howard. NATIVISM IN ALBERTA, 1925-1930. *Can. Hist. Assoc. Hist. Papers 1974: 183-212.* Discusses attitudes toward immigration and ethnic minorities in Alberta society 1925-30.

3081. Parai, Louis. CANADA'S IMMIGRATION POLICY. *Int. Migration Rev. 1975 9(4): 449-477.* Discusses economic and employment factors of Canada's immigration policy during 1962-74.

3082. Passaris, Constantine. "INPUT" OF FOREIGN POLICY TO IMMIGRATION EQUATION. *Int. Perspectives [Canada] 1976 (6): 23-28.* Examines population and skilled labor concerns in Canada's immigration policy and its relationship to foreign policy and refugees, from the 1950's-70's.

3083. Richmond, Anthony H. and Rao, G. Lakshmana. RECENT DEVELOPMENTS IN IMMIGRATION TO CANADA AND AUSTRALIA: A COMPARATIVE ANALYSIS. *Int. J. of Comparative Sociol. [Canada] 1976 17(3-4): 183-205.* Analyzes immigration to Canada and Australia during 1967-75. Considers the numbers involved, racial and national discrimination, educational and occupational selection, opposition to immigration, and government sponsored studies. Government immigration policy is debated in the political arena and forms an accommodation of conflicting interests and ideologies. The most influential opposition to immigration in Australia and Canada now comes from those concerned with the environmental consequences of population growth. Counteracting them are those who support moderate growth. Even in the face of high unemployment, immigration has continued. In both countries fertility has declined, and continued immigration is seen as a means of avoiding future population decline and ameliorating the consequences of an otherwise aging population. Primary and secondary sources; 5 tables, 7 notes, biblio.   R. G. Neville

3084. Russell, Robert. CANADIAN IMMIGRATION POLICY AND THE CIRCULATION OF LABOUR-POWER. *Catalyst [Canada] 1978 (12): 1-11.* Discusses present considerations of growth in the labor force and the power of labor in the economy which dictate and influence immigration policy in Canada, 1978.

3085. St. John, Edward S. THE IMAGE OF THE FRENCH CANADIAN IN GLENGARRY LITERATURE. *Ontario Hist. [Canada] 1973 65(2): 69-80.* The image of French Canadians in Glengarry County novels usually is basically negative. Details the major exception. Primary and secondary sources; 52 notes.   W. B. Whitham

3086. Schwartz, Mildred A. CITIZENSHIP IN CANADA AND THE UNITED STATES. *Tr. of the Royal Soc. of Can. [Canada] 1976 14: 83-96.* Defines citizenship and compares attitudes in Canada and the United States concerning that status. Notes the efforts in Canada to pass a Citizenship Act and a Bill of Rights, and discusses the British tradition in Canada and the effect of the Citizenship Act on British subjects. Compares treatment of Japanese in the United States and Canada during World War II. 8 notes, biblio.   J. D. Neville

9. IMMIGRANTS AND ETHNICS: BY GROUPS

French Canadians

General

3087. Angers, François-Albert. LA LANGUE FRANÇAISE AU QUÉBEC (1774-1974) [The French language in Quebec: 1774-1974]. *Action Natl. [Canada] 1974 63(8/9): 618-628.* The Act of Quebec (1774), reestablishing French laws and language, has been the justification for a sovereign Quebec for 200 years and is the basis for the establishment of French as the official language.

3088. Angers, François-Albert. LIONEL GROULX, NOTRE LIBÉRATEUR [Lionel Groulx, our liberator]. *Action Natl. [Canada] 1978 67(9): 697-709.* Lionel Groulx, the foremost historian of French Canada, may be compared to Gandhi in his devotion to the achievement of national autonomy by nonviolence. Quebec nationalism had been checked by the repercussions of the rebellions of 1837, and Quebecois saw themselves as an ethnic minority in an Anglicized nation. Groulx helped establish the journal *Action Française* in 1917, signalling the renaissance of a national spirit directly antecedent to contemporary separatism, and a departure from the Bourassa tradition which sought protection of minority rights in the context of confederation. Paper presented at a conference in Quebec on 21 January 1978 commemorating the centenary of Groulx's birth. A. W. Novitsky

3089. Arès, Richard. LES MINORITÉS FRANCO-CANADIENNES: ÉTUDE STATISTIQUE [The French Canadian minority: a statistical study]. *Tr. of the Royal Soc. of Can. 1975 13: 123-132.* Presents a statistical study of the French-speaking minority in Canada, first defining what a French Canadian is and making a distinction between French Canadian and French Quebecois. Shows trends 1871-1971 and notes that although most French Canadians continue to live in Quebec, a greater percentage of them now live in other sections of the country. In the other areas—the Maritimes, Ontario, and the Western Provinces—French Canadians continue to be a small and declining percentage of the population. Also, whereas in Quebec French is their first language, in the other areas, English increasingly is their first language and an increasing number know no French. The Maritimes, because of the large French population in New Brunswick, have a larger percentage of French-speaking people than other non-Quebec areas, but except for that one province the Maritimes have a small percentage, too. 5 tables. J. D. Neville

3090. Audet, Louis-Philippe. BILAN DE LA CONTRIBUTION DE LA SECTION DES LETTRES ET DES SCIENCES HUMAINES AUX ÉTUDES CANADIENNES, 1952-72 [Perspective on the contribution of the Letters and Social Sciences Section on Canadian studies, 1952-72]. *Tr. of the Royal Soc. of Can. 1973 11: 131-146.* Offers a comprehensive inventory of studies presented to the Letters and Social Sciences Section of the Royal Society of Canada, 1952-72; the studies are an important contribution to the knowledge of French civilization in Canada.

3091. Belliveau, J. E. THE ACADIAN FRENCH AND THEIR LANGUAGE. *Can. Geographical J. [Canada] 1977 95(2): 46-55.* Discusses the Acadian presence in Canada (especially the Maritime Provinces), 1605-1800, and the enforced migration of many of the group, 1755-67, because of the outbreak of hostilities between Britain and France.

3092. Bonenfant, Jean-Charles. LA FÉODALITÉ A DÉFINITIVEMENT VÉCU... [The feudal system is definitely dead...]. *Rev. de l'U. d'Ottawa [Canada] 1977 47(1-2): 14-26.* French feudalism, which had been brought into Quebec with some changes and confirmed by the Quebec Act (1774), was abolished in 1854, but rental duties remained in effect with possibility of redemption. After subsequent laws gradually improved the procedure, these duties became extinct in 1971. The Canadian feudal system was then, definitely ended. Primary and secondary sources; 39 notes. G. P. Cleyet

3093. Bouchard, Gerard. DÉMOGRAPHIE ET SOCIÉTÉ RURALE AU SAGUENAY, 1851-1935 [Demography and rural society in the Saguenay, 1851-1935]. *Recherches Sociographiques [Canada] 1978 19(1): 7-31.* Demographic, economic, and cultural realities of a developing rural community throw into question many aspects of rural life in 19th century Quebec. Fertility increased despite extreme material privation. The family structure survived within a context of instability. Finally, the society developed with the minimum of structure although with a maximum of cohesion. Based on a computerized demographic analysis of Laterrière, Quebec, and secondary sources; 8 tables, 4 graphs, 35 notes. A. E. LeBlanc

3094. Bouchard, Gérard. FAMILY STRUCTURE AND GEOGRAPHIC MOBILITY AT LATERRIÈRE, 1851-1935. *J. of Family Hist. 1977 2(4): 350-369.* Using both family reconstitution and census records, examines demographic trends in Laterrière, Quebec. There was a high degree of population turnover and net migration was the key determinant of the rate of population change. Examines the influence of the community's hybrid system of farming and lumbering on its general economic development. Map, 8 tables, 4 graphs, 26 notes, biblio. T. W. Smith

3095. Bouchard, Gérard. INTRODUCTION A L'ÉTUDE DE LA SOCIÉTÉ SAGUENAYENNE AUX XIXᵉ ET XXᵉ SIÈCLES [Introduction to the study of Saguenayan society in the 19th and 20th centuries]. *Rev. d'Hist. de l'Am. Française [Canada] 1977 31(1): 3-27.* Relates developments in agriculture and industry to the mobility of various classes of Saguenayan society since the late 19th century. Secondary works; map, graph, 43 notes. L. B. Chan

3096. Bouchard, Gérard and La Rose, André. LA RÉGLEMENTATION DU CONTENU DES ACTES DE BAPTÊME, MARIAGE, SÉPULTURE, AU QUÉBEC, DES ORIGINES A NOS JOURS [Regulation of the contents of the acts of baptism, marriage, and burial in Quebec from the beginning to our day]. *Rev. d'Hist. de l'Am. Française [Canada] 1976 30(1): 67-77.* From the 16th century to the present, both the Church and the state have been concerned with registering baptisms, marriages, and burials. Church regulation of these practices has always been more detailed than that of the state. Vicars have been recording performances of these acts, and the state has benefited from such assistance. Based on published Church and state documents and secondary works; 6 tables, 37 notes. L. B. Chan

3097. Bouchard, Gerard and Brard, Patrick. LE PROGRAMME DE RECONSTITUTION AUTOMATIQUE DES FAMILLES SAGUENAYENNES: DONNÉES DE BASE ET RESULTATS PROVISOIRES [The automatic reconstitution program of Saguenay families: basic principles and provisional results]. *Social Hist. [Canada] 1979 12(23): 170-185.* The Saguenay population social history project, begun in 1972, studies the population of the Saguenay district, north of Quebec City, from 1842 to 1941. The objective is to develop a comprehensive register, entirely computerized, of the region. The data extracted from these sources helps to create individualized family cards, and to include there, for the first time, key demographic data, which will be integrated with economic, social, cultural, and medical information. 19 notes. D. F. Chard

3098. Bouchard, Gérard. L'HISTOIRE DE LA POPULATION ET L'ÉTUDE DE LA MOBILITÉ SOCIALE AU SAGUENAY, XIXᵉ-XXᵉ SIÈCLES [History of the population and a study of social mobility in Saguenay, 19th-20th centuries]. *Recherches Sociographiques [Canada] 1976 17(3): 353-372.* Studies more than 125,000 birth, marriage, and death records of the Saguenay region. The underemployment and the socioprofessional instability recorded almost from the beginning are characteristic of a sick society and economic base. 2 tables, 3 charts, diagram, 22 notes. A. E. LeBlanc

3099. Bouchard, Gérard. UN ESSAI D'ANTHROPOLOGIE RÉGIONALE: L'HISTOIRE SOCIALE DU SAGUENAY AUX XIXᵉ ET

XXe SIÈCLES [A study in regional anthropology: the social history of Saguenay in the 19th and 20th centuries]. *Ann.: Écon., Soc., Civilisations [France] 1979 34(1): 106-125.* There can be no doubt that between 1960 and 1970 the advances made in social history, particularly in France, did not entirely match expectations. To start with, the method of reconstructing the family has been used solely for demographic purposes. In addition, only sporadic use has been made of the continual advances in computer techniques, and data retrieval and analysis methods have not always been able to match the scope of the more comprehensive problematic issues. Likewise, close-knit and stable research teams have been the exception rather than the rule. These are some of the many reasons why it seemed worthwhile undertaking a collective experiment in regional history, combining all the material and personal conditions required to implement genuinely interdisciplinary research and covering the main lines followed in social history. This project, which has been in progress since 1972 at the University of Quebec-Chicoutimi, has now become designated as the Social history project on the population of Saguenay. In this paper, the co-ordinator presents the aims and methods of this project, and the results thus far achieved. J

3100. Boucher, Neil. THE SURETTES OF EEL BROOK AND THEIR DESCENDANTS. *Nova Scotia Hist. Q. [Canada] 1979 9(1): 15-24.* Reviews briefly the history of the Surette family in Nova Scotia through the lives of Pierre (1679-1749), the first settler, and his son Pierre II (1709-?). Grandsons of Pierre II settled on Surrette's Island between 1801 and 1804. Descendants of the family are still on the island. Primary and secondary sources; 19 notes, biblio. H. M. Evans

3101. Byers, G. THE NORTH SHORE LANGILLES OF NOVA SCOTIA. *Nova Scotia Hist. Q. [Canada] 1977 7(3): 267-289.* Traces the history and descendants of the Langille family through David Langille (1718-1804), who left France with his son, a half-brother, and two cousins to escape persecution. They arrived in Halifax in 1752. Primary and secondary sources; biblio. H. M. Evans

3102. Choquette, Robert. L'EGLISE D'OTTAWA SOUS MGR GUIGUES, 1848-1874 [The church of Ottawa under Monseigneur Guigues, 1848-74]. *Sessions d'Étude: Soc. Can. d'Hist. de l'Église Catholique [Canada] 1977 44: 57-62.* The Ottawa diocese was administered by Joseph-Eugène Guigues during 1848-74, where he actively pursued French Canadian colonization in Ontario, church funding, and spiritual and social programs.

3103. Coolhaas, W. Ph. DE FRANS-CANADEZEN [The French Canadians]. *Historia [South Africa] 1976 21(1): 37-54.* Outlines French Canadian history for the purpose of showing its similarities with, and differences from, that of South Africa.

3104. Cormier, Clement. LA SOCIÉTÉ ACADIENNE D'AUJOURD'HUI [Acadian society today]. *Tr. of the Royal Soc. of Can. 1975 13: 73-90.* Discusses the survival of the Acadian population in Canada from its first colonization in 1604 until today. Emphasizes a demographic study of French-speaking Canadians showing a decline in the percentage of the population outside of Quebec which has French as its first or only language. Centers on the Maritime Provinces which have had little immigration which is neither British nor French in origin. More people of French origin are bilingual than are those of English origin, but in North America there are only six million French-speaking people and 250 million English-speaking ones. Utilizes the work of the Laurendeau-Dunton Commission and suggests that the French-speaking population holds its own in areas where there is some population density, especially in the areas with close proximity to Quebec. Cites aids to survival of French culture. 12 tables, 12 notes. J. D. Neville

3105. Cotnam, Jacques. AMERICANS VIEWED THROUGH THE EYES OF THE FRENCH-CANADIANS. *J. of Popular Culture 1977 10(4): 784-796.* Examines French Canadians' attitudes toward Americans, during 1837-1973.

3106. Dagneau, G. H. À LA MÉMOIRE DE GUY FRÉGAULT [In memory of Guy Fregault]. *Action Natl. [Canada] 1978 68(2): 167-171.* Guy Frégault mirrored the subject of his last book on Lionel Groulx. Frégault completed *Lionel Groulx tel qu'en meme* just before his death, and exhibited the qualities of intelligence, clear analysis, honesty, literary grace, and love of his tradition. A. W. Novitsky

3107. Deffontaines, Pierre. ULTIMES VICTOIRES SUR L'HIVER AU CANADA FRANÇAIS [Ultimate victories over winter in French Canada]. *Rev. de l'U. d'Ottawa [Canada] 1977 47(1-2): 61-64.* The extremely severe climate of French Canada has impelled settlers to find ways of struggling against its inconveniences and dangers. Beginning with gradually perfecting the structures of houses and improving the heating systems, today, central heating allows the discontinuance of the former work of preparing logs for the winter and a conversion of many wooden areas into pastures or farming zones. Note. G. P. Cleyet

3108. DeKoninck, Rodolphe and Langevin, Jean. LA PERENNITE DES PEUPLEMENTS INSULAIRES LAURENTIENS: LE CAS DE L'ILE SAINT-IGNACE ET DE L'ILE DUPAS [Settlement permanency on the islands of the St. Lawrence River: the case of St. Ignace and Dupas Islands]. *Cahiers de Géographie de Québec [Canada] 1974 18(44): 317-336.*

3109. Desmeules, Jean. STATISTIQUES DE LA POPULATION DE QUEBEC SUR LA BASE DES BASSINS VERSANTS HYDROGRAPHIQUES [Population statistics of Quebec based on hydrographic regions]. *Cahiers de Géographie de Québec [Canada] 1974 18(44): 367-370.*

3110. Doyle-Frenière, Murielle. LES ARCHIVES DE LA VILLE DE QUEBEC [The archives of the city of Quebec]. *Urban Hist. Rev. [Canada] 1977 (1): 33-37.* Describes the historical background and contents of the Quebec city archives and lists general information on the facilities available and their use by researchers. C. A. Watson

3111. Dumont-Johnson, Micheline. LES COMMUNAUTÉS RELIGIEUSES ET LA CONDITION FÉMININE [Religious communities and the feminine condition]. *Recherches Sociographiques [Canada] 1978 19(1): 79-102.* As far back as the French Regime, women's religious communities played an important role in the social and cultural development of Quebec. In the second half of the 19th century one discerns the first manifestations of feminism in Quebec within the structures of these religious communities. With the present one sees their influence and importance disappear since the "Quebecoise" more and more lives within a society that offers avenues for self-development and expression unknown in the past. Based on an analysis of recent monographs; 5 tables, 4 graphs, 76 notes. A. E. LeBlanc

3112. Dussault, Gabriel. L'UTOPIE COLONISATRICE CONTRE L'ORDRE ÉCONOMIQUE [The colonization utopia as counter to the economic order]. *Recherches Sociographiques [Canada] 1978 19(1): 55-78.* Colonization in the second half of the 19th century was perceived in Quebec as a utopian and pacific expansion to reconquer the patrimony. In reality, as seen in the Ottawa Valley, the movement was continually at odds with the economic forces, represented by the forest industry, already in place. Based on a variety of primary and secondary sources including the writings of A. Labelle; map, table, 78 notes. A. E. LeBlanc

3113. Falaise, Noël. BIOGRAPHIE ET BIBLIOGRAPHIE DE BENOÎT BROUILLETTE [Biography and bibliography of Benoit Brouillette]. *Cahiers de Géographie de Québec [Canada] 1973 17(40): 5-34.* Benoit Brouillette, first Quebec geographer of international repute, was a professor at Montreal's École des Hautes Études Commerciales, 1931-69. He was responsible for establishing the Montreal Geographical Society and was a member of the Commission of Geography in Education. Biblio. A. E. LeBlanc

3114. Falardeau, Jean-Charles. ANTÉCÉDENTS, DÉBUTS ET CROISSANCE DE LA SOCIOLOGIE AU QUÉBEC [Antecedents, beginnings and growth of sociology in Quebec]. *Recherches Sociographiques [Canada] 1974 15(2-3): 135-165.* Until the late 1930's sociology in French-speaking Quebec was dominated by theological and doctrinal preoccupations. This was followed by a period of broader and more scientific activity. It was not until the late 1940's, under the impact of American influences, that sociology came into its own. In close relationship to the rapid modernization of Quebec, sociology was to know a rapid maturation and diversification. A. E. LeBlanc

3115. Faucher, Albert. EXPLICATION SOCIO-ÉCONOMIQUE DES MIGRATIONS DANS L'HISTOIRE DU QUÉBEC [Socioeconomic explication of migrations in the history of Quebec]. *Tr. of the Royal Soc. of Can. 1975 13: 91-107*. Discusses the causes of emigration in Quebec in the 19th and 20th centuries, noting several explanations. One was by contemporaries such as the Chicoyne Committee which noted the depopulation of rural areas caused by the industrial revolution. Most emigrants sought both a job and a better life as they left the agricultural areas of Quebec where there were fewer chances for economic advancement, especially as its two primary employers, agriculture and forestry, went into a decline. French Canadians moved both to other areas of Canada and to the United States, leaving an area which had a high birth rate and an economy that could not absorb new people. Thus, Quebec had to industrialize in order to find a solution to its decline in population, which had affected the entire province rather than just the rural areas. By contrast, areas such as Ontario with diversified economies grew rapidly in population during the same period. 76 notes.
                                                                J. D. Neville

3116. Faucher, Albert. LA NOTION DE LUXE CHEZ LES CANADIENS FRANÇAIS DU DIX-NEUVIÈME SIÈCLE [The concept of luxury among French Canadians in the 19th century]. *Tr. of the Royal Soc. of Can. 1973 11: 175-180*. The outlook on luxury in Quebec 1849-1900 was derived in large part from moralistic literature of the time, such as the writings of David Hume; clarifies the economic reality, and studies the social consequences, of the luxury concept.

3117. Faucher, Albert. PSUEUDO-MARXISME ET RÉVOLUTION AU QUÉBEC: RÉFLEXIONS SUR LA PROPAGANDE DE LÉANDRE BERGERON [Pseudo-Marxism and revolution in Quebec: Reflections on Léandre Bergeron's propaganda]. *Action Natl. [Canada] 1975 64(6): 487-508*. Sees in Léandre Bergeron's *Petit Manuel d'Histoire du Québec* (Editions Québecoises, 1970) an oversimplified Marxist interpretation of Quebec history.

3118. Foster, J. E. THE METIS: THE PEOPLE AND THE TERM. *Prairie Forum [Canada] 1978 3(1): 79-90*. Traces the history of the Métis, a group that originated with the fur trade in the Prairie Provinces, with Indian and Euro-Canadian roots, 17c-20c.

3119. Fournier, Marcel. LA SOCIOLOGIE QUÉBÉCOISE CONTEMPORAINE [Contemporary Quebec sociology]. *Recherches Sociographiques [Canada] 1974 15(2-3): 167-199*. The 1960's and 1970's were characterized by a rapid development in sociology departments at French-language universities in Quebec. This expansion was dictated by the demand of government, unions, and other organizations for university graduates to fill numerous posts. The result was not necessarily good for the profession even though it was to serve immediate needs within the province.
                                                                A. E. LeBlanc

3120. Gagné, Suzanne. LIONEL GROULX: HISTORIEN D'HIER OU D'AUJOURDHUI [Lionel Groulx: a historian of the present or the past]. *Rev. d'Hist. de l'Amerique Française [Canada] 1978 32(3): 455-462*. The writings of Lionel Groulx (1878-1967), the prominent French Canadian historian, are still relevant. "They call people to freedom. Lionel Groulx was a great historian who understood the thoughts of the nation, an historian not only of yesterday but also of our time." 9 notes.
                                                                M. R. Yerburgh

3121. Gagnon, Serge. LE XVIᵉ SIÈCLE CANADIEN DE NARCISSE-EUTROPE DIONNE À MARCEL TRUDEL (1891-1963) [The Canadian 16th century of Narcisse-Eutrope Dionne to Marcel Trudel, 1891-1963]. *Rev. de l'U. d'Ottawa [Canada] 1977 47(1-2): 65-83*. Examines the social and ideological framework of the knowledge of 16th-century Canada through the analysis of two representative authors who reconstituted the epoch with practically the same material: Narcisse-Eutrope Dionne (1891), whose work reflected a religious and conservative nationalism, and Marcel Trudel (1963), who gave a liberal interpretation which showed the change in the Quebec collective memory after World War I and identified the retrospective vision of the national destiny shared by the 1950's and 1960's protesters. Primary and secondary sources; 58 notes.
                                                                G. P. Cleyet

3122. George, Pierre. LA CONTRIBUTION DES GÉOGRAPHES FRANÇAIS À LA CONNAISSANCE DU QUÉBEC DES ANNÉES 1930-1950 [French geographers' contribution to the knowledge of Quebec in years 1930-50]. *Rev. de l'U. d'Ottawa [Canada] 1977 47(1-2): 95-113*. Analyzes the works of three outstanding French observers of Canada who contributed to the knowledge of Quebec: Raoul Blanchard, a rationalist and technocrat, who wrote a comprehensive work which is basically historical and descriptive; André Siegfried, professor at the Collège de France, who oriented his studies toward the political geography of the entire territory of Canada; and Pierre Deffontaines, whose observations were based more on a point of view close to ethnology. Primary and secondary sources; 52 notes.
                                                                G. P. Cleyet

3123. Gérin-Lajoie, Henri. LES ARCHIVES MUNICIPALES DE LA VILLE DE MONTRÉAL [Municipal archives in the city of Montreal]. *Urban Hist. Rev. [Canada] 1974 74(2): 2-4*. Chronicles the Montreal city archives, 1913-74; mentions library facilities, collections, and research possibilities.

3124. Germain, Annick. HISTOIRE URBAINE ET HISTOIRE DE L'URBANISATION AU QUÉBEC: BRÈVE REVUE DES TRAVAUX REALISÉS AU COURS DE LA DECENNIE [Urban history and the history of urbanization in Québec: brief review of work accomplished in the past decade]. *Urban Hist. Rev. [Canada] 1979 (3): 3-22*. Traditional historiography of the cities of Quebec was mostly anecdotal monographs of parishes and small cities and some "urban biographies" of Montreal. A review of the literature since 1968 shows that the more recent writing examines the forgotten majorities, the working classes, the women, and the poor. Not only subjects but research practices are changing too: new groups of researchers are often interdisciplinary, work together over a long time, and use quantitative methods. Greater interest is shown in urban history by local communities and some professions, such as architects. There is a new sensitivity to the usefulness of historical research in urban studies, particularly in urban politics. Secondary sources; 68 notes.
                                                                C. A. Watson

3125. Gervais, Gaetan. LORENZO CADIEUX, S.J., 1903-1976. *Ontario Hist. [Canada] 1977 69(4): 214-218*. Father Cadieux was born in Granby, Quebec, educated in Montreal and Edmonton, and closely associated with the study of northern Ontario. Outlines his career as a teacher, and mentions organizations he was associated with. Gives examples of his work, and lists some titles of his publications. The obituary is in English and French.
                                                                W. B. Whitham

3126. Giguère, Georges-Émile. LIONEL GROULX, SON MYTHE ET SES MYTHES [Lionel Groulx: his myth and his myths]. *Sessions d'Étude: Soc. Can. d'Hist. de l'Église Catholique [Canada] 1978 45: 19-39*. Surveys authors' opinions about Lionel Groulx, Catholic cleric, Quebec nationalist, and fascist sympathizer.

3127. Gill, Robert M. FRENCH CANADA'S SEARCH FOR A HOMELAND: A LITERARY PERSPECTIVE. *Am. Rev. of Can. Studies 1978 8(2): 102-115*. Historically the French Canadian novel has reflected the French Canadians' determination to survive and find a homeland in spite of "foreign" domination. Beginning in the mid-19th century, the *roman du terroir* viewed rural Quebec as the true French Canadian homeland. Rural society was threatened by technology and urbanization, and, by the 1930's, French Canada was forced to resume its literary search for a homeland, arriving in the poorer sections of Montreal. In the 1960's, the French Canadian novel had achieved a more cosmopolitan outlook indicating that French Canada had achieved a sense of identity that transcended geographical boundaries. 32 notes.
                                                                G.-A. Patzwald

3128. Godfrey, William G. SOME THOUGHTS ON THE *DICTIONARY OF CANADIAN BIOGRAPHY* AND MARITIME HISTORIOGRAPHY. *Acadiensis [Canada] 1978 7(2): 107-115*. Volumes I, II, and III, covering the period 1000 to 1770, provide "a blend of gentle revision and polite reconciliation." They say little about Indian leadership, but effectively discuss French missionaries, and offer illuminating glimpses of Acadia's relationship to France and New France. Volumes IX and X deemphasize Acadians and Indians, and devote much attention to Maritime politics, in Prince Edward Island and New Brunswick, as contests between elites. The treatment of Maritime economic and intellectual development suggests that the legendary mid-19th-century Golden Age was only a veneer. 4 notes.   D. F. Chard

3129. Grant, John N. THE DEVELOPMENT OF SHERBROOKE VILLAGE TO 1880. *Nova Scotia Hist. Q. [Canada] 1972 2(1): 1-15.* Traces the development of the St. Mary's River Valley in the eastern part of Nova Scotia beginning in 1655 when Forte Sainte Marie was built by the French trader LaGiraudiere.

3130. Greer, Allan. THE PATTERN OF LITERACY IN QUEBEC, 1745-1899. *Social Hist. [Canada] 1978 11(22): 293-335.* Parish registers, petitions, censuses, and the Buller Commission's report of 1838 suggest that before the mid-19th century French-Canadian literacy was extremely low in rural areas, but relatively high in Montreal and Quebec. In the first half of the 19th century English Canadians and their children were much more literate than French Canadians. Literacy rates among French Canadians were low before the Conquest and remained low until the 1840's and 1850's. Progress thereafter was impressive, particularly among women and in the Montreal area. 17 illus., 66 notes.   D. F. Chard

3131. Guitard, Michelle. POUR UNE HISTOIRE DE L'INSTITUT CANADIEN DE MONTRÉAL [On behalf of a history of the Canadian Institute of Montreal]. *R. d'Hist. de l'Amérique Française [Canada] 1973 27(3): 403-407.* Expresses the desire to collect the names of members of the Canadian Institute of Montreal, 1845-73, as a basis for a social history of the institute.

3132. Hautecoeur, Jean-Paul. NATIONALISME ET DEVELOPPEMENT EN ACADIE [Nationalism and development in Acadia]. *Recherches Sociographiques [Canada] 1976 17(2): 167-188.* The traditional nationalism fostered by the Acadian elites and reinforced by the principal national institutions setup over the years came into contact with a neonational movement in the 1960's. Constructed to establish new social structures to bring about development, the neonational ideology conflicted with the small bourgeoisie class of the dominant elites. Based on writings of Acadian leaders and contemporary political theorists; 44 notes.
A. E. LeBlanc

3133. Hayne, David M. NATIONAL IDENTITY IN QUEBEC LITERATURE AND THEATRE. *Tr. of the Royal Soc. of Can. [Canada] 1978 16: 279-291.* Discusses literary development among French Canadians, 1534-1978, dividing Canadian literature into seven periods: the French regime, 1534-1760; the post conquest period, 1760-1830; the beginnings of literature, 1830-60; the Quebec Movement, 1860-90; the School of Montreal, 1890-1935; the postwar period, 1935-60; and the Quiet Revolution, 1960-78.   J. D. Neville

3134. Houde, Pierre et al. LA PROPRIÉTÉ FONCIÈRE AU SAGUENAY, 1840-1975: ORIENTATION DE LA RECHERCHE [Land ownership in Saguenay, 1840-1975: Research directions]. *Protée [Canada] 1975 4(1): 67-86.* Defines types, problems, and present basic techniques of research in regional land ownership in Saguenay, including exploitation of local historical resources and the construction of spatial graphs and geographical matrices.

3135. Koshelev, L. V. KANADSKAIA ISTORIOGRAFIIA NOVOI FRANTSII [Canadian historiography of New France]. *Novaia i Noveishaia Istoriia [USSR] 1970 (4): 177-184.* Surveys works relating to New France published in French and English from the 1940's to the late 1960's. It also mentions Soviet works on the same theme. Connected with this is an analysis of trends in historiography and of new centers for the study of Canadian history. Agrees with Professor Ryerson that New France was defeated because it was headed by a feudal monarchy, whilst Britain was at a more developed bourgeois stage of historical development. French colonial policy was one not of colonization but of open plunder. Based on published secondary sources; 48 notes.
D. N. Collins

3136. Lacroix, Benoît. LIONEL GROULX CET INCONNU [The unknown Lionel Groulx]. *Rev. d'Hist. de l'Amérique Française [Canada] 1978 32(3): 325-346.* An intimate portrait of Father Lionel Groulx (1878-1967), the eminent French Canadian historian. During an incredibly long and productive career, Father Groulx wrote more than 30 books and hundreds of articles. Though his world consisted primarily of

books, libraries, and research, he often wrote in a popular style so that history could be enjoyed by a much larger audience. He taught for more than 50 years. 7 notes.   M. R. Yerburgh

3137. Lamonde, Yvan. INVENTAIRE DES ÉTUDES ET DES SOURCES POUR L'ÉTUDE DES ASSOCIATIONS "LITTÉRAIRES" QUÉBÉCOISES FRANCOPHONES AU 19ᵉ SIÈCLE (1840-1900) [Inventory of monographs and sources for the study of Quebec French-language "literary" associations in the 19th century (1840-1900)]. *Recherches Sociographiques [Canada] 1975 16(2): 261-275.* The inventory includes an introductory bibliography of studies involving various forms of voluntary associations in Quebec, Canada, the United States, and Europe. This is followed by an inventory of sources, both manuscript and secondary, on French language literary associations that existed in Quebec during 1840-1900.   A. E. LeBlanc

3138. Lamonde, Yvan. LES ARCHIVES DE L'INSTITUT CANADIEN DE MONTRÉAL (1844-1900)—HISTORIQUE ET INVENTAIRE [The archives of the Canadian Institute of Montreal (1844-1900)—a history and an inventory]. *Rev. d'Hist. de l'Amérique Française [Canada] 1974 28(1): 77-94.* Gives a history of the archives of the Canadian Institute of Montreal in terms of documents destroyed and preserved, and its locations, methods, and ideological and financial crises.

3139. Laperrière, Guy. LES ATTITUDES DEVANT LA MORT: SUR DEUX OUVRAGES RÉCENTS [Two recent works regarding attitudes before death]. *Rev. d'Hist. de l'Amérique Française [Canada] 1978 32(2): 251-255.* Briefly traces changing attitudes toward death as presented by Philippe Ariès in his massive work *L'Homme Devant La Mort* (Paris: Seuil, 1977). Though Quebec historians have shown little sustained interest in the subject, Paul Jacob, an ethnologist, has prepared a masterful little volume entitled *Les Revenants de la Beauce* (Montreal: Boréal express, 1977).   M. R. Yerburgh

3140. Lefebvre, Jean-Jacques. LA FAMILLE PAGE, DE LAPRAIRIE, 1763-1967 [The Page Family of Laprairie, 1763-1967]. *Tr. of the Royal Soc. of Can. [Canada] 1976 14: 209-220.* Notes that earlier genealogical studies were of families of men knighted by the British monarch and suggests the other French Canadians have been ignored. Studies the genealogy of the family of Page, from Laprairie, beginning with Jean Page who was born in 1730 and probably came to Canada as a soldier during the Seven Years War. He married Madeleine Circe. Traces the family up to the present. 11 notes.   J. D. Neville

3141. Lefebvre, Jean-Jacques. LA LIGNÉE CANADIENNE DE L'HISTORIEN SIR THOMAS CHAPAIS (1946) [The Canadian line of the historian Sir Thomas Chapais (1946)]. *Tr. of the Royal Soc. of Can. 1975 13: 151-168.* Studies the family of the historian Sir Thomas Chapais, beginning with a discussion of the lack of genealogical information in many biographical dictionaries. Notes Sir Thomas's father, Jean-Charles Chapais, one of the "Fathers of the Confederation." Discusses the members of Sir Thomas's family from the 17th through the 19th centuries and shows, for the most part, their marriages, descendants, occupations, etc. Concludes with Sir Thomas' marriage to Miss Hectorine Langevin in 1884. She died in 1934 and he in 1946 without issue. 42 notes.
J. D. Neville

3142. Lévesque, Delmas. L'EXPÉRIENCE QUÉBÉCOIS [The Quebec experience]. *Action Natl. [Canada] 1978 68(2): 91-115.* I. ESSAI SUR NOTRE CULTURE [Part I. Essay on our culture]. Demography has been a major factor in Quebec history: on an anglicized continent, there are only 6,000,000 Quebecois descended from 10,000 immigrants. The collective psyche has also been dominated by the immensity of the land, rigorous climate, abundant natural resources, and a sense of isolation and dependence. Major events included the British conquest, the rebellion of the 1830's, the great depression of the 1930's, and the quiet revolution of the 1960's. While Quebec has been an urban province since the 1920's, only in the 1950's did the contradictions between traditional institutions and society appear. While the clergy were a major factor in maintaining a French identity, their power was destroyed by the resulting transformation. Primary and secondary sources; 6 notes. Part II. The preservation of French traditions in the face of modernization depends on the provincial government of Quebec, a revitalized Catholicism, and co-operative economic institutions. 7 notes.   A. W. Novitsky

3143. Linteau, Paul-André. LA SOCIETE MONTREALAISE AU 19ᵉ SIECLE: BILAN DES TRAVAUX [Montreal society in the 19th century: balance of workers]. *Urban Hist. Rev. [Canada] 1973 (3): 17-19.* Explores the work of the Research Group on Montreal Society of the 19th century which set about, in 1971, to write a social history of Montreal during the era when commercial capitalism was changing into industrial capitalism.

3144. Little, J. I. THE PARISH AND FRENCH CANADIAN MIGRANTS TO COMPTON, QUEBEC, 1851-1891. *Social Hist. [Canada] 1978 11(21): 134-143.* The Catholic Church in Quebec clearly wanted a society of small independent landowners because of fear that landless laborers would eventually abandon French and Catholicism. In Compton County rural communities were the most stable and homogeneous, reinforcing this bias, but the parish was still an effective institution in towns and where French Canadian farmers were a minority. Studies of a colonization parish, a mixed rural parish, and an industrial parish confirm this. 30 notes.
D. F. Chard

3145. Menard, Johanne. L'INSTITUT DES ARTISANS DU COMTÉ DE DRUMMOND, 1856-1890 [The Drummond County Mechanics Institute, 1856-1890]. *Recherches Sociographiques [Canada] 1975 16(2): 207-218.* Established in 1856, the Drummond County Mechanics Institute was largely composed of farmers and by 1861, French-Canadian Roman Catholics were in the majority. Until 1880 the institute was a vital part of the community; however, the changing composition of its membership brought an end to this dynamism.
A. E. LeBlanc

3146. Miron, Gaston. ROBERT-LIONEL SÉGUIN, HISTORIEN DE L'IDENTITÉ ET DE L'APPARTENANCE [Robert-Lionel Séguin, historian of identity and roots]. *Action Natl. [Canada] 1976 65(8): 539-546.* Robert-Lionel Séguin, historian, ethnologist and professor, has devoted his life to the explication of French Canadian identity in over 200 articles and 17 books, including *La civilisation traditionelle de "l'Habitant" aux 17ᵉ et 18ᵉ siècles* (1972) and *L'injure en Nouvelle-France* (1975). He founded and directs the Centre de documentation en civilisation traditionelle at the University of Quebec at Trois-Rivières. Adapted from a speech given 9 February 1975.
A. W. Novitsky

3147. Monet, Jacques. COMMUNAUTÉ ET CONTINUITÉ: VERS UN NOUVEAU PASSÉ [Community and continuity: toward a new past]. *Can. Hist. Assoc. Hist. Papers [Canada] 1976: 1-11.* Quebec's approach to the gradual transformation of her *ancien regime* has been incorporated in the original experience of Canada among New World republics based on revolution. Having concentrated on the study of their particular past, French Canadian historians have much to learn from and to contribute to the history of their neighbors. By providing them with a new past, Quebec's historians will have changed their present and future as well.
G. E. Panting

3148. Morissonneau, Christian. LA COLONISATION ÉQUIVOQUE [An uncertain colonization]. *Recherches Sociographiques [Canada] 1978 19(1): 33-53.* The colonist who opened up the Mattawinie district of Quebec formed part of a nomadic tradition that goes back to the early history of French Canada. This tradition was integrated into the geopolitical strategy, the religious project, and the economic development plan of Father T. S. Provost. Covers 17c-1890. Based on the writings of T. S. Provost and other primary and secondary sources; 27 notes.
A. E. LeBlanc

3149. Ouellet, Fernand. HISTORIOGRAPHIE CANADIENNE ET NATIONALISME [Canadian historiography and nationalism]. *Tr. of the Royal Soc. of Can. 1975 13: 25-39.* Discusses the development of Canadian historiography and the influence of nationalism on it ever since J. Viger, the first mayor of Montreal, began to accumulate historical sources (1810). Notes Ramsay Cook's study of historians and nationalism and discusses the effect of historians on attitudes in both English-speaking and French-speaking Canada. Deals first with nationalism and narrative history, discussing the effect of such historians as Garneau, David, Chapais, Groulx, McMullen, Christie, Innis, Creighton, Lower, Burton, Landon, Underhill, and Morton. Discusses the development of history departments at the universities of Laval and Montreal, and the varying interrelation of Canadian history as seen by the different schools of thought.
J. D. Neville

3150. Ouellet, Fernand. PROPRIÉTÉ SEIGNEURIALE ET GROUPES SOCIAUX DANS LA VALLÉE DU SAINT-LAURENT (1663-1840) [Manorial property and social groups in the St. Lawrence Valley, 1663-1840]. *Rev. de l'U. d'Ottawa [Canada] 1977 47(1-2): 183-213.* The manorial system in the St. Lawrence Valley colony was the privilege of the nobility, but the bourgeoisie gradually pervaded the system. In 1760, the English conquest brought a serious decline in the nobility's political power allowing the bourgeoisie to become more autonomous and increase its manorial ownership. The clergy, not experiencing the nobility's vicissitudes, dominated the society during 17th-18th centuries, even after the partial abolition of the manorial system which kept its social meaning in the 19th century. Secondary sources; 40 notes.
G. P. Cleyet

3151. Phillips, Paul. LAND TENURE AND ECONOMIC DEVELOPMENT: A COMPARISON OF UPPER AND LOWER CANADA. *J. of Can. Studies 1974 9(2): 35-45.* The seigneurial system of New France and Lower Canada did not provide a potential investment frontier because there was a limited total income unequally distributed with secondary economic institutions concentrated in Montreal and Quebec. By contrast, in Upper Canada the method of land tenure led to high labor productivity among widely distributed small independent landholders. Secondary sources; 2 tables, 40 notes.
G. E. Panting

3152. Porter, John R. L'HÔPITAL-GÉNÉRAL DE QUÉBEC ET LE SOIN DES ALIÉNÉS (1717-1845) [General Hospital of Quebec and the care of the insane (1717-1845)]. *Sessions d'Étude: Soc. Can. d'Hist. de l'Église Catholique [Canada] 1977 44: 23-56.* Discusses establishing the General Hospital of Quebec during 1692-1717 by the Augustinians and assesses methods of treating the insane, their acceptance within the local community, and the role of the Catholic Church during 1717-1845. Biblio.

3153. Porter, John R. UN PROJET DE MUSÉE NATIONAL À QUÉBEC À L'ÉPOQUE DU PEINTRE JOSEPH LÉGARÉ (1833-1853) [A proposed National Museum in Quebec during the era of painter Joseph Légaré, 1833-1853]. *Rev. d'Hist. de l'Am. Française [Canada] 1977 31(1): 75-82.* The painter Joseph Légaré (1795-1855) was one of the first promoters of a national museum in Quebec. He suggested such a project in 1833, but the public was indifferent. The National Gallery was not established until 1880, in Ottawa instead of Quebec. In 1874, Laval University purchased the old collection of Légaré's paintings. When the provincial Museum of Quebec opened in 1933, the university's collections were not integrated with it. Based on periodicals and secondary works; 23 notes.
L. B. Chan

3154. Pouyez, Christian and Bergeron, Michel. L'ÉTUDE DES MIGRATIONS AU SAGUENAY (1842-1931): PROBLÈMES DE MÉTHODE [The study of migrations to the Saguenay (1842-1931): methodological problems]. *Social Hist. [Canada] 1978 11(21): 26-61.* This study, part of a social history project on the population of Quebec's Saguenay district, relies on four main sources: federal censuses (available for only 1852, 1861, and 1871), parish censuses and annual reports, and civil registers (misleading where parishes and municipalities were subdivided, thereby suggesting moves where none occurred). Methods devised to identify such problems justify the research, and show that the problem of the equivalence of territories needs resolution to put the study of migrations on a solid methodological basis. 3 tables, 62 notes.
D. F. Chard

3155. Rioux, Albert. DE LIONEL GROULX À MARCEL RIOUX [From Lionel Groulx to Marcel Rioux]. *Action Natl. [Canada] 1978 68(3): 251-254.* In a review of Marcel Rioux, *La Question du Quebec, Action Nationale,* 1978 68(1), it was noted that the author had omitted Lionel Groulx in a list of liberators of Quebec. Similar oversights occurred in the fourth centennial celebration at Gaspé in 1934, and in Alphonse Désilets, "Notre Héritage Nationale," *Culture,* March, 1952. More seriously, it appears that contemporary college students are unaware of the role of this historian in the renaissance of Quebec nationalism.
A. W. Novitsky

3156. Savard, Pierre. UN QUART DE SIÈCLE D'HISTORIOGRAPHIE QUÉBÉCOISE, 1947-1972 [A quarter century of Quebec historiography, 1947-72]. *Recherches Sociographiques [Canada] 1974 15(1):*

77-96. With the establishment of historical institutes at Laval University and at the University of Montreal in 1947, the quantitative and qualitative development of historical writing in French-speaking Quebec entered into a quarter century period of impressive production. Until this point historical writing glorified the past and sought to defend French Canada's traditional way of life. This gave way in the late 1940's to a varied methodological and ideological exploration of the reality of French Quebec.

A. E. LeBlanc

3157. Séguin, Norman. COLONISATION ET IMPLANTATION RELIGIEUSE AU LAC SAINT-JEAN, DANS LA SECONDE MOITIÉ DU XIXᵉ SIÈCLE [Settlement and the establishment of religion around Lake Saint John, in the second half of the 19th century]. *Protée [Canada] 1976 5(2): 55-59.* The Catholic Church was eminently successful in establishing its influence in the region of Lake St. John, Quebec, beginning with the settlement of Hébertville in 1840.

3158. Séguin, Norman. L'ÉCONOMIE AGRO-FORESTIÈRE: GENÈSE DU DÉVELOPPEMENT AU SAGUENAY AU XIXᵉ SIÈCLE [The agricultural-forestry economy: genesis of development in Saguenay in the 19th century]. *Rev. d'Hist. de l'Amérique Française [Canada] 1976 29(4): 559-565.* Discusses the principal characteristics of the economy and the process of settlement of Saguenay in the 19th century. Concentrates on the production of timber for export and subsistence agriculture. Saguenay was a hinterland of Quebec and Montreal. Economic control over the region was in the hands of interests located in the two cities. Instead of establishing a new frontier society, the settlers of Saguenay merely reproduced the type of rural society to be found elsewhere in 19th-century Quebec. A summary of a part of the author's *La conquête du sol au XIXᵉ siècle* (The conquest of the soil in the 19th century).

L. B. Chan

3159. Simard, Sylvain. LES FRANÇAIS ET LE CANADA, 1850-1914: IDENTITÉ ET PERCEPTION [The French and Canada, 1850-1914: identity and perception]. *Rev. d'Hist. de l'Amérique Française [Canada] 1975 29(2): 209-239.* More than 700 books and brochures about Canada were published in late 19th-century France. Their authors were chiefly interested in Quebec for ethnic and linguistic reasons. They attributed the survival and development of the French in Canada to the leadership of the French-speaking Roman Catholic clergy. Secondary works; 10 tables, 26 notes.

L. B. Chan

3160. Stauffer, Anne Tholen. THE FRENCH-AMERICANS AND THE FRENCH-CANADIANS: A SELECT BIBLIOGRAPHY OF MATERIALS IN THE LIBRARY OF THE VERMONT HISTORICAL SOCIETY. *Vermont Hist. 1976 44(2): 110-114.* Includes 30 titles on Quebec, 7 on Samuel de Champlain, 10 on New England, 14 on Vermont, 4 periodicals, 3 maps, and 2 genealogies.

T. D. S. Bassett

3161. Sylvain, Philippe. UN FRÈRE MÉCONNU D'ANTOINE GÉRIN-LAJOIE: ELZÉAR GÉRIN [Elzéar Gérin, Antoine Gérin-Lajoie's brother not rightly recognized]. *Rev. de l'U. d'Ottawa [Canada] 1977 47(1-2): 214-225.* Because of adverse circumstances and a premature death, Elzéar Gérin 1843-87 was not as well-known as his brother, journalist, poet, novelist, and historian, Antoine Gérin-Lajoie. A talented, alert, and witty journalist with a combative spirit, Elzéar contributed to various important French Canadian newspapers and had many faithful readers; he was involved in political dissensions, once between the Vatican and the French government because of his publication of a confidential document. He founded his own newspaper and was elected a deputy of Quebec. Primary and secondary sources; 41 notes.

G. P. Cleyet

3162. Theriault, Leon. CHEMINEMENT INVERSE DES ACADIENS ET DES ANGLOPHONES DES MARITIMES [Inverse progress among Acadians and the English-speaking population of the Maritimes]. *Tr. of the Royal Soc. of Can. [Canada] 1977 15: 145-168.* Discusses the change in status of French-speaking people in the Maritime Provinces from the defeat of France in 1763 to the present. For the first century, especially after the influx of American Loyalists, the English-speaking population dominated the area. Gradually, the Acadians developed an identity and began to play a more active role. The Catholic Church expanded until it was able to establish dioceses in the area. Conflict between French parishoners and an Irish hierarchy was a prob-

lem. Henry Wadsworth Longfellow's poem "Evangeline" and Napoleon Bourassa's novel *Jacques et Marie* helped create an Acadian identity. Colleges such as Saint Anne's founded in 1890 and Sacred Heart founded in 1899 also helped. By the 1970's the Acadians had become an important force in the area, the economy of which had declined. In New Brunswick they have achieved a bilingual province. 55 notes, biblio.

J. D. Neville

3163. Torrelli, Maurice. CHARLES MAURRAS ET LE NATIONALISME CANADIEN FRANÇAIS [Charles Maurras and French Canadian nationalism]. *Action Natl. [Canada] 1977 67(2): 102-113.* Despite the lack of any direct connection between the two, there are many similarities in the thought of French royalist nationalist Charles Maurras and French Canadian nationalist Lionel Groulx. Both founded journals entitled *L'Action française.* Both emphasized the French national heritage, favoring a corporative rather than an individualistic view of society. Both emphasized the concept of a nation as a natural society founded on blood, history, faith, and culture, repudiating the liberal contract theory. Both questioned the value of democratic forms of government, and asserted that only history could provide the basis for the discovery and verification of natural laws of society which individualism neglected. Covers 1910-40. Primary and secondary sources; 39 notes.

A. W. Novitsky

3164. Tremblay, Marc-Adelard. EXISTE-T-IL DES CULTURES REGIONALES AU QUEBEC [Do regional cultures exist in Quebec?]. *Tr. of the Royal Soc. of Can. [Canada] 1977 15: 137-144.* Notes that Quebec has a regional culture made up of subregions. Makes use of the disciplines of geography, economics, political science, sociology and anthropology. Suggests that the French language draws together about eight distinct regions. Notes the criteria for identifying regional cultures. Concludes that with limitations there are distinct regional cultures within Quebec.

J. D. Neville

3165. Trépanier, Pierre. NOTRE PREMIER XIXᵉ SIÈCLE (1790-1890) [Our first 19th century (1790-1890)]. *Action Natl. [Canada] 1978 67(9): 745-751.* Quebec has produced a prodigious number of historians since the time of Perrault, Viger, Bibaud, and Garneau. Since the 1950's, Fernand Ouellet and his colleagues have reoriented Quebec historiography on the model of the French *Annales* school, with great reliance on statistical methods, integration of sociology, psychology, and politics, and an emphasis on economics. Recent studies of 19th-century Quebec history in this tradition include: Ouellet, *Le Bas-Canada, 1791-1840, Changements structuraux et crise* (Ottawa, 1976), Richard Chabot, *Le Curé de campagne et la contestation locale au Québec* (Montreal, 1975), and Jean-Louis Roy, *Édouard-Raymond Fabre, libraire et patriote canadien (1799-1854)* (Montreal, 1974). 10 notes.

A. W. Novitsky

3166. Trépanier, Pierre. POUR MIEUX CONNAÎTRE GROULX [To know Groulx better]. *Action Natl. [Canada] 1978 68(3): 209-218.* Reviews G.-É. Giguère, *Lionel Groulx, Biographie, "Notre État français, nous l'aurons!..."* (Montreal, 1978); M. Filion, ed., *Hommage à Lionel Groulx,* (Montreal, 1978); and Guy Frégault, *Lionel Groulx tel qu'en lui-même,* (Montreal, 1978). These biographies of Lionel Groulx reveal that the historian of French Canada refrained from endorsing Quebec independence through prudence as a priest, a political figure, and a leader who recognized the need for the broadest possible support for Quebec nationalism. He was more an activist than a scholar, writing history to prepare for the future. The influence of Charles Maurras and his Action Française on Groulx can no longer be doubted.

A. W. Novitsky

3167. Trépanier, Pierre. RUMILLY ET SON PAPINEAU [Rumilly and his Papineau]. *Action Natl. [Canada] 1978 67(9): 727-736.* For 50 years, Robert Rumilly has published several volumes per year on Quebec history, including his monumental *Histoire de la province de Québec.* He has recently published his second biography of Louis-Joseph Papineau, *Papineau et son temps* (Montreal, 1977, 2 vols.). There are some modifications from Rumilly's earlier *Papineau* (Paris, 1934), but the author's ideological position remains the same. The rebellions of 1837-38 were ideological, a local manifestation of the struggle which agitated the West since the French Revolution of 1789 and subsequent counterrevolution. Ethnic, cultural, and economic conflicts were secondary. For Trepanier, Rumilly's interpretation is somewhat narrow and simplistic. 40 notes.

A. W. Novitsky

3168. Trudel, Marcel. LES DÉBUTS DE L'INSTITUT D'HIS-TOIRE À L'UNIVERSITÉ LAVAL [The beginnings of the Institute of History at Laval University]. *Rev. d'Hist. de l'Amérique Française [Canada] 1973 27(3): 397-402.* Discusses the founding of the Institute of History at Laval University in 1947 which effectively established the study of history as an academic discipline.

3169. Trudel, Marcel. L'HOMME DE MA GÉNÉRATION, HOMME DE L'ANCIEN RÉGIME [The man of my generation, the man of the old order]. *Rev. de l'U. d'Ottawa [Canada] 1977 47(3): 251-269.* Commentary on the liberalizing changes in Quebec society during the lifetime of the author, with frequent references to secular and religious life during the 17th century.
G. J. Rossi

3170. Veltman, Calvin J. DEMOGRAPHIC COMPONENTS OF THE FRANCISATION OF RURAL QUEBEC: THE CASE OF RAW-DON. *Am. Rev. of Can. Studies 1976 6(2): 22-41.* Explores francization of the village of Rawdon about 40 miles from Montreal. The population was divided into groups based on ethnic and religious characteristics and each was studied in terms of 19th- and 20th-century patterns of marriage, family size, and migration. The study concludes that the Irish emigrated and were replaced by French Canadians whose higher marriage rate and tendency to have larger families produced a predominance of franco-phones. The relatively stable Anglican population became the most sig-nificant part of the anglophone community. 5 tables, 11 notes, biblio.
G. A. Patzwald

3171. Wallot, Jean-Pierre. GROULX HISTORIOGRAPHIE [Groulx historiography]. *Rev. d'Hist. de l'Amérique Française [Canada] 1978 32(3): 407-433.* An historiographic analysis of the writings of Fr. Lionel Groulx (1878-1967), distinguished Canadian historian. 95 notes.
M. R. Yerburgh

3172. Wawrzysko, Aleksandra. A BIBLIOGRAPHIC GUIDE TO FRENCH-CANADIAN LITERATURE. *Can. Lib. J. [Canada] 1978 35(2): 115-117, 119-121, 123-131, 133.* Covers not only French Canadian literature but also other disciplines that study the French in Canada. Focuses on reference works in the humanities and fine arts. Emphasizes writings since the late 19th century but contains some from the early 17th century. Encompasses catalogs, translations (from French into English and vice versa), biobibliographies, dictionaries of quotations, encyclope-dias, indexes and abstracts, dissertations, literary history, drama, fiction, poetry, and literary periodicals. Annotates 108 works and 41 journals.
D. J. Mycue

3173. Weiss, Jonathan M. ACADIA TRANSPLANTED: THE IM-PORTANCE OF *EVANGÉLINE DEUSSE* IN THE WORK OF AN-TONINE MAILLET. *Colby Lib. Q. 1977 13(3): 173-185.* Discusses Antonine Maillet's 1976 play *Evangéline Deusse* and its importance to her literary career as well as what it represents in terms of the transplanta-tion of the Acadians' culture of New Brunswick into the urban setting of Quebec.

3174. White, Stephen A. THE LAVACHE FAMILY OF ARI-CHAT, CAPE BRETON. *Nova Scotia Hist. Q. 1977 7(1): 69-85.* Gives a genealogy of the LaVache family beginning in 1774. Traces the name changes from LaVache, Lavache, to Lavash. Primary and secondary sources; 9 notes.
H. M. Evans

3175. Zinman, Rosalind. SELECTED BIBLIOGRAPHY ON QUE-BEC. *Can. Rev. of Sociol. and Anthrop. [Canada] 1978 15(2): 246-251.* A selection of English and French books, research articles, government publications written during 1968-78, and some classic works about the province of Quebec. Includes bibliographies, history, demography, econ-omy, social classes, government, politics, the state and the natinal ques-tion.
G. P. Cleyet

3176. —. [FRENCH-CANADIAN LITERARY HISTORY AND CRITICISM]. *Recherches Sociographiques [Canada] 1964 5(1-2): 11-74.*
Wyczynski, Paul. HISTOIRE ET CRITIQUE LITTÉRAIRES AU CANADA FRANCAIS: ÉTAT DES TRAVAUX [Literary his-tory and criticism in French Canada: work state], *pp. 11-69.* French-Canadian literary history and criticism is a difficult subject

to pursue due to incomplete references and sources, and its division into two stages; offers a historical perspective, ideas, and bibliogra-phy, although further research and compilation are still greatly needed; covers 1860's-20th century.
Lacroix, Benoît. COMMENTAIRE [Commentary], *pp. 70-74.* French-Canadian literature has its own place in universal literature and is unique to the French-Canadian character, historical, and cultural experience, 18th-20th centuries.

3177. —. [IDEOLOGICAL CURRENTS IN 19TH CENTURY FRENCH-CANADIAN LITERATURE]. *Recherches Sociogra-phiques [Canada] 1964 5(1-2): 101-121.*
Lamontagne, Leopold. LES COURANTS IDÉOLGIQUES DANS LA LITTÉRATURE CANADIEN-FRANÇAISE DU XIX SIÈCLE [Ideological currents in French-Canadian literature of the 19th century], *pp. 101-119.* Like French romanticism, 19th century French-Canadian literature dealt with similar themes, but it was more objective and focused on religion and patriotism, central to the French-Canadian experience.
Bonenfant, Jean-Charles. COMMENTAIRE [Commentary], *pp. 120-121.* Although Lamontagne offers a detailed historical perspective to understanding 19th-century French-Canadian literature, a more sociological standpoint is needed for further research into the sub-ject.

Early Settlement

3178. Baudry, René. CHARLES D'AULNAY ET LA COMPAG-NIE DE LA NOUVELLE-FRANCE [Charles d'Aulnay and the Com-pagnie de la Nouvelle-France]. *Rev. d'Hist. de l'Amérique Française [Canada] 1957 11(2): 218-241.* Describes Charles d'Aulnay's role in the Compagnie de la Nouvelle-France, also known as the Hundred Asso-ciates, and in the coming of French settlement to Acadia and Quebec in the early 17th century.

3179. Bideaux, Michel. CULTURE ET DÉCOUVERTE DANS LES *RELATIONS DES JÉSUITES* [Culture and discovery in the *Relations of the Jesuits*]. *Dix-Septième Siècle [France] 1976 (112): 3-30.* Examines the view of French missionaries toward American Indians, from the perspectives of a Christian, a humanist, and a 17th-century Frenchman. Based on the 41 little volumes of the *Rélations des Jésuites de la Nouvelle-France* published annually from 1632 to 1672, and other printed primary and secondary works; 108 notes.
W. J. Roosen

3180. Bideaux, Michel. LE DISCOURS DE L'ORDRE ET LE SÉISME DE 1663 [The order report and earthquake of 1663]. *Rev. de l'U. d'Ottawa [Canada] 1978 48(1-2): 62-83.* Analyzes the *Relation de 1663*, a Jesuit report in which there is a description of the theological and psychological implications of an earthquake which struck Quebec on 5 February 1663. Text of a paper presented at the conference Travel Writ-ings Related to New France, at York University, Toronto, 20-22 Febru-ary 1979. Primary sources; 99 notes.
G. J. Rossi

3181. Blain, Jean. ÉCONOMIE ET SOCIÉTÉ EN NOUVELLE-FRANCE: L'HISTORIOGRAPHIE DES ANNÉES 1950-1960—GUY FRÉGAULT ET L'ÉCOLE DE MONTRÉAL [Economy and society in New France: Historiography during 1950-60—Guy Frégault and the school of Montreal]. *Rev. d'Hist. de l'Amérique Française [Canada] 1974 28(2): 163-186.* The study of history in Montreal after 1950 became more scientific thanks to the work of Guy Frégault.

3182. Blain, Jean. ÉCONOMIE ET SOCIÉTÉ EN NOUVELLE-FRANCE: L'HISTORIOGRAPHIE AU TOURNANT DES ANNÉES 1960 [Economy and society in New France: historiography at the begin-ning of the 1960's]. *Rev. d'Hist. de l'Amérique Française [Canada] 1976 30(3): 323-362.* In 1957, Guy Frégault wrote that the period of French colonial rule was not Canada's golden age, but only a normal evolutionary period. A contemporary, Marcel Rioux, also identified the minority status of the French Canadians, Roman Catholicism, and the French language as the basic forces contributing to a romanticization of the French colonial period. Writers such as Frégault and Rioux distinguished between social history and nationalistic history, and along with others of the Montreal school helped to rejuvenate French Canadian historiography. Secondary works; 124 notes. L. B. Chan

3183. Blain, Jean. LA MORALITÉ EN NOUVELLE-FRANCE: LES PHASES DE LA THÈSE ET DE L'ANTITHÈSE [Morality in New France: thesis and antithesis]. *Rev. d'Hist. de l'Amérique Française [Canada] 1973 27(3): 408-416.* Examines the historiographical problem of conveying an accurate sense of the life of New France in the 17th and 18th centuries and finds a scientific analysis of the society's morals inadequate.

3184. Bosher, J. F. A FISHING COMPANY OF LOUISBOURG, LES SABLES D'OLONNE, AND PARIS: LA SOCIÉTÉ DU BARON D'HUART, 1750-1775. *French Hist. Studies 1975 9(2): 263-277.* Describes the general character and circumstances of a fishing company organized by Baron d'Huart formed to exchange goods for fish at Louisbourg, Cape Breton. It points out the role of the nobility in capitalistic enterprises. Based on archival materials; 37 notes. H. T. Blethen

3185. Bosher, J. F. FRENCH PROTESTANT FAMILIES IN CANADIAN TRADE 1740-1760. *Social Hist. [Canada] 1974 7(14): 179-201.* Protestant merchants in Quebec increased in number after the end of the War of Austrian Succession in 1748. By the time Quebec fell in 1759 they may have been preponderant in Franco-Canadian trade. Information on the origins, family ties, and business connections of the 16 identifiable Protestant firms indicates they came from and maintained ties with southwestern France (La Rochelle, Bordeaux, and Montauban) and were willing to trade with anyone, but formed companies and married only with other Protestants. Based on secondary sources and on documents in the Archives nationales, Public Record Office, Bibliothèque de l'Arsenal (Paris), Public Archives of Canada, and departmental and town archives in France; 82 notes. W. K. Hobson

3186. Bosher, J. F. A QUEBEC MERCHANT'S TRADING CIRCLES IN FRANCE AND CANADA: JEAN-ANDRÉ LAMALETIE BEFORE 1763. *Social Hist. [Canada] 1977 10(19): 24-44.* The trading merchants of 18th-century Quebec depended on a particular network of associates in other ports and cities of the trading region. These trading circles were usually composed of family members and close friends. This study of the trading circle of Jean-André Lamaletie, a merchant in Quebec from 1741 to 1758, reveals the nature of these business relationships. Lamalatie was not one of the merchants arrested by the French government in 1761 for profiteering and fraud (the *affaire du Canada),* although probably he was not completely innocent. Based on documents in the Public Record Office (London), Quebec Archives, and national and department archives in France; 2 tables, 3 charts, 50 notes. W. K. Hobson

3187. Brière, Jean-François. LE REFLUX DES TERRE-NEUVIERS MALOUINS SUR LES COTES DU CANADA DANS LA PREMIÈRE MOITIÉ DU XVIIIᵉ SIÈCLE: RÉPONSE À UN CHANGEMENT DU CLIMAT? [The movement of St. Malo fishermen from Newfoundland to the Canadian coasts in the first half of the 18th century: a response to a change of climate?]. *Social Hist. [Canada] 1979 12(23): 166-169.* From 1717 to 1734 St. Malo fishermen largely abandoned Newfoundland waters in favor of the Canadian coast. Then, beginning in 1734, they returned to Newfoundland. Parallel developments have been noted in the English fishery. In 1928 the oceanographer Beauge discovered that years of bad fishing in Newfoundland waters corresponded to a decline in the cold Labrador current. By analyzing fishing patterns, we may reconstitute the history of the climate of the oceans. 9 notes. D. F. Chard

3188. Brière, Jean-François. LE TRAFIC TERRE-NEUVIER MALOUIN DANS LA PREMIÈRE MOITIÉ DU XVIIIᵉ SIÈCLE 1713-1755 [St. Malo trade in the New World in the first half of the 18th century, 1713-55]. *Social Hist. [Canada] 1978 11(22): 356-374.* Although St. Malo before the French Revolution was best known for privateering, some 67% of its vessels in the 18th century pursued the North American fisheries. During 1713-55 the fisheries involved about 2,400 vessels and 3,000 men annually, while tonnage doubled. The fishing fleet comprised about 40% of France's North American fleet. During the Anglo-French detente the fishery shifted from Newfoundland to Île Royale, Labrador,

and the Gaspe, then back to Newfoundland by the 1730's. Based on records of the Archives of the Marine, Brest, and printed sources; 9 tables, 31 notes. D. F. Chard

3189. Campeau, Lucien. LE COMMERCE DES CLERCS EN NOUVELLE-FRANCE [Trade by the clergy in New France]. *Rev. de l'U. d'Ottawa [Canada] 1977 47(1-2): 27-35.* In New France, the clergy was forbidden to exercise trade, which was defined as the resale for a profit of merchandise purchased at a smaller price, without any transformation increasing its value beyond the social service rendered. Members of the clergy, who handled a considerable amount of furs which they used only as currency to pay for imports necessary to church administration activities, were often falsely accused of trading in the manner prohibited by the law. G. P. Cleyet

3190. Campeau, Lucien. MGR DE LAVAL ET LE CONSEIL SOUVERAIN 1659-1684 [Monseigneur Laval and the Sovereign Council 1659-84]. *Rev. d'Hist. de l'Amérique Française [Canada] 1973 27(3): 323-360.* Discusses the relationship between the ecclesiastical and commercial authorities in New France in the late 17th century and how the provincial governors exploited both.

3191. Carcassonne, Marcel. LA JONQUIÈRE ET LES ORIGINES DE TORONTO [La Jonquière and the origins of Toronto]. *R. Française d'hist. d'Outre-Mer [France] 1974 61(224): 366-394.* Toronto, a city with a population of more than two million, was originally established in 1750 as a fortified French fur trading station. Pierre-Jacques de Taffanel (1685-1752), the Marquis de La Jonquière, and governor of New France from 1749-52, suggested that the post be established. Based on documents in the Archives nationales de France, and secondary works; 48 notes. L. B. Chan

3192. Charbonneau, Hubert and Landry, Yves. LA POLITIQUE DÉMOGRAPHIQUE EN NOUVELLE-FRANCE [Demographic policy in New France]. *Ann. de Demógraphique Hist. [France] 1979: 29-57.* In the 17th century, the French government sought to encourage immigration to Canada, but it did not provide itself with the means, for it wanted to reserve the major part of human and economic resources for the mother country. It encouraged the settling of indentured servants, former soldiers, and *filles du Roy,* but not of Protestants; facilitated marriages and offered fiscal exemptions to large families, but posed unrealistic conditions. It was unable to prevent returns, effected few naturalizations, and did not succeed in assimilating the least part of the Indian population. In the last analysis, if the Canadian population reached a high level of natural growth under the French regime, it was in no way a consequence of demographic policy. J

3193. Charbonneau, Hubert; Desjardins, Bertrand; and Beauchamp, Pierre. LE COMPORTEMENT DEMOGRAPHIQUE DES VOYAGEURS SOUS LE REGIME FRANÇAIS [The demographic behavior of the Voyageurs in the French regime]. *Social Hist. [Canada] 1978 11(21): 120-133.* Scanty sources prevent thorough research on the voyageurs of Canada, but an analysis of the genealogical work of Archange Godbout indicates that some 16.4% of adult males were involved in the fur trade, with higher proportions from western regions. Godbout's *Nos ancetres au xviiᵉ siecle,* a veritable encyclopedia of first Canadians, thereby helps remedy the traditionally neglected demographic history of migrants such as the voyageurs, usually ignored in favor of their sedentary contemporaries. 12 fig., 12 notes. D. F. Chard

3194. Charbonneau, Hubert. RECONSTITUTION DE LA POPULATION DU CANADA AU 30 JUIN 1663 SUIVANT MARCEL TRUDEL [The reconstitution of the population of Canada on 30 June 1663 according to Marcel Trudel]. *Rev. d'Hist. de l'Amérique Française [Canada] 1973 27(3): 417-424.* Marcel Trudel's *La population du Canada en 1663* (Montreal: les Editions Fides, 1973) is representative of a new approach to demographic history based on numerous archival manuscripts and printed materials.

3195. Charbonneau, Hubert. RÉFLEXIONS EN MARGE D'HABITANTS ET MARCHANDS DE MONTRÉAL DE LOUISE DECHÊNE [Marginal reflections about *Habitants et marchands de Montréal,* by Louise Dechêne]. *Rev. d'Hist. de l'Am. Française [Canada] 1976 30(2): 263-269.* Reviews Louise Dechêne's *Habitants et marchands* de Montréal au XVIIᵉ siècle (Paris, 1974) in light of Hubert Charbonneau's Vie et mort des nos ancêtres (Montréal, 1975). Discusses migrations, births, deaths, and family structures in Québec, Trois-Rivières, and Montréal between 1660 and 1713. Secondary works; 14 notes.

L. B. Chan

3196. Cliche, Marie-Aimée. LES ATTITUDES DEVANT LA MORT D'APRÈS LES CLAUSES TESTAMENTAIRES DANS LE GOUVERNEMENT DE QUÉBEC SOUS LE RÉGIME FRANÇAIS [Attitudes before death as evidenced by wills filed with the government of Quebec during the French regime]. Rev. d'Hist. de l'Amérique Française [Canada] 1978 32(1): 57-94. Analysis of 799 wills registered in Quebec during 1663-1760 clearly reveals the deep religious convictions of their authors and a fundamental conformity to the teachings of the Catholic Church. Men and women of all socioeconomic classes were more concerned with salvation than with details of burial. Legacies providing for the celebration of Masses and the propagation of good works were favored. 13 tables, 66 notes.

M. R. Yerburgh

3197. D'Allaire, Micheline. LES INVENTAIRES DES BIENS DE DENIS-JOSEPH RUETTE D'AUTEUIL [Inventories of Denis-Joseph Ruette d'Auteuil's property]. Rev. de l'U. d'Ottawa [Canada] 1977 47(1-2): 36-45. The inventory of an estate, besides establishing an individual's financial situation, may reveal the vicissitudes of his life and career. A comparative analysis of an evaluation of Quebec's Denis-Joseph Ruette d'Auteuil's property following his separation from his wife (1661), and an inventory of his estate at his death (1680), shows an important deterioration of his fortune and discloses the difficulties born from his matrimonial separation. Primary and secondary sources; 26 notes.

G. P. Cleyet

3198. Dickinson, John A. COURT COSTS IN FRANCE AND NEW FRANCE IN THE EIGHTEENTH CENTURY. Can. Hist. Assoc. Hist. Papers [Canada] 1977: 48-65. A comparative study of the administration of justice in New France and France, emphasizing the traditional tendency to drag out judicial processes in order to increase the income of judges and other court personnel. The study examines not only the relative level of fees but also the wealth of potential litigants and concludes that the colonial judicial process was not as great an improvement as has been supposed. Canadian justice was relatively expeditious but inaccessible because of potential court costs. 2 tables, 3 fig., 41 notes.

R. V. Ritter

3199. Dickinson, John A. LA JUSTICE SEIGNEURIALE EN NOUVELLE-FRANCE: LE CAS DE NOTRE-DAME-DES-ANGES [Seigneurial justice in New France: the case of Notre Dame des Anges]. R. d'Hist. de l'Amérique Française 1974 28(3): 323-346. In the fief of Notre Dame des Anges (New France), granted to the Jesuits in 1626, feudal justice was practiced and covered serious crimes. Conflicts between feudal law and the Provost Court of Quebec were settled by an ordinance of 2 August 1706 confirming the competence of feudal lords in the administration of justice, including commerce, inheritances, guardianship, and taxes. Based on primary and secondary sources; 4 tables, 111 notes.

C. Collon

3200. Dubé, Jean-Claude. COLBERT ET L'INTENDANCE DE QUEBEC [Colbert and the administration of Quebec]. Rev. de l'U. d'Ottawa [Canada] 1977 47(3): 292-306. An essential element of 17th-century political life in France was a patronage that mirrored the feudal relationship between suzerain and vassal. Just as Cardinal Mazarin had made Jean Baptiste Colbert his protégé, so did Colbert develop a network of political patronage, usually based upon family ties. Some of his administrative appointees to Quebec were very closely connected with him, but all had at least an indirect association. This phenomenon persisted after Colbert's death. Based on documents in the Archives Nationales, Bibliothèque Nationale, and the departmental archives of Indre-et-Loire, and secondary works; 69 notes.

G. J. Rossi

3201. Dubé, Jean-Claude. LES INTENDANTS DE LA NOUVELLE-FRANCE ET LA RELIGION. [The intendants of New France and religion]. Sessions d'Étude: Soc. Can. d'Hist. de l'Église Catholique [Canada] 1978 45: 5-17. The 15 royal intendants in Quebec during 1663-1760 were generally sincere believers in the Catholic faith.

3202. Dubé, Jean-Claude. LES INTENDANTS DE LA NOUVELLE-FRANCE ET LA RÉPUBLIQUE DES LETTRES [The intendants of New France and the intellectuals]. R. d'Hist. de l'Amérique Française 1975 29(1): 31-48. A series of 15 royal intendants were appointed to administer New France during 1663-1760, all with strong intellectual backgrounds. Notarial documents concerning their personal furnishings attest to their sober tastes and their extensive libraries in theology, jurisprudence, art, science, literature, and history. Based on primary and secondary sources; table, 71 notes.

C. Collon

3203. Dunn, James Taylor. DU LUTH'S BIRTHPLACE: A FOOTNOTE TO HISTORY. Minnesota Hist. 1979 46(6): 228-232. Many historians have incorrectly indicated that the birthplace of Daniel Greysolon, Sieur Du Luth, was Saint-Germain-en-Laye, a suburb of Paris. In the early 1950's, a Canadian historian, Gerald Malchelosse, and a French local historian, Doctor Attale Boël, correctly identified Saint-Germain-Laval in the Forez region as the birthplace of this 17th-century French explorer of the New World. The lack of extant records makes an exact date of birth impossible to ascertain, but evidence strongly suggests that Greysolon was born in that town between 1636 and 1640. His family was of the petty nobility.

N. Lederer

3204. Eccles, W. J. DENONVILLE ET LES GALÉRIENS IROQUOIS [Denonville and the Iroquois galley slaves]. Rev. d'Hist. de l'Amérique Française [Canada] 1960 14(3): 408-429. Reexamines the historical evidence pertaining to the incident in New France in the summer of 1687, and the outcome of the Indian prisoners.

3205. Eccles, W. J. NEW FRANCE AND THE FRENCH IMPACT ON NORTH AMERICA. Am. Rev. of Can. Studies 1973 3(1): 56-64. Examines French colonial efforts in Canada from the early 17th century to 1760, including the life and government of the Canadians under France, as well as social, political, economic, and cultural institutions influenced by the French; highlights France's loss of power and eventual expulsion from the New World, 1757-60.

3206. Eisen, George. VOYAGEURS, BLACK-ROBES, SAINTS, AND INDIANS. Ethnohistory 1977 24(3): 191-205. Examines the earliest historical sources of Indian games and sport activities as well as the attitudes of the chroniclers toward these diversions. The scope of this study, therefore, is limited to a selection of early works, memoirs and journals of voyageurs, colonial officials and missionaries dating back to the 16th and 17th centuries. Many of these writings remained in manuscript form for centuries and were not previously presented in sporthistorical studies.

J

3207. Frégault, Guy. ESSAI SUR LES FINANCES CANADIENNES (1700-1750) [An essay on Canadian finances (1700-50)]. Rev. d'Hist. de l'Amérique Française [Canada] 1958 12(3): 307-322. An illumination of Canadian history in the 18th century through a study of Canadian financial documentation of that period.

3208. Gagnon, Serge. THE HISTORIOGRAPHY OF NEW FRANCE, 1960-1974: JEAN HAMELIN TO LOUISE DECHÊNE. J. of Can. Studies [Canada] 1978 13(1): 80-99. Jean Hamelin's Economie et société en Nouvelle-France (1960) and Louise Dechêne's Habitants et marchands de Montréal au XVIIᵉ siècle (1974), which frame this wide-ranging discussion, are both admirable examples of the Annales school of quantitative, nonnarrative historiography, which has only recently made its appearance in Canada. Hamelin's thesis, that preconquest Canada possessed no real bourgeoisie and Dechêne's attack on the popular image of the inhabitant as improvident and more inclined to engage in the fur trade than to farm his land effectively, take their place in the continuing debate between proponents and opponents of the Liberal tradition in Quebec politics. Sound methodology can render polemic intent harmless to effective scholarship. 83 notes.

L. W. Van Wyk

3209. Gaucher, M.; Delafosse, M.; and Debien, G. LES ENGAGÉS POUR LE CANADA AU XVIIIᵉ SIÈCLE [The volunteers for Canada in the 18th century]. Rev. d'Hist. de l'Amérique Française [Canada] 1959 13(2): 247-261, (3): 402-421; 1960 13(4): 550-561; 14(1): 87-108, (2): 256-258, (3): 430-440; 1961 14(4): 583-602. Part I. A list of the French volunteers who enlisted to go to Canada for their military service from 1714 to 1719, including their names, ages, and professions. Part II. A list of the French volunteers who enlisted to go to Canada for their military service in the Company of St. Jean's Isle, 1719-24. Part III. More volunteers, 1719-24. Part IV. More volunteers, 1719-24. Part V. Lists French volunteers for military service in Canada during 1727-49. Part VI. Covers volunteers, 1743-48. Part VII. Covers volunteers, 1751-58, with an overall demographic interpretation of the migration of the volunteers from 1714 to 1758.

3210. Gilman, Carolyn. PERCEPTIONS OF THE PRAIRIE: CULTURAL CONTRASTS ON THE RED RIVER TRAILS. *Minnesota Hist. 1978 46(3): 112-122.* The French and Métis hunters, farmers, trappers, and fishermen living around present-day Winnipeg saw the Red River trails as a means to transport goods to St. Paul and in this manner obtain those few commodities necessary for their comfort or survival in their near-subsistence economy. As St. Paul developed American traders visualized the Red River trails from a south to north vantage point instead of the north to south perception of the Métis. They saw the trails as a means of generating commerce with the growing settlements in Manitoba. The Métis visualized the prairie as a sea, employing French nautical terms to describe natural phenomena. They were highly conscious of the dangers of the trails, especially in regard to the menace of storms, drought, and prairie fires. Later Americans on the scene began to comment on the beauty of the environment along the trail and especially its potential as a site for agricultural progress and the building of towns and cities. While the Métis favored Red River trails that would provide the most rapid form of transportation with available provisions, the Americans saw the trails as linkages between settlements. N. Lederer

3211. Goossen, N. Jaye. A WEARER OF MOCCASINS: THE HONOURABLE JAMES MC KAY OF DEER LODGE. *Beaver [Canada] 1978 309(2): 44-53.* James McKay, a Red River Métis, was born at Fort Edmonton in 1828 to an employee of the Hudson's Bay Company. By the time he joined the Company in 1853, McKay was fluent and literate in English and French, and knew Cree, Ojibwa, Assiniboine, and Sioux dialects. He remained with the company until 1860, being important in negotiating with the Métis and Indians, and was a local expert on transportation. He married Margaret Roward, who inherited substantial money and land. By the late 1860's, McKay had become part of the local landed gentry and built a remarkable home at Deer Lodge on his Assiniboine tract. In later years McKay was a key figure in many Indian treaties. In the 1870's he held several positions in the new Manitoba government. McKay died in 1879, having risen from a Métis odd-job man to a leading businessman, government leader, and a man of tremendous respect in Manitoba. 11 illus. D. Chaput

3212. Goulding, Stuart D. FRANCIS PARKMAN AND THE JESUITS. *Hist. Today [Great Britain] 1974 24(1): 22-31.* Gives biographical data on historian Francis Parkman (1823-93) and discusses his treatment of 17th-century Jesuit missionaries in *The Conspiracy of Pontiac: Pioneers of New France in the New World* (1865) and *Jesuits* (1867).

3213. Greer, Allan. MUTINY AT LOUISBOURG, DECEMBER 1744. *Social Hist. [Canada] 1977 10(20): 305-336.* This mutiny is noteworthy because it occurred in wartime (during King George's War) and involved nearly all of the Fortress of Louisbourg soldiers. Provoked by rotten vegetables, and irritated by other injustices, Swiss troops protested and French troops then rebelled. When New Englanders attacked in 1745, French troops performed well, but later many surviving rebels were punished. Misery and hardship are often given as explanations of the rebellion, but the gap in outlook, background, and material interests between the Louisbourg soldiers and their officers also was important. 134 notes. D. F. Chard

3214. Gridgeman, N. T. CHAMPLAIN'S ASTROLABE RE-EXAMINED. *Can. Geographical J. 1977 94(1): 24-27.* Examines facts surrounding Samuel de Champlain's 1613 inland exploration of Canada, especially the contested fact of whether he actually employed the Cobden astrolabe (1603) during this time.

3215. Groulx, Lionel. LE LIEU DE L'EXPLOIT DU LONG-SAULT [The scene of Long Sault's exploit]. *Rev. d'Hist. de l'Amérique Française [Canada] 1960 14(3): 353-369.* Discusses the search for the location of Fort Orange, where the battle of Long Sault between French and Iroquois took place in May 1660, citing the Carillon rapids, Point-Fortune and the Bay des Sauvages as possible locations.

3216. Groulx, Lionel. UN SEIGNEUR EN SOUTANE [A lord in a cassock]. *Rev. d'Hist. de l'Amérique Française [Canada] 1957 11(2): 201-217.* Discusses the Compagnie de Saint-Sulpice (the Sulpician order), whose members were drawn from the nobility, in New France, 17th-18th centuries.

3217. Hamilton, Raphael N. WHO WROTE *PREMIER ÉTABLISSEMENT DE LA FOY DANS LA NOUVELLE FRANCE* [Who wrote *The First Establishment of the Faith in New France?*] *Can. Hist. Rev. [Canada] 1976 57(3): 265-288.* Examines evidence about the authorship by others than Crestien Le Clercq who is named on the title page. A Parisian savant, Abbe Claude Bernou, and Eusèbe Renaudot, editor of the *Gazette de France*, seem to have edited the work with the purpose of promoting Robert Cavelier de la Salle and the Comte de Frontenac. Based on the 1691 edition, contemporary printed sources, and unpublished documents from the archives in Montreal (Canada), Paris (France), and Seville (Spain). A

3218. Harris, Jane E. GLASSWARE EXCAVATED AT BEAUBASSIN, NOVA SCOTIA. *Can. Historic Sites 1975 (13): 127-142.* Approximately 200 glass objects, mostly bottles for wine, snuff or medicine, were recovered from the Acadian townsite of Beaubassin, Nova Scotia. The settlement was occupied by the French from the 1670's to about 1750, and by the British from the 1750's to the early 1800's. The French occupation is represented by fragments of bottles, tumblers, and stemware bowls; the British period by bottles, a small amount of plain stemware and a decanter stopper. J

3219. Heidenreich, Conrad E. AN ANALYSIS OF CHAMPLAIN'S *MAPS* IN TERMS OF HIS ESTIMATES OF DISTANCE, LATITUDE AND LONGITUDE. *Rev. de l'U. d'Ottawa [Canada] 1978 48(1-2): 12-45.* Detailed analysis of the maps of Samuel de Champlain (1567-1635) based upon his scientific explorations during 1603-1616 along the North American coast from Cape Cod to Cape Race and inland to the Georgian Bay and Eastern Lake Ontario. Text of a paper presented at the conference Travel Writings Related to New France, at York University, Toronto, 20-22 February 1979. Primary sources; 8 tables, 3 fig., 58 notes. G. J. Rossi

3220. Hynes, Gisa I. SOME ASPECTS OF THE DEMOGRAPHY OF PORT ROYAL, 1650-1755. *Acadiensis [Canada] 1973 3(1): 3-17.* Emphasizes immigration to Port Royal, Nova Scotia, from France.

3221. Jaenen, Cornelius J. AMERINDIAN VIEWS OF FRENCH CULTURE IN THE SEVENTEENTH CENTURY. *Can. Hist. R. [Canada] 1974 55(3): 261-291.* Examines the traditional interpretation that the Amerindians admired French civilization and welcomed policies of Christianization and assimilation. Despite the paucity of Amerindian sources, there is evidence to indicate selective adaptation of some European technology and cultural patterns, outright rejection of much of French culture and belief systems, development of counter-innovative devices and behavior, and maintenance of native convictions of superiority to European life-style. Based on French travel literature and unpublished archival materials. S

3222. Jaenen, Cornelius J. THE PERSISTENCE OF THE PROTESTANT PRESENCE IN NEW FRANCE, 1541-1760. *Pro. of the Ann. Meeting of the Western Soc. for French Hist. 1974 (2): 29-40.* Outlines the varying fortunes of the Huguenots in New France and examines the small Protestant community of 1759. The Catholic Recollet missionaries and the Jesuits successfully campaigned to exclude Protestants from colonial administration and from further settlement in New France by 1627. Protestants continued to trickle in and during 1669-78 Jean Baptiste Colbert's policy of tolerance outweighed the clergy's demand for exclusion of all Huguenots, but Louis XIV's much harsher policy culminated in the Edict of Fontainebleau. Under the Regency and Louis XV, Huguenots reestablished contacts with Canada. In 1759 there were about 1,000 Protestants of whom 471 are identified by name. Their various national origins, their economic and occupational status, and the number of and reasons for abjurations are cited. Protestantism, although not a major factor, continued to be important in the history of New France. Based on Canadian and French archives and other primary sources; 31 notes. J. D. Falk

3223. Jennings, Francis. THE SAVAGE WHO CAME TO NEW FRANCE. *Rev. in Am. Hist. 1976 4(4): 513-519.* Review article prompted by Cornelius J. Jaenen's *Friend and Foe: Aspects of French-Amerindian Cultural Contact in the Sixteenth and Seventeenth Centuries* (New York: Columbia U. Pr., 1976); discusses each culture's impact on the other, as well as evangelism and trade.

3224. Keyes, John. UN COMMIS DES TRÉSORIERS GÉNÉRAUX DE LA MARINE À QUEBEC: NICOLAS LANOULLIER DE BOISCLERC [A clerk of the Admiralty's general treasury in Quebec: Nicolas Lanoullier of Boisclerc]. *Rev. d'Hist. de l'Amérique Française [Canada] 1978 32(2): 181-202.* Lanoullier was the Admiralty's general treasury clerk in Quebec during 1720-30. An analysis of his career sheds considerable light on details of colonial government and finance. The position entailed the disbursement of funds to meet the salaries and expenses of soldiers and administrative personnel. Sufficient monies rarely arrived from France. Amidst a flurry of allegations, Lanoullier was fired for financial malfeasance. He spent the rest of his life attempting to honor his obligations. 98 notes.   M. R. Yerburgh

3225. Kleber, Louis C. BRITAIN AND FRANCE IN NORTH AMERICA. *Hist. Today [Great Britain] 1974 24(12): 819-826.* Discusses the variant natures of British and French colonization in North America and traces developments up to the capitulation of New France to the British in 1760.

3226. Koyen, Kenneth. FRENCH CANADA'S COLONIAL FORT IS BEING BUILT ANEW. *Smithsonian 1973 4(2): 76-83.* Discusses the restoration of the 18th-century French fortress of Louisbourg, Nova Scotia.   S

3227. Lachance, André. LA DÉSERTION ET LES SOLDATS DÉSERTEURS AU CANADA DANS LA PREMIÈRE MOITIÉ DU XVIIIᵉ SIÈCLE [Desertion and soldiers who deserted in Canada in the first half of the 18th century]. *Rev. de l'U. d'Ottawa [Canada] 1977 47(1-2): 151-161.* Military desertions were frequent in New France; soldiers deserted most often because of the fear of getting caught after committing a misdemeanor, on account of unfriendly relations with their officers, or because of a decision made while being drunk. They usually chose the summer months for running away, were 20-24 years old, of varied appearance and good size. They were rarely caught because the environment was favorable to hiding and they had help from the country people. The most frequent punishment was the death penalty. Primary and secondary sources; 4 tables, 50 notes.   G. P. Cleyet

3228. Lachance, André. UNE ÉTUDE DE MENTALITÉ: LES INJURES VERBALES AU CANADA AU XVIIIᵉ SIECLE (1712-1748) [A study of mental attitudes: verbal abuse in Canada in the eighteenth century (1712-1748)]. *Rev. D'Hist. De L'Amérique Française [Canada] 1977 31(2): 229-238.* Judicial records reveal a significant number of cases involving slander, defamation, and other verbal indignities in French Canadian society. Neighborhood women, for example, might question each other's morality; an intoxicated card player might accuse another of cheating. The various "insults" of that era provide a unique view of the contemporary social fabric and strongly suggest that French Canadians placed great emphasis on maintaining their honor and their reputations. 26 notes.   M. R. Yerburgh

3229. Laflèche, Guy. LE NARRATEUR DES PREMIÈRES *RELATIONS* [The narrator in the early *Relations*]. *Rev. de l'U. d'Ottawa [Canada] 1978 48(1-2): 46-61.* Discusses the narrative function of early writers of the *Jesuit Relations*. Text of a paper presented at the conference Travel Writings Related to New France at York University, Toronto, 20-22 February 1979. Primary sources; 55 notes.   G. J. Rossi

3230. Lafrance, Marc. ÉVOLUTION PHYSIQUE ET POLITIQUES URBAINES: QUÉBEC SOUS LE RÉGIME FRANÇAIS [Physical evolution and urban policies: Quebec under the French]. *Urban Hist. Rev. [Canada] 1975 (3): 3-22.* Quebec, capital of New France, grew rapidly in the century and a half between its founding and the British conquest; the French authorities did their best to plan this development according to the city planning ideas of the day.

3231. Lamontagne, Roland. PRISE DE CONTACT DE LA GALISSONIÈRE AVEC LA NOUVELLE-FRANCE [La Galissonière's preliminary contact with New France]. *Rev. d'Hist. de l'Amérique Française [Canada] 1960 14(3): 384-394.* Describes the initial phase of the government of Roland Michel Barrin, Comte de la Galissonière, in New France, fall 1747.

3232. Lanctot, Gustave. POSITION DE LA NOUVELLE-FRANCE EN 1663 [The position of New France in 1663]. *Rev. d'Hist. de l'Amérique Française [Canada] 1958 11(4): 517-532.* Describes New France in 1663, when the commercial companies were suppressed; it then numbered some 2,500 inhabitants along the St. Lawrence River.

3233. Leefe, John. NOVA SCOTIA AND THE ACADIAN PROBLEM 1710-1755. *Nova Scotia Hist. Q. [Canada] 1974 4(4): 327-343.* Discusses the causes and background of the expulsion of the Acadians from Nova Scotia. In 1710 Great Britain conquered Port Royal, the capital of Acadia. Inhabitants living within three miles of the fort were given two years to change their allegiance from French to British. The dispute was not settled until 1755 when 6,000 Acadians were dispersed among the English colonies in the South. 34 notes.   H. M. Evans

3234. Légaré, Jacques; La Rose, André; and Roy, Raymond. RECONSTITUTION OF THE 17TH CENTURY CANADIAN POPULATION: AN OVERVIEW OF A RESEARCH PROGRAM. *Hist. Methods Newsletter 1975 9(1): 1-8.* Using parish registers and the censuses of 1666, 1667, and 1681 as data, the authors outline their methodology, which uses particulary the Henry Code. They believe that their work has merit for both demographers and historians.

D. K. Pickens

3235. Liebel, Jean. ON A VIEILLI CHAMPLAIN [The aging of Champlain]. *Rev. d'Hist. de l'Amérique Française [Canada] 1978 32(2): 229-237.* For more than a century, Samuel de Champlain's biographers have claimed that he was born about 1567. In actuality, his birth date was probably closer to 1580. Champlain refers to a friend born in 1560 as being "like a father to me." Furthermore, he first went to sea in 1594; it is inconceivable that he was 27 years old at the time. Champlain's biographers have unwittingly aged him. 27 notes.   M. R. Yerburgh

3236. Lindsay, Charles S. LOUISBOURG GUARDHOUSES. *Can. Historic Sites 1975 (12): 47-100.* Louisbourg guardhouses are studied from two aspects, architectural and functional, by bringing together primary historical and archaeological evidence from Louisbourg, secondary historical evidence from France, and pictorial evidence of surviving French guardhouses. The results have shown that Louisbourg guardhouses were parallel in building techniques and materials with the simpler guardhouses used in lesser positions in France. In layout and function they were consistent with the principles applied to all French guardhouses. The evidence also shows that, consistent with much of the other construction work at Louisbourg, few concessions were made to the climatic differences between France and North America.   J

3237. Marmier, Jean. LE RÉCIT DE M. DE COURCELLES AU LAC ONTARIO (1671), ET DOLLIER DE CASSON [The account of de Courcelles at Lake Ontario and Dollier de Casson]. *Rev. d'Hist. de l'Amérique Française [Canada] 1978 32(2): 239-250.* In 1671, the governor of New France, Remy de Courcelles, travelled to Lake Ontario to prevent the Iroquois Indians from further disrupting colonial life. Authorship of the document relating this event has never been clearly revealed. Though it had been attributed to François Dollier de Casson, the evidence is highly implausible. For all intents and purposes, the author remains anonymous. 36 notes.   M. R. Yerburgh

3238. Massicotte, Jean-Paul and Lessard, Claude. LA CHASSE EN NOUVELLE-FRANCE AU XVIIᵉ SIÈCLE [Hunting in New-France in the 17th century]. *Can. J. of Hist. of Sport and Physical Educ. 1974 5(2): 18-30.* In 17th century Canada, the European hunted for pleasure while the Indians were encouraged to hunt for trading which would benefit the mother country. Describes the Indian's skill at hunting various animals, which supplemented grain cultivation and provided a sportive event. Based on contemporary accounts and secondary literature; 42 notes.   L. R. Atkins

3239. Massio, Roger. LES SOURCES PRIVÉES DE L'HISTOIRE COLONIALE DANS LE PAYS DE BIGORRE [Private sources of colonial history in the country of Bigorre]. Rev. d'Hist. de l'Amérique Française [Canada] 1958 12(3): 407-410. Observes the major problems of New France in the 18th century through the private papers of Lacaye, LaPorte, and François de Carrere, on the colonial history of Canada.

3240. McLeod, Carol. TRAILS AND TORMENT: THE STORY OF TWO STALWARTS. Nova Scotia Hist. Q. [Canada] 1979 9(1): 37-45. Nicholas Denys and his brother Simon settled in Acadia in 1632. Although they were granted a tract of land on Miscou Island, their efforts to establish a successful fur trade were thwarted by more powerful traders. Twice Nicholas' ships were confiscated. King Louis XIV of France granted him letters of patent so that he could continue his life in Nova Scotia. Secondary sources; biblio. H. M. Evans

3241. Miquelon, Dale. HAVY AND LEFEBVRE OF QUEBEC: A CASE STUDY OF METROPOLITAN PARTICIPATION IN CANADIAN TRADE, 1730-1760. Can. Hist. R. 1975 56(1): 1-24. The business papers of a French trading company, Robert Dugard et Cie of Rouen, housed in the Archives nationales, Paris, and Canadian private papers and notarial archives have been used to reconstruct the day-to-day business of these 18th-century factors, answering some questions regarding Canadian economic history while posing the larger one of the influence of French business society on Canada. A

3242. Monière, Denis. L'UTILITÉ DU CONCEPT DE MODE DE PRODUCTION DES PETITS PRODUCTEURS POUR L'HISTORIOGRAPHIE DE LA NOUVELLE-FRANCE [The utility of the concept of mode of production of the small producers for the historiography of New France]. Rev. d'Hist. de l'Amérique Française [Canada] 1976 29(4): 483-502. The concept of "mode of production of the small producers" is applicable to New France, and helps to describe the complexity of the transition process from feudalism to capitalism under colonialism. The theory regarding the destruction of the Canadian colonial bourgeoisie and its replacement by an English bourgeoisie, by itself, cannot explain adequately the formation of Canadian society after 1760. The MPSP concept clarifies the importance of the petty bourgeoisie in the historical development of Quebec's society. Based on secondary works; 28 notes. L. B. Chan

3243. Moogk, Peter N. IN THE DARKNESS OF A BASEMENT: CRAFTSMEN'S ASSOCIATIONS IN EARLY FRENCH CANADA. Can. Hist. Rev. [Canada] 1976 57(4): 399-439. Provides an historical explanation for the scarcity of self-constituted, secular associations among the French Canadians in Quebec before the First World War. The failure of the colonists to transplant the corporate traditions of old France to North America is attributed to the Bourbon administration's hostility to private and unsanctioned groups and gatherings and to the colonists' preoccupation with self-employment and family autonomy. The government attitude is evident from the history of three artisans' religious brotherhoods and a shipwright's strike. The colonists' values are shown by the number and nature of partnerships and journeymen's indentures among craftsmen. Based on the administrative, judicial, and notarial records of New France. A

3244. Moogk, Peter N. RANK IN NEW FRANCE: RECONSTRUCTING A SOCIETY FROM NOTARIAL DOCUMENTS. Social Hist. [Canada] 1975 8(15): 34-53. The social status of occupations in New France closely paralleled the social status of occupations in France but the hierarchy of occupations did not correlate so closely with wealth in New France as it did in France. Requirements of rank led those in high social standing to conspicuous consumption no matter what their relative wealth, whereas those in low social standing could save. The wealth hierarchy was reconstructed from estate inventories; the social status hierarchy was reconstructed from marriage contracts. Based on documents in Archives Nationales de France, archives judiciaires de Montréal, archives de Québec, archives judiciaires de Trois-Rivières, and secondary sources; 2 tables, 38 notes. W. K. Hobson

3245. Moogk, Peter N. RÉEXAMEN DE L'ÉCOLE DES ARTS ET MÉTIERS DE SAINT-JOACHIM [Another look at the School of Arts and Crafts of St. Joachim]. R. d'Hist. de l'Amérique Française 1975 29(1): 3-29. Reexamines historian Auguste-Honoré Gosselin's study of the School of Arts and Crafts of St. Joachim (New France). Gosselin attributed creation of the school to Bishop François de Laval (ca. 1668) and supposed it an extension of the Petit Séminaire of Quebec. The St. Joachim school, an alternative to traditional apprenticeship, lacked the structure and importance of a modern technical school. Translation of article in English based on primary and secondary sources; 68 notes. C. Collon

3246. Moogk, Peter N. "THIEVING BUGGERS" AND "STUPID SLUTS": INSULTS AND POPULAR CULTURE IN NEW FRANCE. William and Mary Q. 1979 36(4): 524-547. The mentality and values of a cultural group can be determined from verbal conflicts—name-calling, etc. Analyzes 136 insult cases in the courts of Montreal, Trois-Rivières, Quebec, and Louisbourg before 1760. Unlike France, complainants in Canada were usually from the lower classes. Considers mitigating circumstances accepted by the courts. Various instances are discussed to show that the conservatism in the vocabulary of abuse is due to the traditionalism of the Canadians in their social values and folk beliefs. The amusing case involving the Chesnay-Feret brawl in 1743 is emphasized. Uses court and other local records; table—Scale of Frequency for Insults Used in New France; 65 notes. H. M. Ward

3247. Moon, Robert. RESTORING 17TH CENTURY LOWER TOWN QUEBEC. Can. Geographical J. 1975 91(3): 38-45. Describes the historic restoration of 17th-century buildings in Lower Town Place Royale, Quebec. S

3248. Morel, André. RÉFLEXIONS SUR LA JUSTICE CRIMINELLE CANADIENNE, AU 18e SIÈCLE [Reflections on Canadian criminal justice, in the 18th century]. Rev. d'Hist. de l'Amérique Française [Canada] 1975 29(2): 241-253. The great severity of justice can be an indication of the real values which people strove to protect. Banishment was the punishment invariably retained during the 17th century for all crimes except rape; in the 18th century, it was only enforced against adulterous men. Secondary works; 2 tables, 13 notes. L. B. Chan

3249. Morgan, Robert J. and MacLean, Terrence D. SOCIAL STRUCTURE AND LIFE IN LOUISBOURG. Can.: An Hist. Mag. 1974 1(4): 60-75 Social classes and daily life of the inhabitants of Louisbourg, 1713-50. One of five articles in this issue on the National Historic Park at Louisbourg. S

3250. Morrison, Kenneth M. NATIVE AMERICAN HISTORY: THE ISSUE OF VALUES (REVIEW ESSAY). J. of Ethnic Studies 1978 5(4): 80-89. Analyzes Cornelius Jaenen's Friend and Foe: Aspects of French-Amerindian Cultural Contact in the Sixteenth and Seventeenth Centuries (1976), and Bruce Trigger's The Children of Aataentsic: A History of the Huron People to 1660 (1976). Both add important new dimensions to Indian history by focusing on Native American values and their relation to ordering intercultural relations, but Trigger is far more successful in explaining the experience of particular Indian peoples at specific times. Jaenen focuses on the French and their ideological postures, and thus does not appreciate the ordered nature of tribal life and repeated Indian rejections of French policies. Trigger is a truer ethnohistorian, who reassesses each stage of Huron history in light of its own values and shows that direct contact with the French "did not alter the direction or nature of cultural change." Internal disunity, as much as Iroquoian aggressions, led to the Hurons' collapse. 4 notes. G. J. Bobango

3251. Neave, Judith Chamberlin. LAHONTAN AND THE LONG RIVER CONTROVERSY. Rev. de l'U. d'Ottawa [Canada] 1978 48(1-2): 124-147. In Letter XVI of his work Nouveaux voyages de Mr le Baron de Lahontan dans l'Amérique septentrionale (1703), Louis-Armand de Lom d'Arce Lahontan (1666-1715) described his discovery in 1688-1689 of the Long River which flowed into the Upper Mississippi from the west. This discovery has never been proved definitively. Based upon stylistic comparisons with other travel writings, Lahontan quite possibly borrowed information from these sources, especially The Journal of Jean Cavelier. Text of a paper presented at the conference Travel Writings Related to New France, at York University, Toronto, 20-22 February 1979. Based on primary sources; 2 maps, 97 notes, biblio. G. J. Rossi

3252. Nish, Cameron. LA BANQUEROUTE DE FRANÇOIS-ÉTIENNE CUGNET, 1742 [The bankruptcy of François-Étienne Cugnet, 1742]. *Actualité Écon. [Canada] 1965 41(1): 146-202.* Presents the documents relevant to the bankruptcy of François-Étienne Cugnet in 1742—inventories of personal and business effects—to provide information on economic conditions in New France during this period.

3253. Olivier-Lecamp, Gaël and Légaré, Jacques. QUELQUES CARACTERISTIQUES DES MENAGES DE LA VILLE DE QUEBEC ENTRE 1666 ET 1716 [Some characteristics of Quebec City households between 1666 and 1716]. *Social Hist. [Canada] 1979 12(23): 66-78.* Quebec City grew from a market-town of 550 people in 1666 to a small city of 2,500 inhabitants in 1716. Its households also changed in this period. In the first 20 years of the period French immigration to Canada reached a peak. In these years Quebec City differed considerably from 17th and 18th century Europe. In 1716 Quebec was closer to European norms. This is clear from studying the censuses of 1666, 1667, 1681, and 1716. 5 tables, 17 notes.   D. F. Chard

3254. Pichette, Robert and Lussier, Jean Jacques. ARMORIAL DES CHEVALIERS DE MALTE FRANÇAIS EN TERRE D'AMERIQUE [Heraldry of the French Knights of Malta in America]. *Rev. de l'U. d'Ottawa [Canada] 1976 46(1): 40-67.* The Knights of Malta were involved in the founding, development, and defense of the French colonies in America and in the American Revolution. Although the Canadian order of Malta was not founded until 1950, its roots are deep in both America and Canada. Lists some of the more important knights and provides a history of their coat of arms. Primary and secondary sources; biblio.   M. L. Frey

3255. Pilgrim, Donald G. FRANCE AND NEW FRANCE: TWO PERSPECTIVES ON COLONIAL SECURITY. *Can. Hist. Rev. [Canada] 1974 55(4): 381-407.* A critique of the theses of William J. Eccles in his *Canada under Louis XIV, 1663-1701* (Toronto, 1964) and *Frontenac: The Courtier Governor* (Toronto, 1962) in explanation of France's claimed neglect of New France. Eccles exaggerated the degree of neglect of the Marquis de Seignelay's (1651-90) administration, has given an unbalanced portrait of the secretary of state himself, and his analysis is incomplete, being "based on a conceptual framework which does not take into account the multitude of factors and considerations which determined French foreign policy during the 1680's." His interpretation overemphasizes New France's isolation. 89 notes.   R. V. Ritter

3256. Plamondon, Lilianne. UNE FEMME D'AFFAIRES EN NOUVELLE-FRANCE: MARIE-ANNE BARBEL, VEUVE FORNEL [A business woman in New France: Marie-Anne Barbel, the widow Fornel]. *Rev. D'Hist. De L'Amérique Française [Canada] 1977 31(2): 165-185.* There has been virtually no systematic examination of the role of women in business and financial affairs during the French hegemony in Canada. Individuals such as Marie-Anne Barbel, however, provide a more realistic portrait of women in colonial society and the ways in which they helped shape that society. Barbel (Widow Fornel) inherited her husband's business holdings and under her management those holdings grew, diversified, and prospered. Partially in response to the military intrusions of the English, she liquidated her assets in 1759 and lived in retirement for another 31 years. 54 notes.   M. R. Yerburgh

3257. Pritchard, James S. THE PATTERN OF FRENCH COLONIAL SHIPPING TO CANADA BEFORE 1760. *Rev. Française d'Hist. d'Outre-mer [France] 1976 63(2): 189-210.* Between 1640 and 1720 maritime trade between France and Canada was dominated by La Rochelle armament suppliers and merchants. As French colonial commerce grew during the 18th century and the colonial population doubled, the volume of trade with Canada remained stable. Canadians entered the intercolonial trade to Louisbourg and the West Indies, but Canada was becoming self-sufficient with few interests outside of North America and fewer attractions for French merchants. After 1738 maritime traffic to Canada increased greatly; poor harvests led to demands for flour. Five years later the struggle for empire led French authorities to view Canada and Canadians as a fortress and garrison that had to be maintained. By the 1740's most shipping was carried on from Bordeaux. 6 tables, 2 graphs, 25 notes.   A. W. Howell

3258. Proulx, Gilles. SOLDAT À QUÉBEC, 1748-1759. [Soldiers in Quebec, 1748-59]. *Rev. d'Hist. de l'Amérique Française [Canada] 1979 32(4): 535-563.* During the years leading up to the fall of Quebec, distinctions must be made between the two forces assigned to its defense—the civilian militia and the soldiers sent from France. The latter were of very limited assistance; for the most part, they were young and inexperienced, adapted poorly to the rigorous climate, and lacked total commitment to the French Canadians' cause. 102 notes.   M. R. Yerburgh

3259. Rousseau, François. HÔPITAL ET SOCIÉTÉ EN NOUVELLE-FRANCE: L'HÔTEL-DIEU DE QUÉBEC À LA FIN DU XVIIᵉ SIÈCLE [Hospital and society in New France: the chief hospital of Quebec at the end of the 17th century]. *Rev. d'Hist. de l'Am. Française [Canada] 1977 31(1): 29-47.* Quebec's first hospitals were established in the 1640's as part of the policy of evangelizing the American Indians. By 1700, however, Indians accounted for less than four percent of total admissions. Most patients were Canadian colonists. Illness records were started in 1689. From such records, it is possible to study the chief hospital in society, and popular perception of it. Based on published documents and secondary works; 4 tables, 4 graphs, 37 notes.   L. B. Chan

3260. Rousseau, Jacques. "L'AFFAIRE DOLLARD," DE FORT ORANGE AU LONG-SAULT ["The Dollard Affair," from Fort Orange to Long Sault]. *Rev. d'Hist. de l'Amérique Française [Canada] 1960 14(3): 370-377.* Views the Dollard affair of May 1660, in which Adam Dollard des Ormeaux's party held out for a week before succumbing to a large force of Iroquois Indians at Long Sault, as an economic, not a spectacular, event in Canada's history.

3261. Roy, Raymond and Charbonneau, Hubert. LE CONTENU DES REGISTRES PAROISSIAUX CANADIENS DU XVIIᵉ SIÈCLE [The contents of Canadian parish registers of the 17th century]. *Rev. d'Hist. de l'Am. Française [Canada] 1976 30(1): 85-97.* From about 1616 to 1700, more than 26,000 acts of baptism, marriage, and burial affecting Europeans were recorded in Quebec's parish registers. Attempts to analyze Canada's 17th-century population from parish registers. Based on parish registers and secondary works; 3 figs., 12 notes.   L. B. Chan

3262. Roy, Raymond; Landry, Yves; and Charbonneau, Hubert. QUELQUES COMPORTEMENTS DES CANADIENS AU XVIIᵉ SIÈCLE D'APRÈS LES REGISTRES PAROISSIAUX [Some comportments of 17th-century Canadians according to parish registers]. *Rev. d'Hist. de l'Am. Française [Canada] 1977 31(1): 49-73.* The Department of Demography of the University of Montreal has attempted to reconstitute the whole population of Quebec during the 17th century based on parish records. Surviving records show more than 31,000 acts of baptism, marriage, and burial. Scholars may certainly attempt to make conclusions about the social and cultural nature of the early colonial population from such statistics. Based on parish records, published documents, and secondary works; 9 tables, 3 figs., 23 notes, appendix.   L. B. Chan

3263. Runte, Roseann. ROBERT CHALLE: AN EARLY VISITOR TO ACADIA AND QUEBEC. *Nova Scotia Hist. Q. [Canada] 1979 9(3): 201-214.* Robert Challe (b. 1659) accompanied an expedition to the coast of Acadia in 1681. The company chose a site at Chedabucto at the head of the Bay of Canso to establish a settlement. Challe's journal (Journal de Voyage), written 25 years later, presents a history of the settlement and includes descriptions of the country, a plan for colonizing the area, criticisms of the French management of the colony, and his own personal experiences. 17 notes.   H. M. Evans

3264. Salter, Michael A. L'ORDRE DE BON TEMPS [The Order of Good Times]. *Nova Scotia Hist. Q. [Canada] 1975 5(2): 143-154.* An account of the founding of L'Ordre de Bon Temps, the first social club in the new world, at Port Royal in 1606. The idea of Samuel de Champlain, its purpose was to help while away the dreary evening hours of the bleak Nova Scotian winter, and, more seriously, to save the colonists from the devastation suffered from disease the previous winter. By this means were avoided poor diets, a passive existence, and a failure in esprit de corps that would again bring disaster. The experiment was successful. 38 notes.   R. V. Ritter

3265. Salter, Michael A. L'ORDRE DE BON TEMPS: A FUNCTIONAL ANALYSIS. *J. of Sport Hist. 1976 3(2): 111-119.* In 1606 Samuel de Champlain proposed that a social group be established in New France to while away the evening hours of the Nova Scotian winter. It was to be called L'Ordre de Bon Temps, the first social club structured by Caucasians in North America. The club and its activities are described. 44 notes.   M. Kaufman

3266. Schlesier, Karl H. EPIDEMICS AND INDIAN MIDDLEMEN: RETHINKING *THE WARS OF THE IROQUOIS,* 1609-1653. *Ethnohistory 1976 23(2): 129-146.* In discussions of historians and ethnohistorians, George T. Hunt's book, *The Wars of the Iroquois,* continues to loom prominently. His interpretation of events in northeastern North America during the seventeenth century, which proposed that the Iroquois fought the French colonials and French-dominated tribes for economic reasons, is widely accepted. This paper re-examines the period. It finds, contrary to Hunt and his followers, that the Iroquois did not fight for economic causes, and that the destruction or dispersal of many tribes around the middle of the seventeenth century did not result from the fur trade. A new look at the period reveals a set of forces destructive to tribes from Quebec to Wisconsin, including the Iroquois. Smallpox emerges as the most significant among those forces. This paper suggests that much of the historical and ethnohistorical literature before and after Hunt propounds biases which not only do injustice to the Iroquois, but prevent a deeper understanding of the historical truth.   J

3267. Séguin, Robert-Lionel. LES DIVERTISSEMENTS AU QUÉBEC AUX XVIIᵉ ET XVIIIᵉ SIÈCLES [Amusements in Quebec during the 17th and 18th centuries]. *Rev. Française d'Hist. d'Outre-Mer [France] 1974 61(222): 5-17.* The social and cultural conditions in New France did not favor parties and amusements. War with the Indians was a real danger. The Church did not approve of balls, dancing, or the theater. Despite the attitudes of secular and ecclesiastical authorities, the people of New France knew how to amuse themselves by dancing, laughing, and singing. Based on notarial registries in the Archives nationales du Québec and secondary works; biblio.   L. B. Chan

3268. Vachon, André. INVENTAIRE CRITIQUE DES NOTAIRES ROYAUX DES GOUVERNEMENTS DE QUÉBEC, MONTRÉAL ET TROIS-RIVIÈRES (1663-1764): CHAPITRE TROISIÈME [Critical inventory of royal notaries of the governments of Québec, Montréal and Trois-Rivières, 1663-1764: Chapter 3]. *Rev. d'Hist. de l'Amérique Française [Canada] 1957 11(1): 93-106, (2): 270-276, (3): 400-406.* Part VI. Covers 31 royal notaries in French Canada. Part VII. Describes careers of 18 royal notaries in French Canada. Part VIII. Discusses the careers of eight of the 103-127 royal notaries in New France during 1663-1764; most were French-born, with only 28.5% born in Canada. (Chapters 1 and 2, which include Parts I-V, appear in *Rev. d'Hist. de l'Amérique Française* 1955-56 9: 423-438, 546-561; and 1956-57 10: 93-103, 257-263, 381-390).

3269. Wakefield, Theodore D. A VIEW OF THE LAKES IN 1648: A TRIBUTE TO THE *JESUIT RELATIONS. Inland Seas 1976 32(3): 184-191, 206-207.* Reprints with introduction the 16 April 1648 covering letter of Father Paul Ragueneau and excerpts from Chapters I and X of his description of the Huron country around the southern end of Georgian Bay. Illus., 17 notes.   K. J. Bauer

3270. Warwick, Jack. OBSERVATION, POLEMICS AND POETIC VISION IN GABRIEL SAGARD'S NARRATION. *Rev. de l'U. d'Ottawa [Canada] 1978 48(1-2): 84-92.* Gabriel Sagard (?-1650), a Recollect monk, wrote of his travels in New France in *Grand voyage au pays des Hurons* (1632) and *Histoire du Canada* (1636). Although there are doubts as to the accuracy of Sagard's writing, it deserves recognition for its literary elements. Text of a paper presented at the conference Travel Writings Related to New France, at York University, Toronto, 20-22 February 1979.   G. J. Rossi

3271. —. [THE SCHOOL OF ARTS AND CRAFTS OF ST. JOACHIM]. *Rev. d'Hist. de l'Amérique Française [Canada] 1976 29(4): 567-576.*
Campeau, Lucien. À PROPOS DE L'ÉCOLE DES ARTS ET MÉTIERS DE SAINT-JOACHIM [With respect to the School of Arts and Crafts of Saint-Joachim], *pp. 567-570.* A critical commen-

tary regarding Peter N. Moogk's study of this school of New France.
Moogk, Peter N. RÉPLIQUE AU COMMENTAIRE DU PÈRE CAMPEAU [Reply to the commentary of Father Campeau], *pp. 571-576.* When a researcher as remarkable as Father Lucien Campeau defends the traditional version of the history of the School of Arts and Crafts of Saint Joachim, his comments merit attention. Father Campeau, however, misunderstood several portions of the earlier article.   L. B. Chan

From British Conquest to Confederation

3272. Barthe, Joseph-Guillaume. LE CANADA RECONQUIS PAR LA FRANCE [Canada reconquered by France]. *Études Françaises [Canada] 1973 9(3): 257-263.* Increased intellectual and commercial ties between France and French Canada would allow the democratic institutions already established in the New World to continue to flourish, based on an expansion of French immigration to Canada and the continuance of Anglo-French cooperation. Extracted from *Le Canada reconquis par la France,* Paris, Ledoyen, 1855, p. 291-302; illus.   G. J. Rossi

3273. Bernard, Jean-Paul; Linteau, Paul-André; and Robert, Jean-Claude. LA STRUCTURE PROFESSIONNELLE DE MONTRÉAL EN 1825 [The professional structure of Montreal in 1825]. *Rev. d'Hist. de l'Amérique Française [Canada] 1976 30(3): 383-415.* In 1825, Montreal was a mercantile city uninfluenced by the industrial revolution. Petty bourgeois merchants and artisans competed for the business of a small commercial economy. Based on published government statistics and on secondary works; 4 tables, 28 notes, appendix.
L. B. Chan

3274. Bernier, Jacques. LA CONSTRUCTION DOMICILIAIRE À QUÉBEC 1810-1820 [House construction in Quebec 1810-20]. *Rev. d'Hist. de l'Amérique Française [Canada] 1978 31(4): 547-561.* Examines domestic building contracts in Quebec during a period of sustained population growth. Details the geographical and architectural development of the city. Contracts, for example, reveal type, size, and location of house, name of builder, mode of payment, etc. These documents provide little information on the daily life of the construction worker, but are a valuable source of information in their own right. 12 notes.
M. R. Yerburgh

3275. Bouchard, Gérard. L'HISTOIRE DÉMOGRAPHIQUE ET LE PROBLÈME DES MIGRATIONS: L'EXEMPLE DE LATERRIÈRE [Historical demography and the problem of geographical mobility: the example of Laterrière]. *Social Hist. [Canada] 1975 8(15): 21-33.* Family reconstitution studies at the parish level for the 19th century are seriously hampered by the high rate of geographical mobility. Prior to the 19th century, the parish was a more natural unit; for later periods the historical demographer should focus on larger units. These problems were discovered in the study of the village of Laterrière in Québec during 1855-70. Less than 10 per cent of the families were sedentary enough to permit a complete family reconstitution study. Based on parish records and secondary sources; 3 tables, graph, 15 notes.
W. K. Hobson

3276. Brasser, T. J. METIS ARTISANS. *Beaver [Canada] 1975 306(2): 52-57.* Canadian Plains Indians originally had decorative arts emphasizing geometric patterns, yet by the mid-1800's circular, floral patterns predominated. Examines the origins of such changes, especially the influence of Chippewa-Cree-Métis groups which originated around the Straits of Mackinac and Sault Sainte Marie, then by the early 1800's settled around Pembina. From there, the Métis hunted, traveled, and explored a wide territory, probably thus spreading the floral-circular styles. 12 illus.   D. Chaput

3277. Byrne, Cyril. THE MARITIME VISITS OF JOSEPH-OCTAVE PLESSIS, BISHOP OF QUEBEC. *Nova Scotia Hist. Soc. Collections [Canada] 1977 39: 23-48.* Translated parts of travel journals of Joseph-Octave Plessis, Catholic bishop in Quebec, 1812-15, offer his impressions of the Maritime Provinces, primarily Cape Breton, Nova Scotia, and New Brunswick.

3278. Chaput, Donald. CHARLOTTE DE ROCHEBLAVE: MÉTISSE TEACHER OF THE TEACHERS. *Beaver [Canada] 1977 308(2): 55-58.* Daughter of prominent fur trader Noel de Rocheblave, Charlotte moved from Manitoulin Island to Oka (Lake of Two Mountains), Quebec, in 1813. In the following decades, because of her fluency in French, English, and the various Algonquian dialects, she became the most important instructor of the many priests who studied at Oka in preparation for work in the Red River country, Labrador, and among the Nipissings. Based on ecclesiastical and linguistic sources; 5 illus.   A

3279. Chaput, Donald. THE "MISSES NOLIN" OF RED RIVER. *Beaver [Canada] 1975 306(3): 14-17.* Discusses the story of two daughters of Jean-Baptiste Nolin, and the origin of the first school for girls in western Canada, St. Boniface, in 1829. Also includes data on the role of the Métis Nolin family in the Red River country, as well as the Earl of Selkirk's plans for utilizing key merchants such as Nolin, who had previously lived in the United States. Based on church records and Lord Selkirk's Papers; 4 illus.   A

3280. Dechêne, Louise. LA CROISSANCE DE MONTRÉAL AU XVIIIᵉ SIÈCLE [The growth of Montreal in the 18th century]. *Rev. d'Hist. de l'Amérique Française [Canada] 1973 27(2): 163-180.* In spite of the proportionately large number of people inhabiting the cities of New France in the 18th century, the population of the cities did not tend to increase during this period at a significantly higher rate than that of the countryside.

3281. Dessaules, Louis-Antoine. CONTRE LES DÉTRACTEURS DE L'INSTITUT CANADIEN [Against the detractors of the Canadian Institute]. *Études Françaises [Canada] 1973 9(3): 197-204.* Ostensibly addressed to Canadian ecclesiastics, refutes the legitimacy of the *Index* in determining the suitability of a book for inclusion in a library. Extracted from *Le Pays*, March 11, 1862.   G. J. Rossi

3282. Dorge, Lionel. THE METIS AND CANADIEN COUNCILLORS OF ASSINIBOIA: PART III. *Beaver [Canada] 1974 305(3): 51-58.* Continued from a previous article. Emphasizes the 1860's as a prelude to the Riel Rebellion. The Council of Assiniboia, faced with problems of famine, peace-keeping, road building, and Sioux presence, was unable to keep pace with political changes. A key factor in their failures was the composition of the Council. Métis and Canadiens were included, but in inadequate numbers, and the men chosen were often too closely allied to the Hudson's Bay Co. The tendency to rank all "French speaking" members as a unit was fallacious, as the Metis did not always agree with Canadien policies or plans. The Council could not govern, but the Metis and Canadien members learned some of the intricacies of governing, and they were later active in municipal and provincial affairs in Manitoba. 7 illus., map.   D. Chaput

3283. Dorge, Lionel. THE METIS AND THE CANADIEN COUNCILLORS OF ASSINIBOIA. *Beaver [Canada] 1974 305(1): 12-19, (2): 39-45.* Part I traces type of legislation and policies favored by the French-Métis representatives governing Assiniboia in the Northwest Territories. Part II discusses the growing influences of the French-speaking Métis population of the Red River settlement. 9 illus.   D. Heermans

3284. Galarneau, Claude. L'ENSEIGNEMENT DES SCIENCES AU QUÉBEC ET JÉRÔME DEMERS (1765-1835) [Teaching sciences in Quebec and Jérôme Demers, 1765-1835]. *Rev. de l'U. d'Ottawa [Canada] 1977 47(1-2): 84-94.* Discusses scientific education in Quebec, especially at the Quebec seminary, mentioning professors' names, subject matter, and methods. Stresses that, in the 18th century, philosophy and sciences were not separate disciplines, but united under the name of sciences-philosophy, including mathematics, physics, chemistry and philosophy. Analyzes the career of Jérôme Demers, one of the most brilliant men of the time, as a professor of sciences-philosophy at the Quebec seminary during 1800-35. Primary and secondary sources; 52 notes.   G. P. Cleyet

3285. Hare, John E. LA FORMATION DE LA TERMINOLOGIE PARLEMENTAIRE ET ÉLECTORALE AU QUÉBEC, 1792-1810 [The formation of parliamentary and electoral terminology in Quebec: 1792-1810]. *Rev. de l'Université d'Ottawa [Canada] 1976 46(4): 460-475.* As a result of the Constitutional Act of 1791, Quebec, then known as

Lower Canada, was given its own Parliament to be elected by the voters of the province. Parliamentary institutions were strange to the French-speaking Québécois, because France lacked parliamentary bodies when Canada was ruled by the French. Some of the terminology used in the electoral process and the new Quebec Parliament were pure French, but much was borrowed, either in the form of calques or of direct loaning, from English electoral and parliamentary terminology. Many of these borrowings have persisted. Canadian French electoral and parliamentary vocabulary is quite different from that of the mother country, whose history has been a good deal less stable and tranquil than that of Quebec. 56 notes, biblio.   J. C. Billigmeier

3286. Hare, John E. LA POPULATION DE LA VILLE DE QUÉBEC, 1795-1805. [The population of the city of Québec, 1795-1805]. *Social Hist. [Canada] 1974 7(13): 23-47.* Parish censuses of 1795 and 1805 reveal a strong pattern of religious group residential segregation and high rates of geographic mobility. The special occupational and ethnic character of each of the city's four districts is also apparent. Ethnic differences strongly influenced patterns of social stratification in 1795. Based on published census schedules; 9 maps, 17 tables, 3 graphs, 31 notes.   W. K. Hobson

3287. Hare, John E. SUR LES IMPRIMÉS ET LA DIFFUSION DES IDÉES [Printed matter and the diffusion of ideas]. *Ann. Hist. de la Révolution Française [France] 1973 45(3): 407-421.* Describes the spread of Enlightenment ideas in Canada. Between 1764 and 1810, 11 newspapers were established and hundreds of pamphlets were printed. *La Gazette de Quebec*, the first newspaper, espoused republican ideas and was sympathetic to the French Revolution. Primary and secondary sources; 31 notes.   S. R. Smith

3288. Harvey, Robert Paton. WHEN VICTOR HUGO'S DAUGHTER WAS A HALIGONIAN. *Nova Scotia Hist. Q. [Canada] 1977 7(3): 243-256.* Recounts the story of Adèle Hugo, daughter of Victor Hugo, the circumstances of her residence in Nova Scotia (1863-66), and her later history. Primary and secondary sources; biblio.   H. M. Evans

3289. Hodgson, Maurice. BELLOT AND KENNEDY: A CONTRAST IN PERSONALITIES. *Beaver [Canada] 1974 305(1): 55-58.* In 1851, Joseph René Bellot, a lieutenant in the French Marines, and William Kennedy, a métis from Rupert's Land, led an expedition to the Arctic on the *Prince Albert* to search for Sir John Franklin. Bellot was an educated Roman Catholic Frenchman, inexperienced in Arctic travel, whereas Kennedy was an intolerant Protestant, well-schooled in frontier life. They eventually found mutual respect and completed an amazing sled journey of 1,100 miles, traveling west of Prince of Wales Island, north to Cape Walker, around North Somerset, then to quarters at Batty Bay. Claims that Bellot was more interested in glory and future promotion than in finding Franklin. 4 illus., map.   D. Chaput

3290. Igartua, José E. THE MERCHANTS OF MONTREAL AT THE CONQUEST: SOCIO-ECONOMIC PROFILE. *Social Hist. [Canada] 1975 8(16): 275-293.* Of the 200 merchants and traders who can be identified in Montreal 1750-75, 92 form a core group of those in business for an extended period of time. Examinations of the core group reveals that they were not wealthy, their social mobility was restricted, and a distinct hierarchy existed among them. Importers and wholesale merchants formed the highest group; they married within their group or one notch below. Fifty-five fur trade outfitters formed the second category. They also tended to marry within their group, but had few social or business connections with the colony's governing elite. The third category, "shopkeepers," was not a socially cohesive group. The fourth category consisted of assorted traders, artisans, and one moneylender. Based on published primary sources and documents in the Public Archives of Canada and the National Archives of Quebec. 82 notes, 2 appendixes.   W. K. Hobson

3291. Jarrell, R. A. THE RISE AND DECLINE OF SCIENCE AT QUEBEC, 1824-1844. *Social Hist. [Canada] 1977 10(19): 77-91.* The marked interest during the first half of the period declined after 1836 because of a split in the social elite between the English and French. Also, elite interests shifted to politics from the mid-1830's on. The French elite, especially, came to find literature, history, journalism, and the arts more important than science in their fight for cultural survival. Based on published primary and secondary sources; 2 tables, 41 notes.

W. K. Hobson

3292. LaBrèque, Marie-Paule. LES ÉGLISES DANS LES CANTONS DE L'EST, 1800-1860 [The churches in the Eastern Townships, 1800-1860]. *Sessions d'Étude: Soc. Can. d'Hist. de l'Eglise Catholique 1974 41: 87-103.* A history of the establishment of churches in the Eastern Townships of Quebec, including the great material obstacles and the psychological and moral difficulties faced in French settlement. Analyzes the problem of maintaining French education and religion in the isolated colony after the establishment of other settlers (American, Scotch, Irish). Studies the decline of colonization and validity of French rule on Anglo-Saxon land. Describes the establishment of Catholicism and the propagation of the faith under various bishops. Regional and diocesan archives and secondary sources; 49 notes.

S. Sevilla

3293. LaFrance, Marc and Ruddell, Thiery. ELEMENTS DE L'URBANISATION DE LA VILLE DE QUEBEC: 1790-1840 [Elements of urbanization in the city of Quebec: 1790-1840]. *Urban Hist. Rev. [Canada] 1975 75(1): 22-30.* Discusses urbanization in Quebec, Quebec, 1790-1840, examining the rapid physical expansion and the military, administrative, and commercial functions in the city; one of eight articles in this issue on the Canadian city in the 19th century.

3294. Lambert, James H. "LE HAUT ENSEIGNEMENT DE LA RELIGION": MGR BOURGET AND THE FOUNDING OF LAVAL UNIVERSITY. *R. de l'U. d'Ottawa [Canada] 1975 45(3): 278-294.* Concentrates "solely on the role of Mgr. Ignace Bourget, second bishop of Montreal," in founding Laval University. "The founding of Laval must be seen in the context of a Catholic ultramontane reaction to a liberal and secularist outburst during and following the French Revolution." Bourget saw the university as the principal instrument for "wresting the elite from the clutches of liberalism." Based on primary and secondary sources; 72 notes.

M. L. Frey

3295. Lamonde, Yvan. LE MEMBERSHIP D'UNE ASSOCIATION DU 19ᵉ SIÈCLE: LE CAS DE L'INSTITUT CANADIEN DE LONGUEUIL (1857-1860) [The membership of a 19th century association: The case of the Canadian Institute of Longueuil, 1857-1860]. *Recherches Sociographiques [Canada] 1975 16(2): 219-240.* In the Canadian Institute of Longueuil the membership came from a variety of occupations, although the leadership was assumed by a merchant-commercial group rather than by individuals coming from the liberal profession. This rendered the Longueuil institute more practically-oriented than other such associations. The study utilizes occupational classification techniques for analytical purposes.

A. E. LeBlanc

3296. Lamonde, Yvan. LES ASSOCIATIONS AU BAS-CANADA: DE NOUVEAUX MARCHÉS AUX IDÉES (1840-1867) [Literary associations of Lower Canada: new markets of ideas (1840-1867)]. *Social Hist. [Canada] 1975 8(16): 361-369.* The literary association movement in Lower Canada was promoted by lawyers and journalists, members of the liberal bourgeoisie. They saw the movement as a solution to the problems faced by the younger generation of a society in transition from a subsistence to a market economy. They considered education via literary associations as a solution to the distinctions of class, wealth, race, and religion, and as a solution to the political isolation of young French Canadians. They believed old institutions were no longer capable of performing such functions. The promotional literature for the associations was permeated with applications of free-market idiom to the discussion of education. Based on literary association promotional periodicals. Graph, 51 notes.

W. K. Hobson

3297. Landry, Yves. ÉTUDE CRITIQUE DU RECENSEMENT DU CANADA DE 1765 [Critical study of the census of Canada of 1765]. *Rev. d'hist. de l'Amérique française [Canada] 1975 29(3): 323-351.* The census of 1765, ordered by the imperial government, was taken with the help of the Catholic clergy. A total population of 76,675 persons was reported. The census was not taken in all parishes, and approximately 10% of the population were not counted. A total figure of 80,000 is more realistic. Criticism of statistical sources is an essential prerequisite in determining historical reality. Based on documents in the Public Record Office (London), Archives Publiques du Canada, Archives Nationales du Québec, and secondary works; 5 tables, 47 notes.

L. B. Chan

3298. Lejeunesse, Marcel. LES CABINETS DE LECTURE À PARIS ET À MONTRÉAL AU 19ᵉ SIÈCLE [Reading rooms in Paris and Montreal in the 19th century]. *Recherches Sociographiques [Canada] 1975 16(2): 241-247.* The reading room was one of the major sociocultural forces at work in Paris during the first half of the 19th century, but its popularity only began in Montreal in the late 1850's. Its development in Montreal was closely related to the interests of the Roman Catholic Church.

A. E. LeBlanc

3299. Little, J. I. MISSIONARY PRIESTS IN QUEBEC'S EASTERN TOWNSHIPS: THE YEARS OF HARDSHIP AND DISCONTENT, 1825-1853. *Study Sessions: Can. Catholic Hist. Assoc. [Canada] 1978 45: 21-35.* During 1825-53, missionary priests in southeastern Quebec around Sherbrooke close to the American border ministered to a population which, though white, lived much as did the Indians; they were poor, dispersed, backward, and the priests among them had a hard and unglamorous life.

3300. Ouellet, Fernand. DUALITÉ ÉCONOMIQUE ET CHANGEMENT TECHNOLOGIQUE AU QUÉBEC (1760-1790) [Dual economy and technological change in Quebec, 1760-1790]. *Social Hist. [Canada] 1976 9(18): 256-296.* The rise in wages for fur trappers in New France during 1760-90 is explained by the increasing commercialization of agriculture in the period and by the growing competition among fur trading companies. Fur trapping was seasonal work for about one-third of New France's peasants. After the Seven Years' War, the number of fur traders increased when Englishmen began to compete with the established francophone traders. During the American Revolution the prices of imported goods rose steeply, squeezing out individual francophone traders, stimulating technological changes, and encouraging the growth of the larger enterprises. Based on statistical analysis of data on trading expeditions, investments, prices, wages, and exports in Public Archives of Quebec and Canada; 53 tables, 70 notes, appendix.

W. K. Hobson

3301. Paquet, Gilles and Wallot, Jean-Pierre. LES INVENTAIRES APRÈS DÉCÈS À MONTRÉAL AU TOURNANT DU XIXᵉ SIÈCLE: PRÉLIMINAIRES À UNE ANALYSE [Inventories after death in Montreal at the turn of the 19th century: preliminaries to an analysis]. *Rev. d'Hist. de l'Am. Française [Canada] 1976 30(2): 163-221.* At the turn of the 19th century, Lower Canada's role in the trans-Atlantic commercial economy was transformed by external and internal forces. Presents research regarding wealth distribution, social stratification, and behavioral adjustment. Based on notarial documents and secondary works; 3 tables, 96 notes, 2 appendixes.

L. B. Chan

3302. Pouliot, Léon. UNE LETTRE DE M. FAILLON À MGR. BOURGET [A letter by M. Faillon to Mgr. Bourget]. *Rev. d'Hist. de l'Amérique Française [Canada] 1957 11(1): 107-110.* Presents a letter written in 1850 by Etienne-Michel Faillon to Monseigneur Ignace Bourget about writing a religious history of Montreal.

3303. Proulx, Georges-Étienne. LES CANADIENS ONT-ILS PAYÉ LA DÎME ENTRE 1760 ET 1775? [Did the Canadians pay the *dîme* between 1760 and 1775?]. *Rev. d'Hist. de l'Amérique Française [Canada] 1958 11(4): 533-562.* The *dîme* in New France was a tithe or ecclesiastical tax of 1/13 of each inhabitant's harvest, paid to the local priest. Imposed by French law before 1760 and by the Québec Act after 1774, it was paid voluntarily by most French Canadians during the period of British military rule, (1760-75).

3304. Ray, Arthur J. SMALLPOX: THE EPIDEMIC OF 1837-38. *Beaver [Canada] 1975 306(2): 8-13.* The smallpox epidemic that smashed the Mandans and other Upper Missouri tribes in 1837 soon crossed to the prairies of Canada. The Hudson's Bay officials were better prepared, as they had on hand a vaccine, and several knowledgeable surgeons. Many Indians, Métis, and traders were inoculated, but those who refused or neglected to receive such preventatives died. Examines the geographical flow of the epidemic and the work of officials such as William Todd who controlled the vaccination program. 6 illus.

D. Chaput

3305. Schonberger, Vincent L. LE JOURNALISME LITTÉRAIRE DE MICHEL BIBAUD [The literary journalism of Michel Bibaud]. *Rev. de l'U. d'Ottawa [Canada] 1977 47(4): 488-506.* Between the cession of French-Canada to Britain in 1760 and the arrival of the *Capricieuse*

to Canada in 1855, the rationalist and intellectual literary tradition in the French language gave way to a more sentimental, moral, and patriotic literature. This movement spread mainly by means of the newspaper and other periodicals, especially in Quebec and Montreal. Michel Bibaud (1782-1857) was one journalist who, through various publications such as the *Spectateur* and the *Aurore,* contributed to the rise of this type of literature and worked to advance the moral and intellectual level of the people. Primary and secondary sources; 62 notes, bibliography of works by Bibaud.
G. J. Rossi

3306. Tousignant, Pierre. LE CONSERVATISME DE LA PETITE NOBLESSE SEIGNEURIALE [The conservatism of the petit seigneurial nobility]. *Ann. Hist. de la Révolution Française [France] 1973 45(3): 322-343.* Under French rule in Canada, a class of small landowning gentry developed. British policy cultivated the support of this class and during both the American and French Revolutions, they remained loyal to Great Britain in the hope of maintaining and consolidating their status. The article was originally presented in 1969 at the University of Montreal and includes a transcript of part of a discussion that followed. Primary and secondary sources; 42 notes.
S. R. Smith

3307. Tulchinsky, Gerald. UNE ENTREPRISE MARITIME CANADIENNE-FRANÇAISE—LA COMPAGNIE DU RICHELIEU 1845-1854 [A French Canadian maritime enterprise—the Richelieu Company 1845-54]. *Rev. d'Hist. de l'Amérique Française [Canada] 1973 26(4): 559-582.* The French Canadian Richelieu shipping company created in 1845 successfully competed against the English Canadian companies, in the region of Montreal and notably along the Richelieu River. First involved with freight, it later offered a passenger service. Most of the shareholders of this company were French Canadians and sound businessmen. Based on primary and secondary sources; 91 notes.
C. Collon

3308. Vernon, Howard A. THE JOURNAL OF J. DUFAUT. *Beaver [Canada] 1974 305(2): 23-27.* J. Dufaut's journal describes the daily life and transactions of a fur trader for the XY Company during the winter of 1803-04. Dufaut recorded the weather, game caught, and goods traded with the Indians, as well as notes on life in the bush of Prince Rupert's Land. 5 illus.
D. Heermans

3309. Wade, Mason. AFTER THE *GRAND DERANGEMENT*: THE ACADIANS' RETURN TO THE GULF OF ST. LAWRENCE AND TO NOVA SCOTIA. *Am. Rev. of Can. Studies 1975 5(1): 42-65.* Despite numerous attempts by the colonial government of Nova Scotia to remove Acadians, some groups remained in the Gulf of St. Lawrence area and eventually returned to Nova Scotia, 1756-95.

3310. Wallot, Jean-Pierre. RÉVOLUTION ET RÉFORMISME DANS LE BAS-CANADA (1773-1815) [Revolution and reformism in Lower Canada (1773-1815)]. *Ann. Hist. de la Révolution Française [France] 1973 45(3): 344-406.* During the American Revolution, most French-speaking Canadians adopted an attitude of neutrality, despite American propaganda. Several reasons for this are suggested. However, Canadians were generally familiar with the trends of Enlightenment thought and many hailed the beginning of the French Revolution as the dawn of a new era. Despite the zeal of some revolutionaries and several local uprisings against the established government, reformers saw greater hope in expanding their influence within a British-style parliamentary system. Local issues and anticlericalism played major roles. Primary and secondary sources; 213 notes.
S. R. Smith

3311. —. ACCROISSEMENT ET STRUCTURE DE LA POPULATION À QUÉBEC AU DÉBUT DU XIXᵉ SIÈCLE [Growth and structure of the Quebec population at the beginning of the 19th century]. *Social Hist. [Canada] 1976 9(17): 187-196.*
Paillé, Michel P. ACCROISSEMENT ET STRUCTURE DE LA POPULATION À QUÉBEC AU DÉBUT DU XIXᵉ SIÈCLE (À PROPOS D'UN ARTICLE DE JOHN HARE) [Growth and structure of the Quebec population at the beginning of the 19th century (with respect to an article by John Hare)], *pp. 187-193.* Reviews John Hare's article on the population of the city of Quebec during 1795-1805. Corrects several compilation errors, defines several concepts, and illustrates methodology for studying population growth and age structure. 3 tables, 33 notes.

Hare, John E. À PROPOS DES COMMENTAIRES DE MICHEL PAILLÉ [Response to Michel Paillé], *pp. 193-196.* Michel Paillé's reexamination is flawed because he relies on the published census' summary tables, which do not correspond to the census' details when examined street by street and house by house. Studying the age structure cannot be as exact as Paillé believes because it must be based on census data using the age of communicants. During 1703-1840, the age for communion was not precise; it was allowed to vary between 10 and 14 years old. 3 tables.
W. K. Hobson

3312. —. [THE AGRICULTURAL CRISIS IN LOWER CANADA]. *Can. Hist. R. 1975 56(2): 133-168.*
Paquet, Gilles and Wallot, Jean-Pierre. THE AGRICULTURAL CRISIS IN LOWER CANADA, 1802-12: MISE AU POINT. A RESPONSE TO T. J. A. LE GOFF, *pp. 133-161.* Assesses Le Goff's contribution to the debate over the thesis of a crisis in Lower Canadian agriculture starting circa 1802 and giving rise to the "first French-Canadian nationalism" (F. Ouellet). The authors assert that Le Goff's statistical exercises are based on insufficient and biased data and that his demography-oriented interpretation, although valuable in some European contexts, does not take into account the extension of colonization in a North American setting. Finally, they stress that the struggles of the 1800's are simply another round in the more-and-more insistent struggle for global power (political, economic, social).

Le Goff, T. J. A. A REPLY, *pp. 162-168.* Maintains that Paquet and Wallot fail to refute his criticisms of their work. Their analytical model of foreign demand for Lower Canadian produce is meaningless in a preindustrial economy; their description of domestic demand is based only on impressions; their discussion of supply shows ignorance of the limitations on good accessible and available land in the colony. There was a "structural" crisis after the turn of the century. Expresses a general lack of interest in Paquet and Wallot's global models of socio-economico-political transformations drawn from systems analysis, etc., but suggests that those models may be undercut by the flimsiness of the evidence presented by Paquet and Wallot on the state of the agricultural economy and of people in the countryside.
A

Since Confederation

3313. Angers, François-Albert. ESDRAS MINVILLE ET L'ÉCOLE DES HAUTES ÉTUDES COMMERCIALES [Esdras Minville and the School of Higher Commercial Studies]. *Action Natl. [Canada] 1976 65(9-10): 643-676.* Esdras Minville was the first Canadian to direct the École des Hautes Études Commerciales. He was appointed in 1938 and succeeded the Belgians A.-J. Bray, who served during 1910-16, and Henry Laureys, who served during 1916-38. Minville stressed faculty research, academic freedom, and rigorous standards for admission and degrees.
A. W. Novitsky

3314. Angers, François-Albert. LA PENSÉE ÉCONOMIQUE D'ESDRAS MINVILLE [The economic thought of Esdras Minville]. *Action Natl. [Canada] 1976 65(9-10): 727-761.* Esdras Minville opposed liberal capitalism, but was not an agrarian. He sought a balanced industrialization for Quebec. He saw in *Rerum Novarum* and *Quadragesimo Anno* support for his corporatism and personalism. His nationalism was based on respect for French Canadian culture. 7 notes.
A. W. Novitsky

3315. Angers, François-Albert. LE SENS D'UNE VIE [The sense of a life]. *Action Natl. [Canada] 1976 65(9-10): 800-803.* Reprints the funeral oration for Esdras Minville presented at the church of Saint-Pascal Baylon, 12 December 1975. Minville was, above all else, a Christian. His life was devoted exclusively to the common good of the French Canadian people and was based on the Christian virtues of faith, hope, and charity.
A. W. Novitsky

3316. Archibald, Clinton and Paltiel, Khayyam Z. DU PASSAGE DES CORPS INTERMÉDIARES AUX GROUPES DE PRESSION: LA TRANSFORMATION D'UNE IDÉE ILLUSTRÉE PAR LE

MOUVEMENT COOPÉRATIF DESJARDINS [From common interest groups to pressure groups: The transformation of a concept as seen in the Desjardins cooperative movement]. *Recherches Sociographiques [Canada] 1977 18(1): 59-91.* The notion of common interest groups has deep roots in Catholic Quebec and it is one of the foundation stones of the Desjardins cooperative movement. The notion, however, has undergone profound change in the past few decades as the Quebec government has sought to increase its role in all facets of the province's life. Common interest groups have overtly accepted the mantle of a pressure group to achieve their respective ends. Table, 2 graphs, 96 notes.

A. E. Le Blanc

3317. Arès, Richard. LE RECENSEMENT DE 1976: LA LANGUE FRANCAISE AU CANADA ET AU QUEBEC [The census of 1976: the French language in Canada and in Quebec]. *Action Natl. [Canada] 1978 68(4): 331-338.* Comparison of the 1971 and 1976 Canadian censuses indicates that the percentage of the population considering French as their maternal language declined in every province except the Yukon Territory, where it remained stable. In the province of Quebec, 16 counties had populations over 98% of French origin, an additional 20 over 95%, an additional 13 over 90%, 11 more over 80%, and 11 more over 50%. Only Brome (47.1%) and Pontiac (39.2%) have French in the minority. The Montreal region shows larger percentages of English background. Based on the 1971 and 1976 Canadian census; 8 tables.

A. W. Novitsky

3318. Arès, Richard. LES MINORITÉS FRANCO-CANADIENNES: ÉTUDE STATISTIQUE [French-Canadian minorities: A statistical study]. *Action Natl. [Canada] 1976 66(1): 34-47.* Census returns of 1971 indicate that outside the province of Quebec, francophones tend to become strongly anglicized. Ethnic French tend to consider English as their maternal language and to speak English within the family. The trend is most pronounced in the western provinces. It is also strong in Ontario and appears in the Maritime provinces where only New Brunswick maintains a strong French influence. 5 tables.   A. W. Novitsky

3319. Babcock, Robert. SAMUEL GOMPERS AND THE FRENCH-CANADIAN WORKER, 1900-1914. *Am. Rev. of Can. Studies 1973 3(2): 47-66.* Discusses Samuel Gompers and the American Federation of Labor's policy toward trade unions and the organization of the working class in Quebec 1900-14.

3320. Backeland, Lucille and Frideres, James S. FRANCO-MANITOBANS AND CULTURAL LOSS: A FOURTH GENERATION. *Prairie Forum [Canada] 1977 2(1): 1-18.* French Manitobans have maintained their cultural identity, although some loss is noted; corroborates Frank Vallee's hypothesis concerning the necessity of regional research.

3321. Bakvis, Herman. FRENCH CANADA AND THE "BUREAUCRATIC PHENOMENON." *Can. Public Administration [Canada] 1978 21(1): 103-124.* Identifies characteristics of bureaucracy structure and behavior among French Canadians in order to understand organization, policymaking, and dispute settlement in Quebec, 1969-77.

3322. Barrett, F. A. THIS CHANGING WORLD: THE RELATIVE DECLINE OF THE FRENCH LANGUAGE IN CANADA: A PRELIMINARY REPORT. *Geography [Great Britain] 1975 60(Part 2): 125-129.* The number of French-speaking people in Canada, notably in Montreal, has been declining during the past decade, partly because of decreasing birth rates in the French population.

3323. Baudoux, Maurice. LES FRANCO-CANADIENS DE L'OUEST: CONSTITUTIFS D'UNE SOCIÉTÉ FRANCOPHONE CANADIENNE [The French Canadians in the West: elements of a French-speaking Canadian society]. *Tr. of the Royal Soc. of Can. 1975 13: 141-149.* "The West" consists of both the coast and the prairies, the latter being the object of this article. Several generations of French Canadians have now lived in this area. Gradually they are declining in number as younger generations assimilate into English-speaking Canada. Schools and universities are predominantly English-speaking, as are radio and television. In intercultural marriages the children frequently speak only English. The French Canadians in the prairies are separated from Quebec both geographically and psychologically, the result being more assimilation.

J. D. Neville

3324. Bauer, Charles. RECOLLECTIONS OF PHILIPPE VAILLANCOURT. *Can. Labour 1977 22(2): 39-43.* Philippe Vaillancourt discusses his role in the labor movement in Quebec during 1936-76.

3325. Behiels, Michael. L'ASSOCIATION CATHOLIQUE DE LA JEUNESSE CANADIENNE-FRANÇAISE AND THE QUEST FOR A MORAL REGENERATION, 1903-1914. *J. of Can. Studies [Canada] 1978 13(2): 27-41.* The Association catholique de la jeunesse canadienne-française was founded (1903) when many developments (e.g., increased immigration, urbanization, and foreign control) gave rise to fears that the French Canadian nation faced imminent demoralization and assimilation. The ACJC's founders promised Archbishop Bruchési of Montreal to remain aloof from politics, and in general the organization's emphasis was moral rather than political. But it did become involved in the drive for increased bilingualism at the national level, and in promoting the interest of French-speaking minorities outside Quebec. ACJC spokesmen opposed Jewish immigration, and the drive (spearheaded by members of the Masonic lodge Emancipation) to reduce the Church's role in education. They also advocated various industrial reforms, most of them voluntaristic in nature. Based on the ACJC organ *Le Semeur,* other primary, and secondary sources; 88 notes.   L. W. Van Wyk

3326. Bergevin, André. NOTES BIOGRAPHIQUES ET RÉPERTOIRE BIBLIOGRAPHIQUE DES OEUVRES D'ESDRAS MINVILLE [Biographic notes and bibliography of the works of Esdras Minville]. *Action Natl. [Canada] 1976 65(9-10): 762-783.* Lists Esdras Minville's academic career, activities, awards, books, pamphlets, articles for *L'Action Française, L'Action Canadienne-Française, L'Action Nationale, L'Actualité Économique,* and other publications.

A. W. Novitsky

3327. Bernier, Bernard. THE PENETRATION OF CAPITALISM IN QUEBEC AGRICULTURE. *Can. Rev. of Sociol. and Anthrop. [Canada] 1976 13(4): 422-434.* The transformation of Quebec agriculture under the impact of capitalism has not resulted in the use of wage labour in agriculture, i.e. has not followed the "classic" English case analysed by Marx. Rather, smallholding agriculture has been established and maintained in Quebec, despite an accelerated rate of dispossession of peasants. This type of agricultural development, resulting in a real crisis in the 1970's, has its cause in the preference of monopoly capital (whether industrial, commercial, or financial) in an indirect exploitation of peasants effected through the market.   J

3328. Besner, Jacques and Bertrand, Louis Claude. LA COOPÉRATIVE FÉDÉRÉE DE QUÉBEC [The federated cooperative in Quebec]. *Action Natl. [Canada] 1973 62(9): 746-756.* Discusses the diverse activities of the Coopérative Fédérée de Québec, a federation of farming cooperatives, focusing on the extent of its enterprise, its ideology, present problems, and future directions.

3329. Bouchard, Gérard. SUR L'ÉGLISE CATHOLIQUE ET L'INDUSTRIALISATION AU QUÉBEC: LA RÉLIGION DES EUDISTES ET LES OUVRIERS DU BASSIN DE CHICOUTIMI, 1903-1930 [The Catholic Church and the industrialization of Quebec: religion as practiced by the Eudists and the workers of the Chicoutimi Basin, 1903-30]. *Protée [Canada] 1976 5(2): 31-43.* A tacit alliance between the Church and the working class helped shape religious practices in a working-class parish.

3330. Bowman, Ian. THE LAURENTIAN LINE OF THE CANADIAN PACIFIC RAILWAY. *Transport History [Great Britain] 1978 9(3): 223-228.* The writer journeyed from Montreal to Lac Manitou, in the Laurentian Mountains of Eastern Canada, during 1922. Describes the history of the Mont Laurier section of the Canadian Pacific Railway, which was laid between 1880-1915. The extension of the railway network in the region was chiefly the result of agitation by Antoine Labelle, Curé of St. Jerome, who wished to improve the lives of the French Canadian Quebecois. The writer also describes the train in which he travelled and the towns, forests, and mountains he passed, and compares them with the railroad and region as they exist today.   G. M. Alexander

3331. Cabatoff, Kenneth. RADIO-QUÉBEC: UNE INSTITUTION PUBLIQUE À LA RECHERCHE D'UNE MISSION [Radio-Québec: a public institution looking for a mission]. *Can. Public Administration*

[Canada] 1976 19(4): 542-551. Radio-Québec, an educational television service, 1969-76, is seeking public access to the airwaves and self-regulation status from the federal government.

3332. Caldwell, Gary and Czarnocki, B. Dan. UN RATTRAPAGE RATÉ: LE CHANGEMENT SOCIAL DANS LE QUÉBEC D'APRÈS-GUERRE, 1950-1974: UNE COMPARAISON QUÉBEC-ONTARIO [Failure to recover: social change in Quebec after World War II, 1950-1974: a comparison of Quebec/Ontario]. Recherches Sociographiques [Canada] 1977 18(1): 9-58. Compares 96 socioeconomic variables for Ontario and Quebec. From this analysis, it appears that a major structural change has taken place in Quebec since World War II. Quebec's modernization during this period was at the expense of its industrial development, which may mean future compromising social advances. 3 tables, 71 notes.　　　　　　　　　　　　　A. E. Le Blanc

3333. Castonguay, Charles. EXOGAMIE ET ANGLICISATION CHEZ LES MINORITÉS CANADIENNES-FRANÇAISES [Exogamy and anglicization among the French Canadian minorities]. Can. Rev. of Sociol. and Anthrop. [Canada] 1979 16(1): 21-46. Relying on data derived from the 1971 census, the causal relations between linguistic exogamy and assimilation among the nine provincial minorities of French mother tongue are investigated. Rates of anglicization, matrimonial cohabitation, exogamy, and precocious anglicization are first defined, then calculated for different age groups. Anglicization rates for francophone spouses in linguistically homogeneous and heterogeneous marriages are also established for each province. It is observed that among those minorities which best resist anglicization, mixed marriages indeed appear to be the principal factor initiating transfer to English as the home language. Among the less resistant minorities, however, this causal relation is less evident, if not outright reversed, with exogamy appearing instead to accompany, or even to follow from a number of other anglicizing factors which lead the minorities towards a type of language transfer which is rather more evolutionary in nature than catastrophic. 6 tables, ref.　J

3334. Castonguay, Charles. LA MONTÉE DE L'EXOGAMIE CHEZ LES JEUNES FRANCOPHONES HORS QUÉBEC [The increase in exogamy among young Francophones outside Quebec]. Action Natl. [Canada] 1978 68(3): 219-224. The 1971 census shows that in all Canadian provinces outside Quebec except New Brunswick, more than 90% of French Canadians with non-French spouses had adopted English as their primary language. In addition, the tendency for Francophones to enter such mixed marriages has increased each decade. The 1976 census shows, for the first time in Canada's history, an absolute decline in the French population outside Quebec. It appears that neither federal nor provincial policies will be able to preserve a French minority in any province except New Brunswick. Based on the 1971 and 1976 Canadian censuses; table.　　　　　　　　　　　　A. W. Novitsky

3335. Castonguay, Charles and Marion, Jacques. L'ANGLICISATION DU CANADA [The Anglicization of Canada]. Action Natl. [Canada] 1974 63(8/9): 733-749. A study comparing language usage in Canada, 1961-71, indicates a trend toward the assimilation of French-speaking Canadians to English, even in Quebec.

3336. Caulais, Jacques. LE CANADA ET L'UTOPIE [Canada and Utopia]. Année Pol. et Écon. [France] 1975 47(242): 338-351. Reports on problems of thought-instinct duality, human alienation, and the degradation of civilization in Canada—especially Quebec—due to population growth and industrialization of society in modern times, commenting on the quest for utopia concept in popular Canadian consciousness.

3337. Chouinard, Denys. ALFRED CHARPENTIER FACE AU GOUVERNEMENT DU QUÉBEC, 1935-1946 [Alfred Charpentier in relation to the Quebec government, 1935-1946]. Rev. d'Hist. de L'Amérique Française [Canada] 1977 31 (2): 211-227. Though the Confederation of Catholic Workers of Canada (CTCC) has been the subject of intense scrutiny, its ideological/philosophical moorings can be appreciated fully only by examining the relationship between its leadership and the Quebec government. President of the CTCC during 1935-46, Alfred Charpentier imbued the movement with a fresh sense of mission and morality, but his concepts of corporatism and worker-employer entente never caught on. His moderate stance vis-à-vis the provincial government alienated the more radical elements in the movement. 44 notes.
　　　　　　　　　　　　　　　M. R. Yerburgh

3338. Contandriopoulos, A. P.; Lance, J. M.; and Meunier, C. UN REGROUPEMENT DES COMTÉS DE LA PROVINCE DE QUÉBEC EN RÉGIONS HOMOGÈNES [A regrouping of the counties of the province of Quebec into homogeneous regions]. Actualité Écon. [Canada] 1974 50(4): 572-586. Presents a method of identifying the regions of Quebec and proposes a classification of its counties into homogeneous regions for use in the administration of medical services and in planning socioeconomic development. Proposes eight regional groupings. 3 tables, 5 notes, biblio.　　　　　　　　J. C. Billigmeier

3339. Côté, Andre and McComber, Marie. SOURCES DE L'HISTOIRE DU SAGUENAY-LAC-SAINT-JEAN: INVENTAIRE DU FONDS DUBUC [Historical resources of Saguenay-Lac-Saint-Jean: inventory of the Dubuc Estate]. Protée [Canada] 1976 4(1): 129-153. Gives an inventory of the Dubuc family papers of three generations, 1892-ca. 1963, dealing with some 50 pulp and paper companies founded and directed by J.-E. Alfred Dubuc of Chicoutimi and by his son Antoine Dubuc, with personal correspondence of his wife and family.

3340. Dagg, Michael A. SOURCES OF MATERIALS ON THE NATIVE PEOPLES OF CANADA. Can. Lib. J. 1975 32(2): 122-126. Bibliography of publications and list of national organizations representing native peoples of Canada. Indicates ways to acquire materials reflecting Indian, Métis, and Eskimo (Inuit) viewpoints.
　　　　　　　　　　　　　　　L. F. Johnson

3341. Delude-Clift, Camille and Champoux, Edouard. LE CONFLIT DES GÉNÉRATIONS [The generations conflict]. Recherches Sociographiques [Canada] 1973 14(2): 157-201. An analysis of the perceptions of adults and adolescents with respect to family, religion, and education shows that the socioeconomic milieu of the individual determines attitudes concerning social integration, whereas age is an important factor in the quest for identity. Intergenerational tension is largely due to this emergence of a private self among members of the younger generation. Based on 196 interviews conducted in Québec City.
　　　　　　　　　　　　　　　A. E. LeBlanc

3342. Dominique, Richard. L'ETHNOHISTOIRE DE LA MOYENNE-CÔTE-NORD [The ethnohistory of the middle North Shore of the St. Lawrence estuary]. Recherches Sociographiques [Canada] 1976 17(2): 189-220. The testimony of numerous inhabitants of the middle North Shore of the St. Lawrence estuary is used to provide a retrospective. Concepts such as economy, work, politics, family, education, religion, and leisure show a way of life that has been radically transformed since the turn of the century. Map, 3 tables.
　　　　　　　　　　　　　　　A. E. LeBlanc

3343. Driedger, Leo. MAINTENANCE OF URBAN ETHNIC BOUNDARIES: THE FRENCH IN ST. BONIFACE. Sociol Q. 1979 20(1): 89-108. Discusses the reasons for the segregation of French Canadians in St. Boniface, Manitoba, and the recent attempts to get the French to assimilate, based on studies done in the 1970's dating to 1871.

3344. Dumais, François. JOCELYNE LORTIE: UNE ARTISTE-PEINTRE [Jocelyne Lortie: Painter]. Action Natl. [Canada] 1978 67(8): 644-653. Lortie, born in 1939 at La Tuque, Quebec, is a foremost contemporary interpreter of the Laurentian landscape: forests, mountains and rivers. Influenced by Sisley and the impressionists, she especially admires the simplicity and space of Corot and the luminous technique of Rembrandt.　　　　　　　　　　　　　A. W. Novitsky

3345. Durocher, René. L'HISTOIRE PARTISANE: MAURICE DUPLESSIS ET SON TEMPS VUS PAR ROBERT RUMILLY ET CONRAD BLACK [Partisan history: Maurice Duplessis and his times as seen by Robert Rumilly and Conrad Black]. Rev. d'Hist. de l'Amérique Française [Canada] 1977 31(3): 407-426. A comparison of Conrad Black's Duplessis (Toronto: McClelland and Stewart, 1976) and Robert Rumilly's Maurice Duplessis et Son Temps (Montreal: Fides, 1973). Duplessis was the controversial Prime Minister of Quebec during 1936-39 and 1944-59. These two massive studies are the first to incorporate materials from the Duplessis archives. Though Black's treatment is somewhat more critical than Rumilly's, neither presents a clear or convincing portrait of their fascinating subject.　　　　　　M. R. Yerburgh

3346. Finn, Jean-Guy. LA SITUATION SOCIO-POLITIQUE DES ACADIENS: AUJOURD' HUI ET DEMAIN [The socio-political situation of the Acadians: today and tomorrow]. *Tr. of the Royal Soc. of Can. [Canada] 1977 15: 197-205.* Discusses the role of the French-speaking population of New Brunswick, noting that, although they have increased at a rate higher than the English-speaking population, emigration has reduced their number. They make up about 40% of the population. They are also rural; thus, their influence is less than the urbanized English-speaking population. Gradual assimilation also reduces their number. Moncton is the center of French-speaking culture in the Maritimes. 12 notes.   J. D. Neville

3347. Foggin, Peter M. L'ACCESSIBILITÉ À L'ENSEIGNEMENT COLLÉGIAL: UNE ANALYSE GÉOGRAPHIQUE DE LA FRÉQUENTATION DES CEGEP DU SAGUENAY [The accessibility of the college education: A geographical analysis of the attendance of Saguenay's CEGEP's]. *Protée [Canada] 1975 4(1): 20-37.* Researches the nature of student populations in six secondary schools (CEGEP) in Saguenay, including the origin of the students, their attendance and behavior, and the phenomenon of democratization in college education, with some comparison of American high schools and the colleges of Ile de Montréal.

3348. Frigon, F. J. CATHOLICISM AND CRISIS: L'ECOLE SOCIALE POPULAIRE AND THE DEPRESSION IN QUEBEC, 1930-1940. *R. de l'U. d'Ottawa 1975 45(1): 54-70.* Analyzes the Roman Catholic Church's reaction to the depression and stresses the importance of the École Sociale Populaire "in promoting a profound reexamination of the church's relationship to the other institutions of French Canada and in encouraging the growth of new ones such as labor unions." Based on primary and secondary sources; 62 notes.   M. L. Frey

3349. Gagnon, Marcel-Aimé. ESDRAS MINVILLE ET L'ACTION NATIONALE [Esdras Minville and *Action Nationale*]. *Action Natl. [Canada] 1976 65(9-10): 677-688.* In 1933, under the direction of Esdras Minville, the Ligue d'Action Nationale established *L'Action Nationale,* successor to *L'Action Française* and *L'Action Canadienne-Française,* as an organ of thought and action to serve the religious and national traditions of the French element in America. Its major inspiration was the papal encyclical *Rerum Novarum,* and its philosophy was corporatist.   A. W. Novitsky

3350. Gagnon, Serge. L'HISTOIRE DES IDÉOLOGIES QUÉBÉCOISES: QUINZE ANS DE REÁLISATIONS [The history of ideas in Quebec: Fifteen years of development]. *Social Hist. [Canada] 1976 9(17): 17-20.* Before the 1950's the study of the history of ideas in Quebec utilized categories drawn from European intellectual history and traced the influence of European ideas in Quebec. Since then there has been increasing emphasis on the social and class context of ideas in Quebec, but many works have suffered from an inadequate analysis of social structure. Secondary sources; 8 notes.   W. K. Hobson

3351. Gauvin, Lise. LES REVUES LITTÉRAIRES QUÉBÉCOISES DE L'UNIVERSITÉ À LA CONTRE-CULTURE [Quebec literary magazines from the university to the counterculture]. *Études Françaises [Canada] 1975 11(2): 161-183.* Describes various contemporary Quebec literary magazines and their histories within an intellectual context. Primary and secondary sources; 15 notes.   G. J. Rossi

3352. Gauvin, Michel. THE REFORMER AND THE MACHINE: MONTREAL CIVIC POLITICS FROM RAYMOND PRÉFONTAINE TO MÉDÉRIC MARTIN. *J. of Can. Studies [Canada] 1978 13(2): 16-26.* Focuses on machine politicians Préfontaine and Martin and on reform leader Hormisdas Laporte; reviews Montreal city politics 1894-1921. Early in the period, Alderman Préfontaine dispensed much patronage as chairman of the Roads Committee. Laporte's Reform Party came to power in 1900, but the Roads Committee soon became a stronghold of ward politics again. Discusses the Royal Commission investigation of political corruption in Montreal (1909) and the problem of undue influence by the Montreal Light, Heat and Power Company. A watchdog Board of Control, established in 1909, itself became a center of corruption with the electin of the demagogic machine politician Martin to the mayoralty (1914). Concludes that the dominant themes in Montreal politics were those most prominent throughout urban North America. Primary sources; 72 notes.   L. W. Van Wyk

3353. Genest, Jean-Guy. LES PIONNIERS DE L'ENSEIGNEMENT UNIVERSITAIRE AU SAGUENAY (1948-1969) [Pioneers of university instruction in Saguenay (1948-1969)]. *Protée [Canada] 1977 6(1): 15-128.* Chronicles the beginnings of university education, with L'Ecole de Génie (1949) and L'Ecole de Commerce (1950) in Saguenay-Lac-Saint-Jean, Quebec and discusses the development of educational programs and administrative policy during 1948-69.

3354. Gourd, Benoît-Beaudry. APERÇU CRITIQUE DES PRINCIPAUX OUVRAGES POUVANT SERVIR À L'HISTOIRE DU DÉVELOPPEMENT MINIER DE L'ABITIBI-TÉMISCAMINGUE (1910-1950) [Critical survey of the principal works relating to the history of mining development in Abitibi-Témiscamingue, 1910-50]. *Rev. d'Hist. de l'Am. Française [Canada] 1976 30(1): 99-107.* The Abitibi-Témiscamingue region was developed much later than the rest of Quebec. Most historical studies have dealt with its agricultural development. Mining activity, however, was a major factor in populating the region. Presents critical summaries of basic works: Raoul Blanchard, *L'Ouest du Canada français* (Montréal: Beauchemin, 1954), Pierre Bays, *Les marges de l'oekoumène dans l'Est du Canada* (Québec: Presses de l'Université Laval, 1964), Marcien Villemure, *Les villes de la Faille de Cadillac* (Rouyn: Conseil économique régional du Nord-Ouest québécois, 1971), E. S. Moore, *American Influence in Canadian Mining* (Toronto: U. of Toronto Pr., 1941), Leslie Roberts, *Noranda* (Toronto: Clarke and Irwin, 1952), Émile Benoist, *L'Abitibi, pays de l'or* (Montréal: Éditions du Zodiaque, 1938), and Evelyn Dumas, *Dans le sommeil de nos os* (Montréal: Leméac, 1971). 14 notes.   L. B. Chan

3355. Grenier, Manon; Roy, Maurice, and Bouchard, Louis. L'EVOLUTION DE LA POPULATION DES ENFANTS AU CENTRE DE LA VILLE DE QUEBEC ET EN BANLIEU, 1951-1971 [The evolution of the population of children in downtown Quebec City and the suburbs, 1951-71]. *Cahiers de Géographie de Québec 1974 18(45): 541-552.*

3356. Guitard, Michelle. LA ROLANDERIE. *Saskatchewan Hist. [Canada] 1977 30(3): 110-114.* Examines an estate near Whitewood in Eastern Assiniboia, its founder, Rudolf Meyer, and his successor owner, Count Yves de Roffignac, who came to Saskatchewan with Meyer in 1886. The economic ventures of a series of French owners were disasters; however, the culture and social manners these French aristocrats provided were talked about in the district for several decades. 30 notes.   C. Held

3357. Harvey, Pierre. LES IDÉES ÉCONOMIQUES D'ESDRAS MINVILLE DES DÉBUTS À LA MATURITE (1923-1936) [The economic ideas of Esdras Minville from the beginning to maturity (1923-36)]. *Action Natl. [Canada] 1976 65(9-10): 626-642.* Esdras Minville's primary concern was the economic development of Quebec and the institution of a corporative order to replace liberal capitalism. He believed that forestry would play a major role in the province, and was one of the first authors to note the domination of Quebec by American multinational corporations. 23 notes.   A. W. Novitsky

3358. Henripin, Jacques. L'AVENIR DES FRANCOPHONES AU CANADA [The future of French-speaking people in Canada]. *Tr. of the Royal Soc. of Can. 1975 13: 133-139.* Discusses French-speaking Canadians, noting that they have retained their percentage of the population because of their much higher birthrate. Each year the percentage of Canadians whose primary language is French declines as they emigrate or assimilate. Assimilation is greater in areas far from Quebec, areas in which the French-speaking population is very small. Discusses Robert Maheu's predictions concerning French-speaking Canadians. Also, even in Quebec the percentage of the population which is French-speaking is declining gradually. 2 notes.   J. D. Neville

3359. Huel, Raymond. THE FRENCH LANGUAGE PRESS IN WESTERN CANADA: *LE PATRIOTE DE L'OUEST,* 1910-41. *Rev. de l'Université d'Ottawa [Canada] 1976 46(4): 476-499.* The newspaper *Le Patriote de l'Ouest* was founded in Saskatchewan in 1910 with the encouragement of the Roman Catholic bishop and clergy, who regarded the maintenance of the French language and of the Catholic faith as inseparable. *Le Patriote* was located at first in remote Duck Lake, and after 1913 in Regina. The newspaper faced constant financial difficulties.

It had to be subsidized constantly by Catholic clergymen, and had a difficult time capturing the imagination of French-speakers in Saskatchewan. In 1933, the Oblates of Mary Immaculate of the Province of Alberta-Saskatchewan took over the newspaper and its publishing company to save it from the Depression. In 1941, *Le Patriote* was merged with *La Liberté* of Winnipeg in the hope that the new, merged journal would survive and help preserve the French language in the West. 142 notes.
J. C. Billigmeier

3360. Humphrys, Ruth. DR. RUDOLF MEYER AND THE FRENCH NOBILITY OF ASSINIBOIA. *Beaver [Canada] 1978 309(1): 17-23.* Rudolf Meyer, a German fluent in French, came to Pipestone Creek, Saskatchewan, in 1885, with backing from French capitalists. He started an agricultural settlement with modest success. Soon around a dozen members of the French nobility and their families arrived. They continued with their aristocratic airs, dancing, dressing well, riding, and hunting. They even created the Whitewood town band, which included a marquis, a count, and a viscount. They tried a variety of farming and business ventures, but their inexperience and lack of direction led to constant failures. The colony disappeared after a few years. The only moderate success was Viscount de Langle, who operated a store in Whitewood. 7 illus., map.
D. Chaput

3361. Jacob, Paul. CROIX DE CHEMIN ET DÉVOTIONS POPULAIRES DANS LA BEAUCE [Roadside crosses and popular devotions in La Beauce]. *Sessions d'Étude: Soc. Can. d'Hist. de l'Église Catholique [Canada] 1976 43: 15-34.* Studies 17 roadside shrines in La Beauce County as a key to popular devotion, religious practice, and social customs of the area.

3362. Johnstone, John W. C. SOCIAL CHANGE AND PARENT-YOUTH CONFLICT: THE PROBLEM OF GENERATIONS IN ENGLISH AND FRENCH CANADA. *Youth and Soc. 1975 7(1): 3-26.* The high degree of tension between Quebec French Canadian youth and their parents is based primarily on the decline of the Roman Catholic Church as a dominant force and significant changes in the educational system. Conflicts are strongest over dating and religion, and are strong also over politics and occupational plans. There is much less tension in English Canadian families. Based on a 1965 sample of Canadian youth (ages 13-20), and on primary and secondary sources; 5 tables, 8 notes, biblio.
J. H. Sweetland

3363. Lalonde, André N. ARCHBISHOP O. E. MATHIEU AND FRANCOPHONE IMMIGRATION TO THE ARCHDIOCESE OF REGINA. *Study Sessions: Can. Catholic Hist. Assoc. [Canada] 1977 44: 45-60.* Olivier-Elzéar Mathieu, Archbishop of the Regina Archdiocese during 1911-31, promoted the immigration of Catholic French Canadians, French, and Americans to Canada's Prairie Provinces, especially Manitoba and Saskatchewan.

3364. Lamontagne, Maurice. LA FACULTÉ DES SCIENCES SOCIALES DE LAVAL: PRELUDE DE LA RÉVOLUTION TRANQUILLE [The faculty of social sciences at Laval: prelude to the quiet revolution]. *Social Hist. [Canada] 1977 10(19): 146-151.* The history of Quebec has been marked by an opposition between the sources and orientation of economic growth (external), on the one hand, and the tenor of the dominant ideology of the traditional elites on the other hand. Ideology has opposed the trends of economic growth and proposed impossible alternatives. The Faculty of Social Sciences of Laval University, founded by R.-P. Lévesque, has sought to develop a more realistic and positive approach to the problems of contemporary Quebec society. As a result, a new educated elite is emerging and is inspiring a new dynamic in the popular movements.
W. K. Hobson

3365. Lapointe, Michelle. LE SYNDICAT CATHOLIQUE DES ALLUMETTIÈRES DE HULL, 1919-1924 [The Catholic matchmakers' union in Hull, 1919-24]. *Rev. d'Hist. de l'Amerique Française [Canada] 1979 32(4): 603-628.* Analysis of the matchmakers' union in Hull, Quebec, enables the researcher to develop much-needed perspective on the female Catholic workers' movement. It was a vigorous union; membership was impressive. Two strike actions were conducted in a very conservative milieu. The union played an important role in raising the consciousness of its membership and in ensuring, on a modest scale, that the needs of female workers in Canada would receive additional attention in years to come. 40 notes.
M. R. Yerburgh

3366. Lapointe, Pierre-Louis. LA NOUVELLE EUROPÉENNE ET LA PRESSE QUÉBÉCOISE D'EXPRESSION FRANÇAISE (1866-1871) [European news and the French-language press of Quebec (1866-1871)]. *R. d'hist. de l'Amérique française [Canada] 1975 28(4): 517-537.* During the Austro-Prussian and Franco-Prussian Wars, the French-language newspapers of Quebec covered events in Europe mainly by reproducing published French-language articles from European and American sources. After completion of the trans-Atlantic cable, some of Quebec's French-language newspapers subscribed to the Associated Press dispatch system, and received news from Europe in English on a two-days delayed basis via New York. Most French newspapers in Quebec lacked the funds to subscribe, and had to be content with reproducing articles. Based on newspapers and secondary works; 5 tables, 84 notes.
L. B. Chan

3367. Larivière-Derome, Céline. UN PROFESSEUR D'ART AU CANADA AU XIXᵉ SIÈCLE: L'ABBÉ JOSEPH CHABERT [An art teacher in 19th-century Canada: Abbé Joseph Chabert]. *R. d'Hist. de l'Amérique Française 1974 28(3): 347-366.* Describes the history of the National Institute for Arts and Crafts of Montreal founded in 1870 and directed by the French Abbé Joseph Chabert. Courses in engraving, sculpture, architecture, drafting, and various scientific subjects were offered to the working classes. The school declined following the Abbé's involvement in a scandal, later changed location several times, and finally disappeared after his death in 1894. Based on primary and secondary sources; 126 notes.
C. Collon

3368. Larocque, Paul. LES PÊCHEURS GASPÉSIENS ET LA MOUVEMENT COOPÉRATIF (1939-1948) [Gaspé fishermen and the cooperative movement (1939-1948)]. *Social Hist. [Canada] 1975 8(16): 294-313.* Gaspé Peninsula (Québec) fishermen, who suffered economic hardship in the 1930's, united during World War II in more than 30 local producers' cooperatives, which federated into the Pêcheurs-Unis. Promotion by the government and clergy were important factors in the cooperatives' founding and success, as was the wartime economic boom. The rapid growth of the cooperatives created an unstable structure, which partially collapsed when the boom ended. Based on documents in Pêcheurs-Unis du Québec Archives (Montreal) and published primary sources; 126 notes.
W. K. Hobson

3369. Lavigne, Marie et al. LA FÉDÉRATION NATIONALE SAINT-JEAN-BAPTISTE ET LES REVENDICATIONS FÉMINISTES AU DÉBUT DU XXᵉ SIÈCLE [The Saint John the Baptist National Federation and feminist demands at the start of the 20th century]. *R. d'hist. de l'Amérique française [Canada] 1975 29(3): 353-373.* Surveys the history of the Fédération Nationale Saint-Jean-Baptiste from 1907-33, and discusses the role of its founder, Marie Gérin-Lajoie (1867-1945). In order to develop in French-Canadian society, the Fédération, a feminist group, had to make alliances with the Catholic clergy and compromises with the prevailing ideology. While calling for increased political rights for women, it supported the integrity of the family and the traditional female familial role. The organization did not succeed in synthesizing these paradoxical interests, and its influence declined after 1933. Based on documents in the Archives de la Fédération Nationale Saint-Jean-Baptiste (Montréal), Archives de la Communauté des Soeurs de Notre-Dame-du-Bon Conseil (Montréal), and secondary sources; 31 notes.
L. B. Chan

3370. Lavigne, Marie and Stoddart, Jennifer. LES TRAVAILLEUSES MONTRÉALAISES ENTRE LES DEUX GUERRES [Women in the workforce of Montreal between the wars]. *Labour [Canada] 1977 2: 170-183.* Examines the participation of women in the Montreal workforce where they constituted at least 25% of the total throughout the period. Includes an analysis of their distribution in various occupations and the problem of wage discrimination. Comparisons are made with men workers in Montreal and with men and women in Toronto. The unique influence of large numbers of religious women, especially in teaching, is also examined. Most employed women were young (15-twenty-four), single, and most worked in jobs which did not damage their role and traditional function in the family. Census reports, primary and secondary sources; 3 tables, 34 notes.
W. A. Kearns

3371. LeMoignan, Michel. LA VISION AUDACIEUSE DE MGR. F.-X. ROSS, PREMIER ÉVÊQUE DE GASPÉ [The audacious vision of Monsignor F.-X. Ross, first bishop of Gaspé]. *Sessions d'Étude: Soc.*

Can. d'Hist. de l'Église Catholique [Canada] 1976 43: 35-47. A biography of Bishop-founder François Xavier Ross (1869-1945), emphasizing his contributions to the educational system, medical facilities, and socioeconomic organization of Gaspé and its environs, 1923-45, and stressing the importance of his writings to the historian.

3372. Létourneau, Firmin. ESDRAS MINVILLE. *Action Natl. [Canada] 1976 65(9-10): 621-625.* Esdras Minville wrote his first article for *Action Française* (Canada) in 1922. Later he became a director of the Ligue d'Action Français. In 1928, with Gerard Parizeau, Fortunat Fortier, François Vézina, and others, he founded *Actualité Économique,* the official publication of the École des Hautes Études Commerciales in Montreal. A. W. Novitsky

3373. Lévesque, Georges-Henri. PRÉLUDE À LA RÉVOLUTION TRANQUILLE AU QUÉBEC: NOTES NOUVELLES SUR D'ANCIENS INSTRUMENTS [Prelude to the quiet revolution in Quebec: New notes on old instruments]. *Social Hist. [Canada] 1977 10(19): 134-146.* Personal comments on the historial background to the "quiet revolution" in Quebec. From its founding in 1903 until the 1930's the A.C.J.C. was the only movement of young French Canadians. Its focus was on both Catholicism and nationalism. The dual emphasis was not compatible with the needs of the 1930's, and purely nationalist and purely Catholic youth movements were formed. The author adopted the nationalist position, and a major controversy developed over an article he planned to publish outlining these views in the *Revue Dominicaine* in 1935. 10 notes. W. K. Hobson

3374. Levitt, Joseph. IMAGES OF BOURASSA. *J. of Can. Studies [Canada] 1978 13(1): 100-113.* The attitudes of Canadian historians, both Anglophone and Francophone, toward Henri Bourassa (1868-1952) consistently have been colored by the position of each on the major issues Bourassa addressed during his more than 40 years in public life (1890's-1930's). Goldwin Smith, a fellow anti-imperialist, introduced him into historical literature in 1902. The isolationism of the 30's and the biculturalism of the 60's (Bourassa, while a champion of Francophone rights, always opposed separatism) occasioned favorable treatment of Bourassa among Anglophones, while Lionel Groulx, his onetime foe, described him in 1971 as "l'incomparable Éveilleur." Bourassa's position on social issues —Catholic, moderately reformist, emphasizing the family and agricultural values—likewise has called forth praise and blame. Calls for a view of Bourassa that is truer to the man himself. Primary sources; 120 notes. L. W. Van Wyk

3375. Little, John I. LA PATRIE: QUEBEC'S REPATRIATION COLONY, 1875-1880. *Can. Hist. Assoc. Hist. Papers [Canada] 1977: 66-85.* A study of the reaction of Quebec's lay and clerical leaders to the massive exodus of French-speaking Canadians to the United States in the second half of the 19th century. The antidote promoted was reform of the land-holding system, building of colonization roads, and establishing new settlements. To encourage return from New England, the new ministry in 1874 launched its repatriation colony society proposing use of crown lands. Investigates the nature of the considerations involved, how practical were they, and what religious and agrarian values entered into the structuring and operation of the colonies. The Repatriation Act (1875) became the basis for implementation, with the village of La Patrie as headquarters and Jérôme-Adolphe Chicoyne in charge. The effort was only a partial success, for a variety of reasons. 111 notes. R. V. Ritter

3376. Little, John I. LES INVESTISSEURS FRANÇAIS ET LE NATIONALISME CANADIEN-FRANÇAISE: LA COMPAGNIE DE COLONISATION ET DE CRÉDIT DES CANTONS DE L'EST, 1881-1893 [French investors and French-Canadian nationalism: the company of colonization and credit of the eastern townships, 1881-1893]. *Rev. d'Hist. de l'Amérique Française [Canada] 1978 32(1): 19-39.* Toward the end of the 19th century, French investors sought new opportunities in eastern Quebec. La Compagnie de Colonisation et de Credit des Cantons de l'Est, for example, settled unpopulated areas in return for the right to exploit natural resources. Though sawmills were erected and farms were established, initial financial outlays were too great. La Compagnie ceased its activities in 1893. It had built an impressive network of roads and attracted a permanent population to a formerly undeveloped area. 81 notes. M. R. Yerburgh

3377. Louder, Dean R.; Bisson, Michel; and La Rochelle, Pierre. ANALYSE CENTROGRAPHIQUE DE LA POPULATION DE QUEBEC DE 1951 A 1971 [Centrographic analysis of Quebec population, 1951-1971]. *Cahiers de Géographie de Québec 1974 18(45): 421-444.*

3378. Lussier, A. S. THE METIS: CONTEMPORARY PROBLEM OF IDENTITY. *Manitoba Pageant [Canada] 1978 23(3): 12-15.* Discusses psychological, economic, ethnic, and cultural factors that define Western Canada's Métis' identity. 14 notes. R. V. Ritter

3379. Maloof, George. CLAUDE HENRI GRIGNON A LA DEFENSE DE LA LANGUE CANADIENNE-FRANCAISE [Claude Henri Grignon in defense of Canadian-French language]. *Rev. de Louisiane 1977 6(1): 77-85.* Discusses French Canadians in the 20th century, especially the Anglicization of the French language; that is, incorporation of English words, with the addition of accent and verb endings.

3380. Migner, Robert Maurice. LE BOSSISME POLITIQUE À MONTRÉAL: CAMILLIEN HOUDE REMPLACE MÉDERIC MARTIN (1923-1929) [Bossism politics in Montreal: Camillien Houde replaces Méderic Martin (1923-1929)]. *Urban Hist. Rev. [Canada] 1974 74(1): 2-8.* Examines bossism in Montreal politics; rivalry between Méderic Martin and Camillien Houde led to Houde's replacement of Martin as local government "boss" in 1928.

3381. Montpetit, Raymond. UN EXEMPLE DE PEINTURE D'HISTOIRE AU QUÉBEC: CHARLES HUOT À L'ASSEMBLÉE NATIONALE [An example of historical paintings in Quebec: Charles Huot at the National Assembly]. *Rev. d'Hist. de l'Amérique Française [Canada] 1977 31(3): 397-405.* Analyzes three paintings by Charles Huot (1855-1930) on display at Quebec's Legislative Assembly. Historical paintings such as these contribute to an understanding of intellectual history and should not be judged by contemporary aesthetic standards. 16 notes. M. R. Yerburgh

3382. Moreau, Jean-Paul. VINGT-QUATRE HEURES AVEC MARCEL OUIMET [Twenty-four hours with Marcel Ouimet]. *Can. Oral Hist. Assoc. J. [Canada] 1978 3(1): 10-21.* Discusses Marcel Ouimet's career with Radio Canada, 1939-75.

3383. Muir, Margaret. PROFESSIONAL WOMEN AND NETWORK MAINTENANCE IN A FRENCH AND AN ENGLISH CANADIAN FISHING VILLAGE. *Atlantis [Canada] 1977 2(2, pt. 2): 45-55.* Describes employment patterns in two small villages on the Magdalen Islands, Quebec, to compare women in professional careers with women who work in the villages in the traditional role of housewife and mother.

3384. Munro, Kenneth. L'OUEST DANS LA PENSÉE POLITIQUE DE CHAPLEAU [The west in the political thought of Chapleau]. *Rev. de l'U. d'Ottawa [Canada] 1977 47(4): 413-426.* Joseph Adolphe Chapleau (1840-98) was one French-Canadian politician who saw in the opening and development of the Canadian west an opportunity for French Canadians to play an important role there. One of his projects toward this end was to see completed a Montreal terminus on the transcontinental railroad. Much of his political life was directed at claiming for French Canadians a more effective voice in national politics, in order that their interests might be advanced in the developing western areas of the country. Primary and secondary sources; 62 notes. G. J. Rossi

3385. Painchaud, Robert. FRENCH-CANADIAN HISTORIOGRAPHY AND FRANCO-CATHOLIC SETTLEMENT IN WESTERN CANADA, 1870-1915. *Can. Hist. Rev. [Canada] 1978 59(4): 447-466.* Critically analyzes the usual explanations for the large number of French Canadians who quit Quebec, to become not homesteaders in the Canadian Prairies but rather factory workers in New England or farmers in the American West. It has been common to attribute this to discriminatory measures and attitudes on the part of English Canadians to discourage settlement in western Canada. However such explanations are far too simple, not recognizing the complexity of the forces at work. Nor can it be attributed only to the lack of support of Catholic coreligionists in Quebec. The disagreements indicate a need to reassess the motivations and conclusions which underlie Quebec historiography on the subject. 60 notes. R. V. Ritter

3386. Painchaud, Robert. LES ORIGINES DES PEUPLEMENTS DE LANGUE FRANÇAISE DANS L'OUEST CANADIEN, 1870-1920: MYTHES ET RÉALITÉS [The origins of the French-speaking people in the Canadian West, 1870-1920: Myths and realities]. *Tr. of the Royal Soc. of Can. 1975 13: 109-121.* Discusses the origins of French-speaking people in Western Canada, with emphasis on Manitoba, and describes the efforts, especially by ecclesiastical leaders, to get them to settle there. In Manitoba they settled largely in a contiguous area; hence, they were concentrated and retained their identity. They came from three major areas—Quebec, the United States, and French-speaking Europe (i.e., France, Belgium, and Switzerland). Many of them were farmers; however, some of them worked in the coal mines. 30 notes.

J. D. Neville

3387. Parenteau, Roland. L'INFLUENCE ÉTATSUNIENNE DANS LES ÉCOLES D'ADMINISTRATION AU CANADA ET PLUS PARTICULIÈREMENT AU QUÉBEC [US influence on management schools in Canada and especially in Quebec]. *Tr. of the Royal Soc. of Can. 1973 11: 109-118.* Outlines the catastrophic proportions of Americanization in Canadian business education, stressing the influence of US-educated professors, US textbooks, and US ideological inspiration on business schools in Quebec, where the language barrier protects to some extent, but cultural alienation is still strongly felt.

3388. Payment, Diane. MONSIEUR BATOCHE. *Saskatchewan Hist. [Canada] 1979 32(3): 81-103.* Attempts to disprove the assumption of many historians that the Métis were a defeated people after 1885 and could only be reabsorbed into the parent Indian society or assimilated by the white man's culture and society. Using the family of François-Xavier Letendre (or Batoche), presents arguments for the survival of at least some Métis, well documented by family, church, and government files. Letendre was successful in business, acquired social status and provided political leadership in Saskatchewan. 4 photos, 2 maps, genealogy chart, 97 notes.

C. Held

3389. Rocher, Guy. L'INFLUENCE DE LA SOCIOLOGIE AMÈRICAINE SUR LA SOCIOLOGIE QUÉBECOISE [The influence of American sociology on Quebec sociology]. *Tr. of the Royal Soc. of Can. 1973 11: 75-79.* Compares American and French influence on the field of sociology in Quebec, blaming these two elements for the indetermination, weakness, and lack of creativity in Quebec sociology, and for its failure to develop its own potential.

3390. Rogel, Jean-Pierre. LA PRESSE QUEBECOISE ET L'INFORMATION SUR LA POLITIQUE INTERNATIONALE [Quebec's press and information on international politics]. *Études Int. [Canada] 1974 5(4): 693-711.* Analyzes foreign news coverage in three major Quebec daily newspapers, *La Presse, Le Soleil,* and *Le Devoir.* Discusses the sources for foreign news, notably the impact of the US press, international news agencies, and journalists. Examines the treatment afforded foreign developments, including editorials. Covers 1962-74. Primary and secondary sources; 3 tables, 25 notes, biblio.

J. F. Harrington, Jr.

3391. Saguin, André-Louis. TERRITORIALITÉ, ESPACE MENTAL ET TOPOPHILIE AU SAGUENAY [Territorialism, mental space and topophilia in Saguenay]. *Protée [Canada] 1975 4(1): 53-66.* Studies collective and individual behaviorism regarding spatial perception in Saguenay County 1969-74, and the emergence of strong territorialism of a topographical, circulatory, urban, and landscape nature, which opens new promising avenues toward establishment of a political geography in the area.

3392. St. Amant, Jean-Claude. LA PROPAGANDE DE L'ÉCOLE SOCIALE POPULAIRE EN FAVEUR DU SYNDICALISME CATHOLIQUE 1911-1949 [The propaganda of the Social Popular School in favor of Catholic Syndicalism]. *Rev. d'Hist. de l'Amérique Française [Canada] 1978 32(2): 203-228.* Founded by Jesuits in Montreal, the Social Popular School was an educational agency whose primary purpose was to promote improved conditions for workers. It published numerous pamphlets, tracts, and journals on a wide variety of related topics, e.g., the dangers of communism, the perils of alcohol, and the restoration of social order. The School encouraged a brand of unionism that was grounded in the Catholic faith, one that would alleviate the traditional tensions that existed between the working and proprietary classes. 76 notes.

M. R. Yerburgh

3393. Schenck, Ernest. EUGÈNE LAPIERRE, MUSICIEN ET NATIONALISTE [Eugène Lapierre, musician and nationalist]. *Action Natl. [Canada] 1974 64(2): 154-169.* The late Eugène Lapierre, a musician and a fervent nationalist, was president of the Historical Society of Montreal (Société historique de Montréal).

3394. Séguin, Norman. HERBERTVILLE AU LAC SAINT-JEAN, 1850-1900: UN EXEMPLE QUEBECOIS DE COLONISATION AU XIXᵉ SIECLE [Herbertville in the Lake St. John Region, 1850-1900: An example of 19th-century Quebec colonization]. *Can. Hist. Assoc. Hist. Papers 1973: 251-268.* Herbertville was a traditional market center for the sawmill industry founded in a remote area. It was dominated by the parish priest and a group of families who provided local functionaries: the merchants and moneylenders who throve on the indebtedness of subsistence farmers. The railway, in 1893, tightened the commercial and financial connections with larger centers, while after 1896 a paper mill marked a shift to intensified industrialization and an urban work force. Based on provincial archives, church archives, and secondary sources; 36 notes.

G. E. Panting

3395. Simard, Jean Paul and Riverin, Bérard. ORIGINE GÉOGRAPHIQUE ET SOCIAL DES ETUDIANTS DU PETIT-SÉMINAIRE DE CHICOUTIMI ET LEUR ORIENTATION SOCIO-PROFESSIONNELLE: 1873-1930 [Geographic and social origins of the students of the Petit-Séminaire de Chicoutimi and their socioprofessional orientation: 1873-1930]. *Sessions D'Étude: Soc. Can. d'Hist. de l'Eglise Catholique 1973 40: 33-54.*

3396. Spigelman, Martin S. SURVIVAL: NEW VIEWS ON THE FRANCOPHONE MINORITIES IN CANADA. *Acadiensis [Canada] 1978 7(2): 141-150.* Many recent works on French minorities outside Quebec suggest that their assimilation is inevitable. Richard Joy's *Language in Conflict* (1972) reveals continued language loss while Thomas R. Maxwell's *The Invisible French, the French in Metropolitan Toronto* reveals divisions among Toronto's French, and a general acceptance of assimilation. Similarly, Robert Choquette's work explores divisions between Ontario's French and Irish. These and other works suggest that lessening self-consciousness, not Anglo-Protestant pressure, has weakened French culture outside Quebec. 4 notes.

D. F. Chard

3397. Sutherland, Ronald. YVON DESCHAMPS: NEW LIFE FOR AN OLD FORM. *Colby Lib. Q. 1977 13(3): 165-172.* Discusses the topical humor of Yvon Deschamps, a Quebec comedian who has performed 1968-77, in the tradition known as "Le Monologue quebeçois," a form of social, political, and cultural commentary.

3398. Sylvain, Philippe. LES CHEVALIERS DU TRAVAIL ET LE CARDINAL ELZÉAR-ALEXANDRE TASCHEREAU [The Knights of Labor and Cardinal Elzéar-Alexandre Taschereau]. *Tr. of the Royal Soc. of Can. 1973 11: 31-42.* Records the history of Cardinal Taschereau's condemnation and later pardon of the Noble and Holy Order of the Knights of Labor for secretiveness, 1884-94, suggesting that this secret society, founded in Philadelphia in 1869, had some influence on the history of French Canadian labor unions.

3399. Tremblay, Marc-Adélard. LES QUÉBÉCOIS À LA RECHERCHE DE LEUR IDENTITÉ CULTURELLE [Quebecers in search of their cultural identity]. *Action Natl. [Canada] 1973 62(6): 439-450.* French-speaking Quebecers suffer from cultural alienation brought about by rapid change in their historical roots and by the adoption of the North American material value system. Unless redressed, this process of alienation will lead to complete assimilation of the French-language group.

A. E. LeBlanc

3400. Tremblay, Rodrigue. LES QUÉBÉCOIS ET LEUR ÉCONOMIE [The people of Quebec and their economy]. *Action Natl. [Canada] 1975 64(10): 801-809.* Examines the causes for lack of participation by French Canadians in Quebec industry and proposes solutions to the problem.

3401. Trépanier, Pierre. DUPLESSIS PARMI NOUS [Duplessis among us]. *Action Natl. [Canada] 1978 68(2): 127-132.* There has been rising interest in Maurice Duplessis recently. Robert Rumilly's *Maurice Duplessis et son temps* (Montreal, 1973) provides a favorable view of the former Quebec premier, while Conrad Black's *Duplessis* (Toronto and Montreal, 1977) emphasizes the power of the church and the infantilism of the Quebecois. For Black, the hallmarks of the Duplessis system were autonomy, frugality, fidelity, and paternalism, based on an alliance between the premier and the church to assure the docility of the people. Biblio. A. W. Novitsky

3402. Trépanier, Pierre. SIMÉON LE SAGE ET L'AFFAIRE DU TÉMISCAMINGUE (1884-1902) [Simeon le Sage and the Temiscamingue affair (1884-1902)]. *Rev. de l'U. d'Ottawa [Canada] 1977 47(3): 365-376.* Describes the role of Simeon Le Sage (1835-1909) in the development and colonization of lands in the Témiscamingue area of Quebec. Based on documents in the Archives nationales du Québec, and in the Archives Deschatelets (JH 401 C21R), and secondary works; 77 notes. G. J. Rossi

3403. Trépanier, Pierre. SIMÉON LE SAGE (1835-1909): UN NOTABLE D'AUTREFOIS DANS L'INTIMITÉ [Simeon Le Sage (1835-1909): the personal life of a notable of the past]. *Action Natl. [Canada] 1978 67(6): 469-496.* Biographical sketch and study of the social mobility of a Quebec lawyer and public official in the late 19th century. His father was an unlettered craftsman, but Simeon Le Sage completed classical studies, became a lawyer, and married into a landed family. Although defeated twice in legislative elections (1862 and 1867) he was appointed deputy director of the Department of Agriculture and Public Works by Quebec premier P.-J.-O. Chauveau. A staunch conservative and French Canadian nationalist, he was a patron of the arts and letters, especially French Canadian history. Primary and secondary sources; 150 notes. A. W. Novitsky

3404. Trépanier, Pierre. VICTOR BARBEAU ET ALBINY PAQUETTE [Victor Barbeau and Albiny Paquette]. *Action Natl. [Canada] 1978 68(4): 324-330.* Although best known as a writer, linguist, and critic, Victor Barbeau was a prophet of the Quebec consumer cooperative movement. He urged its extension throughout the world as a model for a new society based on rationality of service rather than profit. Albiny Paquette was a medical doctor, mayor, prefect, deputy, provincial secretary, minister of health under Maurice Duplessis, and legislative councillor. He launched crusades against tuberculosis and infant mortality, and was both a political conservative and a staunch Catholic. Covers ca. 1900-45. Review of "Victor Barbeau, hommages et tributes," *Cahiers de l'Académie canadienne-française,* No. 15 (Montreal, Fides, 1978), and Paquette, *33 années à la législature de Québec, Soldat—médecin—maire —député—ministre, Souvenirs d'une vie de travail et de bonheur* (1977). 11 notes. A. W. Novitsky

3405. Trifiro, Luigi. UNE INTERVENTION À ROME DANS LA LUTTE POUR LE SUFFRAGE FÉMININ AU QUÉBEC (1922) [An appeal to Rome in the struggle for woman suffrage in Quebec (1922)]. *Rev. d'Hist. de l'Amérique Française [Canada] 1978 32(1): 1-18.* By 1922, Quebec was the only Canadian province that still denied women the right to vote. Facing strong opposition from the conservative Catholic hierarchy, a prosuffrage group launched a direct appeal to the Congress of the International Union of Catholic Women's Leagues in Rome. Despite a somewhat sympathetic hearing, the women of Quebec were refused the franchise for another 20 years. 48 notes. M. R. Yerburgh

3406. Trofimenkoff, Susan Mann. HENRI BOURASSA AND "THE WOMAN QUESTION." *J. of Can. Studies 1975 10(4): 3-11.* Discusses the opposition of writer Henri Bourassa to feminism, woman suffrage and divorce in Canada, 1913-25.

3407. Turmel, Antoine. LE DÉVELOPPEMENT DE PROVIGO [The development of Provigo]. *Action Natl. [Canada] 1978 68(4): 279-293.* The author, president of Provigo, founded the Denault grocery company at Sherbrooke, Quebec, in 1945. Through 1950, sales increased by 50% annually. Since 1968, the company has pursued aggressively a policy of mergers with Jato in the Quebec metropolitan area, Dionne in Montreal, La Baie on the North Coast, Weston, Ltd., and Loeb, expanding its markets throughout Canada and the states of California, Virginia, and Maryland. Vertical integration was accomplished, and more than 130 Provi-Soir convenience food and fuel stations were established in cooperation with Shell, Gulf, Esso, Fino, and Texaco oil companies. Address before the Montreal Chamber of Commerce, 31 October 1978. A. W. Novitsky

3408. Tusseau, Jean-Pierre. LA FIN "ÉDIFIANTE" D'ARTHUR BUIES [The "edifying" end of Arthur Buies]. *Études Françaises [Canada] 1973 9(1): 45-54.* Discusses the return of French Canadian pamphleteer Arthur Buies to the Catholic Church. Based on works of Buies, newspapers, and works of Gagnon; illus., 31 notes. C. Bates

3409. Veltman, Calvin J. ETHNIC ASSIMILATION IN QUEBEC: A STATISTICAL ANALYSIS. *Am. Rev. of Can. Studies 1975 5(2): 104-129.* Examines linguistic transfers in 1971 census reports to determine whether the use of the French language in Quebec is really in danger of extinction; there is some linguistic transfer, but the French-speaking community is presently growing.

3410. Vigod, B. L. BIOGRAPHY AND POLITICAL CULTURE IN QUEBEC. *Acadiensis [Canada] 1977 7(1): 141-147.* Three recent biographies of Quebec political leaders during the 19th-20th centuries are discussed in this review article prompted by Alastair Sweeny's *George-Etienne Cartier* (Toronto: McClelland and Stewart, 1976), Robert Rumilly's *Maurice Duplessis et son temps* (2 vols., Montreal: Fides, 1973), and Conrad Black's *Duplessis* (Toronto: McClelland and Stewart, 1973), plus an analytical work by Jean-Louis Roy *La Marche des Québécois: le temps des ruptures 1945-1960* (Montreal: Leméac, 1967).

3411. Waterston, Elizabeth. HOWELLS AND THE CITY OF QUEBEC. *Can. Rev. of Am. Studies [Canada] 1978 9(2): 155-167.* Travel accounts, a flourishing literary genre of the 1800's, often covered Quebec. But accounts by Americans differed from the writings of others, because American men-of-letters mostly were impressed by Quebec's rich imperial heritage and monuments of past wars, its Catholic cultural milieu, and its quaint preindustrial setting. In *Their Wedding Journey* (1871) and *A Chance Acquaintance* (1872), William Dean Howells (1837-1920) pictured Quebec as charming for the same reasons as did other Americans. However, Howells preferred the "rawer countryside" surrounding that "antique city." Based on Howells's writings; 4 photos, 9 notes. H. T. Lovin

3412. Weiss, J. M. IMAGES DES ETATS-UNIS DANS LE ROMAN QUEBECOIS MODERNE [Images of the United States in contemporary Quebec novels]. *Am. Rev. of Can. Studies 1975 5(2): 82-103.* Examines images of the United States in Quebec novels, especially those of Ringuet, Roger Lemelin, and Anne Hébert; discusses themes expressed through the use of US imagery in much French Canadian literature, 1940's-70's.

3413. —. LES RÉPERTOIRES DES INDUSTRIES FRANCOPHONES [Lists of francophone industries]. *Action Natl. [Canada] 1978 67(8): 624-643.* The Conseil d'expansion économique studies the food, furniture, wood-working, leather, metal fabrication, printing, machine, transportation, electrical, paper, chemical, textile, clothing, and other industries in Quebec 1961-71, updated to 1975, in terms of numbers of establishments and employees, value of salaries and products, and percentage of Canadian production. Corporate headquarters and major manufacturing centers outside of Quebec are noted for the leading companies in each industry, and preferential purchase of the products of Quebec manufacturers is urged. Primary and secondary sources; 14 tables, note. A. W. Novitsky

British Canadians

General

3414. Schultz, J. A. CANADIAN ATTITUDES TOWARD EMPIRE SETTLEMENT, 1919-1930. *J. of Imperial and Commonwealth Hist. [Great Britain] 1973 1(2): 237-251.* Analyzes Canadian attitudes towards immigration into British Columbia after World War I. Fear of American growth, a renewed closeness with Great Britain, and altered public opinion all contributed to a pervasive sentiment which encouraged Britons to come to Canada. The details of various settlement schemes and the impact of the movement, which attracted relatively few British immigrants, are described. Based on printed and manuscript sources; 67 notes.
J. A. Casada

3415. Turner, Wesley B. MISS RYE'S CHILDREN *Ontario Hist. [Canada] 1976 68(3): 169-203.* Discusses the attitudes of the press toward the immigration of more or less officially sponsored British pauper children into Ontario, following the publication in Great Britain of a highly critical report on such immigration. This began in 1869 with the work of a Miss Rye; discusses her life and activities. In general, the Ontario press favored the movement. 89 notes.
W. B. Whitham

English

3416. Brooks, W. H. THE PRIMITIVE METHODISTS IN THE NORTH-WEST. *Saskatchewan Hist. [Canada] 1976 29(1): 26-37.* The branch of evangelical Methodists known as Primitive Methodists since their origin in early 19th-century England, founded an agricultural colony near Grenfell, Saskatchewan, in 1882. Mentions early leaders such as Hugh Bourne, William Clowes, and Lorenzo Dow, as well as a very active leader of the colony, the Reverend William Bee. Presents excerpts from Reverend Bee's letters. Photos, 65 notes.
C. Held

3417. Cameron, Wendy. THE PETWORTH EMIGRATION COMMITTEE: LORD EGREMONT'S ASSISTED EMIGRATIONS FROM SUSSEX TO UPPER CANADA, 1832-37. *Ontario History [Canada] 1973 65(4): 231-246.* Describes the activities of the Petworth Emigration Committee and the emigrations from Petworth to Upper Canada during 1832-37. Notes that there were six emigrant groups sent at annual intervals, but major attention is paid to the first. Its progress from Sussex to York, Upper Canada, is described, and the problems it encountered are outlined. 68 notes.
W. B. Whitham

3418. Cauthers, Janet, ed. NUMBERS OF PROSPEROUS PEOPLE: THE SMALL, ELEGANT WORLD OF THE BRITISH COLONISTS. *Sound Heritage [Canada] 1978 7(3): 32-45.* Describes the lives and activities of the affluent British colonists who lived in Victoria, B.C., between 1880 and 1914, from the reminiscences of Victoria residents.

3419. Criddle, Percy. THE CRIDDLES OF AWEME. *Beaver [Canada] 1978 308(4): 15-19.* In 1882, Percy Criddle of London migrated to Canada and settled at Aweme, southeast of Brandon, Manitoba. With him were his wife Alice, friend Elise Vane, and nine children. Criddle kept a diary for over 35 years, excerpts of which appear here. He discusses various homestead situations, including digging a well, cutting logs, hosting guests, and earning a living from the land. He was particularly impressed with that great Canadian predator, the field mouse, an "all-devouring monster." 6 illus.
D. Chaput

3420. Doerksen, A. D. "Tony". THE BRANDON WHEAT KINGS —1887 VINTAGES. *Manitoba Pageant [Canada] 1976 22(1): 11-17.* Immigrants from eastern Canada and England began farming in the Brandon district of Manitoba during 1879-80. Wheat was the principal crop. By 1887, even with single-furrow plows and hand-broadcast seeding, the area produced 1,920,000 bushels. In 1881 General Rosser of the Canadian Pacific Railway selected the site of Brandon for a major divisional point. The Great North West Central and the Northern Pacific and Manitoba Railways both connected with Brandon making it become the commercial center of the Northwest. 2 illus.
B. J. Lo Bue

3421. Essar, D. A LETTER FROM AN EARLY SASKATCHEWAN SETTLER. *Saskatchewan Hist. [Canada] 1976 29(2): 65-72.* Reprints a letter from Septimus Alfred Clark, of "Ardencroft, Township 19-Range 19, N. Regina, Assiniboia, Canada" to his sister, Lady Mary Radcliffe of Liverpool, written in 1884. It describes the journey from Great Britain the previous year and the hardships of Western Canadian life for a man trained to be an architect in England. He ultimately became a successful hardware merchant in Saskatoon and died there in 1909. 11 notes.
C. Held

3422. Goodwin, Theresa. RECOLLECTIONS AND REMINISCENCES OF AN ENGLISH SCHOOL MARM IN SASKATCHEWAN. *Saskatchewan Hist. [Canada] 1974 27(2): 103-107.* The author writes of her teaching experiences in Chaplin and Duval, 1912-13. Photo.
C. Held

3423. Guay, Donald. PROBLEMES DE L'INTÉGRATION DU SPORT DANS LA SOCIETÉ CANADIENNE 1830-1865: LE CAS DES COURSES DE CHEVAUX [Problems of sport's integration in Canadian society in 1830-1865: the case of horse races]. *Can. J. of Hist. of Sport and Physical Educ. 1973 4(2): 70-92.* Horse racing, introduced to Canadian society by Englishmen in the second half of the 18th century, was accepted as a sport by Canadians not sooner than the first decades of the 19th century. There was strong moral, ideological, and cultural resistance against horse racing, because it was viewed as an affair of the high bourgeoisie and aristocracy. Canadian nationalism, primarily anti-English, developed later (about 1860) in a nationalism of conciliation. The attitude toward this English-imported sport changed then. Based on secondary sources; 103 notes.
G. E. Pergl

3424. Humphrys, Ruth. [THE SHINY HOUSE].
THE SHINY HOUSE... AND THE MAN WHO BUILT IT. *Beaver [Canada] 1977 307(4): 49-55.* James Humphrys, retired British naval architect, moved to Assiniboia in 1888 for his health. There he acquired land for a farm. Within a few months he erected a large, comfortable home for his family of eight children and his wife, who remained in England until the home was completed. The Humphrys home was at Cannington Manor in southeastern Saskatchewan. Humphrys adjusted well, helped initiate medical and educational services, and looked forward to life in a progressive community. 8 illus.
EARLY DAYS IN THE SHINY HOUSE. *Beaver [Canada] 1977 308(1): 20-28.* Concludes the story of the family of James Humphrys. Discusses education, church life, entertainment, and other social affairs. 17 illus.
D. Chaput

3425. Lambert, Augustine. LIFE ON THE FARM. *Beaver [Canada] 1975 306(1): 19-23.* The 13 sketches and accompanying description were done by Augustine Lambert in 1913-14, while he farmed at Arelee, northwest of Saskatoon. The materials were then sent to his family in England. Lambert drew animals, wagons, harvesting and loading scenes, and social views such as Sunday church services and the family gathered around the pot-bellied stove. Lambert then joined the First Canadian Mounted Rifles and was killed at Vimy Ridge in 1917. Map, 13 illus.
D. Chaput

3426. Lischke-McNab, Ute and McNab, David. PETITION FROM THE BACKWOODS. *Beaver [Canada] 1977 308(1): 52-57.* Catherine Parr Traill, an English settler who lived near Peterborough, wrote several popular emigrant guides, especially *The Backwoods of Canada* (1836). In 1854, she petitioned Queen Victoria for a "reward" for her literary services to the Empire. Various administrative and colonial officials considered the petition and even brought it to the Queen's attention. No land was granted Traill, however, mostly due to Colonial Office lethargy and a shifting colonial policy for Canada. In succeeding years, the author wrote other emigrant travel works. In the 1860's she received a small cash grant from British Prime Minister Lord Palmerston, but for her fern collecting and research, and not her literary efforts. 5 illus.
D. Chaput

3427. MacCallum, Elizabeth. CATHERINE PARR TRAILL: A NINETEENTH-CENTURY ONTARIO NATURALIST. *Beaver [Canada] 1975 306(2): 39-45.* Catherine Parr Traill married in England and emigrated to Canada with several family members in the 1830's. Until her death in 1899, she lived mostly near Peterborough. After the death of her husband she devoted most of her time to collecting botanical types and publishing. Her most notable works are *Studies of Plant Life in Canada* (1885) and *Pearls and Pebbles*. Includes family history as well as aspects of botanical research. 12 illus., map.   D. Chaput

3428. Rees, Ronald. ECCENTRIC SETTLEMENTS IN THE CANADIAN WEST, 1882-1900. *Hist. Today [Great Britain] 1977 27(9): 607-614.* Discusses the settlement of Cannington, Saskatchewan, which, unlike most frontier towns, was settled by a group of British who enjoyed the hunt, tennis, cricket, horseracing, and rugby, 1882-1900.

3429. Smith, Donald B. THE BELANEYS OF BRANDON HILLS: GREY OWL'S CANADIAN COUSINS. *Beaver [Canada] 1975 306(3): 46-50.* Biography of Grey Owl, born Archibald Stansfeld Belaney in England. He moved to Canada in 1906 and concocted a new identity, claiming he was Scotch and Apache. Until his death in 1938 he was a well-known spokesman for various conservation movements. Discusses the family connections of Grey Owl in England and in Canada, his successful attempt at covering his identity tracks, his success as an early environmentalist. 6 illus.   D. Chaput

Scottish (including Scotch-Irish)

3430. Bumsted, J. M. HIGHLAND EMIGRATION TO THE ISLAND OF ST. JOHN AND THE SCOTTISH CATHOLIC CHURCH, 1769-1774. *Dalhousie Rev. [Canada] 1978 58(3): 511-527.* The Catholic Church in Scotland systematically attempted to resettle persecuted Highlanders in what is now called Prince Edward Island between the Seven Years War and the American Revolution; for that reason there is an unusual amount of contemporary documentation. This is a rare thing in the history of Highland emigration. It began with Colin MacDonald of Boysdale's attempts to Protestantize his tenants on South Uist in 1769. The planning for this Hebridean exodus was done by two Edinburgh bishops, George Hay and John MacDonald. Illustrates the Scottish persecutions and the economic problems of the movement. 58 notes.
C. H. Held

3431. Bumsted, J. M. LORD SELKIRK'S HIGHLAND REGIMENT AND THE KILDONAN SETTLERS. *Beaver [Canada] 1978 309(2): 16-21.* During the War of 1812 Selkirk tried to interest the government in a Highland regiment to serve at Red River of the North. The Duke of York resisted; there had been poor precedents. Selkirk learned of the parish of Kildonan, where the owners were shifting from farming to sheep grazing. The villagers were receptive to the regimental plans. Through misunderstandings (Selkirk did not get governmental approval) he was faced with hundreds of residents of Kildonan ready to go to Red River. He finally arranged for several hundred men to settle there, and for some others to work for Hudson's Bay Company. They arrived during 1813-14, but only after many deaths at sea. During later troubles, the villagers from Kildonan were not among Selkirk's major backers. 5 illus.
D. Chaput

3432. Bumsted, J. M. SETTLEMENT BY CHANCE: LORD SELKIRK AND PRINCE EDWARD ISLAND. *Can. Hist. Rev. [Canada] 1978 59(2): 170-188.* Gives background information to the 5th Earl of Selkirk's (1771-1820) successful transplantation of Scottish Highland emigrants to Prince Edward Island in 1803.

3433. Campbell, Douglas F. and Bouma, Gary D. SOCIAL CONFLICT AND THE PICTOU NOTABLES. *Ethnicity 1978 5(1): 76-88.* Pictou County's per capita representation in four editions of *Who's Who in Canada* and two editions of *Canadian Men and Women of the Times* during 1898-1966 is preeminent among Nova Scotia counties. Yet Pictou is not unique in size, educational facilities, economic development, ethnic composition, or in the dominant position of Scottish Presbyterians. Seeks the explanation for the county's dynamism in the almost equal distribution of local Presbyterians into Kirk and non-Kirk factions, in the resultant conflict, and in the fact that this conflict was almost entirely verbal, thus fostering the skills which make for notability. Secondary sources; 5 tables, 14 notes, 27 ref.   L. W. Van Wyk

3434. Currie, Justice L. D. THE EMIGRANTS OF ST. ANN'S. *Nova Scotia Hist. Soc. Collections [Canada] 1973 38: 113-126.* Against the background of chaos produced by the abolition of the ancient landholding system of the clans, the dynamic and courageous Norman MacLeod (1780-1866) vowed he would be college-educated. After attending Aberdeen University where he acquired an M.A. and a gold medal in philosophy, as a lay preacher he traveled to Middle River, Nova Scotia, with about 400 Scottish settlers. In 1820, after intending to travel to Ohio, MacLeod and supporters were shipwrecked at St. Ann's Bay, Cape Breton, where one year later they built the first Presbyterian Church in Cape Breton. The Nova Scotia government soon appointed MacLeod schoolmaster, Justice of the Peace, and postmaster. In the fall of 1851, MacLeod led 140 people from St. Ann's to Adelaide, South Australia; then to Waipu, New Zealand. Favorable comments later caused more than 1,000 people to follow MacLeod's example.   E. A. Chard

3435. Frost, S. B. A TRANSATLANTIC WOOING. *Dalhousie Rev. [Canada] 1978 58(3): 458-470.* Discusses the correspondence between a young Scottish girl, Margaret Mercer, and William Dawson, the future famous geologist who was the son of a merchant of Pictou, Nova Scotia. The letters began following a visit to Edinburgh in 1840 and continued until 1847 when they married. 7 notes.   C. H. Held

3436. Graves, Ross. THE WEATHERHEAD FAMILY OF UPPER RAWDON. *Nova Scotia Hist. Q. [Canada] 1975 5(2): 177-188.* Presents a genealogy of the James Weatherhead (ca. 1802-67) family from the late 1820's when he came to Hants County as a weaver from southern Scotland; carries the line down to 1946.   R. V. Ritter

3437. Hughes, Ken. POET LAUREATE OF LABOUR. *Can. Dimension [Canada] 1976 11(4): 33-40.* Describes the life of the radical Alexander McLachlan, who was born in Scotland in 1818 and died in Ontario, Canada, in 1896; discusses his poetry on the working class and social reform.

3438. Hunter, William A. THE REUNION. *Modern Age 1979 23(2): 178-182.* Founded in 1891 and having seen service in both World Wars, the 48th Highlanders of Canada is the only regiment in the Commonwealth which still parades in ceremonial doublets and bonnets. Its strong allegiance to ceremony and tradition have both reflected and nurtured high morale. The author recalls his service with the unit in World War II and laments the influence of "leftist" and liberal elements which he argues have morally and spiritually weakened Canada.
C. D'Aniello

3439. Inglis, R. E. LOCHABER: A TYPICAL RURAL COMMUNITY. *Nova Scotia Hist. Soc. Collections [Canada] 1977 39: 89-106.* Discusses the Lochaber region through a portion of the descriptive poem "Acadie" by Joseph Howe. This geographical region is used as a prototype of "what has happened in many rural districts of eastern Nova Scotia since [the] arrival of the first white settlers." Immigration may have commenced as early as 1795 so that by 1830, the pattern of settlement was almost complete. The next 20 years witnessed many important changes such as the replacement of log cabins with frame houses, central heating, and the development of small orchards. During 1850-80, the Lochaber region "reached the zenith of its progress," yet by 1880 in retrospect, a downward trend was noted as the youth began to move to the Boston States, and later to Western Canada, creating a lack of interest in the land. Discusses Lochaber churches, schools, industries, and professionals. 16 notes.   E. A. Chard

3440. Jones, Huw R. MODERN EMIGRATION FROM SCOTLAND TO CANADA. *Scottish Geographical Mag. [Great Britain] 1979 95(1): 4-12.* Discusses the trends in emigration from Scotland to Canada, 1960's-70's.

3441. Kennedy, Roy M. SOME CAME TO NOVA SCOTIA. *Nova Scotia Hist. Q. [Canada] 1979 9(2): 99-112.* Outlines the economic and social conditions in Scotland which influenced emigration overseas. In the first three years of the 1800's, some 10,000 people left parts of Scotland for Nova Scotia and Upper Canada; by 1820, some 25,000 had settled in Cape Breton. Primary and secondary sources; biblio.
H. M. Evans

3442. Lower, Thelma Reid. GENERAL JOHN REID. *Nova Scotia Hist. Q. [Canada] 1979 9(2): 113-136.* Reviews the life and career of John Reid (1721-1807), military man, settler, flautist, and composer. His service in the 42nd Regiment, known as the Black Watch or Royal Highlanders of Scotland, took him to North America where he acquired a wife and extensive property holdings. Land disputes forced him to return to Scotland in 1775. There he published his musical compositions—largely regimental marches. Much of his property in Nova Scotia was sold to endow a "Chair of Music" at the University of Edinburgh which included a music building, a library, instruments, and faculty. Primary and secondary sources; biblio.   H. M. Evans

3443. MacLaren, George. PASSENGER LIST OF THE SHIP *HECTOR*. *Nova Scotia Hist. Q. 1973 3(2): 121-129.* Recalls the hardships endured by the immigrants who sailed from Scotland to Pictou Harbor in 1773. They arrived in September, too late in the year to erect shelters or plant crops, and barely managed to survive the first cold winter. A passenger list is appended. (Quoted from an article by Alexander Mackenzie, "First Highland Emigrant to Nova Scotia," *Celtic Magazine*, Jan. 1883, pp. 141-144.)   H. M. Evans

3444. Marble, Al Everett. JAMES MC CABE GENEALOGY. *Nova Scotia Hist. Q. 1975 5(4): 411-422.* The genealogy of James McCabe, native of Belfast who emigrated to Philadelphia about 1743, and came to Pictou on 10 June 1767. Descendants are traced to 1917. Lists sources.   R. V. Ritter

3445. Marble, Allan E. THE BURNS FAMILY OF WILMOT TOWNSHIP: SCOTCH-IRISH FOLK IN ANNAPOLIS COUNTY. *Nova Scotia Hist. Q. [Canada] 1978 8(2): 171-180.* Traces the genealogy of the Burns family through four generations; Francis Burns (d. 1789) came to Wilmot Township with his brother William (1733-1818) from the North of Ireland in 1764. Primary and secondary sources.   H. M. Evans

3446. Marble, Allan E. and Punch, Terrence M. SIR J. S. D. THOMPSON: A PRIME MINISTER'S FAMILY CONNECTIONS. *Nova Scotia Hist. Q. [Canada] 1977 7(4): 377-388.* Outlines the genealogy of John S. D. Thompson (1844-94), a native of Halifax and Prime Minister of Canada 1892-94. The listings trace the family from 1796 in Waterford, Ireland, to 1903 and include both female and male lines. Primary and secondary sources.   H. M. Evans

3447. Neatby, Hilda. QUEEN'S COLLEGE AND THE SCOTTISH FACT. *Queen's Q. [Canada] 1973 80(1): 1-11.* Discusses the educational and religious controversies behind the founding of Queen's College in 1842. William Morris was the key figure in leading the struggle for Scottish Presbyterians' rights in Canada against the Anglican establishment. His inability to win acceptable concessions for Presbyterian participation on King's College Council led to the decision to found a separate university and thus provided the first chapter in the history of Queen's University. An adaptation of a portion of the author's forthcoming history of Queen's University.   J. A. Casada

3448. Reid, John G. THE SCOTS CROWN AND THE RESTITUTION OF PORT ROYAL, 1629-1632. *Acadiensis [Canada] 1977 6(2): 39-63.* Several historians have accused Charles I of stupidity or duplicity in returning Port Royal to France in 1632. Yet Charles sought arguments to justify retention, and asserted Scotland's claim at some length. But the issue threatened to jeopardize peace, as France insisted on restitution. Scotland agreed to withdraw, while maintaining its claims. French reoccupation and Scottish lack of capital then rendered Scotland's claims futile, and dealt a death-blow to Scottish colonization in North America. 95 notes.   D. F. Chard

3449. Scotland, James. EDUCATION IN OLD AND NEW SCOTLAND. *Nova Scotia Hist. Q. 1974 4(4): 355-371.* Reviews the early history of formal education in Nova Scotia from its beginnings with Thomas McCullouch's Pictou Grammar School (established in 1811).   H. M. Evans

3450. Shaw, Edward C. THE KENNEDYS—AN UNUSUAL WESTERN FAMILY. *Trans. of the Hist. and Sci. Soc. of Manitoba [Canada] 1972/73 Series 3(29): 69-79.* Traces the origins of the Kennedy family from their Scottish ancestry and devotes considerable attention to the activities of those who settled in Canada in the late 18th and early 19th centuries. 2 charts.   J. A. Casada

3451. Sherwood, Roland H. THE FOUNDING OF PICTOU. *Nova Scotia Hist. Q. [Canada] 1971 1(4): 325-334.* Traces the founding and history of Pictou, Nova Scotia, in 1773 by Scottish emigrants.

3452. Sherwood, Roland H. LANDING OF THE *HECTOR*. *Nova Scotia Hist. Q. 1973 3(2): 87-97.* In 1773 the brig *Hector* brought 200 Scottish immigrants from Loch Broom to Pictou Harbor. The passengers experienced smallpox, dysentery, food shortages, and a dwindling water supply on the 11-week voyage.   H. M. Evans

3453. Sherwood, Roland Harold. PICTOU'S PIONEER MINISTER. *Nova Scotia Hist. Q. 1975 5(4): 337-352.* Describes the primitive way of life and the hardships patiently accepted for the sake of his calling by the Reverend James MacGregor, sent to the "Township of Pictou" in 1786 as a missionary by the Presbyterian Church of Scotland. Records the main events in his 44-year ministry in this parish, until his death on 3 March 1830.   R. V. Ritter

3454. Sinclair, D. M. REV. DUNCAN BLACK BLAIR, D.D. (1815-1893): PIONEER PREACHER IN PICTOU COUNTY, GAELIC SCHOLAR AND POET. *Nova Scotia Hist. Soc. Collections [Canada] 1977 39: 155-168.* Duncan Black Blair's poem "Eas Niagara" is regarded as one of the "two most celebrated Gaelic poems composed on Canadian soil." His Gaelic *Diary* provides not only interesting information on society but also on the youthful author's education, including 1834-38, when he was enrolled at the University of Edinburgh. In 1846 he came to Nova Scotia as a Free Church [Presbyterian] missionary, remained slightly more than one year, only to return in 1848 to accept the call of the congregation at Barney's River-Blue Mountain where he remained until his death in 1893. Regarded as "the best Gaelic scholar in America, in his time" Blair wrote *Rudiments of Gaelic Grammar,* "a most complete Gaelic dictionary," as well as some poetry, examples of which are provided in this article.   E. A. Chard

3455. Sunter, Ronald. THE SCOTTISH BACKGROUND TO THE IMMIGRATION OF BISHOP ALEXANDER MACDONNELL AND THE GLENGARRY HIGHLANDERS. *Study Sessions: Can. Catholic Hist. Assoc. 1973 40: 11-20.* The British Navy attempted to impress Catholics emigrating to Canada where Bishop Alexander Macdonnell and the Glengarry Highlanders settled and figured prominently in the history of Ontario. Covers the period 1770's-1814.

3456. White, Gavin. SCOTTISH TRADERS TO BAFFIN ISLAND, 1910-1930. *Maritime Hist. [Great Britain] 1977 5(1): 34-50.* Outlines the history of the free traders, particulary the Scots, in Baffin Island. Names ships, discusses the nature of the trade, and assesses its effects on the Eskimos. Based on Public Record Office company documents and on secondary sources; 2 photos, map, 32 notes.   C. A. McNeill

3457. Young, R. S. MINERALS AND THE FUR TRADE. *Alberta Hist. 1976 24(3): 20-24.* Extensive records of the Hudson's Bay Company reveal that the company had little impact on mineral discoveries. Examines reasons for this, such as little native knowledge and use of metals, company interests in immediate riches from fur trade, and personnel from Scotland, rather than from the mineral-rich regions of Cornwall and Wales. Even when some minerals were found and identified, there was no use for them until the 20th century. Based on Hudson's Bay Co. records; 2 illus.   D. Chaput

Welsh

3458. Thomas, Lewis H. WELSH SETTLEMENT IN SASKATCHEWAN, 1902-1914. *Western Hist. Q. 1973 4(4): 435-449.* Part of a Welsh settlement in southern Argentina migrated to east-central Saskatchewan in 1902. Some 200 immigrants were closely knit by language, Protestantism, and customs, but they had no illusion that they could maintain their national identity. Previous experience on the Argentine pampas helped them to adjust rapidly and successfully to farming the prairies. 37 notes.   D. L. Smith

Other Immigrant Groups

Baltic (Estonian, Latvian, Lithuanian)

3459. Wukasch, Peter. BALTIC IMMIGRANTS IN CANADA, 1947-1955. *Concordia Hist. Inst. Q. 1977 50(1): 4-22.* Fleeing Russian expansion, a number of people from Estonia, Latvia, and Lithuania entered Canada during 1947-55. To assist these immigrants the Lutheran Church responded with a multifaceted program led by Rev. Ernest Hahn and Rev. Donald Ortner of St. John's Lutheran Church in Toronto. The church involved itself in social, economic, cultural, and political efforts to safeguard the interests of the displaced Baltic people. Primary sources; 28 notes. W. T. Walker

Basque

3460. Barkham, Selma. THE BASQUES: FILLING A GAP IN OUR HISTORY BETWEEN JACQUES CARTIER AND CHAMPLAIN. *Can. Geographical J. [Canada] 1978 96(1): 8-19.* Some of the earliest Europeans to settle on the coasts of Labrador were Basques, who set up whaling stations in the 16th century.

3461. Barkham, Selma and Grenier, Robert. DIVERS FIND SUNKEN BASQUE GALLEON IN LABRADOR. *Can. Geographic [Canada] 1978-79 97(3): 60-63.* Research in Spanish archives confirmed the presence of a Basque whaling ship, the *San Juan*, in Labrador's Red Bay where it sank in 1565.

3462. Barkham, Selma. TWO DOCUMENTS WRITTEN IN LABRADOR, 1572 AND 1577. *Can. Hist. Rev. [Canada] 1976 57(2): 235-238.* Discusses the predominance of Basque as a spoken language in 16th-century Labrador. Documents about the Labrador whaling industry tend to be written in Spanish, since French Basques were more concerned with codfishing prior to 1580. A thorough grounding in Spanish palaeography is a basic requirement for further research in Spain. Based on a 1572 bond and a 1577 will found in the notarial archives of the Province of Guipuzcoa which house the earliest known civil documents written in Canada. A

Belgian

3463. Loudfoot, Raymonde. THE NUYTTENS OF BELGIAN TOWN. *Manitoba Pageant [Canada] 1974 19(3): 15-18.* Discusses Edmund and Octavia Nuytten and other Belgian immigrants who settled in the East St. Boniface area of Winnipeg. Appended is a list of over 300 Belgian families who arrived in Winnipeg, 1880-1914. Illus. D. M. Dean

German

3464. Bauckman, Frank A. JOHN BAPTIST BACHMAN OF LUNENBURG TOWNSHIP, NOVA SCOTIA. *Nova Scotia Hist. Q. [Canada] 1975 5(3): 297-306.* A genealogy of John Baptist Bachman (1720-94), who arrived in Halifax in 1752 among a company of German immigrants. Mentions his descendants down to 1952. R. V. Ritter

3465. Becker, A. THE GERMANS IN WESTERN CANADA. *Study Sessions: Can. Catholic Hist. Assoc. 1975 42: 29-49.* A history of the oldest and largest German settlements of western Canada, ca. 1891-1931, using modern census figures on population and ethnic division, which appear inaccurate due to inadequate wording of questions and coverups by German descendants during the racially tense atmosphere of World War I.

3466. Bird, Michael. ONTARIO FRAKTUR ART: A DECORATIVE TRADITION IN THREE GERMANIC SETTLEMENTS. *Ontario Hist. [Canada] 1976 68(4): 247-272.* Fraktur art is "the embellishment of a written or printed text . . . to produce a pleasing and often personalised work of art within a religio-ethnic tradition." This tradition is associated with Pennsylvania Germans. Points out minor variations and analyzes the background in Europe and Pennsylvania. Details the arrival and development of this art form in Ontario. Discusses specific artists and analyzes characteristic applications. 36 illus., notes. W. B. Whitham

3467. Fingard, Judith. HOW THE "FOREIGN" PROTESTANTS CAME TO NOVA SCOTIA, 1749-1752. *Can. Geographical J. [Canada] 1976/77 93(3): 54-59.* Discusses German immigrants who settled in Nova Scotia, 1749-52.

3468. Patterson, Nancy-Lou. THE IRON CROSS AND THE TREE OF LIFE: GERMAN-ALSATIAN GRAVEMARKERS IN THE WATERLOO REGION AND BRUCE COUNTY ROMAN CATHOLIC CEMETERIES. *Ontario Hist. [Canada] 1976 68(1): 1-16.* Gravemarkers throw light on social values and beliefs. In the Roman Catholic districts of Ontario settled by German Alsatians iron working was an art and iron gravemarkers are characteristic examples of this skill. Discusses the distribution and location of iron gravemarkers in these areas and analyzes the basic characteristics and variations in the design of markers and associated appendages. 8 illus., 55 notes. W. B. Whitham

3469. Punch, Terrence M. THE WESTS OF HALIFAX AND LUNENBURG. *Nova Scotia Hist. Q. [Canada] 1976 6(1): 69-84.* Traces the history and genealogy of the family of Johann Wendel Wuest, or Wiest (1724-1811). Born in Hesse-Darmstadt, a small German state, he emigrated to Halifax in 1751 and was one of the founders of Lunenburg. The family name was changed to West in the second generation. Primary sources; 9 notes. H. M. Evans

3470. Threinen, Norman J. EARLY LUTHERANISM IN WESTERN CANADA. *Concordia Hist. Inst. Q. 1974 47(3): 110-117.* Discusses the role (ca. 1870) of William Wagner, a German immigrant, in establishing Township Berlin, in Manitoba, and his relation to the Lutheran Church, Missouri Synod. S

3471. White, Clinton O. LANGUAGE, RELIGION, SCHOOLS AND POLITICS AMONG GERMAN-AMERICAN CATHOLIC SETTLERS IN ST. PETER'S COLONY, SASKATCHEWAN, 1903-1916. *Study Sessions: Can. Catholic Hist. Assoc. [Canada] 1978 45: 81-99.* Details efforts of German Catholics in St. Peter's Colony to maintain their language and religion in a largely Protestant and English-speaking environment, using their own school system.

Greek

3472. Polyzoi, Eleoussa. THE GREEK COMMUNAL SCHOOL AND CULTURAL SURVIVAL IN PRE-WAR TORONTO. *Urban Hist. Rev. [Canada] 1978 78(2): 74-94.* Communal language schools, often ignored by historians, were established to maintain an immigrant group's cultural heritage. Toronto had a growing Greek population in the early decades of this century concerned that their children retain their ethnic and religious heritage. After one Greek school was founded and failed in the early 1920's, a permanent After-Four school was established in 1926. It grew in numbers and received strong parental and community support. The school was successful in helping Greek immigrants become an ethnic group although some former students remembered resentment at extra hours spent in school. Interviews, census reports, and secondary sources; 5 illus., diagram, 53 notes. C. A. Watson

Hungarian

3473. Dégh, Linda. TWO LETTERS FROM HOME. *J. of Am. Folklore 1978 91(361): 808-822.* Examines two letters from Hungarian peasants to Canadian relatives. Such letters from the home country reinforce ethnicity, and the folklore they contain symbolizes the native land for the emigrant community. Based on letter texts and secondary sources; 31 notes. W. D. Piersen

3474. Dojcsak, G. V. THE MYSTERIOUS COUNT ESTERHAZY. *Saskatchewan Hist. 1973 26(2): 63-72.* The Saskatchewan town of Esterhazy bears the name of Count Paul O. d'Esterhazy (1831-1912), who founded a colony of Hungarian immigrants in 1886. This Esterhazy, however, was born as, and for his first 35 years was known as, Johan Baptista Packh. Illus., 30 notes.   D. L. Smith

3475. Dreisziger, N. F. WATSON KIRKCONNELL: TRANSLATOR OF HUNGARIAN POETRY AND A FRIEND OF HUNGARIAN-CANADIANS. *Canadian-American Rev. of Hungarian Studies [Canada] 1977 4(2): 117-143.* A biography of Watson Kirkconnell, via a historical description of Hungarians in Canada, 1895-1977.

Irish

3476. Baker, William M. AN IRISH-CANADIAN JOURNALIST-POLITICIAN AND CATHOLICISM: TIMOTHY ANGLIN OF THE SAINT JOHN FREEMAN. *Study Sessions: Can. Catholic Hist. Assoc. [Canada] 1977 44: 5-24.* Timothy Warren Anglin during 1849-83 supported Catholicism while acting as editor of the *Freeman,* a newspaper in Saint John, New Brunswick.

3477. Baker, W. M. TURNING THE SPIT: TIMOTHY ANGLIN AND THE ROASTING OF D'ARCY MC GEE. *Can. Hist. Assoc. Hist. Papers 1974: 135-155.* Discusses debates between Irish Catholic leaders Timothy Warren Anglin and Thomas D'Arcy McGee in Canada, 1863-68, on the character of Irish Canadians, and on McGee's proposed British North American Union, support for Confederation, and attacks on the Fenians.

3478. Houston, Cecil and Smyth, William J. THE ORANGE ORDER AND THE EXPANSION OF THE FRONTIER IN ONTARIO, 1830-1900. *J. of Hist. Geography 1978 4(3): 251-264.* The Orange Order, with its two main tenets, anti-Catholicism and loyalty to Britain, flourished in Ontario. Largely coincident with Protestant Irish settlement, its role pervaded the political, social and community as well as religious lives of its followers. Spatially, Orange lodges were founded as Irish Protestant settlement spread north and west from its original focus on the Lake Ontario plain. Although the number of active members, and thus their influence, may have been overestimated, the Orange influence was considerable and comparable to the Roman Catholic influence in Quebec. Primary and secondary sources; 3 maps, table, graph, 34 notes.   A. J. Larson

3479. Kesteman, Jean-Pierre. LES TRAVAILLEURS À LA CONSTRUCTION DU CHEMIN DE FER DANS LA RÉGION DE SHERBROOKE (1851-1853) [The railway construction workers in the Sherbrooke region (1851-53)]. *Rev. d'Hist. de l'Amérique Française [Canada] 1978 31(4): 525-545.* Construction of the railroad connecting Montreal with Portland, Maine, attracted many migrant laborers. The census reports issued for the Sherbrooke region of Quebec in 1851 and 1852 enable the historian to more clearly understand the lives, conditions, and activities of this traditionally "invisible" group. Most of the workers were young Irishmen who, with their wives and children, lived in overcrowded railway camps. Local newspaper accounts reveal their most sensational activities, e.g., drinking, brawling, and resisting arrest, but the census materials represent a richer, more systematic vein of information. 8 tables, 45 notes.   M. R. Yerburgh

3480. Martin, Ged. CONVICT TRANSPORTATION TO NEWFOUNDLAND IN 1789. *Acadiensis [Canada] 1975 5(1): 84-99.* In 1789 authorities in Ireland transported 114 convicts to Newfoundland. Authorities there seized and returned 80. The affair threatened to upset Anglo-Irish relations, because the British government had ceased transporting convicts to America after 1783. The authorities in Ireland actually had not violated this policy because Newfoundland technically was not a colony then. The affair confirmed inadequacies of the system and ended convict transportation to British North America. 90 notes.   D. F. Chard

3481. Millar, Jan L. THE LIFE AND TIMES OF JAME BOYLE UNIACKE. *Nova Scotia Hist. Q. [Canada] 1979 9(3): 225-233.* Richard John Uniacke (1755-1830) emigrated to Nova Scotia from Ireland in 1775 and was elected to the Provincial Assembly in 1781. His fifth son, James Boyle Uniacke (1800-1858), obtained his law degree in London and entered politics in 1830 as a member of the General Assembly from Cape Breton. He was elected Premier and Attorney General in 1848. Primary sources from Public Archives of Nova Scotia; 37 notes.   H. M. Evans

3482. O'Gallagher, Marianna. CARE OF THE ORPHAN AND THE AGED BY THE IRISH COMMUNITY OF QUEBEC CITY, 1847 AND YEARS FOLLOWING. *Study Sessions: Can. Catholic Hist. Assoc. [Canada] 1976 43: 39-56.* Indicates the history and development of St. Bridget's Home in Quebec, and the work of Father Patrick McMahon, Irish immigrants, and the Catholic Church to provide for the needy, 1847-1972.

3483. Parr, G. J. THE WELCOME AND THE WAKE: ATTITUDES IN CANADA WEST TOWARD THE IRISH FAMINE IMMIGRATION. *Ontario Hist. [Canada] 1974 66(2): 101-113.* The initial reaction to Irish immigration into the Canadas in the late 1840's was sympathetic in Canada West and the concept of immigration allied to settlement was favorably received. But the scale of the problem was not realized at first, so that when available funds were exhausted a backlash developed, especially when the problem of disease became public knowledge. Yet even in this situation there was marked public sympathy, although the situation forced the reappraisal of some basic concepts. Canadian anger was directed less at the immigrants than at the landlords and others in Ireland who were seen as exploiting the famine. Concludes that the incident produced a marked shift in the attitude toward immigration in the province. 76 notes.   W. B. Whitham

3484. Pennefather, R. S. THE ORANGE ORDER AND THE UNITED FARMERS OF ONTARIO, 1919-1923. *Ontario Hist. [Canada] 1977 69(3): 169-184.* Discusses the attitudes of the Orange Order, and the United Farmers of Ontario toward the Ontario election of 1920. Issues were the "Keep Ontario British" campaign, and "Regulation 17", as well as the role of Orangemen in the legislature. Mentions the Orange attitude to the Federal Conservative party and their policies. Concludes that in the 1924 election, which saw the United Farmers (who had won in 1920) badly defeated, Orangeism and the Orange Order had some influence, but the extent is debatable. 73 notes.   W. B. Whitham

3485. Punch, Terrence M. BEAMISH OF KILVURRA AND HALIFAX. *Nova Scotia Hist. Q. [Canada] 1979 9(3): 269-278.* Traces the genealogy of the Beamish family through five generations. Thomas Beamish (ca. 1743-ca. 1792), second son of John Beamish emigrated from Ireland to Halifax in 1765. He was the first Port Warden appointed in Halifax. His descendants include teachers, lawyers, farmers, ministers, and merchants.   H. M. Evans

3486. Punch, Terrence M. TOBIN GENEALOGY. *Nova Scotia Hist. Q. [Canada] 1975 5(1): 71-82.* Contains a genealogy of Thomas Tobin (d. 1783), merchant tailor, who established his home in Halifax about 1759. He came from Newfoundland and, earlier, Ireland. Mentions his descendants down to 1936.   R. V. Ritter

3487. Senior, H. OGLE GOWAN, ORANGEISM, AND THE IMMIGRANT QUESTION 1830-1833. *Ontario Hist. [Canada] 1974 66(4): 193-210.* Discusses the effect of Irish immigration and Irish influence on the political life of Upper Canada in the early 19th century, with an emphasis on the continuing contest between reformers and the governing circles, popularly known as the "Family Compact."

3488. Smith, Dorothy Blakey. "POOR GAGGIN": IRISH MISFIT IN THE COLONIAL SERVICE. *BC Studies [Canada] 1976-77 (32): 41-63.* John Boles Gaggin sailed from Ireland in 1859 to seek his fortune in newly established British Columbia. He served as a minor cog in the civil service machine. He always gave his colleagues concern and eventually provoked a confrontation with the governor of the colony. 78 notes.   D. L. Smith

3489. Toner, Peter M. THE UNSTRUNG HARP: CANADA'S IRISH. *Acadiensis [Canada] 1978 7(2): 156-159.* Two recent works illuminate the Irish experience in 19th-century Canada. W. S. Neidhardt's

Fenianism in North America (1975) is the first work on the Fenians in the Canadian context, but fails to explain the phenomenon of Fenianism or the reaction of Canadian Irish. W. M. Baker's *Timothy Warren Anglin* (1977) emphasizes Anglin's search for power through respectability, and his inability to decide who to represent: Irish, Catholics, or Liberals. As a result, when he lost his seat in 1882, his political career was virtually over.   D. F. Chard

3490. Turner, Wesley. "80 STOUT AND HEALTHY LOOKING GIRLS." *Canada 1975 3(2): 36-49.* Discusses the immigration of approximately 80 penniless Irish girls and women sent to Canada from Irish workhouses by British Poor Law Commissioners in 1865, the demoralization and victimization of some of them, their eventual employment as domestic servants, and official investigation in Ireland and Canada.
                                                                      S

3491. Tweed, Tommy. ON THE TRAIL OF MR. O'B. *Alberta Hist. [Canada] 1975 23(2): 4-13.* An account of the scholarly hitch-hiker Eugene Francis O'Beirne from Ireland, who went to the Red River country in 1863 after wearing out his welcome in Wisconsin and Minnesota. O'Beirne figures prominently in travel narratives of the time as a fraud, interesting conversationalist, and alcoholic. Recent research in archives in Ireland confirms his background as a youth expelled from school and a young adult who gave inflammatory anti-Catholic lectures. After his Red River experiences, O'Beirne went to Queensland, Australia. 5 illus.
                                                                      D. Chaput

Italian

3492. Battistelli, Fabrizio. L'AUTONOMIA CULTURALE COME STRUMENTO DI ASSIMILAZIONE: I MASS MEDIA ITALIANI NELLA COMMUNITÀ IMMIGRATA DI TORONTO, [Cultural autonomy as means of assimilation: Italian mass media in the Toronto immigrant community]. *Rassegna Italiana di Sociologia [Italy] 1975 16(3): 449-465.* A study of Italian mass media in Toronto during the 1970's shows that the media, by carrying the message of Anglo-Canadian capitalism to immigrants, tends to assimilate and thus eradicate the minority community.

3493. Harney, Robert F. BOARDING AND BELONGING. *Urban Hist. Rev. [Canada] 1978 78(2): 8-37.* A recent study of immigrants has focused on the relationship between ethnic colonies and their acculturation or lack of it. There is now a need to make comparative studies of the migration of immigrants, their sojourning, and finally their settling patterns. The boardinghouse as an institution in the acculturation process of sojourners is described with an emphasis on the Italian boardinghouse in Toronto. Interviews, published government reports, and secondary sources; illus., 59 notes.   C. A. Watson

3494. Harney, Robert F. CHIAROSCURO: ITALIANS IN TORONTO 1885-1915. *Italian Americana 1975 1(2): 143-167.* Discusses the settlement of Italian immigrants who lived and found employment in Toronto before World War II.
                                                                      S

3495. Rayfield, J. R. MARIA IN MARKHAM STREET: ITALIAN IMMIGRANTS AND LANGUAGE-LEARNING IN TORONTO. *Ethnic Groups 1976 1(2): 133-150.* An account of the sociocultural and psychological problems faced by monolingual Italian working-class housewives in Toronto, Ontario, and their efforts to overcome these problems by enrolling in an English-language school for immigrants run by the Ontario Citizenship Board.   M. J. Clark

3496. Sturino, Franc. A CASE STUDY OF A SOUTH ITALIAN FAMILY IN TORONTO, 1935-60. *Urban Hist. Rev. [Canada] 1978 78(2): 38-57.* City directories are used to trace the occupational and residential history of one immigrant family. Part of a larger research project, the history of this one family seems typical. The family was upwardly mobile in residence, moving from a working-class to a middle-class district, and in occupation, the sons moving from factory to white collar jobs. Many of the upward moves were a result of aid given because of kinship ties. Interviews, city directories, and secondary sources; illus., 2 tables, fig., 18 notes.   C. A. Watson

3497. Sturino, Franc. ORAL HISTORY IN ETHNIC STUDIES AND IMPLICATIONS FOR EDUCATION. *Can. Oral Hist. Assoc. J. [Canada] 1979 4(1): 14-21.* Describes using oral testimony in a doctoral study on the chain migration of people from the southwestern Cosenza province in southern Italy to North America during 1880-1940's. Discusses the value of oral history as a source for social history, as a tool in immigrant and minority education, and as an indirect means of integrating ethnic groups into Canadian society.

3498. Tomasi, Lydio F. THE ITALIAN COMMUNITY IN TORONTO: A DEMOGRAPHIC PROFILE. *Int. Migration Rev. 1977 11(4): 486-513.* Examines Italian immigration during 1946-72; Italian Canadians are a cohesive, socially active group in Toronto.

3499. Yeo, W. B. CANADA'S CURIOUS USAGE OF ITALIAN PLACE NAMES. *Can. Geographic [Canada] 1979 98(1): 58-61.* Though some were chosen for their romantic associations or flowing sounds, most Italian-inspired place names came from Italian immigrants to Canada, 1850's-1910's.

3500. Ziegler, Suzanne. THE FAMILY UNIT AND INTERNATIONAL MIGRATION: THE PERCEPTIONS OF ITALIAN IMMIGRANT CHILDREN. *Int. Migration Rev. 1977 11(3): 326-333.* Examines through a series of interviews with children of Italian immigrants the postwar migratory process to Canada, the centrality of the 20th-century family, and the importance of intergenerational ties and commitments; family ties have survived migration and even been fortified because of it.

Jewish

3501. Abella, Irving, ed. PORTRAIT OF A JEWISH PROFESSIONAL REVOLUTIONARY: THE RECOLLECTIONS OF JOSHUA GERSHMAN. *Labour [Canada] 1977 2: 184-213.* Gershman came to Canada from Europe in 1921. He soon began his association with the labor movement. In 1923 he joined the Communist Party and remained a member for 54 years. His memoir provides insights on left-wing Jewish unionism, Zionism, cultural life, and Communist activity in Winnipeg, Toronto, Montreal, and Chicago. He left the CP because of differences on the Jewish and national questions. Introduction gives historical perspective and emphasizes uniqueness of Jewish labor movement because of its dominance in the garment industry and its support of "progressive candidates and causes." Based on interviews; 3 notes.
                                                                      W. A. Kearns

3502. Arnold, A. J. THE EARLIEST JEWS IN WINNIPEG 1874-1882. *Beaver [Canada] 1974 305(2): 4-11.* Describes the settlement of Russian Jews in Winnipeg. Disappointed at first because most failed to receive land grants or find employment, many eventually moved out of the city to find or create employment opportunities. For those who stayed, the city offered closer ties with Jewish cultural institutions. 11 illus.   D. Heermans

3503. Arnold, A. J. JEWISH PIONEER SETTLEMENTS. *Beaver [Canada] 1975 306(2): 20-26.* A series of settlements of Russian Jews was started in the 1880's at the instigation of Sir Alexander Galt. Three bad crop years led to dissatisfaction; some of the Jews went to Manitoba, others began "peddling." Mentions other contemporary Jewish settlements, occupations, travel problems, family life, and relations with neighboring communities. Provides details on the family of Alter Kaplun of Wapella, who settled there in 1891 and whose descendants are still on the farm. 12 illus., map.   D. Chaput

3504. Astrachan, Anthony. ON THE BROAD PRAIRIE: IN WINNIPEG, MANITOBA: A JEWISH PHENOMENON. *Present Tense 1975 2(4): 31-35.* History and description of the flourishing Jewish community in Winnipeg, Manitoba.   S

3505. Betcherman, Lita-Rose. CANADA'S HUMAN RIGHTS AFTER THE QUEBEC ELECTIONS. *Patterns of Prejudice [Great Britain] 1977 11(3): 23-27.* The 1 April 1977 promulgation of the French Language Charter by the Parti Quebecois government of René Levesque disturbs the province's 116,000 Jews, who sense anti-Semitism is implied in the law, in a climate of extreme French-Canadian nationalism.

3506. Erideres, James S. ATTITUDE AND BEHAVIOUR: PREJUDICE IN WESTERN CANADA. *Patterns of Prejudice [Great Britain] 1973 7(1): 17-22.* Summarizes research on Canadian anti-Semitism to the early 1960's and explores continued anti-Semitism, and its causes and its study. Active anti-Semitism continues in Canada; a large percentage of Canadians have strong anti-Semitic attitudes. Based on secondary sources and a study of 315 randomly selected households in an urban location; 2 tables, 36 notes.   G. O. Gagnon

3507. Farb, Judith and Farb, Nathan. THEY CAN'T GO HOME AGAIN. *Present Tense 1973 1(1): 59-61.* Jewish deserters and exiles in Canada.   S

3508. Frideres, James S. OFFSPRING OF JEWISH INTERMARRIAGE: A NOTE. *Jewish Social Studies 1973 35(2): 149-156.* In sociological investigation of a Jewish community in the Canadian Midwest, the author found that the incidence of intermarriage could be correlated with the size of the Jewish community, the previous pattern of intermarriage, and the availability of Jewish education. Based on primary and secondary sources; 21 notes.   P. E. Schoenberg

3509. Friedler, Egon et al. JEWS WITHOUT MONEY TODAY. *Present Tense 1975 2(2): 62-67.* Discusses Jews currently living in poverty in Uruguay, Canada, France, and Great Britain.

3510. Gruneir, Robert. THE HEBREW MISSION IN TORONTO. *Can. Ethnic Studies [Canada] 1977 9(1): 18-28.* Focuses primarily on the Presbyterian Church and the Protestant-supported Jewish mission founded in 1912. Examines efforts to convert immigrant Jews to Protestantism. Though presented as an aid to social assimilation, conversion (even the hybrid Hebrew-Protestant variety which allowed maintenance of ethnic identity), failed to attract large numbers of Jews. The movement faded after World War I.   K. S. McDorman

3511. Gutwirth, Jacques. HASSIDIM ET JUDAÏCITÉ À MONTRÉAL [Hasidism and Judaicity in Montreal]. *Recherches Sociographiques 1973 14(3): 291-325.* The Hasidic groupings that established themselves in Montreal during 1941-52 have, through their sociocultural and religious presence, had a direct and salutary impact on the Jewish community of the city. This has become possible through common reference points of Judaism where institutional collaboration takes place. In turn, Montreal's Jewish faction has permitted the Hasidic groupings to implant themselves. Based on field research and secondary sources; 87 notes.   A. E. LeBlanc

3512. Hayes, Saul. CANADIAN JEWISH CULTURE: SOME OBSERVATIONS. *Queen's Q. [Canada] 1977 84(1): 80-88.* Canadian Jews have been affected by the broader culture and are heterogeneous, but their "all important propulsion is an *élan vital* of folk, group, [and] people."   J. A. Casada

3513. Kalter, Bella Briansky. A JEWISH COMMUNITY THAT WAS: ANSONVILLE, ONTARIO, CANADA. *Am. Jewish Arch. 1978 30(2): 107-125.* "Oh, it was lovely, lonely, lighted with snow in the wintertime. . . ." So begins the author's poignant memoir of Jewish life in the harsh climate of Canada's northern Ontario province. There are glimpses in her recollection of an existence which many North American Jews have forgotten or never experienced: a sense of community, traditional in nature, which put its emphasis upon sharing and caring; a life of hardship modified by the celebration of simple joys; a sense of continuity, uninterrupted by the geographic rootlessness of our time.   J

3514. Kardonne, Rick. MONTREAL, QUEBEC. *Present Tense 1975 2(2): 50-55.* Discusses the social and religious life of the Jews of Montreal, Quebec during the 1970's and the problems presented by the emigration of Jews from Morocco in the 1960's.

3515. Kayfetz, Ben. NEO-NAZIS IN CANADA. *Patterns of Prejudice [Great Britain] 1979 13(1): 29-31, 34.* Since 1963 a rash of neo-Nazi organizations have been formed, especially in the Toronto area, and they have engaged in the publication of Hitlerite material and antisemitic acts of destruction, for some of which the participants have been caught, tried and sentenced according to the provisions of Canada's new (1970) "anti-hate" law.

3516. Lander, Clara. SASKATCHEWAN MEMORIES OR HOW TO START A JEWISH CEMETERY. *Am. Jewish Arch. 1975 27(1): 5-7.*

3517. Levin, Arthur. A SOVIET JEWISH FAMILY COMES TO CALGARY. *Can. Ethnic Studies [Canada] 1974 6(1-2): 53-66.* Describes the experience of the first Soviet Jewish family to come to Calgary, Alberta, during the post-1971 wave of Jewish emigration from the USSR, as reported in interviews held in September and October 1974.

3518. Medovy, Harry. THE EARLY JEWISH PHYSICIANS IN MANITOBA. *Tr. of the Hist. and Sci. Soc. of Manitoba 1972/73 Series 3(29): 23-39.* Discusses the development of medical practice among Jewish doctors in Manitoba. Thirteen doctors are described in biographical sketches which include anecdotal material. These were men who "helped the community come of age."   J. A. Casada

3519. Richtik, James M. and Hutch, Danny. WHEN JEWISH SETTLERS FARMED IN MANITOBA'S INTERLAKE AREA. *Can. Geographical J. [Canada] 1977 95(1): 32-35.* In an effort to escape persecution in tsarist Russia, Jews migrated to Canada in 1884, settling primarily in the interlake districts of Manitoba; in the 1920's they set up agricultural communities in Saskatchewan and Alberta.

3520. Shack, Sybil. THE IMMIGRANT CHILD IN THE MANITOBA SCHOOLS IN THE EARLY TWENTIETH CENTURY. *Tr. of the Hist. and Sci. Soc. of Manitoba [Canada] 1973-74 (30): 17-32.* Discusses the history of the public schools in Winnipeg during 1900-20, concentrating on the educational difficulties of Jewish Central European immigrant children. Examines the school attendance records. The lack of incentive was due in part to the academic program reflecting a strong Protestant British tradition taught by English-speaking teachers who paid little attention to the children's heritage, and to the clash with the impoverished home situation. Primary and secondary works; 14 notes.   S. R. Quéripel

3521. Shaffir, William. THE ORGANIZATION OF SECULAR EDUCATION IN A CHASSIDIC JEWISH COMMUNITY. *Can. Ethnic Studies [Canada] 1976 8(1): 38-51.* Examines how the religious community of Lubavitcher chassidim in Montreal, Quebec, attempts to minimize their children's exposure to contradictive materials during their secular learning; covers late 1969 to 1971.

3522. Weinfeld, Morton. LA QUESTION JUIVE AU QUÉBEC [The Jewish question in Quebec]. *Midstream 1977 23(8): 20-29.* With the victory of René Levesque's Parti Québecois in the Quebec provincial elections in 1976, many Quebec Jews (most of whom are English-speaking) began to fear that the separatist philosophy of the P.Q. would lead to disenfranchisement for non-French residents of Quebec (even those able to speak French).

3523. Weinfeld, Morton. A NOTE ON COMPARING CANADIAN AND AMERICAN JEWRY. *J. of Ethnic Studies 1977 5(1): 95-103.* Evaluates the two factors usually cited to account for the greater communal identification of Canadian Jews compared with their American brethren: 1) that the Canadian community is one generation younger or closer to Europe and 2) the Canadian mosaic is more accepting and supportive of ethnic diversity than is the conformity of the American melting pot ethos. Sees the major empirical differences between the two groups as somewhat misleading because of variations in statistical criteria between the United States and Canada. Still, Canadian Jews rate of intermarriage is much lower, day school enrollment far exceeds that in the United States, retention of Yiddish is stronger in Canada, and religious affiliation of Canadian synagogues leans more to Orthodoxy than does that of American Jews. Canada's new national preoccupation with fostering national sentiment, its official multiculturalism, and its government expenditures to promote ethnic maintenance, which are four times those of the United States explain the greater sense of Jewish identity in Canada. Primary and secondary sources; 3 tables, 13 notes.   G. J. Bobango

3524. Wisse, Ruth R. and Cotler, Irwin. QUEBEC'S JEWS: CAUGHT IN THE MIDDLE. *Commentary 1977 64(3): 55-59.* With the rise of Quebec's separatist movement and the 1976 *Quebecois* victory, the prevailing French-English tension, formerly a stimulant to Jewish cohesiveness, began to cause uncertainty in the Jewish community. Sympathetic toward French Canadian aspirations, yet fearful of negative repercussions, Jews in Montreal face a crisis of conscience. Should they strive to adapt to the new political situation in order to preserve and nuture their many achievements? Or should they accept their latest difficulty as evidence corroborating the Zionist judgment that the Diaspora will never treat Jews altogether kindly?   D. W. Johnson

Rumanian

3525. Woywitka, Anne B. A ROUMANIAN PIONEER. *Alberta Hist. R. 1973 21(4): 20-27.* Recounts the struggles of pioneer Rumanian homesteaders in Alberta, particularly of Mrs. Veronia Kokotailo (b. 1894) whose family migrated in 1898. 3 illus.   D. L. Smith

Scandinavian

3526. Bjork, Kenneth O. SCANDINAVIAN MIGRATION TO THE CANADIAN PRAIRIE PROVINCES, 1893-1914. *Norwegian-American Studies 1974 26: 3-30.* Discusses the work of government agents, railroad, steamship, and land companies in promoting the emigration of Scandinavians from Denmark, Sweden, Finland, Norway, and the United States, 1893-1914, to Canada's Prairie Provinces. While some unfavorable press reports intimated that the Canadian government's plan would cause indebtedness among the settlers, financial life was made simple by Canadian payment of mortgages and cheapened land prices. 16 notes.   G. A. Hewlett

3527. Dahlie, Jorgen, ed. LETTERS HOME FROM A DANISH FAMILY ON THE PRAIRIES. *Can. Ethnic Studies [Canada] 1976 8(2): 93-95.* Prints a 1913 letter from Canada by a Danish settler, Julie Feilberg, describing domestic events such as the construction of an artificial Christmas tree.

3528. Elford, Jean. THE ICELANDERS—THEIR ONTARIO YEAR. *Beaver [Canada] 1974 304(4): 53-57.* Describes the 1872 arrival and first year of life in Ontario, Canada for 352 immigrants from Iceland.   S

3529. Ewanchuk, Michael. LORD DUFFERIN TRAIL AT GIMLI. *Manitoba Pageant [Canada] 1975 20(2): 5-9.* Examines Dufferin's 1877 trip to Gimli, Manitoba; attempts to ferret out the route taken and the farms in the Icelandic community which Dufferin visited.

3530. Finnie, Richard Sterling. MY FRIEND STEFANSSON. *Alaska J. 1978 8(1): 18-25, 84-85.* In 1931 the author met Vilhjalmur Stefansson (1879-1962), Canadian-born Arctic explorer and researcher. The author worked under him during World War II for the Office of the Coordinator of Information, which later became the OSS and much later the CIA. Having a brilliant intellect, Stefansson finished a four-year arts program at the State University of Iowa in one year, and later developed the very rare skill of speaking one of the Eskimo languages correctly as well as fluently. He made a few enemies, for example Roald Amundsen, who denounced him as a charlatan, but in general he was and is highly respected as an Arctic expert and pioneer. 8 illus., map.
                                          L. W. Van Wyk

3531. Kolehmainen, John I. THE LAST DAYS OF MATTI KURIKKA'S UTOPIA: A HISTORICAL VIGNETTE. *Turun Hist. Arkisto [Finland] 1976 31: 388-396.* The collapse of the Finnish American utopian colony at Harmony Island, British Columbia, active 1901-05, was due largely to the unrealistic ideas of its founder, Matti Kurikka (1863-1913).   R. G. Selleck

3532. Lund, Rolf T. SKIING IN CANADA: THE EARLY YEARS. *Beaver [Canada] 1977 308(3): 48-53.* The first printed reference to skiing in Canada appeared in 1879. Skiing was the result of Norwegian and Finnish influence and developed in Canada on a regional basis. In the east the sport became formalized in 1904 with the founding of the Montreal Ski Club. In the west, mining engineer Olaus Jeldness, a Norwegian, won the first downhill event at Red Mountain, British Columbia, in 1897. In most places in Canada, ski-jumping became popular before racing. The friction between groups from eastern and western Canada was quieted somewhat in 1920 with the founding of the Canadian Amateur Ski Association, but only in 1935 was the association representative of all clubs in the country. 8 illus.   D. Chaput

3533. McKnight, Roger, transl. and ed. ANDERS OLSSON IN BRITISH COLUMBIA: SIX LETTERS, 1906-1908. *Swedish Pioneer Hist. Q. 1979 30(2): 94-102.* Anders Olsson was a young Swedish immigrant from Jämtland, Sweden, to British Columbia who found employment in a smelter. The first five letters printed were from him to his brother, Axel, in Sweden. They show increasing despair about working conditions and crowded living conditions. The last letter printed is from "B. Lindblom, a relative in America," who visits Olsson's grave and writes to his sister. The translator writes that these letters parallel the letters in the short story, *"En av dem,"* by Swedish novelist Henning Berger (Berger, *"En av dem. En Historia i fyra brev,"* Där ute; Stockholm, 1923).   C. W. Ohrvall

3534. Patterson, R. S. and Wilson, Leroy R. THE INFLUENCE OF THE DANISH FOLK HIGH SCHOOL IN CANADA. *Paedagogica Historica [Belgium] 1974 14(1): 64-79.* In the three decades following World War I, the Danish folk school concept had a significant impact on the growth of adult education in Canada, beginning in the western part of the nation and proceeding eastward.   J. M. McCarthy

3535. Theberge, C. B. and Theberge, Henry. HIGH ADVENTURE IN THE HIGH ARCTIC. *Canada 1975 2(3): 44-57.* Vilhjalmur Stefansson (1879-1962) spent his youth exploring the Canadian Arctic and attempting to advertise its wealth and its ability to sustain human life. A single disastrous expedition to Wrangel Island defeated his plans, but time has vindicated his theories. 7 photos, map, biblio., 9 notes.
                                          W. W. Elison

3536. Wonders, William C. SCANDINAVIAN HOMESTEADERS. *Alberta Hist. 1976 24(3): 1-4.* Scandinavian settlement in the Prairie Provinces and British Columbia was secondary to the initial thrust, homesteading in the United States. However, after completion of the Calgary & Edmonton Railroad in 1891, and the immigrant quotas in the United States in the 1920's, Scandinavian population in central Canada increased markedly. Examines reasons for settlements, homesteading policies, and percentages of population. Unanswered questions are many and must be asked now, as assimilation is so rapid that there is seldom any second Scandinavian generation. 2 illus., 6 notes.   D. Chaput

3537. Youe, Christopher. EAU CLAIRE, THE COMPANY AND THE COMMUNITY. *Alberta Hist. [Canada] 1979 27(3): 1-6.* The Eau Claire district of Calgary was named after the lumber company headed by Isaac Kerr. In 1886, at the urging of K. N. MacFee of Ottawa, Kerr moved his operations from Eau Claire, Wisconsin, to Calgary. This was indeed a transplanted outfit: personnel, machinery, and the Scandinavian work force from Wisconsin moved to Alberta. Kerr was born in Ontario, and the manager of the Calgary operation, Peter Prince, was from Quebec. The company flourished, as Calgary's housing needs were taken care of by the Eau Claire Co., with mills on the Bow River, and large forests nearby. The district of Eau Claire retained its overall appearance until the early 1970's, when high-rise apartment units began to replace the common one- and two-story residential structures. Based on company records, newspapers, and printed sources; illus., map.   D. Chaput

Slavic

Czechoslovakian

3538. Behuncik, Edward V. FORTIETH ANNIVERSARY CANADIAN SLOVAK LEAGUE. *Slovakia 1973 23(46): 48-52.* Speech by Edward J. Behuncik, President of the Slovak League of America, on the 40th anniversary of the founding of the Canadian Slovak League (5

August 1972). Calls upon all Slovaks to support the Slovak World Congress organized in New York in 1970.   J. Williams

3539. Kirschbaum, J. M. JESUITS FIND A HOME IN CANADA. *Jednota Ann. Furdek 1977 16: 107-109.* Jesuits from Czechoslovakia came to Canada in 1950 following the dissolution of religious communities under Communism.

3540. Kirschbaum, J. M. SLOVAK AMERICAN ORGANIZATIONS IN CANADA. *Jednota Ann. Furdek 1977 16: 233-238.* Discusses Slovak American organizations which were transplanted to Canada with immigration; discusses the labor, political, and community organizing aspects of these immigrant associations, 1890-1964.

3541. Kirschbaum, J. M. SLOVAKS HELP SET PACE IN CANADA. *Jednota Ann. Furdek 1977 16: 109-114.* Discusses Slovak Canadians and their contribution to public life, politics, sports, and fine arts in Canada, 1950-77.

3542. Kirschbaum, J. M. SLOVAKS IN CANADA. *Jednota Ann. Furdek 1977 16: 97-101.* Of the three waves of immigration of Slovaks to Canada, the first two were for economic reasons, the last for political ones; describes settlement and acculturation.

3543. Kirschbaum, J. M. SOME OF CANADA'S SLOVAK PARISHES. *Jednota Ann. Furdek 1977 16: 114-117.* Discusses 10 Catholic parishes having a majority of Slovakian parishioners.

3544. —. A PARISH BORN IN THE GREAT DEPRESSION. *Jednota Ann. Furdek 1977 16: 101-106.* Catholic Slovak Canadians founded Saints Cyril and Methodius Parish in Toronto, Ontario, in 1934; a church was completed in 1941.

3545. —. A SHORT HISTORY OF THE SLOVAK CATHOLICS OF THE BYZANTINE PARISH OF THE ASSUMPTION OF THE B.V.M. *Jednota Ann. Furdek 1977 16: 207-209.* This Uniate parish in Hamilton, Ontario, was founded in 1952, and in 1963 the Shrine of Our Lady of Klococov was dedicated there; Father Francis J. Fuga has been pastor since 1954.

Polish

3546. Budakowska, Elżbieta. STRUKTURA DEMOGRAFICZNA POLONII KANADYJSKIEJ [Demographic structure of the Poles in Canada]. *Kultura i Społeczeństwo [Poland] 1976 20(1): 107-116.* The largest center of the Canadian Polonia is still Toronto, followed by Winnipeg, Montreal, Edmonton, Hamilton, Vancouver, Calgary, and Ottawa. The Canadian Polonia, hindered by foreign heritage and low income, shows a considerable rise in its professional structure since World War II. The educated or partly educated pre- and postwar Polish emigration greatly influenced this because it increased the number of intellectuals and scholars. The number of Polish students at Canadian universities also has risen considerably.   M. Swiecicka-Ziemianek

3547. Grabowski, Yvonne. SOME FEATURES OF POLISH AND OTHER SLAVIC LANGUAGES IN CANADA. *Polish Rev. 1977 22(2): 62-72.* Many of the changes in Polish, as spoken in Canada, are the results of extralinguistic factors shared with other tongues. Among these are the size and length of residence of a given language group, its level of education and social class, and its time of arrival. The changes in Polish are stabilized by the second generation, but its use tends to disappear entirely by the third generation. Primary and secondary sources; 20 notes.   E. M. McLendon

3548. Kapiszewski, Andrzej. PROBLEMS IN CANADIAN MULTICULTURALISM AND THE POLISH-CANADIAN COMMUNITY. *Polish Western Affairs [Poland] 1976 17(1-2): 145-151.* The Canadian Commission on Bilingualism and Biculturalism Affairs reported that Polish Canadians actively participate in Canadian cultural life. Polish schools are the third most numerous among ethnic groups. Poles received substantial subsidies to develop cultural enterprises. In November 1972, Dr. Stanley Haidasz, a Polish Canadian, was appointed Minister of State responsible for multiculturalism.
                    M. Swiecicka-Ziemianek

3549. Kraszewski, Piotr. POLSKA GRUPA ETNICZNA W KANADZIE [The Polish ethnic group in Canada]. *Przegląd Zachodni [Poland] 1975 31(5-6): 129-159.* Discusses the periodization and the social and professional structure of immigration to Canada during 1900-65, with special reference to the Polish immigrant group—its geographical distribution and its social mobility, in relation to other ethnic groups.

3550. Matejko, Alexander. MULTICULTURALISM: THE POLISH-CANADIAN CASE. *Polish Rev. 1976 21(3): 177-194.* Discusses the presence of Polish immigrants in Canada, their incorporation into the predominantly Anglo culture, 1945-75, and their efforts to be both Poles and Canadians ethnically.

3551. Matejko, Joanna and Matejko, Alexander. POLISH PIONEERS IN THE CANADIAN PRAIRIES. *Ethnicity 1978 5(4): 351-369.* In the late 1920's Poles became numerically significant in Canada when they totaled about 2.2% of the population. Their importance was considerable in rural areas of Manitoba, Alberta, and Saskatchewan where they began settling during the 1890's. Not considered desirable immigrants by the majority population, the Poles endured prejudice, discrimination, and extreme economic hardship in their early years of settlement. They clung to the Catholic Church as their major social institution. Early good relations with their Ukrainian immigrant neighbors deteriorated following the rise in nationalism during World War I and after. The Depression had a devastating impact on the Polish Canadians in the Prairie Provinces. Many lost their land and moved to urban areas to find work. Those who remained eventually found economic well-being in the 1940's and later. Primary, secondary and oral interview sources.   N. Lederer

Russian and Ukrainian

3552. Goresky, Isidore, transl. MINUTES OF THE FOUNDING OF ONE OF THE FIRST UKRAINIAN GREEK CATHOLIC CHURCHES IN ALBERTA, MARCH 1900. *Can. Ethnic Studies [Canada] 1974 6(1-2): 67-69.* Translates the minutes of this founding by Ukrainians in the colony of Rabbit Hill, Alberta.

3553. Hughes, Kenneth. ASESSIPPI EVERYWHERE! *Can. Dimension [Canada] 1978 13(3): 26-37.* Analyzes the work of contemporary Canadian artist Don Proch, in relation to his roots in Ukrainian cultural tradition.

3554. Klymasz, Robert B. FROM IMMIGRATION TO ETHNIC FOLKLORE: A CANADIAN VIEW OF PROCESS AND TRANSITION. *J. of the Folklore Inst. 1973 10(3): 131-139.* Examines dissolution as well as acquisition techniques of immigrant folklore in terms of Ukrainian folklore in Western Canada; maintains that study of such change must be evaluated and a new framework for observation formulated.

3555. Klymasz, Robert B. and Porter, James. TRADITIONAL UKRAINIAN BALLADRY IN CANADA. *Western Folklore 1974 33(2): 89-132.* Discusses the function, content, poetics, structure, and style of traditional Ukrainian balladry still popular among Ukrainian immigrants in the prairie provinces of Canada. Includes the music, text, and translations of 11 ballads. Based on primary and secondary sources and oral interviews; 18 notes, 7 music examples (in addition to the ballads), appendix.   S. L. Myres

3556. Lehr, John C. CHANGING UKRAINIAN HOUSE STYLES. *Alberta Hist. [Canada] 1975 23(1): 25-29.* Transformation of immigrant architecture as a reflection of Anglo-Canadian assimilation from the late 19th century to the present.   S

3557. Lehr, John C. UKRAINIAN HOUSES IN ALBERTA. *Alberta Hist. R. 1973 21(4): 9-15.* Ukrainian pioneer cottages in Alberta are distinctive cultural expressions of generations of practical experience of the homeland. The Ukrainian area of settlement in Alberta became distinctive visually as well as culturally. 3 illus., 15 notes.
                    D. L. Smith

3558. Lehr, John C. THE UKRAINIAN PRESENCE ON THE PRAIRIES. *Can. Geographic [Canada] 1978 97(2): 28-33.* Chronicles the immigration and settlement of Ukrainians in Canada's Prairie Provinces, 1910-31.

3559. Mitchell, John Fletcher and Driedger, Leo. CANADIAN ETHNIC FOLK ART: AN EXPLORATORY STUDY IN WINNIPEG. *Ethnicity 1978 5(3): 252-265.* A survey of 12 Latvian and 38 Ukrainian artists working in Winnipeg seeking to ascertain sociocultural complexity employed a general schema of folk art emphasizing art forms, role of the artist, distribution and reward systems, the art consuming public, and principles of judgment. In art forms design and use of colors were indicated as important, along with employment of symbols and patterns. The role of the artist included ethnic loyalty and a general interest in other ethnic activities. Art created was used in the home with some artists entering contests and selling their creations at exhibitions and fairs. The ethnic group to which the artist adhered was the most responsive to the art created. N. Lederer

3560. Penner, Norman. RECOLLECTIONS OF THE EARLY SOCIALIST MOVEMENT IN WINNIPEG, BY JACOB PENNER. *Social Hist. [Canada] 1974 7(14): 366-378.* Recollections of Jacob Penner (1880-1965), a Communist member of the Winnipeg City Council, 1933-60, except for a two-year period when jailed during World War II. Covers his youth and early manhood in Russia where he developed a Marxist consciousness, his migration to Canada in 1904, and the development of the Socialist movement in Winnipeg between 1906 and the General Strike of 1919. 10 notes. W. K. Hobson

3561. Pinczuk, J. R. MANITOBA—CENTRE OF UKRAINIAN STUDIES. *Ukrainian R. [Great Britain] 1974 21(4): 85-95.*

3562. Wagner, J. Richard and O'Neill, Daniel J. THE GOUZENKO AFFAIR AND THE CIVILITY SYNDROME. *Am. Rev. of Can. Studies 1978 8(1): 31-42.* The theory that Canadian political culture has provided a more humane and decent tradition than the American can be tested by comparing the two countries' responses to the same situation, employing a norm called the "civility syndrome" which examines: moderation in style and policy; conformity to law; and respect for the rights of others. Using as an example the American attempt to pressure Canada into permitting a US congressional committee to interview Soviet defector Igor Gouzenko in 1953, Canadian political culture appears superior to American in terms of the "civility syndrome." Primary and secondary sources; 28 notes. G.-A. Patzwald

3563. Woywitka, Anne B. HOMESTEADER'S WOMAN. *Alberta Hist. [Canada] 1976 24(2): 20-24.* Dominka Roshko, born in 1893 in the Ukraine, came to Manitoba with her family in 1900. In 1912 she married Monoly Zahara, and they went to homestead in the Peace River country. Examines frontier living, such as clearing the land, farming, lack of medical facilities, and education. 2 illus. D. Chaput

3564. Woywitka, Anne B. LABOURING ON THE RAILROAD. *Alberta Hist. [Canada] 1979 27(1): 25-33.* Nick Gill, born in the Ukraine in 1894, moved to Canada in 1912 to escape service in the Austro-Hungarian Army. For the next few years he worked on railroad gangs in western Canada, moving ties, shifting dirt, and working at odd jobs during the winters. Includes details of food service, clothing needs, company policies, and multiethnic work crews. 4 illus. D. Chaput

3565. Woywitka, Anne B. A PIONEER WOMAN IN THE LABOUR MOVEMENT. *Alberta Hist. [Canada] 1978 26(1): 10-16.* Teklia Chaban was born in the Ukraine. She moved to Alberta in 1914, the year of her marriage. Her husband worked in the Cardiff coal mines, 15 miles north of Edmonton. Follows the family for the next 10 years, with agitation for a labor organization, dealings with the United Mine Workers of America, and strikes and violence in the early 1920's. She was active in Ukrainian cultural movements that were part of the labor efforts. In the mid-1920's the family moved to Edmonton, and again was involved in agitation for labor recognition, spending some time in jail and suffering periodic unemployment for their efforts. 2 illus. D. Chaput

3566. Woywitka, Anne B. RECOLLECTIONS OF A UNION MAN. *Alberta Hist. [Canada] 1975 23(4): 6-20.* Peter Kyforuk, a Ukrainian immigrant, came to Canada in 1912 at the age of 18. In the next decades he worked as a woodsman and railroad hand from Ontario to British Columbia. In the 1920's he became active in the Ukrainian Labour-Farmer Association in Manitoba. Later active in Farmers Unity League, he played a key role in the Hunger March on Edmonton in December 1932 and with many other leaders was arrested. By the mid-1930's Kyforuk had settled in Alberta, became a successful farmer, and remained active in the Farmer's Union of Alberta. 8 photos. D. Chaput

Yugoslavian

3567. Harney, Robert F. A NOTE ON SOURCES IN URBAN AND IMMIGRANT HISTORY: (INCLUDING EXCERPTS FROM PRIMARY MATERIALS ON MACEDONIANS IN TORONTO). *Can. Ethnic Studies [Canada] 1977 9(1): 60-76.* Of the three major sources on immigrants in Toronto (municipal statistics, "caretakers' " records, and immigrant literature), the last has been the most ignored and offers the greatest enrichment to urban history. Provides four types of immigrant sources: a description of the Canadian Baptist mission for Macedonians, the actual records of a Macedonian church, a community historian's depiction of the founding of a Macedonian church in Toronto, and an interview with Gina Petroff, a Macedonian immigrant. Interviews with living immigrants will better document the ethnic community's experience. K. S. McDorman

3568. Petroff, Lillian. MACEDONIANS: FROM VILLAGE TO CITY. *Can. Ethnic Studies [Canada] 1977 9(1): 29-41.* Because they believed that Slavic peoples were inferior immigrants, Canadian Protestants, educators, and health officials urged major programs of Canadization upon the Macedonian community in Toronto's East End. Though aided by elementary language education and nursing services, most of Toronto's first-generation Macedonian population refused to adopt Protestantism or surrender their unique traditions. By World War I second-generation Macedonian Canadians had begun to accept their adopted country's culture. Despite some assimilation a distinct ethnic community remains. K. S. McDorman

3569. Rasporich, Anthony W. A CROATIAN IMMIGRANT ON THE FRONTIER. *Can. Ethnic Studies [Canada] 1976 8(2): 95-102.* Translates and reprints an excerpt entitled "My Discovery of Canada," from *A Memoir on the Twentieth Anniversary of the Croatian Peasant Party in Canada* (Winnipeg, 1952), by Stjepan Bradica, an activist in the Croatian Peasant Party in the 1930's.

United States (including Loyalists)

3570. Barkley, Murray. THE LOYALIST TRADITION IN NEW BRUNSWICK: THE GROWTH AND EVOLUTION OF AN HISTORICAL MYTH, 1825-1914. *Acadiensis [Canada] 1975 4(2): 3-45.* Examines the New Brunswick loyalist tradition from 1825 to 1914, including the loyalists' elitist origins, their loyalty to England, their suffering and self-sacrifice, and a recurring anti-Americanism, which usually emerged during periods of crisis and weakness in New Brunswick. The loyalist tradition has been seriously undercut by 20th-century historical scholarship. Primary and secondary sources; 133 notes. E. A. Churchill

3571. Bawtinhimer, R. E. THE DEVELOPMENT OF AN ONTARIO TORY: YOUNG GEORGE DREW. *Ontario Hist. [Canada] 1977 69(1): 55-75.* Presents the major influences in George Drew's early career and analyzes his development into a leading Tory. Outlines his Loyalist family background. He served in the army in World War I before being invalided home. His early postwar career was devoted to the family law practice, until he entered local politics. Analyzes his attitudes and campaigns, along with his election in 1925 as mayor of Guelph. 72 notes. W. B. Whitham

3572. Bird, Lilah Smith. MY ISLAND HOME. *Nova Scotia Hist. Q. 1975 5(4): 323-336.* Contains nostalgic recollections of early years on Port Hood Island off the coast of Cape Breton. Describes the simple, and, in some ways, primitive manner of life during the first part of the 20th century. The first English settlers, David Smith and family (the author's ancestor), came from New England in 1786.　　　R. V. Ritter

3573. Brown, Wallace. 'VICTORIOUS IN DEFEAT': THE AMERICAN LOYALISTS IN CANADA. *Hist. Today [Great Britain] 1977 27(2): 92-100.* Discusses the settlement of British Loyalists in Nova Scotia, New Brunswick, Prince Edward Island and Quebec near the end of the American Revolution, 1782-90's.

3574. Clark, S. D. THE ATTACK ON THE AUTHORITY STRUCTURE OF THE CANADIAN SOCIETY. *Tr. of the Royal Soc. of Can. [Canada] 1976 14: 3-15.* Discusses the effect of the protest movements of the 1960's on Canadian society. In Canada the middle class was more narrowly based than in the United States; hence, there was less opportunity for individual advancement. Dissatisfied Canadians, both working class and middle class, sought opportunities to the south. After World War II there were more economic opportunities in Canada with the resulting population shift from rural to urban; but, in the 1960's, more young people entered the work force than there were positions. At the same time, dissatisfied Americans emigrated to Canada where they became leaders in opposition to the old order. Although in the United States the protest movement was more violent, in Canada it had a more lasting effect because many Canadian officials had little experience in running newly created educational and governmental agencies and more readily yielded to pressure. 2 notes.　　　J. D. Neville

3575. Colhoun, Jack. THE EXILE'S ROLE IN WAR RESISTANCE. *Monthly Rev. 1979 30(10): 27-42.* Reviews the history of the anti-Vietnam War and amnesty activities of Americans exiled in Canada after 1965, especially the 1968 founding of the Union of American Exiles and the publication of their magazine, *Amex-Canada Magazine.*

3576. Crowson, E. T. JOHN SAUNDERS: AN EXILED VIRGINIA LOYALIST AND A FOUNDER OF NEW BRUNSWICK. *Virginia Cavalcade 1977 27(2): 52-57.* John Saunders, a determined loyalist forced to flee his native Virginia in 1782, helped found New Brunswick and lived in that British colony, 1784-1834.

3577. Day, John M. TORY OR LOYALIST? A MODEL FOR CURRICULUM DEVELOPMENT IN NEW ENGLAND AND THE ATLANTIC PROVINCES. *Am. Rev. of Can. Studies 1979 9(1): 52-55.* The Canadian-American Center (University of Maine-Orono) and the Atlantic Institute of Education (Halifax) sponsored an international student-developed program designed to help high school classes in New Brunswick and Maine understand the Loyalists in the American Revolution. Employing exploratory exercises, readings, videotapes, and instructional games, the students examined issues related to loyalty and revolution and attempted to develop an appreciation of the Loyalist position and the effect of 18th-century thought on present differences between the United States and Canada. The program's apparent success has led to proposals for other international curricula. Based on personal experience; note.　　　G.-A. Patzwald

3578. Duffy, Dennis. UPPER CANADIAN LOYALISM: WHAT THE TEXTBOOKS TELL. *J. of Can. Studies [Canada] 1977 12(2): 17-26.* Discusses the mythology of Loyalism in Upper Canada, as depicted in history textbooks. Describes the changing attitudes toward the Loyalist heritage, and discusses different viewpoints. Suggests the need in Canada's national mythology for the civilized character of Loyalism. Based on primary and secondary school history textbooks approved by the educational authorities of Ontario; 36 notes.　　　J. B. Reed

3579. Dunton, Davidson. THE RESPONSE TO CULTURAL PENETRATION. *Pro. of the Acad. of Pol. Sci. 1976 32(2): 63-74.* Analyzes US cultural influence in Canada, which is pervasive. Most Canadians are within easy reach of American cultural attractions. Original cultural productions are costly, and Canada has but a small population to support the cost, whereas distribution of cultural productions is rather inexpensive. American television and radio, newspapers and magazines, are everywhere. Many American professors staff the universities. Canadian talent has difficulty becoming known. There is no movement to a closed society, but the government should increase support for Canadian efforts.　　　V. L. Human

3580. Fellows, Jo-Ann. THE "BRITISH CONNECTION" IN THE JALNA NOVELS OF MAZO DE LA ROCHE: THE LOYALIST MYTH REVISITED. *Dalhousie Rev. [Canada] 1976 56(2): 283-290.* The idea that the "Loyalists" or "Tories" of the American Revolution were monolithic in their ideologies is a myth which did not survive the First World War except in fantasy, patriotic speeches, bad poetry, and the Jalna novels. Through analysis of several novels in the series the author declares that "Jalna is the Loyalist Myth." However, the "Loyalist tradition is only one of many in the pantheon of Canadian national ethics or myths." 29 notes.　　　C. Held

3581. Johnson, Arthur H. COMING TO ALBERTA. *Alberta Hist. [Canada] 1976 24(1): 23-27.* Discusses turn-of-the-century homesteading near Red Deer-Halrirk by a family of North Dakota farm boys. Examines means of acquiring land, type and use of tools, neighborhood work sessions to harvest and plant, and early adjustments to the Alberta frontier. 2 illus.　　　D. Chaput

3582. Keyes, Jane. MARRIAGE PATTERNS AMONG EARLY QUAKERS. *Nova Scotia Hist. Q. [Canada] 1978 8(4): 299-307.* Economic factors persuaded Quakers from Nantucket, Massachusetts, to settle in Dartmouth, Nova Scotia, in 1786; Friends meetings continued until 1789 when most of the settlers returned to Nantucket. Examination of the Minutes of the Dartmouth Friends Meetings for Business revealed that only four marriages of the 10 recorded were between members of the Society of Friends following prescribed procedures. Two were between two members of the Meeting but were not sanctioned, and four were between a member and a non-member. Based on Minutes of the Dartmouth Friends Meetings for Business; table.　　　H. M. Evans

3583. Lambert, Robert S. A LOYALIST ODYSSEY: JAMES AND MARY CARY IN EXILE, 1783-1804. *South Carolina Hist. Mag. 1978 79(3): 167-181.* Forced to leave the United States in 1781 because of his commitment to the British cause, James Cary spent the remainder of his life in Jamaica, Great Britain and Nova Scotia seeking compensation for losses suffered because of this loyalty.

3584. Lambert, Ronald D. and Curtis, James. NATIONALITY AND PROFESSIONAL ACTIVITY CORRELATES AMONG SOCIAL SCIENTISTS: DATA BEARING ON CONVENTIONAL WISDOMS. *Can. Rev. of Sociol. and Anthrop. 1973 10(1): 62-80.* Analysis of data from a recent CSAA survey of sociologists and anthropologists provides perspective on the Americanization of academe in Canada. Similarities and differences between American and English-Canadian sociologists are explored for a range of professional background and professional activity characteristics. Nationality is operationalized in terms of birthplace, citizenship, and places of BA and highest degrees. Comparisons are also made for 'pure' Canadians and "pure" Americans and for Canadian- and American-born sociologists controlling for highest degree.　　　J/S

3585. MacKinnon, Neil. THE ENLIGHTENMENT AND TORYISM: A LOYALIST PLAN FOR EDUCATION IN BRITISH NORTH AMERICA. *Dalhousie Rev. [Canada] 1975 55(2): 307-314.* Outlines the growth of governmental responsibility for education in Nova Scotia, noting the optimistic concept of education and its potential in the age of Enlightenment. Financial inducements were necessary to encourage the most able students into the teaching profession. Based on "A Plan of Liberal Education for the Youth of Nova Scotia and the Sister Province in North America" in *Nova Scotia Magazine* (1789) and probably authored by Professor William Cochran of the then newly founded King's College.　　　C. Held

3586. MacNutt, W. S. THE LOYALISTS: A SYMPATHETIC VIEW. *Acadiensis [Canada] 1976 6(1): 3-20.* Throughout the American Revolution, many Loyalists suffered severe persecution. Eventually, those who had too openly sided with the British crown left for Nova Scotia and Canada. Struggling against shortages, resentful of their fate, and critical of British aid, some Loyalists returned home while those who remained clung to marginal settlements for decades. For 30 years they were the principal English-speaking element in British North America, and they assured the language's continuance. 50 notes.　　　D. F. Chard

3587. McLeod, Carol. PRIVATEERS AND PETTICOATS. *Nova Scotia Hist. Q. [Canada] 1978 8(3): 205-214.* The fishing village of

Lockport, on the southern coast of Nova Scotia, was settled by Americans from New England searching for new homes and good fishing. Their loyalties were to their former home rather than the British Crown or their new government. During the American Revolution the community profited from trade goods supplied by American privateers. By 1779 sympathy had changed and the privateers began to raid the settlements on the coast. One raid was discouraged by the women of Lockport who draped red petticoats on trees to simulate British soldiers. The privateers withdrew. Biblio.   H. M. Evans

3588. McLeod, Evelyn Slater. OUR SOD HOUSE. *Beaver [Canada] 1977 308(2): 12-15.* Wesley Williams came from North Dakota in 1909 to settle west of Stettler, Alberta. Explains methods and materials used in construction of a sod house. Provides a photo of the completed sod house, plus floor plan, cut-away view, and sod slabbing diagrams. 5 illus.
                                                                      D. Chaput

3589. McLeod, Evelyn Slater. RESTLESS PIONEERS. *Beaver [Canada] 1976 307(1): 34-41.* As a six-year-old, the author arrived at Stettler, Alberta, with her North Dakota family. Relates pioneer experiences such as building a sod-house, farming, gopher problems, and schooling. 10 illus.   D. Chaput

3590. Morgan, Robert J. THE LOYALISTS OF CAPE BRETON. *Dalhousie R. [Canada] 1975 55(1): 5-22.* The loyalists of Cape Breton, though relatively unknown because of later Scottish migration, played an important role in the history of the area from their arrival in 1784 until its annexation to Nova Scotia in 1820. Some of the important early settlers mentioned are Abraham Cuyler, Jonathan Jones, David Smith, Jacob Sparling, David Mathews, and Neil Robertson. The Cape Breton loyalists were generally either officials, farmers, or soldiers from northern New England. Includes a seven page list of Cape Breton loyalists. 46 notes.
                                                                      C. Held

3591. Ogmundson, Rick and Dasko, Donna. AMERICANIZATION AND HIGHER EDUCATION IN CANADA: RECENT DEVELOPMENTS IN THE ARTS FACULTY AT THE UNIVERSITY OF MANITOBA. *Can. Ethnic Studies [Canada] 1976 8(1): 71-76.* Discrimination against Canadian academics continues, due to the increased hiring of Americans, as based on statistics from the University of Manitoba from 1970 to 1972.

3592. Osborne, Brian S. THE CEMETERIES OF THE MIDLAND DISTRICT OF UPPER CANADA: A NOTE ON MORTALITY IN A FRONTIER SOCIETY. *Pioneer Am. 1974 6(1): 46-55.* Illustrates demographic information that can be taken from gravestones. The Midland District of Upper Canada (fronting onto the Bay of Quinte at the eastern end of Lake Ontario) was selected for study because little is known of the birth rate, death rate, life expectancy, etc., of the Americans who left the former colonies following the War of Independence to settle in this region. Since this was a pioneer society which predated the major advancements in science and technology, the analysis bore out the hypotheses that the hardships associated with this life accounted for the high infant and female mortality and peak years of mortality associated with outbreaks of epidemics. Primary and secondary sources; 3 photos, map, 4 tables, 2 figs., 20 notes.   C. R. Gunter, Jr.

3593. Petrone, Gerard S., ed. AN IOWAN IN THE KLONDIKE GOLD RUSH: SELECTIONS FROM THE DIARY OF MARVIN MARSH. Dodd, Horace L. and Long, Robert W., ed. *People of the Far West* (Brand Book no. 6; San Diego: Corral of the Westerners, 1979): 119-130. Excerpts from the diary of Marvin Sanford Marsh indicate the splendor and the hardship of participating in the Klondike Stampede of 1898.

3594. Punch, Terrence M. and Marble, Allan E. JOHN HOWE GENEALOGY. *Nova Scotia Hist. Q. [Canada] 1976 6(3): 317-328.* Gives the genealogy of John Howe, a Loyalist in Nova Scotia and King's printer in Halifax, in the 18th and 19th centuries.

3595. Punch, Terrence M. LOYALISTS ARE STUFFY, EH? *Nova Scotia Hist. Q. [Canada] 1978 8(4): 319-343.* John M'Alpine (1748-1827) was a Scotsman who had a varied career in New York and Halifax. He supplied horses and fuel to the British troops during the American

Revolution. After the war he moved to Nova Scotia and was an innkeeper, undertaker, drover, road builder, cattle dealer, father of six children and husband to four wives. Based on diaries and secondary sources; 47 notes, genealogical appendix.   H. M. Evans

3596. Robertson, Allen B. THE FAMILY OF ROLEN ROGERS, A NEW ENGLAND PLANTER IN KING'S COUNTY. *Nova Scotia Hist. Q. [Canada] 1979 9(2): 177-187.* Traces the descendants of Rolen Rogers (d. 1805) to the fifth generation. Rolen emigrated from Connecticut to Nova Scotia in 1760, acquired land, and became involved in community affairs. He reared eight children, three of whom founded families in Horton. Church, census, and cemetery records; 9 notes.
                                                                      H. M. Evans

3597. Schneck, Rodney. THE AMERICANIZATION OF CANADIAN FACULTIES OF BUSINESS. *J. of Can. Studies [Canada] 1978 13(2): 100-108.* In recent years, Canadian business schools have not been able to supply sufficient Ph.D.'s for their own collective growth requirements. As of 1974-75, 85% of the Ph.D.'s held by members of 13 selected Canadian business faculties were from US colleges and universities. The quality of these members, however, appears to be high: 57% were from universities rated (on the basis of contributions to scholarly business journals) among the USA's top 10, and 90% from the top 20. Teachers of Canadian origin still were in the majority (56%), but this figure was down from 62% in 1970-71. Discusses possible areas of research aimed at clarifying the problem of adapting Canadian business education to Canadian needs. Canadian business faculties must not be "branch plants," but must develop their own intellectual capital. Based mainly on 1974-75 calendars of Canadian business faculties; 4 tables, 21 notes.
                                                                      L. W. Van Wyk

3598. Sutherland, David. HALIFAX MERCHANTS AND THE PURSUIT OF DEVELOPMENT, 1783-1850. *Can. Hist. Rev. [Canada] 1978 59(1): 1-17.* The American War of Independence caused an exodus of settlers to Halifax, Nova Scotia, who were determined to convert the town into another New England. Appeals to England brought only limited assistance. The Napoleonic Wars brought great prosperity, thought to be lasting, but the following peace treaty hurt the Halifax cause. Hard times set in. A Chamber of Commerce was created to explore new avenues to prosperity. Halifax's isolation from the rest of Canada was underscored, and demands were voiced for a railroad, which was not soon in coming. Halifax's real problem was its merchants, who preferred traditional commerce and failed to establish an industrial base. 63 notes.
                                                                      V. L. Human

3599. Temperly, Howard. FRONTIERISM, CAPITAL, AND AMERICAN LOYALISTS IN CANADA. *J. of Am. Studies [Great Britain] 1979 13(1): 5-27.* Of the 40,000 Loyalists who fled to British possessions during the American Revolution, generally they avoided pioneering a virgin frontier. When Loyalists went to Canada, many took resources with them, and Britain then expended over 1,300,000 pounds compensating them for their loyalty. In so doing, Great Britain established an English-speaking colonial elite which, loyal to the motherland, helped it control Canada. Based on British archival sources and secondary works; 6 tables, 49 notes.   H. T. Lovin

3600. Thomas, C. E. THE WORK OF THE S.P.G. IN NOVA SCOTIA, SECOND HALF-CENTURY. *Nova Scotia Hist Soc. Collections [Canada] 1973 38: 63-90.* The Loyalists' arrival opened a new chapter in the history of the Society for the Propagation of the Gospel in Foreign Parts as 18 of the 31 Church of England clergymen who came as Loyalists remained in the Maritime Provinces. In 1787, Charles Inglis became the first Anglican bishop of Nova Scotia; in 1788, King's College, Windsor was founded; and thereafter new missionary stations were established. All increased the S.P.G.'s work so that hardships were ever present, notably after 1833 when the British government drastically reduced its support to overseas missionaries. A new missionary society from England, The Colonial Church Society, arose; then in 1864, the Nova Scotian Diocesan Synod.   E. A. Chard

3601. Vincent, Thomas Brewer. KEEPING THE FAITH: THE POETIC DEVELOPMENT OF JACOB BAILEY, LOYALIST. *Early Am. Literature 1979 14(1): 3-14.* Traces the development of the style and form in the poetry of Jacob Bailey (1731-1808), one of the most prolific poets in 18th-century North America. Bailey's early poems were lyrical, sentimental, and moral in tone, and were concerned with local subjects. Forced to leave Maine during the American Revolution, Bailey began writing satiric poetry that reflected a broader concern for social order and the stability of civilization. From Canada, he viewed the American Revolution as part of a decivilizing movement in human history. 23 notes.

T. P. Linkfield

3602. Young, Murray. W. STEWART MAC NUTT, 1908-1976. *Can. Hist. Assoc. Hist. Papers [Canada] 1976: 271-273.* Obituary of a Professor Emeritus of the University of New Brunswick and Chairman of the International Programme for Loyalist Studies. He received awards for local history from the American and Canadian Historical Associations and was noted as an interpreter of the Atlantic Provinces.

G. E. Panting

3603. —. [MORMONS ON VANCOUVER ISLAND].
McCue, Robert J. THE CHURCH OF JESUS CHRIST OF LATTER-DAY SAINTS AND VANCOUVER ISLAND: THE ESTAB-LISHMENT AND GROWTH OF THE MORMON COMMUNITY. *BC Studies [Canada] 1979 (42): 51-64.* Brigham Young considered Vancouver Island, British Columbia, as a possible haven for the Mormons when they were leaving Illinois. They settled in Utah instead. In 1875, a trickle of Mormon families arrived on Vancouver Island. In tracing the history of the Mormon community of the island, reasons for the scarcity of converts in the early years are suggested, the origins and dates of arrival of Mormon immigrants and missionaries are determined, and the reasons for their choice of the island are examined. 2 tables, 40 notes.
Warburton, T. Rennie. A COMMENT. *BC Studies 1979 (43): 94-97.* Robert J. McCue's article does not make use of the social sciences in its analysis. It does not consider the psychological values and social conditions that help to explain Mormon growth. It does not, therefore, concern itself with the explanation of why people became Mormons. 13 notes.
McCue, Robert J. A REPLY. *BC Studies 1979 (43): 98.* The "why do people join" question does need further investigation. This matter, however, was beyond the scope of the author's intention.

D. L. Smith/S

10. IMMIGRANTS AND ETHNICS: BY TOPICS

Religion

General

3604. Hanrahan, James. A CURRENT BIBLIOGRAPHY OF CANADIAN CHURCH HISTORY. *Study Sessions: Can. Catholic Hist. Assoc. 1973 40: 69-93.*

3605. Hogan, Brian F. A CURRENT BIBLIOGRAPHY OF CANADIAN CHURCH HISTORY. *Study Sessions: Can. Catholic Hist. Assoc. [Canada] 1977 44: 111-144.* Alphabetical listing of articles, books, and general sources, published during 1970-77.

3606. Hogan, Brian F. A CURRENT BIBLIOGRAPHY OF CANADIAN CHURCH HISTORY. *Study Sessions: Can. Catholic Hist. Assoc. [Canada] 1978 45: 101-141.* Lists recent works on the history of the Catholic, Protestant, and Eastern Orthodox churches, and smaller groups such as Jews, Mennonites, and Hutterites.

3607. Lucas, Glenn. CANADIAN PROTESTANT CHURCH HISTORY TO 1973. *Bull. of the United Church of Can. [Canada] 1974 (23): 5-50.* Outlines the history of the Methodist, Presbyterian, Anglican, Baptist, Congregational, and Lutheran churches in Canada and the United Church of Canada since 1825; includes bibliographies and historiography.

3608. Vipond, Mary. CANADIAN NATIONAL CONSCIOUSNESS AND THE FORMATION OF THE UNITED CHURCH OF CANADA. *Bull. of the United Church of Can. 1975 24: 4-27.* Examines "the extent to which a feeling of national consciousness and a sense of national responsibility motivated the unionists in the post World War I period." The movement for church union was directly related to the heavy European immigration and the need to evangelize and 'Canadianize' the west." Concludes that the United Church was intended "to accomplish a double mission for a nation whose unity was threatened by ethnic and geographic divisions.... The unity of the three Protestant churches was a religious goal, but it was also a national one." Based on United Church archival material, newspapers, and secondary sources; illus., 82 notes. B. D. Tennyson

Amish, Hutterite, and Mennonite

3609. Bergey, Lorna L. MENNONITE CHANGE: THE LIFE HISTORY OF THE BLENHEIM MENNONITE CHURCH, 1839-1974. *Mennonite Life 1977 32(4): 23-27.* Pennsylvania Germans settled Waterloo and Oxford Counties in southwest Ontario 1830-50, forming a prosperous agricultural community. In 1839 they organized the Blenheim Mennonite Church. Jacob Hallman was pastor. Membership in the church averaged 50 people for 135 years until it merged with the Biehn congregation to form the Nith Valley Mennonite Church in 1975. Reasons for its lack of growth are its location on the fringe of the Waterloo County settlement, the appeal of the livelier Methodist Church, a schism which led to the formation of the Missionary Church, and population changes in the area. B. Burnett

3610. Brado, Edward B. MENNONITES ENRICH THE LIFE OF MANITOBA. *Can. Geographic [Canada] 1979 99(1): 48-51.* Drawn by the offer of land, exemption from military service, and lack of objection to their use of the German language in the schools, Mennonites settled in two areas of Manitoba, the East Reserve and the West Reserve, 1875.

3611. Clark, Peter. LEADERSHIP SUCCESSION AMONG THE HUTTERITES. *Can. Rev. of Sociol. and Anthrop. [Canada] 1977 14(3): 294-302.* Forty-two Hutterite colonies were examined in order to determine the degree to which succession to leadership positions departs from a model of complete equality of opportunity. Variation in political

mobility patterns within colonies is explained by utilizing a 'demography of opportunity' hypothesis. This hypothesis posits that the degree of inequality of opportunity exhibited by a colony varies directly with the degree to which population growth (growth in the supply of potential position holders) exceeds organizational expansion (expansion in the supply of positions). J

3612. Devlin, T. P. HOMESTEADING IN NORTHERN BRITISH COLUMBIA. *Mennonite Life 1976 31(4): 21-27.* In the late 1930's drought conditions in southern Saskatchewan forced many farm families on government relief. The Canadian government assisted relocation of some families to an area approximately 65 miles south of Burns Lake, British Columbia. Twenty-five families and 17 carloads of effects arrived in Burns Lake by rail on 7 May 1940. They proceeded by trucks and ferries to the homestead area, where they build log houses at an average cost of $15 and planted crops. Twenty-five additional families joined the settlers in 1941. All the families were self-sufficient by 1942. The successful program would have continued, but World War II intervened. 13 photos. B. Burnett

3613. Dick, Ernest J. RESOURCES ON MENNONITE HISTORY IN THE PUBLIC ARCHIVES OF CANADA. *Mennonite Life 1975 30(4): 26-28, 1976 31(1): 19-22.* Covers research tools since the 19th century. In two parts.

3614. Driedger, Leo. CANADIAN MENNONITE URBANISM: ETHNIC VILLAGERS OR METROPOLITAN REMNANT? *Mennonite Q. R. 1975 49(3): 226-241.* Presents a study of the effect of urbanization on traditional Mennonite beliefs and practices in an attempt to determine the amount of erosion, if any, on urban Mennonites in contrast to those in rural areas. Urban Mennonites are lost to other groups in lesser numbers. Institutions (colleges, etc.) are shifting to urbanized areas successfully. The study shows that Canadian Mennonites have suffered less than their American counterparts in urbanization. 3 charts, 19 notes. E. E. Eminhizer

3615. Driedger, Leo. MENNONITE CHANGE: THE OLD COLONY REVISITED, 1955-1977. *Mennonite Life 1977 32(4): 4-12.* Comparison of studies of the Hague-Osler area of Saskatchewan shows that six of the original 15 villages disappeared between 1955 and 1977, and that six more are in decline. The role of the village committee and *Schultze* has been downgraded and Pentecostal evangelism has altered the old conservative religion. Other changes: consolidation of small schools, smaller families, more frequent use of English, more modern and colorful clothing, and introduction of nontraditional foods. Four processes have caused the changes: migration out of the area by the most conservative Mennonites, improved transportation to Saskatoon, influence of industrialization and capitalism, and a general liberalization in education and religion. 9 photos, map, 2 notes, biblio. B. Burnett

3616. Driedger, Leo and Zehr, Dan. THE MENNONITE STATE-CHURCH TRAUMA: ITS EFFECTS ON ATTITUDES OF CANADIAN STUDENTS AND LEADERS. *Mennonite Q. Rev. 1974 48(4): 515-526.* Discusses some of the social causes for the Canadian Mennonites' perception of social issues, and gives a 1970 statistical analysis of the views of differing Mennonite Conference leaders and university students. S

3617. Driedger, Leo. NATIVE REBELLION AND MENNONITE INVASION: AN EXAMINATION OF TWO CANADIAN RIVER VALLEYS. *Mennonite Q. R. 1972 46(3): 290-300.* Discusses how Mennonites have reaped settlement benefits from government eviction of Métis and Indian groups, specifically in the Red River Valley of Manitoba and the Saskatchewan River Valley (1869-95). S

3618. Dyck, Peter J. THE DIARY OF ANNA BAERG. *Mennonite Life 1973 28(4): 121-125.* Anna Baerg and other Russian Mennonites emigrated to Canada after the Russian Revolution; excerpts from her diary, 1917-23, detail Russian life, the Revolution, and the trip to Canada.

3619.　Ens, Adolph and Penner, Rita.　QUEBEC PASSENGER LISTS OF THE RUSSIAN MENNONITE IMMIGRATION, 1874-1880. *Mennonite Q. R. 1974 48(4): 527-531.*

3620.　Epp, Frank H.　1923: THE BEGINNINGS OF THE GREAT MIGRATION. *Mennonite Life 1973 28(4): 101-103.* Economic depression and cholera in the Ukraine inspired a group of Russian Mennonites to begin immigration to Canada, a country ripe for settlement.

3621.　Evans, Simon.　SPATIAL BIAS IN THE INCIDENCE OF NATIVISM: OPPOSITION TO HUTTERITE EXPANSION IN ALBERTA. *Can. Ethnic Studies [Canada] 1974 6(1-2): 1-16.* Examines the spatial variation in the incidence of overt hostility between the Hutterites and the host population in rural Alberta between 1918 and 1972, as revealed in a study of 50 Hutterite colonies.

3622.　Fretz, J. Winfield.　THE PLAIN AND NOT-SO-PLAIN MENNONITES IN WATERLOO COUNTY, ONTARIO. *Mennonite Q. Rev. 1977 51(4): 377-385.* The Mennonite community in Waterloo County, Ontario, is unique for its mixture of liberal and conservative elements and diversity of ethnic origin. Describes 12 grades of social action ranging from ultraconservative to ultraliberal. However, all factions work together surprisingly well as a result of a governing committee that is loose and resilient. In fact, the groups are not very different beneath the surface, except in their methods. This fact makes accommodation possible. The various groups cooperate if movement by an individual or a family from one group to another is desired. 4 tables.
　　　　　　　　　　　　　　　　　　　V. L. Human

3623.　Gross, Leonard, ed.　"PREPARING FOR '76": A CANADIAN-MENNONITE PERSPECTIVE. *Mennonite Hist. Bull. 1974 35(2): 2-4.* Though "many Canadian and 'American' Mennonites share a common Pennsylvania heritage, "some evidence suggests that from the American Revolution through the War of 1812 many Mennonites left Pennsylvania for Canada because of their allegiance to the British Crown. Prints excerpts from the introduction and text of Ezra E. Eby's *A Biographical History of Waterloo Township . . .* (Berlin, Ontario, 1895).
　　　　　　　　　　　　　　　　　　　S

3624.　Klassen, Henry C.　THE MENNONITES OF THE NAMAKA FARM. *Mennonite Life 1975 30(4): 8-14.* Describes farming on the Namaka Farm, a 13,000-acre communal Mennonite settlement east of Calgary, 1920's-40's.

3625.　Klippenstein, Lawrence.　AELTESTER DAVID STOESZ AND THE BERGTHAL STORY: SOME DIARY NOTES. *Mennonite Life 1976 31(1): 14-18.* Chronicles the years 1872-76 in the life of David Stoesz, a bishop of the Bergthaler Mennonites, during his immigration from the Ukraine to Manitoba. Article to be continued.

3626.　Klippenstein, Lawrence.　DIARY OF A MENNONITE DELEGATION (1873). *Manitoba Pageant 1973 18(2): 18-23.* A delegation of 12 Russian Mennonites visited Manitoba during the summer of 1873. They travelled by steamboat from Moorhead, Minnesota, to Fort Garry and then visited the East Reserve and the Assiniboine River district from Winnipeg West. Records brief observations of their survey. The favorable findings of the delegation were instrumental in sending thousands of Mennonite families to North America. Illus., 4 notes.　D. M. Dean

3627.　Klippenstein, Lawrence.　MANITOBA METIS AND MENNONITE IMMIGRANTS: FIRST CONTACTS. *Mennonite Q. R. 1974 48(4): 476-488.* Discusses the first experiences of Russian Mennonites who immigrated to Manitoba in 1873, especially their relationship to the Chippewa Indians and the Métis, natives of mixed blood.　S

3628.　Klippenstein, Lawrence.　MANITOBA SETTLEMENT AND THE MENNONITE WEST RESERVE. *Manitoba Pageant 1975 21(1): 13-24.* Seven thousand Russian Mennonites entered Manitoba 1870-80. The peak year was 1875. Many of the Mennonites arriving that year settled on the plains west of the Red River, an area not dissimilar to what they had just left in Russia. Based on secondary works; 7 notes.
　　　　　　　　　　　　　　　　　　　B. J. LaBue

3629.　Klippenstein, Lawrence and Friesen, John.　THE MENNONITE HERITAGE CENTRE FOR RESEARCH AND STUDY. *Mennonite Life 1978 33(4): 19-22.* The new Mennonite Heritage Centre at Canadian Mennonite Bible College in Winnipeg, Manitoba, offers the largest public Mennonite archival deposit in the country. The files include several series of German and English newspapers published for Mennonite communities, microfilm records from European points of origin, a 5,000-item photograph collection, and the personal papers of nearly 50 Mennonite leaders (e.g., David Toews, J. J. Thiessen, Benjamin and Heinrich Ewert, H. M. Epp). Works-in-progress include a photo album of Mennonite conscientious objectors in World War II, translations of Russian documents relating to migration, and a detailed catalog of the entire Mennonite studies literary holdings. 7 photos.　B. Burnett

3630.　Klippenstein, Lawrence.　MOVING TO MANITOBA: JACOB Y. SHANTZ, ONTARIO BUSINESSMAN, PROMOTED SETTLEMENT ON THE PRAIRIE. *Mennonite Life 1974 29(3): 51-53.* Discusses efforts of Jacob Y. Shantz to encourage friends of his remaining in the Ukraine to come to Manitoba, 1870's; includes excerpts from Shantz' letters.

3631.　Klippenstein, Lawrence.　A VISIT TO MANITOBA IN 1873: THE RUSSIAN MENNONITE DELEGATION. *Canada 1975 3(1): 48-61.* Discusses a visit by Russian Mennonites to Manitoba for the purpose of investigating settlement possibilities in 1873, emphasizing the role of Mennonite Reverend John F. Funk.

3632.　Krahn, Cornelius.　A CENTENNIAL CHRONOLOGY. *Mennonite Life 1973 28(1): 3-9, (2): 40-45.* Part I. Describes Mennonite immigration from Russia to the American prairies, noting the underlying causes of the migration and the chronology of the key events in the movement. 9 illus., biblio. Part II. Chronology of events among Mennonite immigrants in Manitoba, Canada, 1871-74.
　　　　　　　　　　　　　　　　　　　J. A. Casada/G. A. Hewlett

3633.　Kreider, Robert.　1923: THE YEAR OF OUR DISCONTENT, THE YEAR OF OUR PROMISE. *Mennonite Life 1973 28(4): 99-101.* Describes the immigration of 408 Russian Mennonites to Rosthern, Saskatchewan, in 1923, focusing on the prevailing social conditions in Canada at that time.

3634.　MacDonald, Robert James.　HUTTERITE EDUCATION IN ALBERTA; A TEST CASE IN ASSIMILATION, 1920-1970. *Can. Ethnic Studies [Canada] 1976 8(1): 9-22.* Hutterites in Alberta have resisted assimilation through the public schools since 1920, viewing the schools as a threat to their culture.

3635.　Mackie, Marlene.　OUTSIDERS' PERCEPTION OF THE HUTTERITES. *Mennonite Q. Rev. 1976 50(1): 58-65.* Asks "How is a sacred community perceived by members of the containing society?" and "Do outsiders withhold acceptance of a people which refuses to be integrated?" The study is based on a sample of 590 persons around Edmonton, Alberta. The conclusions are that most appreciate Hutterite uniqueness. Social distance is not based on stereotyped prejudice. 4 tables, 12 notes.　E. E. Eminhizer

3636.　Patterson, Nancy-Lou.　ANNA WEBER HAT DAS GEMACHT: ANNA WEBER (1814-1888)—A *FRAKTUR* PAINTER OF WATERLOO COUNTY, ONTARIO. *Mennonite Life 1975 30(4): 15-19.*

3637.　Penner, Peter.　BY REASON OF STRENGTH: JOHANN WARKENTIN, 1859-1948. *Mennonite Life 1978 33(4): 1-9.* Johann Warkentin (1859-1948), a little-known leader of the Mennonite Brethren Church in Canada, was born in South Russia and migrated to Manitoba in 1879. In 1881 he married Sara Krahn Loewen (d. 1930). Eventually he became a prosperous farmer and they had 19 well-spaced children. Converted from Old Colony Mennonite to Mennonite Brethren, Warkentin served in the Sunday School, directed the choir, and studied theology. Ordained in the Gospel ministry in 1895, he became assistant moderator to the Reverend David Dyck in the Winkler congregation, and moderator in 1906. As part of his missionary outreach interest, he helped establish a MB group in Winnipeg. Warkentin continued active church leadership until 1931 and remained influential for 10 more years. Based on unpublished material by Ben Warkentin; 6 photos, 15 notes.
　　　　　　　　　　　　　　　　　　　B. Burnett

3638. Penner, Peter. MENNONITES IN THE ATLANTIC PROVINCES. *Mennonite Life 1976 31(4): 16-20.* Mennonites did not settle in the Canadian Atlantic Provinces until after World War II. Three motivations brought Mennonites to the area after 1954: a desire to withdraw from crowded metropolitan life, an orientation toward social and evangelical service in underdeveloped areas, and the availability of jobs in teaching, engineering, research, and medicine. 5 photos, map, 7 notes.
B. Burnett

3639. Regeher, Ted D. MENNONITE CHANGE: THE RISE AND DECLINE OF MENNONITE COMMUNITY ORGANIZATIONS AT COALDALE, ALBERTA. *Mennonite Life 1977 32(4): 13-22.* Russian German immigrants settled Coaldale, Alberta, 1920-30, but because they came as individuals rather than as a colony, they were subject to Canadian regulations and could not transplant distinctly Mennonite institutions and social structures. Organizations evolving from the settlement included churches, a German library, a language preservation society, and Saturday schools. Settlers founded a cooperative cheese factory, a Savings and Credit Union, and a society to provide medical care. Although prosperous, Mennonites at Coaldale had become assimilated into the larger Canadian society by 1976, largely because of the decline of the German language, economic consolidation, superiority of government welfare services, and internal divisions involving religious splits and inadequate leadership. Primary sources; 13 photos.
B. Burnett

3640. Sawatzky, H. L. MANITOBA MENNONITES PAST AND PRESENT. *Mennonite Life 1974 29(1-2): 42-46.* Covers Mennonites in Manitoba 1870-1900.

3641. Shantz, Jacob Y. NARRATIVE OF JOURNEY TO MANITOBA. *Manitoba Pageant 1973 18(3): 2-6.* In 1873 Jacob Y. Shantz, at the request of the Canadian government, travelled with Bernard Warkentin of South Russia to see what the Manitoba prairies offered Russian Mennonites who wished to migrate. Shantz described the villages and the burgeoning town of Winnipeg. He visited farms owned by recent immigrants and recorded crop prices. His account was translated into several languages and distributed to prospective settlers.
D. M. Dean

3642. Tanaka, Hiroshi. ALBERTAN GIFT TO ASIA: HUTTERITES IN JAPAN. *Can. Geographic [Canada] 1979 98(2): 70-73.* Following the example of, and aided by funds from Hutterites in Alberta, a group of Japanese became Hutterites and established an agricultural community in Owa, Honshu, Japan, 1972.

3643. Wagner, Jonathan F. TRANSFERRED CRISIS: GERMAN VOLKISH THOUGHT AMONG RUSSIAN MENNONITE IMMIGRANTS TO WESTERN CANADA. *Can. Rev. of Studies in Nationalism [Canada] 1974 1(2): 202-220.* In 1917, a group of German Mennonite settlers left Russia to relocate in Saskatchewan, western Canada. In 1924, they established *Der Bote,* a German-language newspaper to inform and thus bind the Mennonite community more closely together. *Der Bote* enthusiastically supported Hitler after his advent to power in 1933. Earlier research has largely ignored this sympathy, and has emphasized instead the Mennonites' religious and ethnic diversity, or their contribution to the Canadian mosaic. This revision clears up the Mennonites' Nazi affinities by explaining their devotion to German völkisch thought, actually a mark of insecurity and a revolt against the chaotic conditions of modern living as well as a result of Mennonite hostility to the USSR, which had persecuted them. 55 notes.
T. Spira

3644. —. MENNONITE BEGINNINGS AT ROSTHERN. *Mennonite Life 1976 31(4): 4-15.* Presents an anonymous personal account, perhaps by Peter Klassen, of the first years of the Russian Mennonite settlement in Rosthern, Saskatchewan. In early spring 1892, 27 families staked out homesteads and began planting crops, building homes, and establishing a community. A split between Old Colony Mennonites and liberal Mennonites prevented the establishment of a church until Elder Peter Regier united factions in 1894. Despite frequent prairie fires, a food shortage during the harsh winter of 1892-93, and an 1895 shoot-out with rebellious Cree chief Almighty Voice, morale remained high. Settlers continued to arrive, crop yield was good, and the area prospered. Based on material in the archives of the Conference of Mennonites in Canada; 5 photos, map.
B. Burnett

Catholic

3645. Allaire, Georges. INFLUENCE DU MILIEU ÉTUDIANT QUÉBÉCOIS SUR L'ACTION DE L'ÉGLISE CATHOLIQUE [The influence of Quebec student culture on the action of the Catholic Church]. *Action Natl. [Canada] 1978 67(9): 737-744.* In the 1970's, Quebec university students dramatically have abandoned the practice of Catholicism, and many have adopted agnosticism as well. Students generally are indifferent to the Church, and strongly support total freedom of religion, opposing indoctrination in schools. In response, Catholic college chaplains have developed a mission of evangelization, attempting to form Christian campus communities capable of attracting more sophisticated student participation. Biblio.
A. W. Novitsky

3646. Arès, Richard. L'INFLUENCE DE L'ESPACE SUR L'ÉVANGÉLISATION DU PAYS [The influence of space on the evangelization of the country]. *Tr. of the Royal Soc. of Can. [Canada] 1976 14: 163-172.* Defines space and evangelization. Notes negative influences such as the great distance required to cross the Atlantic. Once in Canada, one found an immense territory and nomadic indigenous tribes. Great spaces allowed expansion. Priests were among the early explorers, and there was regional development of the Catholic Church. In 1820 British authorities allowed the development of four dioceses: in the Maritimes, at Montreal, at Kingston, and at the Red River. Earlier there had been one diocese of Quebec. Other dioceses were created later. 11 notes.
J. D. Neville

3647. Beck, Jeanne M. HENRY SOMERVILLE AND SOCIAL REFORM: HIS CONTRIBUTION TO CANADIAN CATHOLIC SOCIAL THOUGHT. *Study Sessions: Can. Catholic Hist. Assoc. 1975 42: 91-108.* Henry Somerville, editor of the *Catholic Register* 1933-53, provided an impetus for his generation through his contributions to the development of Catholic social thought and action in Canada by combining the influences of Edwardian England and his own Canadian immigrant experiences since his arrival in 1915.

3648. Begnal, Calista. THE SISTERS OF THE CONGREGATION OF NOTRE DAME, NINETEENTH-CENTURY KINGSTON. *Study Sessions: Can. Catholic Hist. Assoc. 1973 40: 27-34.* Examines the efforts of religious women during 1841-48, important years in the history of religious education.
S

3649. Bélanger, Noël. MGR. COURCHESNE ET L'ACTION CATHOLIQUE [Monsignor Courchesne and Action Catholique]. *Sessions d'Étude: Soc. Can. d'Hist. de l'Église Catholique [Canada] 1976 43: 49-67.* Studies Monsignor Georges Courchesne's work in the Rimouski diocese, 1940-67, with an outline of major dates in the organization of Action Catholique and his rupture with the Church in 1942.

3650. Boileau-DeSerres, Andrée. LES COLLECTIONS RELIGIEUSES DU MUSÉE HISTORIQUE DE VAUDREUIL [The religious collections of the Historical Museum of Vaudreuil]. *Sessions d'Étude: Soc. Can. d'Hist. de l'Église Catholique [Canada] 1978 45: 41-56.* The Musée Historique de Vaudreuil, Quebec, contains a sizable collection of French Canadian popular religious art, 17th-20th centuries.

3651. Byrne, Cyril. THE MARITIME VISITS OF JOSEPH-OCTAVE PLESSIS, BISHOP OF QUEBEC. *Nova Scotia Hist. Soc. Collections [Canada] 1977 39: 23-47.* The diary of the Bishop of Quebec, Joseph-Octave Plessis, provided considerable detail of the visits which he undertook in 1812 and 1815 to his diocese in Prince Edward Island, Cape Breton, and mainland Nova Scotia, as well as New Brunswick. Several outstanding characteristics of Plessis's attitude are noted: his implicit and explicit acceptance of the British dominance; his adverse judgment of the Acadians; his observation of the "most perfect harmony [which] existed" between the Scotch and Acadian Catholics on Prince Edward Island; his consciousness of his episcopal office and the dignity which it deserved together with the respectfulness due the performance of the sacred offices of the Church. Interesting details of daily life of the whites and Indians are delineated, as are frequent references to the geography and topography of the Maritime Provinces.
E. A. Chard

3652. Carrière, Gaston, transl. LETTER FROM BISHOP ALEXANDRE TACHÉ TO HIS MOTHER, CONCERNING HIS LIFE WITH THE CHIPEWYAN NATION. *Prairie Forum [Canada] 1978 3(2): 131-156.* Reprints a letter by Bishop Alexandre Antonin Taché to his mother in 1851 describing his experiences with the Chipewyan Indians at the Mission St. Jean-Baptiste on Île-à-la-Crosse in Saskatchewan, and gives a very brief background of Bishop Taché from his birth in 1823 until 1854.

3653. Charron, Marguerite. MARIE D'AQUIN ET LE NOUVEAU DÉPART DE L'INSTITUT JEANNE D'ARC (1914-1919) [Marie d'Aquin and the new start of the Joan of Arc Institute (1914-19)]. *Sessions d'Étude: Soc. Can. d'Hist. de l'Église Catholique [Canada] 1977 44: 63-80.* The Joan of Arc Institute was established during 1903-14 by Ottawa Catholic nuns for young employment-seeking women who needed security or lodgings. Examines the growth of the Institute during 1914-19 under the leadership of Marie Thomas d'Aquin and the eventual establishment of the Congregation of Sisters of the Institute of Joan of Arc in 1919.　　　　　　　　　　　　　　　　　G. A. Hewlett

3654. Choquette, Robert. ADÉLARD LANGEVIN ET L'ÉRECTION DE L'ARCHIDIOCÈSE DE WINNIPEG [Adélard Langevin and the establishment of the archdiocese of Winnipeg]. *Rev. d'Hist. de l'Amérique Française [Canada] 1974 28(2): 187-208.* Recounts the conflicts which arose after 1905 in Winnipeg between French Catholics and English-speaking Catholics over the administration of Monsignor Louis Philippe Adélard Langevin.

3655. Choquette, Robert. JOHN THOMAS MC NAILLY ET L'ERECTION DU DIOCÈSE DE CALGARY [John Thomas McNailly and the establishment of the diocese of Calgary]. *Rev. de l'U. d'Ottawa [Canada] 1975 45(4): 401-416.* John Thomas McNailly (1871-1952), the first bishop of Calgary, was an anglophone who defended the interests of the Catholic anglophiles in Calgary, particularly the Irish. The Pope, in selecting McNailly, believed that western Canada was English in both language and culture. Provides brief sketch of McNailly's life and accomplishments and discusses his problems as bishop, particularly with the French Canadians. Primary and secondary sources; 84 notes.
　　　　　　　　　　　　　　　　　　　　　M. L. Frey

3656. Choquette, Robert. PROBLÈMES DES MOEURS ET DE DISCIPLINE ECCLÉSTIASTIQUE: LES CATHOLIQUES DES PRAIRIES CANADIENNES DE 1900 À 1930 [Problem of morality and ecclesiastical discipline: Catholics of the Canadian prairies from 1900 to 1930]. *Social Hist. [Canada] 1975 8(15): 102-119.* During 1900-30 the Catholic minority (20 per cent of the population) in the Canadian prairies was split between francophone and anglophone, with the latter in the majority. Francophone clerics were more intransigent than anglophones in enforcing their authority, interpreting doctrine, and in relations with the Protestant majority on such matters as dancing, clerical dress, public schools, and mixed marriages. Adélard Langevin, archbishop of Saint-Boniface, Manitoba (1895-1915), and Monsignor Legal de Saint-Albert of Edmonton provide examples of especially intransigent francophone clerics. John Thomas McNally (1871-1952), archbishop of Calgary, 1913-1924, provides an example of a more liberal anglophone cleric. Based on Edmonton and Saint Boniface archbishopric archives and Calgary diocese archives; table, 55 notes.　　　　　　　W. K. Hobson

3657. Cliche, Marie-Aimée. LA CONFRÉRIE DE LA SAINTE-FAMILLE À QUÉBEC SOUS LE RÉGIME FRANÇAIS, 1663-1760 [The Brotherhood of the Holy Family in Quebec under the French regime, 1663-1760]. *Sessions d'Étude: Soc. Can. d'Hist. de l'Église Catholique [Canada] 1976 43: 79-93.* Describes the formation, recruitment, and nature of the elitist society, the Brotherhood of the Holy Family, founded through collaboration among Bishop François de Laval, Pierre Joseph Marie Chaumonot, and followers in Montreal, and its important influence on religious activities in colonial Canadian society.

3658. Cosette, Joseph. ARCHIVES DE LA COMPAGNIE DE JÉSUS, PROVINCE DU CANADA-FRANÇAIS [Archives of the Jesuits, Province of French Canada]. *Manuscripta 1979 23(1): 26-30.* The archives have been at St. Jérôme, Quebec, since 1968. Presents a short history of this institution, which was started by Father Superior Martin in 1842. It became an important source in the history of the Jesuits in Canada since the 17th century.　　　　　　　　G. E. Pergl

3659. Côté, André. LE MONASTÈRE DE MISTASSINI: SA SUPPRESSION OU SA FORMATION EN PRIEURÉ, 1900-1903 [The monastery of Mistassini: its suppression or formation in the priory, 1900-03]. *Sessions D'Étude: Soc. Can. d'Hist. de l'Église Catholique 1973 40: 92-111.* Examines the religious controversy between Cistercian authorities and the Archbishop of Quebec, Monseigneur Bégin (and his successor Msgr. Labrecque) over the establishment of a monastery for Trappists.　　　　　　　　　　　　　　　　　　　　S

3660. DeBonville, Jean. LA LIBERTÉ DE PRESSE À LA FIN DU XIXᵉ SIÈCLE: LE CAS DE *CANADA-REVUE* [Freedom of the press at the end of the 19th century: the case of *Canada-Revue*]. *Rev. d'Hist. de l'Amérique Française [Canada] 1978 31(4): 501-523.* The short life of the journal *Canada-Revue* (1890-94) clearly illustrates the capacity of the Catholic Church in French Canada to limit the freedom of the press. When the editors of *Canada-Revue* used their accusation of immoral activities against one cleric to declare that clerical reform was needed, the Archbishop of Montreal declared a total boycott against the journal. *Canada-Revue* eventually won damages in court, but never was able to reverse its financial losses. 63 notes.　M. R. Yerburgh

3661. de Valk, Alphonse. INDEPENDENT UNIVERSITY OR FEDERATED COLLEGE?: THE DEBATE AMONG ROMAN CATHOLICS DURING THE YEARS 1918-1921. *Saskatchewan Hist. [Canada] 1977 30(1): 18-32.* Deals with the complicated and often quarrelsome discussions of English-speaking Western Canadian Catholics attempting to establish a location for a college with degree-granting powers in Saskatchewan. The struggle centered on Regina and Saskatoon with the eventual victory going to Saskatoon through the federated college of St. Thomas More and the university there. J. J. Leddy, Father Henry Carr, President Murray (University of Saskatchewan), Archbishop Mathieu, Father Daly, and Father MacMahon played prominent roles in the eventual establishment of the federated college in Saskatoon. 54 notes.
　　　　　　　　　　　　　　　　　　　　　C. Held

3662. Drolet, Jean Claude. UNE MOUVEMENT DE SPIRITUALITÉ SACERDOTALE AU QUEBEC AU XXᵉ SIÈCLE (1931-1950): LE LACOUTURISME [A movement of priestly spirituality in Quebec in the 20th century (1931-50): Lacouturism]. *Sessions D'Étude: Soc. Can. d'Hist. de l'Eglise Catholique 1973 40: 55-91.* Researches the spiritual movement provoked by Jesuit priest Onésime Lacouture during 1931-39 as it emerged in Quebec.　　　　　　　　　　　　　　　　　S

3663. Flynn, Louis J. THE HISTORY OF SAINT MARY'S CATHEDRAL OF THE IMMACULATE CONCEPTION, KINGSTON, ONTARIO, 1843-1973. *Study Sessions: Can. Catholic Hist. Assoc. 1973 40: 35-40.*

3664. Huel, Raymond. THE IRISH-FRENCH CONFLICT IN CATHOLIC EPISCOPAL NOMINATIONS: THE WESTERN SEES AND THE STRUGGLE FOR DOMINATION WITHIN THE CHURCH. *Study Sessions: Can. Catholic Hist. Assoc. 1975 42: 51-69.* Describes the bitter competition and internal rivalry between the French-speaking minority and the aggressive Irish Catholics in western Canada for ascendancy in the hierarchy of the Church, showing how the problem went beyond episcopal nomination to concern the nature of Catholicism in Canadian society today (1900-75).

3665. Hurtubise, Pierre. L'ORIGINE SOCIALE DES VOCATIONS CANADIENNES DE NOUVELLE-FRANCE [The social origin of Canadian vocations in New France]. *Sessions d'Étude: Soc. Can. d'Hist. de l'Église Catholique [Canada] 1978 45: 41-56.* Between 1650 and 1762, 841 Canadians became priests, monks, or nuns, of whom 630 were women; they were drawn from all social classes.

3666. Hurtubise, Pierre. NI JANSENIST, NI GALLICAN, NI ULTRAMONTAIN: FRANÇOIS DE LAVAL [Neither Jansenist, nor Gallican, nor Ultramontane: François de Laval]. *R. d'Hist. de l'Amérique Française [Canada] 1974 28(1): 3-26.* Attempts to place the late-17th-century bishop of Quebec, François de Laval, in relationship to the men and ideas of his time, particularly Jansenism and Ultramontanism.

3667. Jones, Richard R. L'IDÉOLOGIE DE L'ACTION CATHOLIQUE, 1917-1939 [The ideology of the *Action Catholique*, 1917-39].

R. d'Hist. de l'Amérique Française [Canada] 1973 27(1): 63-78. The French Canadian newspaper *L'Action Catholique* steadily defended Catholic ideology 1917-39, criticizing the Bolshevik Revolution of 1917 and the Socialist and Communist organizations of Canada. It did not support Nazism but attacked the Jews and their immigration to Canada (1936-39), for they appeared as natural enemies of the Catholic Church. It supported private enterprise and all the traditional moral principles of the Catholic Church, notably the Sabbath. Based on the *Action Catholique* and secondary sources; 27 notes. C. Collon

3668. Kennedy, Estella. IMMIGRANTS, CHOLERA, AND THE SAINT JOHN SISTERS OF CHARITY, 1854-1864. *Study Sessions: Can. Catholic Hist. Assoc. [Canada] 1977 44: 25-44.* Following a cholera epidemic in 1854, the Sisters of Charity of the Immaculate Conception, was founded in Saint John, New Brunswick, to care for orphaned children, but expanded to include education of youth and care for the elderly during 1854-64.

3669. Langlais, Antonio. MESSIEURS DE SAINT-SULPICE DEVANT LE CONSEIL SOUVERAIN EN 1667 (LEUR TITRES DE PROPRIÉTÉ) [The gentlemen of Saint-Sulpice before the Sovereign Council in 1667: their titles of property]. *Rev. d'Hist. de l'Amérique Française [Canada] 1957 11(3): 393-399.* In 1667, the Sovereign Council, a judicial body in French Canada, confirmed the members of the Compagnie de Saint-Sulpice (the Sulpician order) in possession of property to which they held titles.

3670. LaPalm, Loretta. THE HÔTEL-DIEU OF QUEBEC: THE FIRST HOSPITAL NORTH OF THE RIO GRANDE UNDER ITS FIRST TWO SUPERIORS. *Study Sessions [Canada] 1974 41: 53-64.* Gives a history of the Hôtel-Dieu, a hospital founded in 1639 by nuns to provide medical care for the Indians. A paper read at the 1974 annual meeting of the Canadian Catholic Historical Association. S

3671. Laperrière, Guy. L'ÉGLISE ET L'ARGENT: LES QUÊTES COMMANDÉES DANS LE DIOCÈSE DE SHERBROOKE, 1893-1926 [The church and money: the collections ordered in the diocese of Sherbrooke, 1893-1926]. *Sessions d'Etude: Soc. Can. d'Hist. de l'Eglise Catholique 1974 41: 61-86.* Studies the financial sources of the Church in the Quebec diocese of Sherbrooke, based on the collections ordered during the episcopate of Bishop Paul LaRocque. Seeks an explanation for changes in church income and in financial administration. Draws conclusions on the development of the population and agricultural production during this time, as well as on the mentality and the religiousness of the ministers and congregation. Based on diocesan archives and secondary sources; 4 tables, 11 graphs, 55 notes. S. Sevilla

3672. Lavallée, Jean-Guy. L'ÉGLISE DE SHERBROOKE ET LES TRAPPISTES (1880-1948) [The Sherbrooke Church and the Trappists]. *Sessions d'Étude: Société Can. d'Histoire de l'Église Catholique [Canada] 1974 41: 9-24.* A history of relations between the Sherbrooke Church and the Trappist Order. Touches on the great anticlerical and secular crises in France in the 19th and 20th centuries, the internal structure and formation of the Order, and broader problems such as the emigration of French-Canadians to the United States, their repatriation in Quebec, and the colonization of less developed regions of the province. The Trappists failed in their attempt to establish a permanent order in Quebec. Based on Archives of the Sherbrooke Arch-diocese; 41 notes. S. Sevilla

3673. Lemieux, Lucien. LA PREMIÈRE CAISSE ECCLÉSIASTIQUE DU CLERGÉ CANADIEN [The first ecclesiastical fund of the Canadian clergy]. *Sessions d'Étude: Soc. Can. d'Hist. de L'Église Catholique [Canada] 1977 44: 5-22.* Discusses the establishment and administration of a fund for ill and aged priests of the Canadian Catholic Church during the 1790's, as well as further financial aid during the 1830's.

3674. Maurault, Olivier. LES DIVERS MOTIFS QUI ONT AMENÉ SAINT-SULPICE A MONTRÉAL [The diverse motives which led Saint-Sulpice to Montreal]. *Rev. d'Hist. de l'Amérique Française [Canada] 1957 11(1): 3-9.* Discusses the motives which led the Compagnie de Saint-Sulpice (the Sulpician order) to establish itself in the new French settlement of Montreal in the 1630's-50's, stressing the role of Jean Jacques Olier.

3675. Miller, James R. HONORÉ MERCIER, LA MINORITÉ PROTESTANTE DU QUÉBEC ET LA LOI RELATIVE AU RÈGLEMENT DE LA QUESTION DES BIENS DES JÉSUITES [Honoré Mercier, the Protestant minority of Quebec, and the law governing the question of the properties belonging to the Jesuits]. *Rev. d'Hist. de l'Amérique Française [Canada] 1974 27(4): 483-508.* Recounts the attempt of Honoré Mercier, First Minister of Quebec, to resolve the problems occasioned by legislation governing the disposition of lands once granted to the Jesuits, following his rise to power in 1886.

3676. Nearing, Peter. REV. JOHN R. MAC DONALD, ST. JOSEPH'S COLLEGE AND THE UNIVERSITY OF ALBERTA. *Study Sessions: Can. Catholic Hist. Assoc. 1975 42: 70-90.* John Roderick MacDonald (b. 1891), a Basilian Father, undertook Archbishop O'Leary's 1922-23 project of organizing a Catholic university in Edmonton, thus working toward the evangelization of the large immigrant population of the West, despite his own failing health.

3677. Noppen, Luc. L'ÉVOLUTION DE L'ARCHITECTURE RELIGIEUSE EN NOUVELLE-FRANCE [The evolution of religious architecture in New France]. *Sessions d'Étude: Soc. Can. d'Hist. de l'Église Catholique [Canada] 1976 43: 69-78.* Discusses the principal architectural types characteristic of the period, 1600-1760.

3678. Paré, Marius. LE ROLE DES ÉVÊQUES DE CHICOUTIMI DANS L'OEUVRE DU SÉMINAIRE [The role of the bishops of Chicoutimi in the work of the seminary]. *Sessions D'Étude: Soc. Can. d'Hist. de l'Eglise Catholique 1973 40: 113-124.* Gives a history of the bishops of the Séminaire de Chicoutimi in Quebec from its foundation in 1873 to the present. S

3679. Poelzer, Irene A. THE CATHOLIC NORMAL SCHOOL ISSUE IN THE NORTHWEST TERRITORIES, 1884-1900. *Study Sessions: Can. Catholic Hist. Assoc. 1975 42: 5-28.* The real reason behind the loss of the Catholic Church's right to separate normal schools was not its inability to meet legitimate requirements, but political opportunism and growing intolerance in the North-West during 1884-1900.

3680. Price, Brian J. THE ARCHIVES OF THE ARCHDIOCESE OF KINGSTON. *Study Sessions: Can. Catholic Hist. Assoc. 1973 40: 21-26.* Describes material in Kingston archives, including information on bishops of the Archdiocese of Kingston, beginning with Alexander Macdonell (1760?-1840). S

3681. Savard, Pierre. SUR LES NOMS DE PAROISSES AU QUÉBEC, DES ORIGINES À 1925 [On parish names in Quebec, from the beginning until 1925]. *Sessions d'Étude: Soc. Can. d'Hist. de l'Eglise Catholique 1974 41: 105-113.* Studies the religious orientation of town and parish names in Quebec, and evaluates the evolution of religious feeling during 1600-1925. Discusses the question of the origin of church names, stressing chronology as a key to recurring themes particular to Quebec: Irish names accompanying emigration, and Jesuit and Franciscan cycles. Catalogues names by number and subject. Based on departmental archives and secondary sources; 9 notes. S. Sevilla

3682. Simard, Jean. CULTES LITURGIQUES ET DÉVOTIONS POPULAIRES DANS LES COMTÉS DE PORTNEUF ET DU LAC-SAINT-JEAN [Liturgical cults and popular devotions in the counties of Portneuf and Lac-Saint-Jean]. *Sessions d'Études: Soc. Can. d'Hist. de l'Église Catholique [Canada] 1976 43: 5-14.* Presents the results of research and surveys on the close relation between liturgical cults and popular devotions in Quebec, comparing them to similar developments in France.

3683. Simard, Ovide-D. SÉMINAIRE DE CHICOUTIMI, 1873-1973: COUP D'OEIL SUR LE SIÈCLE ECOULÉ [Séminaire de Chicoutimi, 1873-1973: a glance at the past century]. *Sessions D'Étude: Soc. Can. de l'Eglise Catholique 1973: 40: 125-130.* The oldest living Superior of the Chicoutimi seminary reflects on its hundred-year existence. S

3684. Spigelman, Martin S. RACE ET RELIGION: LES ACADIENS ET LA HIÉRARCHIE CATHOLIQUE IRLANDAISE DU NOUVEAU-BRUNSWICK [Race and religion: the Acadians and the

Irish Catholic hierarchy of New Brunswick]. *R. d'Hist. de l'Amérique Française 1975 29(1): 69-85.* In 1900, increasing population and economic power led the French-speaking Acadians of New Brunswick to vie for high clerical positions in the Irish dominated Catholic Church. The conflict centered on racial and linguistic issues. The Irish feared the Acadians might reach a compromise with the English Protestant population of New Brunswick and sabotaged attempts to teach the French language and to publish French language newspapers. Based on primary and secondary sources; 62 notes.　　　　　C. Collon

3685. Stortz, Gerald J. ARCHBISHOP LYNCH AND THE TORONTO SAVINGS BANK. *Study Sessions: Can. Catholic Hist. Assoc. [Canada] 1978 45: 5-19.* John Joseph Lynch, the first Roman Catholic archbishop of Toronto, helped set up the Toronto Savings Bank to aid the poor of the city, but was unable to prevent the bank from being used for more secular, profit-oriented aims during the 1870's.

3686. Voisine, Nive. L'ÉPISCOPAT QUÉBÉCOIS AU MOMENT DE LA FORMATION DU DIOCÈSE DE SHERBROOKE, 1874 [The Quebec episcopate at the time of the formation of the diocese of Sherbrooke, 1874]. *Sessions d'Étude Soc. Can. d'Hist. de l'Eglise Catholique 1974 41: 25-41.* A biographical sketch of six bishops of the Sherbrooke Diocese studying conflicts dividing the episcopate, such as opposition to modern thought, to liberalism, and to changes in education. A reunion (1872) to celebrate the bicentennial of the Quebec seat became a confrontation between the two rival clans of bishops, the "idealists": Taschereau, La Rocque, and Langevin; and the "realists": Bourget, and Laflèche. Based on correspondence and publications in Diocese Archives; 43 notes.　　　　　S. Sevilla

3687. Voisine, Nive. UN DIOCÈSE DIVISÉ CONTRE LUI-MÊME, TROIS-RIVIÈRES (1852-1885) [A diocese divided against itself: Trois-Rivières, 1852-85]. *Rev. de l'U. d'Ottawa [Canada] 1977 47(1-2): 226-236.* The Trois-Rivières diocese which extended north and south of the St. Lawrence River was divided in 1885, the southern part becoming the Nicolet diocese. It ended a 15 year feud inside the diocese between the north and the south among the clergy of opposite philosophies, added to financial difficulties, and the threat of the transfer of the Nicolet seminary. Primary and secondary sources; 51 notes.　　　　　G. P. Cleyet

3688. Zink, Ella. CHURCH AND IMMIGRATION: THE SISTERS OF SERVICE, ENGLISH CANADA'S FIRST MISSIONARY CONGREGATION OF SISTERS, 1920-1930. *Study Sessions: Can. Catholic Hist. Assoc. [Canada] 1976 43: 23-38.* Sketches the broad background against which the Sisters of Service were founded and developed, beginning in Toronto, and working especially among the largely Protestant populations of new settlers in Western Canada.

3689. —. TABLE RONDE [Round table]. *Sessions d'Étude: Soc. Can. d'Hist. de l'Église Catholique [Canada] 1971 (38): 85-98.*
Hurtubise, Pierre. LE CENTRE DE RECHERCHE EN HISTOIRE RELIGIEUSE DU CANADA [Center for research on the religious history of Canada], *pp. 85-88.* Discusses objectives of the Center for Research on the Religious History of Canada for the Canadian Catholic Historical Association, including an inventory of sources and annual congresses.
Lacroix, R. P. Bernard. UN CENTRE D'ÉTUDE DES RELIGIONS POPULAIRES [A center for the study of popular religions], *pp. 88-94.* Discusses objectives of the Center for the Study of Popular Religions for the Canadian Catholic Historical Association, including the founding of a museum of ecclesiastical artifacts and a public archives.
Hardy, M. René. LES INSTITUTS D'HISTOIRE [Historical Institutes], *pp. 94-98.* Discusses objectives of the Historical Institutes for the Canadian Catholic Historical Association, including the publication of documents whose access is difficult and the participation of university faculty in the work of the Association.

Dukhobor

3690. Becker, A. THE LAKE GENEVA MISSION: WAKAW, SASKATCHEWAN. *Saskatchewan Hist. [Canada] 1976 29(2): 51-64.* In 1903 when the Presbyterian Church of Canada decided to establish a medical mission to serve the Dukhobors and Galicians of Western Canada they selected the Reverend George Arthur, originally from Hazel Grove, Prince Edward Island. He served in that position at the Lake Geneva Mission on Crooked Lake until 1908 when he was replaced by Reverend Robert George Scott, M.D., who served until the hospital and mission closed in 1942. A description of hospital problems during World War I and the Depression in Western Canada provides the bulk of the article. 6 photos, 34 notes.　　　　　C. Held

3691. Betke, Carl. THE MOUNTED POLICE AND THE DOUKHOBORS IN SASKATCHEWAN, 1899-1909. *Saskatchewan Hist. [Canada] 1974 27(1): 1-14.* Following the initial need for the Royal Canadian Mounted Police to safeguard the province from the Indians, the force faced the necessity of being drastically reduced or changing its mission. The latter was the case and many new kinds of services were given by the officers to the settlers in the prairie West. Police comments on the suitability of certain ethnic groups for agricultural pursuits were not required but were made by the constables in their reports. These reports shed light upon the social and economic problems of the period. Personal antipathy toward certain ethnic groups was often overcome if they were successful as farmers. This was true in the case of the Galicians, Mennonites, and Mormons, and particularly the Doukhobors. The Doukhobors' tradition to "submit to no human authority" sorely tried the tolerance of the Mounted Police during their first decade in Canada. The major reason for the problems that did exist is the change in policy toward the Doukhobor settlement, by the federal government. 2 illus., 60 notes.　　　　　C. Held

3692. Legebokoff, Peter P. PORTRAIT OF DOUKHOBORS: INTRODUCTION. *Sound Heritage [Canada] 1977 6(4): 12-21.* Offers a history, 1652-1908, of the Christian Community of Universal Brotherhood, also known as Dukhobors; recounts early oppression in Russia and immigration to Nova Scotia in 1899, Saskatchewan in 1905, and British Columbia in 1908.

3693. Lyons, John. THE (ALMOST) QUIET EVOLUTION: DOUKHOBOR SCHOOLING IN SASKATCHEWAN. *Can. Ethnic Studies [Canada] 1976 8(1): 23-37.* Describes efforts to bring public education to the Saskatchewan Dukhobors since 1905 and the circumstances surrounding their eventual acceptance of public schools.

3694. McCormick, P. L. THE DOUKHOBORS IN 1904. *Saskatchewan Hist. [Canada] 1978 31(1): 12-19.* The year 1904 was pivotal in the early history of the Doukhobors in Canada. The earliest groups came from three different backgrounds and had varying commitments to communal life. They also lacked leadership. The arrival of Peter Verigin in the Yorkton colonies in December 1902 solved the leadership problem and brought a vigorous move to reimpose communalism. A major objective in this, self-sufficiency, was nearly achieved in 1904. The same year, however, saw the arrival of the railway in the area of some of the settlements and the isolation the group had sought was gone forever. Photo, map, 35 notes.　　　　　C. Held

3695. Mealing, F. M. PORTRAITS OF DOUKHOBORS: PREFACE AND CHRONOLOGY. *Sound Heritage [Canada] 1977 6(4): 1-11.* Discusses the social structure, economic conditions, values, and religious beliefs of the Christian Community of Universal Brotherhood, or Dukhobors, a communalistic religious sect which migrated from Russia to Saskatchewan and eventually settled in British Columbia; includes a chronology, 1652-1976.

3696. Woodcock, George. THE SPIRIT WRESTLERS: DOUKHOBORS IN RUSSIA AND CANADA. *Hist. Today [Great Britain] 1977 27(3): 152-158; (4): 249-255.* Part I. Outlines the history of the Dukhobor sect in Russia 1654-1890's and their emigration to Canada in 1898-99 because of religious persecution. Part II. Describes the Dukhobors as a militant religious sect led by Peter Nerigin, and their emigration from tsarist Russia to Canada, 1898-1902.

3697. —. THE DOUKHOBORS. *Sound Heritage [Canada] 1977 6(4): 23-77.* Fourteen members of the Christian Community of Universal Brotherhood, also known as Dukhobors, reminisce about immigration, the early days in Russia, and daily life in British Columbia, 1880's-1976.

Lutheran

3698. Schwermann, Albert H. MY DEBT OF GRATITUDE TO THE U.S.A. *Concordia Hist. Inst. Q. 1977 50(1): 23-31.* The author was born in Jefferson City, Missouri, in 1891. He became a Lutheran minister in 1913 and served in Mellowdale, Alberta, before becoming the president and a faculty member of Concordia College in Edmonton. His career at Concordia spanned 42 years. Expresses gratitude for the upbringing and educational experiences he enjoyed in the United States. 6 notes.
W. T. Walker

3699. Threinen, Norman J. THE STUERMER UNION MOVEMENT IN CANADA. *Concordia Hist. Inst. Q. 1973 46(4): 148-157.* An early (1922) attempt at unity among Lutheran synods in Western Canada.
S

Politics

Responses to Specific Events and Political Leaders

3700. Brennan, J. William. WOOING THE "FOREIGN VOTE": SASKATCHEWAN POLITICS AND THE IMMIGRANT, 1905-1919. *Prairie Forum [Canada] 1978 3(1): 61-77.* The power of the Liberal Party was based on its ability to attract the votes of both the native-born and the immigrant.

3701. Galarneau, France. L'ÉLECTION PARTIELLE DU QUARTIER-OUEST DE MONTRÉAL EN 1832: ANALYSE POLITICO-SOCIALE [The special election of Montreal's western quarter in 1832: a social and political analysis]. *Rev. d'Hist. de l'Amerique Française [Canada] 1979 32(4): 565-584.* The resignation of a representative to the Assembly prompted a special election in Montreal's western quarter. The election exacerbated the social, economic, and ethnic tensions of the city; threats, violence, and deaths resulted. Though the French Canadian party defeated the British party, the real significance of the election lay in its stimulation of French Canadian bitterness regarding British immigration, British land monopolization, and frequent interference from the British Parliament. 4 tables, 35 notes.
M. R. Yerburgh

3702. Jones, Frederick. BISHOPS IN POLITICS: ROMAN CATHOLIC V. PROTESTANT IN NEWFOUNDLAND 1860-2. *Can. Hist. R. 1974 55(4): 408-421.* Adds to what has already been written about the ousting of the Liberal government in Newfoundland in 1861 by detailing the several newspaper interventions of the Anglican Bishop, Edward Feild. Describes how these interventions so upset the Roman Catholic Bishop, John Thomas Mullock, an influential reformer, that he lost his growing misgivings about the Liberals and worked for their victory with such imprudence that he facilitated their downfall. Based mainly on Colonial Office correspondence, Society for the Propagation of the Gospel letters and records, and Newfoundland newspapers.
A

3703. Jones, Frederick. THE EARLY OPPOSITION TO BISHOP FEILD OF NEWFOUNDLAND. *J. of the Can. Church Hist. Soc. 1974 16(2): 30-41.* Newfoundland was torn between two rival groups when Edward Feild became Anglican bishop there in 1844. The liberals included most of the fishermen, Roman Catholic in religion and Irish in nationality, while the conservatives were Anglican, of English background and included a majority of the merchants. The Protestant Dissenters, Methodists and Presbyterians, were ambivalent in their attitude towards the two groups. Feild's appointment was unfortunate, since the new bishop was High Church and ritualistic while most Anglicans in Newfoundland were Low Church and evangelical. Thus a new source for dispute arose. Feild fought the evangelicals on many issues, and his

relations with Roman Catholics and Methodists were not good, either. The conflict between Feild and his Anglican flock typifies the division in the Church of England as a whole. Primary sources; 74 notes.
J. A. Kicklighter

3704. Jones, Frederick. JOHN BULL'S OTHER IRELAND—NINETEENTH-CENTURY NEWFOUNDLAND. *Dalhousie Rev. [Canada] 1975 55(2): 227-235.* Compares the role of sectarian religion in the politics of 19th-century Newfoundland with that of Ireland, evaluating the reasons for the dissimilar outcome. From early predictions of disaster for Protestants if responsible government should come, to being considered a model at a later date, the fate of Newfoundland is followed through the careers of three important leaders of the day, Roman Catholic bishop John Thomas Mullock, politician Philip Little, and Anglican bishop Edward Feild. 21 notes.
C. Held

3705. Miller, James R. "THIS SAVING REMNANT": MACDONALD AND THE CATHOLIC VOTE IN THE 1891 ELECTION. *Study Sessions [Canada] 1974 41: 33-52.* Discusses the issues involved in the 1891 election in Canada and shows how conservative John A. Macdonald retained the Catholic vote. A paper read at the 1974 annual meeting of the Canadian Catholic Historical Association.
S

3706. Robertson, Ian Ross. THE BIBLE QUESTION IN PRINCE EDWARD ISLAND FROM 1856 TO 1860. *Acadiensis [Canada] 1976 5(2): 3-25.* In 1856 the head of Prince Edward Island's teachers' college suggested daily Bible lessons. The Board of Education rejected the suggestion, but evangelical Protestants launched a campaign for public school Bible-reading. Supported by most Tories, the campaign became the colony's most important political issue until 1860. Sectarian animosity replaced class and ideological divisions as the moving force in Island politics and resulted in an all-Protestant government in a nearly half-Catholic colony. 99 notes.
D. F. Chard

3707. Robertson, Ian Ross. PARTY POLITICS AND RELIGIOUS CONTROVERSIALISM IN PRINCE EDWARD ISLAND FROM 1860 TO 1863. *Acadiensis [Canada] 1978 7(2): 29-59.* Sectarian bitterness erupted in Prince Edward Island with a debate over Board of Education membership and the Prince of Wales College Act (1860), seen as a Protestant effort to gain state funds for their college. Feuding escalated from 1861, with attempts to incorporate the Grand Orange Lodge, and because of measures threatening Acadian schools. In 1863 bickering declined. Although verbal, not physical, the battles further divided Islanders and diverted attention from land reform. 132 notes.
D. F. Chard

3708. Tousignant, Pierre. LA PREMIÈRE CAMPAGNE ÉLECTORALE DES CANADIENS EN 1792 [The first Canadian electoral campaign in 1792]. *Hist. sociale—Social Hist. [Canada] 1975 8(15): 120-148.* In the first electoral campaign in Canada, in 1792, the francophone majority elected a disproportionately anglophone Legislative Assembly. Although corruption may have played some role, an analysis of the available returns of the propaganda disseminated prior to the election suggests that the anglophone candidates' appeal to colonial unity and loyalty had a stronger attraction than the francophone candidates' appeal to ethnic loyalty, especially among the French-speaking upper and middle classes. Based on newspapers and documents in Canadian Public Archives, Quebec Seminary Archives, and National Library of Quebec; 77 notes, appendix.
W. K. Hobson

3709. Trépanier, Pierre. LE 2 MARS 1878 [March 2, 1878]. *Action Natl. [Canada] 1977 66(5): 372-390.* On 2 March 1878 Lieutenant Governor Luc Letellier de Saint-Just, a Liberal, dismissed the Conservative Prime Minister Boucherville of Quebec and called upon Liberal Henri-Gustave Joly to form a new government. The dismissal was precipitated by the provincial government's railroad and fiscal policies, but the major issues of the following election campaign were the validity of the dismissal as well as religious and ethnic conflicts. Election results demonstrated the continuing rise of the Liberal Party in Quebec, supported by Anglo-Protestants. The replacement of Letellier by Théodore Robitaille as Lieutenant-Governor in July, however, may be seen as a victory of Canadian federalism over Quebec autonomy. Chart, 50 notes.
A. W. Novitsky

Political Elites

3710. Campbell, Colin. "THE PROTESTANT ETHIC," "RATIO-NALITY" AND CANADA'S POLITICAL ELITE: ETHNIC AND RELIGIOUS INFLUENCE ON SENATORS. *Soc. Sci. J. 1976 12(3): 159-173.* Analyzes the religious and ethnic values held by Canadian senators in a 1971 study.

3711. Ogmundson, Rick. A SOCIAL PROFILE OF MEMBERS OF THE MANITOBA LEGISLATURE: 1950, 1960, 1970. *J. of Can. Studies [Canada] 1977 12(4): 79-84.* Studies the religious, ethnic, and occupational makeup of the legislative contingents of the three major Manitoba political parties in 1950 when the Liberals were in power, in 1960 when the Progessive Conservatives held office, and in 1970 after the surprise 1969 victory of the New Democratic Party. Tests the validity of popular views about the composition of each of these parties. The NDP, despite its working-class rhetoric, is now represented mainly by members of the professional class. Concludes that systematic scrutiny of this kind is useful, because several widely accepted ideas on this subject were not supported. Based on the *Parliamentary Guide* and secondary sources; 5 tables, 6 notes.   L. W. Van Wyk

Voting Behavior

3712. Curtis, James E. and Lambert, Ronald D. VOTING, ELECTION INTEREST, AND AGE: NATIONAL FINDINGS FOR ENGLISH AND FRENCH CANADIANS. *Can. J. of Pol. Sci. 1976 9(2): 293-307.* Analysis from a sample survey conducted in 1968 shows that, contrary to prevailing notions, there is no drop-off in political interest with age and perhaps even some modest increases. 3 tables, 18 notes.   R. V. Kubicek

3713. Hamilton, Richard and Pinard, Maurice. THE BASES OF PARTI QUÉBÉCOIS SUPPORT IN RECENT QUEBEC ELECTIONS. *Can. J. of Pol. Sci. 1976 9(1): 3-26.* Based on a cross-sectional sample of eligible voters in the 1973 election. Excludes for methodological reasons anglophone population and distinguishes between Montreal and the rest of the province. Voters who in terms of socioeconomic status should be most attracted the the PQ give the party either the same or less support than do the more privileged. 9 tables, 30 notes.   R. V. Kubicek

3714. Hare, John. L'ASSEMBLÉE LÉGISLATIVE DU BAS-CANADA, 1792-1814: DÉPUTATION ET POLARISATION POLITIQUE [The legislature of Lower Canada, 1792-1814: the deputies and political polarization]. *Rev. d'Hist. de l'Amérique Française [Canada] 1973 27(3): 361-396.* Analyzes the membership of the legislative assembly of Lower Canada in the late 17th and early 18th century, and assesses its conduct and voting patterns.

3715. Piva, Michael J. WORKERS AND TORIES: THE COLLAPSE OF THE CONSERVATIVE PARTY IN URBAN ONTARIO, 1908-1919. *Urban Hist. Rev. [Canada] 1976 (3): 23-39.* Examines the Canadian election of 1919 with regard to the major losses by Conservative Party candidates in southern Ontario urban areas as compared with the prewar elections of 1908, 1911, and 1914. The analysis shows that class was more important in determining voting patterns than either ethnicity or religion and that the class patterns of voting in 1919 represent a culmination of prewar social and political trends rather than an aberration in working class voting behavior. Based on papers in the Public Archives of Canada and on secondary sources; 2 tables, 20 notes.   C. A. Watson

3716. Richert, Jean Pierre. POLITICAL PARTICIPATION AND POLITICAL EMANCIPATION: THE IMPACT OF CULTURAL MEMBERSHIP. *Western Pol. Q. 1974 27(1): 104-116.* Examines and tests a hypothesis using Quebec as an example that suggests how two cultural groups differ in the formation of political attitudes.   S

3717. Richert, Jean Pierre. POLITICAL SOCIALIZATION IN QUEBEC: YOUNG PEOPLE'S ATTITUDES TOWARD GOVERNMENT. *Can. J. of Pol. Sci. 1973 6(2): 303-313.* English- and French-Canadian children differed in their perception of the character and purpose of government but held similar views about its performance. Based on data gathered from a survey of elementary school children; 8 tables, 42 notes.   R. V. Kubicek

3718. Rudin, Ronald. REGIONAL COMPLEXITY AND POLITICAL BEHAVIOUR IN A QUEBEC COUNTY, 1867-1886. *Social Hist. [Canada] 1976 9(17): 92-110.* Examines voting patterns on the parish level within the strongly Liberal county of Saint-Hyacinthe in Quebec, 1867-86, not previously revealed in earlier county studies. The city's Liberal tradition developed largely because of the political stance of local church leaders. Saint-Denis parish's anti-Liberal tradition can be traced to that parish's subordinate position within the Saint-Hyacinthe regional economy. Based on sessional papers of Canada and Quebec and other published primary sources; 48 notes, appendix.   W. K. Hobson

3719. Taylor, K. Wayne and Wiseman, Nelson. CLASS AND ETHNIC VOTING IN WINNIPEG: THE CASE OF 1941. *Can. Rev. of Sociol. and Anthrop. [Canada] 1977 14(2): 174-187.* A unique opportunity to assess the relative strengths of class versus ethnic determinants of voting in provincial elections was offered by the historical development of class and ethnic relations in Winnipeg and the fact that the entire city was a multiple-member constituency for purposes of representation in the provincial legislature. Data analyses were carried out on areal units using census social area data, poll-by-poll voting results, and party and campaign literature. Class factors were found to be only marginally less important than ethnic factors in accounting for voting patterns despite a Liberal/Conservative/CCF party coalition and the lowest voter turnout in a provincial election historically recorded in Manitoba—factors which would tend to minimize class factors in voting. These results were corroborated by an analysis of transferable ballot data. Apart from minor differences in the relative weighting of class and ethnic factors, these results support the conclusions of an earlier similar study of Winnipeg voting patterns in the 1945 provincial election.   J

3720. Wiseman, Nelson and Taylor, K. Wayne. CLASS AND ETHNIC VOTING IN WINNIPEG DURING THE COLD WAR. *Can. Rev. of Sociol. and Anthrop. [Canada] 1979 16(1): 60-76.* Using a combination of poll and census tract data, this paper examines the relative strength of ethnic and class determinants of the voting patterns of three Winnipeg multiple member constituencies in the provincial elections of 1949 and 1953. Compared to the patterns in the provincial elections of 1941 and 1945, class voting remained high in Winnipeg South and Winnipeg Centre, but ethnic voting became stronger in Winnipeg North—the strongest base for left-wing parties in previous elections. We argue that these changes can be explained as a local effect of the larger changes in international relations between the capitalist and communist blocs during the Cold War. 4 tables, biblio.   J

3721. Wiseman, Nelson and Taylor, K. Wayne. ETHNIC VS CLASS VOTING: THE CASE OF WINNIPEG, 1945. *Can. J. of Pol. Sci. 1974 7(2): 314-328.* Based on census and electoral returns and using multiple regression analyses, shows class voting to be exceptionally high and ethnicity a confounding factor disguising class voting behavior. 6 tables, fig, 33 notes.   R. V. Kubicek

Labor, Unions, and Radicalism

3722. Avery, Donald. CONTINENTAL EUROPEAN IMMIGRANT WORKERS IN CANADA 1896-1919: FROM 'STALWART PEASANTS' TO RADICAL PROLETARIAT. *Can. R. of Sociol. and Anthrop. 1975 12(1): 53-64.* This paper challenges the traditional interpretation of European immigration to Canada between 1896 and 1919 and the Canadian experience of these immigrants in this period. The author rejects the view that most of the European immigrants settled on the land; instead, he concludes that large numbers became unskilled industrial workers. The author also emphasizes the serious class and ethnic tension which developed between the 'foreign' worker and the Anglo-Canadian business community, especially during the First World War and the 'Red Scare' of 1919. Indeed, in response to the apparent radicalism of many immigrant workers the Immigration Act was

dramatically altered in the spring of 1919. Immigrants who advocated Bolshevist ideas were not only excluded from the country, but were also subject to rapid deportation. Ethnic, cultural, and ideological acceptability became temporarily a more important factor than economic utility in determining Canadian immigration policy.
J

3723. Comeau, Robert. L'HISTOIRE OUVRIÈRE AU QUÉBEC: QUELQUES NOUVELLES AVENUES [The working class history of Quebec: some new avenues]. *R. d'hist. de l'Amérique française [Canada] 1975 28(4): 579-583.* Recent histories of Quebec's working class emphasize the exploitation of workers. New approaches are needed in retracing and interpreting the evolution of political consciousness among members of that class. Geographic precision, specific job descriptions, accurate wage and salary scales, and full knowledge about living conditions are necessary. A good history of Quebec's working class should be integrated with the general social and economic history of Quebec. Based on secondary works; 7 notes.
L. B. Chan

3724. Cook, George L. ALFRED FITZPATRICK AND THE FOUNDATION OF FRONTIER COLLEGE (1899-1922). *Canada 1976 3(4): 15-39.* To combat the brutal conditions in Canadian railroad, mining, and lumber camps, and to help assimilate immigrant laborers into Canadian society, Alfred Fitzpatrick (1862-1932) established the Frontier College. In its final development the laborer-teachers of the Frontier College faculty traveled and worked side-by-side with the camp laborers during the day and taught them evenings or Sundays. 12 photos, 43 notes, biblio.
W. W. Elison

3725. Kothari, Vinay. A CROSS-CULTURAL STUDY OF WORKER ATTITUDES IN A BICULTURAL ECONOMIC ENVIRONMENT. *Industrial Relations [Canada] 1973 28(1): 150-163.* Examines the attitudes of French and English workers of New Brunswick to show similarities and differences in the attitudes of the two cultural groups. Specifically, the worker's attitudes towards his coworkers, economic benefits, administrative practices, physical conditions, and the work itself are examined and analyzed. Overall, there are no significant differences between the attitudes of French and those of English.
J

3726. Larocque, Paul. APERÇU DE LA CONDITION OUVRIÈRE À QUÉBEC, 1896-1914 [A look at the condition of workers in Quebec, 1896-1914]. *Labour [Canada] 1976 1: 122-138.* Examines workers' lives in Quebec City's Lower Town when industries were diversifying, growing, and becoming mechanized. In crowded neighborhoods near the factories and commercial areas, workers lived in or close to misery and were plagued by poor working conditions and pay, disease, unemployment, fires, and monotony. In frustration, many turned to alcohol. Despite efforts by charitable organizations such as the St. Vincent de Paul Society and some feeble action by government, neither the law nor the social system provided much to alleviate conditions which produced a fundamental alienation of the working class. Primary and secondary sources; 93 notes.
W. A. Kearns

3727. McCormack, A. Ross. THE INDUSTRIAL WORKERS OF THE WORLD IN WESTERN CANADA: 1905-1914. *Can. Hist. Assoc. Hist. Papers [Canada] 1975: 167-190.* Assesses the contribution of the Industrial Workers of the World (IWW) to the radical tradition. In a continental and regional setting the IWW organized unskilled, itinerant, ethnically heterogeneous, and nonpolitical workers outside the classic labor movement. This situation led to friction with the American Federation of Labor, the Trades and Labour Congress of Canada, and the Socialist Party of Canada. Although it sought immediate improvements for workers, the IWW stood for sabotage and the general strike as weapons to defeat capitalism. Based on Frontier College Papers in the Public Archives of Canada, Public Records in the Public Archives of British Columbia, union proceedings, and secondary sources; 119 notes.
G. E. Panting

3728. Scott, Stanley. A PROFUSION OF ISSUES: IMMIGRANT LABOUR, THE WORLD WAR AND THE COMINCO STRIKE OF 1917. *Labour [Canada] 1977 2: 54-78.* Labor-management relations in Trail, British Columbia, were characterized by poor working conditions, poor wages, and poor living conditions. The Consolidated Mining and Smelting Company (controlled by the Canadian Pacific Railray) used various methods to maintain a nonunionized, subservient work force

ideally composed of a "mixture of races which includes a number of illiterates." Nonetheless, a majority of workers joined the International Union of Mine, Mill, and Smelter Workers local in 1916 and negotiated an agreement. That pact, inflation, xenophobia, wages, hours, the Wartime Elections Act, conscription, and the paternalistic antiunion stance of management were factors behind the strike, which ended in a company victory. Primary and secondary sources, and interviews; 92 notes.
W. A. Kearns

3729. Seager, Allen. THE PASS STRIKE OF 1932. *Alberta Hist. [Canada] 1977 25(1): 1-11.* The depression in the coal district by the British Columbia-Alberta border started in the early 1920's, with a decline in the price of coal. The worldwide depression led to confrontations between management and labor. In 1932, violence erupted in several mining communities, and the Mounties were called in. Management tried unsuccessfully to separate the Eastern European workers from the Canadians. An unusual aspect of the strike was the participation of women and children in parades and other demonstrations. By the mid-1930's the workers had the upper hand, and in 1936 they joined the United Mine Workers of America. 5 illus., 53 notes.
D. Chaput

3730. Snow, Duart. THE HOLMES FOUNDRY STRIKE OF MARCH, 1937: "WE'LL GIVE THEIR JOBS TO WHITE MEN!" *Ontario Hist. [Canada] 1977 69(1): 3-31.* The Holmes strike grew out of the Depression and was one of the few sitdown strikes in Canadian labor history. Presents the origins of the strike, its course, and its resolution. There were significant anti-immigrant, antilabor sentiments as well as simple antiunionism. 3 illus., 90 notes.
W. B. Whitham

3731. Weiermair, Klaus. THE ECONOMIC EFFECTS OF LANGUAGE TRAINING TO IMMIGRANTS: A CASE STUDY. *Internat. Migration R. 1976 10(2): 205-219.* Discusses the role of English language training in the employment and economic assimilation of immigrants in Toronto, Ontario, 1968-70.

3732. Williamson, Eileen. BUSH WIFE. *Beaver [Canada] 1975 306(3): 40-45.* In 1932, the author and her family flew to Casummit Lake in northern Ontario where the family had discovered gold. Discusses the weather, living conditions, food, and camp personnel, which consisted mostly of Swedes and Irishmen. Improvements were made at the mine in 1932, and the company, bought out by Jason Gold Mines, continued in operation until 1952. 5 illus., map.
D. Chaput

Foreign Policy Involvement

General

3733. Balthazar, Louis. LE STYLE CANADIEN ET LA POLITIQUE ÉTRANGÈRE [Canadian style and foreign policy]. *Pol. Étrangère [France] 1973 38(2): 131-148.* Outlines a few traits of Canadian national style to show how it determines and affects foreign policy, defining style as the British Canadian historical perspective, and speculating on the curious lack of French Canadian interest or influence, 1973.

3734. Miller, Carman. ENGLISH CANADIAN OPPOSITION TO THE SOUTH AFRICAN WAR AS SEEN THROUGH THE PRESS. *Can. Hist. R. 1974 55(4): 422-438.* Examines the English Canadian opposition to Canadian participation in the Boer War, 1899-1902, attempting to suggest the intellectual and social pattern of dissent. English Canadian opposition, though neither large nor widespread, found its strongest support among farmers, radical labour, Protestant clergy and anglophobic Canadians notably of Irish and German descent who defended their cause with a mélange of arguments from isolationism to Socialism and Christian pacifism. Based primarily on English language Canadian newspaper sources.
A

3735. Painchaud, Paul. FÉDÉRALISME ET THÉORIES DE POLITIQUE ÉTRANGÈRE [Federalism and theories of foreign policy]. *Études Internationales [Canada] 1974 5(1): 25-44.* Examines the theories of foreign policy as a facet of international relations. Questions whether federalism is a legitimate vehicle to discuss foreign policy. Notes the problem in federalism which permits the coexistence of individual state relations and national foreign policy. Examines the types of international activity a federal state may embrace; uses Canada as a model. Secondary sources; chart, 51 notes.   J. F. Harrington

French

3736.   Baker, Donald N.   QUEBEC ON FRENCH MINDS.   *Queen's Q. [Canada] 1978 85(2): 249-265.* Attempts to explain the reversal of French public opinion between Charles deGaulle's controversial behavior in Canada in 1967 and the Parti Québécois's electoral victory in 1976, resulting in widespread and apparently exclusive sympathy for separatism. Gaullists have embraced a cause whose successes underline the prescience of their hero, present a low-budget way of expanding French influence, and suggest affecting parallels with their own concern for French independence. A growing segment of the French left, deeply concerned with the "cultural question," has likewise taken an interest in Québécois politics. Cultural relations have greatly expanded since the Franco-Canadian agreement of 1965, and French tourism in Quebec has increased exponentially in recent decades. 2 notes.
L. W. Van Wyk

3737.   Chapdelaine, Jean.   ESQUISSE D'UNE POLITIQUE EXTERIEURE D'UN QUEBEC SOUVERAIN: GENESE ET PROSPECTIVE   [Outline of a sovereign Quebec's foreign policy: origins and prospects]. *Études Int. [Canada] 1977 8(2): 342-355.* Discusses the possibility of Quebec adopting an independent foreign policy. Examines the influence Paris and Ottawa would have as models for Quebec and considers the ramifications of an independent Quebec in relation to the United States and NATO and other international bodies.
J. F. Harrington, Jr.

3738.   De Goumois, Michel.   LE CANADA ET LA FRANCOPHONIE   [Canada and "Francophonie"]. *Études Internationales [Canada] 1974 5(2): 355-366.* Discusses Canada's bilateral relations with France, Belgium, and the French-speaking African states as well as Ottawa's involvement with multinational francophone institutions, especially the Agency for Cultural and Technical Cooperation, the Conference of Education Ministers (1960), the Conference of Ministers for Youth and Sports (1969), and various private French-speaking associations.
J. F. Harrington

3739.   Filion, Jacques.   DE GAULLE, LA FRANCE ET LE QUEBEC   [de Gaulle, France and Quebec]. *Rev. de l'U. d'Ottawa [Canada] 1975 45(3): 295-319.* Analyzes Charles de Gaulle's views of French Canadians and their political milieu. All Frenchmen, according to de Gaulle, represent a particular interest in the world. Primary and secondary sources; 66 notes.   M. L. Frey

3740.   Fontaine, André.   LA FRANCE ET LE QUEBEC   [France and Quebec]. *Études Int. [Canada] 1977 8(2): 393-402.* Discusses foreign relations between France and Canada from the 18th century to 1967. Reflects on the effect of deGaulle's 1967 Montreal address calling for a free Quebec and notes the new relationship between Pierre Elliott Trudeau and Valery Giscard d'Estaing. Secondary sources; 3 notes.
J. F. Harrington, Jr.

3741.   Gay, Daniel.   LA PRESSE D'EXPRESSION FRANÇAISE DU QUÉBEC ET L'AMÉRIQUE LATINE INVENTAIRE D'EDITORIAUX ET DE PARA-EDITORIAUX, 1959-1973   [The French press of Quebec on Latin America: an inventory of editorials, 1959-73]. *Études Int. [Canada] 1976 7(3): 359-392.* This subject-author inventory of signed and unsigned editorials appearing daily in *l'Action Catholique* and *Le Soleil* of Quebec, and *Le Devoir* and *La Presse* of Montreal, 1959-73, facilitates the study of Canadian-Latin American and Quebec-Latin American relations. Secondary sources; 3 notes.
J. F. Harrington, Jr.

3742.   Léger, Jean-Marc.   BUILDING THE FRENCH-SPEAKING COMMUNITY: AN EXCITING VENTURE IN THE ART OF COOPERATION.   *Int. Perspectives [Canada] 1975 (6): 50-57.* Discusses attempts to form cooperative bonds between French-speaking nations in international relations, 1950's-70's, including France, regions of Africa, and Quebec, Canada.

3743.   Painchaud, Paul.   LE ROLE INTERNATIONAL DU QUEBEC: POSSIBILITES ET CONTRAINTES   [Quebec's international role: possibilities and constraints]. *Études Int. [Canada] 1977 8(2): 374-392.* Notes the problems of dealing with a state that has not yet determined its form of independence. Nonetheless, two criteria are useful in anticipating foreign policy: first, states are influenced by their commercial, scientific, technical, and cultural environment, and second, they are influenced by ideology. Quebec must determine its affiliation with NATO and NORAD as well as its cultural alliances with such areas as Francophonia, the African states, and Latin America. Concludes by examining the methods available to implement an independent foreign policy. Primary and secondary sources; 21 notes.
J. F. Harrington, Jr.

3744.   Portes, Jacques.   "LA CAPRICIEUSE" AU CANADA   [The *Capricieuse* in Canada]. *Rev. d'Hist. de l'Amérique Française [Canada] 1977 31(3): 351-370.* Details an official visit by the French warship *La Capricieuse* to the ports of Montreal and Quebec during the summer of 1855. Though the anticipated result of increased Franco-Canadian commercial cooperation did not materialize, the voyage of *La Capricieuse* marked the initial resumption of ties between France and its former colony. 70 notes.   M. R. Yerburgh

3745.   Portes, Jacques.   LA REPRISE DES RELATIONS ENTRE LA FRANCE ET LE CANADA APRÈS 1850   [The revival of relations between France and Canada after 1850]. *Rev. Française d'Hist. d'Outre-Mer [France] 1975 62(3): 447-461.* Before 1850 France and Canada were linked only by a few private contacts. In 1855 a French warship, the *Capricieuse*, visited Quebec City. A French consulate was established there in 1858, and trade between the two countries started to grow. However, the French had no Canadian policy, and wished to avoid arousing British suspicions. Therefore the volume of trade was kept at a low level. Such ties as existed were mainly cultural and sentimental. Based on documents in the Archives nationales, the Archives du Ministère des Affaires étrangères, and secondary works; 40 notes.   L. B. Chan

3746.   Roy, Jean-Louis.   THE FRENCH FACT IN NORTH AMERICA: QUEBEC-UNITED STATES RELATIONS.   *Int. J. [Canada] 1976 31(3): 470-487.* Accounts for and describes Quebec government initiatives to establish a presence in the US. 9 notes.
R. V. Kubicek

3747.   Sabourin, Louis.   QUEBEC'S INTERNATIONAL ACTIVITY RESTS ON IDEA OF COMPETENCE.   *Int. Perspectives [Canada] 1977 Mar.-Apr.: 3-7.* Discusses attempts of Quebec to initiate foreign relations as a separate entity within Canada; examines the ascension of the Parti Québécois in politics and the aims of the French speaking populace, 1960-76.

3748.   Silver, A. I.   SOME QUEBEC ATTITUDES IN AN AGE OF IMPERIALISM AND IDEOLOGICAL CONFLICT.   *Can. Hist. Rev. [Canada] 1976 57(4): 440-460.* Uses French-Quebec newspapers, pamphlets, and other printed material to examine late 19th- and early 20th-century attitudes toward world affairs. Finds considerable sympathy for the "civilising mission" in colonial imperialism and for the Catholic, conservative camp in a perceived division of the world on ideological grounds. These sympathies and perceptions seem to have influenced attitudes toward French Canada's place in Canada and in the British Empire.
A

3749.   Vaugeois, Denis.   LA COOPÉRATION DU QUÉBEC AVEC L'EXTÉRIEUR   [Quebec and cooperation with the outside world]. *Études Internationales [Canada] 1974 5(2): 376-387.* Reviews Quebec's relations with Belgium, the French-speaking African states, and France. Primary and secondary sources; chart, 7 notes.
J. F. Harrington

3750.   —.   [FRANCO-CANADIAN RELATIONS].   *Internat. Perspectives [Canada] 1975 (1): 3-11.*
Halstead, John G. H.   RESTORING RELATIONS WITH FRANCE AND OPENING NEW DOORS TO EUROPE, *pp. 3-6.* Tru-

deau's visit to Europe promoted "new levels of mutual understanding and awareness on both sides of the Atlantic" and emphasized Canada's concern with the problems of security and detente.

Painchaud, Paul. THE NEW TRIANGLE: CANADA-FRANCE-QUEBEC, *pp. 6-11.* The renewed entente between Paris and Ottawa will affect Franco-Quebec relations. De Gaulle's visit in 1967 initiated a rapid growth in Franco-Quebec relations. Quebec must now "adopt a strategy and soundly-based doctrine on the international level."

L. S. Frey

Wars and Responses to Wars

World War I

3751. Boudreau, Joseph A. INTERNING CANADA'S "ENEMY ALIENS," 1914-1919. *Can.: An Hist. Mag. 1974 2(1): 15-28.* At the outbreak of World War I, roughly 200,000 "Austrians," mainly of Ukrainian descent, resided in Canada. Until the government released or paroled them, they constituted the majority of enemy aliens interned. The main camps were at Amherst, Nova Scotia; old Fort Henry at Kingston, Ontario; Kapuskasing, Ontario; and Vernon, British Columbia. Administration of the internment camps was unimaginative and bureaucratic. Based on primary materials in the Public Archives of Canada; 8 illus., 24 notes.

D. B. Smith

3752. Cameron, Brian. THE BONNE ENTENTE MOVEMENT, 1916-1917: FROM COOPERATION TO CONSCRIPTION. *J. of Can. Studies [Canada] 1978 13(2): 42-55.* In the summer of 1916, Canadian recruitment was falling sharply, and a widely discussed study declared that Quebec, with 40% of potential recruits, had contributed only 4.5% as of 1 January 1916. John Godfrey, a top recruiting official, who was determined to "bring Quebec into line," founded the "Bonne Entente" movement with the help of Arthur Hawkes, a journalist and expert on French Canada. Well-publicized visits were exchanged by delegations from Ontario and Quebec, but even at the banquets given for these delegations, little real rapprochement either on the War or on the Ontario schools question was in evidence. Godfrey ruined whatever benefits had resulted, by fraudulently luring a Quebec delegation to what was effectively a "Win the War" convention in May 1917. Archival and other primary sources; 70 notes.

L. W. Van Wyk

3753. Entz, W. THE SUPPRESSION OF THE GERMAN LANGUAGE PRESS IN SEPTEMBER 1918. *Can. Ethnic Studies [Canada] 1976 8(2): 56-70.* Explains the reasons behind the 25 September 1918 Order-in-Council prohibiting the printing of "any publication in any enemy language," with special emphasis on German language newspapers in Western Canada, including *Der Nordwesten* and *Der Saskatchewan Courier.*

3754. Hogan, Brian F. THE GUELPH NOVITIATE RAID: CONSCRIPTION, CENSORSHIP AND BIGOTRY DURING THE GREAT WAR. *Study Sessions: Can. Catholic Hist. Assoc. [Canada] 1978 45: 57-80.* On 7 June 1918, three Jesuit novices were arrested by military police at the Novitiate of St. Stanislaus, near Guelph, Ontario, for evading military service. Protestant militants' refusal to consider novices as clergy entitled to exemption from military service led to the incident and subsequent legal moves and investigation, during which Protestant leaders denounced the raid.

3755. Morton, Desmond. THE SHORT, UNHAPPY LIFE OF THE 41ST BATTALION CEF. *Queen's Q. [Canada] 1974 81(1): 70-80.* The 41st Canadian Expeditionary Force was the second French Canadian battalion to be sent overseas during the First World War and its story lends poignant insight into divisive forces at work in Canadian society prior to the war's outbreak. The Battalion's experiences symbolized the failure of Canada's military forces to attract competent French Canadians in the pre-war era and exemplifies a recurrent military problem in Canada. Based on printed and manuscript sources. 27 notes.

J. A. Casada

3756. Morton, Desmond. SIR WILLIAM OTTER AND INTERNMENT OPERATIONS IN CANADA DURING THE FIRST WORLD WAR. *Can. Hist. Rev. 1974 55(1): 32-58.* During World War I, more than 8,500 German, Austrian, and Turkish subjects were interned in Canada. Examines the work of the director of internment operations amidst the cross-pressures of official reluctance to act and a rising hysteria of anti-alien feeling. Based on records of the Canadian Departments of Justice and of Militia & Defence, and on the newly available papers of General Sir William Otter; 100 notes.

A

World War II

3757. Betcherman, Lita-Rose. THE EARLY HISTORY OF CANADA'S ANTI-DISCRIMINATION LAW. *Patterns of Prejudice [Great Britain] 1973 7(6): 19-23.* Discusses the passing of anti-discrimination legislation in Canada in the 1930's as a reaction against the anti-Semitism of Nazism.

3758. Granatstein, J. L. LE QUÉBEC ET LE PLÉBISCITE DE 1942 SUR LA CONSCRIPTION [Quebec and the Plebiscite of 1942 regarding conscription]. *R. d'Hist de l'Amérique Française [Canada] 1973 27(1): 43-62.* Quebec voted against conscription on 27 April 1942, while English-speaking provinces voted in favor of it. The LPDC (Ligue pour la Défense du Canada) actively worked against conscription. Premier William Lyon Mackenzie King, who had initiated the plebiscite, respected Quebec's decision until 1944, when limited conscription was decided upon. 62 notes.

C. Collon

3759. Gravel, J. Yves. LE CANADA FRANÇAIS ET LA GUERRE 1939-1945 [French Canada and the war, 1939-45]. *Rev. d'Hist. de la Deuxième Guerre Mondiale [France] 1976 26(104): 31-47.* World War II accentuated the differences between the English and French Canadians. In general, the French opposed conscription and participation in overseas warfare. As a compromise, only volunteers went overseas but conscription was instituted for home defense. Anglo Canadians tended to volunteer and readily supported the Commonwealth, but French Canadians tended to wait for conscription. Officers' schools and entrance exams were conducted in English only. French-speaking officers came from a different class (bilinguals or teachers) than the English-speaking officers. Before 1941 the air force ignored French Canadians, but after that some classes were taught in English and French, and courses in mechanics were offered in French. One of 85 squadrons was French Canadian. The navy modeled itself after the British fleet and gave no chance to French-speaking volunteers. 107 notes.

G. H. Davis

3760. Kelly, John Joseph. INTELLIGENCE AND COUNTER-INTELLIGENCE IN GERMAN PRISONER OF WAR CAMPS IN CANADA DURING WORLD WAR II. *Dalhousie Rev. [Canada] 1978 58(2): 285-294.* About 40,000 German prisoners of war and civilian internees were held at 25 sites in Canada on behalf of the British government, 1940-47. The decision to establish a Psychological Warfare Committee in Canada in 1943 followed obviously well-organized riots in camps at Ozada (Alberta) and Espanola (Ontario). Gestapo elements within the camps were responsible for many of the problems experienced in Canada. One of the major goals of the Canadian authorities was to reeducate the young, physically fit, thoroughly indoctrinated Nazis before they were returned to Germany following the war. Murder, even mass murder, plotted by the Gestapo, was one of the major worries of Canadian officials. 15 notes.

C. Held

3761. Martens, Hildegard M. ACCOMMODATION AND WITH-DRAWAL: THE RESPONSE OF MENNONITES IN CANADA TO WORLD WAR II. *Social Hist. [Canada] 1974 7(14): 306-327.* Canadian Mennonite response to World War II was primarily in the direction of assimilation. There was no united Mennonite policy. Church leaders divided over whether to try and protect baptized members only or to include adherents. They also divided over whether to accept alternative service. The Conference of Historic Peace Churches was formed to negotiate agreements with the Government on matters affecting pacifists. Some individual Mennonites chose jail when unable to satisfy a Mobilization Board of their conscientious objection. Many others, especially recent immigrants, volunteered for active duty. Based on secondary sources and the Conrad Grebel Archives; 79 notes.

W. K. Hobson

3762. Massicotte, Guy. LES ÉDITORIALISTES CANADIENS-FRANÇAIS ET LES ORIGINES DE LA SECONDE GUERRE MONDIALE [French Canadian editorialists and the origins of World War II]. *Recherches Sociographiques [Canada] 1976 17(2): 139-165.* Juxtaposes the opinions of eight contemporary historians concerning the origins of World War II with the perceptions of French Canadian editorialists writing in five newspapers during 1938-39. The editorialists perceived the movement of international politics in the same light as the contemporary historians. 91 notes.   A. E. LeBlanc

3763. Stokes, Lawrence D. CANADA AND AN ACADEMIC REFUGEE FROM NAZI GERMANY: THE CASE OF GERHARD HERZBERG. *Can. Hist. Rev. [Canada] 1976 57(2): 150-170.* Examines Gerhard Herzberg's experience in coming to Canada in 1935 as a visiting Carnegie Fellow and in later obtaining landed immigrant status. Refugees, including displaced scholars, had great difficulty entering Canada before 1945 because of high unemployment, antiforeign sentiment, narrow university hiring practices, and restrictive immigration policies. Only those refugees were successful whose cases were energetically presented to the government, as was Herzberg's by University of Saskatchewan president Walter Murray.   A

3764. Wagner, Jonathan F. BRITISH COLUMBIA'S ANTI-NAZI GERMANS: THE TUPPER CREEK REFUGEES. *BC Studies [Canada] 1978 (39): 3-19.* When Nazi Germany absorbed Czechoslovakian Sudetenland in 1938, many anti-Nazi Germans living there fled. Thirty-seven single men and 152 families were settled the next year in the Peace River district near Tupper, British Columbia. The Sudeten settlement was a successful venture. The dissatisfied and unqualified left for urban attractions or military service. Families were eventually located on their own farms. They soon took over and directed their own communities and affairs. 82 notes.   D. L. Smith

3765. Wagner, Jonathan. THE *DEUTSCHER BUND CANADA* 1934-39. *Can. Hist. Rev. [Canada] 1977 58(2): 176-200.* The Deutscher Bund Canada was a radical movement which conducted a propaganda campaign to convert German Canadians to Nazism.

3766. Wagner, Jonathan F. THE DEUTSCHER BUND CANADA IN SASKATCHEWAN. *Saskatchewan Hist. [Canada] 1978 31(2): 41-50.* The Deutscher Bund Canada, founded in Waterloo, Ontario, during January 1934, was closely linked to the pan-German movement sponsored by Hitler's Germany. Its move into western Canada began in the summer of 1934 with a tour by Karl Gerhard, the first national leader. Explains organizational terms such as *Gau, Gebeit, Bezirke, Ortsgrupper,* and *Stutzpunkt.* The number of members was relatively small, representing less than one percent of Saskatchewan's German population. The attempts to propagandize the Nazi ideology through German cultural programs and the speeches of Bernhard Bott, Horst Jerosch, and Henrich Seelheim were overt, and probably telling, until the summer of 1938. At that time the mood all over Canada began to change toward fear of Hitler's Germany. By late 1939 the movement had notably failed. Photo, map, 55 notes.   C. H. Held

3767. Wagner, Jonathan F. HEIM INS REICH: THE STORY OF LOON RIVER'S NAZIS. *Saskatchewan Hist. [Canada] 1976 29(2): 41-50.* Describes a group of 20 German families who settled in the Loon River area of Saskatchewan in 1929 and returned to Germany in 1939. Explores the difficulties they encountered in the Depression/Drought period of Western Canadian history, the role of the Deutscher Bund Canada, and the resultant reaction of anti-German neighbors. Hugo von Schilling's letters and articles provide source material. 3 photos, 53 notes.   C. Held

Social Organization

Family

3768. Andrews, Margaret W. REVIEW ARTICLE: ATTITUDES IN CANADIAN WOMEN'S HISTORY 1945-1975. *J. of Can. Studies [Canada] 1977 12(4): 69-78.* A consistently polemic intent characterizes recent literature on Canadian women's history. From 1945 to 1970, English-language authors emphasized the compatibility of a life inside and outside the home, and sought to recall women to the activism of earlier years through the example of those whose lives they described. French-language writers praised the traditional roles of mother and nun, especially as they helped to preserve French Canadian culture. In the 70's, trends in the two literatures tended to converge. Canadian writing on women tended to be less devoted to great individuals, and to be influenced by the ideas and rhetoric of a revitalized but much-changed women's movement. Based on the texts reviewed and secondary sources; 55 notes.   L. W. Van Wyk

3769. Denton, Frank T. and George Peter J. SOCIO-ECONOMIC CHARACTERISTICS OF FAMILIES IN WENTWORTH COUNTY, 1871: SOME FURTHER RESULTS. *Social Hist. [Canada] 1974 7(13): 103-110.* Study of 429 urban and 671 rural families in Wentworth County, Ontario in 1871 reveals that most occupational, religious, birthplace, and ethnic origin variables were not significantly related to number of children; only the wife's birthplace was. The observed urban-rural difference in family size was not due to the differences in socio-economic characteristics of rural and urban families. School attendance was significantly related to father's occupation, parental birthplace, and to basic urban-rural differences, but not to religion or ethnic origin. Based on manuscript census; 2 tables, 6 notes.   W. K. Hobson

3770. Doucet, Michael J. DISCRIMINANT ANALYSIS AND THE DELINEATION OF HOUSEHOLD STRUCTURE: TOWARD A SOLUTION TO THE BOARDER/RELATIVE PROBLEM ON THE 1871 CANADIAN CENSUS. *Hist. Methods Newsletter 1977 10(4): 149-157.* Using knowledge about Hamilton's boarders and relatives during 1851-71 it is possible to distinguish between the two groups in 1871. Many of the boarders were female Catholics of Irish birth. "In the final analysis, most of the associations seem to be inherently logical." 5 tables, 12 notes.   D. K. Pickens

3771. Gagan, David. LAND, POPULATION, AND SOCIAL CHANGE: THE "CRITICAL YEARS" IN RURAL CANADA WEST. *Can. Hist. Rev. [Canada] 1978 59(3): 293-318.* Competition for land among a rural community's families in the 1850's to increase productivity and provide landed inheritances for children created a land shortage, wildly fluctuating land prices and increased rural indebtedness during a period of general economic and agricultural instability. The land and economic crises resulted in the adoption of a more restrictive system of inheritance, later ages of marriage and lower marital fertility. But because these adjustments were essentially unpalatable an alternative prospect—emigration to a new farming frontier—proved more attractive; hence agrarian support for the creation of the new Canadian nation in 1867 and its territorial objectives—westward expansion. A microanalysis which employs manuscript census returns, aggregate census data, probate and real property records, record linkage, family reconstitution and quantitative analysis.   A

3772. Gagan, David. THE PROSE OF LIFE: LITERARY REFLECTIONS OF THE FAMILY, INDIVIDUAL RESPONSES AND SOCIAL STRUCTURE IN NINETEENTH CENTURY CANADA. *J. of Social Hist. 1976 9(3): 367-381.* Travel and immigration records offer clues to the quest for a one-class society in early Ontario. The unity of the family, children, servants, relatives, land, labor, and emotional outlook are explored.   M. Hough

3773. Masse, Jacqueline C. ATTRACTION INTERPERSONNELLE DANS UN GROUPE MUTLI-ETHNIQUE [Interpersonal attraction among a multiethnic group]. *Can. Rev. of Sociol. and Anthrop. 1973 10(2): 160-170.* Studies interpersonal attraction among a multiethnic group composed of 324 students, men and women, who lived in a university residence. Shows the relationship between different levels of attraction in pairs of individuals (these pairs being the unit of analysis), and degrees of homogeneity in these pairs with regard to nationality, length of residence, and proximity of residence. Interpersonal attraction is linked with similarity and reciprocity of choice. Relationships between men and women depend on different types of similarity.   J

3774.   Silverman, Elaine Leslau.   PRELIMINARIES TO A STUDY OF WOMEN IN ALBERTA, 1890-1929.   *Can. Oral Hist. Assoc. J. [Canada] 1978 3(1): 22-26.* Discusses 130 interviews with women who migrated to or were born in rural Alberta during 1890-1929, in order to assess the importance of oral history; concludes that history of exceptional women does not represent the cross section, that social hierarchy which related men to each other separated women from one another, that historical assessments of men's lives does not necessarily pertain to women's lives, and that historical periodization formed by men does not hold true for women.

3775.   Tepperman, Lorne.   ETHNIC VARIATIONS IN MARRIAGE AND FERTILITY: CANADA, 1871.   *Can. R. of Sociol. and Anthrop. 1974 11(4): 324-343.* The Canadian census of 1871 provided data for the estimation of ethnic variations in marriage and fertility. These variations largely account for the observed provincial variations in mean age at marriage, marital fertility, and birth rate, in 1871. Ethnic identity exercised an extremely strong influence on nuptiality and fertility, both directly and indirectly through the impact of ethnic custom on land distribution. Customs of inheritance and land partibility affected land inequality and mean size of landholdings, which in turn increased or decreased the feasibility of high levels of nuptiality and fertility. However, nuptiality was less influenced by land distribution than was fertility, implying that ethnic customs of nuptiality continued to predominate in the direct determination of marriage levels. It is concluded that regional and provincial variations in nuptiality and fertility can be satisfactorily accounted for by variations in ethnic composition and, perhaps secondarily, by historical patterns of land settlement. Ethnic reproductive practices were part of the cultural heritage brought to Canada by its immigrants, and they continued largely unaffected by the changed environment. Their continuity signified and maintained ethnic distinctiveness in Canadian society, but may also have had implications for the development of the Canadian "vertical mosaic."   J

Social Mobility and Social Status

3776.   Acheson, T. W.   CHANGING SOCIAL ORIGINS OF THE CANADIAN INDUSTRIAL ELITE, 1880-1910.   *Business Hist. Rev. 1973 47(2): 189-216.* Two groups of Canada's manufacturing elites are compared and contrasted, 1880-85 and 1905-10. The latter group tended to be organization men rather than owner-entrepreneurs, and social mobility seems to have decreased for them. Overall, differences between the two groups outweighed any continuity. Based primarily on standard biographical sources; 18 tables, 50 notes.   C. J. Pusateri

3777.   Anderson, Michael.   FAMILY AND CLASS IN NINE-TEENTH-CENTURY CITIES.   *J. of Family Hist. 1977 2(2): 139-149.* Reviews the first book-length product of the Canadian Social History Project at the University of Toronto, Michael B. Katz's *The People of Hamilton, Canada West: Family and Class in a Mid-Nineteenth-Century City.* Analyzes each of Katz's main themes: the distribution of wealth and power, social and geographic mobility, and the structure and role of the family. 10 notes, biblio.   T. W. Smith

3778.   Burley, Kevin.   OCCUPATIONAL STRUCTURE AND ETH-NICITY IN LONDON, ONTARIO, 1871.   *Social Hist. [Canada] 1978 11(22): 390-410.* London grew rapidly in the three decades before 1871. Its population of 15,826 made it the fourth largest town in Ontario. The foreign-born, particularly those from Great Britain, dominated London's work force. London's percentage of foreign-born (54%) was well below the national average, but typical of western Ontario towns. The Canadian-born were more active in the city's commercial sector and in some professions. Occupations apparently differed widely between ethnic groups, but the distribution by socioeconomic class was remarkably alike for all ethnic groups. Based on the 1871 census and on other primary and secondary sources; 9 tables, 45 notes.   D. F. Chard

3779.   Clement, Wallace.   INEQUALITY OF ACCESS: CHARAC-TERISTICS OF THE CANADIAN CORPORATE ELITE.   *Can. Rev. of Sociol. and Anthrop. 1975 12(1): 33-52.* Modelled after John Porter's 1951 corporate elite study, this paper updates an analysis of the social characteristics of this elite to 1972. By comparing means of mobility into the elite and class of origin for the two periods it finds that access to dominant corporations has become increasingly confined to members of the upper class. Mobility from working class origins has declined. Compradorization, the elite reflection of foreign penetration of Canada's economy, has provided more mobility for middle class Canadians than has the indigenous elite. There remains a powerful core of indigenous Canadian capitalists firmly rooted in the upper class. The private world of powerful people is examined as a means of elite interaction and selection. It is shown that traditional social forces tend to become more exclusive while new social forces bring new social types to power.   J

3780.   Cross, L. Doreen.   LOCATING SELECTED OCCUPA-TIONS: OTTAWA, 1870.   *Urban Hist. Rev. [Canada] 1974 74(2): 5-14.* The city directory and a historical atlas provide the basis for an examination of the occupational structure in Ottawa, Ontario, 1870; focuses on professional and skilled labor.

3781.   Cuneo, Carl J. and Curtis, James E.   SOCIAL ASCRIPTION IN THE EDUCATIONAL AND OCCUPATIONAL STATUS AT-TAINMENT OF URBAN CANADIANS.   *Can. Rev. of Sociol. and Anthrop. 1975 12(1): 6-24.* Applies the Blau-Duncan model of the process of social stratification to urban Canadian samples and additional independent variables. Focuses on the nature and extent of social ascription—the effect of family background, language, and gender on the educational and occupational status attainment of respondents, comparing francophone men and women and anglophone men and women. Social ascription is strong in that family background has rather strong and different effects on occupational attainment, through its influence on respondent's education, among women and men and among franco-phones and anglophones. Mother's education has, of all family background variables, the strongest effect on respondent's education among French males; family size has a greater negative impact on education among anglophones than among francophones; respondent's education has greater effects on occupation among francophones than among anglo-phones, and among men than among women.   J/S

3782.   Curtis, James E. and Lambert, Ronald D.   STATUS DISSATIS-FACTION AND OUT-GROUP REJECTION: CROSS-CULTURAL COMPARISONS WITHIN CANADA.   *Can. R. of Sociol. and An-throp. 1975 12(2): 178-192.* An analysis of data on negative affect towards selected religious, racial, and ethnic out-groups. The analysis is for working subsamples of English-speaking Catholics and Protestants and French-speaking Catholics, all native born. The independent variable, status dissatisfaction, is measured by four alternative procedures. Education and occupational status are control variables, employed in analyses within each of the three linguistic-religious groups. There are some slight, but statistically significant, direct relationships between status dissatisfaction and negative affect toward Jews and Blacks in evaluations by French Catholics. This trend was not found for the other groups.   J

3783.   Fox, Richard W.   "MODERNIZING" MOBILITY STUDIES.   *Hist. of Educ. Q. 1977 17(2): 203-209.* Reviews Michael B. Katz's *The People of Hamilton, Canada West: Family and Class in a Mid-Nineteenth Century City* (Cambridge, Mass: Harvard U. Pr., 1975), an important work comparable to Stephen Thernstrom's *Progress and Poverty* (1964) and one that takes a major step in more fully understanding social mobility. Argues against using occupations as a surrogate for class and analyzes the social structure of mobility. Includes work on poor Irish Catholics in Hamilton. 2 notes.   L. C. Smith

3784.   Gagan, David.   GEOGRAPHICAL AND SOCIAL MOBIL-ITY IN NINETEENTH-CENTURY ONTARIO: A MICROSTUDY.   *Can. Rev. of Soc. and Anthrop. 1976 13(2): 152-164.* This microstudy focuses on geographical mobility in a mid-nineteenth-century rural Cana-dian community and seeks to explain it in terms of levels of vocational opportunity. Levels of migration were as high in this rural community as they were in contemporary urban societies as individuals moved into and out of the community seeking to improve their economic status. But it is also shown that vocational mobility was a function of displacement or replacement and not of an expanding demand for goods and services. Thus the limited opportunities for vertical mobility were predicated on persistence; however, emigration was the usual response in the face of limited opportunities. Within this context 19th-century rural communities were able to assimilate, however temporarily, large numbers of transient employables.　　　　　　　　　　　　　　J/S

3785.　Gagan, David and Mays, Herbert.　HISTORICAL DEMOGRAPHY AND CANADIAN SOCIAL HISTORY: FAMILIES AND LAND IN PEEL COUNTY, ONTARIO.　*Can. Hist. Rev. 1973 54(1): 27-45.* The authors discuss population studies and quantitative methodology as an approach to Canadian social history. Describe the Peel County History Project and examine its findings on transiency among one township's population. The rate and persistence of transiency among all social and economic groups 1840-80 seems to contradict previous assumptions about the stability of rural society in Upper Canada and suggests the need for more quantitative, microanalytical studies of Canadian populations and social structures.　　　　　　　　　　　A. R. Shipton

3786.　Goyder, John C. and Curtis, James E.　OCCUPATIONAL MOBILITY IN CANADA OVER FOUR GENERATIONS.　*Can. Rev. of Sociol. and Anthrop. [Canada] 1977 14(3): 303-319.* Occupational mobility over three and four generations is examined in order to provide additional perspective on Canada's mobility processes and especially to test hypotheses of cumulative family ascription. Direct links between occupational status scores over three generations are found but, as would be expected, the effects here are relatively low compared to those between fathers and sons. Perhaps surprisingly the occupations of great-grandfathers and great-grandsons are found to show no association. Among other findings, there is some evidence of a status consistency effect (for family status in two earlier generations) on respondents' status attainments. White-collar respondents with white-collar fathers and grandfathers are more numerous than would be expected according to a simple additive model. Results also suggest that the effect of grandfather's status on occupation in the third generation is channelled through the grandson's education.　　　　　　　　　　　　　　J

3787.　Harvey, Edward B. and Charner, Ivan.　SOCIAL MOBILITY AND OCCUPATIONAL ATTAINMENTS OF UNIVERSITY GRADUATES.　*Can. Rev. of Sociol. and Anthrop. 1975 12(2): 134-149.* An analysis of the changing rates of social mobility and the changes in occupational attainment patterns of 2137 Ontario males who received BA or BSC degrees in 1960, 1964, and 1968. Although some findings are mixed, there is general support for hypotheses that a declining proportion of recent university graduates are likely to be upwardly mobile and that this decline will be more pronounced for graduates from middle level socioeconomic backgrounds than for those from lower socioeconomic backgrounds. Hypotheses relating the effect of socioeconomic background, year of graduation, major field of study, and postgraduate training on occupational attainment are also tested.　　　　　　　　　J

3788.　House, J. Douglas.　ENTREPRENEURIAL CAREER PATTERNS OF RESIDENTIAL REAL ESTATE AGENTS IN MONTREAL.　*Can. Rev. of Sociol. and Anthrop. 1974 11(2): 110-124.* Real estate agents are best understood as a type of modern entrepreneur. Provides model of their entrepreneurial behavior and distinguishes five career patterns: abortives, marginals, regulars, upwardly mobiles, and perennial high producers. Explains these patterns in terms of sales success through implementing productive entrepreneurial strategies; mobility opportunities or structurally imposed barriers to mobility, which in turn depend upon ascribed ethnicity and sex status; and individual decisions at crucial career phases.　　　　　　　　　　　J/S

3789.　Johnson, J. K.　THE U.C. CLUB AND THE UPPER CANADIAN ELITE, 1837-1840.　*Ontario Hist. [Canada] 1977 69(3): 151-168.* Mentions some of the historiographic problems that once existed around the early years of the Upper Canada Club. Discusses its origins and early years. Comments on the characteristics and interests of some early members. The picture of the club as excluding businessmen is not valid. In appendixes, lists the names of the politically significant in Toronto 1837-40, public offices held by members, some business directorships and interests, and the memberships of the management committees of the club in those years. There is considerable overlapping of the lists. Mainly secondary sources; 50 notes.　　　　　　　　　W. B. Whitham

3790.　Kaestle, Carl F.　MOBILITY AND ANXIETY IN A COMMERCIAL CITY.　*Rev. in Am. Hist. 1976 4(4): 504-512.* Review article prompted by Michael B. Katz's *The People of Hamilton, Canada West: Family and Class in a Mid-Nineteenth-Century City* (Cambridge, Mass.: Harvard U. Pr., 1975); discusses family organization and class structure in Hamilton, 1851-61.

3791.　Katz, Michael B.　THE ENTREPRENEURIAL CLASS IN A CANADIAN CITY.　*J. of Social Hist. 1975 8(2): 1-29.* Although an entrepreneurial elite ruled Hamilton, Ontario, in the mid-19th century, the individual members of the elite often varied—"the identity of its members swirled with the vicissitudes of commerce, the whims of creditors, the logic of character and the vagaries of chance." 2 tables, 42 notes.　　　　　　　　　　　　　　L. Ziewacz

3792.　Katz, Michael B.; Doucet, Michael J.; and Stern, Mark J.　POPULATION PERSISTENCE AND EARLY INDUSTRIALIZATION IN A CANADIAN CITY: HAMILTON, ONTARIO, 1851-71.　*Social Sci. Hist. 1978 2(2): 208-229.*

3793.　Lanphier, C. M. and Morris, R. N.　STRUCTURAL ASPECTS OF DIFFERENCES IN INCOME BETWEEN ANGLOPHONES AND FRANCOPHONES.　*Can. Rev. of Sociol. and Anthrop. 1974 11(1): 53-66.* Compares the data on French-British income differences presented by Raynauld et al. with more recent survey data. Comparisons between data gathered in 1961 and 1968 indicate a levelling of the income differences during that period. Although the nation-wide ration of francophone to anglophone incomes is now closer to unity, the income disparity has increased for persons in lower-skilled occupations. These and other findings invite various interpretations of discrimination as a variable related to income.　　　　　　　　　　　　　　J

3794.　Li, Peter S.　THE STRATIFICATION OF ETHNIC IMMIGRANTS: THE CASE OF TORONTO.　*Can. Rev. of Sociol. and Anthrop. [Canada] 1978 15(1): 31-40.* Recent developments in the study of ethnic stratification have placed a greater emphasis on differential opportunities by way of explanation, as opposed to the more traditional interpretation of motivational variations. Building on the basic stratification model of Blau and Duncan, this research evaluates the theory of differential opportunities with regard to occupational status differences among eight European immigrant groups in Toronto. A wide range of gross status differences exist among the various immigrant groups, and that inequality persists despite adjusting for intergroup differences in social origin, education, and prior achieved occupational status. To the extent that immigrants with similar qualifications are received differently in the occupational structure on the basis of ethnic origin, this study gives support to the theory of differential opportunities.　　　　　J

3795.　Linteau, Paul-André.　QUELQUES RÉFLEXIONS AUTOUR DE LA BOURGEOISIE QUÉBÉCOISE, 1850-1914　[Some reflections about the Quebec bourgeoisie, 1850-1914].　*Rev. d'Hist. de l'Am. Française [Canada] 1976 30(1): 55-66.* Examines the Quebec bourgeoisie at three levels: upper, middle, and lower. The upper bourgeoisie was primarily English-speaking, and directed the banks, insurance companies, trusts, railroads, steamship lines, and other major business enterprises of a national or international nature headquartered in Montreal. The middle bourgeoisie included a greater number of French Canadians, and concentrated on regional business and finance. The lower bourgeoisie served in clerical and managerial capacities at the municipal or parish levels. Based on unpublished theses and secondary works; 8 notes.　　　L. B. Chan

3796.　Moore, Larry F. and Daly, William G.　OCCUPATIONAL CHARACTERISTICS OF LEADING CANADIAN EXECUTIVES.　*Industrial Relations [Canada] 1973 28(1): 110-123.* Investigates the geographic origins, the social and educational backgrounds and the occupational and career patterns of top executives in Canadian companies.　　　　　　　　　　　　　　J

3797.　Piédalue, Gilles.　LES GROUPES FINANCIERS AU CANADA 1900-1930—ÉTUDE PRÉLIMINAIRE　[The financial groups of Canada, 1900-30: A preliminary study].　*Rev. d'Hist. de l'Am. Française [Canada] 1976 30(1): 3-34.* During 1900-30, Canadian economic activity was divided into four major sectors: financial, industrial, mining, and public services. The administrators of companies in these sectors formed an economic elite. Few of the men were self-made. Most were born in Quebec or Ontario, English-speaking, very well-educated, and from successful business families. They began their careers as managers or company lawyers. Based on published statistics and secondary works; 15 tables, 8 figs., 35 notes.

L. B. Chan

3798. Rich, Harvey. THE VERTICAL MOSAIC REVISITED: TOWARD A MACROSOCIOLOGY OF CANADA. *J. of Can. Studies [Canada] 1976 11(1): 14-31.* John Porter's *The Vertical Mosaic: An Analysis of Class and Power in Canada* (U. of Toronto Pr., 1965) presented a caricature of Canadian society. Refutes Porter's assertions concerning equality of opportunity and upward mobility. Lacking a coherent theoretical framework Porter reached a series of incompatible conclusions. Radicals accepted the conclusions because Canadian society as presented seemed to have a high potential for radicalism. Secondary works; 4 tables, 52 notes.

G. E. Panting

3799. Robert, Jean-Claude. LES NOTABLES DE MONTRÉAL AU XIXᵉ SIÈCLE [Montreal's "worthies" in the 19th century]. *Social Hist. [Canada] 1975 8(15): 54-76.* In 1892 J. Douglas Bothwick (1832-1912) published the *History and Biographical Gazetteer of Montreal to the Year 1892.* It includes usable biographical sketches of 491 Montreal notables. "Intellectuals" and professionals are overrepresented and businessmen are underrepresented, but it is otherwise a good source on the social composition of the 19th century Montreal elite. Almost 50% of the notables were born outside Lower Canada, in Great Britain for the most part. The elite was proportionally more English-speaking than the population. Occupations showed ethnic specialization. British-born tended to be in business; Canadian-born tended to be doctors or lawyers. Francophones formed the majority of the political class. Anglophones formed the majority of the business class. 4 tables, 28 notes.

W. K. Hobson

3800. Sheriff, Peta. PREFERENCES, VALEURS ET DIFFERENTIATION INTRAPROFESSIONNELLE SELON L'ORIGINE ETHNIQUE [Preferences, values, and intraoccupational distribution according to ethnic origin]. *Can. R. of Sociol. and Anthrop. 1974 11(2): 125-137.* Using a sample of French- and English-speaking engineers of the city of Montreal, the author tests the hypothesis that their occupational values influence their distribution within the profession. The values of the two ethnic groups are similar; however, their occupational preferences, which reflect social constraints, are more closely linked to their professional situation.

J/S

3801. Smith, David and Tepperman, Lorne. CHANGES IN THE CANADIAN BUSINESS AND LEGAL ELITES, 1870-1970. *Can. R. of Sociol. and Anthrop. 1974 11(2): 97-109.* Examines the social origins and activities of two Canadian elites, those of business and law, in the 19th and 20th centuries. It attempts a provisional explanation of the changes in access to wealth, authority, prominence, and influence that have occurred in the last hundred years.

J

3802. Tandon, B. B. EARNING DIFFERENTIALS AMONG NATIVE BORN AND FOREIGN BORN RESIDENTS OF TORONTO. *Int. Migration Rev. 1978 12(3): 406-410.* Immigrants entering the Canadian labor market start with lower earnings than native born residents, but their earnings equalize within a period of five years.

3803. Tandon, B. B. and Tandon, K. K. WAGE DIFFERENTIALS BETWEEN NATIVE AND FOREIGN BORN CANADIANS. *Industrial Relations [Canada] 1977 32(2): 202-214.* Estimates the extent of male-female wage differential in a local labor market among the native born and foreign born Canadians.

J

3804. Vaillancourt, François. REVENUS ET LANGUES, QUEBEC, 1961-1971 [Incomes and languages, Quebec, 1961-1971]. *J. of Can. Studies [Canada] 1978 13(1): 63-69.* The Laurendeau-Dunton Commission reported in 1969 that the incomes of French Canadians were among the lowest for ethnic groups in Quebec, and that Quebecers of British origin who could not speak French earned slightly higher incomes than those who could. Comparing figures for 1961 and 1971, the author finds that the former situation has shifted in favor of French Canadians, while the latter has worsened. The decade witnessed a sharp rise, both absolutely and relative to other groups, in the level of education of French

Canadians, and this, plus a slight increase in the proportion of the economy under Francophone control, helps explain the group's income gains. Based on census data, surveys by other researchers, and secondary sources; 26 notes.

L. W. Van Wyk

3805. —. [CANADIANS, IMMIGRANTS, AND OCCUPATIONAL STATUS]. *Can. Rev. of Sociol. and Anthrop. 1973 10(4): 366-372.*
Warburton, T. Rennie. CANADIANS, IMMIGRANTS, AND OCCUPATIONAL STATUS: A COMMENT, *pp. 366-370.* Criticizes article by Bernard Blishen on the regional class distribution of Canadian-born and immigrant males in the labor force, claiming he omitted a vast array of potential cultural influences, restricting occupational levels to those entered on coming to Canada. The author offers a proposition which incorporates some of the factors Blishen omits including important social structural variables. Biblio.
Blishen, Bernard R. CANADIANS, IMMIGRANTS, AND OCCUPATIONAL STATUS: A REJOINDER, *pp. 370-372.* States that the point of his previous article is that the level of education has an important influence on the class distribution of immigrants. Biblio.

E. P. Stickney

Health and Social Welfare

3806. Bilson, Geoffrey. THE FIRST EPIDEMIC OF ASIATIC CHOLERA IN LOWER CANADA, 1832. *Medical Hist. [Great Britain] 1977 21(4): 411-433.* In 1832, Lower Canada faced an epidemic of cholera. Canadian doctors learned of British and French treatments, and debated whether cholera was contagious. French doctors were more likely to see a link between emigrant ships and the disease, while English doctors were more inclined to think that climatic conditions created the disease. Doctors exposed their patients to a variety of treatments, leaning heavily on calomel, opium, and bleeding. Doctors faced some hostility, but no violence. There were some accusations, however, that cholera had been introduced to kill off the French Canadians. Quarantine was tried, but it did not prevent the spread of the disease. When disease struck, people fled the cities. Cholera contributed to the tensions of a year marked by ethnic and political divisions. 118 notes.

M. Kaufman

3807. Fingard, Judith. THE RELIEF OF THE UNEMPLOYED POOR IN SAINT JOHN, HALIFAX AND ST. JOHN'S, 1815-1860. *Acadiensis [Canada] 1975 5(1): 32-53.* Overseas immigration, economic recession, and other factors forced urban poverty to the forefront of public attention in the major centers of eastern British North America after the Napoleonic Wars. Responses were influenced by "interest in economy, order, and the wider welfare of the town. . . ." Heavy outdoor labor, such as stonebreaking, and indoor factory work were seen as solutions. Generally, however, organizations dispensed charity rather than campaigning for economic reform, and capitalists exploited patterns of unemployment. 101 notes.

D. F. Chard

3808. Keywan, Zonia. MARY PERCY JACKSON: PIONEER DOCTOR. *Beaver [Canada] 1977 308(3): 41-47.* In 1929, Dr. Mary Percy left England to practice medicine in northern Alberta. She began near Manning, among new immigrants from Eastern Europe who knew little English. After her marriage to Frank Jackson, they moved to the farm near Keg River. Most of her service here was with local Indians and Métis. With few medical supplies, inadequate transportation, and rarely any income from patients, she continued to provide medical service to the local population until her retirement in 1974. In the past few decades she has become a nationally known spokeswoman for Indian and Métis causes. 6 illus.

D. Chaput

3809. Negrete, J. C. CULTURAL INFLUENCES ON SOCIAL PERFORMANCE OF ALCOHOLICS: A COMPARATIVE STUDY. *Q. J. of Studies on Alcohol 1973 34 (3, pt. A): 905-916.* The records of 3 groups of men alcoholics, patients in a residential treatment center in Montreal, were studied: 34 English-speaking Protestants, 28 English-speaking Catholics, and 29 French Catholics. It seems that the social manifestations of alcoholism are influenced by cultural attitudes toward drinking and alcoholism and toward role expectations. Definitions of alcoholism in English-speaking cultures emphasize the sociopathic characteristics of alcoholism; French-speaking cultures put more emphasis on the physical consequences of excessive drinking. The Catholic alcoholics of the present study tended to adopt an 'incapacitated' role while the Protestants adopted a "sociopathic" role.　　　　　J

Education

3810. Choquette, Robert. ADÉLARD LANGEVIN ET LES QUESTIONS SCOLAIRES DU MANITOBA ET DU NORD-OUEST 1895-1915 [Adélard Langevin and questions concerning the school system in Manitoba and the North-West, 1895-1915]. *Rev. de l'Université d'Ottawa [Canada] 1976 46(3): 324-344.* In 1890, the Liberal government of Manitoba passed a law which abolished church schools; all children were to be educated in the public schools. The Catholic Church, with its own school system, opposed this. The national Conservative Party promised, if victorious in federal elections, to overturn the decision of the provincial government. Instead, the Liberal Party under Wilfrid Laurier won the 1896 elections. Laurier, though French-speaking and Catholic himself, engineered a compromise with Thomas Greenway, the Manitoba premier. All schools would be public, but there would be religious education for those who wished it between 3:30 and 4:00 PM. In addition, the French language would be used where 10 or more pupils were French-speaking (the same rights were given to other non-English-speaking groups), thus partially reversing Greenway's abolition of French as one of the official languages. Most Catholic prelates accepted the compromise, and were suported in this by the Vatican, but Louis Philippe Adélard Langevin, Archbishop of the Diocese of St. Boniface, which included the Prairie Provinces, refused to go along. He accused Laurier of being a traitor to his language and his faith, and continued to demand separate schools for Catholic students throughout his episcopate. 98 notes.
　　　　　J. C. Billigmeier

3811. Eid, Nadia F. EDUCATION ET CLASSES SOCIALES: ANALYSE DE L'IDÉOLOGIE CONSERVATRICE—CLÉRICALE ET PETITE-BOURGEOISE—AU QUEBEC AU MILIEU DU 19ᵉ SIÈCLE [Education and social class: an analysis of conservative ideology —clerical and lower middle class—in Quebec during the middle of the nineteenth century]. *Rev. d'Hist. de l'Amérique Française [Canada] 1978 32(2): 159-179.* Two conservative elements shaped the direction of Quebec's public educational system as it emerged during 1840-75. The clergy linked up with representatives of the lower middle classes to ensure an educational structure that was denominational, non-obligatory, and underutilized. Their intentions were transparent; children of the working classes were "kept in their places." 2 tables, 44 notes.
　　　　　M. R. Yerburgh

3812. Graff, Harvey J. WHAT THE 1861 CENSUS CAN TELL US ABOUT LITERACY: A REPLY. *Social Hist. [Canada] 1975 8(16): 337-349.* Replies to criticism by H. J. Mays and H. F. Manzl that the census is an unsatisfactory source for the systematic study of literacy in Canada in comparison to signatory documents. Contemporary literacy research in several countries has established a high level of accuracy in census self-reports. Proof that admission of illiteracy on census forms was not random can be found in the fact that literacy rates were quite similar in four cities of Upper Canada, and that the rates varied by age, sex, ethnicity, occupation, and wealth in a predictable manner. Although signatures are a direct indication of the ability to read and perhaps of some ability to write, nonsigners cannot immediately be classed as nonreaders. Using signatory documents alone poses a serious problem of unrepresentativeness in terms of sex, wealth, and probably ethnicity and occupation. 20 notes.　　　　　W. K. Hobson

3813. Hatfield, Michael. H. H. PITTS AND RACE AND RELIGION IN NEW BRUNSWICK POLITICS. *Acadiensis [Canada] 1975 4(2): 46-65.* In 1871 New Brunswick adopted a free nonsectarian school system, avoiding an Acadian rebellion only by allowing "a sectarian bias within the non-sectarian system." The dispute resurfaced in 1890 when the Catholic-dominated Bathurst board of trustees began reinstituting strong sectarian policies in their local schools. Herman H. Pitts, a newspaper editor and radical Protestant reformer, cited Bathurst excesses in prodding the province's Protestant majority to institute a "British cul-

tural hegemony." His militant approach failed as the people refused to rekindle the sectarian conflict. Primary and secondary sources; 3 tables, 80 notes.　　　　　E. A. Churchill

3814. Huel, Raymond. THE ANDERSON AMENDMENTS AND THE SECULARIZATION OF SASKATCHEWAN PUBLIC SCHOOLS. *Study Sessions: Can. Catholic Hist. Assoc. [Canada] 1977 44: 61-76.* Dedicated to educational reform, Premier James T. M. Anderson advanced two major amendments to Saskatchewan's School Act which prohibited religious garb and symbols in the public schools (1930) and suppressed the French language in grade one (1931). These actions occurred in a climate of anti-Catholicism and spurred nationalism among French-speaking Catholics, including those in Quebec. Covers 1929-34.
　　　　　G. A. Hewlett

3815. Huel, Raymond. PASTOR VS. POLITICIAN: THE REVEREND MURDOCH MACKINNON AND PREMIER WALTER SCOTT'S AMENDMENT TO THE SCHOOL ACT. *Saskatchewan Hist. [Canada] 1979 32(2): 61-73.* Originally a private exchange of letters between Presbyterian minister Murdoch MacKinnon and Premier Walter Scott, of the Liberal Party, concerning an amendment to the School Act which would force Catholics to support separate schools (thus enhancing the status of those schools) and to which MacKinnon was opposed, the controversy became a vicious public debate from 1913 to 1916. Scott wished to guarantee language and school rights to French Canadians and immigrants, while MacKinnon wished to impose Anglo-Protestant assimilation on them. Details personal vituperations on both sides. Follows MacKinnon's career up to the Church Union and his acceptance of a pastorate in Toronto in 1925. Delineates the preparation of an anti-French, anti-Catholic atmosphere which would lead to the appearance of the Ku Klux Klan in Saskatchewan in 1926. 65 notes.
　　　　　C. H. Held

3816. Jackson, James A. RAILWAYS AND THE MANITOBA SCHOOL QUESTION. *Tr. of the Hist. and Sci. Soc. of Manitoba [Canada] 1973-74 (30): 81-87.* Examines the Railway Disallowance Question and how this issue accelerated and intensified Manitoba's controversial School Question of the 1890's. Liberal Party legislator Thomas Greenway and his Attorney-General Joseph Martin, in an effort to rally Manitobans' support in a period when they were accused of corrupt bargaining with the Northern Pacific Railway after achieving the withdrawal of the Canadian Pacific Railway monopoly through Manitoba, reintroduced the issue of abolishing French-English school segregation which had a history of long dissatisfaction. The school question was a huge success and "the Liberal party held a monolithic control of the government of Manitoba." Primary and secondary works; 16 notes.
　　　　　S. R. Quéripel

3817. Jaenen, Cornelius J. AN INTRODUCTION TO EDUCATION AND ETHNICITY. *Can. Ethnic Studies [Canada] 1976 8(1): 3-8.* The concept of this special issue of *Canadian Ethnic Studies* is to provide a historical overview with essays from various relevant domains and areas of concern, with emphasis on the history of education as it relates to ethnic groups.

3818. Katz, Michael B. THE ORIGINS OF PUBLIC EDUCATION: A REASSESSMENT. *Hist. of Educ. Q. 1976 16(4): 381-408.* Assesses the expectations for and outcomes of public schools as tools for socialization in Hamilton, Ontario, during 19th-century industrialization.

3819. Lamonde, Yvan. CLASSES SOCIALES, CLASSES SCOLAIRES: UNE POLÉMIQUE SUR L'ÉDUCATION EN 1819-1820 [Social classes, scholarly classes: A controversy on education in 1819-1820]. *Sessions d'Étude: Soc. Can. d'Hist. de l'Eglise Catholique 1974 41: 43-60.* A history of the educational controversy raised by French-Canadian priest Abbot de Calonne on the importance of doctrinal vigilance by counter-revolutionary clergy in Canada against liberal "Lancastrian" schools modeled after British secular teaching. Studies de Calonne's letters to the *Trois-Rivieres Gazette* against public schools. Debate centers on the control of schools, the extent of modernization, and protection of the existing social order. Failure of the liberal primary schools was due to clerical efforts. Based on a previous study by Fernand Ouellet, *Éléments d'Histoire Sociale du Bas-Canada* (Cahiers du Quebec, 1972). 49 notes.　　　　　S. Sevilla

3820. Miller, James R. D'ALTON MCCARTHY, EQUAL RIGHTS, AND THE ORIGINS OF THE MANITOBA SCHOOL QUESTION. *Can. Hist. R. 1973 54(4): 369-392.* Examines the historiography of the origins of provincial legislation in Manitoba to eliminate Catholic denominational education in 1890. Offers a revised view of the role of Conservative Member of Parliament D'Alton McCarthy and the Equal Rights Association in this process. There was little connection between McCarthy and the schools legislation. The 1890 Acts were the result of the social transformation of Manitoba, 1870-90. Based on newspaper, pamphlet, and manuscript sources in the Public Archives of Canada, the Public Archives of Manitoba, and the Archiepiscopal Archives of St. Boniface. A

3821. Spigelman, Martin S. "DES PAROLES EN L'AIR": QUEBEC, MINORITY RIGHTS AND THE NEW BRUNSWICK SCHOOLS QUESTION. *Dalhousie Rev. [Canada] 1978 58(2): 329-345.* The New Brunswick Schools question vexed Canada during most of the 1870's. The Common Schools Act (1871) ordered taxation of all, including Catholics, for public schools, but withdrew long-standing grants to Catholic schools. That Quebec gave vocal support to the Acadians was to be expected; but that little real support was forthcoming greatly disappointed the French-speaking New Brunswickers. Catholic newspapers and politicians gave vocal support to the Acadians and Irish Catholics in New Brunswick but always stopped short of changing their political allegiance to the governing Conservative Party. Names such as Georges Cartier, Hector Langevin, and John A. Macdonald appear frequently, as do references to the newspapers *La Minerve, L'Opinion Publique,* and *Le Nouveau Monde.* Quebec's first concern was not a Catholic minority in another province but its own security. 70 notes. C. Held

3822. Troper, Harold. NATIONALITY AND HISTORY EDUCATION: NATIONALISM AND THE HISTORY CURRICULUM IN CANADA. *Hist. Teacher 1978 12(1): 11-27.* A study of the recent changes in the history curriculum in Ontario reflects some basic changes in attitudes toward Canada's multicultural heritage. Instead of an attempt at unity through assimilation into an Anglo-oriented culture there is now a recognition and acceptance of the multicultural heritage, and an attempt at mutual understanding and continuation of this multiplicity as a desirable characteristic of Canadian self-understanding. 33 notes. R. V. Ritter

Law, Crime, and the Courts

3823. Graff, Harvey J. "PAUPERISM, MISERY, AND VICE": ILLITERACY AND CRIMINALITY IN THE NINETEENTH CENTURY. *J. of Social Hist. 1977 11(2): 245-268.* A study of the Middlesex County, Ontario, gaol registers of 1867-68 indicates that the popular concept that crime is committed by the uneducated is in error. Instead, such crimes as property offenses and prostitution were committed by some of the most literate members of society. Judging from this study, it was really "social inequality" that was the "prime determinant of criminality . . . Stratification by ethnic or sexual factors influenced the hierarchy of class, status, and wealth; in similar fashion, they turned the wheels of justice. Rather than illiteracy or ignorance leading directly to lives of crime, ethnicity, class, and sex lay behind and strongly mediated the relationships most commonly drawn." 6 tables, 62 notes. L. E. Ziewacz

Economic and Business Activities

3824. Deschênes, Gaston. ASSOCIATIONS COOPÉRATIVES ET INSTITUTIONS SIMILAIRES AU XIXᵉ SIÈCLE [Cooperative associations and similar institutions in the 19th century]. *Rev. d'Hist. de l'Amérique Française [Canada] 1976 29(4): 539-554.* Agricultural, mutual aid, fire protection, and construction cooperatives were first started by English Canadians during the 19th century. They were subsequently adopted and often transformed by the French Canadians. There was a minimum of cooperation among and continuity between cooperatives. Based on newspapers, published government documents, and monographic studies; 87 notes. L. B. Chan

3825. Passaris, Constantine. THE COST-BENEFIT IMPACT OF IMMIGRANTS ON ECONOMY. *Int. Perspectives [Canada] 1975 (5): 9-13.* Discusses the effect of immigration on the economics of Canada in the 1970's, emphasizing employment and wages.

Culture, the Arts, and Ideas (including Popular Culture)

3826. Arès, Richard. LANGUES MATERNELLES ET LANGUES D'USAGES AU QUÉBEC [Mother tongue and idiom in Quebec]. *Action Natl. [Canada] 1973 63(3): 228-234.* Discusses the extent to which mother tongues are commonly used by various social classes in Quebec and forecasts the possibility of complete anglicization.

3827. Bernard, Léon. LES ARCHIVES DE FOLKLORE DE L'UNIVERSITÉ LAVAL [The folklore archives from the Laval University]. *Culture Vivante [Canada] 1971 (23): 3-11.* An interview with M. Luc Lacorcière, founder and director of the Archives de Folklore de L'Université Laval, in order to study its history and projects.

3828. Henderson, M. Carole. FOLKLORE SCHOLARSHIP AND THE SOCIOPOLITICAL MILIEU IN CANADA. *J. of the Folklore Inst. 1973 10(1-2): 97-107.* Canada's folklore studies have been overly selective in concentrating on Anglo regional subculture studies, French, Indian, and ethnic traditions, and oral tradition, and have been influenced more by social, political, and economic factors than by scholarship.

3829. Juneau, Pierre. CULTURE ET SUPERCULTURE [Culture and superculture]. *Tr. of the Royal Soc. of Can. [Canada] 1978 16: 153-160.* Compares Canadian cultural expenditures with those of the United States. Notes that Canada is a new country with a small population. Few who speak English also speak French, and one-seventh of the population has a native language other than English or French. Notes the extent to which companies, ideas, and products from the United States are on Canadian television. 5 notes. J. D. Neville

3830. Mackey, William F. LANGUAGE POLICY AND LANGUAGE PLANNING. *J. of Communication 1979 29(2): 48-53.* Discusses government policy and options in nation-states affected by bilingualism, including the United States and Canada.

3831. McLean, Hugh J. CANADA: ITS MUSICAL UNITY AND DIVERSITY. *Tr. of the Royal Soc. of Can. [Canada] 1978 16: 251-258.* Discusses nationalism in music and notes two kinds of nationalism: defending and aggressive. Defending nationalism includes work of such people as Mendelsson, Brahms, and John Philip Sousa, and supports cultural identity. Aggressive nationalism tries to impose an identity on someone else. Suggests that Canadian music finds its unity in its diversity. 6 notes. J. D. Neville

3832. Wonders, William C. LOG DWELLINGS IN CANADIAN FOLK ARCHITECTURE. *Ann. of the Assoc. of Am. Geographers 1979 69(2): 187-207.* Some log construction techniques were borrowed from natives of Canada, but most were from Europe: French-speaking Acadians brought methods to maritime Canada, English-speaking Ontario settlers imported many techniques from Pennsylvania, and settlers in the Prairie Provinces represented many northern European countries; 16th-19th centuries.

11. FRENCH ENGLISH RELATIONS

General

3833. Balthazar, Louis. LE NATIONALISME AU QUÉBEC [Nationalism in Quebec]. *Études Int. [Canada] 1977 8(2): 266-281.* Quebec's nationalism has been present for more than two hundred years through tradition, religion, and language. Emphasizes the more recent manifestations of this nationalism, particularly in the 1960's. Primary and secondary sources; 19 notes. J. F. Harrington, Jr.

3834. Brunet, Michel. LA MINORITÉ ANGLOPHONE DU QUÉBEC: DE LA CONQUÊTE À L'ADOPTION DU BILL 22 [The English-speaking minority of Quebec: from the conquest to the passing of Bill 22]. *Action Natl. [Canada] 1975 64(6): 452-466.* Reviews the struggle of French-speaking Canadians, first in Lower Canada and then in Quebec, against the English-speaking population, now a minority, and the consequences of Bill 22 (the Official Language Act, 1974) for the French-speaking community.

3835. Claval, Paul. ARCHITECTURE SOCIALE, CULTURE ET GÉOGRAPHIE AU QUÉBEC: UN ESSAI D'INTERPRÉTATION HISTORIQUE [Social structure, culture and geography in Quebec: an essay of historical interpretation]. *Ann. de Géographie [France] 1974 458: 394-419.* How can be explained Quebec's persistent originality within North America? Its isolation, its peripheric situation are often cited but are not sufficient reasons. The analysis of the spatial organization systems and of the types of social relations that create them allows to go further in the explanation and to take into account the historic and cultural data. It seems the difficulty French Canadians experience when trying to create modern bureaucracies explains at the same time their resistance to the Anglo-Saxon world and their dominated position. The fragile equilibrium which had built itself little by little is jeopardized by the ever larger opening of Quebec's economy and society. J

3836. Codignola, Luca. VINCITORI E VINTI NELLA STORIA AMERICANA: IL CONFLITTO ANGLO-FRANCESE [Winners and losers in American history: The Anglo-French conflict]. *Ponte [Italy] 1975 31(10): 1112-1125.* Considers the historiography of the relations of France and Great Britain as reflected in their respective American colonies and suggests that the distance and independence of Italian historians of the period has allowed them to study the century-long conflict in a new light, one that does not corroborate the traditional interpretation that every American expansionist victory was a victory for progress and civilization.

3837. Corry, J. A. NOTES TO ENGLISH CANADIANS. *J. of Can. Studies [Canada] 1977 12(3): 33-38.* English Canadians need to be more tolerant and understanding of the position of the Québécois. The cultural community that is Quebec has a history of 300 plus years along the banks of the St. Lawrence, and must be respected. If equality of the two cultures in Canada were guaranteed, in reality as well as in word, and if much wider autonomy were given the government of Quebec, and other Canadian provincial governments, the wind might be taken out of the sails of the Parti Québécois. By cherishing and cultivating their diversity, Canadians would find a larger, more spacious unity than they had before. J. C. Billigmeier

3838. Gagnon, Jean-Louis. CONCEPT D'ÉGALITÉ ENTRE LES PEUPLE FONDATEURS [The concept of equality between the founding races]. *Tr. of the Royal Soc. of Can. [Canada] 1978 16: 103-109.* Compares the French concept of equality between the two "founding races" with the English concept of partnership between them, and shows the problems that result from these two different ideas. J. D. Neville

3839. Goldberg, Steve. CANADIAN "CIVIL WAR": SEPARATISM VS. FEDERALISM IN MODERN CANADA. *Strategy and Tactics 1977 (64): 25-35.* Summarizes Canadian history, providing background on the possible separation of Quebec; combines an analysis of political and military factors, concluding that Canadian union deserves preservation.

3840. Kattan, Naim. LA DIMENSION CULTURELLE DES DEUX SOLITUDES [The cultural dimension of the two solitudes]. *Études Int. [Canada] 1977 8(2): 337-341.* Discusses the parallel development of the British and French cultures in Canada, noting especially the dissimilarities in their historical origins, religious orientation, and cosmology. J. F. Harrington, Jr.

3841. Kerwin, Larkin. PROVINCIALISME INTELLECTUEL AU CANADA [Intellectual provincialism in Canada]. *Tr. of the Royal Soc. of Can. [Canada] 1977 15: 3-7.* Presidential address to the Royal Society based on a similar speech by Monseigneur Camille Roy in 1929. Notes that societies are rarely monolithic and homogeneous; instead most of them are pluralist. Some have accepted ideas from several cultures from which they have then created their own culture such as Italian, English, Dutch, French, and Spanish. Canada, of course benefits from two of these cultures. Cautions against the division of countries into many small regions and notes that Quebec is not the only Canadian area with this tendency. Also notes the role of the Royal Society of Canada in bringing together the two cultures in Canada. J. D. Neville

3842. Neatby, H. Blair. POLITICAL PARTIES AND CULTURAL DUALITY: THE SQUARING OF THE CIRCLE. *Tr. of the Royal Soc. of Can. [Canada] 1978 16: 59-70.* Discusses how Canadian political parties have attempted to deal with the dual culture of Canada and asserts that distinctively Canadian qualities result from this cultural dualism. The government bilingual coalition is a special case. 19 notes. J. D. Neville

3843. Painchaud, Paul. TERRITORIALIZATION AND INTERNATIONALISM: THE CASE OF QUEBEC. *Publius 1977 7(4): 161-175.* Describes the historical existence and development of a French political identity within the Canadian population. The present conflict developed slowly because of Canadian nationalism and a widely spread French population. Quebec maintains that its development requires access to the international system. Predicts that other individual territorial components will wish to share sovereignty on both the internal and external levels. Canadians and Quebecois are creating a new type of federalism, "diplomatic federalism" and suggests that it may "provide a solution to the growing problems posed by the polyethnic character of liberal and industrialized societies." 10 notes. R. S. Barnard

3844. Richert, Jean Pierre. THE IMPACT OF ETHNICITY ON THE PERCEPTION OF HEROES AND HISTORICAL SYMBOLS. *Can. R. of Sociol. and Anthrop. 1974 11(2): 156-163.* Seeks to verify the Royal Commission on Bilingualism and Biculturalism hypothesis that there are two Canadian historical traditions, one Anglophone, the other Francophone, and that they are mutually exclusive. The data were derived from a survey of 960 English- and French-Canadian elementary pupils, essays written by children, and in-depth interviews and observations. The findings generally confirmed the hypothesis and showed, first of all, that children overwhelmingly identified with historical symbols of their own culture, and that their ethnocentric perception of historical figures increased with age. Second, the data showed that Francophone and Anglophone children identified with different eras of Canadian history. The former identified primarily with the pre-1760 era, while the latter identified mostly with the post-1760 era. There are few reconciliation symbols in Canadian history which was, therefore, viewed as a divisive rather than a binding force. J

Before Confederation

3845. Angers, François-Albert. LE DOSSIER DE L'ACTE DE QUEBEC [The Quebec Act file]. *Action Natl. [Canada] 1974 64(1): 871-922.* Comments on the Quebec Act, 1774, which marked the official founding of Quebec, with documents by three great Canadian historians, Thomas Chapais, François Xavier Garneau, and Lionel Groulx.

3846. Baker, Raymond R. A CAMPAIGN OF AMATEURS: THE SIEGE OF LOUISBOURG, 1745. *Canadian Hist. Sites [Canada] 1978 18: 5-58.* On the morning of 11 May 1745, some 90 transport vessels under escort of a British naval squadron sailed into Gabarus (Gabarouse) Bay on Cape Breton Island. Aboard the transports were nine regiments of hastily raised citizen soldiers from the colonies of Massachusetts, New Hampshire, and Connecticut. They had come to conquer the great French fortress of Louisbourg; in 47 days they were to do just that, and shatter the myth of invincibility that had begun to surround the fortress.

3847. Banks, Margaret A. UPPER AND LOWER CANADA OR CANADA WEST AND EAST, 1841-67? *Can. Hist. R. 1973 54(4): 475-482.* Seeks to determine the official names of the constituent parts of the Province of Canada. There was no uniform official terminology until April 1849, but from then until the end of the union, Upper Canada and Lower Canada were the names authorized for use in the statutes and generally employed in official documents. It would therefore be preferable for historians to use these names instead of calling the constituent parts of the province Canada West and East, as many of them do. Based on statutes, journals of the Legislative Assembly, and other contemporary sources.   A

3848. Beattie, Judith and Pothier, Bernard. THE BATTLE OF THE RESTIGOUCHE. *Can. Hist. Sites [Canada] 1977 (16): 5-34.* The battle of the Restigouche, 1760, was fought between the remnants of a French relief fleet bound for Montreal and a British squadron. The three French ships, only half the number that had sailed from Bordeaux in the spring, captured six British vessels in the Gulf of St. Lawrence. On learning that the British had already reached the St. Lawrence River, the French fleet sought refuge in Chaleur Bay and the Restigouche River where its numbers were further increased by 25 to 30 Acadian sloops and schooners. A British fleet from the Fortress of Louisbourg made contact with the French on 22 June. By 8 July, the final day of the engagement, the French had lost, in addition to 10 vessels sunk across channels in the river to halt the British advance, 22 or 23 vessels, most of which the French destroyed to prevent the British from taking them. The loss of the French fleet and its supplies contributed to the fall of New France. The battle was the last naval engagement between France and Great Britain for the possession of North America.   J

3849. Bédard, Marc-André. LA PRÉSENCE PROTESTANTE EN NOUVELLE-FRANCE [The Protestant presence in New France]. *Rev. d'Hist. de l'Amérique Française [Canada] 1977 31(3): 325-349.* A few Protestants had always dwelt in French Canada, but they led a precarious existence before the permanent arrival of the English in 1759. Totally disorganized, the Protestants were subjected to a series of sectarian excesses designed to force their conversion to Catholicism. During the early years of British hegemony, the Catholic majority was subjected to similar abuses. 69 notes.   M. R. Yerburgh

3850. Brown, Desmond H. FOUNDATIONS OF BRITISH POLICY IN THE ACADIAN EXPULSION: A DISCUSSION OF LAND TENURE AND THE OATH OF ALLEGIANCE. *Dalhousie Rev. [Canada] 1977-78 57(4): 709-725.* Searches for the roots of the idea of personal loyalty to the king. Traces the development of oaths from Normandy through Saxon England and the writings of jurists such as Henry de Bracton (d. 1268), Sir Thomas Littleton in his 1481 treatise, and Edward Coke in his 1628 interpretation of Littleton. Examines the meaning of the oath of allegiance as it was intended at the time of the 1755 expulsion of the Acadians and as expounded by William Blackstone (1755). Trying to understand the meaning of the oath in today's society is difficult, because no writer has sufficiently explained why the right to possess title to land depended upon allegiance to the crown. Quotes from Nova Scotia Lieutenant Governors Thomas Caulfield (1715), Lawrence Armstrong (1726), Paul Mascarene (1736), and Charles Lawrence (1753). 96 notes.   C. H. Held

3851. Chard, Donald F. CANSO, 1710-1721: FOCAL POINT OF NEW ENGLAND-CAPE BRETON RIVALRY. *Nova Scotia Hist. Soc. Collections [Canada] 1977 39: 49-77.* The pivotal geographical location of Canso rendered it vital in the establishment of attitudes of officials in Great Britain, France, and New England. New England's problem was "to ensure the effective control of the area without disrupting trade with Cape Breton, or the entente which developed between France and Britain" after 1710. New England representatives such as Cyprian Southack sought to defend Canso as the gateway to the French Colony and to insure that the delineation of imperial policy insofar as the French in Acadia (Nova Scotia) were concerned took place in Canso and in Boston. In short, the establishment of colonial-imperial policy by New Englanders for their own ends was aided and abetted (in ignorance) by the British officials. Based on the *Calendar of State Papers, Colonial Series; Public Archives of Nova Scotia papers; Colonial Office Papers,* and secondary sources; 107 notes.   E. A. Chard

3852. Cuthbertson, Brian C. THOMAS BEAMISH AKINS: BRITISH NORTH AMERICA'S PIONEER ARCHIVIST. *Acadiensis: J. of the Hist. of the Atlantic Region [Canada] 1977 7(1): 86-102.* Thomas Beamish Akins (1809-91), Commissioner of Public Records for Nova Scotia (1857-91), was largely responsible for the proper preservation of early Nova Scotian public records. Previous efforts only organized small parts of the public records. Akins's *Selections from the Public Documents of the Province of Nova Scotia* (1869) occasioned considerable controversy because its incomplete nature appeared deliberately selective concerning the Acadian expulsion, but Akins took pains to publish all relevant documents as they came to light. 74 notes.   D. F. Chard

3853. Dessaules, Louis-Antoine. PREMIÈRE "LECTURE" SUR L'ANNEXION [First "reading" on annexation]. *Études Françaises [Canada] 1973 9(3): 205-236.* Far from being the freest people on earth as claimed by Great Britain, 19th-century inhabitants of Lower Canada were subjected to the oppressive political policies of the British colonial administration. To free themselves of this oppression, they ought to seek unification with the United States of America. Extracted from *Six lectures aur l'annexion du Canada auz États-Unis*, Montreal, Gendron, 1851, p. 42-54.   G. J. Rossi

3854. Duffy, John and Muller, H. Nicholas. THE GREAT WOLF HUNT: THE POPULAR RESPONSE IN VERMONT TO THE *PATRIOTE* UPRISING OF 1837. *J. of Am. Studies [Great Britain] 1974 8(2): 153-169.* Chronicles the failure of the *patriote* in Vermont to assist Canadian rebels in their 1837-38 rebellion against British rule of Canada. Governor Silas Jennison and other Vermont authorities condemned the *patriote*. President Martin van Buren (1782-1862) intervened and used force to curb *patriote* activities along the Vermont-Canada border. Based on American and British archival materials; 49 notes.

H. T. Lovin

3855. Dunnigan, Brian Leigh. VAUBAN IN THE WILDERNESS: THE SIEGE OF FORT NIAGARA, 1759. *Niagara Frontier 1974 21(2): 37-52.* Describes the battle plans and action of the British Army in its takeover of Fort Niagara, 1759, during the French and Indian War.

3856. Fahmy-Eid, Nadia. ULTRAMONTANISME, IDÉOLOGIE ET CLASSES SOCIALES [Ultramontanism, ideology and social classes]. *R. d'Hist. de l'Amérique Française 1975 29(1): 49-68.* During the 19th century, the French middle class of Lower Canada united with the ultramontane clergy against the economic power being wielded by the English middle class of Upper Canada. The clergy of Lower Canada aimed at a state governed by the Church and effectively influenced education and government until Lower Canada became a modern capitalist state. Based on primary and secondary sources; 25 notes.

C. Collon

3857. Farrell, David R. ANCHORS OF EMPIRE: DETROIT, MONTREAL AND THE CONTINENTAL INTERIOR, 1760-1775. *Am. Rev. of Can. Studies 1977 7(1): 33-54.* After the conquest of New France, Great Britain attempted to insure the military defense, political stability, and economic exploitation of the interior by direct imperial control through regional garrison towns. These outposts were subject to strict military and economic regulations which prevented their developing into urban centers. By 1770, changing trade patterns and unrest in the eastern colonies altered British policy, concentrating interest in the Great Lakes. Some garrison towns were abandoned and the fur-trading centers of Detroit and Montreal became the logical anchors for the realigned empire. Primary and secondary sources; map, 37 notes.

G.-A. Patzwald

3858. Gibson, James A. POLITICAL PRISONERS, TRANSPORTATION FOR LIFE, AND RESPONSIBLE GOVERNMENT IN CANADA. *Ontario Hist.* [Canada] 1975 67(4): 185-198. Argues that the Colonial Office conceded "responsible government" to the Canadas during 1838-45, less as a result of the Earl of Durham's report on the two provinces, than as an effort to divert attention from penal transportation from the Canadas as punishment for the 1837-38 uprisings. Analyzes events in Upper Canada only, and sees a trend in public opinion initially forcing the substitution of transportation for execution, and then against transportation. In passing, comments on the treatment of transportees in Australia. Based on primary sources; 33 notes. W. B. Whitham

3859. Greenwood, E. Murray. ANALYSE DE L'EXPOSÉ DE N.-E. DIONNE SUR LE DISCOURS DE PIERRE BÉDARD AU SUJET DE LA LANGUE OFFICIELLE, 1793 [Analysis of N.-E. Dionne's account about Pierre Bédard's discourse on the subject of the official language, 1793]. *Rev. d'Hist. de l'Am. Française* [Canada] 1976 30(2): 259-262. In his analysis of the linguistic conflict of 1792-93 in the Legislative Assembly of Lower Canada, Mason Wade cites a discourse of Pierre-Stanislas Bédard. The *Gazette de Québec* did not publish it, nor do historians F.-X. Garneau and Thomas Chapais refer to it. Wade cites Narcisse-Eutrope Dionne, *Pierre Bédard et ses fils* (Québec, 1909). Dionne's views were probably based on Hugh Gray's francophobic public commentary published in the newspaper *Le Canadien* on 30 December 1809. Based on letters in the Public Archives of Canada and secondary works; 10 notes. L. B. Chan

3860. Griffiths, Naomi. ACADIANS IN EXILE: THE EXPERIENCES OF THE ACADIANS IN THE BRITISH SEAPORTS. *Acadiensis* [Canada] 1974 4(1): 67-84. Caught between the French and English, the Acadians of Nova Scotia remained neutral, developing their own distinctive character by the time of their dispersion in 1755. Those sent to England maintained their separate identity; French officials, emphasizing similarities in language and religion and ignoring cultural differences, saw these Acadians as dislocated loyal French and got them resettled in France in 1763. The Acadians proved unhappy, uncooperative and troublesome and many later emigrated to New Orleans. Based on materials in the British and French Archives, published primary and secondary sources; 86 notes. E. A. Churchill

3861. Gwyn, Julian. WAR AND ECONOMIC CHANGE: LOUISBOURG AND THE NEW ENGLAND ECONOMY IN THE 1740'S. *Rev. de l'U. d'Ottawa* [Canada] 1977 47(1-2): 114-131. An economic survey of New England showing the changes brought by King George's War which ended in 1745 by the capture of the fortress of Louisbourg and its restoration to the French by the British in 1749. In spite of New England's costly war effort, 1745-49 were years of prosperity, but these were followed by a deflation bringing financial insecurity to citizens already embittered by Britain's restoration of Louisbourg to the French. Based on primary and secondary sources; 11 tables, 49 notes.

G. P. Cleyet

3862. Hardy, René. LA RÉBELLION DE 1837-38 ET L'ESSOR DU PROTESTANTISME CANADIEN-FRANÇAIS [The rebellion of 1837-38 and the scope of French-Canadian Protestantism]. *Rev. d'Hist. de l'Amérique Française* [Canada] 1975 29(2): 163-189. English and Swiss Protestant evangelists considered the rebellion of 1837-38 in Lower Canada as a good opportunity to destroy the influence of the Catholic clergy. The English residents of Montreal thought that the conversion of the French-Canadians to Protestantism would guarantee cohesion between the two ethnic groups. Colonial administrators, however, considered the Catholic clergy indispensable to the maintenance of law and order. Based on documents in the Archives de la paroisse Notre-Dame de Québec, Archives de la Chancellerie de l'Archevêché de Montréal, Archives de l'Université du Québec à Trois-Rivières, and secondary works; 106 notes. L. B. Chan

3863. Hare, John E. LE COMPORTEMENT DE LA PAYSANNERIE RURALE ET URBAINE DE LA RÉGION DE QUÉBEC PENDANT L'OCCUPATION AMÉRICAINE, 1775-1776 [The behavior of the rural and urban peasantry of the Quebec region during the American occupation]. *Rev. de l'U. d'Ottawa* [Canada] 1977 47(1-2): 145-150. During the American occupation of the province of Quebec (1775-76), a minority of the rural, peasant militiamen responded favorably to Governor Guy Carleton's appeal to resistance; however, the majority of them remained neutral with sometimes a friendly attitude toward Americans and a small group of activists rebelled against the governor's orders. In the city of Quebec, an equal lack of enthusiasm to resistance was shown by the urban peasantry. The expulsion of the American army from the province proved for the rebels a humiliating defeat which ensured the clergy and the gentry a favorable position toward the British government. Primary and secondary sources; 2 tables, 15 notes.

G. P. Cleyet

3864. Igartua, José. A CHANGE IN CLIMATE: THE CONQUEST AND THE *MARCHANDS* OF MONTREAL. *Can. Hist. Assoc. Hist. Papers* 1974: 115-134. Discusses the change from French to British commercial ascendancy among the middle classes of Montreal, Quebec, 1750-92, emphasizing the fur trade.

3865. Kaulback, Ruth E. A JOURNAL OF THE PROCEEDINGS ... (SIR WM. PHIPPS' EXPEDITION TO PORT ROYAL APRIL 23-MAY 30, 1690). *Nova Scotia Hist. Q.* 1973 3(2): 131-143. Recounts the destruction of the French fort at Port Royal with excerpts from the journal of Sir William Phipps, leader of the English expedition. All inhabitants of the area were required to swear allegiance to King William and Queen Mary of England. 9 notes. H. M. Evans

3866. Kesteman, Jean-Pierre. LES PREMIERS JOURNAUX DU DISTRICT DE SAINT-FRANÇOIS (1823-1845) [The first newspapers in the district of Saint Francis (1823-1845)]. *Rev. D'Hist. De L'Amérique Française* [Canada] 1977 31(2): 239-253. An overview of the principal newspapers published in a single district of Lower Canada's (Quebec's) Eastern Townships. Though many of these pioneering ventures, e.g., the *British Colonist* and the *Farmer's Advocate* were initiated by Americans, they clearly reflected the social, political, and economic polarization that developed before the French Canadians' Rebellion of 1837. 82 notes. M. R. Yerburgh

3867. Lanctot, Gustave. CANADA 1759: BĂTĂLIA ȘESURILOR [Canada 1759: The Battle of the Plains]. *Magazin Istoric* [Romania] 1975 9(12): 11-16. An extract from *Histoire du Canada*, vols. 1-3 (Montreal, 1966-67), translated into Romanian with an introduction by Cristina Corciorescu, describing events leading up to the defeat of the Marquis de Montcalm by General James Wolfe in the British capture of Quebec City.

3868. Martin, Ged. THE CANADIAN REBELLION LOSSES BILL OF 1849 IN BRITISH POLITICS. *J. of Imperial and Commonwealth Hist.* [Great Britain] 1977 6(1): 3-22. Examines the Canadian Rebellion Losses Bill of 1849, which was to compensate for losses resulting from the rebellions of 1837-38 in Lower Canada, from the standpoint of its impact on British politics. William Ewart Gladstone and Lord Henry Peter Brougham were the key figures in attempting to have the bill vetoed, and in so doing they brought into question the whole definition of responsible government and imperial authority. In the end parliament did not intervene in Canadian affairs and thus gave responsible government a chance to mature as a constitutional concept. 71 notes.

J. A. Casada

3869. Muller, H. Nicholas, III. TROUBLE ON THE BORDER, 1838: A NEGLECTED INCIDENT FROM VERMONT'S NEGLECTED HISTORY. *Vermont Hist.* 1976 44(2): 97-102. "During the ... winter of 1837-1838, ... nearly the entire population of northern Vermont showed "frenzied excitement" over the Canadian Rebellion of 1837. The 1 March letter of N. R. Woods of Potton, north of Troy, Vermont, in the Eastern Townships of Lower Canada, in the Vermont Historical Society, here edited with introduction, described a raid of some 60 *patriotes* which seized arms. By November the excitement died down. 16 notes. T. D. S. Bassett

3870. Neagle, Marjorie Spiller. THE LONGEST DAY. *New-England Galaxy 1975 16(4): 43-48.* The French and Indian attack on Storer Garrison in Wells, Maine, 6 June 1692, was repelled by the local militia.

3871. Nourry, Louis. L'IDÉE DE FÉDÉRATION CHEZ ÉTIENNE PARENT 1831-1852 [The idea of federation in Étienne Parent's thinking 1831-52]. *R. d'Hist. de l'Amérique Française [Canada] 1973 26(4): 533-557.* French Canadian politician Étienne Parent defended the idea of an almost independent Canada, with more or less protectorate status in the British Empire, in his newspaper *Le Canadien.* Parent felt such status would enable Canada to win its independence gradually from England, rather than be absorbed by the United States. Based on primary and secondary sources; 102 notes. C. Collon

3872. Ojala, Jeanne A. IRA ALLEN AND THE FRENCH DIRECTORY, 1796: PLANS FOR THE CREATION OF THE REPUBLIC OF UNITED COLUMBIA. *William and Mary Q. 1979 36(3): 436-448.* Ira Allen visited London to interest the British in building a canal linking Lake Champlain and the St. Lawrence River and also Paris to secure arms for the Vermont militia. Undoubtedly Allen intended to foment rebellion in Quebec. He was not successful in England. The second objective is discussed at length, including comment on the 16 documents in the French archives relating to his planned republic in Canada. Allen signed a contract with the French Secretary of War. Allen's plans came to naught, as he and a shipment of arms from France were captured at sea by the British. Allen returned to the United States in 1801. Reproduces Allen's report on conditions in Canada and advantages of a republic. Based on Allen's writings and correspondence and several monographs; 18 notes. H. M. Ward

3873. Ouellet, Fernand. L'ÉCHEC DU MOUVEMENT INSURRECTIONNEL: 1837-1839 [The failure of the insurrectional movement: 1837-39]. *Recherches Sociographiques [Canada] 1965 6(2): 135-161.* Failure of the Rebellion of 1837 in Lower Canada can be attributed to personal ambition, immediate interests of the liberal professionals, the weak economy of the French Canadians, and the unpredictable behavior of Louis Joseph Papineau; discusses Great Britain's appointment of the 1st Earl of Durham in 1838.

3874. Ouellet, Fernand. RÉGIONALISMES ET UNITÉ POLITIQUE AVANT 1867: ESSAI DE GÉO-POLITIQUE [Regionalism and political unity before 1867: a study of geopolitics]. *Tr. of the Royal Soc. of Can. [Canada] 1978 16: 39-58.* Discusses regionalism in Canada before 1867, noting the development of the different areas, 1608-1840, comparing the centralism of the French Empire with the decentralism of the British Empire, discussing the events leading to confederation in 1867, and showing the influence of the commercial classes on unification. 23 notes. J. D. Neville

3875. Papineau, Louis-Joseph. UN TESTAMENT POLITIQUE [A political testament]. *Études Françaises [Canada] 1973 9(3): 237-255.* Praises Aristotle's political thought as the best explication of the science of government. Unlike Montesquieu, who allowed his social position to affect his writings, Aristotle searched for the truth. Describes the outrages of the English victory in the battle of Quebec and rejects the justice of the 1867 Act of Confederation. Calls for liberty of political, religious, and scientific thought. Text of *Discours de l'Honorable Louis-Joseph Papineau devant l'Institut canadien, à l'occasion du 23 anniversaire de la fondation de l'Institut canadien, le 17 décembre 1867,* Montréal, Imprimerie du journal *Le Pays,* 1868, 20p. G. J. Rossi

3876. Read, Colin. THE DUNCOMBE RISING, ITS AFTERMATH, ANTI-AMERICANISM, AND SECTARIANISM. *Social Hist. [Canada] 1976 9(17): 47-69.* The Duncombe Rising of 1837 was a haphazard and disorganized revolt in Upper Canada, resulting from political discord. Rebels came from isolated agrarian townships populated largely by people born in North America. Although religion was not important in the revolt, most churches suffered setbacks in the aftermath of the rebellion because accusations were made against their members. Many church-going settlers fled the area. The smaller sects and the American sects suffered the most. Based on papers in public and church archives, on church periodicals, and on published primary sources; 3 maps, 88 notes. W. K. Hobson

3877. Read, Colin. THE SHORT HILLS RAID OF JUNE, 1838, AND ITS AFTERMATH. *Ontario Hist. [Canada] 1976 68(2): 93-115.* Discusses the events of the Short Hills raid, a minor incident following the rebellion of 1837. Comments on the organization of the raid and some of the persons involved. Suggests the participants' motives. The trials subsequent to the capture of the raiders also are remarked upon. Posttrial appeals and the international atmosphere of the time are mentioned. 111 notes, 3 appendixes. W. B. Whitham

3878. Rudé, George. IDEOLOGY AND POPULAR PROTEST. *Hist. Reflections [Canada] 1976 3(2): 69-77.* The American and French Revolutions of the 18th century and the Lower Canada Rebellions of 1837-38 show that revolutions and rebellions involve a distinctive popular element. In the American Revolution the common people shared the dominant ideology which the revolutionary elites transmitted. The French Revolution also suggest the impact of the ideology of the revolutionary middle class and liberal aristocracy on the common people. The common people of France added something of their own to the notions of the French bourgeoisie. The Canadian rebellions show a popular ideology distinguishable from that of the leadership. P. Travis

3879. Salagnac, Georges Cerbelaud. LA REPRISE DE TERRE-NEUVE PAR LES FRANCAIS EN 1762 [The reconquest of Newfoundland by the French in 1762]. *Rev. Française d'Hist. d'Outre-mer [France] 1976 63(2): 211-222.* Recounts the 1762 attempt to recapture Newfoundland by a French naval division commanded by the Chevalier d'Arsac de Ternay and 600 French troops led by the Count of Haussonville. The division left Brest on 8 May and succeeded in taking Saint John's without a shot. English resistance, led by Sir Jeffrey Amherst, forced the small flotilla of de Ternay to escape 15 September. Haussonville had no choice but to yield the last fort to the English 18 September. Primary sources; note. A. W. Howell

3880. Senior, Elinor. THE BRITISH GARRISON IN MONTREAL IN THE 1840'S. *J. of the Soc. for Army Hist. Res. 1974 52 (210): 111-127.* From its capitulation (1760) until 1870, "Montreal was a British garrison town" and was "never without a regiment of the line, a battery of Royal Artillery and some Royal Engineers." For those 110 years it rivalled "Quebec as the major British military station" in Canada. For much of the 1840's, in fact, "when the city was also the political capital of the united province of Canada, Montreal resembled a European metropolis, having the seat of government and military headquarters located in the most important commercial city of the country," and "it is difficult to touch any aspect of Montreal history without encountering the influence or, at least, the presence of the military." Probably the most important duty of the British garrison was aiding the civil authorities in times of disturbance—"and the forties in Montreal proved exceptionally disturbing"—and particularly during the annual municipal elections, the provincial elections in 1844 and 1848, and the troubles during the summer of 1849 "as the house of assembly debated the Rebellion Losses Bill." 110 notes. A. N. Garland

3881. Senior, Elinor. THE GLENGARRY HIGHLANDERS AND THE SUPPRESSION OF THE REBELLIONS IN LOWER CANADA 1837-38. *J. of the Soc. for Army Hist. Res. [Great Britain] 1978 56(227): 143-159.* The Glengarry Highlanders attempted to assist Sir John Colborne in suppressing internal disorders in Lower Canada during 1837-38.

3882. Senior, Elinor. THE PROVINCIAL CAVALRY IN LOWER CANADA, 1837-50. *Can. Hist. Rev. [Canada] 1976 57(1): 1-24.* Examines the colonial cavalry's role assisting British regulars during the insurrections of 1837-38, its use as frontier guards in the post-rebellion period, and its aid to civil power in Montreal during the turbulent 1840's. Although its disbandment in 1850 was owing partly to alleged annexationist sympathies among its officer corps, no evidence of such sympathies was found. Based on documents in the military "C" series, the memoirs of Sydney Bellingham and Thomas Wily, in the Public Archives in Ottawa, and the McCord Papers in the McCord Museum, Montreal. A

3883. Stewart, Catharine McArthur. QUEBEC CITY IN THE 1770'S. *Hist. Today [Great Britain] 1973 23(2): 116-121.* "Life in Quebec was considerably changed by the arrival of merchants from Britain and by the effects of the American Revolution."

3884. Tishkov, V. A. K ISTORII VOZNIKNOVENIIA FRANKO-KANADSKOGO NATSIONAL'NOGO VOPROSA [On the history of the origin of the French Canadian national problem]. *Voprosy Istorii [USSR] 1974 (1): 76-90*. Drawing on archive materials and historical documents, the author traces the origin of the national question among French Canadians in connection with the British conquest of Canada. The article contains a critical analysis of the various trends existing in the bourgeois historiography of Canada, which give widely differing interpretations to this question. The origin of the national question in Canada should be directly attributed to the policy pursued by Britain and her colonial top crust in relation to the indigenous French-speaking population. He makes a point of stressing that from the very outset the national question in Canada was distinguished by its class character, for it concerned relations between the privileged English minority and the ruthlessly exploited and disfranchised mass of colonists of French extraction.
J

3885. Tishkov, V. A. VOSSTANIE 1837-1838 GODOV V KANADE (OBZOR LITERATURY) [The Canadian Rebellion of 1837-1838: a review of the literature]. *Novaia i Noveishaia Istoriia [USSR] 1970 (5): 171-180*. Claims that this rebellion was essentially a bourgeois, anticolonialist revolution. It regrets that it has been little studied in the USSR, and it reviews Canadian literature. Traditionally the rebellion has been seen as essentially either a nationalist struggle between progressive English Canadians and backward French Canadians, or as a justified struggle by French Canadians. More recent works have unsystematically attempted to relate economic factors and the political attitudes of the mass of the population. Major themes still to be studied in depth include the ideas of the revolutionary leaders, and the reasons for the defeat of the rebellion. Secondary sources; 67 notes.
C. I. P. Ferdinand

3886. Tousignant, Pierre. PROBLÉMATIQUE POUR UNE NOUVELLE APPROCHE DE LA CONSTITUTION DE 1791 [Thoughts toward a new approach concerning the Constitution of 1791]. *Rev. d'Hist. de l'Amérique Française [Canada] 1973 27(2): 181-234*. Attempts to place in a new perspective the establishment of a parliamentary government in Lower Canada which takes into account the ambitions of the Scottish-English middle class, the sociopolitical concepts of British leaders, and the peculiar problems raised by the "Old Colonial System."

3887. Trudel, Marcel. LE DESTIN DE L'ÉGLISE SOUS LE RÉGIME MILITAIRE [The destiny of the Church under the military regime]. *Rev. d'Hist. de l'Amérique Française [Canada] 1957 11(1): 10-41*. Great Britain's conquest of French Canada during the French and Indian War ushered in a period of military government in Quebec. The French-speaking Catholic Church felt oppressed by the Protestant English authorities, and the Church passed through its most difficult period.

3888. Trudel, Pierre. LA PROTECTION DES ANGLO-QUÉBÉCOIS ET LA PRESSE CONSERVATRICE (1864-1867) [The protection of the Anglo-Quebecans and the Conservative Press (1864-1867)]. *Rev. de L'U. d'Ottawa [Canada] 1974 44(2): 137-157*. Analyzes the economic and political power of the "Anglo-Québécois" and their desire, as a minority, to retain their rights. The conservative press argued for the majority of the Franco-Québécois by stressing the importance of the French language, the Catholic religion, and the basic institutions of lower Canada. Based on primary and secondary sources; 133 notes.
M. L. Frey

3889. Wallot, Jean Pierre. THE LOWER CANADIAN CLERGY AND THE REIGN OF TERROR (1810). *Study Sessions: Can. Catholic Hist. Assoc. 1973 40: 53-60*. Studies the Catholic clergy's reactions and conduct during the crisis of 1810, in which Governor Sir James Craig implemented repressive measures to fend off the threat of democracy and French Canadian nationalism.
S

3890. Whiteley, W. H. NEWFOUNDLAND, QUEBEC, AND THE ADMINISTRATION OF THE COAST OF LABRADOR, 1774-1783. *Acadiensis [Canada] 1976 6(1): 92-112*. Merchants in Quebec and England argued over the Labrador fisheries from the conquest in 1763 until the implementation of the Quebec Act in 1775, when Labrador reverted to Quebec. British fishermen retained the right to fish cod where there were no Canadian posts. During the American Revolution, Quebec lacked the means to administer Labrador. The Newfoundland governors assumed primary responsibility for the coast and regularly sent warships there, although American privateers inflicted considerable damage to the fishery. 77 notes.
D. F. Chard

After Confederation

3891. Angers, François-Albert. LE QUÉBEC: ÉCONOMIQUEMENT ACCULÉ À L'INDÉPENDANCE [Quebec: economically forced to independence].
LE QUÉBEC EST ACCULÉ À L'INDÉPENDANCE [Quebec is forced toward independence]. *Action Natl. [Canada] 1973 63(1): 7-22*. Gives the history of Canadian federalism since 1867 as an appeal for the independence of Quebec.
LA THÈSE FÉDÉRALISTE [The federalist thesis]. *Action Natl. [Canada] 1973 63(3): 188-205*. The political liberation of Quebec must precede its economic expansion and raise its standard of living.
LES DÉMENTIS DE L'EXPÉRIENCE VÉCUE À LA THÈSE FÉDÉRALISTE [The denials of life under federalism]. *Action Natl. [Canada] 1973 63(4): 268-277*. Present worldwide economic conditions have cast doubt on the liberal theory of international economic relations and, by analogy, on the validity of the federalist thesis in Canada.
LE FÉDÉRALISME CANADIEN: UNE THÉORIE NON SEULEMENT PAR LES FAITS, MAIS THÉORIQUEMENT RETARDATAIRE [Canadian federalism: both actually and theoretically regressive]. *Action Natl. [Canada] 1974 63(7): 523-538*. The preconceptions of politicians and theoreticians toward political centralization prevent them from adapting their federalist economic theory to new scientific knowledge.

3892. Arès, Richard. LE COMMISSAIRE ROYAL [The royal commissary]. *Action Natl. [Canada] 1976 65(9-10): 689-705*. Richard Arès served with Esdras Minville on the Tremblay Commission (Commission royale d'enquête sur les problèmes constitutionnels) during 1953-56. Minville stressed that Quebec's primary concern must be security for the French tradition in a bicultural Canada. 5 notes.
A. W. Novitsky

3893. Brown, D. H. THE MEANING OF TREASON IN 1885. *Saskatchewan Hist. [Canada] 1975 28(2): 65-73*. In 1885 Louis Riel, then a naturalized US citizen living in Saskatchewan, was charged with treason against the British crown. Examines whether the charge was legitimate, and the evolving nature of treason in British law from 1352 to 1885. Also examines whether Riel could renounce his British citizenship by taking US citizenship. 69 notes.
C. Held

3894. Campbell, Murray. DR. J. C. SCHULTZ. *Tr. of the Hist. and Sci. Soc. of Manitoba [Canada] 1965 3(20): 7-12*. Provides the background to and events after John Christian Schultz's escape from Louis Riel and Upper Fort Garry during the Red River Rebellion on 23 January 1870.

3895. Carr, W. K. and Belanger, J. A. THE UNEASY UNION. *Conflict 1979 1(3): 161-170*. Discusses regionalism in Canada since Confederation in 1867, in particular, French nationalism in Quebec, 19th-20th centuries.

3896. Choquette, Robert. OLIVIER-ELZÉAR MATHIEU ET L'ÉRECTION DU DIOCÈSE DE REGINA, SASKATCHEWAN [Olivier-Elzear Mathieu and the establishment of the diocese of Regina, Saskatchewan]. *R. de l'U. d'Ottawa 1975 45(1): 101-116*. Discusses the conflict between Anglophiles and Francophiles in Saskatchewan and Mathieu's attempt to reconcile the two groups. Based on primary and secondary sources; 58 notes.
M. L. Frey

3897. Clark, S. D. THE POST SECOND WORLD WAR CANADIAN SOCIETY. *Can. R. of Sociol. and Anthrop. 1975 12(1): 25-32*. The primary concern of this paper is with what has happened to Canadian society since the Second World War. In seeking to understand the changes that have been taking place in this society, however, the author argues that it is necessary to go back and examine the way in which

Canadian society developed over the years before the Second World War. One can speak of an 'old order' of Canadian society, not simply of an old order of the society of French Canada, and what has happened since the war, in English-speaking as well as French-speaking Canada, can be described as a 'quiet revolution.'   J

3898. Clark, W. Leland. ASSIGNMENT: "THE 1885 REBELLION." *Manitoba Pageant [Canada] 1978 23(2): 11-17.* An account of the part played by George A. Flinn, a reporter for the *Winnipeg Sun,* during the North West Rebellion of Métis and Indians under the leadership of Louis Riel, against the Canadian government. They had defeated the North West Mounted Police, and the government sent a military force under the command of Major General Middleton to put down the rebellion. Flinn accompanied the expedition to Batoche and, when Riel had been captured, made a 70-mile journey to Clarke's Crossing to telegraph his report, doing several important interviews enroute. 34 notes.
R. V. Ritter

3899. Codignola, Luca. LOUIS RIEL E LE RIVOLTE DELL'OVEST CANADESE (1870-1885) [Louis Riel and the West Canadian revolts (1870-1885)]. *Riv. Storica Italiana [Italy] 1976 88(1): 127-142.* In 1869 the Hudson's Bay Company gave up its possessions to the government in Ottawa. This action provoked revolts in North Western Canada and in particular Red River. These revolts were the culmination of important themes in American history; the colonization of Western Canada and the Western United States, agrarian protest movements in the West, the history of the Indians, the history of relations between Canada and the United States, and the conflict between the French and English in North America. Louis Riel (1844-1885) was the leader of the major part of these revolts. On 15 May 1885, Riel was arrested by Canadian authorities and the entire movement was suppressed. Refusing to allow his lawyers to plead insanity, he was condemned to death and was hung in Regina on 16 November 1885. Primary and secondary sources; 85 notes.
M. T. Wilson

3900. Cody, Howard. THE EVOLUTION OF FEDERAL-PROVINCIAL RELATIONS IN CANADA: SOME REFLECTIONS. *Am. Rev. of Can. Studies 1977 7(1): 55-83.* The strong centralized federation envisioned at the time of Canadian Confederation has never materialized because of the absence of a sense of national allegiance, constitutional allocation of significant responsibilities to the provinces, the disproportionate strength of Ontario and Quebec, and Quebec's cultural individuality. An initial period of provincial ascendancy ended about 1910 when fiscal difficulties forced the provinces to accept federal aid and accompanying federal control over provincial programs. Since 1960, the increasing importance of certain provincial responsibilities, such as natural resources has fostered a system under which national policy is negotiated through federal-provincial conferences. Based on government publications and secondary sources; 58 notes.
G. A. Patzwald

3901. Flanagan, Thomas. LOUIS "DAVID" RIEL: PROPHET, PRIEST-KING, INFALLIBLE PONTIFF. *J. of Can. Studies 1974 9(3): 15-25.* Louis Riel's letters, written after his entry into a mental hospital, reveal a traditional Christian eschatological faith with the overtones of a Joachimite dispensation. The letters are well organized rather than demented ravings. During the 1885 Rebellion, Riel tried to put his messianic religious convictions into practice. Based on Public Archives of Canada, and of Manitoba, Archives of the Archdiocese of Montreal and the Seminary of Quebec, periodicals, monographs; 54 notes.
G. E. Panting

3902. Flanagan, Thomas E. LOUIS RIEL'S RELIGIOUS BELIEFS: A LETTER TO BISHOP TACHÉ. *Saskatchewan Hist. [Canada] 1974 27(1): 15-28.* Louis Riel (1844-85) claimed to be a religious prophet in addition to being a separatist leader. Argues that Riel's religious leadership was "an essential part of the attempt to recover the integrity of the Métis way of life," and that his religious theories were not as fantastic or nonsensical as missionaries and his defense attorneys pointed out. Too much information is gathered from hostile sources. His letter to Bishop Alexandre Antonin Taché tends to ameliorate this condition despite Bishop Taché's opinion that Riel was hopelessly insane. 2 portraits, 16 notes.
C. Held

3903. Flanagan, Thomas. THE MISSION OF LOUIS RIEL. *Alberta Hist. [Canada] 1975 23(1): 1-12.* Examines visionary Louis Riel's conception of the North-West Rebellion as a messianic religious movement.   S

3904. Flanagan, Thomas. POLITICAL THEORY OF THE RED RIVER RESISTANCE: THE DECLARATION OF DECEMBER 8, 1869. *Can. J. of Pol. Sci. [Canada] 1978 11(1): 153-164.* The document, written by a missionary and inspired by the Métis [people of French-Canadian and Amerindian descent] led by Louis Riel, is presented in English and French. 16 notes.
R. V. Kubicek

3905. Flanagan, Thomas. THE RIEL "LUNACY COMMISSION": THE REPORT OF DR. VALADE. *Rev. de l'U. d'Ottawa [Canada] 1976 46(1): 108-127.* Discusses the report of Dr. François-Xavier Valade on the insanity of Louis Riel, who was hanged for high treason at Regina, Saskatchewan, 1885. Dr. Valade's appointment and subsequent report were "meaningless political sop." The government misinterpreted and later forged a telegram by Valade, in an attempt to disguise Valade's original opinion that Riel could not "distinguish between right and wrong on political and religious questions." Includes the published text of the report. Primary and secondary sources; 59 notes.
M. L. Frey

3906. Genest, Jean. LE PROCÈS DE M. CASTONGUAY [The trial of M. Castonguay]. *Action Natl. [Canada] 1974 63(5): 353-375.* The views of Claude Castonguay, minister of social welfare, regarding Canadian federalism versus Quebec nationalism are blind to the long history of Ottawan dominance over the provincial autonomy of Quebec. Based on Michel Roy's interview of Castonguay in *Le Devoir,* 20 November 1973.

3907. Guy, L. et al. A SYMPOSIUM ON BICULTURALISM IN MANITOBA. *Tr. of the Hist. and Sci. Soc. of Manitoba [Canada] 1965 3(20): 71-83.* Provides an account of the Symposium on Biculturalism in Manitoba with the Manitoba Historical Society and La Societe Historique de Saint-Boniface, regarding French and English culture in Canada from 1870 to 1965.

3908. Hall, D. J. "THE SPIRIT OF CONFEDERATION": RALPH HEINTZMAN, PROFESSOR CREIGHTON, AND THE BICULTURAL COMPACT THEORY. *J. of Canadian Studies 1974 9(4): 24-42.* Discusses the government of Canada from the 1850's to the 1890's, political problems between the French Canadian minority and English Canadians, and the work of Ralph Heintzman and D. G. Creighton on this subject.   S

3909. Hallett, Mary E. THE QUEBEC TERCENTENNIAL: LORD GREY'S IMPERIAL BIRTHDAY PARTY. *Can. Hist. R. 1973 54(3): 341-352.* Governor General Lord Grey (Albert Henry George Grey, 4th Earl Grey), tried to foster imperial feeling in Canada and in particular to win French Canadians to the imperial cause by using the occasion of Quebec City's tercentennial for a display of imperial pageantry and power. The long-term results were probably negligible. This episode in relations between Canadians of English and French descent (1904-06) had an amusing imperial involvement. Based on the Grey and Laurier papers in the Public Archives of Canada, newspapers and periodicals.   A

3910. Lalonde, André N. THE NORTH-WEST REBELLION AND ITS EFFECTS ON SETTLERS AND SETTLEMENT IN THE CANADIAN WEST. *Saskatchewan Hist. [Canada] 1974 27(3): 95-102.* The positive effects of a completed railroad and cash for their crops to support the troops brought in by the rebellion were more than offset in the minds of the settlers by the violence occasioned by Riel's men. While actual casualties were light the widespread rumors of violence, often erroneous, effected a serious reduction in immigration for the remaining years of the 1880's. 38 notes.
C. Held

3911. Lamonde, Pierre and Julien, Pierre André. ECONOMIE ET NOUVEAU NATIONALISME: DE LA NOSTALGIE AGRICULTURISTE AU SOUVERAINISME [The economy and the new nationalism: from agricultural nostalgia to sovereignty]. *Can. Rev. of Studies in Nationalism [Canada] 1978 5(2): 208-236.* Compares the old and the new views of nationalism in Quebec. The former, rural, Catholic, and traditional, was supported by the French-Canadian elite in an effort to overcome Anglo-Saxon economic control and exploitation. Since 1940 Quebec's economic structure has undergone considerable change, and with it has come a new nationalism. Based on a vastly increased urban force, it insists on a unique "Québécois" culture and maintains a social-democratic ideology. Printed primary and secondary sources; 74 notes.

J. A. Kicklighter

3912. Lévesque, Delmas. UN QUÉBEC EN REDÉFINITION [Quebec in redefinition]. *Action Natl. [Canada] 1977 67(1): 16-33.* At the turn of the 20th century, English Canadians saw Quebec as a backward, priest-ridden province dominated by the Catholic Church. Quebec was transformed only by industrialization imported from New England and Ontario, which absorbed the excess farm population. In 200 years, the hegemony of the Catholic Church was challenged only during the 1830's. Catholicism thwarted modernization, but also protected Quebec from the American cultural imperialism which conquered English Canada. In an independent Quebec, the state would be expected to assume the role formerly held by the Church. The text is a lecture prepared for students of L'École Internationale de Bordeaux at the École des Hautes Études Commerciales, Montreal, August, 1972. 5 notes.

A. W. Novitsky

3913. McLean, W. J. TRAGIC EVENTS AT FROG LAKE AND FORT PITT DURING THE NORTHWEST REBELLION. *Manitoba Pageant 1972 18(1): 22-24, 1973 18(2): 4-8, (3): 11-16.* Continued from a previous article. Part III. Diary account by the author, Chief Factor of the Hudson Bay Company, of his captivity by the Plains Cree during the Riel Rebellion in 1885. The Plains Cree failed to induce the Wood Cree to join the fight against government troops at the Battle of Frenchman's Butte. In this encounter the cannonfire caused the Indians to flee. Part IV. Held captive, McLean and his family had to accompany the Cree on an arduous flight after the battle. He urged his captors to free him so that he could negotiate a peace settlement. Part V. McLean successfully urged his captors to free all their white prisoners so that he could negotiate a peace settlement. Details the return journey of 140 miles to Fort Pitt.

D. M. Dean

3914. McRoberts, Kenneth. QUEBEC AND THE CANADIAN POLITICAL CRISIS. *Ann. of the Am. Acad. of Pol. and Social Sci. 1977 433: 19-31.* For the first 90 years of Canada's existence, political conflict between the French-Canadian minority and the English-Canadian majority embraced electoral politics, government policies, and federal-provincial relations, but there was no major challenge to the Canadian political community itself. At the same time, there was only limited accommodation of French Canadians in federal institutions and virtually none in provinces other than Quebec. Apparently, the existence of a Quebec provincial government sufficed to prevent the rise of a strong secessionist movement. With the modernization of Quebec, however, such a movement has now emerged. The large difference in size between the English-speaking majority and the French-speaking minority appears to preclude mutual veto arrangements or general parity of representation in federal institutions. It has even hindered the attainment of proportional representation in federal power structures. Attempts to reinforce the French-Canadian presence outside Quebec have also been frustrated by demographic factors. Meanwhile, intensification of ethnic conflict within Quebec and preference for French-Canadian controlled institutions have strengthened demands by French Canadians to make Quebec their primary political community.

J

3915. Miller, J. R. "EQUAL RIGHTS FOR ALL": THE E.R.A. AND THE ONTARIO ELECTION OF 1890. *Ontario Hist. [Canada] 1973 65(4): 211-230.* Discusses one manifestation of Ontario reaction to Quebec legislation that seemed to breach the principle of separation of church and state. Shows that some of the motivation for the violence of this reaction to a sister-province's internal business came from unresolved Ontario problems which touched the same principle. Particular attention is paid to the "Anti-Jesuit Convention," and the Equal Rights Association which emerged from the convention. Examines the activities of the ERA in relation to provincial politics, especially the 1890 election. Concludes that the ERA had less influence than had been expected. 2 photos, 96 notes.

W. B. Whitham

3916. Miller, James R. UNITY/DIVERSITY: THE CANADIAN EXPERIENCE. *Dalhousie R. [Canada] 1975 55(1): 63-82.* Reviews the ideas behind the Canadian union as expressed by such men as George-Etienne Cartier, Donald Creighton, and Arthur Lower. Discusses the formula "Unity for diversity" used by the Fathers of Confederation, and terms such as dualism, biculturalism, centralization, disallowance, and bilingual. Early unity was based upon pursuit of common economic goals, which began to erode in the 1880's. New ideas focusing national unity on language and culture by such men as D'Alton McCarthy and Goldwin Smith, and massive immigration from Europe in the 1890's meant trouble for the doctrine of diversity. The solution proposed by Protestant Anglo-Saxons, "a good English education," met with French opposition. The most recent facet of the problem is the Trudeau government's move toward multiculturalism in 1971. 46 notes.

C. Held

3917. Minville, Esdras. LA VOCATION ÉCONOMIQUE DE LA PROVINCE DE QUÉBEC [The economic vocation of the province of Quebec]. *Action Natl. [Canada] 1976 65(9-10): 784-799.* Quebec's natural resources are appropriate for industrialization, so the province cannot remain agrarian. However, the wise use of forests will guarantee success for Quebec agriculture. A commission of scholars should set forth Quebec's position on Canadian federalism. Includes a letter from Minville to Maurice Duplessis, Premier of Quebec, 15 November 1945.

A. W. Novitsky

3918. Minville, Esdras. QUELQUES ASPECTS D'UN GRAND PROBLÈME [Several aspects of a major problem]. *Action Natl. [Canada] 1978 67(9): 779-787.* At the time of Confederation, Ontario and Quebec formed a geological and topographic unity, as did Nova Scotia and New Brunswick. The social and political fact of ethnic contrasts, however, prevents the two central provinces from sharing common interests. As additional Anglo-Canadian provinces were created, Quebec became the sole defense for a threatened minority. Reprinted from *L'Actualité économique,* November 1937.

A. W. Novitsky

3919. Morton, W. L. TWO YOUNG MEN, 1869: CHARLES MAIR AND LOUIS RIEL. *Tr. of the Hist. and Sci. Soc. of Manitoba [Canada] 1973-74 (30): 33-43.* Discusses political tension between the nationalist group Canada First and the Red River Rebellion, 1869-70. Poet Charles Mair, seen as a representative of Canada First, "the forerunner of Canadian Manifest Destiny," believed the future of the new nation was to be assumed by annexing the Northwest. Canada's future martyr, poet Louis Riel, defended the rights of the Métis and Indian groups occupying the area. The 1879 decision of Sir John MacDonald would create the province of Manitoba on the basis of Riel's Bill of Rights, but for now Riel was forced into exile while Mair returned to the Northwest and continued his literary career. Primary and secondary works; 9 notes.

S. R. Quéripel

3920. Murray, Donald. THE RALLIEMENT DES CREDITISTES IN PARLIAMENT, 1970-1971. *J. of Can. Studies 1973 8(2): 13-31.* Chronicles the origins of the Ralliement des Creditistes during the 1930's-70 and their participation in Canada's Parliamentary politics, 1970-71.

3921. Neatby, H. Blair. MACKENZIE KING AND FRENCH CANADA. *J. of Can. Studies [Canada] 1976 11(1): 3-13.* William Lyon Mackenzie King (1874-1950), as Liberal Party leader, understood that French Canada was a society with a collective identity. He developed an organizational structure for ascertaining the political situation within that society. His closest and most trusted colleague was always a French Canadian, first Ernest Lapointe and then Louis St. Laurent. This arrangement goes far to explain the dominance of the Federal Liberal Party in Quebec during King's years as its leader. Based on King Papers and secondary sources; 22 notes.

G. E. Panting

3922. Owram, Doug. "CONSPIRACY AND TREASON": THE RED RIVER RESISTANCE FROM AN EXPANSIONIST PERSPECTIVE. *Prairie Forum [Canada] 1978 3(2): 157-174.* Describes the French Canadian resistance to English Canadian expansionists which culminated in the Red River Rebellion of 1869 and 1870, from the point of view of the expansionists.

3923. Pennefather, John P. A SURGEON WITH THE ALBERTA FIELD FORCE. *Alberta Hist. [Canada] 1978 26(4): 1-14.* Reminiscences of Pennefather, a British surgeon who moved to Manitoba in the early 1880's. During the Second Riel Rebellion in 1885, he served as surgeon of the Winnipeg Light Infantry. Discusses some of the fighting, means of transportation and communication, and general dealing with and treatment of the Métis and Indians. Material extracted here is from a rare pamphlet published in 1892. 5 illus. D. Chaput

3924. Portes, Jacques. LE PROBLÈME DES IDÉOLOGIES DU CANADA FRANÇAIS À LA FIN DU XIXe SIÈCLE ET AU DÉBUT DU XXe SIÈCLE [The problem of the ideologies of French Canada at the end of the 19th century and at the beginning of the 20th century]. *Rev. d'Hist. Écon. et Sociale [France] 1975 53(4): 574-577.* Review article prompted by J. P. Bernard's *Les idéologies au Canada français, 1900-1929* (Quebec, 1974), A.-J. Bélanger's *L'apolitisme des idéologies québécoises, le Grand Tournant de 1934-36* (Quebec, n.d.), and G. Laloux-Jain's *Les manuels d'Histoire du Canada, au Québec et en Ontario (de 1867 à 1914)* (Quebec, 1973). The ideological response of French Canadians to British hegemony was ambiguous and did not lead to serious demands for separatism. The books under review give no clue about how French Canadian nationalism survived in spite of this ambiguity and how it could subsequently influence policy and economic development. 4 notes. U. Wengenroth

3925. Rayside, David M. THE IMPACT OF THE LINGUISTIC CLEAVAGE ON THE "GOVERNING" PARTIES OF BELGIUM AND CANADA. *Can. J. of Pol. Sci. [Canada] 1978 11(1): 61-97.* Discusses why there is less disagreement between English and French Canadians in the Liberal Party in Canada than between Flemings and francophones in Belgium's Social Christian Party. Covers 1880's-1973. 8 tables, fig., 27 notes, appendix. R. V. Kubicek

3926. Roy, Jean-Louis. DYNAMIQUE DU NATIONALISME QUÉBÉCOIS (1945-1970) [The dynamics of Quebecois nationalism (1945-70)]. *Can. Rev. of Studies in Nationalism [Canada] 1973 1(1): 1-13.* Quebec nationalism obtained its postwar dynamism from complex social, economic, and political forces. The cultural isolation of French Canadian Catholic life has broken down, forcing a redefinition of Quebec's identity in a secular, nationalist sense. The centralizing tendencies of Canadian federal bureaucrats and planners have provoked strong reactions from inside Quebec. 36 notes. J. C. Billigmeier

3927. Ryerson, Stanley B. SOCIAL CREDIT IN QUEBEC. *Queen's Q. [Canada] 1974 81(2): 278-283.* Reviews Maurice Pinard's *The Rise of a Third Party: A Study in Crisis Politics* (New York: Prentice-Hall, 1971) and Michael B. Stein's *The Dynamics of Right-wing Protest: A Political Analysis of Social Credit in Quebec* (Toronto: U. of Toronto Pr. 1973), which discuss the works in comparison with others dealing with the rise of the *Créditiste* movement in French Canada. Both works are accorded qualified praise with the reservation that much work remains to be done in the field. J. A. Casada

3928. Trépanier, Lise and Trépanier, Pierre. NATIONALISME ET PARTISANERIE: LOUIS ARCHAMBEAULT (1815-1890) [Nationalism and partisanism: Louis Archambeault (1815-1890)]. *Action Natl. [Canada] 1975 64(8): 649-655.* Studies the views of Louis Archambeault on the Confederation and Canadian unity, as seen during his long career of public official and spokesman for Canadian politics, stressing his evolution from the Conservative to the Liberal Party.

3929. Trépanier, Pierre. L'OPINION PUBLIQUE ANGLO-QUÉBÉCOISE ET L'AUTONOMIE PROVINCIALE (1945-1946) [Anglo-Quebec public opinion and provincial autonomy (1945-46)]. *Action Natl. [Canada] 1977 67(1): 34-55.* The depression and World War II prompted the Canadian federal government to formulate social welfare proposals. At a federal-provincial conference during August 1945-May 1946, the William Lyon Mackenzie King government proposed to assume taxation powers previously reserved to the provinces in exchange for fixed, per capita, welfare grants. Ontario and Quebec opposed the plan, citing an infringement on provincial sovereignty. Two conservative Anglo-Canadian newspapers in Quebec, the Montreal *Daily Star* and the *Gazette*, deplored the failure of the conference. The *Star* supported new fiscal arrangements increasing federal responsibility and power and blamed the provincial autonomists for the lack of results. The *Gazette*, less favorable to social security and more influenced by economic liberalism, de-emphasized the controversy over autonomy and blamed the federal government for the deadlock. Based on newspapers and secondary sources; 52 notes. A. W. Novitsky

3930. Trépanier, Pierre. SIMÉON LE SAGE (1835-1909): L'IDÉOLOGIE D'UN HAUT FONCTIONNAIRE NATIONALISTE [Simeon LeSage (1835-1909): the ideology of a nationalist government official]. *Action Natl. [Canada] 1978 67(8): 654-684.* The nationalism of Le Sage was essentially defensive. It reflected a faith in the providential mission of French Canada to maintain the traditions and faith of *ancien régime* France. Quebec civilization was to be based on agriculture fortified by religion. While a loyal member of the Conservative party, Le Sage had reservations about confederation and especially the Anglo-Protestant policies of John A. MacDonald. The Riel Rebellion posed a conflict between his conservatism and his nationalism. While he supported clemency for Louis Riel, Le Sage opposed the transformation of his execution into martyrdom. While accepting the dogma of papal infallibility, Le Sage rejected ultramontanism. He supported church control of education and condemned anticlericalism. Based on primary sources, especially the Simeon Le Sage collection of the Archives nationale du Québec, and secondary sources; 149 notes. A. W. Novitsky

3931. Vigod, B. L. ALEXANDRE TASCHEREAU AND THE NEGRO KING HYPOTHESIS. *J. of Can. Studies [Canada] 1978 13(2): 3-15.* The term "Negro king," coined in the 1950's to attack Quebec's then-Premier Maurice Duplessis, has been applied retroactively to his predecessor Louis Alexandre Taschereau (1920-36). Challenges this second application of the epithet, which implies that Taschereau was a colonial puppet, subservient and illicitly beholden to foreign capitalists. Taschereau perceived economic progress as a necessary condition of cultural survival and, like his mentor Simon-Napoleon Parent, saw the need to offer realistic incentives to foreign capital and to foreigners with the entrepreneurial skills that Quebecers lacked. If his exit from public life was ungraceful, this largely was due to the common problem of an overlong period in office. Based on archival, press, other primary, and secondary sources; 87 notes. L. W. Van Wyk

3932. Weiss, Jonathan M. *LES PLOUFFE* ET L'AMERICANISME AU QUÉBEC [*Les Plouffe* and Americanism in Quebec]. *Can. Rev. of Studies in Nationalism [Canada] 1976 3(2): 226-230.* Discusses Roger Lemelin's 1948 novel *Les Plouffe* and the author's attitude toward the Americanism in Quebec nationalism, 1938-45.

Contemporary

General

3933. Adamson, Christopher R.; Findlay, Peter C.; Oliver, Michael K.; and Solberg, Janet. THE UNPUBLISHED RESEARCH OF THE ROYAL COMMISSION ON BILINGUALISM AND BICULTURALISM. *Can. J. of Pol. Sci. 1974 7(4): 709-720.* Provides a reference to more than 100 unpublished reports deposited in mimeographic form in the Public Archives of Canada, Ottawa. 2 notes, appendix. R. V. Kubicek

3934. Albinski, Henry S. CURRENTS IN CANADIAN POLITICS. *Current Hist. 1977 72(426): 158-161, 178.* Discusses political parties in Canada, 1975-77, emphasizing the continuing rift between French-speaking and English-speaking Canadians and the threatened separatism of Quebec.

3935. Angers, François-Albert. LES ORIGINES DE L'INDÉPENDANTISME CONTEMPORAIN AU QUÉBEC: L'ALLIANCE LAURENTIENNE DE RAYMOND BARBEAU [The origins of contemporary independence in Quebec: the Alliance Laurentienne of Raymond Barbeau]. *Action Natl. [Canada] 1975 65(3): 234-244.* Reproduces Pierre Guillemette's "Raymond Barbeau, l'alliance Laurentienne et le début du Souverainisme Quebécois" *Le Jour* (14 August 1975), dealing with the Alliance Laurentienne, a Quebec movement for independence.

3936. Arès, Richard. QUI FERA L'AVENIR DES MINORITÉS FRANCOPHONES AU CANADA? [Who will be responsible for the future of French-speaking minorities in Canada?]. *Action Natl. [Canada] 1973 62(5): 349-377.* The French "fact" has influenced Canadian history.

This influence, however, is not such that it can assure the normal development of French language minorities throughout Canada. Quebec, with 84 percent of Canada's French-speaking population, is able to assure its own destiny but it is not necessarily able or willing to do the same for French minority groups. The future of these minorities is a collective responsibility.   A. E. LeBlanc

3937. Aubéry, Pierre. NATIONALISME ET LUTTE DES CLASSES AU QUEBEC [Nationalism and class struggle in Quebec]. *Am. Rev. of Can. Studies 1975 5(2): 130-145.* Intellectuals in Quebec are trying to help the proletariat French-speaking community bring about social, political, and economic equality for all Quebecois, 1960's-70's.

3938. Bernier, Paul. LE QUÉBEC DANS LA PRESSE ANGLO-PHONE [Quebec in the English-language press]. *J. of Can. Studies [Canada] 1978 13(2): 79-99.* Analyzes front-page treatment of Quebec by three English-language newspapers—the *Globe and Mail*, the *Winnipeg Free Press*, and the *Vancouver Sun*—for September 1974 to August 1975. The same tendency—to highlight crime, disorder, corruption, and fiscal waste, and to suggest a general atmosphere of immaturity—is evident in headlines, editorials, commentary, photos, and cartoons, as well as among all three papers. "Trouble" is a key word, and one rather symptomatic title announces that "A Gallic shrug greets Quebec's swing towards anarchy." 5 charts, 9 tables.   L. W. Van Wyk

3939. Bourgeault, Guy. LE NATIONALISME QUEBECOIS ET L'EGLISE [Quebecois nationalism and the Church]. *Can. Rev. of Studies in Nationalism [Canada] 1978 5(2): 189-207.* Discusses the difficulties of the Catholic Church in Quebec in dealing with the contemporary nationalism movement there. Traditionally the Church associated itself with French Canadian aspirations, but it has felt uncomfortable with contemporary expressions of those feelings, characterized as they are by secularism and socialism. The Church's problem in this connection is bound fundamentally to the larger question of the role of the Church in Quebec society today. Secondary sources; 52 notes.   J. A. Kicklighter

3940. Boutet, Odina. LA GRENOUILLE BICULTURELLE ET LE BOEUF UNICULTUREL [The bicultural frog and the unicultural bull]. *Action Natl. [Canada] 1977 67(1): 61-73.* Canadian federalism and biculturalism are opportunities for English Canadians to retain their identity while assimilating and destroying the identity of French Canadians. Quebec's weakness has been caused not only by the strength of English culture in North America but also by the absence of a French culture even within the province. French Canadian educational institutions and news media have been especially negligent in preserving French culture. While presenting a facade of seeking unity to the outside world, internally English Canadians have exercised a policy of intimidation and deprived French Canadians of perspective and a sense of accomplishment.   A. W. Novitsky

3941. Courchene, Thomas J. ECONOMICS AND FEDERALISM. *Tr. of the Royal Soc. of Can. [Canada] 1978 16: 71-87.* Discusses Canada in an economic framework, and describes Anglophones as unilingual, because their language dominates the Western world. Notes the gradual westward shift of Canada's economic center and shows how policies of the federal government encourage the provinces to take unrealistic approaches to economic matters. Compares "gap closing" with "adjustment accommodating" programs. 8 notes.   J. D. Neville

3942. Craig, A. W. BRITAIN, CANADA AND EUROPE FACE RESURGENT REGIONALISM. *Int. Perspectives [Canada] 1977 (July-August): 37-42.* Examines the phenomenon variously described as regionalism, separatism, home-rule, devolution, subnationalism, or minority nationalism in Great Britain and Canada. Such movements may be the result of excessive centralization (e.g., Scotland, Wales) or weakness of national identity (e.g., Quebec), but neglect of perceived regional needs is a common factor. Governments must respond to such regional pressures. Federal systems, such as Canada's, appear better equipped to make the required adjustments. Secondary sources; photo, 6 notes.   E. S. Palais

3943. Dion, Léon. ANTI-POLITICS AND MARGINALS. *Government and Opposition [Great Britain] 1974 9(1): 28-41.* Discusses

the political stability of liberal democracy and the Canadian government's tolerance of dissent in Quebec in the 1960's-70's.

3944. Dion, Léon and deSeve, Micheline. QUEBEC: INTEREST GROUPS AND THE SEARCH FOR AN ALTERNATIVE POLITICAL SYSTEM. *Ann. of the Am. Acad. of Pol. and Soc. Sci. 1974 413: 124-144.* Nearly 15 years ago Quebec entered an active period of socio-political unrest. A people who had undergone considerable changes in their objective conditions of living without a corresponding change in their social consciousness suddenly found themselves forced, by their political leaders, to realize the extent of their maladjustment to a predominantly urban and highly industrialized society and pressured to readjust their position. The Union Nationale Party was thrown into temporary disarray by the sudden deaths of Maurice Duplessis—uncontested master of the province—on August 30 1959 and of his successor, Paul Sauvé, scarcely four months after he came to power. The Liberal Party under Jean Lesage was thus able to win the provincial election in June 1960. This event precipitated what has been labelled the quiet revolution. The Lesage program manifested a new desire to modernize the mechanisms of the state and to seize the initiative in policies of economic and social development. This set off a reform movement that went beyond the ambitions of its initiators. The process of rationalizing the administrative mechanisms of a modern bureaucratic state created a wave of cultural shock which was felt at all levels of the society. Such changes could not occur without putting great pressures on the population or without having unexpected consequences, the most important being the rebirth of the Quebec nationalist ideology as a political movement and the formation of various kinds of popular movements.   J

3945. Doucet, Paul. ENGLISH CANADIAN NATIONALISM: A QUEBEC VIEW. *Queen's Q. [Canada] 1975 82(2): 259-262.* Analyzes developing nationalism among the English-origin people of Canada. Persons of French origin went through the same process 25 years ago. Oil has provided the economic impetus. It will no longer be exported to the United States unless all other markets fail. Americans will soon be forbidden to purchase certain properties in Canada. The old ideal of a single continent with single aims is dead. The most important remaining task is to create an English Canadian culture, the burden of which will fall on the universities.   V. L. Human

3946. Dunton, Davidson. RECOGNIZED, EQUITABLE DUALITY. *J. of Can. Studies [Canada] 1977 12(3): 106-108.* The attitudes of English-speaking Canadians have had much to do with the rise of Québécois nationalism. Anglophones have tended to consider Canada as an English-speaking country, with a small, quaint pocket of French in Quebec. Tolerated there, the French language was actively discouraged elsewhere. Maybe it is too late, but Canadians from coast to coast should make a real effort to put French on an equal level with English at the provincial level. Rather than talking of Canadian unity, we might speak of Canadian duality—recognized, equitable duality from which could come immense strength and quality.   J. C. Billigmeier

3947. Glazier, Kenneth M. THE SURGE OF NATIONALISM IN CANADA TODAY. *Current Hist. 1974 66(392): 150-154.*

3948. Gourevitch, Peter. THE REEMERGENCE OF "PERIPHERAL NATIONALISMS": SOME COMPARATIVE SPECULATIONS ON THE SPATIAL DISTRIBUTION OF POLITICAL LEADERSHIP AND ECONOMIC GROWTH. *Comparative Studies in Soc. and Hist. [Great Britain] 1979 21(3): 303-322.* Analyzes the separatist movements in Western European countries, Yugoslavia, and Canada in the 20th century.

3949. Guindon, Hubert. LA MODERNISATION DU QUÉBEC ET LA LÉGITIMITÉ DE L'ÉTAT CANADIEN [The modernization of Quebec and the legitimacy of the Canadian state]. *Recherches Sociographiques [Canada] 1977 18(3): 337-366.* The foundation of the present Canadian crisis flows from the modernization of the political economy of Quebec. The rise of a new middle class, supported by the expanding role of the Quebec provincial government, created a new series of expectations. With time the question of language was to surface as a political issue and the federal government established its language policy to cope with the new expectations. This has proven inadequate and a renegotiation of the Canadian federal structure is now a necessity. Based on studies on the

Royal Commission on Bilingualism and Biculturalism and secondary sources; table, 58 notes. A. E. LeBlanc

3950. Guindon, Hubert. THE MODERNIZATION OF QUEBEC AND THE LEGITIMACY OF THE CANADIAN STATE. *Can. Rev. of Sociol. and Anthrop. [Canada] 1978 15(2): 227-245.* Examines the process of modernization in Quebec and its legitimacy as a Canadian state. Political discontent in Quebec is the consequence of modernization because a new middle class has emerged, which is confined to the public sector and is limited to the management and control of the private sector by virtue of language. The language policy is irrelevant to modernization of Quebec and considers the need for a renegotiation of the "unequal union." Primary and secondary sources; table, 9 notes, biblio.
G. P. Cleyet

3951. Hodgins, Bruce W. and Smith, Denis. CANADA AND QUÉBEC: FACING THE REALITY. *J. of Can. Studies [Canada] 1977 12(3): 124-126.* English-speaking Canada and Quebec-French Canada are really separate nations, though the Anglophones are not as aware of their identity as are the French. Whether the result of the current confrontation is sovereignty for Quebec or some new type of confederation, English-speaking Canadians should become more aware and confident of their own purpose and will to survive as a distinct entity.
J. C. Billigmeier

3952. Holmes, Jean. A NOTE ON SOME ASPECTS OF CONTEMPORARY CANADIAN AND AUSTRALIAN FEDERALISM. *J. of Commonwealth and Comparative Pol. [Great Britain] 1974 12(3): 313-322.* Examines the constitutional crises in Canada and Australia resulting from a breakdown in the relations between the state and federal governments and compares the constitutional conferences prompted in Canada by Quebec and in Australia by Victoria. Discusses the importance of bargaining in a federal system, the freedom of action of political leaders as compared with their counterparts in unitary systems, and the problems inherent in financial policymaking and the allocation of revenue. Based on extracts from newspapers; 112 notes. C. Anstey

3953. Hurley, Jefferson. "THE NATIONAL FILM BOARD OF CANADA IS FRIGHTENED OF ITS OWN IMAGES." *Communist Viewpoint [Canada] 1973 5(3): 36-42.* The National Film Board's attempts to censor French-language documentaries from Quebec. S

3954. Hutchison, Bruce. CANADA'S TIME OF TROUBLES. *Foreign Affairs 1977 56(1): 175-189.* Though the 1976 provincial victory of René Lévesque and his Parti Quebecois added new momentum to the cause of French Canadian separatism, an independent Quebec is by no means inevitable. After years of indecision and hesitation, the federal government clearly has committed itself to a bicultural and bilingual Canada. M. R. Yerburgh

3955. Kwavnick, David. QUEBEC AND THE TWO NATIONS THEORY: A RE-EXAMINATION. *Queen's Q. [Canada] 1974 81(3): 357-376.* A critical rejoinder to Hugh Thorburn's article "Needed: A New Look at the Two-Nation Theory." Suggests that English Canadian reactions to separatism in the 1960's had irrational bases, particularly those that centered on the "More Power to Quebec" theory, and that Quebec was a nation in a "sociological" sense. 15 notes.
J. A. Casada

3956. Latouche, Daniel. LES PROGRAMMES ÉLECTORAUX LORS DE L'ÉLECTION PROVINCIALE DE 1973: UNE DESCRIPTION QUANTITATIVE [The electoral programs during the provincial elections of 1973: a quantitative description]. *Can. Rev. of Studies in Nationalism [Canada] 1974 1(2): 263-275.* Analyzes Quebec's four major parties: the secessionist Parti Québécois, the Liberals, Crédit Social, and Union Nationale, and their positions on social, economic, environmental, and constitutional questions, including the issue of Quebec's ties to Canada. The Parti Québécois, despite its secessionist views, stressed social issues more in its campaign literature, relegated Quebec's independence to third place, and appealed to voters as a general party of the Left. The Union Nationale discussed its main issue, Québec's relationship to the federal government, more than did any other party. 2 fig., 9 tables, 6 notes.
J. C. Billigmeier

3957. Lemieux, Pierre. WHAT'S HAPPENING IN QUEBEC. *Reason 1978 10(3): 24-27, 36.* Examines political attitudes of the Parti Québécois, 1976-78, toward French language, separatism, statism, socialism, and anti-capitalism.

3958. Lithwick, N. H. and Winer, Stanley L. FALTERING FEDERALISM AND FRENCH CANADIANS. *J. of Can. Studies [Canada] 1977 12(3): 44-52.* The current debate over Quebec's relationship to Canada consists of two separable but closely interwoven themes: one concerns the meaning of and role for French Canada, and the second involves the nature of Canadian federalism. 14 notes.
J. C. Billigmeier

3959. Loh, Wallace D. NATIONALIST ATTITUDES IN QUEBEC AND BELGIUM. *J. of Conflict Resolution 1975 19(2): 217-249.* Nationalist attitudes were studied in relation to ethnicity and social class in Quebec and Belgium, two bilingual multiethnic societies, during the 1970's.

3960. Macleod, Alex. NATIONALISM AND SOCIAL CLASS: THE UNRESOLVED DILEMMA OF THE QUEBEC LEFT. *J. of Can. Studies 1973 8(4): 3-15.*

3961. Mallory, J. R. AMENDING THE CONSTITUTION BY STEALTH. *Queen's Q. [Canada] 1975 82(3): 394-401.* Canada's Representation Act of 1974 attempted to solve the historical constitutional conflict between proportional representation by population favored by English-speaking Canadians in the larger provinces, and equitable representation of minorities, espoused by French Canadians in Quebec and in the smaller provinces. Although the reapportionment act amended the constitution by altering the legislated formula for representation in the House of Commons, this fact was not openly debated, probably to facilitate a practical political compromise. 6 notes. T. Simmerman

3962. Nappi, Carmine. DES MÉTHODES QUANTITATIVES APPLIQUÉES AU SECTEUR DES EXPORTATIONS QUÉBÉCOISES, 1969 [Quantitative methods and the Quebec export sector, 1969]. *Actualité Écon. [Canada] 1974 50(4): 491-511.* Measures the degrees of specialization of exports for 50 goods, the interprovincial and international export intensity indices for the five Canadian regions, and the export performance indices for the provinces under study. The conclusion highlights the importance of the east-west Canadian trade, specially for the internal provinces. Finally, the Quebec commercial characteristics in relation with those of other Canadian provinces are outlined and stressed.
J

3963. Ornstein, Michael D.; Stevenson, Michael H.; and Williams, A. Paul M. PUBLIC OPINION AND THE CANADIAN POLITICAL CRISIS. *Can. Rev. of Sociol. and Anthrop. [Canada] 1978 15(2): 158-205.* Analyzes public opinion concerning the relations between French and English communities in Quebec, and between Quebec and the other Canadian provinces. Concludes that the constraints in public opinion influence English Canadian political elites toward a less adversarial confrontation with Quebec. Based on data gathered on a national sample survey, May-June 1977; 17 tables, biblio. G. P. Cleyet

3964. Ossenberg, Richard J. UNITY IN SPITE OF OURSELVES. *Queen's Q. [Canada] 1974 81(3): 431-436.* Examines separatism in Quebec and alienation in Canada's hinterlands, suggesting that, somewhat paradoxically, conflict forces are a factor making for national unity. Biblio.
J. A. Casada

3965. Rayside, David M. FEDERALISM AND THE PARTY SYSTEM: PROVINCIAL AND FEDERAL LIBERALS IN THE PROVINCE OF QUEBEC. *Can. J. of Pol. Sci. [Canada] 1978 11(3): 499-528.* A study of provincialism vs. federalism in Canada, particularly in relation to Quebec and the ethnic and language issues. "In a curious way, the Canadian political system and party system accentuates regionalism, and then stifles the expression of regional concerns in the national arena." It results in Quebec Liberals in Ottawa clearly disagreeing with their counterparts in the provincial legislative halls, a conflict which could be creative but in fact becomes destructive, because it becomes a tool in the hands of elected politicians tempted thereby to act from self-interest rather than in the interests of the people of Quebec. 4 tables, fig., 42 notes.

3966. Rich, Harvey. THE CANADIAN CASE FOR A REPRESENTATIVE BUREAUCRACY. *Pol. Sci. [New Zealand] 1975 27(1-2): 97-110.* Discusses representative bureaucracies as they relate to the Canadian Public Service; considers the anglophone and francophone communities as well as the corresponding binational character of the Canadian national government, 1944-75.

3967. Richert, Jean Pierre. CANADIAN NATIONAL IDENTITY: AN EMPIRICAL STUDY. *Am. Rev. of Can. Studies 1974 4(1): 89-98.* Examines differences in Canadian children and American children as they experience feelings of nationalism; further, discusses the tendency of Canadian anglophone children to identify with Canada, while Francophone children identify with Quebec; examines tendency for nationalistic feelings to weaken with age, 1971-72.

3968. Roback, Léo and Tremblay, Louis-Marie. LE NATIONALISME AU SEIN DE SYNDICATS QUEBECOIS [Nationalism among Québecois labor organizations]. *Can. Rev. of Studies in Nationalism [Canada] 1978 5(2): 237-257.* Analyzes the changing views of nationalism in Quebec's largest labor organizations, the Fédération des Travailleurs du Québec (Quebec Federation of Labor) and the Confédération des Syndicats Nationaux (Confederation of National Trade Unions). The former, much older than the latter, supported a homogenous Canadian nationalism; only in 1960 did there begin to emerge a nationalistic ideology based on belief in class conflict and a call for an end to all forms of socioeconomic exploitation. The much younger Confederation was originally hostile to all forms of nationalism but today believes a substantial increase of power to the Quebec state would substantially improve the lot of the working people there. Secondary sources; 25 notes.
J. A. Kicklighter

3969. Robertson, R. Gordon. DIVERSITY WITH UNITY IN CANADA: POSSIBILITIES AND LIMITS. *Tr. of the Royal Soc. of Can. [Canada] 1978 16: 269-278.* Notes the differences in perception between French- and English-speaking Canadians. Francophones see themselves as a nation and are frustrated because there is no equivalent feeling among the Anglophones, who are used to the idea that their ancestors came from many nations and that their point of unity is that they are Canadians. Anglophones are pan-Canadian and geographical in their nationalism, rather than particular and linguistic. Before World War II, however, they became blurred into the British Empire, and their geographical emphasis makes those in the Maritimes feel closer to Boston than to Vancouver.
J. D. Neville

3970. Rotstein, Abraham. IS THERE AN ENGLISH-CANADIAN NATIONALISM? *J. of Can. Studies [Canada] 1978 13(2): 109-118.* Deplores English Canadians's indifference to their own economic and cultural autonomy, threatened with "quiet erosion" from the United States. Reviews developments since the publication of George Grant's seminal *Lament for a Nation* (1965). Adduces a number of facts suggesting that English Canadian nationalism largely is concerned with simple territorial integrity, which places it on a collision course with the separatist aspirations of the Parti Québécois. Notes the refusal of several provincial premiers to consider economic union with an independent Quebec. Calls for a more cooperative attitude based on a more profound kind of English Canadian nationalism. 60 notes. Translation of an address delivered in French at Université Laval, 26 January 1978.
L. W. Van Wyk

3971. Ryan, Claude. ANDRÉ LAURENDEAU. *J. of Can. Studies 1973 8(3): 3-7.* Discusses the thought of André Laurendeau, a French Canadian from Quebec who urged his fellow French Canadians to gain knowledge and understanding of English Canadians.

3972. Saint-Germain, Maurice. DÉPENDANCE ÉCONOMIQUE ET FREINS AU DÉVELOPPEMENT: LE CAS DU QUÉBEC [Economic dependence and curbs on development: the Quebec case]. *Recherche Sociale [France] 1974 49: 93-98.* The present economic structure of Quebec suffers from double domination by English Canada and the United States, and from the juxtaposition of two unequal economic sectors having different dynamics and objectives. This dependence and dualism, which are manifested at various levels of the economy and society, are the major obstacles to the development of Quebec.
J. D. Falk

3973. Sirois, Antoine. LITTÉRATURE ET NATIONALISME [Literature and nationalism]. *J. of Can. Studies [Canada] 1976 11(4): 54-56.* Discusses the T. H. B. Symons report (1975) on Canadian higher education, as it relates to Quebec; the report does not adequately deal with national educational needs or with the needs of those who are not strictly English Canadian.

3974. Smiley, Donald V. THE DOMINANCE OF WITHINPUTS?: CANADIAN POLITICS. *Polity 1973 6(2): 276-281.* A review article of John Meisel's *Working Papers on Canadian Politics* (Montreal: McGill-Queen's U. Press, 1972) and Richard Simeon's *Federal-Provincial Diplomacy; The Making of Recent Policy in Canada* (Toronto: U. of Toronto Pr. 1972). The longest of Meisel's papers are interim reports on the study of the 1968 federal general elections, while others deal with linguistic groups and with relations between the English and the French in Canada. Examines intensively three sets of federal-provincial interactions in the middle and late 1960's. Speculates that "there are relatively weak linkages between political decision makers and their environment." 10 notes.
E. P. Stickney

3975. Srebnik, Henry. THE LIBERAL PARTY: CANADA'S PROTECTION RACKET. *Can. Dimension [Canada] 1978 13(1): 22-27.* Concludes that the popularity of Canada's Liberal Party, which has maintained national rule for 43 years, is due to its basic unifying nature, and that though many French Canadians vote in the Liberal Party nationally and in the Parti Québécois locally and provincially, such votes allow them to protect their collective interests vis-à-vis English Canada

3976. Teeple, Gary. LIMITS TO NATIONALISM. *Can. Dimension [Canada] 1977 12(6): 27-36.* Examines the presence of nationalism in Canadian national politics, 1957-75; discusses several political movements spawned by it and the possibility of social change because of nationalistic feelings.

3977. Thorburn, Hugh G. CANADIAN PLURALIST DEMOCRACY IN CRISIS. *Can. J. of Pol. Sci. [Canada] 1978 11(4): 723-738.* Canada reconciles political democracy and the control of society by an established elite consisting mainly of business leaders. The people are led to believe in the system and accept their differences with the elite. When the differences cannot be settled they become exacerbated, as in the case of the different ethnic and cultural levels between the English and the French groups whose mutual relations are impaired. Presidential address to the Canadian Political Association, London, May 1978; 6 notes.
G. P. Cleyet

3978. Thorburn, Hugh. NEEDED: A NEW LOOK AT THE TWO-NATION THEORY. *Queen's Q. [Canada] 1973 80(2): 268-273.* The disaffection of French Canada has introduced a malaise into Canadian politics, with increasing sentiment in Quebec for a permanent separation. Too much Americanization and too rapid a depletion of economic resources pose economic problems for the country. Canada must solve these problems to have a successful future by tackling existing constitutional arrangements which cause frustrations and animosities.
J. A. Casada

3979. Tremblay, Arthur. LES NATIONALISMES ET LES ÉTATS [Nationalisms and states]. *Tr. of the Royal Soc. of Can. [Canada] 1978 16: 141-149.* Notes loyalties in Canada to the federal and to the provincial governments. Discusses where in Canada one finds nationalism and where one finds two forms of it.
J. D. Neville

3980. Walsh, Jeannette. 50 YEARS OF THE U.S.S.R. AND THE NATIONAL QUESTION IN CANADA. *Communist Viewpoint [Canada] 1972 4(6): 12-15.* Examines the initial Soviet attitude toward ethnic groups and then discusses French Canadians.

3981. —. L'ÉCONOMIE ET LES DISPARITÉS RÉGIONALES [The economy and regional disparities]. *Action Natl. [Canada] 1978 67(8): 607-623.* Despite favorable rhetoric, Canada remains far from genuine biculturalism. The English sector is strongly influenced and supported by the United States. The maintenance of French culture in North America requires a stronger Quebec economy, and the leveling of regional economic disparity in which Quebec suffers in comparison with Ontario. Since 1951, Montreal has increased its dominance over Quebec, while falling farther behind Toronto on the national scale. Primary and secondary sources; 7 tables, 13 notes.   A. W. Novitsky

Quebec Separatism

3982. Albinski, Henry S.   QUEBEC AND CANADIAN UNITY. *Current Hist.* 1974 66(392): 155-160. Discusses Quebec's position within Canada and the problems of unifying Quebec with the nine other Canadian provinces.   S

3983. Alessandri, Giuseppe.   UN'ALTERNATIVA PER IL QUEBEC [An alternative for Quebec]. *Affari Esteri [Italy]* 1973 5(20): 150-161. The alternative for Quebec in contemporary Canada is to maintain its social and cultural identity within the Canadian confederation.   A. R. Stoesen

3984. Allen, Patrick.   LES JEUX OLYMPIQUES: ICEBERGS OU RAMPES DE LANCEMENTS? [The Olympic Games: icebergs or launching pads?]. *Action Natl. [Canada]* 1976 65(5): 271-323. Pierre de Coubertin proposed the reestablishment of the Olympic Games at a conference at the Sorbonne on 25 November 1892. The first games in the modern series took place four years later at Athens, and they have been held every four years since, except in 1916, 1940, and 1944 during major wars. Canadians have participated since 1900, but the 1976 games at Montreal were the first to be held in Canada. The entire province of Quebec prepared for the games and allied activities and there has been a resurgence of amateur athletic participation throughout the province. The spirit of cooperation in the preparations may be a manifestation of Quebec nationalism. 8 tables.   A. W. Novitsky

3985. Angers, François-Albert.   UN DOCUMENT À MÉDITER SUR LE PLAN NATIONAL FRANÇAIS OU QUÉBÉCOIS: COMPARAISON ENTRE LA POLOGNE ET LE QUÉBEC [Meditations on a document on the French or Quebec national plan: a comparison between Poland and Quebec]. *Action Natl. [Canada]* 1973 63(4): 324-344. Evaluates Quebec's future as a nation capable of resisting foreign influences and of maintaining its national identity, based on Marcel Mermoz's "Pologne Vivante sous les Contraintes," *La France Catholique* (18 May 1973), here reproduced.

3986. Bauer, Julien.   ATTITUDE DES SYNDICATS [The political position of unions]. *Études Int. [Canada]* 1977 8(2): 307-319. Examines the relationship of workers' movements and unions with the Parti Québécois before and after the 15 November 1976 elections. Explains differences in attitude among the labor organizations. Primary and secondary sources; 30 notes.   J. F. Harrington, Jr.

3987. Beaudoin, Gerald.   LES ASPECTS CONSTITUTIONNELS DE REFERENDUM [The constitutional aspects of a referendum]. *Études Int. [Canada]* 1977 8(2): 197-207. Discusses the legal basis for and the political ramifications of a referendum in connection with Quebec's aspirations for independence. Secondary sources; 20 notes, biblio.   J. F. Harrington, Jr.

3988. Benjamin, Jacques.   CONSÉQUENCES DE L'ÉLECTION DU 15 NOVEMBRE 1976 AU QUÉBEC: DE NOUVELLES FLAMBÉES DE VIOLENCE? [The consequences of the elections of 15 November 1976 in Quebec: some new flare-ups of violence?]. *J. of Can. Studies [Canada]* 1977 12(3): 85-92. During 1960-68, under the Union Nationale, Quebec was a consensual society, moving to modernize its traditional institutions; this was the so-called Révolution Tranquille (Quiet Revolution). During 1969-76, it was a conflictual society, in which forces desiring change, some violent (the FLQ), some nonviolent (labor unions, the PQ) opposed the ruling Liberals and each other. With the election of the Parti Québécois, Quebec has become more of a consensus society again; opposition to the PQ comes from the federal government and marginal groups (English-speakers, corporations). The PQ government does not stress its independence plank, but rather social reform; it is this that is winning it support from the Québécois. 43 notes.   J. C. Billigmeier

3989. Bergeron, Gerard.   PROJECT D'UN NOUVEAU COMMONWEALTH CANADIEN [Proposal for a new Canadian commonwealth]. *Études Int. [Canada]* 1977 8(2): 240-253. Rejoices in the 15 November 1976 vote and wants to insure that Quebec's victory is lasting. Suggests as an alternative to Ottawa's federalism and Quebec's separatism, a "Commonwealth *Canadien*" which reflects the bilingual and distinctive nature of the British and French parts of Canada. Discusses the political design of the proposed Commonwealth, emphasizing its two-state construction: one would be federative and English-speaking and the other would be unitary and French-speaking.   J. F. Harrington, Jr.

3990. Blanchard, Guy.   LA POSITION DE FAIBLESSE DU "FRENCH POWER" [The weak position of "French power"]. *Action Natl. [Canada]* 1973 62(10): 810-815. The sense of French inferiority to the English and superior English economic power are at the base of the separatist movement in Quebec.

3991. Bonenfant, Joseph.   GASTON MIRON ET L'IDENTITE POLITIQUE DU QUEBEC [Gaston Miron and Quebec's political identity]. *Am. Rev. of Can. Studies* 1974 4(2): 46-54. Examines the poetry of Gaston Miron, a Québécois poet whose belief in linguistic, cultural, and political sovereignty for Quebec has come to be represented in his work, identifying him as the national poet of Quebec, 1969-74.

3992. Bourgault, Jacques.   L'ATTITUDE DES MASS MEDIA VIS-À-VIS DU GOUVERNEMENT QUÉBECOIS [The attitude of the mass media toward the Quebec government]. *Études Int. [Canada]* 1977 8(2): 320-336. Analyzes the attitudes of the Montreal press toward René Levesque's government. Examines the coverage of *La Presse, Le Devoir, Montreal-Matin, Dimanche-Matin,* and one English-language paper, the *Montreal Star,* on eight political events during 16 November 1976-1 April 1977. The topics included the result of the elections, the new Council of Ministers, the first two sessions of the legislature, the Prime Minister's trip to New York and his automobile accident, the budget, and the French White Book. Primary sources; 11 notes.   J. F. Harrington, Jr.

3993. Boutet, Odina.   LA CULTURE ET L'INDÉPENDANCE DU QUÉBEC [Culture and the independence of Quebec]. *Action Natl. [Canada]* 1974 63(10): 838-849. The goals of the Parti Québécois are to develop French culture, promote the idea of a viable Quebec currency, and secure the independence of Quebec.

3994. Brossard, Jacques.   LE DROIT DE PEUPLE QUÉBECOIS A L'AUTODETERMINATION ET A L'INDEPENDANCE [The right of the people of Quebec to self-determination and independence]. *Études Int. [Canada]* 1977 8(2): 151-171. Examines the constitutional aspect of Quebec's legal right to self-determination and to secede from Ottawa's control. Considers the establishment of a French-Canadian state from the viewpoint of international law and UN precedents. Concludes that the Quebec people have the legal right to determine their own form of government and that their wishes can be discerned easily through a referendum. Primary and secondary sources; 26 notes.   J. F. Harrington, Jr.

3995. Chouinard, Jean-Yves.   ÉGALITÉ DE DROITS POUR LES PEUPLES CANADIENS ET QUÉBÉCOIS [Equality of rights for Canadians and Quebecois]. *Action Natl. [Canada]* 1978 68(3): 234-239. French Canadians in Quebec constitute a nation with historical, cultural, linguistic, ethnic, and demographic attributes, as defined in the United Nations Charter and various declarations; the pronouncements of Woodrow Wilson; the final act of the Helsinki Conference (1975); and statements of ecclesiastical authorities, notably Pope John XXIII's "Pacem in Terris." This distinct nation has been recognized implicitly and explicitly by adherents of Canadian biculturalism, and this must lead to self-determination in any Canadian constitutional revision. 2 notes.   A. W. Novitsky

3996. Chouinard, Jean-Yves.   L'AUTODÉTERMINATION ET LES LAURENTIENS [Self-determination and the Laurentians]. *Action Natl. [Canada]* 1977 66(6): 410-422. Since 1957 the Alliance Laurentienne has provided intellectual support for Quebec separatism with the publication of a reprint of Wilfred Morin's *L'Indépendance du Québec,* first published in 1938 as *Nos Droits a l'indépendence politique*; 20 issues of the *Revue Laurentie*; and three books written by the Director of the Alliance, Raymond Barbeau. The Alliance asserts that Quebec has moral, legal, and constitutional rights to autonomy, and is particularly critical of Pierre Elliott Trudeau, André Laurendeau, and other proponents of a reformed federalism. 6 notes.   A. W. Novitsky

3997. Clarke, Harold.   PARTISANSHIP AND THE PARTI QUEBECOIS: THE IMPACT OF THE INDEPENDENCE ISSUE. *Am. Rev. of Can. Studies 1978 8(2): 28-47.* The Parti Québécois has been principal beneficiary of affiliation changes in the Quebec electorate during the 1970's. It has attracted young, better-educated, politically active voters who tend to be strongly oriented toward provincial politics. Although the PQ's favoring of separatism has been the most significant factor in attracting adherents, in 1976 the PQ changed its emphasis to good government in a successful attempt to secure additional support. However, the PQ must still convince the majority of Quebec voters that independence is desirable. Based on interviews with 702 Quebec voters in the 1974 Canadian national election survey. 8 tables; graph; 33 notes.
                                                        G.-A. Patzwald

3998. Cody, Howard.   THE ONTARIO RESPONSE TO QUEBEC'S SEPARATIST CHALLENGE. *Am. Rev. of Can. Studies 1978 8(1): 43-55.* Since the election of Quebec's separatist government, Ontario Premier William Davis has employed overtures of friendship, economic arguments, and a new concern for Franco-Ontarians in his attempt to convince the Quebec people of the advantages of continued confederation. Further, Davis has proposed creation of a Federal-Provincial Secretariat to resolve inter-provincial conflicts. Ontario's opposition parties, both opposed to separation, "have been jockeying against the Premier and each other for the position of Ontario's champion of a united Canada." Primary and secondary sources including interviews with unidentified persons; 57 notes.   G.-A. Patzwald

3999. Cuneo, Charles J. and Curtis, James E.   QUEBEC SEPARATISM: AN ANALYSIS OF DETERMINANTS WITHIN SOCIAL-CLASS LEVELS. *Can. R. of Sociol. and Anthrop. 1974 11(1): 1-29.* Surveys 1968 data on the extent and correlates of separatist opinion among French-speaking adults in Quebec. The analysis focuses on determinants of separatism within new middle-class occupational levels, but some comparative data are provided for the lower classes and farmers as well. The author's model of separatist support fits the new middle class best and explains 40 percent of the variance in the dependent variable for professionals and semi-professionals and 43 percent for managers, officials, and proprietors. The effect of the independent variables on separatist support varied by occupational level. For example, French-Canadian ethnic consciousness, distrust of the federal government and personal dissatisfaction had their strongest independent effects within the new middle class, while economic insecurity and left politico-economic orientation generally had their strongest effects on separatist support among unskilled workers and farmers.   J

4000. Dion, Léon and Seve, Micheline de.   QUEBEC OU L'EMERGENCE D'UNE FORMULE POLITIQUE ALTERNATIVE [Quebec or the emergence of an alternative political formula]. *Can. Rev. of Studies in Nationalism [Canada] 1978 5(2): 258-283.* For 15 years Quebec has undergone significant sociopolitical shocks with vast urbanization and industrialization. Simultaneously, Quebec's political leaders initiated major reform movements in the government, which had the effect of awakening the people to the great cultural changes around them. From this awakening came the Québécois nationalist ideology as a popular political movement. Printed primary and secondary sources; 39 notes.
                                                        J. A. Kicklighter

4001. Dobell, Peter C.   QUÉBEC SEPARATISM: DOMESTIC AND INTERNATIONAL IMPLICATIONS. *World Today [Great Britain] 1977 33(4): 149-159.* Examines separatism among French Canadians in Quebec, 1974-76.

4002. Glazier, Kenneth M.   SEPARATISM AND QUEBEC. *Current Hist. 1977 72(426): 154-157, 178-179.* Examines economic issues in Quebec separatism, the breakdown of minorities in the province, and the militant French-speaking population.

4003. Gonick, Cy.   THE NEW PATRIOTS. *Can. Dimension [Canada] 1977 12(2): 32-36.* Traces the historical development of nationalism in Quebec and analyzes the relations among nationalism, the Parti Québécois, the business community, and the working class in the 1970's.

4004. Gudmundson, Fred and Gonick, Cy.   A REFERENDUM STRATEGY FOR THE LEFT. *Can. Dimension [Canada] 1979 13(6): 38-41.* Discusses the unofficial position of the Canadian Left regarding the question of Quebec sovereignty which will be voted on in 1979.

4005. Hamel, Jacques.   LE MOUVEMENT NATIONAL DES QUÉBÉCOIS À LA RECHERCHE DE LA MODERNITÉ [The Quebecers national movement and the search for modernity]. *Recherches Sociographiques [Canada] 1973 14(3): 341-361.* The movement has directed its attention to the emergence of a political objective, the state of Québec. Since the movement is an outgrowth of the St. John the Baptist Society of a preceeding era, this has led to significant problems. The latter, concerned with the French-Canadian family and the Church, created a distinct mode of thinking and action. The former has found it necessary to turn to other sources for inspiration and elite support. Based on interviews and official pronouncements of both groups; 44 notes.
                                                        A. E. LeBlanc

4006. Hero, Alfred, Jr.   QUELQUES REACTIONS AMERICAINES AU REGIME DU PARTI QUÉBÉCOIS DEPUIS LE 15 NOVEMBRE 1976 [American reactions to the Parti Québécois government since 15 November 1976]. *Études Int. [Canada] 1977 8(2): 356-373.* Few Americans ever have been interested in Canada. Those presently interested are the influential; they are concerned by the 15 November 1976 Quebec vote. That much of their information on Canada comes from English Canadians colors their perceptions of the economic, cultural, and collective security ramifications in Ottawa and Washington of an independent Quebec. Examines the future of Canadian-US relations, noting that Quebec's separatism could make the Maritime Provinces US satellites. Secondary sources; 6 notes.   J. F. Harrington, Jr.

4007. Hudon, Raymond.   THE 1976 QUEBEC ELECTION. *Queen's Q. [Canada] 1977 84(1): 18-30.* Analyzes the 1976 provincial election in Quebec in terms of both French and English Canada. Details causes of the election, the nature of the campaign, and recent developments. Clearly the election marks a new era in Quebec politics, but the question of the long-term impact of the victorious Parti Québécois remains. 15 notes.   J. A. Casada

4008. Idrissi.   QUÉBEC DE L'AN DEUX: LA GENÈSE D'UNE NATION [Quebec in year two: the genesis of a nation]. *Défense Natl. [France] 1977 33(11): 43-60.* Traces the history of Quebec nationalism and of the Parti Québécois, detailing the sources of discontent among French Canadians, and suggests a solution to the political conflict in Quebec and the establishment of a new 'Quebec nation' with reference to France's responsibilities. 3 notes.

4009. Kopkind, Andrew.   QUEBEC: A DECLARATION OF INDEPENDENCE BUT NO REVOLUTION. *Working Papers for a New Soc. 1978 6(5): 32-40.* Discusses the aims of the Parti Québécois which seeks cultural and lingual hegemony for French-speaking citizens, placing political and economic ends in a secondary position, 1973-78.

4010. Kwavnick, David.   QUÉBECOIS NATIONALISM AND CANADA'S NATIONAL INTEREST. *J. of Can. Studies [Canada] 1977 12(3): 53-68.* Quebec nationalism, whether separatist or "moderate," has been damaging to Canada's national interest. In fact, the "moderates" are worse, for they want to remain in Canada, while making other Canadians repay them for this magnanimity by giving them all sorts of special privileges. Canada's national interest lies in minimizing Quebec nationalism in Canada at the least possible cost to Canada. 5 notes.
                                                        J. C. Billigmeier

4011. Laczko, Leslie.   ENGLISH CANADIANS AND QUÉBECOIS NATIONALISM: AN EMPIRICAL ANALYSIS. *Can. Rev. of Sociol. and Anthrop. [Canada] 1978 15(2): 206-217.* Analyzes the English-speaking Québécois's reactions to French Canadian nationalism, as they vary according to the degree to which French Canadians' demands and aspirations are legitimate. The more highly educated English Canadians in

Quebec have a greater awareness of the situation the French Canadian nationalist movement aims at improving, and are more sympathetic to the movement than the working class. Primary and secondary sources; 3 tables, 2 fig., biblio., appendix. G. P. Cleyet

4012. Lamontagne, Maurice. FEDERALISME OU ASSOCIATION D'ETATS INDEPENDANTS [Federalism or an association of independent states]. *Études Int. [Canada] 1977 8(2): 208-230.* A Canadian senator reviews the arguments supporting Quebec's independence and examines alternatives to such separation, including an association of independent states, and federalism (his own preference). J. F. Harrington, Jr.

4013. Latouche, Daniel. IT TAKES TWO TO... DIVORCE AND REMARRY. *J. of Can. Studies [Canada] 1977 12(3): 24-32.* Canadians, both Anglophone and Francophone, should calm down and realize that neither independence for Quebec nor continued federalism would be the end of the world. Independence is not inevitable, and it isn't the only alternative to federalism. Québécois and English Canadians need to discuss all alternatives. 5 notes. J. C. Billigmeier

4014. Latouche, Daniel. QUEBEC AND THE NORTH AMERICAN SUBSYSTEM: ONE POSSIBLE SCENARIO. *Int. Organization 1974 28(4): 931-960.* Examines, in a special issue on US-Canadian foreign relations, the history of Quebec (1950's-73) to determine if the province could become independent and what the impact of independence would be on Quebec's relations with the US and the rest of Canada.

4015. LeDuc, Lawrence. CANADIAN ATTITUDES TOWARD QUEBEC INDEPENDENCE. *Public Opinion Q. 1977 41(3): 347-355.* Using data from a national election study and from recent public opinion polls in Quebec, this article examines the strength and stability of support for independence in Quebec and of electoral support for the Parti Québécois which led to its victory. The data suggest that support for the Parti Quebecois is neither a transient phenomenon nor unrelated to support for independence, which has remained relatively constant over a number of years. Finds that support for both independence and the Parti Quebecois is highest among younger, better educated respondents. J

4016. Legaré, Anne. LES CLASSES SOCIALES ET LE GOUVERNEMENT PQ À QUEBEC [Social classes and the PQ government in Quebec]. *Can. Rev. of Sociol. and Anthrop. [Canada] 1978 15(2): 218-226.* Analyzes the difficulties or misunderstandings of the Parti Québécois in its relations with the various social classes in Canada. Examines the new elements in class structure in the province of Quebec, and views the future place of the PQ in the Canadian confederation as a political structural representative of non-monopoly capital in the province of Quebec. Primary and secondary sources; biblio. G. P. Cleyet

4017. Lemieux, Vincent. QUEL ETAT DU QUEBEC? [What type of state for Quebec?]. *Études Int. [Canada] 1977 8(2): 254-265.* Discusses the social, cultural, political and economic implications of statehood for Quebec. Mentions three political functions a state can assure: It can maintain order, it can be a benefactor to citizens, and it can provide organizational structures. Secondary sources; 5 notes. J. F. Harrington, Jr.

4018. Lévesque, René. FOR AN INDEPENDENT QUEBEC. *Foreign Affairs 1976 54(4): 734-744.* Briefly discusses the historical position of the French of Quebec from the beginning of English domination in 1763 to the present. The Québécois remained outside the national development carried on by the Anglo-Saxons and assimilated immigrant groups, but their prolific numbers ensured them a continued presence on the land and the use of their own language. After World War II, nationalism took hold; by the 1960's it had become the Quiet Revolution. The author, president of the Parti Québécois, argues for sovereignty with a new kind of healthy association with Canada. C. W. Olson

4019. Levine, Marc V. INSTITUTION DESIGN AND THE SEPARATIST IMPULSE: QUEBEC AND THE ANTEBELLUM AMERICAN SOUTH. *Ann. of the Am. Acad. of Pol. and Social Sci. 1977 433: 60-72.* Regional autonomy and separatist movements severely test the conflict management capacities of a nation's political system. Following Calhoun, a series of institutional arrangements and political practices which depart from majority rule decision making have been identified in the literature as contributing to the peaceful management of subcultural cleavages. In Canada and the antebellum U.S., failure to set up "formal modes of sectional self-protection" led to conflict regulation failure and the emergence of separatist movements in Quebec and the South. Without mechanisms of the type noted above and in the context of mass politics, the machinery of national political parties and intersubcultural elite accommodation which had held regional cleavages in check simply proved inadequate. J

4020. Levitt, Joseph. THE FEDERAL N.D.P. AND QUÉBEC. *J. of Can. Studies [Canada] 1977 12(3): 118-123.* Canada's social democratic New Democratic Party (NDP) favors a strong federal government. The Parti Québécois (PQ) is also social democratic, but wants Quebec to be independent. The NDP, with its social democratic program, may be able to win Québécois from support of the PQ to a renewed, reformed federalism. If Quebec does secede, the NDP may be crucial in ensuring that secession is peaceful. J. C. Billigmeier

4021. Mallory, J. R. CONFEDERATION: THE AMBIGUOUS BARGAIN. *J. of Can. Studies [Canada] 1977 12(3): 18-23.* Confederation, as an alternative to federalism and to the division of Canada into two independent states, one Anglophone, the other (Quebec) Francophone, has many disadvantages. Rather, the solution to the present impasse between the governments of Canada and Quebec lies in a renewal and revitalization of federalism, a federalism that will pay more attention to the needs of Quebec and Francophone Canadians generally. 6 notes. J. C. Billigmeier

4022. Manor, F. S. CANADA'S CRISIS: THE CAUSES. *Foreign Policy 1977-78 (29): 43-55.* The Canadian crisis is due less to political nationalism in Quebec than to economic nationalism among English-speaking Canadians which has taken the form of a socialistic assault on the American-dominated business system. The resulting flight of foreign capital has wrecked the economy, encouraging Quebec's separatism. T. L. Powers

4023. McKinsey, Lauren S. DIMENSIONS OF NATIONAL POLITICAL INTEGRATION AND DISINTEGRATION, THE CASE OF QUEBEC SEPARATISM, 1960-75. *Comparative Pol. Studies 1976 9(3): 335-360.* Discusses Canadian government attempts to maintain centralization and political stability to counteract separatist movements in Quebec 1960-75.

4024. McRoberts, Kenneth. ENGLISH CANADA AND THE QUEBEC REFERENDUM: THE STAKES AND THE DANGERS. *J. of Can. Studies [Canada] 1977 12(3): 108-113.* The accession to power of the Parti Québécois (with its program of separation from Canada) has created a tremendous potential for destructive conflict between English and French Canada. J. C. Billigmeier

4025. Monière, Denis. THE *PARTI-QUEBECOIS* AND SOCIAL CHANGE IN QUEBEC. *Australian and New Zealand J. of Sociol. [Australia] 1978 14(3, Part 2): 340-346.* Since its founding in 1968, the Parti Québécois has been funded through its own members' contributions (unique in a country where the traditional parties—the Liberal Party and the *Union Nationales*—rely on the "gifts" of the large commercial enterprises they serve) and has advocated participatory democracy in political and social life to implement its program of independence (but not secession) for Quebec, guarantees of an independent school system for the anglophone minority, humanistic capitalism, redistribution of wealth, etc.

4026. Moore, Marie-France. NATIONALISME ET CONTRE-CULTURE AU QUEBEC [Nationalism and the counter culture in Quebec]. *Can. Rev. of Studies in Nationalism [Canada] 1978 5(2): 284-306.* Discusses the possible influence of the nationalist, separatist movement in Quebec on the emergence of the counter culture there, as demonstrated in the literary organ, *Mainmise*. The counter culture's practical beliefs involved a kind of ecological nationalism, anti-American in focus, with a rejection of political patriotic nationalism. With its theoretical support for utopian internationalism always present, the counter culture movement in Quebec possessed a serious contradiction in its ideology. Covers 1970-75. Printed primary and secondary sources; 28 notes. J. A. Kicklighter

4027. Nuechterlein, Donald E. AN AMERICAN LOOKS AT CANADA. *Int. Perspectives [Canada] 1978 (July-Aug.): 31-35.* Americans no longer take Canada for granted, particularly since 1972, when Prime Minister Pierre Elliott Trudeau adopted the Third Option as a basis for economic and foreign policy decisions. A more serious concern to US citizens is the threat to Canadian unity from René Lévesque's Parti Québécois. Photo. E. S. Palais

4028. Orban, Edmond. CANADA-QUÉBEC: POUR UN PROCESSUS ACCÉLÉRÉ DE CRÉATIVITÉ [Canada-Quebec: for an accelerated process of creativity]. *J. of Can. Studies [Canada] 1977 12(3): 39-43.* Calls for creative thinking to deal with the problems between Quebec and the Canadian federal government. 14 notes. J. C. Billigmeier

4029. Pageau, René. L'IDÉOLOGIE POLITIQUE DE GUSTAVE LAMARCHE [The political ideology of Gustave Lamarche]. *Action Natl. [Canada] 1975 64(9): 758-777.* Surveys the political philosophy of Catholic Father Gustave Lamarche, an active supporter of the independence of Quebec.

4030. Penner, Norman. QUEBEC EXPLODES A BOMBSHELL: RENÉ LEVESQUE AND THE CHALLENGE OF SEPARATISM. *Round Table [Great Britain] 1977 (266): 153-160.* Examines the growth of the Parti Québécois, focusing on its separatism and René Levesque's success in the November 1976 election. Discusses the position of Prime Minister Pierre Elliott Trudeau and the options open to separatists and federalists. C. Anstey

4031. Pinard, Maurice and Hamilton, Richard. THE INDEPENDENCE ISSUE AND THE POLARIZATION OF THE ELECTORATE: THE 1973 QUEBEC ELECTION. *Can. J. of Pol. Sci. [Canada] 1977 10(2): 215-259.* Uses data acquired by a telephone poll conducted shortly after the 1973 Quebec election to examine the forces which led to the rapid polarization of the electorate between the Liberals and the Parti Québécois. Findings anticipated the results of the 1976 election. 10 tables, 71 notes. R. V. Kubicek

4032. Pinard, Maurice and Hamilton, Richard. THE PARTI QUÉBÉCOIS COMES TO POWER: AN ANALYSIS OF THE 1976 ELECTION. *Can. J. of Pol. Sci. [Canada] 1978 11(4): 739-775.* The Parti Québécois's (PQ) decision to dissociate the election from a choice on the independence of Quebec attracted support mainly from the French Canadians who rejected independence and the Liberal Party for its corruption and bad administration. However, the PQ's victory was limited in terms of popular votes, because of many voters' fear of its leading to Quebec's independence, in spite of this dissociation. Primary and secondary sources; 18 tables, 68 notes, appendix. G. P. Cleyet

4033. Sabourin, Louis. LA RECHERCHE D'UN STATUT ENDOGENE QUÉBECOIS: TROIS STADES DE CONNAISSANCE MUTUELLE [Quebec's search for an endogenous statute: Three stages of mutual understanding]. *Études Int. [Canada] 1977 8(2): 231-239.* Analyzes the perceptions, fears, and understandings that affect Quebec-Ottawa relations as a result of that French-speaking province's demand for independence. Primary and secondary sources; 17 notes. J. F. Harrington, Jr.

4034. Saint-Germain, Maurice. LE QUÉBEC ET "L'INDÉPENDANCE TRANQUILLE" [Quebec and "peaceful independence"]. *Esprit [France] 1977 (4-5): 277-283.* Reflects on the significance of the victory of the Parti Québécois in the 1976 provincial election, and describes the first official actions of the new government.

4035. Sigler, John. STABILITE, CHANGEMENT SOCIAL ET SEPARATISME DANS LES SOCIETES DEVELOPPEES: LE CAS QUEBECOIS [Stability, social change and separatism in developed societies: the case of Quebec]. *Études Int. [Canada] 1977 8(2): 282-291.* Examines the political and sociological implications of Quebec's separatism. Gives considerable attention to the work of the Norwegian sociologist Johan Galtung and shows the average salary of male workers in Quebec in 1961 according to their ethnic origin. Primary and secondary sources; chart, 6 notes. J. F. Harrington, Jr.

4036. Singer, Howard L. INTERNAL CONFLICTS WITHIN THE PARTI QUEBECOIS. *Dalhousie Rev. [Canada] 1977 57(1): 5-17.* The Parti Québécois has had two major sources of cleavage since its founding in 1968. The first was an ideological one between radical and moderate members, and the second was an institutional one between the executive council and the parliamentary wing. René Lévesque represents the moderate group and has thus far defeated radical attempts by Pierre Bourgault and André Larocque to gain supremacy. The several crises of the party during 1969-73 are explained. Following the 29 October 1973 election and the pequiste position of official opposition in the National Assembly, the move to tone down the separatist issue caused several more party quarrels including a renewed questioning of Lévesque's party leadership. The position of holding a referendum on independence should the party form a government was a reassuring one for the moderates in the party. If the referendum on independence votes to remain in confederation, the conflict within the party will severely escalate. 36 notes. C. Held

4037. Smiley, Donald V. AS THE OPTIONS NARROW: NOTES ON POST-NOVEMBER 15 CANADA. *J. of Can. Studies [Canada] 1977 12(3): 3-7.* The elections of 15 November 1976, in which the Parti Québécois (PQ), led by René Lévesque, captured a majority in the provincial Parliament of Quebec with a program based on independence from Canada, have irreversibly altered the situation in Canada. Either the federal system has to be reformed—and explained to the people more clearly—or Quebec will leave Canada. Intensified resistance to the PQ independence policy could result in either a retreat from independence by the relatively moderate Lévesque leadership, or replacement of that leadership by extremists. A purely English Canada would be born in an atmosphere of rejection and failure. 6 notes. J. C. Billigmeier

4038. Starnes, John. QUEBEC, CANADA, AND THE ALLIANCE. *Survival [Great Britain] 1977 19(5): 212-215.* Speculates about the effects of successful Quebec separatism on its relations with Canada and in the Western Alliance.

4039. Stein, Michael. LE ROLE DES QUÉBECOIS NON FRANCOPHONES DANS LE DEBAT ACTUEL ENTRE LE QUÉBEC ET LE CANADA [The role of non-Francophone Quebecers in the current Canadian debate]. *Études Int. [Canada] 1977 8(2): 292-306.* More than one million non-French-speaking people live in Quebec province. Discusses the historic self-perception of these people, and the impact of Bill 22 which made French the official language in Quebec and the landmark vote of 15 November 1976. Examines the role these people can play in Quebec's future. Secondary sources; 31 notes. J. F. Harrington, Jr.

4040. Stein, Michael. QUÉBEC AND CANADA: THE CHANGING EQUILIBRIUM BETWEEN "FEDERAL SOCIETY" AND "FEDERAL POLITICAL SYSTEM." *J. of Can. Studies [Canada] 1977 12(3): 113-117.* In 1968, just before Pierre Elliott Trudeau became Prime Minister and René Lévesque formed the Parti Québécois, the author argued that Canada is a "federal society" supported and shaped by a "federal political system." Since then, both "society" and "system" have changed radically, and there has arisen a severe disjunction between them. Reform of the federal system is needed to create a bilingual or plurilingual "federal society" as in Belgium and Switzerland. 3 notes. J. C. Billigmeier

4041. Stethem, Nicholas. CANADA'S CRISIS: THE DANGERS. *Foreign Policy 1977-78 (29): 56-64.* The independence of Quebec would disrupt the strong and united North America which has been so vital in the East-West balance of power. Strategically important, Quebec lies athwart the major bombing route from the Soviet Union to the most populous and industrialized areas of Canada and the United States. The loss of that province would cripple the NORAD system of continental defense. There are domestic dangers involved as well, for the question already may have gone far enough to make inevitable some form of internal violence, whether from separatists, the federal government, or antiseparatist minorities within Quebec. Note. T. L. Powers

4042. Thomson, Dale C. QUEBEC AND THE BICULTURAL DIMENSION. *Pro. of the Acad. of Pol. Sci. 1976 32(2): 27-39.* Analyzes the present position and possible future of French Quebec in Canada. The present provincial government is committed to the Canadian federation, supporting separatist sentiment just enough to remain in power. Separation is unlikely. French Canadians are primarily concerned with making English Canada endure what they have endured, at least in Quebec, and in wringing financial and other concessions from the federal government. Declining birthrates augur ill for the future, though this trend will probably reverse.   V. L. Human

4043. Treddenick, J. M.   QUEBEC AND CANADA: SOME ECONOMIC ASPECTS OF INDEPENDENCE.   *J. of Can. Studies 1973 8(4): 16-31.* Discusses Quebec's desire for economic independence, the political influence of the Parti Québécois, and United States influence in political and social affairs in Canada and Quebec.

4044. Tremblay, Marc-Adélard.   LE 15 NOVEMBRE ET SES LENDEMAINS: LES DÉFIS DE LA SOUVERAINETÉ POLITIQUE [The 15th of November and after: the challenges of political sovereignty]. *J. of Can. Studies [Canada] 1977 12(3): 100-105.* The government of the Parti Quebecois seems to underestimate the problems associated with accession to sovereignty. The PQ should concentrate on political reform and on building a strong economic infrastructure for Quebec. If it succeeds—and if other necessary conditions are present—then independence will be a viable option, which it is not at present. 2 notes.
J. C. Billigmeier

4045. Trent, John.   TERRAIN D'ENTENTE ET TERRITOIRES CONTESTES: LES POSITIONS FEDERALES ET PROVINCIALES A L'EGARD DE L'AVENIR CONSTITUTIONNEL DU CANADA [Common ground and disputed territory: federal and provincial positions concerning Canada's constitutional future]. *Études Int. [Canada] 1977 8(2): 172-197.* Discusses arguments and constitutional debates concerning federalism and provincialism in Canada and relates these issues to Quebec's quest for independence. Graphically contrasts the theories and positions of Trudeau and Levesque and illustrates in tabular form the proposals for constitutional reform from 1968-77. Primary and secondary sources; 2 tables, 25 notes.   J. F. Harrington, Jr.

4046. Vaillancourt, Jean-Guy and Vaillancourt, Pauline.   CONTEMPORARY QUEBEC NATIONALISM AND THE LEFT.   *Australian and New Zealand J. of Sociol. [Australia] 1978 14(3, Part 2): 329-339, 346.* Reviews Canadian (and chiefly Québécois) francophone political groups and parties across a broad spectrum (from conservative to liberal to social-democrat to socialist to extreme left) from 1960 to 1978 and finds that sentiment for and against total independence or separation for Quebec—and all the positions between—can be found among all the political groupings with no definite pattern of a particular sentiment for a particular political philosophy.

4047. Walsh, Sam.   FOR RECOGNITION OF THE FRENCH-CANADIAN NATION.   *World Marxist Rev. [Canada] 1974 17(10): 126-133.* Oppression of French Canadians can be ended by making Quebec a separate nation in a confederated republic.   S

4048. Young, R. A.   NATIONAL IDENTIFICATION IN ENGLISH CANADA: IMPLICATIONS FOR QUEBEC INDEPENDENCE.   *J. of Can. Studies [Canada] 1977 12(3): 69-84.* English-speakers among Canadians may be divided into four groups, according to their attitudes on the possibility of Quebec's separation from Canada and other issues: Dogmatists, Locals, Cosmopolitans, and Individualists. Dogmatists oppose separation, being strong Canadian nationalists, but they might accept it if a corridor to the Maritime Provinces were left within Canada. Locals, being oriented toward local and provincial entities, would let the Québécois go if they wished, while considering it a mistake. Cosmopolitans will tolerate secession if economic and communications links are maintained unimpaired. Individualists, wrapped up in themselves, seem to care little about any public issues. 21 notes.
J. C. Billigmeier

4049. —.   CANADA AND QUEBEC NATIONALISM.   *Can. Dimension 1975 10(7): 32-37.*
Piotte, Jean-Marc.   A QUESTION OF STRATEGY, pp. 32-34.
Resnick, Philip.   STRATEGY AND ITS DISCONTENTS, pp. 35-37.

4050. —.   THE MOUNTING CLASS STRUGGLE IN QUEBEC.   *Int. Socialist Rev. 1973 34(7): 36-62.* Discusses socialists' potential for exploiting the politicization of the working class and class struggle in Quebec, and for establishing an independent socialist state in the 1970's.

Bilingualism

4051. Albrecht-Carrie, Rene.   COMMENTARY: THE CANADIAN DILEMMA.   *J. of Can. Studies 1974 9(1): 53-62.* The historic trend to the identification of the nation and the state may not apply everywhere. Bilingualism would give Canada an identity separate from the United States and demonstrate that the "Second Hundred Years' War" has ended in North America as it has in Europe. Secondary works; 8 notes.
G. E. Panting

4052. Allard, Jean-Louis.   LES FRANCO-ONTARIENS ET L'EDUCATION POSTSECONDAIRE [French Ontarians and postsecondary education]. *R. de l'U. d'Ottawa [Canada] 1973 43(4): 518-531.* Analyzes education problems, especially in postsecondary schools, and the progress in making Canada, especially Ontario, bilingual and bicultural. Based on secondary sources; 5 notes.   M. L. Frey

4053. Angers, François-Albert.   LA SITUATION LINGUISTIQUE AU QUÉBEC APRÈS LA LOI 22 [The language situation in Quebec after Law 22].
LA SITUATION DE DROIT DU FRANÇAISE [The de jure situation of French]. *Action Natl. [Canada] 1974 64(3): 207-228.*
APRÈS L'ÉTAT DE DROIT, L'ÉTAT DE FAIT [After the de jure situation, the de facto situation]. *Action Natl. [Canada] 1974 64(4): 287-301.*
Law 22, the Official Language Act (Quebec, 1974), "establishes" French as the official language in Quebec but still favors the English-speaking because of intrinsic differences between written law and common law. Law 22 does not make French the only official language of Quebec.

4054. Angers, François Albert.   MOUVEMENT QUÉBEC FRANÇAIS: À PROPOS DU BILL 22 [French Quebec Movement: On the Bill 22]. *Action Natl. [Canada] 1974 64(1): 923-946.* A declaration of outrage by the President of the French Quebec Movement concerning the Official Language Act (1974), passed by the Canadian government, and affirming the use of English in French-speaking Quebec.

4055. Angle, John.   MAINLAND CONTROL OF MANUFACTURING AND REWARD FOR BILINGUALISM IN PUERTO RICO.   *Am. Sociol. R. 1976 41(2): 289-307.* The literature on language group relations in the economy of Quebec Province suggests that more French Canadians are bilingual than English Canadians because many businesses use English and are owned or operated by English Canadians. Bilingual French Canadians are rewarded, on the average, by placement into better occupations. The hypothesis is made that a similar reward exists for bilingualism in English in the Spanish mother tongue labor force in Puerto Rico.   J

4056. Anglejan, Alison d'.   FRENCH IN QUEBEC.   *J. of Communication 1979 29(2): 54-63.* Quebec's Bill 101, the Charter of the French Language, enacted in 1977, is "designed to make Quebec both institutionally and socially a unilingual French state" and "contains measures to prevent the growth of the English-speaking community and to diminish its status."

4057. Beaupré, Viateur.   LA LOI 22 LE FRANGLAIS OU LA SCHIZOPHRÉNIE [Law 22, "Frenglish" or schizophrenia]. *Action Natl. [Canada] 1974 64(3): 229-238.* Law 22 (the Official Language Act, 1974) institutionalized "Frenglish" (franglais) while theoretically making French the official language of Quebec.

4058. Castonguay, Charles.   POUR UNE POLITIQUE DES DISTRICTS BILINGUES AU QUEBEC [Toward a policy for bilingual districts in Quebec]. *J. of Can. Studies [Canada] 1976 11(3): 50-59.* The role of bilingual districts is intended to be largely symbolic. Federal census data from 1971 reveal that everywhere in Canada, including Quebec, the French language is losing ground to English. Therefore, at present, there is no point in establishing bilingual districts in order to protect the English language in Quebec. Such action should be postponed until the census data reveal that, in certain areas of Quebec, English has lost its power to attract users. Based on census data and language reports; 4 tables, ref.   G. E. Panting.

4059. Garon-Audy, Muriel and Vandycke, Robert. LA CHARTE DU FRANÇAIS ET LES DROITS DES MINORITÉS [The Charter of the French language and the rights of minorities]. *J. of Can. Studies [Canada] 1977 12(4): 85-94.* Argues in favor of *Projet no.* 1 (or 101), also called the *Charte du Français,* regulations proposed by the new provincial government for strengthening the French language in Quebec. The rhetoric of "free competition" in language, employed by the new law's opponents (e.g. Canadian Prime Minister Trudeau), is interested and inapplicable to the Canadian situation. Discusses parts of the proposed legislation which limit the right to an English-language education, arguing that they are not, in international law, discriminatory. Compares *Projet no.* 1 with its "timid" predecessor, Law 22, passed by the former Liberal government of Quebec. Based on government documents, publications of international bodies, newspaper articles, and secondary sources; 14 notes.   L. W. Van Wyk

4060. Gaulin, André. LE RAPPORT GENDRON [The Gendron Report]. *Action Natl. [Canada] 1973 62(9): 716-721.* Criticizes the report of the Gendron commission, its recognition of Quebec as a bilingual area, and its recommendation of bilingual instruction in the schools.

4061. Légaré, Jacques. LES GROUPES ETHNIQUES ET LINGUISTIQUES AU CANADA [Ethnic and linguistic groups in Canada]. *Can. R. of Sociol. and Anthrop. 1973 10(1): 81-84.* Report on three recent studies of bilingualism and biculturalism in Canada by authors of differing origins. Apart from the original contribution of each, all agree that outside of Quebec and an encircling zone, French has little chance of survival as an everyday language in Canada. 3 notes.
L. R. Atkins

4062. McRoberts, Kenneth. BILL 22 AND LANGUAGE POLICY IN CANADA. *Queen's Q. [Canada] 1976 83(3): 464-477.* Surveys the struggles for language equality throughout all the Canadian provinces and the federal government's support of such programs. Bill 22 seems a reversal of the language equality policy for the Province of Quebec because it calls for the primacy of French over English within Quebec. For some it does not go far enough, for others it violates the general equality of language ideal. An analysis of the bill indicates some weaknesses, especially at operational levels. 23 notes.   R. V. Ritter

4063. Stein, Michael. LE BILL 22 ET LA POPULATION NON-FRANCOPHONE AU QUEBEC: LES ATTITUDES DU GROUPE MINORITAIRE FACE A LA LEGISLATION DE LA LANGUE [Bill 22 and the non-Francophone populace in Quebec: the attitudes of a minority group encountering language legislation]. *Can. Rev. of Studies in Nationalism [Canada] 1978 5(2): 163-188.* Describes the reactions of English speakers and immigrants to the Official Language Act (1974), which made French the official language there. Opposing the legislation in an emotional and negative fashion, non-Francophones indicated that they thought of themselves as the majority party in Quebec. Their future success lies in their acceptance of their minority status and their willingness to work for their goals within the political system. Printed primary and secondary sources; 45 notes.   J. A. Kicklighter

4064. Veltman, Calvin J. THE EVOLUTION OF ETHNO-LINGUISTIC FRONTIERS IN THE UNITED STATES AND CANADA. *Social Sci. J. 1977 14(1): 47-58.* Examines the political and ethnic implications of linguistic nationalism in the Official Language Act (1974) in Quebec restricting the use of the English language in favor of French; the United States and Canada should provide government services in minority languages in any region where the minority language population is sufficiently numerous.

4065. Yuzyk, Paul. THE NEW CANADIAN CONSTITUTION AND THE RIGHTS OF ETHNIC GROUPS. *Ukrainian Q. 1978 34(1): 61-66.* Reviews the report of the Special Joint Committee of the Canadian Senate and House of Commons to review the Canadian constitution, particularly in regard to language rights. The Committee recommended that French and English be recognized as the two official languages of Canada but that other languages be given official recognition at the provincial level when appropriate.   K. N. T. Crowther

4066. —. [FRENCH LANGUAGE CHARTER AND COMMENTS]. *Can. Rev. of Sociol. and Anthrop. [Canada] 1978 15(2): 115-147.*
Laurin, Camille. FRENCH LANGUAGE CHARTER, *pp. 115-132.* Canadian Minister of State for cultural development Camille Laurin, in an address to the Quebec National Assembly analyzes the history of French Quebec, its evolution, the resistance of its French-speaking community to the anglicization of the province, and the maintenance of a territory with French traditions, language, culture, history, and a collective purpose. Notes that the bill heralds a French educated, and modern Quebec.
Blishen, Bernard R. PERCEPTIONS OF NATIONAL IDENTITY, *pp. 128-132.* Collects data which shows identification with Canada, or province by province, or regional language group, national identification of francophone respondents in Quebec by age, education, and income. 4 tables, biblio.
Dorais, Louis-Jacques. LA LOI 101 ET LES AMÉRINDIENS [The 101 law and the Amerindians], *pp. 133-135.* Analyzes Dr. Laurin's address and other statements, concentrating on his opinion that, since the Indians have the right to be distinct from the Quebec francophones, Laurin is implying that the motivations of his ideological address are political and that the francophones want to "divide and conquer." Biblio.
Jackson, John D. NATIONAL CONSCIOUSNESS AND CLASS: A COMMENT ON LAURIN'S VIEW OF THE HISTORY OF QUEBEC, *pp. 136-141.* Analyzes the English Quebec responses to Laurin's views of the history of Quebec, his concepts and interpretations of collectivity, leading to a theory of Quebec development which justifies the "French language charter." Biblio.
Rioux, Marcel. BILL 101: A POSITIVE ANGLOPHONE POINT OF VIEW, *pp. 142-144.* Clarifies the meaning of Bill 101; explains that, as a francophone and a Canadian, he considers that the language situation should be corrected by a repatriation in Quebec of political and economic centers of decision, agrees with the contents of the brief presented by the Comité anglophone pour un Québec unifié (June 1977). Note.
Ossenberg, Richard J. COLONIALISM, LANGUAGE, AND FALSE CONSCIOUSNESS: THE MYTHOLOGY OF NATIONALISM IN QUEBEC, *pp. 145-147.* Analyzes Laurin's statements on the history of Quebec as a manifesto imprinted with emotionalism and subjectivity which are a form of false consciousness; yet still supports it and notes that the academicians of anglophone Canada are no less subjective. Biblio.   G. P. Cleyet

SUBJECT INDEX

Subject Profile Index (ABC-SPIndex) carries both generic and specific index terms. Begin a search at the general term but also look under more specific or related terms. Cross-references are included.

Each string of index descriptors is intended to present a profile of a given article; however, no particular relationship between any two terms in the profile is implied. Terms within the profile are listed alphabetically after the leading term. The variety of punctuation and capitalization reflects production methods and has no intrinsic meaning; e.g., there is no difference in meaning between "History, study of" and "History (study of)."

Cities, towns, and counties are listed following their respective states or provinces; e.g., "Ohio (Columbus)." Terms beginning with an arabic numeral are listed after the letter Z. The chronology of the bibliographic entry follows the subject index descriptors. In the chronology, "c" stands for "century"; e.g., "19c" means "19th century."

Note that "United States" is not used as a leading index term; if no country is mentioned, the index entry refers to the United States alone. When an entry refers to both Canada and the United States, both "Canada" and "USA" appear in the string of index descriptors, but "USA" is not a leading term. When an entry refers to any other country and the United States, only the other country is indexed.

The last number in the index string, in italics, refers to the bibliographic entry number.

A

Abolition Movement *See also* Antislavery Sentiments; Emancipation.
—. Conservatism. German Americans. Pennsylvania. Religion. 1779-88. *549*
—. German Americans. Labor Unions and Organizations. Political Participation. 19c. *581*
—. Gurowski, Adam. Polish Americans. Radicals and Radicalism. 1849-66. *2041*
—. Negroes. Pennsylvania (Philadelphia). Riots. 1830-50. *2886*
Abolitionists. Irish Americans. Nationalism. ca 1830's-50's. *765*
Abramson, Harold J. Catholic Church. Ethnicity (review article). Hays, Samuel P. Politics. 1973. *2333*
Academic freedom. Concordia Seminary. Lutheran Church (Missouri Synod). Missouri (St. Louis). Teachers. Tenure. 1968-74. *2428*
—. Hebrew Union College. Judaism, Reform. Kohler, Kaufmann. Ohio (Cincinnati). Zionism. 1903-07. *1562*
Acadians *See also* Cajuns; Creoles; French Canadians.
—. Acculturation. Exiles. France. Great Britain. Nova Scotia. 18c. *3860*
—. Assimilation. Emigration. Minorities in Politics. New Brunswick (Moncton). 1871-1971. *3346*
—. Assimilation. Massachusetts (Gloucester). Nova Scotia (Arichat region). 1850's-1900. *480*
—. Canada. Emigration. 1605-1800. *3091*
—. Canada. France. Great Britain. Immigration. Louisiana. Spain. 1755-85. *382*
—. Canada. Louisiana. 17c-20c. *388*
—. Catholic Church. Discrimination. Irish Canadians. New Brunswick. 1860-1900. *3684*
—. Catholic Church. English Canadians. Maritime Provinces. Social Conditions. 1763-1977. *3162*
—. Charities. Friends, Society of. German Americans. Irish Americans. Pennsylvania Hospital for the Sick Poor. Pennsylvania (Philadelphia). 18c. *2834*
—. Colonial Government. Documents. Louisiana (St. Gabriel). Spain. 1767. *380*
—. Colonial Government. Exiles. Great Britain. Land tenure. Loyalty. Nova Scotia. Oaths of allegiance. 11c-1755. *3850*
—. Colonial Government. Louisiana (New Orleans). Mississippi (Natchez). Settlement. Spain. 1768. *381*
—. Creoles. Human Relations. Interethnic Relations. Louisiana (Lafourch Parish). Smallpox. 1766-90. *371*
—. Drama. Maillet, Antoine (*Evangéline Deusse*). Quebec. Social Customs. 1976. *3173*
—. Environment. Louisiana. 18c-19c. *387*
—. Exiles. Great Britain. Nova Scotia. 1710-55. *3233*
—. Exiles. Nova Scotia. St. Lawrence, Gulf of. 1756-95. *3309*
—. Folklore. Louisiana. Social customs. 18c-1978. *454*
—. Genealogy. LaVache family. Nova Scotia (Cape Breton; Arichat). 1774-20c. *3174*
—. Institutions. Nationalism. Nova Scotia. Social Organization. 1700's-1970. *3132*

—. Leisure. Louisiana, southern. Plantations. 1839-59. *396*
—. Louisiana (Cabanocey). Population. 1766-70. *475*
Accademia (association). Americanism. Catholic Church. Clergy. New York. 1865-1907. *2323*
Accolti, Michael. California. Jesuits. Santa Clara, University of. 1849-51. *2344*
Account books. German Americans. Lutheran Church. Pennsylvania, central. Stock, Daniel. 1850-67. *494*
Acculturation *See also* Assimilation.
—. Acadians. Exiles. France. Great Britain. Nova Scotia. 18c. *3860*
—. Agriculture. Immigration. Lutheran Church. Minnesota (Isantic County). Social customs. Swedish Americans. 1840-1910. *1842*
—. Alberta (Calgary). Woman's Canadian Club. 1911-20's. *3062*
—. Alienation. French Canadians. Quebec. 1950-73. *3399*
—. Americanization. Catholic Church. Leo XIII, Pope (*Testem Benevolentiae*). Periodicals. Protestantism. 1899. *2368*
—. Amish. Mennonites. Revivals. 1860-90. *2273*
—. Artifacts. Material Culture. Scandinavian Americans. Social Customs. Utah (Sanpete, Sevier counties). 1849-1979. *1670*
—. Artists. California, southern. Exiles. German Americans. Intellectuals. 1933-50. *164*
—. Bellow, Saul. Illinois (Chicago). Immigrants. ca 1937-74. *2937*
—. Bianco, Carla. Catholic Church. Family. Gambino, Richard. Italian Americans (review article). Pennsylvania (Rosetos). Social Organization. Tomasi, Silvano. 20c. *865*
—. Bibliographies. Dissertations. Italian Americans. 1921-75. *861*
—. Bicentennial Celebrations. Human Rights. Slovakian Americans. 19c-20c. *1916*
—. Boardinghouses. Immigrants. Italian Canadians. Ontario (Toronto). 20c. *3493*
—. Brethren in Christ. Individualism. 1870-1910. *2280*
—. British Americans. Colorado (Denver). German Americans. Irish Americans. 1860-90. *124*
—. Cajuns. Louisiana (Houma). Negroes. Texans. 1945-73. *479*
—. California (Los Angeles). Ethnicity. Race. Social status. Voting and Voting Behavior. 1973. *2509*
—. Canada. Ethnicity. Jews. USA. 1961-74. *3523*
—. Canada. French Canadians. Language. 1971. *3318*
—. Canada. Immigrants. Polish Canadians. 1945-75. *3550*
—. Canada. Immigration. Settlement. Slovak Canadians. 1885-1970's. *3542*
—. Catholic Church. Immigration. Slovakian Americans. 1860's-1970's. *1937*
—. Catholic Church. Irish Americans. Pennsylvania (Pittsburgh). St. Andrew Parish. 1863-90. *726*
—. Charters. Institutionalization. Mennonites (Franconia Conference). Protestant Churches. 1840-1940. *2222*
—. City Life. Indians. Migration, Internal. 1945-75. *127*

—. City Life. Kral, Tonka. Northeastern or North Atlantic States. Reminiscences. Slovakian Americans. 20c. *1902*
—. Clothing industry. Jews. May brothers. Oklahoma (Tulsa). Retail Trade. 1889-1970. *1505*
—. Conservatism. Irish Americans. Political Attitudes. 19c. *745*
—. Drama. Language. Literature. Malm, G. N. (*Charli Johnson, Svensk-Amerikan, Härute*). Swedish Americans. 1909-19. *1799*
—. Dutch Americans. New Jersey. 1860-1918. *334*
—. Education. Immigrants. Massachusetts (Boston). Negroes. Social status. 1850. *2820*
—. Educational Reform. Ideology. Immigrants. Industrialization. Pennsylvania. Social control. 1880-1910. *2859*
—. Educational reform. Immigrants. Public Schools. 19c-1910's. *2867*
—. Ethnicity. 1970's. *2972*
—. Ethnicity. German Americans. Neighborhoods. 1840's-1970's. *100*
—. Ethnicity. Religion. 19c-20c. *2181*
—. Ethnicity. Social change. 1740-1976. *2988*
—. Farms. Jews. New Jersey (Farmdale). Settlement. 1919-70's. *1183*
—. Folk art. Frontier and Pioneer Life. Swedish Americans. 1638-1976. *1771*
—. French Canadians. Nationalism. New England. ca 1610-1975. *445*
—. Frontier and Pioneer Life. Immigrants. Protestantism. Rølvaag, Ole Edvart (*Giants in the Earth*). South Dakota. 1870. 1927. *1734*
—. Georgia, Southeastern. Scottish Americans. 1746-1860. *308*
—. German Americans. 19c. *512*
—. German Americans. Italian Americans. Michigan. Polish Americans. Scandinavian Americans. Voluntary Associations. 1850's-1950's. *2756*
—. German Americans (image of). Ohio (Toledo). Press. 1850-90. *492*
—. Immigrants. Italian Americans. Labor. Padrone system. Virginia (Wise County). 1900-20. *897*
—. Immigrants. Italian Americans. Utah (Salt Lake City). Voluntary Associations. 1897-1934. *859*
—. Immigrants. Jews. Jews. Novels. 1900-17. *947*
—. Immigrants. Jews. New York City. Yiddishe Arbeiten Universitett. 1921-39. *1191*
—. Immigrants. Ontario (Toronto). 1950's-70's. *3047*
—. Italian Americans. Jews. Pennsylvania (Pittsburgh). Slavic Americans. Women. 1900-45. *2736*
—. Jewish Theological Seminary. Kaplan, Mordecai M. New York City. Theology. 1920's. *1100*
—. Labor. Polish Americans. 1860-1960. *1976*
—. Language. Swedish language. 1870-1970. *1812*
—. New England. Politics. Portuguese Americans. Research. Social Customs. 18c-20c. *1654*
—. Pennsylvania. Reminiscences. Sapak, Theresa. Slovakian Americans. 20c. *1923*
Act of Sexual Sterilization (Alberta, 1928). Canada, western. Eugenics. Immigration. Press. Woodsworth, James S. 1900-28. *3061*

Beiliss, Mendel. California (Oakland, San Francisco). Jews. Newspapers. Russia. Trials. 1911-13. *1619*

Beissel, Johann Conrad. Communalism. Eckerlin, Emmanuel. Ephrata Cloister. German Americans. Pennsylvania (Conestoga Valley). 1732-68. *514*

Belaney, Archibald S. (Grey Owl). Canada. Conservation movements. English Canadians. Great Britain. 1906-38. *3429*

Belgian Americans. French Canadians. Independent Textile Union. Rhode Island (Woonsocket). Working Class. 1931-50's. *2564*

Belgian Canadians. Immigrants. Manitoba (St. Boniface, Winnipeg). Nuytten, Edmund. Nuytten, Octavia. 1880-1914. *3463*

Belgium. Africa, French-speaking. Canada. Foreign Relations. France. French Canadians. French Language. Institutions. 1960-74. *3738*

—. Africa, French-speaking. Foreign Relations. France. French Canadians. Quebec. 1964-74. *3749*

—. Canada. English Canadians. French Canadians. Liberal Party. Social Christian Party. 1880's-1973. *3925*

—. Ethnicity. Nationalism. Quebec. Social Classes. 1970's. *3959*

Belkin, Samuel. Brown University. Jews. Reminiscences. Rhode Island (Providence). 1932-35. *1356*

Bell Tavern. Huling, Tom. Irish Americans. Land transactions. Meagher, Paddy. Tennessee (Memphis). 1775-1918. *772*

Bell, Thomas. Labor Unions and Organizations. Novels. Slovakian Americans. 1920's-63. *1887*

Bellot, Joseph René. Arctic. Canada. Franklin, John. Kennedy, William. Métis. *Prince Albert* (vessel). Voyages. 1851. *3289*

Bellow, Saul. Acculturation. Illinois (Chicago). Immigrants. ca 1937-74. *2937*

—. History. Novels. 1976. *1057*

— . Nobel Prize. Novels. 1976. *914*

Bellow, Saul *(Henderson The Rain King)*. American dream. Jews. Literature. Technology. 1965. *1075*

Bellow, Saul *(Mr. Sammler's Planet)*. Jews. Literature. Mailer, Norman *(Armies of the Night)*. Political Theory. 1975. *1011*

Ben-Amos, Dan. Folklore (review article). Jews. Mintz, Jerome R. Rappoport, Angelo S. 1937-72. *980*

Benedict, N. B. Blood transfusion. Choppin, Samuel. French Americans. Louisiana (New Orleans). Medicine (practice of). 1853-58. *441*

Benedictine High School. Boys. Catholic Church. Church Schools. Ohio (Cleveland). Slovakian Americans. 1928-78. *2374*

Benedictine Sisters. Immigration. Missouri (Conception). Renggli, M. Beatrice. Swiss Americans. Travel Accounts. 1874. *2353*

Benedictines. Americanization. Germany. Switzerland. 1846-1900. *2354*

—. Australia (Sydney). German Americans. Letters. Missions and Missionaries. Polding, John Bede. Wimmer, Boniface. 1847-55. *2358*

—. Bankruptcy. Hoenerbach, Placid. North Dakota (Richardton). St. Mary's Abbey. 1915-25. *2348*

—. Catholic Church. Frontier and Pioneer Life. German Americans. Oetgen, Jerome (review article). Wimmer, Boniface. 1809-87. *2316*

—. German Americans. Illinois (New Cluny). Missions and Missionaries. Monasticism. Moosmüller, Oswald. 1832-1901. *584*

Benedictines (review articles). German Americans. Monasteries. 19c. 1960's-70's. *2335*

Benevent, Prince de. *See* Talleyrand-Perigord, Charles Maurice de.

Bengston, Henry. Illinois (Chicago). Publishers and Publishing. Swedish Americans. 1887-1974. *1816*

Benjamin, Judah. Confederate States of America. Jews. 1861-68. *1422*

Benjamin, Philip S. Feldberg, Michael. Miller, Richard G. Pennsylvania (Philadelphia; review article). Sinclair, Bruce. 1790-1920. 1974-76. *183*

Bennett, James Gordon. Catholic Church. Immigration. *New York Herald* (newspaper). 1835-70. *2363*

Benson, Elmer A. Anti-Semitism. Minnesota. Political Campaigns (gubernatorial). 1930's. *1602*

Bentrup, H. A. Deafness. Duemling, Enno A. Ephphatha Conference. German Americans. Lutheran Church. Reinke, Augustus H. 1893-1976. *2385*

Ben-Zion (Ben-Zion Weinman). Judaism. Painting. 1933-73. *1142*

Berdahl Family. Norwegian Americans. Rølvaag, Ole Edvart *(Giants in the Earth)*. South Dakota. 1873-1900. *1748*

Bergel, Siegmund. California (San Bernardino). Jews. Private Schools. 1868-1912. *1307*

Bergendorff, Conrad. Reminiscences. Swedish Pioneer Historical Society. 1945-48. *1777*

Berger, Carl. Brebner, J. B. Canada. French Canadians. Historiography. 17c-18c. 20c. *3030*

Berger, Elmer. Jews. Reminiscences. Zionism (opposition to). ca 1945-75. *1522*

Berger, Henning. Illinois (Chicago). Immigrants. Literature. Swedish Americans. Travel Accounts. USA. 1872-1924. *1788*

Bergeron, Léandre (review article). French Canadians. Historiography. Marxism. Quebec. 1970-75. *3117*

Bergman, Andrew. Cynicism. Jews. Novels, detective. Simon, Roger. 1970's. *1129*

Bergner, Peter. Bethel Ships. Evangelism. Merchant Marine. Methodist Church. New York City. Swedish Americans. 1832-66. *1869*

Bergson, Henri. Federal government. Intergovernmental Relations. Quebec. 1970's. *4028*

Bernays, Karl Ludwig. Civil War. Diplomacy. German Americans. Journalism. Switzerland. 1815-79. *544*

—. Civil War. German Americans. Missouri. 1862-70's. *543*

Bernou, Claude. Canada. France. LeClercq, Crestien. *Premier Établissement de la Foy dans la Nouvelle France* (book). Renaudot, Eusèbe. 1691. *3217*

Bernstein, Max. California. Development. Gold rushes. International Company of Mexico. Jews. Mexico (Baja California). 1854-1971. *1482*

Berrien, John M. Georgia. Know-Nothing Party. Letters. Nativism. Political Attitudes. 1854-56. *192*

Bertarelli, Pier Giuseppe. Business. California. Gold Rushes. Immigration. Italian Americans. 1849-53. *855*

Beth Ha Medrosh Hagodol Synagogue. Colorado (Denver). Judaism (Orthodox). Kauvar, Charles E. H. Progressivism. 1902-71. *1460*

—. Colorado (Denver). Judaism (Orthodox). Kauvar, Charles E. H. Zionism. 1902-71. *1459*

Beth Olam Cemetery. California (San Jose). Congregation Bickur Cholim. Jews. 1850-1900. *1230*

Bethel Ships. Bergner, Peter. Evangelism. Merchant Marine. Methodist Church. New York City. Swedish Americans. 1832-66. *1869*

Betten, Neil. Catholic Church (review article). Dolan, Jay P. Labor. 1830-1978. *2320*

Bevis Marks Synagogue. Architecture. Great Britain (London). Harrison, Peter. Rhode Island (Newport). Touro Synagogue. 1670-1775. *1285*

Beware (film). Anti-German Sentiment. Films. Gerard, James W. German Americans. Propaganda. World War I. 1918-19. *2634*

Bianco, Carla. Acculturation. Catholic Church. Family. Gambino, Richard. Italian Americans (review article). Pennsylvania (Rosetos). Social Organization. Tomasi, Silvano. 20c. *865*

Bibaud, Michel. French language. Journalism. Language. Quebec. 1760-1857. *3305*

Bible. Imber, Naphtali Herz *(The Fall of Jerusalem: Reflecting upon the Present Condition of America)*. Myths and Symbols. Populism. 1856-1909. *1379*

Bible reading. Catholic Church. Desmond, Humphrey. Protestantism. Religion in the Public Schools. *State of Wisconsin ex rel. Frederick Weiss et al.* v. *District School Board of School District 8* (1890). Wisconsin. 1888-90. *218*

—. Catholic Church. Politics. Prince Edward Island. Protestants. Public Schools. 1856-60. *3706*

Bibliographies. Acculturation. Dissertations. Italian Americans. 1921-75. *861*

—. American Revolution. Bicentennial Celebrations. Mennonites. 1776. 1975-76. *2217*

—. Ammann, Othmar Hermann. Bridges. Engineering. Swiss Americans. 1915-77. *2154*

—. Anabaptists. Dissertations. Mennonites. 1975-76. *2242*

—. Anthologies. Jews. Literature. 1950's-70's. *920*

—. Architecture. German Americans. Pennsylvania. ca 1818-1970. *633*

—. Archives. Canadian Institute of Montreal. Quebec. 1844-1900. *3138*

—. Artists. Orłowski, Alexander. Poles. 1777-1832. 20c. *1970*

—. Authors. Collectors and Collecting. Deinard, Ephraim. Newspapers. Zionism. 1846-1930. *1542*

—. Autobiography. Fiction. History Teaching. 1800-1960. 1976. *29*

—. Bilingualism. Canada. Pluralism. Research. 1964-67. *3933*

—. Brouillette, Benoit. French Canadians. Geography. Quebec (Montreal). 1903-73. *3113*

—. Canada. Church history. 17c-1973. *3604*

—. Canada. Church history. 17c-20c. *3605*

—. Canada. Church history. 17c-20c. *3606*

—. Canada. Eskimos. Indians. Métis. 1975. *3340*

—. Canada. French Canadians. Literature. 1606-1977. *3172*

—. Canada. Historiography. Protestant churches. 1825-1973. *3607*

—. Canada. Pluralism. Public Policy. 1967-76. *3019*

—. Canada. Population. 17c-20c. 1977. *3025*

—. Captivity narratives. Indian-White Relations. 19c. *57*

—. Catholic Church. Catholic University of America. Hogan Schism. Parsons, Wilfrid. Pennsylvania (Philadelphia). 1785-1825. 1975. *2361*

—. Catholic Church. Clergy. Irish Americans. Keane, John J. (writings). 1838-1918. *2372*

—. Colleges and Universities. Dissertations. Italian Americans. 1908-77. *862*

—. Curricula. Ethnic studies. Public Schools. 1908-70's. *18*

—. Danish Americans. 1886-1976. *1681*

—. Economic Theory. French Canadians. Minville, Esdras. Quebec. 20c. *3326*

—. Editorials. French Canadians. Latin America. Newspapers. Quebec. 1959-73. *3741*

—. Education. Social reform. 1960's-70's. *2847*

—. Ethnicity. Family. 1970's. *2955*

—. Ethnicity. French Americans. French Canadians. New England. 1755-1973. *466*

—. Europe. French Language. Literary associations. Quebec. USA. Voluntary associations. 1840-1900. *3137*

—. Fiction. Immigration. Jews. 1867-1920. *1008*

—. Folklore. 20c. *2915*

—. French. LaHarpe, Jean-Baptiste Bénard de. Louisiana. Pioneers. 1718-22. *476*

—. French Americans. French Canadians. Vermont Historical Society Library. 1609-1975. *3160*

—. French Canadians. Literary history. Quebec. 18c-20c. *3176*

—. French Canadians. Quebec. 1968-78. *3175*

—. Gingerich, Melvin. Historians. Mennonites. 1921-75. *2241*

—. Immigration. Law. 1970-77. *263*

—. Immigration. Scott, Franklin D. 1925-74. *31*

—. Israel. Jews. Noah, Mordecai Manuel. 1785-1851. 1930's-76. *1403*

—. *Jewish Social Studies* (periodical). 1964-78. *959*

—. Jews. 1960-74. *939*

—. Jews. 1960-75. *940*

—. Jews. 1960-75. *941*

—. Jews. 1974-75. *997*

—. Jews. 1960-76. *998*

—. Jews. 1960-78. *999*

—. Jews. 16c-1978. *1000*

—. Jews. 1960-79. *1001*

—. Jews. 1960-73. *1402*

—. Judaism (Reform). 1883-1973. *1125*

—. Literature. Nationalism. Paučo, Joseph (obituary). Politics. Slovakian Americans. 1930's-75. *1900*

—. Models. Research. Social Mobility. 1969-73. *2766*

—. Polish Americans. 1918-77. *1961*

Buczek, Daniel Stephen (review article). Bójnowski, Lucyan. Catholic Church. Connecticut (New Britain). Polish Americans. 1895-1960. *2042*

Budgets *See also* Public Finance.

—. Decisionmaking. Family. Pennsylvania (Philadelphia). 1870-80. *2716*

Buenker, John D. (review article). Metropolitan areas. Political reform. Progressive Movement. 1910's. *2455*

Buettner, George L. Concordia Publishing House. Lutheran Church (Missouri Synod). Missouri (St. Louis). Reminiscences. 1888-1955. *2383*

Buffalo hunting. Fur trade. Gingras, Antoine Blanc. Indian-White Relations. Red River of the North. Settlement. 1845-73. *484*

Buies, Arthur. Catholic Church. French Canadians. 1880's-1901. *3408*

Buildings *See also* Architecture.

—. Bricks, yellow. Dutch Americans. Pennsylvania. Swedish Americans. 17c. *40*

—. Grand Opera House. Jews. Judah, Abraham. Missouri (Kansas City). Theater. 1883-1926. *1180*

—. Quebec (Quebec City; Lower Town Place Royale). Restorations. 17c. 1975. *3247*

Buildings (iron front). California (San Luis Obispo). Jews. Sinsheimer, Aaron Zachary (and family). 1878-1956. *1490*

Bulgaria. Illinden Uprising. Macedonian Americans. Press. Public opinion. 1903. *2120*

Bureau of Social Morals. Hertz, Rosie. Jews. Law Enforcement. New York City. Prostitution. 1912-13. *1209*

Bureaucracies. Anglophones. Canada. Civil Service. French Canadians. 1944-75. *3966*

—. Assimilation. Catholic Church. Irish Americans. Voluntary associations. 19c. *704*

—. Attitudes. Educational Administration. National Characteristics. Pluralism. Public Schools. ca 1850-1970's. *2865*

—. Colonial Government. Commissaire ordonnateur. French. Louisiana. 1712-69. *432*

—. French Canadians. Quebec. 1969-77. *3321*

Burgenland. Austrian Americans. Immigration. Poetry. Riessner, Johann. 1856-1939. *266*

Burgheim, Max. Authors. Bode, August H. Bruehl, Gustav. Fick, Heinrich H. German Americans. Ohio (Cincinnati). Rattermann, Heinrich A. VonWahlde, Hermann. Zeydel, Edwin Herman. 19c-20c. *629*

Burials. American Cemetary. French Americans. Louisiana (Natchitoches). St. Denis, Louis Antoine Juchereau de. 1744-1974. *478*

Burns family. Immigration. Nova Scotia (Annapolis County; Wilmot Township). Scotch Irish. 1764-20c. *3445*

Burthe, Charles André. Civil-Military Relations. Colonial Government. French. Laussat, Pierre Clément. Louisiana. 1802-03. *376*

Business *See also* Advertising; Banking; Corporations; Management; Marketing; Multinational Corporations; Real Estate Business.

—. Adler, Lewis. California (Sonoma). Jews. 1840's-96. *1342*

—. Advertisements. American Revolution. Jews. Newspapers. Salomon, Haym. 1777-85. *1401*

—. Alaska. Gold Rushes. Jews. Reminiscences. Rozenstain, Yael. 1900-44. *1456*

—. Alaska. Jews. Reminiscences. Ripinsky, Sol. 1867-1909. *1267*

—. Banking. California (Ventura County). Levy, Achille. 1853-1936. *1415*

—. Barbel, Marie-Anne. French Canadians. New France. Women. 18c. *3256*

—. Bertarelli, Pier Giuseppe. California. Gold Rushes. Immigration. Italian Americans. 1849-53. *855*

—. California (Anaheim). Democratic Party. Dreyfus, Benjamin. Jews. Winemaking. 1854-86. *1491*

—. California (Fort Bragg). Jews. Russia. Shafsky family. 1889-1976. *1516*

—. California (Los Angeles). Housing. Jews. Middle Classes. Social Mobility. 1880's. *1195*

—. California (San Diego). City Government. Jews. Mannasse, Joseph Samuel. Schiller, Marcus. 1853-97. *1407*

—. California (San Francisco; San Bruno Avenue). Esther Hellman Settlement House. Jews. Neighborhoods. 1901-68. *1239*

—. Canada. Elites. Lawyers. 19c-1974. *3801*

—. Cities. Elites. Historiography. Iron Industry. Social classes. 1874-1900. *2788*

—. Confederate States of America. Jews. Levy, Jonas Phillips. Merchant marine. North Carolina (Wilmington). 1830's-60's. *1449*

—. Demens, Peter. Political Commentary. Russian Americans. 1881-1919. *2055*

—. Economic Growth. Jews. 18c-20c. *929*

—. Elites. Illinois (Chicago). Social Backgrounds. 1830-1930. *2771*

—. Elites. Ontario (Toronto). Upper Canada Club. 1835-40. *3789*

—. Filene, Edward A. Jews. Leadership. Massachusetts (Boston). Philanthropy. 1860-1937. *1372*

—. French Americans. Lewis, Meriwether. Missouri (St. Louis). US Military Academy. 1803-38. *383*

—. French Canadians. Nationalism. Parti Québécois. Quebec. Working class. 1970's. *4003*

—. French Canadians. Quebec (Montreal). 1825. *3273*

—. Godchaux, Leon. Jews. Louisiana (New Orleans). 19c. *1501*

—. Great Britain (London). Immigration. Jews. Labor Unions and Organizations. New York City. 19c-20c. *1266*

—. Illinois (Chicago; Englewood district). Osberg, Edward E. Reminiscences. Swedish Americans. 1926. *1841*

—. Immigration Policy. Labor. Legislation. 1870's-1920's. *245*

—. Jacobs, James. Jews. Rhode Island (Providence). 1820's-30's. 1850's. *1469*

—. Jews. Memoirs. Resnik, Bezalel Nathan. Rhode Island (Providence). 1891-1971. *1446*

—. Jews. New York City. 1654-1820. *1217*

—. Jews. Photographs. Washington (Seattle). 1890-1920. *1325*

—. Jews. Social Change. Women. 18c-20c. *1049*

—. Letendre, François-Xavier (and family). Métis. Political leadership. Saskatchewan. Social status. 1870-1900. *3388*

Business education. Americanization. Canada. Colleges and universities. Faculty. USA. 1971-75. *3597*

—. Americanization. French Canadians. Quebec. 1972. *3387*

Businessmen *See also* Entrepreneurs; Merchants.

—. Cooperatives. Nelson, Nelson O. Norwegian Americans. Profit-sharing. Social Reform. 1886-1904. *1740*

—. Democratic Party. Elections. Immigrants. Negroes. New York City (Brooklyn). Racism. Suffrage. 1860. *2460*

Busing. Civil disobedience. Irish Americans. Massachusetts (Boston; South Boston). 19c-1974. *753*

Butzel, Magnus. Attitudes. Isaacs, Meyer Samuel. Jews. Letters. Social Organizations. 1885. *1635*

Byrnes, James F. Federal Government. Germany. Hungarian Americans. Memoirs. Nuclear Science and Technology. Szilard, Leo. 1898-1945. *686*

C

Cabala. Counter Culture. Jews. Mysticism. Rationalism. Tradition. 1940's-70's. *1074*

—. Friends, Society of. Jews. 17c-20c. *1038*

Cabet, Étienne. Documents. French Americans. Icarians. Missouri (Cheltenham). Utopias. 1849-62. *368*

—. French Americans. Icaria (colony). Illinois (Nauvoo). Utopias. 1848-56. *377*

Cabet, Étienne *(Voyage to Icaria)*. French Americans. Icarians. Utopias. 1830's-56. *394*

Cable, George Washington ("Jean-ah Poquelin"). Creoles. Dialects. Fiction. 1875-99. *400*

Cable, George Washington *(Old Creole Days)*. Creoles. Literature. Louisiana. 1879-1925. *474*

Cadieux, Lorenzo (obituary). French Canadians. Jesuits. Ontario, northern. Scholarship. 1903-76. *3125*

Cahan, Abraham. Cities. Crane, Stephen. Fiction. Jews. Romanticism. 1890's. *946*

—. *Jewish Daily Forward* (newspaper). Palestine. Socialism. Zionism. 1925. *1593*

Cajuns *See also* Creoles.

—. Acculturation. Louisiana (Houma). Negroes. Texans. 1945-73. *479*

—. Alabama, south. Rural settlements. Social change. 1960's. *472*

—. Creoles. Language. Louisiana, southern. Social Customs. Texas (Gulf Coast). 17c-1977. *469*

—. Economic Growth. Louisiana. Social Organization. 1830-60. *51*

California *See also* Far Western States.

—. Accolti, Michael. Jesuits. Santa Clara, University of. 1849-51. *2344*

—. Advertising. Jews. *Ketubot* (contract). Marriage certificates. San Francisco *Weekly Gleaner* (newspaper). 1850-61. *1024*

—. Agricultural Industry. Immigration. 1880's-1939. *90*

—. Agricultural Industry. Wine. ca 1830-1975. *2901*

—. Agriculture. Alien Land Law (California, 1913). Exclusion Act (US, 1882). Immigration Policy. 1880-1940. *88*

—. Agriculture. Fort Ross. Fur Trade. Lumber and Lumbering. Russian-American Company. Shipbuilding. 1812-41. *2104*

—. Agriculture. Hamburg, Sam. Israel. Jews. 1898-1976. *1385*

—. Agriculture. Immigrants. 1850's-1945. *84*

—. Anti-Semitism. Banking. Norris, Frank (*The Octopus*). Novels. Pollasky, Marcus. S. Behrman (fictional character). 1880's-1901. *1614*

—. Anti-Semitism. Freemasons. Hyam, Benjamin Daniel. 1850-93. *1488*

—. Anti-Semitism. Newspapers. 1849-53. *1641*

—. Arguello, Maria de la Concepcion. Catholic Church. Orthodox Eastern Church, Russian. Rezanov, Nikolai. Russians. 1806. *2119*

—. Arizona. Copper Mines and Mining. Jews. Newman, John B. (Black Jack). Real estate. 1880's-1920's. *1481*

—. Arts. Catholic Church. Gold Rushes. Immigration. Irish Americans. Politics. 1849-90's. *748*

—. Assimilation. Ethnicity. Polish Americans. 1860-1971. *2037*

—. Auerbach's Department Store. Jews. Retail Trade. Utah (Salt Lake City). 1857-1977. *1461*

—. Australian Americans. Demography. ca 1850-52. *326*

—. Bancroft, Hubert Howe ("Pioneer Register and Index"). Scottish Americans. 1542-1848. *316*

—. Behavior. Black, Esther Boulton. Jews (review article). *Los Angeles Daily News* (newspaper). Pitt, Leonard. 1869. *1310*

—. Bernstein, Max. Development. Gold rushes. International Company of Mexico. Jews. Mexico (Baja California). 1854-1971. *1482*

—. Bertarelli, Pier Giuseppe. Business. Gold Rushes. Immigration. Italian Americans. 1849-53. *855*

—. Bloch, Ernest. Jews. Music. San Francisco Conservatory of Music. 1922-30. *1445*

—. California (Hollywood). DeMille, Cecil B. Film Industry. Jews. Lasky, Jesse L. Paramount-Publix Corporation. Vaudeville. 1890's-1930. *1400*

—. Catholic Church. German Americans. Intellectuals. Ramm, Charles A. 1863-1951. *2371*

—. Charities. Disaster relief. Economic aid. Jews. Nieto, Jacob. San Francisco Earthquake and Fire. 1906. *1256*

—. Croatian Americans. Nevada. 1680-1977. *2127*

—. Democratic Party. Gould, Lewis L. Political Factions (review article). Progressivism. Texas. Williams, R. Hal. 1880-1919. 1973. *2534*

—. Disaster relief. Jews. San Francisco Earthquake and Fire. 1906. *1245*

—. English Americans. Gold Rushes. Harrold family. Letters. 1847-51. *297*

—. Frank, Leo M. Georgia. Jews. Lynching. Progressivism. Trials. 1913-15. *1620*

—. Frank, Leo M. Georgia (Atlanta). Jews. Newspapers. Trials. 1913-15. *1630*

—. Franklin, Harvey B. Jews. Rabbis. Reminiscences. 1916-57. *1376*

—. Fur Trade. Russians. Travel Accounts. Zavalishin, Dmitry. 1823-24. *2068*

—. Gold Rushes. Lumber and Lumbering. Norwegian Americans. Week, Andrew. Week, John. Wisconsin. 1838-60. *1752*

—. Haraszthy family. Hungarian Americans. New England. Wine (Zinfandel). 1850-90. *685*

—. Heydenfeldt, Solomon. Jews. Lyons, Henry A. Supreme courts, state. 1850's. *1048*

D

E

—. Educational reform. Nativism. Niles Bill (Ohio, 1898). Ohio (Toledo). Progressive Era. School boards. 1890's. *2459*

—. English Canadians. Federal Government. French Canadians. Politics. Public opinion. Quebec. 1977. *3963*

—. Entrepreneurs. Ingraham, John N. (review article). Iron industry. Ohio (Youngstown). Pennsylvania (Philadelphia, Pittsburgh). West Virginia (Wheeling). 1874-1965. *2800*

—. Entrepreneurs. Ontario (Hamilton). 1850's. *3791*

—. French Canadians. Quebec. Science. 1824-44. *3291*

—. Intellectuals. Jews. 1945-78. *1060*

—. Jews. Social Classes. 20c. *1089*

—. Photography. Stereotypes. 20c. *2952*

—. Political Parties. Social Classes. Tennessee (Davidson County). 1835-61. *2473*

—. Working class. 19c-20c. *2553*

Elkin, Mendel. Immigrants. Jews. Yidisher Visnshaftlekher Institut (Library). 1918-63. *1431*

Emancipation. Assimilation. Jewish studies. 18c-1974. *1005*

—. Ghettos. Jews. Negroes. 15c-20c. *1015*

Emanuel Lutheran Church. German Americans. Lutheran Church. New York City (Queens). Reminiscences. Wyneken, Frederick G. 1887-1907. *2427*

Emanu-El (newspaper). Anti-Semitism. California (San Francisco). Editorials. Immigrants. Jews. Slavic Americans. Voorsanger, Jacob. 1905. *1080*

Embroidery. Folklore. Immigrants. Women. ca 1890's-1900's. 1970's. *2918*

Emigrants. America (image). Folklore. Hungary. 19c-20c. *676*

—. Illinois. Janssonists. Sects, Religious. Social Classes. Sweden. 1845-47. *1831*

—. Jews. USSR. 1974. *1604*

Emigration *See also* Demography; Immigration; Population; Race Relations; Refugees.

—. Acadians. Assimilation. Minorities in Politics. New Brunswick (Moncton). 1871-1971. *3346*

—. Acadians. Canada. 1605-1800. *3091*

—. America (image). Great Britain. London *Times* (newspaper). 19c. *287*

—. American studies. Yugoslavia. -1973. *2129*

—. Anti-Semitism. Famines. Foreign Relations. Russia. 1891-92. *1122*

—. Australia. Gold Rushes. Train, George Francis. USA. 1850's. *170*

—. Canada. Epp, Johann. Germans, Russian. Letters. Mennonites. Russia. USA. 1875. *2213*

—. Canada. Population. 1961-71. *3022*

—. Cary, Austin F. Forests and Forestry. German Americans. Germany. Schenck, Carl A. World War I. 1910's-20's. *2614*

—. Catholic Church. Immigration. Persecution. Prince Edward Island. Scotland. Scottish Canadians. 1769-74. *3430*

—. Centennial Exposition of 1876. France. Labor delegation. Pennsylvania (Philadelphia). Travel Accounts (French). 1876. *404*

—. Depressions. Maritime Provinces. Massachusetts (Boston). New England. 1860-1900. *328*

—. Economic Conditions. Expatriation. Politics. 1946-70's. *169*

—. Economic Conditions. Greece. 1945-75. *662*

—. Economic Development. French Canadians. Quebec. 1837-1930. *3115*

—. Finland. Research. Sweden. 19c-20c. 1962-76. *1810*

—. French Canadians. New England. Quantitative Methods. Quebec. 1870-1910. *448*

—. French Canadians. Quebec. USA. 1850's-1900's. *401*

—. Genealogy. Germany (Palatinate; Lambsheim). Pennsylvania. 1832-77. *598*

—. German Americans. Norway. Religious dissenters. 1817-25. *1757*

—. Great Britain. Letters. Mormons. Richards, Willard. Young, Brigham. 1840. *305*

—. Great Britain. Letters-to-the-editor. *London Times* (newspaper). Nebraska. 1872. *307*

—. Greece. 1900-70. *669*

—. Hawaii. Jews. 1850-1913. *1202*

—. Israel. Jews. 1970's. *1585*

—. Italian Americans. Italy, southern. 1964-68. *810*

—. Jackson, Henry M. Jews. Legislation. Most-Favored-Nation status. USSR. 1972-74. *1637*

—. Jews. Morocco. Quebec (Montreal). 1960's-70's. *3514*

—. Jews. Russia. 1881-1914. *1016*

—. Norway (Hegra). Norwegian Americans. 1865-90. *1738*

—. Norway (Land Parish). Norwegian Americans. 1866-75. *1753*

—. Reminiscences. Sweden. Vontver, May. ca 1900. *1866*

—. Strindberg, August. Sweden. 1890-1912. *1791*

—. Sweden. Unonius, Gustaf. 1858-63. *1851*

—. Sweden (Blekinge province). 1851-70. *1870*

Emigration agents. Immigration. Michigan. Thomson, Edward H. 1849. *72*

—. Immigration. Steamship companies. ca 1850's-1914. *14*

Emmert, Paul. Hawaii. Sutter, John. Swiss Americans. 1778-1975. *2152*

Emmet, Joseph Kline. Acting. Gayler, Charles (*Fritz, Our Cousin German*). German Americans. Immigration. Irish Americans. Missouri (St. Louis). Stereotypes. 1858-91. *2914*

—. Acting. German Americans. Irish Americans. Missouri (St. Louis). Stereotypes. 1858-91. *2912*

Employment *See also* Discrimination, Employment; Occupations; Unemployment.

—. *Ambach* v. *Norwick* (US, 1979). *Foley* v. *Connelie* (US, 1978). *Graham* v. *Richardson* (US, 1971). Immigrants. Supreme Court. 1971-79. *253*

—. Assimilation. English Language. Immigrants. Income. Ontario (Toronto). 1968-70. *3731*

—. Assimilation. Immigration. Israel. Jews. 1967-70's. *958*

—. Attitudes. Family. Rhode Island. Women. 1968-69. *2709*

—. Canada. Economic Conditions. Immigration policy. 1962-74. *3081*

—. Canada. Economics. Immigrants. Wages. 1970's. *3825*

—. Canada. Immigration Bill. Management. 1976. *3070*

—. Cities. Federal Government. Integration. 1967-73. *2949*

—. College graduates. Ontario. Social Mobility. 1960-71. *3787*

—. Colorado (Denver). Geographic mobility. Immigrants. Social Mobility. 1870-92. *2813*

—. Cost of living. German Americans. Income. Irish Americans. Pennsylvania (Philadelphia). Poverty. 1880. *2772*

—. Discrimination. Higher Education. Italian Americans. 1960-72. *793*

—. Economic Conditions. New Brunswick. Nova Scotia. Rural Settlements. 1961-76. *3049*

—. Economic opportunity. Education. Immigrants. Jews. Urbanization. 1880-1914. *1154*

—. Ethnic Studies. German Americans. Irish Americans. Land Tenure. Methodology. Philadelphia Social History Project. 1850-80. 1973. *13*

—. Fishing. French Canadians. Marriage. Quebec (Magdalen Islands). Sex roles. Women. 1977. *3383*

—. Greek Americans. Massachusetts (Springfield). Politics. Social Conditions. 1884-1944. *654*

—. Illinois (Chicago). Industry. Negroes. Polish Americans. Stereotypes. Violence. 1890-1919. *2031*

—. Immigrants. Italian Canadians. Ontario (Toronto). 1885-1915. *3494*

—. Immigration. Jews. New York City. Social Organization. 1970's. *1017*

—. Immigration. Nativism. Negroes (free). Politics. 1830-60. *195*

—. Income. 1970. *2764*

—. Italian Americans. New York City. Women. 1880-1905. *2731*

—. Italian Americans. Oral history. Pennsylvania (Pittsburgh). Slavic Americans. Women. ca 1900-20. 1976. *2735*

—. New York (Buffalo, Poughkeepsie). Ontario (Kingston). Pennsylvania (Philadelphia). Property ownership. Social Classes. 19c. *2782*

Energy. Anti-Semitism. Public opinion. 1970's. *1627*

Engel, Jacob. Brethren in Christ. Canada. Pennsylvania (Lancaster County). 1775-1964. *2299*

Engineering *See also* Military Engineering.

—. Ammann, Othmar Hermann. Bibliographies. Bridges. Swiss Americans. 1915-77. *2154*

—. Ammann, Othmar Hermann. Bridges. 1893-1954. *2155*

Engineers. Occupations. Quebec (Montreal). Values. 1974. *3800*

—. Radzimovsky, Eugene. Ukrainian Americans. 1930-73. *2107*

England, John. Catholic Church. Ireland. Voluntarism. 1808-50. *699*

England, Robert. Canada, western. Reminiscences. Settlement. 1920-76. *3045*

Engle, Paul. Attitudes. Iowa (Cedar Rapids). Jews. Reminiscences. 1900-60. *1186*

English Americans *See also* British Americans.

—. Agriculture. Appalachia. Mining. Pollard, Thomas. 19c. *290*

—. Andros, Edmund (recall). Colonial Government. Dutch Americans. Economic Policy. Merchants. New York. Political change. Trade. 1674-80. *349*

—. Appalachia. Copper Mines and Mining. 1830-90. *289*

—. Architecture. Cultural diffusion. German Americans. Limestone. Maryland (Washington County). Scotch Irish. Wood. 1736-1840. *2930*

—. Architecture. German Americans. Masonry, dry stone. 1700-1975. *498*

—. Barns. Cultural diffusion. German Americans. Ohio, northeast. Silos. 19c. *83*

—. Birkbeck, Morris. Diaries. Flower, George. Illinois (Albion). Letters. Westward Movement. 1816-17. *301*

—. Birkbeck, Morris. Flower, George. Health. Illinois (Albion). Settlement. 1818-29. *299*

—. Blaine, James G. Cleveland, Grover. Dicey, Albert Venn. Godkin, Edwin L. Ireland. Irish Americans. Political Campaigns. 1884. *2450*

—. Boston Finance Commission. Democratic Party. Irish Americans. Massachusetts (Boston). Matthews, Nathan. Mayors. Political Reform. 1890-1910. *2462*

—. California. Gold Rushes. Harrold family. Letters. 1847-51. *297*

—. California (San Diego). Hutchinson, Allen. Sculpture. 1888-1929. *298*

—. Capps, Samuel J. Colorado. Immigration. Strange family. Westward Movement. 1850-1912. *304*

—. City Politics. Irish Americans. Massachusetts (Boston). 1884-1933. 1978. *2449*

—. Clayton, William. Illinois (Nauvoo). Immigration. Letters. Mormons. 1840. *291*

—. Clayton, William. Immigration. Letters. Moon, John. Mormons. 1840. *292*

—. Coal Mines and Mining. Illinois. Labor Unions and Organizations. Legislation. Lobbying. Scottish Americans. 1861-72. *285*

—. Colonial Government. Dutch Americans. Intergovernmental Relations. Local Government. New Netherland. 1624-63. *356*

—. Crisp, John. Letters. Pennsylvania (Brownsville). Playford, Robert W. 1830. *295*

—. Delaware. Dutch Americans. Indentured Labor. Labor. Swedish Americans. 1681-1921. *2900*

—. Environment. Farmers. Kansas (Ellis County). Rural Settlements. Russian Americans. 1870's. *49*

—. German Americans. Pennsylvania. Political Participation. 1700-55. *631*

—. Irish Americans. Kansas (Runnymede). Post offices. Ranching. Rural Settlements. Scottish Americans. Turnly, Francis J. S. Watmough, Robert W. 1886-90. *286*

—. Mining. Western States. 19c. *296*

—. Mormons. Staines, William C. Utah. 1818-81. *294*

—. Mormons. Utah. Watt, George D. 1840's-81. *306*

—. North Central States. Primitive Methodist Church. 1842-1976. *303*

English Canadians *See also* British Canadians.

—. Acadians. Catholic Church. Maritime Provinces. Social Conditions. 1763-1977. *3162*

—. Age. Canada. French Canadians. Political Participation. Voting and Voting Behavior. 1968. *3712*

—. Agricultural production. Culture. Economic Development. French Canadians. Quebec (Compton, Winslow townships). 1851-70. *3051*

—. Agriculture. Bee, William. Bourne, Hugh. Clowes, William. Dow, Lorenzo. Grenfell Colony. Primitive Methodist Church. Saskatchewan. 1882. *3416*

—. Agriculture. Duplessis, Maurice. Federalism. Industrialization. Letters. Minville, Esdras. Natural resources. Quebec. 20c. *3917*

—. Cary, Austin F. Emigration. German Americans. Germany. Schenck, Carl A. World War I. 1910's-20's. *2614*

—. Economic development. French Canadians. Minville, Esdras. Multinational corporations. Quebec. USA. 1923-36. *3357*

Formisano, Ronald P. Hackney, F. Sheldon. Kleppner, Paul. Methodology. Political history (review article). 1827-1900. 1969-71. *2522*

—. Holt, Michael F. Politics (review article). Shade, William G. 1827-65. 1969-72. *2524*

Formosa. *See* Taiwan.

Forrest, Edwin. Actors and Actresses. Astor Place Opera House. Macready, William Charles. Nativism. New York City. Riots. 1849. *191*

Fort Caroline. Florida. Huguenots. Settlement. 1562-65. 1976. *430*

Fort Garry. Escapes. German Canadians. Manitoba (Winnipeg). Métis. Red River Rebellion. Riel, Louis. Schultz, John Christian. 1869-70. *3894*

Fort Keogh. Catholic Church. Chaplains. Diaries. French Americans. Frontier and Pioneer Life. Lindesmith, Eli. Montana. Wibaux, Pierre. 1855-1922. *2349*

Fort Niagara (battle). Armies. French and Indian War. Great Britain. 1759. *3855*

Fort Orange. French-Indian Relations. Indian Wars. Iroquois Indians. Long Sault (battle). Quebec. 1660. 1960. *3215*

Fort Phil Kearney. Indian Wars. Jews. Littmann, Max. Wagon Box Fight. Wyoming. 1865-1921. *1410*

Fort Pitt. Cree Indians (Plains, Wood). Diaries. Frenchman's Butte, Battle of. Indians (captivities). Manitoba. McLean, W. J. North West Rebellion. Scottish Canadians. 1885. *3913*

Fort Ross. Agriculture. California. Fur Trade. Lumber and Lumbering. Russian-American Company. Shipbuilding. 1812-41. *2104*

—. California, northern. Colonization. Kuskov, Ivan A. Russian-American Company. 1808-41. *2095*

—. California, northern. Colonization. Kuskov, Ivan A. Russian-American Company. 1808-41. *2096*

Fort St. Louis. Colonization. French. LaSalle, Sieur de. Texas (Aransas, Matagorda bays). 1684-85. *412*

Forts. *See* Military Camps and Forts.

Foster homes. Child Welfare. Immigrants. Jews. New York City. Working class. 1900-05. *1271*

Foucault, Denis-Nicolas. Colonial Government. Coups d'Etat. French. Louisiana. 1762-68. *372*

Founding Fathers. Constitutions. Declaration of Independence. 1775-89. *2468*

Fourierist movement. Communes. Considérant, Victor Prosper. French Americans. Texas (La Réunion). 1854-59. *393*

Fowler, Charles Lewis. Georgia (Atlanta). Ku Klux Klan. Lanier Unviersity. 1917-22. *214*

Fox, Kenneth. Allswang, John M. City Politics (review article). Dorsett, Lyle W. Ebner, Michael H. Tobin, Eugene M. 1850's-1970's. *2463*

Fraktur. Art. German Canadians. Ontario. 1976. *3466*

—. Birth and baptismal certificates. Folk art. German Americans. Pennsylvania. 1750-1850. *635*

—. Calligraphy. German Americans. Pennsylvania. 19c. *547*

—. Eisenbrown, John Daniel. Folk Art. German Americans. Pennsylvania. 1820-74. *523*

—. Folk Art. Mennonites. Ontario (Waterloo County). Weber, Anna. 1825-88. *3636*

—. German Americans. Mennonites. Pennsylvania. 1740's-1860's. *651*

Fram, Harry. California (Los Angeles). Zionism. 1900-44. *1530*

Fram, Leon. Anti-Nazi Movements. Boycotts. Jews. League for Human Rights. Michigan (Detroit). Reminiscences. 1930's-40's. *2670*

France *See also* French Revolution.

—. Acadians. Acculturation. Exiles. Great Britain. Nova Scotia. 18c. *3860*

—. Acadians. Canada. Great Britain. Immigration. Louisiana. Spain. 1755-85. *382*

—. Africa, French-speaking. Belgium. Canada. Foreign Relations. French Canadians. French Language. Institutions. 1960-74. *3738*

—. Africa, French-speaking. Belgium. Foreign Relations. French Canadians. Quebec. 1964-74. *3749*

—. Africa (French-speaking). Foreign relations. French Canadians. Quebec. 1950's-70's. *3742*

—. Allen, Ira. Canada. Filibusters. French Canadians. Great Britain. 1795-1801. *3872*

—. American Revolution. Canada. French Canadians. Heraldry. Knights of Malta. 1600's-1976. *3254*

—. Anti-Semitism. Dreyfus, Alfred. Editorials. Press. Public opinion. Trials. 1895-1906. *1613*

—. Assimilation. Immigrants. Italian Americans. 19c-20c. *882*

—. Bernou, Claude. Canada. LeClercq, Crestien. *Premier Établissement de la Foy dans la Nouvelle France* (book). Renaudot, Eusèbe. 1691. *3217*

—. Blanchard, Raoul. Deffontaines, Pierre. Geography. Quebec. Siegfried, André. 1930-50. *3122*

—. Books. Canada. Catholic Church. Clergy. French Canadians. 1850-1914. *3159*

—. California (San Francisco). Immigrants. Jews. Meyer, Eugene. Reminiscences. 1842-60. *1434*

—. Canada. Catholic Church. Catholic Church. Great Britain. Law. Tithes. 1760-75. *3303*

—. Canada. Colonization. Discovery and Exploration. Great Britain. Vikings. War. Prehistory-19c. *3037*

—. Canada. Colonization. Immigration Policy. Population. 17c. *3192*

—. Canada. Conservatism. French Canadians. French Canadians. Groulx, Lionel. Maurras, Charles. Nationalism. 1910-40. *3163*

—. Canada. Cultural relations. French Canadians. International Trade. 1760-1870. *3745*

—. Canada. Democracy. Foreign Relations. French Canadians. Immigration. 1855. *3272*

—. Canada. Foreign Relations. French Canadians. Quebec. 1967-75. *3750*

—. Canada. French Canadians. Trade. 1640-1760. *3257*

—. Canada. Great Britain. Jews. Poverty. Uruguay. 1975. *3509*

—. *Capricieuse* (vessel). Foreign Relations. French Canadians. International Trade. Official visits. Quebec. 1855. *3744*

—. Centennial Exposition of 1876. Emigration. Labor delegation. Pennsylvania (Philadelphia). Travel Accounts (French). 1876. *404*

—. Charles I. Colonization. Great Britain. Nova Scotia (Port Royal). Scotland. 1629-32. *3448*

—. Colonial Government. French Canadians. Notaries, royal. Quebec. 1663-1764. *3268*

—. Colonial Government. Great Britain. New England. Nova Scotia (Canso, Cape Breton). 1710-21. *3851*

—. Colonies. Great Britain. Historiography. Italy. North America. 1663-1763. *3836*

—. Compagnie de Colonisation et de Credit des Cantons de l'Est. Foreign Investments. French Canadians. Natural resources. Quebec, eastern. Settlement. 1881-93. *3376*

—. Courts. French Canadians. New France. Trials (costs). ca 1685-1753. *3198*

—. Creoles. Louisiana. 17c-20c. *373*

—. deGaulle, Charles. Foreign Relations. French Canadians. Public opinion. Quebec. Separatist Movements. 1967-76. *3736*

—. deGaulle, Charles. French Canadians. Quebec. 1940-67. *3739*

—. Denonville, Marquis de. French. Galley slaves. Indians. Iroquois Indians. New France. 1687. *3204*

—. Elections. French Canadians. Language. Parliaments. Quebec. 1792-1810. *3285*

—. Foreign relations. French Canadians. Quebec. 1763-1976. *3740*

—. French and Indian War. Great Britain. New Brunswick. Restigouche River (battle). 1760. *3848*

—. French Canadians. Lamaletie, Jean-André. Merchants. Quebec. 1741-63. *3186*

—. French-Indian Relations (review article). Huron Indians. Jaenen, Cornelius J. Trigger, Bruce G. Values. 1600-60. 1976. *3250*

—. Jews. Levy, Jonas (deposition). 1780. *1451*

—. Quebec. Sociology. USA. 1970's. *3389*

France (Paris). Catholic Church. French Canadians. Quebec (Montreal). Reading rooms. Social Customs. 19c. *3298*

France (Poitou; Les Sables d'Olonne). Fishing. Huart, Christophle-Albert-Alberic d'. Nobility. Nova Scotia (Louisbourg). 1750-75. *3184*

France (Saint-Germaine-Laval). Boël, Attale. Discovery and Exploration. Duluth, Daniel Greysolon, Sieur (birthplace). French. Malchelosse, Gerald. North America. 1636-40. 1950's. *3203*

France (St. Malo). Atlantic Provinces. Climate. Fishing. French. Newfoundland. Oceans. 1717-34. *3187*

—. Canada. Commerce. Fishing. French. 1713-55. *3188*

Franchise. *See* Citizenship; Suffrage.

Franciscan Sisters. Catholic Church. Irish Americans. Minnesota (Winona). Molloy, Mary Aloysius. St. Teresa, College of. Women. 1903-54. *739*

Franciscan Sisters of Chicago. Addams, Jane. Dudzik, Mary Theresa. Illinois. Polish Americans. Social Work. 1860-1918. *1989*

Francke, Gottfried. Austria (Salzburg). Georgia (Ebenezer). Kiefer, Theobald, II. Letters. Orphanages. Settlement. Whitefield, George. 1738. 1750. *553*

Francophiles. Anglophiles. Catholic Church. Mathieu, Olivier-Elzéar. Saskatchewan (Regina). 1905-30. *3896*

Franco-Prussian War. California (Los Angeles). Jews. Universal Jewish Alliance. 1868-70. *1309*

Frank, Leo M. California. Georgia. Jews. Lynching. Progressivism. Trials. 1913-15. *1620*

—. California. Georgia (Atlanta). Jews. Newspapers. Trials. 1913-15. *1630*

—. Conley, James. Georgia (Atlanta). Jews. Negroes. Press. Trials. 1913-15. *1624*

—. Discrimination. Georgia (Atlanta). Jews. 1865-1915. *1218*

Frankenstein, Abraham Frankum. California (Los Angeles). Conductors. Jews. 1897-1934. *1390*

Frankfurter, Felix. Brandeis, Louis D. Jews. New Deal. Politics. Roosevelt, Franklin D. World War I. 1917-33. *1368*

Franklin and Marshall College. Gerhardt, Emanuel V. German Americans. Pennsylvania (Lancaster). Reformed German Church. Theology. 1840-1904. *2381*

Franklin and Marshall College Library. German Americans. Imprints. Pennsylvania (Lancaster County). 1745-1888. *517*

Franklin, Harvey B. California. Jews. Rabbis. Reminiscences. 1916-57. *1376*

Franklin, John. Arctic. Bellot, Joseph René. Canada. Kennedy, William. Métis. *Prince Albert* (vessel). Voyages. 1851. *3289*

Franklin, Leo M. Jews. Nebraska (Omaha). Rabbis. Temple Israel. 1892-99. *1370*

Franklin, Lewis Abraham. California (San Diego). Franklin, Maurice Abraham. Frontier and Pioneer Life. Merchants. 1851-65. *1485*

—. California (San Francisco). Jews. Sermons. 1850. *1192*

Franklin, Maurice Abraham. California (San Diego). Franklin, Lewis Abraham. Frontier and Pioneer Life. Merchants. 1851-65. *1485*

Fraud. German Americans. Indiana (New Harmony). Owen, Robert. Rapp, Frederick. Real Estate. 1825. *488*

Freedom of Assembly *See also* Freedom of Speech; Riots.

—. American Civil Liberties Union. Illinois (Skokie). Jews. Nazism. 1977-78. *1618*

—. American Civil Liberties Union. Illinois (Skokie). Jews. Nazism. 1977-78. *1621*

Freedom of Speech *See also* Freedom of the Press.

—. Anti-Communist movements. Anti-Semitism. Immigration. National self-image. Ontario (Toronto). 1928-29. *3075*

—. Anti-Semitism. Elites. Mencken, H. L. Public opinion. 1917-41. *2654*

—. Attitudes. Child-rearing. Social Organization. 1950's-70's. *2933*

Freedom of the Press *See also* Censorship.

—. Anticlericalism. Boycotts. *Canada-Revue* (newspaper). Catholic Church. Quebec (Montreal). 1890-94. *3660*

Freemasons. Anti-Semitism. California. Hyam, Benjamin Daniel. 1850-93. *1488*

—. California (Los Angeles, San Diego). Cave, Daniel. Dentistry. Jews. Leadership. 1873-1936. *1413*

Freemasons (King David's Lodge). Jews. Rhode Island (Newport). Washington, George. 1780-90. *1272*

—. American Revolution. British Canadians. Economic Conditions. Quebec. 1770's. *3883*

—. American Revolution. Canada. France. Heraldry. Knights of Malta. 1600's-1976. *3254*

—. American Revolution. Canada. French Revolution. Ideology. Popular movements. Rebellion of 1837. 1775-1838. *3878*

—. American Revolution. Canada. Military officers. 1763-80. *384*

—. American Revolution. French Revolution. Quebec (Lower Canada). Reform. 1773-1815. *3310*

—. Americanization. Business education. Quebec. 1972. *3387*

—. Americanization. Canada. Constitutions. Economic Conditions. Quebec. Separatist Movements. 1973. *3978*

—. Anderson, James T. M. Anti-Catholicism. Language. Public schools. Saskatchewan. School Act (amendment). Secularization. 1929-34. *3814*

—. Anglicization. Canada. French language. Grignon, Claude Henri. 20c. *3379*

—. Anglicization. Canada, western. Immigration Policy. MacDonald, John A. 1860-1900. *3023*

—. Anglophones. Bureaucracies. Canada. Civil Service. 1944-75. *3966*

—. Anglophones. Canada. Children. National Identity. USA. 1971-72. *3967*

—. Anglophones. Canada. Ethnicity. Heroes. 1974. *3844*

—. Anglophones. Canada. House of Commons. Language. Population. Representation Act (1974). 1974. *3961*

—. Anglophones. Canada. National Self-image. 1978. *3969*

—. Anglophones. Canada. Political Parties. Separatist Movements. 1975-77. *3934*

—. *Annales* school. Dechène, Louise. Hamelin, Jean. Historiography. New France. 1600-1760. 1960-74. *3208*

—. Anti-Catholicism. Assimilation. Education, Finance. MacKinnon, Murdoch. Saskatchewan. School Act (amendment). Scott, Walter. Scottish Canadians. 1913-26. *3815*

—. Anti-Catholicism. New Brunswick. Pitts, Herman H. Religion in the Public Schools. 1871-90. *3813*

—. Anticolonialism. Canada. English Canadians. Historiography. Middle Classes. Rebellion of 1837. 1815-1965. *3885*

—. Archambeault, Louis. Canada. Politics. 1815-90. *3928*

—. Architecture. Barns. Dutch Americans. Scottish Americans. 17c-1978. *80*

—. Architecture. Catholic Church. New France. 1600-1760. *3677*

—. Architecture. Guardhouses. Louisbourg, Fortress of. Military Camps and Forts. Nova Scotia. 1713-68. *3236*

—. Archives. Canada. Jesuits. 17c-1978. *3658*

—. Arès, Richard. Minville, Esdras. Quebec. Tremblay Commission. 1953-56. *3892*

—. Aristocracy. Estates. French. Meyer, Rudolf. Roffignac, Yves de. Saskatchewan (Assiniboia; Whitewood). 1885-1900. *3356*

—. Aristocracy. German Canadians. Meyer, Rudolf. Saskatchewan (Pipestone Creek, Whitewood). Settlement. 1880's. *3360*

—. Armies. Desertion. New France. 1700-63. *3227*

—. Armies. French and Indian War. Militia. Quebec. 1748-59. *3258*

—. Art. Catholic Church. Musée Historique de Vaudreuil. Quebec. 17c-20c. *3650*

—. Art. Chabert, Joseph. Education. National Institute for Arts and Crafts. Quebec (Montreal). Working Class. 1861-94. *3367*

—. Artisans. Labor Unions and Organizations. Quebec. 17c-18c. *3243*

—. Assimilation. Canada. Indians. 17c. *3221*

—. Assimilation. Canada. Language. 1961-71. *3335*

—. Assimilation. Catholic Church. Clergy. Dufresne, Andre B. Massachusetts (Holyoke). 1869-87. *409*

—. Assimilation. Catholic Church. Hendricken, Thomas F. Irish Americans. Massachusetts (Fall River). 1870's-85. *463*

—. Assimilation. Catholic Church. Language. Vermont. 1917-75. *444*

—. Assimilation. Catholic Church. Vermont (Winooski). 1867-1900. *369*

—. Assimilation. Maine (Lewiston). 1810's-1960's. *449*

—. Assimilation. Manitoba (St. Boniface). Residential Segregation. 1871-1971. *3343*

—. Assimilation. Nationalism. Religion. Rhode Island (Woonsocket). 1924-29. *468*

—. Assimilation. Prairie Provinces. 1871-1975. *3323*

—. Assiniboia, Council of. Manitoba. Métis. Minorities in Politics. 1860-71. *3282*

—. Association catholique de la jeunesse canadienne-française. Catholic Church. Morality. Quebec. 1903-14. *3325*

—. Astrolabes. Canada. Champlain, Samuel de. Discovery and Exploration. 1613. *3214*

—. Atlantic Provinces. Catholic Church. Diaries. Plessis, Joseph-Octave. Quebec Archdiocese. 1812-15. *3651*

—. Atlantic Provinces. Catholic Church. Plessis, Joseph-Octave. Travel (accounts). 1812-15. *3277*

—. Atlantic Provinces (review article). Historiography. Missions and Missionaries. Politics. 1000-1770. 19c. *3128*

—. Attitudes. Canada. National Characteristics. USA. 1837-1973. *3105*

—. Attitudes. Canada. Slander. 1712-48. *3228*

—. Attitudes. Catholic Church. Death and Dying. Quebec. Wills. 1663-1760. *3196*

—. Attitudes. Children. English Canadians. Government. Political socialization. Quebec. 1970-71. *3717*

—. Attitudes. Colonial Government. Explorers. Games. Indians. Missions and Missionaries. 16c-17c. *3206*

—. Attitudes. English Canadians. Nationalism. Quebec. Social Classes. 1978. *4011*

—. Attitudes. English Canadians. New Brunswick. Working conditions. 1973. *3725*

—. Balance of power. Defense Policy. Quebec. Separatist Movements. 1970's. *4041*

—. Banishment. Canada. Criminal Law. 1648-1748. *3248*

—. Bankruptcy. Cugnet, François-Étienne. Economic conditions. Quebec. 1742. *3252*

—. Barbeau, Victor. Cooperatives. Medical Reform. Paquette, Albiny. Politics. Quebec. 1900-45. *3404*

—. Barbel, Marie-Anne. Business. New France. Women. 18c. *3256*

—. Bédard, Pierre. Dionne, Narcisse-Eutrope. Language, official. Quebec (Lower Canada). 1792-1809. 1909. *3859*

—. Behaviorism. Political geography. Quebec (Saguenay County). Spatial perception. Territorialism. 1969-74. *3391*

—. Belgian Americans. Independent Textile Union. Rhode Island (Woonsocket). Working Class. 1931-50's. *2564*

—. Belgium. Canada. English Canadians. Liberal Party. Social Christian Party. 1880's-1973. *3925*

—. Berger, Carl. Brebner, J. B. Canada. Historiography. 17c-18c. 20c. *3030*

—. Bergeron, Léandre (review article). Historiography. Marxism. Quebec. 1970-75. *3117*

—. Bibliographies. Brouillette, Benoit. Geography. Quebec (Montreal). 1903-73. *3113*

—. Bibliographies. Canada. Literature. 1606-1977. *3172*

—. Bibliographies. Economic Theory. Minville, Esdras. Quebec. 20c. *3326*

—. Bibliographies. Editorials. Latin America. Newspapers. Quebec. 1959-73. *3741*

—. Bibliographies. Ethnicity. French Americans. New England. 1755-1973. *466*

—. Bibliographies. French Americans. Vermont Historical Society Library. 1609-1975. *3160*

—. Bibliographies. Literary history. Quebec. 18c-20c. *3176*

—. Bibliographies. Quebec. 1968-78. *3175*

—. Bilingual Education. Colleges and Universities. Ontario. 1946-73. *4052*

—. Black, Conrad. Duplessis, Maurice. Historiography. Political Leadership. Quebec. Rumilly, Robert. 1936-59. *3345*

—. Black, Conrad. Duplessis, Maurice (review article). Provincial Government. Quebec. Rumilly, Robert. 1930's-77. *3401*

—. Black, Conrad. Political Leadership (review article). Quebec. Ray, Jean-Louis. Rumilly, Robert. Sweeny, Alastair. 19c-20c. 1967-76. *3410*

—. "Bonne Entente" movement. Godfrey, John. Military Recruitment. Quebec. World War I. 1916-17. *3752*

—. Books. Canada. Catholic Church. Clergy. France. 1850-1914. *3159*

—. Books. Canadian Institute. Catholic Church. Censorship. Clergy. *Index of Prohibited Books.* 1862. *3281*

—. Bossism. Houde, Camillien. Local government. Martin, Médéric. Quebec (Montreal). 1923-29. *3380*

—. Bothwick, J. Douglas (*History and Biographical Gazetteer of Montreal to the Year 1892*). British Canadians. Elites. Quebec (Montreal). Social Classes. 19c. *3799*

—. Boucherville, Charles Eugène Boucher de. British Canadians. Federalism. Joly, Henri-Gustave. Liberal Party. Political Campaigns. Provincial government. Quebec. 1878. *3709*

—. Bourassa, Henri. Canada. Divorce. Feminism. Woman suffrage. 1913-25. *3406*

—. Bourassa, Henri. Historiography. Politics. Provincial Government. Quebec. 1902-71. *3374*

—. Bourget, Ignace. Catholic Church. Colleges and Universities. Laval University. Quebec (Quebec City). 1840's-50's. *3294*

—. Bourgmont, Etienne Veniard de. Discovery and Exploration. DuTisne, Charles Claude. LaVerendrye, Sieur de. Louisiana. St. Denis, Louis Antoine Juchereau de. Trans-Mississippi West. 18c. *437*

—. Bowman, Ian. Canadian Pacific Railway. Labelle, Antoine. Quebec (Laurentian Mountains). Reminiscences. Travel. 1880-1978. *3330*

—. British Canadians. Commerce. Fur trade. Middle classes. Quebec (Montreal). 1750-92. *3864*

—. British Canadians. Demography. Quebec (Rawdon). Rural Settlements. 1791-1970. *3170*

—. British Canadians. Elections (provincial). Ethnicity. Quebec (Montreal). 1832. *3701*

—. British Empire. Canada. *Canadien* (newspaper). Confederation. Parent, Étienne. Political Theory. 1831-52. *3871*

—. British Empire. Canada. Commerce. Confederation. English Canadians. Regionalism. Social Classes. 1608-1867. *3874*

—. British Empire. Catholic Church. Ideology. Imperialism. Quebec. 19c-20c. *3748*

—. British North America Act (1867). Canada. Papineau, Louis-Joseph. Political Theory. 1759-1867. *3875*

—. Brotherhood of the Holy Family. Catholic Church. Chaumonot, Pierre Joseph Marie. Elites. Laval, François de. Quebec (Montreal). 1663-1760. *3657*

—. Buies, Arthur. Catholic Church. 1880's-1901. *3408*

—. Bureaucracies. Quebec. 1969-77. *3321*

—. Business. Nationalism. Parti Québécois. Quebec. Working class. 1970's. *4003*

—. Business. Quebec (Montreal). 1825. *3273*

—. Cadieux, Lorenzo (obituary). Jesuits. Ontario, northern. Scholarship. 1903-76. *3125*

—. Calonne, Abbot de. Canada. Catholic Church. Clergy. Conservatism. Letters. Public schools. 1819-20. *3819*

—. Canada. 1871-1971. *3089*

—. Canada. 1970's. *3358*

—. Canada. 20c. *3936*

—. Canada. 1970-72. *3980*

—. Canada. Catholic Church. Clergy. Craig, James Henry. Government repression. Nationalism. Quebec (Lower Canada). 1810. *3889*

—. Canada. Catholic Church. Knights of Labor. Labor Unions and Organizations. Taschereau, Elzéar Alexandre. 1884-94. *3398*

—. Canada. Census. 1761-90. *3297*

—. Canada. Cities. International trade. 1730-60. *3241*

—. Canada. Colleges and Universities. Historiography. Nationalism. 1810-1967. *3149*

—. Canada. Colonial Government. Conservatism. Seigneurialism. Social Classes. 1763-1815. *3306*

—. Canada. Colonialism. English Canadians. Social Classes. 18c. *3884*

—. Canada. Confederation. Creighton, D. G. English Canadians. Heintzman, Ralph. Minorities in Politics. 1850's-90's. *3908*

—. Canada. Conservatism. France. French Canadians. Groulx, Lionel. Maurras, Charles. Nationalism. 1910-40. *3163*

—. Canada. Conservatism. France. French Canadians. Groulx, Lionel. Maurras, Charles. Nationalism. 1910-40. *3163*

Fvrvhjelm, Enoch Hjalmar. Alaska (Kenai). Coal Mines and Mining. Letters. Russian Americans. 1788-1863. *2091*

G

Gaebelein, Arno C. Attitudes. Fundamentalism. *Our Hope* (periodical). Stroeter, Ernst F. Zionism. 1894-97. *1567*

—. Fundamentalism. Methodist Episcopal Church. Missions and Missionaries. *Tiqweth Israel* (periodical). Zionism. 1893-1945. *1566*

Gaelic language. Blair, Duncan Black. Language. Nova Scotia (Pictou County). Poetry. Scholars. Scottish Canadians. 1846-93. *3454*

Gaggin, John Boles. British Columbia. Civil service. Irish Canadians. 1859-66. *3488*

Galicians. Dukhobors. Lake Geneva Mission. Missions and Missionaries. Presbyterian Church. Russian Canadians. Saskatchewan (Wakaw). 1903-42. *3690*

Gallaway, Lowell. British Americans. Irish Americans. Settlement. Vedder, Richard. 1897-98. *283*

Galley slaves. Denonville, Marquis de. France. French. Indians. Iroquois Indians. New France. 1687. *3204*

Galt, Alexander. Jews. Kaplun, Alter (family). Saskatchewan. Settlement. 1880's-90's. *3503*

Galtung, Johan. Quebec. Separatist Movements. Social change. 1961-75. *4035*

Galvanized Yankees. Courts Martial and Courts of Inquiry. Indian Wars. Saltiel, Emanuel H. (pseud. of Joseph Isaacs). 1866. *1497*

Galveston Plan. Canada. Immigration. Jews. Schiff, Jacob H. USA. 1907-14. *911*

—. Charities. Immigrants. Industrial Removal Office. Jews. Migration, Internal. New York City. 1890-1914. *1076*

Gálvez, Bernardo de. Colonial Government. Creoles. Documents. Gottschalk, Louis M. Historic New Orleans Collection. Louisiana (New Orleans). Manuscripts. 18c-20c. *378*

Gambino, Richard. Acculturation. Bianco, Carla. Catholic Church. Family. Italian Americans (review article). Pennsylvania (Rosetos). Social Organization. Tomasi, Silvano. 20c. *865*

Gambling. Illinois (Chicago). Irish Americans. O'Leary, Jim. 1892-1925. *731*

Games *See also* Physical Education and Training; Sports.

—. Attitudes. Colonial Government. Explorers. French Canadians. Indians. Missions and Missionaries. 16c-17c. *3206*

—. Bocce ball. Ethnicity. Immigrants. Italian Americans. Pennsylvania (Philadelphia). 1974. *850*

—. Nipsy (game). Pennsylvania (Eckley). 1972. *2925*

Games, children's. German Americans. Learning. Pennsylvania. Social Organization. Values. 1955-74. *501*

Garment Industry *See also* Clothing.

—. Factories. Fire. New York City. Safety. 1911. *2577*

—. Illinois (Chicago). Immigrants. O'Reilly, Mary. Socialist Party. Strikes. Women. Zeh, Nellie M. 1910. *2558*

—. Jews. Labor Unions and Organizations. 1920's-30's. *915*

Garrison Towns. French Canadians. Great Britain. Military. Quebec (Montreal). Rebellion Losses Bill. Riots. 1840's. *3880*

—. Fur Trade. Michigan (Detroit). Military Camps and Forts. Quebec (Montreal). 1760-75. *3857*

Garvett, Morris (obituary). Jews. Leadership. Michigan (Detroit). ca 1919-71. *1504*

Gasoline. Canada. Grocery trade. Provigo (company). Reminiscences. Turmel, Antoine. USA. 1945-78. *3407*

Gay, Peter. German Americans. Immigration. National Characteristics. Reminiscences. 1930's-76. *531*

Gayarré, Charles. Creoles. Historians. King, Grace. Letters. Louisiana. 1867-95. *375*

Gayler, Charles (*Fritz, Our Cousin German*). Acting. Emmet, Joseph Kline. German Americans. Immigration. Irish Americans. Missouri (St. Louis). Stereotypes. 1858-91. *2914*

Gehman, John B. Diaries. Education. Mennonites. Pennsylvania (Hereford). Speak Schools. 1853. *2310*

Geiger, Abraham. Holdheim, Samuel. Judaism, Reform. 19c. *1055*

Gendron Report. Bilingualism. Quebec. Schools. 1973. *4060*

Genealogical Society of Utah. Archives. Family history. Mormons. 1500-1900. *2755*

Genealogists. Historians. Research. 1975. *2737*

Genealogy *See also* Heraldry.

—. 1890-1978. *2726*

—. Acadians. LaVache family. Nova Scotia (Cape Breton; Arichat). 1774-20c. *3174*

—. Archives. Interdisciplinary Studies. Research. Social history. 1975. *2729*

—. Assimilation. Delaware (Lewes). Jews. Nunez family. 18c. *1448*

—. Beamish family. Irish Canadians. Nova Scotia (Halifax). 1765-1970's. *3485*

—. Brigham Young University Library. Immigration. Libraries. Mormons. Utah (Provo). 1830-1978. *36*

—. Brunk family. German Americans. Immigrants. Mennonites. 1750-1850. *2193*

—. Canada. Irish Canadians. Prime Ministers. Thompson, John S. D. 1796-1903. *3446*

—. Catholic Church. Church records. 19c-20c. *37*

—. Conte, Stephen G. Italian Americans. Italy (Andretta). Travel Accounts. 1971. *811*

—. Croatians. Dominis, John Owen. Hawaii. Liliuokalani, Queen. 1437-1891. *2126*

—. Dutch Americans. Iowa. Mennonites. Settlement. Swiss Americans. 1839-1974. *2209*

—. Emigration. Germany (Palatinate; Lambsheim). Pennsylvania. 1832-77. *598*

—. Family history. National Characteristics. 18c-20c. *2753*

—. French Canadians. Fur trade. Godbout, Archange. New France. Population. 1608-1763. *3193*

—. French Canadians. Page Family. Quebec (Laprairie). 1763-1967. *3140*

—. German Americans. Inventories. Pennsylvania (Tulpehocken area). Property. 18c. *559*

—. German Canadians. Nova Scotia (Halifax, Lunenburg). West family. Wuest, Johann Wendel. 17c-20c. *3469*

—. Germany. Methodology. 1600's-1978. *632*

—. Goranson, Greta K. Immigration. Reminiscences. Swedish Americans. 1832-1973. *1797*

—. Hershey family. Land Tenure. Mennonites. Pennsylvania (Lancaster County). 1730's-1870's. *2231*

—. History teaching. 1978. *2887*

—. Howe, John (and family). Loyalists. Nova Scotia (Halifax). 18c-19c. *3594*

—. Huguenots. 16c-20c. *457*

—. Immigrants. Missions and Missionaries. Mormons. Utah. 1885-1900. *2713*

—. Immigration. Matus, Margaret. Slovakian Americans. 1919-78. *1904*

—. Immigration. Minnesota (Sunrise). Research. Swedish Americans. 1890-1972. *1847*

—. Inventories. Pennsylvania (Philadelphia, Lower Merion). Property. Welsh Americans. Wills. 1650-1750. *321*

—. Nova Scotia (Hants County). Scottish Canadians. Weatherhead family. ca 1820-1946. *3436*

General Hospital of Quebec. Catholic Church. French Canadians. Mental Illness. Quebec. 1692-1845. *3152*

Generation Gap. Catholic Church. Education. Family. French Canadians. Quebec. Social change. 1960-70. *3362*

—. French Canadians. Identity. Quebec (Quebec City). Socialization. 1968. *3341*

Generations. Assimilation. Attitudes. Jews. 1925-75. *1084*

—. Attitudes. Genocide (survivors). Jews. 1939-45. ca 1960-76. *2664*

—. Canada. Family. Immigrants. Italian Canadians. 20c. *3500*

—. Jews. Language. Residential patterns. Rhode Island. Yiddish Language. 1910-70. *1208*

Generations hypothesis. Ethnicity. Hansen, Marcus Lee. Herberg, Will. Religion. 1960's. *2158*

Genes. Children (sibling). Environment. IQ. 1970's. *2862*

Genêt, Edmond Charles. Diplomatic correspondence. DuPont de Nemours, Victor. French. Mangourit, Michel de. South Carolina (Charleston). 1793. 1797. *442*

—. French Americans. French Revolution. Jacobin societies. Pennsylvania (Philadelphia). Politics. 1792-94. *425*

Genocide. Anti-Semitism. Christianity. Toynbee, Arnold. World War II. ca 1940-1975. *1626*

—. Attitudes. Israel. Jews. World War II. Youth. 1939-45. ca 1970's. *2705*

—. Authors. Fiction. Jews. 1945-74. *2695*

—. Christianity. Jews. Theology. World War II. 1945-74. *2663*

—. Comparative History. History Teaching. Indians. Jews. Negroes. Racism. 20c. *2675*

—. Concentration camps. Germany. Jews. Press. World War II. 1939-42. *2678*

—. Europe. Foreign Policy. Jews. World War II. 1938-45. *2652*

—. Foreign Policy. Jews. Palestine. Zionism. 1945. *2680*

—. Foreign Policy. Jews. World War II. 1939-45. *2669*

—. Friedman, Saul S. (review article). Jews. Public Policy. Refugees. Roosevelt, Franklin D. (administration). World War II. 1938-45. 1973. *2694*

—. Fund raising. Joint Distribution Committee. Judaism (Orthodox). Rescue work. World War II. Yeshiva Aid Committee. 1939-41. *2704*

—. Germany. Immigration Policy. Jews. Refugees. Roosevelt, Franklin D. (administration). 1933-45. *2666*

—. Immigrants. Jews. Kremer, Charles H. Rumanian Americans. Trifa, Valerian. World War II. 1941-74. *1628*

—. Immigration Policy. Jews. Prejudice. World War II. 1880's-1940's. *2687*

—. Jews. Pell, Herbert Claiborne. State Department. UN War Crimes Commission. World War II. 1943-45. *2656*

—. Jews. Psychology. World War II. 1940's. *2684*

Genocide (survivors). Attitudes. Generations. Jews. 1939-45. ca 1960-76. *2664*

Geographic Mobility *See also* Migration, Internal.

—. Census. Cities. Immigration. Methodology. Soundex indexes. 1880-1900. *2811*

—. Census. Methodology. Migration, Internal. 1880-1900. *2810*

—. Colorado (Denver). Employment. Immigrants. Social Mobility. 1870-92. *2813*

—. Demography, historical. Methodology. Ontario. Peel County History Project. Social History. 1840-80. 1973. *3785*

—. Economic development. Family. French Canadians. Quebec (Laterrière). 1851-1935. *3094*

—. Farmers. French Canadians. Frontier and Pioneer Life. Kansas. Mennonites. Swedish Americans. 1875-1925. *82*

—. Georgia (Atlanta). Immigrants. Jews. Settlement. 1870-96. *1220*

—. Immigrants. Texas (Houston). 1850-60. *2789*

—. Jews. Maryland (Baltimore). Population. 1810-20. *1278*

—. Jews. Religion. 1952-71. *1052*

—. Massachusetts (Chelsea). Social Organization. 1915. *120*

—. Ontario. Rural settlements. Social mobility. 19c. *3784*

Geography *See also* Boundaries; Maps; Voyages.

—. Agriculture. Pennsylvania (Lancaster County). 1758-72. *79*

—. Bibliographies. Brouillette, Benoit. French Canadians. Quebec (Montreal). 1903-73. *3113*

—. Blanchard, Raoul. Deffontaines, Pierre. France. Quebec. Siegfried, André. 1930-50. *3122*

—. Canada. Catholic Church. Church Administration. Missions and Missionaries. Regionalism. 1615-1851. *3646*

—. Canada. Communications. Great Britain. Regionalism. 1976. *3027*

—. Canada. Historiography. Settlement. USA. 17c-19c. *12*

—. Folklore. 1971-73. *2927*

—. French Canadians. Quebec. Regionalism. Urbanization. 1930-73. *3039*

Geopolitics *See also* Boundaries; Demography.

—. Catholic Church. Colonization. Economic development. French Canadians. Provost, T. S. Quebec (Mattawinie district). 17c-1890. *3148*

Georgia *See also* South; Southeastern States.

—. American Revolution. Religion. 1733-90. *2185*

—. Berrien, John M. Know-Nothing Party. Letters. Nativism. Political Attitudes. 1854-56. *192*

—. California. Frank, Leo M. Jews. Lynching. Progressivism. Trials. 1913-15. *1620*

—. Beck, Karl. Curricula. Follen, Karl. Gymnastics. Lieber, Francis. Massachusetts. Physical education and training. 1825-28. 532

—. Beck, Karl. Follen, Karl. Gymnastics. Lieber, Francis. New England. Physical Education and Training. 1820's. 533

—. Beckford Parish. Church of England. Clergy. Muhlenberg, John Peter Gabriel. Virginia (Dunmore County). 1772-76. 601

—. Beer. West Virginia (Wheeling). 17c-1917. 620

—. Behavior. Hutterites. Social theory. Utopias. ca 1650-1977. 2192

—. Behavior. Lewin, Kurt. Phenomenology. Psychology. Social change. 1917-78. 520

—. Behnke, Henry. Indian Wars. Minnesota (New Ulm). Sioux Indians. 1833-79. 511

—. Beissel, Johann Conrad. Communalism. Eckerlin, Emmanuel. Ephrata Cloister. Pennsylvania (Conestoga Valley). 1732-68. 514

—. Benedictines. Catholic Church. Frontier and Pioneer Life. Oetgen, Jerome (review article). Wimmer, Boniface. 1809-87. 2316

—. Benedictines. Illinois (New Cluny). Missions and Missionaries. Monasticism. Moosmüller, Oswald. 1832-1901. 584

—. Benedictines (review articles). Monasteries. 19c. 1960's-70's. 2335

—. Bentrup, H. A. Deafness. Duemling, Enno A. Ephphatha Conference. Lutheran Church. Reinke, Augustus H. 1893-1976. 2385

—. Bernays, Karl Ludwig. Civil War. Diplomacy. Journalism. Switzerland. 1815-79. 544

—. Bernays, Karl Ludwig. Civil War. Missouri. 1862-70's. 543

—. Birth and baptismal certificates. Folk art. Fraktur. Pennsylvania. 1750-1850. 635

—. Boehm, Martin. Mennonites. Newcomer, Christian. Pennsylvania. Revivals. 1740-1850. 2291

—. Book Industries and Trade. Minnesota. 1850-1935. 628

—. Brethren churches. Pennsylvania, southeastern. Quilting. 1700-1974. 624

—. Brigham Young Academy. Educators. Maeser, Karl G. Mormons. 1828-56. 1876. 627

—. Brunk family. Genealogy. Immigrants. Mennonites. 1750-1850. 2193

—. California. Catholic Church. Intellectuals. Ramm, Charles A. 1863-1951. 2371

—. California (Los Angeles). Editors and Editing. Jacoby, Conrad. Jews. *Sud-California Post* (newspaper). 1874-1914. 1176

—. California (San Francisco). Clothing. Jews. Strauss, Levi. 1850-1970's. 1444

—. Calligraphy. Fraktur. Pennsylvania. 19c. 547

—. Canada. Eby, Ezra E. Loyalism. Mennonites. 18c-1835. 3623

—. Carus, Paul. Clifford, William Kingdon. Letters. Mach, Ernst. Philosophy. 1890-1900. 626

—. Cary, Austin F. Emigration. Forests and Forestry. Germany. Schenck, Carl A. World War I. 1910's-20's. 2614

—. Casey, Louise Theresa Rauchle. Reminiscences. Tennessee (Germantown). 1880-1941. 597

—. Catholic Church. Civil War. Copperheads. Dissent. Irish Americans. Ohio (Cincinnati). 1861-65. 2604

—. Catholic Church. Dolan, Jay P. (review article). Irish Americans. New York. Social Conditions. 1815-65. 1975. 2341

—. Catholic Church. Ethnicity. Fundamentalists. Rural Settlements. Texas (Cooke, Denton counties). 1860-1976. 555

—. Catholic Church. Ethnicity. Irish Americans. New Jersey (Newark). 1840-70. 2351

—. Catholic Church. Language. Politics. St. Peter's Colony. Saskatchewan. Schools. 1903-16. 3471

—. Catholic Church (hierarchy). Irish Americans. Ohio (Cleveland). Rappe, Louis Amadeus. 1847-70. 2340

—. Cawein, Madison Julius. Kentucky. Poetry. Translating and Interpreting. 1865-1914. 610

—. Cemeteries. Kansas (Lyon County). Mennonites. 1870-1925. 2216

—. Cherokee Indians. Colonial Government. Georgia. Kingdom of Paradise colony. Political Imprisonment. Priber, Christian Gottlieb. Utopias. 1730's-ca 1744. 572

—. Chicago Fire. Illinois. Reminiscences. Stamm, Martin. 1871. 596

—. Chorale book. Helmuth, Justus Henry Christian. Hymns. Lutheran Church. 1786-1813. 2425

—. Christian Socialism. Rauschenbusch, Walter. Social Gospel. Theology. 1891-1918. 550

—. *Christliche Apologete* (periodical). Methodist Church. Neutrality. World War I. 1914-18. 2616

—. Cities. Irish Americans. Italian Americans. Nativism. Negroes. Riots. 19c-20c. 2890

—. City Politics. Irish Americans. Nativism. Ohio (Cincinnati). Temperance. 1845-60. 2500

—. City Politics. Kempster, Walter. Polish Americans. Public health. Smallpox. Wisconsin (Milwaukee). 1894-95. 2831

—. Civil War. Conscription, Military. Letters. New York City. Riots. Schlegel, Jacob. 1861-63. 619

—. Civil War. Ethnicity. Massacres. Missouri (Concordia). 1864. 530

—. Civil War. Indiana Volunteers, 32d. Ohio (Cincinnati). Willich, August. 1861-65. 493

—. Civil War. Irish Americans. Labor. Negroes. 1780-1860. 2602

—. Civil War. Irish Americans. Military General Staff. Schurz, Carl. 1861-65. 2603

—. Civil War. McRae, C. D. Nueces (battle). Texas. 1862. 609

—. Clark, Bertha W. Culture. Hutterites. Manuscripts. South Dakota. 1921. 2232

—. Class Consciousness. Irish Americans. Labor Unions and Organizations. Ohio (Cincinnati). Working Class. 1893-1920. 2581

—. Clergy. Concordia Seminary. Daily Life. Kansas (Clay Center). Lutheran Church. Missouri (St. Louis). Mueller, Peter. Students. 1883-89. 2403

—. Clergy. Lutheran Church. Schulze, Ernst Carl Ludwig. Steup, Henry Christian. 1852-1931. 2416

—. Clothing Industry. Entrepreneurs. Social Mobility. Wisconsin (Milwaukee). 1840-80. 2814

—. Coal miners. Germer, Adolph. Illinois (Virden). Socialism. Strikes. United Mine Workers of America. 1893-1900. 502

—. Colonial Government. Louisiana (Pointe Coupee Parish). Slave Revolts. Spain. Taxation. 1795. 491

—. Colorado. World War I. 1917-18. 2615

—. Communalism. Frontier and Pioneer Life. Hutterites. Western States. 1874-1977. 2284

—. Communalism. Leon, Elisa. Louisiana (Germantown). 1830's-60's. 552

—. Communism. Eisler, Hanns. House Committee on Un-American Activities. 1933-47. 612

—. Communism ("Council"). Mattick, Paul. 1918-39. 2557

—. Compulsory Education. Culture. Hutterites. Legislation. South Dakota. 1700-1970's. 2225

—. Concordia Historical Institute. Farms. Lutheran Church (Missouri Synod). Missouri (Perry County). Preservation. Saxon Lutheran Memorial. 1958-64. 563

—. Concordia (Junior) College. Indiana (Fort Wayne). Lutheran Church (Missouri Synod). Reminiscences. Schmidt, George P. 1906-09. 2412

—. Concordia Seminary. Illinois (Hahlen, Nashville). Lutheran Church. St. Peter's Church. Scharlemann, Ernst K. (interview). 1905-18. 2409

—. Concordia Seminary. Illinois (Springfield). Loehe, Wilhelm. Lutheran Church (Missouri Synod). Missouri (St. Louis). Seminaries. Sihler, Wilhelm. Wynecken, Friedrich. 1846-1938. 2384

—. Conscription, military. Mennonites. Pacifism. World War I. 1914-18. 2646

—. Cost of living. Employment. Income. Irish Americans. Pennsylvania (Philadelphia). Poverty. 1880. 2772

—. Country Life. North Dakota. Teachers. Vaagen, Esther (interview). World War I. 1900-18. 623

—. Country stores. Louisiana (Germantown). Slaves. 1851-61. 566

—. Courtship. Diaries. Indiana. Mennonites. Sprunger, David. 1893-95. 2287

—. Cows, milk. Farmers. Germany. North Dakota. Relief efforts. South Dakota. Wisconsin. 1921. 2642

—. Cumberland Valley. Folk art. Pennsylvania. Schimmel, Wilhelm. Wood carving. 1865-90. 545

—. Daily life. Diaries. Schirmer, Jacob Frederick. South Carolina (Charleston). 1845-46. 615

—. Daily Life. Diaries. Schirmer, Jacob Frederick. South Carolina (Charleston). 1847. 616

—. Daily life. Diaries. Schirmer, Jacob Frederick. South Carolina (Charleston). 1826-76. 617

—. Daily Life. Eichholtz, Leonard (family). Pennsylvania (Lancaster). 1750-1817. 607

—. Democratic Party. Irish Americans. New York City. Prohibition. Tammany Hall. 1840-60. 2461

—. Democratic Party. Isolationism. Kentucky (Kenton County). 1930-40. 2662

—. Depressions. Meat Industry. North Dakota (Williston). Norwegian Americans. Soup kitchens. Vohs, Al J. (interview). 1900's-30's. 2906

—. Diamond, Sander A. (review article). Nazism. 1924-41. 1974. 2667

—. Diaries. Schirmer, Jacob Frederick. South Carolina. 1846. 618

—. Dissent. Government Repression. Oklahoma State Council of Defense. Patriotism. Violence. World War I. 1917-18. 2620

—. DuBois, W. E. B. Education. Ethnic studies. Irish Americans. Woodson, Carter G. 1649-1972. 2848

—. Dutch Americans. Ethnicity. Norwegian Americans. Polish Americans. Wisconsin. 19c-20c. 2967

—. Ecumenism. Lutheran Church. Periodicals. Schmucker, Samuel Simon. 1838. 2404

—. Editors and Editing. Mennonites. Miller, Samuel H. Pro-German sentiments. Trials. World War I. 1917-18. 2628

—. Education. Family. Income. Occupations. 1969-70. 650

—. Education. Iowa. Novels. Olerich, Henry. Utopias. 1870-1902. 537

—. Educators. Exiles. Johns Hopkins University. Scholarship. Veterans. 1945-50. 162

—. Ehrenberg, Herman. Indians. Map drawing. Western States. 1816-66. 608

—. Eisenbrown, John Daniel. Folk Art. Fraktur. Pennsylvania. 1820-74. 523

—. Elections (mayoral). Hylan, John F. Irish Americans. Mitchell, John Purroy. New York City. Patriotism. World War I. 1917. 2612

—. Elections (presidential). Iowa. Roosevelt, Franklin D. 1936-40. 2538

—. Elections (presidential). Ohio. Political Parties. Scotch Irish. Voting and Voting Behavior. 1824. 2535

—. Emanuel Lutheran Church. Lutheran Church. New York City (Queens). Reminiscences. Wyneken, Frederick G. 1887-1907. 2427

—. Emigration. Norway. Religious dissenters. 1817-25. 1757

—. Employment. Ethnic Studies. Irish Americans. Land Tenure. Methodology. Philadelphia Social History Project. 1850-80. 1973. 13

—. English Americans. Pennsylvania. Political Participation. 1700-55. 631

—. Eschatology. Folk Art. Myths and Symbols. Pennsylvania. Spirituality. 18c-20c. 638

—. Espionage. Ethnicity. Germany. 1933-41. 2665

—. Ethnicity. 1750-ca 1974. 579

—. Ethnicity. Kamp, Henry. Oklahoma (Oklahoma City). 1906-57. 519

—. Ethnicity. Lutheran Church (Missouri Synod). Theology. 1847-1970. 573

—. Ethnicity. Presbyterian Church. Synod of the West. 1912-59. 499

—. Evangelical Alliance. Lutheran Church. Schmucker, Samuel Simon. 1843-51. 2417

—. Evangelical Association. Ohio. United Brethren in Christ. 1806-39. 2376

—. Evangelical United Brethren Church. Social history. Theology. 1800-1968. 2379

—. *Evangelische Kirchen-Zeitung* (newspaper). Fister, W. Lutheran Church (Missouri Synod). 1866. 2401

—. Family. Local history. Pennsylvania (Philadelphia; Germantown). Population. Social Organization. Wolf, Stephanie Grauman (review article). 1683-1800. 1976. 505

—. Farmers. Iowa (Riceville). Memoirs. Paul, Matilda Peitzke. Pioneers. Women. 1865-1936. 602

—. Farmers. Minnesota. Standke family. 1873-1978. 575

—. Feminism. Literature. Martin, Helen Reimensnyder. Pennsylvania. Social Classes. Socialism. Stereotypes. 1904-39. 621

—. Fire department, volunteer. Institutions. Irish Americans. New York City (Morrisania). 1884-87. 141

Good, Merle (interview). Authors. Ethnicity. German Americans. Mennonites. Pennsylvania. 1975. *2260*

Goodwin, Theresa. English Canadians. Reminiscences. Saskatchewan (Chaplin, Duval). Teaching. 1912-13. *3422*

Goranson, Greta K. Genealogy. Immigration. Reminiscences. Swedish Americans. 1832-1973. *1797*

Gosselin, Auguste-Honoré (review article). French Canadians. Laval, François de. New France. School of Arts and Crafts of St. Joachim. Vocational Education. 1668-1730. *3245*

Gottlieb Storz (home). German Americans. Nebraska (Omaha). Preservation. 1907-79. *587*

Gottschalk, Louis M. Colonial Government. Creoles. Documents. Gálvez, Bernardo de. Historic New Orleans Collection. Louisiana (New Orleans). Manuscripts. 18c-20c. *378*

Gouffon, Auguste. Letters. Settlement. Swiss Americans. Tennessee (Beverly). 1848-61. *2146*

Gould, Lewis L. California. Democratic Party. Political Factions (review article). Progressivism. Texas. Williams, R. Hal. 1880-1919. 1973. *2534*

Gouzenko, Igor. Canada. Civility syndrome. Political culture. Refugees. Russian Canadians. USA. 1953-54. *3562*

Government *See also* City Government; Civil Service; Constitutions; Federal Government; Local Government; Military Government; Political Science; Politics; Provincial Government; Public Administration; State Government.

—. Alienation. Charities. French Canadians. Quebec (Quebec City; Lower Town). Social Problems. Working Class. 1896-1914. *3726*

—. American Christian Palestine Committee. Palestine. Zionism. 1940's. *1592*

—. Architecture. Povstenko, Oleksa. Russian Americans. 1949-68. *2084*

—. Attitudes. Children. English Canadians. French Canadians. Political socialization. Quebec. 1970-71. *3717*

—. Canada. Politics. Regionalism. 1974. *3035*

—. Catholic Church. Church and State. Economic Development. French Canadians. Quebec (Lower Canada). Social classes. Ultramontanism. 19c. *3856*

—. Catholic Church. French Canadians. Parish registers. Quebec. 1539-1973. *3096*

—. Commerce. Croatians. Dominis family. Hawaii. Liliuokalani, Queen. 1838-1910. *2122*

—. Cooperatives. Desjardins cooperative movement. French Canadians. Interest groups. Quebec. 18c-1973. *3316*

—. Family. Morality. Religion. 1960's-70's. *2743*

—. French Canadians. Independence. Quebec. 1960-76. *4017*

—. French Canadians. Parti Québécois. Quebec. Social classes. 1978. *4016*

—. Human rights agencies. Ontario. Racism. 1973-77. *3074*

Government Employees. *See* Civil Service.

Government, provisional. French Canadians. Gray, William. Oregon Territory. 1843. *434*

Government, Resistance to *See also* Revolution.

—. Fenians. Funerals. Ireland. Irish Americans. McManus, Terence Bellew. 1848-61. *691*

Governors. Alexander, Moses. Democratic Party. Idaho. Jews. Retail Trade. 1914-32. *1506*

—. Bamberger, Simon. Jews. Utah. 1916. *1371*

—. Bartlett, Washington. California (San Francisco). Jews. 1886. *1483*

Governors, provincial. Catholic Church. Laval, François de. New France. Sovereign Council. 1659-84. *3190*

Gowan, Ogle. Immigration. Irish Canadians. Ontario (Upper Canada). Orange Order. Politics. 1830-33. *3487*

Graham v. *Richardson* (US, 1971). *Ambach* v. *Norwick* (US, 1979). Employment. *Foley* v. *Connelie* (US, 1978). Immigrants. Supreme Court. 1971-79. *253*

Grain. Agriculture. German Americans. Virginia. Tidewater. Waterways. 1730-1860. *535*

Grand Opera House. Buildings. Jews. Judah, Abraham. Missouri (Kansas City). Theater. 1883-1926. *1180*

Grape Day. California (Escondido). Jews. Politics. Steiner, Sigmund. 1886-1912. *1464*

Grappe, François. Creoles. Indians. Louisiana (northern). Pioneers. 1760-1835. *406*

Gravemarkers *See also* Historical markers.

—. Catholic Church. German Canadians. Iron work. Ontario (Bruce County; Waterloo). 1850-1910. *3468*

Gray, William. French Canadians. Government, provisional. Oregon Territory. 1843. *434*

Great Awakening. German Americans. Missions and Missionaries. Northeastern or North Atlantic States. Protestant Churches. 1720-60. *528*

Great Britain *See also* British Empire; Ireland; Northern Ireland; Scotland.

—. Acadians. Acculturation. Exiles. France. Nova Scotia. 18c. *3860*

—. Acadians. Canada. France. Immigration. Louisiana. Spain. 1755-85. *382*

—. Acadians. Colonial Government. Exiles. Land tenure. Loyalty. Nova Scotia. Oaths of allegiance. 11c-1755. *3850*

—. Acadians. Exiles. Nova Scotia. 1710-55. *3233*

—. Alexander I. Foreign Relations. Noncolonization principle. Pacific Coast (north). Russo-American Convention of 1824. 1821-25. *2058*

—. Allen, Ira. Canada. Filibusters. France. French Canadians. 1795-1801. *3872*

—. America (image). Emigration. London *Times* (newspaper). 19c. *287*

—. American Revolution. Anti-British sentiment. Foreign Relations. Irish Americans. Politics. War of 1812. 1865-90's. *769*

—. American Revolution. Canada. Elites. Loyalists. Settlement. 1776-83. *3599*

—. American Revolution. Jews. Rhode Island. Touro, Isaac. 1782. *1428*

—. Anti-Catholicism. Irish Canadians. Loyalty. Ontario. Orange Order. 1830-1900. *3478*

—. Anti-Semitism. Conspiracy theories. Intellectual History. *Protocols of the Elders of Zion* (document). 20c. *1642*

—. Archdeacon, Thomas J. (review article). Colonial Government. Dutch Americans. New York City. Social Organization. 1664-1710. 1976. *342*

—. Armies. Fort Niagara (battle). French and Indian War. 1759. *3855*

—. Australia. Jews. Marriage, interfaith. 1960-74. *1046*

—. Balfour Declaration. Palestine. Wilson, Woodrow. World War I. Zionism. 1917. *1589*

—. Belaney, Archibald S. (Grey Owl). Canada. Conservation movements. English Canadians. 1906-38. *3429*

—. Boer War. Irish Americans. Public Opinion. South Africa. 1898-1903. *719*

—. Brougham, Henry Peter. Canada. Gladstone, William Ewart. Home Rule. Political Theory. Rebellion Losses Bill. Rebellion of 1837. 1849. *3868*

—. Brownson, Orestes A. Catholic University of Ireland. Ireland. Newman, John Henry. USA. 1853-54. *196*

—. California, image of. Public Opinion. Travel Accounts. 1800-75. *282*

—. Canada. Catholic Church. Catholic Church. France. Law. Tithes. 1760-75. *3303*

—. Canada. Colonization. Discovery and Exploration. France. Vikings. War. Prehistory-19c. *3037*

—. Canada. Communications. Geography. Regionalism. 1976. *3027*

—. Canada. France. Jews. Poverty. Uruguay. 1975. *3509*

—. Canada. French Canadians. Regionalism. 1969-77. *3942*

—. Canada. French Canadians (review article). Ideology. 1867-1936. *3924*

—. Canada. Germans. Prisoners of war. World War II. 1940-47. *3760*

—. Cape Florida Society. DeBrahm, William Gerard. Florida, southeastern. Immigration. Legge, William (Lord Dartmouth). Settlement. 1773-80. *42*

—. Cary, James. Jamaica. Loyalists. Nova Scotia. 1781-1804. *3583*

—. Catholic Church. French Canadians. Military government. Protestantism. Quebec. 18c. *3887*

—. Catholic Church. Irish Americans. Propaganda. USA. World War I. 1918. *2623*

—. Charles I. Colonization. France. Nova Scotia (Port Royal). Scotland. 1629-32. *3448*

—. Colonial Government. France. New England. Nova Scotia (Canso, Cape Breton). 1710-21. *3851*

—. Colonial policy. English Canadians. Guidebooks. Land grants. Ontario (Peterborough). Traill, Catherine Parr. 19c. *3426*

—. Colonies. France. Historiography. Italy. North America. 1663-1763. *3836*

—. Colonization. Florida (Campbell Town). Huguenots. West Florida. 1763-70. *470*

—. Durham, 1st Earl of. French Canadians. Papineau, Louis-Joseph. Rebellion of 1837. 1837-39. *3873*

—. Emigration. Letters. Mormons. Richards, Willard. Young, Brigham. 1840. *305*

—. Emigration. Letters-to-the-editor. *London Times* (newspaper). Nebraska. 1872. *307*

—. Foreign Policy. Palestine. World War II. Zionism. 1941-45. *1526*

—. France. French and Indian War. New Brunswick. Restigouche River (battle). 1760. *3848*

—. French Canadians. Garrison Towns. Military. Quebec (Montreal). Rebellion Losses Bill. Riots. 1840's. *3880*

—. French Canadians. Iroquois Indians. Jesuits. Missions and Missionaries. Netherlands. New York. 1642-1719. *45*

—. Independence Movements. Ireland. Irish Americans. Self-determination. Wilson, Woodrow. World War I. 1914-20. *2637*

—. Irish. Keating, James. Michigan. Michilimackinac (battle). War of 1812. 1814. *730*

Great Britain (Isle of Jersey). Assimilation. Huguenots. Massachusetts (Essex County). 1572-1692. *429*

Great Britain (London). Architecture. Bevis Marks Synagogue. Harrison, Peter. Rhode Island (Newport). Touro Synagogue. 1670-1775. *1285*

—. Authority. New York City. Police. Social classes. 1830-70. *2888*

—. Business. Immigration. Jews. Labor Unions and Organizations. New York City. 19c-20c. *1266*

—. Famines. Immigration. Irish Americans. Pennsylvania (Philadelphia). Urbanization. 1840's-60. *741*

Great Britain (Salford). Connecticut (New Haven). Dahl, Robert A. Elites. Local politics. Political leadership. 19c-20c. *2474*

Great Plains. Agriculture. Irish. Landlords and Tenants. Scully, William. 1843-1976. *777*

—. Agriculture. Mennonites. Wheat, Turkey. 1880-1922. *2279*

—. Armies. Custer, George A. Indian Wars. Italian Americans. Martini, Giovanni (Martin, John). 1870's. *889*

—. Autobiography. Fiction. Frontier and Pioneer Life. Prairie Provinces. Women. 1804-1978. *2714*

—. Chouteau, Pierre. French Americans. Indian-White relations. Missouri. Osage Indians. Westward movement. 1804-18. *403*

—. Conscription, military. Germans, Russian. Immigration. Mennonites. 1880-84. *2190*

—. Country life. Mennonites. Photographs. 1870-1974. *2308*

—. Germans, Russian. Immigration. Manitoba. Mennonites. 1871-74. *3632*

—. Institutions. Mennonites. Missions and Missionaries. Photographs. Social customs. 1880-1940. *2246*

—. Settlement. 1860-1910. *58*

Greece. Congress. Cyprus. Foreign policy. Greek Americans. NATO. Pressure groups. Turkey. 1960-76. *668*

—. Dictatorship. Greek Americans. Public Opinion. 1967-75. *652*

—. Economic Conditions. Emigration. 1945-75. *662*

—. Emigration. 1900-70. *669*

Greek Americans. Agnew, Spiro T. Public Opinion. 1960's-70's. *667*

—. Arab Americans. Attitudes. Irish Americans. Negroes. Polish Americans. Zionism (opposition to). 1912-41. *1544*

—. Armenian Americans. Foreign Relations. Middle East. 1820's-1970's. *2595*

—. Assimilation. Colorado (Denver). 20c. *666*

—. Assimilation. Elections (presidential). Republican Party. 1968. *658*

—. Assimilation. Moskos, Charles C., Jr. Reminiscences. 1898-1976. *660*

—. Assimilation. New York City. Orthodox Eastern Church, Greek. St. Demetrios Church. St. Markela Church. 1970's. *671*

—. Assimilation. Orthodox Eastern Church, Greek. 1918-73. *670*

—. Immigration. Tapes. Teaching Aids and Devices. 1978. *1*

—. Jews. Michigan Department of Education. Textbooks. 1966-73. *1032*

—. Nationalism. Ontario. Pluralism. ca 1975-78. *3822*

—. Ontario (Upper Canada). Textbooks. 19c-20c. *3578*

Hlinka, Andrew. Ethnicity. Furdek, Stephen. Hungary. Political repression. Slovakia. Slovakian Americans. 1906. *1907*

Hodur, Francis. Catholic Church. Ethnicity. Polish National Catholic Church. 1875-1975. *1974*

Hoenerbach, Placid. Bankruptcy. Benedictines. North Dakota (Richardton). St. Mary's Abbey. 1915-25. *2348*

Hogan Schism. Bibliographies. Catholic Church. Catholic University of America. Parsons, Wilfrid. Pennsylvania (Philadelphia). 1785-1825. 1975. *2361*

Hohmann, Walter H. Hertzler, A. E. Kansas. Kaufman, E. G. Krehbiel, C. E. Lagenwalter, J. H. Letters. Mennonites. Physicians. 1920-46. *2276*

Hokanson, Nels M. Historiography. Immigration. Minnesota. Swedish Americans. 20c. *1853*

—. Illinois. Language. Liberty Loan Campaign (Foreign Language Division). Reminiscences. World War I. 1917-18. *2624*

Holdheim, Samuel. Geiger, Abraham. Judaism, Reform. 19c. *1055*

Holiness Movement. Brethren in Christ. Canada. North Central States. Wesleyanism. 1910-50. *2297*

—. Brethren in Christ. Kansas. Mennonites. Wesleyanism. 1870-1910. *2298*

Hollman, Frederick G. Autobiography. Frontier and Pioneer Life. Wisconsin. 1790-1875. *571*

Holmes Foundry. Antilabor sentiments. Immigrants. Nativism. Ontario. Strikes. 1935-40. *3730*

Holocaust (program). Attitudes. Jews. Television. 1974-79. *2691*

—. Jews. Public opinion. Television. 1978. *2659*

Holt, Benjamin M. Lutheran Church. Minnesota. Reminiscences. 1882-1974. *2395*

Holt, Michael F. Formisano, Ronald P. Politics (review article). Shade, William G. 1827-65. 1969-72. *2524*

Holth, Walborg Strom. Illinois (Chicago). Letters. Norwegian Americans. South Dakota. Travel accounts. 1882. *1735*

Holubnychyi, Vsevolod (obituary). Economics. Historians. Politics. Ukrainian Americans. 1940's-77. *2078*

Holy Cross Parish. Assimilation. Catholic Church. Connecticut (New Britain). Polish Americans. 1928-76. *1949*

Home of Peace Cemetery. California (Los Angeles). Cemeteries. Congregation B'nai B'rith. Jews. 1902. *1331*

—. California (Los Angeles; Chavez Ravine). Cemeteries. Hebrew Benevolent Society of Los Angeles. Jews. Photographs. 1855-1910. *1335*

Home Rule. Brougham, Henry Peter. Canada. Gladstone, William Ewart. Great Britain. Political Theory. Rebellion Losses Bill. Rebellion of 1837. 1849. *3868*

—. Durham, 1st Earl of. French Canadians. Ontario (Upper Canada). Political prisoners. Public opinion. Rebellion of 1837. Transportation. 1835-50. *3858*

Homeland (concept). French Canadians. Novels. Quebec. Self-perception. 1664-1970's. *3127*

Homesteading and Homesteaders. Alberta. Kokotailo, Veronia. Rumanian Canadians. 1898- . *3525*

—. Alberta. Peace River country. Ukrainian Canadians. Zahara, Dominka Roshko. 1900-30. *3563*

—. Alberta (Red Deer-Halrirk). American Canadians. Farms. 1900-15. *3581*

—. Anderson, John A. Nebraska (Cherry County). Reminiscences. Roosa, Alma Carlson. Swedish Americans. 1880's. *1849*

—. British Columbia. Immigration. Prairie Provinces. Scandinavian Canadians. 1850's-1970's. *3536*

—. British Columbia (northern). Mennonites. Public Welfare. Resettlement. 1940-42. *3612*

—. Criddle, Percy. Diaries. English Canadians. Manitoba (Aweme). 1882-1900's. *3419*

—. Daily Life. Danish Americans. Erickson, Ann. Erickson, Ethel. Letters. North Dakota (Hettinger County). 1910-11. *1717*

—. Immigrants. Jews. North Dakota (Fargo). 1870's-1920's. *1190*

—. Immigration. Minnesota. North Dakota (Sheyenne River Valley). Norwegian Americans. Skrien, Johnson. 1870's-1930's. *1758*

—. Montana (Dutton). Real Estate Business. Scandinavian Americans. Sollid, George. 1909-28. *1665*

Homicide. *See* Murder.

Honcharenko, Agapius. *Alaska Herald* (newspaper). Clergy. Far Western States. Ukrainian Americans. 1832-1916. *2059*

Honorary Degrees. *See* Degrees, Academic.

Hook, Sidney. Anti-Semitism. Columbia University. Educators. New York City. Reminiscences. Trilling, Lionel. 1920's-70's. *1622*

Hoover, Herbert C. Elections (presidential). Immigration Policy. Racism. Smith, Al. Tennessee, west. 1928. *2454*

—. Political Campaigns (presidential). Smith, Al. Tennessee, west. 1928. *2453*

Hornborg, Axel Gustaf. Alaska Colonization and Development Company. Finnish Americans. Immigrants. Port Axel (proposed town). 1903-40. *1707*

Horologium Achaz. Astronomy. German Americans. Pennsylvania. Pietists. Witt, Christopher. 1578-1895. *643*

Horowitz, Helen. Catholic Church. Ethnic Groups (review article). Illinois (Chicago). Kessner, Thomas. New York City. Sanders, James W. 1883-1965. 1970's. *149*

Horse racing. Canada. Nationalism. 1830-65. *3423*

Hospers, Henry. Dutch Americans. Iowa, northwest. Settlement. 1860-72. *343*

Hospitals. California (Los Angeles). Cedars of Lebanon Hospital. Jews. Schlesinger, Jacob. 1901-30. *1212*

—. Catholic Church. Church schools. Illinois (Chicago). Immigrants. Mental Hospitals. Wisconsin (Milwaukee). 19c. *151*

—. Catholic Church. French Canadians. Hôtel-Dieu. Indian-White Relations. Quebec. 1635-98. *3670*

—. French-Indian Relations. Missions and Missionaries. Quebec. 1633-1703. *3259*

Hôtel-Dieu. Catholic Church. French Canadians. Hospitals. Indian-White Relations. Quebec. 1635-98. *3670*

Hotels. Bishop Hill Colony. Illinois. Janssonists. Swedish Americans. 1846-1978. *1855*

Houde, Camillien. Bossism. French Canadians. Local government. Martin, Médéric. Quebec (Montreal). 1923-29. *3380*

House Committee on Un-American Activities. Communism. Eisler, Hanns. German Americans. 1933-47. *612*

House of Commons. Anglophones. Canada. French Canadians. Language. Population. Representation Act (1974). 1974. *3961*

House of Representatives *See also* Legislation; Senate.

—. Czech Americans. Illinois (Chicago). Legislation. Sabath, Adolph Joachim. 1920-52. *1889*

—. Czech Americans. Illinois (Chicago). Politics. Sabath, Adolph Joachim. 1907-32. *1890*

—. Glove factory. Jews. Littauer, Lucius Nathan. New York. Philanthropy. Politics. 1859-1944. *1354*

—. Italian Americans. Marcantonio, Vito. New York. Puerto Ricans. Republican Party. 20c. *840*

Households. Canada. Census. Irish Canadians. Ontario (Hamilton). 1851-71. *3770*

—. Family. History. Kinship. Methodology. 1970's. *2889*

—. Family cycle. Massachusetts (Worcester). Social Change. Urbanization. 1860-80. *2708*

—. French Canadians. Immigration. Quebec (Quebec City). 1666-1716. *3253*

—. Life cycles. New York (Buffalo). 1855. *2715*

Houses *See also* specific types of houses, e.g. sod houses.

—. Alberta. Ukrainian Canadians. 1890's-1915. *3557*

—. Architecture. Ethnicity. Germans, Russian. Kansas, western. Kniffen, Fred. 1890-1940. 1976. *589*

—. Architecture. French Americans. Missouri (Sainte Genevieve). Settlement. 1750-1820. *420*

—. California. Jews. Leow, Jacob. Levy, Edward R. Meyberg, Max. Neustader, David. Neustader, Jacob. Photographs. Stern, Jacob. 1890's. *1510*

—. Cultural Diffusion. Irish Americans. Mexico. Rio Grande. Texas. 19c. *757*

Houses, Brick. German Americans. Ohio (Columbus; German Village). Preservation. 19c. 1960-78. *591*

Housework. Pennsylvania (Pittsburgh). Social Conditions. Technology. Women. Working class. 1870-1900. *2733*

Housing *See also* terms beginning with the word Residential; City Planning; Discrimination, Housing; Landlords and Tenants; Urban Renewal.

—. Agriculture. Barns. Churches. Dutch Americans. New Jersey, northern. 1740's-80's. *353*

—. Alberta. American Canadians. Construction. Settlement. Sod Houses. Williams, Wesley. 1909. *3588*

—. Alberta. Architecture. Assimilation. Ukrainian Canadians. 1891-1970's. *3556*

—. Alberta (Calgary; Eau Claire district). Eau Claire Company. Kerr, Isaac. Lumber and Lumbering. Prince, Peter. Scandinavian Canadians. 1886-1970's. *3537*

—. Architecture. Cultural Diffusion. Pennsylvania. 1800-50. *2929*

—. Business. California (Los Angeles). Jews. Middle Classes. Social Mobility. 1880's. *1195*

—. Canada, eastern. French Canadians. Heating. Winter. 1958-77. *3107*

—. City Government. Economic Conditions. Polish Americans. Wisconsin (Milwaukee; 14th ward). 1880-1910. *2040*

—. City planning. Neighborhoods. Population. Public policy. 1890-1979. *106*

—. Construction. Contracts. French Canadians. Population. Quebec (Quebec City). 1810-20. *3274*

—. Daily Life. Family. Irish Americans. Massachusetts (Holyoke). 1860-1910. *2710*

—. Methodology. New York City (East Village). Social Classes. 1899. *2793*

Howe, Fanny Quincy. Davidson, Sue. Jews. Pinzer, Maimie. Rosen, Ruth. Social Classes. Women (review article). 1910-22. 1977. *1085*

Howe, Irving (review article). Immigration. Jews. Language. Social Customs. Socialism. Yiddish Language. 1880-1975. *982*

Howe, John (and family). Genealogy. Loyalists. Nova Scotia (Halifax). 18c-19c. *3594*

Howe, Joseph ("Acadie"). Immigration. Nova Scotia (Lochaber). Rural Development. 1795-1880. *3439*

Howells, William Dean. French Canadians. Quebec (Quebec City). Travel accounts. 1871-72. *3411*

Hricko, George A. First Catholic Slovak Union. Pennsylvania. Slovakian Americans. State politics. 1883-1963. *1913*

Hrušovský, Francis. Research. Slovak League of America. 1903-56. *1906*

Huart, Christophle-Albert-Alberic d'. Fishing. France (Poitou; Les Sables d'Olonne). Nobility. Nova Scotia (Louisbourg). 1750-75. *3184*

Hudson's Bay Company. Canada. Fur trade. Mineral Resources. Scottish Canadians. 17c-20c. *3457*

—. Indians. Manitoba. McKay, James. Métis. Provincial Government. 1853-79. *3211*

Hugo, Adèle. French. Nova Scotia (Halifax). 1863-66. *3288*

Huguenots. Artists. Colonization. Florida. French. LeMoyne, Jacques De Morgues. 1564-65. *415*

—. Assimilation. Great Britain (Isle of Jersey). Massachusetts (Essex County). 1572-1692. *429*

—. Colonization. Florida (Campbell Town). Great Britain. West Florida. 1763-70. *470*

—. Florida. Fort Caroline. Settlement. 1562-65. 1976. *430*

—. French Canadians. New France. 1541-1760. *3222*

—. Genealogy. 16c-20c. *457*

Huling, Tom. Bell Tavern. Irish Americans. Land transactions. Meagher, Paddy. Tennessee (Memphis). 1775-1918. *772*

Hull House. Addams, Jane. Education. Illinois (Chicago). Immigrants. Working class. 1890's. *117*

Human Relations *See also* Discrimination; Family; Interpersonal relations; Labor; Marriage; Race Relations.

—. Acculturation. Ontario (Toronto). 1950's-70's. *3047*

—. Addams, Jane. Education. Hull House. Illinois (Chicago). Working class. 1890's. *117*

—. Adult Education. Assimilation. Canada. Fitzpatrick, Alfred. Frontier College. Labor. 1899-1922. *3724*

—. Adultery. Boardinghouses. Hungarian Americans. Illinois. Landlords and Tenants. 1899-1914. *687*

—. Agricultural Labor. Louisiana. Slavery. 1790-1820. *2902*

—. Agriculture. 1776-1960. *87*

—. Agriculture. California. 1850's-1945. *84*

—. Alaska Colonization and Development Company. Finnish Americans. Hornborg, Axel Gustaf. Port Axel (proposed town). 1903-40. *1707*

—. Alpert, Abraham. Jews. Massachusetts (Boston). 20c. *1343*

—. *Ambach* v. *Norwick* (US, 1979). Employment. *Foley* v. *Connelie* (US, 1978). *Graham* v. *Richardson* (US, 1971). Supreme Court. 1971-79. *253*

—. Americanization. Assimilation. Language (instruction). Roberts, Peter. Young Men's Christian Association. 1907-17. *231*

—. Americanization. Baptists. 1890-1925. *246*

—. Americanization. Educational Reform. New York (Buffalo). Public Schools. 1890-1916. *2881*

—. Americanization. Income. Men. 1970. *2763*

—. Americanization. Indiana (Gary). Public welfare. 1906-40. *2833*

—. Americanization. Interior Department (Bureau of Education). Labor Department (Bureau of Naturalization). National Americanization Committee. 1915-24. *233*

—. Amish. Mennonites. Pennsylvania. 1693-1803. *2255*

—. Anarchist Scare (1908). Patriotism. Radicals and Radicalism. 1900-10. *221*

—. Anti-Catholicism. Chicago *Tribune* (newspaper). Editors and Editing. Illinois. Political Parties. 1853-61. *189*

—. Antilabor sentiments. Holmes Foundry. Nativism. Ontario. Strikes. 1935-40. *3730*

—. Anti-Semitism. California (San Francisco). Editorials. *Emanu-El* (newspaper). Jews. Slavic Americans. Voorsanger, Jacob. 1905. *1080*

—. Antiwar sentiment. Labor Unions and Organizations. Socialism. World War I. 1914-17. *2626*

—. Archives. Ontario (Toronto). Photographs. 1900-30. 1974. *3056*

—. Arizona (Phoenix). Economic Development. Jews. 1870-1920. *1237*

—. Art. Ghettos. Jews. 1880-1930. *1143*

—. Art, modern. Exhibits and Expositions. 1876-1976. *2922*

—. Assimilation. California (Los Angeles). Jews. Marriage. 1910-13. *1069*

—. Assimilation. Canada. Ethnic studies. Sociology. 1960's-70's. *3021*

—. Assimilation. Canada. Pluralism. Psychology. 1970's. *3024*

—. Assimilation. City life. Public schools. 1890's-1920. *2856*

—. Assimilation. Drama. Jews. Zangwill, Israel (*The Melting Pot*). 1908. *1106*

—. Assimilation. Education. Negroes. Racism. 1890-1966. *2857*

—. Assimilation. Employment. English Language. Income. Ontario (Toronto). 1968-70. *3731*

—. Assimilation. Films. Jews. Stereotypes. 1900's-20's. *924*

—. Assimilation. France. Italian Americans. 19c-20c. *882*

—. Assimilation. Italian Americans. 19c. *808*

—. Assimilation. Italian Americans (review article). 1970-71. *816*

—. Assimilation. Literature. Public schools. 19c-20c. *2858*

—. Assimilation. Macedonian Canadians. Ontario (Toronto). 1900-20. *3568*

—. Assimilation. Mining. Quebec. 1941-71. *3050*

—. Assimilation. Nebraska. Swiss Americans. 1975. *2142*

—. Assimilation. Pennsylvania (Philadelphia). Polish Americans. Polish Emigration Land Company. Smolinski, Joseph. Virginia. 1860's. 1917-18. *1985*

—. Atlantic Provinces. Charities. Cities. Poverty. Unemployment. 1815-60. *3807*

—. Auren, Harold G. (interview). Country Life. North Dakota (Griggs County). Sod houses. 1897-1900's. *71*

—. Australia. Catholic Church. O'Farrell, Patrick (review article). 17c-1977. *2329*

—. Baltic Canadians. Canada. Lutheran Church. 1947-55. *3459*

—. Baseball. Negroes. Social mobility. 1900-16. *2803*

—. Belgian Canadians. Manitoba (St. Boniface, Winnipeg). Nuytten, Edmund. Nuytten, Octavia. 1880-1914. *3463*

—. Berger, Henning. Illinois (Chicago). Literature. Swedish Americans. Travel Accounts. USA. 1872-1924. *1788*

—. Boardinghouses. Labor. Minnesota (Minneapolis). Women's Christian Association. 1880's-1979. *153*

—. Bocce ball. Ethnicity. Games. Italian Americans. Pennsylvania (Philadelphia). 1974. *850*

—. Brunk family. Genealogy. German Americans. Mennonites. 1750-1850. *2193*

—. Businessmen. Democratic Party. Elections. Negroes. New York City (Brooklyn). Racism. Suffrage. 1860. *2460*

—. California. Medicine. Mental Illness. Morality. 1860-80. *2839*

—. California (Napa Valley). Winemaking. 1840-1900. *2895*

—. California (San Francisco). Charities. Voluntary Associations. ca 1850-60. *2759*

—. California (San Francisco). City life. Education. Libraries. Mercantile Library Association. Missouri (St. Louis). 1840-56. *2868*

—. California (San Francisco). Commitment, civil. Mental Illness. Social Conditions. 1906-29. *2825*

—. California (San Francisco). Diaries. Irish Americans. Labor. Roney, Frank. 1875-76. *774*

—. California (San Francisco). France. Jews. Meyer, Eugene. Reminiscences. 1842-60. *1434*

—. California (San Francisco). Politics. 1849-56. *125*

—. Canada. Economics. Employment. Wages. 1970's. *3825*

—. Canada. Education. Occupations. Social Classes. 1973. *3805*

—. Canada. Family. Generations. Italian Canadians. 20c. *3500*

—. Canada. Finnish Americans. Labor Unions and Organizations. Radicals and Radicalism. USA. 1918-26. *1701*

—. Canada. Italian Americans. Toponymy. 1850's-1910's. *3499*

—. Canada. Occupations. Statistics. USA. Women. 1964-71. *2898*

—. Carroll, John. Catholic Church. Nativism. Protestants. 1790-1820. *178*

—. Cassel, Peter. Iowa (New Sweden). Swedish Americans. 1845-1912. *1826*

—. Catholic Church. Charities. Cholera. New Brunswick (Saint John). Sisters of Charity of the Immaculate Conception. 1854-64. *3668*

—. Catholic Church. Church schools. Hospitals. Illinois (Chicago). Mental Hospitals. Wisconsin (Milwaukee). 19c. *151*

—. Catholic Church. Culture region. Minnesota (St. Cloud Diocese). 1860-1973. *2369*

—. Catholic Church. Journalism. 1822-1975. *2352*

—. Charities. Galveston Plan. Industrial Removal Office. Jews. Migration, Internal. New York City. 1890-1914. *1076*

—. Charities Organization Society Movement. Illinois (Chicago). 1880-1930. *2830*

—. Child Welfare. Foster homes. Jews. New York City. Working class. 1900-05. *1271*

—. Children. Jews. Manitoba (Winnipeg). Public schools. 1900-20. *3520*

—. Church records. Italian Americans. Methodology. Pennsylvania (Philadelphia). 1789-1900. *836*

—. Cities. New York. Philanthropy. Social problems. Voluntary Associations. 1830-60. *2827*

—. City Politics. Economic Conditions. Pennsylvania (Philadelphia). Social Mobility. 1681-1776. *2798*

—. Civil War. Irish Americans. Negroes. Race Relations. 1830's-90's. *735*

—. Coal Mines and Mining. Economic Development. Kansas. 1870-1940. *65*

—. Coal Mines and Mining. Labor Unions and Organizations. Strikebreakers. Utah, eastern. 1875-1929. *2584*

—. Coal Mines and Mining. Negroes. West Virginia. 1880-1917. *2552*

—. Coal Mines and Mining. Ohio (Hocking Valley). Strikebreakers. Violence. 1884-85. *2559*

—. Colorado (Denver). Employment. Geographic mobility. Social Mobility. 1870-92. *2813*

—. Communist Party (Central Committee). Political Leadership. Women. 1921-61. *2573*

—. Community Participation in Politics. New York City. People's Institute of New York City. Social Reform. Working Class. 1910-20. *104*

—. Compulsory education. Missouri (St. Louis). Public Schools. Truancy. 1905-07. *2861*

—. Construction. Labor Unions and Organizations. Skill differential. Wages. 1907-72. *2904*

—. Conzen, Kathleen Neils (review article). Wisconsin (Milwaukee). 1836-60. 1976. *121*

—. Craftsmanship. Delaware. Furnituremaking. Industrialization. 1850-70. *2899*

—. Daily Life. Nova Scotia (Lochaber). Rural Settlements. 1830-1972. *3048*

—. Demography. Economic conditions. Settlement. 1900. *10*

—. Demography. Negroes. Retail Trade. Urbanization. 1890-1910. *2786*

—. Dewey, John. Ethnicity. 1902-27. *215*

—. Discrimination. Intelligence testing. 1905-74. *227*

—. Discrimination. Italian Americans. Louisiana. 1871-1905. *880*

—. Discrimination. Wages. Women. 1890-1911. *2768*

—. Discrimination, Employment. Income. Labor (skilled). Methodology. 1840-1920. *2808*

—. Discrimination, Employment. Industry. Wages. 1880-1914. *2578*

—. Documents. Macedonian Canadians. Ontario (Toronto). Urban history. 20c. *3567*

—. Economic opportunity. Education. Employment. Jews. Urbanization. 1880-1914. *1154*

—. Economic opportunity. Occupational mobility. Population. Settlement. 19c. *2790*

—. Education. Hackett, Francis. Irish Americans. Literature. Religion. 1880's-1901. *768*

—. Education. Jews. Pennsylvania (Pittsburgh). 1862-1932. *1289*

—. Education. Women. 1900-35. *2882*

—. Educational associations. Jews. Libraries. New York City. Newspapers. 1880-1914. *1168*

—. Educational history (review article). Greer, Colin. Katz, Michael B. Revisionism. Spring, Joel H. 1973. *2866*

—. Educational policy. Race relations. 1970's. *2841*

—. Elections. New York (43rd Congressional District). Townsend Movement. 1936. *2446*

—. Elkin, Mendel. Jews. Yidisher Visnshaftlekher Institut (Library). 1918-63. *1431*

—. Embroidery. Folklore. Women. ca 1890's-1900's. 1970's. *2918*

—. Employment. Italian Canadians. Ontario (Toronto). 1885-1915. *3494*

—. English Canadians. Farms. Manitoba (Brandon). Railroads. Wheat. 1880-87. *3420*

—. Entrepreneurs. Frontier thesis. Mining. Social mobility. Western states. 1870-1900. *2801*

—. Ethnic Relations. Manitoba (Winnipeg). Population. Prejudice. 1874-1974. *3013*

—. Ethnicity. 19c-20c. *2979*

—. Ethnicity. Hungarian Americans (interviews). Ohio (Cleveland). 1900-20. *688*

—. Family. Irish Americans. Pennsylvania (Scranton). Social mobility. Welsh Americans. 1880-90. *2707*

—. Family. Ontario. Social Conditions. 1820-60. *3772*

—. Federal policy. Prairie Provinces. Settlement. USA. 1870-80. *3055*

—. Fertility. Frontier and Pioneer Life. Land. Rural Settlements. 1860. *2711*

—. Fiction, juvenile. Stereotypes. 1900-45. *2924*

—. Finnish Americans. Mining. North Central States. Radicals and Radicalism. Social Conditions. Swedish Americans. 1865-1920. *1692*

—. Florida East Coast Railway. Italian Americans. Labor recruitment. Padrone system. Railroad construction. ca 1890-1901. *871*

—. Folklore. Scholarship. ca 1960-78. *2916*

—. Garment Industry. Illinois (Chicago). O'Reilly, Mary. Socialist Party. Strikes. Women. Zeh, Nellie M. 1910. *2558*
—. Genealogy. Missions and Missionaries. Mormons. Utah. 1885-1900. *2713*
—. Genocide. Jews. Kremer, Charles H. Rumanian Americans. Trifa, Valerian. World War II. 1941-74. *1628*
—. Geographic mobility. Georgia (Atlanta). Jews. Settlement. 1870-96. *1220*
—. Geographic Mobility. Texas (Houston). 1850-60. *2789*
—. German Canadians. Nova Scotia. Protestants. 1749-52. *3467*
—. Germans, Russian. Manitoba. Mennonites. Russians. Shantz, Jacob Y. 1873. *3641*
—. Gutman, Herbert G. (review article). Industrialization. Labor. Social Conditions. 19c. 1976. *2580*
—. *Hector* (vessel). Mackenzie, Alexander. Nova Scotia (Pictou Harbor). Passenger lists. Scottish Canadians. 1773. 1883. *3443*
—. Historiography. Social mobility. 1979. *2799*
—. Homesteading and Homesteaders. Jews. North Dakota (Fargo). 1870's-1920's. *1190*
—. Illinois. Janssonists. Swedish Americans. Utopias. 1846-60. *1789*
—. Illinois (Chicago). *Italia* (newspaper). Italian Americans. Labor. Letters-to-the-editor. Padrone system. 1886. *858*
—. Income. Labor (skilled). 1870-1920. *2787*
—. Income. Ontario (Toronto). 1971. *3802*
—. Indiana (New Harmony). Letters. Norwegian Americans. Pennsylvania (Harmony). Rapp, George. 1816-26. *1716*
—. Industrial Revolution. Technology transfer. 1750-1820. *2896*
—. Industry. Occupational status. Pennsylvania (Philadelphia). 1850-80. *2792*
—. Intellectuals. Jews. Social Customs. 1890-1910. *988*
—. International Brotherhood of Pulp, Sulphite, and Paper Mill Workers. Negroes. Pacific Northwest. South. Women. 1909-40. *2594*
—. Irish Americans. Labor Unions and Organizations. Leadership. McCarthy, Patrick Henry. Youth. 1863-80. *760*
—. Irish Americans. Macomb, Alexander. New York. 1748-1841. *707*
—. Irish Americans. New York. Tradition. Women. 1840-60. *732*
—. Israel. Jews. Scientists. USSR. 1930's. 1970's. *1066*
—. Italian Americans. Labor Unions and Organizations. ca 1880-1927. *894*
—. Italian Americans. Louisiana. Negroes. Race Relations. Sugar cane industry. 1880-1910. *879*
—. Italian Americans. New York City (Greenwich Village). Presbyterian Church. 1900-30. *842*
—. Italian Americans. Oral history. 20c. *873*
—. Italian Americans. Pecorini, Alberto. Self-help guides. 1911. *876*
—. Jews. Literature. Values. 19c-20c. *1107*
—. Jews. Minnesota (St. Paul; Lower West Side). Settlement. ca 1860-1920. *1259*
—. Jews. Sex roles. Women. 1880's-1979. *992*
—. Kentucky (Louisville). Migration, Internal. Ohio (Cincinnati). 1865-1901. *119*
—. Labor. 1973. *2582*
—. Labor Unions and Organizations. Steel industry. 1888-1912. *2570*
—. Law. Venue. 1789-1976. *251*
—. Manitoba (Winnipeg). Melnyk, George. Reminiscences. 1949. 1977. *3053*
—. Michigan (Holland). Migration. Occupations. Social mobility. 1850-80. *2791*
—. *National Labor Tribune* (newspaper). Strikebreakers. 1878-85. *2563*
—. National Miners Union. Strikes. United Mine Workers of America. Utah (Carbon County). 1900-39. *2583*
—. New Jersey (Jersey City). Progressivism. Social reform. Whittier House. 1890-1917. *2480*
—. New York City (Greenwich Village). Radicals and Radicalism. Social Backgrounds. 1900-20. *2795*
—. Ontario (Toronto). Stereotypes. Urban history. 19c-20c. *3046*
—. Pennsylvania (Philadelphia). Vital Statistics. 1720-75. *2836*
—. Refugees. Social Problems. 20c. *160*
—. Social Classes. Swedish Americans. Women. 1850-90. *1772*
—. Western States. 1850-1900. *76*
Immigrants' Protective League. Illinois (Chicago). Social Reform. 1908-21. *123*

Immigrants (review article). Barton, Josef J. Cities. Esslinger, Dean R. Kantowicz, Edward R. 19c-20c. 1976. *135*
—. California (Hollywood). Films. 1920-60's. *165*
Immigration *See also* Aliens; Assimilation; Demography; Deportation; Emigration; Naturalization; Population; Race Relations; Refugees; Social Problems.
—. Acadians. Canada. France. Great Britain. Louisiana. Spain. 1755-85. *382*
—. Acculturation. Agriculture. Lutheran Church. Minnesota (Isantic County). Social customs. Swedish Americans. 1840-1910. *1842*
—. Acculturation. Canada. Settlement. Slovak Canadians. 1885-1970's. *3542*
—. Acculturation. Catholic Church. Slovakian Americans. 1860's-1970's. *1937*
—. Act of Sexual Sterilization (Alberta, 1928). Canada, western. Eugenics. Press. Woodsworth, James S. 1900-28. *3061*
—. Acting. Emmet, Joseph Kline. Gayler, Charles (*Fritz, Our Cousin German*). German Americans. Irish Americans. Missouri (St. Louis). Stereotypes. 1858-91. *2914*
—. Agricultural Cooperatives. Jews. New Jersey (Alliance, Woodbine). Rosenthal, Herman. Russian Americans. Socialism. 1880-92. *984*
—. Agricultural Industry. California. 1880's-1939. *90*
—. Agricultural labor. Farmers. Midwest. National Origins Act (1924). South. 1924. *247*
—. Agricultural labor. Italian Americans. Negroes. Newspapers, black. South. 1880-1915. *884*
—. Agriculture. Germans, Russian. Kansas. Wheat. 1874-77. *611*
—. Agriculture. Historiography. 19c-20c. *86*
—. Agriculture. Kalehaven. Peder Nielsen. Letters. Missouri (Buchanan County). Norwegian Americans. 1848. *1746*
—. Agriculture. Missions and Missionaries. Politics. Sects, Religious. Settlement. South Dakota. 1850-1900. *55*
—. Alabama (Mobile). French Americans. Iberville, Pierre Le Moyne d'. Women. 1702-04. *411*
—. Alberta. Nativism. 1925-30. *3080*
—. Alberta (Calgary). Jews. 1974. *3517*
—. American Federation of Labor. Fascism. Gompers, Samuel. Jingoism. Racism. 1850-1924. *2579*
—. American Revolution. City Life. Colonial government. Economic development. New York City. 17c-20c. *115*
—. American Revolution. Military Service. Politics. Scotch Irish. 1600-1785. *315*
—. Americanization. Foreign Language Information Service. News releases. Public Relations. 1918-39. *249*
—. Americas (North and South). Historiography. Italian Americans. 19c-20c. *818*
—. Andersson, Joris Per. Letters. Minnesota (Chisago Lake). Swedish Americans. 1851-53. *1804*
—. Andrews, C. C. Lewenhaupt, Carl (report). Norwegian Americans. Swedish Americans. 1870. *1675*
—. Anglo-Saxonism. Anthropology, cultural. Assimilation. Polish Americans. 18c-20c. *4*
—. Anti-Catholicism. Ku Klux Klan. Protestants. Saskatchewan. 1927-30. *3060*
—. Anti-Communist movements. Anti-Semitism. Freedom of speech. National self-image. Ontario (Toronto). 1928-29. *3075*
—. Anti-Communist Movements. Christianity. Clergy. Lithuanian Americans. 1945-75. *267*
—. Anti-Semitism. Congress. Displaced Persons Act (US, 1948). Germans. World War II. 1945-48. *2660*
—. Aquino, Salvatore A. City Life. Family. Italian Americans. New York City. Reminiscences. 1914. *792*
—. Archives. Ethnicity. Research. 1970's. *32*
—. Archives. Foreign Relations. Jozef Pilsudski Institute. Polish Americans. 19c-20c. *2008*
—. Archives. Immigration History Research Center. Labor history. Minnesota, University of (St. Paul). 1890-1960. *33*
—. Arizona (Phoenix). Italian Americans. Migration, Internal. Social Organization. 1880's. *848*
—. Arkansas. Boosterism. 1865-74. *74*

—. Arkansas. German Americans. Germans. Guidebooks. Texas. 1830's-40's. *500*
—. Arts. California. Catholic Church. Gold Rushes. Irish Americans. Politics. 1849-90's. *748*
—. Asians. Conservatism. Methodist Episcopal Church. Social Gospel. 1865-1908. *226*
—. Assimilation. Attitudes. Canada. Federal Policy. USA. 1880's-1978. *175*
—. Assimilation. Diaries. Jonsson, Jonas (John Johnson). Minnesota. Swedish Americans. 1864-95. *1803*
—. Assimilation. Employment. Israel. Jews. 1967-70's. *958*
—. Assimilation. German Americans. Jews. 1880-1920. *1103*
—. Assimilation. Historiography. 19c-20c. *7*
—. Assimilation. Historiography. Slovakian Americans. 1880's-1940's. *1926*
—. Assimilation. Negroes. Pennsylvania (Philadelphia). 1850-1970. *111*
—. Assimilation. Rumanian Americans. Union and League of Romanian Societies. 1900-39. *1656*
—. Atellis, Orazio de. *Correo Atlántico* (newspaper). Independence Movements. Italian Americans. Texas. 1824-47. *877*
—. Attitudes. Irish Canadians. Ontario (Canada West). Potato famine. 1845-50. *3483*
—. Australia. Canada. Federal Policy. Population. 1967-75. *3083*
—. Australia. Politics. 1810-1976. *20*
—. Austria. Kreve, Vincas. Letters. Lithuanians. Refugees. 1947. *274*
—. Austrian Americans. Burgenland. Poetry. Riessner, Johann. 1856-1939. *266*
—. Autobiography. Colorado (South Platte Valley). Ehrlich, Clara Hilderman. Farmers. Frontier and Pioneer Life. Germans, Russian. 1890-ca 1907. *518*
—. Baerg, Anna. Canada. Diaries. Germans, Russian. Mennonites. Russian Revolution. 1917-23. *3618*
—. Banking. Illinois (Chicago). Isaacson, John A. Swedish Americans. 1892-1974. *1801*
—. Baptists. Swedish Americans. Travel (accounts). Wiberg, Anders. 1852-53. *1835*
—. Benedictine Sisters. Missouri (Conception). Renggli, M. Beatrice. Swiss Americans. Travel Accounts. 1874. *2353*
—. Bennett, James Gordon. Catholic Church. *New York Herald* (newspaper). 1835-70. *2363*
—. Bertarelli, Pier Giuseppe. Business. California. Gold Rushes. Italian Americans. 1849-53. *855*
—. Bibliographies. Fiction. Jews. 1867-1920. *1008*
—. Bibliographies. Law. 1970-77. *263*
—. Bibliographies. Scott, Franklin D. 1925-74. *31*
—. Borglum, Gutzon. Dana College. Danish Americans. Riis, Jacob. Settlement. Wisconsin. 1741-20c. *1684*
—. Bradica, Stjepan. Croatian Peasant Party. Prairie Provinces. 1930's. *3569*
—. Brain drain. Labor. 1963-66. *2897*
—. Brigham Young University Library. Genealogy. Libraries. Mormons. Utah (Provo). 1830-1978. *36*
—. British Canadians. British Columbia. Public opinion. 1919-30. *3414*
—. British Canadians. Children. Ontario. Poor. Press. Rye, Miss. 1865-1925. *3415*
—. British Canadians. Coal Mines and Mining. Labor. 1860-70. *284*
—. British Columbia. Daily life. Dukhobors. Reminiscences. Russian Canadians. 1880's-1976. *3697*
—. British Columbia. Homesteading and Homesteaders. Prairie Provinces. Scandinavian Canadians. 1850's-1970's. *3536*
—. British Columbia (Vancouver Island). Converts. Missions and Missionaries. Mormons. 1875-1979. *3603*
—. Burns family. Nova Scotia (Annapolis County; Wilmot Township). Scotch Irish. 1764-20c. *3445*
—. Business. Great Britain (London). Jews. Labor Unions and Organizations. New York City. 19c-20c. *1266*
—. California. 1850-1976. *61*
—. California (Los Angeles). Greek Americans. Jews. Sephardic Hebrew Center. 1900-74. *1214*
—. California (San Francisco). Italian Americans. 1890-1977. *890*

—. California (San Francisco). Italian Swiss Colony Wine Company. Sbarboro, Andrea. 1881-1923. *825*

—. Canada. Czech Canadians. Jesuits. Refugees. 1950. *3539*

—. Canada. Democracy. Foreign Relations. France. French Canadians. 1855. *3272*

—. Canada. Dukhobors. Nerigin, Peter. Persecution. Russian Canadians. 1654-1902. *3696*

—. Canada. Dukhobors. Russian Canadians. 1652-1908. *3692*

—. Canada. Education. Jews. Reminiscences. Segal, Beryl. USA. 1900-70's. *1468*

—. Canada. Ethnicity. USA. 1974. *2959*

—. Canada. Galveston Plan. Jews. Schiff, Jacob H. USA. 1907-14. *911*

—. Canada. Germans, Russian. Mennonites. 1922-23. *3620*

—. Canada. Irish Canadians. Poor Law Commissioners. Servants. Women. 1865. *3490*

—. Canada. Italian Americans. Italian Canadians. USA. 1870-1977. *829*

—. Canada. Mennonites. Surnames. Swiss Brethren. USA. 1680-1880. *2270*

—. Canada. National Identity. Protestant churches. United Church of Canada. 1902-25. *3608*

—. Canada. Polish Canadians. 1900-65. *3549*

—. Canada. Political Attitudes. Settlement. Ukrainian Americans. Ukrainian Canadians. USA. ca 1750-1975. *2111*

—. Canada. Scottish Canadians. 1960's-70's. *3440*

—. Canada. Slovak Americans. Voluntary Associations. 1890-1964. *3540*

—. Canada, Western. Catholic Church. Missions and Missionaries. Sisters of Service. 1920-30. *3688*

—. Canada, Western. Folklore. Ukrainian Canadians. 1945-75. *3554*

—. Cape Florida Society. DeBrahm, William Gerard. Florida, southeastern. Great Britain. Legge, William (Lord Dartmouth). Settlement. 1773-80. *42*

—. Cape Verdean Americans. Ethnicity. Massachusetts. 1850-1977. *1652*

—. Capps, Samuel J. Colorado. English Americans. Strange family. Westward Movement. 1850-1912. *304*

—. Catholic Church. Converts. French Americans. Louisiana. 1753-59. *389*

—. Catholic Church. Dutch Americans. Wisconsin. 1845-75. *350*

—. Catholic Church. Emigration. Persecution. Prince Edward Island. Scotland. Scottish Canadians. 1769-74. *3430*

—. Catholic Church. French Americans. Manitoba. Mathieu, Olivier-Elzéar. Regina Archdiocese. Saskatchewan. 1911-31. *3363*

—. Catholic Church. Glengarry Highlanders. Macdonnell, Alexander. Ontario. Scottish Canadians. 1770's-1814. *3455*

—. Census. Cities. Geographic Mobility. Methodology. Soundex indexes. 1880-1900. *2811*

—. Chicopee Manufacturing Company. Irish Americans. Massachusetts (Chicopee). Mills. Nativism. 1830-75. *711*

—. Cholera. Diaries. Illinois (Chicago). Jönsson, Peter Johan. New York. Voyages. 1866. *1808*

—. Cities. Family. Italian Americans. Jews. Rhode Island. 1880-1940. *2751*

—. City government. Irish Americans. Massachusetts (Boston area). 16c-1979. *759*

—. City Life. Jews. Manitoba (Winnipeg). 1874-82. *3502*

—. Clayton, William. English Americans. Illinois (Nauvoo). Letters. Mormons. 1840. *291*

—. Clayton, William. English Americans. Letters. Moon, John. Mormons. 1840. *292*

—. Colleges and Universities. Mennonites. Ohio (Median County). Wadsworth Institute. 1825-80. *2244*

—. Colorado (Denver). Jews. Shwayder family. 1865-1916. *1350*

—. Colorado (Denver). Saloons. 1865-1933. *134*

—. Conscription, military. Germans, Russian. Great Plains. Mennonites. 1880-84. *2190*

—. Crime and Criminals. Irish Canadians. Newfoundland. Public Policy. 1789. *3480*

—. Danish Americans. Letters. Missouri. 1839. *1685*

—. Delaware River Valley. Indians. Settlement. 17c. *41*

—. Democracy. Israel. Jews. USSR. 1971-76. *960*

—. Depressions. Legislation. Social Conditions. 1918-24. *228*

—. Depressions. Pennsylvania (Pittsburgh). Wages. 1908. *2905*

—. Deutscher Bund Canada. German Canadians. Saskatchewan (Loon River area). 1929-39. *3767*

—. Diaries. Florida. Sjöborg, Sofia Charlotta. Swedish Americans. 1871. *1858*

—. Discrimination. Economic Conditions. Italian Americans. Oregon (Portland). 1880-1920. *823*

—. Discrimination, Employment. 1960's-70's. *260*

—. Dutch Americans. 1820-77. *352*

—. Dutch Americans. Ethnicity. Inbreeding. Kinship. Oregon (Verboort). 19c-20c. *339*

—. Dutch Americans. Jews. 1852-77. *1153*

—. Dutch Americans. Michigan, Lake. *Phoenix* (vessel, burning). Wisconsin (Sheboygan). 1847. *358*

—. Economic conditions. 1840-1950. *22*

—. Economic Conditions. 1955-76. *161*

—. Economic Development. Missouri, southwest. Social change. 1865-73. *47*

—. Economic growth. Industrialization. ca 1840-1910. *30*

—. Economic Growth. Industrialization. Labor. 1870-1910. *2908*

—. Economic Growth. Irish Americans. Michigan (Detroit). 1850. *781*

—. Economic opportunity. Settlement. 19c. *9*

—. Education. Hungary. Slovakian Americans. Social mobility. 1890's-1930's. *1928*

—. Elazar, Daniel. Illinois. Politics. 19c-1970's. *2530*

—. Emigration agents. Michigan. Thomson, Edward H. 1849. *72*

—. Emigration agents. Steamship companies. ca 1850's-1914. *14*

—. Employment. Jews. New York City. Social Organization. 1970's. *1017*

—. Employment. Nativism. Negroes (free). Politics. 1830-60. *195*

—. English Canadians. Ontario (Upper Canada; York). Petworth Emigration Committee. 1830-40. *3417*

—. Erickson, George F. Letters. Michigan. Sweden. 1891-1950. *1793*

—. Ethnic Fraternal Project. Immigration History Research Center. International Institutes Project. Minnesota, University of (St. Paul). Organizations. 1976-78. *35*

—. Ethnicity. Greek Canadians. Ontario (Toronto). Private Schools. 1900-40. *3472*

—. Ethnicity. Jews. Niger, Shmuel. Slavic Americans. 1920-33. *1054*

—. Ethnicity. Language. Slovakian Americans. Social Customs. 1780-1903. *1927*

—. Europe. Foreign Policy. McDonald, James G. Palestine. Taylor, Myron. Zionism. 1930's-40's. *2697*

—. Europe, Northern. Sects, religious. South. 1820's-50's. *62*

—. Exiles. Polish Americans. 1608-1860's. *2049*

—. Fallenius, Carl Johan. Massachusetts (Boston). Swedish Americans. 1811-69. *1765*

—. Family. Lindbäck, Ola. Lindbäck, Verner. Minnesota (Minneapolis). Research. Swedish Americans. 1906-76. *1781*

—. Family. Norwegian Americans. Semmingsen, Inge (review article). Social conditions. 1815-1930. *1750*

—. Famines. Great Britain (London). Irish Americans. Pennsylvania (Philadelphia). Urbanization. 1840's-60. *741*

—. Famines. Irish Americans. 1845-50's. *743*

—. Farms. Frontier and Pioneer Life. New River. North Carolina. Social Organization. Virginia. 1684-1820. *39*

—. Fertility. Walker, Francis A. 1800-60. *24*

—. Films. *Hester Street* (film). *Lies My Father Told Me* (film). 1896-1920's. 1974-75. *2920*

—. French Canadians. Households. Quebec (Quebec City). 1666-1716. *3253*

—. French Canadians. Nova Scotia (Port Royal). Population. 1650-1755. *3220*

—. Frontier and Pioneer Life. New York. Pennsylvania. Scotch Irish. Virginia (Shenandoah Valley). 17c-1776. *311*

—. Frost, Max. New Mexico Bureau of Immigration. State Government. 1880-1912. *56*

—. Gay, Peter. German Americans. National Characteristics. Reminiscences. 1930's-76. *531*

—. Genealogy. Goranson, Greta K. Reminiscences. Swedish Americans. 1832-1973. *1797*

—. Genealogy. Matus, Margaret. Slovakian Americans. 1919-78. *1904*

—. Genealogy. Minnesota (Sunrise). Research. Swedish Americans. 1890-1972. *1847*

—. Georgia (Atlanta). Haas (family). Jews. Leadership. Levi, Henry. Mayer, David. 1845-65. *1281*

—. German Americans. 17c-20c. *551*

—. German Americans. 1818-1970. *561*

—. German Americans. 1742-49. *565*

—. German Americans. Jews. Lobbying. Russian Americans. 1880-1924. *1132*

—. German Americans. Kentucky. Lemcke, Heinrich. Travel Accounts. 1885. *636*

—. German Americans. Louisiana (Acadia Parish). 1870's-1917. *562*

—. Germans, Russian. 1870's. *516*

—. Germans, Russian. Great Plains. Manitoba. Mennonites. 1871-74. *3632*

—. Germans, Russian. Kansas. Mennonites. Nebraska. 1884-93. *2189*

—. Germans, Russian. Kansas. Mennonites. Warkentin, Bernhard. 1847-1908. *2218*

—. Germans, Russian. Kansas. Mennonites. Warkentin, Bernhard. 1872-1908. *2219*

—. Germans, Russian. Manitoba. Mennonites. 1873. *3626*

—. Germans, Russian. Manitoba. Mennonites. Shantz, Jacob Y. 1870's. *3630*

—. Germans, Russian. Manitoba. Mennonites. Stoesz, David. 1872-76. *3625*

—. Germans, Russian. Mennonites. 1923. *2227*

—. Germans, Russian. Mennonites. 1870's-1920's. *2234*

—. Germans, Russian. Mennonites. Passenger lists. Quebec. 1874-80. *3619*

—. Germans, Russian. Mennonites. Saskatchewan (Rosthern). Social conditions. 1923. *3633*

—. Germans, Russian. Mennonites. South Dakota. Unruh, Daniel. 1820-82. *2294*

—. Gowan, Ogle. Irish Canadians. Ontario (Upper Canada). Orange Order. Politics. 1830-33. *3487*

—. *Hector* (vessel). Nova Scotia (Pictou Harbor). Scottish Canadians. Voyages. 1773. *3452*

—. Herberg, Will. Historiography. Religion. 1790's-1970's. *2186*

—. Historians. Wittke, Carl Frederick (tribute). 1892-1971. *16*

—. Historical Societies. Research. Swedish Americans. 1977. *1773*

—. Historiography. 1960-78. *28*

—. Historiography. Hokanson, Nels M. Minnesota. Swedish Americans. 20c. *1853*

—. Historiography. Italian Americans. 1900's-20's. *881*

—. History Teaching. Tapes. Teaching Aids and Devices. 1978. *1*

—. Homesteading and Homesteaders. Minnesota. North Dakota (Sheyenne River Valley). Norwegian Americans. Skrien, Johnson. 1870's-1930's. *1758*

—. Howe, Irving (review article). Jews. Language. Social Customs. Socialism. Yiddish Language. 1880-1975. *982*

—. Howe, Joseph ("Acadie"). Nova Scotia (Lochaber). Rural Development. 1795-1880. *3439*

—. Icelandic Canadians. Ontario. 1872-75. *3528*

—. Indian Territory. Population. 19c. *48*

—. Industrialization. Morality. Muckraking. Periodicals. 1900-09. *239*

—. Influenza. Mortality. 1918-19. *2829*

—. Irish Americans. Italian Americans. Jews. Social Mobility. 1820's-1970's. *15*

—. Irish Americans. McCaffrey, Lawrence J. (review article). 17c-1976. *709*

—. Israel. Jews. Scholars. USSR. 1960's-70's. *1584*

—. Italian Americans. Italian Americans. Marolla Family. Reminiscences. Wisconsin (Horicon). 1893. 1970's. *847*

—. Italian Americans. New York City. 1924-70's. *834*

—. Italian Americans. Novels. 20c. *891*

—. Italian Americans. Novels. Stonecutters. Tomasi, Mari. Vermont. 1909-65. *874*

—. Italian Americans. Pascoli, Giovanni. Poetry. 1904. *821*

—. Italian Americans. Social conditions. 1859-1963. *837*

—. Italian Americans. Women. 1830-1920. *807*

—. Alberta (Calgary Diocese). Catholic Church. French Canadians. McNailly, John Thomas. 1871-1952. *3655*

—. American Canadians. McCabe, James (and descendants). Nova Scotia (Pictou). Pennsylvania (Philadelphia). ca 1743-1917. *3444*

—. Anglin, Timothy Warren. Canada. Fenians. McGee, D'Arcy. Political Speeches. 1863-68. *3477*

—. Anglin, Timothy Warren. Catholic Church. New Brunswick. Newspapers. St. John *Freeman* (newspaper). 1849-83. *3476*

—. Anti-Catholicism. Great Britain. Loyalty. Ontario. Orange Order. 1830-1900. *3478*

—. Attitudes. Immigration. Ontario (Canada West). Potato famine. 1845-50. *3483*

—. Beamish family. Genealogy. Nova Scotia (Halifax). 1765-1970's. *3485*

—. Bishops. Catholic Church. Lynch, John Joseph. Ontario. Poor. Toronto Savings Bank. 1870's. *3685*

—. Boer War. Canada. English Canadians. German Canadians. Peace Movements. 1899-1902. *3734*

—. British Canadians. Canada. Minorities. Prejudice. 1970's. *3065*

—. British Columbia. Civil service. Gaggin, John Boles. 1859-66. *3488*

—. Canada. Census. Households. Ontario (Hamilton). 1851-71. *3770*

—. Canada. Genealogy. Prime Ministers. Thompson, John S. D. 1796-1903. *3446*

—. Canada. Immigration. Poor Law Commissioners. Servants. Women. 1865. *3490*

—. Canada, western. Catholic Church. Episcopal nominations. French Canadians. 1900-75. *3664*

—. Catholic Church. Charities. McMahon, Patrick. Poor. Quebec (Quebec City). St. Bridget's Home. 1847-1972. *3482*

—. Catholic Church. Church of England. English Canadians. Feild, Edward. Methodist Church. Newfoundland. Presbyterian Church. 1765-1852. *3703*

—. Catholic Church. French Canadians. New Brunswick. Politics. Public Schools. Quebec. Taxation. 1871-73. *3821*

—. Catholic Church. Katz, Michael B. (review article). Occupations. Ontario (Hamilton). Social mobility. 1850-75. 1975. *3783*

—. Census. Construction. Migrant labor. Quebec (Sherbrooke area). Railroads. 1851-53. *3479*

—. Crime and Criminals. Immigration. Newfoundland. Public Policy. 1789. *3480*

—. Elections. Farmers. Ontario. Orange Order. Political Attitudes. United Farmers of Ontario. 1920-25. *3484*

—. English Canadians. Feild, Edward. Little, Philip. Mullock, John Thomas. Newfoundland. Politics. Religion. 19c. *3704*

—. Family. Katz, Michael B. (review article). Ontario (Hamilton). Social Classes. 1850-80. *3777*

—. Frontier and Pioneer Life. Gold Mines and Mining. Ontario (Casummit Lake). Reminiscences. Swedish Canadians. William, Eileen. 1930's. *3732*

—. Gowan, Ogle. Immigration. Ontario (Upper Canada). Orange Order. Politics. 1830-33. *3487*

—. Manitoba. O'Beirne, Eugene Francis. Red River of the North. Travel. 1860's. *3491*

—. Nova Scotia. Political Leadership. Uniacke, James Boyle. Uniacke, Richard John. 1775-1858. *3481*

—. Nova Scotia (Halifax). Tobin, Thomas (and descendants). ca 1759-1936. *3486*

Irish Canadians (review article). Anglin, Timothy Warren. Baker, W. M. Canada. Fenians. Neidhardt, W. S. 19c. 1970's. *3489*

Iron Industry *See also* Steel Industry.

—. Business. Cities. Elites. Historiography. Social classes. 1874-1900. *2788*

—. Elites. Entrepreneurs. Ingraham, John N. (review article). Ohio (Youngstown). Pennsylvania (Philadelphia, Pittsburgh). West Virginia (Wheeling). 1874-1965. *2800*

—. Finnish Americans. Labor Unions and Organizations. Minnesota (Mesabi Range). Radicals and Radicalism. 1914-17. *1705*

—. Italian Americans. Labor recruitment. Letters. Negroes. Pennsylvania (Reading). Robesonia Iron Company. Slavic Americans. 1915-23. *2556*

Iron work. Catholic Church. German Canadians. Gravemarkers. Ontario (Bruce County; Waterloo). 1850-1910. *3468*

Iron workers. New York (Troy). Social Customs. Statistics. Working Class. 1860-80. *2593*

Iroquois Indians. Courcelles, Remy de. Documents (authorship). Dollier de Casson, François. French-Indian Relations. New France. Ontario, Lake. 1671. *3237*

—. Denonville, Marquis de. France. French. Galley slaves. Indians. New France. 1687. *3204*

—. Dollard des Ormeaux, Adam. French Canadians. Indian Wars. Long Sault (battle). New France. 1660. *3260*

—. Epidemics. French Canadians. Fur Trade. Hunt, George T. *(The Wars of the Iroquois)*. Indians. 1609-53. *3266*

—. Fort Orange. French-Indian Relations. Indian Wars. Long Sault (battle). Quebec. 1660. 1960. *3215*

—. French Canadians. Great Britain. Jesuits. Missions and Missionaries. Netherlands. New York. 1642-1719. *45*

Irrigation. Ice harvesting. Mills. Norwegian Americans. Tjossem, Rasmus Peder. Washington (Ellensburg). 1841-1922. *1763*

Isaacs, Meyer Samuel. Attitudes. Butzel, Magnus. Jews. Letters. Social Organizations. 1885. *1635*

Isaacson, John A. Banking. Illinois (Chicago). Immigration. Swedish Americans. 1892-1974. *1801*

Isaak, Gottlieb. Autobiography. Germans, Russian. South Dakota. 1870's. *639*

Iselin, Isaac. Diaries. *Maryland* (vessel). Swiss Americans. Voyages. 1805-08. *2137*

Isolationism. Democratic Party. German Americans. Kentucky (Kenton County). 1930-40. *2662*

—. Foreign relations. Germans, Russian. Lubell, Samuel. North Dakota (McIntosh County). Political Theory. 1936-40. *2498*

Israel *See also* entries under Palestinian; Palestine.

—. Agriculture. California. Hamburg, Sam. Jews. 1898-1976. *1385*

—. Alienation. Chomsky, Noam. Jews. Liberalism. 1975. *918*

—. American Israel Public Affairs Committee. Foreign Policy. Jews. Lobbying. 1922-76. *1520*

—. Anti-Defamation League of B'nai B'rith. Anti-Semitism. 1913-75. *953*

—. Arab States. Congress. Foreign Policy. Jews. 1973-74. *1533*

—. Assimilation. Discrimination. 1954-77. *172*

—. Assimilation. Employment. Immigration. Jews. 1967-70's. *958*

—. Attitudes. Ethnicity. Jews. Northeastern or North Atlantic States. Students. Zionism. 1973-76. *1595*

—. Attitudes. Genocide. Jews. World War II. Youth. 1939-45. ca 1970's. *2705*

—. Bibliographies. Jews. Noah, Mordecai Manuel. 1785-1851. 1930's-76. *1403*

—. Christianity. Jews. 1975. *1594*

—. Civil rights. Education. Jews. Marriage, mixed. 1950's-70's. *955*

—. Defense budget. Foreign Policy. Jews. Liberals. Senate. 1975. *1553*

—. Democracy. Immigration. Jews. USSR. 1971-76. *960*

—. Diplomatic recognition. Jews. Politics. Truman, Harry S. ca 1945-49. *1525*

—. Emigration. Jews. 1970's. *1585*

—. Eris, Alfred. Jews. New York City. Reminiscences. Six-Day War. 1967. *1527*

—. Foreign policy. Jews. Public opinion. 1967-74. *1565*

—. Foreign Policy. Protestantism. Zionism (review article). 1945-48. *1588*

—. Friends, Society of. Palestinians. 1977. *1555*

—. Immigrants. Jews. Scientists. USSR. 1970's. *1066*

—. Immigration. Jews. Scholars. USSR. 1960's-70's. *1584*

—. Jews. 1492-1976. *1568*

—. Jews. Population. 1970-77. *910*

—. Jews. Religion. Secularization. Self-perception. 1957-77. *1014*

—. Jews. Social Conditions. 1960's-75. *964*

Israel (Jerusalem). Hebrew University (Institute of Contemporary Jewry). Jewish studies. 1972-74. *925*

Israelite (periodical). Anti-Semitism. *The Asmonean* (periodical). *The Occident* (periodical). Periodicals. 1840-59. *921*

Issacs, Samuel Meyer. California (Sacramento, San Francisco). Henry, Henry Abraham. Jews. Letters. Rabbis. Travel (accounts). 1858. *1392*

Italia del Popolo (newspaper). Italians. Papa, Dario. Populism. 1881-94. *803*

Italia (newspaper). Illinois (Chicago). Immigrants. Italian Americans. Labor. Letters-to-the-editor. Padrone system. 1886. *858*

Italian Americans. 1970's. *895*

—. Acculturation. Bibliographies. Dissertations. 1921-75. *861*

—. Acculturation. German Americans. Michigan. Polish Americans. Scandinavian Americans. Voluntary Associations. 1850's-1950's. *2756*

—. Acculturation. Immigrants. Labor. Padrone system. Virginia (Wise County). 1900-20. *897*

—. Acculturation. Immigrants. Utah (Salt Lake City). Voluntary Associations. 1897-1934. *859*

—. Acculturation. Jews. Pennsylvania (Pittsburgh). Slavic Americans. Women. 1900-45. *2736*

—. Agricultural labor. Immigration. Negroes. Newspapers, black. South. 1880-1915. *884*

—. Alessandro, Antonietta Pisanelli. Czech Americans. Pesotta, Rose. Stereotypes. Women. Zeman, Josephine Humpel. 1880-1924. *2748*

—. American Committee on Italian Migration. Immigration and Nationality Act (US, 1965). Lobbying. Political participation. 1951-65. *809*

—. American Revolution. 1773-83. *797*

—. American Revolution. Mazzei, Philip. Propaganda. 1773-1816. *820*

—. American Revolution. Mazzei, Philip. Vigo, Francis. 1775-83. *795*

—. American Revolution. Mazzei, Philip. Vigo, Francis. 1773-84. *824*

—. Americas (North and South). Historiography. Immigration. 19c-20c. *818*

—. Anarchism and Anarchists. Florida (Tampa). Social Customs. Socialism. 1890-1902. *869*

—. Anti-Fascist Movements. Foreign Relations. Sforza, Carlo. World War II. 1940-43. *2688*

—. Aquino, Salvatore A. City Life. Family. Immigration. New York City. Reminiscences. 1914. *792*

—. Arizona (Phoenix). Immigration. Migration, Internal. Social Organization. 1880's. *848*

—. Armies. Custer, George A. Great Plains. Indian Wars. Martini, Giovanni (Martin, John). 1870's. *889*

—. Assimilation. Autobiography. Connecticut. D'Antonio, William V. Ethnicity. ca 1926-73. *813*

—. Assimilation. Catholic Church. Folk religion. 1880's-1920's. *893*

—. Assimilation. Derrico family. 1904-1970's. *806*

—. Assimilation. France. Immigrants. 19c-20c. *882*

—. Assimilation. Immigrants. 19c. *808*

—. Assimilation. Missouri (St. Louis). World War I. 1914-18. *2636*

—. Atellis, Orazio de. *Correo Atlántico* (newspaper). Immigration. Independence Movements. Texas. 1824-47. *877*

—. Barzini, Luigi (review article). Journalism. National Characteristics. 1925-77. *856*

—. Bayor, Ronald H. (review article). Conflict and Conflict Resolution. German Americans. Irish Americans. Jews. New York City. 1929-41. 1978. *152*

—. Behavior. Irish Americans. 1960's. *2950*

—. Bertarelli, Pier Giuseppe. Business. California. Gold Rushes. Immigration. 1849-53. *855*

—. Bibliographies. Colleges and Universities. Dissertations. 1908-77. *862*

—. Bocce ball. Ethnicity. Games. Immigrants. Pennsylvania (Philadelphia). 1974. *850*

—. California. Reminiscences. Teiser, Ruth. Wine industry. 1890's-1977. *2903*

—. California (San Francisco). Immigration. 1890-1977. *890*

—. California (San Francisco). Pisanelli, Antonietta. Theater, variety. 1905-32. *826*

—. California (San Francisco Bay). Fishing. Tarantino, Gaetano. 1850's-1940's. *827*

—. Canada. Immigrants. Toponymy. 1850's-1910's. *3499*

—. Canada. Immigration. Italian Canadians. USA. 1870-1977. *829*

—. Capone, Al. Crime and Criminals. Illinois (Chicago). 1919-47. *853*

—. American Dream. Ethnicity. Literature. 20c. *957*

—. American Federation of Labor. International Ladies' Garment Workers' Union. Labor Unions and Organizations. 1930's. *903*

—. American Israel Public Affairs Committee. Foreign Policy. Israel. Lobbying. 1922-76. *1520*

—. *American Israelite* (newspaper). Letters. Nevada (Eureka). 1875. *1337*

—. *American Jewess* (periodical). Sonnenschein, Rosa. Women. 1895-99. *1063*

—. American Jewish Committee. American Jewish Congress. Anti-Defamation League of B'nai B'rith. Arab-Israeli conflict. Boycotts. Legislation. 1975-77. *1554*

—. American Jewish Committee. Foreign relations. Immigration Policy. Lobbying. Russia. 1915-17. *967*

—. American Jewish Committee. Kishinev pogrom. Russia. 1903. *1097*

—. American Jewish Congress. Nationalism. Socialism. 1914-18. *956*

—. American Jewish Historical Society. Collections. Rhode Island. 1692-1975. *1322*

—. American Jewish Joint Distribution Committee. Diplomacy. Mayer, Saly. World War II. 1944-45. *2655*

—. American Revolution. Commerce. Georgia (Savannah). Memoirs. Sheftall, Levi. 1739-1809. *1480*

—. American Revolution. Diaries. Military Finance. Morris, Robert. Solomon, Haym. 1781-84. *1092*

—. American Revolution. Documents. Letters. 1775-90. *1035*

—. American Revolution. Equal Opportunity. 1760's-1876. *1160*

—. American Revolution. Georgia (Savannah). Sheftall (family). 1730-1800. *1437*

—. American Revolution. Great Britain. Rhode Island. Touro, Isaac. 1782. *1428*

—. American Revolution. Military finance. Military Service, Enlistees. Politics. Solomon, Haym. 1775-83. *993*

—. American Revolution. Rhode Island (Newport). 1763-76. *1244*

—. Amish. Hutterites. Women. 1977. *2747*

—. Anthologies. Bibliographies. Literature. 1950's-70's. *920*

—. Anti-Nazi Movements. Boycotts. Fram, Leon. League for Human Rights. Michigan (Detroit). Reminiscences. 1930's-40's. *2670*

—. Anti-Semitism. ca 1800-1970. *1607*

—. Anti-Semitism. California (San Francisco). Editorials. *Emanu-El* (newspaper). Immigrants. Slavic Americans. Voorsanger, Jacob. 1905. *1080*

—. Anti-Semitism. Diplomats. Immigration Policy. 1918-25. *1130*

—. Anti-Semitism. Ethnicity. Liberals. Negroes. 1969. *917*

—. Anti-Semitism. German Americans. Midwest. Press. 1919-33. *2698*

—. Anti-Semitism. Negroes. Race Relations. 1970. *1643*

—. Antiwar sentiment. Religion. Vietnam War. Youth. 1960's. *1124*

—. Arab States. Congress. Foreign Policy. Israel. 1973-74. *1533*

—. Arab-Israeli conflict. Foreign policy. Interest groups. Public opinion. 1970's. *1586*

—. Arab-Israeli conflict. Newspapers. Periodicals. Public opinion. 1966-75. *1521*

—. Ararat Colony. German Americans. Greenberg, Gershon. New York. Noah, Mordecai Manuel. Wise, Isaac Mayer. 1820's-50's. 1978. *1466*

—. Ararat Colony. New York. Noah, Mordecai Manuel. Rhode Island (Newport). 1813-21. *1207*

—. Architecture. California (Los Angeles). Insurance. Marks, David X. Marks, Joshua H. Philanthropy. 1902-77. *1511*

—. Archives. Detroit Public Library (Burton Historical Collection). Michigan. 19c-20c. *1123*

—. Arizona. Barth, Solomon. Frontier and Pioneer Life. Mormons. 1856-1928. *1388*

—. Arizona. California. Copper Mines and Mining. Newman, John B. (Black Jack). Real estate. 1880's-1920's. *1481*

—. Arizona. Capitalism. Frontier and Pioneer Life. Wormser, Michael. 19c. *1384*

—. Arizona (Phoenix). Economic Development. Immigrants. 1870-1920. *1237*

—. Armies. Germany. Military Occupation. Refugees. 1946. *2661*

—. Art. Einstein, Albert. Intellectuals. Religion. ca 1900-55. *1397*

—. Art. Europe. Stereotypes. 1870-1976. *1601*

—. Art. Ghettos. Immigrants. 1880-1930. *1143*

—. Art. New York City. Sculpture. 1905-45. *1144*

—. Artists. Assimilation. Individualism. Modernism. Universalism. 1900-70's. *989*

—. Artists. Ezekiel, Moses Jacob. Virginia (Richmond). 1844-60. *1360*

—. Assimilation. 1880-1976. *1117*

—. Assimilation. Attitudes. Generations. 1925-75. *1084*

—. Assimilation. California (Los Angeles). Immigrants. Marriage. 1910-13. *1069*

—. Assimilation. California (Los Angeles). Reminiscences. Sichel, Carolyn Meyberg. 1902-31. *1474*

—. Assimilation. Converts. Ontario (Toronto). Presbyterian Church. 1912-18. *3510*

—. Assimilation. Delaware (Lewes). Genealogy. Nunez family. 18c. *1448*

—. Assimilation. Drama. Immigrants. Zangwill, Israel (*The Melting Pot*). 1908. *1106*

—. Assimilation. Duelling. Feinberg, Siegmund. Schwartz, Benedict. Texas. 1857. *1404*

—. Assimilation. Education. Labor Unions and Organizations. Socialism. 1880's-1945. *1134*

—. Assimilation. Employment. Immigration. Israel. 1967-70's. *958*

—. Assimilation. Films. Immigrants. Stereotypes. 1900's-20's. *924*

—. Assimilation. German Americans. Immigration. 1880-1920. *1103*

—. Assimilation. Literature. ca 1900-20. *1151*

—. Assimilation. Negroes. 1974. *923*

—. Assimilation. Novels. Values. 1917-70. *974*

—. Assimilation. October War. Public opinion. 1973. *1557*

—. Assimilation. Political Attitudes. South Carolina (Charleston). 1970's. *1258*

—. Assimilation. Self-identity. Social Organization. 1954-74. *1003*

—. Assimilation. Sociologists. 1930-73. *1119*

—. Association of Jewish Book Publishers. Publishers and Publishing. USSR. 1977-78. *1640*

—. Association of Jewish Libraries. Libraries. 1965-67. *1150*

—. Attitudes. 1970-75. *1623*

—. Attitudes. Bowman, Isaiah. Europe, Eastern. League of Nations. Letters. Royse, Morton W. 1927. *1625*

—. Attitudes. Butzel, Magnus. Isaacs, Meyer Samuel. Letters. Social Organizations. 1885. *1635*

—. Attitudes. California (San Francisco). Earthquakes. 1906. *1241*

—. Attitudes. California (San Francisco). Reese, Michael. 1850-78. *1421*

—. Attitudes. Cleaver, Eldridge. 1968-70's. *1524*

—. Attitudes. Colleges and Universities. Northwestern University. Students. Yale University. 1968-69. *1062*

—. Attitudes. Engle, Paul. Iowa (Cedar Rapids). Reminiscences. 1900-60. *1186*

—. Attitudes. Ethnicity. Israel. Northeastern or North Atlantic States. Students. Zionism. 1973-76. *1595*

—. Attitudes. Generations. Genocide (survivors). 1939-45. ca 1960-76. *2664*

—. Attitudes. Genocide. Israel. World War II. Youth. 1939-45. ca 1970's. *2705*

—. Attitudes. *Holocaust* (program). Television. 1974-79. *2691*

—. Attitudes. Literature. Tyler, Royall. ca 1777-1826. *1605*

—. Attitudes. Philosophy. 1970's. *1056*

—. Attitudes. Social Conditions. South. 1890-1977. *1058*

—. Auerbach's Department Store. California. Retail Trade. Utah (Salt Lake City). 1857-1977. *1461*

—. Australia. Great Britain. Marriage, interfaith. 1960-74. *1046*

—. Authors. Colorado (Denver). Physicians. Social work. Spivak, Charles. ca 1880-1927. *1399*

—. Authors. Family. Mothers. Olsen, Tillie. Schaeffer, Susan Fromberg. Stereotypes. Yezierska, Anzia. 20c. *1044*

—. Authors. Fiction. Genocide. 1945-74. *2695*

—. Authors. Memoirs. Socialism. Winchevsky, Morris. ca 1890-1932. *1509*

—. Authors. Negroes. Race Relations. 1956-70. *1026*

—. Autobiography. Kazin, Alfred. Literature. National Characteristics. New York City (Brooklyn). 1940-76. *933*

—. Autobiography. Literature. 1975. *1079*

—. Ballet. California (San Francisco). Clar, Reva. Hirsch-Arnold Ballet School. Pavlova, Anna. Reminiscences. 1924. *1362*

—. Ballin, Max. Harper Hospital. Medical Education. Michigan (Detroit). 1906-24. *1369*

—. Bamberger, Simon. Governors. Utah. 1916. *1371*

—. Banking. 17c-19c. *975*

—. Banking. California (Los Angeles). Farmers' and Merchants' Bank. Hellman, Isaias W. 1868-85. *1430*

—. Banking. Finance. German Americans. New York City. 19c. *1178*

—. Bartlett, Washington. California (San Francisco). Governors. 1886. *1483*

—. Bayor, Ronald H. (review article). Conflict and Conflict Resolution. German Americans. Irish Americans. Italian Americans. New York City. 1929-41. 1978. *152*

—. Beiliss, Mendel. California (Oakland, San Francisco). Newspapers. Russia. Trials. 1911-13. *1619*

—. Belkin, Samuel. Brown University. Reminiscences. Rhode Island (Providence). 1932-35. *1356*

—. Bellow, Saul (*Mr. Sammler's Planet*). Literature. Mailer, Norman (*Armies of the Night*). Political Theory. 1975. *1011*

—. Ben-Amos, Dan. Folklore (review article). Mintz, Jerome R. Rappoport, Angelo S. 1937-72. *980*

—. Benjamin, Judah. Confederate States of America. 1861-68. *1422*

—. Bergel, Siegmund. California (San Bernardino). Private Schools. 1868-1912. *1307*

—. Berger, Elmer. Reminiscences. Zionism (opposition to). ca 1945-75. *1522*

—. Bergman, Andrew. Cynicism. Novels, detective. Simon, Roger. 1970's. *1129*

—. Bernstein, Max. California. Development. Gold rushes. International Company of Mexico. Mexico (Baja California). 1854-1971. *1482*

—. Beth Olam Cemetery. California (San Jose). Congregation Bickur Cholim. 1850-1900. *1230*

—. Bibliographies. 1960-74. *939*

—. Bibliographies. 1960-75. *940*

—. Bibliographies. 1960-75. *941*

—. Bibliographies. 1974-75. *997*

—. Bibliographies. 1960-76. *998*

—. Bibliographies. 1960-78. *999*

—. Bibliographies. 16c-1978. *1000*

—. Bibliographies. 1960-79. *1001*

—. Bibliographies. 1960-73. *1402*

—. Bibliographies. Fiction. Immigration. 1867-1920. *1008*

—. Bibliographies. Israel. Noah, Mordecai Manuel. 1785-1851. 1930's-76. *1403*

—. Bloch, Ernest. California. Music. San Francisco Conservatory of Music. 1922-30. *1445*

—. B'nai B'rith. California (Los Angeles). 1905. *1330*

—. B'nai B'rith. Modernization. Oregon (Portland). Social Change. Voluntary Associations. 1920's. *1313*

—. B'nai B'rith (Judah Touro Lodge No. 998). Rhode Island (Newport). 1924-74. *1235*

—. *B'nai B'rith Messenger* (newspaper). California (Los Angeles). Newspapers. 1895-1929. *1304*

—. B'nai B'rith (Paradise Lodge No. 237). California (San Bernardino). Choynski, Isidor Nathan. 1875-1975. *1255*

—. Boxing. California (San Francisco). Choynski, Joe. ca 1884-1904. *1420*

—. Boy Scouts of America. Rhode Island. 1910-76. *1223*

—. Brandeis, Louis D. Frankfurter, Felix. New Deal. Politics. Roosevelt, Franklin D. World War I. 1917-33. *1368*

—. Brandeis, Louis D. Freund, Paul A. Law. Reminiscences. Supreme Court. 1932-33. *1377*

—. Braude, William G. Rabbis. Reminiscences. Wolfson, Harry Austryn. 1932-54. *1355*

—. Brin, Fanny Fligelman. Minnesota (Minneapolis). Peace. Women. 1913-60's. *1492*

—. Buildings. Grand Opera House. Judah, Abraham. Missouri (Kansas City). Theater. 1883-1926. *1180*

—. Buildings (iron front). California (San Luis Obispo). Sinsheimer, Aaron Zachary (and family). 1878-1956. *1490*
—. Bureau of Social Morals. Hertz, Rosie. Law Enforcement. New York City. Prostitution. 1912-13. *1209*
—. Business. California (Anaheim). Democratic Party. Dreyfus, Benjamin. Winemaking. 1854-86. *1491*
—. Business. California (Fort Bragg). Russia. Shafsky family. 1889-1976. *1516*
—. Business. California (Los Angeles). Housing. Middle Classes. Social Mobility. 1880's. *1195*
—. Business. California (San Diego). City Government. Mannasse, Joseph Samuel. Schiller, Marcus. 1853-97. *1407*
—. Business. California (San Francisco; San Bruno Avenue). Esther Hellman Settlement House. Neighborhoods. 1901-68. *1239*
—. Business. Confederate States of America. Levy, Jonas Phillips. Merchant marine. North Carolina (Wilmington). 1830's-60's. *1449*
—. Business. Economic Growth. 18c-20c. *929*
—. Business. Filene, Edward A. Leadership. Massachusetts (Boston). Philanthropy. 1860-1937. *1372*
—. Business. Godchaux, Leon. Louisiana (New Orleans). 19c. *1501*
—. Business. Great Britain (London). Immigration. Labor Unions and Organizations. New York City. 19c-20c. *1266*
—. Business. Jacobs, James. Rhode Island (Providence). 1820's-30's. 1850's. *1469*
—. Business. Memoirs. Resnik, Bezalel Nathan. Rhode Island (Providence). 1891-1971. *1446*
—. Business. New York City. 1654-1820. *1217*
—. Business. Photographs. Washington (Seattle). 1890-1920. *1325*
—. Business. Social Change. Women. 18c-20c. *1049*
—. Cabala. Counter Culture. Mysticism. Rationalism. Tradition. 1940's-70's. *1074*
—. Cabala. Friends, Society of. 17c-20c. *1038*
—. Cahan, Abraham. Cities. Crane, Stephen. Fiction. Romanticism. 1890's. *946*
—. California. California (Hollywood). DeMille, Cecil B. Film Industry. Lasky, Jesse L. Paramount-Publix Corporation. Vaudeville. 1890's-1930. *1400*
—. California. Charities. Disaster relief. Economic aid. Nieto, Jacob. San Francisco Earthquake and Fire. 1906. *1256*
—. California. Disaster relief. San Francisco Earthquake and Fire. 1906. *1245*
—. California. Frank, Leo M. Georgia. Lynching. Progressivism. Trials. 1913-15. *1620*
—. California. Frank, Leo M. Georgia (Atlanta). Newspapers. Trials. 1913-15. *1630*
—. California. Franklin, Harvey B. Rabbis. Reminiscences. 1916-57. *1376*
—. California. Heydenfeldt, Solomon. Lyons, Henry A. Supreme courts, state. 1850's. *1048*
—. California. Houses. Leow, Jacob. Levy, Edward R. Meyberg, Max. Neustader, David. Neustader, Jacob. Photographs. Stern, Jacob. 1890's. *1510*
—. California. Marks, Bernhard. Pioneers. 1852-1913. *1439*
—. California. San Francisco Earthquake and Fire. 1906. *1179*
—. California (Escondido). Grape Day. Politics. Steiner, Sigmund. 1886-1912. *1464*
—. California (Los Angeles). 1799-1910. *1512*
—. California (Los Angeles). Cedars of Lebanon Hospital. Hospitals. Schlesinger, Jacob. 1901-30. *1212*
—. California (Los Angeles). Cemeteries. Congregation B'nai B'rith. Home of Peace Cemetery. 1902. *1331*
—. California (Los Angeles). Census. Clothing. Retail Trade. 1870's. *1301*
—. California (Los Angeles). Charities. Chicago fire. 1871. *1302*
—. California (Los Angeles). Charities. Civic associations. Lazard, Solomon. 1826-1916. *1424*
—. California (Los Angeles). Conductors. Frankenstein, Abraham Frankum. 1897-1934. *1390*
—. California (Los Angeles). Congregation B'nai B'rith. Finance. Political Factions. Rabbis. 1897. *1326*
—. California (Los Angeles). Congregation B'nai B'rith. Letters. Newmark, Joseph. Rabbis. 1881. *1518*

—. California (Los Angeles). Editors and Editing. German Americans. Jacoby, Conrad. *Sud-California Post* (newspaper). 1874-1914. *1176*
—. California (Los Angeles). Federation of Jewish Charities. 1916-17. *1254*
—. California (Los Angeles). Films. Myers, Carmel. Reminiscences. 1902-30. *1438*
—. California (Los Angeles). Franco-Prussian War. Universal Jewish Alliance. 1868-70. *1309*
—. California (Los Angeles). Greek Americans. Immigration. Sephardic Hebrew Center. 1900-74. *1214*
—. California (Los Angeles). Hattem, Isadore M. Supermarkets. 1913-66. *1391*
—. California (Los Angeles). Hebrew Benevolent Society of Los Angeles. Labatt, Samuel K. 1851-54. *1416*
—. California (Los Angeles). Letters. Marriage. Newmark, Rosa Levy. Social customs. 1867. *1442*
—. California (Los Angeles). Letters. Newmark, Abraham. 1883. *1440*
—. California (Los Angeles). Lissner, Henry H. Physicians. 1895-1968. *1493*
—. California (Los Angeles). Mesmer, Joseph. Newmark, Joseph. Reminiscences. 1824-1947. *1249*
—. California (Los Angeles). Political Campaigns (mayoral). Social Classes. Voting and Voting Behavior. 1969. *1034*
—. California (Los Angeles; Chavez Ravine). Cemeteries. Hebrew Benevolent Society of Los Angeles. Home of Peace Cemetery. Photographs. 1855-1910. *1335*
—. California (Los Angeles, San Diego). Cave, Daniel. Dentistry. Freemasons. Leadership. 1873-1936. *1413*
—. California (Mariposa County). Gold Rushes. Merchants. 1850-82. *1294*
—. California (Oakland). 1852-91. *1232*
—. California (Oakland). Disaster relief. Refugees. San Francisco Earthquake and Fire. Synagogues. 1906. *1334*
—. California (Oakland). Rosenbaum, Fred (review article). 1920's-70's. *1233*
—. California (Orangevale, Porterville). Lilienthal, Philip Nettre. Lubin, David. Settlement. Weinstock, Harris. 1890's. *1306*
—. California (Oroville, Woodland). Messing, Aron J. Temple Beth Israel. Travel. 1879. *1333*
—. California (Petaluma). Chickens. Farmers. Socialists. 1900-77. *1357*
—. California (Pomona). Childhood. Cole, Sylvan. People's Store. Reminiscences. Retail Trade. 1886-1901. *1366*
—. California (Rincon). Goldsmith, Simon. Kallman, George. Murder. 1875-1903. *1489*
—. California (Sacramento, San Francisco). Henry, Henry Abraham. Issacs, Samuel Meyer. Letters. Rabbis. Travel (accounts). 1858. *1392*
—. California (San Bernardino). Cohn, Isaac. Cohn, Wolff. Cole, Dick. Murder. 1862. *1295*
—. California (San Diego). Divorce. Green family. Murder. Suicide. 1863-88. *1484*
—. California (San Diego). Interethnic Relations. Pioneers. 1850-60. *1098*
—. California (San Diego). Population. Temple Beth Israel. 1889-1978. *1287*
—. California (San Diego). Purim Ball. Social Customs. 1888. *1167*
—. California (San Francisco). California, University of, Berkeley. Colleges and Universities. Journalism. Lawyers. Newmark, Nathan. 1853-1928. *1417*
—. California (San Francisco). Cemeteries. First Hebrew Benevolent Society. Funerals. Johnson, Henry D. 1849-50. *1297*
—. California (San Francisco). Charities. Cholera. Neustadt, Samuel I. 1850. *1296*
—. California (San Francisco). Choynski, Harriet. Letters. 1850-72. *1358*
—. California (San Francisco). Clothing. German Americans. Strauss, Levi. 1850-1970's. *1444*
—. California (San Francisco). Congress. Kahn, Julius. Political Leadership. Public Policy. Republican Party. 1898-1924. *1352*
—. California (San Francisco). Dyer, Leon. Leadership. Maryland (Baltimore). 1820's-75. *1453*
—. California (San Francisco). Earthquakes. Food supply. Voorsanger, Jacob. 1906. *1317*
—. California (San Francisco). Economic Conditions. 1860's. *1170*
—. California (San Francisco). Ethnicity. Synagogues. 1848-1900. *1234*

—. California (San Francisco). France. Immigrants. Meyer, Eugene. Reminiscences. 1842-60. *1434*
—. California (San Francisco). Franklin, Lewis Abraham. Sermons. 1850. *1192*
—. California (San Francisco). Mount Zion Hospital. 1887-1978. *1270*
—. California (San Francisco). Mount Zion Hospital. Rosenstirn, Julius. 1897. *1316*
—. California (San Francisco). Nieto, Jacob. Rubin, Max. Temple Sherith Israel. 1893. *1308*
—. California (San Francisco). Women. 1896. *1210*
—. California (Santa Monica). Resorts. 1875-1939. *1329*
—. California, southern. Choynski, Isidor Nathan. Cities. Journalism. Travel (accounts). 1881. *1476*
—. California (Temecula Valley). Entrepreneurs. Indians. Jackson, Helen Hunt. Wolf, Louis. 1852-87. *1486*
—. Canada. 1977. *3512*
—. Canada. Communist Party. Gershman, Joshua. Labor Unions and Organizations. Reminiscences. 1913-77. *3501*
—. Canada. Deserters. USA. Vietnam War. 1969-70. *3507*
—. Canada. Education. Immigration. Reminiscences. Segal, Beryl. USA. 1900-70's. *1468*
—. Canada. France. Great Britain. Poverty. Uruguay. 1975. *3509*
—. Canada. Galveston Plan. Immigration. Schiff, Jacob H. USA. 1907-14. *911*
—. Carigal, Hakham Raphael Haim Isaac. Rabbis. Rhode Island (Newport). 1771-77. *1443*
—. Catholic Church. Drinan, Robert. Elections (congressional). Massachusetts. 1970-76. *1022*
—. Cavaignac, Louis. Mann, A. Dudley. Switzerland. Treaties. 1850-55. *1629*
—. Cemeteries. Congregation Beth El. Historical markers. Letters. Michigan (Detroit). 1850-1971. *1328*
—. Cemeteries. Saskatchewan. 1975. *3516*
—. Charities. Galveston Plan. Immigrants. Industrial Removal Office. Migration, Internal. New York City. 1890-1914. *1076*
—. Charities. Hannah Schloss Old Timers. Michigan (Detroit). 1903-73. *1211*
—. Charities. Michigan (Detroit). Odessa Progressive Aid Society. 1915-18. *1319*
—. Charities. Michigan (Detroit). Reminiscences. Simons, Leonard N. 1901-75. *1475*
—. Charities. Nebraska (Omaha). Political Leadership. Refugees. Settlement. 1820-1937. *1197*
—. Child Welfare. Foster homes. Immigrants. New York City. Working class. 1900-05. *1271*
—. Children. Council of Jewish Women. Neighborhood House. Oregon (Portland). Women. 1895-1905. *1172*
—. Children. Immigrants. Manitoba (Winnipeg). Public schools. 1900-20. *3520*
—. Christianity. Converts. Daland, William C. Friedlaender, Herman. New York City. *Peculiar People* (newspaper). 1880's-90's. *1102*
—. Christianity. Genocide. Theology. World War II. 1945-74. *2663*
—. Christianity. Israel. 1975. *1594*
—. Christianity. Marriage, Interfaith. 1962-79. *1112*
—. Church schools. Documents. Education, Finance. Public Policy. Religion in the Public Schools. 1961-71. *922*
—. Cincinnati Union Bethel. Ohio. Settlement houses. Social reform. 1838-1903. *1187*
—. Cities. Family. Immigration. Italian Americans. Rhode Island. 1880-1940. *2751*
—. Cities. Poor. 1967-77. *1110*
—. City Life. Immigration. Manitoba (Winnipeg). 1874-82. *3502*
—. City Politics. Koehl, Matt. National Socialist White People's Party. Nazism. Wisconsin (Milwaukee). 1974-76. *1632*
—. Civil Rights. Colonization. Europe. Florida. Levy, Moses Elias. 1825. *1314*
—. Civil rights. Education. Israel. Marriage, mixed. 1950's-70's. *955*
—. Civil Rights. Ethnicity. Riis, Jacob. Social Organization. 1870-1914. *1615*
—. Civil rights. Liberals. Minorities in Politics. New York City. Social reform. 1963-70's. *985*

Khlebnikov, Kirill. Natural History. Pacific Coast. Russian-American Company. Travel Accounts. 1817-32. *2069*

Kiefer, Theobald, II. Austria (Salzburg). Francke, Gottfried. Georgia (Ebenezer). Letters. Orphanages. Settlement. Whitefield, George. 1738. 1750. *553*

King, Edward Smith (1848-96). Jews. New York City (Old East Side). Novels. 19c. *1221*

King family. Amish. Daily Life. Diaries. Farms. Loomis, Charles P. Pennsylvania (Lancaster County). 1940. *2251*

King George's War. Economic Conditions. French Canadians. Louisbourg, fortress of. New England. Nova Scotia. 1745-50. *3861*

—. French. Louisbourg, Fortress of. Mutinies. Nova Scotia. 1744-45. *3213*

—. French Canadians. Louisbourg (siege). Military Service (enlistees). New England. Nova Scotia (Cape Breton Island). 1745. *3846*

King, Grace. Creoles. Gayarré, Charles. Historians. Letters. Louisiana. 1867-95. *375*

King, William Lyon Mackenzie. Canada. Intergovernmental Relations. Newspapers. Public opinion. Public Welfare. Taxation. 1945-46. *3929*

—. Conscription, Military. Elections. French Canadians. Ligue pour la Défense du Canada. Quebec. World War II. 1942-44. *3758*

—. French Canadians. Lapointe, Ernest. Liberal Party. Politics. Quebec. St. Laurent, Louis. 1919-50. *3921*

King-Crane Report. Christianity. Palestine. Zionism (opposition to). 1919. *1549*

Kingdom of Paradise colony. Cherokee Indians. Colonial Government. Georgia. German Americans. Political Imprisonment. Priber, Christian Gottlieb. Utopias. 1730's-ca 1744. *572*

Kingston, Archdiocese of. Archives. Bishops. Catholic Church. Ontario. 1800-1966. *3680*

Kinship. Dutch Americans. Ethnicity. Immigration. Inbreeding. Oregon (Verboort). 19c-20c. *339*

—. Family. History. Households. Methodology. 1970's. *2889*

Kirkconnell, Watson. Canada. Hungarian Canadians. Poetry. 1895-1977. *3475*

Kishinev pogrom. American Jewish Committee. Jews. Russia. 1903. *1097*

Kissinger, Henry A. Balance of power. Foreign policy. German Americans. Mazlish, Bruce (review article). 1973-76. *595*

—. German Americans. James, Henry. Values. World view. 19c-20c. *567*

—. Jews. Political Leadership. Psychohistory. 1923-73. *1503*

Klasmer, Benjamin. Conductors. Jews. Maryland (Baltimore). Music. 1909-49. *1364*

Klassen, John P. Artists. Ukrainian Americans. 1909-33. *2238*

Klein, Milton M. Bonomi, Patricia U. New York (review article). Provincial Government. Religion. 1690's-1770's. 1971-74. *2441*

Kleppner, Paul. Bogue, Allan G. Flanigan, William H. Hammarberg, Melvyn. Political history (review article). Silbey, Joel. Voting and Voting Behavior. 19c-20c. 1970's. *2511*

—. Formisano, Ronald P. Hackney, F. Sheldon. Methodology. Political history (review article). 1827-1900. 1969-71. *2522*

—. Jensen, Richard. North Central States. Politics. Religion. 1850-1900. *2486*

Kliewers, Warren. Brackett, Lee. Epp, Peter. Juhnke, James. Mennonites. Moyer, Harold. Novels. Pacifism. Reed, Kenneth. 20c. *2290*

Klondike Stampede. American Canadians. Diaries. Marsh, Marvin Sanford. Yukon Territory. 1898. *3593*

Knickerbocker (vessel). Dutch Americans. Michigan (Zeeland). Trade. 1847. *357*

Kniffen, Fred. Architecture. Ethnicity. Germans, Russian. Houses. Kansas, western. 1890-1940. 1976. *589*

Knights of Columbus. Catholic Church. Commodore Barry Country Club. Illinois (Chicago). Irish Americans. Wisconsin (Twin Lakes). 1907-20's. *728*

Knights of Labor. Canada. Catholic Church. French Canadians. Labor Unions and Organizations. Taschereau, Elzéar Alexandre. 1884-94. *3398*

—. Irish Americans. Labor Unions and Organizations. Pennsylvania (Scranton). Politics. Powderly, Terence Vincent. 1876-1900. *736*

Knights of Malta. American Revolution. Canada. France. French Canadians. Heraldry. 1600's-1976. *3254*

Knott, William V. Anti-Catholicism. Catts, Sidney J. Elections (gubernatorial). Florida. Guardians of Liberty. Sturkie Resolution. 1916. *216*

Know-Nothing Party. Anti-Catholicism. Political Leadership. Thompson, Richard W. 1850's. *193*

—. Anti-Catholicism. Religious Liberty. 1770's-1840's. *200*

—. Antislavery Sentiments. Massachusetts. Nativism. Republican Party. Voting and Voting Behavior. 1850's. *179*

—. Arkansas. Elections (presidential). 1855-56. *199*

—. Berrien, John M. Georgia. Letters. Nativism. Political Attitudes. 1854-56. *192*

—. Democratic Party. Elections. Irish Americans. Local Politics. Missouri (St. Louis). Riots. 1844-56. *198*

—. German Americans. Illinois (Chicago). Law. Local Politics. Riots. Temperance. 1855. *194*

—. Nativism. Political Parties. 1853-56. *188*

Koehl, Matt. City Politics. Jews. National Socialist White People's Party. Nazism. Wisconsin (Milwaukee). 1974-76. *1632*

Koehler, J. P. ("Gesetzlich Wesen Unter Uns"). German Americans. Lutheran Church. Theology. 1880's-1915. *2400*

Kogan, Michael S. Brandeis, Louis D. Gompers, Samuel. Judaism. Labor Unions and Organizations. 1880's-1975. *1147*

Kohler, Kaufmann. Academic Freedom. Hebrew Union College. Judaism, Reform. Ohio (Cincinnati). Zionism. 1903-07. *1562*

—. Judaism, Reform. Michigan (Detroit). 1869-1926. *1408*

Kohut, George Alexander. Book Collecting. Judaism. Yale University Library (Kohut Collection). 1901-33. *919*

Kokotailo, Veronia. Alberta. Homesteading and Homesteaders. Rumanian Canadians. 1898- . *3525*

Köllner, Augustus (Staten Island drawings). Artists. German Americans. New York City. 19c. *649*

Kollontai, Aleksandra. Communism. Norway. Propaganda. Russians. World War I. 1915-16. *2089*

Kosciusko, Thaddeus. American Revolution. Armies. Poles. Public opinion. Pulaski, Casimir. 1775-83. *2019*

—. American Revolution. Military engineering. Poles. 1746-1817. *1972*

—. American Revolution. Polish Americans. Pulaski, Casimir. Salomon, Haym. Settlement. 1608-1780. *2051*

—. Citizenship. Jefferson, Thomas. Poles. Supreme Court. Wills. 1798-1852. *2029*

Kostelanetz, Richard (review article). Jews. Literature. 1970's. *902*

Kovats, Michael. American Revolution. Hungarian Americans. Military Service. 1775-83. *682*

Kowalsky, Henry I. Zangwill, Israel. Zionism. 1904. *1598*

Kral, Tonka. Acculturation. City Life. Northeastern or North Atlantic States. Reminiscences. Slovakian Americans. 20c. *1902*

Kramer, William A. German Americans. Lutheran Church. Missouri (Perry County). Reminiscences. ca 1890-1910. *564*

Krasovich family. Colorado (Pueblo). Mines. Olyejar family. Slovakian Americans. Slovenian Americans. 1900's-10's. *1880*

Kraus, William. Jews. Mayors. Ohio (Toledo). 1869-76. *1345*

Krauskopf, Joseph. Agriculture. Judaism. Reform. 1880's-1923. *1495*

Krehbiel, C. E. Hertzler, A. E. Hohmann, Walter H. Kansas. Kaufman, E. G. Lagenwalter, J. H. Letters. Mennonites. Physicians. 1920-46. *2276*

Krehbiel, H. P. Dunkards. Friends, Society of. Historic Peace Churches. Kansas (Newton). Mennonites. Pacifism. 1935-36. *2245*

Kremer, Charles H. Genocide. Immigrants. Jews. Rumanian Americans. Trifa, Valerian. World War II. 1941-74. *1628*

Krenitsyn, Petr Kuz'mich. Alaska (Aleutian Islands). Discovery and Exploration. Eskimos. Levashov, Mikhail Dmitrievich. Russians. 1769. *2071*

Kreve, Vincas. Austria. Immigration. Letters. Lithuanians. Refugees. 1947. *274*

Krivitsky, Walter (death). Anti-Communism. Defectors. Military Intelligence. Russian Americans. USSR. 1937-41. *2070*

Kruzenshtern, Ivan Fedorovich. Arctic. Romanov, Vladmir Pavlovich. Russians. Scientific Expeditions. 1819-25. *2056*

Krzycki, Leo. Labor Unions and Organizations. Polish Americans. Radicals and Radicalism. Socialist Party. 1900's-66. *2009*

Krzyzanowski, Jerzy (review article). Literature. Poland. Polish Americans. Reymont, Wladyslaw. 1867-1925. *2011*

Ku Klux Klan. Alley, Jim. Memphis *Commercial Appeal* (newspaper). Mooney, Charles Patrick Joseph. Pulitzer Prize. Tennessee. 1920-25. *206*

—. Anti-Catholicism. Elections (provincial). Legislation. Saskatchewan. Schools. 1929. *3058*

—. Anti-Catholicism. Immigration. Protestants. Saskatchewan. 1927-30. *3060*

—. Antilabor sentiments. Canada, western. Elections, local. Immigration Policy. Labor Unions and Organizations. 1921-30's. *3073*

—. Arizona. Mexican Americans. 1921-25. *203*

—. Attitudes. Morality. Ohio (Youngstown). Reform. 1920's. *225*

—. California (Anaheim). City Government. Political Participation. ca 1923-25. *234*

—. Colorado. State Politics. 1920-26. *230*

—. Columbus *Enquirer-Sun* (newspaper). Georgia. Harris, Julian LaRose. 1920's. *238*

—. Columbus *Enquirer-Sun* (newspaper). Georgia. Harris, Julian LaRose. Racism. 1920's. *241*

—. Democratic Party. Elections (gubernatorial). Johnston, Henry S. Oklahoma. 1926. *207*

—. Educational policy. Law and order campaign. Patriotism. Reform. Stereotypes. Textbooks. Wisconsin (Madison). 1922-27. *220*

—. Fowler, Charles Lewis. Georgia (Atlanta). Lanier Unviersity. 1917-22. *214*

—. Georgia. Political Power. Simmons, William Joseph. 1915-25. *237*

—. Georgia (Macon). Morality. Nativism. Violence. Yarbrough, C. A. 1919-25. *224*

—. Indiana (Gary, Valparaiso). Nativism. 1920's. *205*

—. Kansas. State Government. White, William Allen. 1922-27. *242*

—. Kansas (Emporia). Political Campaigns (gubernatorial). Republican Party. White, William Allen. 1924. *244*

—. Oklahoma (Lawton). 1921-29. *209*

Kubašek, John J. Catholic Church. Independence Movements. New York (Yonkers). Slovakian Americans. 1902-50. *1932*

Kubiak, Hieronim (review article). Assimilation. Polish National Catholic Church. 1897-1965. *1997*

Kudirka, Simas. Asylum, Right of. Diplomacy. Lithuanian Americans. USSR. 1970-75. *270*

Kudlich, Hans. Antislavery Sentiments. Germans, Sudeten. Journalism. Missions and Missionaries. Neumann, John Nepomucene. Ottendorfer, Oswald. Postl, Karl (pseud. Charles Sealsfield). Republican Party. 19c-20c. *593*

Kuehn, Ernst Ludwig Hermann. German Americans. Lutheran Church. Michigan. Missions and Missionaries. 1850-98. *2429*

Kuhn, Fritz. German-American Bund. Germany. Nazism. 1936-41. *2679*

Kuhnle, Howard A. Lutheran Church. Necrology. 1950-73. *2398*

Kumlien, Thure. Brewer, Thomas M. Natural history. Swedish Americans. Wisconsin. 1843-88. *1865*

Kurikka, Matti. British Columbia. Finnish Americans. Harmony Island colony. Utopias. 1901-05. *3531*

Kuskov, Ivan A. California, northern. Colonization. Fort Ross. Russian-American Company. 1808-41. *2095*

—. California, northern. Colonization. Fort Ross. Russian-American Company. 1808-41. *2096*

Kutztown Folk Festival. Folk festivals. German Americans. Pennsylvania. Social Customs. 1950-74. *647*

Kuusinen, Aino (pseud. A. Morton). Comintern. Communist Party. Finnish Workers' Federation. 1930-33. *1696*

Kyforuk, Peter. Alberta (Edmonton). Farmer's Union of Alberta. Manitoba. Political Participation. Ukrainian Labour-Farmer Association. 1912-30's. *3566*

—. English Canadians. French Canadians. Official Language Act (1974). Quebec. 1750's-1974. *3834*

—. Federal government. French Language. Official Language Act (1974). Quebec. 1960-76. *4062*

—. Federal government. Middle Classes. Modernization. Provincial government. Quebec. 1960-76. *3949*

—. French language. Official Language Act (1974). Quebec. 1974. *4053*

—. French language. Official Language Act (1974). Quebec. 1974. *4057*

—. French Language. Official Language Act (1974). Quebec. USA. 1970's. *4064*

Lanier Unviersity. Fowler, Charles Lewis. Georgia (Atlanta). Ku Klux Klan. 1917-22. *214*

Lanoullier, Nicolas. Colonial government. Finance. French. Quebec. 1720-30. *3224*

LaPatrie (colony). French Canadians. New England. Quebec. Repatriation Act (1875). ca 1875-80. *3375*

Lapierre, Eugène (obituary). French Canadians. Historical Society of Montreal. Nationalism. Quebec. 1927-70's. *3393*

Lapointe, Ernest. French Canadians. King, William Lyon Mackenzie. Liberal Party. Politics. Quebec. St. Laurent, Louis. 1919-50. *3921*

Laporte, Hormisdas. City politics. French Canadians. Martin, Médéric. Political corruption. Préfontaine, Raymond. Quebec (Montreal). 1894-1921. *3352*

LaRocque, Paul. Catholic Church. Church Finance. Economic Development. French Canadians. Quebec (Sherbrooke). 1893-1926. *3671*

Larson, Agnes. Bacteriologists. Education. Historians. Larson, Henrietta. Larson, Nora. Minnesota. Norwegian Americans. Women. 1883-1972. *1736*

Larson, Henrietta. Bacteriologists. Education. Historians. Larson, Agnes. Larson, Nora. Minnesota. Norwegian Americans. Women. 1883-1972. *1736*

Larson, Nora. Bacteriologists. Education. Historians. Larson, Agnes. Larson, Henrietta. Minnesota. Norwegian Americans. Women. 1883-1972. *1736*

LaSalle, Sieur de. Colonization. Fort St. Louis. French. Texas (Aransas, Matagorda bays). 1684-85. *412*

Lasch, Christopher (review article). Family history. Modernization theory. Women. ca 1400-1976. *2727*

Laski, Harold. Zionism. 1910-46. *1537*

Lasky, Jesse L. California. California (Hollywood). DeMille, Cecil B. Film Industry. Jews. Paramount-Publix Corporation. Vaudeville. 1890's-1930. *1400*

Latin America. Bibliographies. Editorials. French Canadians. Newspapers. Quebec. 1959-73. *3741*

Lattarpe, Jean-Baptiste Bénard de. Discovery and Exploration. French. Oklahoma. 1690's-1763. *461*

Lattimer Massacre. Coal miners. Martin, James. Pennsylvania. Slovakian Americans. Strikes. Trials. 1897-98. *1924*

—. Coal miners. Pennsylvania. Press. Slovakian Americans. Strikes. 1897. *1892*

—. Coal miners. Pennsylvania. Slovakian Americans. Strikes. 1897. *1935*

Latvian Canadians. Ethnicity. Folk art. Manitoba (Winnipeg). Ukrainian Canadians. 1978. *3559*

Latvians. Communism. Propaganda. *Strädnieks* (newspaper). 1904-19. *273*

Lauchheimer, Charles. Anti-Semitism. Lobbying. Marines. Taft, William H. (administration). 1910-12. *1646*

Laurendeau, André. English Canadians. French Canadians. Nationalism. Quebec. 1945-66. *3971*

Laurens, Levy L. (death). Duelling. Jews. Newspapers. Texas. 1837. *1454*

Laurier, Wilfrid. Catholic Church. Church schools. French language. Langevin, Louis Philippe Adélard. Liberal Party. Prairie Provinces. Religion in the Public Schools. 1890-1915. *3810*

Laurin, Camille. Charter of the French Language (1977). English Canadians. Indians. Language Policy. Quebec. 1760-1978. *4066*

Laussat, Pierre Clément. Burthe, Charles André. Civil-Military Relations. Colonial Government. French. Louisiana. 1802-03. *376*

LaVache family. Acadians. Genealogy. Nova Scotia (Cape Breton; Arichat). 1774-20c. *3174*

Laval, François de. Brotherhood of the Holy Family. Catholic Church. Chaumonot, Pierre Joseph Marie. Elites. French Canadians. Quebec (Montreal). 1663-1760. *3657*

—. Catholic Church. French Canadians. Jansenism. Quebec. Ultramontanism. 17c. *3666*

—. Catholic Church. Governors, provincial. New France. Sovereign Council. 1659-84. *3190*

—. French Canadians. Gosselin, Auguste-Honoré (review article). New France. School of Arts and Crafts of St. Joachim. Vocational Education. 1668-1730. *3245*

Laval University. Bourget, Ignace. Catholic Church. Colleges and Universities. French Canadians. Quebec (Quebec City). 1840's-50's. *3294*

—. Economic growth. Elites. Ideology. Lévesque, R.-P. Quebec. Social sciences. 1930's-70's. *3364*

—. Institute of History. Quebec (Quebec City). 1947. *3168*

Laval University (Folklore Archives). Folklore. French Canadians. Lacorcière, Luc. Quebec (Quebec City). 1939-70. *3827*

LaVerendrye, Sieur de. Bourgmont, Etienne Veniard de. Discovery and Exploration. DuTisne, Charles Claude. French Canadians. Louisiana. St. Denis, Louis Antoine Juchereau de. Trans-Mississippi West. 18c. *437*

Law *See also* Constitutional Law; Courts; Criminal Law; Judges; Lawyers; Legislation; Police.

—. Arbitration. Dutch Americans. New Netherland. Trade. Women. 1662. *330*

—. Autobiography. Solomon, Joseph. 1905-28. *1478*

—. Bibliographies. Immigration. 1970-77. *263*

—. Brandeis, Louis D. Freund, Paul A. Jews. Reminiscences. Supreme Court. 1932-33. *1377*

—. Canada. Catholic Church. Catholic Church. France. Great Britain. Tithes. 1760-75. *3303*

—. Conspiracy theories. Italian Americans. Mafia. Public opinion. 1798-1970. *886*

—. Dargo, George (review article). French Americans. Louisiana. Minorities in politics. 1803-08. 1975. *414*

—. Feudalism. New France (Notre Dame des Anges). Provost Court of Quebec. 1626-1750. *3199*

—. French Canadians. New France. Property. Sulpicians. 1667. *3669*

—. German Americans. Illinois (Chicago). Know-Nothing Party. Local Politics. Riots. Temperance. 1855. *194*

—. Gribetz, Lewis J. Jews. New York City. Poultry Industry. Walker, James J. 1888-1940. *1193*

—. Immigrants. Venue. 1789-1976. *251*

—. Immigration and Nationality Act (US, 1952). Immigration policy. Morality. Sexual conduct, private. 1952-70's. *264*

—. McCarran, Patrick A. Nevada. Supreme Courts, state. 1913-18. *713*

—. Naturalization. 1673-1978. *177*

Law and order campaign. Educational policy. Ku Klux Klan. Patriotism. Reform. Stereotypes. Textbooks. Wisconsin (Madison). 1922-27. *220*

Law and Society. Jews. Judges. 17c-20c. *1047*

Law Enforcement. Alien Anarchist Act (US, 1918). Anti-Communist Movements. Congress. Leftism. Post, Louis F. 1919-20. *208*

—. Bureau of Social Morals. Hertz, Rosie. Jews. New York City. Prostitution. 1912-13. *1209*

—. Ohio (Niles). Riots. State government. 1924. *213*

Law Enforcement (raids). Communist Party. Michigan (Bridgman). 1922. *2572*

Law schools. Admissions Policies. *DeFunis* v. *Odegaard* (US, 1974). Discrimination. Jews. Washington. 1970's. *906*

Lawsuits. French Canadians. Insults. New France. 1658-1760. *3246*

Lawyers. Business. Canada. Elites. 19c-1974. *3801*

—. California (San Francisco). California, University of, Berkeley. Colleges and Universities. Jews. Journalism. Newmark, Nathan. 1853-1928. *1417*

—. French Canadians. LeSage, Simeon. Provincial Government. Quebec. 1835-1909. *3403*

—. Jews. Social mobility. 20c. *904*

—. Szold, Robert. Zionism. 1910's-70's. *1381*

Laxness, Halldór (*Paradise Reclaimed*). Brúnum, Eiríkur á. Icelandic Americans. Mormons. Novels. 1870-1900. 1960. *1713*

Lazard, Solomon. California (Los Angeles). Charities. Civic associations. Jews. 1826-1916. *1424*

Leadership. Business. Filene, Edward A. Jews. Massachusetts (Boston). Philanthropy. 1860-1937. *1372*

—. California (Los Angeles, San Diego). Cave, Daniel. Dentistry. Freemasons. Jews. 1873-1936. *1413*

—. California (San Francisco). Dyer, Leon. Jews. Maryland (Baltimore). 1820's-75. *1453*

—. Garvett, Morris (obituary). Jews. Michigan (Detroit). ca 1919-71. *1504*

—. Georgia (Atlanta). Haas (family). Immigration. Jews. Levi, Henry. Mayer, David. 1845-65. *1281*

—. Immigrants. Irish Americans. Labor Unions and Organizations. McCarthy, Patrick Henry. Youth. 1863-80. *760*

—. Immigration. Scholarship. Stachiw, Matthew (obituary). Ukrainian Americans. 1910's-78. *2115*

—. Jews. Levi, Abraham. Texas (Victoria). 1850-1902. *1473*

—. Jews. Students. Women. 1968-77. *1018*

—. Labor Unions and Organizations. New Deal. 1933-40. *2575*

—. Laity. New York (Kingston). Political Leadership. Protestant Churches. Social Status. 1825-60. *2162*

Leadership recruitment. American Revolution. Elites. Pennsylvania. Philadelphia Resistance Committee. Political mobilization. 1765-76. *2478*

Leadership succession. Hutterites. Population. Prairie Provinces. Social Organization. 1940's-70's. *3611*

League for Human Rights. Anti-Nazi Movements. Boycotts. Fram, Leon. Jews. Michigan (Detroit). Reminiscences. 1930's-40's. *2670*

League of Nations. Attitudes. Bowman, Isaiah. Europe, Eastern. Jews. Letters. Royse, Morton W. 1927. *1625*

—. Economic Conditions. Ireland. Irish Americans. Labor. Massachusetts. 1918-19. *737*

—. Germany. High Commission for Refugees. McDonald, James G. Nazism. Refugees. 1933-35. *2672*

LeClercq, Crestien. Bernou, Claude. Canada. France. *Premier Établissement de la Foy dans la Nouvelle France* (book). Renaudot, Eusèbe. 1691. *3217*

Lectures *See also* Speeches, Addresses, etc.

—. Borg, Selma Josefina. Centennial Exposition of 1876. Finnish Americans. Music. Pennsylvania (Philadelphia). Women's rights. 1858-90. *1704*

Lederer, Henry. Jews. Michigan (Lansing). Settlement. 1850-1918. *1227*

Leeser, Isaac. Georgia (Macon). Judaism. Letters. Loewenthal, Henry. Rabbis. 1854-70. *1012*

Leftism *See also* Communism; New Left; Radicals and Radicalism; Socialism.

—. Alien Anarchist Act (US, 1918). Anti-Communist Movements. Congress. Law Enforcement. Post, Louis F. 1919-20. *208*

—. Alienation. Intellectuals. Jews. New Deal. Roosevelt, Franklin D. 1930's. *1152*

—. Canada. Highlanders, 48th. Hunter, William A. Liberalism. Military Service. Reminiscences. Scottish Canadians. World War II. 1939-45. *3438*

—. French Canadians. Nationalism. Quebec. Social classes. 1970's. *3960*

—. French Canadians. Politics. Quebec. Referendum. Separatist Movements. 1979. *4004*

—. Jews. 1880's-1970's. *1028*

Légaré, Joseph. Art Galleries and Museums. Painting. Quebec. 1824-1933. *3153*

Legends. Catholic Church. New York (Buffalo). Polish Americans. 1870-1973. *1944*

Legge, William (Lord Dartmouth). Cape Florida Society. DeBrahm, William Gerard. Florida, southeastern. Great Britain. Immigration. Settlement. 1773-80. *42*

Legislation *See also* Congress; Law.

—. American Jewish Committee. American Jewish Congress. Anti-Defamation League of B'nai B'rith. Arab-Israeli conflict. Boycotts. Jews. 1975-77. *1554*

Lutheran Church, Swedish. Assimilation. Episcopal Church, Protestant. Swedish Americans. 1630-1850. *1868*

Luxury, concept of. French Canadians. Hume, David. Morality. Quebec. 1849-1900. *3116*

Lynch, John Joseph. Bishops. Catholic Church. Irish Canadians. Ontario. Poor. Toronto Savings Bank. 1870's. *3685*

Lynching. California. Frank, Leo M. Georgia. Jews. Progressivism. Trials. 1913-15. *1620*

Lynn, Washington Frank. Canada. Landscape Painting. Reporters and Reporting. USA. 1860's-70's. *293*

Lyon, Marcus. Anti-Catholicism. Anti-Irish sentiments. Cheverus, Jean Louis Lefebvre de. Irish Americans. Massachusetts (Northampton). Murder. Trials. 1805-06. *182*

Lyons, Henry A. California. Heydenfeldt, Solomon. Jews. Supreme courts, state. 1850's. *1048*

Lyser, Gustav. German Americans. Hewitt, Abram S. Illinois (Chicago). Legislative Investigations. Satire. *Vorbote* (newspaper). Working Class. 1878. *548*

M

MacDonald, John A. Anglicization. Canada, western. French Canadians. Immigration Policy. 1860-1900. *3023*

—. Canada. Catholic Church. Scottish Canadians. Voting and Voting Behavior. 1850's-91. *3705*

MacDonald, John Roderick. Alberta (Edmonton). Catholic Church. Colleges and Universities. St. Joseph's College (Alberta). Scottish Canadians. 1922-23. *3676*

Macdonnell, Alexander. Catholic Church. Glengarry Highlanders. Immigration. Ontario. Scottish Canadians. 1770's-1814. *3455*

Macedonian Americans. Bulgaria. Illinden Uprising. Press. Public opinion. 1903. *2120*

—. City Life. Croatian Americans. Folklore. Indiana, northwestern. Serbian Americans. 1976. *1882*

Macedonian Canadians. Assimilation. Immigrants. Ontario (Toronto). 1900-20. *3568*

—. Documents. Immigrants. Ontario (Toronto). Urban history. 20c. *3567*

Macedonian National Association. Dimitrov, Georgi. Letters. 1934. *2125*

MacGregor, James. Missions and Missionaries. Nova Scotia (Pictou). Presbyterian Church of Scotland. Scottish Canadians. 1786-1830. *3453*

Mach, Ernst. Carus, Paul. Clifford, William Kingdon. German Americans. Letters. Philosophy. 1890-1900. *626*

Machinists. Irish Americans. Pennsylvania (Carbondale, Scranton). Powderly, Terence Vincent. Working Class. 1866-77. *782*

Mack, Julian. Brandeis, Louis D. Cleveland Conference. Weizmann, Chaim. Zionist Organization of America. 1921. *1559*

Mackenzie, Alexander. *Hector* (vessel). Immigrants. Nova Scotia (Pictou Harbor). Passenger lists. Scottish Canadians. 1773. 1883. *3443*

MacKinnon, Murdoch. Anti-Catholicism. Assimilation. Education, Finance. French Canadians. Saskatchewan. School Act (amendment). Scott, Walter. Scottish Canadians. 1913-26. *3815*

MacLeod, Norman. Migration. Nova Scotia (St. Ann's). Presbyterian Church. Scottish Canadians. ca 1800-50's. *3434*

MacNutt, W. Stewart (obituary). Local history. Loyalist Studies. New Brunswick, University of. 1935-76. *3602*

Macomb, Alexander. Immigrants. Irish Americans. New York. 1748-1841. *707*

Macready, William Charles. Actors and Actresses. Astor Place Opera House. Forrest, Edwin. Nativism. New York City. Riots. 1849. *191*

Madison, Harry T. Jewish War Veterans of the United States. Michigan (Detroit). Veterans. 1938-50's. *1450*

Madog ab Owain Gwynedd (legend). Americas (North and South). Discovery and Exploration. Indians. Missions and Missionaries. Myths and symbols. Welsh. 16c-18c. *325*

Maeser, Karl G. Brigham Young Academy. Educators. German Americans. Mormons. 1828-56. 1876. *627*

Mafia. Conspiracy theories. Italian Americans. Law. Public opinion. 1798-1970. *886*

—. Crime and Criminals. Hennessy, David. Italian Americans. Louisiana (New Orleans). Murder. 1890. *857*

—. Crime and Criminals. Italian Americans. Stereotypes. 1870's-1920's. *833*

—. Italian Americans. Literature, popular. 1969-76. *887*

—. Italian Americans. Violence. 20c. *863*

Magazines. *See* Periodicals.

Magnes, Judah L. Hebrew University (Jerusalem). Palestine. Zionism. 1900-25. *1535*

Mailer, Norman (*Armies of the Night*). Bellow, Saul (*Mr. Sammler's Planet*). Jews. Literature. Political Theory. 1975. *1011*

Maillet, Antoine (*Évangéline Deusse*). Acadians. Drama. Quebec. Social Customs. 1976. *3173*

Maine *See also* New England; Northeastern or North Atlantic States.

—. American Revolution. Bailey, Jacob. Canada. Loyalists. Poetry. Satire. 1751-1808. *3601*

—. Champlain, Samuel de. French. Military Camps and Forts. Monts, Sieur de. New Brunswick. St. Croix Island. 1603-05. *464*

—. French Canadians. ca 1870-20c. *360*

Maine (Ellsworth). Bapst, John. Chaney, William Henry. Jesuits. Nativism. 1853-54. *202*

Maine (Lewiston). Assimilation. French Canadians. 1810's-1960's. *449*

Maine (New Sweden). Immigration. Swedish Americans. 1870's-1973. *1856*

—. Immigration. Swedish Americans. Thomas, William Widgery. 1850-80. *1815*

—. Letters. Settlement. Swedish Americans. 1873-88. *1828*

—. Letters. Södergren family. Swedish Americans. 1880-1913. *1829*

Maine, University of, Orono (Canadian-American Center). Atlantic Institute of Education. High Schools. History Teaching. Loyalists. Nova Scotia (Halifax). 1775-83. 1977-79. *3577*

Maine (Waldoboro). German Americans. Missions and Missionaries. Moravian Church. Soelle, Georg. 1762-70. *2434*

Maine (Wells). French Canadians. Indian Wars. Militia. Storer Garrison, attack on. 1692. *3870*

Mainmise (periodical). Counter culture. French Canadians. Nationalism. Quebec. 1970-75. *4026*

Mair, Charles. Canada First, group. Expansionism. Métis. Red River Rebellion. Riel, Louis. 1869-70. *3919*

Maksutov, Dmitri Petrovich. Alaska. Colonial Government. Russian-American Company. 1849-89. *2090*

Malamud, Bernard. Colleges and Universities. Curricula. Ethnic studies. Jews. Literature. Roth, Henry. 20c. *991*

Malamud, Bernard (*The Tenants*). Jews. Novels. 1971. *1031*

Malchelosse, Gerald. Boël, Attale. Discovery and Exploration. Duluth, Daniel Greysolon, Sieur (birthplace). France (Saint-Germaine-Laval). French. North America. 1636-40. 1950's. *3203*

Malkiel, Theresa Serber. Jews. Labor Unions and Organizations. New York City. Socialist Party. Women. 1900's-14. *1436*

Malm, G. N. (*Charli Johnson, Svensk-Amerikan, Härute*). Acculturation. Drama. Language. Literature. Swedish Americans. 1909-19. *1799*

M'Alpine, John. Loyalists. New York. Nova Scotia. Occupations. 1748-1827. *3595*

Management *See also* Industrial Relations.

—. Canada. Elites. Social mobility. 1880-85. 1905-10. *3776*

—. Canada. Employment. Immigration Bill. 1976. *3070*

Mangourit, Michel de. Diplomatic correspondence. DuPont de Nemours, Victor. French. Genêt, Edmond Charles. South Carolina (Charleston). 1793. 1797. *442*

Manifest Destiny. Gurowski, Adam. Pan-Slavism. Polish Americans. 1830-66. *2046*

Manitoba *See also* Prairie Provinces.

—. Alberta (Edmonton). Farmer's Union of Alberta. Kyforuk, Peter. Political Participation. Ukrainian Labour-Farmer Association. 1912-30's. *3566*

—. Assiniboia, Council of. French Canadians. Métis. Minorities in Politics. 1860-71. *3282*

—. Batoche (battle). Flinn, George A. Métis. North West Rebellion. Riel, Louis. *Winnipeg Sun* (newspaper). 1885. *3898*

—. Catholic Church. Church Schools. Legislation. McCarthy, D'Alton. 1870-90. *3820*

—. Catholic Church. French Americans. Immigration. Mathieu, Olivier-Elzéar. Regina Archdiocese. Saskatchewan. 1911-31. *3363*

—. Chippewa Indians. Germans, Russian. Mennonites. Métis. 1872-73. *3627*

—. Cree Indians (Plains, Wood). Diaries. Fort Pitt. Frenchman's Butte, Battle of. Indians (captivities). McLean, W. J. North West Rebellion. Scottish Canadians. 1885. *3913*

—. Documents. Métis. Political theory. Red River Rebellion. Riel, Louis. 1869. *3904*

—. English Canadians. French Canadians. Liberal Party. Politics. Railroads. Schools. 1870's-90's. *3816*

—. English Canadians. French Canadians. Pluralism symposium. 1870-1965. *3907*

—. French Canadians. Settlement. 1870-1920. *3386*

—. French Canadians. Social Customs. Vallee, Frank. 1970-74. *3320*

—. Funk, John F. Germans, Russian. Mennonites. Settlement. 1873. *3631*

—. German Canadians. Mennonites. Pioneers. 1875. *3610*

—. Germans, Russian. Great Plains. Immigration. Mennonites. 1871-74. *3632*

—. Germans, Russian. Immigrants. Mennonites. Russians. Shantz, Jacob Y. 1873. *3641*

—. Germans, Russian. Immigration. Mennonites. 1873. *3626*

—. Germans, Russian. Immigration. Mennonites. Shantz, Jacob Y. 1870's. *3630*

—. Germans, Russian. Immigration. Mennonites. Stoesz, David. 1872-76. *3625*

—. Germans, Russian. Mennonite Brethren Church. Warkentin, Johann. 1879-1948. *3637*

—. Germans, Russian. Mennonites. Settlement. 1870-80. *3628*

—. Hudson's Bay Company. Indians. McKay, James. Métis. Provincial Government. 1853-79. *3211*

—. Indians. Mennonites. Métis. Red River of the North. Removal, forced. Saskatchewan River Valley. 1869-95. *3617*

—. Irish Canadians. O'Beirne, Eugene Francis. Red River of the North. Travel. 1860's. *3491*

—. Jews. Physicians. 19c. *3518*

—. Mennonites. 1870-1900. *3640*

—. Military Recruitment. Red River of the North. Scottish Canadians. Selkirk, 5th Earl. Settlement. War of 1812. 1812-14. *3431*

—. Ukrainian studies. 1949-74. *3561*

Manitoba (Aweme). Criddle, Percy. Diaries. English Canadians. Homesteading and Homesteaders. 1882-1900's. *3419*

Manitoba (Brandon). English Canadians. Farms. Immigrants. Railroads. Wheat. 1880-87. *3420*

Manitoba (Gimli). Dufferin and Ava, 1st Marquis of. Icelandic Canadians. Travel. 1877. *3529*

Manitoba (Red River Settlement). Local Government. Métis. Saskatchewan (Assiniboia). 1857-65. *3283*

Manitoba (St. Boniface). Assimilation. French Canadians. Residential Segregation. 1871-1971. *3343*

Manitoba (St. Boniface, Winnipeg). Belgian Canadians. Immigrants. Nuytten, Edmund. Nuytten, Octavia. 1880-1914. *3463*

Manitoba (St. Boniface, Winnipeg; North End). Boundaries. Neighborhoods. 19c-1978. *102*

Manitoba (Township Berlin). German Canadians. Lutheran Church, Missouri Synod. Wagner, William. ca 1870. *3470*

Manitoba, University of. Americanization. Discrimination, Employment. Higher education. 1970-75. *3591*

Manitoba (Winnipeg). Children. Immigrants. Jews. Public schools. 1900-20. *3520*

—. City Life. Immigration. Jews. 1874-82. *3502*

—. City Politics. Penner, Jacob. Russia. Socialism. 1900-65. *3560*

—. Cold War. Social Classes. Voting and Voting Behavior. 1949-53. *3720*

—. Escapes. Fort Garry. German Canadians. Métis. Red River Rebellion. Riel, Louis. Schultz, John Christian. 1869-70. *3894*

—. Ethnic Relations. Immigrants. Population. Prejudice. 1874-1974. *3013*

—. Ethnicity. Folk art. Latvian Canadians. Ukrainian Canadians. 1978. *3559*

—. French Canadians. Métis. Minnesota (St. Paul). Prairies. Red River of the North. Trade. Trails. 19c. *3210*

—. Fallenius, Carl Johan. Immigration. Swedish Americans. 1811-69. *1765*
—. Family. Historiography. 19c. *2721*
—. Filene, Edward A. Industrial democracy. Jews. Reform. 1890-1937. *1432*
—. Greek Americans. Oral history. Social Classes. 1974. *653*
—. Irish Americans. Kelley, William D. "Pig-Iron". Political Attitudes. 1830's. *727*
—. Jewish Student Movement. Radicals and Radicalism. Social Change. Youth Movements. 1960-75. *1279*
—. New York (Poughkeepsie). Occupational mobility. Pennsylvania (Philadelphia). 19c. *2780*
—. Ohio (Cleveland). Residential patterns. Washington (Seattle). 1930-70. *109*
—. Palestine. Tobin, Maurice Joseph. Zionism. 1926-48. *1550*
—. Religion. Social classes. Wealth. 1880-1920. *2794*
—. Settlement houses. South End House. Woods, Robert A. 1891-1900's. *142*
—. Social mobility. Thernstrom, Stephan (review article). Working class. 1880-1970. *2776*
Massachusetts (Boston area). City government. Immigration. Irish Americans. 16c-1979. *759*
—. Jews. Social change. Suburbs. 1965-75. *1280*
Massachusetts (Boston; North End). Italian Americans. Neighborhoods. Urban Renewal. 1960's-79. *815*
Massachusetts (Boston; Roxbury). Hentoff, Nat. Jews. Neighborhoods. Reminiscences. 1930's. *1215*
Massachusetts (Boston; South Boston). Busing. Civil disobedience. Irish Americans. 19c-1974. *753*
—. Ethnicity. Irish Americans. Social Classes. 19c-20c. *752*
Massachusetts (Boston; South Boston, South End). Birth Rate. Ethnicity. Marriage. Occupations. 1880. *2720*
Massachusetts (Boylston, West Boylston). Construction. French Canadians. Hungarian Americans. Italian Americans. Social Change. Wachusett reservoir. 1889-1902. *93*
Massachusetts (Chelsea). Geographic mobility. Social Organization. 1915. *120*
Massachusetts (Chicopee). Chicopee Manufacturing Company. Immigration. Irish Americans. Mills. Nativism. 1830-75. *711*
Massachusetts (Concord). Attitudes. Irish Americans. Thoreau, Henry David. 1840's-50's. *773*
Massachusetts (Essex County). Assimilation. Great Britain (Isle of Jersey). Huguenots. 1572-1692. *429*
Massachusetts (Fall River). Assimilation. Catholic Church. French Canadians. Hendricken, Thomas F. Irish Americans. 1870's-85. *463*
—. French Canadians. Labor Unions and Organizations. Polish Americans. Portuguese Americans. Textile industry. 1890-1905. *2589*
Massachusetts (Gardner). Nyman, Gustaf. Sculpture. Swedish Americans. Violins. 1864-1954. *1811*
Massachusetts (Gloucester). Acadians. Assimilation. Nova Scotia (Arichat region). 1850's-1900. *480*
Massachusetts (Holyoke). Assimilation. Catholic Church. Clergy. Dufresne, Andre B. French Canadians. 1869-87. *409*
—. Canadians. Family. Irish Americans. 1880. *2742*
—. Daily Life. Family. Housing. Irish Americans. 1860-1910. *2710*
—. French Canadians. Proulx, Nicholas. Working Class. 1850-1900. *366*
Massachusetts (Leicester). American Revolution. Jews, Sephardic. Rhode Island (Newport). 1777-83. *1320*
Massachusetts (Lowell). Anderson, Peder. Cultural Relations. Norway. 1838-74. *1731*
—. French Canadians. Irish Americans. Labor. Textile Industry. Women. 1833-57. *2592*
—. French Canadians. Occupational mobility. Quebec. Working Class. 1870-80. *399*
Massachusetts (Northampton). Anti-Catholicism. Anti-Irish sentiments. Cheverus, Jean Louis Lefebvre de. Daley, Dominic. Halligan, James. Irish Americans. Trials. 1805-06. *180*
—. Anti-Catholicism. Anti-Irish sentiments. Cheverus, Jean Louis Lefebvre de. Irish Americans. Lyon, Marcus. Murder. Trials. 1805-06. *182*

Massachusetts (Springfield). Cotton mills. Demography. French Canadians. 1870. *379*
—. Employment. Greek Americans. Politics. Social Conditions. 1884-1944. *654*
Massachusetts (Waltham). Brandeis University. Educators. Students. 1948-79. *1083*
—. Cook, Adrian. Gitelman, Howard M. New York City. Social Mobility. Urban history (review article). Working Class. 1850-90. *155*
—. Discrimination. Irish Americans. Labor. 1850-90. *724*
Massachusetts (Worcester). Family cycle. Households. Social Change. Urbanization. 1860-80. *2708*
Massacres. Agriculture. French-Indian Relations. Louisiana. Natchez Indians. 1700-31. *482*
—. Civil War. Ethnicity. German Americans. Missouri (Concordia). 1864. *530*
—. Indians. Mennonites. Pacifism. Paxton Boys. Pennsylvania. Politics. Presbyterian Church. 1763-68. *2293*
Masson, Paul. California (Santa Clara Valley). French Americans. Winemaking. 1878-1976. *390*
Mast, Daniel E. Amish. Clergy. German Language. *Herald der Wahrheit* (newspaper). Kansas (Reno County). Language. 1886-1930. *2254*
Match industry. French Canadians. Labor Unions and Organizations. Quebec (Hull). Syndicat Catholique des Allumettières. Women. 1919-24. *3365*
Material Culture. Acculturation. Artifacts. Scandinavian Americans. Social Customs. Utah (Sanpete, Sevier counties). 1849-1979. *1670*
—. Iowa (Decorah). Museums. Norwegian-American Museum (Vesterheim). Pioneers. 1890-1975. *1723*
Materialism. Assimilation. Croatian Americans. Education. Morality. Polish Americans. Slovakian Americans. Ukrainian Americans. 1890-1940. *1875*
—. Morality. Public Schools. Slovakian Americans. Working Class. 1890-1940. *1888*
Mathieu, Olivier-Elzéar. Anglophiles. Catholic Church. Francophiles. Saskatchewan (Regina). 1905-30. *3896*
—. Catholic Church. French Americans. Immigration. Manitoba. Regina Archdiocese. Saskatchewan. 1911-31. *3363*
Matthews, Nathan. Boston Finance Commission. Democratic Party. English Americans. Irish Americans. Massachusetts (Boston). Mayors. Political Reform. 1890-1910. *2462*
Mattick, Paul. Communism ("Council"). German Americans. 1918-39. *2557*
Mattson, Hans. Autobiography. Lundeberg, Axel Johan Sigurd Mauritz. Swedish Americans. 1880-91. *1862*
Mattson, Hans *(Minnen)*. Armies. Journalism. Minnesota. Swedish Americans. 1850's-93. *1818*
Matus, Margaret. Family History. Slovakian Americans. 1910-70's. *1903*
—. Genealogy. Immigration. Slovakian Americans. 1919-78. *1904*
Maurras, Charles. Canada. Conservatism. France. French Canadians. French Canadians. Groulx, Lionel. Nationalism. 1910-40. *3163*
Maxwell, Thomas R. Assimilation. Canada. Choquette, Robert. French Canadians (review article). Joy, Richard. 18c-20c. 1970's. *3396*
May brothers. Acculturation. Clothing industry. Jews. Oklahoma (Tulsa). Retail Trade. 1889-1970. *1505*
Mayer, David. Georgia (Atlanta). Haas (family). Immigration. Jews. Leadership. Levi, Henry. 1845-65. *1281*
Mayer, Saly. American Jewish Joint Distribution Committee. Diplomacy. Jews. World War II. 1944-45. *2655*
Mayors. Boston Finance Commission. Democratic Party. English Americans. Irish Americans. Massachusetts (Boston). Matthews, Nathan. Political Reform. 1890-1910. *2462*
—. Jews. Kraus, William. Ohio (Toledo). 1869-76. *1345*
Mazlish, Bruce (review article). Balance of power. Foreign policy. German Americans. Kissinger, Henry A. 1973-76. *595*
Mazzei, Philip. American Revolution. Italian Americans. Propaganda. 1773-1816. *820*
—. American Revolution. Italian Americans. Vigo, Francis. 1775-83. *795*
—. American Revolution. Italian Americans. Vigo, Francis. 1773-84. *824*

—. Diplomacy. Italian Americans. Jefferson, Thomas. Poland. Stanislaus II Poniatowski. Virginia. ca 1764-95. *844*
Mazzuchelli, Samuel *(Memoirs)*. Catholic Church. Church and state. Democracy. Dominicans. Italian Americans. Old Northwest. 1806-63. *2343*
McCabe, James (and descendants). American Canadians. Irish Canadians. Nova Scotia (Pictou). Pennsylvania (Philadelphia). ca 1743-1917. *3444*
McCaffrey, Lawrence J. (review article). Immigration. Irish Americans. 17c-1976. *709*
McCarran, Patrick A. Law. Nevada. Supreme Courts, state. 1913-18. *713*
McCarthy, D'Alton. Catholic Church. Church Schools. Legislation. Manitoba. 1870-90. *3820*
McCarthy, Patrick Henry. Immigrants. Irish Americans. Labor Unions and Organizations. Leadership. Youth. 1863-80. *760*
McCauly, Mary Hays (Molly Pitcher). American Revolution. Irish Americans. Monmouth (battle). New Jersey. Women. 1778. *775*
McCormack, John. Irish Americans. Music. 1900's-45. *740*
McCullouch, Thomas. Education. Nova Scotia. Pictou Grammar School. Scottish Canadians. 19c. *3449*
McDonald, James G. Documents. Europe. Jews. Refugees. Resettlement. World War II. 1938-43. *2668*
—. Europe. Foreign Policy. Immigration. Palestine. Taylor, Myron. Zionism. 1930's-40's. *2697*
—. Germany. High Commission for Refugees. League of Nations. Nazism. Refugees. 1933-35. *2672*
—. Jews. Refugees. Roosevelt, Franklin D. (administration). State Department. 1933-40's. *2673*
McDonough, Madrienne C. Catholic Church. Church Schools. Girls. Irish Americans. Mount St. Mary Convent. New Hampshire (Manchester). Reminiscences. 1902-09. *2342*
McElroy, Robert M. Education. National Security League. Patriotism. Propaganda. World War I. 1917-19. *2618*
McFarland, Gerald W. (review article). Mugwumps. New York City. Political Attitudes. 1884-1920. 1975. *2472*
McGee, D'Arcy. Anglin, Timothy Warren. Canada. Fenians. Irish Canadians. Political Speeches. 1863-68. *3477*
McGovern, George S. Elections (presidential). Nixon, Richard M. 1972. *2531*
McHale, Tom. Irish Americans. Novels. O'Hara, John. 1934-77. *696*
McKay, James. Hudson's Bay Company. Indians. Manitoba. Métis. Provincial Government. 1853-79. *3211*
McLachlan, Alexander. Ontario. Poetry. Radicals and Radicalism. Scottish Canadians. Social reform. Working class. 1818-96. *3437*
McLean, Mildred Evans. Daily Life. Finnish Americans. Reminiscences. Teaching. Washington (Deep River). 1913-14. *1702*
McLean, W. J. Cree Indians (Plains, Wood). Diaries. Fort Pitt. Frenchman's Butte, Battle of. Indians (captivities). Manitoba. North West Rebellion. Scottish Canadians. 1885. *3913*
McLeod, Evelyn Slater. Alberta (Stettler). American Canadians. Frontier and Pioneer Life. Personal Narratives. Reminiscences. 1900's. *3589*
McMahon, Patrick. Catholic Church. Charities. Irish Canadians. Poor. Quebec (Quebec City). St. Bridget's Home. 1847-1972. *3482*
McManus, Terence Bellew. Fenians. Funerals. Government, Resistance to. Ireland. Irish Americans. 1848-61. *691*
McNailly, John Thomas. Alberta (Calgary Diocese). Catholic Church. French Canadians. Irish Canadians. 1871-1952. *3655*
McRae, C. D. Civil War. German Americans. Nueces (battle). Texas. 1862. *609*
Meagher, Paddy. Bell Tavern. Huling, Tom. Irish Americans. Land transactions. Tennessee (Memphis). 1775-1918. *772*
Mears, Otto. Colorado. Jews. Lobbyists. Republican Party. State Politics. 1876-89. *1405*
—. Colorado (San Juan Mountains). Jews. Mines. Tollroads. 1881-87. *1406*

Miller, Richard G. Benjamin, Philip S. Feldberg, Michael. Pennsylvania (Philadelphia; review article). Sinclair, Bruce. 1790-1920. 1974-76. *183*

Miller, Samuel H. Editors and Editing. German Americans. Mennonites. Pro-German sentiments. Trials. World War I. 1917-18. *2628*

Mills. Chicopee Manufacturing Company. Immigration. Irish Americans. Massachusetts (Chicopee). Nativism. 1830-75. *711*

—. Ice harvesting. Irrigation. Norwegian Americans. Tjossem, Rasmus Peder. Washington (Ellensburg). 1841-1922. *1763*

Millworkers. Ethnicity. Fishermen. New England. Wages. 1972. *2585*

Mine, Mill, and Smelter Workers, International Union of. British Columbia (Trail). Consolidated Mining and Smelting Company. Strikes. World War I. 1916-17. *3728*

Mineral Resources. Canada. Fur trade. Hudson's Bay Company. Scottish Canadians. 17c-20c. *3457*

Miners. Italian Americans. Oklahoma (Krebs). Robertson, J. B. A. Strikes. 1890-1920. *800*

Mines. Agriculture. Colorado. Czech Americans. Migration, Internal. Slovakian Americans. 1860-1920. *1899*

—. Anti-Semitism. Higher Education. Interest Groups. Levine, Louis. Montana State University. 1916-20. *1617*

—. Census. Colorado (San Juan Mountains). 1880-85. *2590*

—. Colorado (Pueblo). Krasovich family. Olyejar family. Slovakian Americans. Slovenian Americans. 1900's-10's. *1880*

—. Colorado (San Juan Mountains). Jews. Mears, Otto. Tollroads. 1881-87. *1406*

Mining *See also* specific types of mining, e.g. Silver Mining.

—. Agriculture. Appalachia. English Americans. Pollard, Thomas. 19c. *290*

—. Assimilation. Immigrants. Quebec. 1941-71. *3050*

—. California (Sonora). Discrimination. Nativism. Newspapers. 1850-60. *190*

—. Economic Development. French Canadians. Quebec (Abitibi, Timiskaming). 1885-1950. *3354*

—. English Americans. Western States. 19c. *296*

—. Entrepreneurs. Frontier thesis. Immigrants. Social mobility. Western states. 1870-1900. *2801*

—. Finnish Americans. Immigrants. North Central States. Radicals and Radicalism. Social Conditions. Swedish Americans. 1865-1920. *1692*

—. Investments. Jews. Marks, Anna. Real estate. Utah (Eureka City). 1880-1900. *1463*

Ministers. See Clergy.

Minnesota *See also* North Central States.

—. Anti-Semitism. Benson, Elmer A. Political Campaigns (gubernatorial). 1930's. *1602*

—. Armies. Journalism. Mattson, Hans *(Minnen)*. Swedish Americans. 1850's-93. *1818*

—. Artists. Dehn, Adolph. Ethnicity. German Americans. Radicals and Radicalism. Satirists. 1895-1968. *508*

—. Assimilation. Diaries. Immigration. Jonsson, Jonas (John Johnson). Swedish Americans. 1864-95. *1803*

—. Bacteriologists. Education. Historians. Larson, Agnes. Larson, Henrietta. Larson, Nora. Norwegian Americans. Women. 1883-1972. *1736*

—. Book Industries and Trade. German Americans. 1850-1935. *628*

—. Diaries. Peterson, Andrew. Swedish Americans. 1849-1972. *1825*

—. Elementary Education. Johnson, Emeroy. Lutheran Church. Reminiscences. Swedish Americans. ca 1854-ca 1920. *1805*

—. Evjen, John O. Lutheran Church. Theologians. 1874-1942. *2392*

—. Farmers. German Americans. Standke family. 1873-1974. *575*

—. Federal Writers' Project. Finnish Americans. Interviews. 1930's. *1697*

—. Finnish Americans. Loyalty. Political Repression. Socialism. Syndicalism. 1917-20. *2638*

—. Finnish Americans. Sauna. 1867-1937. *1694*

—. German Americans. Lutheran Church (Missouri Synod). Missouri. Swedish Americans. Wihlborg, Niels Albert. 1893-1918. *2407*

—. Historiography. Hokanson, Nels M. Immigration. Swedish Americans. 20c. *1853*

—. Holt, Benjamin M. Lutheran Church. Reminiscences. 1882-1974. *2395*

—. Homesteading and Homesteaders. Immigration. North Dakota (Sheyenne River Valley). Norwegian Americans. Skrien, Johnson. 1870's-1930's. *1758*

—. Immigration. Johnson, Nils Johan ("Wood-John"). Swedish Americans. 1828-1909. *1807*

—. Immigration. Persson, Johan. Settlement. Swedish Americans. 1874-75. *1806*

—. Lundeberg, Axel Johan Sigurd Mauritz. Swedish Americans. Theology. 1852-1940. *1863*

Minnesota (Chicago Lake area). Karl Oskar (fictional character). Linnell, Magnus Jonasson. Moberg, Vilhelm. Novels. Sweden (Kronsberg area). Swedish Americans. 1820-75. 20c. *1764*

Minnesota (Chisago County). Ethnicity. Population. Swedish Americans. 1885-1905. *1843*

Minnesota (Chisago Lake). Andersson, Joris Per. Immigration. Letters. Swedish Americans. 1851-53. *1804*

Minnesota (Chisago Lakes area). Moberg, Vilhelm. Novels. Swedes. Tourism. 1948. *1834*

Minnesota (Gentilly). Catholic Church. French Canadians. Settlement. Theillon, Elie. 1870's-1974. *364*

Minnesota (Isantic County). Acculturation. Agriculture. Immigration. Lutheran Church. Social customs. Swedish Americans. 1840-1910. *1842*

Minnesota (Kandiyohi County). Dutch Americans. Federal government. Land policy. Settlement. Swedish Americans. ca 1850-1900's. *68*

Minnesota (Mesabi Range). Finnish Americans. Iron Industry. Labor Unions and Organizations. Radicals and Radicalism. 1914-17. *1705*

Minnesota (Minneapolis). Americanization. North East Neighborhood House. Progressivism. Settlement houses. Social Reform. 1910's-20's. *95*

—. Boardinghouses. Immigrants. Labor. Women's Christian Association. 1880's-1979. *153*

—. Brin, Fanny Fligelman. Jews. Peace. Women. 1913-60's. *1492*

—. Deinard, Samuel N. Ethnicity. Jews. 1915-21. *1265*

—. Family. Immigration. Lindbäck, Ola. Lindbäck, Verner. Research. Swedish Americans. 1906-76. *1781*

—. Immigration. *Svenska Bröderna* (Swedish Brothers organization). Swedish Americans. Voluntary Associations. 1876-88. *1840*

—. Norwegian Americans. Novels. Social Conditions. 1887-89. *1760*

Minnesota (New Ulm). Behnke, Henry. German Americans. Indian Wars. Sioux Indians. 1833-79. *511*

Minnesota (St. Cloud Diocese). Catholic Church. Culture region. Immigrants. 1860-1973. *2369*

Minnesota (St. Paul). Catholic Church. Irish Americans. North Dakota (Jamestown Diocese). Shanley, John. 1852-1909. *2326*

—. French Canadians. Manitoba (Winnipeg). Métis. Prairies. Red River of the North. Trade. Trails. 19c. *3210*

—. Irish Americans. O'Brien, Alice. Philanthropy. Women. 1914-62. *750*

Minnesota (St. Paul; Lower West Side). Immigrants. Jews. Settlement. ca 1860-1920. *1259*

Minnesota (Sunrise). Genealogy. Immigration. Research. Swedish Americans. 1890-1972. *1847*

Minnesota, University of (St. Paul). Archives. Immigration. Immigration History Research Center. Labor history. 1890-1960. *33*

—. Ethnic Fraternal Project. Immigration. Immigration History Research Center. International Institutes Project. Organizations. 1976-78. *35*

—. Immigration History Research Center. Microfilm. Newspapers. Polish Microfilm Project. 1975. *1990*

Minnesota (Winona). Catholic Church. Franciscan Sisters. Irish Americans. Molloy, Mary Aloysius. St. Teresa, College of. Women. 1903-54. *739*

Minorities *See also* Discrimination; Ethnicity; Nationalism; Nationalities; Population; Racism; Segregation.

—. British Canadians. Canada. Irish Canadians. Prejudice. 1970's. *3065*

—. Charter of the French Language (1977). French language. Language Policy. Quebec. 1913-77. *4059*

—. Economic Conditions. French Canadians. Quebec. Separatist Movements. 1976. *4002*

—. Education. North Carolina. Prejudice. Religious orthodoxy. World view. 1957-73. *262*

—. Ethnic studies. Sociology. 1960's-70's. *3003*

—. Italian Americans. LaGuardia, Fiorello H. Marginalism. New York City (Harlem). 1944. *805*

—. Jews. Lewin, Kurt. Social psychology. 1935-70. *1053*

Minorities in Politics. Acadians. Assimilation. Emigration. New Brunswick (Moncton). 1871-1971. *3346*

—. Assiniboia, Council of. French Canadians. Manitoba. Métis. 1860-71. *3282*

—. Canada. Confederation. Creighton, D. G. English Canadians. French Canadians. Heintzman, Ralph. 1850's-90's. *3908*

—. Civil rights. Jews. Liberals. New York City. Social reform. 1963-70's. *985*

—. Dargo, George (review article). French Americans. Law. Louisiana. 1803-08. 1975. *414*

Mintz, Jerome R. Ben-Amos, Dan. Folklore (review article). Jews. Rappoport, Angelo S. 1937-72. *980*

Minville, Esdras. *Action Nationale* (periodical). French Canadians. Quebec. 1933. *3349*

—. Agriculture. Duplessis, Maurice. Federalism. Forests and Forestry. Industrialization. Letters. Natural resources. Quebec. 20c. *3917*

—. Arès, Richard. French Canadians. Quebec. Tremblay Commission. 1953-56. *3892*

—. Bibliographies. Economic Theory. French Canadians. Quebec. 20c. *3326*

—. École des Hautes Études Commerciales. Economics. Educators. French Canadians. Quebec (Montreal). 20c. *3313*

—. Economic development. Forests and Forestry. French Canadians. Multinational corporations. Quebec. USA. 1923-36. *3357*

—. Economic Theory. French Canadians. Quebec. 20c. *3314*

—. Economics. French Canadians. Periodicals. Quebec (Montreal). 1922-28. *3372*

Minville, Esdras (eulogy). Catholic Church. French Canadians. Quebec. 1975. *3315*

Miranda, Francisco de. Germany (Berlin). Intellectuals. Jews. Mendelssohn, Moses. Smith, William Stephens. 1785. *1059*

Miron, Gaston. French Canadians. Poetry. Quebec. Sovereignty. 1969-74. *3991*

Mission Festival Sunday. German Americans. Lutheran Church. Missions and Missionaries. Reminiscences. Schreiber, Clara Seuel. Wisconsin (Freistadt). 1900. *2414*

Mission St. Jean-Baptiste. Catholic Church. Chipewyan Indians. French Canadians. Indian-White Relations. Letters. Saskatchewan (Île-à-la-Crosse). Taché, Alexandre Antonin. 1823-54. *3652*

Missions and Missionaries. Africa. Dutch Americans. German Americans. Protestant churches. 19c-20c. *2377*

—. Agriculture. Immigration. Politics. Sects, Religious. Settlement. South Dakota. 1850-1900. *55*

—. Alaska. Diaries. Indian-White Relations. Library of Congress (Alaska Church Collection). Orlov, Vasili. Orthodox Eastern Church, Russian. 1886. *2106*

—. Americas (North and South). Discovery and Exploration. Indians. Madog ab Owain Gwynedd (legend). Myths and symbols. Welsh. 16c-18c. *325*

—. Antislavery Sentiments. Germans, Sudeten. Journalism. Kudlich, Hans. Neumann, John Nepomucene. Ottendorfer, Oswald. Postl, Karl (pseud. Charles Sealsfield). Republican Party. 19c-20c. *593*

—. Arapaho Indians. German Americans. Haury, Samuel S. Indian Territory. Letters. Mennonites. 1876-80. *2220*

—. Arndt, E. L. China. Lutheran Church. 1913-29. *2422*

—. Atlantic Provinces (review article). French Canadians. Historiography. Politics. 1000-1770. 19c. *3128*

—. Attitudes. Colonial Government. Explorers. French Canadians. Games. Indians. 16c-17c. *3206*

—. Attitudes. French. Indians. Jesuits. New France. 1611-72. *3179*

—. German-American Bund. Germany. Kuhn, Fritz. 1936-41. *2679*

—. Germany. High Commission for Refugees. League of Nations. McDonald, James G. Refugees. 1933-35. *2672*

—. Judaism, Reform. Zionism. 1917-41. *1545*

Near East. *See* Middle East.

Nebraska *See also* Western States.

—. Assimilation. Immigrants. Swiss Americans. 1975. *2142*

—. Colorado. Daily Life. Frontier and Pioneer Life. Ouren, Hogan. Reminiscences. 1861-66. *1725*

—. Emigration. Great Britain. Letters-to-the-editor. *London Times* (newspaper). 1872. *307*

—. Frontier and Pioneer Life. Swedish Americans. 1870-90. *1786*

—. Germans, Russian. Immigration. Kansas. Mennonites. 1884-93. *2189*

Nebraska (Cherry County). Anderson, John A. Homesteading and Homesteaders. Reminiscences. Roosa, Alma Carlson. Swedish Americans. 1880's. *1849*

Nebraska Council of Defense. Church Schools. German language. Language. Lutheran Church (Missouri Synod). Supreme Court. 1917-23. *2627*

Nebraska (Lincoln). Clerks. Courts. Jews. Newmark, Nellie. 1888-1978. *1514*

Nebraska (Omaha). Artists. German Americans. Portraits. Sloan, John. Storz, Gottlieb. 1912. *546*

—. Charities. Jews. Political Leadership. Refugees. Settlement. 1820-1937. *1197*

—. Economic Conditions. Race Relations. Riots. Social Conditions. 1919. *122*

—. Franklin, Leo M. Jews. Rabbis. Temple Israel. 1892-99. *1370*

—. German Americans. Gottlieb Storz (home). Preservation. 1907-79. *587*

—. Judaism. Temple Israel. 1867-1908. *1196*

—. Residential patterns. 1880-1920. *98*

Nebraska (Saunders County). Gibson, Peter. Pioneers. Swedish Americans. 1836-1924. *1848*

Nebraska (Weyerts). German Americans. Helmreich, Christian. Letters. Lutheran Church. 1887-88. *2394*

Necrology. Kuhnle, Howard A. Lutheran Church. 1950-73. *2398*

Neff, Christian. Mennonite World Conference. 1910-78. *2203*

Négrin, Jean-Jacques. Daudet, Charles Alexis. French Americans. *Hémisphère. Journal des Dames.* Literature. New York City. Pennsylvania (Philadelphia). Periodicals. *Petit Censeur.* Political Commentary. 1805. *423*

"Negro King" hypothesis. Foreign Investments. French Canadians. Politics. Provincial Government. Quebec. Taschereau, Louis Alexandre. 1920-36. *3931*

Negroes *See also* Black Power; Civil War; Confederate States of America; Discrimination; Race Relations; Racism; Reconstruction; Slavery.

—. Abolition Movement. Pennsylvania (Philadelphia). Riots. 1830-50. *2886*

—. Acculturation. Cajuns. Louisiana (Houma). Texans. 1945-73. *479*

—. Acculturation. Education. Immigrants. Massachusetts (Boston). Social status. 1850. *2820*

—. Affirmative action. Anti-Semitism. Bakke, Allan. *Regents of the University of California* v. *Allan Bakke* (US, 1978). 1964-78. *1140*

—. Affirmative Action. Discrimination. Health, Education, and Welfare Department. Jews. 1973. *978*

—. Affirmative action. Ethnic studies. Ideology. 1964-73. *2878*

—. Africa. Foreign policy. Lobbying. Polish Americans. 1944-73. *2600*

—. Agricultural labor. Immigration. Italian Americans. Newspapers, black. South. 1880-1915. *884*

—. Anti-Semitism. 20c. *1631*

—. Anti-Semitism. Ethnicity. Jews. Liberals. 1969. *917*

—. Anti-Semitism. Jews. Race Relations. 1970. *1643*

—. Anti-Semitism. Middle Classes. Political Leadership. 1965-79. *1616*

—. Arab Americans. Attitudes. Greek Americans. Irish Americans. Polish Americans. Zionism (opposition to). 1912-41. *1544*

—. Arab Americans. Six-Day War. Zionism. 1941-70's. *1546*

—. Assimilation. City Life. Migration. Occupations. Pennsylvania (Pittsburgh). Polish Americans. 1900-30. *1951*

—. Assimilation. Education. Immigrants. Racism. 1890-1966. *2857*

—. Assimilation. Immigration. Pennsylvania (Philadelphia). 1850-1970. *111*

—. Assimilation. Jews. 1974. *923*

—. Attitudes. Poverty programs. 1960-72. *2995*

—. Authors. Jews. Race Relations. 1956-70. *1026*

—. Barthé, Richmond. Creoles. Sculpture. 1901-75. *435*

—. Baseball. Immigrants. Social mobility. 1900-16. *2803*

—. Businessmen. Democratic Party. Elections. Immigrants. New York City (Brooklyn). Racism. Suffrage. 1860. *2460*

—. Cities. German Americans. Irish Americans. Italian Americans. Nativism. Riots. 19c-20c. *2890*

—. Civil War. German Americans. Irish Americans. Labor. 1780-1860. *2602*

—. Civil War. Immigrants. Irish Americans. Race Relations. 1830's-90's. *735*

—. Coal Mines and Mining. Immigrants. West Virginia. 1890-1917. *2552*

—. Colleges and Universities. Educational reform. Ethnicity. Teaching. 1950's-70's. *2992*

—. Colleges and Universities. Jews. Literature. Stereotypes. Students. 1933-69. *968*

—. Comparative History. Genocide. History Teaching. Indians. Jews. Racism. 20c. *2675*

—. Conley, James. Frank, Leo M. Georgia (Atlanta). Jews. Press. Trials. 1913-15. *1624*

—. Demography. Immigrants. Retail Trade. Urbanization. 1890-1910. *2786*

—. Dever, William. Elections (mayoral). Illinois (Chicago). Prohibition. 1923-27. *2445*

—. Discrimination. Folklore. Jews. Stereotypes. 18c-1974. *990*

—. Discrimination. Jews. Racism. 1890-1915. *952*

—. Economic Conditions. Jews. Race Relations. Social Organization. 1940's-70's. *1141*

—. Education. Levy, William. Northwest Texas Colored Citizens College. Social Mobility. Speeches, Addresses, etc. Texas (Sherman). 1890. *1025*

—. Elections (presidential). Tennessee. Voting and Voting Behavior. 1928. *2458*

—. Emancipation. Ghettos. Jews. 15c-20c. *1015*

—. Employment. Illinois (Chicago). Industry. Polish Americans. Stereotypes. Violence. 1890-1919. *2031*

—. Ethnicity. Ghettos. Jews. Literature. 20c. *1095*

—. Ethnicity. Illinois (Chicago). Neighborhoods. Polish Americans. 1920-70. *2018*

—. Ethnicity. Jews. Lumbee Indians. South Carolina (Robeson County). Stereotypes. 1967-68. *912*

—. Ghettos. Social Problems. 1890-1940. *139*

—. Immigrants. International Brotherhood of Pulp, Sulphite, and Paper Mill Workers. Pacific Northwest. South. Women. 1909-40. *2594*

—. Immigrants. Italian Americans. Louisiana. Race Relations. Sugar cane industry. 1880-1910. *879*

—. Immigration. Washington, Booker T. (Atlanta Exposition Address). 1895. *222*

—. Intellectuals. Jews. Race Relations. 1970's. *1645*

—. Iron Industry. Italian Americans. Labor recruitment. Letters. Pennsylvania (Reading). Robesonia Iron Company. Slavic Americans. 1915-23. *2556*

—. Italian Americans. Occupational mobility. Pennsylvania (Steelton). Slavic Americans. 1880-1920. *2555*

—. Italian Americans. Press (black). 1886-1936. *883*

—. Jews. 1960's-70's. *994*

—. Jews. Kaplan, Kivie (obituary). NAACP. Race Relations. 1975. *1395*

—. Jews. Literature. 1975. *1087*

—. Jews. New York (Syracuse). Race Relations. 1787-1977. *1324*

—. Jews. Politics. Race Relations. Social Conditions. 1930's-79. *1065*

—. Jews. Race Relations. 1960-74. *1091*

—. Jews. Race Relations. 1800-1940. *1145*

—. Louisiana (Opelousas, Washington). Residential patterns. 1860-80. *131*

—. Missouri (St. Louis). Neighborhoods. Segregation. 1850-1930. *146*

—. New Jersey. Political candidates. Voting and Voting Behavior. 1960's-70's. *2497*

—. School Integration. 1964-78. *3006*

—. Social Status. Women. 19c-20c. *2985*

Negroes (free). Employment. Immigration. Nativism. Politics. 1830-60. *195*

Neidhardt, W. S. Anglin, Timothy Warren. Baker, W. M. Canada. Fenians. Irish Canadians (review article). 19c. *3489*

Neighborhood House. Children. Council of Jewish Women. Jews. Oregon (Portland). Women. 1895-1905. *1172*

Neighborhoods. Acculturation. Ethnicity. German Americans. 1840's-1970's. *100*

—. Boundaries. Manitoba (St. Boniface, Winnipeg; North End). 19c-1978. *102*

—. Business. California (San Francisco; San Bruno Avenue). Esther Hellman Settlement House. Jews. 1901-68. *1239*

—. Catholic Church. Cities. Protestant ethic. Segregation. Social mobility. Values. 1970's. *145*

—. Cities. 1979. *113*

—. City life. Pennsylvania (Philadelphia; Fairmount). Social Change. 1960's-70's. *101*

—. City planning. Housing. Population. Public policy. 1890-1979. *106*

—. Ethnicity. Illinois (Chicago). Negroes. Polish Americans. 1920-70. *2018*

—. Farrell, James T. Illinois (Chicago; Washington Park). Irish Americans. Novels. Social history. 1904-79. *718*

—. Hentoff, Nat. Jews. Massachusetts (Boston; Roxbury). Reminiscences. 1930's. *1215*

—. Italian Americans. Massachusetts (Boston; North End). Urban Renewal. 1960's-79. *815*

—. Maryland (Baltimore). 1850-70. *105*

—. Michigan (Detroit). Population. 1880-85. *156*

—. Missouri (St. Louis). Negroes. Segregation. 1850-1930. *146*

—. New York City. Residential patterns. 1730. *154*

—. New York City. Socialism. Working class. 1908-18. *2574*

Neiman-Marcus Company. Clothing. Department stores. Jews. Marketing. Texas (Dallas). 1900-17. *1389*

—. Fashion. Marketing. Texas (Dallas). 1880-1970. *1363*

Nelson, Bersven. Civil War. Diaries. Norwegian Americans. Wisconsin Regiment, 15th. 1861-63. *1744*

Nelson, E. Clifford. Ecumenism. Lutheran Church. 1945-69. *2410*

Nelson, Edward O. Reminiscences. Salvation Army (Scandinavian Corps). Scandinavian Americans. 1877-1977. *1668*

Nelson, Nelson O. Businessmen. Cooperatives. Norwegian Americans. Profit-sharing. Social Reform. 1886-1904. *1740*

Nerigin, Peter. Canada. Dukhobors. Immigration. Persecution. Russian Canadians. 1654-1902. *3696*

Netherlands. Congregation Shearith Israel. Jews. New York. Pinto, Joseph Jesurun. Travel. 1759-82. *1465*

—. French Canadians. Great Britain. Iroquois Indians. Jesuits. Missions and Missionaries. New York. 1642-1719. *45*

Netherlands (Amsterdam). Bibliotheca Rosenthaliana. Book Collecting. Felsenthal, Bernard. Illinois (Chicago). Letters. Roest, Meyer. Rosenthal, George. 1868-96. *1365*

Neumann, John Nepomucene. Antislavery Sentiments. Germans, Sudeten. Journalism. Kudlich, Hans. Missions and Missionaries. Ottendorfer, Oswald. Postl, Karl (pseud. Charles Sealsfield). Republican Party. 19c-20c. *593*

—. Beatification. Catholic Church. Germans, Sudeten. Pennsylvania (Philadelphia). 1830's-1963. *2338*

—. Canonization. Germans, Sudeten. Vatican Council II. 19c. 1962-65. *2355*

—. Catholic Church. Czech Americans. Pennsylvania (Philadelphia). 1811-1977. *1942*

Neustader, David. California. Houses. Jews. Leow, Jacob. Levy, Edward R. Meyberg, Max. Neustader, Jacob. Photographs. Stern, Jacob. 1890's. *1510*

Neustader, Jacob. California. Houses. Jews. Leow, Jacob. Levy, Edward R. Meyberg, Max. Neustader, David. Photographs. Stern, Jacob. 1890's. *1510*

Neustadt, Samuel I. California (San Francisco). Charities. Cholera. Jews. 1850. *1296*

—. Berdahl Family. Rølvaag, Ole Edvart (*Giants in the Earth*). South Dakota. 1873-1900. *1748*

—. Businessmen. Cooperatives. Nelson, Nelson O. Profit-sharing. Social Reform. 1886-1904. *1740*

—. California. Gold Rushes. Lumber and Lumbering. Week, Andrew. Week, John. Wisconsin. 1838-60. *1752*

—. Choral societies. Ethnicity. Iowa (Decorah). Luren Quartet. Politics. 1868-1911. *1722*

—. Civil War. Diaries. Nelson, Bersven. Wisconsin Regiment, 15th. 1861-63. *1744*

—. Clergy. Education. Ethnicity. Evangelical Lutheran Synod. Midwest. 1853-80. *1743*

—. Community Participation in Politics. Danish Americans. Naturalization. Public Records. Swedish Americans. Wisconsin (Milwaukee). 1837-1941. *1658*

—. Country Life. Iowa. Langland, Joseph (interview). Poetry. Youth. 1917-30's. 1977. *1726*

—. Country Life. Iowa. Oral History Project. 1900-60. *1761*

—. Daily Life. Letters. 1867-96. *1751*

—. Danish Americans. Democratic Party. Finnish Americans. Progressive Movement. Republican Party. Swedish Americans. Voting and Voting Behavior. Wisconsin. 1900-50. *2490*

—. Depressions. German Americans. Meat Industry. North Dakota (Williston). Soup kitchens. Vohs, Al J. (interview). 1900's-30's. *2906*

—. Dutch Americans. Ethnicity. German Americans. Polish Americans. Wisconsin. 19c-20c. *2967*

—. Editors and Editing. Iowa. Settlement. South Dakota. 1865-1941. *1729*

—. Emigration. Norway (Hegra). 1865-90. *1738*

—. Emigration. Norway (Land Parish). 1866-75. *1753*

—. Ethnicity. Lovoll, Odd Sverre (review article). Settlement. 1899-1939. *1754*

—. Family. Immigration. Semmingsen, Inge (review article). Social conditions. 1815-1930. *1750*

—. Folklore. Happiness, search for. Literature. Rølvaag, Ole Edvart. 1925-37. *1733*

—. Gjerset, Knut. Historians. Publishers and Publishing. Social Organizations. 1873-1935. *1745*

—. Haakon VII. Independence. Norway. Press. Public opinion. 1905-1906. *1737*

—. Hansen, Marcus Lee. Historiography. Puritans. Temperance movements. 19c. 1920's-30's. *1727*

—. Holth, Walborg Strom. Illinois (Chicago). Letters. South Dakota. Travel accounts. 1882. *1735*

—. Homesteading and Homesteaders. Immigration. Minnesota. North Dakota (Sheyenne River Valley). Skrien, Johnson. 1870's-1930's. *1758*

—. Ice harvesting. Irrigation. Mills. Tjossem, Rasmus Peder. Washington (Ellensburg). 1841-1922. *1763*

—. Immigrants. Indiana (New Harmony). Letters. Pennsylvania (Harmony). Rapp, George. 1816-26. *1716*

—. Indians. Lutheran Church. Missions and Missionaries. Morstad, Eric O. Wisconsin. 1895-1920. *1741*

—. Iowa (Decorah). Literature. Prestgard, Kristian. *Smyra* (periodical). Wist, Johannes B. 1905-15. *1730*

—. Iowa (Decorah). Luther College. Reminiscences. Veblen, Andrew A. 1877-81. *1762*

—. Kendall Colony. Migration, Internal. New York. 1830-1925. *1719*

—. Literature. Wisconsin (Madison). Ygdrasil Literary Society. 1896-1971. *1742*

—. Migration, Internal. Mordt, Anders L. Settlement. Texas (Hansford County; Oslo). 1908-50. *1749*

—. Minnesota (Minneapolis). Novels. Social Conditions. 1887-89. *1760*

—. Mormons. Polygamy. 1840's-1904. *1756*

—. Odegard, Ethel J. Reminiscences. Wisconsin (Merrill). 1874-1974. *1747*

—. Postal Service. Sierra Madre Mountains. Skiing. Thompson, John A. "Snowshoe". Western States. 1827-76. *1724*

—. Shipbuilding. Wisconsin (Milwaukee). 19c. *1715*

Norwegian Canadians. Canada. Finnish Canadians. Skiing. 1879-1935. *3532*

Norwegian Lutheran Church. Frontier and Pioneer Life. Letters. Montana, eastern. Thorpe, Christian Scriver. 1906-08. *1714*

Norwegian Lutheran Church of America. Name change. Nativism. World War I. 1918-20. *1721*

Norwegian-American Historical Association. Historical societies. Swedish Pioneer Historical Society. 1974-75. *1661*

Norwegian-American Museum (Vesterheim). Iowa (Decorah). Material Culture. Museums. Pioneers. 1890-1975. *1723*

Norwegians. Attitudes. Christianity. 1830-1972. *1718*

Notaries, royal. Colonial Government. France. French Canadians. Quebec. 1663-1764. *3268*

Notre Dame, University of. Catholic Church. Indiana. Political Theory. *Review of Politics* (periodical). 1938-78. *2365*

Nova Scotia *See also* Atlantic Provinces.

—. Acadians. Acculturation. Exiles. France. Great Britain. 18c. *3860*

—. Acadians. Colonial Government. Exiles. Great Britain. Land tenure. Loyalty. Oaths of allegiance. 11c-1755. *3850*

—. Acadians. Exiles. Great Britain. 1710-55. *3233*

—. Acadians. Exiles. St. Lawrence, Gulf of. 1756-95. *3309*

—. Acadians. Institutions. Nationalism. Social Organization. 1700's-1970. *3132*

—. Akins, Thomas Beamish. French Canadians. Public Records. 1857-91. *3852*

—. American Canadians. Rogers, Rolen (and family). 1760-1979. *3596*

—. Architecture. French Canadians. Guardhouses. Louisbourg, Fortress of. Military Camps and Forts. 1713-68. *3236*

—. Aulnay-Charnisay, Charles d'. Hundred Associates. Quebec. Settlement. 17c. *3178*

—. Cary, James. Great Britain. Jamaica. Loyalists. 1781-1804. *3583*

—. Champlain, Samuel de. French Canadians. L'Ordre de Bon Temps. Voluntary Associations. 1606-07. *3265*

—. Church of England. Loyalists. Society for the Propagation of the Gospel. 1787-1864. *3600*

—. Cochran, William. Education. Enlightenment. Loyalists. 1789. *3585*

—. Composers. Land. Military. Reid, John. Scottish Canadians. 1740's-1807. *3442*

—. Denys brothers. French Canadians. Fur trade. Shipping. 17c. *3240*

—. Economic Conditions. Employment. New Brunswick. Rural Settlements. 1961-76. *3049*

—. Economic Conditions. French Canadians. King George's War. Louisbourg, fortress of. New England. 1745-50. *3861*

—. Education. McCullouch, Thomas. Pictou Grammar School. Scottish Canadians. 19c. *3449*

—. French. King George's War. Louisbourg, Fortress of. Mutinies. 1744-45. *3213*

—. French Canadians. Langille family. 1718-1804. *3101*

—. French Canadians. Louisbourg, fortress of. Military Camps and Forts. Restorations. 1654-1745. 1928-73. *3226*

—. French Canadians. Surette family. 18c-1979. *3100*

—. German Canadians. Immigrants. Protestants. 1749-52. *3467*

—. Immigration. Scottish Canadians. 1800-20. *3441*

—. Irish Canadians. Political Leadership. Uniacke, James Boyle. Uniacke, Richard John. 1775-1858. *3481*

—. Loyalists. M'Alpine, John. New York. Occupations. 1748-1827. *3595*

Nova Scotia (Annapolis County; Wilmot Township). Burns family. Immigration. Scotch Irish. 1764-20c. *3445*

Nova Scotia (Arichat region). Acadians. Assimilation. Massachusetts (Gloucester). 1850's-1900. *480*

Nova Scotia (Beaubassin). Excavations. French Canadians. Glassware. Settlement. Towns. ca 1670-1800's. *3218*

Nova Scotia (Canso, Cape Breton). Colonial Government. France. Great Britain. New England. 1710-21. *3851*

Nova Scotia (Cape Breton; Arichat). Acadians. Genealogy. LaVache family. 1774-20c. *3174*

Nova Scotia (Cape Breton Island). Daily life. French Canadians. Historical Sites and Parks. Louisbourg, Fortress of. Social classes. 1713-50. *3249*

—. French Canadians. King George's War. Louisbourg (siege). Military Service (enlistees). New England. 1745. *3846*

—. Loyalists. Settlement. 1784-1820. *3590*

Nova Scotia (Cape Breton; Port Hood Island). American Canadians. Bird, Lilah Smith. Daily Life. Reminiscences. ca 1907-70. *3572*

Nova Scotia (Chedabucto). Challe, Robert. Colonization. French Canadians. Quebec. Travel Accounts. 1681. *3263*

Nova Scotia (Dartmouth). American Canadians. Friends, Society of. Marriage. 1786-89. *3582*

Nova Scotia (Halifax). Atlantic Institute of Education. High Schools. History Teaching. Loyalists. Maine, University of, Orono (Canadian-American Center). 1775-83. 1977-79. *3577*

—. Beamish family. Genealogy. Irish Canadians. 1765-1970's. *3485*

—. French. Hugo, Adèle. 1863-66. *3288*

—. Genealogy. Howe, John (and family). Loyalists. 18c-19c. *3594*

—. Irish Canadians. Tobin, Thomas (and descendants). ca 1759-1936. *3486*

—. Loyalists. Trade. 1783-1850. *3598*

Nova Scotia (Halifax, Lunenburg). Genealogy. German Canadians. West family. Wuest, Johann Wendel. 17c-20c. *3469*

Nova Scotia (Hants County). Genealogy. Scottish Canadians. Weatherhead family. ca 1820-1946. *3436*

Nova Scotia (Lochaber). Daily Life. Immigrants. Rural Settlements. 1830-1972. *3048*

—. Howe, Joseph ("Acadie"). Immigration. Rural Development. 1795-1880. *3439*

Nova Scotia (Lockport). American Canadians. American Revolution. Fishing. Privateers. 18c. *3587*

Nova Scotia (Louisbourg). Fishing. France (Poitou; Les Sables d'Olonne). Huart, Christophle-Albert-Alberic d'. Nobility. 1750-75. *3184*

Nova Scotia (Lunenburg Township). Bachman, John Baptist (and descendants). German Canadians. 1752-1952. *3464*

Nova Scotia (Pictou). American Canadians. Irish Canadians. McCabe, James (and descendants). Pennsylvania (Philadelphia). ca 1743-1917. *3444*

—. Dawson, William. Letters. Mercer, Margaret. Scottish Canadians. 1840-47. *3435*

—. MacGregor, James. Missions and Missionaries. Presbyterian Church of Scotland. Scottish Canadians. 1786-1830. *3453*

—. Scottish Canadians. Settlement. 1773-1971. *3451*

Nova Scotia (Pictou County). Blair, Duncan Black. Gaelic language. Language. Poetry. Scholars. Scottish Canadians. 1846-93. *3454*

—. Presbyterian Church. Scottish Canadians. Social Conditions. 1898-1966. *3433*

Nova Scotia (Pictou Harbor). *Hector* (vessel). Immigrants. Mackenzie, Alexander. Passenger lists. Scottish Canadians. 1773. 1883. *3443*

—. *Hector* (vessel). Immigration. Scottish Canadians. Voyages. 1773. *3452*

Nova Scotia (Port Royal). Champlain, Samuel de. French Canadians. L'Ordre de Bon Temps. Voluntary Associations. 1606. *3264*

—. Charles I. Colonization. France. Great Britain. Scotland. 1629-32. *3448*

—. Diaries. French Canadians. Military Campaigns. Phipps, William. 1690. *3865*

—. French Canadians. Immigration. Population. 1650-1755. *3220*

Nova Scotia (St. Ann's). MacLeod, Norman. Migration. Presbyterian Church. Scottish Canadians. ca 1800-50's. *3434*

Nova Scotia (St. Mary's River Valley). French Canadians. Settlement. 1655-1880. *3129*

Novak, Michael (review article). 1960's-70's. *2976*

Novels. Acculturation. Immigrants. Jews. Jews. 1900-17. *947*

—. America (image). French Canadians. Hébert, Anne. Lemelin, Roger. Panneton, Philippe (Ringuet, pseud.). Quebec. 1940's-70's. *3412*

—. Americanization. Lemelin, Roger (*Les Plouffe*). Nationalism. Quebec. 1938-45. *3932*

—. Anti-Catholicism. Anti-Irish sentiments. Breslin, Jimmy. Flaherty, Joe. Hamill, Pete. Irish Americans. New York City (Brooklyn). 1960's-70's. *701*

—. Anti-Semitism. Banking. California. Norris, Frank (*The Octopus*). Pollasky, Marcus. S. Behrman (fictional character). 1880's-1901. *1614*

P

Pietists. Astronomy. German Americans. *Horologium Achaz.* Pennsylvania. Witt, Christopher. 1578-1895. *643*

Pinard, Maurice (review article). French Canadians. Quebec. Social Credit Party. Stein, Michael (review article). 1971-74. *3927*

Pinto, Joseph Jesurun. Congregation Shearith Israel. Jews. Netherlands. New York. Travel. 1759-82. *1465*

Pinzer, Maimie. Davidson, Sue. Howe, Fanny Quincy. Jews. Rosen, Ruth. Social Classes. Women (review article). 1910-22. 1977. *1085*

Pioneer Band. Aurora Colony. German Americans. Music. Oregon. Utopias. 1855-1920's. *585*

Pioneers *See also* Frontier and Pioneer Life; Homesteading and Homesteaders; Voyages.
—. Bibliographies. French. LaHarpe, Jean-Baptiste Bénard de. Louisiana. 1718-22. *476*
—. California. Jews. Marks, Bernhard. 1852-1913. *1439*
—. California. Jews, Sephardic. 1850-1900. *1300*
—. California (San Diego). Interethnic Relations. Jews. 1850-60. *1098*
—. Charbonneau, Toussaint. French Canadians. Sacagawea (Shoshoni Indian). Westward Movement. 1759-1839. *446*
—. Chauvin brothers. French Americans. Louisiana. 1699-1760. *438*
—. Creoles. Grappe, François. Indians. Louisiana (northern). 1760-1835. *406*
—. Farmers. German Americans. Iowa (Riceville). Memoirs. Paul, Matilda Peitzke. Women. 1865-1936. *602*
—. German Americans. Germans, Russian. North Dakota. Scandinavian Americans. Settlement. 1875-1915. 1930's. *53*
—. German Canadians. Manitoba. Mennonites. 1875. *3610*
—. Gibson, Peter. Nebraska (Saunders County). Swedish Americans. 1836-1924. *1848*
—. Iowa (Decorah). Material Culture. Museums. Norwegian-American Museum (Vesterheim). 1890-1975. *1723*
—. Irish Americans. Montana. O'Keeffe, Cornelius C. 1853-83. *758*
—. Jews. Manitoba (Winnipeg). 1860's-1975. *3504*
—. Saskatchewan. Welsh Canadians. 1902-14. *3458*

Pious Fund. California (San Francisco). Casserly, Eugene. Catholic Church. Daily Life. Documents. Doyle, John T. Irish Americans. *Letters.* 1773-1871. *742*

Pisanelli, Antonietta. California (San Francisco). Italian Americans. Theater, variety. 1905-32. *826*

Pitass, John. Catholic Church. New York (Buffalo). Polish Americans. 1890-1934. *1958*

Pitt, Leonard. Behavior. Black, Esther Boulton. California. Jews (review article). *Los Angeles Daily News* (newspaper). 1869. *1310*

Pittman, Clara. Anti-Socialist Law. Christianity. German Americans. Harmony Society. Pennsylvania (Economy). Utopias. 1878-79. *487*

Pitts, Herman H. Anti-Catholicism. French Canadians. New Brunswick. Religion in the Public Schools. 1871-90. *3813*

Pittsburgh Agreement. Czechoslovakia. Independence Movements. Pennsylvania. Slovakian Americans. 1918. *1893*

Pittsburgh Platform (1885). Judaism (Reform). Voorsanger, Jacob. 1872-1908. *1071*

Pittsburgh Survey (1909). Industrialization. Pennsylvania. Social Surveys. 1907-14. *129*

Pius IX, Pope. Nativism. Pennsylvania (Philadelphia). Public Opinion. 1848. *197*

Pixley, Frank M. Anti-Semitism. California (San Francisco). D'Ancona, David Arnold. Letters-to-the-editor. Newspapers. 1883. *1606*

Place Names. *See* Toponymy.

Plains of Abraham (battle). French and Indian War. Quebec (Quebec City). 1759. *3867*

Plank, D. Heber. Amish. Church History. Documents. Pennsylvania (Morgantown). 1668-1790's. 20c. *2237*

Plantations. Acadians. Leisure. Louisiana, southern. 1839-59. *396*
—. Barre, Marie-Catherine. Chaumont, Antoine. Company of the West. French Americans. Louisiana (Pascagoula River). 1717-32. *410*

Playford, Robert W. Crisp, John. English Americans. Letters. Pennsylvania (Brownsville). 1830. *295*

Plessis, Joseph-Octave. Atlantic Provinces. Catholic Church. Diaries. French Canadians. Quebec Archdiocese. 1812-15. *3651*
—. Atlantic Provinces. Catholic Church. French Canadians. Travel (accounts). 1812-15. *3277*

Plural establishment, theory of. Arnold, Matthew. Ethnicity. Religion. 19c-20c. *2166*

Pluralism. 1880's-1976. *2961*
—. Adamic, Louis. Assimilation. Slovenian Americans. Social Conditions. 1913-51. *6*
—. Adamic, Louis. Literature. Slovenian Americans. 1935-45. *5*
—. Ahlstrom, Sydney E. (review article). Religious history. 1974. *2167*
—. American Studies. Folklore. Regionalism. Scholars. 19c-20c. *2911*
—. Assimilation. Canada. Immigrants. Psychology. 1970's. *3024*
—. Assimilation. German Americans. Michigan (Ann Arbor). Protestantism. 1830-1955. *485*
—. Assimilation. New England. Portuguese Americans. 1840-1975. *1655*
—. Attitudes. Bureaucracies. Educational Administration. National Characteristics. Public Schools. ca 1850-1970's. *2865*
—. Baptists. Ethnicity. Melting pot theory. 1870-1976. *2993*
—. Bibliographies. Bilingualism. Canada. Research. 1964-67. *3933*
—. Bibliographies. Canada. Public Policy. 1967-76. *3019*
—. Canada. Confederation. Political theory. 1860's-1970's. *3916*
—. Canada. English Canadians. French Canadians. Royal Society of Canada. 1929-78. *3841*
—. Canada. Haidasz, Stanley. Polish Canadians. 1975. *3548*
—. Canada. Libraries. 1957-73. *3040*
—. Canada. Music. Nationalism. 1879-1978. *3831*
—. Canada. Political parties. 1857-1978. *3842*
—. Canada. Public Policy. 1970's. *3042*
—. Christianity. Economic growth. Michigan (Detroit). 1880-1940. *2169*
—. City Life. Ethnicity. Social Customs. 1977. *2941*
—. Civil rights. Migration, internal. Polish Americans. 1946-76. *1979*
—. Cosmopolitanism. Intellectuals. Liberalism. 1930's-40's. *2956*
—. Curricula. Educational Reform. Ideology. 1976. *2842*
—. Curricula. Educational Reform. Public schools. Social studies. 1975. *2880*
—. English Canadians. Federalism. French Canadians. Quebec. 20c. *3940*
—. Ethnicity. 1908-74. *2954*
—. Ethnicity. 1970's. *2978*
—. Ethnicity. Race. Social organization. 1978. *2943*
—. Ethnicity. Religion. 17c-20c. *2183*
—. Federal government. French Canadians. Public Policy. Quebec. Separatist Movements. 1976. *3954*
—. French Canadians. Quebec. 1970's. *3951*
—. History Teaching. Nationalism. Ontario. ca 1975-78. *3822*
—. Idealism. National characteristics. Religion. 1620's-1940's. *2159*
—. Ideology. Social Sciences. 17c-20c. 1960's-70's. *2989*
—. Jews (review article). Liberalism. Political Participation. Social Classes. 1945-70's. *932*
—. Language. 1865-1975. *2923*
—. Political Participation. 1950's-70's. *2951*
—. Sects, Religious. Social Organization. 1850's-1970's. *2964*

Pluralism symposium. English Canadians. French Canadians. Manitoba. 1870-1965. *3907*

Poetry. American Revolution. Bailey, Jacob. Canada. Loyalists. Maine. Satire. 1751-1808. *3601*
—. Austrian Americans. Burgenland. Immigration. Riessner, Johann. 1856-1939. *266*
—. Bahn, Rachel. Christianity. German Americans. Paraplegia. Pennsylvania. 1829-1902. *569*
—. Blair, Duncan Black. Gaelic language. Language. Nova Scotia (Pictou County). Scholars. Scottish Canadians. 1846-93. *3454*
—. Bogan, Louise. Catholic Church. Irish Americans. Women. 1920's-70's. *771*
—. Canada. Hungarian Canadians. Kirkconnell, Watson. 1895-1977. *3475*

—. Cawein, Madison Julius. German Americans. Kentucky. Translating and Interpreting. 1865-1914. *610*
—. Country Life. Iowa. Langland, Joseph (interview). Norwegian Americans. Youth. 1917-30's. 1977. *1726*
—. Creoles. Henriot, Paroles de Jean. Hurricanes. Louisiana (Chénière). 1893. *450*
—. French Canadians. Miron, Gaston. Quebec. Sovereignty. 1969-74. *3991*
—. Immigration. Italian Americans. Pascoli, Giovanni. 1904. *821*
—. McLachlan, Alexander. Ontario. Radicals and Radicalism. Scottish Canadians. Social reform. Working class. 1818-96. *3437*

Poets. Banér, Johan Gustav Runeskeold. Michigan (Ironwood). Swedes. 1861-1938. *1792*
—. Brodsky, Joseph. Russian Americans. Social Customs. Students. 1973. *2075*
—. Landfors, Arthur. Swedish Americans. ca 1910-73. *1857*

Poland. Banking. Foreign Investments. Harriman, W. Averell. Polish Americans. 1920-39. *2006*
—. Conrad, Joseph. Foreign Aid. Intervention. National Campaign Committee, Polish Government Loan. Polish Americans. USSR. 1919-23. *1984*
—. Dewey, John. Foreign policy. Polish Americans. Wilson, Woodrow (administration). World War I. 1918. *2052*
—. Diplomacy. Italian Americans. Jefferson, Thomas. Mazzei, Philip. Stanislaus II Poniatowski. Virginia. ca 1764-95. *844*
—. Elections (presidential). Polish Americans. Roosevelt, Franklin D. 1942-44. *1981*
—. Ethnicity. Independence movements. Polish Americans. 1870-1925. *1973*
—. Exiles (review article). Politics. Stasik, Florian. 1831-64. 1976. *1965*
—. Foreign Investments. Polish Americans. 1918-39. *2053*
—. French Canadians. National identity. Quebec. 1970's. *3985*
—. Hauptmann, Gerhart (*The Weavers*). Jews. Working class. 1899-1902. *1013*
—. Immigration. Peasants. Polish Americans. Social Organizations. 20c. *1960*
—. Jews. Literature. Singer, Isaac Bashevis (interview). Singer, Israel Joshua. 20c. *1111*
—. Jews. Press. Warsaw ghetto uprising. World War II. 1942-43. *2677*
—. Krzyzanowski, Jerzy (review article). Literature. Polish Americans. Reymont, Wladyslaw. 1867-1925. *2011*

Poland, eastern. Communism. Diplomacy. Lange, Oscar. Polish Americans. Roosevelt, Franklin D. USSR. 1941-45. *2036*

Poland: Historical, Literary, Monumental, Picturesque (periodical). Copernicus, Nicolaus. Polish Americans. Publishers and Publishing. Sobolewski, Paul. 1830's-40's. *2047*

Polding, John Bede. Australia (Sydney). Benedictines. German Americans. Letters. Missions and Missionaries. Wimmer, Boniface. 1847-55. *2358*

Poles. American Revolution. 1776-84. *1980*
—. American Revolution. Armies. Kosciusko, Thaddeus. Public opinion. Pulaski, Casimir. 1775-83. *2019*
—. American Revolution. Historiography. 1776-83. 1976. *2020*
—. American Revolution. Kosciusko, Thaddeus. Military engineering. 1746-1817. *1972*
—. Artists. Bibliographies. Orłowski, Alexander. 1777-1832. 20c. *1970*
—. Canada. Exiles. Spaniards. USA. ca 1936-78. *163*
—. Citizenship. Jefferson, Thomas. Kosciusko, Thaddeus. Supreme Court. Wills. 1798-1852. *2029*

Police *See also* Crime and Criminals; Criminal Law; Law Enforcement; Prisons.
—. Authority. Great Britain (London). New York City. Social classes. 1830-70. *2888*
—. Coal Mines and Mining. Labor. Pennsylvania (Scranton). Violence. 1866-84. *2894*
—. Conflict and Conflict Resolution. Military. 18c. 1960's-70's. *2885*
—. Pennsylvania (Philadelphia). Violence. 1834-44. *2891*

Polish American Congress. Foreign policy. Illinois (Chicago). Roosevelt, Franklin D. World War II. 1944. *2035*

Polish Americans. 1870-1970. *1993*
—. 1776-1976. *2004*
—. Abolition Movement. Gurowski, Adam. Radicals and Radicalism. 1849-66. *2041*

—. Hutterites. Leadership succession. Population. Social Organization. 1940's-70's. *3611*

—. Immigration. Public policy. Scandinavian Canadians. 1893-1914. *3526*

—. Jews. Marriage, mixed. 1957-69. *3508*

—. Letters. Métis. Religion. Riel, Louis. Taché, Alexandre Antonin. 1880's. *3902*

—. Letters. Millenarianism. North West Rebellion. Riel, Louis. 1876-78. 1885. *3901*

—. Métis. Migration, Internal. North West Rebellion. 1885. *3910*

—. Métis. Millenarianism. North West Rebellion. Rebellions. Religion. Riel, Louis. 1869-85. *3903*

—. Métis. Nolin, Jean-Baptiste (and daughters). Red River of the North. St. Boniface School. 1760-1840. *3279*

—. Métis. North West Rebellion. Rebellions. Red River Rebellion. Riel, Louis. 1870-85. *3899*

—. Settlement. Ukrainian Canadians. 1910-31. *3558*

Prairie States. *See* Great Plains.

Prairies. French Canadians. Manitoba (Winnipeg). Métis. Minnesota (St. Paul). Red River of the North. Trade. Trails. 19c. *3210*

Préfontaine, Raymond. City politics. French Canadians. Laporte, Hormisdas. Martin, Médéric. Political corruption. Quebec (Montreal). 1894-1921. *3352*

Prejudice. *All in the Family* (program). Race Relations. 1971-75. *3010*

—. British Canadians. Canada. Irish Canadians. Minorities. 1970's. *3065*

—. Canada. Immigration Policy. Physicians. 1920's. *3066*

—. Education. Minorities. North Carolina. Religious orthodoxy. World view. 1957-73. *262*

—. Ethnic Relations. Immigrants. Manitoba (Winnipeg). Population. 1874-1974. *3013*

—. Genocide. Immigration Policy. Jews. World War II. 1880's-1940's. *2687*

Premier Établissement de la Foy dans la Nouvelle France (book). Bernou, Claude. Canada. France. LeClercq, Crestien. Renaudot, Eusèbe. 1691. *3217*

Presbyterian Church. American Revolution. Georgia (Savannah). Loyalists. Political Repression. Swiss Americans. Zubly, John Joachim. 1766-81. *2150*

—. American Revolution. Georgia (Savannah). Loyalists. Zubly, John Joachim. 1770-81. *2148*

—. American Revolution. Scotch Irish. Scottish Americans. 1700-75. *312*

—. Assimilation. Converts. Jews. Ontario (Toronto). 1912-18. *3510*

—. Catholic Church. Church of England. English Canadians. Feild, Edward. Irish Canadians. Methodist Church. Newfoundland. 1765-1852. *3703*

—. Church of England. Morris, William. Ontario (Kingston). Queen's College. Scots. Scottish Canadians. 1836-42. *3447*

—. Dukhobors. Galicians. Lake Geneva Mission. Missions and Missionaries. Russian Canadians. Saskatchewan (Wakaw). 1903-42. *3690*

—. Ethnicity. German Americans. Synod of the West. 1912-59. *499*

—. Georgia (Savannah). Swiss Americans. Zubly, John Joachim. 1724-58. *2144*

—. Immigrants. Italian Americans. New York City (Greenwich Village). 1900-30. *842*

—. Indians. Massacres. Mennonites. Pacifism. Paxton Boys. Pennsylvania. Politics. 1763-68. *2293*

—. MacLeod, Norman. Migration. Nova Scotia (St. Ann's). Scottish Canadians. ca 1800-50's. *3434*

—. Nova Scotia (Pictou County). Scottish Canadians. Social Conditions. 1898-1966. *3433*

Presbyterian Church of Scotland. MacGregor, James. Missions and Missionaries. Nova Scotia (Pictou). Scottish Canadians. 1786-1830. *3453*

Preservation *See also* Restorations.

—. Architecture. German Americans. Harmony Society. Indiana (New Harmony). Pennsylvania (Economy, Harmony). Rapp, George. Restorations. 1804-25. 20c. *590*

—. Attitudes. German Americans. Historical Sites and Parks. Ohio (Columbus; German Village). 19c-20c. *527*

—. California (Los Angeles). Culture. Lummis, Charles F. Newmark, Harris. Newmark, Marco. Newmark, Maurice. Southwest Museum. 1859-1930. *1386*

—. Concordia Historical Institute. Farms. German Americans. Lutheran Church (Missouri Synod). Missouri (Perry County). Saxon Lutheran Memorial. 1958-64. *563*

—. German Americans. Gottlieb Storz (home). Nebraska (Omaha). 1907-79. *587*

—. German Americans. Houses, Brick. Ohio (Columbus; German Village). 19c. 1960-78. *591*

—. German Americans. Kentucky (Louisville; Butchertown). 1967-78. *542*

—. Immigration. New York City (Ellis Island). Restore Ellis Island Committee. 17c-20c. *8*

Presidents *See also* names of individual presidents.

—. Foreign policy. Lobbying. Zionism. 1912-73. *1543*

Press *See also* Editors and Editing; Journalism; Newspapers; Periodicals; Reporters and Reporting.

—. Acculturation. German Americans (image of). Ohio (Toledo). 1850-90. *492*

—. Act of Sexual Sterilization (Alberta, 1928). Canada, western. Eugenics. Immigration. Woodsworth, James S. 1900-28. *3061*

—. Anti-Semitism. Dreyfus, Alfred. Editorials. France. Public opinion. Trials. 1895-1906. *1613*

—. Anti-Semitism. German Americans. Jews. Midwest. 1919-33. *2698*

—. British Canadians. Children. Immigration. Ontario. Poor. Rye, Miss. 1865-1925. *3415*

—. Bulgaria. Illinden Uprising. Macedonian Americans. Public opinion. 1903. *2120*

—. Canada. French Canadians. Historiography. World War II (antecedents). 1938-39. *3762*

—. Civil Wars. Jews. Spain. 1934-39. *1116*

—. Coal miners. Lattimer Massacre. Pennsylvania. Slovakian Americans. Strikes. 1897. *1892*

—. Concentration camps. Genocide. Germany. Jews. World War II. 1939-42. *2678*

—. Conley, James. Frank, Leo M. Georgia (Atlanta). Jews. Negroes. Trials. 1913-15. *1624*

—. Conservatism. Economic Conditions. English Canadians. French Canadians. Political power. Quebec. 1864-67. *3888*

—. Ethnicity. Greek Americans. 1892-1978. *663*

—. Haakon VII. Independence. Norway. Norwegian Americans. Public opinion. 1905-1906. *1737*

—. Haymarket Riot. Nativism. Norway. Pullman Strike. Thrane, Marcus. 1886-94. *2550*

—. Illinois (Chicago; Swede Town). Swedish Americans. 1870-80. *1774*

—. Italian Americans. Louisiana (New Orleans). Stereotypes. 1880-1920. *845*

—. Jews. Michigan (Detroit). 1823-1973. *1229*

—. Jews. Poland. Warsaw ghetto uprising. World War II. 1942-43. *2677*

—. Lithuanian Americans. 1875-1975. *268*

—. Polish Americans. 1863-1977. *2015*

—. Ukraine. Ukrainian Americans. Women. 1924-74. *2081*

—. Ukrainian Americans. Women. 1850's-1974. *2118*

Press (black). Italian Americans. Negroes. 1886-1936. *883*

Presse. Devoir. French Canadians. News, foreign. Newspapers. Quebec. *Soleil.* 1962-74. *3390*

Pressure Groups *See also* Interest Groups.

—. Arab-Israeli Conflict. Foreign policy. 1970's. *1539*

—. Congress. Cyprus. Foreign policy. Greece. Greek Americans. NATO. Turkey. 1960-76. *668*

Prestgard, Kristian. Iowa (Decorah). Literature. Norwegian Americans. *Smyra* (periodical). Wist, Johannes B. 1905-15. *1730*

Priber, Christian Gottlieb. Cherokee Indians. Colonial Government. Georgia. German Americans. Kingdom of Paradise colony. Political Imprisonment. Utopias. 1730's-ca 1744. *572*

Price, C. A. Canada. Huttenback, Robert A. Immigration (review article). 1830-1970. *3079*

Primaries *See also* Elections; Voting and Voting Behavior.

—. Democratic Party. Political Campaigns. Smith, Al. South Dakota. 1928. *2457*

Primaries (mayoral). Jones, Arthur. National Socialist White People's Party. Nominations for Office. Petition signing. Wisconsin (Milwaukee). 1976. *1603*

Primary Education. *See* Elementary Education.

Prime Ministers. Canada. Genealogy. Irish Canadians. Thompson, John S. D. 1796-1903. *3446*

Primitive Methodist Church. Agriculture. Bee, William. Bourne, Hugh. Clowes, William. Dow, Lorenzo. English Canadians. Grenfell Colony. Saskatchewan. 1882. *3416*

—. English Americans. North Central States. 1842-1976. *303*

Prince Albert (vessel). Arctic. Bellot, Joseph René. Canada. Franklin, John. Kennedy, William. Métis. Voyages. 1851. *3289*

Prince Edward Island. Bible reading. Catholic Church. Politics. Protestants. Public Schools. 1856-60. *3706*

—. Catholic Church. Emigration. Immigration. Persecution. Scotland. Scottish Canadians. 1769-74. *3430*

—. Church and State. English Canadians. French Canadians. Political Parties. Prince of Wales College Act (1860). School Boards. 1860-63. *3707*

—. Scottish Canadians. Selkirk, 5th Earl. Settlement. 1803. *3432*

Prince of Wales College Act (1860). Church and State. English Canadians. French Canadians. Political Parties. Prince Edward Island. School Boards. 1860-63. *3707*

Prince, Peter. Alberta (Calgary; Eau Claire district). Eau Claire Company. Housing. Kerr, Isaac. Lumber and Lumbering. Scandinavian Canadians. 1886-1970's. *3537*

Prisland, Marie. Adamic, Louis. Baraga, Frederick. Ethnic studies. Slovenian Americans. 1687-1975. *2124*

Prisoners of War *See also* Concentration Camps.

—. Aliens, enemy. Austrians. Canada. Internment camps. World War I. 1914-19. *3751*

—. Canada. Germans. Great Britain. World War II. 1940-47. *3760*

—. Germany. Jews. Reminiscences. Winograd, Leonard. World War II. 1944-45. *2701*

—. Italians. Labor. World War II. 1943-45. *2689*

Prisons *See also* Crime and Criminals; Criminal Law; Police.

—. California. Jewish Committee for Personal Service in State Institutions. Mental hospitals. Meyer, Martin A. Psychiatry. Shirpser, Elsie. 1920-60. *1045*

Private Schools *See also* Church Schools.

—. Bergel, Siegmund. California (San Bernardino). Jews. 1868-1912. *1307*

—. Catholic Church. Family. Judaism. 1960's-70's. *2165*

—. Ethnicity. Greek Canadians. Immigration. Ontario (Toronto). 1900-40. *3472*

Privateers. American Canadians. American Revolution. Fishing. Nova Scotia (Lockport). 18c. *3587*

Proch, Don. Art. Canada. Ukrainian Canadians. 1970's. *3553*

Production, mode of. Economic Development. French Canadians. New France. Social Classes. 17c-18c. *3242*

Professions. Greek Americans. 1820's-1970's. *659*

Profit-sharing. Businessmen. Cooperatives. Nelson, Nelson O. Norwegian Americans. Social Reform. 1886-1904. *1740*

Pro-German sentiments. Editors and Editing. German Americans. Mennonites. Miller, Samuel H. Trials. World War I. 1917-18. *2628*

Progressive education. Ethnicity. Race. 1929-45. *256*

Progressive Era. Educational reform. Elites. Nativism. Niles Bill (Ohio, 1898). Ohio (Toledo). School boards. 1890's. *2459*

Progressive Movement. Buenker, John D. (review article). Metropolitan areas. Political reform. 1910's. *2455*

—. Danish Americans. Democratic Party. Finnish Americans. Norwegian Americans. Republican Party. Swedish Americans. Voting and Voting Behavior. Wisconsin. 1900-50. *2490*

Progressivism. Aloe, Louis Patrick. Anti-Semitism. Elections (mayoral). Jews. Missouri (St. Louis). 1910-25. *1353*

—. Americanization. Minnesota (Minneapolis). North East Neighborhood House. Settlement houses. Social Reform. 1910's-20's. *95*

—. Beth Ha Medrosh Hagodol Synagogue. Colorado (Denver). Judaism (Orthodox). Kauvar, Charles E. H. 1902-71. *1460*
—. Biography, collective. Historiography. Political Leadership. Quantitative Methods. Social Status. 1950's-77. *2470*
—. California. Democratic Party. Gould, Lewis L. Political Factions (review article). Texas. Williams, R. Hal. 1880-1919. 1973. *2534*
—. California. Frank, Leo M. Georgia. Jews. Lynching. Trials. 1913-15. *1620*
—. California (San Francisco). Catholic Church. City Politics. Irish Americans. Yorke, Peter C. 1900's. *785*
—. Cities. Institutions. Social Organization. Violence. 1880's-1910's. *2892*
—. Ethnicity. Middle Classes. Reform. Religion. Voting and Voting Behavior. Wisconsin. 1890's-1917. *2549*
—. Immigrants. New Jersey (Jersey City). Social reform. Whittier House. 1890-1917. *2480*
Progresso Italo-Americano (newspaper). Italian Americans. Journalism. Linguistics. 1976-78. *828*
Prohibition. Capone, Al. Heroes. Italian Americans. Myths and Symbols. 1925-47. *804*
—. Cities. Saloons. Values. Working Class. 1890-1920. *118*
—. Democratic Party. German Americans. Irish Americans. New York City. Tammany Hall. 1840-60. *2461*
—. Dever, William. Elections (mayoral). Illinois (Chicago). Negroes. 1923-27. *2445*
—. Ethnicity. Local option. Michigan. 1889-1917. *2501*
—. Illinois (Chicago). Liquor industry. Saloons. 1880's-1920. *103*
—. Ontario. Racism. Reform. 1890-1915. *3063*
Proletariat. *See* Working class.
Propaganda *See also* Advertising; Public Opinion.
—. American Revolution. Italian Americans. Mazzei, Philip. 1773-1816. *820*
—. Anti-German Sentiment. *Beware* (film). Films. Gerard, James W. German Americans. World War I. 1918-19. *2634*
—. Canada. Deutscher Bund Canada. German Canadians. Nazism. 1934-39. *3765*
—. Canada. Elections. Political Factions. Provincial legislatures. 1792. *3708*
—. Catholic Church. Great Britain. Irish Americans. USA. World War I. 1918. *2623*
—. Catholic Church. Quebec (Montreal). Social Popular School. Syndicalism. Working Class. 1911-49. *3392*
—. Civilian preparedness organizations. Patriotism. Prowar sentiments. Vigilantes. World War I. 1916-18. *2617*
—. Comic books. 20c. *2928*
—. Communism. Kollontai, Aleksandra. Norway. Russians. World War I. 1915-16. *2089*
—. Communism. Latvians. *Strädnieks* (newspaper). 1904-19. *273*
—. Conant, James B. Exiles. Germany. Harvard University. Hasidism. Higher education. Nazism. 1930's. *166*
—. Czechoslovakia. Czechs. Independence Movements. Masaryk, Tomáš. 1918. *1898*
—. Education. McElroy, Robert M. National Security League. Patriotism. World War I. 1917-19. *2618*
—. Fascism. Italian Americans. Liberalism. Loyalty. Office of War Information. 1939-40. *2599*
Property *See also* Income; Real Estate.
—. Aliens. Civil War. International claims commissions. Louisiana. Neutrality. Red River Campaign. 1861-84. *2606*
—. Auteuil, Denis-Joseph Ruette d'. Inventories. Quebec. 1661-80. *3197*
—. French Canadians. Law. New France. Sulpicians. 1667. *3669*
—. Genealogy. German Americans. Inventories. Pennsylvania (Tulpehocken area). 18c. *559*
—. Genealogy. Inventories. Pennsylvania (Philadelphia, Lower Merion). Welsh Americans. Wills. 1650-1750. *321*
Property ownership. Employment. New York (Buffalo, Poughkeepsie). Ontario (Kingston). Pennsylvania (Philadelphia). Social Classes. 19c. *2782*
Prostitution. Bureau of Social Morals. Hertz, Rosie. Jews. Law Enforcement. New York City. 1912-13. *1209*
Protest Marches. *See* Demonstrations; Political Protest.
Protestant Churches *See also* names of churches, e.g. Methodist Church, etc.; Protestantism.

—. Acculturation. Charters. Institutionalization. Mennonites (Franconia Conference). 1840-1940. *2222*
—. Africa. Dutch Americans. German Americans. Missions and Missionaries. 19c-20c. *2377*
—. Bibliographies. Canada. Historiography. 1825-1973. *3607*
—. Canada. Immigration. National Identity. United Church of Canada. 1902-25. *3608*
—. Catholic Church. Church attendance. Religion. 1974. *2160*
—. French Canadians. Jesuits. Land Tenure. Legislation. Mercier, Honoré. Quebec. 1886. *3675*
—. German Americans. Great Awakening. Missions and Missionaries. Northeastern or North Atlantic States. 1720-60. *528*
—. German language. Language. Pennsylvania. Sermons. 18c. *603*
—. Laity. Leadership. New York (Kingston). Political Leadership. Social Status. 1825-60. *2162*
—. Michigan (Detroit). Social organization. 1880-1940. *114*
Protestant ethic. Canada. Elites. Ethnicity. Rationality. Senators. Values. 1971. *3710*
—. Catholic Church. Cities. Neighborhoods. Segregation. Social mobility. Values. 1970's. *145*
—. Johnson, Benton. Political Parties. 1960's-70's. *2537*
Protestantism *See also* Evangelism; Fundamentalism.
—. Acculturation. Americanization. Catholic Church. Leo XIII, Pope (*Testem Benevolentiae*). Periodicals. 1899. *2368*
—. Acculturation. Frontier and Pioneer Life. Immigrants. Rølvaag, Ole Edvart (*Giants in the Earth*). South Dakota. 1870. 1927. *1734*
—. Anti-Catholicism. Conscription, Military. Jesuits. Novitiate of St. Stanislaus. Ontario (Guelph). World War I. 1918-19. *3754*
—. Assimilation. German Americans. Michigan (Ann Arbor). Pluralism. 1830-1955. *485*
—. Bible reading. Catholic Church. Desmond, Humphrey. Religion in the Public Schools. *State of Wisconsin ex rel. Frederick Weiss et al. v. District School Board of School District 8* (1890). Wisconsin. 1888-90. *218*
—. Catholic Church. 1972-73. *2182*
—. Catholic Church. English Canadians. Evangelism. French Canadians. Quebec (Lower Canada). Rebellion of 1837. Swiss Canadians. 1766-1865. *3862*
—. Catholic Church. French Canadians. Great Britain. Military government. Quebec. 18c. *3887*
—. Catholic Church. New France. ca 1625-1760's. *3849*
—. Family. French Canadians. Quebec. Trade. 1740-60. *3185*
—. Foreign Policy. Israel. Zionism (review article). 1945-48. *1588*
—. Fundamentalism. Jews. 17c-1976. *973*
—. German Americans. Harmony Society. Indiana. Pennsylvania. Rapp, George. Utopias. 1804-47. *604*
—. German Americans. Niebuhr, Reinhold. Theology. World War I. 1915-18. *2613*
—. Scandinavian Americans. 1849-1900. *1666*
Protestantism (review article). Cities. Muhlenberg, Augustus. Politics. Social Problems. 1812-1900. *2180*
Protestants. American Revolution. Canada. French Americans. USA. Whaling industry and Trade. 17c-20c. *398*
—. Anti-Catholicism. Immigration. Ku Klux Klan. Saskatchewan. 1927-30. *3060*
—. Bible reading. Catholic Church. Politics. Prince Edward Island. Public Schools. 1856-60. *3706*
—. Canada. English Canadians. Jesuits' Estates Act. Political Protest. 1880-90. *3078*
—. Carroll, John. Catholic Church. Immigrants. Nativism. 1790-1820. *178*
—. Catholic Church. Colleges and Universities. Intellectuals. 1960's-70's. *2823*
—. Catholic Church. Migration, Internal. Religion. Rhode Island. 1926-71. *2184*
—. German Americans. Settlement. Spotswood, Alexander. Virginia (Germanna). 1714-21. *577*
—. German Canadians. Immigrants. Nova Scotia. 1749-52. *3467*
—. Illinois (Chicago). Jews. 1960's-70's. *2170*
—. Jews. National Council of Churches (General Assembly). 1969-74. *1583*

Protocols of the Elders of Zion (document). Anti-Semitism. Conspiracy theories. Great Britain. Intellectual History. 20c. *1642*
Proulx, Nicholas. French Canadians. Massachusetts (Holyoke). Working Class. 1850-1900. *366*
Provigo (company). Canada. Gasoline. Grocery trade. Reminiscences. Turmel, Antoine. USA. 1945-78. *3407*
Provincial Government. Black, Conrad. Duplessis, Maurice (review article). French Canadians. Quebec. Rumilly, Robert. 1930's-77. *3401*
—. Bonomi, Patricia U. Klein, Milton M. New York (review article). Religion. 1690's-1770's. 1971-74. *2441*
—. Boucherville, Charles Eugène Boucher de. British Canadians. Federalism. French Canadians. Joly, Henri-Gustave. Liberal Party. Political Campaigns. Quebec. 1878. *3709*
—. Bourassa, Henri. French Canadians. Historiography. Politics. Quebec. 1902-71. *3374*
—. Canada. Economic Policy. English Language. Federal government. Language. 1969-74. *3941*
—. Canada. English Canadians. Federalism. French Canadians. Public Policy. 1867-1977. *3900*
—. Canada. Federal Government. Nationalism. 1976. *3979*
—. Charpentier, Alfred. Confederation of Catholic Workers of Canada. French Canadians. Industrial Relations. Quebec. 1935-46. *3337*
—. Confederation. French Canadians. Ontario. Quebec. 1867-1937. *3918*
—. Constitutions. Federal Government. French Canadians. Quebec. Separatist Movements. 1968-76. *4045*
—. Elections. French Canadians. Parti Québécois. Quebec. 1976-77. *4034*
—. Federal government. French Canadians. Parti Québécois. Quebec. Reform. Social Change. 1960-77. *3988*
—. Federal government. Language policy. Middle Classes. Modernization. Quebec. 1960-76. *3949*
—. Foreign Investments. French Canadians. "Negro King" hypothesis. Politics. Quebec. Taschereau, Louis Alexandre. 1920-36. *3931*
—. French Canadians. Lawyers. LeSage, Simeon. Quebec. 1835-1909. *3403*
—. French Canadians. Lévesque, René. Newspapers. Parti Québécois. Quebec (Montreal). 1976-77. *3992*
—. Hudson's Bay Company. Indians. Manitoba. McKay, James. Métis. 1853-79. *3211*
—. Intergovernmental Relations. Quebec. Separatist Movements. 1955-75. *4042*
Provincial legislatures. Canada. Elections. Political Factions. Propaganda. 1792. *3708*
—. Federalism. French Canadians. Liberal Party. Parliaments. Quebec. Regionalism. ca 1917-77. *3965*
—. French Canadians. Huot, Charles. Intellectual History. Painting, historical. Quebec. 1870's-1930. 1977. *3381*
—. French Canadians. Quebec (Lower Canada). Voting and Voting Behavior. 1792-1814. *3714*
—. Political parties. Social Conditions. 1950-70. *3711*
Provisional Executive Committee for General Zionist Affairs. Americanism. Brandeis, Louis D. Zionism. 1900-74. *1597*
Provost Court of Quebec. Feudalism. Law. New France (Notre Dame des Anges). 1626-1750. *3199*
Provost, T. S. Catholic Church. Colonization. Economic development. French Canadians. Geopolitics. Quebec (Mattawinie district). 17c-1890. *3148*
Prowar sentiments. Civilian preparedness organizations. Patriotism. Propaganda. Vigilantes. World War I. 1916-18. *2617*
Psychiatry *See also* Mental Illness; Psychology.
—. California. Jewish Committee for Personal Service in State Institutions. Mental hospitals. Meyer, Martin A. Prisons. Shirpser, Elsie. 1920-60. *1045*
Psychohistory. DeLeon, Daniel. Socialism. Wandering Jew (concept). 1872-1914. *1470*
—. Georgia. Jews. Nativism. State Politics. Watson, Thomas E. 1856-1922. *217*
—. Jews. Kissinger, Henry A. Political Leadership. 1923-73. *1503*
Psychology *See also* Behaviorism; Psychiatry; Social Psychology.
—. Assimilation. Canada. Immigrants. Pluralism. 1970's. *3024*

—. Behavior. German Americans. Lewin, Kurt. Phenomenology. Social change. 1917-78. *520*

—. Colleges and Universities. Jews. Solomons, Leon Mendez. 1873-1900. *1500*

—. Genocide. Jews. World War II. 1940's. *2684*

Public Administration *See also* Bureaucracies; Civil Service; Civil-Military Relations; Government.

— French Canadians. Interest groups. Political Systems. Quebec. Reform. 1970's. *3944*

Public Finance *See also* Budgets.

—. Public Opinion. 1970. *2546*

Public Health *See also* Cemeteries; Diseases; Epidemics; Hospitals; Medicine.

—. City Politics. German Americans. Kempster, Walter. Polish Americans. Smallpox. Wisconsin (Milwaukee). 1894-95. *2831*

— Federal government. Legislation. Louisiana (New Orleans). Yellow fever. 1830's-79. *2824*

—. Social Sciences. Urbanization. 20c. *2835*

Public Opinion *See also* Propaganda; Public Relations.

—. Agnew, Spiro T. Greek Americans. 1960's-70's. *667*

—. Alberta (Edmonton). Ethnicity. Hutterites. 1966-75. *3635*

—. American Revolution. Armies. Kosciusko, Thaddeus. Poles. Pulaski, Casimir. 1775-83. *2019*

—. Amish, Old Order. Literature. Pennsylvania (Lancaster County). Tourism. 1910-78. *2194*

—. Anti-Semitism. Dreyfus, Alfred. Editorials. France. Press. Trials. 1895-1906. *1613*

—. Anti-Semitism. Elites. Freedom of speech. Mencken, H. L. 1917-41. *2654*

—. Anti-Semitism. Energy. 1970's. *1627*

—. Arab-Israeli conflict. Foreign policy. Interest groups. Jews. 1970's. *1586*

—. Arab-Israeli conflict. Jews. Newspapers. Periodicals. 1966-75. *1521*

—. Assimilation. Jews. October War. 1973. *1557*

—. Boer War. Great Britain. Irish Americans. South Africa. 1898-1903. *719*

—. Books (donated). Colorado. Denver, University of. Germany. 1936. *2692*

—. British Canadians. British Columbia. Immigration. 1919-30. *3414*

—. Bulgaria. Illinden Uprising. Macedonian Americans. Press. 1903. *2120*

—. California, image of. Great Britain. Travel Accounts. 1800-75. *282*

—. Canada. Green Paper. Immigration policy. O'Connell, Martin. 1975. *3064*

—. Canada. Intergovernmental Relations. King, William Lyon Mackenzie. Newspapers. Public Welfare. Taxation. 1945-46. *3929*

—. City government. Decentralization. New York City. 1974. *140*

—. Congress. Eisenhower, Dwight D. (administration). Hungarian Americans. Immigration policy. Refugees. 1956-57. *680*

—. Conspiracy theories. Italian Americans. Law. Mafia. 1798-1970. *886*

—. deGaulle, Charles. Foreign Relations. France. French Canadians. Quebec. Separatist Movements. 1967-76. *3736*

—. Dictatorship. Greece. Greek Americans. 1967-75. *652*

—. District of Columbia. Feuer, Leon I. Lobbying. Reminiscences. Zionism. 1940's. *1529*

—. Durham, 1st Earl of. French Canadians. Home Rule. Ontario (Upper Canada). Political prisoners. Rebellion of 1837. Transportation. 1835-50. *3858*

—. Education. Ethnicity. Mass Media. Ohio (Cleveland). Social Status. 1976. *2962*

—. Elites. English Canadians. Federal Government. French Canadians. Politics. Quebec. 1977. *3963*

—. Ethnicity. Foreign Relations. Polish Americans. Wisconsin (Milwaukee). 1970's. *2024*

—. Ethnicity. Intellectuals. National Characteristics. 1930's. *265*

—. Foreign policy. Israel. Jews. 1967-74. *1565*

—. German Americans. Hüssy, John. *Oklahoma Vorwärts* (newspaper). World War I. 1914-18. *2611*

—. Haakon VII. Independence. Norway. Norwegian Americans. Press. 1905-1906. *1737*

—. Historiography. Immigration Policy. Slavic Americans. 1800-1976. *1884*

—. *Holocaust* (program). Jews. Television. 1978. *2659*

—. Jews. Labor Unions and Organizations. Stereotypes. 1880's-1915. *962*

—. Nativism. Pennsylvania (Philadelphia). Pius IX, Pope. 1848. *197*

—. October War. Six-Day War. Zionism. 1967-73. *1540*

—. Public Finance. 1970. *2546*

Public Policy. Affirmative Action. Ethnicity. Health, Education, and Welfare Department. 1970. *2945*

—. Bibliographies. Canada. Pluralism. 1967-76. *3019*

—. Bilingualism. Canada. 1970's. *3830*

—. California (San Francisco). Congress. Jews. Kahn, Julius. Political Leadership. Republican Party. 1898-1924. *1352*

—. Canada. English Canadians. Federalism. French Canadians. Provincial Government. 1867-1977. *3900*

—. Canada. Pluralism. 1970's. *3042*

—. Church schools. Documents. Education. Finance. Jews. Religion in the Public Schools. 1961-71. *922*

—. City planning. Housing. Neighborhoods. Population. 1890-1979. *106*

—. Colonization companies. Economic growth. Railroads. Saskatchewan (Yorkton). Settlement. 1882-1905. *3052*

—. Crime and Criminals. Immigration. Irish Canadians. Newfoundland. 1789. *3480*

—. Culture. Language, foreign. Mass media. 1970's. *2963*

—. Federal government. French Canadians. Pluralism. Quebec. Separatist Movements. 1976. *3954*

—. Federalism. 1750-1977. *173*

—. Friedman, Saul S. (review article). Genocide. Jews. Refugees. Roosevelt, Franklin D. (administration). World War II. 1938-45. 1973. *2694*

—. Immigration. Population. Social Classes. 1970-77. *259*

—. Immigration. Prairie Provinces. Scandinavian Canadians. 1893-1914. *3526*

Public Records *See also* Archives.

—. Akins, Thomas Beamish. French Canadians. Nova Scotia. 1857-91. *3852*

—. Community Participation in Politics. Danish Americans. Naturalization. Norwegian Americans. Swedish Americans. Wisconsin (Milwaukee). 1837-1941. *1658*

— Dutch Americans. New Netherland. New York State Library. Translations. 17c-1975. *336*

— Jews. Ohio (Columbus). Quantitative methods. 1880-1915. *1264*

Public Relations *See also* Advertising; Public Opinion.

—. Americanization. Foreign Language Information Service. Immigration. News releases. 1918-39. *249*

Public Schools *See also* High Schools; Schools.

—. Acculturation. Educational reform. Immigrants. 19c-1910's. *2867*

—. Americanization. Educational Reform. Immigrants. New York (Buffalo). 1890-1916. *2881*

— Anderson, James T. M. Anti-Catholicism. French Canadians. Language. Saskatchewan. School Act (amendment). Secularization. 1929-34. *3814*

—. Assimilation. City life. Immigrants. 1890's-1920. *2856*

—. Assimilation. Immigrants. Literature. 19c-20c. *2858*

—. Attitudes. Bureaucracies. Educational Administration. National Characteristics. Pluralism. ca 1850-1970's. *2865*

—. Bible reading. Catholic Church. Politics. Prince Edward Island. Protestants. 1856-60. *3706*

—. Bibliographies. Curricula. Ethnic studies. 1908-70's. *18*

—. Calonne, Abbot de. Canada. Catholic Church. Clergy. Conservatism. French Canadians. Letters. 1819-20. *3819*

—. Catholic Church. French Canadians. Irish Canadians. New Brunswick. Politics. Quebec. Taxation. 1871-73. *3821*

—. Children. Immigrants. Jews. Manitoba (Winnipeg). 1900-20. *3520*

—. Citizenship. Historiography. 1930-74. *2846*

—. Clergy. Conservatism. French Canadians. Middle classes. Quebec. Working class. 1840-75. *3811*

—. Compulsory education. Immigrants. Missouri (St. Louis). Truancy. 1905-07. *2861*

—. Curricula. Educational Reform. Pluralism. Social studies. 1975. *2880*

—. Curricula. Maryland. Slavic studies. 1970's. *1878*

—. Dukhobors. Russian Canadians. Saskatchewan. 1905-50. *3693*

—. Greer, Colin (review article). Social Mobility. 1900-70. 1972. *2855*

—. Ideology. Missouri (St. Louis). Troen, Selwyn K. (review article). 1838-1920. 1975. *2864*

—. Industrialization. Ontario (Hamilton). Socialization. 19c. *3818*

—. Jews. New York City. Social mobility. 1880-1920. *1171*

—. Materialism. Morality. Slovakian Americans. Working Class. 1890-1940. *1888*

—. New York City. Strikes. 1968. *2879*

—. Racism. 1970's. *2875*

Public Schools (review article). Assimilation. Kaestle, Carl F. Massachusetts (Boston). New York City. Schultz, Stanley K. 1750-1860. *2863*

Public Welfare *See also* Charities; Child Welfare; Children; Hospitals; Social Work.

—. Americanization. Immigrants. Indiana (Gary). 1906-40. *2833*

—. British Columbia (northern). Homesteading and Homesteaders. Mennonites. Resettlement. 1940-42. *3612*

—. Canada. Intergovernmental Relations. King, William Lyon Mackenzie. Newspapers. Public opinion. Taxation. 1945-46. *3929*

—. Jews. Voluntary Associations. 1776-1976. *909*

Publishers and Publishing *See also* Books; Editors and Editing; Press.

—. Assimilation. Danish Americans. North Central States. 1870-1900. *1683*

—. Association of Jewish Book Publishers. Jews. USSR. 1977-78. *1640*

—. Autobiography. California (San Francisco). DeYoung, Michael H. 1813-1925. *1455*

—. Bengston, Henry. Illinois (Chicago). Swedish Americans. 1887-1974. *1816*

—. Copernicus, Nicolaus. *Poland: Historical, Literary, Monumental, Picturesque* (periodical). Polish Americans. Sobolewski, Paul. 1830's-40's. *2047*

—. Finnish Americans. 1858-1970. *1698*

—. French Americans. Nancrede, Joseph. 1761-1841. *471*

—. Gjerset, Knut. Historians. Norwegian Americans. Social Organizations. 1873-1935. *1745*

Puck (periodical). Anti-Irish sentiments. Cartoons and Caricatures. Irish Americans. Politics. Social Conditions. 1880-94. *714*

Puerto Ricans. House of Representatives. Italian Americans. Marcantonio, Vito. New York. Republican Party. 20c. *840*

Pulaski, Casimir. American Revolution. Armies. Kosciusko, Thaddeus. Poles. Public opinion. 1775-83. *2019*

—. American Revolution. Heroes. Polish Americans. 1779-1976. *2021*

—. American Revolution. Kosciusko, Thaddeus. Polish Americans. Salomon, Haym. Settlement. 1608-1780. *2051*

Pulitzer Prize. Alley, Jim. Ku Klux Klan. Memphis *Commercial Appeal* (newspaper). Mooney, Charles Patrick Joseph. Tennessee. 1920-25. *206*

Pullman Strike. Haymarket Riot. Nativism. Norway. Press. Thrane, Marcus. 1886-94. *2550*

Purim Ball. California (San Diego). Jews. Social Customs. 1888. *1167*

Puritans *See also* Church of England; Congregationalism.

—. Hansen, Marcus Lee. Historiography. Norwegian Americans. Temperance movements. 19c. 1920's-30's. *1727*

Puzo, Mario. Coppola, Francis Ford. Crime and Criminals. *Godfather* (novel, film). Italian Americans. 1970's. *885*

Quakers. *See* Friends, Society of.

Q

Quantitative Methods *See also* Methodology.

—. Biography, collective. Historiography. Political Leadership. Progressivism. Social Status. 1950's-77. *2470*

—. Carnegie-Mellon University. History Teaching. Social mobility. Urban history. 1975. *2816*

Reusser, Christian (home). Architecture. Iowa. Social Customs. Swiss Americans. 1890-1905. *2149*

Review of Politics (periodical). Catholic Church. Indiana. Notre Dame, University of. Political Theory. 1938-78. *2365*

Revivals *See also* Great Awakening.

—. Acculturation. Amish. Mennonites. 1860-90. *2273*

—. Antislavery Sentiments. Ethnicity. Ohio. Political attitudes. Voting and Voting Behavior. 1825-70. *2510*

—. Boehm, Martin. German Americans. Mennonites. Newcomer, Christian. Pennsylvania. 1740-1850. *2291*

—. Laity. 1858. *2179*

Revolution *See also* specific revolutions by name, e.g. American Revolution; Coups d'Etat; Government, Resistance to; Radicals and Radicalism; Rebellions; Riots.

—. Chile. Diplomacy. Egan, Patrick. Irish Americans. Republican Party. 1880's-93. *725*

—. Jews. Levy, Jonas Phillips. Merchant Marine. Mexican War. Peru. 1823-48. *1447*

Reymont, Wladyslaw. Krzyzanowski, Jerzy (review article). Literature. Poland. Polish Americans. 1867-1925. *2011*

Rezanov, Nikolai. Arguello, Maria de la Concepcion. California. Catholic Church. Orthodox Eastern Church, Russian. Russians. 1806. *2119*

Rhode Island *See also* New England; Northeastern or North Atlantic States.

—. American Jewish Historical Society. Collections. 1692-1975. *1322*

—. American Revolution. Great Britain. Jews. Touro, Isaac. 1782. *1428*

—. Attitudes. Employment. Family. Women. 1968-69. *2709*

—. Boy Scouts of America. Jews. 1910-76. *1223*

—. Catholic Church. Migration, Internal. Protestants. Religion. 1926-71. *2184*

—. Cities. Family. Immigration. Italian Americans. Jews. 1880-1940. *2751*

—. Democratic Party. Nativism. Republican Party. Voting and Voting Behavior. Whig Party. 1850-61. *184*

—. Generations. Jews. Language. Residential patterns. Yiddish Language. 1910-70. *1208*

—. Illness, perceptions of. Medical care. Portuguese Americans. 1960-77. *1653*

—. Italian Americans. Labor. Radicals and Radicalism. 1905-30. *802*

—. Jews. Orphanages. 1909-42. *1250*

—. Jews. Voluntary Associations. Women. ca 1877-1975. *1226*

—. Nardella, Luigi (interview). Strikes. Textile Industry. 1922. *801*

Rhode Island Jewish Historical Association. Jews. Local History. 1951-74. *1206*

Rhode Island (Newport). American Revolution. Jews. 1763-76. *1244*

—. American Revolution. Jews, Sephardic. Massachusetts (Leicester). 1777-83. *1320*

—. Ararat Colony. Jews. New York. Noah, Mordecai Manuel. 1813-21. *1207*

—. Architecture. Bevis Marks Synagogue. Great Britain (London). Harrison, Peter. Touro Synagogue. 1670-1775. *1285*

—. Artifacts. Moravian Church. 1767-1835. *2432*

—. B'nai B'rith (Judah Touro Lodge No. 998). Jews. 1924-74. *1235*

—. Carigal, Hakham Raphael Haim Isaac. Jews. Rabbis. 1771-77. *1443*

—. Catholic Church. Church of St. John the Evangelist. Construction. 1883-1934. *2325*

—. Demonstrations. Jews. Touro Synagogue. 1893-1902. *1236*

—. Freemasons (King David's Lodge). Jews. Washington, George. 1780-90. *1272*

—. Jews. Letters. Religious Liberty. Seixas, Moses. Washington, George. 1790. 1974. *1248*

—. Jews. Merchants. 1740-90. *1228*

—. Jews. Touro Synagogue. 1902. *1177*

—. Jews. Touro Synagogue. 1658-1963. *1243*

Rhode Island (Providence). Belkin, Samuel. Brown University. Jews. Reminiscences. 1932-35. *1356*

—. Business. Jacobs, James. Jews. 1820's-30's. 1850's. *1469*

—. Business. Jews. Memoirs. Resnik, Bezalel Nathan. 1891-1971. *1446*

—. Catholic Church. Conflict and Conflict Resolution. Italian Americans. Parishes. 1890-1930. *794*

—. Clothing. Outlet Company Store. Retail Trade. Samuels, Joseph. Samuels, Leon. 1894-1974. *1225*

—. Congregation Sons of Zion. Finesilver, Moses Ziskind. Judaism. Rabbis. 1880-83. *1409*

—. Education. Jews. 1854-1946. *1288*

—. Education. Politics. 1974. *2870*

—. *Ezra* (periodical). Jews. Order of Ezra. 1911-77. *1173*

—. Family. Jews. Social Organization. 1882-1978. *1251*

—. Finance. Jews. Ladies' Hebrew Free Loan Association. Women. 1931-65. *1222*

—. German Americans. Marx, Eleanor. Political Speeches. Socialism. 1886. *2565*

—. Jews. 1900-12. *1224*

—. Jews. Medicine (practice of). Starr, Samuel. 1910-50. *1452*

—. Jews. Touro Synagogue. 1654-1977. *1321*

Rhode Island (West Warwick). Congregation Ahavath Shalom. Judaism. 1912-38. *1315*

Rhode Island (Woonsocket). Assimilation. French Canadians. Nationalism. Religion. 1924-29. *468*

—. Belgian Americans. French Canadians. Independent Textile Union. Working Class. 1931-50's. *2564*

Richards, Willard. Emigration. Great Britain. Letters. Mormons. Young, Brigham. 1840. *305*

Richelieu Company. French Canadians. Quebec (Montreal). Transportation. 1845-54. *3307*

Rickles, Don. Allen, Woody. Comedians. Humor. Jews. Steinberg, David. Stereotypes. 1960's-70's. *1067*

Riel, Louis. Batoche (battle). Flinn, George A. Manitoba. Métis. North West Rebellion. *Winnipeg Sun* (newspaper). 1885. *3898*

—. Canada. Citizenship. Métis. North West Rebellion. Rebellions. Treason. USA. 1885. *3893*

—. Canada First, group. Expansionism. Mair, Charles. Métis. Red River Rebellion. 1869-70. *3919*

—. Conservatism. French Canadians. LeSage, Simeon. Nationalism. Quebec. 1867-1909. *3930*

—. Documents. Manitoba. Métis. Political theory. Red River Rebellion. 1869. *3904*

—. Escapes. Fort Garry. German Canadians. Manitoba (Winnipeg). Métis. Red River Rebellion. Schultz, John Christian. 1869-70. *3894*

—. Letters. Métis. Prairie Provinces. Religion. Taché, Alexandre Antonin. 1880's. *3902*

—. Letters. Millenarianism. North West Rebellion. Prairie Provinces. 1876-78. 1885. *3901*

—. Mental Illness. Saskatchewan (Regina). Treason. Trials. Valade, François-Xavier (medical report). 1885. *3905*

—. Métis. Millenarianism. North West Rebellion. Prairie Provinces. Rebellions. Religion. 1869-85. *3903*

—. Métis. North West Rebellion. Prairie Provinces. Rebellions. Red River Rebellion. 1870-85. *3899*

Riessner, Johann. Austrian Americans. Burgenland. Immigration. Poetry. 1856-1939. *266*

Riis, Jacob. Borglum, Gutzon. Dana College. Danish Americans. Immigration. Settlement. Wisconsin. 1741-20c. *1684*

—. Civil Rights. Ethnicity. Jews. Social Organization. 1870-1914. *1615*

—. Immigration. Jews. Nativism. Slavic Europeans. 1890-1914. *1644*

Rio Grande. Cultural Diffusion. Houses. Irish Americans. Mexico. Texas. 19c. *757*

Riots *See also* Demonstrations; Strikes.

—. Abolition Movement. Negroes. Pennsylvania (Philadelphia). 1830-50. *2886*

—. Actors and Actresses. Astor Place Opera House. Forrest, Edwin. Macready, William Charles. Nativism. New York City. 1849. *191*

—. Anti-Catholicism. Ideology. Massachusetts (Boston). Social Classes. 1834-35. *187*

—. Cities. German Americans. Irish Americans. Italian Americans. Nativism. Negroes. 19c-20c. *2890*

—. Civil War. Conscription, Military. German Americans. Letters. New York City. Schlegel, Jacob. 1861-63. *619*

—. Civil War. Conscription, Military. New York City. 1863. *2601*

—. Democratic Party. Elections. Irish Americans. Know-Nothing Party. Local Politics. Missouri (St. Louis). 1844-56. *198*

—. Economic Conditions. Nebraska (Omaha). Race Relations. Social Conditions. 1919. *122*

—. Ethnicity. Social Change. 1960-70's. *2981*

—. French Canadians. Garrison Towns. Great Britain. Military. Quebec (Montreal). Rebellion Losses Bill. 1840's. *3880*

—. German Americans. Illinois (Chicago). Know-Nothing Party. Law. Local Politics. Temperance. 1855. *194*

—. German Americans. Irish Americans. Local politics. New York City. Temperance. 1857. *201*

—. Hanson, Alexander Contee. Maryland (Baltimore). State Politics. War of 1812. 1812. *181*

—. Law enforcement. Ohio (Niles). State government. 1924. *213*

—. Missouri (St. Francois County). Modernization. Nativism. World War I. 1917. *2621*

Rioux, Marcel. Colonial Government. Frégault, Guy. French Canadians. Historiography. New France. 1615-1763. 1957-60's. *3182*

Ripinsky, Sol. Alaska. Business. Jews. Reminiscences. 1867-1909. *1267*

—. Alaska (Haines Mission). Jews. Teachers. 1850-1905. *1515*

Risser, Johannes. Democratic Party. Letters. Mennonites. Politics. Slavery. 1856-57. *2305*

Rites and Ceremonies. Attitudes. Lancaster Mennonite High School. Mennonites. Pennsylvania. Students. 1974-78. *2196*

—. Commercialism. Folk art. Greek Americans. Pennsylvania. Religion. 1970's. *672*

—. Episcopal Church, Protestant. Illinois (Chicago). Pamphlets. Swedish Americans. Swope, Cornelius E. Unonius, Gustaf. 1850-51. *1790*

Rittenhouse, David. Astrology. Astronomy. German Americans. Pennsylvania. 1750-96. *644*

Rizzo, Saverio. Fire. Italian Americans. Labor Unions and Organizations. Padrone system. Reminiscences. Triangle Waist Company. 1900-30. *838*

Roberts, Peter. Americanization. Assimilation. Immigrants. Language (instruction). Young Men's Christian Association. 1907-17. *231*

Roberts, W. Adolphe. Creoles. Journalism. Louisiana. Novels. 1929-49. *367*

Robertson, J. B. A. Italian Americans. Miners. Oklahoma (Krebs). Strikes. 1890-1920. *800*

Robesonia Iron Company. Iron Industry. Italian Americans. Labor recruitment. Letters. Negroes. Pennsylvania (Reading). Slavic Americans. 1915-23. *2556*

Rochambeau, Comte de. American Revolution. French Americans. Military Campaigns. 1781. *424*

Rocheblave, Charlotte de. Catholic Church. Language. Métis. Missions and Missionaries. Quebec (Oka). Religious Education. 19c. *3278*

Rodino, Peter W., Jr. Aliens, Illegal. Ethnic Heritage Studies Act (1972). 1972-73. *257*

Roest, Meyer. Bibliotheca Rosenthaliana. Book Collecting. Felsenthal, Bernard. Illinois (Chicago). Letters. Netherlands (Amsterdam). Rosenthal, George. 1868-96. *1365*

Roffignac, Yves de. Aristocracy. Estates. French. French Canadians. Meyer, Rudolf. Saskatchewan (Assiniboia; Whitewood). 1885-1900. *3356*

Rogers, Rolen (and family). American Canadians. Nova Scotia. 1760-1979. *3596*

Roll-call voting. City Government. Constitutional conventions, state. Democratic Party. Illinois (Chicago). Political machines. 1970. *2447*

—. Ethnicity. Political Parties. State Legislatures. Wisconsin. 1893. *2494*

—. Michigan. Political parties. Religion. State Legislatures. 1837-61. *2536*

—. Quantitative Methods. Rural-Urban Studies. State legislatures (review article). 1880-1930. *2495*

Rølvaag, Ole Edvart. Folklore. Happiness, search for. Literature. Norwegian Americans. 1925-37. *1733*

Rølvaag, Ole Edvart (*Giants in the Earth*). Acculturation. Frontier and Pioneer Life. Immigrants. Protestantism. South Dakota. 1870. 1927. *1734*

—. Norwegian Americans. South Dakota. 1873-1900. *1748*

Roman Catholic Church. *See* Catholic Church.

Romanov, Vladimir Pavlovich. Arctic. Kruzenshtern, Ivan Fedorovich. Russians. Scientific Expeditions. 1819-25. *2056*

Sandberg, Neil C. (review article). California (Los Angeles). Ethnicity. Methodology. Polish Americans. 1968-74. *2013*

Sanders, James W. Catholic Church. Ethnic Groups (review article). Horowitz, Helen. Illinois (Chicago). Kessner, Thomas. New York City. 1883-1965. 1970's. *149*

Sanders, James W. (review article). Catholic Church. Church Schools. Illinois (Chicago). 1833-1965. 1977. *2324*

Sang, Philip David (obituary). Illinois State Historical Society. Jews. 1902-75. *1502*

Santa Clara, University of. Accolti, Michael. California. Jesuits. 1849-51. *2344*

Sapak, Theresa. Acculturation. Pennsylvania. Reminiscences. Slovakian Americans. 20c. *1923*

Sarna, Jan. Arkansas (Marche). Polish Americans. Reminiscences. Settlement. Social Customs. 1877-1977. *2038*

Sartorio, Enrico C. Catholic Church. Historiography. Italian Americans (review article). Tomasi, Silvano. 1918. 1975. *852*

Saskatchewan *See also* Prairie Provinces.

—. Agriculture. Bee, William. Bourne, Hugh. Clowes, William. Dow, Lorenzo. English Canadians. Grenfell Colony. Primitive Methodist Church. 1882. *3416*

—. Anderson, James T. M. Anti-Catholicism. French Canadians. Language. Public schools. School Act (amendment). Secularization. 1929-34. *3814*

—. Anti-Catholicism. Assimilation. Education, Finance. French Canadians. MacKinnon, Murdoch. School Act (amendment). Scott, Walter. Scottish Canadians. 1913-26. *3815*

—. Anti-Catholicism. Elections (provincial). Ku Klux Klan. Legislation. Schools. 1929. *3058*

—. Anti-Catholicism. Immigration. Ku Klux Klan. Protestants. 1927-30. *3060*

—. *Bote* (newspaper). Germans, Russian. Mennonites. Nazism. 1917-39. *3643*

—. British Columbia. Dukhobors. Russian Canadians. 1652-1976. *3695*

—. Business. Letendre, François-Xavier (and family). Métis. Political leadership. Social status. 1870-1900. *3388*

—. Catholic Church. French Americans. Immigration. Manitoba. Mathieu, Olivier-Elzéar. Regina Archdiocese. 1911-31. *3363*

—. Catholic Church. French language. Language. *Patriote de l'Ouest* (newspaper). 1910-41. *3359*

—. Catholic Church. German Americans. Language. Politics. St. Peter's Colony. Schools. 1903-16. *3471*

—. Cemeteries. Jews. 1975. *3516*

—. Communalism. Dukhobors. Russian Canadians. 1904. *3694*

—. Deutscher Bund Canada. German Canadians. Nazism. 1934-39. *3766*

—. Dukhobors. Public schools. Russian Canadians. 1905-50. *3693*

—. Dukhobors. Royal Canadian Mounted Police. Russian Canadians. Settlement. 1899-1909. *3691*

—. Galt, Alexander. Jews. Kaplun, Alter (family). Settlement. 1880's-90's. *3503*

—. Liberal Party. Voting and Voting Behavior. 1905-19. *3700*

—. Pioneers. Welsh Canadians. 1902-14. *3458*

Saskatchewan (Arelee). Country Life. Drawings. Lambert, Augustine. 1913-14. *3425*

Saskatchewan (Assiniboia). Local Government. Manitoba (Red River settlement). Métis. 1857-65. *3283*

Saskatchewan (Assiniboia; Whitewood). Aristocracy. Estates. French. French Canadians. Meyer, Rudolf. Roffignac, Yves de. 1885-1900. *3356*

Saskatchewan (Cannington). British Canadians. Settlement. Sports. 1882-1900. *3428*

Saskatchewan (Cannington Manor). Daily Life. English Canadians. Humphrys, James (and family). 1880's-1908. *3424*

Saskatchewan (Chaplin, Duval). English Canadians. Goodwin, Theresa. Reminiscences. Teaching. 1912-13. *3422*

Saskatchewan (Esterhazy). Esterhazy, Paul O. d' (Johan Baptista Packh). Hungarian Canadians. 1831-1912. *3474*

Saskatchewan (Hague-Osler area). Mennonites. Settlement. Social Change. 1895-1977. *3615*

Saskatchewan (Île-à-la-Crosse). Catholic Church. Chipewyan Indians. French Canadians. Indian-White Relations. Letters. Mission St. Jean-Baptiste. Taché, Alexandre Antonin. 1823-54. *3652*

Saskatchewan (Loon River area). Deutscher Bund Canada. German Canadians. Immigration. 1929-39. *3767*

Saskatchewan (Pipestone Creek, Whitewood). Aristocracy. French Canadians. German Canadians. Meyer, Rudolf. Settlement. 1880's. *3360*

Saskatchewan (Regina). Anglophiles. Catholic Church. Francophiles. Mathieu, Olivier-Elzéar. 1905-30. *3896*

—. Clark, Septimus Alfred. English Canadians. Frontier and Pioneer Life. Letters. Radcliffe, Mary. 1884-1909. *3421*

—. Mental Illness. Riel, Louis. Treason. Trials. Valade, François-Xavier (medical report). 1885. *3905*

Saskatchewan (Regina, Saskatoon). Catholic Church. Colleges and Universities. St. Thomas More College. 1918-21. *3661*

Saskatchewan River Valley. Indians. Manitoba. Mennonites. Métis. Red River of the North. Removal, forced. 1869-95. *3617*

Saskatchewan (Rosthern). Germans, Russian. Immigration. Mennonites. Social conditions. 1923. *3633*

—. Germans, Russian. Mennonites. Settlement. 1891-1900. *3644*

Saskatchewan (Wakaw). Dukhobors. Galicians. Lake Geneva Mission. Missions and Missionaries. Presbyterian Church. Russian Canadians. 1903-42. *3690*

Saskatchewan (Yorkton). Colonization companies. Economic growth. Public Policy. Railroads. Settlement. 1882-1905. *3052*

Satire. American Revolution. Bailey, Jacob. Canada. Loyalists. Maine. Poetry. 1751-1808. *3601*

—. German Americans. Hewitt, Abram S. Illinois (Chicago). Legislative Investigations. Lyser, Gustav. *Vorbote* (newspaper). Working Class. 1878. *548*

Satirists. Artists. Dehn, Adolph. Ethnicity. German Americans. Minnesota. Radicals and Radicalism. 1895-1968. *508*

Saturday Evening Post (periodical). Immigration. Mexicans. Nativism. 1914-33. *236*

Sauna. Finnish Americans. Minnesota. 1867-1937. *1694*

—. Finnish Americans. Social Customs. 1970's. *1700*

Saunders, John. American Revolution. Loyalists. New Brunswick. Virginia. 1774-1834. *3576*

Saxon Lutheran Memorial. Concordia Historical Institute. Farms. German Americans. Lutheran Church (Missouri Synod). Missouri (Perry County). Preservation. 1958-64. *563*

Sbarboro, Andrea. California (San Francisco). Immigration. Italian Swiss Colony Wine Company. 1881-1923. *825*

Scandinavia. Canada. Education, nonformal. Income. Self Realization. 1975. *2874*

Scandinavian Americans. Acculturation. Artifacts. Material Culture. Social Customs. Utah (Sanpete, Sevier counties). 1849-1979. *1670*

—. Acculturation. German Americans. Italian Americans. Michigan. Polish Americans. Voluntary Associations. 1850's-1950's. *2756*

—. Alaska. Economic Development. 1877-1965. *1669*

—. Americanization. Domesticity. Washington (Seattle). Women. 1888-1900. *1676*

—. American-Scandinavian Foundation. Culture. 1911-76. *1673*

—. Architecture. City Planning. Country Life. Mormons. Utah (Spring City). 1851-1975. *1671*

—. Bibliographies. 1972. *1674*

—. Decisionmaking. Family. Friendship. Settlement. 1890's. *1663*

—. Folklore. Mormons. Utah (Sanpete, Sevier counties). 1849-1979. *1678*

—. German Americans. Germans, Russian. North Dakota. Pioneers. Settlement. 1875-1915. 1930's. *53*

—. Homesteading and Homesteaders. Montana (Dutton). Real Estate Business. Sollid, George. 1909-28. *1665*

—. Literature. 1847-1945. *1672*

—. Nelson, Edward O. Reminiscences. Salvation Army (Scandinavian Corps). 1877-1977. *1668*

—. Protestantism. 1849-1900. *1666*

Scandinavian Canadians. Alberta (Calgary; Eau Claire district). Eau Claire Company. Housing. Kerr, Isaac. Lumber and Lumbering. Prince, Peter. 1886-1970's. *3537*

—. British Columbia. Homesteading and Homesteaders. Immigration. Prairie Provinces. 1850's-1970's. *3536*

—. Immigration. Prairie Provinces. Public policy. 1893-1914. *3526*

Scandinavian studies. Colleges and Universities. 1970-73. *1659*

Scandinaviska Sällskapet i San Francisco. California (San Francisco). Lütbeck, Karl Wilhelm. Voluntary Associations. Wetterman, August. 1850-1917. *1664*

Scanlan, Laurence. Catholic Church. Clergy. Salt Lake City Parish. Utah. 1875-79. *2373*

Schaeffer, Susan Fromberg. Authors. Family. Jews. Mothers. Olsen, Tillie. Stereotypes. Yezierska, Anzia. 20c. *1044*

Scharlemann, Ernst K. (interview). Concordia Seminary. German Americans. Illinois (Hahlen, Nashville). Lutheran Church. St. Peter's Church. 1905-18. *2409*

Schenck, Carl A. Cary, Austin F. Emigration. Forests and Forestry. German Americans. Germany. World War I. 1910's-20's. *2614*

Schiavo, Giovanni. Historiography. Italian Americans. 18c-20c. 1924-62. *796*

Schiff, Jacob H. California (El Centro). Letters. Schireson, Bernard. Wolffson, David. Zionism. 1914. *1596*

—. Canada. Galveston Plan. Immigration. Jews. USA. 1907-14. *911*

Schiller, Marcus. Business. California (San Diego). City Government. Jews. Mannasse, Joseph Samuel. 1853-97. *1407*

Schimmel, Wilhelm. Cumberland Valley. Folk art. German Americans. Pennsylvania. Wood carving. 1865-90. *545*

Schireson, Bernard. California (El Centro). Letters. Schiff, Jacob H. Wolffson, David. Zionism. 1914. *1596*

Schirmer, Jacob Frederick. Daily life. Diaries. German Americans. South Carolina (Charleston). 1845-46. *615*

—. Daily Life. Diaries. German Americans. South Carolina (Charleston). 1847. *616*

—. Daily life. Diaries. German Americans. South Carolina (Charleston). 1826-76. *617*

—. Diaries. German Americans. South Carolina. 1846. *618*

Schisms. American Revolution. Funk, Christian. Mennonites. Pennsylvania (Indian Field). 1760-1809. *2215*

—. Amish. Pennsylvania (Lancaster County). Stoltzfus, John. Theology. 1850-77. *2301*

Schlegel, Jacob. Civil War. Conscription, Military. German Americans. Letters. New York City. Riots. 1861-63. *619*

Schlesinger, Jacob. California (Los Angeles). Cedars of Lebanon Hospital. Hospitals. Jews. 1901-30. *1212*

Schlutius, Emma. California (Santa Cruz). Converts. Judaism. 1877. *1375*

Schmidt, C. B. German Americans. Historiography. Mennonites. 1525-1974. *2264*

Schmidt, George P. Concordia (Junior) College. German Americans. Indiana (Fort Wayne). Lutheran Church (Missouri Synod). Reminiscences. 1906-09. *2412*

Schmidt, Johann Friederich. Astronomy. German Americans. Pennsylvania. 1785-1812. *641*

Schmucker, Samuel Simon. Ecumenism. German Americans. Lutheran Church. Periodicals. 1838. *2404*

—. Evangelical Alliance. German Americans. Lutheran Church. 1843-51. *2417*

Scholars. Alaska. Foreign Relations. Russian Americans. 1867. 1979. *2113*

—. American Studies. Folklore. Pluralism. Regionalism. 19c-20c. *2911*

—. Blair, Duncan Black. Gaelic language. Language. Nova Scotia (Pictou County). Poetry. Scottish Canadians. 1846-93. *3454*

—. Canada. German Canadians. Herzberg, Gerhard. Immigration Policy. Murray, Walter. 1935-37. *3763*

—. Catholic Church. 1973. *2775*

—. Immigration. Israel. Jews. USSR. 1960's-70's. *1584*

Scholarship. Cadieux, Lorenzo (obituary). French Canadians. Jesuits. Ontario, northern. 1903-76. *3125*

—. Canada. Folklore studies. ca 1900-75. *3828*

—. Educators. Exiles. German Americans. Johns Hopkins University. Veterans. 1945-50. *162*

—. Faculty. Religion. Secularization. 1969. *2163*

—. Feuer, Lewis S. Jews. Reminiscences. Teaching. Wolfson, Harry Austryn. ca 1900-74. *1374*

—. Folklore. Immigrants. ca 1960-78. *2916*

—. Historiography. Jews. 1948-76. *981*

—. Immigration. Leadership. Stachiw, Matthew (obituary). Ukrainian Americans. 1910's-78. *2115*

—. Jews. New York City. Yidisher Visnshaftlekher Institut. 1920-76. *1200*

—. Shevchenko Scientific Society. Ukrainian Americans. 1947-76. *2060*

School Act (amendment). Anderson, James T. M. Anti-Catholicism. French Canadians. Language. Public schools. Saskatchewan. Secularization. 1929-34. *3814*

—. Anti-Catholicism. Assimilation. Education, Finance. French Canadians. MacKinnon, Murdoch. Saskatchewan. Scott, Walter. Scottish Canadians. 1913-26. *3815*

School Boards. Church and State. English Canadians. French Canadians. Political Parties. Prince Edward Island. Prince of Wales College Act (1860). 1860-63. *3707*

—. Educational reform. Elites. Nativism. Niles Bill (Ohio, 1898). Ohio (Toledo). Progressive Era. 1890's. *2459*

School Busing. See Busing.

School Integration See also Busing.

—. Negroes. 1964-78. *3006*

School of Arts and Crafts of St. Joachim. French Canadians. Gosselin, Auguste-Honoré (review article). Laval, François de. New France. Vocational Education. 1668-1730. *3245*

—. New France. Vocational Education. 1668-1715. *3271*

Schools See also Church Schools; Colleges and Universities; Education; High Schools; Private Schools; Public Schools; Students; Teaching.

—. Adolescence. Economic conditions. North Central States. Northeastern or North Atlantic States. Social Status. 19c. *2883*

—. Anti-Catholicism. Elections (provincial). Ku Klux Klan. Legislation. Saskatchewan. 1929. *3058*

—. Bilingualism. Gendron Report. Quebec. 1973. *4060*

—. Catholic Church. German Americans. Language. Politics. St. Peter's Colony. Saskatchewan. 1903-16. *3471*

—. Curricula. Ethnicity. Race Relations. 1974. *2852*

—. Daily Life. Interethnic relations. Jews. New York. Religion. 18c. *1182*

—. English Canadians. French Canadians. Liberal Party. Manitoba. Politics. Railroads. 1870's-90's. *3816*

Schools (attendance). Illinois (Chicago). Working Class. 1880-1930. *2854*

Schreiber, Clara Seuel. German Americans. Lutheran Church. Mission Festival Sunday. Missions and Missionaries. Reminiscences. Wisconsin (Freistadt). 1900. *2414*

—. German Americans. Lutheran Church. Palm Sunday. Reminiscences. Wisconsin (Freistadt). 1898. *2415*

Schreiber, Emanuel. California (Los Angeles). Judaism (Reform). Rabbis. 1881-1932. *1414*

Schultz, John Christian. Escapes. Fort Garry. German Canadians. Manitoba (Winnipeg). Métis. Red River Rebellion. Riel, Louis. 1869-70. *3894*

Schultz, Stanley K. Assimilation. Kaestle, Carl F. Massachusetts (Boston). New York City. Public Schools (review article). 1750-1860. *2863*

Schulze, Ernst Carl Ludwig. Clergy. German Americans. Lutheran Church. Steup, Henry Christian. 1852-1931. *2416*

Schurz, Carl. Civil War. German Americans. Irish Americans. Military General Staff. 1861-65. *2603*

Schwan, Henry C. Luther, Martin (Small Catechism). Theology. 1893-1912. *2408*

Schwartz, Auguste von. Germans, Russian. Iowa. Wartburg College. 1861-77. *570*

Schwartz, Benedict. Assimilation. Duelling. Feinberg, Siegmund. Jews. Texas. 1857. *1404*

Schweizer, Max. Dietsch, Andreas. Immigration (review article). Swiss Americans. 1844-50's. 1978. *2145*

Schwermann, Albert H. Alberta (Edmonton, Mellowdale). Concordia College. German Canadians. Lutheran Church. Reminiscences. USA. 1891-1976. *3698*

Science See also headings beginning with the word scientific; Astronomy; Botany; Natural History.

—. Demers, Jerôme. French Canadians. Philosophy. Quebec. Teaching. 1765-1835. *3284*

—. Elites. French Canadians. Quebec. 1824-44. *3291*

—. Irish Americans. 17c-20c. *761*

Scientific Expeditions See also names of specific expeditions.

—. Alaska. Russians. Voznesenski, Il'ia. 1816-71. *2092*

—. Arctic. Kruzenshtern, Ivan Fedorovich. Romanov, Vladmir Pavlovich. Russians. 1819-25. *2056*

Scientists See also names of individual scientists.

—. Immigrants. Israel. Jews. USSR. 1930's. 1970's. *1066*

Sciranka, John Coleman. Historiography. Journalism. Slovakian Americans. Voluntary Associations. 1924-78. *1931*

Scorsese, Martin (*Mean Streets*). Films. Italian Americans. 1973. *872*

Scotch Irish. Alabama. German Americans. Irish Americans. Scottish Americans. Welsh Americans. 18c-20c. *60*

—. American Revolution. Immigration. Military Service. Politics. 1600-1785. *315*

—. American Revolution. Presbyterian Church. Scottish Americans. 1700-75. *312*

—. Architecture. Cultural diffusion. English Americans. German Americans. Limestone. Maryland (Washington County). Wood. 1736-1840. *2930*

—. Burns family. Immigration. Nova Scotia (Annapolis County; Wilmot Township). 1764-20c. *3445*

—. Elections (presidential). German Americans. Ohio. Political Parties. Voting and Voting Behavior. 1824. *2535*

—. Frontier and Pioneer Life. Immigration. New York. Pennsylvania. Virginia (Shenandoah Valley). 17c-1776. *311*

Scotland. Catholic Church. Emigration. Immigration. Persecution. Prince Edward Island. Scottish Canadians. 1769-74. *3430*

—. Charles I. Colonization. France. Great Britain. Nova Scotia (Port Royal). 1629-32. *3448*

Scots. Church of England. Morris, William. Ontario (Kingston). Presbyterian Church. Queen's College. Scottish Canadians. 1836-42. *3447*

—. Eskimos. Northwest Territories (Baffin Island). Trade. 1910-30. *3456*

Scott, Franklin D. Bibliographies. Immigration. 1925-74. *31*

—. Historians. Johnson, E. Gustav (obituary). Letters. Swedish Americans. Swedish Pioneer Historical Society. 1893-1974. *1770*

—. Historians. Swedish Americans. 1901-74. *2*

Scott, Walter. Anti-Catholicism. Assimilation. Education, Finance. French Canadians. MacKinnon, Murdoch. Saskatchewan. School Act (amendment). Scottish Canadians. 1913-26. *3815*

Scottish Americans. Acculturation. Georgia, Southeastern. 1746-1860. *308*

—. Alabama. German Americans. Irish Americans. Scotch Irish. Welsh Americans. 18c-20c. *60*

—. American Revolution. Jones, John Paul. Military Service. St. Clair, Arthur. 1729-85. *309*

—. American Revolution. Presbyterian Church. Scotch Irish. 1700-75. *312*

—. Appalachia. Land. 1717-1977. *314*

—. Architecture. Barns. Dutch Americans. French Canadians. 17c-1978. *80*

—. Bancroft, Hubert Howe ("Pioneer Register and Index"). California. 1542-1848. *316*

—. Brownson, Orestes A. Cumming, William. Letters. 1850's. *2312*

—. Coal Mines and Mining. English Americans. Illinois. Labor Unions and Organizations. Legislation. Lobbying. 1861-72. *285*

—. Colorado. Fergus, James. Gold Mines and Mining. Montana. 1860-61. *310*

—. Danish Americans. Flagler, Henry Morrison. Florida East Coast Railway. Settlement. 1865-1910. *66*

—. English Americans. Irish Americans. Kansas (Runnymede). Post offices. Ranching. Rural Settlements. Turnly, Francis J. S. Watmough, Robert W. 1886-90. *286*

—. German Americans. Social status. Sports clubs. Voluntary Associations. 19c. *2761*

—. Mormons. Ross, James. 1842-1900. *313*

Scottish Canadians. Alberta (Edmonton). Catholic Church. Colleges and Universities. MacDonald, John Roderick. St. Joseph's College (Alberta). 1922-23. *3676*

—. Anti-Catholicism. Assimilation. Education, Finance. French Canadians. MacKinnon, Murdoch. Saskatchewan. School Act (amendment). Scott, Walter. 1913-26. *3815*

—. Blair, Duncan Black. Gaelic language. Language. Nova Scotia (Pictou County). Poetry. Scholars. 1846-93. *3454*

—. Canada. Catholic Church. MacDonald, John A. Voting and Voting Behavior. 1850's-91. *3705*

—. Canada. Constitution of 1791. Parliaments. Quebec (Lower Canada). 1791. *3886*

—. Canada. Ethnicity (review article). Polish Canadians. Portuguese Canadians. 18c-20c. 1976. *3034*

—. Canada. Fur trade. Hudson's Bay Company. Mineral Resources. 17c-20c. *3457*

—. Canada. Highlanders, 48th. Hunter, William A. Leftism. Liberalism. Military Service. Reminiscences. World War II. 1939-45. *3438*

—. Canada. Immigration. 1960's-70's. *3440*

—. Canada. Kennedy family. 18c-1973. *3450*

—. Catholic Church. Emigration. Immigration. Persecution. Prince Edward Island. Scotland. 1769-74. *3430*

—. Catholic Church. Glengarry Highlanders. Immigration. Macdonnell, Alexander. Ontario. 1770's-1814. *3455*

—. Church of England. Morris, William. Ontario (Kingston). Presbyterian Church. Queen's College. Scots. 1836-42. *3447*

—. Composers. Land. Military. Nova Scotia. Reid, John. 1740's-1807. *3442*

—. Cree Indians (Plains, Wood). Diaries. Fort Pitt. Frenchman's Butte, Battle of. Indians (captivities). Manitoba. McLean, W. J. North West Rebellion. 1885. *3913*

—. Dawson, William. Letters. Mercer, Margaret. Nova Scotia (Pictou). 1840-47. *3435*

—. Education. McCullouch, Thomas. Nova Scotia. Pictou Grammar School. 19c. *3449*

—. Genealogy. Nova Scotia (Hants County). Weatherhead family. ca 1820-1946. *3436*

—. *Hector* (vessel). Immigrants. Mackenzie, Alexander. Nova Scotia (Pictou Harbor). Passenger lists. 1773. 1883. *3443*

—. *Hector* (vessel). Immigration. Nova Scotia (Pictou Harbor). Voyages. 1773. *3452*

—. Immigration. Nova Scotia. 1800-20. *3441*

—. MacGregor, James. Missions and Missionaries. Nova Scotia (Pictou). Presbyterian Church of Scotland. 1786-1830. *3453*

—. MacLeod, Norman. Migration. Nova Scotia (St. Ann's). Presbyterian Church. ca 1800-50's. *3434*

—. Manitoba. Military Recruitment. Red River of the North. Selkirk, 5th Earl. Settlement. War of 1812. 1812-14. *3431*

—. McLachlan, Alexander. Ontario. Poetry. Radicals and Radicalism. Social reform. Working class. 1818-96. *3437*

—. Nova Scotia (Pictou). Settlement. 1773-1971. *3451*

—. Nova Scotia (Pictou County). Presbyterian Church. Social Conditions. 1898-1966. *3433*

—. Prince Edward Island. Selkirk, 5th Earl. Settlement. 1803. *3432*

Scully, William. Agriculture. Great Plains. Irish. Landlords and Tenants. 1843-1976. *777*

—. Illinois. Irish. Landlords and Tenants. 1843-90's. *776*

Sculptors. Italian Americans. 1776-1876. *888*

Sculpture See also Monuments.

—. Art. Jews. New York City. 1905-45. *1144*

—. Barthé, Richmond. Creoles. Negroes. 1901-75. *435*

—. California (San Diego). English Americans. Hutchinson, Allen. 1888-1929. *298*

—. Massachusetts (Gardner). Nyman, Gustaf. Swedish Americans. Violins. 1864-1954. *1811*

Sears, Roebuck and Company. Jews. Philanthropy. Rosenwald, Julius. 19c-20c. *1347*

Secondary Education See also Adult Education; High Schools; Private Schools; Public Schools.

—. Immanuel Lutheran School. Lutheran Church. Wisconsin (Milwaukee). 1903-78. *2430*

Secret Societies. Kallen, Horace M. *Parushim.* Zionism. 1913-1920. *1575*

Sects, Religious. Agriculture. Immigration. Missions and Missionaries. Politics. Settlement. South Dakota. 1850-1900. *55*

—. American Canadians. Anti-Americanism. Ontario (Upper Canada). Rebellion of 1837. 1837. *3876*
—. Brethen, Old Order River. Love feast. Pennsylvania. ca 1773-1973. *2223*
—. California (San Francisco). Ethnicity. Molokans. 1906-76. *2063*
—. Chinese Americans. Nativism. Pacific Northwest. Racism. ca 1840-1945. *171*
—. Emigrants. Illinois. Janssonists. Social Classes. Sweden. 1845-47. *1831*
—. Europe, Northern. Immigration. South. 1820's-50's. *62*
—. Mennonites. Mormons. ca 19c-20c. *2176*
—. Pluralism. Social Organization. 1850's-1970's. *2964*
Secularization. Amana Colony. Communalism. German Americans. Iowa. 1843-1932. *600*
—. Anderson, James T. M. Anti-Catholicism. French Canadians. Language. Public schools. Saskatchewan. School Act (amendment). 1929-34. *3814*
—. Faculty. Religion. Scholarship. 1969. *2163*
—. Israel. Jews. Religion. Self-perception. 1957-77. *1014*
Segal, Beryl. Canada. Education. Immigration. Jews. Reminiscences. USA. 1900-70's. *1468*
Segregation *See also* Discrimination; Minorities; Negroes; Residential Segregation.
—. Catholic Church. Cities. Neighborhoods. Protestant ethic. Social mobility. Values. 1970's. *145*
—. Missouri (St. Louis). Negroes. Neighborhoods. 1850-1930. *146*
Séguin, Robert-Lionel. Centre de documentation en civilisation traditionelle. French Canadians. Historians. Identity. Quebec, University of. 1959-75. *3146*
Seigel, Sheldon. Bombings. Civil rights. Informers. Jewish Defense League. Trials. 1972-73. *928*
Seignelay, Marquis de. Colonial policy (review article). Eccles, William J. French Canadians. New France. ca 1663-1701. 1962-64. *3255*
Seigneurialism. Canada. Colonial Government. Conservatism. French Canadians. Social Classes. 1763-1815. *3306*
—. Economic development. Land tenure. Ontario (Upper Canada). Quebec (Lower Canada). 1700-1854. *3151*
—. French Americans. Michigan (Detroit). Social Classes. 1701-1837. *413*
Seixas, Gershom Mendes. Noah, Mordecai Manuel. Zionism. 1800-47. *1570*
Seixas, Moses. Jews. Letters. Religious Liberty. Rhode Island (Newport). Washington, George. 1790. 1974. *1248*
Self-determination *See also* Home Rule.
—. French Canadians. Quebec. 1960's-78. *3995*
—. French Canadians. Quebec. Separatist Movements. 1970-76. *3994*
—. Great Britain. Independence Movements. Ireland. Irish Americans. Wilson, Woodrow. World War I. 1914-20. *2637*
Self-help guides. Immigrants. Italian Americans. Pecorini, Alberto. 1911. *876*
Self-identity. Assimilation. Jews. Social Organization. 1954-74. *1003*
—. Social Classes. 1974. *2773*
Self-perception. Canada, Western. Métis. ca 1870-1978. *3378*
—. Ethnicity. 1965-78. *2987*
—. French Canadians. Homeland (concept). Novels. Quebec. 1664-1970's. *3127*
—. French Canadians. Quebec. Social Customs. Values. 17c-1978. *3142*
—. Israel. Jews. Religion. Secularization. 1957-77. *1014*
—. Italian Americans. Mass media. Stereotypes. 20c. *864*
—. Jews. Social studies. Teaching. Textbooks. 1880-1920. 1945-65. *1099*
Self-Realization. Canada. Education, nonformal. Income. Scandinavia. 1975. *2874*
Self-respect. American dream. Illinois (Chicago). Inequality. Labor. 1972. *2806*
Selkirk, 5th Earl. Manitoba. Military Recruitment. Red River of the North. Scottish Canadians. Settlement. War of 1812. 1812-14. *3431*
—. Prince Edward Island. Scottish Canadians. Settlement. 1803. *3432*
Semantics. *See* Linguistics.
Seminaries. Catholic Church. Irish Americans. Kenrick, Peter Richard. Missouri (Carondelet, St. Louis). St. Mary's of the Barrens (seminary). 1840-48. *2356*

—. Concordia Seminary. German Americans. Illinois (Springfield). Loehe, Wilhelm. Lutheran Church (Missouri Synod). Missouri (St. Louis). Sihler, Wilhelm. Wynecken, Friedrich. 1846-1938. *2384*
—. Curricula. Hebrew Union College. Jews. Ohio (Cincinnati). Wise, Isaac Mayer. 1817-90's. *1042*
—. Lifestyles. Lutheran Church. Miller, H. Earl. Missouri (St. Louis). Reminiscences. Students. 1922-28. *2402*
Semmingsen, Inge (review article). Family. Immigration. Norwegian Americans. Social conditions. 1815-1930. *1750*
Senate *See also* House of Representatives; Legislation.
—. Defense budget. Foreign Policy. Israel. Jews. Liberals. 1975. *1553*
—. Foreign policy. Ideology. Voting and Voting Behavior. 1965-68. *2489*
Senators. Canada. Elites. Ethnicity. Protestant ethic. Rationality. Values. 1971. *3710*
Senyshyn, Ambrose (obituary). Pennsylvania (Philadelphia Archeparchy). Ukrainian Americans. Uniates. 1903-76. *2064*
Separatist Movements. Alliance Laurentienne. Federalism. French Canadians. Quebec. 1957-70's. *3996*
—. Americanization. Canada. Constitutions. Economic Conditions. French Canadians. Quebec. 1973. *3978*
—. Anglophones. Canada. French Canadians. Political Parties. 1975-77. *3934*
—. Anglophones. Canada. National identity. Political Attitudes. Quebec. 1970's. *4048*
—. Australia. Canada. Constitutional conferences. Federalism. 1965-74. *3952*
—. Balance of power. Defense Policy. French Canadians. Quebec. 1970's. *4041*
—. Canada. Economic growth. Europe, Western. French Canadians. Political leadership. Yugoslavia. 20c. *3948*
—. Canada. Federal Government. French Canadians. Political Theory. Quebec. 1976-77. *3989*
—. Canada. Foreign Relations. French Canadians. Parti Québécois. Quebec. USA. 1973-77. *4006*
—. Canada. French Canadians. Parti Québécois. Quebec. 1970's. *4044*
—. Catholic Church. French Canadians. Lamarche, Gustave. Political theory. Quebec. 1922-75. *4029*
—. Centralization. Federal Government. French Canadians. Political Integration. Quebec. 1960-75. *4023*
—. Class struggle. French Canadians. Quebec. Socialists. 1970's. *4050*
—. Conflict and Conflict Resolution. French Canadians. Institutions. Quebec. Regionalism. South. 19c-1970. *4019*
—. Constitutions. Federal Government. French Canadians. Provincial Government. Quebec. 1968-76. *4045*
—. Davis, William. French Canadians. Ontario. Politics. Quebec. 1976-77. *3998*
—. deGaulle, Charles. Foreign Relations. France. French Canadians. Public opinion. Quebec. 1967-76. *3736*
—. Economic Conditions. French Canadians. Minorities. Quebec. 1976. *4002*
—. Economic Conditions. French Canadians. Quebec. 1960's-70's. *3990*
—. Economic Conditions. Nationalism. Quebec. Socialism. USA. 1970's. *4022*
—. Elections, provincial. Jews. Parti Québécois. Quebec. 1976. *3522*
—. English Canadians. French Canadians. Interethnic Relations. Parti Québécois. Quebec. 1970's. *4024*
—. English Canadians. French Canadians. Modernization. Political Change. Quebec. 19c-1970's. *3914*
—. Europe. Federal Government. Foreign Relations. French Canadians. Quebec. USA. 1977. *4038*
—. Federal Government. French Canadians. Intergovernmental Relations. Quebec. 1960-77. *4033*
—. Federal government. French Canadians. New Democratic Party. Parti Québécois. Quebec. 1960's-70's. *4020*
—. Federal Government. French Canadians. Parti Québécois. Quebec. 1976-77. *4037*
—. Federal government. French Canadians. Pluralism. Public Policy. Quebec. 1976. *3954*

—. Federal Government. French Canadians. Quebec. ca 1970-74. *3964*
—. Federal Government. French Canadians. Quebec. 20c. *4013*
—. Federalism. French Canadians. Quebec. 1759-1977. *3839*
—. Federalism. French Canadians. Quebec. 1867-1976. *4012*
—. Federalism. Lévesque, René. Parti Québécois. Quebec. Trudeau, Pierre Elliott. 1970's. *4030*
—. Filion, M. Frégault, Guy. French Canadians. Giguère, G.-É. Groulx, Lionel (review article). Quebec. 1920's-78. *3166*
—. Foreign policy. French Canadians. Quebec. 1690-1976. *3737*
—. Foreign Policy. French Canadians. Quebec. USA. 1972-78. *4027*
—. Foreign relations. French Canadians. Quebec. 1960-76. *3747*
—. French Canadians. Groulx, Lionel. Historians. Quebec. 1970's. *3155*
—. French Canadians. Jews. Quebec. Social Conditions. 1976-77. *3524*
—. French Canadians. Leftism. Politics. Quebec. Referendum. 1979. *4004*
—. French Canadians. Lévesque, René. Parti Québécois. Quebec. 1968-70's. *4036*
—. French Canadians. Mouvement National des Québécois. Quebec. St. John the Baptist Society. 1834-1972. *4005*
—. French Canadians. National Characteristics. Quebec. 1971-74. *3982*
—. French Canadians. Nationalism. Quebec. 1763-1976. *4018*
—. French Canadians. Parti Québécois. Political Attitudes. Quebec. Voting and Voting Behavior. 1968-76. *3997*
—. French Canadians. Political Attitudes. Quebec. 1960's-70's. *4015*
—. French Canadians. Political Parties. Quebec. 1960-78. *4046*
—. French Canadians. Quebec. 1974-76. *4001*
—. French Canadians. Quebec. 1774-1975. *4047*
—. French Canadians. Quebec. 1975. *4049*
—. French Canadians. Quebec. Referendum. 1867-1976. *3987*
—. French Canadians. Quebec. Regionalism. 19c-20c. *3895*
—. French Canadians. Quebec. Self-determination. 1970-76. *3994*
—. French Canadians. Quebec. Social classes. 1968. *3999*
—. Galtung, Johan. Quebec. Social change. 1961-75. *4035*
—. Intergovernmental Relations. Provincial government. Quebec. 1955-75. *4042*
—. Mennonites. Politics. Social Reform. 1840's-1930's. *2272*
—. Political Theory. Quebec. 1960's. *3955*
Sephardic Hebrew Center. California (Los Angeles). Greek Americans. Immigration. Jews. 1900-74. *1214*
Serbia. Habsburg Empire. Military recruitment. Slavic Americans. World War I. Yugoslav Committee. 1914-18. *2121*
Serbian Americans. City Life. Croatian Americans. Folklore. Indiana, northwestern. Macedonian Americans. 1976. *1882*
Serfdom. Slavic. 19c-20c. *2982*
Serfs. Alaska. Colonization. Russian-American Company. Shelekhov-Golikov Company. 1794-1823. *2099*
Serials. *See* Periodicals.
Sermons. California (San Francisco). Franklin, Lewis Abraham. Jews. 1850. *1192*
—. German language. Language. Pennsylvania. Protestant Churches. 18c. *603*
Servants. Canada. Immigration. Irish Canadians. Poor Law Commissioners. Women. 1865. *3490*
Seton, Elizabeth Ann. Catholic Church. Church Schools. 1774-1821. *2328*
Settlement *See also* Colonization; Frontier and Pioneer Life; Homesteading and Homesteaders; Pioneers; Resettlement; Rural Settlements.
—. Acadians. Colonial Government. Louisiana (New Orleans). Mississippi (Natchez). Spain. 1768. *381*
—. Acculturation. Canada. Immigration. Slovak Canadians. 1885-1970's. *3542*
—. Acculturation. Farms. Jews. New Jersey (Farmdale). 1919-70's. *1183*
—. Agriculture. California (Ripon). Economic Development. 19c-1976. *63*
—. Agriculture. Farmers. Jewish Agriculturists' Aid Society of America. Levy, Abraham R. North Dakota (central). Reminiscences. Slavic Americans. 1903. *1242*

Sollid, George. Homesteading and Homesteaders. Montana (Dutton). Real Estate Business. Scandinavian Americans. 1909-28. *1665*

Solomon, Haym. American Revolution. Diaries. Jews. Military Finance. Morris, Robert. 1781-84. *1092*

—. American Revolution. Jews. Military finance. Military Service, Enlistees. Politics. 1775-83. *993*

Solomon, Joseph. Autobiography. Law. 1905-28. *1478*

Solomons, Leon Mendez. Colleges and Universities. Jews. Psychology. 1873-1900. *1500*

Solzhenitsyn, Alexander. Foreign Relations. National Self-image. Russian Americans. Slavophilism. USSR. ca 1830-1978. *2088*

Sombart, Werner. Immigration. Socialism. Standard of Living. Working class. 1890's-1900's. *2591*

Somerville, Henry. British Canadians. Canada. Catholic Church. Journalism. Social theory. 1915-53. *3647*

Songfests. German Americans. West Virginia (Wheeling). 1860. 1885. *645*

Sonnenschein, Rosa. *American Jewess* (periodical). Jews. Women. 1895-99. *1063*

Sorge, Friedrich Adolph. German Americans. International, 1st. Marxism. 1852-1906. *526*

Sorokin, Elena. Colleges and Universities. Memoirs. Russian Americans. Sociology. Sorokin, Pitirim A. USA. 1889-1959. *2110*

Sorokin, Pitirim A. Colleges and Universities. Memoirs. Russian Americans. Sociology. Sorokin, Elena. USA. 1889-1959. *2110*

—. Russian Americans. Sociology. 20c. *2086*

Soundex indexes. Census. Cities. Geographic Mobility. Immigration. Methodology. 1880-1900. *2811*

Soup kitchens. Depressions. German Americans. Meat Industry. North Dakota (Williston). Norwegian Americans. Vohs, Al J. (interview). 1900's-30's. *2906*

South *See also* individual states; Southeastern States.

—. Agricultural labor. Farmers. Immigration. Midwest. National Origins Act (1924). 1924. *247*

—. Agricultural labor. Immigration. Italian Americans. Negroes. Newspapers, black. 1880-1915. *884*

—. Attitudes. Jews. Social Conditions. 1890-1977. *1058*

—. Civil rights movement. Jews. 1954-70. *930*

—. Civil War. Jews. Levy, Richard. Levy, Rosena Hutzler. Reminiscences. 1860-65. *1499*

—. Conflict and Conflict Resolution. French Canadians. Institutions. Quebec. Regionalism. Separatist movements. 19c-1970. *4019*

—. Europe, Northern. Immigration. Sects, religious. 1820's-50's. *62*

—. Immigrants. International Brotherhood of Pulp, Sulphite, and Paper Mill Workers. Negroes. Pacific Northwest. Women. 1909-40. *2594*

South Africa. Boer War. Great Britain. Irish Americans. Public Opinion. 1898-1903. *719*

—. Canada. French Canadians. 18c-20c. *3103*

South Carolina *See also* South; Southeastern States.

—. Agriculture. Happyville Colony. Jews. 1900-08. *1293*

—. Barnwell, John. Indian Wars. Irish Americans. Tuscarora Indians. Yamassee War. 1701-24. *749*

—. Bosc, Louis Augustin Guillaume. Consular service. Delaware (Wilmington). DuPont de Nemours, Victor. French Americans. Michaux, Andre. Natural History. 1796-98. *363*

—. Diaries. German Americans. Schirmer, Jacob Frederick. 1846. *618*

—. German Americans. Libraries. Lutheran Church. Theological Seminary Library of Lexington, South Carolina. 1832-59. *2391*

South Carolina (Camden). Friends, Society of. Irish Americans. Milhouse, Robert. Wyly, Samuel. 1751-93. *700*

South Carolina (Charleston). Assimilation. Jews. Political Attitudes. 1970's. *1258*

—. Daily life. Diaries. German Americans. Schirmer, Jacob Frederick. 1845-46. *615*

—. Daily Life. Diaries. German Americans. Schirmer, Jacob Frederick. 1847. *616*

—. Daily life. Diaries. German Americans. Schirmer, Jacob Frederick. 1826-76. *617*

—. Diplomatic correspondence. DuPont de Nemours, Victor. French. Genêt, Edmond Charles. Mangourit, Michel de. 1793. 1797. *442*

—. Foreign Relations. French Americans. Jacobin Club. 1789-1800. *426*

—. Jews. Kahal Kadosh Beth Elohim (synagogue). 1695-1978. *1174*

South Carolina (Robeson County). Ethnicity. Jews. Lumbee Indians. Negroes. Stereotypes. 1967-68. *912*

South Dakota *See also* Western States.

—. Acculturation. Frontier and Pioneer Life. Immigrants. Protestantism. Rølvaag, Ole Edvart (*Giants in the Earth*). 1870. 1927. *1734*

—. Agriculture. Immigration. Missions and Missionaries. Politics. Sects, Religious. Settlement. 1850-1900. *55*

—. Autobiography. Germans, Russian. Isaak, Gottlieb. 1870's. *639*

—. Berdahl Family. Norwegian Americans. Rølvaag, Ole Edvart (*Giants in the Earth*). 1873-1900. *1748*

—. Canada. Communalism. Hutterites. 1874-1975. *2211*

—. Clark, Bertha W. Culture. German Americans. Hutterites. Manuscripts. 1921. *2232*

—. Compulsory Education. Culture. German Americans. Hutterites. Legislation. 1700-1970's. *2225*

—. Country life. Mennonites. 1944. *2282*

—. Cows, milk. Farmers. German Americans. Germany. North Dakota. Relief efforts. Wisconsin. 1921. *2642*

—. Cows, milk. Germans, Russian. Germany. North Dakota. Relief efforts. 1918-22. *2643*

—. Democratic Party. Political Campaigns. Primaries. Smith, Al. 1928. *2457*

—. Dutch Americans. Ethnicity. North Dakota. 1880's-1951. *333*

—. Editors and Editing. Iowa. Norwegian Americans. Settlement. 1869-1941. *1700*

—. Eureka (colony). Germans, Russian. Settlement. 1889-90. *541*

—. Germans, Russian. Immigration. Mennonites. Unruh, Daniel. 1820-82. *2294*

—. Holth, Walborg Strom. Illinois (Chicago). Letters. Norwegian Americans. Travel accounts. 1882. *1735*

—. Settlement. Swedish Americans. 1859-1976. *1864*

South Dakota (Deadwood). Colman, Blanche. Colman, Nathan. Frontier and Pioneer Life. Jews. 1877-1977. *1344*

South End House. Massachusetts (Boston). Settlement houses. Woods, Robert A. 1891-1900's. *142*

Southeastern States *See also* individual states.

—. Folklore. Irish Americans. Language. Travel. 1840-1955. *734*

—. Industrial Removal Office. Jews. Migration, Internal. Northeastern or North Atlantic States. Ohio (Columbus). 1901-16. *1262*

Southern Baptist Convention Home Missions Board. Language. Missions and Missionaries. Northeastern or North Atlantic States. 1950-75. *2178*

Southern Baptists *See also* Baptists.

—. Anti-Catholicism. 1920's. *243*

Southwest Museum. California (Los Angeles). Culture. Lummis, Charles F. Newmark, Harris. Newmark, Marco. Newmark, Maurice. Preservation. 1859-1930. *1386*

Sovereign Council. Catholic Church. Governors, provincial. Laval, François de. New France. 1659-84. *3190*

Sovereignty. Federalism. French Canadians. Quebec. 1760-1977. *3843*

—. French Canadians. Miron, Gaston. Poetry. Quebec. 1969-74. *3991*

—. French language. Language. Quebec Act (1774). 1774-1974. *3087*

Spain. Acadians. Canada. France. Great Britain. Immigration. Louisiana. 1755-85. *382*

—. Acadians. Colonial Government. Documents. Louisiana (St. Gabriel). 1767. *380*

—. Acadians. Colonial Government. Louisiana (New Orleans). Mississippi (Natchez). Settlement. 1768. *381*

—. Archives. Basques. Labrador (Red Bay). *San Juan* (vessel). Shipwrecks. 1565. 1978. *3461*

—. Bouligny, Francisco. Creoles. Immigration policy. Letters. Louisiana. 1776-78. *395*

—. Civil Wars. Jews. Press. 1934-39. *1116*

—. Colonial Government. German Americans. Louisiana (Pointe Coupee Parish). Slave Revolts. Taxation. 1795. *491*

—. Immigration policy. Louisiana. 1792-1803. *43*

Spaniards. Canada. Exiles. Poles. USA. ca 1936-78. *163*

—. Discovery and Exploration. French. Mississippi River Valley. 16c-17c. *465*

—. Discovery and Exploration. French. Romanticism. Trans-Mississippi West. 1540-1800. *370*

Spanish Language. Basque language. Documents. Labrador. 1572-77. *3462*

Spatial perception. Behaviorism. French Canadians. Political geography. Quebec (Saguenay County). Territorialism. 1969-74. *3391*

Speak Schools. Diaries. Education. Gehman, John B. Mennonites. Pennsylvania (Hereford). 1853. *2310*

Special Interest Groups. *See* Interest Groups; Pressure Groups; Lobbying; Political Factions.

Speech *See also* Dialects; Language; Linguistics.

—. Georgia, middle. Humor. Johnston, Richard Malcolm. Rural Settlements. 89

Speeches, Addresses, etc. *See also* Lectures; Political Speeches.

—. Education. Levy, William. Negroes. Northwest Texas Colored Citizens College. Social Mobility. Texas (Sherman). 1890. *1025*

—. Friedlander, Alice G. Jews. Oregon (Portland). Woman Suffrage. 1893. *1378*

—. Ireland, John. Irish Americans. St. Patrick's Day Orations. 1840's-70's. *762*

Spiegelberg, Flora Langermann. Metropolitan Protective Association. New Mexico (Santa Fe). New York City. Reform (movements). 1875-1943. *1425*

Spiritual movement. French Canadians. Jesuits. Lacouture, Onésime. Quebec. 1931-50. *3662*

Spirituality. Eschatology. Folk Art. German Americans. Myths and Symbols. Pennsylvania. 18c-20c. *638*

Spivak, Charles. Authors. Colorado (Denver). Jews. Physicians. Social work. ca 1880-1927. *1399*

Sport, illegal. Cockfighting. 3000BC-1975. *2760*

Sports *See also* Games; Physical Education and Training.

—. British Canadians. Saskatchewan (Cannington). Settlement. 1882-1900. *3428*

Sports clubs. German Americans. Scottish Americans. Social status. Voluntary Associations. 19c. *2761*

Spotswood, Alexander. German Americans. Protestants. Settlement. Virginia (Germanna). 1714-21. *577*

Spring, Joel H. Educational history (review article). Greer, Colin. Immigrants. Katz, Michael B. Revisionism. 1973. *2866*

Sprunger, David. Courtship. Diaries. German Americans. Indiana. Mennonites. 1893-95. *2287*

St. John, J. Hector. *See* Crevecoeur, Michel de.

Stachiw, Matthew (obituary). Immigration. Leadership. Scholarship. Ukrainian Americans. 1910's-78. *2115*

Staines, William C. English Americans. Mormons. Utah. 1818-81. *294*

Stamm, Martin. Chicago Fire. German Americans. Illinois. Reminiscences. 1871. *596*

Standard of Living *See also* Cost of Living.

—. Immigration. Socialism. Sombart, Werner. Working class. 1890's-1900's. *2591*

Standke Family. Farmers. German Americans. Minnesota. 1873-1978. *575*

Staniokovich, M. N. Alaska. Indians. Mikhailov, Pavel. Painting. Russians. Voyages. 1826-29. *2108*

Stanislaus II Poniatowski. Diplomacy. Italian Americans. Jefferson, Thomas. Mazzei, Philip. Poland. Virginia. ca 1764-95. *844*

Starr, Samuel. Jews. Medicine (practice of). Rhode Island (Providence). 1910-50. *1452*

Stasik, Florian. Exiles (review article). Poland. Politics. 1831-64. 1976. *1965*

—. Exiles (review article). Polish Americans. 1831-64. *1964*

Stasik, Florian (review article). Exiles. Polish Americans. 1831-64. *1999*

State Department. Documents. Immigration Policy. Jews. Morgenthau, Henry, Jr. Refugees. Treasury Department. World War II. 1942-44. *2686*

—. Genocide. Jews. Pell, Herbert Claiborne. UN War Crimes Commission. World War II. 1943-45. *2656*

—. Jews. McDonald, James G. Refugees. Roosevelt, Franklin D. (administration). 1933-40's. *2673*

State Government *See also* Governors; State Legislatures; State Politics.

—. Frost, Max. Immigration. New Mexico Bureau of Immigration. 1880-1912. *56*

—. Agnosticism. Catholic Church. French Canadians. Quebec. 1970-78. *3645*
—. Assimilation. Attitudes. Behavior. Catholic Church. 1961-71. *2346*
—. Attitudes. Canada. Church and State. Mennonite Conference (leaders). Social issues. 1917-74. *3616*
—. Attitudes. Colleges and Universities. Jews. Northwestern University. Yale University. 1968-69. *1062*
—. Attitudes. Ethnicity. Israel. Jews. Northeastern or North Atlantic States. Zionism. 1973-76. *1595*
—. Attitudes. Lancaster Mennonite High School. Mennonites. Pennsylvania. Rites and Ceremonies. 1974-78. *2196*
—. Brandeis University. Educators. Massachusetts (Waltham). 1948-79. *1083*
—. Brodsky, Joseph. Poets. Russian Americans. Social Customs. 1973. *2075*
—. Canada. Identity. 1971. *3015*
—. Canada (western). Colleges and Universities. Identity. Nationalism. Regionalism. 1960-77. *3017*
—. Catholic Church. Chicoutimi, Séminaire de. Quebec (Saguenay County). Religious Education. 1873-1930. *3395*
—. Clergy. Concordia Seminary. Daily Life. German Americans. Kansas (Clay Center). Lutheran Church. Missouri (St. Louis). Mueller, Peter. 1883-89. *2403*
—. Colleges and Universities. Ethnicity. Religion. 1972. *2948*
—. Colleges and Universities. Interpersonal Relations. 1973. *3773*
—. Colleges and Universities. Jews. Literature. Negroes. Stereotypes. 1933-03. *300*
—. Counter culture. Ethnicity. Jews. 1960's-70's. *961*
—. Ethnicity. Jews. Maryland, University of. Parents. Religion. 1949-71. *1020*
—. French Canadians. High Schools. Quebec (Saguenay County). 1975. *3347*
—. Illinois, University of. Jews. Political Participation. Social backgrounds. 1930's. 1960's. *927*
—. Intercollegiate Menorah Association. Jews. 1906-30. *995*
—. Jews. Leadership. Women. 1968-77. *1018*
—. Lifestyles. Lutheran Church. Miller, H. Earl. Missouri (St. Louis). Reminiscences. Seminaries. 1922-28. *2402*
Stuermer, Herbert. Canada, Western. Ecumenism. Lutheran Church. 1922. *3699*
Sturkie Resolution. Anti-Catholicism. Catts, Sidney J. Elections (gubernatorial). Florida. Guardians of Liberty. Knott, William V. 1916. *216*
Stutz, George M. Jews. Memoirs. Michigan (Detroit). 1920's-70's. *1494*
Stuyvesant, Peter. Dutch Americans. New York City. 1640's-60's. *355*
Suburbs. Institutions. Pennsylvania (Philadelphia). Residential patterns. Social Classes. 1880-1900. *128*
—. Jews. Massachusetts (Boston area). Social change. 1965-75. *1280*
Success. American Dream. Swedish Americans. 1870's-1910's. *1860*
Sud-California Post (newspaper). California (Los Angeles). Editors and Editing. German Americans. Jacoby, Conrad. Jews. 1874-1914. *1176*
Sudetenland. British Columbia (Tupper). Czechoslovakia. German Canadians. Refugees. Settlement. World War II. 1938-44. *3764*
Suffrage *See also* Naturalization; Voting and Voting Behavior; Woman Suffrage.
—. Businessmen. Democratic Party. Elections. Immigrants. Negroes. New York City (Brooklyn). Racism. 1860. *2460*
Sugar cane industry. Immigrants. Italian Americans. Louisiana. Negroes. Race Relations. 1880-1910. *879*
Sugar production. Elections (presidential, gubernatorial). Ethnicity. Louisiana. Slavery. Voting and Voting behavior. 1828-44. *2508*
Suicide. California (San Diego). Divorce. Green family. Jews. Murder. 1863-88. *1484*
Sullivan, John. American Revolution. Barry, John. Carroll, John. Irish Americans. Military Service. Read, George. Thompson, Charles. 1775-83. *733*
Sulpicians. Catholic Church. French Canadians. New France. Nobility. 17c-18c. *3216*
—. Catholic Church. French Canadians. Olier, Jean Jacques. Quebec (Montreal). 1630's-50's. *3674*

—. French Canadians. Law. New France. Property. 1667. *3669*
Supermarkets. California (Los Angeles). Hattem, Isadore M. Jews. 1913-66. *1391*
Supreme Court. Aliens. Permanent resident status. 1974. *254*
—. *Ambach* v. *Norwick* (US, 1979). Employment. *Foley* v. *Connelie* (US, 1978). *Graham* v. *Richardson* (US, 1971). Immigrants. 1971-79. *253*
—. Brandeis, Louis D. Freund, Paul A. Jews. Law. Reminiscences. 1932-33. *1377*
—. Church Schools. Federal Aid to Education. 1947-71. *2876*
—. Church Schools. German language. Language. Lutheran Church (Missouri Synod). Nebraska Council of Defense. 1917-23. *2627*
—. Citizenship. Jefferson, Thomas. Kosciusko, Thaddeus. Poles. Wills. 1798-1852. *2029*
—. Criminal cases. Judges. Social backgrounds. 1947-56. *2481*
Supreme courts, state. California. Heydenfeldt, Solomon. Jews. Lyons, Henry A. 1850's. *1048*
—. Judges. Mormons. Social backgrounds. Utah. 1896-1976. *2476*
—. Law. McCarran, Patrick A. Nevada. 1913-18. *713*
Surette family. French Canadians. Nova Scotia. 18c-1979. *3100*
Surnames. American Revolution. Brennan family. Irish Americans. Military Service. War of 1812. 1775-83. 1812-14. *694*
—. Brennan family. Irish Americans. Military Service. 1745-1918. *693*
—. Canada. Immigration. Mennonites. Swiss Brethren. USA. 1680-1880. *2270*
—. Dutch Americans. Massachusetts (Berkshire County). Settlement. 1670-1823. *340*
Sutter, John. Emmert, Paul. Hawaii. Swiss Americans. 1778-1975. *2152*
Svenska Bröderna (Swedish Brothers organization). Immigration. Minnesota (Minneapolis). Swedish Americans. Voluntary Associations. 1876-88. *1840*
Sverdrup, Georg. Augsburg Seminary. Curricula. Lutheran Church. Norwegian Americans. St. Olaf College. 1869-1907. *1728*
Swastek, Joseph Vincent (obituary). Historians. Polish Americans. 1913-77. *2005*
Swede Point (colony). Dalander family. Iowa (Madrid). 1846-71. *1859*
Sweden *See also* Scandinavia.
—. American Studies. Uppsala, University of. USA. 1860-20c. 1962-75. *1784*
—. Attitudes. Erickson, Lars. Swedish Americans. 1882-1929. *1820*
—. Emigrants. Illinois. Janssonists. Sects, Religious. Social Classes. 1845-47. *1831*
—. Emigration. Finland. Research. 19c-20c. 1962-76. *1810*
—. Emigration. Reminiscences. Vontver, May. ca 1900. *1866*
—. Emigration. Strindberg, August. 1890-1912. *1791*
—. Emigration. Unonius, Gustaf. 1858-63. *1851*
—. Erickson, George F. Immigration. Letters. Michigan. 1891-1950. *1793*
—. Immigration. Johansson, Anders. Letters. Quebec. Swedish Americans. 1854. *1802*
Sweden (Blekinge province). Emigration. 1851-70. *1870*
Sweden (Kronsberg area). Karl Oskar (fictional character). Linnell, Magnus Jonasson. Minnesota (Chicago Lake area). Moberg, Vilhelm. Novels. Swedish Americans. 1820-75. 20c. *1764*
Swedes. Banér, Johan Gustav Runeskeold. Michigan (Ironwood). Poets. 1861-1938. *1792*
—. Minnesota (Chisago Lakes area). Moberg, Vilhelm. Novels. Tourism. 1948. *1834*
Swedish Americans. Acculturation. Agriculture. Immigration. Lutheran Church. Minnesota (Isanti County). Social customs. 1840-1910. *1842*
—. Acculturation. Drama. Language. Literature. Malm, G. N. (*Charli Johnson, Svensk-Amerikan, Härute*). 1909-19. *1799*
—. Acculturation. Folk art. Frontier and Pioneer Life. 1638-1976. *1771*
—. American Dream. Success. 1870's-1910's. *1860*
—. American Revolution. Clergy. Delaware River Valley. Episcopal Church, Protestant. Lutheran Church. 1655-1831. *1768*

—. American Revolution. Congress. Hanson, George A. Hanson, John. Maryland. 1740-83. 1876. *1783*
—. American Revolution. Hanson, John. Military Service. Morton, John. Norwegian Americans. 1770-85. *1662*
—. Anderson, B. Frank. Anderson family. Illinois (Geneseo). Iowa (Madrid). Reminiscences. Westward Movement. 1868. *1766*
—. Anderson, John A. Homesteading and Homesteaders. Nebraska (Cherry County). Reminiscences. Roosa, Alma Carlson. 1880's. *1849*
—. Andersson, Joris Per. Immigration. Letters. Minnesota (Chisago Lake). 1851-53. *1804*
—. Andrews, C. C. Immigration. Lewenhaupt, Carl (report). Norwegian Americans. 1870. *1675*
—. Armies. Journalism. Mattson, Hans *(Minnen)*. Minnesota. 1850's-93. *1818*
—. Arvedson, Peter. Episcopal Church, Protestant. Illinois. 1822-80. *1839*
—. Assimilation. Connecticut (Woodstock). Daily life. District of Columbia. 1906-70. *1787*
—. Assimilation. Diaries. Immigration. Jonsson, Jonas (John Johnson). Minnesota. 1864-95. *1803*
—. Assimilation. Episcopal Church, Protestant. Lutheran Church, Swedish. 1630-1850. *1868*
—. Assimilation. Historiography. 19c-1978. *1852*
—. Assimilation. Lutheran Church. Muhlenberg, Henry Melchior. Pennsylvania. Politics. Wrangel, Carl Magnus. 1749-69. *1827*
—. Attitudes. Erickson, Lars. Sweden. 1882-1929. *1820*
—. Augustana Book Concern. Illinois (Rock Island). Lutheran Church. 1830-1967. *1800*
—. Augustana College. Augustana Seminary. Colleges and Universities. Illinois (Paxton). Osborn, William H. Railroads. 1853-73. *1824*
—. Augustana College. Colleges and Universities. Illinois (Rock Island). Lutheran Church. 1855-1956. *1775*
—. Augustana Evangelical Lutheran Church. Lutheran Church. 1860-1973. *1776*
—. Autobiography. Lundeberg, Axel Johan Sigurd Mauritz. Mattson, Hans. 1880-91. *1862*
—. Bäck, Olof. Esbjörn, Lars Paul. Janssonists. Letters. Methodism. 1846-49. *1837*
—. Banking. Illinois (Chicago). Immigration. Isaacson, John A. 1892-1974. *1801*
—. Baptists. Immigration. Travel (accounts). Wiberg, Anders. 1852-53. *1835*
—. Bengston, Henry. Illinois (Chicago). Publishers and Publishing. 1887-1974. *1816*
—. Berger, Henning. Illinois (Chicago). Immigrants. Literature. Travel Accounts. USA. 1872-1924. *1788*
—. Bergner, Peter. Bethel Ships. Evangelism. Merchant Marine. Methodist Church. New York City. 1832-66. *1869*
—. Bibliographies. Utah. 19c-1979. *1779*
—. Bibliographies. Washington. 1844-1972. *1780*
—. Bishop Hill Colony. Communalism. Economic growth. Illinois. Westward Movement. 1846-59. *1833*
—. Bishop Hill Colony. Communalism. Illinois. Janssonists. Letters. 1847. *1836*
—. Bishop Hill Colony. Daily life. Illinois. Jansson, Erik H. Letters. 1847-56. *1854*
—. Bishop Hill Colony. Engstrand, Stuart (review article). Illinois. Jansson, Erik H. 1846-50. 20c. *1871*
—. Bishop Hill Colony. Hotels. Illinois. Janssonists. 1846-1978. *1855*
—. Brewer, Thomas M. Kumlien, Thure. Natural history. Wisconsin. 1843-88. *1865*
—. Bricks, yellow. Buildings. Dutch Americans. Pennsylvania. 17c. *40*
—. Business. Illinois (Chicago; Englewood district). Osberg, Edward E. Reminiscences. 1926. *1841*
—. California, northern. Economic growth. Ericson, Augustus William. Frontier and Pioneer Life. Social change. 1880's-1920's. *1844*
—. Cassel, Peter. Immigrants. Iowa (New Sweden). 1845-1912. *1826*
—. Christmas. Farmers. Festivals. Iowa (Pomeroy). 1900's. *1778*
—. Clergy. Episcopal Church, Protestant. Lutheran Church. Unonius, Gustaf. Wisconsin (Pine Lake). 1841-58. *1795*
—. Colonization. Delaware River. Penn, William. Pennsylvania. 1637-53. *1809*

U

—. Alberta. Homesteading and Homesteaders. Peace River country. Zahara, Dominka Roshko. 1900-30. *3563*

—. Alberta. Houses. 1890's-1915. *3557*

—. Alberta. Orthodox Eastern Church, Greek. Rabbit Hill Colony. 1900. *3552*

—. Alberta (Cardiff, Edmonton). Chaban, Teklia. Coal mines and Mining. Labor Unions and Organizations. 1914-20's. *3565*

—. Art. Canada. Proch, Don. 1970's. *3553*

—. Ballads. Prairie provinces. 1900-74. *3555*

—. Canada. French Canadians. Social Organization. 1970's. *3029*

—. Canada. Immigration. Political Attitudes. Settlement. Ukrainian Americans. USA. ca 1750-1975. *2111*

—. Canada, Western. Folklore. Immigration. 1945-75. *3554*

—. Canada, western. Gill, Nick. Labor. Railroads. 1894-1918. *3564*

—. Ethnicity. Folk art. Latvian Canadians. Manitoba (Winnipeg). 1978. *3559*

—. Prairie Provinces. Settlement. 1910-31. *3558*

Ukrainian Institute of Music. Music. New York. 1952-73. *2101*

Ukrainian Labour-Farmer Association. Alberta (Edmonton). Farmer's Union of Alberta. Kyforuk, Peter. Manitoba. Political Participation. 1912-30's. *3566*

Ukrainian language. Language. 1920's-77. *2085*

Ukrainian Quarterly. Periodicals. 1944-74. *2062*

—. 1944-74. *2065*

Ukrainian studies. Manitoba. 1949-74. *3561*

Ultramontanism. Catholic Church. Church and State. Economic Development. French Canadians. Government. Quebec (Lower Canada). Social classes. 19c. *3856*

—. Catholic Church. French Canadians. Jansenism. Laval, François de. Quebec. 17c. *3666*

UN War Crimes Commission. Genocide. Jews. Pell, Herbert Claiborne. State Department. World War II. 1943-45. *2656*

Underdeveloped Nations. *See* Developing Nations.

Unemployment *See also* Employment.

—. Atlantic Provinces. Charities. Cities. Immigrants. Poverty. 1815-60. *3807*

—. Canada. Immigration Policy. 1950-77. *3076*

Uniacke, James Boyle. Irish Canadians. Nova Scotia. Political Leadership. Uniacke, Richard John. 1775-1858. *3481*

Uniacke, Richard John. Irish Canadians. Nova Scotia. Political Leadership. Uniacke, James Boyle. 1775-1858. *3481*

Uniates. Clergy. Pennsylvania (Shenandoah). Ukrainian Americans. 1884-1907. *2094*

—. Fuga, Francis J. Ontario (Hamilton). Shrine of Our Lady of Klococov. Slovak Canadians. 1952-77. *3545*

—. Ortynsky, Soter. Ukrainian Americans. 1907-16. *1883*

—. Pennsylvania (Philadelphia Archeparchy). Senyshyn, Ambrose (obituary). Ukrainian Americans. 1903-76. *2064*

Unification Church. Anti-Semitism. Moon, Sun Myung. 1946-76. *1638*

Uniforms, Military. French Americans. Louisiana. Military Ground Forces. Weapons. 1699-1769. *385*

Union and League of Romanian Societies. Assimilation. Immigration. Rumanian Americans. 1900-39. *1656*

Union Nationale. Elections, provincial. French Canadians. Liberal Party. Nationalism. Parti Québécois. Quebec. Social Credit Party. Social issues. 1973. *3956*

Union of American Exiles. *Amex-Canada Magazine.* Antiwar sentiment. Canada. Vietnam War. 1965-77. *3575*

Union of American Hebrew Congregations. Fund raising. Hebrew Union College. Western States. Wise, Isaac Mayer. 1873-75. *1155*

—. Jews. Religion. 1873-1973. *1157*

—. Judaism (Reform). 1873-1973. *935*

—. Judaism (Reform). 1873-1973. *1158*

Union (USA 1861-65). *See* Civil War; also names of US Government agencies, bureaus, and departments, e.g., Bureau of Indian Affairs, War Department.

Unions. *See* Labor Unions and Organizations.

United Brethren in Christ. Evangelical Association. German Americans. Ohio. 1806-39. *2376*

United Church of Canada. Canada. Immigration. National Identity. Protestant churches. 1902-25. *3608*

United Farmers of Ontario. Elections. Farmers. Irish Canadians. Ontario. Orange Order. Political Attitudes. 1920-25. *3484*

United Hebrew Charities. Immigration. Jews. Lipsitch, I. Irving. New York City (Ellis Island). 1891-1910. *1070*

United Hebrew Trades. Jews. New York City. Social Classes. Socialism. 1877-1926. *1094*

United Jewish Charities. Hexter, Maurice B. Jews. Ohio (Cincinnati). Reminiscences. Social Work. 1910's. *1394*

United Jewish Fund. Jews. Ohio (Columbus). Philanthropy. 1904-48. *1260*

United Mine Workers of America. Coal miners. German Americans. Germer, Adolph. Illinois (Virden). Socialism. Strikes. 1893-1900. *502*

—. Immigrants. National Miners Union. Strikes. Utah (Carbon County). 1900-39. *2583*

United States. *See* entries beginning with the word American; US; states; regions, e.g. New England, Western States, etc.; British North America; also names of government agencies and departments, e.g., Bureau of Indian Affairs, State Department, etc..

United States Steel Corporation. Americanization. Indiana (Gary). Labor Unions and Organizations. Polish Americans. 1906-20. *1948*

—. City government. College Graduates. Indiana (Gary). Middle Classes. Monopolies. 1905-76. *108*

United Synagogue of America. Judaism (Conservative). 1910-13. *1078*

Universal Jewish Alliance. California (Los Angeles). Franco-Prussian War. Jews. 1868-70. *1309*

Universalism. Artists. Assimilation. Individualism. Jews. Modernism. 1900-70's. *989*

Universalists. Dutch Americans. Mennonites. New Netherland (New Amsterdam). Shecut, John L. E. W. (*The Eagle of the Mohawks*). 17c. 1800-36. *2200*

Unonius, Gustaf. Clergy. Episcopal Church, Protestant. Lutheran Church. Swedish Americans. Wisconsin (Pine Lake). 1841-58. *1795*

—. Emigration. Sweden. 1858-63. *1851*

—. Episcopal Church, Protestant. Illinois (Chicago). Pamphlets. Rites and Ceremonies. Swedish Americans. Swope, Cornelius E. 1850-51. *1790*

—. Episcopal Church, Protestant. Letters. Wisconsin (Nashotah). 1884. *1767*

—. Episcopal Church, Protestant. Swedish Americans. Wisconsin (Manitowoc). 1848-49. *1796*

Unruh, Daniel. Germans, Russian. Immigration. Mennonites. South Dakota. 1820-82. *2294*

Upper Canada Club. Business. Elites. Ontario (Toronto). 1835-40. *3789*

Upper classes. Canada. Corporations. Social Mobility. 1951-72. *3779*

—. Illinois (Chicago). Libraries. Newberry Library. Values. 1880's. *2851*

Uppsala, University of. American Studies. Sweden. USA. 1860-20c. 1962-75. *1784*

Urban history. 1930's-70's. *148*

—. Carnegie-Mellon University. History Teaching. Quantitative Methods. Social mobility. 1975. *2816*

—. Documents. Immigrants. Macedonian Canadians. Ontario (Toronto). 20c. *3567*

—. Historiography. Interdisciplinary Studies. Quebec. 1968-78. *3124*

—. Illinois (Chicago). 1837-1977. *138*

—. Immigrants. Ontario (Toronto). Stereotypes. 19c-20c. *3046*

Urban History (review article). Clark, Dennis. Connecticut (Stamford). Davis, Allen F. Feinstein, Estelle F. Haller, Mark H. Pennsylvania (Philadelphia). 1700-1970. 1965-74. *133*

—. Cook, Adrian. Gitelman, Howard M. Massachusetts (Waltham). New York City. Social Mobility. Working Class. 1850-90. 1975. *155*

—. Methodology. Ohio (Columbus). Ontario (Hamilton). Pennsylvania (Warren). Wisconsin (Milwaukee). 1830's-1910's. 1970's. *136*

Urban Renewal *See also* Housing.

—. Czech Americans. Illinois (Chicago; Pilsen neighborhood). Polish Americans. 1970-78. *1873*

—. Italian Americans. Massachusetts (Boston; North End). Neighborhoods. 1960's-79. *815*

Urbanization *See also* City Planning; Modernization; Rural-Urban Studies.

—. Canada. Mennonites. Social Customs. USA. 1961-71. *3614*

—. Demography. Immigrants. Negroes. Retail Trade. 1890-1910. *2786*

—. Economic opportunity. Education. Employment. Immigrants. Jews. 1880-1914. *1154*

—. Family. Industrialization. 1800-1977. *2722*

—. Family cycle. Households. Massachusetts (Worcester). Social Change. 1860-80. *2708*

—. Famines. Great Britain (London). Immigration. Irish Americans. Pennsylvania (Philadelphia). 1840's-60. *741*

—. French Canadians. Geography. Quebec. Regionalism. 1930-73. *3039*

—. French Canadians. Industrialization. Nationalism. Political Reform. Quebec. Social Change. 1960's-78. *4000*

—. French Canadians. Quebec (Quebec City). 1790-1840. *3293*

—. Industrialization. Pennsylvania. Philadelphia Social History Project. Research. 1976. *2784*

—. Public Health. Social Sciences. 20c. *2835*

Urbanization (review article). German Americans. Polish Americans. Wisconsin (Milwaukee). 1836-1977. *144*

Urofsky, Melvin I. (review article). Zionism. ca 1900-48. *1528*

—. Zionism. 1880-1930. *1551*

Ursulines. Catholic Church. French Canadians. Louisiana (New Orleans). Marie Madeleine of St. Stanislaus, Sister. Women. 1727-60. *455*

Uruguay. Canada. France. Great Britain. Jews. Poverty. 1975. *3509*

US Military Academy. Business. French Americans. Lewis, Meriwether. Missouri (St. Louis). 1803-38. *383*

Ushin, Stepan M. Alaska. Citizenship. Russian Americans. 1867-95. *2105*

USSR *See also* Russia.

—. Anti-Communism. Defectors. Krivitsky, Walter (death). Military Intelligence. Russian Americans. 1937-41. *2070*

—. Anti-Semitism. Attitudes. 1948-78. *1600*

—. Association of Jewish Book Publishers. Jews. Publishers and Publishing. 1977-78. *1640*

—. Asylum, Right of. Diplomacy. Kudirka, Simas. Lithuanian Americans. 1970-75. *270*

—. Communism. Diplomacy. Lange, Oscar. Poland, eastern. Polish Americans. Roosevelt, Franklin D. 1941-45. *2036*

—. Conrad, Joseph. Foreign Aid. Intervention. National Campaign Committee, Polish Government Loan. Poland. Polish Americans. 1919-23. *1984*

—. Democracy. Immigration. Israel. Jews. 1971-76. *960*

—. Detente. Europe, Eastern. Ford, Gerald R. Political Campaigns (presidential). 1976-77. *2596*

—. Emigrants. Jews. 1974. *1604*

—. Emigration. Jackson, Henry M. Jews. Legislation. Most-Favored-Nation status. 1972-74. *1637*

—. Europe, Eastern. Foreign policy. Politics. Slavic Americans. 1970's. *2597*

—. Foreign Relations. Jewish Defense League. Kahane, Meir. ca 1950's-75. *1009*

—. Foreign Relations. National Self-image. Russian Americans. Slavophilism. Solzhenitsyn, Alexander. ca 1830-1978. *2088*

—. Foreign Relations. Polish Americans. 1939-48. *1983*

—. Immigrants. Israel. Jews. Scientists. 1930's. 1970's. *1066*

—. Immigration. Israel. Jews. Scholars. 1960's-70's. *1584*

—. Immigration. Jews. New York City (Brooklyn). ca 1900-1975. *1508*

Utah *See* Far Western States.

—. Bamberger, Simon. Governors. Jews. 1916. *1371*

—. Bibliographies. Swedish Americans. 19c-1979. *1779*

—. Brooks, Juanita. Jews (review article). Settlement. Watters, Leon L. 1864-65. 1952-73. *1298*

—. Catholic Church. Church Schools. Higher Education. 1875-1975. *2327*

—. Catholic Church. Clergy. Salt Lake City Parish. Scanlan, Laurence. 1875-79. *2373*

—. Danish Americans. Mormons. Morrisites. 1862. *1682*

—. Diaries. Mormons. Musser, Elise Furer. Political Leadership. Social Reform. Swiss Americans. 1897-1967. *2136*

—. English Americans. Mormons. Staines, William C. 1818-81. *294*

—. English Americans. Mormons. Watt, George D. 1840's-81. *306*

—. Genealogy. Immigrants. Missions and Missionaries. Mormons. 1885-1900. *2713*

W

AUTHOR INDEX

LIST OF PERIODICALS

A

AAUP Bulletin (see Academe: Bulletin of the AAUP)
Academe: Bulletin of the AAUP
Acadiensis: Journal of the History of the Atlantic Region [Canada]
Acta Poloniae Historica [Poland]
Action Nationale [Canada]
Actualité Économique [Canada]
Administration and Society
Adventist Heritage
Affari Esteri [Italy]
Afro-Americans in New York Life and History
Agricultural History
AHA Newsletter
Alabama Historical Quarterly
Alabama Review
Alaska Journal (ceased pub 1980)
Alberta Historical Review (see Alberta History) [Canada]
Alberta History [Canada]
Amerasia Journal
American Archivist
American Art and Antiques (see Art and Antiques)
American Art Journal
American Behavioral Scientist
American Benedictine Review
American Book Collector (ceased pub 1976)
American Economic Review
American Heritage
American Historical Review
American History Illustrated
American Jewish Archives
American Jewish Historical Quarterly (see American Jewish History)
American Jewish History
American Journal of Economics and Sociology
American Journal of International Law
American Journal of Legal History
American Journal of Political Science
American Journal of Sociology
American Neptune
American Political Science Review
American Politics Quarterly
American Preservation
American Quarterly
American Review of Canadian Studies
American Scandinavian Review (superseded by Scandinavian Review)
American Scholar
American Society of International Law. Proceedings (issues for 1970-73 appeared under the title American Journal of International Law)
American Sociological Review
American Speech
American Studies International
American Studies (Lawrence, KS)
American Studies (Washington, DC) (see American Studies International)
American West
Américas (Organization of American States)
Amerikastudien/American Studies [German Federal Republic]
Annales de Démographie Historique [France]
Annales de Géographie [France]
Annales: Économies, Sociétés, Civilisations [France]
Annales Historiques de la Révolution Française [France]
Annali della Fondazione Luigi Einaudi [Italy]
Annals of Iowa
Annals of the American Academy of Political and Social Science
Annals of the Association of American Geographers
Année Politique et Économique (ceased pub 1975) [France]
Antioch Review
Appalachian Journal
APT Bulletin [Canada]
Arbitration Journal
Arizona and the West
Arkansas Historical Quarterly
Army Quarterly and Defence Journal [Great Britain]
Art & Antiques
Asupoth [Israel]
Atlantis: A Women's Studies Journal [Canada]
Australian and New Zealand Journal of Sociology [Australia]
Australian Economic History Review [Australia]
Australian Journal of Politics and History [Australia]
Aztlán

B

Balkan Studies [Greece]
Baptist History and Heritage
BC Studies [Canada]
Beaver [Canada]
Behind the Headlines [Canada]
Beiträge zur Geschichte der Arbeiterbewegung [German Democratic Republic]
Bitzaron *
Biuletyn Żydowskiego Instytutu Historycznego w Polsce [Poland]
Bohemia [German Federal Republic]
Brigham Young University Studies
British Heritage [Great Britain]
Bulletin de la Société de l'Histoire du Protestantisme Français [France]
Bulletin des Séances de l'Académie Royale des Sciences d'Outre-mer [Belgium]
Bulletin of Bibliography
Bulletin of Research in the Humanities
Bulletin of the Atomic Scientists (briefly known as Science and Public Affairs)
Bulletin of the History of Medicine
Burgenländische Heimatblätter [Austria]
Business History Review

C

Cahiers de Géographie de Québec [Canada]
California Historical Quarterly (see California History)
California History
California Librarian (suspended pub 1978)
Canada: An Historical Magazine (ceased pub 1976) [Canada]
Canadian Dimension [Canada]
Canadian Ethnic Studies = Études Ethniques au Canada [Canada]
Canadian Geographic [Canada]
Canadian Geographical Journal (see Canadian Geographic) [Canada]
Canadian Historic Sites [Canada]
Canadian Historical Association Historical Papers (see Canadian Historical Papers) [Canada]
Canadian Historical Review [Canada]
Canadian Journal of History = Annales Canadiennes d'Histoire [Canada]
Canadian Journal of History of Sport = Revue Canadienne de l'Histoire des Sports [Canada]
Canadian Journal of Political Science = Revue Canadienne de Science Politique [Canada]
Canadian Labour [Canada]
Canadian Library Journal [Canada]
Canadian Oral History Association Journal = Journal de la Société Canadienne d'Histoire Orale [Canada]
Canadian Public Administration = Administration Publique du Canada [Canada]
Canadian Review of American Studies [Canada]
Canadian Review of Sociology and Anthropology = Revue Canadienne de Sociologie et d'Anthropologie [Canada]
Canadian Review of Studies in Nationalism = Revue Canadienne des Études sur le Nationalisme [Canada]
Canadian-American Review of Hungarian Studies [Canada]
Capitol Studies (see Congressional Studies)
Caribbean Quarterly [Jamaica]
Caribbean Review
Catalyst [Canada]
Catholic Historical Review
Centennial Review
Center Magazine
Change
Chicago History
Chronicle
Chronicles of Oklahoma
Church History
Cincinnati Historical Society Bulletin
Civil Liberties Review (ceased pub 1979)
Civil War History
Clio Medica [Netherlands]
Colby Library Quarterly
Colorado Magazine
Colorado Quarterly
Columbia Journal of Transnational Law
Commentary
Communautés: Archives Internationales de Sociologie de la
Communist Viewpoint [Canada]
Comparative Political Studies

Comparative Studies in Society and History [Great Britain]

Comparative Studies in Society and History [Great Britain]
Computers and the Humanities
Comunità [Italy]
Concordia Historical Institute Quarterly
Conflict
Congress and the Presidency: A Journal of Capital Affairs
Congressional Studies (see Congress and the Presidency)
Crisis
Critical Inquiry
Culture Vivante [Canada]
Cultures [France]
Current History

D

Daedalus
Dalhousie Review [Canada]
Daughters of the American Revolution Magazine
Défense Nationale [France]
Delaware History
Dialogue: A Journal of Mormon Thought
Dissent
Dix-Septième Siècle [France]
Durham University Journal [Great Britain]

E

Early American Life
Early American Literature
East European Quarterly
Education and Urban Society
Eesti NSV Teaduste Akadeemia. Toimetised. Ühiskonnateadused [Union of Soviet Socialist Republic]
Éire-Ireland
Encounter [Great Britain]
Esprit [France]
Essex Institute Historical Collections
Estudios del Departamento de Historia Moderna (IHE) [Spain]
Ethnic Groups
Ethnicity
Ethnohistory
Études [France]
Études Françaises [Canada]
Études Internationales [Canada]
Europa Archiv [German Federal Republic]
Explorations in Economic History
Explorations in Ethnic Studies

F

Family Heritage (ceased pub 1979)
Feminist Studies
Fides et Historia
Film and History
Filson Club History Quarterly
Florida Historical Quarterly
Foreign Affairs
Foreign Policy
Foundations: A Baptist Journal of History and Theology
Frankfurter Hefte [German Federal Republic]
Freedom at Issue
French Historical Studies
French-American Review
Frontiers

G

Gal-Ed: On the History of the Jews in Poland [Israel]
Gateway Heritage
Gazette: International Journal for Mass Communication Studies [Netherlands]
Geographical Review
Geography [Great Britain]
Georgia Historical Quarterly
Geschichte in Wissenschaft und Unterricht [German Federal Republic]
Government and Opposition [Great Britain]
Great Plains Journal
Greek Orthodox Theological Review

H

Harvard Educational Review
Hawaiian Journal of History
Hebrew Union College Annual
Heimen [Norway]
Histoire Sociale (see Social History = Histoire
   Sociale) [Canada]
Historia [South Africa]
Historiallinen Aikakauskirja [Finland]
Historian
Historic Preservation
Historical Archaeology
Historical Journal of Massachusetts
Historical Journal of Western Massachusetts (see
   Historical Journal of Massachusetts)
Historical Magazine of the Protestant Episcopal
   Church
Historical Methods
Historical Methods Newsletter (see Historical
   Methods)
Historical New Hampshire
Historical Reflections = Réflexions Historiques
   [Canada]
Historijski Zbornik [Yugoslavia]
History of Childhood Quarterly: The Journal of
   Psychohistory (see Journal of Psychohistory)
History of Education [Great Britain]
History of Education Quarterly
History of Religions
History Teacher
History Today [Great Britain]
History Workshop Journal [Great Britain]
Horizon
Human Organization

I

Idaho Yesterdays
Immigration History Newsletter
Indian Review [India]
Indiana Folklore
Indiana History Bulletin
Indiana Magazine of History
Indiana Social Studies Quarterly
Industrial and Labor Relations Review
Industrial Relations = Relations Industrielles
   [Canada]
Inland Seas
Innes Review [Great Britain]
International Affairs [Union of Soviet Socialist
   Republic]
International Journal [Canada]
International Journal of Comparative Sociology
   [Canada]
International Journal of Contemporary Sociology
International Journal of Women's Studies [Canada]
International Migration = Migrations
   Internationales = Migraciones Internacionales
   [Netherlands]
International Migration Review
International Organization
International Perspectives [Canada]
International Review of History and Political
   Science [India]
International Review of Social History
   [Netherlands]
International Social Science Journal [France]
International Socialist Review
Internationale Wissenschaftliche Korrespondenz zur
   Geschichte der Deutschen Arbeiterbewegung
   [German Federal Republic]
Irish Historical Studies [Republic of Ireland]
Irish Sword: Journal of the Military History Society
   of Ireland [Republic of Ireland]
Isis
Istoriia SSSR [Union of Soviet Socialist Republic]
Italia Contemporanea [Italy]
Italian Americana
Italian Quarterly (ceased pub 1977-79)

J

Jahrbuch des Instituts für Deutsche Geschichte
   [Israel]
Jahrbuch für Geschichte [German Democratic
   Republic]
Jahrbücher für Geschichte Osteuropas [German
   Federal Republic]
Jednota Annual Furdek
Jerusalem Journal of International Relations [Israel]
Jerusalem Quarterly [Israel]
Jewish Social Studies
Journal of American Folklore
Journal of American History
Journal of American Studies [Great Britain]

Journal of Arizona History
Journal of Baltic Studies
Journal of Canadian Studies = Revue d'Études
   Canadiennes
Journal of Church and State
Journal of Commonwealth and Comparative Politics
   [Great Britain]
Journal of Communication
Journal of Conflict Resolution
Journal of Croatian Studies
Journal of Economic History
Journal of Ecumenical Studies
Journal of Ethnic Studies
Journal of Family History: Studies in Family,
   Kinship, and Demography
Journal of Forest History
Journal of General Education
Journal of Historical Geography
Journal of Imperial and Commonwealth History
   [Great Britain]
Journal of Interdisciplinary History
Journal of Intergroup Relations
Journal of Libertarian Studies
Journal of Library History, Philosophy, and
   Comparative Librarianship
Journal of Mexican American History
Journal of Mississippi History
Journal of Negro Education
Journal of Palestine Studies [Lebanon]
Journal of Political Economy
Journal of Politics
Journal of Popular Culture
Journal of Popular Film (see Journal of Popular
   Film and Television)
Journal of Popular Film and Television
Journal of Presbyterian History
Journal of Psychohistory
Journal of Religious History [Australia]
Journal of San Diego History
Journal of Social History
Journal of Social Issues
Journal of Southern History
Journal of Sport History
Journal of Studies on Alcohol
Journal of the American Academy of Religion
Journal of the American Historical Society of
   Germans from Russia
Journal of the Canadian Church Historical Society
   [Canada]
Journal of the Folklore Institute
Journal of the Hellenic Diaspora: Critical Thoughts
   on Greek
Journal of the History of Medicine and Allied
   Sciences
Journal of the History of the Behavioral Sciences
Journal of the Illinois State Historical Society
Journal of the Lancaster County Historical Society
Journal of the Society for Army Historical Research
   [Great Britain]
Journal of the West
Journal of Urban History
Journalism Quarterly
Judaica [Switzerland]

K

Kalendar Jednota
Kansas Historical Quarterly (superseded by Kansas
   History)
Kansas Quarterly
Kultura i Społeczeństwo [Poland]
Kwartalnik Historyczny [Poland]

L

Labor History
Labour = Travailleur [Canada]
Latvijas PSR Zinãtnu Akademijas Vestis [Union of
Leo Baeck Institute. Year Book [Great Britain]
Lietuvos TSR Mokslu Akademijos. Darbai. Serija A:
   Visuomenes Mokslai [Union of Soviet Socialist
   Republic]
Lincoln Herald
Lituanus
Louisiana History
Louisiana Review = Revue de Louisiane
Louisiana Studies (see Southern Studies: An
   Interdisciplinary Journal of the South)
Luso-Brazilian Review
Lutheran Quarterly (ceased pub 1977)

M

Macedonian Review [Yugoslavia]
Magazin Istoric [Romania]

Magyar Könyvszemle [Hungary]
Maine Historical Society Quarterly
Manitoba History [Canada]
Manitoba Pageant (superseded by Manitoba History)
   [Canada]
Mankind
Manuscripta
Manuscripts
Maritime History [Great Britain]
Marxist Perspectives
Maryland Historian
Maryland Historical Magazine
Massachusetts Historical Society Proceedings
Massachusetts Review
Masterkey
Medical History [Great Britain]
Mennonite Historical Bulletin
Mennonite Life
Mennonite Quarterly Review
Methodist History
Michael: On the History of the Jews in the Diaspora
   [Israel]
Michigan History
Michigan Jewish History
Mid-America
Middle East Journal
Midstream
Midwest Quarterly
Midwestern Archivist
Military Affairs
Military Collector and Historian
Milwaukee History
Minnesota History
Missionalia Hispanica [Spain]
Mississippi Quarterly
Missouri Historical Review
Missouri Historical Society. Bulletin (superseded by
   Gateway Heritage)
Modern Age
Montana: Magazine of Western History
Monthly Labor Review
Monthly Review
Mouvement Social [France]
Movimento Operaio e Socialista [Italy]

N

National Civic Review
Nationalities Papers
Nebraska History
Negro History Bulletin
Nevada Historical Review
Nevada Historical Society Quarterly
New England Historical and Genealogical Register
New England Quarterly
New England Social Studies Bulletin
New Hungarian Quarterly [Hungary]
New Jersey History
New Mexico Historical Review
New York Affairs
New York Folklore
New York Folklore Quarterly (superseded by New
   York Folklore)
New York History
New York University Journal of International Law
   and Politics
New-England Galaxy
Newport History
New-York Historical Society Quarterly
Niagara Frontier
North Carolina Historical Review
North Dakota History
North Dakota Quarterly
North Louisiana Historical Association Journal
Northwest Ohio Quarterly: a Journal of History and
   Norwegian-American Studies
Nouvelle Revue des Deux Mondes [France]
Nova Scotia Historical Quarterly [Canada]
Nova Scotia Historical Society Collections [Canada]
Novaia i Noveishaia Istoriia [Union of Soviet
   Socialist Republic]
Nowe Drogi [Poland]

O

Ohio History
Old Northwest
Ontario History [Canada]
Oregon Historical Quarterly

P

Pacific Historian
Pacific Historical Review
Pacific Northwest Quarterly

Pacific Northwesterner
Pacific Sociological Review
Paedagogica Historica [Belgium]
Palimpsest
Panhandle-Plains Historical Review
Papers in Slovene Studies (see Slovene Studies)
Papers of the Bibliographical Society of America
Partisan Review
Párttörténeti Közlemények [Hungary]
Past and Present [Great Britain]
Patterns of Prejudice [Great Britain]
Peace and Change
Peasant Studies
Peasant Studies Newsletter (see Peasant Studies)
Pennsylvania Folklife
Pennsylvania History
Pennsylvania Magazine of History and Biography
Pennsylvania Mennonite Heritage
Perspectives in American History
Phylon
Pioneer America
Plains Anthropologist
Plural Societies [Netherlands]
Policy Studies Journal
Polish American Studies
Polish Perspectives [Poland]
Polish Review
Polish Western Affairs [Poland]
Political Science [New Zealand]
Political Science Quarterly
Political Studies [Great Britain]
Politico [Italy]
Politics & Society
Politique Étrangère [France]
Polity
Ponte [Italy]
Population Studies [Great Britain]
Present Tense
Problemi di Ulisse [Italy]
Proceedings of the Academy of Political Science
Proceedings of the American Antiquarian Society
Proceedings of the American Philosophical Society
Proceedings of the Annual Meeting of the Western
   Society for French History
Proceedings of the Huguenot Society of London
   [Great Britain]
Prologue: the Journal of the National Archives
Protée [Canada]
Przegląd Historyczny [Poland]
Przegląd Zachodni [Poland]
Psychiatry: Journal for the Study of Interpersonal
   Processes
Public Interest
Public Opinion Quarterly
Publius

Q

Quaker History
Quarterly Journal of Studies on Alcohol (see Journal
   of Studies on Alcohol)
Quarterly Journal of the Library of Congress
Quarterly Review of Historical Studies [India]
Queen's Quarterly [Canada]

R

Radical History Review
Rassegna Italiana di Sociologia [Italy]
Reason
Recherche Sociale [France]
Recherches Sociographiques [Canada]
Records of the American Catholic Historical Society
   of Philadelphia
Red River Valley Historical Review
Register of the Kentucky Historical Society
Relations Industrielles (see Industrial Relations =
   Relations Industrielles) [Canada]
Religion in Life (ceased pub 1980)
Research Studies
Review of Politics
Review of Radical Political Economics
Review of Social Economy
Reviews in American History
Revue de Louisiane-Louisiana Review (see Louisiana
   Review = Revue de Louisiane)
Revue de l'Université d'Ottawa (see University of
   Ottawa Quarterly = Revue de l'Université
   d'Ottawa) [Canada]
Revue d'Histoire de la Deuxième Guerre Mondiale
   [France]
Revue d'Histoire de l'Amérique Française [Canada]
Revue d'Histoire Économique et Sociale (suspended
   pub 1977) [France]
Revue d'Histoire Moderne et Contemporaine
   [France]

Revue Française d'Histoire d'Outre-mer [France]
Revue Internationale de Droit Comparé [France]
Revue Internationale d'Histoire de la Banque
   [Italy]
Rhode Island History
Richmond County History
Risorgimento [Italy]
Rivista Militare [Italy]
Rivista Storica Italiana [Italy]
Rochester History
Round Table [Great Britain]
Rural Sociology
Russian Review

S

Saskatchewan History [Canada]
Sborník Historický [Czechoslovakia]
Scandinavian Economic History Review [Denmark]
Scandinavian Journal of History [Sweden]
Scandinavian Review
Scandinavian Studies
Schweizerische Zeitschrift für Geschichte = Revue
   Suisse d'Histoire = Rivista Storica Svizzera
   [Switzerland]
Science and Public Affairs (see Bulletin of the
   Atomic Scientists)
Science and Society
Scottish Geographical Magazine [Great Britain]
Scottish Historical Review [Great Britain]
Scottish Journal of Political Economy [Great
   Britain]
Serials Librarian
Sessions d'Étude: Société Canadienne d'Histoire de
   l'Église Catholique (published simultaneously in
   one volume with Study Sessions: Canadian
   Catholic Historical Association) [Canada]
Shvut [Israel]
Signs: Journal of Women in Culture and Society
Slavic Review: American Quarterly of Soviet and
   East European Studies
Slavonic and East European Review [Great Britain]
Slovakia
Slovanský Přehled [Czechoslovakia]
Slovene Studies
Smithsonian
Social Education
Social Forces
Social History = Histoire Sociale [Canada]
Social Policy
Social Problems
Social Research
Social Science
Social Science History
Social Science Journal
Social Science Quarterly
Social Science Research Council Items
Social Service Review
Social Studies
Societas
Society
Sociological Analysis
Sociological Quarterly
Sociology and Social Research
Sociology of Education
Sound Heritage [Canada]
Soundings (Nashville, TN)
South Atlantic Quarterly
South Carolina Historical Magazine
South Dakota History
Southern California Quarterly
Southern Exposure
Southern Folklore Quarterly
Southern Literary Journal
Southern Studies: An Interdisciplinary Journal of the
   South
Southwest Review
Southwestern Art (ceased pub 1978)
Southwestern Historical Quarterly
Sovetskaia Etnografiia [Union of Soviet Socialist
   Republic]
Sovetskoe Gosudarstvo i Pravo [Union of Soviet
   Socialist Republic]
Soviet Jewish Affairs [Great Britain]
Special Libraries
Spiegel Historiael [Netherlands]
Stadion [German Federal Republic]
Staten Island Historian *
Storia Contemporanea [Italy]
Strategy and Tactics
Studia Hibernica [Republic of Ireland]
Studia Rosenthaliana [Netherlands]
Studies: An Irish Quarterly Review of Letters,
   Philosophy and Science [Republic of Ireland]
Studies in Bibliography and Booklore
Studies in Comparative Communism
Studies in History and Society (suspended pub 1977)

Study Sessions: Canadian Catholic Historical
   Association (published simultaneously in one
   volume with Sessions d'Étude: Société
   Canadienne d'Histoire de l'Église Catholique)
   [Canada]
Sučasnist [German Federal Republic]
Sudetenland [German Federal Republic]
Survey [Great Britain]
Survival [Great Britain]
Swedish Pioneer Historical Quarterly
Swiss American Historical Society Newsletter

T

Teachers College Record
Teaching History [Great Britain]
Tennessee Folklore Society Bulletin
Tennessee Historical Quarterly
Tequesta
Terrae Incognita
Texana (ceased pub 1974)
Texas Quarterly (ceased pub 1978)
Transactions of the Historical and Scientific Society
   of Manitoba (superseded by Manitoba History)
   [Canada]
Transactions of the Moravian Historical Society
Transactions of the Royal Society of Canada =
   Mémoires de la Société Royale du Canada
   [Canada]
Transport History [Great Britain]
Turun Historiallinen Arkisto [Finland]

U

Ukrainian Quarterly
Ukrainian Review [Great Britain]
Ukraïns'kyi Istoryk
University of Ottawa Quarterly = Revue de
   l'Université d'Ottawa [Canada]
University of Turku, Institute of General History.
   Publications [Finland]
Upper Ohio Valley Historical Review
Urban Affairs Quarterly
Urban and Social Change Review
Urban History Review = Revue d'Histoire Urbaine
   [Canada]
Urban Review
Utah Historical Quarterly

V

Veltro [Italy]
Vermont History
Vesnik Vojnog Muzeja — Beograd [Yugoslavia]
Vestnik Moskovskogo Universiteta, Seriia 8: Istoriia
   [Union of Soviet Socialist Republic]
Vierteljahrshefte für Zeitgeschichte [German
   Federal Republic]
Viewpoints: Georgia Baptist History
Virginia Cavalcade
Virginia Magazine of History and Biography
Virginia Quarterly Review
Voprosy Istorii [Union of Soviet Socialist Republic]

W

Washington Monthly
Welsh History Review = Cylchgrawn Hanes Cymru
   [Great Britain]
West Georgia College Studies in the Social Sciences
West Tennessee Historical Society Papers
West Virginia History
Western Folklore
Western Historical Quarterly
Western Illinois Regional Studies
Western Pennsylvania Historical Magazine
Western Political Quarterly
Western States Jewish Historical Quarterly
Westways
Wiener Library Bulletin [Great Britain]
William and Mary Quarterly
Winterthur Portfolio
Wisconsin Magazine of History
Women's Studies
Working Papers for a New Society
Working Papers from the Regional Economic
   History Center
World Marxist Review [Canada]
World Today [Great Britain]
Worldview

Y

Yad Vashem News [Israel]
Yad Vashem Studies on the European Jewish
    Catastrophe and Resistance [Israel]
Yale University Library Gazette

Yalkut Moreshet Periodical [Israel]
Yivo Annual of Jewish Social Science
Yivo Bleter
York State Tradition (ceased pub 1974)
Youth and Society

Z

Z Pola Walki [Poland]
Zeitschrift für Geschichtswissenschaft [German
    Democratic Republic]
Zeitschrift für Kirchengeschichte [German Federal
    Republic]

LIST OF ABSTRACTERS

A

Aimone, A. C.
Alcock, A.
Alexander, G. M.
Alltmont, R. C.
Alvis, R.
Andrew, J. A.
Anstey, C.
Athey, L. L.
Atkins, L. R.
Atkinson, J. L. B.
Auffenberg, T. L.

B

Bailey, E. C.
Balmuth, D.
Barkan, E. R.
Barnard, R. S.
Bassett, T. D. S.
Bassler, G.
Bates, C.
Bauer, K. J.
Baylen, J. O.
Beaber, P. A.
Beck, P. J.
Beecher, L. N.
Belles, A. G.
Benson, J. A.
Billigmeier, J. C.
Blethen, H. T.
Blum, G. P.
Bobango, G. J.
Bowers, D. E.
Bradford, J. C.
Broussard, J. H.
Burckel, N. C.
Burnett, B.
Buschen, J.
Butchart, R. E.

C

Calkin, H. L.
Cameron, D. D.
Campbell, E. R.
Carp, E. W.
Carr, S. P.
Casada, J. A.
Chan, L. B.
Chaput, D.
Chard, D. F.
Chard, E. A.
Churchill, E. A.
Clark, M. J.
Cleyet, G. P.
Clive, A.
Coleman, P. J.
Collins, D. N.
Collon, C.
Correia-Afonso, J.
Crowther, K. N. T.
Curtis, G. H.

D

D'Aniello, C.
Davis, D. G.
Davis, G. H.
Davison, S. R.
Dean, D. M.
de Leonardis, M.
Dewees, A. C.
Dibert, M. D.
Dodd, D.
Driggs, O. T.

E

Egerton, F. N.
Eiel, C. G.
Elison, W. W.
Eminhizer, E. E.
Engler, D. J.
Evans, A. J.
Evans, H. M.

F

Fahl, R. J.
Faissler, M.
Falk, J. D.
Ferdinand, C. I. P.
Findling, J. E.
Fitzgerald, C. B.
Forgus, S. P.
Fox, J. P.
Frame, R. M., III
Frenkley, N.
Frey, L. S.
Frey, M. L.
Fulton, R. T.

G

Gagnon, G. O.
Gammage, J.
Garfinkle, R. A.
Garland, A. N.
Gassner, J. S.
Geyer, M.
Gibson, E.
Gillam, M. R.
Glasrud, B. A.
Grant, C. L.
Grant, H. R.
Gunter, C. R.

H

Hapak, J. T.
Hardacre, P. H.
Harling, F. F.
Harrington, J. F.
Harrow, S.
Hartford, D. A.
Hartig, T. H.
Hazelton, J. L.
Heermans, D.
Heitzman-Wojcicka, H.
Held, C. H.
Henry, B. W.
Herbst, J.
Herstein, S. R.
Hetzron, R.
Hewlett, G. A.
Hidas, P. I.
Hillje, J. W.
Hively, W. R.
Hobson, W. K.
Hočevar, T.
Hoffman, A.
Holsinger, J. C.
Homan, G. D.
Hough, M.
Howell, A. W.
Howell, R.
Huff, A. E.
Human, V. L.
Hunley, J. D.
Hyslop, E. C.

J

Jennison, E. W.
Jeyes, U. G.
Johnson, B. D.
Johnson, D. W.
Johnson, L. F.
Jordan, D. P.

K

Kalinowski, L.
Kaufman, M.
Kearns, W. A.
Kennedy, P. W.
Kerens, S.
Khan, R. O.
Kicklighter, J. A.
Klein, B.
Knafla, L. A.
Krenkel, J. H.
Kubicek, R. V.
Kuntz, N. A.
Kurland, G.

L

LaBue, B. J.
Larson, A. J.
Layton, R. V.
LeBlanc, A. E.
Ledbetter, B. D.
Lederer, N.
Lee, J. M.
Leedom, J. W.
Legan, M. S.
Lester, E. R.
Levy, D. N.
Libbey, G. H.
Lifka, M. L.
Lindgren, R. E.
Linkfield, T. P.
Lokken, R. N.
Lovin, C. R.
Lovin, H. T.
Lowitt, R.
Lubelski, B.
Lucas, M. B.
Lukaszewski, W. J.

M

Marks, H. S.
Marr, W. L.
Marshall, P. C.
McCarthy, E.
McCarthy, J. M.
McDonald, D. R.
McDorman, K. S.
McElroy, K.
McGinnis, D.
McGinty, G. W.
McIntyre, W. D.
McKinney, G. B.
McKinstry, E. R.
McLendon, E. M.
McNeill, C. A.
McQuilkin, D. K.
Meier, H. K.
Mendel, R. B.
Miller, R. M.
Moen, N. W.
Moody, C.
Moore, J.
Moriarty, T. F.
Mulligan, W. H.
Murdoch, D. H.
Murdock, E. C.
Mycue, D. J.
Myers, R. C.
Myres, S. L.

N

Neville, J. D.
Neville, R. G.
Newton, C. A.
Newton, P. T.

Nielson, D. G.
Niven, A. C.
Noble, R. E.
Novitsky, A. W.

O

Oaks, R. F.
OHainle, C. G.
Ohrvall, C. W.
Olbrich, W. L.
Olson, C. W.
Olson, G. L.
Orr, R. B.
Oser, A. K.
Osur, A. M.

P

Palais, E. S.
Panting, G. E.
Papalas, A. J.
Parker, H. M.
Patterson, S. L.
Patzwald, G. A.
Paul, B. J.
Paul, J. F.
Pergl, G. E.
Petersen, P. L.
Pickens, D. K.
Piersen, W. D.
Pliska, S. R.
Porter, B. S.
Powell, L. N.
Powers, T. L.
Pragman, J. H.
Prowe, D.
Puffer, K. J.
Pusateri, C. J.

Q

Quéripel, S. R.

R

Raife, L. R.
Reed, J. B.
Rilee, V. P.
Ritter, R. V.
Robitaille, S.
Roosen, W. J.
Rosenthal, F.
Rossi, G. J.

S

Sassoon, T.
Savitt, T. L.
Schermerhorn, D. L.
Schoenberg, P. E.
Schoonover, T. D.
Schroeder, G. R.
Schulz, C. B.
Selleck, R. G.
Senn, A. E.
Sevilla, S.
Shapiro, E. S.
Shergold, P. R.
Shipton, A. R.
Simmerman, T.
Sindermann, R. P.
Slavutych, Y.
Sliwoski, R. S.
Smith, D. B.
Smith, D. L.
Smith, J. D.
Smith, L.

Smith, L. C.
Smith, S. R.
Smith, T. W.
Smoot, J. G.
Snow, K. C.
Solodkin, P. L.
Spira, T.
Sprague, S. S.
Stack, R. E.
Stickney, E. P.
Stocker, E. F.
Stoesen, A. R.
Storey, B. A.
Street, J. B.
Street, N. J.
Strom, S. C.
Stromberg, R.
Summers, N.
Susskind, J. L.
Svengalis, K. F.
Sweetland, J. H.
Swiecicka-Ziemianek, M.
Swift, D. C.
Szewczyk, M. W.

T

Talley, K. A.
Tate, M. L.
Tennyson, B. D.
Tomlinson, R. H.
Travis, P.
Trickey, D. J.
Tull, J.
Tutorow, N. E.

V

Van Wyk, L. W.
Vance, M. M.
Vexler, R. I.
Vivian, J. F.

W

Wagnleitner, R.
Walker, J. T.
Walker, W. T.
Walsh, J. M.
Ward, G. W. R.
Ward, H. M.
Watson, C. A.
Wechman, R. J.
Welisch, S. A.
Weltsch, R. E.
Wendel, T. H.
Wengenroth, U.
West, K. B.
White, J. L.
Whitham, W. B.
Wiederrecht, A. E.
Wiegand, W. A.
Williams, J.
Williamson, N. A.
Wilson, M. T.
Woehrmann, P. J.
Woodward, R. L.

Y

Yanchisin, D. A.
Yerburgh, M. R.
Yntema, S. G.

Z

Zabel, O. H.
Ziewacz, L. E.
Zornow, W. F.

LIST OF ABBREVIATIONS

A.	Author-prepared Abstract
Acad.	Academy, Academie, Academia
Agric.	Agriculture, Agricultural
AIA	Abstracts in Anthropology
Akad.	Akademie
Am.	America, American
Ann.	Annals, Annales, Annual, Annali
Anthrop.	Anthropology, Anthropological
Arch.	Archives
Archaeol.	Archaeology, Archaeological
Art.	Article
Assoc.	Association, Associate
Biblio.	Bibliography, Bibliographical
Biog.	Biography, Biographical
Bol.	Boletim, Boletin
Bull.	Bulletin
c.	century (in index)
ca.	circa
Can.	Canada, Canadian, Canadien
Cent.	Century
Coll.	College
Com.	Committee
Comm.	Commission
Comp.	Compiler
DAI	Dissertation Abstracts International
Dept.	Department
Dir.	Director, Direktor
Econ.	Economy, Econom-.
Ed.	Editor, Edition
Educ.	Education, Educational
Geneal.	Genealogy, Genealogical, Genealogique
Grad.	Graduate
Hist.	History, Hist-.
IHE	Indice Historico Espanol
Illus.	Illustrated, Illustration
Inst.	Institute, Institut-.
Int.	International, Internacional, Internationaal, Internationaux, Internazionale
J.	Journal, Journal-prepared Abstract
Lib.	Library, Libraries
Mag.	Magazine
Mus.	Museum, Musee, Museo
Nac.	Nacional
Natl.	National, Nationale
Naz.	Nazionale
Phil.	Philosophy, Philosophical
Photo.	Photograph
Pol.	Politics, Political, Politique, Politico
Pr.	Press
Pres.	President
Pro.	Proceedings
Publ.	Publishing, Publication
Q.	Quarterly
Rev.	Review, Revue, Revista, Revised
Riv.	Rivista
Res.	Research
RSA	Romanian Scientific Abstracts
S.	Staff-prepared Abstract
Sci.	Science, Scientific
Secy.	Secretary
Soc.	Society, Societe, Sociedad, Societa
Sociol.	Sociology, Sociological
Tr.	Transactions
Transl.	Translator, Translation
U.	University, Universi-.
US	United States
Vol.	Volume
Y.	Yearbook

Abbreviations also apply to feminine and plural forms.
Abbreviations not noted above are based on *Webster's Third New International Dictionary*
and the *United States Government Printing Office Style Manual*.